THE CAMBRIDGE
URBAN HISTORY OF BRITAIN

VOLUME III
1840–1950

The third volume in *The Cambridge Urban History* examines the process of urbanisation and suburbanisation in Britain from the early Victorian period to the twentieth century. Twenty-eight leading scholars provide a coherent, systematic, historical investigation of the rise of cities and towns in England, Scotland and Wales, examining not only the evolving networks and types of towns, but their economic, demographic, social, political, cultural and physical development. The contributors discuss pollution and disease, the resolution of social conflict, the relationships between towns and the surrounding countryside, new opportunities for leisure and consumption, the development of local civic institutions and identities, and the evolution of municipal and state responsibilities.

Part I looks at circulation and networks within the urban environment through pollution, migration and transport. Part II investigates the structures of government and the provision of services. Part III examines urban construction and planning. Parts IV and V focus on the market and economy including consumerism, leisure and the visual arts. This comprehensive volume gives unique insights into the development of the urban landscape. Its detailed overview and analyses of the problems and opportunities which arise shed historical light on many of the issues and challenges that we face today.

The editor MARTIN DAUNTON is Professor of Economic History at the University of Cambridge and a Fellow of Churchill College. He has written extensively on British social, economic and urban history, and is a Fellow of the British Academy.

THE CAMBRIDGE
URBAN HISTORY OF BRITAIN

GENERAL EDITOR

PROFESSOR PETER CLARK (*University of Leicester*)

The three volumes of *The Cambridge Urban History of Britain* represent the culmination of a tremendous upsurge of research in British urban history over the past thirty years. Mobilising the combined expertise of nearly one hundred historians, archaeologists and geographers from Britain, continental Europe and North America, these volumes trace the complex and diverse evolution of British towns from the earliest Anglo-Saxon settlements to the mid-twentieth century. Taken together they form a comprehensive and uniquely authoritative account of the development of the first modern urban nation. *The Cambridge Urban History of Britain* has been developed with the active support of the Centre for Urban History at the University of Leicester.

VOLUME I 600–1540
EDITED BY D. M. PALLISER (*University of Leeds*)
ISBN 0 521 44461 6

VOLUME II 1540–1840
EDITED BY PETER CLARK (*University of Leicester*)
ISBN 0 521 43141 7

VOLUME III 1840–1950
EDITED BY MARTIN DAUNTON (*University of Cambridge*)
ISBN 0 521 41707 4

Advisory committee

Caroline M. Barron	*Royal Holloway College, University of London*
Jonathan Barry	*University of Exeter*
Peter Borsay	*St David's College, Lampeter, University of Wales*
Peter Clark	*University of Leicester*
Penelope Corfield	*Royal Holloway College, University of London*
Martin Daunton	*Churchill College, University of Cambridge*
Richard Dennis	*University College London*
Patricia Dennison	*University of Edinburgh*
Vanessa Harding	*Birkbeck College, University of London*
Gordon Jackson	*University of Strathclyde*
Derek Keene	*Institute of Historical Research, University of London*
Michael Lynch	*University of Edinburgh*
D. M. Palliser	*University of Leeds*
David Reeder	*University of Leicester*
Richard Rodger	*University of Leicester*
Gervase Rosser	*St Catherine's College, University of Oxford*
Paul Slack	*Linacre College, University of Oxford*
Richard Trainor	*University of Greenwich*
Sir Tony Wrigley	*Corpus Christi College, University of Cambridge*

THE
CAMBRIDGE
URBAN HISTORY
OF
BRITAIN

VOLUME III

1840–1950

EDITED BY

MARTIN DAUNTON

CAMBRIDGE
UNIVERSITY PRESS

PUBLISHED BY THE PRESS SYNDICATE OF THE UNIVERSITY OF CAMBRIDGE
The Pitt Building, Trumpington Street, Cambridge, United Kingdom

CAMBRIDGE UNIVERSITY PRESS
The Edinburgh Building, Cambridge CB2 2RU, UK
40 West 20th Street, New York, NY 10011–4211, USA
10 Stamford Road, Oakleigh, VIC 3166, Australia
Ruiz de Alarcón 13, 28014 Madrid, Spain
Dock House, The Waterfront, Cape Town 8001, South Africa

http://www.cambridge.org

First published 2000

Printed in the United Kingdom at the University Press, Cambridge

Typeface Bembo 10/12½pt.   *System* QuarkXPress™ [SE]

A catalogue record for this book is available from the British Library

ISBN 0 521 41707 4 hardback

Contents

Contents

Contents

Plates

Maps

Figures

Tables

Contributors

John Armstrong: Professor of Business History, Thames Valley University

Caroline Arscott: Lecturer in Victorian Art, Courtauld Institute of Art, University of London

Abigail Beach: formerly of University College London

Martin Daunton: Professor of Economic History, University of Cambridge and Fellow of Churchill College

John Davis: Fellow, Tutor and Praelector in History, The Queen's College, Oxford

Barry M. Doyle: Lecturer in History, University of Teesside

Richard Dennis: Reader in Geography, University College London

Marguerite Dupree: Lecturer in the History of Medicine, Wellcome Unit for the History of Medicine, University of Glasgow

David Feldman: Senior Lecturer in History, Birkbeck College, University of London

David Gilbert: Senior Lecturer in Geography, Royal Holloway College, University of London

Anne Hardy: Historian of Modern Medicine, Wellcome Institute for the History of Medicine

Lynn Hollen Lees: Professor of History, University of Pennsylvania

Bill Luckin: Professor of Urban and Cultural Studies at Bolton Institute

Robert Millward: Professor of Economic History, University of Manchester

R. J. Morris: Professor of Economic and Social History, University of Edinburgh

Sarah Palmer: Professor of Maritime History and Director, Greenwich Maritime Institute, University of Greenwich

Colin G. Pooley: Professor of Historical and Social Geography, University of Lancaster

David Reeder: Senior Research Associate, Centre for Urban History, University of Leicester

Douglas A. Reid: Senior Lecturer in Social History, University of Hull

Richard Rodger: Professor of Urban History and Director of the Centre for Urban History, University of Leicester

Stephen A. Royle: Senior Lecturer in Geography, The Queen's University of Belfast

Peter Scott: Senior Lecturer in Economic History, University of Portsmouth

Humphrey Southall: Reader in Geography, University of Portsmouth

Simon Szreter: University Lecturer in History, University of Cambridge, and Fellow of St John's College

Nick Tiratsoo: Senior Research Fellow, University of Luton

Richard Trainor: Vice-Chancellor and Professor of Social History, University of Greenwich

J. A. Yelling: Senior Lecturer in Geography, Birkbeck College, University of London

John K. Walton: Professor of Social History, University of Central Lancashire

Preface by the General Editor

British cities and towns at the end of the twentieth century are at a turning-point: their role, developed over hundreds of years, is being challenged. The redevelopment of bigger city centres in the 1960s, and of many small county and market towns during subsequent decades, has eroded much of the ancient palimpsest, the mixture of public and private buildings, high streets and back lanes, which has given them for so long a sense of place, of physical coherence and individual communal identity.[1] The decline of traditional urban industries, increasingly at the mercy of global forces, has been partially redressed by the expansion of the service sector, but the recent arrival of American-style out-of-town shopping malls has contributed to the contraction of retailing in the old central areas of towns, even affecting the business of their medieval markets, while shopping parades in the suburbs are littered with empty premises.

Just as economic activity has begun to decamp from the city, so the cultural and leisure life of town centres is being threatened by the migration of cinemas and other entertainment to the urban periphery, and the decay of municipal provision. Fundamental to the weakening position of British cities in recent times has been the erosion of municipal power and autonomy, first through the transfer of key civic functions to the state during and after the second world war, and, more recently, through a brutal assault by Conservative governments of the 1980s and 1990s on the financial position of town halls and their ability to sustain their civic responsibilities. It is little wonder that, in this problematic urban world, issues of social exclusion and environmental degradation seem increasingly stark, their effects impacting on the whole of national society.

Of course, the decline of the city is not a uniquely British phenomenon. Throughout much of Western Europe there has been a loss of momentum, a

---

[1] Such changes have also destroyed much of the archaeological record, the buried archives of towns, so essential for understanding their early history.

decay of confidence, manifested but hardly resolved by the endless spate of European conferences, research programmes and official reports on the subject, almost an industry in itself. However, the problems and pressures seem particularly acute in Britain, raising questions about how far their current difficulties reflect longer-term structural factors related to the processes by which Britain became the first modern urban nation. Is the peripheralisation of economic and cultural activity the logical conclusion of the spatial fragmentation of British cities, including suburbanisation, which has been occurring since 1800? Why have so many of Britain's great cities fared so badly in the twentieth century? Is this related to the nature of the rapid urbanisation and industrialisation from the late eighteenth century, based on low human capital formation and cheap fuel, which made it difficult to maintain growth once other countries began to exploit cheap fuel as well?

And yet if at least some of the problems of Britain's present-day cities and towns may be rooted in the past, the historic experience of our urban communities encourages us to believe that, given greater autonomy both of leadership and funding, they can generate an effective response to many of the current challenges. As we shall see in this series, past periods of urban decline, with all their attendant social, political and other difficulties, have often been reversed or moderated by changes of economic direction by towns, whether in the late middle ages through the expansion of service trades, in the seventeenth century through the development of specialist manufacturing and leisure sectors or in the early twentieth century through the rise of new, often consumer-oriented industries. At the present time, general images of urban decline and dereliction are countered, however selectively, by the rise of the Docklands area as the new international financial quarter of the capital, by the renewed vitality of Glasgow, Manchester and Newcastle as regional capitals, by the tourist success of towns like Bath and York marketing their civic heritage, by the social harmony and cultural vibrancy of a multi-ethnic city such as Leicester. Propelled by a strong sense of civic pride, Britain's urban system has shown, over time, a powerful capacity to create new opportunities from changing circumstances, a capacity that remains as crucial now as in the past. Certainly if many of the modern challenges to society have an urban origin then urban solutions are imperative.

Undoubtedly, Britain is an ancient urban country, remarkable for the longevity and, for much of the time, relative stability of its urban system. Though the early city barely outlasted the Romans' departure from these shores, after the seventh and eighth centuries a skeleton of urban centres developed in England, which was fully fleshed out by the start of the fourteenth century, headed by London, already a great European city, but with a corpus of established shire and market towns: the pattern established by 1300 was remarkably stable until the start of the nineteenth century. Scottish and Welsh towns were slower to become fully established and even in the early modern period new market burghs were founded in Scotland, but by the eighteenth century the island had a strong, generally affluent and increasingly integrated network of towns, which was to provide the essential springboard for the urban and industrial take-off of the nineteenth century. From the Georgian era cities and towns were centres of manufacturing and commercial expansion, public improvement and enlightenment; they were the centre stage for the enactment of a British identity. In Victoria's reign the city with its political rallies, crafts and factories, railways, gothic town halls, societies and civic amenities threatened to swallow up the country. Whether one should see the growing fascination with the countryside after 1918, that fashionable, if fanciful pursuit of Ambridge, as a new kind of anti-urbanism, or rather as the ultimate post-urban annexation of the countryside and its incorporation into the cultural hinterland of the city, remains in hot debate.[2] But the interwar period was, despite the problems of the biggest industrial cities, a time of considerable prosperity and community pride for many cities and towns up and down the country. Even in the aftermath of the second world war, many of the traditional functions and relationships of the British urban system survived – at least until the 1960s.

This is a good time for a systematic historical investigation of the rise of British cities and towns over the *longue durée*. Not just because understanding urban society is too important a task to be left to contemporary sociologists, geographers and planners, but because of the flourishing state of British urban history. Though earlier scholarly works existed, the last thirty years have seen a revolution in our understanding of the complexity of the social, political and other functions of towns in the past, of the social groups and classes that comprised the urban population, of the relationships within the urban system and between cities and the wider society, whether countryside, region or state. Initially most sonorous for the Victorian period and orchestrated by that brilliant academic conductor, H. J. (Jim) Dyos, in company with Asa Briggs and Sydney Checkland, the new concert of urban historians has increasingly embraced the early modern and medieval periods, a historiographical story explained in detail in the introductions to the separate volumes. The result is that for the first time we can follow the comparative evolution of English, Scottish and Welsh towns from the seventh to the twentieth century, traversing those conventional divisions of historical labour, particularly at the close of the middle ages and the end of the eighteenth century. Mobilising the expertise of historians, geographers, archaeologists, landscape historians and others, the modern study of urban history has always sought to pursue a wide-ranging agenda, aiming, so far as possible, to comprehend communities in the round, to see the interrelation of the different parts, even if such ambitions cannot always

---

[2] P. Mandler, 'Against "Englishness": English culture and the limits to rural nostalgia', *TRHS*, 6th series, 7 (1997), 155–75.

be fully achieved. Here urban history offers an important methodological alternative to the more fragmented study of specific urban themes, which, through micro-studies focusing on the most interesting sources and communities, runs the risk of seeing issues, social groups or particular towns in isolation, out of meaningful context. Thickets of knowledge of this type are the bane of sustained and innovative scholarly research, and have contributed much to the distancing of academic literature from the public domain. Strikingly, the last few years have seen a renewed or enhanced recognition of the overarching importance of the urban variable, both dependent and independent, in the many different areas of social, business, demographic and women's history.

In the fertile tradition of urban history, the three volumes of the *Cambridge Urban History of Britain* are the product of a collaborative project, with a good deal of friendship, fellowship, hard talking and modest drinking amongst those involved. The idea for such a series was discussed at Leicester as early as 1977, at a convivial lunch hosted by Jim Dyos, but it was not until 1990 that a proposal was made to launch the series. An advisory board was established, editors agreed, and several meetings held to plot the structure of the volumes, the contributors and the publishing arrangements. Since then regular meetings have been held for particular volumes, and the discussions have not only produced important dividends for the coherence and quality of the volumes, but have contributed to the better understanding of the British city in general. The involvement of colleagues working on Scotland has been particularly fruitful.

This series of volumes has had no earmarked funding (though funding bodies have supported research for individual chapters), and the editors and contributors are grateful to the many British and several North American universities for funding, directly and indirectly, the research, travel and other costs of contributors to the enterprise. Through its commitment to the Centre for Urban History, which has coordinated the project, the University of Leicester has been a valued benefactor, while Cambridge University Press, in the friendly guise of Richard Fisher, has been enormously helpful and supportive over the long haul of preparation and publication. The fact that the series, involving nearly ninety different contributors, has been published broadly on schedule owes a great deal to the energy, high commitment and fathomless interpersonal skills of my fellow editors, David Palliser and Martin Daunton (to whom I have been heavily indebted for wise and fortifying counsel), to the collective solidarity of the contributors, as well as to the generous support and patience of partners and families.

Thirty years ago in his introduction to *The Study of Urban History* Dyos declared that 'the field is as yet a very ragged one, and those in it are a little confused as to what they are doing'.[3] Plausibly, the volumes in the present series show that current students of urban history are less confused and somewhat

---

[3] H. J. Dyos, ed., *The Study of Urban History* (London, 1968), p. 46.

better dressed intellectually, having access to an extensive wardrobe of evidence, arguments and ideas, with a broad comparative and temporal design. The picture of the British town becomes ever more complex, as our greater knowledge recognises variety where once only uniformity was evident. However, we are at last nearer the point of uncovering the spectrum of historical processes, which have shaped our many cities and towns, making the urban past more intelligible and accessible, not just to academics, but to those townspeople whose identification with their own contemporary communities at the turn of the millennium is being so constantly and fiercely questioned.

Acknowledgements

The gestation period of a large collaborative volume is long and its birth is difficult. The eventual delivery of this third volume owes a great deal to Peter Clark as the general editor, who provided a sense of purpose and commitment to keep the project on track, even when contributors pulled out or seemed destined never to deliver. The meetings with him and with David Palliser to shape the three volumes were always stimulating and productive. I am particularly grateful to Peter Clark for his comments on the Introduction, as well as on the general shape of the volume. The task of editing a large volume provides many opportunities for friction with authors who do not deliver on time or who ignore the publisher's conventions. There were some tense moments, but there was also a sense of engagement and commitment, based on an exchange of ideas and testing of approaches. The early planning meetings of authors at the Institute of Historical Research were highly enjoyable, intellectually challenging events which provided a good foundation for our subsequent writing. I am grateful to the authors for their willingness to come to meetings in London, and to put up with my constant demands for revision and rewriting. At the Press, Richard Fisher was a constant source of reassurance and optimism over the ten years from the initial negotiating of the contract to the final publication. The intimidating task of copy-editing such a long and complex book was handled with great care and efficiency by Linda Randall. The bibliography was compiled by Eleanor O'Keeffe and the index by Auriol Griffith-Jones, and I am very grateful to them for their major contributions to the volume.

The editor, contributors and publisher are indebted to the following copyright owners for giving permission for illustrations to be reproduced: the Syndics of Cambridge University Library (1); Martin Daunton (2, 12, 14, 22); Ironbridge Gorge Museum (3); Manchester City Council, Department of Libraries and Theatres (5, 20); Coalville Publishing Group (7); National Monuments Record (8, 21); R. J. Morris (9, 10); Liverpool Libraries (11, 15, 16); Centre for Urban

History, University of Leicester (13); Richard Dennis (17); London Transport Museum (18); Alan Jackson (19); the Syndics of Cambridge University Press (24); East Sussex County Library (25); Selfridges and Co. and the History of Advertising Trust (26); Midlands Co-operative Society Ltd (27); Guildhall Library, Corporation of London (28, 32); Guildhall Art Gallery, Corporation of London (29); Birmingham Museums and Art Gallery (30); British Council (31); Tate Gallery (33, 34, 36, 39); British Museum (35); Courtauld Institute of Art (37, 40, 45, 51); Museum of London (38, 47, 48, 49, 50); Victoria and Albert Museum (41); Delaware Art Museum (42); Scottish National Portrait Gallery (43); Manchester City Art Galleries (44, 46); Toledo Museum of Art, Ohio (52); Musée des Beaux Arts, Rouen (53). Similarly, we are grateful for permission to reproduce the following maps and figures: the Syndics of Cambridge University Library (Figures 1.1, 17.1, 17.2); Routledge (Maps 2.1, 2.2, 2.3); University College London, Department of Geography Drawing Office (Maps 3.1, 3.2, 3.3); B. T. Robson (Maps 5.4, 5.5); Department of Geography, University of Liverpool (Figure 14.1); Hertfordshire Archives and Local Studies (Figure 15.1); the Syndics of Cambridge University Press (Map 23.1).

Abbreviations

Bull. IHR	Bulletin of the Institute of Historical Research (now Historical Research)
CMH	Centre for Metropolitan History
Ec.HR	Economic History Review
HJ	Historical Journal
HR	Historical Research
JEcc.Hist.	Journal of Ecclesiastical History
JEc.Hist.	Journal of Economic History
JUH	Journal of Urban History
LJ	London Journal
MOAR	Medical Officer's Annual Report
NHist.	Northern History
PEP	Political and Economic Planning
PP	Parliamentary Papers
P&P	Past and Present
PRO	Public Record Office
RGSR	Registrar General's Statistical Review for England and Wales
SHist.	Southern History
SHR	Scottish Historical Review
Soc. Hist.	Social History
TRHS	Transactions of the Royal Historical Society
UH	Urban History
UHY	Urban History Yearbook
VCH	Victoria County History

Introduction

MARTIN DAUNTON

(i) CIRCULATIONS

IN 1850, Charles Dickens received a gruesome gift from his brother-in-law, Herbert Austin – the *Report on a General Scheme for Extra-Mural Sepulture*. This nauseating account of densely packed urban graveyards exuding noxious gases, secreting foul fluids, turning the soil 'black and pitchy' and making the boundary wall 'damp, glutinous and spongy' led Dickens to dream of putrefaction. But his imagination had been stimulated even before reading Austin's sickening report, for his novels were obsessed with graveyards and slaughterhouses, sewers and cess pits, their textures and secretions, described in the same language as the reports of sanitary reformers. Dickens portrayed early Victorian London as permeated with notions of decay, corruption, stench and stickiness.[1] The city of Dickens and the sanitary reformers, at the beginning of the period covered by this third volume of the *Cambridge Urban History*, was rotten, stagnant, putrefying – a place of blockage where the frustration of circulation resulted in secretions and miasmas. The language of Dickens and sanitary reformers provided imaginative force to a real and alarming crisis in British towns and cities at the opening of Victoria's reign, bringing a variety of problems together into a single frame of reference and uniting otherwise disparate issues in a way which justified action and intervention. As Christopher Hamlin has remarked, the monumental infrastructure of sanitation inserted into Victorian towns was 'even more remarkable as an achievement of public persuasion than one of bricks and mortar'.[2]

The physical form of cities prevented circulation, and led to both ill-health

---

[1] D. Trotter, *Circulation* (Basingstoke, 1988), pp. 103–12; D. E. Nord, *Walking the Victorian Streets* (Ithaca, 1995), pp. 98–9. The connections between sanitary reforms and the literary forms of novelists is also discussed in J. W. Childers, *Novel Possibilities: Fiction and the Formation of Early Victorian Culture* (Philadelphia, 1995), for the way in which Chadwick utilised the novelist's language.
[2] C. Hamlin, *Public Health and Social Justice in the Age of Chadwick* (Cambridge, 1998), p. 337.

and crime. William Strange was one of many writers who expressed concern about the lack of circulation of air in 'the dense and intricate masses of buildings inhabited by the poorer classes . . . The atmosphere of these places is charged with the exhalations from the persons and dwellings of the crowded population, and is rendered still more infectious by the effluvia from the cesspools, dungheaps, pigsties, etc., which abound therein.'[3] The inhabitants of these districts were themselves 'immortal sewerage'. In 1853, the Reverend S. G. Osborne expressed his alarm at the 'living nastiness and offensive living matter which we have been content to allow to accumulate in streets, a very small distance from our doors; matters not only offensive, repulsive, and pernicious when viewed in detail, but in their aggregated masses acting to the deep permanent injury of mankind in general'. People were refuse or sewerage with a difference: they had souls and immortality. But the problem was the same: how to purify stagnation and pollution which led to disease and moral contamination? As Osborne commented, 'there are moral miasmas just as there are physical. The mind – the soul of man – can be just as polluted as to its springs of healthy life by external, removable causes, as can the human physical constitution: – there is a mental typhus.'[4] The metaphor extended to administrative reform and economic policy. The trade monopolies of the East India Company or the navigation laws giving preference to British ships were restrictions on circulation which created inefficiencies and corruption. The outmoded practices of the law courts and government – the legal cases festering in the court of Chancery and the administrative decisions delayed in the Circumlocution Office – were linked together in a single frame of reference.[5]

The ecology of the large cities – the handling of flows of wastes and pollution – was breaking down. In the conclusion to Volume II of the *Cambridge Urban History*, Peter Clark commented that the urban system was facing crisis.[6] In provincial cities of 100,000 and above, life expectancy at birth dropped from thirty-five years in the 1820s to twenty-nine in the 1830s, a marked break in the previous trend of improvement of life expectancy in towns and cities.[7] Here is a theme explored in Bill Luckin's chapter on pollution, and commented on in

---

[3] W. Strange, *Address to the Middle and Working Classes on the Causes and Preventions of the Excessive Sickness and Mortality Prevalent in Large Towns* (London, 1845), quoted in Trotter, *Circulation*, p. 73. For an account of the contest between miasma and contagion, see R. J. Morris, *Cholera 1832* (London, 1976), pp. 170–84.

[4] S. G. Osborne, 'Immortal sewerage', *Meliora*, 2nd series (1853), 7, quoted in Trotter, *Circulation*, p. 73; for the way in which the poor and prostitutes were treated as moral sewage, see also Nord, *Walking the Streets*, ch. 3; J. R. Walkowitz, *City of Dreadful Delight* (London and Chicago, 1992), p. 22; L. Nead, *Myths of Sexuality* (Oxford, 1988), pp. 126–7.   [5] Trotter, *Circulation*, pp. 108–9.

[6] P. Clark, ed., *The Cambridge Urban History of Britain*, vol. II: *1540–1840* (Cambridge, 2000), p. 835.

[7] S. Szreter and G. Mooney, 'Urbanisation, mortality and the standard of living debate: new estimates of the expectation of life at birth in nineteenth-century cities', *Ec.HR*, 2nd series, 51 (1998), 84–112, and below, p. 634; the mortality pattern in the eighteenth century is covered in Clark, ed., *Cambridge Urban History*, II, pp. 503–13.

Simon Szreter and Anne Hardy's discussion of mortality at the beginning of our period. As Szreter and Hardy point out in their chapter, life expectancy in the slums of the 1830s and 1840s was the lowest since the Black Death. Although cities grew rapidly in the late eighteenth and early nineteenth centuries, with a larger proportion of an ever increasing population, investment in the urban infrastructure did not keep pace. British urbanisation in the late eighteenth and early nineteenth centuries was undertaken 'on the cheap'.[8] The grim consequences were apparent in the 1830s and 1840s, with blockages in the circulation of water and wastes, stagnation of foul cess pits and graveyards, and densely packed courtyards.

In the late eighteenth and early nineteenth centuries, the number of houses more or less kept pace with the rapid increase in the urban population, but only by subdividing property and packing more houses into courtyards and alleys, creating a maze of dead-ends and blockages where sanitary reformers feared that crime and disease flourished.[9] In Liverpool in 1841, for example, about a quarter of the population lived in courts entered through a narrow passage, with houses packed around a tiny open space containing a common privy and ashpit 'with its liquid filth oozing through their walls, and its pestiferous gases flowing into the windows'.[10] The installation of water closets might simply transfer the problem elsewhere, and possibly make things worse by pouring excrement into the water supply, as happened in London in the early nineteenth century.[11] Indeed, many people scarcely *had* a water supply: the Royal Commission on the Health of Towns of 1843/5 found that only 5,000 people out of 130,000 in Bristol had piped water.[12] The recycling of waste products was a major problem

---

[8] J. G. Williamson, *Coping with City Growth during the British Industrial Revolution* (Cambridge, 1990), especially ch. 10; N. F. R. Crafts, 'Some dimensions of the "quality of life" during the British Industrial Revolution', *Ec.HR*, 2nd series, 50 (1997), 617–39; S. Szreter, 'Economic growth, disruption, deprivation, disease and death: on the importance of the politics of public health for development', *Population and Development Review*, 23 (1997), 693–728; and below, pp. 634, 671.

[9] C. W. Chalklin, *The Provincial Towns of Georgian England* (London, 1974), pp. 225, 307; M. J. Daunton, *House and Home in the Victorian City* (London, 1983).

[10] Daunton, *House and Home*, pp. 22–3; A. Errazurez, 'Some types of housing in Liverpool, 1785–1890', *Town Planning Review*, 19 (1943–7), 57–68; I. Taylor, 'The court and cellar dwelling: the eighteenth-century origin of the Liverpool slum', *Transactions of the Historical Society of Lancashire and Cheshire*, 122 (1970), 67–90. On the general change in urban form of the city, see Daunton, *House and Home*, p. 12, and 'Public place and private space: the Victorian city and the working-class household', in D. Fraser and A. Sutcliffe, eds., *The Pursuit of Urban History* (London, 1983), 212–33. See Plates 11 and 43.

[11] S. Halliday, *The Great Stink of London* (Stroud, 1999), pp. 33, 35–47. The problem arose from a change in policy, to permit householders to connect to sewers, which were designed to discharge storm water into the Thames; the interests of the water companies in increasing their income clashed with those of the commissioners of sewers, who did not have the financial resources to increase the capacity of the system.

[12] M. Falkus, 'The development of municipal trading in the nineteenth century', *Business History*, 19 (1977), 61–88; and below, p. 219.

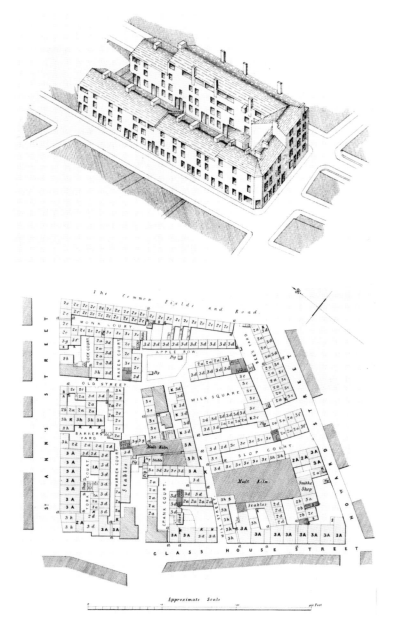

Figure 1.1 Courts in Nottingham 1844. The plan shows the internal, shared space with communal privies, a lack of privacy and an absence of through circulation.
Source: PP 1844 XVIII, *First Report of the Commissioners for Inquiring into the State of Large Towns and Populous Districts.*

for the Victorian city, as materials came in to sustain the urban economy and were transformed into goods and waste products.[13] Animals were slaughtered for meat, leaving blood, bone and hides to be converted into leather, glue and tallow – processes of overpowering stench which were located in 'dirty' areas of the city. The livestock market at Smithfield, with its noise, dirt and smell, horrified Dickens, and as Pip remarked in *Great Expectations* 'the shameful place, being all asmear with filth and fat and blood and foam, seemed to stick to me'.[14] The tanning yards and glue works on the south bank of the Thames at Bermondsey, where hides and bones were processed, were even worse.[15] Coal for domestic fuel and industrial processes created a pall of smoke which led to bronchial problems and blocked out the sun, so contributing to rickets as a result of vitamin deficiency.[16] In the major industrial cities, raw materials were imported on a vast scale and often poisoned the landscape and the people, most notoriously the chemical and copper industries around Swansea and St Helens where 'the landscape of Hell was foreshadowed'.[17] What could be done about these problems, which raised major issues of how to prevent one party imposing costs on another, and required large-scale investment in the infrastructure?

The initial concern of sanitary reformers was water-borne pollution, and their solution was simple: '*continuous circulation*'. As Edwin Chadwick put it, 'the main conveyance of pure water into towns and its distribution into houses, as well as the removal of foul water by drains from the houses and from the streets into the fields for agricultural production, should go on without cessation and without stagnation either in the houses or the streets'.[18] A constant flow was essential so that putrefaction did not set in before the wastes were removed from the city. This was also a statement of what was *not* part of public health – adequate food or healthy working conditions, a sense of the economic causes of disease and the political rights asserted by the radicals and Chartists. The public health movement, as defined by Chadwick, was also about political stability, moral reform and control. Courts and alleys should be opened up to circulation by driving new roads through the worst slums to bring air and the light of civilisation into

---

[13] On one such flow – the use of ashes from London to mix with clay for brick production in Middlesex, which were then returned to London, see P. Hounsell, 'Cowley stocks: brickmaking in west Middlesex from 1800' (PhD thesis, Thames Valley University, 2000; and below, p. 234.

[14] Quoted in Trotter, *Circulation*, p. 104; Dickens attacked Smithfield in *Household Words*, 4 May 1850. On Smithfield, see A. B. Robertson, 'The Smithfield cattle market', *East London Papers*, 4 (1961), 80–7.

[15] On Bermondsey, see G. Dodd, *Days at the Factory; or The Manufacturing Industry of Great Britain Described* (London, 1843), p. 175.

[16] On the link between sunlight and rickets, see A. Hardy, *The Epidemic Streets* (Oxford, 1993), pp. 19–20, 26, 238, 284; and below, p. 642. On smoke pollution, see P. Brimblecombe, *The Big Smoke* (London, 1987), and also A. S. Wohl, *Endangered Lives* (London, 1983); see below, pp. 222–6 and Plate 4.

[17] W. G. Hoskins, *The Making of the English Landscape* (London, 1955), p. 171

[18] B. Ward Richardson, ed., *The Health of Nations*, vol. II (London, 1887), pp. 297–8, quoted in Trotter, *Circulation*, p. 71.

their gloomy depths, so dispelling both physical and moral miasmas. The same process would contribute to the health of the nation as to the wealth of the nation: its effluent could be turned to profitable use, and blockages in the free circulation of trade could be removed by repealing the corn laws and navigation laws, sweeping away the corporate privileges of the East India Company and regulating the circulation of bank notes by the Bank Charter Act of 1844. Circulation of information and knowledge would be improved by the cheap and efficient carriage of mail by the penny post, by the construction of railways and telegraphs, by itinerant lecturers and circulating libraries.[19]

The notion of 'continuous circulation' implied a particular vision of urban life. Arteries should be kept free of blockages or the city – like an individual – would suffer apoplexy:

> the streets of London are choked by their ordinary traffic, and the life blood of the huge giant is compelled to run through veins and arteries that have never expanded since the days and dimensions of its infancy. What wonder is it that the circulation is an unhealthy one? That the quantity carried to each part of the frame is insufficient for the demands of its bulk and strength, that there is dangerous pressure in the main channels and morbid disturbance of the current, in all causing daily stoppages of the vital functions.[20]

The street was not a place to loiter, but to move. In Paris, the great boulevards of Baron Haussman combined movement and parade: the centre of the street was dedicated to fast, cross-town traffic; at the side, separate lanes catered for slower, local traffic; and wide, tree-lined pavements allowed pedestrians to stroll or sit at cafés. Here was the Paris of Baudelaire, of people displaying themselves before a parade of strangers and watching others as a spectacle.[21] As a British visitor to the Paris exhibition of 1867 remarked, the Frenchman 'lives in his streets and boulevards, is proud of them, loves them, and will spend his money on their beauty and decoration'. By contrast, Londoners lived indoors or in more private spaces, and streets were 'simply and solely a means of transit from one point to another'.[22] The aim of urban improvements was to create free movement of goods and people. When Joseph Bazalgette constructed the Embankment along the Thames, it was not as a place to saunter or sit; it was an artery rather than a public space, with a road above and a railway below, alongside gas mains and sewers.[23]

---

[19] Hamlin, *Public Health and Social Justice*, pp. 338–9; he notes the difference between Chadwick's 'sanitarianism' and William Pultney Alison's medical critique of industrialism in Scotland, see pp. 74–83; Trotter, *Circulation*, pp. 101–2.

[20] *Illustrated London News*, 1846, quoted in J. Winter, *London's Teeming Streets, 1830–1914* (London, 1993), p. 6.

[21] M. Berman, *All That Is Solid Melts into Air* (New York, 1982); on the reconstruction of Paris, see N. Evanson, *Paris: A Century of Change, 1878–1978* (New Haven, 1979).

[22] Winter, *London's Teeming Streets*, p. 20; see also D. Olsen, *The City as a Work of Art* (London and New Haven, 1986).

[23] Winter, *London's Teeming Streets*, pp. 29–31; Halliday, *Great Stink*, pp. 144–63. See Plates 2 and 49.

The metaphor of illness led to a negative response to street life. Reformers looked for clots and infection; movement of sewage or traffic had priority over multiple uses as a source of vitality. And reform of the fabric of the city was linked to reforming the culture and morals of the people; the health and care of the city was at one with the health and care of the body.[24]

The process of creating free movement of people and air in the city led to a growing concern for the layout of towns, in order to prevent the continued construction of courts and dead-ends. From the 1840s, Liverpool town council started to impose regulations on the construction of courts so that they were more easily cleaned and open to inspection, with individual backyards and separate sanitation for each house. Nationally, the Public Health Act of 1875 led to the development of 'by-law' housing, with open grids of streets, and separate yards and sanitation for each house.[25] This change in the form of the city was not simply a result of public regulation, but also of falling land prices after the Napoleonic wars, the onset of gains in real income around the middle of the century and a slow improvement in urban transport. In addition to a greater concern for the layout of streets and the internal structure of housing, steps were taken to prevent pollution and nuisances. Landowners attempted to limit offensive trades on their urban estate developments through clauses in leases, in an effort to maintain the amenity and value of their property. Their efforts were usually in vain, for it was difficult to contain wider processes within the urban economy.[26] Public controls were also introduced. The Public Health (London) Act, 1891, for example, gave the London County Council (LCC) power to regulate slaughterhouses, cowhouses and knackers' yards, and to prevent nuisances. From 1896, even dogs were not immune, and the LCC slaughtered 32,000 strays within a year.[27]

More difficult was control over the quality of air, beyond ensuring that expensive developments were up-wind from the worst pollution. The first legislation against smoke in 1821 dealt with the limited case of steam engines. In 1852, smoke emissions in London were controlled, and in 1875 all local authorities were given power to adopt anti-smoke measures. They had little effect, for domestic coal was not covered until the clean air legislation of 1956. The pall of

---

[24] Winter, *London's Teeming Streets*, p. 15; on street clearances, see A. S. Wohl, *The Eternal Slum* (London, 1977); H. J. Dyos, 'Urban transformation: a note on the objects of street improvement in Regency and early Victorian London', *International Review of Social History*, 2 (1957), 259–65; G. Stedman Jones, *Outcast London* (Oxford, 1971), on debates over housing and the theories of urban degeneration.

[25] See Errazurez, 'Some types of housing', and Taylor, 'Court and cellar dwelling'.

[26] For the failure of control in one area of Camberwell, see H. J. Dyos, *Victorian Suburb* (Leicester, 1961), p. 111, and for strict leases on a large estate, p. 97; see also the attempts of the Bedford estate to preserve Bloomsbury in D. J. Olsen, *Town Planning in London* (New Haven, 1964), and the Calthrope estate in Edgbaston, in D. Cannadine, *Lords and Landlords* (Leicester, 1980), pp. 81–220. For an assessment of the significance of landowners' controls, see D. Cannadine, 'Victorian cities: how different?', *Soc. Hist.*, 4 (1977), 457–82.

[27] S. D. Pennybacker, *A Vision for London, 1889–1914* (London, 1995), p. 179.

coal hanging over British towns and cities was bad enough; even worse were the so-called 'noxious vapours' from industrial processes. Polluters could be taken to court under the private or public law of nuisance. Property owners might take factory owners to court on the grounds that they were committing a nuisance, such as the aggrieved owners of Park Square, Leeds, who were offended by the smoke from Mr Gott's factory.[28] In some towns, local landowners took action against the urban authority itself for causing a nuisance by polluting the river, and so forced an improvement in sewage treatment.[29] But actions against industrial pollution were rare, limited by cost and the realisation that the industries involved were vital to the prosperity of the local economy. The courts adopted the notion of 'reasonableness', accepting that a degree of discomfort was acceptable given the economic benefits to the community and the nature of the area involved. After all, as one judge remarked, 'what would be a nuisance in Belgrave Square would not necessarily be one in Bermondsey'. When legislation was introduced against noxious vapours in the Alkali Acts of 1863, 1874 and 1881, the worst pollution from copper was still excluded. Essentially, legislation covered only processes where regulation was economically feasible – a narrow definition which did not place a cost on the damaged health of the inhabitants.[30] The issue continues with the problems of petro-chemical pollution in cities and the difficulties of taking political action against car owners.

Urban spaces were increasingly controlled, and Dickens' concern for circulation gave way to a new interest in surveillance and observation.[31] Medical officers of health inspected insanitary housing, mapping 'plague spots' in order to excise them from the urban fabric.[32] They inspected individuals, who could similarly pollute the city with their physical and moral contamination. The power of doctors over the bodies of urban residents increased in the mid-nineteenth century, with compulsory vaccination of children by poor law medical officers.[33] They monitored infectious disease, isolated individuals and disinfected their

[28] M. W. Beresford, 'Prosperity Street and others: an essay in visible urban history', in M. W. Beresford and G. R. J. Jones, eds., *Leeds and its Region* (Leeds, 1967), pp. 186–97.

[29] For example, Merthyr Tydfil and Birmingham: see C. Hamlin, 'Muddling in bumbledom: on the enormity of large sanitary improvements in four British towns, 1855–1885', *Victorian Studies*, 33 (1988–9), 55–83.

[30] On smoke and noxious fumes, see Brimblecombe, *Big Smoke*; Pennybacker, *Vision for London*, pp. 179–80; E. Newell, 'Atmospheric pollution and the British copper industry, 1690–1920', *Technology and Culture*, 38 (1997), 655–89; R. Rees, 'The south Wales copper-smoke dispute, 1833–1895', *Welsh History Review*, 10 (1981), 480–96; on nuisance law, J. F. Brenner, 'Nuisance law and the Industrial Revolution', *Journal of Legal Studies*, 3 (1974), 403–33; J. P. S. McClaren, 'Nuisance law and the Industrial Revolution: some lessons from social history', *Oxford Journal of Legal Studies*, 3 (1983), 155–221; and J. H. Baker, *An Introduction to English Legal History* (London, 1990), pp. 478–93.   [31] Trotter, *Circulations*, pp. 112–18.

[32] J. A. Yelling, *Slums and Slum Clearance in Victorian London* (London, 1986).

[33] Hardy, *Epidemic Streets*, ch. 5; the use of compulsion was contentious – see R. M. Macleod, 'Law, medicine and public opinion: the resistance to compulsory health legislation, 1870–1907', *Public Law* (1967), 107–28, 189–211.

homes, clothes and possessions to prevent its spread.[34] The Contagious Diseases
Acts of 1864–9 gave power to inspect and confine women with sexual diseases, to
prevent them from polluting the soldiers and sailors of garrison towns.[35] Cities
were divided into 'beats' for the police, inspected by school board visitors, anat-
omised in statistical tables and maps.[36] In his chapter, Douglas Reid shows how
fairs and pleasure gardens, with their mixing and moral dangers, or recreations of
bull running and street football, were attacked by the movement for the reformation of manners, the Royal Society for the Prevention of Cruelty to Animals and
the temperance movement, often with the support of businessmen and councillors eager to create an orderly workforce and urban environment. Public spaces
previously used for demonstrations and meetings – Spa Fields and Kennington
Common in London, for example – were built over or turned into parks.[37]
Tyburn, the site of public executions and their associated crowds, became merely
another part of Hyde Park. In 1868, hangings retreated behind the walls of prisons,
away from the passion of crowds and the threat to urban decorum.[38] As Mark
Harrison points out, the trend was away from the city as an open stage for the
enactment of civic rituals and disputes, to a controlled set of enclosed spheres.[39]

However, as Colin Pooley remarks, the transition from a chaotic early nineteenth-century city to a controlled twentieth-century city was never smooth.
Travel itself entailed social collisions and dangers. The horse omnibus produced

---

[34] Hardy, *Epidemic Streets*, pp. 194–5, 207, 273, 277–8; S. Szreter, 'The importance of social intervention in Britain's mortality decline, *c.* 1850–1914: a reinterpretation of the role of public health',
Social History of Medicine, 1 (1988), 1–37.
[35] J. R. Walkowitz, *Prostitution and Victorian Society* (Cambridge, 1980); on London, see R. D. Storch,
'Police control of street prostitution in Victorian London: a study in the context of police action',
in D. H. Bayley, ed., *Police and Society* (Beverly Hills, 1977), pp. 49–72.
[36] On school board visitors, who provided the data for Charles Booth's detailed mapping of poverty
in London, see D. Rubinstein, *School Attendance in London, 1870–1914* (Hull, 1969); on the police,
see C. Steedman, *Policing and the Victorian Community* (London, 1984); D. Phillips, *Crime and
Authority in Victorian England* (London, 1977); R. D. Storch, 'The plague of the blue locusts: police
reform and popular resistance in northern England, 1840–57', *International Review of Social History*,
20 (1975), 61–91; R. D. Storch, 'The policeman as domestic missionary: urban discipline and
popular culture in northern England, 1850–80', in R. J. Morris and R. Rodger, eds., *The Victorian
City* (London, 1993), pp. 281–306; C. Elmsley, *Policing in Context, 1750–1870* (London, 1983). For
the notion of a 'policeman state', under surveillance and the gaze of authority, see V. Gatrell,
'Crime, authority and the policeman state', in F. M. L. Thompson, ed., *The Cambridge Social
History of Britain, 1750–1950*, vol. III: *Social Agencies and Institutions* (Cambridge, 1990), pp. 243–310.
[37] D. A. Reid, 'The decline of Saint Monday', *P&P*, 71 (1976), 76–101; H. Cunningham, 'The metropolitan fairs: a case study in the social control of leisure', in A. P. Donajgrodzki, ed., *Social
Control in Nineteenth Century Britain* (London, 1977), pp. 163–84; R. W. Malcolmson, *Popular
Recreations in English Society, 1700–1850* (Cambridge, 1973); A. Taylor, '"Commons-stealers",
"land-grabbers", and "jerry-builders": space, popular radicalism and the politics of public access
in London, 1848–80', *International Review of Social History*, 40 (1995), 383–407; see below, p. 118.
[38] V. A. C. Gatrell, *The Hanging Tree: Execution and the English People, 1770–1868* (Oxford, 1994), pp. 23–4.
[39] M. Harrison, 'Symbolism, ritualism and the location of crowds in early nineteenth-century
English towns', in D. Cosgrove and S. Daniels, eds., *The Iconography of Landscape* (Cambridge,
1988), pp. 194–213, cited by Pooley, p. 441.

unwelcome intimacies (see Plate 39), and railway companies tried to avoid the embarrassments of social mixing by the provision of carriages for different classes, and separate trains for workmen. Even so, dirty, uncouth workers might loiter at stations waiting for their cheap train, and offend respectable passengers.[40] The process of 'sterilising' the street, creating neutral or 'dead' spaces, was contested. The police, local by-laws and the Metropolitan Traffic Act of 1867 sought to clarify the use of the street and remove ambiguities but one person's freedom was another person's nuisance, and the policing of the streets remained controversial.[41] When Lord Montagu defended the motorists' freedom to use the king's highway, claiming that 'the right to use the road, that wonderful emblem of liberty, is deeply ingrained in our history and character',[42] he was continuing a battle waged by costermongers with their barrows, hawkers selling their wares, heavy drays unloading, itinerant musicians entertaining and annoying in equal measure, omnibuses picking up passengers, or women soliciting men and vice versa. Streets were contested in terms of class: a top hat invited deference at one place and time, ridicule at another. They were contested in terms of gender: a lady commanded respect here and importunity there, the lines shifting between day and evening. Streets changed their identity over the day, as they were appropriated by different social groups for a variety of purposes – for male commuters rushing to work, for women shopping, or (as Reid notes) young men and women in the 'monkey parade', walking and bantering to attract attention.[43] Men – or at least bourgeois men – were privileged spectators, urban explorers who could 'stroll across the divided spaces of the metropolis', a subjectivity reflected in literature and in social surveys by Henry Mayhew and Charles Booth.[44] By the 1880s, women were starting to claim greater access to public spaces of the city, so triggering alarm at their transgressions of boundaries. As Judith Walkowitz points out, the 'imaginary landscape' of London shifted 'from one that was geographically bounded to one where boundaries were indiscriminately and dangerously transgressed'. The murders committed by Jack the Ripper in 1888 became a cautionary tale for women, 'a warning that the city was a dangerous place when they transgressed the narrow boundary of home and hearth to enter public space'.[45] For all the efforts of control and surveillance, the city still remained a place for imagination, encounters and collisions, with new possibilities for freedom and self-expression.

Transport within towns was only slowly transformed, as John Armstrong shows in his chapter. At the beginning of the period, the only method of transport for most people was walking, and the destruction of inner-city housing for

---

[40] Below, p. 441, J. Richards and J. M. MacKenzie, *The Railway Station* (Oxford, 1986); W. Schivelbusch, *The Railway Journey* (Oxford, 1980).   [41] Winter, *London's Teeming Streets*, pp. 42–9.
[42] *Ibid.*, p. 9.   [43] *Ibid.*, *passim*; and below, p. 762.
[44] *Ibid.*, pp. 177–89; Nord, *Walking the Streets*, pp. 1–3; Walkowitz, *City of Dreadful Delight*, p. 16.
[45] Walkowitz, *City of Dreadful Delight*, pp. 3, 11, 29; see also Nord, *Walking the Streets*, ch. 6.

commerce, industry, railway lines and stations simply led to an ever denser packing of the poor in adjacent areas.[46] The pattern of urban development by individual estates, the subdivision of inner-city property to pack more accommodation into a small area, the insertion of railway lines into the existing fabric, meant that circulation was constricted. And the surface of the roads was a source of continued difficulty: how could it be kept clean of animal waste and refuse which provided a breeding ground for flies and a vector for the spread of disease? An act of 1817 tried to ban dumping of mud, dirt, dung, blood – the evocatively named 'slop' – on the streets of London. These good intentions were of little effect, for Henry Mayhew calculated that animals deposited 39,592 tons of manure a year on the streets of the metropolis by the mid-1850s. William Farr, the registrar general, was impressed by the stickiness of this 'highly agglutinative compound' which could pull up paving stones when attached to cart wheels – and became treacherously slippery after rain. Different road surfaces produced more or less dirt, and were more or less easy to clean. They also affected the noise of the city, and the chance of accident to pedestrians and horses. From the 1820s, gravel was replaced on main thoroughfares by macadam, a concave, impermeable surface made from uniform, small pieces of granite – often produced by paupers as the labour test in workhouses. The surface was difficult to clean, and the wheels of heavy carts of omnibuses soon created ruts so that a new layer of stone was laid on the busiest streets three times a year. The alternative was granite paving stones or setts, set in ballast or cement. The surface could be more easily cleaned; on the other hand, it was appallingly noisy from the clatter of horses' hooves and iron-rimmed wheels. By the 1870s, two new surfaces were becoming available. The quietest was wooden blocks: the Society of Arts reported in 1874 that the rent of lodgings rose on streets with wooden paving. The second was asphalt, which was reasonably quiet and clean, with the additional virtue that it could be easily opened for access to cables and pipes. The choice of surface was contentious, for residents preferred wood for the sake of quietness, whereas hauliers were more concerned with traction. Granite setts gave a better grip to horses' hooves and so reduced the amount of traction power; macadam demanded most energy, followed by wood and asphalt which were slippery after rain. On Cheapside in the City of London in 1873, horses suffered from an average of 18.64 accidents a day. They could only be slaughtered by specialist, licensed firms which kept carts on call to destroy horses, and carry the carcasses to specialist cat-meat suppliers at Wandsworth – another part of the ecology of the city. The choice of surface therefore reflected a contest between different interests, and also a changing calculation of cost by town councils. The

---

[46] H. J. Dyos, 'Railways and housing in Victorian London', *Journal of Transport History*, 2 (1955), 11–21, 90–100; H. J. Dyos, 'Some social costs of railway building in London', *Journal of Transport History*, new series, 3 (1957), 3–30; Stedman Jones, *Outcast London*, ch. 8; J. R. Kellett, *The Impact of Railways on Victorian Cities* (London, 1969).

initial capital cost of macadam was low, but it was expensive to maint[...]
and asphalt imposed heavy capital costs but saved on repairs. A drop[...]
rates in the late nineteenth century meant that borrowing for capita[...]
ture became more attractive than higher running costs of maintena[...]
construction of roads is by no means a trivial issue. It was central [...]
nomenology of the city, to the cacophony of noise and the experi[...]
to the spread of disease through the vector of flies, and the cost [...]
was one of the largest expenditures of local authorities, ahead of [...]
health and education until overtaken by education in the e[...]
century.[48]

Indeed, cost was central to the entire project of 'continuous circula[...]
Expenditure on improved paving and street cleaning was only one part of a wider
investment in demolition and the construction of new thoroughfares, on drains
to clear away storm water, on networks of sewers and water mains, on gas,
electricity and trams. Glasgow corporation, for example, received royal assent to
construct a massive scheme to draw on the waters of Loch Katrine in 1855, at an
estimated cost of £540,000 which escalated to nearer £1m. The scale of the
investment exceeded any of the great engineering and shipbuilding works along
the Clyde – and it was undertaken with great speed. The completed works were
opened by Queen Victoria in 1859 with elaborate pomp and ceremony. The
waterworks became a symbol of civic purpose, indicating a restoration of the
balance of nature in a dangerous environment.[49] In London, the new system of
sewers designed and built by Joseph Bazalgette for the Metropolitan Board of
Works cost £4.1m; the construction of the Embankment along the Thames and
the removal of tolls from private bridges across the river in order to ease the circulation of traffic cost a further large sum.[50] At the same time, the Metropolitan
Board of Works drove new roads through the worst slums in central London, such
as Shaftesbury Avenue cutting through Soho to Piccadilly Circus. The new road
provided a main traffic artery, and opened up the area to inspection – it was a
response to moral as well as physical miasmas, its very name reflecting the evangelical reforming zeal of Lord Shaftesbury who was commemorated in the statute
of Eros at Piccadilly Circus.[51] The cost of these schemes in London and the great

---

[47] Winter, *London's Teeming Streets*, ch. 7; R. Turvey, 'Street mud, dust and noise', *LJ*, 21 (1996), 131–48; F. M. L. Thompson, 'Nineteenth-century horse sense', *Ec.HR*, 2nd series, 29 (1976), 60–81.

[48] R. Millward and S. Sheard, 'The urban fiscal problem, 1870–1914: government expenditure and finances in England and Wales', *Ec.HR*, 2nd series, 48 (1995), 505–6, tables 1, 3, 4, A1–3; below, p. 632 on flies.

[49] W. H. Fraser and I. Maver, eds., *Glasgow*, vol. II: *1830 to 1912* (Manchester, 1996), pp. 409, 454–7, however, the sewers were not improved until the late 1880s, see below, p. 214.

[50] Halliday, *Great Stink*; on the Embankment, see D. Owen, *The Government of Victorian London, 1855–1889* (Cambridge, Mass. and London, 1982), ch. 4.

[51] On Shaftesbury Avenue, see Owen, *Government of Victorian London*, pp. 108, 114–15, and the corruption over leases for redevelopment, pp. 177–9.

provincial cities was formidable, and investment in the urban infrastructure formed a rising proportion of capital formation between 1850 and 1900. The value of the net stock of domestic reproducible fixed assets in water, gas, trams and electricity (at constant 1900 prices) rose from £17.7m in 1850 to £175.1m in 1900, a 9.9-fold increase. By contrast, fixed assets in manufacturing rose from £165.7m to £478.7m or 2.9-fold.[52] As Marguerite Dupree points out, investment in social overhead capital – hospitals, orphanages, asylums, schools, museums and galleries, prisons and reformatories – was also considerable. One of the major issues in the history of British towns and cities in the mid-Victorian period is: how were these problems of investment in the economic and social infrastructure resolved, how was collective spending on public goods liberated so that urban health and life started to recover from the nadir of the early Victorian period?

Such a question turns attention to the issue of urban governance, which is considered in Part II of this volume. But before analysing the ways in which public and private investment in cities was freed from constraints, we need to consider the changing networks of towns at the regional, national and international level. The changing form of these networks affected the ability of towns to cope with their problems. Individual towns were part of a wider system of governance within the nation-state, which shaped the duties of local authorities, and influenced the level of their resources. Cities varied in the extent of their social problems – the quality of the housing stock, the level of unemployment, the incidence of disease – and the worst areas often had fewer resources. How far should the central state redirect resources? How readily could labour and capital flow from areas of surplus to shortage? To what extent were profits retained in the cities where they were earned, or withdrawn? The circulation of resources and power within the urban system is vitally important.

(ii) NETWORKS

During the eighteenth century, investment in turnpikes, rivers, canals and harbours meant that goods and information flowed more easily between towns. By 1840, railways and the penny post were further speeding and cheapening communication, and they were soon joined by the telegraph and telephone. In her chapter, Lynn Lees outlines the development of an urban network, in part in response to technological changes. She examines the interconnections between cities from the early railways at the start of the period, to telephones, the electricity grid, broadcasting and motor cars at the end. Networks were also shaped by economic interests. Regional urban networks revolved around a major city, which coordinated the activities of towns within a specialised economy. Manchester, for example, provided financial and marketing services for the spinning, weaving and finishing trades of the cotton industry throughout Lancashire.

---

[52] C. Feinstein and S. Pollard, eds., *Studies in Capital Formation in the United Kingdom, 1750–1920* (Oxford, 1988), pp. 300, 304–6, 330.

Leeds fulfilled similar functions in the West Riding, and Birmingham in the West Midlands, for the woollen industry and small metal trades. These regions and their 'capitals' developed distinctive cultural and political lives, which were confident and powerful in the Victorian period, expressed through political movements, local newspapers, distinctive patterns of recreation and dialect.[53] These regional urban systems were nevertheless part of a larger national urban network which was, as Lees shows, shaped by the actions of the state.

The state needs to collect information and communicate resources, messages or personnel across space; the geography of the state is therefore important. The creation of systems of information-gathering, allocation and inspection was contested, in a continuing process which never reached a settled form.[54] The New Poor Law of 1834, for example, grouped together medieval parishes into a new administrative geography of unions, so enabling a more efficient transfer of standard procedures. Ideally, the unions were based on market towns but neat order was subverted by the survival of existing 'incorporations' created by local initiative before 1834, and by the challenge of anti-poor law agitation. In Huddersfield, for example, an alliance of radicals and Tories exploited a rhetoric of local autonomy; the central government countered by appointing new magistrates. The tussle over the geography of the state did not end, for opponents of the poor law in Huddersfield side-stepped the Board of Guardians by providing welfare through different institutions, whether charitable hospitals and dispensaries or model lodging houses supplied by the town council.[55] The poor law was merely the most contentious example of a wider process of monitoring of administration by centrally-based inspectorates. Between 1832 and 1875, more than twenty central inspectorates were created to enforce local administration of laws or standards.[56] Increasingly, control was also exercised through grants paid to authorities on condition that certain standards of efficiency were achieved, which raised a further question: how trustworthy were local authorities in spending the money of the central state?[57]

---

[53] J. Langton, 'The Industrial Revolution and the regional geography of England', *Transaction of the Institute of British Geographer*, new series, 9 (1984), 145–67.

[54] See M. Mann, 'The autonomous power of the state', *Archives Européennes de Sociologie*, 25 (1984), 185–213; M. Mann, *The Sources of Social Power*, vol. II: *The Rise of Classes and Nation States 1760–1914* (Cambridge, 1986); A. Giddens, *A Contemporary Critique of Historical Materialism*, vol. II: *The Nation State and Violence* (Cambridge, 1985); M. Ogborn, 'Local power and state regulation in nineteenth-century Britain', *Transactions of the Institute of British Geographers*, 17 (1992), 215–26; R. Paddison, *The Fragmented State: The Political Geography of Power* (Oxford, 1983). These ideas are applied to the example of the poor law by F. Driver, *Power and Pauperism* (Cambridge, 1993).

[55] See below, p. 361, on the development of voluntary hospitals in Huddersfield, citing H. Marland, *Medicine and Society in Wakefield and Huddersfield 1780–1870* (Cambridge, 1987); the town was also one of the main centres of opposition to compulsory vaccination against smallpox, and a pioneer of infant welfare: see H. Marland, 'A pioneer in infant welfare: the Huddersfield scheme, 1903–20', *Social History of Medicine*, 6 (1993), 25–50.

[56] Driver, *Power and Pauperism*, pp. 28–9, 31.

[57] J. Bulpitt, *Territory and Power in the United Kingdom* (Manchester, 1983), pp. 3, 60–6, 143–61.

A continuing theme throughout the period covered by this volume was the extent to which the central government should allow local authorities auton- omy, and how far they should be controlled. This is the focus of John Davis' chapter on central–local government relations, and it is also a significant issue in Dupree's analysis of welfare provision. On the one hand, granting local author- ities discretion meant that the centre did not need to find revenue, so reducing pressure on the Treasury and delegating potentially explosive issues to the local arena where the central state would not be implicated. On the other hand, the central government might wish to enforce the provision of certain services – an efficient police force or poor law – which meant that it provided grants and imposed control. Should the subventions be linked to local expenditure, meeting a proportion of whatever the authority opted to spend, with the danger that 'extravagant' or progressive councils would place demands on central govern- ment, regardless of the concerns of the chancellor for the national budget? Or should subventions be tied to fixed grants which obliged urban authorities to find the revenue for any new initiative? Such a policy was justified on the grounds that it was safe to grant more autonomy to the localities, for additional costs fell on local taxpayers and there was less need for constant government inspection to protect its interests. It could also be justified as a means of redress- ing inequalities within the urban system. The poorest areas, with the greatest social problems, had the smallest local revenue and were therefore less likely to benefit from grants proportionate to their own spending. Block grants could be awarded according to a formula taking account of the fiscal resources of each council and the demand for various services indicated by demographic meas- ures. A related point was the appropriate tier of local government to provide ser- vices: the central government might prefer larger authorities as more efficient and trustworthy, and move responsibility up the hierarchy, against the wishes of smaller bodies. The transfer or circulation of resources within the urban system – the tension between local autonomy and redistribution – was a major theme throughout the period.[58]

One possible outcome was to transfer responsibility for social services away from the localities and pass them directly to the central government, as in the provision of old-age pensions in 1908 or the National Health Service in 1948. The justification could be equity: national taxation allowed redistribution both between income levels and between parts of the country, unlike local, regressive rates. But it might arise from a desire to impose control from Whitehall. In 1834, the creation of poor law unions in place of parishes was intended to prevent deci- sions on relief being 'warped by private interests'. The creation of plural voting for large ratepayers was designed to take control away from the beneficiaries and

---

[58] C. Bellamy, *Administering Central–Local Relations, 1871–1919* (Manchester, 1988); Bulpitt, *Territory and Power*. These issues were fought out at the time of the reconstruction of local government in 1929: see below, p. 279.

transfer it to those who provided tax revenues.[59] However, central government confidence in the local system was weakened in the early twentieth century. In 1894, multiple votes for Boards of Guardians were abolished and the beneficiaries might have a larger say than taxpayers in local policy, especially with the extension of the franchise in 1918 and the rise of Labour. The response of the government was to pass control of the poor law to larger, more 'responsible', multi-function local authorities, and then in 1934 to transfer relief payments to non-elected, government-appointed bodies.[60] This loss of local responsibility for relief could be seen as an attack on the autonomy of urban authorities, but Dupree suggests it could be seen in a more positive light. By passing the costs of unemployment from the poorest areas to the centre, local authorities were then free to provide better hospitals or infant and maternity care. Local authority spending on welfare was still 40 per cent of government spending on social services between the wars, with wide variations in provision. For example, the provision of infant and maternal care varied between local authorities, reflecting different political decisions and cultural attitudes with clear consequences for patterns of infant and maternal mortality.[61]

Similarly, the geography of voluntary hospitals reflected the assumptions of the local middle class as much as the need for treatment, as Dupree indicates in her comparison of Wakefield and Huddersfield.[62] The geography of health provision remained a contentious issue, fought over by local authorities and the medical profession. A wider regional coordination of hospital services made sense, as did a comprehensive system of local medical services within each district. Should this be achieved by bringing together all health services under the control of the local authority, as many argued in the 1930s? But doctors were fearful of local political control, and preferred a national hospital system which gave them more freedom, and left other medical services to the localities. The tussle over the political geography of health services ran from the end of the First World War to 1948 and the creation of the National Health Service.[63] The map of urban welfare remained highly differentiated up to 1948 and well beyond, for the construction of new hospitals from the late 1950s only slowly removed the long-standing discrepancies of charitable and poor law provision.

---

[59] Driver, *Power and Pauperism*, p. 41, quoting the Poor Law Report of 1834 and the First Annual Report of the Poor Law Commission.

[60] M. A. Crowther, *British Social Policy, 1914–1939* (Basingstoke, 1988), pp. 46–50, 64–6.

[61] Below, pp. 388–9, 391–3; see L. Marks, *Metropolitan Maternity* (Amsterdam and Atlanta, 1996); E. P. Peretz, 'A maternity service for England and Wales: local authority maternity care in the interwar period in Oxfordshire and Tottenham', in J. Garcia, R. Kilpatrick and M. Richards, eds., *The Politics of Maternity Care* (Oxford, 1990), pp. 30–46.

[62] Below, p. 361, citing Marland, *Medicine and Society*; for similar contrasts in Lancashire, see J. V. Pickstone, *Medicine and Industrial Society* (Manchester, 1985), and M. Powell, 'Hospital provision before the NHS: territorial justice or inverse care law?', *Journal of Social Policy*, 21 (1992), 146–63.

[63] On debates over regional control and the tussle between different authorities and the profession, see C. Webster, 'Conflict and consensus: explaining the British health service', *Twentieth Century British History*, 1 (1990), 121–33.

The circulation of resources for welfare is a central theme in the urban history of Britain, and the terms on which welfare was provided had an immediate effect on another process of circulation: migration within the urban network, as discussed by David Feldman. Whether people could respond to the lure of the urban labour market depended on weakening their attachment to the land. In Britain, the demise of small occupiers or peasants was in strong contrast to France where the Revolution entrenched peasants and urban growth was much slower.[64] Changes in land tenure and the adoption of free trade surrendered the countryside, making it the 'lost domain' for consumption by town dwellers rather than a powerful political presence.[65] In Scotland, large landowners had greater power to clear tenants from their land, forcing them to migrate to the growing towns or to emigrate.[66] In Ireland, landowners failed to 'rationalise' agriculture and the population grew until mass migration after the catastrophe of the potato famine of 1846.[67] Migrants into English towns from Scotland and Ireland – and indeed from other parishes in England – did not have any absolute right to poor relief. At the beginning of the period, entitlement to welfare was 'policed' by the local parish or union through the laws of settlement: access to welfare was determined locally rather than nationally, and migration *within* the country could lead to a loss of entitlement. The result, in the opinion of many political economists, was a 'blockage' in circulation.[68] The laws of settlement were reformed and abolished in the course of the nineteenth century, and in the twentieth century a new pattern emerged. Welfare entitlement came to depend on entry into the country rather than a parish settlement, with the result that circulation within Britain was freer but entry into Britain was controlled.[69]

The process did not run in one direction. Circulation of labour was also affected by the housing market, which in some respects became more rigid. In England, working-class housing was held on short lets up to 1914, usually for one week, and movement was endemic. In Scottish cities, the housing market was less flexible, with all except the poorest houses held on long lets with fixed dates of entry. In 1911, the Scottish system was brought more into line with that of England, but flexibility proved to be short-lived. The introduction of rent controls and security of tenure in 1915 made it difficult for migrants to find accommodation in the free market. This was compounded by access to

[64] See P. K. O'Brien and C. Keyder, *Economic Growth in Britain and France, 1780–1914* (London, 1978).

[65] P. Mandler, 'Against "Englishness": English culture and the limits to rural nostalgia, 1850–1940', *TRHS*, 6th series, 7 (1997), 155–75; J. Harris, *Private Lives, Public Spirit: A Social History of Britain, 1870–1914* (Oxford, 1993), pp. 32–6.

[66] T. M. Devine, 'Social responses to agrarian "improvement": the Highland and Lowland clearances in Scotland', in R. A. Houston and I. D. Whyte, eds., *Scottish Society, 1500–1800* (Cambridge, 1989), pp. 148–68.

[67] C. O'Gráda, *Ireland: A New Economic History, 1780–1939* (Cambridge, 1994), pp. 129–30, 224–35.

[68] J. S. Taylor, 'The impact of pauper settlement, 1691–1834', *P&P*, 73 (1976), 42–74.

[69] D. Feldman, *Englishmen and Jews: Social Relations and Political Culture, 1840–1914* (London, 1994); and below, pp. 200, 376.

public housing, where entitlement remained local. Changes in the housing market could therefore frustrate labour mobility and tie people to areas of deprivation.[70]

Urban networks were partly created by the state in a contested process, which shaped the circulation of resources and labour. They were affected by changes in technology, which were themselves influenced by patterns of political control over railways, telegraphs or roads. The structure of businesses also influenced the circulation of capital, credit and profits within the urban hierarchy. In the early nineteenth century, most businessmen still relied on local sources of capital and credit, but these local and regional networks could only function effectively as part of a wider national network. Lancashire needed an inflow of credit; East Anglia had a surplus after the harvest. They were connected through the bankers of the City of London.[71] Scotland had its own distinct banking system, with Edinburgh fulfilling the same functions as London.[72] At least until the mergers of the 1890s, banks had a strong regional identity with local branch networks. The mergers transferred more power to London, and industrial concerns were floated on the Stock Exchange with a loss of control from the localities.[73] Lees follows the Marxian analysis of David Harvey in suggesting a shift of control over capital and profits to the centre and away from the provinces, so leading to a weakening of provincial cities and a loss of their proud independence. The changing geography of capitalism – the control over retail distribution, banking, insurance and industry – is a vital theme, both within Britain and the international economy.[74]

Here is one of the important points in Richard Dennis' account of London, the largest city in the world at the beginning of the period and still the largest city in Europe at the end. London was the apex of the British urban hierarchy with a vital role in coordinating credit systems, and was increasingly important in control over the media and entertainment. It had an unrivalled position within the international urban system as a port and financial and commercial centre, providing capital, insurance and banking and mercantile services for the rest of the world. Similarly, Liverpool should be located within an Atlantic urban

---

[70] D. Englander, *Landlord and Tenant in Urban Britain, 1838–1918* (Oxford, 1983); Daunton, *House and Home*; on council house building in declining areas, see R. Ryder, 'Council house building in County Durham, 1900–39: the local implementation of national policy', in M. J. Daunton, ed., *Councillors and Tenants* (Leicester, 1984), pp. 39–100.

[71] I. S. Black, 'Geography, political economy and the circulation of finance capital in early industrial England', *Journal of Historical Geography*, 15 (1989), 366–84, and 'Money, information and space: banking in early nineteenth-century England and Wales', *Journal of Historical Geography*, 21 (1995), 398–412.

[72] S. G. Checkland, *Scottish Banking: A History, 1695–1973* (Glasgow, 1975); R. Saville, *Bank of Scotland: A History, 1695–1995* (Edinburgh, 1996).

[73] P. L. Cottrell, *Industrial Finance 1830–1914* (London, 1980), ch. 7.

[74] D. Harvey, *Social Justice and the City* (Oxford, 1973), and A. D. King, *Global Cities* (London, 1990).

system of Boston, Baltimore, New York and New Orleans, symbolised by the offices of Cunard or the great merchant house of Brown Brothers.[75] By the First World War, Liverpool was already losing its position relative to the American cities, and the status of the City of London was increasingly hampered by the loss of Britain's financial dominance to the United States.[76] Sarah Palmer considers the history of ports, liminal cities linking regional urban networks within Britain to their suppliers of raw material and markets, connecting flows of migration within the country to immigration and emigration.

The country was criss-crossed by many geographies, creating different maps in the minds of different people. Judges and barristers travelled around circuits based on assize towns. The ancient dioceses of the Church of England were reordered, creating issues of regional identity. The Catholic Church reinstated its diocesan structure in 1850 with its own geography in part reflecting the pattern of Irish immigration, and the Methodists and other nonconformists had their circuits. The geography of sporting and cultural events – rugby, cricket, football, brass bands and choirs – both defined local loyalties and created a national framework for competition, as shown by Reid.

The boundaries of local government posed major issues for utilities such as water, gas and electricity, so that the geography of the state impacted on technological change. A number of authorities might share a single natural area for water, with all the difficulties that implied for ensuring that one town did not pollute another's water supply with sewage or industrial wastes. The technical solution to sewage disposal was highly politicised: a town might prefer to use rivers to carry away wastes, so polluting the next community downstream or provoking local landowners to secure an injunction. Conflicts arose over the exploitation of water resources. In textile districts, dyers needed soft water from rivers which might be polluted and unfit for consumption; sanitary reformers preferred water from wells, which was hard and unsuitable for dyeing. Neighbouring towns might compete for access to water supplies, or might be able to sell surplus capacity to other authorities. Should new regional authorities be created to handle these conflicting demands, based on the river systems and possibly free from immediate democratic control?[77] The control – and often ownership – of gas and electricity were the responsibility of boroughs, which

---

[75] A. Ellis, *Heir of Adventure: The Story of Brown, Shipley and Co., Merchant Bankers, 1810–1960* (London, 1960).

[76] D. Kynaston, *The City of London*, vol. II: *Golden Years, 1890–1914* (London, 1995), R. C. Michie, *The City of London* (London, 1992).

[77] Hamlin, 'Muddling in bumbledom'; C. Hamlin, *A Science of Impurity* (Bristol, 1990); J. A. Hassan, 'The water industry, 1900–1951: a failure of public policy?', in R. Millward and J. Singleton, eds., *The Political Economic of Nationalisation, 1920–1950* (Cambridge, 1995), pp. 189–211; J. A. Hassan, 'The growth and impact of the British water industry in the nineteenth century', *Ec.HR*, 2nd series, 38 (1985), 531–47; J. Sheail, 'Planning, water supplies and ministerial power in inter-war Britain', *Public Administration*, 61 (1983), 386–95; below, pp. 210, 212.

might create difficulties where the economies of scale outstripped the limits of a single authority. As Robert Millward shows in his chapter, municipalisation of gas companies in part depended on the identity between the boundaries of a borough and the limits of a company's supply. By the interwar period, falling profits increased the case for regionalisation to secure greater economies of scale. This was achieved to some extent by private producers, coming together in holding companies, but progress was limited in the industry as a whole by the jealous independence of local authorities. Although the Gas Regulation Act, 1920, allowed neighbouring municipalities to merge their systems, only five joint bodies were created. The answer was nationalisation in 1948 to force through rationalisation, the creation of regional gas boards by *fiat* from above rather than local initiative.[78] In the case of electricity, the discrepancy between local authority units and the scale of efficient generating plant created even greater problems, for it was easier to distribute electricity over long distances than low-pressure town gas, and the economic scale of generating plant increased. Yet in 1913, London had sixty-five electricity suppliers and seventy generating stations, with forty-nine different supply systems, ten frequencies and twenty-four voltage levels for distribution. Responsibility was left to each metropolitan borough in London to provide its own supply or to license a private concern. At a time of bitter hostility between the LCC and the metropolitan boroughs, and Conservative fear of the progressives, cooperation was scarcely feasible. A similar pattern applied in the provinces, with each urban authority responsible for its own supply. When private companies were given the right to cover wider areas, they were barred from the territory of urban authorities and from any district with an existing distributor. Consequently, most urban-industrial districts repeated the pattern of London, with a plethora of suppliers in each town, and a larger private concern in the surrounding district. The solitary exception was the North-East of England; a large private concern did cover most of the area. Otherwise, private companies were unable to operate over a large area, unlike in America or Germany. The eventual resolution to these inefficiencies was to create a national body, the Central Electricity Board.[79] Similar issues arose with telephones. The government initially granted national licences to private companies, but the Post Office subsequently took over the long-distance trunk lines and encouraged urban authorities to provide local services in competition. But in 1911, the postmaster general felt that the result

[78] J. F. Wilson, 'The motives for gas nationalisation: practicality or ideology?', in Millward and Singleton, eds., *Political Economy of Nationalisation*, pp. 144–63; below, pp. 334–5.
[79] T. P. Hughes, *Networks of Power* (Baltimore, 1983), ch. 9 on London and see pp. 443–60 on the North-East Supply Company. L. Hannah, 'Public policy and the advent of large-scale technology: the case of electricity supply in the USA, Germany and Britain', in N. Horn and J. Kocka, eds., *Law and the Formation of Big Enterprises in the Nineteenth and Early Twentieth Centuries* (Göttingen, 1979), pp. 577–89; L. Hannah, *Electricity before Nationalisation* (London, 1979); below, p. 343.

would simply be friction and inefficiency because of divided responsibility. Above all, he pointed out that the municipality was not the natural area for a telephone service, which covered the town, its suburbs and the surrounding district. The answer was to concentrate services in the hands of a single national – and nationalised – monopoly in 1912, and only one local authority (Hull) managed to cling on to its independence.[80] The mapping of these and many other geographies on to the urban system was a constant process of political contestation, technological change and cultural identities.

Issues of governance were vitally important in resolving the problems created by low levels of investment in the urban infrastructure, and in dealing with the difficulties of transferring resources within urban networks. The creation of strong municipalities might solve one difficulty by permitting higher levels of investment, only to create another by erecting political obstacles to a wider, regional, approach to the provision of water, electricity or transport. A fundamental question, to which the contributors to Part II of this volume of the *Cambridge Urban History* provide an answer, is: how were cities able to invest large sums in the urban infrastructure after the shortcomings at the start of our period?

(iii) GOVERNANCE AND COLLECTIVE ACTION

At the outbreak of the Second World War, John Betjeman gently mocked the congregation praying at Westminster Abbey for protection of everything sacred to middle-class respectability. Democracy and good drains were high on the list of the blessings of Englishness. But, as with most ancient traditions, they were newly created in the second half of the nineteenth century. Early Victorian Britain was an undemocratic nation with bad drains, and reform of the political system in the 1830s hindered rather than assisted investment in sewers and sanitation. One of the major concerns of economists and political scientists is to understand the circumstances in which individual rationality gives way to collective action.[81] The problem was particularly acute in British cities in the early Victorian period: how to secure collective action to control pollution of the water or air; how to make sure that if drains *were* supplied, that some industrialists were not 'free-riders' who took the benefits without paying; how to secure financial resources without inspiring a taxpayers' revolt? What was needed was the creation of a sense of trust both between taxpayers and between taxpayers and local government, so that taxpayers had a credible commitment

---

[80] C. R. Perry, *The Victorian Post Office: The Growth of a Bureaucracy* (Woodbridge, 1992); M. J. Daunton, 'The material politics of natural monopoly: gas in Britain, 1830–1914', in Daunton and M. Hilton, eds., *The Politics of Consumption* (forthcoming).

[81] For example, E. Ostrom, *Governing the Commons: The Evolution of Institutions for Collective Action* (Cambridge, 1990), and D. C. North, *Institutions, Institutional Change and Economic Performance* (Cambridge, 1990).

to municipal enterprise. Taxpayers needed to accept that each was paying a fair amount, for any suggestion that others were free-riders would justify non-payment, and create problems of compliance. It was also necessary to create a general assumption that local government would deliver what it promised. The story of British cities in the mid-Victorian period is how these problems of collective action were resolved, and large-scale investment made possible in the later nineteenth century.

Many of the great cities of England suffered from political and administrative paralysis in the second quarter of the nineteenth century. Scotland was, at least to some extent, an exception, for the strong burghal tradition meant that councils still had considerable control over commerce, prices, building standards and work. The Merchants' House and Traders' House – a form of corporate guild – had *ex officio* representation, and the councils often had assets which gave them more financial freedom. Scottish cities therefore had a greater continuity of effective municipal activity than their English counterparts. In Glasgow, for example, divisive partisanship was short-lived with a powerful professional *cadre* to drive through policy, and a 'close-knit fraternity' of leading councillors.[82] In the case of English cities, the 'disruption' of governance in the second quarter of the nineteenth century was more marked. It could be argued that the unreformed municipal corporations of English towns in the eighteenth century were more capable of responding to the problems of towns, and that reform in the 1830s weakened the long-established basis for civic identity without as yet creating a new sense of municipal dignity.

The point is made by Szreter and Hardy that the 'four Ds' of death, disease, deprivation and disruption marked the 1830s and 1840s. The reform movement of the 1830s – the revision of the franchise in 1832, the creation of the New Poor Law in 1834 and a new form of municipal corporation in 1835 – undermined the responsiveness of towns to environmental problems by driving a wedge between urban employers and propertyless workers.[83] We have noted that reform of the poor law shifted control to larger owners and occupiers. Similarly, the Reform Act of 1832 created a more exclusive franchise which reduced the proportion of electors drawn from the ranks of craftsmen and labourers, and confined the vote to men with modest amounts of property. At the local level, the franchise was dependent on the prompt payment of rates, so that securing the vote was a financial transaction which potential voters might decide to

---

[82] W. H. Fraser and I. Maver, 'Tackling the problems', in Fraser and Maver, eds., *Glasgow*, II, p. 395; the remainder of the chapter provides a good account of the efforts to tackle major problems of public health in Glasgow in the mid-Victorian period; for the lack of partisanship, see I. Maver, 'Glasgow's civic government', in Fraser and Maver, eds., *Glasgow*, II, pp. 442–4.

[83] Szreter, 'Economic growth'; on the divisions within local politics, see E. P. Hennock, *Fit and Proper Persons* (London, 1973); E. P. Hennock, 'Finance and politics in urban local government in England, 1835–1900', *HJ*, 6 (1963), 212–25; D. Fraser, *Urban Politics in Victorian England* (Leicester, 1976), pp. 212–25.

forego. The size of the electorate was also influenced by how the rates were fixed by the local council, for they could control whether any particular property exceeded the threshold for the vote. The franchise was therefore actively constituted rather than passively granted.[84]

The result was to create debilitating internal divisions within towns, and to create the circumstances for dominance by small property owners who were concerned with economy. It was in the interest of small property owners to control local government, and to hold down rates which would fall on their assets and profits. Reform might replace a patrician oligarchy of local gentry and urban merchants who were willing to embark on collective spending on urban improvements; it might weaken collective action and undermine the older civic or corporate culture of the towns. By the late 1830s, patrician ascendancy was toppled, and there was no clear consensus about priorities. As Szreter puts it, 'It was much easier to agree to disagree, and for each to get on with minding his own business, in accordance with the liberal and libertarian precepts of the age.' The emphasis was on retrenchment in both central and local government, and it was more difficult to negotiate a political bargain to promote expensive investment.[85]

In the third quarter of the nineteenth century, the ability of urban authorities to respond to problems was transformed, with a greater sense of trust between taxpayers and in the virtues of public action. One Glaswegian was able to claim that the council did far more than maintain order and preserve property; it provided citizens with services they were unable to undertake for themselves, and ensured that they performed duties in the interests of the community. '[T]he general result seems, without exaggeration, to be that the modern City is reverting in importance to the position of the City-state in classical antiquity.'[86] Urban politics and the increasing role of the municipality are explored by Davis, Barry Doyle and R. J. Morris. The hold of ratepayers' retrenchment was broken with the extension of the franchise by the Second Reform Act of 1867 and the Municipal Franchise and Assessed Rates Acts of 1869. The result was that the local electorate quadrupled, bringing in 60 per cent of working-class men, most of whom did not pay their rates in person but as part of their rent through the landlord. As a result, the electorate was less sensitive to costs than the narrow,

---

[84] F. O'Gorman, *Voters, Patrons and Parties: The Unreformed Electoral System of Hanoverian England, 1734–1832* (Oxford, 1989); for the contestation of this definition of property by artisans, see C. Behagg, *Politics and Production in the Early Nineteenth Century* (London, 1990); P. Salmon, 'Electoral reform at work: local politics and national politics, 1832–41' (DPhil., University of Oxford, 1997); Szreter, 'Economic growth', 705–6; Williamson, *Coping with City Growth*. On the local response to the Municipal Corporation Act, and the nature of pre-reform government, see E. J. Dawson, 'Finance and the unreformed borough: a critical appraisal of corporate finance, 1660–1835, with special reference to the boroughs of Nottingham, York and Boston' (PhD thesis, University of Hull, 1978). [85] Szreter, 'Economic growth'; Hennock, 'Finance and politics'.
[86] J. H. Muir, *Glasgow in 1901* (Glasgow and Edinburgh, 1901), quoted in I. Maver, 'Glasgow's city government', in Fraser and Maver, eds., *Glasgow*, II, p. 441.

property-based electorate after 1832. In some cases, such as museums (1845), washhouses (1846) and libraries (1855), new services could only be undertaken after a plebiscite of ratepayers, and the Borough Funds Act, 1872, required approval from a public meeting of owners and ratepayers before seeking a private bill. These procedures could lead to resistance from 'economists', but they also had the virtue of indicating consent to new forms of spending.[87] It also proved possible to create a new form of cross-class alliance, with what Szreter has called a 'neo-patrician political leadership'.[88] As Morris argues, the period from about 1780 to 1860 was marked by voluntaristic agencies: schools, hospitals, libraries were provided by charities which held public meetings and published accounts, offering membership to anyone who paid a subscription; and paving, lighting and poor relief were supplied by a variety of *ad hoc* agencies and trusts, with their own independent rating powers. From about 1860, the emphasis shifted to municipal activity, which took a larger role alongside voluntary associations, moving to the centre of urban culture. Although the growth of municipal activities did not simply 'crowd out' voluntarism, in the later nineteenth century, a larger number of prosperous businessmen started to seek public office as a mark of honour and dignity, and the culture of voluntary associationalism moved into the municipality. Richard Trainor points out that the involvement of middle-class men in local office was astonishing in the late Victorian period. The municipal arena became the space within which all interests in the town could seek influence, and the municipalities entered a new phase in providing parks, libraries, art galleries, town halls or water works. As Morris remarks, 'the word "municipal" was closely associated with notions of local pride, of improvement and of achievement'. The corporate or civic culture of the eighteenth century, which was disrupted in the era of reform, re-emerged in the 1860s and 1870s in a new guise of an active municipal culture. The new world of free trade and circulation was not simply about individualism; it was also about moralism, about responsible participation in a community or (in the words of J. S. Mill) an 'Athenian democracy' of charities, clubs, friendly societies, unions and public office.[89]

The change was the result of a combination of forces. In part, dissenters and evangelicals transferred their energies from voluntary societies to the municipality, as in the case of Joseph Chamberlain in Birmingham who was elected to the council when it seemed that it would take responsibility for elementary education. In part, it was the result of economic self-interest, for investment in the

---

[87] J. Prest, *Liberty and Locality* (Oxford, 1990), pp. 30, 35, 42–5.
[88] J. Davis and D. Tanner, 'The borough franchise after 1867', *HR*, 69 (1996), 306–27; Szreter, 'Economic growth', 717.
[89] Below, pp. 410–14, 699–702; E. F. Biagini, 'Liberalism and direct democracy: John Stuart Mill and the model of ancient Athens', in E. F. Biagini, ed., *Citizenship and Community* (Cambridge, 1996), pp. 21–44.

infrastructure was often good business sense in securing supplies of cheap water for industrial processes or, more generally, increasing the efficiency of the urban economy at a time when many firms relied on 'externalities', a point to which we shall return. Small, competitive family firms had weak internal managerial hierarchies, and relied on external bodies to provide training or marketing, to deal with labour relations and to cope with social welfare. As a result, a plethora of institutions developed, from Chambers of Commerce to civic universities, from Boards of Conciliation to voluntary hospitals. This myriad activity provided the basis for a strong municipal culture.[90]

Practical action depended on the availability of funds. The willingness of councils to spend might well depend on the availability of cheap loans offered by the central government. Tension was likely to exist here, between the urban authorities and the Local Government Board which favoured low interest rates and long periods for repayment, and the Treasury which wanted stricter terms. The larger authorities had more freedom, by turning to the capital market and issuing bonds. As interest rates dropped in the later nineteenth century, large capital schemes became possible, until the rise in interest rates and the flow of funds overseas from 1905 choked off investment in the urban infrastructure.[91] The central government needed to have a sense of trust in the municipalities; and the local electors also needed to be confident that the huge schemes were justified and economical. A balance had to be drawn between controls which were too strict and frustrated activity and the need to establish the legitimacy of public action by establishing transparency, accountability and trust. During the second and third quarters of the nineteenth century, the *central* state created a much greater sense of trust in taxation, by establishing a set of clear accounting rules which ensured that every item of expenditure was voted annually by parliament, with complete transparency; the aim was to prevent expenditure from running out of control, and to establish trust in the integrity and honesty of government. The same project was carried out in local government.

Investment in the urban infrastructure was private as well as public, which posed serious problems for Victorian cities. Utilities such as gas, water, trams and electricity required large amounts of capital. They did not fit into the norm of control and ownership by a family or partnership, and they might therefore be perceived as unaccountable and 'corrupt', using their power against the consumer without the discipline of competition or political accountability. Utility and railway companies diverged from the model of 'personal capitalism' and were

---

[90] On Chamberlain, Hennock, *Fit and Proper Persons*; on the reliance on externalities and weak internal managerial hierarchies, see, for example, W. Lazonick, *Competitive Advantage on the Shop Floor* (Cambridge, Mass., 1990), and H. F. Gospel, *Markets, Firms, and the Management of Labour in Modern Britain* (Cambridge, 1992).

[91] Millward and Sheard, 'Urban fiscal problem', 503–4; A. Offer, 'Empire and social reform: British overseas investment and domestic politics, 1908–14', *HJ*, 26 (1983), 119–38.

open to the same criticism as the East India Company and the railway companies, that they were self-interested monopolists with the power of 'taxation' of consumers through high charges, without representation. One response to the power of gas companies was to establish rival 'consumer' companies, in which customers and shareholders controlled the concern in the same way as subscribers to voluntary associations or members of cooperatives. Another response was to limit the power of the companies by pitting one against the other, which did not succeed for understandable economic reasons: entry costs were high, and companies formed monopolies to supply a town or (in the case of London) a distinct territory.[92] John Stuart Mill expressed deep unease about the outcome, arguing that monopolistic companies were not accountable. In theory, shareholders had power over the directors of companies; in practice, he feared that their input was minimal. By contrast, government agencies were more accountable to electors. As Mill saw it, any 'delegated management' was likely to be 'jobbing, careless and ineffective' compared with personal management by the owner, but the likelihood of these faults was greater in the case of large companies than the state. Despite the dangers that a powerful bureaucracy would keep citizens in a child-like condition, Mill felt that the threat posed by company control of gas and water was still greater: the companies were more irresponsible and unapproachable than the government, and had the power to levy what was, in effect, a compulsory tax. What was needed, therefore, was strict regulation over private companies, to control their prices and profits or to give the right of public purchase at fixed intervals. On such a view, the companies were a threat to a freely competitive market, and control was needed as a complement to the removal of the heavy hand of the state in the regulation of trade through customs duties or chartered monopolies.[93]

The politics of regulation of public utility companies was a serious issue throughout the period. The Gas Works and Water Works Clauses Acts of 1847 laid down that the dividend paid to shareholders should be limited to 10 per cent; when this level was reached consumers could apply to the Quarter Sessions for a reduction in price. In the 1860s, it was usual to add a maximum price, with the right of the company or corporation to seek a variation by applying to arbitrators appointed by the Board of Trade. There was, in other words, concern to limit the 'taxing' powers of the utilities, and to empower consumers. In the case of gas, the 'maximum dividend' system was increasingly replaced from the mid-1870s by sliding scales by which gas prices and dividends were automatically adjusted: a fall in the price of gas by 1d. would permit an increase in the dividend of 0.25 per cent, and vice versa. The aim was to create a common interest

---

[92] For example, D. A. Chatterton, 'State control of public utilities in the nineteenth century: the London gas industry', *Business History*, 14 (1972), 166–78.

[93] J. S. Mill, *Principles of Political Economy* (1st edn, London, 1848; last major revision, London, 1865), ch. XI of Book IV.

of shareholders and consumers in efficiency and improvements in productivity, which would obviously have deleterious effects on wages and workers. In the case of railways, the government created a commission to protect customers against discriminatory pricing, and in 1883 required companies to provide cheap trains in order to encourage dispersal of workers from the congested areas of London. The use of private companies to deal with urban social problems caused serious difficulties. Railway companies resented providing unprofitable services which might drive away other middle-class commuters, at a time of mounting costs and pressure on profit margins. The result was a conflict with trade unions over wages and recognition. The development of tramways and electricity relied on Mill's alternative method of control by establishing the public's right to a 'reversionary profit'. The Tramways Act of 1870 and the Electricity Act of 1882 gave power to local authorities to grant a licence for a fixed interval of twenty-one years, with the right to purchase at 'then value' when the term expired; the period was increased to forty-two years in 1882 for electricity. A similar system was introduced for telephones in 1881, with licences expiring at the end of 1911 when the postmaster general had the right to purchase. There was, therefore, a deep-seated concern about the powers of these 'natural' monopolies, and the need to create methods of democratic accountability in cases of 'delegated management'.[94]

Municipalisation became increasingly common from the middle of the nineteenth century, as is shown in Millward's chapter. The explanation was, in part, that regulations limited the ability of companies to pursue efficient economic strategies, by reducing their profitability and the long-term security of investment. Above all, the problem facing the utilities was political: consumers were largely coterminous with the voters within a municipality. It seemed to many consumers that the best way of creating participation and democratic accountability was through municipalisation. Such an outcome was attractive because of the shift to a representative municipal corporate structure from 1867, so that the urban resident was a tax (rate) payer and consumer. Municipal ownership offered a resolution of the problems of democratic accountability or informed

---

[94] See T. L. Alborn, *Conceiving Companies* (London, 1998). There is an extensive literature: see Hassan, 'Growth and impact of the British water industry'; D. Matthews, 'Laissez-faire and the London gas industry in the nineteenth century: another look', *Ec.HR*, 2nd series, 39 (1986), 244–73; Chatterton, 'State control of public utilities'; PP 1918 III, Select Committee on Gas Undertakings (Statutory Prices); R. Millward, 'The emergence of gas and water monopolies in nineteenth-century Britain: contested markets and public control', in J. Foreman-Peck, ed., *New Perspectives on the Late Victorian Economy* (Cambridge, 1991), pp. 96–124; J. P. McKay, *Tramways and Trolleys* (Princeton, 1976); J. Foreman-Peck and R. Millward, *Public and Private Ownership of British Industry, 1820–1990* (Oxford, 1994); J. R. Kellett, 'Municipal socialism, enterprise and trading in the Victorian city', *UHY* (1978), 36–45; Falkus, 'Development of municipal trading'; on telegraphs and telephones, Perry, *Victorian Post Office*; on railways, F. Dobbin, *Forging Industrial Policy* (Cambridge, 1994), ch. 4. See below, pp. 236, 240, 332, 334.

consumer control, by making the consumer coterminous with the owner and offering an opportunity, through council elections and meetings, to participate in management.

Ownership of utilities also appealed for a further, related, reason: it offered a solution to the limited tax base of local government, by taking profits from private shareholders and making them available for public purposes. The income might be used in order to reduce rate demands and so circumvent the threat of a ratepayers' revolt; or it might be devoted to other purposes, such as in Birmingham where the profits from the gas undertaking were channelled into the provision of an art gallery. Indeed, Joseph Chamberlain was able to portray municipal ownership as a form of accountable and efficient joint-stock company or voluntary association, where the interests of all were in harmony, and the opportunity of 'corruption' removed:

> The leading idea of the English system of municipal government is that of a joint-stock or co-operative enterprise in which the dividends are received in the improved health and the increase in the comfort and happiness of the community. The members of the Council are the directors of this great business, and their fees consist in the confidence, the consideration, and the gratitude of those amongst whom they live. In no other undertaking, whether philanthropic or commercial, are the returns more speedy, more manifest or more beneficial.[95]

Where utilities did survive in private hands, the explanation, as Millward indicates, was partly the existence of alternative sources of revenue for the council, and low levels of population growth. The explanation was also in part political: a lack of identity between the area served by the company and the limits of the local authority. This was most obviously true in London, where companies covered a larger area than any single vestry or metropolitan borough, and public ownership required national political action. In other cases, the utility covered adjacent authorities, which would need to combine to negotiate terms and administer the service – an outcome which usually defeated jealously independent municipalities.[96] London posed particular difficulties, as a result of the conflict between metropolitan boroughs and the London County Council and central government concern at the massive scale of utilities in the metropolis. As a result, the Metropolitan Water Board in 1904, the Port of London Authority in 1908, and London Passenger Transport Board in 1933 adopted a new organisational form of public corporations, with members appointed by the govern-

---

[95] Quoted in L. Jones, 'Public pursuit of private profit? Liberal businessmen and municipal politics in Birmingham, 1865–1900', *Business History*, 25 (1983), 240–59.

[96] Foreman-Peck and Millward, *Public and Private Ownership*; R. Millward and R. Ward, 'The costs of public and private gas enterprises in late nineteenth-century Britain', *Oxford Economic Papers*, 39 (1987), 719–37; R. Millward and R. Ward, 'From private to public ownership of gas undertakings in England and Wales, 1851–1947: chronology, incidence and causes', *Business History*, 35 (1993), 1–21; Millward and Sheard, 'Urban fiscal problem'; below, pp. 333–4.

ment, unlike the normal pattern in provincial cities of ownership and control by democratically elected councils.

The new form of public corporations reflects a growing unease with the reliability of local democracies, and the mounting concern for the viability of local revenues. At some point, the autonomy of local government started to decline, and the strength of the active municipal culture started to recede. The hostility of Mrs Thatcher to local government, cited by John Davis, was merely an extreme version of a general phenomenon of impatience or even alarm at the doings of politicians in the town halls. The creation of a powerful, municipal culture and expenditure on the urban infrastructure was again disrupted towards the end of our period. We return to this point in the final section of the Introduction.

(iv) CONSTRUCTION

The scale of investment in the infrastructure of urban services – roads, railways, sewers, water, gas, electricity – was huge, and created major problems both of collective action and of regulation of private enterprise. Still greater was investment in residential and commercial buildings. At the beginning of the period, specialisation of property had still not developed very far, and housing often combined residence with shops and workshops. In 1851, a large part of industry still consisted of retail-producers and handicrafts supplying local markets, reflected in the polarity of the industrial structure noted by Richard Rodger and David Reeder.[97] Many merchants and professional men ran their business from their own house. The division of home and work was far from complete in 1840; by the end of the century, housing had changed in form and stood in a new relation to work and other elements of the urban environment.

Most middle-class housing in English cities at the beginning of the period was terraced, often with garden squares shared with neighbours, a sort of semi-private space rather than an entirely private garden. The houses were usually vertical in style, stacking rooms on top of each other from a semi-basement for services and servants, to a raised ground-floor dining room, a first-floor drawing room, with bedrooms on the higher levels, with servants in the attic. Space was gendered, with the dining room a male and the drawing room a female preserve; in the largest houses, children and guests also had their delineated areas. From the middle of the nineteenth century, new middle-class housing took a different form. Although terraces continued for modest middle-class housing up to the First World War, the communal garden square gave way to entirely private, individual gardens. In the last quarter of the nineteenth century, the density of building fell and the urban environment became less 'hard', less dominated by roads

---

[97] E. A. Wrigley, *Continuity, Chance and Change* (Cambridge, 1988), pp. 84–6; below, p. 555.

and railings, with narrower roads, small front gardens with privet hedges, lilac trees and laburnum. Houses were less vertical, with greater depth. These middle-class houses were run by a vast army of female servants, usually young and single; the flow of women from one part of the country to the other resulted in skewed demographic structures, as shown by David Gilbert and Humphrey Southall, Feldman, and Szreter and Hardy. More prosperous middle-class families were able to build larger, detached villas, with space for a carriage and male servants. By the interwar period, the general style for middle-class housing shifted to semi-detached houses, less often with servants and with a greater reliance on 'labour saving' equipment. Of course, Scotland differed from England in the style of middle-class housing, especially before 1914. Many middle-class families lived in tenements, usually in defined areas such as the West End of Glasgow. These solid, stone-built, tall buildings produced a completely different built environment from England, more akin to the large cities of continental Europe.[98]

The housing density of English cities was low and strikingly suburban compared with most European cities. Even in London, few middle-class families lived in apartments, unlike Paris, Berlin or Vienna, where the prosperous middle class continued to live close to the city centre.[99] Despite the existence of music halls, theatres and cinemas, the centre of many English cities had a 'dead' feel after offices and shops closed. To some critics, suburbs were the curse of England, the subtopia condemned by W. H. Auden and Christopher Isherwood of semi-detached houses 'isolated from each other like cases of the fever', where house-wives suffered from suburban neurosis. Contempt is easy, but not everyone would prefer Isherwood's exciting life in Weimar Berlin, or would share the belief of Anthony Bertram that flats created a greater sense of community.[100] For most residents, the slightly mocking yet affectionate poems of Betjeman were closer to the mark. Suburbia was a place of peace and order to shelter wives and children from the stresses of the city, and for men to return to a haven of tranquillity at the end of the day, from the competitive strains of the working world to cultivate a garden or to socialise in a way that was not intrusive or a threat to privacy. By the 1930s, suburbs were largely owner-occupied, an investment and an expression of pride. The availability of cheap and abundant mortgages, a fall in land prices as a result of agricultural depression, and higher real wages for those in work, led to a housing boom and the emergence of new, large-scale developers and builders.[101] Women had a large role in maintaining the social

[98] There is a large literature on the patterns of construction and finance, but less on the social life of suburbs: see Dyos, *Victorian Suburb*; F. M. L. Thompson, ed., *The Rise of Suburbia* (Leicester, 1982); F. M. L. Thompson, *Hampstead* (London, 1974); on Glasgow, below, pp. 449–51, M. A. Simpson, 'The West End of Glasgow, 1830–1914', in M. A. Simpson and T. H. Lloyd, eds., *Middle-Class Housing in Britain* (Newton Abbot, 1977), pp. 44–85; on building cycles, see S. B. Saul, 'House-building in England, 1890–1914', *Ec.HR*, 2nd series, 15 (1962); on the changing design of housing, S. Muthesius, *The English Terraced House* (London and New Haven, 1982).
[99] Olsen, *City as a Work of Art*. [100] See below, p. 203.
[101] See below, pp. 202–3, 444–6, 451–2, 487–8 and Plate 19.

fabric of the suburbs, centred on the activities of children, on tea-parties and coffee mornings. Tennis and golf clubs, whist drives and bridge evenings, church fêtes and jumble sales, created a sense of social connectedness. And it was always possible to get a bus or tram to town in order to shop, visit a café or catch a matinee at the cinema.[102]

Working-class housing in English cities became less cellular and promiscuous in its use of space, and increasingly self-contained in the third quarter of the nineteenth century. Courts and alleyways gave way to a more open grid of 'by-law' housing with separate yards or small gardens, rear access in order to empty privies or ashpits, and individual sanitation. The change was only partly explained by the imposition of stricter controls by local authorities. There was also a fall in land prices as British farmers and landowners felt the full force of competition from foreign grain. Free trade therefore had a significant impact on cities, not simply in providing urban consumers with cheap food but also in reducing the supply cost of land. The result was both a higher level of migration to British towns than in France, as Feldman points out, and an outward march of suburbia on to cheap land. A large part of the unprecedented rise in working-class standards of living after 1873 went on higher quality housing. Unlike most other prices, rents rose in the later nineteenth century, reflecting higher quality accommodation rather than an increase in the profit margin of landlords.

Despite the overall increase in housing standards, and the consequent improvements in urban health and the growth of a more domesticated existence, huge variations remained between towns, both in rents and in the style and quality of accommodation. As with so many other variables, there was a very marked difference between towns. At one extreme was Leicester, where only 1.1 per cent of the population lived in overcrowded accommodation in 1911 (over two persons per room); at the other extreme was Gateshead, with 33.7 per cent of the population overcrowded. In 1905, the index of rent in Leicester was 48 (where London was 100), and wages of skilled building workers 94; in Gateshead, rents were higher at 66 and the wage index lower at 90.[103] Standards of sanitation also varied. In Leicester, about two-thirds of houses had water closets by 1896, and the council obtained powers to require owners to replace remaining privies and pail closets in order to prevent a recurrence of the typhoid epidemic of 1893/4. The task was largely completed by 1902, with the assistance of public subventions. In Nottingham – another town in the East Midlands with a similar economic base – water closets were still under half the sanitary conveniences in the city in 1908, and the medical officer of health estimated that the incidence of typhoid in houses with pail closets was four and a half times as great as in houses with water closets. These variations in housing standards contributed to

---

[102] See R. McKibbin, *Classes and Cultures: England* (Oxford, 1998), on patterns of sociability and recreation.   [103] Daunton, *House and Home*, pp. 39, 67, 81.

the divergence in mortality, not only in the case of typhoid and 'summer diar-rhoea', but also in tuberculosis where overcrowding was an important factor in transmission. Of course, Scotland had its own distinctive style of tenemented accommodation. In Glasgow, the level of overcrowding in 1911 was 55.7 per cent, and the bulk of property had only two rooms, with shared sanitary and laundry facilities on common staircases or courtyards. The Scottish house style created great problems of management for owners and the council, in ensuring the cleanliness of communal areas.[104]

Despite the undoubted improvement in urban housing in the later nineteenth century, problems certainly remained. A large part of the population still lived in poor quality, densely packed housing of the Industrial Revolution, and dem-olition for new commercial buildings or roads and railways meant that the pop-ulation was simply packed into the remaining stock. The poor could not afford higher quality by-law housing, and occupied property vacated by the middle class in their move to newer suburbs. In areas such as Islington, single-family houses built in the first half of the nineteenth century were subdivided, with shared sanitation and all the problems of deterioration resulting from multi-occupancy. The process could be applauded as 'filtering up', allowing the poor to leave squalid slums for newer, better-built houses. Reality could be less com-forting, not least after the First World War when rent control removed the incen-tive to maintain property. In the 1860s, some authorities (for example, Glasgow in 1866) obtained private acts to demolish inner-city housing, and in 1875 the Cross Act gave local authorities general powers of demolition in order to cut out 'plague spots'. The medical metaphor was significant, suggesting that destruc-tion of areas with a high incidence of disease and death would create a healthy urban environment. The slums were not understood in terms of the current structure of urban society, of low wages or casual labour markets, but rather of past error which could be swept away. A number of points followed. One was that the owners of the slums should be compensated at market value as unwit-ting legatees of the mistakes of an earlier generation. The second was that recon-struction should be left to private or philanthropic bodies. Problems were soon to emerge. The cost of compensation proved high, for many slum districts in fact contained valuable commercial property such as public houses or work-shops. The high price of cleared land meant that private enterprise was not attracted to redevelop, so that philanthropic bodies, model dwelling companies or local authorities stepped into the gap. The emergence of council housing on a modest scale after the Housing of the Working Classes Act of 1890 was to trans-form British cities between the world wars.[105]

[104] *Ibid*, pp. 33–4, 55–7, 168–9, 254–5; R. Rodger, *Edinburgh and the Transformation of the Nineteenth-Century City: Land, Property and Trust* (Cambridge, forthcoming).

[105] Wohl, *Eternal Slum*; Yelling, *Slums and Slum Clearance*; C. M. Allan, 'The genesis of British urban redevelopment with special reference to Glasgow', *Ec.HR*, 2nd series, 18 (1965), 598–613.

The urban environment was intensely political. As we have seen, access to space was contested, and by the end of the century land itself was a political issue. Rather than *compensating* the owners of slums, many reformers and radicals argued that public investment increased property values, and owners should therefore pay a 'betterment' levy to the council. Many radicals claimed that the system of short leases found in many towns resulted in slums as the leases came to their close: owners of houses had no incentive to maintain property which reverted to the ground landlords. They also argued that large landowners could impose monopoly prices, holding land off the market and forcing up its price. Of course, these points were contested by ground landlords who argued that the provision of land for a low annual charge *encouraged* building by speculative builders who were short of capital to purchase sites outright. Owners of land claimed that they were investing in roads and drainage, making land available ahead of demand, rather than constraining the supply. By the turn of the century, the case against landowners widened to claim that *all* increases in land values were socially created by the enterprise of the community, and that the burdens of local taxation should be passed to the owners of urban sites. The land campaign appealed to Lloyd George as a political response to the Liberals' need to retain middle-class support and at the same time to respond to the challenge of Labour, by creating a common identity as active producers versus parasitical landowners. This policy was intended both to solve the fiscal problem and to force land on to the market for housing and industry. The approach assumed that more land should be made available, at a cheaper price, for housing and industry, and the first Town and Country Planning Act of 1909 created the framework for coherent development of land around towns.[106]

The policy had more rhetorical force than practical outcome, for rent for land was a small and declining share of national income, and did not offer a large source of revenue. The taxation of land values soon failed, both because of practical problems in assessing the value of sites and because Lloyd George was dependent on Conservative support in the coalition government. Interest in the land question did survive within the Labour party, especially in large urban authorities, and resurfaced in the Second World War with the Uthwatt report. As Jim Yelling shows, this report recommended that the state should be able to withhold permission for development without compensation to the owner; where permission was given, any gain should be taxed away. The Town Planning Act of 1947 showed both continuity and a change in emphasis from the Edwardian policy. It continued the Liberal attack on the 'unearned increment', imposing a 100 per cent tax on property development. But it moved away from the earlier assumption that more land should be available for builders. In the

---

[106] Below, pp. 478–84, 525–35; D. Reeder, 'The politics of urban leaseholds in late Victorian Britain', *International Review of Social History*, 6 (1961), 413–30; A. Offer, *Property and Politics, 1870–1914* (Cambridge, 1981).

1930s, outward expansion was no longer seen as an unequivocal benefit. It was attacked for creating a formless sprawl which threatened the countryside and led to an urban environment without defined centres. The countryside was preserved and made available for urban recreation by the new national parks of 1948 – a culmination of the aspirations of the Ramblers Association, Youth Hostels Association and other urban groups. As Yelling points out, planners such as Patrick Abercrombie argued for an active regional policy, with green belts to create distinct communities and to construct new towns as 'balanced', self-contained communities with a mix of social classes and industry. Abigail Beach and Nick Tiratsoo consider the social assumptions and beliefs of the town planners. Urban Britain was contained by its green belts, which made access to land a major consideration for house builders, and drove up prices.[107]

Landownership and the appropriation of rising values were contentious issues; and so was the tenure of housing. Many owners were drawn from the lower middle class or even working class, investing in a few houses as a safe, local and visible investment to provide a form of pension fund or means of support for dependants. The relationship between landlord and tenant was an important feature of urban society. The relative power of the parties varied over the building cycle, which was a pronounced feature of British towns and cities. Speculative builders tended to over-build, with a spate of bankruptcies, high levels of vacancies and a strong bargaining position for tenants. The glut was slowly removed, and a new boom only started after a period of shortages which gave the advantage to the landlord. The relationship was also affected by the legal system. In England, landlords could summarily evict defaulting tenants under the act of 1837. However, eviction did not allow landlords to recover rent, and most tenants simply did a 'flit' before landlords took action to recover possession. In order to obtain payment of overdue rent, owners relied on the common law of distraint to seize goods, but this was increasingly curtailed by judges who were more sympathetic to the tenants (and particularly women who were usually responsible for payment) than to their landlords. In Scotland, the law of landlord and tenants was much harsher, the courts were used much more frequently, and housing was highly politicised to secure reform of the system of long-lets. By the early twentieth century, the rental market in both England and Scotland was facing a serious erosion of profitability. The burden of local taxation rose, and it proved difficult to pass on the cost to tenants at a time of stable real wages and a glut of housing after the boom at the turn of the century. The emergence

---

[107] P. Hall *et al.*, *The Containment of Urban England*, 2 vols. (London, 1973); D. Massey and A. Catalano, *Capital and Land* (London, 1978); F. Trentmann, 'Civilisation and its discontents: English neo-romanticism and the transformation of anti-modernism in twentieth-century western culture', *Journal of Contemporary History*, 29 (1994), 583–625; J. Sheail, *Rural Conservation in Inter-War Britain* (Oxford, 1981); P. Mandler, 'Politics and the English landscape since the First World War', *Huntington Library Quarterly*, 55 (1992), 459–76; below, pp. 490–2, 525–50.

of other outlets for safe investments – such as local government bonds – without the hassles of managing property and tenants meant that investment in rental property was less appealing prior to the First World War. The situation was transformed by the war, when housing shortages and inflation allowed landlords to increase their rents and recoup some of their lost ground. However, tenant protests and rent strikes – especially in Glasgow where housing was so intensely politicised – threatened to disrupt the war effort, and the government imposed rent and mortgage controls in 1915, which meant that house owners and mortgagors experienced a decline in profitability.[108]

Although rent and mortgage control was intended to expire at the end of the war, decontrol was not feasible at a time of serious unrest and housing shortages, with the alarming prospect of soaring rents. The answer was a massive programme of council house building by local councils with considerable financial aid from central government in order to end the shortage and then to permit decontrol. However, retrenchment meant that the programme was cut and some form of rent control remained in force up to the Second World War, when it was again extended. Council house building resumed in the 1920s, to less generous standards with most of the cost financed by local authorities. In the 1930s, 'general purpose' housing largely ceased and most council housing was for slum clearance. The central government imposed an obligation on local authorities to demolish insanitary housing and rehouse the inhabitants. Owners received much less generous compensation than in earlier clearance programmes, but other problems remained. Residents of the slums could scarcely afford the rents of their new accommodation, and one solution was to increase the rents of 'general purpose' housing – a policy which provoked considerable resentment by 'respectable' towards 'unrespectable' tenants.[109] Although the programme was unprecedented in scale, a backlog still remained at the start of the Second World War, and wartime destruction and low investment in maintenance led to a further deterioration in the older stock. The problem of slum property still remained in 1945, and inspired even greater clearance programmes in the 1950s and 1960s.

The council housing schemes created new difficulties, as Pooley's case study of Liverpool shows. The large suburban estates assumed a single male breadwinner with a defined journey to work, which caused particular problems for women and adolescents who were taken away from the labour market of the inner city. Child care became problematic with the disruption of ties of kin and neighbourhood, and access to cheap inner-city food markets was more difficult. Local authorities lacked financial resources to provide social facilities. In London

---

[108] Daunton, *House and Home*; Englander, *Landlord and Tenant*.

[109] Englander, *Landlord and Tenant*; M. Swenarton, *Homes Fit for Heroes* (London, 1981); J. A. Yelling, *Slums and Redevelopment* (London, 1992); R. Finnegan, 'Council housing in Leeds, 1919–39: social policy and urban change', in Daunton, ed., *Councillors and Tenants*, pp. 101–53.

and other large cities, the problem was compounded when estates were built outside their own boundaries, so putting demands on neighbouring authorities. The difficulties between the LCC and Essex County Council, for example, resulted in a shift to inner-city flats in the 1930s. Some commentators were concerned that residents of the new estates were marginalised from society, a threat to integration and social stability – a sentiment which led the National Council of Social Services to set up the New Estates Committee. This was a further stage in the debate over the form of urban communities and the desire to create social cohesion, which ran from the settlement houses to the garden cities and new towns programme (see Beach and Tiratsoo). The perceived problems of the interwar council housing programme helped to shape post-war attitudes, so that the 'mistakes' of Dagenham and Withenshaw should be avoided at Harlow and Stevenage by mixing social classes and creating self-contained communities.[110]

The volume of local authority housing was one of the most striking and peculiar features of British towns, and only the socialist states of Eastern Europe could rival the level of public housing found in Glasgow or Birmingham. The housing market was highly differentiated by 1950, falling into three main categories. The bulk of new rented property was publicly owned for the working class, and most new middle-class or skilled working-class property was owner-occupied – with a fearful concern that values should not be eroded by proximity to council tenants. Older, poorly maintained private rental property was the only option for those unable to secure a council house because they were migrants or had not yet acquired enough 'points', or were incapable of obtaining a mortgage. Towns were divided by tenurial status, clearly demarcated between public rented housing, private owner-occupied housing and a decaying and neglected stock of rented property – a situation which created great problems after the Second World War and the start of large-scale migration from the Commonwealth.[111]

In addition to investment in housing, towns and cities acquired a growing range of public or charitable buildings. Hospitals, schools, workhouses and churches existed in the eighteenth century, but were now built in increasing numbers and to a more lavish scale. The reform of the funding of the poor law in the 1860s meant that more workhouses were built to enforce the stern discipline of less eligibility and indoor relief, and new institutions were provided for the care of the sick and orphans.[112] Board schools and police stations, workhouses and asylums and isolation hospitals, created a new architecture of power and authority in Victorian cities, replacing a concern for circulation with a drive for surveillance and observation, for mapping and classification. By the end of

[110] K. Young and P. Garside, *Metropolitan London* (London, 1982). The best account of a large estate is A. Olechnowicz, *Working-Class Housing in England between the Wars* (Oxford, 1997); see also the case studies in Daunton, ed., *Councillors and Tenants*; and below, pp. 203–4, 455–64, 537–9.
[111] For example, J. Rex and R. Moore, *Race, Community and Conflict: A Study of Sparkbrook* (London, 1967). [112] See Driver, *Power and Pauperism*, ch. 5.

the nineteenth century, most towns of any size and pretension had a public and cultural core of buildings: a monumental town hall, public library, art gallery and museum, a concert hall and possibly a civic university. In many cases, the initiative started with middle-class voluntarism before moving into the civic sphere, such as at Bristol where the debts of the Museum and Library Society were paid off by Sir Charles Wathen in 1893, on condition that the council then took over the building. The municipality and philanthropy continued to work together, for the new central library was paid for by a bequest, and the new art gallery by the cigarette manufacturer, Sir W. H. Wills.[113]

City centres were also transformed by commercial developments. The construction of great railway stations created a new type of space for interaction and social contamination. The surrounding streets were thronged with traffic, and the growth of hotels.[114] Retailing was transformed with the growth of department stores and chain stores, linked to the suburbs by omnibus, tram and railways. Specialist business premises were constructed. Joint-stock banks used palatial premises to inspire confidence, and branch offices were soon erected in the centre of even modest market towns. Insurance companies were amongst the largest businesses, employing considerable numbers of clerical workers and aspiring to an image of moral probity. In London, the huge offices of the Prudential insurance company dominated Holborn, designed by Alfred Waterhouse who was also architect of Manchester Town Hall and University. He symbolises some of the changes in the Victorian city, with his brothers Edwin – the founder of a leading firm of accountants and one of the creators of the modern profession – and Theodore, a solicitor. Together, they were involved in floating office companies to supply rooms or chambers to professional partnerships or commercial concerns. Peter Scott analyses the development of these property companies, in the provision of both offices and retailing space. By the 1860s, specialised offices were starting to transform the City of London, both as the headquarters of large concerns and as chambers for a plethora of stockbrokers, merchants, accountants, lawyers, engineers and so on. The introduction of hydraulic power allowed easier access to upper floors by means of passenger lifts – as well as providing a source of power for stage machinery, for opening dock gates and operating cranes and hoists. These offices often clustered around an exchange, where goods were bought and sold, and freight and credit arranged. In Manchester and London, large warehouses held stocks of textiles to supply the domestic and international market. In the great import centres of London, Liverpool, Bristol and Hull, bonded warehouses held dutiable commodities such as tobacco, wine and tea, or bulky raw materials such as wool or cotton for sale on the exchanges.

---

[113] The best case study is H. E. Meller, *Leisure and the Changing City, 1870–1914* (London, 1976), from which the example comes (pp. 65–70); also, R. J. Morris, 'Middle-class culture, 1700–1914', in D. Fraser, ed., *A History of Modern Leeds* (Manchester, 1980), pp. 200–22.

[114] Kellett, *Impact of Railways*, especially ch. 10.

Grain was milled and sugar refined in large plants which were amongst the largest users of steam power at the beginning of the period, and amongst the largest industrial buildings.[115]

By the late Victorian period, large factories were much more typical, leading to the stereotype of the northern or Midland town dominated by steam-powered spinning mills, weaving sheds and engineering works, surrounded by grids of by-law housing. But even then, many industrial districts still had small-scale units, such as cutlery in Sheffield, metals in Birmingham or hosiery in Leicester.[116] In Victorian Britain, most industrial concerns had weak internal managerial hierarchies, and relied on systems outside the firm at the level of the town or regional network. Historians of Victorian industrial concerns have pursued a comparison with competitors in America and Germany where productivity started to outstrip Britain by the last quarter of the nineteenth century. Many American industrial firms started to create strong *internal* managerial systems, with closer control over labour discipline and remuneration, and allocation of resources within multi-plant concerns. By contrast, most British industrial concerns remained smaller, with weak managerial hierarchies.[117] But simply to criticise British industrialists for failing to follow the American route to high productivity fails to address the characteristic features of the British pattern of production. In particular, two features stand out, and are of great importance for the history of British towns and cities. One is the connection between the firm and the family, which was mediated by the social networks of industrial towns and districts; the second is the nature of the urban economy which allowed firms with weak internal management to survive and even flourish.

(v) THE ECONOMY OF CITIES

A common view of British history in the nineteenth century assumes a division between industrial capitalism in the North, and a commercial and service economy in the South. According to this school of thought, the industrial bour-

[115] E. Jones, ed., *The Memoirs of Edwin Waterhouse: A Founder of Price Waterhouse* (London, 1988); I. S. Black, 'Symbolic capital: the London and Westminster Bank headquarters, 1836–38', *Landscape Research*, 21 (1996), 55–72; I. S. Black, 'Bankers, architects and the design of financial headquarters in the mid-Victorian City of London', in C. Cunningham and J. Anderson, eds., *The Hidden Ice-Berg of Architectural History: Papers from the Annual Symposium of the Society of Architectural Historians of Great Britain, 1998* (London, 1998), pp. 45–58; I. S. Black, 'Re-building the heart of the empire: bank headquarters in the City of London, 1919–39', in D. Arnold, ed., *The Metropolis and Its Image* (Oxford, 1999), pp. 127–52; J. Summerson, 'The Victorian rebuilding of the City of London', *LJ*, 3 (1977), 163–85; J. Summerson, *The London Building World of the Eighteen-Sixties* (London, 1973); E. Green, *Banking: An Illustrated History* (Oxford, 1989).
[116] S. Pollard, *A History of Labour in Sheffield* (Liverpool, 1959); A. Fox, 'Industrial relations in nineteenth-century Birmingham', *Oxford Economic Papers*, 7 (1955), 57–70.
[117] Gospel, *Markets, Firms and the Management of Labour*; Lazonick, *Competitive Advantage on the Shop Floor.*

geoisie in the factory towns of the North and Midlands had a brief moment of cultural and social self-confidence in the mid-Victorian period, as the heroes of Samuel Smiles' *Self Help* and the critics of the landed aristocracy. But in the late nineteenth century – so the argument runs – they were culturally and politically marginalised by a new social elite, created by a fusion between the prestige of land and the wealth of finance based in London and the South-East. The result, in the opinion of Michael Thompson, was the absence of a confident urban elite: the social structure of towns lacked an 'upper storey', and the civic splendour of the mid-Victorian period was a mere hint of what might have been.[118] How far should this account be accepted?

A regional divide between an industrial North and a service economy in the South *is* clear from Gilbert and Southall's chapter. The service and commercial economy was highly successful. Although Britain dominated world trade in manufactures between 1841 and 1911, over half the new jobs created over the period were in the service sector.[119] And the productivity of the service sector was impressive, compared with the experience in Germany. In the case of manufacturing and construction, German labour productivity caught up with the level of the United Kingdom by the early twentieth century; in utilities and transport, Germany pulled far ahead. But Britain retained, and even widened, its advantage in distribution and finance, and professional and personal services. These trends had a significant urban dimension, which cannot be understood by a simple division of towns between industry and finance or services. There were also important interconnections, with considerable significance for the urban economy.

Utilities were overwhelmingly urban, and their comparative performance may be understood in terms of different patterns of political control. British towns were more successful than their German counterparts in the mid-nineteenth century in resolving the problems of investment in the urban infrastructure, but this advantage was eroded at the end of the century. British cities encountered problems in raising finance for large-scale investments from about 1900, as a result of competition with overseas loans and the failure to reform urban

---

[118] For example, W. D. Rubinstein, 'Wealth, elites and the class structure of modern Britain', *P&P*, 76 (1977), 99–126; P. J. Cain and A. G. Hopkins, 'Gentlemanly capitalism and British overseas expansion, II: new imperialism, 1850–1945', *Ec.HR*, 2nd series, 40 (1987), 1–26; Y. Cassis, 'Bankers in English society in the late nineteenth century', *Ec.HR*, 2nd series, 38 (1985) 210–29; F. M. L. Thompson has made the case in a number of places, including 'Introduction', *Rise of Suburbia*, p. 16; *The Rise of Respectable Society* (London, 1988), pp. 166, 173, 360; 'The landed aristocracy and business elites in Victorian Britain', in G. Delille, ed., *Les noblesses européenes au XIXe siècle* (Rome and Milan, 1988), pp. 270–1, 275, 278–9; 'Town and city', in Thompson, ed., *The Cambridge Social History of Britain, 1750–1950*, vol. I: *Regions and Communities* (Cambridge, 1990), pp. 47–8, 67, 72

[119] Below, p. 623; C. H. Lee, 'Regional growth and structural change in Victorian Britain', *Ec.HR*, 2nd series, 34 (1981), 452.

Table 1.1 *German and UK labour productivity levels 1871–1950 (UK= 100)*

	1871	1891	1911	1929	1950
Manufacturing	92.6	94.0	119.3	104.7	96.0
Construction	76.1	90.1	117.7	50.2	84.2
Utilities	31.3	64.2	103.8	158.6	120.6
Transport and communications	96.8	147.5	216.9	151.2	122.0
Distribution and finance	70.7	45.9	52.5	50.3	50.7
Professional and personal services	89.7	77.0	76.3	99.8	94.2
Agriculture	55.7	53.7	67.3	56.9	41.2

Source: S. N. Broadberry, 'Anglo-German productivity differences, 1870–1990: a sectoral analysis', *European Review of Economic History*, 1 (1997), table 3, p. 251.

taxation. In Germany, cities were able to draw on the state income tax, and fiscal problems were more at the level of the Reich.[120] We have already noted that the small scale of urban authorities hampered economies of scale: institutional or political factors contributed to the relative inefficiency of British utilities by the First World War.

Differences in the productivity of distribution may also be explained by the political and social structures of towns. In Britain, guild regulation had disappeared by the nineteenth century; in Germany, corporate forms survived until the onset of rapid economic change in the later nineteenth century, which led to considerable opposition to large-scale stores and a greater degree of politicisation. In France, guilds were abolished with the Revolution, but the system of *patentes* – a tax based on particular trades and the scale of the firm – gave traders a political identity.[121] In Britain, chains of specialist stores developed in the second half of the nineteenth century, often with long and complex systems of supply. Although British manufacturers were slow to develop multi-plant firms with tight internal managerial controls, the pattern in retailing and financial services was different. W. H. Smith, for example, obtained a monopoly of book and newspaper stalls at railway stations, and developed a national system of distribution. Thomas Lipton, the Glaswegian grocer, set up stores in many British cities to supply cheap tea, bacon, sugar, butter from around the world.[122] Lipton's success was predicated upon the reduction of duties on imports, and a loss of

[120] N. Ferguson, 'Public finance and national security: the domestic origins of the First World War re-visited', *P&P*, 142 (1994), 141–68, and J. von Kruedner, 'The Franckenstein paradox in the intergovernmental fiscal relations of imperial Germany', in P.-C. Witt, ed., *Wealth and Taxation in Central Europe: The History and Sociology of Public Finance* (Leamington Spa, 1987), pp. 111–23.
[121] G. Crossick, 'Shopkeepers and the state in Britain, 1870–1914', in G. Crossick and H.-G. Haupt, eds., *Shopkeepers and Master Artisans in Nineteenth-Century Europe* (London, 1984), pp. 260–1.
[122] C. Wilson, *First with the News* (London, 1985); P. Mathias, *Retailing Revolution* (London, 1967).

protection for British farmers; by contrast, German agriculture was still large, protected and inefficient. In Britain, the efficiency of agriculture allowed the release of large numbers of people from the land in the eighteenth century to live in towns; the countryside was emptied and became the subject of nostalgia, rather than remaining politically significant as in Germany or France. This affected how the countryside was used by town dwellers. Rather than a simple flight from urban and industrial modernity into the embrace of rural nostalgia, urban residents consumed the country in a new way which was reflected in the growth of urban-based clubs and societies such as the Youth Hostels Association, Cyclists' Touring Club and Ramblers Association, or motorists with their Shell guides. By the interwar period, the land campaign had lost its political edge and Conservative politicians could now turn to the country for different political purposes. Stanley Baldwin's portrayal of Englishmen as country dwellers helped to resolve tensions, by suggesting that they were not fundamentally divided between capital and labour, and were not essentially imperialists.[123]

Commerce and finance were not rigidly separated from industry, for each major industrial area had a full complement of commercial and financial services catering for its needs. Scotland had its own distinctive banking and financial system; English industrial regions had a degree of financial autonomy at least until the end of the nineteenth century when bank mergers led to a greater degree of centralisation. As Morris has shown, the commercial and professional middle class provided the leadership for local voluntary associations. Far from turning their backs on industry, they realised that their own prosperity depended on the success of production.[124] In his chapter on the middle class, Trainor suggests that any simple divide between an industrial and financial middle class obscures the differences and similarities of their roles in various towns. He suggests that the commercial and financial middle class was often linked with industry in provincial cities; the middle-class elites of provinces had influence in their own town and could deal with the wealthy elite of London.[125] Of course, the City of London was heavily involved with international finance, but the relationship with the provinces was more complicated than simple ignorance and neglect. The financial system of the City of London formed the hub around which the localities revolved, directing funds from one area to another. And too much should not be made of the failure of the City to invest in provincial industry on the lines of German or American financiers. The involvement of financiers or bankers with industry in Germany and the United States might

---

[123] Mandler, 'Against "Englishness"'; Trentmann, 'Civilisation and its discontents'; D. Cannadine, *G. M. Trevelyan: A Life in History* (London, 1992), ch. 4.

[124] R. J. Morris, *Class, Sect and Party* (Manchester, 1990).

[125] R. H. Trainor, 'The gentrification of Victorian and Edwardian industrialists', in A. L. Beier, D. Cannadine and J. M. Rosenheim, eds., *The First Modern Society* (Cambridge, 1989), pp. 167–97; and below, pp. 688–91, 708–9.

provide an opportunity for rent seeking rather than efficiency, and might distort industrial decisions. British firms were able to rely on retained profits and local networks, and were able to draw on the City of London for trade finance which provided a *different* linkage between finance and industry.[126]

The existence of service or professional occupations might well be vital to the growth of cities. As C. J. Simon and Clark Nardinelli argue, cities can be understood as 'information based human capital' embodied in business professionals such as bankers, accountants and lawyers. They found that the most rapidly growing English cities between 1861 and 1961 had the highest proportions of business professionals, which they characterise as the 'talk of the bourgeoisie'. 'Cities where the "talk is good", meaning that it carries useful information, grow more rapidly than cities where the talk is mostly noise.'[127] On this view, the important factor leading to the growth of towns was not simply the availability of raw material or factories, but face-to-face meetings between people with high human capital. The point was made by Alexis De Tocqueville in his journeys to England. He asked the French consul at Liverpool whether the success of British industrial towns depended on the natural resources of coal and iron. The consul replied that 'intellectual qualities and, in general, practical knowledge and acquired advantages play a much greater part still'. De Tocqueville was struck by two features in comparison with France, which at first glance seemed contradictory. One was the extent to which people joined associations to further science, politics, pleasure and business. The other was a well-developed individuality and competitiveness. De Tocqueville tried to bring the two characteristics together.

> Association is a means suggested by sense and necessity for getting things unattainable by isolated effort. But the spirit of individuality comes in on every side; it recurs in every aspect of things. Perhaps one might suggest that it has indirectly helped the development of the other spirit by inspiring every man with greater ambitions and desires than one finds elsewhere. That being so, the need to club together is more generally felt, because the urge to get things is more general and stronger.[128]

Although these comments tell us much about De Tocqueville's political philosophy, they also provide some insight into the social and economic structures of British cities in the nineteenth century.

As we have noted, 'talk' in the early nineteenth-century city could lead to disruption and to a failure to agree. We have analysed how the circumstances for 'good talk' were recreated in the mid-Victorian period in order to allow investment in the urban infrastructure. This collective action was based on private conversations within chapels and churches, charities and trade associations, creating

---

[126] Cottrell, *Industrial Finance.*

[127] C. J. Simon and C. Nardinelli, 'The talk of the town: human capital, information and the growth of English cities, 1861–1961', *Explorations in Economic History*, 33 (1996), 385, 407.

[128] A. De Tocqueville, *Journeys to England and Ireland*, trans. G. Lawrence and K. P. Mayer, ed. J. Mayer (London, 1958), pp. 113, 87–8.

what may be called 'social capital' or a sense of interconnectedness.[129] The Victorian city was highly innovative in forging new forms of sociability, by both the middle class and the working class, helping to create a sense of stability and trust, which is obscured by emphasising the loss of a confident urban elite and its flight into the embrace of the countryside. In reality, British towns and cities were remarkably successful in constructing a wide range of institutions and social practices. Trainor's analysis of the elite of Glasgow shows how the public life of the city was knit together by interlocking positions within leading public and philanthropic bodies – the council, Infirmary, Merchants' House and Chamber of Commerce. In Glasgow, the overlapping membership had a structural basis, for the head of the Merchants' House was *ex officio* a member of the city council, which in turn appointed representatives to leading institutions. But even in the absence of formal institutional structures, it was common for members of the elite to cross the boundaries between local government, philanthropy and business or professional associations. They could also mingle in the neutral world of choral societies, music festivals, the Volunteers, the court of the university, golf club or Masons.[130] Reid provides many examples of the growth of 'social capital' through religion and recreation and sociability. Women played a major role, mediating relationships through the domestic sphere by invitations to dine, or through the world of charity and religion. Men acquired a reputation as connoiseurs or collectors, as members of literary and scientific societies. Men and women took part in philharmonic societies and music festivals.

The middle class of British cities turned to history, not as a flight from present realities and industrial capitalism, but as a means of establishing the pedigree and pride of their city. As Charles Dellheim has pointed out, 'Victorians reconstructed the past to create a cultural tradition that balanced progress and continuity. Reshaping traditions allowed them to forge connections with their history as they liberated themselves from its social, economic and theological restraints . . . These links to the past were bridges to the future more than detours from the present.' Thus Manchester Town Hall was decorated by paintings of the medieval past, linked in one continuous history to the Industrial Revolution and the emergence of political confidence. Similarly, the wool exchange in Bradford – where John Ruskin denounced the money grubbing philistinism of the merchants – combined images of Bishop Blaise and the medieval wool trade with representations of modern industrialists as elements in the proud story of England. It was a claim to provincial identity and to national significance.[131] History could provide legitimacy, by suggesting cohesion with the past rather than rupture.

---

[129] The phrase is associated with R. D. Putnam: see *Bowling Alone: The Collapse and Revival of American Community Life* (New York, 2000)

[130] R. H. Trainor, *Black Country Elites* (Oxford, 1993); Meller, *Leisure and the Changing City*, ch. 4; R. H. Trainor, 'The elite', in Fraser and Maver, eds., *Glasgow*, II, pp. 233, 235, 246.

[131] C. Dellheim, *The Face of the Past* (Cambridge, 1982); see also M. Hardman, *Ruskin and Bradford* (Manchester, 1986).

Similarly, the art collections of prosperous Victorian businessmen were not simple emulation of the aristocracy and gentry, but means of establishing a distinct identity. As Dianne Sachko Macleod argues, art was central to affirming a middle-class identity. In the mid-Victorian period, narrative detail entertained and instructed, celebrating the virtues and probity of the bourgeoisie; in the late Victorian period, middle-class taste turned to eroto-religious subjects and images of the countryside as an escapist fantasy or to suggest that all was still well in a world of rapid change. Art was made available to a wider public, through municipal galleries and reproduction by print dealers and advertisers. Simply to interpret this taste as anti-urban and anti-industrial misses the crucial point: how was art used to signal cultural acuity and discrimination; how could art educate and inspire the working class and civilise rapidly growing towns?[132] These issues are considered in Caroline Arscott's chapter, where she analyses the related theme of artistic representations of the city.

The development of 'social capital' in Victorian towns was closely related to the nature of the urban economy. One way of reconciling the seeming tension between individualism and associational activity is through the notion of bounded competition. In the absence of limited liability, business activity was highly risky with great dangers for dependants and descendants; assets needed to be held apart from the firm to provide for old age or for widows and dependent children, through a marriage settlement or a family trust. The trustees were male relatives or members of the local business community and professional class – a means of creating social connection within a competitive economic order. Funds were often invested in the urban fabric, by lending money on mortgage or through the ownership of houses. Further, charitable trusts held property to provide revenue for hospitals and education. Hence trusteeship created a social network, cutting across business competition and rivalry.[133]

As Rodger and Reeder show in their chapter, the urban economy had two poles, of fragmented, small-producer capitalism, and a larger, more concentrated, sector. Personal reputation was crucial to the success of small businesses, with their heavy dependence on creditworthiness resting on reputation in commercial dealings and as respectable family men. 'Social capital' was therefore crucial to participation in a competitive market economy. Small-scale enterprise might well be dynamic and flexible, such as scientific instrument and watchmakers in Clerkenwell, cutlers in Sheffield, small metal goods in Birmingham, tailoring in the East End. Sweatshops did exist, but workshop production was not simply anachronistic and exploitative. Rather, it offered 'flexible specialisation', permitting a rapid response to changing markets with reasonable levels of skill and wages for male workers, and an efficient use of capital and labour. Paul Johnson points out that business historians usually explain the emergence of large, integrated

[132] D. S. Macleod, *Art and the Victorian Middle Class* (Cambridge, 1996).
[133] Rodger, *Edinburgh and the Transformation of the Nineteenth-Century City.*

firms by their ability to reduce 'transaction costs' – the time spent in discovering the best source of raw materials or semi-finished goods, in monitoring quality, enforcing contracts and finding markets. This argument could be modified to propose that integrated firms were not needed where the urban economy operated effectively to supply these services, and costs were already low. The external economies of the city could therefore permit the survival of small firms, such as in the highly specialised craft districts producing furniture in Bethnal Green or metal goods in Birmingham. Workers and masters could exchange information in public houses or clubs, and in the daily course of business. The costs of monitoring and enforcement were low, for workshops were clustered together with a high degree of reciprocity and short duration of exchanges. These informal patterns could be supplemented by more formal arrangements, for joint ownership of power plant for small producers, common marketing of finished goods or the provision of schools of design. Problems would arise when a greater effort of research and development was needed within firms rather than through the external urban economy, or where more formal support was needed by public action. In Britain, urban authorities were less successful than their counterparts in some European cities in sustaining flexible specialisation.[134]

Towns were labour markets with large externalities, as Gilbert and Southall show in their chapter. Employers could rely on the external labour market, drawing on a pool of skill within the town or region. Even large industrial concerns followed a similar pattern to small firms. In shipbuilding, for example, specialist subcontractors supplied the shipyards, and much of the training of workers and the terms of their employment were left to skilled unions such as the Boilermakers or Amalgamated Society of Engineers.[135] Large cotton-spinning firms in Oldham did not negotiate with their own workers, but joined together in a board of conciliation to deal with unionised workers, establishing a spinning list which set the framework for wages for all employers in the town. The agreement expired at a fixed time, with upper and lower limits for variation in wages, so limiting competition between firms at least in respect to one major cost – and one with the potentiality for threating the stability of urban society by pitting capital against labour.[136] In some cases, businesses developed an internal labour market, investing in the training of workers and creating clear promotion hierarchies. This pattern emerged in large transport and service companies, such as railways and banks.[137] The precise way in which labour markets operated was a major variable in the nature of cities, affecting patterns of migration, residence

---

[134] C. Sabel and J. Zeitlin, 'Historical alternatives to mass production: politics, markets and technology in nineteenth-century industrialisation', *P&P*, 108 (1985), 133–76; P. Johnson, 'Economic development and industrial dynamism in Victorian London', *LJ*, 21 (1996), 27–37; below, pp. 122–3.   [135] Johnson, 'Economic development'; Sabel and Zeitlin, 'Historical alternatives'.
[136] Lazonick, *Competitive Advantage on the Shop Floor*.
[137] See M. Savage, 'Career, mobility and class formation: British banking workers and the lower middle class', in A. G. Miles and D. Vincent, eds., *Building European Society* (Manchester, 1993), pp. 196–216.

and demography. Casual workers were trapped in neighbourhoods by the need for local information on work, and the need for credit; artisans had more information about opportunities in other towns, but even they became much more residentially stable in the later nineteenth century. As Mike Savage and Andy Miles have argued, neighbourhoods were crucial to the formation of class in the later Victorian city. The middle classes, and even the lower middle classes who had lived alongside workers, moved out to suburbia and left the central city to the working class. Levels of migration dropped, and so did population turnover as a result of changes in the housing market after the First World War. The geographical horizons of many workers were restricted, bound by the neighbourhood. One measure of this phenomenon is patterns of marriage: at the end of the nineteenth century, in 80 per cent of working-class marriages, both the bride and groom came from the same district, compared with 25 per cent in middle-class marriages. Working-class neighbourhoods matured and gained in solidarity, with dense patterns of sociability through hobbies and clubs, or female bonds of support and sharing, which were important components of the provision of welfare. They might become part of the wider urban society and national networks, for friendly societies or brass bands or football teams were part of city and national affiliations, but the experience was rather different from middle-class families, who had ties of personal friendship and acquaintance, of education and business, at a regional or national level.[138]

The flow of young migrants into towns and cities in search of jobs, in addition to the high birth rates, meant that towns at the beginning of the period were youthful, in comparison with the more elderly age structure at the end.[139] Whether children were able to obtain work varied between towns. In the textile towns of the North, children were able to work from an early age; even when compulsory education was introduced, they were still allowed to leave school when they reached a minimum standard. In other districts, such as London, there were fewer openings for children and many attended school as a means of filling their time and keeping them off the streets.[140] Juvenile crime, and the attempt to provide 'moral' activities for adolescents and young adults in the city, was a serious concern. Ragged schools and orphanages, school board visitors and truancy schools, the Scouts and Boys Brigade attempted to reform and save children. The dangerous, corrupting influence of the city – its public houses and music halls, its prostitutes and vice – on young men and women was countered

---

[138] M. Savage and A. Miles, *The Remaking of the British Working Class, 1840–1940* (London, 1994), pp. 62–72; M. Savage, 'Urban history and social class: two paradigms', *UH*, 20 (1993), 61–77; H. MacLeod, *Class and Religion in the Late Victorian City* (London, 1974); E. Ross, 'Survival networks – women's neighbourhood sharing in London before World War I', *History Workshop*, 15 (1983), 4–27; C. Chinn, *They Worked All Their Lives* (Manchester, 1988); on the strength of working-class culture, see R. McKibbin, *The Ideologies of Class* (Oxford, 1990). [139] See below, pp. 630, 640.

[140] H. Cunningham, 'The employment and unemployment of children in England, *c.* 1680–1851', *P&P*, 126 (1990), 115–50.

by the Young Men's Christian Association and Young Women's Christian Association.[141]

The ability of women to find paid work outside the home varied between towns, from a high level of participation in textile towns to the low levels in mining and heavy industrial districts. As Szreter and Hardy show, the age and rate of marriage varied between towns. Where women could find work, they had less reason to marry early and a pregnancy would mean loss of income; where work was less available, early marriage was more likely and childbirth did not involve a loss of female earnings. The variation between towns in age and rates of marriage was not simply a matter of economistic calculation, for the labour market could affect attitudes to masculinity. The culture of the coalfields was more dominated by men with their experience of common danger in the hidden world of the pit, than the textile towns where men and women often worked in the same mill. The reduction in the birth rate at the end of the nineteenth century depended on a changing definition of masculinity and male restraint in reducing the frequency of sexual intercourse. Social norms changed, from a large family indicating virility and manhood, to fecklessness and lack of restraint. Labour markets were one important influence on these changes, but simple economic determinism should be modified to take account of social and cultural assumptions. Recent research has suggested that marriage and fertility were influenced not only by occupation and class, but also by locally based communities and their norms.[142]

Urban labour markets also influenced patterns of welfare provision. As we have noted, local provision of welfare by public bodies and charities remained important. A similar point applies to self-help organisations, which varied in their form and level of membership between towns, in part reflecting the differences in employment. The shipbuilding districts of the Tyne, for example, had a marked cycle of boom and slump. As a result, unions of relatively well-paid workers provided unemployment assistance to cover periods of depression, linked to the requirement that men did not accept work at a low wage and undermine the union rate. Although textile districts did experience serious slumps – above all during the cotton famine of the 1860s – and were affected by the trade cycle, the amplitude of fluctuations was generally less than in industries producing capital goods. Workers received reasonably steady and secure wages, which allowed them to pay weekly contributions to friendly societies to provide sick pay and medical treatment. The large, affiliated friendly societies such as the Rechabites and Oddfellows started in the mill towns of Lancashire.

---

[141] Meller, *Leisure and the Changing City*, chs. 6 and 7.

[142] On child care patterns in two contrasting towns in Lancashire, see E. Roberts, 'Working class standards of living in Barrow and Lancaster, 1890–1914', *Ec.HR*, 2nd series, 30 (1977), 306–21; on the decline of fertility, see S. Szreter, *Fertility, Class and Gender in Britain, 1860–1940* (Cambridge, 1996); and below, pp. 651–66.

In the coalfields, the dangers of injury and disaster led to the creation of accident funds and medical facilities, and the provision of pensions or homes for miners forced out of the pit by accidents and age. The exact pattern varied between coalfields, and provides a warning against any simple determinism. In the North-East of England, welfare provision concentrated on pensions and homes for retired miners; in South Wales, miners developed medical services which started to provide maternal and infant welfare, and used building clubs to become owner-occupiers. These decisions reflected different institutional structures and cultural assumptions between the two coalfields. The 'mix' of welfare provision therefore differed between towns, with different priorities and patterns of spending which influenced the life chances of residents. Of course, these patterns of provision came under serious pressure during the industrial depression and mass unemployment of the interwar period, and the newer industrial districts of the Midlands and South did not have anything like the same level of membership.

British cities were a complex balance between the diseconomies of pollution and disease, and the economies of information and knowledge. The diseconomies needed large-scale investment in the urban infrastructure, which was provided in the later nineteenth century. The external economies of information and knowledge, the creation of 'social capital', meant that Victorian cities combined competition with an active associational life. As Lees suggests, social tensions were less in larger towns, with their well-developed institutions to mediate disputes.[143] However, at some point this institutional structure and web of social connections ceased to cope, and the external economies of the city became much less significant. Chambers of Commerce or boards of conciliation could do very little to restructure the economy of industrial towns when their major industry collapsed in the interwar period. And large, capital-intensive industrial concerns placed more emphasis on internal management and research, with considerably less interest in the economies of the city. The relationship between the economy of cities and of industrial firms started to shift between the wars. But before returning to consider the strains within the system of urban governance and adaptability, we should note one further aspect of the economy of cities: they were sites for consumption as well as production.

(vi) CONSUMING THE CITY: IDENTITY AND SUBJECTIVITY

Charles Dickens understood London as a system of circulation, where disease could be spread from one place or social group to another. Baudelaire had a very different image of Paris, less as a system than as a dream of anonymity and

---

[143] L. H. Lees, 'The study of social conflict in English industrial towns', *UHY* (1980), 34–43.

disconnection. These cultural responses to the two capital cities did reflect the physical realities of streets and boulevards, whose construction was shaped by different social and cultural assumptions. However, the contrast should not be overdrawn. British cities were sites of consumption, and were themselves consumed; they were stages where subjectivity and identity were explored. These themes are explored by John Walton's chapter on consumption, and by Richard Dennis in the case of London. As Charles Lamb, the essayist, remarked 'London itself is a pantomime and a masquerade', and he 'cried with fulness of joy at the multitudinous scenes of life in the crowded streets of ever dear London'.[144] The increase in circulation and surveillance within cities was not all loss and control; it also meant safety from disease and crime, a greater opportunity to consume the city. Marshall Berman has suggested that the nineteenth-century city was a site for experimentation, of 'fractured subjectivity' and the 'mystification of modern life'. Despite the efforts of sanitary reformers and the spread of surveillance, the 'moving chaos' of the nineteenth-century city, with its congestion, noise and complexity, was alive and exciting.[145]

A history of the city could be written in phenomenological terms, its onslaught on the senses of sight, sound and smell.[146] The work of the sanitary reformers meant that cities were 'deodorised' by the end of the nineteenth century. Smells are elusive, and not easily measured or categorised; as we have seen, the sanitary reformers expressed the stench of cities by textures, touch and sight. Odours might well have become worse – most notoriously in the 'great stink' of 1858 when Disraeli was driven from the Commons, and the curtains were soaked in chloride of lime to keep the stench of the Thames at bay.[147] Certainly, smells were more keenly perceived or less tolerated, both in the urban environment and to the individual body. The construction of sewers and water supplies, the improvement of roads and refuse collection, meant that cities were cleaner. The provision of piped water and water closets in houses, the provision of public urinals, laundries and bathhouses, meant that individual standards of cleanliness changed. New building codes required builders to insert damp-proof courses to prevent bricks sucking up the emanations of the soil. Air bricks and grilles were required to permit a renewal of air in houses; and architects devised complicated systems of drawing foul air from public buildings. Glazed tiles, linoleum and paintwork allowed walls and floors to be washed, and soap and scouring powders were amongst the first mass advertised goods.[148]

As space was redefined in British cities, the street became more a place of transit and the home more a place for private pleasures. Nevertheless, there were

---

[144] Winter, *London's Teeming Streets*, p. 8.   [145] Berman, *All That is Solid*.
[146] See S. Connor, 'The modern auditory', in R. Porter, ed., *Rewriting the Self: Histories from the Middle Ages to the Present* (London, 1997), pp. 203–23.   [147] Halliday, *Great Stink*, pp. 17–18.
[148] On the history of smell in Paris, see A. Corbin, *The Foul and the Fragrant*, trans. M. L. Kochan (Leamington Spa, 1996).

places to linger and stroll, to sit and spectate. Londoners lacked grand boulevards; they, and their provincial counterparts, did have open spaces where inhabitants could parade and observe. On the crown estate in central London, Hyde Park, Regents Park and St James Park allowed members of Society to drive or ride, observing and being observed, with rules for entry and acceptance.[149] Victoria Park opened to the residents of east London in 1845, offering the pleasures of promenading and observing to a wider section of society, under the gaze of the park keeper and his injunctions to keep off the grass. By 1892, Victoria Park received 303,515 visitors on a single day.[150] The park was designed by James Pennethorne who also planned New Oxford Street as an artery to cut through the slums of St Giles and relieve the flow of traffic on the Strand and Fleet Street. In a sense, the two projects were connected: restricting the street to a neutral space for transit was complemented by the creation of specialised spaces for rec-reation – public parks, football stadia and cricket grounds – with defined rules for access and use, enforced by park keepers and stewards. Reid shows the emer-gence of a clearer definition of time for work and recreation than in the past, when football or fairs spilled over into the streets and blurred the line between work and leisure time. And some towns specialised in recreation. Most famous and demotic was Blackpool where the workers of the Lancashire mill towns spent their week of release from toil; more genteel, with their palm courts and orchestras, were Eastbourne and Bournemouth.[151]

The campaigns to preserve open spaces such as Hampstead Heath and Epping Forest, the pressure from the Commons Preservation Society and the National Trust, were part of a much wider consumption of the countryside by urban res-idents, escaping on bicycles or by train and motor car to hike and visit beauty spots. This was less a sign of a rejection of urbanism, a backward looking nostal-gia for the countryside, than the emergence of a new form of urban consump-tion of the countryside which was now a 'lost domain'. Historic towns themselves started to become centres for tourism, and the architectural 'heritage' a source of pride and celebration. The historic cities of York, Bath, Chester, Edinburgh and the many market and cathedral towns were interpreted in print and in tussles over renovation. In Bath, for example, the discovery of the Roman baths at the end of the nineteenth century posed the question of the relationship with its Georgian fabric, which was generally held in low esteem. What should be destroyed in order to 'modernise' the city? These issues came up in an acute form when the Georgian pump rooms were destroyed in a bombing raid in the war: should they be rebuilt, or replaced by some more 'useful' and 'modern' facil-ity? Should new roads be driven through the city in order to cope with new volumes of motor traffic? In these debates, the writings of urban historians

---

[149] L. Davidoff, *The Best Circles* (London, 1973).   [150] Winter, *London's Teeming Streets.*
[151] J. K. Walton, *The English Seaside Resort* (Leicester, 1983); Cannadine, *Lords and Landlords*, part III on Eastbourne.

became important, with the early work of John Summerson on Georgian London during the Second World War, and the emergence of conservation societies.[152]

As cities were 'deodorised', so they started to blaze with light. At the beginning of the period, the nocturnal city posed problems for security; darkness provided a cover for vice and crime, an escape from the respectability of day time. Night was a time to retreat into safety from the public spaces of the city, behind closed doors. The law recognised the difference. Bailiffs could not enter the home of debtors to seize their goods between sunset and sunrise; by contrast, presence on the streets after dark was good reason for suspicion. The authorities wished to control the night, tightening up closing times of public houses, herding the homeless into night shelters and reforming the system of night watchmen. When the Metropolitan Police was established in 1829, one reason was the 'nightly indecorum and danger of the London streets'. The provision of light was an aid to surveillance, making the city – or at least parts of it – safe at night. The pleasures of the evening and night were democratised, extended from those who could afford a carriage and torch bearer to penetrate the gloom, or could attend balls and dinners in private houses glittering with candle light. The first gas street lighting in London dates from 1807, on a small scale; by the mid-nineteenth century, it was commonplace on streets, in public buildings, shops, public houses and theatres, as well as in the homes of the middle class. Until the installation of prepayment meters in the 1880s, gas was not found in working-class houses, which were lit by cheap tallow candles and, at the end of the century, paraffin lamps. The lack of cheap gas light in working-class houses was seen as a serious problem in the 1840s – how could workers keep themselves and their houses clean, and would they not be tempted by bright gin palaces in contrast with their 'dark and comfortless homes'?[153] By the 1880s, gas was starting to be replaced by electricity, at least in public buildings. Gas and electricity extended the pleasures of music halls, gin palaces, theatres, cinemas, to a larger number of people, and transformed city centres with advertising and window displays. Electricity powered underground railways and tramcars from the turn of the century, carrying people to and from the suburbs in comfort and speed, and lighting them on their way home. Town centres were transformed into spaces for pleasure by night, taking on a new existence as offices and factories closed.[154]

The emergence or extension of specialised shopping districts in London's West End and the major provincial cities connected with debates over gender and morality. Was there a danger that the lavish new stores seduced women to pledge their husbands' credit on luxuries, so threatening the household

---

[152] Mandler, 'Against "Englishness"'; Dellheim, *Face of the Past*; P. Borsay, *The Image of Georgian Bath, 1700–2000* (Oxford, 2000).　[153] Quoted in Falkus, 'Development of municipal trading', 159.
[154] J. Schlör, *Nights in the Big City* (London, 1998).

economy? Samuel Smiles feared that women's 'rage for dress and finery' rivalled the 'corrupt and debauched age of Louis XV', to the ruination of husbands. Judges were inclined to agree, arguing that men should only be responsible for their wives spending on household necessaries. This created difficulties for the owners of the new department stores, with their largely female clientele. In 1880, the owners of Whiteley's store took Mr Sharpe, the keeper of records at the Guildhall in the City of London, to court for the recovery of £12 owed for a sealskin coat bought by his wife. Sharpe argued that the coat was extravagant, and the judge accepted that it could not be termed a necessity; he was absolved from the debt. Large department stores were therefore open to attack for encouraging irrational consumption and de-stabilising gender relations – a case seized upon by their small specialist competitors who could portray themselves as more responsible. The owners of department stores countered that they offered havens of respectability and safety rather than temptation, a sign of a healthy rather than a pathological urban economy. Retailers needed to 'moralise' the city centre, offering women rest rooms and restaurants, even reading and writing rooms, employing door keepers and floor-walkers to maintain decorum and exclude unsuitable customers. By the 1880s, the department store and the shopping streets of the city centre were widely considered to be acceptable places for women, one of the pleasures of the late Victorian city.[155]

Music halls and theatres faced a similar debate, fought between the advocates of temperance and morality, and the desire for freedom and enjoyment. Caught in the middle were the local authorities which licensed music halls and public houses. They had a practical concern for public safety in case of fire or overcrowding, and their regulations helped to determine the form of new buildings and their layout. But these regulations could easily extend into concerns for morality and social behaviour – or prudery and interference in harmless pleasures. The result was a tussle over the number of public houses or standards of acceptable behaviour in the music halls. The LCC, for example, employed a team of inspectors to visit halls, noting the behaviour of the audience (especially women) and recording *risqué* lyrics. In 1894, the council refused any new application for a music hall licence which served alcohol, and closed down the Empire music hall on Leicester Square because of the conduct of women soliciting members of the audience. This interference of Progressive councillors in the pleasures of other people was not welcomed by those who wished to have a drink on their evening of relaxation, and these issues could spill over into local elections. Although the local authorities had powers to license cinemas, the film

---

[155] E. Rappaport, '"A husband and his wife's dresses": consumer credit and the debtor family in England, 1864–1914', in V. De Grazia and E. Furlough, eds., *The Sex of Things* (Berkeley and London, 1996), pp. 163–87; and E. Rappaport, '"The halls of temptation": gender, politics and the construction of the department store in late Victorian London', *Journal of British Studies*, 35 (1996), 58–83. See Plate 26.

industry did manage to free itself from local control over its films, which would obviously cause serious difficulties for distribution. The industry successfully argued for self-regulation by the British Board of Film Censors, which was established in 1912 to ensure that nothing was shown to demoralise the public. The cost of music halls and cinemas was high, and owners were concerned to encourage as wide an attendance as possible, so there was a degree of self-interest in ensuring that performers and films did not overstep certain standards of acceptability.[156] Cities were places of contestation over morality and pleasure, between surveillance and transgression.

(vii) CHALLENGING THE URBAN VARIABLE

We have argued that the Victorian and Edwardian city was successful in accumulating 'social capital', in creating the conditions for collective action to deal with urban diseconomies and in establishing the conditions for powerful external economies. But at some point problems did set in: urban self-confidence was eroded, and the political, social and economic importance of cities declined. Contributors to this volume agree on the main changes, but not on when the change started and how far it had proceeded by 1950.

In his account of the middle class, Trainor suggests that the elite started to distance itself from urban government compared to the remarkable degree of involvement in the later nineteenth century, so leaving the lower middle class and Labour to battle over scraps of urban power. In his account, the interwar years disrupted middle-class leadership in towns. Indeed, it could even be argued that the trend started before the First World War. By the end of the nineteenth century, the banking system was consolidated in the hands of a number of large concerns, so weakening the financial autonomy of the local urban economy. The shift in the control over banks from the localities to head offices in London meant a reduction in sensitivity to local needs, with less involvement in local social networks and economic regeneration. Similarly, the emergence of national legislation on health and unemployment insurance in 1911 obliged trade associations to negotiate with the central government, marking the beginning of a shift from local concerns for poor law provision and charity. The pressures of wartime shortages, with controls over resources and higher levels of business taxation, led to the formation of the first major national employers' organisation, the Federation of British Industry.

These trends went still further between the wars. The concern of the Treasury to control local spending, and the fear that urban authorities were less trustworthy, meant the loss of a degree of local autonomy. And Neville Chamberlain feared that the partial derating of industry in 1929 would remove any incentive

---

[156] On the LCC, see Pennybacker, *Vision for London*, pp. 210–40.

for industrialists to serve on town and city councils. Unlike many continental European countries, national politicians did not continue to rely on a local power base. In France, the prime minister might well serve as the mayor of a town, retaining a foothold in both local and national politics. In Britain, Neville Chamberlain and Herbert Morrison were exceptional in moving into national politics after a significant involvement in the government of Birmingham and London. The growth of larger industrial concerns, with merger waves and flotations at the end of the First World War and again around 1929, weakened the identity between industrialists and the local town. The external labour market and sources of information declined in importance, with the growth of internal training and career structures, and the development of research and development within the firm. In all of these ways, a strong case can be made for an erosion of the urban variable by 1939.

However, Rodger and Reeder claim that the extent of change should not be exaggerated in the interwar period. Although they accept that an independent civic culture was being eroded in the northern industrial cities, they believe that the character of industrial districts survived to the end of the period, and the decomposition of local capital should not be exaggerated. Much depended on the local economic base of towns. In Leicester and Nottingham, with relatively small-scale firms in hosiery and lace, and a prosperous domestic market, the vitality of the urban economy and politics continued throughout the interwar period. Of course, in areas of deep economic depression, urban authorities with straitened finances could do little to restructure the local economy. Even so, local or regional issues should not be overlooked. The so-called 'rationalisation' of industry to reduce excess capacity provided many opportunities for bargaining between industrialists over the location of cuts, with their devastating consequences for the urban community. These tussles were usually within trade associations, acting through a national framework involving the Bank of England or the central government, with little or no involvement by democratically accountable town and city councils.

Where urban authorities did have a significant role was in the allocation of resources for different social policies, with measurable effects on infant or maternal mortality, or educational opportunity. The urban authorities were involved in slum clearance schemes on a large scale, and were major house builders and owners; they operated transport services and utilities, schools and libraries. Indeed, the retreat of the middle class from urban government could be looked at in a different and more positive way: it gave an opportunity for the working class to take power, and to use the municipality to develop social services. The Labour party had an important role in increasing the functions of urban government between the wars. As Savage and Miles argue, the Labour party built up support in the working-class neighbourhoods which had emerged in the late nineteenth century, developing a ward organisation with female membership, and so compensating for the difficulties experienced by trade unions during the depression. This ward structure, and female participation, turned attention to the provision of municipal services, especially for women and children. The retreat of the urban elite meant that Labour was now the main supporter of an active municipal culture, against the opposition of 'ratepayers' concerned about local spending. Above all, Herbert Morrison presented a vision of efficient urban services in London, providing consumers with high standards of transport, housing and health services. Labour could present itself as a party of effective urban government, rather than of trade union self-interest.[157]

What urban authorities could not do was generate an efficient urban economy in the face of massive depression. Declining industrial sectors such as cotton reduced excess capacity throughout Lancashire, rather than operating at the level of the town to restructure the local economy. Any positive action was the result of central government policy, on a modest scale from the 1930s and more powerfully after the Second World War, to relocate industry or service employment from the prosperous South-East and Midlands. The response was national, an attempt to rectify the problems of distribution of employment and wealth from outside rather than within the urban system.

(viii) CONCLUSION

Despite the loss of urban autonomy and the mounting challenge to the urban variable by the end of our period, the chapters in this third volume of the *Cambridge Urban History* provide a convincing case that towns and cities matter. Demographic historians realise that the decline in mortality varied between areas, and reflected local political decisions; they accept the importance of communities in explaining the fall in birth rates. Historians of welfare – of charity, public spending and self-help – are increasingly interested in the different 'mix' of provision at the local as well as national level, and realise that local resources remained vitally important throughout the period. The resolution of problems of collective action to allow investment in the infrastructure, and to regulate 'free riders' and natural monopolies, is central to the political history of the period. The changing balance between urban diseconomies and economies helps to explain the economic performance of Britain, and the nature of the business concern. The ability of towns and cities to create 'social capital' – patterns of sociability and associations – helped to mediate conflicts and create social stability and economic efficiency.

These issues, amongst many others, are giving a new interest to urban history

---

[157] Savage and Miles, *Remaking of the British Working Class*, pp. 68–9, 82–5; see also M. Savage, 'Urban politics and the rise of the Labour party, 1919–39', in L. Jamieson and H. Corr, eds., *State, Private Life and Political Change* (Basingstoke, 1990), pp. 204–23. On the debate on local autonomy, see below, pp. 278–86, 339, 389, 416–19, 583–92, 676.

which was to some extent lost in the 1970s and 1980s, when sociologists such as Philip Abrams cast doubt on the importance of towns as an independent variable. In his view, towns were mere containers for more important explanatory variables. Historians were warned of the dangers of 'reification' of the city, making it a distinct entity; they were urged to study wider processes. But the problem was also from within urban history, at least for the Victorian period. Much attention was paid to the construction of towns, to the operation of the land market and the explanation of building cycles; much less attention was paid to the social experience of life in the new suburbs, or the ways in which different parts of the town fitted together – how space was contested and gendered. The rise of town planning, usually portrayed as a force for progress, lost its appeal at a time of mounting criticism of the impact of planners on British towns and cities. Although urban history did flourish in the 1970s and 1980s in the study of medieval and early modern towns, it seemed much less exciting and challenging to modern historians.

This introduction has shown that the urban variable is again important to modern historians, in a way which connects with the work of historians of gender, of culture and consumption. Demographic historians are aware of the importance of specific patterns of investment in public health and the impact on mortality; and the distinctive patterns of marriage or fertility arising from local labour markets and cultures. Historians of business realise that the performance of an individual firm is shaped by the urban economy, and by the accumulation of reputation and social capital within urban society. Historians of welfare have abandoned a teleological account of the rise of the welfare state, and are interested in the particular mixtures of charity, self-help and public provision within specific localities. And cultural historians, with their concern for subjectivities and identities, are fascinated by the experience of the city. The built form is important in terms of its iconography, the use made of the street or parks, or the experience of travel by bus and tube. Instead of narrow accounts of the politics of this town council or that Board of Guardians, historians are now aware of the importance of the urban variable in understanding major issues of collective action and investment, of dealing with market failure and the problems of externalities. As R. J. Morris has argued, nineteenth-century cities were 'a vast laboratory which tested the effectiveness of market mechanisms to the limit and then tested the operation of other ways of producing and delivering goods and services'.[158]

---

[158] R. J. Morris, 'Externalities, the market, power structure and the urban agenda', *UHY*, 17 (1990), 99–109.

PART I

Circulation

Urban networks

LYNN HOLLEN LEES

Nature prepares the site, and man organizes it in such fashion as meets his desires and wants.

Vidal de la Blache, 1898

I N 1950, a spider-web of railways overlay the British landmass from western Cornwall to the eastern tip of Caithness. Tracks fanned out from London through cities to the coastal settlements of Wales and Scotland, while branch lines moved from mills, mines, resorts and ports to the county towns (see Map 2.1). Commuters rushed from suburbs into London, Glasgow and Manchester, metropolitan centres surrounded by a dense penumbra of roads and rails. Threadlines of transport connected a human geography of settlement. In the eyes of the mapmaker, cities and their interconnections had tamed a world of mountain and plain, turning natural spaces into corridors, making the remote accessible. A century earlier, the transport network had a more truncated shape. Around 1840, railways linked London only to the largest county towns and the industrial centres of the North; they had scarcely reached Cornwall, Wales or the Scottish Highlands (see Map 2.2). A decade later, many new lines connected East and West, North and South, but large sections of Britain remained unreachable by railway (see Map 2.3).[1] Moreover, roads had not yet swollen to accommodate automobiles and the needs of suburban residents. Cities, other than London and a few regional centres, remained small in size. The urban had not yet dwarfed the rural.

Those who mapped the growing railway network pictured British space as organised by central cities and transport. Built landscapes dominated natural ones. Resolutely secular and insular, they privileged the systems of exchange and control that had arisen in a domestic capitalist economy and a nation-state. The

---

[1] F. Celoria, 'Telegraphy changed the Victorian scene', *Geographical Magazine* (1982), 159–64.

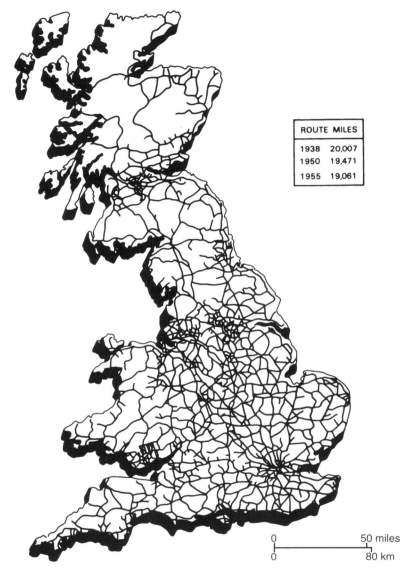

ROUTE MILES	
1938	20,007
1950	19,471
1955	19,061

Map 2.1 The railway network *c.* 1950
Source: Michael Freeman and Derek Aldcroft, *Atlas of British Railway History*
(London, 1985), p. 105.

A   Grand Junction
B   London & Birmingham
C   Great Western
D   Bristol & Exeter
E   London & Southampton
F   London & Brighton
G   Birmingham & Gloucester
H   North Midland
J   Hull & Selby
K   Great North of England
L   Newcastle & Carlisle

Map 2.2 The railway network *c.* 1840
Source: Michael Freeman and Derek Aldcroft, *Atlas of British Railway History*
(London, 1985), p. 14.

Map 2.3 The railway network *c.* 1850
Source: Michael Freeman and Derek Aldcroft, *Atlas of British Railway History*
(London, 1985), p. 20.

urban Britain they sketched captures a particular type of organisation, one that implies stability and centrality, in which size signals complexity and influence and in which London directed the flows of people, information and capital. Moreover, they announce closure at the borders, as if water were a barrier rather than a medium of circulation.

Yet urban networks transcend national borders, reaching out to Ireland and North America, to Europe and to the rest of the globe. In contrast to closure, these maps also signal possibility, fluidity; the pathways they depict permitted multiple systems of circulation which could be adapted, bypassed, extended as need and inclination dictated. Capitalist economies depend upon the mobility of capital, labour and information, as well as the ability of capitalists to restructure modes of production and location. The continuous reshaping of urban geographies to keep pace with economic restructuring has proved both an urban boon and a burden. In the words of David Harvey, 'We look at the material solidity of a building, a canal, a highway, and behind it we see always the insecurity that lurks within a circulation process of capital, which always asks: how much more time in this relative space?'[2]

These railway maps demarcate a particular period of urban and regional development in Britain, the era of high industrialism, which was tied to specific technologies, investment choices and political arrangements. In slightly over one hundred years, the urbanism of coal-based manufacturing for export moved through a cycle of expansion, restructuring and decline, driven by shifts in the capitalist economy and by changing sources of power. Large-scale industry moved along with steam engines into an array of British cities, particularly those near the coalfields in the North and the Midlands. Manufacturing cities, which captured a major share of capital investment, first reaped the benefits of industrial growth and then paid penalties for overinvestment in obsolescence. As Britain industrialised and then de-industrialised, substantial changes took place in the spatial organisation of capitalist relations of production, which were reflected in the functioning of local geographies of manufacturing, consumption and distribution, as well as in local social relations and hierarchies of power.

Unlike most of Western Europe, Britain's urban system in the industrial era included several manufacturing centres in its top ranks. Shifting geographies of production as well as trade cycles have therefore had an atypically large impact on major cities in Britain. Along with the decline of shipbuilding, coal mining, textile production and steel manufacturing has come the relative decline of Glasgow, Wolverhampton, Bradford and Sheffield. Whereas Manchester was the 'shock city' of the 1840s because of its growth, Liverpool and Wigan filled that function in the 1930s as a result of rampant unemployment. Although the modern cycle of urban industrial growth and decline extends slightly beyond the

---

[2] D. Harvey, *Consciousness and the Urban Experience* (Oxford, 1985), p. 28.

period captured by the maps of 1840 and 1950, those dates are useful benchmarks for the era of urban industrialism. Fuelled by the railroads which linked pithead to factory to port, this cycle of development encompasses the rapid urbanisation of the 1830s and 1840s, the economic boom of the period 1850 to 1873, the 'climacteric' of the late nineteenth century, the regional shifts and inflation of the early twentieth and the declines in production and employment of the 1920s and early 1930s, and the growth of the later 1930s and postwar decade. By the 1950s and early 1960s shrinking employment in the export industries of the North testified to the erosion of urban prosperity in the heartland of the Industrial Revolution. Then by the later 1960s and 1970s urban employment shifted toward services while many jobs relocated outside the conurbations, testifying to a dynamic that went far beyond regional boundaries.[3]

The urbanisation of the industrial period is not a placid story of progress and easy growth. The leap from the Barchester of Anthony Trollope to the Bradford of J. B. Priestley required more than a change of clothes and class. Contrasting types of urbanity, of cultural identification, of work and play came along with the growth and decline of industrial cities. Struggles for political and cultural control came along with the railroad and the music hall, the board schools and the labour exchange. Local identities contended with national ones and with the alluring appeal of the capital. Cities created multiple ties as they offered multiple choices.

This chapter explores the changing shapes of British urban networks during the era of high industrialism. On the one hand it is a story of economic growth and decline; on the other it is a tale of adaptation and development, as many manufacturing towns added a range of administrative and cultural functions, which strengthened their regional importance. The combination of capitalist investment strategies with the growth of state welfare service in a period of high consumption has given cities multiple functions, and helped the centres of British urbanism survive the economic shocks of the twentieth century.

(i) URBAN INTERCONNECTIONS AND BOUNDARIES

Not only is the completely isolated city unviable, but it is a contradiction in terms. As points of exchange for people, goods and information, linkage is the major urban function. To say, as Brian Berry did, that 'cities are systems within systems of cities', only makes explicit this assumption of flows and reciprocal influence. Not only are cities interdependent, but significant changes in the attributes or functioning of one member of a set triggers changes in its other members.[4]

---

[3] R. Floud and D. McCloskey, eds., *The Economic History of Britain since 1700*, 2nd edn (Cambridge, 1994), vol. I, p. 249, vol. II, p. 321; D. Massey, *Spatial Divisions of Labour* (London, 1984), pp. 134–5.

[4] B. J. L. Berry, 'Cities as systems within systems of cities', *Papers and Proceedings of the Regional Science Association*, 13 (1964), 147–63; A. Pred, *Urban Growth and City-Systems in the United States, 1840–1860* (Cambridge, Mass., 1980), p. 2.

Moreover, cities are differentiated; their systemic links are fostered by their need to rely on other places for certain specialisations and functions. Geographers can map the circulations of goods and people that link simpler to more complex settlements, and doing so helps them to describe urban hierarchies, as well as to trace the outlines of regions.

Marketing functions have had a central role in shaping urban systems and intensifying differences. Because levels of demand for goods and services vary as do the distances customers are willing to travel to obtain them, more settlements house, for example, bakeries and filling stations than universities or hospitals. The larger cities and towns will offer higher level goods and services, as well as simpler ones, and will draw people from longer distances. This variance results in a hierarchy of settlements in space: the capital city would offer a complete range of goods and services, some of them to an entire region or country, while a second order of central places would supply a more truncated list of goods and services to a smaller area.[5] In the real world, of course, more than one urban function shapes linkages – for example, communications, administration, culture – and each set of locational decisions has longer-run consequences. Railroads and road systems stream traffic and bring locational advantages as well as disadvantages. Administrative hierarchies generate investment, migration and employment.[6] In practice, the largest cities became larger as they captured the benefits of past investments in communications, governance, culture and commerce, which were generated in part because of a city's initial size and regional importance. As we shall see, technological change during the nineteenth century tended to reinforce centrality and hierarchy, giving an advantage to the first-comers in regional races for resources and influence, although many technologies of the twentieth century have proved compatible with the decentralisation of recent decades.

But the first-comers also have an inherent disadvantage over the longer run. Investment can bring obsolescence. As cycles of investment shifted among regions, so too did the dynamism of technological innovation, expansion and profitability. During the nineteenth century, successive waves of capital investment in the iron industry moved from South Wales and the West Midlands to Scotland, then to the North-East, and finally to the East Midlands, driving a dynamic of both industrial and urban growth, followed by relative decline.[7]

Urban networks operate on multiple levels for multiple purposes. Even if London politics and the London season outranked local varieties for people of

---

[5] W. Christaller, *Central Places in Southern Germany*, trans. C. W. Baskin (Englewood Cliffs, N. J., 1966).

[6] William Skinner has argued this point most persuasively using the case of China. See his 'Regional urbanization in nineteenth-century China', in G. W. Skinner, ed., *The City in Late-Imperial China* (Stanford, 1976).

[7] R. A. Dodgshon and R. A. Butlin, eds., *An Historical Geography of England and Wales*, 2nd edn (London, 1990), p. 274.

national status and ambition, other places retained much independence. Not only did county towns remain vital hubs of political and cultural life but so did regional centres, such as Newcastle, Bristol and York. In fact, industrialisation in its early phases might well have intensified regional identities and interactions.[8] The dialect literature of Lancashire spread far and wide during the mid-nineteenth century. The increase in functional linkages brought by new technologies of transportation made local and regional exchanges easier, binding together local producers and consumers, as well as their long-distance cousins. Far from erasing differences in localities, industrial urbanism helped to solidify rich regional identities that linked together urban and rural worlds. Even if some urban linkages ran to and from London, others were oriented to Birmingham, Manchester or Cardiff. Still others remained resolutely local – to and from a market town or a county capital, where the area's bishop, its major chamber of commerce and trade society were located.

In 1840, the British central-place system of cities reflected several centuries of locational decisions by producers, consumers, workers and the state, but in no sense had a stable system been created.[9] In the first place, networks operated in different ways for different people. Mail carriers and marquises, soldiers and servants, spinners and sailors quite literally moved along different roads. Certain occupations bound a person within regional networks, and others did not. Second, the structure of the capitalist economy produces regular change. Capitalist production is technologically dynamic, which implies new investments of capital and labour not necessarily in the same spaces and forms. Struggles for control of decision making, economic cycles of depression and boom, as well as resistance to disinvestment and unemployment, intensify instability.[10] Finance capital is footloose, as many firms and industrial towns have discovered in recent decades, and its locus of possibilities regularly overleapt national borders. Third, the growth of the state bureaucracy in the twentieth century added a long-term pressure for centrality and congruence of service functions that dampened regional differences.[11] Urban networks at any given moment therefore have to be conceptualised in terms of the particular purpose for which the network is being used and the social and economic status of the

[8] J. Langton, 'The Industrial Revolution and the regional geography of England', *Transactions of the Institute of British Geographers*, new series, 9 (1984), 156–7.

[9] Hierarchy within a central-place system can be demonstrated in several ways, but is commonly done in terms of town size. Larger populations are assumed to signal larger hinterlands, wider influence and greater complexity of functions, an assumption encouraged by the fact that demographic data are much more readily available than information on marketing networks or the distribution of functions and services. Although a radical reductionist method, ranking by population at least offers an approximation of a town's relative local importance.

[10] D. Harvey, 'The geopolitics of capitalism', in D. Gregory and J. Urry, eds., *Social Relations and Spatial Structures* (Basingstoke, 1985), p. 131.

[11] A. de Swaan, *In Care of the State: Health Care, Education and Welfare in Europe and the USA in the Modern Era* (New York, 1988).

people using the network. In their nation-wide campaign for universal male suffrage, Chartists sometimes looked to a town electorate, sometimes to the artisans or factory workers of a region, and sometimes to parliament for support. They reached their audiences through local activities and neighbourhood groups, through itinerant speakers, and through the *Northern Star*. Their campaigns moved within town, region and nation in a tactical sequence, rather than a necessary one. To understand urban interconnections requires a look at structures of possibility and then at patterns of utility.

(ii) THE TOWNS OF BRITAIN

The British system of cities includes all the individual urban units within England, Wales and Scotland, however they are defined. Using part of a political unit to demarcate an urban system is of course highly artificial. What of the rest of the United Kingdom or indeed the empire? Urban contacts do not cease at a border; cities are part of 'open systems' that span geographic boundaries.[12] Wider connections will be explored later in this chapter, but for the moment suspend disbelief and concentrate on the urban places of Great Britain alone.

By the mid-nineteenth century, the clarity of what constituted a 'city' had long since disappeared. Legal, demographic and functional criteria jostled one another in uneasy relation. Demarcation by charter, wall and market had given way in Britain to a motley collection of administrative structures through which parliament conferred urban status. There were municipal boroughs, local board districts, utility companies and settlements with improvement commissions, which produced, according to Adna Weber, 'a chaos of boundaries and officials'.[13] Over time, the problem intensified: annexations, enlargements of areas served by utilities, the addition of new ministries and state functions piled confusion upon confusion. Bowing to functionality, the census counted seaport, watering-places, manufacturing, mining and hardware towns, as well as county capitals and legal centres where the assizes met. To add further complexity, the census labelled settlements with more than 2,000 inhabitants as urban, although few such places had municipal governments or clear, unique geographic boundaries. In the designation of cities, English empiricism finally overrode the results of *ad hoc*, decentralised systems of local government. By 1851, statisticians counted a total of 563 towns with more than 5,000 citizens in England and Wales, and 36 more in Scotland with over 10,000 people.[14] Already a majority of the British were urban dwellers, and over three-quarters lived in cities by 1900, if size of settlement is made the criterion of urbanity. By 1950, only about 20 per cent of the population still lived in places which could be counted as

[12] A. Pred, *City Systems in Advanced Economies* (New York, 1977), p. 13.
[13] A. Weber, *The Growth of Cities in the Nineteenth Century* (Ithaca, 1963) p. 41.
[14] *Ibid.*, pp. 43, 58.

'rural', and many of them commuted into cities to work. In any case, automobiles, buses, radios and newspapers had long since eroded the cultural meaning of place of residence. Britain today is effectively an urbanised society in which towns set the pace and city dwellers imagine the countryside in forms that complement their own modernity.

The British set of central places had ancient origins. It had developed in several phases, starting first in the Iron Age. The Romans, of course, were active founders of towns, but so too were the Anglo-Saxons and the Danes. Forts and castles, bishoprics, markets and administrative centres attracted workers and merchants, and some of them prospered. By the time of the Norman Conquest, the British landmass was covered by an extensive set of settlements, only a few of which had the formal trappings of a town. Then the late medieval consolidation of political control which coincided with long-term population growth triggered another period of town foundation from the eleventh through the thirteenth centuries, one which had an extensive impact in Wales and Scotland as well as the English lowlands.[15]

The next major phase of urban creation began in the eighteenth century along with the rapid growth of industry and trade, and it added large numbers of specialised towns to the array. Ports, spas and manufacturing settlements attracted new citizens at a rapid clip.[16] Mills set along the streams of Yorkshire and Lancashire added housing, stores and churches, transforming themselves quickly into towns. Rural mines needed workers, and entrepreneurs located factories and furnaces nearby to benefit from relatively cheap coal and ore. Soon the industrial growth of the eighteenth and early nineteenth centuries had sorted and reordered regional urban networks, most intensely in South Wales, the Scottish Lowlands, the West Midlands, Lancashire and Yorkshire. People settled near the sources of power in the early phases of British industrialisation. In 1851 urban Britain comprised, therefore, an extensive array of settlements of many sizes, functions, administrative structures and dates of origin, which in several regions differed markedly from that of earlier centuries. History, technology, geography and chance combined to produce this particular set of cities, which remained relatively stable at the top ranks.

Describing this array of towns can be done in several ways: size, function and regions are the most common methods. I will concentrate on size, since it permits an easy charting of demographic changes and introduces the issue of relative scale In 1851, the typical British urban dweller lived in a small town. According to Brian Robson almost half of British towns had fewer than 5,000

[15] See I. H. Adams, *The Making of Urban Scotland* (London, 1978); H. Carter, *The Towns of Wales* (Cardiff, 1966).
[16] H. Carter, 'The development of urban centrality in England and Wales', in D. Denecke and G. Shaw, eds., *Urban Historical Geography: Recent Progress in Britain and Germany* (Cambridge, 1988), p. 207.

inhabitants, and most of the rest had under 40,000 in 1851. Only a handful exceeded 100,000.[17] At that date about 23 per cent of the total English and Welsh and 26 per cent of the Scottish population lived in towns with fewer than 50,000 people (Table 2.1). Of course, metropolitan London with more than 2.6 million people dwarfed the rest, but Liverpool, Glasgow, Manchester and Birmingham had become major cities. Between 1750 and 1850, Glasgow had grown from 32,000 to 345,000; Liverpool had exploded from 22,000 to 376,000 people. Outside the capital, the largest British city in 1750 was Edinburgh, which had only 57,000 inhabitants.[18] But by 1850, a town of that size would not have made it on to the list of the top twenty. By 1900, Liverpool, Glasgow, Manchester and Birmingham had more than 500,000 residents, and London swelled to more than 6,000,000. Cities with more than 100,000 became commonplace, and decade by decade, medium-sized places housed more and more of the English population. By 1950, few English and Welsh urbanites lived in towns of under 10,000 people, and almost 40 per cent had moved into the capital or cities that broke the half million mark (see Table 2.1).

The distribution of city sizes in Scotland is somewhat different. There small towns have continued to be of greater importance. Indeed, over 20 per cent of the Scottish population lived in towns with fewer than 10,000 people in 1951, and relatively few settled in cities of 50,000 to 100,000 people. Only Glasgow became a major metropolis. The period of industrial urbanisation produced in Scotland a great many small towns and few places with six-digit populations (see Table 2.1).

Between 1850 and 1900, the numbers of settlements recognised as towns by census takers and government clerks grew by leaps and bounds. (The 521 counted by Robson in 1851 had become 885 by 1901.) Each decade new small towns appeared, as more and more settlements passed the urban size threshold. At any given moment, of course, most towns were small, the vast majority having fewer than 10,000 inhabitants. At the same time, the numbers of large places rose at the expense of smaller ones, and urbanites slowly concentrated in the bigger cities.[19] During the nineteenth century, once a town had established

---

[17] B. T. Robson, *Urban Growth* (London, 1973), p. 53.

[18] Data for British cities in the eighteenth century come from E. A. Wrigley, *People, Cities, and Wealth* (Oxford, 1987), pp. 160–1. For the period after 1800, I use the urban populations compiled by B. R. Mitchell, *Abstract of British Historical Statistics* (Cambridge, 1962), which are taken from British censuses. For information on changing boundaries, see *ibid.*, pp. 24–7.

[19] The relationship between urban size and growth has been much debated by geographers, since statistical theory points in different directions. Brian Robson has investigated it in detail for nine-teenth-century British cities. After tracing decennial growth rates of towns in all size classes, he found that their variation contracted sharply as town size increased. Although small towns could expand greatly or decline, larger places almost never shrank and tended to grow regularly at comparable rates. Indeed until 1860 town size and growth were positively correlated; bigger cities grew more rapidly than small ones. After 1860, however, average rates of growth became almost uniform for towns of all sizes, although variance in growth was higher among the smaller settlements. Robson, *Urban Growth*, pp. 67–70, 87–9.

Table 2.1 Distribution of city sizes in Britain 1851–1951

	Population (in millions)		Percentage of total population in towns						
	Total	Urban	All	<10,000	10,000–50,000	50,000–100,000	100,000–500,000	>500,000	London
1851									
Eng. & Wales	17.9	9.7	54.0	9.9	13.4	5.8	11.0		13.9
Scotland	2.89	1.50	51.8	19.8	6.9	5.2	19.9		
1871									
Eng. & Wales	22.7	14.8	65.2	10.8	16.2	5.6	13.3	5.0	14.3
Scotland	3.36	1.95	57.4	18.7	7.1	4.3	10.6	16.7	
1891									
Eng. & Wales	29.0	21.6	74.5	10.2	16.2	8.6	20.0	4.8	14.7
Scotland	4.03	2.63	65.4	15.4	12.3	3.2	15.4	19.0	
1911									
Eng. & Wales	36.1	28.5	78.9	8.8	18.3	8.0	24.2	7.0	12.6
Scotland	4.76	3.33	69.9	11.2	16.4	4.9	15.7	21.7	
1951									
Eng. & Wales	43.8	35.6	81.2	3.9	14.5	10.1	13.1	20.9	18.7
Scotland	5.10	4.23	82.9	22.7	17.1	5.5	16.2	21.4	

Source: R. Lawton and C. G. Pooley, *Britain 1740–1950* (London, 1992), p. 91.

itself and moved out of the smallest size category, shrinkage in size was rare. The process of city creation and expansion was sufficiently dynamic during the nineteenth century to embrace settlements of all types and sizes. But there was enough variance in growth, particularly in the early decades of industrialisation, to produce a shift in the higher order central places.

Industrialisation disturbed regional urban hierarchies and catapulted new places to regional prominence. If a list of the largest fifteen British cities for 1750 and 1850 are compared, enormous differences appear over time. Older county towns such as Chester, Coventry and Exeter lost their relative position, while newer manufacturing centres like Sheffield, Bradford and Dundee became major cities. Meanwhile, Manchester, Liverpool, Glasgow and Birmingham gained new prominence. By mid-century, the British urban hierarchy was dominated by the capital, major ports and manufacturing centres. Thereafter, major changes were few. Not only did the top five cities remain the same, but during the next century only three towns – Nottingham, Stoke and Leicester – solidified a place in the top fifteen. Portsmouth and Salford moved briefly into the top ranks before moving down again in their relative ranking. The city systems of advanced societies tend to be quite stable at the upper levels. Note the regional implications of this growth pattern. Although all parts of the country experienced rapid urbanisation, the largest new cities were located in the textile and metalworking counties of the North and the Midlands. The early decades of the century were their period of most rapid growth; only after 1900 did the South-East develop an array of medium-sized towns outside London, when the shifting dynamism of industrial sectors in south and north transformed migration and investment patterns.[20]

Industrial urbanisation not only added great size to great density of towns in Britain, but major cities soon engulfed dozens of their small neighbours, which vanished into new boundaries and statistical categories. In 1915, Patrick Geddes wrote of 'this octopus of London, . . . a vast, irregular growth without previous parallel in the world of life', which devoured 'resistlessly' hundreds of villages and towns. Developers paved over historic divisions, turning subtle mixes of borough, village and field into 'a province covered with houses'. He marked out seven of these city regions, or 'conurbations', which could be found from the Clyde to South Wales. Except for London, each was centred on a coalfield, drawing its sustenance from the power source of the factories, which would fuel continued growth.[21] By the 1890s, the conurbations of the Southeast and the industrial belt housed around 40 per cent of the English and Welsh population, a share that they retained into the 1930s (see Table 2.2). During the industrial period, they formed core areas of intense urbanisation, whose banks, industries and offices made up the heartland of the British economy. Most of these conurbations continued to

[20] *Ibid.*, pp. 53, 88, 113.   [21] P. Geddes, *Cities in Evolution* (London, 1915), pp. 26, 34, 41.

Table 2.2 *Conurbations of England and Wales 1891–1971*

	1891		1911		1931		1951		1971[a]	
	A	B	A	B	A	B	A	B	A	B
Greater London	5,638	19.4	7,256	20.1	8,216	20.6	8,348	19.1	7,379	15.2
S.E. Lancashire	1,894	6.5	2,328	6.5	2,427	6.1	2,423	5.5	2,389	4.9
West Midlands	1,269	4.4	1,635	4.5	1,933	4.8	2,237	5.1	2,369	4.9
West Yorkshire	1,410	4.9	1,590	4.4	1,655	4.1	1,692	3.9	1,726	3.6
Merseyside	908	3.1	1,157	3.2	1,348	3.4	1,382	3.2	1,263	2.6
Tyneside	550	1.9	762	2.1	827	2.1	836	1.9	804	1.7
Total	11,670	40.2	14,726	40.8	16,405	41.1	16,918	38.7	15,928	32.8

Notes:

A = total population in thousands. B = percentage of total population.

[a] Boundary change figures based on 1961 adjusted totals.

Source: P. Hall *et al.*, *The Containment of Urban England* (London, 1973), vol. 1, p. 64.

expand slowly until the 1960s, when flight outside their borders outpaced migration and natural increase. But counter-urbanisation, when rural areas and small towns are the most rapidly growing, has diminished their centrality in post-war decades. The 1950s marked the end of a long phase of urban development, in which manufacturing fostered the expansion of particularly large cities. Since that time, the comparative advantages of smaller places have shifted growth away from the conurbations.

The transformation of town into city, city into metropolis and metropolis into conurbation came about through the simple processes of addition and multiplication: more people, more stores, more services, more land. The calculus of industry produced an ever richer urban function. But investments, whether by the state, by individuals or institutions, were not evenly distributed throughout the urban hierarchy nor across the map of Great Britain for that matter, and their inequality reinforced earlier locational decisions. By 1944, an hour-glass shaped area of intense urbanisation stretched from London and the south coast through Lancashire (see Map 2.4). In fact, David Harvey argues for a continuing shift of surplus value within the urban hierarchy to central levels; urbanisation for him is a process of concentration that stems from the nature of capitalism. Market mechanisms combined with economies of scale, planned obsolescence and the increased importance of fixed capital investment help to centralise surplus value in the contemporary city.[22] Harvey's argument works better for the period before 1945 than more recent decades, however, when automobiles and electronic modes of communication encourage decentralisation of both residences and production. The centralising impulses of capitalist industrialisation have varied according to prevailing technologies and the shifting forms of business organisation.

If the upper levels of urban networks of the early eighteenth century are compared with those of the mid-twentieth, it is easy to see how both capitalism and state formation contributed to greater centrality. Outside London in 1700, the five regional capitals described by Peter Clark and Paul Slack constituted the most complex settlements in Britain.[23] Cathedrals, grammar schools, assembly rooms, hospitals, jails and an array of churches distinguished them from tiny market towns. Nevertheless, their stock of specialised institutions for administration, finance or welfare needs was small. Town halls, market squares and churches served multiple purposes, and they represented high points of public investment. Banks were non-existent, outside Edinburgh, Glasgow and London; firm, family and finance operated symbiotically. Talented amateurs staffed local government, and even the justices, sheriffs and lord lieutenants in charge of county-level governance were drawn from local elites. Moreover, their economies were run

---

[22] D. Harvey, *Social Justice and the City* (Oxford, 1973), pp. 237–9, 273, 311.
[23] P. Clark and P. Slack, *English Towns in Transition, 1500–1700* (Oxford, 1976).

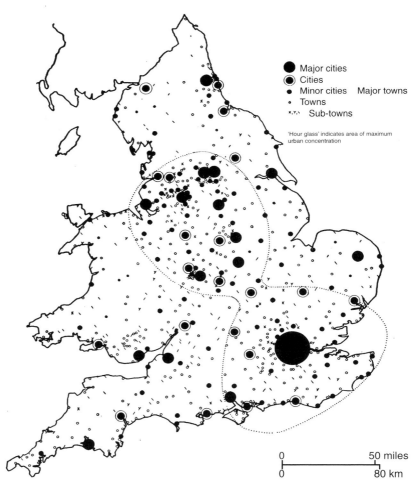

Map 2.4 The urban hierarchy of England and Wales in 1944
Source: Arthur E. Smailes, 'The urban hierarchy in England and Wales',
Geography, 29 (1944).

by local landlords, entrepreneurs and craftsmen. Tighter linkages with London took place during assize week, when judges appeared on regular circuit, but then they quickly moved on. By the 1940s, not only had regional capitals almost tripled in number, but they had acquired a host of new institutions. They housed stock exchanges and branches of the Bank of England, regional post offices, public universities and departments of the national bureaucracy.[24] Thousands of

---

[24] A. E. Smailes, 'The urban hierarchy in England and Wales', *Geography*, no. 144, 29, 2 (1944), 41–51.

their residents lived in municipal housing, used town-supplied water, electricity and trams. They shopped in chain stores, used branch banks and bought standardised goods using state-issued ration coupons. Decisions about production, sale and raw material sources were made outside the region, and investments responded to international opportunities and constraints. Greater centrality went along with larger size and complexity. State and economy operated symbiotically to knit together the localised networks of the early industrial period. Moreover, increased public investment could compensate for the retreat of private capital and economic decline.

(iii) LOCAL SYSTEMS: COUNTY AND REGION

To see an urban network in operation, let us follow interconnections from villages to a county town in the nineteenth century. Leicestershire has a particularly clear-cut central-place system. A ring of market towns – Hinckley, Market Harborough and Melton Mowbray, to name only a few – surround the county capital at a distance of about 15 miles (24 km), and each of the market towns has a penumbra of villages linked to it by road. In the early nineteenth century, both the county's agriculture and its framework knitting industry depended upon these urban markets, which were linked to the villages by extensive carrier services. In 1815 about 100 and in 1884 around 400 village men made weekly trips with a horse and cart into Leicester or one of the country's market towns. They moved along fixed routes, bringing produce in to retailers for sale, delivering packages, carrying passengers, making small purchases and returning home by evening. When they got to town, they crowded into local inns to drink and to trade news, bringing information back home along with yarn, medicine and crockery. Before the appearance of rural omnibus services – in Leicestershire in the 1880s – they provided the only public transport. Where rural industries flourished, the carriers collected raw materials from urban warehouses, delivered them to the artisans and then took back the finished goods. Alan Everitt estimates that in England and Wales around 1880, about 25,000 such carriers moved among villages and market towns, providing necessary transportation and marketing services. In fact, such services increased in frequency during the nineteenth century and were supplemented by scores of light rail lines, which intensified intraregional flows of goods and people.[25] Although trains linked cities and the larger towns by 1850, the transportation and marketing needs of the rural and small-town population, which expanded during the early phases of industrial urbanisation, were not satisfied by the largely intercity routes of the railway.

By the 1840s, in the rapidly industrialising areas, complex transportation services aided the local movements of people and goods. In the Glasgow region

[25] A. Everitt, *Landscape and Community in England* (London, 1985), pp. 281–91.

around 1848, several omnibus and hackney carriage companies linked local towns and suburbs in to the centre. Mail coaches linked Glasgow to about two dozen other more distant Scottish cities, while steamboats left the port regularly for places as far north as Stornoway and west to Ireland. In addition, the Paisley, Monkland, Forth & Clyde canals carried thousands of passengers regularly around the district. In fact, by the 1840s, the early railroad lines had teamed up with coaches and steamers to provide integrated transit services in the region.[26] Urbanisation in Lowland Scotland during the nineteenth century stemmed largely from industrial development: the textile towns of Dunfermline, Hawick, Kilmarnock and Paisley and the coal and iron processing towns of Falkirk, Hamilton, Coatbridge and Motherwell grew faster than older marketing towns. Railway links eased the export of goods and imports of people. Edinburgh supplied higher level financial, educational, medical and religious services, while Glasgow acted as the key city for industry and trade, while developing both middle-class suburbs and industrial satellites like Springburn, which grew around its railway and engineering works.[27] Capital investments flowed into urban infrastructures, as well as into firms.

Elaborate transit systems were needed because of the multiple functions of county capitals, as well as regional geographies of production and distribution. To return to a Midland example, *Thomas Cook's Guide to Leicester* for 1843 pointed out the city's theatre, library, Shakespearean rooms, assembly rooms, New Hall for concerts and public meetings, post office, union workhouse and lunatic asylum. Moreover, the town boasted five banks, eleven schools, eight Anglican parishes, an archdeacon's office, twenty-four dissenting chapels, an excise office, two gaols, four hospitals and a general dispensary that served the poor of the county as well as the town.[28] A host of public institutions, charities, clubs and companies were headquartered in the city. People came to town for race meetings or to see exhibitions from the Leicestershire Floral Society. Others attended elections, assizes or demonstrations. They went to the parks to hear evangelists, to the Temperance hall for testimonal *soirées* or oratorios.[29] For gentry and freeholders, stocking weavers and Chartists, the county town focused political, judicial and cultural concerns. Leicester anchored a 'craft-region' as well as a county community, and the town helped to promote a regional identity through its many institutions and activities.[30]

[26] J. R. Hume, 'Transport and towns in Victorian Scotland', in G. Gordon and B. Dicks, eds., *Scotttish Urban History* (Aberdeen, 1983), pp. 198–202.

[27] D. Turnock, *The Historical Geography of Scotland since 1707* (Cambridge, 1982); J. Doherty, 'Urbanization, capital accumulation, and class struggle in Scotland, 1750–1914', in G. W. Whittington and I. D. Whyte, *An Historical Geography of Scotland* (London, 1983), pp. 239–68.

[28] T. Cook, *Guide to Leicester, Containing the Directory and Almanac for 1843* (Leicester, 1842).

[29] The active social and cultural life of the region is chronicled in the *Leicestershire Mercury*.

[30] A. Everitt, 'Country, county and town: patterns of regional evolution in England', *TRHS*, 5th series, 29 (1979), 94, 106.

Of course, much smaller towns than Leicester could boast flourishing public cultures and industrial establishments, fed by the rising incomes and new demands of consumers in their hinterlands. Even relatively remote, weakly urbanised counties had quite sophisticated central places. The Cumbrian market town of Ulverston, which had 3,000 residents and was the fourth largest town in the county by 1801, served as the central place for a proto-industrial area from the lower Furness Fells to the south-west Cumbrian Dales. Its markets, inns and taverns catered to a large commercial traffic. But the town also had boarding schools for young ladies, hairdressers, confectioners, printers and tea dealers. The town's book club and theatre drew professional people and gentry, while artisans used its friendly societies, savings banks and dissenting chapels. According to J. D. Marshall, Cumbrian market towns expanded markedly along with rural industry in the later eighteenth and early nineteenth centuries. The coming of the railway around 1850 benefited the larger centres by drawing business away from the smaller ones. Although Ulverston maintained its centrality as late as 1900, nearby places such as Bottle and Broughton lost population as did the rural areas.[31] Then during the second half of the nineteenth century, Cumbrian regional networks adjusted to the rapid industrialisation of coastal coal and iron districts. Barrow and Workington turned into boom towns as people left agricultural labour markets for urban ones. By 1881, 60 per cent of the Cumbrian population lived in the coastal strip and its major towns. Rural de-industrialisation and the decline of the local cotton industry undermined the active urban network of the proto-industrial period but produced alternative sets of settlements.[32] The capital investments of the industrial period reworked the spatial organisation of the area, and labour migration followed.

Particularly in industrialising regions, complex geographies of production, merchanting and finance arose on the basis of local social structures and regional ties. Capitalist investment strategies developed in tandem with custom and community. Wool was imported into the major towns of the West Riding, but then shifted by cart to a variety of sites to be processed and reprocessed. Dozens of mechanised carding, scribbling and fulling mills lay along the Calder and Aire rivers, while thousands of clothiers and journeymen wove cloth in small workshops or their homes in the villages and small towns throughout the district. Sales took place in the cloth halls of Leeds, Bradford, Halifax, Huddersfield and Wakefield primarily, each of which served a large, but fluctuating number of producers who brought the finished goods in to the central place. By the mid-1830s, production had become much more concentrated along the Aire near Leeds, along the Calder around and west of Wakefield, in Huddersfield and

---

[31] J. D. Marshall, 'The rise and transformation of the Cumbrian market town, 1660–1900', *NHist.*, 19 (1983), 128–208.

[32] J. D. Marshall, 'Stages of industrialization in Cumbria', in P. Hudson, ed., *Regions and Industries* (Cambridge, 1989), pp. 132–55.

Halifax, and integrated firms handling multiple branches of production grew.[33] Yet the area was not a homogeneous whole: the division between worsted and woollen production rested on different agricultural environments, methods of finance and entrepreneurial control. In the West Riding around Halifax and Bradford, worsted production first developed in upland pastoral areas where early enclosure and a declining manorial system had produced a landless rural proletariat and a small group of putting-out capitalists. The transition to factory production in urban sites took place fairly rapidly after the 1820s with finance supplied by the large putting-out merchants and factory masters from the cotton trade. In contrast, woollen production in the territory around Huddersfield, Dewsbury and Leeds developed amidst more fertile land and a more vital manorial system. The holders of manors and large estates fostered a system of mixed farming and cloth production. In that area, independent weaving households survived and marketed their produce in the large town cloth halls. Jointly financed fulling and carding mills provided local clothiers the services they needed to survive, and local landowners helped to provide capital for mills and workshops.[34]

In the longer run, differential access to credit reshaped the geography of production and trade in both the woollen and worsted districts. After 1826, the growth of banks created a regional capital market, linked to London via the Leeds branch of the Bank of England. The largest firms, whose owners served as bank directors, had easier access to credit and information.[35] Financial services and excellent transportation were part of the comparative advantage of the larger towns. Leeds, for example, was linked by canal to Liverpool in 1816 and by railway to Hull by 1834. Entrepreneurs could get cheap coal from local mines, and raw materials, such as flax from the Baltic region, came via Hull, then by canal and railway. Early investments in steam engines and spinning mills made the city a technological leader. As early as 1800, local engineering firms had begun to supply the steam engines, hackles, gills and combs needed in the textile industry.[36] Its expansion in the area fostered a wave of allied investment in Leeds and other West Riding towns. In the longer run, of course, flax manufacturing virtually disappeared, leaving dozens of empty mills in the town, and woollen manufacture shifted from central areas to outlying townships. But the region's

[33] D. Gregory, *Regional Transformation and Industrial Revolution* (London, 1982), pp. 107, 117, 199.
[34] P. Hudson, 'From manor to mill: the West Riding in transition', in M. Berg, P. Hudson and M. Sonenscher, eds., *Manufacture in Town and Country before the Factory* (Cambridge, 1983), pp. 124–44.
[35] P. Hudson, *The Genesis of Industrial Capital* (Cambridge, 1986); P. Hudson, 'Capital and credit in the West Riding wool textile industry c. 1750–1850', in Hudson, ed., *Regions and Industries*, pp. 69–99. For a discussion of regional organisation in the West Riding in the mid-twentieth century, see R. E. Dickinson, *City and Region* (London, 1964), pp. 273–8.
[36] E. J. Connell and M. Ward, 'Industrial development, 1780–1914', in D. Fraser, ed., *A History of Modern Leeds* (Manchester, 1980), pp. 143–52.

capital was mobile and by 1900 had shifted into clothing, footwear, chemicals and heavy engineering. Networks of supply and marketing had to be reworked, but that was easily done. The next phase of disinvestment and reinvestment took place in the interwar period, when local manufacturing declined precipitously. As old woollen firms disappeared, banks and retail stores enlarged. Commerce, administration and the professions became the city's business, rather than woollen production.[37] The question of why some businessmen manage to react successfully to economic changes and others fail to do so is ultimately unanswerable on a general level. But settings matter. The ability of Leeds entrepreneurs to adapt was facilitated by transportation networks, by the size of the city's consumer market and by a wealth of local institutions that provided capital, technical expertise and commercial information.

Industrial capitalism made even greater changes over the longer run in the urban networks of the mining areas. In a mineral-based energy economy, transportation costs decline because production is punctiform, rather than areal. At limited cost, canals and railroads linked pitheads with the nearby industrial areas and towns. Regional marketing networks, centred on major ports and industrial towns, solidified, and virtually unlimited, cheap energy supplies enabled entrepreneurs to break through earlier ceilings to growth.[38] Interlocking and interacting firms employed the labour and capital that helped to accelerate urbanisation in the industrial regions.

South Wales provides a particularly dramatic example of change. In 1835, South Wales was still primarily an agricultural area dependent upon Bristol for its manufactured goods and marketing services. The Welsh population relied on eleven rather small towns, which acted primarily as service centres. Their bankers, professionals and artisans served interior hinterlands, linked by carriers and a few major roads. Although the presence of theatres, race tracks and poor law unions signalled cultural and administrative importance, they were largely untouched by industrial urbanisation. But coal and iron had already begun to transform South Wales into an industrialised region organised around Merthyr Tydfil and Cardiff. Isolated valleys quickly acquired villages and then towns as the early iron masters and mine owners built housing near their blast furnaces and pitheads. Mining settlements, such as Bargoed and Tonypandy, multiplied after 1850. The Glamorganshire canal after 1811 and the Taff Vale Railway after 1846 brought the rich harvest from the Aberdare and Rhondda valleys out to the coast.[39] Cardiff, one of the major beneficiaries, grew from 10,000 in 1841 to

[37] Michael Meadowcroft, 'The years of political transition, 1914–1939', in Fraser, ed., *Leeds*, pp. 430–1.
[38] Wrigley, *People, Cities and Wealth*, pp. 75–91; see also D. Gregory, 'Three geographies of industrialization', in Dodgshon and Butlin, eds., *Historical Geography*, pp. 362–4.
[39] Carter, *The Towns of Wales*; M. J. Daunton, *Coal Metropolis* (Leicester, 1977).

164,000 in 1900, becoming the region's capital. As more elaborate transport systems eased migration, Swansea and Newport grew into major cities; resorts such as Barry Island and Porthcawl developed, and industrial villages became industrial towns. But Wales paid a price for the heavy dependence of local urban networks upon coal mining. Merthyr declined in importance when the supply of local iron ore became exhausted and the cost of importing it was too high. By 1860, the region turned to the export of coal through Cardiff, but no significant manufacturing or shipbuilding industries ever developed in the regional capital. By late in the century, the city's port needed expansion and modernisation, which was not forthcoming. The major shippers and merchants came from outside the region, and the Bute family by that point had retreated from aggressive municipal leadership. Coal and shipowners built a rival dock and railway at Barry, which siphoned off much trade and left Cardiff with an obsolete, underutilised port. The final blow to the city's major industry came after 1914 with the collapse of coal exporting, as steamships shifted to oil and internal combustion engines, and the British coal industry failed to overcome increasing difficulties of extraction with greater investment and productivity. As local companies went into liquidation, Cardiff turned from 'coal metropolis' to an administrative and retail centre.[40]

The pattern of industrial expansion that dominated Britain during the industrial era was a regional one: firms concentrated all the stages of production of a commodity within one area, mixing management, production and exporting. Regional divisions of labour arose, therefore, from an industrial base – spinners and weavers in Lancashire and the West Riding, miners in the North-East and South Wales, engineers in the West Midlands and the South-East. Regional differentiation increased not only with sectoral collapse but also with nationalisation, which accelerated changes in internal class structure. Upper-level management shifted to the London region; research and development groups could be centralised.[41]

The urban networks created in the era of industrial urbanisation were effective and flexible, but inherently unstable. Many entrepreneurs reacted to technological change and calculations of profitability, shifting money and investment when opportunity beckoned. Roads of entry could easily become roadways of exit for businessmen as well as for their products. Locations had to remain advantageous in either industrial or commercial terms for them to remain attractive to investors. In the longer run, the landscape of industrial urbanism in the north of Britain was reshaped by the transference of much capital investment southward and overseas. After export markets for northern goods collapsed, the lure of potentially higher profits in new industries located elsewhere was difficult to resist.

[40] Daunton, *Coal Metropolis*, pp. 226–8.   [41] Massey, *Spatial Divisions*, pp. 128, 199–201.

(iv) LONDON AND THE REGIONS

Before the Industrial Revolution, Britain had many towns, but only one city. William Cobbett branded it the 'Great Wen', for its density, dominance and draining of national, and indeed international, resources. The largest city in the world by the 1820s, London reached out to India and the Caribbean through its port, to Europe and Latin America through its bankers, to Ireland and Scotland through its parliament, and through the length and breadth of Britain via its newspapers and insatiable demand for workers and consumer goods. London was and remains a primate city, whose size is sustained by its position in economic, cultural and political hierarchies. Yet the growth of the industrial economy and a more centralised state shifted the nature of links within Britain between metropolis and periphery. Not only did London's degree of demographic primacy shrink, but the capital's relative political and economic influence diminished in comparison to that of the new industrial cities of the Midlands and the North during most of the nineteenth century. If London's size is compared to that of the second largest British town, it moved from being more than 10 times as large in 1801 to multipliers of 6 in 1851, 5 in 1901, and 4.8 in 1951. Although London's share of the total British population rose slightly during the nineteenth century, by 1801 more people lived in the textile counties of Lancashire and the West Riding than in the capital. Urbanised regions overtook the metropolis quite early in terms of population, fixed investments in plant and steam power, and in manufacturing for export. In addition, the congruence between relative size and economic or cultural influence that seemed so clear in the seventeenth and eighteenth centuries broke down. In the heyday of industrial urbanisation, British networks of cultural, political and economic exchange were more foot-loose than they had been in the early modern period and the dominance of London was less secure. Regional novels, newspapers, choruses and brass bands had devoted audiences. Culture could be created locally.

The case for a diminished importance of London during the nineteenth century is most easily made in political terms. During the first half of the nineteenth century, most pressure groups arose from regional roots and remained regionally distinctive. Luddism and Chartism took on different colours depending upon the locality observed, and the Anti-Corn Law League, as well as movements for factory reform and for cooperative stores, had strong regional bases. By mid-century, political leadership had migrated northward from the capital. The Anti-Corn Law League's victory in 1846 and John Bright's pronouncement that 'Lancashire, the cotton district, and the West Riding of Yorkshire, must govern England' signalled a fundamental shift of influence in Britain away from London to the Midlands and industrial North.[42] When Elizabeth Gaskell, in

---

[42] D. Read, *The English Provinces, c. 1760–1960* (London, 1964), p. 148.

North and South, contrasted the strong, male producers and innovators of the industrial districts with the effeminate, non-productive residents of London, she was only echoing provincial judgements about social virtue.

Industrialisation gave new power to the British provinces and intensified local loyalties. Cheap print spread regional novels and dialect literature to a large audience; statistical societies counted and measured the people nearby. Not only were trades unions locally based, but factory-owning paternalists worked to turn employees into quasi-families.[43] Despite Marxist predictions, the new proletarians more easily identified with their neighbours than with French or German counterparts.

Pride in regional difference came along with rising integration and uniformity. As football, cricket and rugby professionalised, local teams drew large, proud, socially mixed audiences. The middle-class taste for local antiquarian and folklore societies, for local histories and maps testified to widespread enthusiasm for identities that remained rooted in the nearby, the familiar. When the army shifted to territorial regiments after the Boer War, men rushed to join town-based battalions whose officers came from well-known landed and entrepreneurial families. National and local patriotism fused in groups such as the Lancashire Fusiliers.[44]

The dynamics of political change shifted power back to the metropolis by the later nineteenth century. With expansion of the national suffrage, more and more political energy focused on events in Westminster. After the 1880s, political parties became more and more centralised, bringing effective control into London and the parliamentary party. Meanwhile, city politics lost some of their social drama as major industrialists retreated from town councils late in the century, and the most dynamic regional figures, such as Joseph Chamberlain, James Keir Hardie and David Lloyd George shifted their power base from the provinces to the metropolis.[45] By the mid-twentieth century, the relentless pull of the capital had gone far to undermine regional vitality. The growth of the state combined with that of the media and the financial world to make London the area of innovation and investment. In an information-driven society, there are comparative advantages to being located close to the centres of power and action.

The vital regionalism of the early and mid-nineteenth century raises the issue of integration: how and to what extent were regional urban networks tied together? The spread of the railroad to most corners of the realm in approximately 1850 speeded up local patterns of circulation as well as longer-distance exchanges.[46] London, as the focal point of north–south routes, reinforced its

[43] P. Joyce, *Work, Society and Politics* (Brighton, 1980).
[44] C. B. Phillips and J. H. Smith, *Lancashire and Cheshire from AD 1540* (London, 1994), pp. 290–1.
[45] E. P. Hennock, *Fit and Proper Persons* (London, 1973), pp. 266–70; R. H. Trainor, *Black Country Elites* (Oxford, 1993).
[46] R. Lawton and C. G. Pooley, *Britain 1740–1950* (London, 1992), pp. 195–202.

already privileged position. The railroad illustrates a major point: regionalism and integration into a metropolitan-centred system were parts of a common process of growth. Each fed upon the other.

The credit system of the early industrial period shows how integration and differentiation went hand in hand.[47] Even in the eighteenth century, private country banks had their London agents to settle interregional debts. When joint-stock banking expanded in England after the Banking Act of 1826, firms that grew first spread regionally. But at the same time, the Bank of England set up branches in the major industrial towns, and it remained the central institution for the rediscounting of bills. Banking transactions in the early industrial period therefore operated on several levels: local, within and among regions and between London and the provinces. Bank notes circulated regionally and required regular clearing with banks of issue; commercial intelligence and exchanges of bills flowed to and from multiple cities. Bankers contacted London to buy government securities, to collect dividends and to finance exports to the capital. The flow of capital from agricultural regions to industrial ones or from periphery to the centre required multiple transactions and steps that depended upon both an integrated region and ties to the capital.[48] Paper credit and commercial information helped shape the 'space economy' of the industrial period, operating through urban networks with regional and metropolitan foci. They knit together small regions through a web of daily transactions at the same time as they bound those regions into a national, industrialising economy.

The growth in Britain of an active consumer culture also depended on a complex linkage of capital and provinces. If London was the country's shop window, many of the products displayed had been produced in the Potteries, Birmingham, Lancashire and Sheffield, according to information about mass markets which came from the capital. The symbiotic relationship of metropolis and industrial region rested on fast-flowing commercial news, consumer choices and advertising campaigns. Each side of the exchange was dependent upon the other. The spatial dynamics of retailing linked regionalism with larger networks of supply. To satisfy customer demand for many items at reasonable prices, grocers looked far and wide for goods and then sought out additional customers. To stock his shelves around 1860, John Tuckwood of Sheffield bought from forty different firms in seventeen cities, including London. Starting from a shop in central Sheffield, his firm opened multiple branches in the suburbs and other

---

[47] H. Carter and C. R. Lewis, *An Urban Geography of England and Wales in the Nineteenth Century* (London, 1990), pp. 51–2; J. B. Jeffreys, *Retail Trading in Britain, 1850–1950* (Cambridge, 1954); G. Shaw and M. T. Wild, 'Retail patterns in the Victorian city', *Transactions of the Institute of British Geographers*, new series, 4 (1979), 278–91.

[48] I. S. Black, 'Money, information and space: banking in early nineteenth-century England and Wales,' *Journal of Historical Geography*, 21 (1995), 398–412; I. S. Black, 'Geography, political economy and the circulation of finance capital in early industrial England', *Journal of Historical Geography*, 15 (1989), 366–84.

Yorkshire towns, and it served as a wholesaler to village shops.[49] Thomas Lipton's firm quickly expanded from his main store in Glasgow to local branches and then to a network of shops in Scottish cities, combining wholesale trade with his own retail operations. His chain first developed strong regional roots and linkages before it spread to other areas in the 1880s, when he opened branches in the major cities of England and Wales. As the business spread, he found sources of supply from Ireland to the Antipodes to satisfy the nearly insatiable demand of British consumers for hams, meat pies and tea. From the Glasgow docks, food imports went to warehouses and processing sites before transshipment all over the country. With his entry into the tea trade and contracts with Ceylon and Indian producers, London took on additional importance, and he moved the head offices to London in 1891. But it would be a mistake to see Lipton's as a London-based concern, given its world-wide reach and its regional divisions of labour and distribution, in which Glasgow sites played a major part.[50]

The single most important actor driving the integration of regional urban systems in Britain was the state itself, which used paper, ink and parliament to weave the localities together. By mid-century, railway regulation, factory laws, school inspection and the New Poor Law created a wide paper trail between London and the provinces. After 1834, Edwin Chadwick bombarded poor law unions with endless circulars demanding information and compliance. Clerks at the registrar general's office laboriously transcribed thousands of births, marriages and deaths into huge, black volumes. Mr Podsnap's complaint, 'Centralization. No. Never with my consent. Not English', had already fallen on deaf ears.

British centralisation was, of course, following a much different path from that of France. Driven largely by *ad hoc* improvisation, the reshaping of local government by parliament in the nineteenth century added modest reforms to a grab-bag of residues from the past, resulting in multiple, asymmetrical linkages to London, rather than tightly controlled flows of services and permissions that moved up and down the designated steps of an administrative urban hierarchy from the capital. During the early and mid-nineteenth century, administrative ties between towns and the centre in Britain multiplied, overlapped and competed. Simplification came during the 1880s and after, when intermediary layers of administration were created; finally a rough system of regionalisation emerged from independent decisions to decentralise services.

If we look at the administrative linkages among British towns existing around 1850, several different patterns can be seen. Religious administration privileged Canterbury, York and Edinburgh, with secondary ties to cathedral towns. The judicial system linked royal courts in Westminster to the assize towns within regional circuits. Postal service ran through London until 1865, when procedures

[49] J. Blackman, 'The development of the retail grocery trade in the nineteenth century', *Business History*, 9 (1957), 114. [50] P. Mathias, *Retailing Revolution* (London, 1967), pp. 96–101.

for 'cross-posts' between provincial centres spread.[51] Local government reforms added new, intermediate layers of administration between parish and centre, as hundreds of poor law unions, improvement commissions, rural and urban districts, new boroughs and special boards were created throughout the realm. Overlapping boundaries and confused jurisdictions only added to the complexity, which legislation regularly revised. Greater order came in 1888 and 1894, when large numbers of local authorities were consolidated under county councils, county boroughs, urban and rural districts.[52] Restructuring created series of islands, virtually coequal administrative units, responsible in limited ways to the Local Government Board and parliament in London, but left untouched poor law unions.

The combination of a strong central state with hundreds of weak but direct links to the localities lasted well into the twentieth century. Schemes for formal regionalisation in the interests of efficiency during and after the First World War were largely ignored, but despite parliament's lack of interest, the informal division of Britain into provinces had taken place by the 1940s through a series of independent decisions.[53] The post office set up regional administrative offices in Edinburgh and Leeds in 1936, and added five others in 1938. By 1940, the Ministry of Labour's employment exchange service operated through seven districts with headquarters in Cardiff, Newcastle, Leeds, Birmingham, Manchester, Bristol and London. Telephone service, civil defence, agricultural assistance, road traffic administration, as well as many private organisations, operated through regional offices in major towns linked to the capital. Without official sanction, a series of cities – Birmingham, Manchester, Leeds, Bristol, Newcastle, Nottingham, Edinburgh and Cardiff – emerged as local capitals, anchoring a 'practical regionalism'.[54] A second tier of cities, among them Liverpool, Glasgow, Leicester and Sheffield, also acquired regional functions to a lesser extent. This multiplication of administrative services in the larger cities increased their centrality, further adding to the pressures for their growth.

The meaning of regionalism took a new turn after 1945, when nationalisation, national insurance and national health services both extended the arm of the state and gave London civil servants the whip hand. The rhetoricians of the welfare state spoke with a language of equality and uniformity that belied continued divisions. Indeed, changing social geographies of production intensified regional social differences, as management and white-collar employment shifted to the South-East, leaving low-skilled production jobs in the North and the

[51] M. J. Daunton, *Royal Mail* (London, 1985), p. 123.

[52] V. D. Lipman, *Local Government Areas, 1834–1945* (Oxford, 1949), pp. 142–64.

[53] Early defences of regionalisation came from C. B. Fawcett, 'Natural divisions of England', *Geographical Journal*, 49 (1917), 125–44; and G. D. H. Cole, *The Future of Local Government* (London, 1921).

[54] E. W. Gilbert, 'Practical regionalism in England and Wales', *Geographical Journal*, 94 (1939), 29–44.

Celtic Fringe.[55] The information-based economy of the twentieth century privileged the capital, where bureaucrats, bankers, diplomats and MPs could rub shoulders in the same restaurants and clubs.

(v) URBAN PATHWAYS: MIGRATION AND TECHNOLOGY

Urban networks create multiple pathways – not tracks that confine, but channels none the less – from the core of the island to its periphery. At any given moment, people, products and information are in motion from one site to another. Within central-place systems, transfers normally tend to operate between levels of an urban hierarchy – either toward higher ranking places from lesser centres or from the centre outward to hinterlands and downwards to less complex settlements. But well-articulated urban networks offer multiple choices of destinations.

Skilled workers followed interurban routes when organising their lives. James Beardpark, who joined the Steam Engine Makers' Society in Bolton around 1835, moved through Manchester, Bury, Leeds, Blackburn, Preston and Rochdale in search of a job in 1841. Finding no permanent place, he then shipped to London via Hull. But the capital too did not provide a easy berth, so he moved on to major towns in the South, West, and Midlands, dying in Derby in 1844.[56] Urban networks structured his trips, although he did not follow strictly hierarchical principles or a gradient of distance. News of openings, contacts with friends and relatives probably led him onward, but the organisation of his union in the larger towns provided the fixed points among which he travelled. Yet what is unpredictable for any given person is strongly patterned for groups as a whole. Even if individuals meandered from town to town, the net effect of their seemingly random choices was the ceaseless growth of the larger towns and the continued urbanisation of the British population.

Migration offers a good illustration of hierarchical theories of movement. The British census records a heavy movement of people toward the metropolis and then outward into the Home Counties, particularly after 1881.[57] When people migrated from Wales to England, they chose destinations strongly influenced by the size of town and its distance from their birthplace. By 1851, substantial numbers of Welsh had moved to Liverpool, Chester, Shrewsbury, Bristol, Bath, London and the towns of the Black Country. In the next twenty years, a diffusion from major cities to the smaller towns of their hinterlands took place.[58]

---

[55] Massey, *Spatial Divisions*, pp. 178–9.
[56] H. R. Southall, 'The tramping artisan revisited: labour mobility and economic distress in early Victorian England', *Ec.HR*, 2nd series, 44 (1991), 272–96.
[57] D. Friedlander, 'London's urban transition, 1851–1951', *Urban Studies*, 11 (1974), 127–41.
[58] C. G. Pooley, 'Welsh migration in Great Britain, 1851–1871', *Journal of Historical Geography*, 9, 3 (1983), 287–306.

Hierarchies streamed migration by the Irish too. They entered Britain through the major ports, where many remained and some moved inland; more rapid diffusion down an urban hierarchy – into the Scottish Lowlands from Glasgow, from Liverpool through Lancashire and the West Riding, and from London into the Home Counties – took place in the decades after the famine.[59] These and other similar studies using published census data, which track movement only at decadal intervals, generally confirm linkage of migration paths to urban hierarchies. But such research captures only part of the movement from place to place.

Using other sources, scholars paint a more nuanced picture of population movements. With the aid of census manuscript schedules, Richard Lawton and Colin Pooley have tracked migration into Liverpool. While some newcomers followed the classic stepwise path into the city up a local urban hierarchy, major direct, long-distanced streams of people came into the port from Ireland and Scotland. The unskilled moved to the nearest large market for work, while skilled migrants, who had better sources of information, shifted among the urban labour markets where there was demand for them. As a result, migration into Liverpool had both a rural-to-urban component, particularly large in the early phases of industrialisation, and a substantial city-to-city movement, especially from large towns in the second half of the century. From London came proportionally large numbers of professionals and entrepreneurs, while those from Lancashire and nearby villages worked most typically in agriculture or mining.[60]

Migratory movements in Scotland confirm the mixed origins of newcomers to major cities and their multiple paths. The heavy flows of people from both Highland counties and Lowland agricultural areas into the urban industrial belt included migrants from towns as well as rural parishes. Professionals and artisans from Inverness, St Andrews or Oban tried their luck in the towns of Lanark or the Midlothians. Young Highland women moved directly into the mills in Dundee or took service jobs in Edinburgh, while male labourers trekked to the herring fisheries in east coast ports or became construction workers in Glasgow. Using registers of paupers, Charles Withers and A. J. Watson have tracked Highlanders moving into Glasgow during the second half of the nineteenth century, most of whom came from Argyll and Inverness-shire. All of the movement was hierarchical in nature – by definition, because of Glasgow's relative size. Most migrants had moved directly into Glasgow from the parish of their birth. Of the 30 per cent that had chosen an intermediate destination before entering Scotland's major city, most had lived in a mid-sized town closer to

[59] L. H. Lees and J. Modell, 'The Irish countryman urbanized: a comparative perspective on the famine migration', *JUH*, 3 (1977), 391–408. See also R. Swift and S. Gilley, eds., *The Irish in the Victorian City* (London, 1985).

[60] R. Lawton, 'Mobility in nineteenth-century British cities', *Geographical Journal*, 145 (1979), 206–224; C. G. Pooley and I. D. Whyte, *Migrants, Emigrants and Immigrants* (London, 1991).

Glasgow than the parish of their birth. The urban born – who came from Oban, Inverness, Campbeltown, Stornoway and Rothesay – either went directly to Glasgow or stopped first in a Scottish town of intermediate size.[61]

Technology multiplied the drawing power of the bigger cities, which compounded the prospects of new jobs with the lure of novelty. Alan Pred's analysis of the linkage between urban growth and innovation outlines the process: inventions spur industrial expansion and new construction, and produce continued structural change and invention. As a result workers are drawn into places where changes are introduced.[62] New technology, therefore, has systemic effects that lead to growth. The impact of new technology in the nineteenth century, however, was greatest at the top of urban systems. Brian Robson, who has compared the spatial diffusion of many technologies between 1850 and 1900, argues for 'the hierarchical diffusion down the ranks of the urban size array', as well as a 'neighbourhood spread' of changes to the small towns of a city's hinterland. For the most part, gas works, building societies and telephone exchanges were established first in the largest cities and only later in lower-ranking places. To focus on the example of the telephone, all of the ten largest English and Welsh cities had exchanges by 1881, while adoption was limited among smaller cities and virtually non-existent among small towns at that time. By 1892, almost all of the largest sixty towns had built telephone exchanges, and indeed there was a linear relationship between rank in the urban hierarchy and the acquisition of an exchange. The proportion of towns with a telephone office dropped as urban rank declined.[63] The number of potential customers living within a small radius was a major factor in locational decisions.

The diffusion of the telephone also moved outward from the larger towns into their hinterlands, particularly in the densely urbanised North. Although in the early years of telephone installation licences restricted operations to the radius of a few miles, trunk lines between towns in the vicinity of Manchester, Birmingham, Leeds and Newcastle developed during the 1880s, creating regional networks that were not initially interconnected. The post office, which had tried to protect the monopoly of the telegraph over long-distance communication, gave up its opposition to the expansion of these networks by the mid-1880s, and by 1890, a major trunk line joined London to the already linked cities of the Midlands, Lancashire and Yorkshire.[64] Engineers, entrepreneurs and city officials slowly came to terms with the potential of the telephone for long-distance communication, and the system that they built grew within the confines

[61] J. A. Agnew and K. R. Cox, 'Urban in-migration in historical perspective', *Historical Methods*, 12 (1979), 145–55; R. H. Osborne, 'The movements of people in Scotland, 1851–1951', *Scottish Studies*, 2 (1958), 1–46; C. W. J. Withers and A. J. Watson, 'Stepwise migration and Highland migration to Glasgow, 1852–1898,' *Journal of Historical Geography*, 17 (1991), 35–55.
[62] A. R. Pred, *The Spatial Dynamics of U.S. Urban-Industrial Growth, 1800–1914* (Cambridge, Mass., 1966). [63] Robson, *Urban Growth*, p. 173. [64] *Ibid.*, pp. 175–7.

of a central-place system. Outlying regions – Wales, much of Scotland, East Anglia and most of the South-West – had to wait for exchanges. Where the number of potential customers was a strong influence on the siting of a new technology, the largest cities had an obvious advantage, until such time as economies of scale and rising levels of effective demand meant that smaller places could be profitably serviced.

The extreme flexibility of telephones as a means of communication, however, means that in the longer run interconnections were not confined within any tight, hierarchical structure. Continued urbanisation brings with it dynamic forms of communication, which transcend physical movement and rigid patterns. During the 1950s and early 1960s small towns in Wales became oriented to ever larger cities. While patterns of trunk calls made in mid-Wales in 1958 showed tight linkages between small settlements and Aberystwyth or Hereford, the closest large central place, these same areas in the 1960s moved much more into the orbit of Cardiff. Cultural and economic linkages multiplied between low ranking towns and the regional capital at a time when urbanisation levels were static.[65] The flow of information along urban networks evolves over time and is not a simple function of distance and physical movement.

At any given time, multiple processes of decision-making shape patterns of exchange. They do not necessarily operate in tandem or with consistency. Alongside the pull of markets and entrepreneurial decisions have operated the sometimes contradictory policies of the central government, which through licensing, parliamentary bills and planning decisions shape investment. Early negotiations over the location of airports in Britain illustrate the point. During the First World War aviation shifted from sport to weapon, leading to the building of more than 300 airfields throughout the United Kingdom. After the war, enthusiasts looked forward to the growth of a new transport industry, and hoped for sale of disused Royal Air Force fields to nearby towns. The issues of siting, investment and government control were to be hammered out by the Department of Civil Aviation (DCA) and the Treasury. The head of the DCA, Frederick Sykes, recommended a network of eleven 'key aerodromes' covering the major cities in Britain, plus an additional two in Belfast and Dublin, and in the early 1920s, municipal officials in Manchester, Glasgow and Birmingham worked with London authorities to set up local airports. The lack of financial support from the Treasury combined with insufficient traffic meant that these early experiments soon collapsed, but the DCA persisted in its efforts to link airfields to cities, announcing in 1928 that 'every town of any importance will, sooner or later, find it essential to possess well sited aerodromes as it does today

[65] D. Clark, 'Urban linkage and regional structure in Wales: an analysis of change, 1958–1968', *Transactions of the Institute of British Geographers*, 58 (1973), 41–58; W. K. D. Davies and C. R. Lewis, 'Regional structures in Wales: two studies of interconnectivity', in M. Carter and W. K. D. Davies, eds., *Urban Essays* (London, 1970), pp. 22–48.

to possess railway stations, roads, [and] garages'. By 1939, all the major cities except for Sheffield and Edinburgh, as well as many ports and county towns, had built airfields. In fact after the DCA's early attempt at centralisation failed, many more were built than could be sustained in the longer run.[66] By the later 1930s, traffic in and out of the London airports dwarfed activity in the rest of the kingdom. The fields at Southampton, Portsmouth, Liverpool and Cardiff each serviced over 10,000 passengers per year, but elsewhere the passenger traffic was tiny and ran at a deficit. Profit and usage had trickled uniformly down the British central-place hierarchy. Air service was indeed interurban, but in its early years, it was directed abroad and to offshore islands, rather than to internal destinations. Even if its location conformed to the logic of central-place systems, its early usage did not. Planes pointed to larger networks overseas, overleaping internal hierarchies.

(vi) NETWORKS ABROAD

Urban ties do not stop at national borders. Communications via water – and now air and electricity – allow cities to forge tight links round the world. Indeed, before the era of the railway, it was far easier to get from Hull to Hamburg than to either Leicester or Manchester. Cities, particularly the larger ones and those with access to the sea, have for centuries participated in a network system whose organisational logic is not territorial and geometric but maritime and irregular.[67] With cities as their ports of call, capitalists looked overseas for investments and customers, extending British influence into Latin America, West Africa and the Pacific.[68] As empire added political ties, long-distance city-to-city exchanges of products, people and services changed from the exotic to the everyday. Indeed, the world systems described by Immanuel Wallerstein and Fernand Braudel operated through an 'internationale of cities', whose core included not only London but major Atlantic ports such as Liverpool, Bristol and Glasgow and whose peripheries stretched to Sydney, Capetown and beyond.[69] Moreover, network linkages extended far down the British urban hierarchy; even tiny waterside towns housed a few vessels that crossed the Channel or the Irish Sea, while the many canals and rivers gave much of the country easy access to coastal ports. Waterside settlements were part of a second set of urban linkages that extended to the Antipodes.

Over time, the abundant maritime traffic became more regulated from

---

[66] J. Myerscough, 'Airport provision in the inter-war years', *Journal of Contemporary History*, 20 (1985), 41–70.
[67] P. M. Hohenberg and L. H. Lees, *The Making of Urban Europe*, 2nd edn (Cambridge, 1995).
[68] P. J. Cain and A. G. Hopkins, *British Imperialism: Innovation and Expansion, 1688–1914* and *British Imperialism: Crisis and Deconstruction, 1914–1990* (London, 1993).
[69] I. Wallerstein, *The Modern World System* (New York, 1974); F. Braudel, *Civilization and Capitalism, 15th–18th c.*, 3 vols. (London, 1981–4).

London and the major ports, channelling communication abroad through the existing urban hierarchy. Although in the early nineteenth century, overseas mail moved haphazardly on any vessel from any convenient port, post office steamers also operated out of stations in Dover, Weymouth, Milford, Holyhead, Liverpool and Portpatrick, but fixed contracts with private companies evolved during the 1840s. After the post office determined port-to-port needs and the Treasury approved the schemes, the Admiralty was charged to negotiate terms with bidding shipowners. Cunard won early contracts for the North Atlantic routes beginning with Halifax and Boston, while by the early 1840s, the P & O took the mails to Gibraltar, Alexandria, Madras and Calcutta, soon expanding to the ports of south China and the southern Pacific. The lure of government subsidies and fixed rates brought the Royal Mail Steam Packet Company into existence for service to Latin America and the Caribbean, fattening its coffers for decades. Despite the competition for lucrative contracts, official demands for efficiency and security soon produced a centralised system regulated from London and the largest ports. Monopoly early replaced free competition, streaming the flow of information abroad into a limited number of intercity channels.[70]

The electric web of power that held the Empire together followed a similar spatial logic. To the telegraph lines that fanned out from London along the rail networks, engineers added early underwater cable connections. One of the first, laid in 1850, stretched from Calais to Dover; soon links to Ireland and across the Atlantic followed. The British determination to control secure communications with colonies abroad spurred entrepreneurs to spin out cables to the gateway cities of the globe. During the 1860s, the Falmouth, Gibraltar, Malta Telegraph Company laid the line in nearby waters, while the British Indian Telegraph Company connected Malta to Alexandria, and that city to Suez and Karachi. After 1870, the India Office could send secret cables to the viceroy in Calcutta in a few hours, and receive an almost immediate reply. The Boer War triggered a demand, soon satisfied, for a linkage to South Africa, which was quickly extended to Australia. Although the logic of telecommunications permits decentralised flows of information, the planning, maintenance and finance of such networks is resolutely hierarchical. The spinal cords of the British Empire stretched from London to colonial ports and capitals all over the globe.[71]

Because British companies owned between 40 and 50 per cent of the world's merchant marine in the nineteenth century, her ports captured a major share of international trade. In the 1850s, London claimed the largest maritime business in the world, 'the tidal Thames bringing in its flow the treasure of near and distant nations'.[72] Into its docks came rubber from Brazil, sugar from Jamaica and tea from Ceylon. Schooners and clipper ships sped to Buenos Aires and

---

[70] Daunton, *Royal Mail*, pp. 154–79.

[71] D. R. Headrick, *The Tentacles of Progress* (New York and Oxford, 1988), pp. 99–108.

[72] *The Pictorial Handbook of London* (London, 1854), p. 339.

Kingston, Melbourne and Singapore. Heavily laden steamers left daily for Spain, Germany, France and the Netherlands, exchanging yarn, textiles, metalwork and machinery for food and raw materials. The Liverpool docks opened on to an Atlantic world: fortunes made in the African slave trade later served to purchase sugar from the Caribbean, cotton from the United States, beef from Argentina. Glasgow and Bristol merchants imported food from Ireland and North America; Thomas Lipton, for example, built huge warehouses for the hundreds of thousands of hams he ordered yearly from Chicago and Omaha, for his frozen turkeys from Canada, his consignments of cheese and butter from northern New York State and from Ireland.[73] Hull firms dealt particularly with the Baltic, while other east coast ports cultivated ties with Rotterdam, Hamburg and Bremen. Network connections brought an ever-shifting cornucopia of goods and people into the island's ports. The large liners of the international passenger trade headed for Southampton, as Liverpool became the major port for emigrant departures. Grimsby specialised in the grain and fish trade, and the South Wales ports were configured for coal exports.

Dynasties of shipowning families ran their companies from office palaces in London and Liverpool, commissioning new tramps and liners from builders on the Clyde, Mersey or Thames and dispatching cargoes around the world. As graceful sailing ships gave way to paddle steamers and then to steel vessels driven by propeller and turbine, ports like Boston, Whitby and Whitehaven lost the ability to service major cargoes. Elsewhere, giant wet docks and piers reconfigured riversides to suit the requirements of gargantuan vessels. Investments by railway companies helped Barrow, Tyneside and Southampton outdistance competitors and keep up with changing maritime technology. By 1914, most of the export trade had concentrated in about twelve cities, rather than the hundreds of small ports that had been active a hundred years earlier.[74] Conference agreements to regulate fares, market shares and routes for both freight and passenger travel benefited the larger companies and ports. Until the 1920s, access to cheap coal supplies, to sophisticated finance and to information via the international cable network gave British shipping conglomerates comparative advantages that brought prosperity to Liverpool, Glasgow and Southampton, as well as the capital. The relatively high market shares of Cardiff, Newport and Swansea testified to the continuing power of the Welsh coal trade.

But in the longer run not even a orgy of merger and manoeuvre would save these same ports from foreign competition. By 1938, British ships accounted for only about a quarter of the world's total tonnage, and they had less to carry, after ships shifted from coal to oil as fuel. The market collapsed for South Wales' central export product, while business contracted at all the major ports. Indeed, by 1933 J. B. Priestley saw the Liverpool docks as 'a vast amount of gloom and

[73] Mathias, *Retailing*, pp. 109–11.
[74] H. J. Dyos and D. H. Aldcroft, *British Transport* (Leicester, 1969), pp. 247–55.

emptiness and decay being carefully guarded'.[75] A few cities captured the shrinking pie of British exports and imports. On the eve of the Second World War, over half the value of the UK's foreign trade was channelled through Liverpool and London, and an additional 10 per cent through Hull and Southampton; these proportions remained roughly the same until after 1960.[76]

Air travel and electronic communications have shifted a major share of British network linkages away from the ports in two directions – first up the urban hierarchy into the trinity of cities (London, Manchester, Glasgow) tied to international air traffic and then down the network into ordinary homes. Most physical movement in and out of the country moves through London. In fact, London's international linkages have been reinforced by post-war shifts in economic structures and political power, which thrive on the economies of scale and the rising importance of world trade and finance. During the 1950s, the role of sterling as an international reserve currency second only to the dollar made the Bank of England the centre of a network linking London to the financial capitals of the commonwealth and British colonies, whose object was to regulate trade within the group and restrict competition with the United States. Until sterling became freely convertible into dollars in 1958, London bankers, along with their counterparts in New Delhi, Johannesburg and Hong Kong, made the key decisions about exchange rates and capital flows upon which British trade was based.[77] Although the dimensions of London's role as a world-city have been reconfigured several times since 1600, her position holds firm.

By the 1960s, British cities so dominated the rural that the entire society was effectively urbanised. A spreading consumer culture brought similar goods to Sheffield shop girls and Sloane Rangers. Connected to a wider world through the BBC and London newspapers, citizens from Cornwall to the Highlands found themselves in the same informational universe, which was dominated by the capital. They lived in a radically condensed landscape in which technology and investment had successfully managed 'the annihilation of space by time', and then had collapsed time differences as well. Telegraph, telephone and television brought an illusion of simultaneity, and of the disappearance of distance. Yet the built landscape of industrial urbanism still structured the natural landscape. Mid-twentieth-century cities were linked by the capital investment of the nineteenth and early twentieth – railways, roads and electricity grids, which provided the infrastructures for communications and transport. The historical geography of capitalism, whose waves of investment and disinvestment had transformed the country, endured in multiple forms. Mills and markets, wetdocks and warehouses, town halls and tramways, department stores and schools dominated the

---

[75] J. B. Priestley, *English Journey* (London, 1934), p. 194.

[76] J. W. House, *The UK Space: Resources, Environment, and the Future* (London, 1973), p. 319.

[77] M. Collins, *Money and Banking in the UK: A History* (London, 1988), pp. 540–1.

cityscape and provided destinations for citizens in motion. Urban networks make tangible past choices as they mould present interactions. The reshaping of geographical landscapes in Britain has operated through the interconnections of an urban hierarchy solidified by the combined investments of state and industry in a century of rapid growth and change.

· 3 ·

Modern London

RICHARD DENNIS

It is difficult to speak adequately or justly of London. It is not a pleasant place; it is not agreeable, or cheerful, or easy, or exempt from reproach. It is only magnificent. You can draw up a tremendous list of reasons why it should be insupportable . . . But . . . for one who takes it as I take it, London is on the whole the most possible form of life . . . It is the biggest aggregation of human life – the most complete compendium of the world. The human race is better represented there than any-where else, and if you learn to know your London you learn a great many things.

Henry James, 1881[1]

D ISTILLING THE essence of modern London into a chapter, one cannot help but be selective. I will focus on just four, interrelated aspects of London's history: government, social geography, economy and Empire.[2] It is clearly impossible to understand London without examining the 'problem' of London's government: the relationship between central govern-ment, the Corporation of the City, London-wide authorities such as the Metropolitan Board of Works and its successor, the London County Council, and lower-tier authorities, initially parish vestries and district boards and, subse-quently, metropolitan borough councils. But making sense of debates about appropriate forms of metropolitan government demands a sensitivity to London's changing social geography: a nineteenth-century tension between poor East End and rich West End, subsumed in a twentieth-century contrast

---

[1] F. O. Matthiessen and K. B. Murdock, eds., *The Notebooks of Henry James* (New York, 1947), pp. 27–8.

[2] At the outset it is worth noting two valuable bibliographic essays: J. Davis, 'Modern London 1850–1939', *LJ*, 20 (1995), 56–90, and M. Hebbert, 'London recent and present', *LJ*, 20 (1995), 91–101. For a comprehensive listing of published work on London history, see H. Creaton, ed., *Bibliography of Printed Works on London History to 1939* (London, 1994). See also three general his-tories of London, all with detailed notes and/or bibliographies: R. Porter, *London* (London, 1994); S. Inwood, *A History of London* (London, 1998); F. Sheppard, *London* (Oxford, 1998).

between working-class inner and middle-class outer London. Of course there are numerous qualifications to be made to this caricature, to take account of working-class suburbanisation, the survival of an elite West End and, more recently, a sporadic gentrification of inner London, and a City that shifted from mixed residential to almost exclusively non-residential in its pattern of land use.

Alongside these socio-geographical changes there were also major economic changes: decline of some traditional industries, growth of a service economy and especially of the City as centre of world finance, and interwar manufacturing revival, but in an Americanised and suburban form. Even in the nineteenth century social differentiation was increasing at the same time as the metropolis was becoming economically more integrated. This was also evident in London's continuing evolution as a centre of elite consumption – as reflected in the aristocratic 'season' and its extension into a *nouveau riche* world of grand hotels, restaurants, clubs and theatres – which necessarily depended on low-paid, seasonal and casual labour working what today would be regarded as 'unsocial hours'. So a chapter on London must also pay attention to the city's economy, and to the relationship of London with the rest of the world, especially its role as 'Heart of the Empire'.

Before we can concentrate in detail on these four themes, several other questions merit our attention. First, with regard to the definition and 'knowability' of London.[3] The census first defined a London that was larger than the square mile of the City in 1851. This definition provided the boundary for both the Metropolitan Board of Works, in 1855, and the County of London, in 1888. But the built-up area of London had burst through this boundary long before 1888. 'Greater London' came to be defined statistically in the 1870s as equivalent to the Metropolitan Police District, extending 15 miles (24 km) from Charing Cross (Map 3.1).[4] Although London might be seen as one organic growth, unlike other 'conurbations' that linked several cities of roughly equal importance, its expansion embraced some quite substantial, previously independent settlements. The issue of 'localism' versus 'metropolitanism' continues to the present – do Londoners think of themselves as Londoners, or do they identify with their local borough, or parish; or are all these administrative units artificial impositions cutting across an allegiance to no more than the immediate neighbourhood? To Roy Porter, London is a jigsaw, 'a congregation of diversity' in which the absence of strong metropolitan-wide government meant that 'confusion permitted diversity and interstitial growth', almost a postmodern celebration of an unorganised if not disorganised metropolis.[5]

Secondly, we may question the existence of 'turning points' in the history of

---

[3] On 'knowability' see M. Hebbert, *London* (Chichester, 1998), esp. ch. 1, 'The knowledge'.
[4] P. J. Waller, *Town, City and Nation* (Oxford, 1983), pp. 24–67; P. L. Garside, 'West End, East End: London, 1890–1940', in A. Sutcliffe, ed., *Metropolis, 1890–1940* (London, 1984), p. 242.
[5] Porter, *London*, pp. 10, 186.

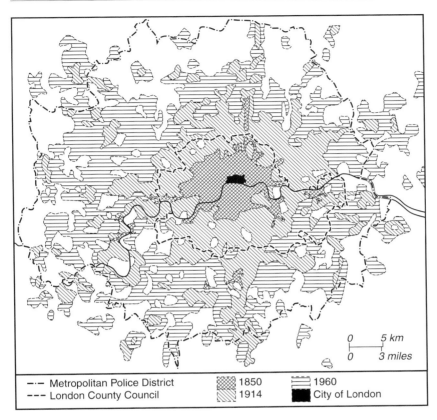

Map 3.1 The boundaries and built-up area of London 1850–1960
Source: modified from H. Clout and P. Wood, eds., *London* (Harlow, 1986).

London. Asa Briggs focused on *fin de siècle* London as a moment when the metropolis particularly exemplified British history.[6] Pat Garside identified critical boundaries at 1870 and 1918, perhaps implying that the whole intervening half-century was one long turning point. Prior to 1870, according to H. J. Dyos' view, 'London was, at one and the same time, central yet peripheral, economically secondary yet socially dominant, culturally inspirational yet parasitic.' Modifying this interpretation, Garside concluded that 'London's economic achievements in the mid-nineteenth century were not derived from, nor even interdependent with provincial manufacturing towns: it was neither parasitic nor ambiotic – it was separate, self-generating and highly successful.' None the less, there was a strong relationship between London and the provinces, in flows of

[6] A. Briggs, *Victorian Cities* (London, 1963), pp. 311–60.

97

both labour and capital, especially for infrastructural projects such as railways, and specialist financial and insurance services. By contrast, after 1870, 'London's own domestic problems were to force themselves forward as *the* national issues of the moment.' National policies were designed to solve metropolitan problems.[7]

The period between 1870 and 1918 may be considered transitional particularly because of the city's novel demographic experience, losing population across an ever wider central area at the same time as it was growing physically and numerically at the periphery. Until 1901, 'Greater London' grew at a faster rate than England as a whole. Until 1881, even the area subject to the Metropolitan Board of Works (later the County of London) was gaining population more rapidly than England, but from 1881 to 1901, the County grew more slowly than the rest of the country. After 1901, the LCC area started to lose population, such that 'Greater London' as a whole failed to keep up with the population growth of the rest of the country, and the proportion of the country's population resident in London peaked in 1901 at 21.4 per cent. The City, of course, had long been in rapid decline as a place of residence: 112,000 residents in 1861, 14,000 sixty years later.[8]

After the First World War, the County continued its gradual population decrease, but outer London now grew so rapidly compared to the sluggish increase elsewhere that in the 1920s population growth in 'Greater London' once again outstripped the rate for England and Wales. Contemporaries concluded that by 1939 London's dominance was contrary to the national interest. Compounding the interpretation of earlier observers, such as William Cobbett, that London was a cancerous growth on the body of the nation, there was now the fear that increasing geographical concentration of wealth and population made the nation more vulnerable to air attack in time of war.[9] But, in most respects, as David Feldman and Gareth Stedman Jones observed, the capital's primacy was just one of the 'striking regularities and recurrences in London's history'. Continuing debates about racism and immigration policy can be compared with agitation that prompted the passage of the Aliens Act in 1905, a piece of national legislation primarily intended to deal with a London problem; and modern ideas of 'underclass' and 'culture of poverty' parallel the Victorian concept of the residuum.[10] Porter, too, points to a congruence between late nineteenth- and late twentieth-century London, for example comparing the diagnoses offered by Mearns' *Bitter Cry of Outcast London* and the Church of

---

[7] The quotations are all from P. L. Garside, 'London and the Home Counties', in F. M. L. Thompson, ed., *The Cambridge Social History of Britain, 1750–1950*, vol. 1: *Regions and Communities* (Cambridge, 1990), pp. 490, 494, 504.   [8] Waller, *Town*, pp. 24–8.

[9] Garside, 'London', p. 525.

[10] D. Feldman and G. Stedman Jones, 'Introduction', in D. Feldman and G. Stedman Jones, eds., *Metropolis* (London, 1989), pp. 1–7.

England's *Faith in the City*.[11] Of course, there are also major differences: in gender relations, in the role of women and as a consequence of the decline of Empire. Such parallels and divergences illustrate how we constantly reinterpret London's history according to our own concerns, whether identifying the origins of postmodern consumption practices in Victorian bazaars and department stores, or re-evaluating the nineteenth-century manufacturing economy in the context of more recent enthusiasm for 'enterprise' and 'flexibility'.

(i) MODERNITY

Whatever else it may be, the period 1840–1950 constitutes the core of what many cultural historians regard as 'modern'. Writing about New York City in the period 1890–1940, David Ward and Olivier Zunz discuss modernity as the combination of rational planning and cultural pluralism, the one creating order – residential segregation, zoning, the efficient use of urban space – the other reflecting the increasing diversity of urban populations.[12] To David Harvey, order, mastery, rationality and planning are characteristics of the modern, in contrast to the apparent chaos, relativism, diversity, even playfulness of the postmodern.[13] But just as it has been argued that postmodernity is but a particular kind of modernity, so we can envisage aspects of the postmodern in the modern city of the late nineteenth century. For Marshall Berman, the roots of *modern* urban life lie in the tension between enlightenment rationality and romanticism. He traces the relationship between the discovery of self, self-knowledge and self-identity on the one hand, and the organisation and ordering of society on the other.[14]

Berman's argument, stressing the double-edged nature of modernity, provides a framework for bringing together disparate themes in the history of London. For example, we may set Charles Booth's application of scientific principles to survey, map and classify the people and places of London alongside George Gissing's novels which show how people experienced those places and constructed their own identities through their use of the city. We can interpret new spaces – new streets like Charing Cross Road or Kingsway, new railway termini and station hotels, department stores and chain stores, office blocks and factories, public parks and cemeteries, music halls and cinemas – as products of rational planning and scientific management, but also as spaces for new kinds of everyday life, and as potential spaces of resistance or subversion. James Winter

[11] Porter, *London*, pp. 383–4.
[12] D. Ward and O. Zunz, 'Between rationalism and pluralism: creating the modern city', in D. Ward and O. Zunz, eds., *The Landscape of Modernity* (New York, 1992), pp. 3–15.
[13] D. Harvey, *The Condition of Postmodernity* (Oxford, 1989), pp. 42–4.
[14] M. Berman, *All That Is Solid Melts into Air* (London, 1983), pp. 13–36. For Berman's ideas critically applied to England, see M. Nava and A. O'Shea, eds., *Modern Times* (London, 1996).

has noted how 'Straighteners, regulators, cleansers, purifiers, conservationists, and promoters of the municipal ideal, liberals most of them, tried to balance their vision of a London that was ordered, rational, efficient, healthy, and safe, in other words, "modern", with a sense that the freedom of the public thoroughfare disclosed what it meant to be English.' It proved difficult to reconcile 'the metaphor of reform and a liberal devotion to individual self-determination'.[15] This is clearly demonstrated in Susan Pennybacker's analysis of the failures of LCC 'Progressivism' prior to the First World War. Far from making space for personal freedom and self-fulfilment, the Progressive programme of regulation and classification, embodied in public health officials, moral guardians, park keepers, housing managers and licensing authorities, and designed to counter fears of moral and physical degeneracy, legitimated the eugenics movement and alienated the lower middle classes. In Pennybacker's words, 'intrusion and supervision were substituted for grander programmes of social amelioration or cultural enlightenment'.[16]

This is not to deny an inherent modernity, which predated and continued independently of the attempts of a modern council to regulate its reluctant citizens. London was 'modern' despite the absence of effective planning. Positing London as much as Paris as 'capital of the nineteenth century', on the basis of 'its exemplary individualism', Richard Sennett has suggested, first, that the power of great landowners, especially in the West End, contrasting with the weakness of metropolitan government, facilitated the development of a city of class-homogeneous but disconnected spaces. London was characterised by estate planning rather than town planning. But London also appeared excessively orderly to Sennett (who has long advocated the positive aspects of disorder) because what 'planning' there was, in the form of new roads and new public transport networks (buses, railways, trams), was designed to encourage the free movement of individuals but discourage the movement of organised groups.[17] It distanced Londoners from the environments through which they passed. Winter noted as much in discussing 'why so many early Victorians came to define the city as a circulatory system rather than a fixed place'. Medical metaphors alluded to the need to remove 'arterial obstructions'. Hence the need to regulate traffic – the first traffic signal erected experimentally, but soon abandoned, in Parliament Square, in 1868, and the eventual introduction of traffic lights in 1929; the appointment of traffic constables from 1869 – and an ambivalence towards street furniture, like drinking troughs and urinals, which utilised new technology in their manufacture but slowed down the flow of both horses and pedestrians. Streets were where one 'walked briskly'. Less purposive behaviour was condemned as 'loafing' or 'sauntering listlessly', or made one liable to

[15] J. Winter, *London's Teeming Streets, 1830–1914* (London, 1993), p. xi.
[16] S. D. Pennybacker, *A Vision for London, 1889–1914* (London, 1995), p. 241.
[17] R. Sennett, *Flesh and Stone* (London, 1994), pp. 317–54.

prosecution under the Vagrancy Act, whereas the same behaviour in a park would be tolerated as 'strolling' or 'promenading'.[18]

While new streets, railway lines and tramways made for faster, more purposive travel, other technological improvements made travel more comfortable. But comfort is associated with rest. Movement became a more passive, as well as a more private experience. Silence in travel was used to protect individual privacy. So, Sennett concluded, drawing on Forster's *Howards End* (1910), London became 'a city that seems to hold together socially precisely because people don't connect personally'.[19] The motto of *Howards End* was 'only connect', and the interpersonal and cross-class connections that eventually occur, which allow Forster's characters to discover their own identities, are the results of displacements and discord in their lives, occurrences which – for Sennett – were all too rare in Edwardian London.

Howards End perfectly captures a dispirited view of London's Faustian development. Margaret Schlegel contemplated the demolition of her own home to make way for a block of 'Babylonian' mansion flats: 'In the streets of the city she noted for the first time the architecture of hurry, and heard the language of hurry on the mouths of its inhabitants – clipped words, formless sentences, potted expressions of approval or disgust. Month by month things were stepping livelier, but to what goal?' When the Schlegels eventually achieved the promised land of *Howards End*, an idyllic converted farmhouse in Hertfordshire, the shadow of the metropolis was still there: '"London's creeping." She pointed over the meadow – over eight or nine meadows, but at the end of them was a red rust.'[20]

(ii) MODERNISING LONDON'S GOVERNMENT

In 1840 London still lacked any semblance of city-wide government. The City Corporation was irrelevant as far as most of London was concerned, and the Municipal Corporations Act had passed London by, though it could be argued that some vestries were at least as efficient as some reformed corporations elsewhere in the country. More often, London historians have condemned the vestries as corrupt and apathetic, dominated by petty-minded tradesmen who resented public spending. However suspicious of such assertions, we must acknowledge that neither elite leadership nor participatory politics was very evident in London's local government.[21]

Worries about public health did lead to some reforms – the creation of a Metropolitan Commission of Sewers in 1847 and, in 1855, the Metropolitan Board of Works (MBW), its members elected by twenty-three ancient vestries and fifteen new district boards which combined groups of small parishes. Briggs

[18] Winter, *London's Teeming Streets*, pp. 5, 34–40, 168–9.   [19] Sennett, *Flesh*, p. 323.
[20] E. M. Forster, *Howards End* (London, 1910; 1983 Penguin edn), pp. 116–17, 329.
[21] J. Davis, *Reforming London* (Oxford, 1988).

claimed that the area governed by the MBW was determined more by the existing network of drains and sewers than by any administrative logic, though a less romantic explanation was that it corresponded to the registrar general's definition of London in the 1851 census. Despite its undoubted achievements – Bazalgette's sewers and the associated pumping stations, the Embankment, Charing Cross Road, Shaftesbury Avenue and the beginnings of slum clearance and rehousing – the indirectly elected MBW, packed with vestrymen of such lengthy experience as to constitute a veritable gerontocracy, was a poor substitute for democratic, London-wide government. Rejection of the latter by a royal commission in 1854, which claimed a lack of sufficient common interest among inhabitants in different parts of the built-up area, represented a triumph for the vestries. The royal commission had, however, suggested the creation of eight large municipalities corresponding to the eight parliamentary boroughs into which the metropolis was then divided, but this too had been turned down on the grounds that they would be too large for effective local government.[22]

When the London County Council eventually came into being as a product of the 1888 Local Government Act, its powers were still quite limited. It had no control over the police, who remained under Home Office authority, or education (which was the responsibility of the London School Board), or administration of the poor law; and it inherited the Board of Works' boundaries, which were now even more illogical, given the physical growth of the metropolis since 1855. From the beginning, therefore, almost all of London's population growth occurred beyond the boundaries of the new county; and from 1901 onwards, the population of the LCC area was in decline. The LCC was established by a Conservative central government, but at the first – now direct – elections, a Liberal-Progressive majority was returned, which retained control until 1907. Lord Salisbury anticipated that the radicals would soon lose popular support, but when this failed to occur, the Conservative-sponsored London Municipal Society was formed to press for decentralisation of the Council's powers to a strengthened lower tier of municipal authorities. The result was the balancing of the LCC by twenty-eight metropolitan boroughs, an arrangement that continued from 1899 into the 1960s.[23]

What was the effect of this arrangement on the LCC, and how far did local populations identify with the new boroughs? According to Garside

> In practice, the new structure did not diminish the power of the LCC. Indeed, it could be argued that the LCC's broader vision was strengthened. With the metropolitan borough councils offering a focus for parochial pride, the LCC could more easily insulate itself from local interests, projecting and developing a London-wide base as a framework for policy and decision-making.[24]

---

[22] Briggs, *Victorian Cities*, p. 322; D. Owen, *The Government of Victorian London, 1855–1889* (Cambridge, Mass., and London, 1982); Davis, *Reforming London*.

[23] K. Young and P. Garside, *Metropolitan London* (London, 1982), pp. 1–101, 343.

[24] Garside, 'London', p. 514.

Yet the LCC's record does not really bear out this strategic role. The Council eventually took control of education, trams and poor law infirmaries. By the 1920s, it owned 10 bridges and 4 tunnels across the Thames, 160 miles of tramway, 115 parks, 66 fire stations, 10 mental hospitals, and more than 1,000 schools. Nevertheless, housing apart, the LCC did little to change the physical structure of London. For example, it laid out far fewer new streets than its supposedly lethargic predecessor, the Metropolitan Board of Works;[25] and the Labour-controlled LCC after 1934 showed no interest in planning that extended beyond its county boundaries. Wider proposals for regional planning were condemned by the chairman of the LCC Town Planning Committee as 'fascist' and 'un-British'.[26] It is difficult to see how the LCC could plan with much vision when it only had responsibility for the declining inner parts of a rapidly expanding whole.

As for the new boroughs, there was some scepticism as to whether their residents would identify with them. H. G. Wells claimed that localism was being eroded by every new form of communication. Philip Waller observes that 'Civic pride in most London districts had to be contrived.' Londoners naturally identified with localities, not with boroughs. Yet in some cases, the construction of local identity was remarkably successful: for example, in the socialist fiefdoms of Poplar and Bermondsey.[27]

For Wells the solution to London's problems lay in a 'Greater London' that would embrace the entire commuting population of the Home Counties. Part of the logic underlying the creation of the LCC had been the need to equalise rates between poor and rich districts, such that the West End would contribute to solving the problems of the East End. Geographically, too, the problems of poor districts were not to be solved *in situ* but elsewhere, in suburbs that lay outside the County of London. In 1871 the richest parish – St James, Piccadilly – had a rateable value per head that was nearly seven times that of the poorest parish – Bethnal Green. To yield an equivalent income, a much higher rate in the pound had to be levied in poor areas. East End vestries also complained that, although they contributed on an equal basis to the MBW, most of the Board's expenditure was concentrated in central London. By 1901, the gap had widened: St Martin-in-the-Fields had a *per capita* valuation thirteen times that of Mile End.[28] By then a programme of rate equalisation and fiscal integration of the City and second-tier authorities had been implemented, but most suburbs with

[25] Porter, *London*, p. 334.   [26] Garside, 'West End', p. 250.
[27] Waller, *Town*, p. 59; for Wells, see Porter, *London*, p. 311, Garside, 'West End', pp. 241–2; on Poplar, see J. Gillespie, 'Poplarism and proletarianism: unemployment and Labour politics in London, 1918–34', in Feldman and Stedman Jones, eds., *Metropolis*, pp. 163–88, G. Rose, 'Locality, politics, and culture: Poplar in the 1920s', *Environment and Planning D: Society and Space*, 6 (1988), 151–68, G. Rose, 'Imagining Poplar in the 1920s: contested concepts of community', *Journal of Historical Geography*, 16 (1990), 425–37; on Bermondsey, see E. Lebas, 'When every street became a cinema: the film work of Bermondsey Borough Council's public-health department, 1923–1953', *History Workshop Journal*, 39 (1995), 42–66.   [28] Davis, *Reforming London*, pp. 33–41.

land to spare and many of the more prosperous middle classes lay beyond the boundaries of the LCC. The Council did have rights to acquire land and develop housing estates outside the County, but the consequence was usually to antagonise out-county authorities who liked to think of themselves as definitely *not* London.

Unsurprisingly, it proved impracticable for the County to expand. After 1918, the urgency of the housing crisis led to shelving of proposals to reform London government, at the expense of striking local bargains with individual out-county authorities prepared to accept LCC housing. But the sight of these new 'Labour colonies', growing up in the fields of Essex, Kent, Surrey and Middlesex, strengthened the resolve of suburban authorities as a whole not to succumb to a 'Greater London'.[29]

One consequence of the continued growth of privately developed, owner-occupied suburbs was that the inner city became more solidly working class. This did not necessarily equate with support for Labour; there was always a strong strand of working-class Toryism, and also the growth of Fascism in parts of the East End in the 1930s. But from 1934 Labour assumed control of the LCC. For Conservatives this heralded a return to the fears of the 1890s: a strong left-leaning municipality challenging the authority of central government. Their solution after the Second World War was to decentralise as much as possible to the boroughs and, reluctantly, acknowledge the need for a modest 'Greater London' in which the weight of suburbia might restore Conservative control; but not as great a 'Greater London' as Wells had envisaged, because such a regional scale of government, even under the Conservatives, would have presented too great a threat to Whitehall. In sum, London government through the nineteenth and twentieth centuries has been a curious mixture of centralised and decentralised, elected and unelected, visionary and routine, a very 'modern' combination of order and diversity.[30]

(iii) MODERNITY AND THE SOCIAL GEOGRAPHY OF LONDON

The scale and character of residential segregation in London was one consequence of its size. Where, in provincial cities, there might be groups of streets, or neighbourhoods, associated with one social or ethnic group, in London – especially in suburban London – there could be whole boroughs in which one class predominated. There was also scope for more gradations in the social hierarchy to be expressed topographically, for example for subtle variations to exist

[29] Garside, 'West End', pp. 245–53.
[30] Young and Garside, *Metropolitan London*, pp. 173–4, 256–330; Porter, *London*, pp. 332–7; C. Husbands, 'East End racism, 1900–1980', *LJ*, 8 (1982), 3–26. On the history of the LCC, see also A. Saint, ed., *Politics and the People of London* (London, 1989).

between estates within lower-middle-class suburbia. A particularly sensitive observer was the novelist, George Gissing. Whereas Wells and Forster wrote about types of places, or at least changed the names to imaginary ones, Gissing often wrote about real streets.

In *In the Year of Jubilee* (1894, but set in 1887 and the years immediately following), much of the story is set in what for urban historians is *the* Victorian suburb: Camberwell.[31] When the honest but dull Samuel Barmby became a partner in a local piano business, his family moved to Dagmar Road, 'a new and most respectable house, with bay windows rising from the half-sunk basement to the second storey. Samuel . . . privately admitted the charm of such an address as "Dagmar Road", which looks well at the head of note-paper, and falls with sonority from the lips.' Less than five minutes' walk away, the Peacheys occupied a villa in De Crespigny Park. Again, the house matched the family. Arthur Peachey was in the business of manufacturing a disinfectant, subsequently proved to be worthless, adulterated, possibly even harmful; the rest of his family were revealed as equally shallow and suspect. As for their home, it was 'unattached, double-fronted . . . a flight of steps to the stucco pillars at the entrance'. Each house in De Crespigny Park 'seems to remind its neighbour, with all the complacence expressible in buff brick, that in this locality lodgings are *not* to let'. Yet higher, both physically and socially, was the residence of Mr Vawdrey, a wealthy City investor, on Champion Hill, 'a gravel byway, overhung with trees; large houses and spacious gardens on either hand . . . One might have imagined it a country road, so profound the stillness and so leafy the prospect.'[32]

What Gissing depicted in words, Charles Booth painted on the map. Booth's portrayal of *Life and Labour of the People in London* began in 1886, with a detailed survey of the East End, based on the reports of school board visitors. Booth's classification of households into one of eight poverty classes facilitated the construction of a poverty map, showing the percentage of households in the four poorest classes in each part of the metropolis (Map 3.2). Alongside this summary map, he also produced a 'Descriptive map of London poverty' in which each street was assigned to one of seven colours, ranging from the black of the 'Lowest class. Vicious, semi-criminal' to the gold of the 'Upper-middle and Upper classes. Wealthy'. Although Booth's focus was on the poor, and most commentators have concentrated on his explanations for poverty and on the somewhat ambiguous relationship between his classifications of households and streets within the four poorest classes, his survey also distinguished between grades of suburban respectability. De Crespigny Park and Champion Hill were both gold, while Dagmar Road was the red of the 'Middle class. Well-to-do'; but adjacent

---

[31] H. J. Dyos, *Victorian Suburb* (Leicester, 1961).
[32] G. Gissing, *In the Year of Jubilee* (London, 1894; 1994 Everyman edn), pp. 177, 5, 42.

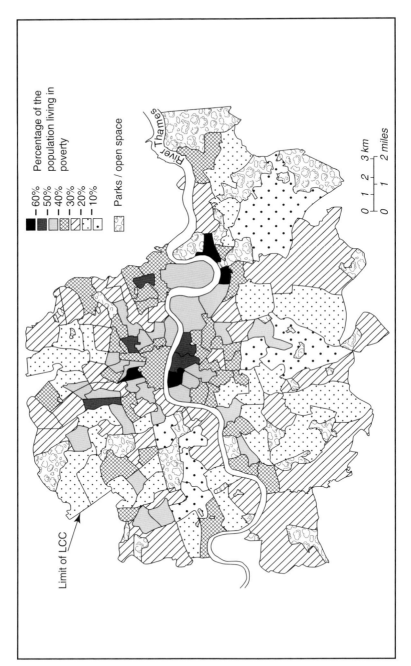

Map 3.2 Charles Booth's poverty map of London 1890
Source: H. Clout, ed., *The Times London History Atlas* (London, 1997).

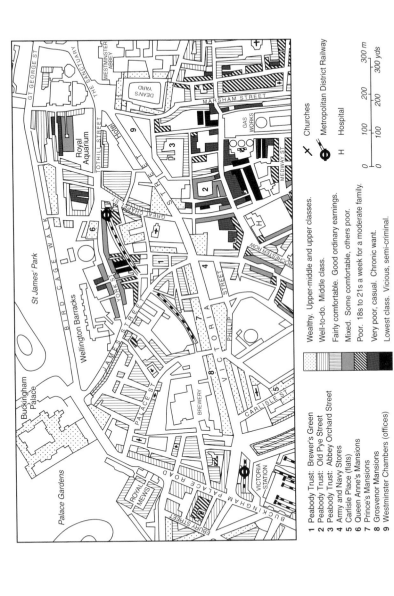

Key:

□ Wealthy. Upper-middle and upper classes.

▥ Well-to-do. Middle class.

▦ Fairly comfortable. Good ordinary earnings.

▨ Mixed. Some comfortable, others poor.

▧ Poor. 18s to 21s a week for a moderate family.

▩ Very poor, casual. Chronic want.

■ Lowest class. Vicious, semi-criminal.

1 Peabody Trust: Brewer's Green
2 Peabody Trust: Old Pye Street
3 Peabody Trust: Abbey Orchard Street
4 Army and Navy Stores
5 Carlisle Place (flats)
6 Queen Anne's Mansions
7 Prince's Mansions
8 Grosvenor Mansions
9 Westminster Chambers (offices)

✠ Churches

Ⓜ Metropolitan District Railway

H Hospital

0   100   200   300 m
0   100   200   300 yds

Map 3.3 Victoria Street 1890: extract from Charles Booth's descriptive map of London poverty streets were only 'Fairly Comfortable' and there were pockets of poverty close to Camberwell Green.[33]

Booth's project has attracted a range of critical evaluations. Christian Topalov discusses Booth's survey, and especially his mapping, as a new and 'modern' way of seeing, arguing that 'the social map owed something both to "slumming", in its attention to social types, and to the panorama in its global vision of the city'. While acknowledging all the subjective aspects of Booth's method of gathering data and of his techniques of mapping, we can recognise the scientific objectives of his survey, contrasting with the anecdotal or picaresque travellers' tales of earlier social explorers. Booth was not just exploring; by classifying and mapping, he was equivalent to a colonial power, with a panoptic vision of the city as a whole. Topalov notes that his poverty maps offered a vision of 'the city of the poor and the city of the rich united within a single space, shown as a whole and therefore open to a coordinated administration'. So, 'when the L.C.C. began work, in 1889, Booth's map was in its in-tray'.[34]

At the conclusion of Gissing's novel, Nancy Tarrant moved across London to Harrow, as remote from Camberwell, morally and culturally, as it was geographically. Compared to the sham pretentiousness of houses in Camberwell, those in the street to which Nancy moved were 'small plain houses, built not long ago, yet at a time when small houses were constructed with some regard for soundness and durability. Each contains six rooms, has a little strip of garden in the rear, and is, or was in 1889, let at a rent of six-and-twenty pounds.'[35] But Harrow was now convenient for London, thanks to the opening of the Metropolitan Railway from Baker Street, which had reached as far as Pinner by 1885.[36] In another of Gissing's novels, *The Whirlpool* (1897), the respectable Harvey Rolfe and his fragile wife, Alma, take a three-year lease on a new house in Pinner, Harvey judging that 'for any one who wished to live practically in London and yet away from its frenzy, the uplands towards Buckinghamshire were convenient ground'.[37] Subsequently, many other Harvey Rolfes opted for the convenience of Metroland. The Metropolitan Railway first established its own development company, promoting an estate in Pinner, then, in 1915, began publication of its

[33] C. Booth, *Life and Labour of the People in London*, 17 vols. (London, 1902–3); for selected extracts, see A. Fried and R. Elman, eds., *Charles Booth's London* (London, 1969); for the original London-wide poverty maps, D. Reeder and the London Topographical Society, *Charles Booth's Descriptive Map of London Poverty 1889* (London, 1987).

[34] C. Topalov, 'The city as terra incognita: Charles Booth's poverty survey and the people of London, 1886–1891', *Planning Perspectives*, 8 (1993), 412. See also M. Bulmer *et al.*, eds., *The Social Survey in Historical Perspective, 1880–1940* (Cambridge, 1991); D. Englander and R. O'Day, eds., *Retrieved Riches* (Aldershot, 1995). [35] Gissing, *Jubilee*, p. 334.

[36] A. A. Jackson, *London's Metropolitan Railway* (Newton Abbot, 1986); T. C. Barker and M. Robbins, *A History of London Transport*, vol. I: *The Nineteenth Century* (London, 1975), pp. 208–14.

[37] G. Gissing, *The Whirlpool* (London, 1897; 1984 edn), p. 183.

annual *Metro-Land* guide, replete with advertisements from leading speculative builders.[38]

Working-class suburbanisation was more limited prior to the First World War. In *The Nether World* (1889), Sidney Kirkwood and his wife attempted to escape the oppressive poverty of Clerkenwell, where he worked as a manufacturing jeweller, by moving to Crouch End. Kirkwood was following exactly the pattern of out-migration prescribed by Booth. Better-off workers in regular employment (Booth's Class E) were to move to the periphery, allowing the occupancy of their old homes by those who were 'immovable'. This was a geographically extended version of what housing reformers referred to as 'levelling up'. It had the advantage of removing the respectable from the potential bad influence of degenerate neighbours, although it also meant there was no hope of improving the latter through the good example of the upwardly mobile.[39]

However, there were few large-scale *industrial* suburbs in late Victorian London, except in east and south-east London, where West Ham, Stratford and Woolwich resembled northern industrial towns, occupied by an artisan elite, mainly employed in large institutions such as Woolwich Arsenal, the Great Eastern Railway works, and some of the food processing and chemical industries close to the Royal Docks and in the lower Lea valley. Self-help agencies that characterised northern towns also flourished here: the Woolwich Building Society dated from 1847, the Royal Arsenal Co-operative Society from 1868.[40]

Most of Victorian and Edwardian suburbia was developed unplanned and piecemeal by small builders: 'in Camberwell, for example, as the local building industry reached its peak between 1878 and 1880, as many as 200 firms, comprising 53 per cent of the total at work in the area, built six houses or fewer over this three-year period; only 15 or less than 4 per cent of the total, built over 60 houses each'. But by the 1890s, these few large firms were responsible for about one third of all new houses: Edward Yates, for example, built more than 2,500 houses in south London between the 1860s and 1900s.[41] There were also a few examples of planned developments prior to the colonisation of the suburbs by local authority housing estates. Bedford Park was laid out from the 1870s as a middle-class garden suburb; a generation later, Hampstead Garden Suburb was

[38] A. A. Jackson, *Semi-Detached London*, 2nd edn (Didcot, 1991), pp. 159, 174–81; Metropolitan Railway, *Metro-Land* (London, 1932; repr. 1987).

[39] G. Gissing, *The Nether World* (London, 1889; 1973 Everyman edn), pp. 364–9; Topalov, 'The city', 403; on levelling up, see R. Dennis, 'The geography of Victorian values: philanthropic housing in London, 1840–1900', *Journal of Historical Geography*, 15 (1989), 40–54.

[40] G. Crossick, *An Artisan Elite in Victorian Society* (London, 1978); J. Marriott, 'West Ham: London's industrial centre and gateway to the world. I: industrialisation, 1840–1910', *LJ*, 13 (1987–8), 121–42.

[41] D. Cannadine and D. Reeder, eds., *Exploring the Urban Past* (Cambridge, 1982), pp. 164–5, 178–89.

envisaged by Henrietta Barnett as a socially mixed community, perhaps building on her experience of East End settlement life, where the working classes were supposed to benefit from the education, example and service of the rich. In practice, Hampstead Garden Suburb evolved as an exclusively middle-class area. Three estates developed by the Artizans', Labourers' and General Dwellings Company, at Shaftesbury Park (1872), Queen's Park (1877) and Noel Park (1881), were more modest in intent, appealing to skilled working-class and lower middle-class families.[42]

The likes of Dagmar Road were still predominantly high-density terraced housing. After the First World War, however, suburbia assumed a different character. Houses became smaller in floor area – usually only two storeys and no basement – but front gardens were larger, and frontages were wider: the predominant house type was semi-detached with side access and, by the 1930s, space for a garage. Between the wars the built-up area of London approximately doubled, although population increased by little more than 10 per cent. Whereas most houses in Victorian Camberwell were rented from private landlords, interwar suburbs were designed for owner-occupation. Building societies flush with funds, cheap money, low building costs (thanks in part to an absence of planning regulations), and the affluence of South-East England compared to the rest of the country, all helped to facilitate suburban sprawl.[43]

Privately developed, owner-occupied suburbia was particularly dependent on further improvements in public transport. Some new 'underground' lines (in practice, often overground by the time they reached suburbia) were financed as public works projects for the unemployed: to Edgware (1924), Stanmore (1932) and Cockfosters (1933). South of the river there was a major programme of railway electrification, extending as far as Dorking by 1925, and reaching to Brighton in 1933, and Portsmouth by 1937.[44]

Apart from council estates, interwar suburbs were mostly socially homogeneous, but nineteenth-century suburbs had contained some slums, such as Sultan Street in Camberwell and parts of North Kensington, while other parts of Kensington which contrasted with the area's predominantly middle-class character were the Potteries and Jennings' Buildings. Jennifer Davis has discussed the social construction of the latter as a slum in terms very similar to the representation of 'problem estates' more recently. For example, many interwar council

---

[42] D. J. Olsen, *The Growth of Victorian London* (London, 1976), pp. 232–5, 287–91; J. N. Tarn, *Five Per Cent Philanthropy* (Cambridge, 1973), pp. 155–6, 171–2, 56–9; Jackson, *Semi-Detached London*, pp. 46–55.

[43] Jackson, *Semi-Detached London*, pp. 61–129, 137–65; M. Turner *et al.*, *Little Palaces: The Suburban House in North London, 1919–1939* (London, 1987); J. H. Johnson, 'The suburban expansion of housing in London, 1918–1939', in J. T. Coppock and H. C. Prince, eds., *Greater London* (London, 1964), pp. 142–66.

[44] Jackson, *Semi-Detached London*, pp. 166–201; T. C. Barker and M. Robbins, *A History of London Transport*, vol. II: *The Twentieth Century to 1970* (London, 1974), pp. 242–60.

estates were castigated by owner-occupier neighbours as 'Little Moscows'; at Downham, in south-east London, a brick wall was built across one road to prevent direct communication between homeowners and tenants. Although the Potteries was the better known district outside Kensington (thanks to Dickens' description of the area), locally Jennings' Buildings had a worse reputation, partly because of its Irishness and partly because of its location close to the commercial heart of Kensington. Davis also shows how the buildings and their inhabitants were an integral part of the Kensington economy, a symbiotic association of wealth and poverty that was even more common in inner and central London.[45]

There were numerous reasons for the absence of residential segregation on a large scale in central London. In the mid-nineteenth century, a labour-intensive middle-class economy required constant access to tradesmen, building workers such as plumbers, tilers and carpenters, and other skilled artisans, including tailors, shoemakers, cabinetmakers and upholsterers, who could provide clothing and furniture to order. Many domestic servants 'lived in' or occupied mews cottages immediately behind their employers' homes. Through most of the West End, aristocratic and ecclesiastical ground landlords continued to own the freehold of large estates and to grant building leases, subject to restrictive covenants designed to maintain the high-status and exclusively residential character of their holdings. But covenants proved difficult to enforce, particularly towards the end of the nineteenth century, as ninety-nine-year leases expired on estates developed during the Georgian and Regency expansion of the West End. This was especially problematic for estates close to the City or to increasingly commercialised areas around Oxford and Regent Streets, as fashionable London moved farther west – to Belgravia, Knightsbridge and Bayswater. The edges of great estates, adjacent to commercial streets like Oxford Street or abutting smaller freehold estates that were less tightly controlled, were most vulnerable to subletting and multi-occupancy. One strategy adopted by several ground landlords, including the duke of Westminster, the marquis of Northampton and the duke of Bedford, was to offer these marginal sites to model dwellings agencies to create a kind of buffer zone or *cordon sanitaire*. Better a closely supervised block of model dwellings than a disorderly slum. The Society for Improving the Condition of the Labouring Classes developed its 'Model Homes for Families' (1850) in Streatham Street on land owned by the duke of Bedford between

---

[45] Dyos, *Victorian Suburb*, pp. 109–13; H. J. Dyos and D. Reeder, 'Slums and suburbs', in H. J. Dyos and M. Wolff, eds., *The Victorian City*, vol. 1 (London, 1973), pp. 359–86; D. Reeder, 'A theatre of suburbs', in H. J. Dyos, ed., *The Study of Urban History* (London, 1968), pp. 262–5; P. Malcolmson, 'Getting a living in the slums of Victorian Kensington', *LJ*, 1 (1975), 28–55; J. Davis, 'Jennings' Buildings and the Royal Borough; the construction of the underclass in mid-Victorian England', in Feldman and Stedman Jones, eds., *Metropolis*, pp. 11–39. On problem estates in inter-war London, see G. Weightman and S. Humphries, *The Making of Modern London 1914–1939* (London, 1984), pp. 107–10.

Bloomsbury and the St Giles rookery; and the duke of Westminster provided sites for several different housing agencies between Oxford Street and Grosvenor Square (the northern edge of Mayfair), and in Pimlico and Chelsea. In practice, the residents of such dwellings, which were invariably oversubscribed, were an elite working class of skilled artisans or regularly employed policemen, postmen and railway workers, rather than the 'poorest of the poor', but they still contrasted in social status with their wealthy neighbours.[46]

Nor was the overlap of different classes confined to 'old' areas of central London. As with many new streets, one motive for Victoria Street – formally opened in 1851 – was to get rid of a notorious slum – the Devil's Acre. As elsewhere, the slum was not eliminated but merely displaced. The Peabody Trust erected one of its first philanthropic housing estates at Brewer's Green (between Victoria Street and St James Park) in 1869; and under the Cross Act (1875) remnants of Devil's Acre on the other side of Victoria Street were replaced by further Peabody estates. Victoria Street itself was lined by a mixture of office blocks (known as 'chambers'), shops (including the Army & Navy department store, opened in 1872) and fashionable apartment buildings (so-called 'French flats').[47] Booth's representation of streets like Victoria Street gives a false picture of social homogeneity because his convention was to colour each street only one colour. But even if Victoria Street was exclusively gold and Abbey Orchard Street all blue, their residents could hardly have avoided contact with one another (Map 3.3).

One consequence of this juxtaposition of slums, model dwellings and fashionable apartments was the need for a more precise language of housing. Apartments were invariably 'Gardens' or 'Mansions' while working-class dwellings were 'Buildings'. In *Howards End*, the Wilcox family took up residence briefly in Wickham Mansions, whereas Leonard Bast, a modest city clerk patronised by the Schlegel sisters, lived in 'what is known to house-agents as a semi-basement, and to other men as a cellar' in Block B of a south London block of flats.[48] More critical still was the language of the 'slum'. The East End was treated as a subject for exploration, 'darkest England' paralleling 'darkest Africa', or apocalyptically, as in references to 'the city of dreadful night', 'the inferno' or 'the people of the abyss'. The sub-human nature of slum dwellers was implied by allusions to 'rookeries' and 'dens', and it was assumed that physical and moral decay went hand-in-hand. The first stage to recovery involved a medical language of incision and dissection to remove cancers and cut new streets. In the process, the term 'slum' itself underwent a shift in meaning. Slums were no longer individual properties in need of improvement or demolition. Under the

[46] D. J. Olsen, *Town Planning in London* (New Haven, 1964; 2nd edn, London, 1982); Olsen, *Growth*, pp. 137–47; Dennis, 'Victorian values', 43–6, 50–1.
[47] I. Watson, *Westminster and Pimlico Past* (London, 1993), pp. 81–6, 100–7, 131–3; J. Tarn, 'French flats for the English in nineteenth-century London', in A. Sutcliffe, ed., *Multi-Storey Living* (London, 1974), pp. 19–40.   [48] Forster, *Howards End*, pp. 59–61, 67–8.

Cross Act (1875) and its subsequent incorporation into Part I of the Housing of
the Working Classes Act (1890), the slum became an *area* for clearance, large
enough to allow redevelopment, but small enough to suggest that the housing
problem was simply a collection of problem *areas*, not a fault of the structure of
housing provision as a whole, let alone an inevitable consequence of the economic system.[49]

Initially, the slum problem was to be solved by individual and corporate philanthropy – a first wave of agencies in the 1840s, followed by the larger scale
Peabody Trust and Improved Industrial Dwellings Company in the early 1860s,
and a third wave of five per cent companies, such as the East End Dwellings
Company and the Four Per Cent Industrial Dwellings Company (which catered
predominantly for Jewish immigrants), in the wake of Mearns' sensationalist tract
on *The Bitter Cry of Outcast London* and the ensuing Royal Commission on the
Housing of the Working Classes (1884–5).[50] They acquired their first sites privately, often from other institutional landlords or aristocratic beneficence, but
the Cross Act provided a new means of acquiring sites cheaply in an otherwise
impossibly expensive central London land market. Indirectly, therefore,
working-class housing was subsidised out of the rates from as early as the 1870s,
since the Metropolitan Board of Works, acting as the agency of slum clearance,
acquired property at market value, but resold the cleared sites to model dwellings agencies for a fraction of the purchase price. Liberals argued that this was
not a subsidy, but rather a shrewd long-term investment which would more than
repay the initial outlay: rateable values and, therefore, revenue to municipal
authorities, would be increased, and the consequence of a healthier and happier
working class, well housed in a sanitary environment, would be a more law-
abiding and economically productive workforce, and a lower poor rate. The secretary of one housing agency protested that his company was 'a commercial
association, and in no wise a charitable institution'. It was the responsibility of
the latter, notably the Peabody Trust, to admit only 'the very lowest order of
self-supporting labourers', while the limited-dividend companies concentrated
on better-paid skilled workers, trusting to the effectiveness of 'levelling up' to
ensure some benefit to the poorest.[51]

Unfortunately, 'levelling up' was limited by the geography of the model dwellings movement. After a few unhappy experiments in dockside areas of the East
End, where estates proved 'hard to let', the major housing agencies preferred to

[49] F. Driver, 'Moral geographies: social science and the urban environment in mid-nineteenth
century England', *Transactions Institute of British Geographers*, new series, 13 (1988), 275–87; S. M.
Gaskell, 'Introduction', in S. M. Gaskell, ed., *Slums* (Leicester, 1990), pp. 1–16; J. A. Yelling, *Slums
and Slum Clearance in Victorian London* (London, 1986); H. J. Dyos, 'The slums of Victorian
London', *Victorian Studies*, 11 (1967), 5–40.
[50] Tarn, *Five Per Cent Philanthropy*; A. S. Wohl, *The Eternal Slum* (London, 1977); J. White, *Rothschild
Buildings* (London, 1980).   [51] Cited in Dennis, 'Victorian values', 41–3.

build in the West End, or around the edges of the City (the so-called 'inner industrial perimeter' where there were plenty of regularly employed artisans who could afford two or three rooms at rents of 2s. to 3s. per room), or on slum clearance sites where they could drive a hard bargain to acquire land relatively cheaply. At the time of Booth's survey, only 2.1 per cent of the population of Tower Hamlets lived in philanthropic block dwellings, compared to 8.1 per cent of the population in Westminster. Yet 12.9 per cent of people in Tower Hamlets fell into Booth's classes A and B (the poorest), compared to only 8.4 per cent in Westminster. 'Levelling up' could only work, therefore, if the poor could be mobile over quite long distances.[52]

Not all MBW sites proved attractive to the model dwellings agencies. The LCC inherited several cleared sites, mostly in the East End, which the MBW had been unable to sell. One interpretation of the origin of council housing in London is, therefore, that the LCC was forced into seeking powers to redevelop clearance sites itself because of the reluctance of the model dwellings movement to work in 'difficult' areas. Under a Progressive LCC the development of council housing took on a more positive character and estates such as Boundary Street in the East End, the Millbank Estate beside the then new Tate Gallery and the Bourne Estate in Holborn included some of the most distinctive domestic architecture in the capital. But the LCC was still reluctant to build in the poorest parts of east and south-east London, for example when required to provide replacement dwellings for those demolished in the approaches to the Blackwall (1897) and Rotherhithe (1908) Tunnels, recognising that local people were too poor to afford the rents charged for new flats under financial constraints that obliged the council to seek some return on its housing investment. The consequence was much higher vacancy and eviction rates on estates near the docks than in central London.[53]

As important as inner-city redevelopment was the adoption of a 'suburban solution'. Under Part III of the 1890 Housing Act local authorities were authorised to acquire green-field sites for public housing, and under a further act in 1900 these powers were extended to include land outside their own boundaries. By the time the Moderates ousted the Progressives from power, the LCC had begun four 'cottage estates', two just inside county boundaries (Totterdown Fields and Old Oak) and two out-county (White Hart Lane and Norbury). Each was dependent on the provision of good public transport: for example, the LCC's own electric trams linked Totterdown to Westminster from 1903. None the less, the estates initially proved hard to let and, in practice, drew tenants from the surrounding districts of Surrey and Middlesex as much as from inner London. The 'suburban solution' was attractive in terms of development costs –

[52] *Ibid.*, 46–9, 51–2.
[53] Wohl, *Eternal Slum*, pp. 250–84; S. Beattie, *A Revolution in London Housing* (London, 1980); R. Dennis, '"Hard to let" in Edwardian London', *Urban Studies*, 26 (1989), 77–89.

land at Totterdown cost £29 per dwelling compared to £454 on LCC estates in central London – and because of the presumed healthiness of the urban periphery, but a problem for working-class suburbanisation before the First World War was the absence of suburban industry on any large scale. In a new wave of interwar council estates, suburban housing was matched by the location of new industries, either on industrial estates, for example at Park Royal and Greenford in west London, at Wembley (on the site of the British Empire Exhibition of 1924–5) and in Collier's Wood in south London, or lining new 'arterial' roads – Western Avenue, the Great West Road, the North Circular Road and the Kingston By-Pass – themselves built ahead of demand as unemployment relief projects. The largest estate, Becontree, was close to Ford's new works at Dagenham; the St Helier estate, on the fringes of Sutton and Merton, was near south London industrial estates, but also served by the southward extension of the Northern Line to Morden in 1926, and by a new electrified branch of the Southern Railway which provided an all-night service to the city termini of Blackfriars and Holborn Viaduct, making the estate popular with postal sorting office workers and newspaper printers who worked unsocial hours.[54]

Families allocated houses on out-county estates were usually an elite among council tenants, who had already proved themselves clean, respectable and reliable rentpayers. But suburban local authorities feared that their presence would raise crime rates, cause increases in local rates (to pay for new educational and welfare facilities) and lower property values, and that they would all vote Labour in otherwise solidly Conservative constituencies. County councils and urban districts combined to purchase vacant land to prevent its falling into the hands of the LCC, for example in Morden, when an extension to the St Helier estate was threatened. Community services, shops, doctors and hospitals often took a long time coming, prompting local residents to organise services themselves – a classic example of local community formation in the face of crisis, as occurred, for example, on the Watling estate in Burnt Oak.[55]

Curiously, given the Moderates' ideological opposition to suburban council housing, all these interwar out-county estates were begun while the LCC was Moderate/Conservative controlled. Under a Labour LCC after 1934, policy changed to favour inner-area redevelopment with blocks of flats, a reflection also of central government's changed priorities under the Greenwood Act (1930). It was assumed that private house builders could look after the suburbs. LCC housing in the 1930s was concentrated in only a few boroughs – those which were happy to cooperate with the LCC. Other boroughs undertook extensive

[54] Jackson, *Semi-Detached London*, pp. 33–6, 235–50; Young and Garside, *Metropolitan London*, pp. 153–65; H. Clout, ed., *The Times London History Atlas* (London, 1997), pp. 108–17.
[55] Weightman and Humphries, *Making 1914–1939*, pp. 102–11; R. Durant, 'Community and association in a London Housing Estate', in R. E. Pahl, ed., *Readings in Urban Sociology* (Oxford, 1968), pp. 159–85; A. Olechnowicz, *Working-Class Housing in England between the Wars* (Oxford, 1997).

rehousing schemes of their own; and some Conservative-controlled boroughs built almost no council housing but encouraged charitable societies to provide working-class dwellings by offering sites at peppercorn rents in return for rights to nominate tenants. For example, the Peabody and Sutton Trusts erected extensive estates in west London boroughs including Kensington, Chelsea and Fulham; while the St Pancras House Improvement Society, founded in 1924 at the initiative of a local clergyman, was active in Somers Town (between Euston and St Pancras Stations).[56]

Overall, local authorities provided 153,000 new dwellings in Greater London between 1919 and 1938, but private developers erected over 600,000, mostly for owner-occupation. Privately rented housing was already in decline, although one kind of private renting that flourished was in response to the popularity of 'mansion flats', usually 'moderne' in style, marketed as efficient, labour-saving homes for single people, newly weds and an increasing number of independent working women. In the late nineteenth century, luxury flats were concentrated mainly in Victoria and Kensington, though there were also some more modest blocks in middle-class suburbs: Gissing's model of a 'new woman', Beatrice French, moved to a bachelor flat in Brixton. Until the First World War, flats were regarded with suspicion by most Londoners, partly because they were too close in appearance to the barrack-like block dwellings of philanthropic agencies, but also because they were associated with a morally suspect, bohemian lifestyle. Beatrice French's sister accused her: 'She lives alone in a flat, and has men to spend every evening with her; it's disgraceful!' In *The Whirlpool*, the extravagant, irresponsible and, significantly, childless Hugh and Sybil Carnaby took a flat in Oxford & Cambridge Mansions (a real block, erected in 1882–3 near Edgware Road station); and in *Howards End*, Forster opined 'flats house a flashy type of person'. But by the 1930s flats had become a less contentious part of London life. The largest new blocks included Du Cane Court in Balham (780 flats) and Dolphin Square, Pimlico (1,250 flats), but altogether, more than 56,000 suites were provided in Greater London in more than 1,300 blocks.[57]

There *were* block dwellings in a few other English cities (and tenements were common in Scottish cities), but philanthropic and council flats and luxury apartments were particularly associated with London. They were a direct consequence of its size and status as capital city. Land values were too high to allow low-density housing except on the urban fringe, but many people needed to live centrally, both artisans and service workers providing for the needs of the

[56] Young and Garside, *Metropolitan London*, pp. 173–98; LCC, *London Housing* (London, 1937), pp. 200–18.
[57] Tarn, 'French flats'; C. Hamnett and B. Randolph, 'The rise and fall of London's purpose-built blocks of privately rented flats: 1853–1983', *LJ*, 11 (1985), 160–75; Gissing, *Jubilee*, pp. 212, 274–5, 319; Gissing, *Whirlpool*, pp. 170–2; Forster, *Howards End*, p. 68.

leisured classes, and entertainers, politicians, bankers and stockbrokers who required *pieds à terre* close to the West End, parliament or the City.

(iv) THE DYNAMICS OF URBAN SPACE

All kinds of multi-family building also presented problems concerning the way in which space was actually *used*. How were the common parts of blocks of flats (staircases, courtyards, shared toilets and sculleries in some working-class buildings) to be administered? Where was the threshold between public and private space? The spatial organisation of London was not just a static matter of where different classes were recorded as 'resident', or where different land uses were located. We must also consider how people used space, how places acquired symbolic significance and how they were appropriated for use by different groups.

There is a wealth of anecdotal and autobiographical evidence on how frequently Londoners moved house. Most households rented from private landlords. There was no security of tenure, but moving costs were minimal. Two surveys in the 1840s of working-class families in Westminster and St-George-in-the-East found that 62 per cent and 50 per cent of families had lived in their present home for less than a year. Yet Charles Booth observed that migration was often circular, people 'cling[ing] from generation to generation to one vicinity, almost as if the set of streets which lie there were an isolated country village'. In Battersea, for example, moves were frequent, but 'seldom further than three streets away, and a year or two will very probably witness the return of the exiles to within a few doors of one of their many forsaken homes'. Almost 40 per cent of applicants for poor relief in St Giles had lived in the district for more than ten years.[58] A graphic example of frequent but short-distance mobility is provided in *A Hoxton Childhood*, an autobiographical account of childhood in East London before and during the First World War. Between 1910 and 1918 the Jasper family lived at nine different addresses, all less than a mile from father's 'local' and from all but one of the places where family members worked. The implication is that, although large numbers passed *through* working-class districts, perhaps en route to suburbia, sufficient remained to develop a cohesive and territorially restricted sense of community, a pattern confirmed by Michael Young and Peter Willmott's survey of family life in Bethnal Green in the 1950s.[59]

It seems likely that rates of residential mobility declined dramatically after 1918. When the Jasper family were forced to leave their Hoxton home in 1919,

---

[58] D. R. Green and A. G. Parton, 'Slums and slum life in Victorian England: London and Birmingham at mid-century', in Gaskell, ed., *Slums*, pp. 31, 76–82; C. Booth, *Life and Labour of the People* (London, 1889), vol. I, p. 27; *Labour and Life of the People* (London, 1891), vol. II, p. 412.

[59] A. S. Jasper, *A Hoxton Childhood* (London, 1969); M. Young and P. Willmott, *Family and Kinship in East London* (London, 1957).

the acute housing shortage obliged them to accept the offer of a house in Walthamstow, 5 miles (8 km) away. For those fortunate enough to have a permanent home, there was little prospect of moving. On one Peabody Trust estate in central London, the tenant turnover rate in the 1920s was less than a third of what it had been in the 1890s.[60] The increasing importance of council housing and owner-occupation made for bureaucratic and financial constraints to frequent mobility, but the availability of affordable public transport also meant that families no longer needed to move whenever household members changed workplaces.

So we can observe a lengthening in journeys to work. Among the employees of a Savile Row tailor, fewer than 5 per cent travelled more than 3 miles (5 km) to work in the 1860s and 1870s compared with more than 50 per cent in the 1890s. Of 2,600 workers at Carreras cigarette factory in Camden Town in 1936, only one third lived within comfortable walking distance, another third made the lengthy trek from east London, and nearly one eighth commuted from parts of the Home Counties outside the London postal area. The number of journeys per annum per Londoner by public transport increased from 166 in 1902 to 496 in 1928, with travel by bus becoming much more significant.[61] So Londoners became familiar with wider areas of the metropolis at the same time as they retreated out of clubs and pubs and into the private home for more of their leisure time.

But urban space was also used more self-consciously. Chartist demonstrators assembled on Kennington Common in south London in 1848. An equivalent locale for political protest north of the river was Copenhagen Fields, near King's Cross. Both places were effectively neutralised during the 1850s. In 1855 Copenhagen Fields became the site for the Metropolitan Cattle Market, while in 1852 Kennington Common was converted into the more decorous Kennington Park, complete with formal walks, flowerbeds, children's playground and a park keeper's lodge that had previously been a prototype set of model dwellings displayed at the Great Exhibition in Hyde Park. Nobody was likely to start a revolution in these surroundings. Victoria Park in east London, opened in 1845, occupied another site of radical political protest. While public meetings continued to be held in the wide open spaces of the park, they now competed with the rational recreation offered by bandstand, bathing pool and boating lakes.[62]

[60] Peabody Trust Archives, Herbrand Street Tenants' Register.
[61] D. R. Green, 'Distance to work in Victorian London: a case study of Henry Poole, bespoke tailors', *Business History*, 30 (1988), 179–94; Clout, *London History Atlas*, p. 91; D. R. Green, 'The metropolitan economy: continuity and change 1800–1939', in K. Hoggart and D. R. Green, eds., *London* (London, 1991), pp. 8–33.
[62] B. Elliott, 'Victorian parks', in M. Galinou, ed., *London's Pride: The Glorious History of the Capital's Gardens* (London, 1990), pp. 150–67; F. Sheppard, *London 1808–1870: The Infernal Wen* (London, 1971), pp. 189, 322–30, 356; C. Poulsen, *Victoria Park* (London, 1976).

Perhaps the most critical site of contestation was Trafalgar Square, a place for ephemeral popular celebration or demonstration, as well as of permanent icono-graphic significance, embracing Nelson's Column (1843), Landseer's lions (1867) and statues to various monarchs, admirals and generals. Following unemploy-ment demonstrations in 1886–7, including the 1886 'invasion' of Pall Mall by 'King Mob' and immediately preceding the following year's 'Bloody Sunday' when a member of the Social Democratic Federation died after clashes between demonstrators and police, the right of public assembly in Trafalgar Square was withdrawn until 1892. Waller comments that the demonstrations 'raised the spectre of sansculottism in clubland. Shopkeepers petitioned the authorities to close the West End to demonstrators; and it was feared that American tourists would shy away from new hotels like the Grand (1880) and Metropole (1885).'[63] We can see here the range of different interest groups laying claim to the same space. For working-class protestors, occupying Trafalgar Square was an act of sol-idarity boosting their own confidence, demonstrating their own power and pub-licising their cause through force of numbers. For local tradesmen their presence undermined the consumer economy (much like terrorist outrages more recently). For members of Pall Mall clubs, it was a violation of the natural order.

At times of celebration, such as Queen Victoria's Golden and Diamond Jubilees, Trafalgar Square was a place to be lost in the crowd, particularly significant for women who might not normally have such freedom. Gissing's Samuel Barmby organised his contingent of Camberwell excursionists: 'We can't be wrong in making for Trafalgar Square', but for Nancy, there was the oppor-tunity to get lost in crowds pressing along Pall Mall: 'No one observed her sol-itary state; she was one of millions walking about the streets because it was Jubilee Day, and every moment packed her more tightly among the tramping populace. A procession, this, greatly more significant than that of Royal person-ages earlier in the day.'[64]

The freedom of women on the city streets has attracted the attention of fem-inist historians, initially propounding a 'separate spheres' argument that in a patriarchal society women were excluded from public and commercial life and confined to an increasingly remote, suburban domestic sphere, but more recently qualifying that thesis by demonstrating the independence that women had attained. By the late nineteenth century, middle-class women could take advan-tage of more comfortable public transport to visit West End department stores. When Selfridge's opened in 1909, it proclaimed itself 'dedicated to the service of women' and offered attractions such as restaurants, writing, reading and rest rooms, and hairdressers, the female equivalent of a gentleman's club. Nor was

[63] Waller, *Town*, p. 40; see also R. Mace, *Trafalgar Square: Emblem of Empire* (London, 1976); G. Stedman Jones, *Outcast London* (Oxford, 1971), pp. 290–6.
[64] Gissing, *Jubilee*, pp. 54, 58. A useful discussion and further illustrations of street life are included in R. Allen, *The Moving Pageant* (London, 1998).

the West End restricted to the wealthiest women and the shopgirls who served them. Carrie Pooter patronised the local Bon Marché in Holloway, but she also visited Shoolbred's in Tottenham Court Road, Liberty's (Regent Street) and Peter Robinson's (Oxford Circus).[65]

From the 1830s lower-middle-class women might travel alone by bus, because they would be under the protective gaze of a conductor. Better-off women might summon their servants to escort them through 'dangerous' areas, apparently oblivious that the servant, probably younger and more attractive to men, might then have to make the return journey on her own. But women's freedom on the streets was still subject to the control of men:

> a fashionably dressed, middle-class Victorian or Edwardian lady could spend a pleasant afternoon shopping on Regent Street and expect to be treated by the police and passers-by with courtesy (provided she knew not to linger too long in front of certain shop windows), but if she remained on that fashionable street, unescorted, after the lamps were lit, she risked insult and loss of reputation.

Women might be prosecuted for soliciting on no more evidence than that they were in the wrong place at the wrong time.[66]

Working-class street life was a good deal more boisterous. A problem of working-class suburbanisation was the loss of this everyday sociability. In the suburbs there were fewer street markets affording opportunities for social interaction as much as for economical shopping; and fewer opportunities for informal employment, such as assisting neighbours with laundry and child-minding; and as Young and Wilmott demonstrated in their studies of family and kinship in the 1950s, suburbanisation reduced the likelihood of living near and making frequent visits to parents, inlaws and siblings.[67]

There were also elite spaces, occupied according to the routine of the 'London Season' – riding in Hyde Park's Rotten Row in the mornings, but driving (in a carriage) in the late afternoon. At various times, the West End expanded to incorporate Ascot (racing), Henley (rowing), Bisley (shooting) or, closer at hand, Hurlingham (polo). These were semi-private gatherings, but the public could view them at a distance: 'pageants of splendour'. Other indoor, and therefore more private, elite spaces reflected the increasing commodification of leisure –

[65] M. Nava, 'Modernity's disavowal: women, the city and the department store', in Nava and O'Shea, eds., *Modern Times*, pp. 38–76; A. Adburgham, *Shopping in Style* (London, 1979), pp. 138–81; Clout, *London History Atlas*, pp. 106–7; for Carrie Pooter, see G. and W. Grossmith, *The Diary of a Nobody* (London, 1892; 1965 Penguin edn), pp. 52, 104, 146, 216. See also E. Rappaport, *Shopping for Pleasure* (Princeton, 2000).

[66] Winter, *London's Teeming Streets*, pp. 11–12, 173–89; J. R. Walkowitz, *City of Dreadful Delight* (London and Chicago, 1992), pp. 46–52, 127–31; see also the discussions in E. Wilson, *The Sphinx in the City* (London, 1991), and D. E. Nord, *Walking the Victorian Streets* (Ithaca, 1995).

[67] Young and Willmott, *Family and Kinship*; P. Willmott and M. Young, *Family and Class in a London Suburb* (London, 1960).

in restaurants, gentlemen's clubs, concentrated along Pall Mall from the 1820s, and concert halls such as Queen's Hall (1893), which accommodated Henry Wood's new Promenade Concerts from 1895 until its destruction in 1941. The Schlegel sisters first encountered Leonard Bast when he sat next to them at a recital in the Queen's Hall, an indication that cultural events might extend across class boundaries, albeit uncomfortably.[68]

Until the 1890s working-class interlopers and passing trade were excluded from elite residential areas by more than 200 privately erected gates. Their eventual dismantling perhaps reflected a democratisation of public space: 'Notions about public rights to the collective consumption of physical infrastructure . . . were indeed developing in the second half of the nineteenth century.'[69] But the rich could maintain their privacy by moving out, to remote suburbs such as Moor Park and Virginia Water, now centred on the golf club rather than the public square, or up, as the penthouse flat became both technologically feasible and fashionable.

(v) A MODERN ECONOMY?

The economy of Victorian London has often been characterised as technologically backward, effectively 'pre-industrial' in its manufacturing, typified by an absence of factories and a continuing preponderance of small-scale workshops. According to the 1851 census, 86 per cent of employers had fewer than ten employees; only eighty firms employed more than 100 workers. But the inference that London's manufacturing was therefore weak, and that London's dependence on services was also a sign of weakness, is unjustified. It reflects a particular ideology, that industry is 'basic' while services are 'non-basic' or even parasitic. It also reflects a misconception of industry elsewhere in nineteenth-century Britain. Steam-powered, large-scale factory production was not so dominant, even in the textile districts.[70]

An alternative interpretation of London's economy is that, far from being parasitic, the growth of services was the foundation for London's success. Between 1841 and 1911 more than half of all new jobs in Britain were in services, one fifth of them in London and Middlesex. The prosperity of the South-East, and the wealth-creating effects of service industry, were indicated by the large numbers of millionaires based in and around London, most owing their wealth to commerce

---

[68] L. Davidoff, *The Best Circles* (London, 1973), pp. 24, 28–32, 65; Forster, *Howards End*, pp. 44–53.

[69] P. J. Atkins, 'How the West End was won: the struggle to remove street barriers in Victorian London', *Journal of Historical Geography*, 19 (1993), 273.

[70] Stedman Jones, *Outcast London*, p. 27; M. J. Daunton, 'Industry in London: revisions and reflections', *LJ*, 21 (1996), 1–8; D. R. Green, 'The nineteenth-century metropolitan economy: a revisionist interpretation', *LJ*, 21 (1996), 17; P. Johnson, 'Economic development and industrial dynamism in Victorian London', *LJ*, 21 (1996), 27–37.

rather than industry.[71] Even if we agree with Paul Johnson that London was not disproportionately endowed with service employment, we cannot deny that London's service economy was a source of strength rather than weakness.

Johnson's own approach focuses on 'the role of incentives, profits, information flows, institutional structures, competition and small-scale enterprise in London's economic development'. He argues that there is nothing new about the enterprise economy. It was flourishing in the 1890s as much as the 1990s, based upon good communications and a fast and efficient flow of information, so that producers, distributors, retailers and consumers could all react quickly to changing conditions; and upon a fluidity and mobility of population that undermined traditional forms of social ranking and class consciousness, promoting an individualistic, materialist culture. So the structure of industries like the East End clothing industry – lots of small workshops and little security of employment – was 'a modern response to competitive pressures rather than a hangover from pre-industrial traditions' and 'the workshop trades of Victorian London had most of the attributes now identified as the key elements of post-modern industrial capitalism'.[72] As final proof of success, Johnson points to relatively low rates of unemployment and an increasingly affluent working class. Even in 1932, in the midst of depression, when the national unemployment rate was 22.1 per cent, London's rate was 13.5 per cent; and between 1870 and 1935 the level of real wages in London more than doubled.[73]

Johnson's thesis is exemplified by the East End garment industry where, particularly in the women's wear industry, firms remained small in order to respond to the vagaries of fashion. No producer could be sure they would have the right design. But if their design flopped, they could always act as subcontractors to firms with successful designs, who would not have the capacity to meet all their orders. The result was a pattern of many small firms, mutually interdependent yet collectively competitive: what Alfred Marshall earlier in the century termed an 'industrial district'.[74]

However, we should not accept so readily that London was so totally dominated by small firms. The 1851 census of employers concentrated on direct employment and ignored subcontracting, yet many subcontractors were effectively the employees of other firms. The census was notoriously incomplete – directory evidence suggests that there were many more firms with more than 100 employees than the census enumerated. What mainly distinguished London

---

[71] C. H. Lee, 'Regional growth and structural change in Victorian Britain', *Ec.HR*, 33 (1981), 438–52; C. H. Lee, 'The service sector, regional specialisation and economic growth in the Victorian economy', *Journal of Historical Geography*, 10 (1984), 139–55; W. D. Rubinstein, *Men of Property* (London, 1981).   [72] Johnson, 'Economic development', 29, 33.

[73] Green, 'Metropolitan economy', pp. 13, 17.

[74] A. Godley, 'Immigrant entrepreneurs and the emergence of London's East End as an industrial district', *LJ*, 21 (1996), 38–45; A. Marshall, *Industry and Trade* (London, 1919).

from other places was the number of masters who failed to state the size of their workforce. Additional evidence often used to support the traditional picture, such as Henry Mayhew's emphasis on small masters, should also be discounted: Mayhew concentrated on the poorest trades and ignored those characterised by more prosperous employers and larger units of production, and he wrote at the end of a long downturn in the economy, when many workers would have turned in desperation to self-employment. In practice, therefore, London's employment structure was bi-polar, with a few large employers dominating some trades.

Johnson's logic assumes that there was a high degree of stability in the London economy, and that large firms developed only in conditions of instability and inefficient market forces. On the surface, it would appear that London's economy was stable. The diversity of different forms of manufacturing should have meant less dramatic boom and bust cycles compared to single-industry regions like the North-West. Finishing trades that predominated in London were also less susceptible to wild fluctuations in demand than producer industries elsewhere. However, David Green shows that London manufacturers *were* vulnerable to downturns in trade and financial dealing. When a speculative bubble burst, as with the collapse of Overend and Gurney in 1866, 'the chill was felt . . . throughout the local economy'. For most of the nineteenth century there were marked cyclical fluctuations in building construction, trade and numbers of bankruptcies, all likely to have knock-on effects on London's manufacturing.[75]

Nor were London workers as apolitical as traditionally claimed. Large numbers of strikes and trade disputes occurred throughout the nineteenth century. For Stedman Jones, a lack of political or community activity on the part of London's working class, a preference for the pub and the music hall rather than the trade union, was a 'culture of consolation';[76] for Johnson it was the individualistic satisfaction of the affluent worker. To Green, they are both trying to explain away an imaginary absence. Some support for his view also comes from John Davis' analysis of radical clubs and London politics at the end of the century. Until the 1880s radical workingmen's clubs continued to be highly political but, thereafter, as the movement grew in numerical strength, so it declined politically. As clubs moved out of rented meeting rooms in pubs and into their own clubrooms, so they faced new financial responsibilities. They needed more members to spend more money at the bar, and could not afford to impose political tests on new members. Meanwhile, the political information and opinions that had previously been dispensed through club lectures were now available through a thriving popular press. To Davis, therefore, the changing emphasis in club activities was consistent with an evolution rather than a simple decline in labour politics. Moreover, the inner suburbs to which artisans were moving were socially

---

[75] Green, 'The nineteenth-century metropolitan economy', 10; see also D. R. Green, *From Artisans to Paupers* (Aldershot, 1995).

[76] G. Stedman Jones, *Languages of Class* (Cambridge, 1983), pp. 179–238.

homogeneous but occupationally mixed: clubs became home- rather than trade-based. None the less, they continued to be electorally active, in sponsoring candidates and canvassing. Most clubs supported a radicalised Liberal party, which slowed down the move to independent Labour politics, and when the Labour party did eventually emerge in interwar London, it was in response to the decline of the Liberal party *nationally*.[77]

Geographically, two principal trends characterised the location of industry in nineteenth-century London. A shift from West End to East End was associated with a relative shift from made-to-measure for wealthy customers who lived nearby to 'slop' manufacture for a generalised mass market of the new lower middle class and skilled working class, with de-skilling through a finer division of labour, and with the employment of more female labour. By mid-century an inner industrial perimeter had emerged, stretching in a semi-circle from Holborn and Clerkenwell, north of the City, to Bow and the Isle of Dogs in the east, then to Deptford and Lambeth in the south. Associated with this pattern, there were separate labour markets, with different traditions of trade union activity, to the north-west, in the East End, and south of the Thames. These divisions reflected the limited mobility of labour and restricted information flows, but later in the century, different trades attempted to establish London-wide wage rates and conditions of employment.[78]

A second geographical trend, developing later, was the beginnings of out-movement, often to escape high rates and an increasing range of LCC controls on the conduct of noxious trades and on workshop conditions. Many manufacturers sought sites outside the jurisdiction of the LCC, especially in West Ham, Stratford and the Lea Valley which, thanks to the peculiar county boundary, were closer to central London than many districts within the County of London.[79]

If London's nineteenth-century economy was 'postmodern', interwar manufacturing was traditionally 'modern'. Marxist geographers like David Harvey have explored the role of suburbanisation and the creation of mass markets as solutions to problems of capital accumulation and a declining rate of profit. They argue that industrial capitalism needed constantly to generate new products and markets, partly through a 'spatial fix'.[80] The suburbs and an associated cult of domesticity were one kind of spatial fix, the Empire was another. Hence the development of new Fordist and scientifically managed assembly-line factories,

[77] J. Davis, 'Radical clubs and London politics, 1870–1900', in Feldman and Stedman Jones, eds., *Metropolis*, pp. 103–28.
[78] D. R. Green, 'A map for Mayhew's London', *LJ*, 11 (1985), 115–26; Green, 'Metropolitan economy', pp. 17–23; E. Hobsbawm, 'The nineteenth-century London labour market', in R. Glass *et al.*, eds., *London* (London, 1964), pp. 3–28.
[79] P. Hall, *The Industries of London since 1861* (London, 1962); Marriott, 'West Ham'.
[80] D. Harvey, *The Urbanization of Capital* (Oxford, 1985), pp. 201–8; R. A. Walker, 'A theory of sub-urbanization', in M. Dear and A. J. Scott, eds., *Urbanization and Urban Planning in Capitalist Society* (London, 1981), pp. 383–429.

producing consumer durables for the home market and generally more robust items, such as buses and lorries, for the colonies. The factories themselves were also modern architecturally, including the Hoover factory in Perivale and a ribbon of art deco constructions such as the Firestone and Gillette buildings lining the Great West Road. Manufacturers took advantage of cheaper electricity – the creation of a Central Electricity Board (1926) and the beginnings of a national grid, which obviated the need for locally and expensively produced electricity – which also benefited the potential purchasers and users of domestic appliances such as vacuum cleaners, refrigerators, irons, washing machines and radios. During the Depression, over 40 per cent of new factories in England and Wales were located in the London region; but while outer London had a net gain of more than 400 factories between 1934 and 1938, the LCC area suffered a net loss of nearly 200.[81]

None the less, London's economy depended more on consumption than production, on retailing than manufacture. William Whiteley, who opened his first store in Bayswater in 1863, soon claimed to be 'the universal provider'. In 1887 his store was described as 'an immense symposium of the arts and industries of the nations and of the world', a phrase which deliberately invited comparison with the Great Exhibition and with more permanent exhibitions of imperial spoils in the South Kensington museums, and which rivalled Harrods' telegraphic address: 'Everything London'. Whiteley's moved to new purpose-built premises in 1911, only two years after the opening of Selfridge's, and the interwar years witnessed a rash of rebuildings as overgrown drapers' re-dressed themselves as modern department stores. Mass consumption was also associated with the growth of chain stores, such as Marks and Spencer. None of these forms of retailing was unique to London, of course, but they assumed particular significance in the London economy as an additional incentive for consumer tourism, from the provinces but also the world.[82]

(vi) CITY AND EMPIRE

If London was a candidate for 'capital of the nineteenth century', it was also – so Londoners were constantly assured – 'the political, moral, physical, intellectual, artistic, literary, commercial and social centre of the world'. From 1884 London was even at the centre of time: the world revolved around the Greenwich meridian and GMT.[83] Sidney Webb appealed to imperial sentiments

[81] Green, 'Metropolitan economy', pp. 23–32; Weightman and Humphries, *Making 1914–1939*, pp. 49–69.
[82] Olsen, *Growth*, pp. 122–5; Clout, *London History Atlas*, pp. 106–7; Porter, *London*, pp. 199–202, 332.
[83] Routledge's Guide (1862), quoted in A. D. King, *Global Cities* (London, 1990), p. 71; Porter, *London*, p. 185.

to gain support for the Fabians' *London Programme* (1891): 'If only for the sake of the rest of the Empire, the London masses must be organised for a campaign against the speculators, vestry jobbers, house farmers, water sharks, market monopolists, ground landlords, and other social parasites now feeding upon their helplessness. Metropolitan reform has become a national, if not an imperial question.'[84] Garside notes that conservative reformers, opposed to municipal socialism and civic expenditure, none the less 'remained receptive to arguments about the need for housing reform in the interests of the Nation, the Race and the Empire'.[85]

Until the mid-nineteenth century, London's trading connections were predominantly with Europe and North America. The first wave of dock building anticipated more than it responded to the growth of imperial trade. By the end of the century, as again in the 1950s, the strength of London's trade with the Empire/Commonwealth reflected a resort to 'easier' export markets, faced with increasing competition from the United States and Western Europe. It was principally after 1870 that trade in the Port of London concentrated on Canada, India, South Africa, Australasia and the Argentine. But trade with the Commonwealth did not reach its peak until after the Second World War, when it accounted for about half of the port's imports and exports. The Commonwealth Preference System, introduced in the 1930s, maintained free trade with the Commonwealth, still very much to the advantage of the home country, while protective tariffs were being reimposed elsewhere. One reason for industrial expansion in 1930s London was that the introduction of tariffs forced international (especially US) firms to locate manufacturing plants in Britain if they wanted to compete in the British and Commonwealth market. So, Tony King notes, 'as late-nineteenth-century London had grown because of free trade so, in the 1930s, her economy grew because of the breakdowns in free trade'.[86]

The imperial connection was expressed in numerous ways in the built environment of London: in Whitehall, in the building of Gilbert Scott's New Government Offices to house the Foreign, Colonial, India and Home Offices (1868–73), the War Office (1899–1906), the extension to the Admiralty (1895) and the raising of Admiralty Arch (1910); in the twentieth century in the succession of new or converted High Commission buildings in the vicinity of Trafalgar Square – Australia House (1914), India House (1924), Canada House (1925), Africa House (1928) and South Africa House (1933). The profits of investment in colonial plantations bore cultural and architectural fruit – the Tate Gallery (1895–7) on the profits of sugar, the Horniman Museum (1896–1901) on tea. The need to train engineers, educators and administrators, and provide them with a London base to which they could return, spawned the Imperial

[84] Quoted in Briggs, *Victorian Cities*, p. 339.   [85] Garside, 'London', p. 518.
[86] King, *Global Cities*, p. 82.

Institute (1887) (later, Imperial College), the Royal Colonial Institute in Whitehall (1868) and a host of clubs and emigration agencies. The Strand became a commercial and administrative gateway to the Empire.[87]

Colonial civil servants were associated with an 'inner colonial perimeter' – from St John's Wood in the north through Bayswater to South Kensington, matching the inner industrial perimeter to the east. Department stores such as Whiteley's in Bayswater and the Army & Navy in Victoria Street sold colonial goods to Londoners and British goods to returning colonists.

Visitors from Europe and America, as well as from the Empire, found accommodation in some imperial hotels: the Russell (1898–1900) and the Imperial (1905–11) in Bloomsbury, the Ritz (1906) on Piccadilly and the Waldorf (1908) on the Aldwych, associated with the one example of a street improvement (Kingsway) that was imperial in scale, if not in execution. London hosted a succession of international exhibitions to display the products and the technological progress of the Empire, starting with the Great Exhibition in 1851, where 6,556 exhibitors from the rest of the world were more than matched by 7,381 from Britain and her dependencies. The former were assigned space east of the transept whereas the products of Empire were consolidated to the west. Visitors were exhorted 'in going through the building, to follow as much as possible the course of the sun', so that they arrived at last at the United Kingdom (where, presumably, the sun never set). Six million tickets were sold for the Great Exhibition, while 27 million attended the British Empire Exhibition at Wembley in 1924–5.[88]

The Empire also arrived more permanently in the form of immigrants. The SS *Empire Windrush*, docking in June 1948, delivered its cargo of 492 Jamaicans to be greeted by the *Evening Standard*'s headline: 'Welcome Home'. But as late as 1952, only 1,500 West Indians, 300 to 400 Indians and Pakistanis, and 1,000 Cypriots were arriving in London each year. More transient imperial visitors were invited to explore imperial London through guidebooks, which directed them to the most obvious imperial sites – the Tower, St Paul's, Westminster Abbey, Buckingham Palace, the Mall, Trafalgar Square and (after 1920) the Cenotaph. But the Empire was also manifest in suburbia, in the proliferation of Mafeking, Ladysmith and Kimberley Streets, at Wembley, and in the *Daily Mail*'s Ideal Home Exhibition which domesticated imperial products for suburban consumption.[89]

[87] *Ibid.*; M. H. Port, *Imperial London* (New Haven and London, 1995); F. Driver and D. Gilbert, 'Heart of empire? Landscape, space and performance in imperial London', *Environment and Planning D: Society and Space*, 16 (1998), 11–28.

[88] C. H. Gibbs-Smith, *The Great Exhibition of 1851* (London, 1981), pp. 20–4.

[89] S. Humphries and J. Taylor, *The Making of Modern London, 1945–1985* (London, 1986), pp. 110–17; Driver and Gilbert, 'Heart of empire?'; D. Gilbert, '"London in all its glory – or how to enjoy London": guidebook representations of imperial London', *Journal of Historical Geography*, 25 (1999), 279–97.

In Niels Lund's famous painting *The Heart of the Empire* (1904), the skyline is dominated by St Paul's, but the foreground is the Bank Junction, between the Mansion House, the Bank of England and the Royal Exchange. For Joseph Chamberlain, the City of London was 'the clearing house of the world', a function that can be measured first by the number of foreign and imperial banks established there, including banks from Hong Kong (1808), Australia (1835), New Zealand (1862), Canada (1867), as well as from Europe (1860s), the USA (1887) and Japan (1898). London directories recorded 86 bankers in 1861, 224 in 1901, of whom 85 were classified as 'foreign and colonial'. While private banks declined in number and importance, London-based clearing banks extended their operations to cover the whole country, and provincial banks moved their headquarters to London.[90]

Insurance became big business: the number of Lloyd's underwriters increased from 189 to 621 between 1849 and 1913, when it was estimated that two-thirds of world marine insurance was handled in the City. By 1948, Lloyd's membership numbered 2,422. At the other extreme of the insurance industry, life assurance for workingmen was wrested from local benefit societies by large-scale agencies such as the Prudential, based in Holborn, which, by 1875, had more than 2 million 'industrial' assurance policies. Membership of the Stock Exchange also rocketed, from 864 in 1850 to 5,567 in 1905.[91]

But the City remained a mixed business community, centred on trade rather than financial services, and still home to manufacturing and warehouses accommodating physical trade in commodities. As late as 1938, 12 per cent of floorspace in the City was occupied by industry, 26 per cent by warehouses, and (only) 45 per cent by offices. The growth of 'office trade' depended on new technology which facilitated the flow of business information and stimulated the concentration of commercial activity. In 1851 London and Paris were linked by cross-Channel cable. Fifteen years later, London was linked to New York and, by 1871, 42,000 telegrams per annum were passing between the two cities. The following year Tokyo and Melbourne were joined to London telegraphically. In 1901 the advent of wireless telegraphy extended the reach of major financial centres, but it was not until 1937 that London and New York were in *telephonic* communication. Meanwhile, *within* the City, information flows were improved by the use of ticker-tape machines (1872) and the publication of specialist financial newspapers, including the *Financial Times* (1888).[92]

---

[90] S. Daniels, *Fields of Vision* (Cambridge, 1993), pp. 13–15, 29–31; Waller, *Town*, p. 54; King, *Global Cities*, p. 89; R. C. Michie, *The City of London* (London, 1992), p. 71; D. Kynaston, *The City of London*, vol. I: *A World of its Own, 1815–1890* (London, 1994), p. 333.

[91] Sheppard, *London 1808–1870*, pp. 196–201; Kynaston, *City*, I, p. 175; Michie, *City*, pp. 134, 150–3, 173.

[92] Michie, *City*, pp. 18, 184; Kynaston, *City*, I, pp. 175, 258, 260; D. Kynaston, *The City of London*, vol. II: *Golden Years, 1890–1914* (London, 1995), p. 260.

Yet the City remained an essentially conservative institution, suspicious of new technology, especially typewriters and telephones, and of 'new women'. Most City businesses were small, effectively family firms. Even Baring's had a staff of less than 100 in the 1870s, when they recruited their first female employee. The pace of life in the City may have been frenetic – 'here everyone seems to run rather than to walk' – but habits were slow to change, exemplified in the continuing uniform of 'bobbing silk hats' in winter, 'straw hats' in summer.[93]

Despite this innate conservatism, the City boomed in the growth of world trade up until the First World War. London's share of Britain's physical trade was already in decline, but office trade and the securities market boomed. Foreign governments and companies raised loans in London to finance development at home; and British companies based in the City ran railways, mines and plantations the world over. Forster's Henry Wilcox typified the 'gentlemanly capitalist', with homes in both the West End (in his case in 'Ducie Street' near Chelsea Embankment) and the country ('Oniton Grange' in Shropshire), his wealth derived from his chairmanship of the Imperial and West African Rubber Company. After 1914, however, the City suffered, partly in competition with rising financial centres such as New York and partly as a consequence of the general decline in international trade during the Depression. The value of Britain's overseas assets declined from £7.3 billion (at 1938 prices) in 1913 to £4.1 billion in 1937. Membership of the Stock Exchange declined below 4,000 by 1938.[94]

Business expansion in the nineteenth century was matched by physical reconstruction. Of every five buildings standing in 1855 only one remained in 1901. New bank offices, such as the headquarters of the London and Westminster Bank, opened in 1838 on Lothbury, facing the Bank of England, were soon overwhelmed by speculatively built 'stacks of office buildings' erected by companies such as the City Offices Company, established in 1864. Mansion House Chambers (1872), on the south side of Queen Victoria Street, itself completed only in 1871, provided 500 rooms. Small businesses seeking a prestigious address would rent no more than one or two rooms in such buildings. Gissing's Luckworth Crewe, engaged in the decidedly 'modern' business of advertising and the promotion of tourist resorts, took three rooms in an office block in Farringdon Street. In 1881 a City Corporation census counted 1,320 lettings in only twenty-six buildings. Speculative developments were mostly in marginal locations, where land values were lower, whereas company headquarters were on high-value frontages on main thoroughfares. There were also separate districts for different kinds of business activity, including an area associated with

[93] Kynaston, *City*, I, pp. 288–90, 312–13; Kynaston, *City*, II, p. 26.
[94] Kynaston, *City*, II, pp. 332–3; Forster, *Howards End*, p. 142; Michie, *City*, pp. 109, 136.

colonial and East India goods around Mincing Lane, and a concentration of textile warehouses and offices between Wood Street and Basinghall Street, close to the Guildhall.[95]

The City's imperial character was also a matter of architectural style and employee sentiment. Building styles evoked past trading empires, especially Renaissance Venice; celebrations of imperial power such as Queen Victoria's Diamond Jubilee and, more spontaneously, to mark the relief of Mafeking, colonised the City's spaces, especially Bank Junction and the Stock Exchange.

As an imperial city, London lacked the grand boulevards and planned assemblages of buildings common in Paris, Vienna or St Petersburg. London resisted the excesses of totalitarian and fascist planning that characterised Rome, Berlin and Moscow in the 1930s. By then, it is not entirely fanciful to think of London as becoming an outpost of the United States. The Americanisation of suburban industry has already been noted. It was American cinema that provided the fantasy world for suburbanites in the 1930s; an American department store – Selfridge's – and an American chain store – Woolworth's – that revolutionised British retailing; and American money that helped to occupy the open spaces left behind by the grand imperial project of Kingsway-Aldwych, where Bush House was developed by the American, Irving T. Bush, between 1919 and 1935. But the Empire struck back. Intended as a trade centre, Bush House became HQ for the External Services Division of the BBC, the still imperious if not imperial 'World Service'.[96]

(vii) CONCLUSION

I have made no attempt in this chapter to be comprehensive. For example, I have ignored the impact of two world wars on either the social life or the built environment of London, nor have I spent much time on either party politics or the mechanics of planning. Rather, I have concentrated on the scale and complexity of London's spatial structure, the implications of that structure in areas of local government, social structure and economic change, and its relevance for everyday life. I have spent more time on change in the West End, the City and suburbia, and paid less attention to the East End,[97] and I have left numerous

[95] Kynaston, *City*, II, p. 245; Kynaston, *City*, I, p. 288; I. S. Black, 'Symbolic capital: the London and Westminster Bank headquarters, 1836–38', *Landscape Research*, 21 (1996), 55–72; R. Thorne, 'Office building in the City of London 1830–1880' (paper to Urban History Group Colloquium, 1984); CMH, 'Progress reports on "From counting-house to office: the evolution of London's central financial district, 1690–1870"', *CMH Annual Reports* (1988–9, 1989–90); CMH, 'Progress report on "The growth and development of the textile marketing district of the City of London, c. 1780–1914"', *CMH Annual Report* (1990–1); Gissing, *Jubilee*, p. 145.
[96] Sheppard, *London*, p. 323; King, *Global Cities*, p. 82.
[97] On the problems of applying the concept of 'modernity' to the East End, see J. Marriott, 'Sensation of the abyss: the urban poor and modernity', in Nava and O'Shea, eds., *Modern Times*, pp. 77–100.

questions unanswered. Why was London so different from other European capitals? Was it simply the absence of strong local government and the dominance
of large estates that prevented either monarchy or mayoralty from restructuring
the city in their own image? Why such enthusiasm for suburbanisation, so many
'cottages', so few flats?

For all the 'progress' of the preceding century, 'modern London' in 1950 was
still a world away from today's London. In 1950–1 there was one car licence for
every 8.7 households in the LCC area, the majority of Londoners rented their
homes from private landlords, and the 'coloured' population was estimated to
number only 27,552.[98] Even in the more extensive Greater London area, only
51 per cent of households had exclusive use of the five basic amenities (piped
water, cooking stove, kitchen sink, water closet, fixed bath); 29 per cent lacked
any access to a fixed bath and another 17 per cent shared access with at least one
other household.[99] As late as 1959 more than 1.4 million Greater Londoners (30
per cent of the workforce) worked in manufacturing, compared to fewer than
0.5 million by the late 1980s. The 1951 census reckoned those 'out of work' in
Greater London to comprise 1.9 per cent of the 'occupied' population; the
Ministry of Labour's more restricted definition estimated the unemployment
rate at 1 per cent.[100] London was not yet 'swinging', 'Docklands' was still docks,
Covent Garden and Spitalfields were still wholesale markets, the Barbican was a
bombsite. For V. S. Pritchett in 1962, London was 'a heavy city' weighed down
by past achievements and lacking in 'Style'. But these characteristics were part
of its charm and distinctiveness; there was little sign of the pessimistic consensus
among authors that developed from the 1980s, 'of a capital city in terminal
decline'.[101] Nor was there any postmodern irony or space for alternative narratives in the plans for post-war reconstruction or the bright optimism of the
Festival of Britain. In 1951 as in 1851 London was the very model of a modern
metropolis.

---

[98] R. Glass, 'Introduction', in Glass *et al.*, eds., *London*, pp. xiii–xlii.

[99] General Register Office, *Census of England and Wales, 1951: Report on Greater London and Five Other Conurbations* (HMSO, 1956).

[100] General Register Office, *Census of England and Wales, 1951: Occupation Tables* (HMSO, 1956); *Ministry of Labour Gazette* (January 1951).

[101] V. S. Pritchett, *London Perceived* (London, 1962), p. 4; J. Coe, 'London: the dislocated city', in M. Bradbury, ed., *The Atlas of Literature* (London, 1996), p. 320.

· 4 ·

Ports

SARAH PALMER

WHILE THE history and the functioning of ports has attracted considerable attention from geographers, economic historians and sociologists, the area of interest has tended either to focus very narrowly on the immediate connections between land and water, such as facilities for shipping or waterfront working conditions, or to be concerned with broad perspectives, such as the value of trade and competitive position.[1] There has been, metaphorically speaking, an inclination to look out to sea rather than inland, or to allow the dock wall to define the limits of investigation. As a result, with the exception of Martin Daunton's study of Cardiff, ports have rarely been treated as urban entities.[2]

This is not to say that the connection between water-based activity on a shoreline or river bank and the growth of permanent settlement has not been a very familiar and well-worked theme. But not every landing place for cargo became a town, still less a city. In 1870 the official returns identify 110 foreign trade ports in the UK. A hundred years later the oil terminals of Milford Haven, Sullom Vo and Orkney ranked high among British ports; reminders that the nature of trade and the state of cargo-handling technology are factors linking, or separating, transhipment needs and populations. Furthermore, for anyone studying ports in a maturing industrialised economy, the enhanced ability to shape the built environment (to dredge, to put up barriers against the sea, readily to take goods into the interior) necessarily shifts the analysis away from a concentration on natural features towards recognition of the human contribution; 'in the beginning the harbour made the trade; but soon the trade began to make the harbour'.[3]

---

[1] D. Hilling, 'Socio-economic change in the maritime quarter: the demise of sailortown', in B. S. Hoyle, D. A. Pinder and M. S. Husain, eds., *Revitalising the Waterfront* (London, 1988), p. 20.
[2] M. J. Daunton, *Coal Metropolis* (Leicester, 1977).
[3] W. Sargent, *Ports and Hinterlands* (London, 1938), p. 88.

A number of studies emphasise the role of political and interest group activity in dock or harbour development, or focus on the relationship between urban resources and port facilities, but in the present context the investigation needs to run also the other way. If a port is more than an interface between land and water, then a port town or city was more than just the settlement behind the waterfront. How much, and in what ways it was more, is the question which forms the subject of this chapter. It is a historical question, but it is also implicitly comparative. What, if anything, was distinctive about the urban experience in British cities which provided port services, as against other cities which did not, and how far did such port cities share common features?

The geographer James Bird, to whom anyone concerned with port history owes an enormous debt, in a detailed investigation of the history of all major British seaports, categorised his subjects under various headings. Under 'Industrial and commercial estuaries' he placed Newcastle, Sunderland and Middlesbrough, stressing the way in which in all three cases the port spread from the original site to produce respectively Tyneside, Wearside and Teesside. Glasgow and Clydeside, as also Belfast, are placed in the same group.

The significance of this categorisation becomes evident when the next of his groupings is considered. Hull and Humberside, Southampton, Bristol and Avonmouth are 'Commercial and industrial estuaries', with the implicit emphasis on their trading functions, rather than industrial developments.

The South Wales ports (Swansea, Milford Haven, Port Talbot, Cardiff, Barry, Newport) are placed in a geographical set of their own, each the end point of different river valley systems leading into the interior. The packet ports (Dover, Harwich, Holyhead), with development based on access to near sea crossings, are similarly seen to have common features. The Port of Manchester, immediately established as a major player when it opened in 1894, stands in a category of its own as an inland port, while London and Liverpool are the 'General cargo giants'.[4]

Bird's analysis stressed the importance of site but other approaches to grouping British ports are possible. Gordon Jackson has emphasised the causative factors in port creation, in particular the role of railway companies, and makes more of the variety of cargoes handled by ports as a defining distinction rather than the physical setting, though the two of course are not unconnected.[5] A related, if somewhat basic, way of looking at ports is to divide them into those which specialised in coasting trades and those in which foreign trade was more

[4] J. H. Bird, *The Major Seaports of the United Kingdom* (London, 1963), pp. 7–9.
[5] See G. Jackson, *The History and Archaeology of Ports* (Tadworth, 1983); and G. Jackson, 'The British port system c. 1850–1913', in A. Guimerá and D. Romero, eds., *Puertos y Sistemas Portuarios (Siglos XVI–XX): Actas del Coloquio Internacional El Sistema Portuario Español, Madrid, 1995* (Madrid, 1996), pp. 76–97.

important. The difference is well drawn out by considering shipping movements in English ports in 1841. The coastwise trade pecking order runs one to ten, London to Hull last, with Newcastle in second place. In contrast, Hull was nearer to the top of the range for foreign trade, coming third. Although coasting business was to prove more resilient in the face of competition from railways than is sometimes assumed, the survival of a port into the twentieth century as a flourishing enterprise was associated with competence in handling foreign-going vessels.[6] Still another mode of categorisation is to distinguish ports according to their system of ownership and control. A variety of forms of port authority developed, all regulated by act of parliament, most of which were some type of public trust, with varying degrees of connection with municipal government, but a number were privately owned, principally by railway companies.

Finally, not all ports had a commercial function. As naval bases Plymouth, Portsmouth and Chatham were in a category of their own. Their sites, initially chosen as sheltered, defensible anchorages, rather than points of entry, proved what have been described as 'frequently idiosyncratic locations' in relation to the naval dockyard function which became dominant. Private developments were hampered by the connection and the comment made in 1840 about one such port, not only applied more generally but held true until the mid-twentieth century: 'Portsmouth, with its surpassing geographical advantages has not kept pace in commercial progress with places far less fortunate in position: indeed the very circumstances of this port being a government arsenal and depot, was prejudicial to it as a place of trade.' The advance of commercial port functions in these towns was deliberately impeded by restrictive Admiralty policies.[7]

It is, then, possible to classify ports, employing alternative criteria to produce groupings which will vary according to the approach and sometimes also over time. Such classifications hint at the range of factors, not all economic, of which an urban history of ports should take account. The overall effect of these considerations is seemingly to highlight the unique character of every port – each of which self-evidently has its own story – but it has also been suggested by Bird that as a result of the need to respond to widespread changes in shipping technology and organisation port development followed a recognisable geographical pattern. Fundamental here was the long-term upward trend, fuelled by demographic increase and the spread of industrialisation, in the quantity of goods being moved by water, with high volume bulk cargoes of raw materials,

[6] J. Armstrong, 'Coastal shipping', in D. H. Aldcroft and M. J. Freeman, eds., *Transport in the Industrial Revolution* (Manchester, 1983), p. 153; J. Armstrong, 'Coastal shipping: the neglected sector of nineteenth-century British transport history', *International Journal of Maritime History*, 6 (1994), 175–88.

[7] R. C. Riley and J. L. Smith, 'Industrialization in naval ports: the Portsmouth case', in B. S. Hoyle and D. A. Pinder, *Cityport Industrialization and Regional Development* (Oxford, 1981), pp. 132–4; PP 1840 XI, Second Report of the Commission of Inquiry into the State of Large Towns and Populous Districts, Appendix II, p. 287.

foodstuffs and fuels becoming of increasing significance. This growth was made possible by an increase in the size and speed of vessels, first discernible when iron hulls began to replace timber, but gathered pace with the application of steam power and with the substitution of oil for coal in the twentieth century. The typical response of a port to the resulting pressure on existing facilities, Bird argued, was the spread of the port downstream, or away from its original urban nucleus, but with earlier facilities continuing to occupy a place in port activity.[8] The eventual abandonment of these, together with the impact of containerisation post-1960, can be added as further stages in this process.[9]

In terms of detail Bird's 'Anyport' model arguably fits some ports better than others, but its central contention, that the course of technological change in shipping meant that port activity within a particular settlement was by its very nature a mobile phenomenon, is helpful in identifying one distinctive urban feature which port cities shared: the need for space. Moreover, as in the larger established seaports each successive wave of investment gave access to deeper and deeper water, greater and greater quay length, the effect was physically to distance the outer limits of the seaport quarter from its older site. As long as traditional, non-mechanised systems of loading and unloading persisted, a corollary of expansion was the need to sustain a large labour force, settled in the area of the facilities. A factor here was the role of ports as storage sites, with warehouses and sheds a common physical feature of the city port urban landscape. Security was an important consideration, so in contrast to the juxtaposition of street and quayside typical in the past, nineteenth- and twentieth-century waterfront areas tended to take on a fortress character, closed to outsiders. Furthermore, the uses to which land was put – the digging out of docks, the construction of quays, the raising of great walls – were so specialised that in the short to medium term they inoculated the port areas against alternative, non-maritime uses, to become in recent times identified with decay and dereliction, though, from a different perspective, also to serve as a means by which inner-city areas came to be reserved for future development.

The process of investment, of course, was not automatic; it required the existence of agencies to implement the required changes, and presented a considerable challenge to local organisation and enterprise. Fundamental conflicts of interest between port users and port operators, as also local competition between rival ports, ensured that the running and the development of dock and harbour facilities were seldom other than a contentious process. Since the capital costs involved in most, though not all, cases put port investment out of the range of private individuals, and given that the rewards were both dispersed and long term, it is understandable that port development was commonly a corporate

[8] J. Bird, *Seaports and Seaport Terminals* (London, 1971).
[9] J. Charlier, 'Dockland regeneration for new port uses', in B. S. Hoyle and D. A. Pinder, eds., *European Port Cities in Transition* (London, 1992), pp. 138–40.

activity. Although many ports had taken the first steps towards improvement within a local government context, by the mid-nineteenth century many port authorities either were, or were about to become, non-profit-making trusts dominated by local maritime and mercantile representatives, with varying degrees of municipal involvement. The success of maritime-based vested interests in persuading parliament to minimise the role of municipalities in running ports was an example of central government suspicion of local authorities evident in other fields, rather than an informed assessment of what was required for efficient port operation or what the public interest might dictate. It is significant here that London was to remain the domain of joint-stock dock companies and private wharves until the docks were transferred in 1909 to a novel type of public corporation, the Port of London Authority (PLA), despite the ambitions of the London County Council to become a port authority. Indeed, among major ports only Bristol was to survive as an entirely municipally owned enterprise, run by a council committee and independent of sectional interests.[10]

Not all harbours or docks were run by public or quasi-public bodies. In 1854 as a government commission reported, there were cases where, 'although apparently a public work and undoubtedly of public importance', port facilities were private property.[11] Examples included the coal trade ports of Seaham Harbour and Cardiff, as well as ports like Southampton, Grimsby and Hull, where quays or docks were in the hands of railway companies.[12] In 1900, out of 113 ports, 67 were operated by trusts; 22 were completely under municipal direction; 7 were run by some other type of public body and 17 were wholly in private, primarily railway, ownership.[13]

Motives for railway company investment in waterfront facilities varied. Sometimes the concern was to provide a terminus for onward shipment from the interior, as in the Tyne and Tees coal ports and the packet ports. At both Hull and Southampton companies took over existing facilities facing financial problems. Local resources often proved inadequate when faced with the need to build a new dock, even when promoted by a public body, hence the power

---

[10] London County Council, Royal Commission on the Port of London, 1900, Statement of Evidence of the Clerk of the London County Council, pp. 29–30; PP 1918 iv, Select Committee on Transport, Second Report, Qq. 3391–469; D. J. Owen, *The Origins and Development of the Ports of the United Kingdom*, 2nd rev. edn (London, 1948), pp. 20–2. On Bristol, see K. P. Kelly, 'Public agencies and private interests: the port transport industry in Bristol, 1918–1939', in I. Blanchard, ed., *New Directions in Economic and Social History* (Edinburgh, 1995).

[11] PP 1854 xxxvii, Commissioners Appointed to Inquire into Local Charges upon Shipping in the Ports of the United Kingdom and the Islands of Guernsey, Jersey, Alderney, Sark and Man, Report, p. vi.

[12] See G. Jackson, 'Shipowners and private dock companies: the case of Hull, 1770–1970', in L. M. Akveld and J. R. Bruijn, eds., *Shipping Companies and Authorities in the 19th and 20th Centuries: Their Common Interest in the Development of Port Facilities* (The Hague, 1989), pp. 47–59.

[13] London County Council, Royal Commission on the Port of London, 1900, Statement of Evidence of the Clerk of the London County Council, pp. 29–30.

railway companies with their greater command of capital were able to exercise. In most cases their interest in docks or quays was ancillary to their main business, though in South Wales where, as one railway company chairman put it, 'dock companies owned little railways', the position was reversed.[14]

With the exception of London and the PLA, Westminster and Whitehall played little active part in promoting port development as such, though intervention in port labour issues was a persistent theme for much of the twentieth century. Although in 1947 a number of ports (together handling a quarter of national trade) were transferred to the state sector, this was a consequence of railway nationalisation rather than an attempt to replace local control by a national ports policy.[15] Even so, in the nineteenth century to be a major commercial port was already routinely to invite the attentions of central government to a degree arguably not experienced by any other type of town or city, other than in relation to the poor law. The state was represented on the quayside not only by customs officers, but in emigrant ports also by officials charged with the implementation of the Passenger Acts and, from 1850, by those operating Board of Trade shipping offices dealing with the signing-on and discharge of seamen.[16] The world enclosed within the dock wall encompassed outposts of central government.

Despite the trend for port facilities to be treated by parliament less as public works and more as the privileged province of special expert interests, links between ports and the wider economic community remained strong. For much of our period, the effect of the movement towards deeper water facilities was site extension, rather than displacement; port and city remained in proximity and maintained a relationship. One factor here, depending on the availability of alternative modes of transport, was the place of a local consumer market in providing custom for incoming goods; the bulk of London's nineteenth-century sea trade, much of it carried coastwise, was destined to feed and warm Londoners. Another was employment; port activity in these towns and cities was a source of jobs, feeding into urban growth via a number of routes. First, there were the demands of the loading and unloading of vessels which took place on the waterfront itself. The number of workers involved, as also when they worked, was determined by both the type of cargo and the flow of business, but in the longer term was also determined by the amount of investment – the size of the enterprise. In large foreign trade ports, like London and Liverpool, dealing with a complex mix of seasonal cargoes, many thousands of labourers were periodically needed on hand to cope with the amount of business, whereas the 'drop' system

[14] PP 1918 IV, Select Committee on Transport, Second Report, Qq. 2063, 2119.
[15] P. Turnbull and S. Weston, 'Employment regulation, state intervention and the economic performance of European ports', *Cambridge Journal of Economics*, 16 (1992), 385.
[16] See O. MacDonagh, *A Pattern of Government Growth 1800–60* (London, 1961); C. H. Dixon, 'Legislation and the seaman's lot', in P. Adam, ed., *Seamen in Society* (Paris, 1981), pp. 96–106.

of loading adopted in the north-eastern coal ports to cope with the steep terrain was less labour intensive. Beyond the immediate transhipment aspects, there were the related demands for special services such as chandling, outfitting, stowage, shipbroking and forwarding. Associated too with the work of every port, though varying in extent, was a distributive sector encompassing whole-saling, merchanting, warehousing and transportation inward and outward. Part of this work was clerical. Indeed, port development meant the creation of two labour forces, one associated with moving cargoes, the other with moving paper-work – one possible reason why mid-nineteenth-century standards of literacy and educational attainment were higher in port towns than elsewhere.[17] In general, it can be said that distribution functions, other than transport, were most significant where trade was diverse and multi-sourced, so that sorting became imperative. Finally, there were maritime related sectors: the industries process-ing sea-borne products, such as sugar, oilseeds and grain, together with, in some cases, shipbuilding and, more commonly, shiprepairing. These activities contrib-uted to what had become by the turn of the century an increasingly industrial-ised, polluted and inhospitable port landscape, with the dock or harbour area inhabited primarily only by those forced to live near their work. Unsurprisingly, merchants, shipowners and other shipping industry professionals, who a century earlier would have been housed close to the port, now chose to have their resi-dences in more salubrious environments.[18]

Not all these functions were of equal weight everywhere. As the following summary survey of the history of ports demonstrates, there is a fundamental dis-tinction, based on the range of overall economic activity, between towns and cities which were also ports (nineteenth-century London, Glasgow, Newcastle, Belfast and twentieth-century Bristol) and those centres (Liverpool, Cardiff, Southampton, Hull, Plymouth) which were port towns or cities in the sense that this dimension was central. This centrality can be demonstrated by the share of port-related employment in the workforce. In 1871, for example, a third of all workers at Cardiff were employed as seamen, dockers or on the railways and in 1931 on Merseyside half of all workers were in shipping, trade or transport.[19] Such dependence meant that these specialised port cities were vulnerable to developments in trade and shipping over which they had little or no influence.

The effects of maritime dominance, however, went deeper than this, becom-ing embedded into the wider urban social structure, influencing such aspects as

---

[17] W. B. Stephens, 'Illiteracy in provincial maritime districts and among seamen in early and mid-nineteenth-century England', in E. Jenkins, ed., *Studies in the History of Education* (Leeds, 1995), pp. 196–219.
[18] See G. Norcliffe, K. Bassett and T. Hoare, 'The emergence of postmodernism on the urban water-front: geographical perspectives on changing relationships', *Journal of Transport Geography*, 4 (1996), 123–34.
[19] Daunton, *Coal Metropolis*, p. 182; University of Liverpool, *Survey of Merseyside, Vol. 2* (Liverpool, 1932), pp. 1–2.

the character and preoccupations of local elites, as also influencing social, religious, political identification at all levels. These are complex matters, which can only be touched on here, but three later nineteenth-century examples may stand as indicative of the types of relationship and their variety. At Liverpool, Liberalism, the creed of the Mersey's shipowning elites, lacked working-class roots in part because the self-help fellowships of cooperation and trade unionism which were its base elsewhere depended on greater permanency of employment than Liverpool offered to much of its working class. At Portsmouth, with a large and skilled workforce, managed by a supervisory stratum, employed by the state, the middle class did not possess the sources of wealth or economic power available to their peers in other port towns, and neighbourhood and locality, rather than class distinction, structured cultural patterns. At Southampton, middle-class control of law enforcement agencies, against a background of regular employment of transport workers and local men as seafarers by railway and liner companies, contributed to its reputation as a quiet, respectable place.[20]

In the mid-nineteenth century London and Liverpool were the giants among English ports, in 1841 together accounting for 58 per cent of all inward shipping, while Glasgow handled 39 per cent of Scotland's import tonnage.[21] These centres were distinct from all others not only in the quantity of cargo handled but also in its range and variety. Import and transhipment business predominated in London, the 'emporium of the world', whereas Liverpool, drawing on the manufacturing and industrial strengths of its hinterland, was export oriented but this distinction should not be overstressed – both ports were general cargo ports. Though their locations as tidal ports were very different, with London inland and Liverpool on an exposed near-coastal site, each port had substantial and extensive dock and quay facilities, with a commensurate range of waterfront ancillary services and maritime-related industries. Each port too had canal links into the interior, but Liverpool was at this time better served by rail and road connections than were the docks and wharves of London.

Such parallels between the two great English ports take too little account of the wider context to be convincing within an urban perspective. London had a long history as the maritime metropolis and the system of the reformed port, with foreign trade docks developed by private companies, had belatedly extended rather than replaced the earlier framework of port activity based on the river. In London the old and the new coexisted, with no authority responsible

[20] See J. Smith, 'Class, skill and sectarianism in Glasgow and Liverpool, 1880–1914', and J. Field, 'Wealth, styles of life and social tone amongst Portsmouth's middle class, 1800–75,' in R. J. Morris, ed., *Class, Power and Social Structure in British Nineteenth-Century Towns* (Leicester, 1986), pp. 173–84, 67–104; V. C. Burton, 'The work and home life of seafarers, with special reference to the port of Southampton, 1871–1921' (PhD thesis, University of London, 1988), p. 362.
[21] PP 1842 XXXIX, Trade and Navigation Accounts.

for the government of the port as a whole. Furthermore, the port, no more than any other type of economic activity, could not claim to be the central feature in the capital's economy, characterised as it was by diversity which included a substantial manufacturing sector. London was a port – but much else besides.[22]

On the Clyde, thanks initially to the improved access provided by steamtugs, Glasgow was just emerging from the shadow of Greenock in serving large ocean-going shipping with further development ensured over the following half-century by an ambitious programme of river deepening and dock construction. Here the pace of urban development was forcing an improvement in communications.[23] In contrast Liverpool in the 1840s was the product of just over a century of trade-related expansion, which drew in population, rapidly extended the area of settlement and both reflected and promoted a continual flow of additional facilities provided by the dock trustees, under the control of the Corporation. Such was the pressure for land close to the waterfront to meet demands for processing of bulk imports that older industries, including shipbuilding, were progressively being displaced. Already Liverpool was defining its longer-term role as a narrowly based, trade-centred port city.[24]

On the east coast, the long-established Baltic port, Hull, was similarly focused on trade, though with less success in expanding its share than Liverpool since handicapped by a difficult site, underinvestment in facilities, poor inland transport links which inhibited exports and the development of other Humberside ports. With the noteworthy exception of cotton manufacture, employing over 2,000 at mid-century, its main industries were small-scale processing or maritime based: shipbuilding, marine engineering, tanning, oilseed crushing and paint manufacture. Whaling was on the decline, and the expansion of the fishing industry still to come.[25]

Bristol, declining as a port from the late eighteenth century with the loss of trade to Liverpool, by the 1840s was at the juncture of a new phase in its development as the city began to gain the benefit of railway links and to find means, administrative as well as technical, of tackling the physical problems of its difficult river access. Its future, however, was to lie in industrial development rather than

---

[22] On the Port of London see J. Broodbank, *History of the Port of London*, 2 vols. (London, 1921); J. H. Bird, *The Geography of the Port of London* (London, 1957); R. D. Brown, *The Port of London* (Lavenham, 1978); R. J. M. Carr and S. K. Al Naib, eds., *Dockland* (London, 1986). On the Port of Liverpool see F. E. Hyde, *Liverpool and the Mersey* (Newton Abbot, 1971); N. Ritchie-Noakes, *Liverpool's Historic Waterfront* (Liverpool, 1984); A. Jarvis, *Liverpool Central Docks, 1799–1905* (Stroud, 1991).

[23] See G. Jackson and C. Munn, 'Trade, commerce and finance', in W. H. Fraser and I. Maver, eds., *Glasgow*, vol. II: *1830 to 1912* (Manchester, 1996), pp. 52–77; D. Turnock, *The Historical Geography of Scotland since 1707* (Cambridge, 1982), pp. 156–7.

[24] See R. Lawton, 'From the Port of Liverpool to the conurbation of Merseyside', in W. T. S. Gould and A. G. Hodgkiss, eds., *The Resources of Merseyside* (Liverpool, 1982), pp. 2–13.

[25] J. Bellamy, 'The Humber estuary and industrial development', in N. V. Jones, ed., *A Dynamic Estuary* (Hull, 1988), pp. 133–41.

in a revival of its past trading tradition.[26] Southampton was also at the beginning of a new phase, but one in which port activity was to come to the fore. Already gaining population on the basis of tourism, in 1840 the opening of the London and South-Western Railway, shortly followed by the first dock, was to form the basis of a passenger business bringing Southampton to the position of fifth port in the country within twenty years.[27]

Of the remaining significant port towns at the start of our period Newcastle and the associated Tyneside settlements were already developing as industrial centres based on proximity to the coalfield, supplementing, though by no means supplanting, a long-established focus on the export of coal. The control of the Tyne itself had long been a cause of dispute between Newcastle and the centres of population at Gateshead, and at South and North Shields, and the river remained in its natural state, with passage hampered by shallows, islands and sandbanks. In 1850 the creation of the Tyne Commission provided the administrative basis for the necessary improvements, in particular the deepening of the river, which also served to promote a growing specialism in the construction of iron vessels.[28] Among the other coal ports, Sunderland was also a major shipbuilding centre, first in timber then in iron, while on the Tees Middlesbrough and Stockton were essentially new ports created by the Stockton and Darlington Railway link to the interior.[29] In the early 1840s Cardiff's role as 'Coal Metropolis' still lay in the future, but its direction had been recently set by the opening of the Taff Vale Railway and the first of the Bute docks.[30]

Over the following decades the railway was to have an increasing impact on port development, reshaping hinterlands and creating new trading opportunities, not least for railway companies themselves. But the most significant influence on port business was the gradual, but relentless, transition from sail to steam once the compound engine had been perfected in the mid-1850s. The associated growth in the size of individual vessels, as also in the quantity of cargo handled by British ports created a need for additional, more extensive dock, quay and storage accommodation and, in established ports, rendered facilities designed to cater for sailing vessels increasingly outdated and inappropriate. By way of response, between 1851 and 1900 over £100 million was invested in English ports and harbours alone.[31]

Though no port of any size was physically unaffected by the change in shipping technology, nor by the continued expansion of trade which characterised

[26] F. Walker, *The Bristol Region* (London, 1972), pp. 240–3.

[27] F. J. Monkhouse, *A Survey of Southampton and its Region* (Southampton, 1964), pp. 232–3.

[28] H. A. Mess, *Industrial Tyneside* (London, 1928), pp. 17–27; Bird, *Major Seaports*, pp. 40–3.

[29] Bird, *Major Seaports*, p. 63.

[30] H. Carter, 'Cardiff, local, regional and national capital', in G. Gordon, ed., *Regional Cities in the UK, 1890–1980* (London, 1986), p. 173.

[31] A. G. Kenwood, 'Port investment in England and Wales, 1851–1913', *Yorkshire Bulletin of Economic and Social Research*, 17 (1965), 156–67.

the later nineteenth century, the consequences varied according to local circumstances. In the case of London the scale of investment in new docks owed as
much to rivalry between dock companies as to the objective needs of shipping,
but, as in the other great ports, Liverpool and Glasgow, the effect was to supplement and extend the reach of earlier maritime activity, with consequent extensions of the area of port-related settlement. The deep water modern facilities of
these three ports made them the main beneficiaries of the development of steel
screw steamers, as the home bases for the main passenger and cargo liner companies. At Bristol viable accommodation for shipping in the city centre was hampered by poor access from the Avon, with the consequence that Avonmouth
(1877) and Portishead (1879) were constructed, effectively serving as outports to
the Port of Bristol, into which they were incorporated.[32] Swansea saw four docks
constructed between 1852 and 1909, though at Cardiff the reluctance of the
Butes to finance new docks, despite the overcrowded state of what was by the
1880s the leading coal export port in the world, meant that the response was
unduly protracted, leading to the opening of rival facilities at Barry (1889).[33]
Southampton's progress was hampered by the tardiness of its dock company in
providing deep water berths, which led to the transfer of P & O's business to
London in 1878–9, but was able to recover its dynamism once the South-
Western Railway Company took control of waterfront facilities.[34] At
Manchester, an inland port brought into being by the completion of the Ship
Canal challenged Liverpool's dominant role in the carriage of cotton.[35] On the
Humber, additional railway connections allowed Goole, another inland port,
and Grimsby to syphon off central England trade from Hull. Both Hull and
Grimsby, in common with Fleetwood were, however, to benefit when the intro-
duction of the steam trawler fostered phenomenal growth in the fishing indus-
try which led to the opening of docks specifically designed to serve its needs.[36]

In general the effect of the change in shipping technology in the later nineteenth century was to encourage the emergence of additional ports without
undermining the position of the former leaders. But whereas earlier port activity had given life to a central business district based on mercantile and commercial activity, providing work opportunities for middle-class professionals,
subsequent development closely linked to railway systems, where goods or
people passed through but did not linger, had no parallel effect.

If in some cities commercial activity initially associated with port-based transactions can subsequently be said to have developed a life and momentum of its

---

[32] Walker, *Bristol Region*, pp. 240–2.
[33] Daunton, *Coal Metropolis*, p. 30; G. Hallett and P. Randall, *Maritime Industry and Port Development in South Wales* (Cardiff, 1970), pp. 37–9.
[34] A. Temple Patterson, 'Southampton in the eighteenth and nineteenth centuries', in Monkhouse, ed., *Survey of Southampton*, p. 235; Burton, 'Work and home life of seafarers', pp. 28–57.
[35] See D. A. Farnie, *The Manchester Ship Canal and the Rise of the Port of Manchester, 1894–1975* (Manchester, 1980).   [36] Bellamy, 'Humber estuary', pp. 142–3.

own, the same can be said of shipbuilding. In the 1840s ships were built in all major ports, with their market primarily but not exclusively local or regional. By 1900 the evolution of the metal-hulled steamship had confined shipbuilding on any scale to the North-East, the Clyde and Belfast. For these centres the specialism in shipbuilding, repairing and engineering, boosted by the armaments race, rendered port services progressively less significant in shaping the physical, social and economic environment of such industrial rivers.[37] In a very different geographical context, the Bristol economy had also been reshaped, with historic port-related industries of tobacco and of cocoa and chocolate redeveloped and joined by a variety of engineering industries, and its port, no longer the leading sector, nevertheless prospering from the handling of foodstuffs and bulk raw materials.[38]

This was not the case for Liverpool, which, drawing its exports from a restricted, highly developed surrounding manufacturing area, did not become a manufacturing centre in its own right. Iron shipbuilding took hold across the Mersey at Birkenhead, but Liverpool's industrial base was rooted in the processing of bulk imported raw materials, where land transport costs discouraged transfer inland. Flour milling, seed crushing, soap making and sugar refining were the dominant industries.[39] Hull also had a somewhat similar bulk-processing profile, with interdependence between traditional industrial and maritime sectors increasing in the second half of the nineteenth century. Its 'new industry', fishing, served to strengthen the maritime basis of the Humber economy, providing a market for the construction of fishing vessels, which served as a lifeline for the shipbuilding industry. A subsequent rapid transition from smack to steam trawling at Hull and the new port, Grimsby, radically restructured the fishing industry and ancillary construction trades.[40] In both Hull and Liverpool, then, maritime-related activity continued to be a major determinant of the wider economic structure, but elsewhere the strength of linkages into the wider urban economy varied. Cardiff's failure, during the period of its greatest success as a port, to widen beyond coal into more general trades or into shipbuilding, despite contemporary identification of the potential and the need, provides an example here.[41] Finally, while naval ports provided the extreme example of maritime domination, the industries promoted were not entirely what might be expected. In Portsmouth it was the clothing industry which benefited in the later nineteenth

[37] See S. Ville, ed., *Shipbuilding in the United Kingdom in the Nineteenth Century* (St Johns, Newfoundland, 1993).   [38] Walker, *Bristol Region*, pp. 277–8.
[39] E. P. Cotter, *The Port of Liverpool, including Birkenhead and Garston: United States Department of Commerce and US Shipping Board Foreign Port Series No. 2* (Washington, 1929), p. 298.
[40] See R. Robinson, 'The development of the British North Sea steam trawling fleet 1877–1900', in L. U. Scholl and J. Edwards, eds., *The North Sea, Resource and Seaway* (Aberdeen, 1996), pp. 365–83; R. Robinson, *A History of the Yorkshire Coast Fishing Industry, 1790–1914* (Hull, 1987); Bellamy, 'Humber estuary', pp. 141–3; E. E. Gillett, *A History of Grimsby* (London, 1970).
[41] See Daunton, *Coal Metropolis*.

century. This employed approaching half of the labour force, almost entirely female. The link here was less with naval tailoring than with the superabundance of low-wage labour, a result of the army and navy presence, which was available to fill orders from London manufacturers.[42]

The outbreak of the First World War had a varied effect on the business of British ports. Liverpool, with its sheltered west coast position and suitability for convoys, in particular benefited at the expense of London which from 1915 was severely affected by the submarine campaign.[43] But the temporary redistribution of trade produced by wartime conditions, followed by the post-war boom, was to prove of minor significance for a number of centres in comparison with the longer term impact of the loss of overseas markets and falling demand for Britain's staple products. The South Wales ports, with their extreme dependence on coal, were hit particularly hard, but in the North-East the effect on trade resulting from the problems of the coal industry were compounded by the crisis in shipbuilding.[44] Yet elsewhere the interwar decline in export volumes, of more significance for port operations than values, was counterbalanced by a rising volume of imports from which London, Hull, Bristol, Southampton and, to a lesser extent, Glasgow benefited.[45] This was not sufficient to exclude these ports from the impact of depression on waterfront employment; in London average daily engagements almost halved between 1920 and 1932.[46] Liverpool's situation, however, stood out as the most dire, with unemployment in the city as a whole rising to 28 per cent in 1932, as against the national average of 22 per cent.[47] It suffered a fall in exports as a result of diminishing demand for the products of its Lancashire hinterland and failed to expand its imports in compensation, with the consequence that every year from 1919 to 1939 on average 1 per cent of its trade was lost to other British ports, mainly in the South. Among other blows, the transfer of much North Atlantic passenger trade to Southampton exemplified Liverpool's changing status.[48] Although there was some diversification of Merseyside's industrial base as a result of these difficulties, the economy remained focused on its traditional port-based concerns.[49]

The effect of the outbreak of war in 1939 was, as earlier in the century, to benefit the trade of western ports at the expense of those on the east (Cardiff in

---

[42] Riley and Smith, 'Industrialization in naval ports', p. 138.

[43] See C. E. Fayle, *The War and the Shipping Industry* (London, 1927).

[44] Michael Barke, 'Newcastle/Tyneside 1890–1980', in Gordon, ed., *Regional Cities*, pp. 129–30; Hallett and Randall, *Maritime Industry*, p. 39.

[45] W. J. Corlett, 'The share of the Port of Liverpool in total imports', in G. Allen *et al.*, eds., *The Import Trade of the Port of Liverpool* (Liverpool, 1946), p. 23; Kelly, 'Port transport industry in Bristol'.   [46] G. Phillips and N. Whiteside, *Casual Labour* (Oxford, 1985), p. 178.

[47] Lawton, 'Port of Liverpool', p. 9.

[48] Corlett, 'Share', pp. 21–3; D. E. Baines, 'Merseyside in the British economy: the 1930s and the Second World War', in R. Lawton and C. M. Cunningham, eds., *Merseyside* (London, 1970), pp. 58–62.   [49] Lawton, 'Port of Liverpool', p. 9.

particular enjoyed a brief remission from decline, handling up to one third of all UK dry cargo), though the extent of physical destruction resulting from enemy attacks posed a need for future investment in reconstruction in all major ports.[50] Even so, the post-war revival of trade provided for some a welcome contrast to the difficulties of the interwar years, and the 1950s saw traffic increasing at both London and Liverpool.[51] There was no salvation for ports specialising in the coal trade, but the rapid development of bulk cargo transportation, particularly of iron ore and oil, advantaged those ports able to invest in deep water specialised facilities to serve these needs.[52] In consequence, Southampton, despite competition from air transport which presaged its demise as an oceanic passenger port, found compensation in oil importing and refining.[53] Southampton, in common with the Channel and east coast ports, was increasingly to benefit from facing towards Europe. Indeed, Hull's prospects, which had diminished with the oceanic emphasis of trade following the war, were transformed by Britain's entry to the European Economic Community (EEC).[54] In the 1960s the spread of new handling methods, including containerisation, were to advantage those ports with waterfront storage space and good road transport connections, as well as to reduce the need for on-site labour.[55] Where docks and quays were hemmed in by urban development, as at London and Liverpool, the effect was to complete the separation between city and port, and between port and employment. From now on ports were gateways, entry and exit points; the port city as the nineteenth century understood it had ceased to exist.[56]

That understanding was not a matter of trade statistics or the amount invested in docks and quays, but involved a perception of a port as possessing special characteristics as a place. Literary evocations of ports are almost a commonplace of Victorian literature, with Charles Dickens, Herman Melville and Joseph Conrad among those attracted by the juxtaposition of shipping and quayside, the exotic and the ordinary. The works of social commentators from Henry Mayhew onwards also testify to other paradoxes including the contrast between valuable cargoes and the poverty of those handling them and the openness to external

---

[50] Hallett and Randall, *Maritime Industry*, p. 39.

[51] Hyde, *Liverpool and the Mersey*, pp. 182–6; S. Palmer, 'From London to Tilbury – the Port of London since 1945', in P. Holm and J. Edwards, eds., *North Sea Ports and Harbours – Adaptations to Change* (Esbjerg, 1992), pp. 189–92.

[52] PP 1962 cmnd 1824, Report of the Committee of Inquiry into the Major Ports of Great Britain (Rochdale Committee), pp. 10–13.

[53] M. E. Witherick, 'Port developments, port-city linkages and prospects for maritime industry: a case study of Southampton', in Hoyle and Pinder, eds., *Cityport*, pp. 115–17.

[54] Jackson, 'Shipowners and private dock companies', p. 58.

[55] See R. E. Takel, 'The spatial demands of ports and related industry and their relationships with the community', in Hoyle and Pinder, eds., *Cityport*, pp. 47–66.

[56] This conclusion draws on B. Hoyle, 'Development dynamics at the port–city interface', in Hoyle, Pinder and Husain, eds., *Revitalising*.

influences, as exemplified by the presence of foreigners, coexisting with a culture of exclusion, as exemplified by the importance of family connection in determining who got waterfront work. It is important to be aware that these concerns or, at a popular level, generalised impressions derived from them have to some extent distorted the picture of what it meant to be a port town or city. Thus we have more awareness of the conditions of port labourers than the characteristics of port elites; the pervasive orderliness of Southampton is less familiar than the squalor of Wapping.

Although port-related employment could extend well beyond the waterfront, the existence of a waterfront maritime quarter, bereft of wealthier occupants, can be seen as one central distinguishing feature of the use of space in the nineteenth-century port city. Not all ports had 'sailortowns' as diverse and wild in reputation as those in London and Liverpool described by Stan Hugill in a well-known popular study but the need for accommodation, not only for seafarers, but also for port labourers, provided the basis for settlement in the surrounding streets, as well as for the provision of services.[57] While sailortown is readily recognisable worldwide as a generic category, the type of seafaring employment influenced its extent and character. In coasting trades, or where voyages were not terminating, crews usually stayed on board so demand for lodgings was less. Liners provided a settled source of employment for 'working men who got wet', who lived locally and were part of wider working-class shore society. Southampton lacked its sailortown because there was no need for one.[58] In contrast, ports such as Cardiff, dominated by tramp shipping, were frequented by seamen tied into systems of payment where credit was a necessity, who looked to the port district to provide them with lodgings, entertainment, clothing and, eventually, an outward berth. The disreputable character of such areas, combined with a view of the sailor as footloose, ignorant, gullible and in need of protection, brought the attention of central and, in the case of Liverpool, municipal government, as also of philanthropists and religious organisations, with the consequence that Board of Trade shipping offices, sailors' homes and seamen's missions became a feature of all ports with an itinerant seafaring population. These institutions failed to alter the behaviour when ashore of other than a minority of seafarers and, by their more permanent, official or semi-official character than lodging houses or slopshops, if anything served to reinforce the seafaring connection with particular districts.[59] The presence of large numbers of sailors gave such areas a particular cultural texture,

[57] See S. Hugill, *Sailortown* (London, 1967); Hilling, 'Socio-economic change'; E. L. Taplin, *Liverpool Dockers and Seamen, 1870–90* (Hull, 1974).

[58] See Burton, 'Work and home life of seafarers', p. 273.

[59] See A. Kennerley, 'British seamen's missions and sailors' homes 1815–1970: voluntary welfare provision for serving seafarers' (PhD thesis, Polytechnic South-West, 1989); M. J. Daunton, 'Jack ashore: seamen in Cardiff before 1914', *Welsh History Review*, 9 (1978); S. Palmer, 'Seamen ashore in late nineteenth-century London: protection from the crimps', in P. Adam, ed., *Seamen in Society* (Paris, 1980).

providing a reminder of a wider world which was to persist in the form of racially and nationally mixed port communities.

Already by the late nineteenth century, however, the demand for sailortown services was no longer expanding commensurately with port business. Not only the greater regularity of employment associated with liner business but also fewer short-term engagements, shorter voyages and the discharge of bulk cargoes away from urban areas progressively reduced the need for shore facilities. Even so, despite a weakening of the force of economic motives, sailors who were not compelled to do so because foreign, still tended to continue to prefer to congregate in port districts. Recent sociologically oriented research has suggested that the occupational characteristics of seafaring (involving periods of living within a highly disciplined work environment, separated from family and social responsibilities, but interspaced with periods of leisure on shore with money to spend) were so different from most other groups that they had the effect of alienating the sailor from society ashore, and encouraged him to seek the company of those with experience of the sea and fewer expectations of a conventional mode of life.[60] Nevertheless, irrespective of such considerations, no sailortown could ultimately survive the decline of the port which had given it life. Cardiff's Tiger Bay, for example, which had a span of just one hundred years, already by 1932 had seen a dramatic fall in the number of seamen's boarding houses and the continued decline of the coal trade ensured its drift into dereliction in the post-war decades.[61]

If seafaring can be seen as engendering attitudes and values which set the sailor apart, a similar claim has frequently been made for the waterside itself.[62] Here the intermittent nature of the work, fundamentally a result of the variety of cargoes and seasonality but accentuated short term by siting of ports on tidal rivers which further militated against regular shifts, was reflected in a casual labour system. Irregularity of employment gave such port workers a freedom to take time off and encouraged a life style based on short-term calculation. In the later nineteenth century it was as much the oversupply of manual labour involved as the irregularity of employment which concerned social reformers but, while port work was the paradigm of casual employment, such a labour market was by no means exceptional among urban workers, nor was the poverty with which it was associated. Other factors were therefore also responsible for creating a distinctive work culture among dock workers.

---

[60] Kennerley, 'Seamen's missions', pp. 9–11; C. J. Forsyth and W. B. Bankston, 'The social and psychological consequences of a life at sea', *Maritime Policy and Management*, 11 (1984).

[61] Hilling, 'Socio-economic change'.

[62] See S. A. Andersen, 'Docker's culture in three north European port cities', in Holm and Edwards, eds., *North Sea Ports*, pp. 133–88, for a discussion of the literature. See also S. Hill, *The Dockers* (London, 1976).

There seems no doubt that ports were associated with a less skilled, low-paid workforce. In Liverpool and Hull, where, as already noted, port-related industry was primarily basic processing, this characteristic extended beyond port operations, affecting the entire urban employment mix. Nevertheless, as a number of studies have demonstrated, the popular picture of an undifferentiated port workforce is misleading; real or constructed occupational distinctions, claims to particular work territories, were a central feature in all ports handling a variety of cargoes.[63] With mechanisation limited, teamwork in lifting and moving cargo using manual labour was essential and even where employment was regular, as in some railway ports, typically workers operated in gangs.[64] A sense of solidarity and interdependence within groups of workers resulted, which encouraged confrontation with those seen as opponents, whether employers or other groups of workers. Unionisation, virtually completed by 1911, failed to subdue the autonomy and individualism of dock workers, and the control of the trade union leadership over the membership frequently proved tenuous. Labour militancy, surfacing in 'wildcat strikes', was a permanent feature in many ports in the twentieth century, though most pronounced after the Second World War. The survival of casual engagement until the 1960s, and the hostility that the introduction in 1947 of the trade union sponsored compulsory national register aroused, in part reflect the strength of established workplace traditions in the workforce.

In their definitive investigation of casual labour, Gordon Phillips and Noel Whiteside warn against seeing dockside inhabitants as a race apart. Nevertheless, developments in the twentieth century tended to enhance differences between waterfront and other types of labour. The survival of casual employment, as also its association with a strongly unionised workforce, was itself unusual, as was a patriarchal family structure, in which recruitment went from father to son, and an older than average age profile for the industry. A factor here was the introduction of labour registers in many ports in the interwar years, which had the effect of encouraging exclusivity by defining the workforce. With fewer jobs available, employment became restricted to a more permanent core of workers – a contrast with the previous century when it had been possible for migrant workers, particularly the Irish, to enter the industry.[65] The residential segregation in dock communities evident in the nineteenth century persisted in the twentieth century, though rehousing following on bomb damage made it less marked after the Second World War.[66] Even so, a 1956 study of the Port of

---

[63] See R. Brown, *Waterfront Organization in Hull, 1870–1900* (Hull, 1972); J. Lovell, *Stevedores and Dockers* (London, 1969); Taplin, *Liverpool Dockers*.

[64] See J. Hovey, *A Tale of Two Ports* (London, 1990), for discussion of differing labour practices between ports. [65] Phillips and Whiteside, *Casual Labour*, pp. 210, 275.

[66] National Dock Labour Board, *Welfare among Dock Workers* (London, 1952), p. 8.

Manchester found 40 per cent of port workers living, apparently by choice rather than necessity, within a mile of the dock gates.[67]

Indeed, even in the mid-1950s British port towns and cities continued to display many of the physical, social and economic features evident at the beginning of the century. There had been no technological revolution in shipping similar to the nineteenth-century transition from sail to steam which would have had an effect of forcing change in the siting or nature of port facilities. On the quayside, cargo handling continued to be a predominantly manual process, though fork lift trucks now supplemented cranes as mechanical aids to dock labour. Altogether there was a settled character to port operations, and likewise to their urban features.

Within little over a decade all was to change. Containerisation and new modes of discharging high volume bulk cargoes would rapidly render much of existing port provision, together with its associated workforce, redundant. In this late twentieth-century world of maritime transport, the connection between city and port was to be finally severed – only to be rediscovered, or reinvented, as an aspect of urban heritage.

[67] Liverpool University, Department of Social Science, *The Dock Worker: An Analysis of Conditions of Employment in the Port of Manchester* (Liverpool, 1956), p. 43.

· 5 ·

The development of small towns in Britain

STEPHEN A. ROYLE

AN EVOCATION of the traditional rural town of the mid-nineteenth century may be found in Anthony Trollope's description of his English West Country county of 'Barsetshire' in *Dr Thorne*:

> There are towns in it, of course; depots from which are bought seeds and groceries, ribbons and fire shovels; in which markets are held and country balls carried on; which return members to parliament, generally – in spite of reform bills, past, present and coming – in accordance with the dictates of some neighbouring land magnate: from whence emanate the country postman, and where is located the supply of post horses necessary for county visitings. But these towns add nothing to the importance of the county; they consist, with the exception of the assize-town, of dull, all but death-like single streets. Each possesses two pumps, three hotels, ten shops, fifteen beer-houses, a beadle and a market-place.[1]

This chapter will trace the evolution of such small urban places over the following century; developments that built upon an already quick pace of change. Peter Borsay concluded that the period from 1688 to 1820 had been 'for towns years of transformation'.[2] 'Transformation' had also been used by Peter Clark to sum up changes experienced by English provincial towns from 1600 to 1800.[3] Clark's research on small towns for this period, not least in his chapter in Volume II of this series, identifies a number of economic trends causing such transformation. These included nascent industrialisation and commercial expansion, transportation evolution and also more localised developments, such as the building of spas and leisure resorts. These developments were minor compared to those to come in the nineteenth century as the full flowering of Clark's nascent trends recast the geography of the British urban scene with regard to

[1] A. Trollope, *Dr Thorne*, new edn (London, 1926), pp. 1–2.
[2] P. Borsay, 'Introduction', in P. Borsay, ed., *The Eighteenth-Century Town* (London, 1990), pp. 1–38.
[3] P. Clark, 'Introduction', in P. Clark, ed., *The Transformation of English Provincial Towns, 1600–1800* (London, 1984), pp. 13–61.

settlement networks and hierarchies, functions and the layout of the urban places themselves. Much of this development was focused on the Victorian industrial cities but the small towns to be studied in this chapter were also affected. This chapter will consider the spatial pattern of urban development as it affected the small town sector and will deal with the functions and internal geographical structure of the small towns themselves for the period from *c.* 1851 to 1951.

The first task is to draw up a list of which places were 'small towns', occupying that niche in the settlement hierarchy which was distinct functionally and in size terms from both non-urban villages and more substantial large towns and cities. One invaluable data set is Clark and Jean Hosking's *Population Estimates of English Small Towns, 1550–1851*,[4] for, from the range of small English places, they identify those which can be regarded as urban. For Wales, Harold Carter's seminal work on the urban geography of that country includes a comprehensive list of towns, with the bonus of a functional classification for 1951.[5] For Scotland, the decision as to what can be regarded as urban can be left to the law; places with the legal status of a 'burgh' were distinct territories whose authorities were responsible for local government, economic policies, public works and services.[6] Burghs were separately identified in the Scottish censuses, that for 1971 usefully listing the population of each from 1851 or 1861.

The urban places listed in these sources were not all small towns, even in England, for Clark and Hosking's catalogue starting in the mid-sixteenth century led to the inclusion by 1851 of such urban giants as Liverpool and Sunderland. So, pruning had to be carried out to discard those places larger than the scale of town to be considered here. The easiest procedure was to impose a population ceiling and remove from this analysis towns that exceeded it. A population of 10,000 has often been used as a benchmark in urban histories,[7] so it seemed appropriate to apply this threshold. This accords with Adna Weber's analysis, too, for he differentiated between 'towns' and 'cities' at 10,000 ('great cities' started at 100,000).[8] No lower threshold population was needed for inclusion here as places in the three national sources have all been identified by scholars or by authority as being functionally and/or legally towns or burghs, whatever their size. This follows Robert Dickinson's ruling that 'the definition of an urban settlement is fundamentally a question of function, not of population . . . the "urban status" of a town depends on the character and variety of functions with which it is endowed'.[9]

[4] P. Clark and J. Hosking, *Population Estimates of English Small Towns 1550–1851*, Centre for Urban History, University of Leicester, Working Paper, 5 (Leicester, 1993).

[5] H. Carter, *The Towns of Wales* (Cardiff, 1966).

[6] G. Gordon and B. Dicks, 'Prolegomena', in G. Gordon and B. Dicks, eds., *Scottish Urban History* (Aberdeen, 1983), pp. 1–22.   [7] J. de Vries, *European Urbanisation 1500–1800* (London, 1984).

[8] A. F. Weber, *The Growth of Cities in the Nineteenth Century* (New York, 1899).

[9] R. E Dickinson, 'The distribution and functions of the smaller urban settlements of East Anglia', *Geography*, 17 (1932), 20.

Those places identified as small towns in 1851 (plus thirty-five Scottish burghs for which the 1971 census report did not record a population total before 1861) were then traced as a cohort through succeeding censuses to 1951. If they reached 10,000 during that period, they were excluded from the analysis from the next census. The resultant data set for Great Britain consisted of 923 small towns in 1851 (958 in 1861 with the additional burghs): 722 in England, 64 in Wales and 137 in Scotland (172 in 1861), falling to 748 by 1951 (567 in England, 43 in Wales and 138 in Scotland) as population growth took 175 of the small towns beyond the 10,000 threshold.

The list and its changes serve as the backbone for the chapter. The operation and economies of the towns will be discussed. Some were mining centres, others ports, resorts or industrial towns although most of them were traditional country and market towns. This was true especially in 1851, but during the study period such places often became more diverse in their economies. In an associated fashion, many towns whose *raison d'être* was, say, mining, assumed also marketing functions to serve their populations. The small towns' society and social geography will also be identified. Particular attention will be paid to the situation in 1851, 1901 (the end of the Victorian era, which falls neatly in the middle of the study period) and 1951. This closing date was chosen for being the first census year after the Second World War, while being prior to the technological, industrial, transportational and social changes, including counterurbanisation, which have had such massive impact on the small towns of Britain in the contemporary era. Material from England, Scotland and Wales will be used throughout the chapter. The population details of the towns mentioned in the text are listed in Table 5.1.

(i) MID–NINETEENTH–CENTURY SMALL TOWNS

During the nineteenth century considerable change took place on the British urban scene, the basic cause summed up as 'steam' by Weber;[10] more fully the processes of industrialisation and modernisation and all that accompanied them. The patterns on the ground in 1851 show some of the initial impact of 'steam' on small towns but whilst few places were not affected ultimately, at mid-century there remained hundreds of towns performing traditional roles as agricultural service centres and central places, part of the traditional symbiosis between town and country.

Map 5.1 presents a distribution map of all 923 small towns in 1851 (the thirty-five Scottish burghs where populations are not given until 1861 are also marked). In addition, Map 5.2 identifies the relationship between the number of people living in small towns and the total population of their county. Three

---

[10] Weber, *Cities*, p. 158.

Table 5.1 *Population figures of small towns mentioned in the text*

Town	1851	1901	1951
Abergavenny	4,797	7,795	8,848
Aberystwyth	5,231	8,014	11,271 (1921)
Ashby de la Zouch	3,762	4,726	6,405
Banbury	4,026	12,072 (1881)	
Bangor	9,564	10,662	
Barry	n/a		
Beaumaris	2,599	2,326	2,134
Beccles	4,398	6,898	6,870
Blaenavon	5,855	11,737 (1891)	
Braintree	2,836	5,330	11,314 (1921)
Brecon	5,673	5,741	6,470
Bridgend	n/a		
Bridgnorth	6,172	6,052	6,250
Briton Ferry	1,737	6,973	8,452
Bromsgrove	4,426	8,418	18,532 (1921)
Bungay	3,841	3,314	3,535
Caernarfon	8,674	10,258 (1881)	
Caerphilly	1,117	15,835	
Cardiff	n/a		
Cardigan	3,876	8,014	11,271 (1921)
Carmarthen	n/a		
Castle Donnington	2,729	2,514	3,140
Chelmsford	6,033	11,008 (1891)	
Chepstow	4,295	3,067	5,283
Chichester	8,662	12,224	
Coalville	n/a		
Coggeshall	3,484	2,578	2,900
Colchester	n/a		
Cowbridge	1,066	1,202	1,055
Cullen	3,165	1,936	1,555
Dingwall	1,990	2,519	3,367
Diss	2,419	3,745	3,503
Dolgellau	2,041	2,437	2,246
Eye	2,587	2,004	1,631
Fakenham	2,240	2,907	2,933
Fishguard	2,316	2,002	4,839
Flint	3,296	4,625	10,091 (1921)
Hallaton	691	602	422
Halstead	5,658	6,073	6,000
Haverfordwest	6,580	6,007	7,267
Helensburgh	2,841	8,554	8,760
Hinckley	6,111	11,304	
Invergordon	1,122 (1861)	1,047	1,514
Ipswich	n/a		
Kelso	4,783	4,008	4,119
Kenninghall	1,648	976	802
Kingston-upon-Thames	6,279	15,263 (1871)	

Table 5.1 (*cont.*)

Town	1851	1901	1951
Kirkwall	2,448	3,711	4,348
Leek	8,877	10,045 (1861)	
Lerwick	2,904	4,541	5,538
Lewes	9,097	10,753 (1871)	
Liverpool	n/a		
Loughborough	n/a		
Ludlow	4,691	4,552	6,456
Lutterworth	2,446	1,734	3,197
Lynn	n/a		
Market Bosworth	1,058	659	1,213
Market Harborough	2,325	7,735	10,400
Marlborough	3,908	3,046	4,557
Melton Mowbray	4,391	7,454	10,540 (1931)
Merthyr Tydfil	n/a		
Millport	1,104 (1861)	1,663	2,012
Mold	3,412	12,237 (1871)	
Monmouth	5,701	5,095	5,438
Newport	n/a		
Newtown	3,784	3,920	5,431
North Berwick	498	2,784	4,001
North Walsham	2,911	3,981	4,733
Norwich	n/a		
Penarth	105	11,103	
Pwllheli	2,709	3,675	3,875
Reigate	1,640	15,916 (1871)	
Richmond	9,065	15,113 (1871)	
Romford	3,791	13,656	
Rothesay	7,104	9,378	15,218 (1921)
Saffron Walden	5,911	5,896	6,828
Stornoway	2,391	3,852	4,954
Stowmarket	3,161	4,162	7,325
Stranraer	3,877	6,036	8,618
Stromness	2,055	2,450	1,503
Sunderland	n/a		
Swaffham	3,858	3,371	2,863
Swansea	n/a		
Swindon	4,876	11,720 (1871)	
Towyn	2,769	3,756	4,491
Welshpool	6,564	6,121	6,036
Woodbridge	5,161	4,640	5,310
Worsborough	n/a		
Yarmouth	n/a		

Those towns with n/a do not feature in the cohort of small towns.
Towns drop out of the cohort if they reach 10,000.
Source: census figures.

Map 5.1 Distribution of small towns (under 10,000) in Great Britain 1851
(with some additional Scottish burghs for 1861)
Source: based on census data.

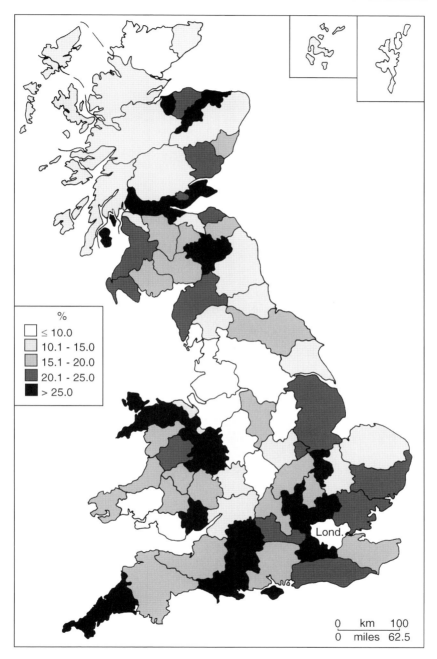

Map 5.2 Proportion of county populations living in small towns in Great
Britain 1851
Source: based on census data.

sorts of area can be identified where small towns were uncommon and/or unimportant.

First, of course, there were few in the London area including Middlesex county. Indeed, following Clark and Hosking's ruling,[11] Middlesex was excluded from this analysis, as were the Scottish 'counties of the town of . . .'. Secondly, small towns were unimportant in counties which industrialised early. These counties formed a wishbone pattern surrounding Derbyshire, running from Nottinghamshire anticlockwise through the West Riding of Yorkshire, Lancashire, Cheshire, Staffordshire and Warwickshire, together with Glamorgan in Wales. Many former market towns in these counties had already assumed industrial functions which attracted migrants and took their population beyond the 10,000 threshold. For example, Nottinghamshire had only six small towns left in contrast to rural Wiltshire which, with a similar total population (254,000 to Nottinghamshire's 270,000), had twenty-five.

A third category of area where small towns were unimportant consisted of sparsely populated rural counties with a limited urban network – Sutherland is the best example. Other rural counties had higher population densities associated with a full network of market towns and these stand out as having a large proportion of their population in small towns. Examples included Dorset, Wiltshire and Shropshire in England; Anglesey and Caernarfon in Wales and Nairn and Banffshire in Scotland. Other high totals were recorded in places being affected by the initial stages of metropolitan growth as in Surrey and Hertfordshire, or the development of small industrial towns as in the Central Valley of Scotland. Indeed, in Scotland, much change was taking place to the overall settlement pattern, though not all of it shows up on Maps 5.1 and 5.2. Shortly before the start of the study period agricultural reform, particularly in north-east Scotland, saw people pushed from their former landholdings to new planned villages but few became even small towns, despite pretensions – New Leeds bears little resemblance to old Leeds.[12] However, during this fashion for rebuilding and improvement, some substantial towns were affected. Ian Adams details the development of Cullen where the landowner, the earl of Seafield, ordered a land surveyor to 'set about the removal of the present town of Cullen and to have a new one gradually erected in order to save the heavy annual expense it costs to keep the swarm of worthless old houses from tumbling about the tenants' heads'.[13] Work began in 1822 and the scale of the project can be gauged from the fact that Cullen was in 1851 the largest of Banffshire's small towns.

Alan Everitt estimated that between one third and half the Victorian English

[11] Clark and Hosking, *Population Estimates*.
[12] D. G. Lockhart, 'Scottish village plans: a preliminary analysis', *Scottish Geographical Magazine*, 96 (1980), 141–57.   [13] I. H. Adams, *The Making of Urban Scotland* (London, 1978), p. 68.

Table 5.2 *British country and market town statistics 1851–1951*

	1851	1901	1951
Great Britain			
Total population[a]	17,786,201	31,821,086	41,702,680
Population in small towns	2,762,075	2,863,730	2,579,369
Number of small towns[b]	923 (958)[c]	851	748
% in small towns	15.5	9.0	6.2
England			
Total population[a]	14,390,863	26,920,852	35,761,009
Population in small towns	2,112,980	2,099,089	1,942,021
Number of small towns[b]	722	641	567
% in small towns	14.6	7.8	5.4
Scotland			
Total population[a]	2,231,929	2,890,728	3,342,996
Population in small towns	435,218	555,570	478,828
Number of small towns[b]	137(172)[c]	156	138
% in small towns	19.5	19.2	14.3
Wales			
Total population[a]	1,163,409	2,009,506	2,598,675
Population in small towns	213,877	209,071	158,523
Number of small towns[b]	64	54	43
% in small towns	18.4	10.4	6.1

[a] The total population excludes London, Middlesex and the Scottish 'counties of the towns of . . . '.
[b] Those identified as towns or burghs in the three lists by 1851 as discussed in the text and whose population was less than 10,000.
[c] Including the thirty-five Scottish burghs whose population was only listed from 1861.
Source: census figures.

population lived in or were dependent upon provincial market towns;[14] the data here show that overall in Great Britain in 1851 2.76 million people lived in the 923 small towns, 15.5 per cent of the total population (Table 5.2). Table 5.3 demonstrates something of the variability of the economic activity of small towns at this time by presenting information on some of those in Leicestershire, taken from census enumerators' books. In 1851 Leicestershire had six main market towns: Ashby de la Zouch, Loughborough, Melton Mowbray, Market Harborough, Hinckley and Lutterworth, arranged, in a symmetry redolent of

[14] A. Everitt, 'Town and country in Victorian Leicestershire: the role of the village carrier', in A. Everitt, ed., *Perspectives in English Urban History* (London, 1973).

Table 5.3 *Occupational structure of selected Leicestershire towns 1851*

% of workforce in:	Coalville	Hinckley	Lutterworth	Melton Mowbray
Primary industry	66.5	3.9	15.8	10.6
Coal mining	65.1	0.0	0.0	0.0
Agriculture	1.4	3.9	15.8	10.6
Secondary industry, including	17.8	75.8	32.2	26.0
Textiles	10.4	67.9	19.5	11.7
Shoemaking	0.0	3.3	3.9	2.6
Tertiary industry, including	14.2	14.4	45.6	52.7
Traders	4.0	5.7	15.2	14.6
Professionals	2.4	2.2	4.3	6.5
Servants	5.4	4.3	14.0	15.1
Grooms	0.0	0.2	1.8	5.7
Others, including	1.4	5.9	6.4	10.7
Labourers	0.8	1.6	0.4	3.7
Out paupers	0.4	2.9	4.7	2.1
Annuitants	0.2	0.4	0.8	3.9
Population	1,449	6,111	2,446	4,391

Source: 1851 census enumerators' books.

the tenets of central-place theory, around the county town of Leicester. Leicestershire's other market towns such as Hallaton, Market Bosworth and Castle Donnington had become less important by this period.[15] Lutterworth's occupational structure in 1851 reveals this town to have had a traditional role. Of its workforce, 16 per cent remained on the land but 46 per cent were in services, a distribution that placed Lutterworth within the parameters for the recognition of a mid-nineteenth-century rural town, rather than just a village.[16] Lutterworth still concentrated on services: 'the local focus of human life and activities, commercial, industrial, administrative and cultural'.[17] Lutterworth's market was (and is) on Thursdays on the spot where it had been held since 1214 and Lutterworth retained its tradition of providing public houses, an activity described as its 'staple business' for the late eighteenth century.[18]

Although it had some textile workers, Lutterworth by 1851 had been little affected by developments that elsewhere in Leicestershire were leading to functional diversification of the small towns.[19] Hinckley, for example, was heavily involved in framework knitting. At that time this was largely a domestic industry

[15] J. M. Lee, 'The rise and fall of a market town: Castle Donnington in the nineteenth century', *Transactions, Leicestershire Archaeological and Historical Society*, 32 (1956), 52–86.
[16] Dickinson, 'East Anglia'.   [17] *Ibid.*, 20.   [18] A. H. Dyson, *Lutterworth* (London, 1913).
[19] S. A. Royle, 'Aspects of nineteenth century small town society: a comparative study from Leicestershire', *Midland History*, 5 (1979–80), 50–62.

and Hinckley might be described as being only proto-industrial. Though it retained its marketing functions, its major economic activity was the processing of American cotton which certainly took it away from being a traditional country town. Elsewhere, Loughborough had also begun to industrialise, but Ashby de la Zouch and Market Harborough remained more traditional. Melton Mowbray had changed, too, but still maintained rural links, its manufacturing related to food processing (pork pies, Stilton cheese and, later, dog food) as well as the servicing and accommodation of the fox-hunting '"gentlemen" as they are called in Melton Mowbray' who stayed here in the season.[20] Hence the large number of grooms in Melton Mowbray. Leicestershire's small towns had been increased in number by the development of a mining town, Coalville, which, as its population grew, added marketing functions to its mining village activities.[21] Everitt points out that the city of Leicester, though it dominated the higher-order central-place activities of the county, with regard to low-order needs attracted only one third of its clientele from the city itself whereas a market town like Melton Mowbray attracted three-quarters of its 'shopping population' from the countryside, evidence of traditional small-town–countryside interaction.[22]

Lerwick, chief town of the Shetland Islands, can serve as an example of a small Scottish town. Lerwick was a port but had also the range of occupations of a central place and market town. The enumerators' returns for 1841 identify some textile working and domestic service among the women whilst 'among the men there were of course a number of merchants, shopkeepers and shop assistants . . . many coopers, carpenters and ships' carpenters. There were masons, joiners, shoemakers, plumbers, tailors, bakers, clerks, blacksmiths, watermen, tobacconists, writers, fishermen and a mixed bag of officials. And of course there were boatmen.'[23]

For Wales, Carter points out that for a town to 'survive depended ultimately on the demand for urban services set up in the surrounding countryside'.[24] He shows how the urban network bequeathed to the principality largely from the Normans' need to subjugate its people was affected later by the local opportunities, the original network having been 'over-elaborate for the economic conditions which characterised the succeeding age'.[25]

By the mid-nineteenth century marketing had developed more and, using data from the 1830s, Carter devised a four tier hierarchy for Welsh towns based on functional criteria. On top were places such as Cardiff, Swansea and Carmarthen. Lower down were small market towns acting in the traditional manner, such as Pwllheli and Dolgellau. A contemporary description of Pwllheli in 1844 remarked that

[20] J. Brownlow, *Melton Mowbray, Queen of the Shires* (Wymondham, 1980), p. 257.
[21] S. A. Royle, 'The development of Coalville, Leicestershire, in the nineteenth century', *East Midland Geographer*, 7 (1978), 32–42.   [22] Everitt, 'Leicestershire'.
[23] J. W. Irvine, *Lerwick* (Lerwick, 1985), p. 84.   [24] Carter, *The Towns of Wales*, p. 29.
[25] *Ibid.*, p. 31

the commerce consists entirely of the importation of coal and shop goods from Liverpool for the supply of which to the surrounding country Pwllheli forms a great depot and is thus, though small, rendered a flourishing place. The market . . . is well supplied . . . with all . . . kinds of provisions . . . and there being no other market held near, it is resorted to by persons living at the furthest extremities of the peninsula of Lleyn.[26]

As Carter notes, 'these towns were carrying out functions very similar in nature but not in order to those of Carmarthen and the other grade 1 towns'.[27]

Lower still were 'a large number of small market towns whose dominance was local and limited'.[28] Everitt identified the mechanism linking the towns and their hinterlands with his estimate that 30,000–40,000 local carriers travelled the English lanes at mid-century.[29]

Town life varied with the type of town. In resort towns patronised by the wealthy it was genteel, doubtless – consider Barsetshire's country balls – but even having aristocrats in residence did not guarantee a quiet life. Thus, in the fox-hunting resort of Melton Mowbray on one occasion in 1837, led by the marquis of Waterford, the 'gentlemen' – hooligans in another age or class – in a particularly baleful drunken spree 'painted the town red', the incident giving rise to the phrase.[30]

By contrast, life within the traditional country town was, for most people, hard. In Lerwick in the first half of the century:

Gross overcrowding was accepted [there were 315 houses in 1833 with an average occupancy of 9.4 persons]. There was no running water, no sewage, little or no drainage, no street lighting, no planning. Every summer there was an acute shortage of water as the wells ran dry. Increasingly the disposal – or lack of disposal – of human excreta became a major problem. Night soil thrown daily in the lanes added to the effluvium of the insanitary little town.[31]

The town council, founded in 1818, attempted to remedy the situation but was handicapped by a lack of finance. They were aided from 1833, as elsewhere in Scotland, by the Commissioners of Police whose duties included also the levying of rates for town improvement. Others shared the insanitary conditions of Lerwick's people. In Worsborough as late as 1910 night soil men were photographed in formal pose, shovels at the ready.[32] Even country towns which had taken on additional functions to support their economy did not necessarily prosper as a result. The present author wanted to entitle a paper on Hinckley in

[26] S. Lewis, *A Topographical Dictionary of Wales*, 3rd edn (London, 1844).
[27] Carter, *The Towns of Wales*, p. 63.   [28] *Ibid.*, p. 66.   [29] Everitt, 'Leicestershire'.
[30] See Nimrod (pseudonym of C. J. Apperly), *The Life of a Sportsman* (London, 1842), for a fictional account of such a life at Melton Mowbray; M. Frewen, *Melton Mowbray and Other Memories* (London, 1924), for the autobiography of one who actually lived that life and Brownlow, *Melton Mowbray*, for the local historian's view.   [31] Irvine, *Lerwick*, p. 72.
[32] Reproduced in the *Local Historian* in 1983.

the 1840s with a contemporary quotation: 'the town is certainly in a stinking state' but was overruled by a sensitive editor who required him to settle for 'the spiritual destitution is excessive – the poverty overwhelming'.[33] The poverty, which presumably worsened the stink, was caused by a downturn in demand for the town's principal product of cotton stockings, made largely on domestic frames. An anonymous poet captured the mood of Hinckley at this period:

> A weaver of 'inckley sot in 'is frame
> 'is children stood mernfully by,
> 'is wife pained with 'unger, near naked with shame,
> As she 'opelessly gazed at the sky.
> The tears rolling fast from 'er famishing eyes
> Proclaimed 'er from 'unger not free,
> And these were the words she breathed with a sigh,
> 'I weep, poor 'inckley, for thee'.[34]

In the same decade the market town and silk manufacturing centre of Leek in Staffordshire was involved in Chartist unrest; in the 1830s there had been strikes by both handloom weavers and mill hands protesting about conditions.[35]

However, perhaps if only to the jaded city dweller, the country town of the nineteenth century had attractions because of its continuing localism. In mid-century it seemed still to have a balance between

> rural backwardness and city discomfort. Here . . . freedom and enterprise would obtain still but viciousness would be neutralised by a stability and civic-minded-ness fed from deep wells of continuity and convention. The reason was that most families would be native to the community. Social and religious teaching would be heeded; personal and class co-operation would be a habit.[36]

Henry James had a fondness for Ludlow in the 1870s, 'a town not disfigured by industry "[which] exhibits no tall chimneys and smoke streamers, no attendant purlieus and slums"',[37] though, by that time, Ludlow, like Hinckley, Leek and others, did have an industrial sector, in malting, glove making and paper manu-facturing. That much small-town industry was often either domestic or traditional and rurally linked (such as food processing, including brewing) did not necessar-ily mean that conditions were good. In Bromsgrove nail making, button making and cloth manufacture in small workshops in courts and rows behind the major streets produced conditions of employment 'generally of the scraping and sweated sort, exploiting in-migrants from the countryside'.[38] This mention of the courts and rows leads into a consideration of the internal layout of these small towns.

---

[33] S. A. Royle, '"The spiritual destitution is excessive – the poverty overwhelming": Hinckley in the mid-nineteenth century', *Transactions, Leicestershire Archaeological and Historical Society*, 54 (1979–80), 51–60.   [34] Cited in H. J. Francis, *A History of Hinckley* (Hinckley, 1930), p. 129.
[35] M. W. Greenslade, 'Leek and Lowe', in *VCH*, Staffordshire, VII, pp. 84–131.
[36] P. J. Waller, *Town, City and Nation* (Oxford, 1983), p. 214.   [37] *Ibid.*, p. 214.   [38] *Ibid.*, p. 215.

Another useful literary extract which details something of the structure of small towns in the mid-nineteenth century is to be found in Thomas Hardy's *Mayor of Casterbridge*. 'Casterbridge' (based on Dorchester) in the 1840s was

> deposited in a block upon a cornfield. There was no suburb in the modern sense, or transitional intermixture between town and down. It stood, with regard to the wide fertile land adjoining, clean-cut and distinct like a chessboard on a green table cloth. The farmer's boy could sit under his barley mow and pitch a stone into the office window of the town clerk; reapers at work among the sheaves nodded to acquaintances on the pavement corner; the red-robed judge, when he condemned a sheep stealer, pronounced sentence to the tune of Baa that floated in at the window from the remainder of the flock browsing hard by; and at executions, the waiting crowd stood in the meadow immediately before the drop, out of which the cows had been temporarily driven to give the spectators room.[39]

This highlights the compact nature of most small towns at mid-century. Within this small space, however, there were considerable social gulfs to be found. Neil Wright describes the social geography of Lincolnshire towns succinctly and his statement is of general applicability: 'In 1845 there were still many people living in the centre of towns – tradesmen or shopkeepers living over their premises and working people in courtyards and lanes behind them.'[40] Early industrialisation reinforced rather than rearranged this pattern. Towns like Bromsgrove and Hinckley located their domestic or workshop industries behind the main streets. In Hinckley the framework knitters mostly resided in terraces or lean-to dwellings in the yards of the inns and farmhouses that had fronted the main streets of the old market town. As their number increased and proper access became necessary, the former farm lanes behind the yards were paved, giving Hinckley a system of parallel streets in its centre, apparent even from the late eighteenth century (Map 5.3). The wealthier people at mid-century still lived on the main streets, some of them in buildings that doubled as shops or other commercial premises.

Change, however, was imminent both to the internal geography of the small towns and to their distribution and function:

> 'Casterbridge' in 1846 was doubtless an odorous town ruled by a brutal code of law in which the desperately poor lived in the shadow of the immoderately rich. But as a town it was still an organic whole . . . an identifiable unit that was greater than the sum of its parts. It would see more change, qualitatively, in the next hundred years than it had in the previous thousand.[41]

In non-fictional Lerwick: 'soon houses would be appearing in the area between Hillhead and Burgh Road [the New Town], gas would illuminate the streets and

---

[39] T. Hardy, *The Life and Death of the Mayor of Casterbridge, a Story of a Man of Character* (London, 1968), p. 105.   [40] N. R. Wright, *Lincolnshire Towns and Industry, 1700–1914* (Lincoln, 1982), p. 225.
[41] R. Chamberlin, *The English Country Town* (Exeter, 1983), p. 96.

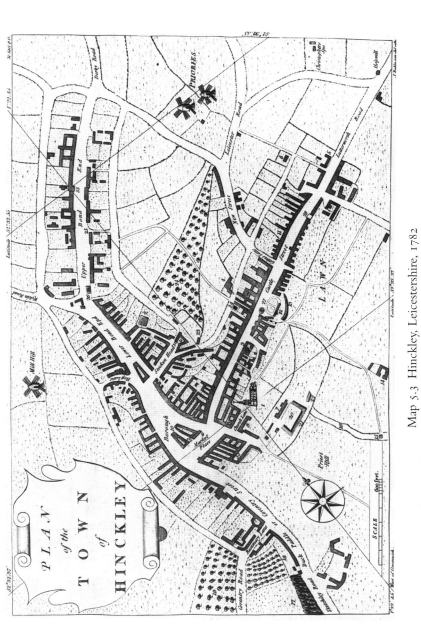

Map 5.3 Hinckley, Leicestershire, 1782

Source: J. Nichols, *The History and Antiquities of Hinckley* (London, 1782).

lanes and tap water was not all that far away. Lerwick was on its way.'[42] For Scotland generally 'the future development of towns lay in the complex and ever-changing interplay of sources of raw materials, markets, labour supply and transport: the industrial town was about to come into being'.[43]

(ii) THE SMALL TOWN AT THE END OF THE NINETEENTH CENTURY

The 1911 census estimated that the urban percentage of the population of England and Wales rose from 50.2 to 77 from 1851 to 1901. The overall spatial pattern of this urban growth was identified by Brian Robson thus: 'the growth of industrial production [and associated urban development] was focused on the mineral bearing and carboniferous areas of "Highland Britain"'.[44] This was somewhat anomalous in British urban history where hitherto urban growth had been in the overwhelmingly dominant London and the South-East of England – lowland Britain. (For much of the twentieth century the pattern of urban growth in lowland Britain reasserted itself.)

Maps 5.4 and 5.5 are taken from Robson's analysis. The former presents the urban pattern (of places above 2,500) of England and Wales at 1851 with details of rates of growth in the previous decade. The latter does the same for 1901 when the imposition of Victorian industrial and urban growth in the mining and manufacturing regions upon the pre-existing, more evenly distributed urban network is clear. In 1901, in addition, the suburbanisation around London stands out and the growth of seaside resorts can also be identified.

Buried within these overall analyses was the development of the small-town sector. Robson's smallest category of town, from 2,500–4,999, though increasing in numbers – 234 in 1851, 290 in 1901 – became proportionately less important, falling from 44.9 per cent of the total urban places in 1851 to 32.8 per cent in 1901. N. Raven stated that '"small towns" shared the fortunes of nineteenth century rural England, experiencing demographic growth and economic expansion up to *c.* 1850 but subsequently suffering from decay in crafts and local industries with the resultant depopulation'.[45] Richard Lawton, too, linked the agricultural areas and the old market towns and showed that there was a general decrease in population of such areas after 1851 because of the concentration of industrial employment, greater mobility brought about by railway development and a relative decline of countryside employment.[46] On decline, Christopher

[42] Irvine, *Lerwick*, p. 85.   [43] Adams, *Urban Scotland*, p. 71.

[44] B. T. Robson, *Urban Growth* (London, 1973), p. 93.

[45] N. Raven, 'Occupational structures of three north Essex towns: Halstead, Braintree and Great Coggeshall, *c.* 1780–1880. Research in progress', *Urban History Newsletter*, 12 (1992), 2.

[46] R. Lawton, 'Population changes in England and Wales in the later nineteenth century: an analysis of trends by registration districts', *Transactions of the Institute of British Geographers*, 44 (1968), 55–74.

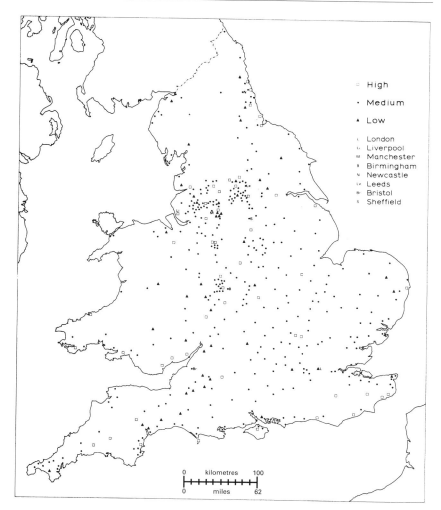

Map 5.4 Urban distribution 1851 and growth 1841–1851, England and Wales
Source: B. T. Robson, *Urban Growth* (London, 1973).

Law identified urban places which between 1801 and 1911 did not experience major urban growth (less than 400 per cent).[47] If this map is compared to a map of urban centres in 1911, it can be seen that outside London and the Home Counties, and the industrial areas, a large proportion of urban settlements come into this category. In the main they are either market centres (not the lowest grade since most of these have already been excluded by the imposition of a

[47] C. M. Law, 'The growth of urban population in England and Wales, 1801–1911', *Transactions of the Institute of British Geographers*, 41 (1967), 125–43.

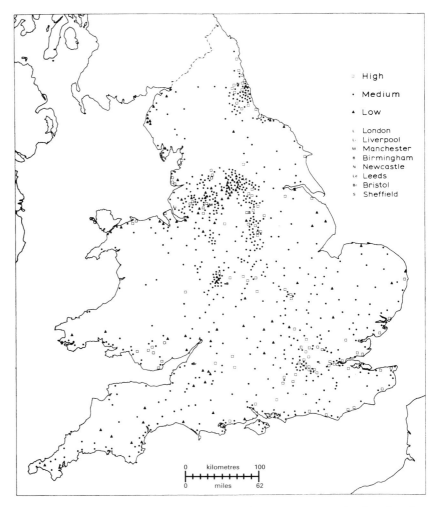

Map 5.5 Urban distribution 1901 and growth 1891–1901, England and Wales
Source: B. T. Robson, *Urban Growth* (London, 1973).

threshold of 2,500) or decayed ports such as Chepstow, Chichester or Lynn which lost trade with the coming of the railways.

More successful were the 107 of the original 958 small towns of 1851 and 1861 which reached 10,000 before 1901. They are located on Map 5.6 and most were either industrial or, alternatively, suburban areas around London, though some were market towns which had grown and prospered by having 'demonstrated an imperial tendency to annex the trade [of other market towns] by virtue of railway connections and superior shopping facilities'.[48] In situations where most towns had a railway connection, however, the comparative advantage a link provided was neutralised. This was the situation in southern Shropshire where it was the smaller towns that benefited most from railways, increasing their range of functions more quickly than the two larger regional centres of Bridgnorth and Ludlow, both of which lost population from 1851 to 1901 (−1.9 per cent and −3 per cent respectively). Transport developments *per se* were another factor that had led to the growth of some of these 107 towns, such as Swindon, a railway town whose 1861 population of 6,856 almost doubled to 11,720 by 1871.

In Scotland more small towns expanded with more than 70 per cent increasing their population between 1851 and 1901. In Scotland they clearly fall into two categories: the rural counties such as Caithness and Inverness and the smaller industrial counties of the Central Valley where small-town growth was associated with industrialisation. There was some suburban growth in central Scotland, too. Helensburgh (which increased 201 per cent from 1851 to 1901) and North Berwick (459 per cent) were 'pleasantly situated towns [which] evolved as residential retreats for the cities because the railways made it possible'.[49] Wales had a similar experience to Scotland in that rural counties like Merionethshire and Radnorshire stood out as did industrial counties such as Flintshire and Glamorgan. Carter specifically separated the 'market principle' which he saw as the factor which best explained the distribution of Welsh towns in an earlier period from the '"industrial principle" whereby the controls of town location are the same factors which determined the location of mining and industry'.[50] Thus, regarding Caerphilly, 'no settlement of any significance had grown around the huge castle [but it] quickly became a mining town of considerable importance and entered the upper ranks of the urban hierarchy [a population increase of 1,317.7 per cent from 1851 to 1901]'.[51]

England, with more of its urbanisation in cities, had fewer counties showing sustained growth in small towns. Some rural counties such as Rutland stood out in 1901 (Map 5.7) and in England there was another category of county whose small towns had grown − those like Surrey close to London which became enmeshed in metropolitan development − 'the modern world . . . submerging it'.[52] All fifteen of Surrey's small towns increased in population from 1851 to 1901, some to become substantial urban places such as Kingston-upon-Thames, Richmond and Reigate.

Accessibility was an important factor in explaining growth. Less accessible country towns and their tributary areas continued to lose population with deleterious effects upon their economies. Within a framework of agricultural

---

[48] Waller, *Town*, p. 231.　　[49] R. J. Naismith, *The Story of Scotland's Towns* (Edinburgh, 1989), p. 123.
[50] Carter, *The Towns of Wales*, pp. 74–5.　　[51] *Ibid.*, p. 71.
[52] G. Bourne (pseudonym of G. Sturt), *Change in the Village* (London, 1912), p. 121.

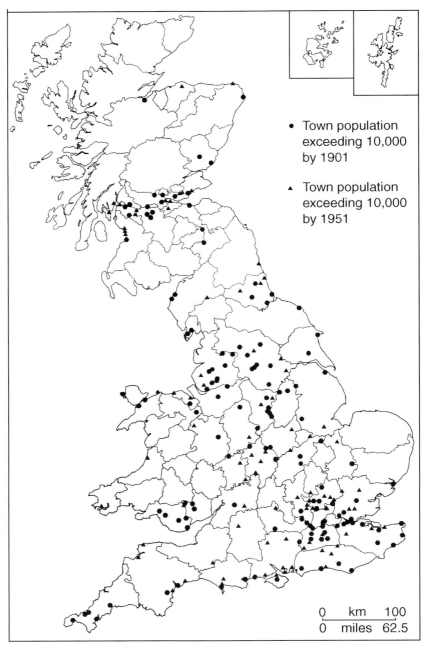

Map 5.6 British small towns reaching 10,000 residents by 1901 and 1951
Source: based on census data.

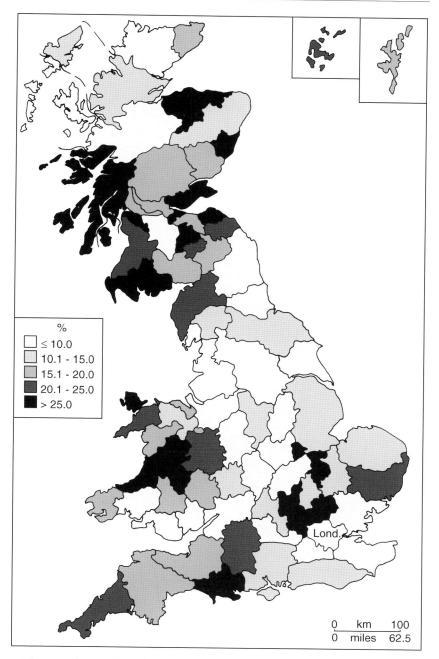

Map 5.7 Proportion of county populations living in small towns in Great
Britain 1901
Source: based on census data.

depression which hastened the decline of some Lincolnshire towns where only twelve of thirty-two in the cohort increased in population between 1851 and 1901, Wright asserted that the fine detail within this pattern was related to accessibility, with those towns with a railway station faring better.[53] In Market Harborough the opening of the railway in 1854 had led to the local tradesmen considering how this increased accessibility could benefit the town. The result was the new Corn Exchange.[54]

Map 5.7 identifies the relative importance of the small towns within their county's population and the national decline from 15.5 per cent to 9 per cent from 1851 to 1901 is reflected in the increase in counties in the lowest category, with the industrial counties being joined by some of the Home Counties where many towns had grown beyond the 10,000 threshold. Many towns in the cohort remaining under 10,000 were traditional market towns that had failed to take on new industries. Others were manufacturing towns whose industry had not prospered in the new era.

In the second half of the nineteenth century, localism which had been the principal characteristic of the traditional market town for centuries, began to decay. 'The intimacy of the small market town suffered invasions, and the local provision of services was encroached upon.'[55] Further, the growth of government regulation and the increase of national legislation 'tipped the scales against the self-sufficiency and individuality of country town life'.[56] Especially significant was the way in which the traditional country town became little more than the agent for city or big firm interests as long-standing local industries collapsed in the face of competition from major capitalist concerns. Philip Waller exemplifies such developments in milling and brewing. Milling had been a locally based activity which in 1851 employed 37,268 people, mainly in small facilities in or just outside country towns. Fifty years on the development of capitalism had seen the growth of large vertically integrated regional, even national, companies dealing with not just milling but also seed crushing, animal feed production and the marketing of end products. These big firms took advantage of the increased importation of grain by erecting huge mills at the ports. New mills employed modern roller grinding techniques which were more efficient than the old mill-stones but to establish a factory using them required major investment beyond the reach of local, traditional millers. Transportation improvements permitted even bulky products like grain to be moved fairly readily and so the big mills could take in grain from a large area. All these developments combined to see the decline of the local miller, unable to compete. 'By 1900 the market was effectively dominated by actual or emerging giants, Joseph Rank, Spillers, Bibby, Thorley, Silcock, the CWS [Co-operative Wholesale Society] and

[53] Wright, *Lincolnshire Towns*.
[54] J. C. Davies and M. C. Brown, *Yesterday's Town* (Buckingham, 1981).   [55] Waller, *Town*, p. 232.
[56] *Ibid.*, p. 238.

BOCM [British Oil and Cake Mills Ltd]. Bibby's alone, for instance, employed 600 people in Liverpool by 1899, 3,000 in 1913.'[57]

With regard to brewing a similar pattern emerged. In 1880 Waller estimated that there were 22,000 breweries and 110,000 private brewers; by 1900 just 7,000 and 13,000 respectively. The decimation of the private brewers is especially significant here for these were likely to have been small-scale local operations characteristic of the market towns. Small towns with an industrial element to their economies thus had to invest or see their economies suffer. In Hinckley, though, there was another depression in the 1860s when the American Civil War cut off the cotton supply. The town's entrepreneurs finally modernised its production facilities from domestic frames into proper factories and were rewarded by Hinckley's population having increased 85 per cent between 1851 and 1901. By contrast, manufacturing towns whose industry was not modernised declined. Dickinson singled out old Norfolk woollen towns such as Diss and Kenninghall and Coggeshall in Essex where there was 'a rapid decline in the formerly prosperous crafts and small industries'.[58] Coggeshall's population declined 26 per cent between 1851 and 1901.

A diverse economy could also be helpful. Melton Mowbray, with food processing and fox-hunting supporting its central-place functions, saw its population rise 69.8 per cent. Nearby, Lutterworth, a more traditional agricultural service town which did not change much, experienced a population fall of 29 per cent. Further down the hierarchy some places fared worse, including Market Bosworth which declined 37.7 per cent. Dickinson pointed out the lack of functional diversification of East Anglian towns which failed to grow such as Swaffham, Norfolk (-12.6 per cent), and the Suffolk towns of Bungay (-13.7 per cent), Eye (-22.5 per cent) and Woodbridge (-10.1 per cent). These were amongst those towns where functions such as livestock markets and/or corn factoring declined in face of larger-scale, more accessible facilities elsewhere.[59]

Thus, it is clear that by the end of the nineteenth century, if a small town could not adapt to change it faced decline. Marlborough had a population fall of 22 per cent from 1851 to 1901, despite the success of its college founded in 1843, for 'it remained as it had been, the capital of an agricultural kingdom', without 'new industries'.[60]

The detail of life in the small towns of late Victorian Britain continued to depend upon the type of town it was. Thus regarding the small towns of Surrey, enmeshed in the growth of the metropolis, George Bourne catalogued, with regret, the change this 'invasion of a new people, unsympathetic to [the old] order' wrought to customary traditions and mores. 'As he [Bourne's labourer] sweats at his gardening, the sounds of piano playing come to him, or of the affected excitement of a tennis party; or the braying of a motor car informs him

---

[57] *Ibid.*, p. 233.   [58] Raven, 'Essex towns', 2.   [59] Dickinson, 'East Anglia'.
[60] Waller, *Town*, p. 230.

that the rich, who are his masters, are on the road.'[61] Not all viewed these changes
to Home County town life with Bourne's gloomy reluctance, of course. *Country
Life* reported of Farnham in 1904 that it was at 'the nadir of its history. But almost
immediately the coming of the motorcar began to raise the town from a decaying agricultural centre to one of increasingly prosperous business and residence.'[62]

One generalisation that can be made about social life in the small towns is that
it can be seen to have developed and institutionalised at this period. The late
Victorian and Edwardian eras were notable for the foundation of sporting and
social clubs and self-improvement societies. In many ways the Edwardian era was
the apogee of British small-town social life. Often dozens of local social activities were available for townsfolk. In Market Harborough there were Sunday
Schools, the Young Men's Friendly Society, the Girls' Friendly Society, the
Church Lads' Brigade, the Young Men's Debating Society of 1892, replaced by
the Mutual Improvement Society in 1905, itself replaced by the Literary and
Debating Society in 1911. There was the Coffee House Reading Room of 1884,
the Reading Society of 1894, refounded as the District Literary and Debating
Society in 1912. There were carnivals, as in 1905, and penny popular concerts.
A choral society was founded in 1893, an operatic society in 1898; the local territorial army contingent had a brass band. There were flower and produce shows,
and shows for birds – the local fanciers' society held its first meeting in 1896.
Market Harborough was second only to Melton Mowbray for fox-hunting and
this was particularly important from the late 1880s. Other equine-related activities were the point to point club, the polo club of 1902 and the horse show, first
held in 1896. There was a cricket club, a football club from 1889; hockey clubs
came and went. The tennis club dates from 1888; the local golf club opened in
1898, with local rules as to how to cope with the cattle that were allowed on the
fairways. A bowls club was founded in 1911, a bicycle club around 1890, an
angling society in 1906; the council built swimming baths in 1896 – galas were
held there from 1900 and the water polo club was based there in 1902. The local
canal was used for boating and skating in hard winters. A roller skating rink
opened in 1906.[63] All these for a local population of 7,735 in 1901. Nor was this
unusual. Eight pages of the *VCH* of Staffordshire are devoted to Leek's social
and cultural activities: sport, music, theatre, arts, friendly societies, political and
social clubs, gardening societies, the embroidery society, volunteers, civic and
historical societies, libraries, museums and galleries, many founded during the
late Victorian and Edwardian periods.[64] Similarly, Margaret Stacey's magisterial
study of small-town life in Banbury, Oxfordshire, identifies 110 formal associations, many of which would have been founded at that time.[65]

[61] Bourne, *Change in the Village*, p. 121.   [62] Cited in Chamberlin, *English Country Town*, p. 197.
[63] Davies and Brown, *Market Harborough*.
[64] N. J. Tringham, 'Social and cultural activities', in *VCH*, Staffordshire, VII, pp. 146–52.
[65] M. Stacey, *Tradition and Change* (London, 1960).

The second half of the century was characterised not just by the development of capitalism but also by that of municipalism as local authorities reacted to the poor environmental and social conditions of the early Victorian period. Across Britain there were massive urban improvement programmes. Additionally, some places invested in projects redolent of civic pride, the town halls of the northern industrial cities being especially notable. Municipalism was not reserved to the great cities such as Birmingham, where Joseph Chamberlain took the concept to its limit, as may be seen from David Gilbert's use of that term to explain community development in English and Welsh mining towns.[66] In small towns, the grandiosity of the Bradford Wool Exchange was hardly to be countenanced. Nevertheless some did erect fine town halls, and many did share in the fashion for municipalism. Thus in Market Harborough the urban district council, established in 1895, within a few years had built public baths, taken over and run the local gas company, built a fire station, a cattle market, recreation grounds, improved the water supply and sewerage arrangements and laid out a new street, having cleared away an old inn to make room.[67]

Lerwick (Map 5.8) provides another example of late century development. The period from 1850 to 1880 was one of consolidation, with gas lighting from 1858 and some minor sanitary improvements. However, from 1880 to 1914, when the herring fishery was buoyant, the town was transformed. These were 'years when the men at the top really broke out from their personal and narrow attitudes which had governed so much of their thinking in the past, and turned their minds to the broader development of their town'.[68] A town hall was opened in 1884, and new harbour works in 1886 which also saw the building of the esplanades. That part of the main street, Commercial Road, to the seaward side of Fort Charlotte was widened and properly surfaced. Further inland came the building of the New Town, first planned in 1862, though little development actually took place until the 1880s when the proposed streets received their names and housing and other properties began to be built: 'handsome and imposing villas, lasting testimonials to the excellence of their builders and silent witnesses to the obvious wealth of their owners'.[69] These wealthy people moved away from the old town centre. As a local correspondent put it in the 1880s:

> The days had gone . . . when merchants and others were prepared to live in houses all of the same pattern, little more than square boxes, with five small holes in the front for windows, a larger one to serve as the door. All the rooms were small, ill-ventilated and low; there were no baths etc., and drains were a matter of secondary importance, often left out altogether.[70]

---

[66] D. Gilbert, 'Community and municipalism: collective identity in late-Victorian and Edwardian mining towns', *Journal of Historical Geography*, 17 (1991), 257–70.
[67] Davies and Brown, *Yesterday's Town*.   [68] Irvine, *Lerwick*, p. 153.   [69] *Ibid.*, p. 175.
[70] *Ibid.*, p. 174.

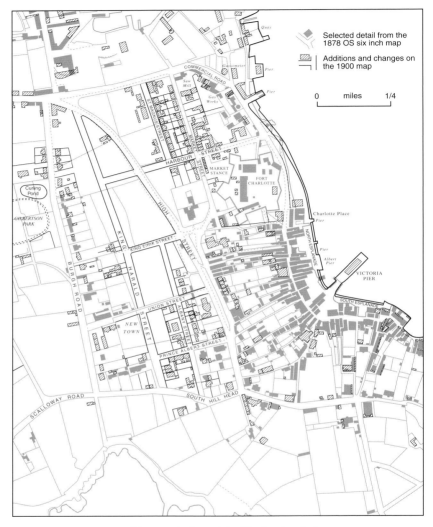

Map 5.8 Changes in Lerwick, Shetland, 1878 to 1900
Source: based largely on information in J. W. Irvine, *Lerwick* (Lerwick, 1985).

Poorer Lerwigians, of course, might be left in insanitary conditions, some in wooden shanties, although there had been improvements in water and sewage arrangements and from the 1870s properties were officially inspected and white-washing ordered where necessary. That it was the chief of police who made such inspections might be seen as a mark of the seriousness with which the author-ities regarded this task, except that this officer was Lerwick's only policeman. Despite the legislative powers available to the authorities by the Housing of the

Working Class Act of 1890 and the Small Dwellings Act of 1899, it was not until 1911 that 'Workmen's Dwellings', Lerwick's first new purpose-built working-class accommodation was provided and that not by the council. It was only after the First World War that Lerwick would be able to take advantage of national planning legislation and begin to be able to provide decent housing for its poor people, with major council schemes of 1923 and 1934.

Some generalities can be garnered from the detail on this most remote of Britain's small towns. Typical were the civic improvements both in hidden areas such as sanitation and for overt show, such as the town hall. Scottish burghs have been commended for statues and monuments erected in the late nineteenth century as well as for splendid commercial buildings and civic facilities, such as courts, libraries, museums and galleries provided by municipalism. Kelso has been singled out in this regard.[71] Lerwick exemplified the slow progress being made with regard to dealing with the conditions endured by the poorer classes. Its developments can be set within the beginnings of a planning framework. In Scotland from 1880 to 1912 the number of burghs with an active dean of guild court (the body responsible for burgh building, amenity and planning matters) rose from 20 to 189 as the need for planning and improvements became more urgent.[72] However, the extensive formal planning of the earlier Scottish urban experience, from the great New Town of Edinburgh to the plethora of planned villages, was not replicated in the late nineteenth century.

The centrifugal movement of the merchant and wealthy class to quieter, more spacious peripheral locations, leapfrogging the poor left in their traditional areas of occupancy, as seen in Lerwick, was typical of the transformation in the socio-spatial structures of urban areas in the late nineteenth century. One factor was the growing commercialisation of the central trading areas, not unrelated to the decline in the localism of the economy. This process served to push people away. As before, Wright's comments on Lincolnshire towns can serve as a general report: 'Towards the end of the century many commercial and professional families moved from such old areas [in the town centres] to new houses on the suburban edges of the towns, either terraced houses with front and back gardens or detached or semi-detached villas in their own grounds'.[73]

(iii) SMALL TOWNS IN THE MIDDLE OF THE TWENTIETH CENTURY

Table 5.2 indicates that another 103 of the cohort of small towns reached the 10,000 threshold between 1901 and 1951. Map 5.6 shows their distribution and the pattern clearly indicates the continuing suburbanisation of the Home Counties: only one out of the fifteen Surrey towns in the original cohort

---

[71] Naismith, *Scotland's Towns.*

[72] R. Rodger, 'The evolution of Scottish town planning', in Gordon and Dicks, eds., *Scottish Urban History*, pp. 71–91.   [73] Wright, *Lincolnshire Towns*, p. 225.

reached 1951 with a population under 10,000. Map 5.9 identifies the location of the surviving small towns in 1951 and should be compared to the 1851 pattern shown in Map 5.1.

England lost seventy-four small towns to the 10,000 threshold, yet the total population in the towns that survive in the cohort remains little changed, indicating that the mean size of the towns has increased. Map 5.10 shows that in mainly rural counties in East Anglia, the Lake District, Herefordshire in the Welsh borderlands and some of the West Country counties small towns remain important.

In Scotland, the situation is similar. The Central Valley lost a large number of small towns whilst many peripheral rural counties had little growth in small towns. A number of them lost population generally. Ross and Cromarty lost 20.8 per cent (76,450 to 60,503) and, whilst its major mainland central place of Dingwall experienced an increase in population of 33.7 per cent and in Stornoway, chief town of the Western Isles, the increase was 28.6 per cent, only Invergordon of the county's other four towns grew (44.6 per cent). In Wigtownshire where the county population fell 3.2 per cent (32,685 to 31,625) only the ferry port of Stranraer increased in population by 42.8 per cent. The county's other three towns in the cohort fell.

In Wales, the industrial counties such as Flintshire and Glamorgan had few small towns left by 1951, and the smaller industrial towns of Monmouthshire continued to grow. In the rural areas, county population declines – Merionethshire fell 15.1 per cent (48,852 to 41,465), Montgomeryshire 16.2 per cent (54,901 to 45,990) – were matched by declines in the small towns with only the resort of Towyn (19.5 per cent) and the regional central place of Newtown growing at all (38.5 per cent) in these counties.

Few English counties now had more than 10 per cent of their population in the surviving small towns. Only the peripheral rural counties and some of those to the north of London were not in this lowest category. In Wales, apart from the industrial counties of Flintshire, Glamorgan and Monmouthshire, the principality's considerable rurality was reflected in higher proportions continuing to live in the small towns, though their overall relative importance was declining. Scotland, generally less urbanised than England, had a more complex pattern with small towns remaining significant proportionately in both some rural and some industrial counties. In the particular circumstances of the insular counties, island central-place burghs continued to dominate the local scene, for instance Rothesay on Bute and Millport on Great Cumbrae. On Orkney, Kirkwall had continued to grow (17.1 per cent) whilst the county's only other burgh, Stromness, had fallen 38.7 per cent. By 1951 Kirkwall accommodated 20.4 per cent of Orkney's population, from only 12.9 per cent in 1901. In Shetland, Lerwick had increased 21.9 per cent and in 1951 it had 28.6 per cent of the county population, up from 16.1 per cent in 1901.

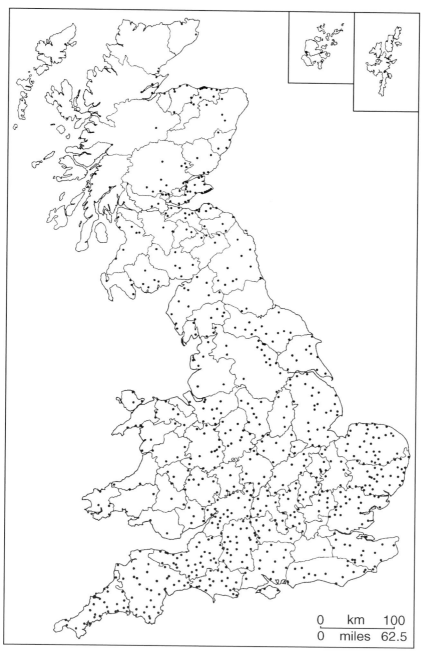

Map 5.9 Distribution of small towns in Great Britain 1951
Source: based on census data.

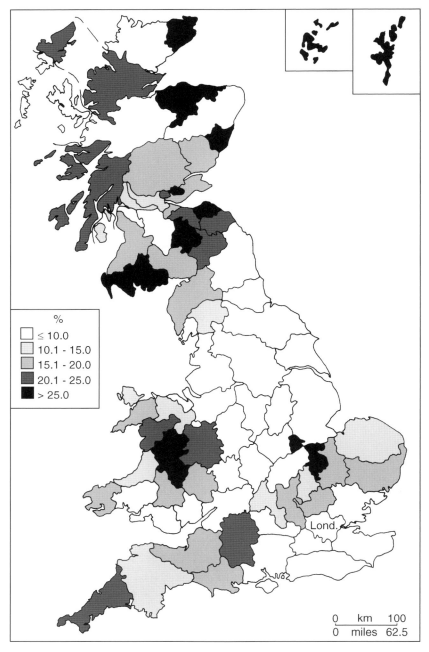

Map 5.10 Proportion of county populations living in small towns in Great
Britain 1951
Source: based on census data.

The economy of the small towns at this period could not be divorced from the national scene: warfare, twice, and the great depression. This last had particular effects on some industrial small towns as well as on market towns and 'a photograph of almost any town centre in the 1930s shows a dreary picture of hoardings covering derelict buildings'.[74] The local basis of the towns' economies continued to decline as products and the outlets that sold them both became more national in character and they faced competition from other places. Dickinson studied the East Anglian urban hierarchy up to 1931. Much of his analysis dealt with either cities or villages, but he did identify a number of small towns where economic difficulties were caused by the decay of their markets. Swaffham, Bungay and Halstead all lost population or gained little from 1901 to 1951 (−15 per cent, +6.7 per cent, −1.2 per cent respectively). Their market functions had declined in a period of improved transportation as a result of competition from the region's traditional large urban centres such as Norwich, Ipswich and Yarmouth and also some of the more successful of the 1851 cohort, including North Walsham (a population increase of 18.9 per cent), Fakenham (0.9 per cent), Saffron Walden (15.8 per cent) and Stowmarket (76 per cent), and the Essex towns of Chelmsford, Romford and Braintree, which all exceeded 10,000 by the early twentieth century. However, two towns singled out by Dickinson did not grow from 1901 to 1951. They were Diss (−6.5 per cent) and Beccles (−0.5 per cent).[75]

A study of small-town services in southern Shropshire postulated that by the 1920s, any equalising effect the development of railway connections had brought in the earlier period had ended and the two regional centres of Bridgnorth and Ludlow began to reassume their former dominance. Certainly Ludlow's growth from 1901 to 1951, at 41.8 per cent, was one of the strongest in the county. The small towns that were losing out in terms of services in some cases only saved their economies by diversification, further evidence of change to the traditional market towns' economy.[76]

A major national study of the Welsh urban hierarchy in 1951 was made by Carter who listed 114 urban places from the capital city of Cardiff down, divided into a hierarchy of six steps, based on functional grounds. That these functions were related to population can be appreciated from the fact that the cohort of towns under 10,000 are found largely in his two lowest categories, E and F, 'local centres' and 'sub-towns', with only a few grade D, 'major local centres'. Some towns originally in the 1851 cohort were grade D, even grade C, 'regional centres', but their populations had risen with their functional significance and they had left the cohort before 1951. Examples are Aberystwyth, Bangor and Caernarfon. Only Haverfordwest was a Grade C regional centre with a

---

[74] Chamberlin, *English Country Town*, p. 187.   [75] Dickinson, 'East Anglia'.
[76] R. Jones, 'Country town survival: some Anglo-Australian comparisons', in M. R. Wilson, ed., *Proceedings of the Prairie Division, Canadian Association of Geographers* (Saskatoon, 1992), pp. 1–19.

population below 10,000. The forty-three Welsh towns that were left in the cohort included eight 'major local centres'. These were Brecon, in its small rural county without a large urban place to dominate trade and Pwllheli, a long-standing central place for the Lleyn peninsula, though elsewhere in its quite densely populated county of Caernarfonshire, as noted, Bangor and Caernarfon were 'regional centres'. Cardigan was the 'major local centre' for its part of Cardiganshire, with Aberystwyth as a 'regional centre'; Dolgellau was the 'major local centre' for rural Merionethshire; Newtown and Welshpool performed similar roles in neighbouring Montgomeryshire; Monmouthshire with its 425,000 population had Abergavenny and Monmouth as 'major local centres' as well as Newport, one of the three biggest places in Wales. The other thirty-five towns in the cohort were mainly still classified as marketing towns and were 'local centres' (sixteen); or the less important 'sub-towns' (seven). Others were assigned to different functional groups, particularly nine 'resorts' including Beaumaris, Anglesey and Towyn. The remaining three towns were the 'industrial/mining' categorisation of Briton Ferry, Blaenavon and 'residential' Fishguard. In sum, thirty-two of forty-three small Welsh towns left in the cohort were functioning largely as market centres which, alongside their isolation, may explain their slow growth.[77]

Similarly for Scotland: 'the small burghs which lie in a rural rather than industrial milieu have, at best, been stagnating',[78] and up to 1961 sixty-five of the ninety-two burghs (70.6 per cent) in the industrial Lowlands had increasing populations whilst sixty-three of 101 (62.3 per cent) elsewhere recorded a decrease. The Lowland burghs were also much bigger.

With regard to the structure and operation of the towns during this fifty-year time span, a number of trends can be identified, though the period was not particularly active as the major thrust of industrialisation had run its course and the poor economic circumstances of Britain for much of the time precluded major investments. However, as everywhere else in Britain, the national planning regulations of the interwar period saw increased activity in sanitary and housing reform. Many towns had their share of council house developments and clearance of some of the worst property: the two interwar council housing developments mentioned for Lerwick can serve as an example. The social geography of the towns changed to only a limited extent. The high class nature of their peripheries, evident by the turn of the century, was reinforced and spread by the development of private transportation which enabled the wealthy to travel to work by car. However, the building of new council property, much of it more space extensive than the housing of earlier eras it supplemented or replaced, could lead to working-class areas also being constructed in some parts of the towns' peripheries.

Small-town life in Britain in mid-century had in some ways remained stable

---

[77] Carter, *The Towns of Wales*.   [78] Adams, *Urban Scotland*, p. 245.

with many of the Victorian and Edwardian societies remaining in existence in this era before mass television. Banbury's 110 formal associations have been mentioned already. This town, although above the 10,000 threshold, was under 19,000 in 1951 and, given the quality of Stacey's classic study, can serve as a useful guide to the operation of town life at this period when the 'key notes' of society were 'conformity, stability, [and the] conservation of established institutions and values'.[79] The society was divided on class lines: 'Middle-class rarely meet working-class Banburians. They go to different pubs or different parts of the same pub; while one group plays squash, the other plays table tennis . . . there are . . . different kinds of houses in different areas, different types of work . . . [and] rules of behaviour.'[80] Further, outsiders were not welcomed by either group: one woman from northern England, 'although she took steps to join all the organisations that her Banburian neighbours belonged to and was assiduous in her attendance, had still not been accepted by them fifteen years later. No reason could be found for this rejection, except her north country origin'. '"All these foreigners"' – people from outside Banbury that is – had 'so altered the town that "you no longer knew where you were"'.[81] If Banbury was typical of small-town Britain around 1951, neither towns nor townspeople were prepared for the more major transformations in both the economies and societies of small towns which were to come in the late twentieth century.

(iv) CONCLUSION

In 1851, except around London and in some of the manufacturing counties, there was a network of small towns, many of them traditional market towns, scattered across Great Britain. Map 5.9 clearly demonstrates that by 1951 the 748 towns left in the cohort from the original 958 were associated with the more rural counties. For example, in the industrial Welsh counties of Glamorgan and Flintshire just two of the ten towns in the original cohort remained under 10,000 – Briton Ferry and Cowbridge. Further, these ten towns had mainly taken on functions outside traditional marketing and central-place activities. Only Mold, a 'major local centre', and tiny Cowbridge, a 'sub-town', were classified as being principally supported by marketing. The others were industrial or mining centres with the exception of Cardiff's suburb, Penarth, which was 'residential'. Around more substantial urban areas than Cardiff such more 'residential' towns would be found, as in the metropolitan ingestion of Surrey.

Thus it seems clear that by 1951 the traditional national distribution of small market towns had, away from the rural areas anyway, broken down in the face of modern conditions: urban and industrial growth and transportation improvements. The interwar period's notable problems with urban sprawl was obviously a factor here, too.

---

[79] Stacey, *Tradition and Change*, p. 168.   [80] *Ibid.*, p. 171.   [81] *Ibid.*, p. 165.

The nature of the small town had also changed. Certainly most of the once-characteristic localism had gone. Social geographical changes would become more pronounced in the post-Second World War period with counterurbanisation seeing in some accessible places the virtual takeover of housing of almost every type by commuters to neighbouring cities. Such developments further destroyed the rural- and country-based nature of some British small towns, transforming them from solitary urban areas to being subsidiary, detached parts of distant, larger, urban centres.

Industrial development was to be another factor bringing post-war changes, such as the policy to set up small factories in the small Scottish burghs to widen their economic base. Commercial development would be significant, too, with the growth of national retail chains and out-of-town shopping centres affecting traditional retailing patterns and structures. The assumption of mass transportation with its effects on movement, not just commuting but shopping, leisure and tourism, would be important. All these factors combined to challenge the traditional nature of the small town. Adams presented a detailed study of how the Scottish burghs whose 'roots lie in the countryside' tried to react to these problems in the 1960s and 1970s.[82] A book on the English country town had a chapter entitled 'The twentieth century: under siege'.[83]

Clark begins his chapter on small towns in Volume II of this series[84] with an interrogation of the diary of Thomas Turner of East Hoathly, Sussex, whose visits to his local small town of Lewes exemplified an 'almost constant interaction between villagers and small towns' in the early Victorian period. Turner's descendants, if they are still in East Hoathly, now probably travel by car to different places for their needs. Nor would Lewes or any other small town still depend on the production and selling of goods for the local market as was often the case in small towns in 1851.

As to whether the traditional small country town still exists at all, even in rural areas, we might consider Lutterworth again. Here its shops are still mainly locally owned, rather than being national chains. The main street is even free of antique shops. However, there are several out-of-town shopping centres within reach of its car-owning population, many of whom are recent in-migrants who work in Leicester or Rugby, and the local Chamber of Trade is engaged in a considerable battle to try to maintain Lutterworth's centuries-old traditions as a 'typical market town'.[85] Its market is still held on a Thursday and generally 'the market is the single strongest uncontaminated link between the twentieth century town and the town at any other period of its perhaps millennium-long past'.[86]

[82] Adams, *Urban Scotland*, p. 258.   [83] Chamberlin, *English Country Town*.
[84] P. Clark, 'Small towns 1700–1840', in P. Clark, ed., *The Cambridge Urban History of Britain*, vol. II; *1540–1840* (Cambridge, 2000), pp. 733–74.
[85] J. Goodacre, *The Transformation of a Peasant Economy* (Aldershot, 1994), p. 6.
[86] Chamberlin, *English Country Town*, pp. 92–3.

· 6 ·

Migration

DAVID FELDMAN

(i) INTRODUCTION

MIGRANTS HAVE been a ubiquitous and, at times, a dominant presence in modern British cities. In 1851, for example, in almost all the
great towns, newcomers outnumbered natives and, among the adult
population, the migrant majority was overwhelming. In cities such as
Manchester, Bradford and Glasgow, more than 75 per cent of the population
over the age of twenty had been born elsewhere and more generally in urban
Britain the proportion was over 66 per cent.[1] The growth of suburban Britain
in the interwar years also gave rise to settlements in which the migrant presence
was spectacular. The population of Hendon, for instance, more than doubled
between 1921 and 1931 to reach 116,000 and migration accounted for 92 per
cent of the increase.[2]

The differences between these two movements – mid-nineteenth-century
migration to industrial and commercial centres and migration out of cities into
suburbs in the twentieth century – should alert us to a further feature of migrants
in modern Britain: namely, their dazzling heterogeneity. A preliminary inventory of migrants would necessarily enumerate the migrant contribution to the
mid-nineteenth-century industrial labour force, as well as the fundholders and
annuitants who congregated in county towns; it would include both village girls

---

I would like to thank Joanna Bourke, Martin Daunton, Dorothy Porter, Simon Szreter and Naomi
Tadmor for their comments on earlier versions of this essay.

[1] A. Redford, *Labour Migration in England, 1800–1850*, 2nd edn (Manchester, 1964), p. 19; R. Dennis,
English Industrial Cities of the Nineteenth Century (Cambridge, 1984), pp. 36–7; E. H. Hunt, *British
Labour History 1815–1914* (London, 1981), p. 144. The figure of 66 per cent is calculated from M.
Anderson, 'Urban migration in Victorian Britain: problems of assimilation?', in *Immigration et
société urbaine en europe occidentale, XVIe–XXe siècle*, sous la direction d'Etienne François (Paris, 1985),
p. 82. Anderson's work is based on census enumerators' books for a widely drawn sample of twenty-
two urban areas.   [2] *Census of England and Wales, 1931*, County of Middlesex, table 2, p. 1.

sent away from home into domestic service, as well as their employers – Victorian suburban and small-town householders in flight from the environmental and social disorder of large cities; it would take note of nineteenth-century artisans moving through well-established tramping networks intending to *return* to their homes, as well as unemployed workers in the late 1920s and 1930s, fleeing from depressed areas and hoping to *settle* in London or the Midlands; it would encompass immigrants from overseas, from places as far apart as Germany and Jamaica; and it would be incomplete without mention of the tens of thousands of itinerants who swelled and then deserted nineteenth-century cities as the seasons changed. Upon examination, this inventory would lead us to question whether migrants had the least thing in common save the fact of their mobility.

Even this criterion of mobility, however, does not provide secure ground for understanding migration, for there has been a great deal of spatial mobility which traditionally has not been analysed as migration. We need to ask, then, what does distinguish migration from mobility? We know, for example, that mid- and late-nineteenth-century slums were inhabited by an intensely mobile population, and we know too that its movement was generally confined within the space of a few streets.[3] Such mobility has not normally been included within studies of 'migration'.[4] In 1961, however, this practice changed. In that year, and subsequently, the census included a question dealing with residential mobility over the previous year. The registrar general's reports on the census have regarded the answers to this question as one index of migration.[5] This is significant for it indicates that at least one part of what distinguishes migration from the myriad other moves made by individuals is that it is a move noted by the government, or by some other formal institution, at either a national or local level.[6]

But it is not only the formal institutions of government that regard some sorts of movement as particularly significant. Informal and cultural boundaries are also important. For the inhabitants of the small Devon town of Colyton, Richard

---

[3] H. J. Dyos, 'The slums of Victorian London', *Victorian Studies*, 11 (1967), 33–4.

[4] An interesting exception is C. Pooley and J. Turnbull, *Migration and Mobility in Britain since the Eighteenth Century* (London, 1998). For examples of the customary approach see A. Cairncross, 'Internal migration in Victorian England', in A. K. Cairncross, *Home and Foreign Investment 1870–1913* (Cambridge, 1953), pp. 65–83; D. Friedlander and R. J. Roshier, 'A study of internal migration in England and Wales: Part 1', *Population Studies*, 19 (1966), 239–79.

[5] D. Coleman and J. Salt, *The British Population: Patterns, Trends and Processes* (Oxford, 1992), p. 397. Only now are British historians beginning to treat all residential moves as a form of migration. See C. G. Pooley and J. Turnbull, 'Migration and mobility in Britain from the eighteenth to the twentieth centuries', *Local Population Studies*, 57 (1996), 50–71. It is interesting, though, that even here the title betrays equivocation over whether mobility and migration are really the same thing.

[6] Indeed, the definitions of what constitutes an urban area used by historians of migration also derive from administrative boundaries. This is acknowledged in D. E. Baines, *Migration in a Mature Economy* (Cambridge, 1985), p. 225. See too J. Williamson, *Coping with City Growth during the Industrial Revolution* (Cambridge, 1990), p. 13.

Wall has suggested, it was not the parochial boundaries but a somewhat wider and, we may presume, unofficial boundary that distinguished 'natives' from 'strangers'.[7] Moreover, the boundaries established by officialdom were also invested with 'unofficial' significance by the people who lived within them. The reception of migrants was informed not simply by the fact that they had arrived from another parish or town or country but by the meanings with which their origins were invested. In 1967, twenty years after the establishment of the new town at Hemel Hempstead, one resident, who claimed to represent 'old Hemel Hempstead', complained resentfuly, 'The newtowners came down here from dusty smoky London and we absorbed them into our culture. But they don't know the minds of us country people.'[8] Likewise, migration, for those who undertook the journey, could be understood as a rupture with their past lives, even if the distance travelled was modest. The *Watling Resident*, the successful local newspaper on a suburban London County Council estate, addressed its readers' predicament thus in its first issue in May 1928: 'we have been torn up by the roots and rudely transplanted to foreign soil', a sentiment that was 'repeated over and over again' by residents on the estate. But these migrants had not been uprooted from distant lands or counties; rather, they were from inner London and more than half had previously lived a few miles away in the north London boroughs of St Pancras, Islington, Finsbury and Paddington.[9] Migrants, then, were not merely people on the move but people on the move who crossed institutionally defined and (or) cultural boundaries.

These considerations hold important revisionist implications for the historical study of migrations and migrants. First, they suggest that studies of migration need not only address the causes and consequences of spatial mobility but should also turn to examine those processes which lead certain sorts of mobility to be defined as migration, and to examine the consequences of this, both in public policy and in social and political discourse. In a necessarily selective and preliminary way, one aim of this chapter will be to do just this.

But it is not only by directing attention to policies, images and debates that attention to the political and cultural dimensions of migration may be useful. It can also illumine some of the long-standing questions in the history of migration. What were the causes of migrations? How did migrants respond to their new environments? What were the responses of established populations? This is particularly the case because the history of migration has often been written as the history of an event whose causes and consequences have been determined by impersonal, 'natural' forces.

The modern study of migration in Britain conventionally is traced to an essay

[7] R. Wall, 'Work, welfare and the family: an illustration of the adaptive family economy', in L. Bonfield, R. Smith and K. Wrightson, eds., *The World We Have Gained* (Oxford, 1986), p. 267.
[8] F. Schaffer, *The New Town Story* (London, 1970), p. 162.
[9] R. Durant, *Watling* (London, 1939), pp. 22, 121.

published in 1876 in the *Geographical Magazine* by E. G. Ravenstein, himself a German immigrant, and elaborated by the same author a decade later in two lengthy contributions to the *Journal of the Royal Statistical Society*. In these essays, Ravenstein enunciated what he termed 'the laws of migration'. As this phrase indicates, his work was animated by an assumption that the investigation of migration could be modelled on the study of phenomena within the field of natural science.[10]

More than a century later these positivist origins continue to influence research.[11] First, following Ravenstein, the causes of migration in the nineteenth century remain widely understood to have been the outcome of the choices of income maximising individuals as they responded to the pushes and pulls of the labour market. Migration is thus seen as the outcome of individual responses to external social forces – a natural process of cause and effect.[12] Second, the history of migrants within cities has often been understood within a similarly mechanistic model. In this case, scholars have set out to assess the migrants' level of adaptation to a new and unfamiliar environment from statistical measures of, for instance, residential and occupational clustering.[13] This emphasis on adaptation further illustrates the influence of natural science on histories of migration. For the concept of adaptation is necessarily predicated on concepts of what is 'normal' and what is 'deviant' whose origins lie in nineteenth-century physiology.[14] The concept of adaptation introduces an emphasis on the ways in which migrant groups, on account of their inherent qualities, responded to an independently given set of circumstances. In this case, scholars emphasise the collective characteristics of the migrants in question – the consequences that follow from their Irish or Jewish origins, for example. At one level, this perspective differs from the one adopted by economic historians who explain the decision to migrate by hypothesising a universal human nature that responds to market

[10] Ravenstein explained that his project had been spurred by William Farr's remark that migration, unlike other demographic events, 'appeared to go on without any definite law'. E.G. Ravenstein, 'The laws of migration', *Journal of the Royal Statistical Society* (1885), 167. The first essay appeared as 'Census of the British Isles, 1871, birthplaces and migration', *Geographical Magazine*, 3 (1876), 173–7.

[11] Acknowledged, for instance, in Pooley and Turnbull, *Migration and Mobility*, p. 17.

[12] See Pooley and Turnbull, *Migration and Mobility*, for an account written within the positivist tradition but which is alive to the wide variety of factors influencing decisions to migrate. But note that for Pooley and Turnbull migration encompasses all residential mobility.

[13] M. Anderson, *Family Structure in Nineteenth-Century Lancashire* (Cambridge, 1971), p. 17. The results are both reductive and uncertain. Thus one study argues that the marked tendency of the nineteenth-century working classes to move residence over only very short distances was caused by their strong sense of community, while another study derives the evidence for sense of community from the very same tendency to move only short distances. R. Dennis, 'Intercensal mobility in a Victorian city', *Transactions of the Institute of British Geographers*, new series, 2 (1977), 350; C. G. Pooley, 'Residential mobility in the Victorian city', *ibid.*, new series, 4 (1979), 274.

[14] I. Hacking, *The Taming of Chance* (Cambridge, 1990), pp. 165–9.

stimuli in uniform and predictable ways. But what both approaches hold in common is a mechanistic view of cause and effect, and a view that impersonal and structural forces, whether the market or ethnicity, determine social outcomes.

But if, instead of regarding migration as a natural event, we take the view that migrations have occurred when people cross boundaries, and that it is this which converts mere mobility into migration, we should be encouraged to investigate whether institutions, policies and perceptions can illumine the causes and consequences of migration. We can ask to what extent political circumstances and cultural practices shaped the pattern of migration, and we can also ask how far the social and political relations within the city itself shaped the opportunities open to migrants. In other words, what this chapter will propose is a more interactive and less mechanistic analysis of the causes and consequences of migration.

(ii) c. 1840–1880

In these decades migration was conceived as a part of the problem of environmental and social order in the face of unprecedented urban growth. The impact of rural migrants on towns and cities was central to social investigation and to social policy. Yet if we look at all mobility in this period we find a different pattern of movement. For instance, the majority of residential moves were not from rural to urban settlements but took place either within a single settlement or were to other settlements of a similar size.[15] This discrepancy between the real pattern of mobility and its representation within policy and discourse underlines the distinction drawn above between mobility and those aspects of mobility which are categorised as migration.

Although rural to urban moves did not typify the pattern of mobility for individuals, from a societal point of view the aggregate net movement away from the countryside is what distinguishes these decades. At least 40 per cent of the demographic growth of urban Britain in the nineteenth century can be attributed to movement away from rural areas.[16] Indeed, from the 1840s net out-migration from agricultural areas was so great that between 1851 and 1911 they suffered an absolute decline in population, and it is only after 1900 that the rate of movement was checked significantly.[17] From 1841 to 1881 London alone received a net increase of 1.1m migrants. Other gains were spread more widely. The eight largest northern towns received, on balance, 800,000 individuals,

---

[15] Pooley and Turnbull, 'Migration and mobility', 62.

[16] Baines, *Migration in a Mature Economy*, p. 219.

[17] R. Lawton, 'Population changes in England and Wales in the later nineteenth century: an analysis of trends by registration district', *Transactions of the Institute of British Geographers*, 44 (1968), 57; Cairncross, 'Internal migration in Victorian England', pp. 74–7.

while the colliery districts and the smaller textile and industrial towns together grew by an additional 600,000.[18]

Why did these migrants leave home? From Arthur Redford writing in the 1920s to Jeffrey Williamson writing in the 1990s the predominant answer portrays migrants as instrumental individualists responding to plentiful opportunities for higher real wages.[19] But can the dynamics of internal migration be grasped by a list of 'push' and 'pull' factors operating on actors governed by individual self-interest? Here I shall suggest that such explanations are not so much misguided as radically incomplete in at least three ways.

The first shortcoming is that they neglect to consider those social relations and institutions in town and country which left individuals free to respond to urban labour markets. To an extent such influences have been discussed, but as residual influences only; alibis hauled into view to explain whatever resists the predicted pull of urban wages. In this spirit, E. H. Hunt has argued that the slow response of labourers in southern agricultural counties of England to higher urban wages can be ascribed to their entitlement to relief under the poor law, tied cottages, security of employment and the influence of local elites over the flow of information on urban conditions.[20]

But social and institutional factors were not only obstacles. Above all, in order to understand why so many people were in a position to respond to the lure of urban wages, we must take account of the radical reduction in the landholding peasantry, the decline of life-course service and the emergence of an agricultural and, more generally, a rural labour force dependent on waged labour. Arthur Redford developed his argument that higher wages pulled migrants into towns, in part, to refute John and Barbara Hammond's view that migrants had been expelled from the land by enclosure. But even if Redford were correct, the Hammonds' insight, that movement away from the land was facilitated by changing social relations in the countryside, and specifically by the long-term erosion of access to land, remains indispensable for understanding why so many people were in a position to respond to urban wages.[21] The contrast with the situation in France is striking. In England and Wales in the late nineteenth century just 11 per cent of the land remained in the hands of peasant proprietors. In France the equivalent figure was 65 per cent and there the capacity of higher urban wages to attract migrants was correspondingly weaker.[22]

---

[18] A. Cairncross, 'Internal migration in Victorian England', pp. 68–71.

[19] See Redford, *Labour Migration in England*, p. 70; Williamson, *Coping with City Growth*, p. 348. See too E. H. Hunt, *Regional Wage Variations in Britain, 1850–1914* (Oxford, 1973), p. 250. For a contrary view, though, see S. Pollard, 'Labour in Great Britain', in P. Mathias and M. Postan, eds., *The Cambridge Economic History of Europe*, vol. VII (Cambridge, 1978), pp. 108–9.

[20] Hunt, *Regional Wage Variations*, pp. 274–81.

[21] Redford, *Labour Migration in England*, pp. 67–80; J. L. Hammond and B. Hammond, *The Town Labourer* (London, 1911), p. 13.

[22] P. O'Brien and C. Keyder, *Economic Growth in Britain and France, 1780–1914* (London, 1978), p. 132.

In France the Revolution advanced and entrenched peasant proprietorship. In Britain too the state and the law were significant in shaping social relations but in this case they promoted a highly concentrated system of landownership. The parliamentary enclosures of the second half of the eighteenth century and early nineteenth century were carried out by a process heavily weighted in favour of large landowners over smaller fry, and in which the wishes of the landless labourers, artisans and small traders who had enjoyed access to the commons were disregarded. These enclosures loosened the hold of rural society on two distinct groups: small landowners – who received land but who were then forced to sell due to the expenses incurred in the business of enclosure – and landless families for whom access to common or waste land had formed a vital element in their livelihood. In the Scottish Lowlands which, far more than the Highlands, provided migrants to urban Scotland in these years, the authority of landlords was still less restrained. Cottars – households provided with a small holding in return for seasonal labour – comprised between a quarter and a third of the Lowland rural population. But they were rapidly and comprehensively transformed into a landless labour force in the late eighteenth and early nineteenth centuries by landowners who were able to evict them at will.[23]

A second shortcoming of most accounts of migration is that they ignore those ways in which the relative attractions of the urban and rural economies were magnified by political decisions. Rural manufacture and retailing, sectors which had expanded dramatically in the first half of the nineteenth century, slipped into decline thereafter in the face of urban competition. This collapse was closely connected to the spread of the railways which promoted the distribution and competitiveness of town-made goods.[24] Railway development was enabled by private acts of parliament, and in many places some interest groups opposed the spread of the locomotive.[25] The response of rural petty producers to railway development, however, has yet to be researched. More securely, we can point to the removal of protection from agriculture as a political development which promoted migration away from the countryside. Free trade was predicated upon the idea that the long-term future of British agriculture lay in low costs and high

[23] J. M. Martin, 'The small landowner and parliamentary enclosure in Warwickshire', *Ec.HR*, 2nd series, 32 (1979), 328–43; M. Turner, *Enclosures in Britain* (London, 1984), pp. 54–6, 67–70, 82–3; J. M. Neeson, *Commoners* (Cambridge, 1993); K. D. M. Snell, *Annals of the Labouring Poor* (Cambridge, 1985), pp. 144–94; T. M. Devine, *The Transformation of Rural Scotland* (Edinburgh, 1994), pp. 140–2.

[24] E. A. Wrigley, 'Men on the land and men in the countryside: employment in agriculture in early nineteenth-century England', in Bonfield, Smith and Wrightson, eds., *The World We Have Gained*, pp. 298–304; J. A. Chartres and G. L. Turnbull, 'Country craftsmen', in G. Mingay, ed., *The Victorian Countryside*, vol. 1 (London, 1981), pp. 314–28.

[25] On landowner opposition see D. Spring, 'English landowners and nineteenth-century industrialism', in J. T. Ward and R. G. Wilson, eds., *Land and Industry: The Landed Estate and the Industrial Revolution* (Newton Abbot, 1971), pp. 18–25.

productivity. Indeed, the total labour force employed in farming shrunk in every decade between 1851 and 1911. The increase in British farmers emigrating to the United States in the decade following repeal suggests that this translated into fewer farmers, less employment and out-migration in the short term as well.[26]

Third, and most important, any adequate explanation of migration must take into account the role of familial decision making. A model of migration which accounts for mobility as a response to real wage differentials is a blunt instrument in so far as it can only account for a general tendency, it cannot address the reasons why some people responded to urban opportunities and others did not.[27] One part of the explanation for such differences lies within the dynamics of family economies. Handloom weavers, for example, remained in their same declining trade once they had moved from village to town in the 1840s. But what made their journey worthwhile was the urban factory employment available for their children.[28] Migration reveals the family economy as a ruthless system of organisation. In Lancashire the non-inheriting sons and daughters of farmers left in droves to join the tide of urban migrants.[29] In Colyton too, the sons of labourers, with nothing to inherit, were the most likely to leave home. Farmers and tradesmen were more likely to retain sons than daughters. Sons could be employed in the family concern, while the collapse of rural trades left girls unable to contribute to family incomes and they, accordingly, were forced by circumstances and by their parents to leave home. In this respect, it is significant that the greatest single contribution to the outflow of rural population were the young girls dispatched into service.[30] This evidence suggests that the calculative element in migration operated at a familial not an individual level, and that the different employment opportunities available for different family members contributed to their different propensities to move.[31]

In these years there was substantial in-migration from Ireland as well as internal migration within Britain. The number of Irish in England and Wales grew from 290,000 in 1841 to 600,000 in 1861 and, over the same period, the Irish population in Scotland rose from 125,000 to 204,000. Although it came to be shaped by its own desperate rhythm, Irish immigration was not entirely *sui generis*. Here too familial behaviour and political influences shaped the pattern and scale of movement. In the case of Ireland, even more than in Britain, the decision to migrate was a familial decision and was closely tied to decisions over

[26] W. E. Van Vugt, 'Running from ruin? The emigration of British farmers to the U.S.A. in the wake of the repeal of the corn laws', *Ec.HR*, 2nd series, 41 (1988), 411–28.
[27] On variation at a village level see A. Howkins, *Reshaping Rural England: A Social History 1850–1920* (London, 1991), pp. 12–13.   [28] Anderson, *Family Structure*, pp. 40–1.   [29] *Ibid.*, pp. 85–6.
[30] W. A. Armstrong, 'The flight from the land', in Mingay, ed., *The Victorian Countryside*, 1, p. 124; Snell, *Annals of the Labouring Poor*, pp. 326–7; Anderson, *Family Structure*, pp. 95–6; Wall, 'Work, welfare and the family', pp. 272–3.   [31] Pooley and Turnbull, *Migration and Mobility.*

the inheritance of land; as David Fitzpatrick has elucidated: 'Since migration normally occurred shortly before marriage became probable, and close to the moment when household control was transferred from one generation to another, the decision to migrate may be treated as the outcome of a choice between marriage and succession, celibacy and dependency in Ireland, and departure.'[32] After 1846, Irish emigration cannot be treated independently from the famine and for the same reason it cannot be treated apart from government policy. Successive years of potato blight can be regarded as a natural disaster; the consequences of this disaster, however, were influenced by ideology and human agencies. The British government contributed £7,000,000 in famine relief. Nevertheless, Whig policy was constrained by a desire to moralise landlords, who had to be taught to employ the poor or support them through rates, and by a fear of demoralising the masses by allowing them to be both idle and in receipt of funds. In other words, government policy served to intensify the crisis in Ireland and one consequence of this was higher levels of emigration.[33]

How, then, did migrants fare in British cities in the mid-nineteenth century? From data for 1851 analysed by Michael Anderson, we can say that the employment chances of British-born migrants and non-migrants were similar. Likewise, the levels of overcrowding in migrant and non-migrant homes were not very different. It is the Irish who fared badly. Irish male immigrants were three times as likely as their British migrant counterparts to be in unskilled employment, their households, on average, were larger and they were more likely to live as a subsidiary household in a shared house.[34] Findings such as these have been used as indices of the degree to which immigrants adapted – or failed to adapt – to urban life. However, this emphasis on adaptation draws attention away from the ways in which the city itself – its social relations, discourses and institutions – interacted with immigrants to shape their behaviour.

In the case of British migrants this means that we need to take account of the open and fragmented character of housing and labour markets. The predominance of rented tenures and, outside of Scotland, short-term leases, meant that housing was easily available. Weak trade unions, the attractions of migrant workers as strike breakers, high rates of labour turnover, casual hiring and internal subcontracting which delegated hiring to some members of the workforce, were all influences that served to fragment labour markets and help migrants to find a niche. In the case of London, for example, while migrants did not on the whole secure a foothold in the older trades located in the inner core of the capital, they were disproportionately well represented in other fields of employment such as the building trades, the police force, in breweries and gas works

---

[32] D. Fitzpatrick, 'Emigration, 1801–70', in W. E. Vaughan, ed., *A New History of Ireland*, vol. v: *Ireland under the Union, I, 1801–70* (Oxford, 1989), p. 606.

[33] C. Kinealy, 'The role of the poor law during the famine', in C. Poirtéir, ed., *The Great Irish Famine* (Cork, 1995), pp. 103–22.   [34] Anderson, 'Urban migration in Victorian Britain', pp. 82–91.

and among transport workers. Here networks based on kinship, patronage and village ties eased the migrants' passage into urban markets.[35]

Why, then, did Irish immigrants fare so poorly? The concept of adaptation inevitably has led some historians to look at the non-adaptive qualities of the Irish themselves. While acknowledging that the Irish may have experienced some discrimination, these researchers have also emphasised their fondness for drink, their preference for leisure rather than work and the low expectations fostered by the Catholic Church.[36] The similarities between this verdict and so much contemporary commentary on Irish migrants may induce us to exercise some caution before accepting it. Moreover, it is an interpretation that fails to take account of the diverse experience of Irish immigrants. In an examination of seven towns, Pooley found that between 17 per cent and 40 per cent of the Irish population were in skilled or higher status occupations and so had access to higher wages and better housing than the small majority in unskilled and semi-skilled jobs. Similarly, in towns such as London, Cardiff and Bradford, the Irish were spread widely through the city as well as clustered in notorious rookeries. Culturally Irish immigrants were a heterogeneous group with diverse origins and included some who tried to break ties to Irish identity, others who strove to transplant Irish culture in Britain, others who helped forge a hybrid, church-oriented immigrant culture.[37]

But though the image of the Irish as a population of unskilled and demoralised slum dwellers can be seen to have been highly partial, it was not without real effects.[38] In view of their reputation, it is easy to see why, disproportionately, the Irish remained concentrated in low-skilled and low-paid employment. It is not that they were regarded by employers and the middle-men of the labour markets as unfit for work; rather, they were seen as fit for only a particular set of tasks. Samuel Hoare, a Liverpool builder, told the 1836 Royal Commission on the Irish Poor in England 'They scarcely ever make good mechanics; they don't look deep into subjects . . . they don't make good millwrights or engineers, or anything which requires thought. They don't even make good bricklayers. This is not because the want of apprenticeship is an obstacle . . . I attribute this not to education but to difference of natural power.'[39] Employers' prejudices also allow us to make sense of the pattern of women's work. For whereas Irish men were simply disadvantaged when compared to both town- and country-born Englishmen, the situation of Irish women was more complex. Their employment

---

[35] *Ibid.*, pp. 87–9; on London see G. Stedman Jones, *Outcast London* (Oxford, 1971), pp. 142–3.

[36] Hunt, *British Labour History*, pp. 166–7; L. H. Lees, *Exiles of Erin* (Manchester, 1979), pp. 193–4.

[37] D. Fitzpatrick, 'A curious middle place: the Irish in Britain, 1871–1921', in R. Swift and S. Gilley, eds., *The Irish in Britain, 1815–1939* (London, 1898), p. 30.

[38] On this see J. Davis, 'Jennings' Buildings and the Royal Borough: the construction of the underclass in mid-Victorian England', in D. Feldman and G. Stedman Jones, eds., *Metropolis London* (London, 1989), pp. 11–39.

[39] PP 1836 xxxiv, Royal Commission on the Irish Poor in England, p. 457.

pattern was broadly similar to that of urban-born women, with a concentration in semi-skilled jobs, whereas domestic migrants were overrepresented among domestic servants. Significant here were both the reluctance of town-born girls to go into service when there was better paid and more congenial work available in factories and, despite difficulties in procuring domestic servants, employers' evident reluctance to employ Irish women in their homes.[40]

What was the impact of this massive movement of population, both within Britain and from Ireland, on public policy and debate? The poor law was the institution which most obviously took note of the mobile population and, in this sense, converted mobility into migration. It did so because the parish set the boundaries of entitlement to welfare. The 1834 Poor Law Amendment Act retained two pillars of the old system of poor relief which continued to shape responses to migration; first, the parish or township remained the unit for setting and collecting the poor rate, and, second, the act retained the Law of Settlement – a complex collection of statutes and precedents which determined where any applicant was entitled to receive poor relief. Migrants did not acquire a new settlement, in this sense of entitlement, simply by arriving in a new poor law jurisdiction; rather, they also had to satisfy other stringent residence or property requirements.[41] As a result, at the beginning of this period many migrants were not entitled to poor relief in the towns to which they had moved.

When migrants applied for poor relief they were examined to determine where their settlement lay. If it was elsewhere they were classified as 'strangers' and liable to be removed to their parish of settlement. Moreover, poor law authorities, anxious to restrict the burden on the poor rates, saw these powers as an essential bulwark against a flood of applications for relief. The Poor Law Commissioners reported that during the depression of 1842 the threat of removal had

> acted most beneficially as a test in preventing the disposition to become chargeable. The Irish and the non-settled poor whom the fear of removal deterred from applying for relief have suffered far the most. The obligation to relieve existed on the spot, but the pauper knew that the receipt of relief would be followed up by removal, and he preferred any extremity to this result.[42]

Removal was expensive and time-consuming. As a result, until the mid-1840s, in some parts of the country, a system of non-resident relief flourished in which the parish of settlement met the bills sent to them for the relief of their non-resident poor. For instance, about 20 per cent of those relieved in the West

[40] Anderson, 'Urban Migration in Victorian England', p. 83; P. Horn, ed., *The Rise and Fall of the Victorian Servant* (Dublin, 1975), pp. 32–3.
[41] M. E. Rose, 'Settlement, removal and the New Poor Law', in D. Fraser ed., *The New Poor Law in the Nineteenth Century* (London, 1976), pp. 25–8; J. S. Taylor, 'The impact of pauper settlement 1691–1834', *P&P*, 73 (1976), 53–4.
[42] Cited in D. Ashforth, 'Settlement and removal in urban areas', in M. E. Rose, ed., *The Poor and the City* (Leicester, 1985), p. 71.

Riding, between 1839 and 1846, were non-resident paupers.[43] But it was the threat of removal which induced poor law authorities to cooperate in this way. From 1846, however, the residential qualifications for receiving poor relief were gradually relaxed and by 1865 the requirement had been reduced to one year's residence. Equally significant was that in 1861 the unit of entitlement had been extended from the parish to the considerably larger unit of the poor law union, thus allowing a wider circle of mobility before entitlement to poor relief was brought into question.[44]

The poor law provides one example of the ways in which a mobile population placed particular demands upon urban institutions. But, in general, migration provoked a fear which dared not speak its name. It was well understood that the environmental crisis of mid-nineteenth-century cities had been created by what one writer accurately described as 'the rapid increase in population, its concentration in towns, and the altered relative proportion of the agricultural and manufacturing communities'.[45] But without bringing this process into question, the difficulties arising from migration in general could not easily be addressed. Instead, the problems were projected upon the most vulnerable fragments of the mobile population: the inhabitants of lodging houses and the Irish.

Sanitary reformers picked out lodging houses as foci of contagious diseases, on account of their filthy bedding, overcrowding and want of ventilation, and as founts of moral depravation on account of 'the indiscriminate intermixture of sexes in the same sleeping apartments' and the character of 'the various orders of tramps and mendicants' who slept and caroused there.[46] In London alone, in the early 1850s the lodging houses contained, perhaps, 100,000 nightly occupants.[47] Lodging houses were the resort of Britain's itinerant population but they were also home to tramping artisans, migrant workers and labouring families down on their luck. But such was not the predominant view. The migrant menace generally was presented as a burden imposed by an outcast, transient population, marginal to the development of civilisation and commerce.[48]

The other group destined to inhabit this role were the Irish. The Irish, like the lodging house population, were widely presented as a fertile source of medical danger and moral decay. The investigations and lamentations of urban Britain produced in the 1830s and 1840s by writers such as J. P. Kay, Cornewall Lewis, Thomas Carlyle and Friedrich Engels repeatedly focused on the degraded

[43] Rose, 'Settlement', pp. 35–6.   [44] *Ibid.*, pp. 29–30.

[45] Anon., *The Health and Sickness of Populations* (London, 1846), p. 1.

[46] PP 1844 XVII, First Report of the Commissioners for Inquiring into the State of Large Towns and Populous Districts, Appendix, pp. 16–17, 31, 84; E. Chadwick, *The Sanitary Condition of the Labouring Population of Great Britain*, ed. M. W. Flinn (Edinburgh, 1965), pp. 411–21.

[47] E. Gauldie, *Cruel Habitations* (London, 1973), p. 246.

[48] PP 1845 XVIII, Second Report of the Commissioners for Inquiring into the State of Large Towns and Populous Districts, pp. 25–7; PP 1852–3 LXXVIII, Copy of a Report Made to the Secretary of State for the Home Department by Captain Hay on the Operation of the Common Lodging-House Act, p. 1.

and degrading state of the Irish population. A small number of Irish were thus instated firmly as one of the main causes of the urban crisis of early Victorian Britain.[49]

This account of the way in which the phenomenon of migration was both grasped and misrepresented by reformers might lead us to regard the Irish as the inevitable scapegoats, the historic 'other', at hand to blame for the dislocations caused by rapid urbanisation. This view of hostility to immigrants as natural and predetermined underestimates the extent to which reactions to their presence in British cities were shaped by institutional pressures and by the analyses and projects of urban reformers, as well as by individual political choices. This becomes clear once we acknowledge that opinion over the Irish was divided. Employers who wanted to continue to enjoy a flow of Irish labour claimed the reformers' pronouncements were alarmist and inaccurate.[50] Moreover, not all medical opinion spoke with one voice. Dr Lyon Playfair, for instance, produced a detailed report on the impact of Irish immigration on mortality in Liverpool. He pointed out, contrary to the claims of the town council, that since the immigrants were largely composed of adults they obscured the impact of infant mortality in the city. He wrote: 'the proportion of the population to deaths is elevated by migrants, and . . . Liverpool is thus rendered apparently more healthy than it really is'.[51]

Sectarianism too was a variable not an inevitable phenomenon, shaped by different urban contexts even where there were large concentrations of Irish immigrants. In Liverpool, at one extreme, city politics was dominated by conflicts between organised Protestantism and Catholicism. Here the weakness of nonconformity, liberalism and the labour movement, amidst a largely casualised working class, left the field open to anti-Irish and anti-Catholic agitation. In Glasgow, by contrast, despite a greater concentration of Irish immigrants, organised anti-Catholicism struggled to make headway in the face of a liberalism that thrived upon a firm base in the institutions of a skilled labour force – the cooperative movement, trade unions and friendly societies.[52]

(iii) C. 1880–1920

In this period, in contrast to the preceding decades, the problem of migration was conceived less often as a problem of urban order and more usually as a facet

---

[49] For a survey see D. M. MacRaid, 'Irish immigration and the "condition of England" question: the roots of an historiographical tradition', *Immigrants and Minorities*, 14 (1985), 67–85.

[50] *Ibid.*, 75.

[51] PP 1845 XVIII Appendix – part II to Second Report of the Commissioners for Inquiring into the State of Large Towns and Populous Districts. Report on the Sanatory Condition of Large Towns in Lancashire, p. 80.

[52] J. Smith, 'Class, skill and sectarianism in Glasgow and Liverpool 1880–1914', in R. J. Morris, ed., *Class, Power and Social Structure in British Nineteenth-Century Towns* (Leicester, 1986), pp. 158–202; F. Neal, *Sectarian Violence* (Manchester, 1987); and see below, pp. 405, 442.

of imperial competition. Rural depopulation, suburbanisation and the influx of Jewish immigrants from Eastern Europe were those aspects of mobility that were seen to be saturated with significance for the nation's imperial future.

In the late nineteenth century migrants left rural Britain at a slower rate than over the preceding forty years. The moment at which the slackening rate of movement was first registered varied. In southern and eastern counties it can be detected from the 1870s, in the case of Wales and the northern counties, the 1870s provided a fresh peak in migration from the countryside but with a sharp diminution thereafter.[53] At the same time there was the beginning of a regional shift in numbers from north to south. Some industrial areas – south-west Durham, parts of east Lancashire and west Yorkshire, the Black Country and the northern fringes of the South Wales coalfield – began to lose numbers. There was also, in these years, a notable inflow to southern residential towns and resorts such as Hastings and Eastbourne.[54] In part, the growth of these places reflected a process of suburbanisation which had become so extensive that it was contributing to the growth of discrete towns. But it was the movement of people from city centres to suburbs that constituted the most significant facet of mobility in this period. Of course, suburbs were not a new phenomenon in the late nineteenth century. From the 1840s the largest cities had all seen the departure of the wealthiest of the middle classes from their centres. But it was only in the 1870s that the central districts of London, Glasgow and Birmingham, for example, began to experience a net loss of population. By the next decade, the fastest growing areas of England and Wales were four north London suburbs.[55]

The other facet of migration in this period which requires comment is immigration; most notably, the immigration of 120,000–150,000 Jews from Eastern Europe.[56] Their impact was slight beyond a few pockets of London, Leeds, Manchester and Glasgow. The public attention devoted to these immigrants, however, was out of all proportion to their number. The problems of sweated labour and of housing, the deterioration of the race and the emergence of a class of violent and amoral criminals were all issues which came to focus on the effects of Jewish immigration.

The attention lavished on Jewish immigrants illustrates, once again, that it was not the sum of all mobility that contemporaries instated as the problem of migration. But it was not only Jewish immigration which received disproportionate attention. For it was in these years, when the pace of migration from country to

---

[53] Cairncross, 'Internal migration in Victorian England', pp. 70–5.

[54] *Ibid.*, p. 74; C. G. Pooley and J. Turnbull, 'Counterurbanization: the nineteenth-century origins of a late twentieth-century phenomenon', *Area*, 28 (1996), 514–24.

[55] The four were West Ham, Leyton, Tottenham and Willesden. A. S. Wohl, *The Eternal Slum* (London, 1977), p. 285.

[56] L. P. Gartner, 'Notes on the statistics of Jewish immigration to England: 1870–1914', *Jewish Social Studies*, 22 (1960), 97–102.

towns was slackening, when, indeed, the decline in the agricultural labour force was checked, that rural depopulation became a central issue in political debate. Both Jewish immigration and rural depopulation were understood in terms of a set of specifically imperial anxieties.

The idea that rural depopulation was at the heart of the social problem had become a commonplace of political debate by the start of the twentieth century. People differed on what to do about the problem, but not the diagnosis. The latter was based on the theory of urban degeneration, which equally pervaded analyses from the political right and the left. It was through the theory of urban degeneration that the rural problem became an urban problem. In a series of articles for the *Daily Express*, later collected in two doorstep volumes titled *Rural England*, Rider Haggard asserted 'rural depopulation can mean nothing less than the progressive deterioration of the race . . . if unchecked it may in the end mean the ruin of the race'.[57] He attributed the reverses of the war in South Africa to 'the putting of town bred bodies and intelligence, both of officers and men, against country bred bodies and intelligence'.[58] He prescribed the protection of agriculture and legislation to promote smallholdings. But this was not a fad of tariff reform Conservatives. Similar diagnoses can be readily found in the Report of the Interdepartmental Committee on Physical Deterioration, which saw one possible solution in the garden city movement, and in the utterances of figures such as Winston Churchill, Ramsay Macdonald and David Lloyd George, whose land campaign drew on this conventional view of the relationship between migration to cities and national strength.[59]

Suburban growth fed these concerns in two ways. First, from the turn of the century there was rising concern at the way the suburbs were robbing the nation of its countryside; at the way in which 'swelling hills and grass pastures' were replaced by 'serrated lines of house tops and slated roofs'.[60] If the nation's strength lay in its fresh air and green fields then the relentless advance of terraced houses was a part of the problem of deterioration. Rider Haggard identified in the new verb 'to maffick' a troubling sign of the change and deterioration in national temperament, and it was with the population of the suburbs that the verb was most clearly associated.[61] Charles Masterman too believed that the suburbs had a degenerative effect. Examining *The Condition of England*, Masterman detected in the suburbs 'a slackening of energy and fibre in a generation which is much occupied with its pleasures'. He dwelt on the intellectual

[57] H. Rider Haggard, *Rural England*, vol. II (London, 1902), p. 540.   [58] *Ibid.*, p. 546.
[59] PP 1904 XXXII, Interdepartmental Committee on Physical Deterioration, pp. 34–5; R. R. James ed., *Winston Churchill: His Complete Speeches, 1897–1963*, vol. I (New York, 1971), p. 779; B. Barker, ed., *Ramsay Macdonald's Political Writings* (London, 1972), p. 136; *Times*, 25 Nov. 1911, p. 12.
[60] S. M. Gaskell, 'Housing and the lower middle class, 1870–1914', in G. Crossick, ed., *The Lower Middle Class in Britain, 1870–1914* (London, 1977), pp. 169–70.
[61] Haggard, *Rural England*, p. 546; from the emotional demonstrations at the 'relief of Mafeking' in 1900.

and moral debasement caused by a diet of the yellow press, vicarious sport and gambling.[62]

The change in the way migration was understood to be a problem can be traced through the successive phases of response to Jewish immigration.[63] In the 1880s, Jewish immigrants were subject to investigation and debate in ways familiar from preceding investigation of the Irish and lodging houses. In 1884 *The Lancet* exposed the intensely overcrowded and insanitary working and living conditions in the Jewish East End of London. Within two years the precise focus of debate shifted from public health to sweated labour but more fundamental continuities remained: first, the several public and private inquiries into the problem drew impetus from the fear for public order in the capital during the depression of the mid-1880s and, second, the consensual prescriptions of this period, which found their way into legislation, extended public health inspection to small workshops. By contrast, at the turn of the century, debate among politicians, social reformers and journalists was animated by the imperial consequences of the immigration of a horde of physically and morally enfeebled Jews. The fact that Jewish immigrants were ousting the native born within labour and housing markets was seen by the opponents of immigration such as William Evans Gordon, the MP for Stepney, as confirmation that in city conditions only a degenerate type would flourish.

The Aliens Act, passed in 1905 with the aim of restricting Jewish immigration, was a legislative landmark in the modern history of migration. Since 1826, and the repeal of legislation passed during the wars with France, there had been free entry to the United Kingdom. In the intervening period, so far as the law was concerned, migration was an internal and local problem; the issues of settlement and removal arose from the local basis of welfare provision. The passage of the Aliens Act was one pioneering (and cheap) contribution to the process through which central government took increasing responsibility for welfare: a process that was widely justified in terms of imperial efficiency. The gradual acquisition by central government of responsibilities for welfare provision necessarily redrew the boundaries of entitlement. Increasingly, it was the boundaries of the state itself, not the parish or the poor law union, which determined the parameters of entitlement. Beginning with the introduction of state contributions to national health insurance in 1911, every provision of government funds for welfare payments had to address the question of whether immigrants were eligible.

The development of state welfare had an important impact on the politics of Jewish immigrants which further brings into question models of adaptation. In the period following the introduction of the Aliens Act, and still more once Lloyd George's National Insurance Bill came into view, Jewish immigrants

---

[62] C. F. G. Masterman, *The Condition of England* (London, 1960 edn), pp. 73–6.
[63] The remainder of this section is based on the fuller account given in part III of my book *Englishmen and Jews* (London, 1994).

organised within the political arena in unprecedented ways. In the case of the National Insurance Bill they lobbied civil servants, MPs, ministers and Lloyd George himself, to elicit a major concession for unnaturalised immigrants. This degree of participation in the British political process was not the culmination of years of integration and adaptation. Instead, it marked a radical discontinuity with previous political habits and was stimulated by changes in the state itself. Jewish immigrants entered the British political arena to pursue their interests as Jews and immigrants, not as part of a flight from them. The more the processes of British politics encroached on Jewish immigrants the greater was their participation within them. Once again, we find not a process of adaptation to a given set of circumstances but one in which immigrant behaviour was shaped by circumstances that were themselves subject to change.

(iv) c. 1920–1950

In these decades, migration continued to provide one focus for public debate and policy. But there was a change in the terms in which the phenomenon was understood. Discussion now concentrated on the decay of 'community' and the decline of industrial Britain. By the end of the period these anxieties had come together and were reflected in wartime and post-war regional and housing policy.

If we look at the experience of individuals, the overall pattern of residential mobility in these decades displays great continuities with the preceding hundred years. Within this stable structure there were some changes. There was probably less residential mobility than in the preceding century. At the same time, the distances moved were on average larger than hitherto, and there were also signs of 'counterurbanisation' – a current of movement from urban to rural England.[64] But despite these changes, it remained the case that most moves were over short distances, either within the same settlement or to one of a similar size. However, as we noted for the period 1840–80, measuring and mapping the dominant pattern of residential mobility for individuals in terms of the size of settlement they have moved to and from, and the distances they have moved, will not necessarily reveal the ways in which migration has interacted most significantly with the dynamics of urban change. In particular, the trend for the populations of central urban districts to decline and for suburbs to grow accelerated in the inter-war years. Between 1921 and 1938, three-quarters of population growth accrued to the suburbs of twenty-seven conurbations.[65] Moreover, the underlying continuity of residential mobility, at the same time as public debate underwent

---

[64] Pooley and Turnbull, *Migration and Mobility*, pp. 65, 98; see M. Anderson, 'The social implications of demographic change', in F. M. L. Thompson, ed., *The Cambridge Social History of Britain*, vol. II: *People and their Environment* (Cambridge, 1990), p. 13.

[65] D. Aldcroft, *The British Economy between the Wars* (Oxford, 1983), p. 25.

significant shifts, draws attention, once again, to the distinction between mobility and that portion of it which has been construed as migration.

The housing that was the stuff of suburban growth was erected from two sources: municipal and private. Almost 4 million houses were built between the wars, 72 per cent of them by private enterprise.[66] How are we to explain this massive growth in the private housing stock? Certainly it was a response to a demand created by the lack of building during the war, the decline in family size, the changing composition of the labour force as the proportion of clerical workers trebled between 1911 and 1951 and the number of supervisory workers doubled, and rising living standards. But these reasons fail to explain why the growth took the form that it did – that is a suburban growth; and not, for example, the erection of modern apartments in the centre of town.

What we need to take account of here is not only the 'natural' force of demand in pushing suburban migration but also utopian fantasies of suburban life and, more materially, the role of the state. The desire for fresher air, larger gardens and a degree of social exclusivity was long-standing. What distinguished the interwar period was the combination of these with an embrace of modernity. The themes, for example, were combined in this Underground advertisement after the extension of the Northern Line in 1924, which strove to convey the attractions of both rusticity and technology:

> Stake your claim at Edgware . . . The loaf of bread, the jug of wine and the book
> of verse may be got there cheaply and easily and . . . a shelter which comprises all
> the latest labour saving and sanitary conveniences. We moderns ask much more
> before we are content than the ancients, and Edgware is designed to give us that
> much more.[67]

Suburbs rejected architectural modernism but embraced the modernity of electrical and gas-powered gadgets which characterised the servantless middle-class suburban home.

Further, this migration of the middle class to their domestic utopias would have been impossible without the support of government. In part this was a matter of helping to provide the utilities upon which suburban life depended. The expansion of London suburbia for example was tied to the parallel expansion of the Underground networks which, in turn, was enabled by Treasury guarantees.[68] The attraction of the modern, gadget-rich life style of the suburbs was enhanced by creation of the national grid and the resulting fall in the price of electricity to domestic consumers.[69] Above all, a policy of cheap money fuelled the housing boom of the 1930s. As interest rates fell from 1932, so the

[66] J. Burnett, *A Social History of Housing*, 2nd edn (London, 1986), p. 252.   [67] *Ibid.*, p. 258.
[68] T. C. Barker and M. Robbins, *A History of London Transport*, vol. II: *The Twentieth Century to 1970* (London, 1974), pp. 206, 218.
[69] L. Hannah, *Electricity before Nationalisation* (London, 1979), pp. 188–204.

amount of new mortgages advanced by building societies rose from £82m per year in 1932 to £140m at the peak of the boom, and in the same period the level of private house building more than doubled.[70]

The other face of suburban growth was the vastly expanded provision of municipal housing, generally on the principle of low-density cottage estates on the outskirts of or beyond city limits. If they could afford the rents, which were high, families took advantage of the new facilities because, as Herbert Morrison put it, 'people are seeking to live under conditions that they conceive to be more pleasant with greater amenity and with more space and light and air about them, and to get rather more modern than old-fashioned conditions'.[71]

The new suburbs displeased many who lived beyond them; the middle-class districts elicited contempt, while concern was reserved for the working-class estates. Anti-suburban prejudice was a time-honoured and protean phenomenon.[72] However, in the interwar period a great deal of the hostility suburbs aroused was on account of their privatised affront to ideals of collective life. W. H. Auden and Christopher Isherwood in this vein described suburban semis as 'isolated from each other like cases of the fever'. And architectural pundits puffed the virtues of more communally oriented designs. In his Pelican paperback on *Design* Anthony Bertram decried suburbs and prescribed flats as the alternative – 'villages, as it were, with some dwellings on top of the others'.[73] According to social workers, women suffered particularly from the spiritual and mental deprivation, and could succumb to 'suburban neurosis'. In the case of the working-class estates a stream of sociologists arrived to investigate and mourn the absence of 'community'. The classic study of this sort was carried out by Ruth Durant at Watling in north London, and the genre reached its best-known expression after the war with the publication of Michael Young and Peter Willmott's *Family and Kinship in East London*. The problem as Durant saw it was how to fashion a community from a diverse migrant population. She was disappointed that after pursuing a vital associational life in the estate's earliest years, Watling residents 'retreated into exclusive domesticity; they had again become isolated human beings'.[74]

These visions of the suburbs have too readily informed later assessments of the lives of the migrants who went there. But eloquent expressions of distaste can divert us from the degree of working-class satisfaction with the cottage estates. This was revealed most clearly by the Mass-Observation study of *People's Homes*,

---

[70] S. Howson, *Domestic Monetary Management in Britain, 1919–38* (Cambridge, 1975), pp. 106–15.

[71] D. E. Pitfield, 'Labour migration and the regional problem in Britain, 1920–39' (PhD thesis, University of Stirling, 1973), p. 153.

[72] H. J. Dyos, *Victorian Suburb* (Leicester, 1961), pp. 24–6.

[73] Cited in P. Oliver, I. Davis and I. Bentley, *Dunroamin* (London, 1981), pp. 11, 18.

[74] Durant, *Watling*, pp. 117–20; M. Young and P. Willmott, *Family and Kinship in East London* (London, 1957).

published in 1943. On three LCC estates the survey found that 86 per cent, 85 per cent and 70 per cent of people liked their homes and that 96 per cent, 63 per cent and 71 per cent liked their neighbourhood.[75] We need also to take account of the diversity of middle-class suburban life. Far from being privatised, middle-class suburbs were characterised by their burgeoning associational club life. And while the tennis club and amateur theatricals may have offered one, perhaps predominant, form of association, by the mid-1930s, as Tom Jeffrey has shown, Left Book Clubs and a host of aid committees provided another. 'In 1937 and 1938', Jeffrey writes, 'the London suburbs hummed with the activity of these groups'.[76]

As well as a move to the suburbs within conurbations, there was also a large net movement from Wales, Scotland and the North-East to London and the South-East, and, to a lesser extent, the Midlands. London and the South-East gained 1.1 million people through migration between 1923 and 1936. This movement was a reflection, albeit a pale one, of the changing labour market; not in the sense of relative wage levels, however, but of relative levels of unemployment.[77] Nevertheless, the movement of people lagged behind the shifting geographical location of industrial output. In part this was because skills were not easily transferable between locations. But as for the period 1840 and 1880, institutional factors were also significant. Above all, the dole, rent control and the advance of council housing with its attendant local residence requirements were major disincentives to mobility.[78] In the face of adversity and with a minimum standard of life guaranteed by the state, large numbers of the unemployed displayed a sensible preference for what was familiar and for minimising risks; they did not migrate.

As a result, the state itself now entered directly as a force actively promoting internal migration. From 1927 the government's policy response was to seek to encourage labour to move from areas with high unemployment, initially colliery areas, by offering financial assistance. By 1938 over 280,000 individuals, some 35,000 households, had transferred using the scheme. The scheme, however, quickly ran into opposition, both from areas of out-migration, which increasingly were left with an ageing and economically dependent population, and from labour interests in receiving areas who objected to the additional competition in the search for scarce jobs. Equally important, the scheme disenchanted those many voices raising alarm at the unremitting expansion of London.[79]

[75] Mass-Observation, *An Enquiry into People's Homes* (London, 1943), pp. 37–46.
[76] T. Jeffery, 'A place in the nation: the lower-middle class in England', in R. Koshar, ed., *Splintered Classes* (New York, 1994), p. 87.
[77] H. Makower, J. Marschak and H. Robinson, 'Studies in mobility of labour: analysis for Great Britain, part 1', *Oxford Economic Papers*, 2 (1939), 70–97.
[78] S. Glynn and A. Booth, 'Unemployment in interwar Britain: a case for relearning the lessons of the 1930s', *Ec.HR*, 2nd series, 36 (1993), 337.
[79] Pitfield, 'Labour migration and the regional problem'; A. D. K. Owen, 'The social consequences of industrial transference', *Sociological Review*, 29 (1937), 331–54.

Accordingly, from the mid-1930s policy began to change. In 1936 the government began to develop measures designed to take industry to the unemployed in what were now designated 'Special Areas', rather than encourage the unemployed to migrate to the South and the Midlands. At the same time, a different migration policy was formulated. In 1934 a government report on the depressed areas had asserted that 'the evils actual and potential of this increasing agglomeration of human beings are so generally recognised as to need no comment'.[80] This opinion was further reinforced by the Political and Economic Planning Report on the Location of Industry, published in 1939, and the Report of the Royal Commission on the Distribution of the Industrial Population – known as the Barlow Report – which was published in 1940.

Both of these reports focused on the environmental hazards arising from migration to conurbations and the limitless capacity of those conurbations to spread outwards. They were concerned with health and housing conditions, the absence of open spaces and playing fields, and the problems of smoke, noise, traffic and industrial waste. The Barlow Report was particularly significant because its major policy recommendations formed the basis of post-war planning policy. So far as migration was concerned, Barlow's key recommendation was for the 'decentralisation or dispersal, both of industries and industrial population' from 'congested urban areas'.[81] During the war this conclusion was reinforced by Patrick Abercrombie whose 1944 *Greater London Plan* met with acclaim and proposed ten satellite towns to relieve pressure from Greater London, and by a similar programme designed for the West Midlands.[82] The upshot was the 1946 New Towns Act. By 1950 fourteen new towns had been established, eight of them around London. In conception, new towns were the apotheosis of interwar thinking on migration: they were designed to arrest migration to existing cities, to disperse the population of those cities, to spread industry and to create an aesthetically pleasing environment and new urban communities. The new town was the planners' riposte to the suburb.

(v) CONCLUSION

In a sense, a century on, public discourse on migration had come full circle; once again migration was thought of as an environmental hazard. But there was one fundamental difference between the debate on migration in 1940 and that in 1840. For now it was not marginal minorities – the lodging house population or the Irish – that were seen to be the problem but the totality of migration itself. This recurrent theme as well as its development over time both serve to underline one

[80] Cited in J. D. McCallum, 'The development of British regional policy', in D. Maclennan and J. Parr, eds., *Regional Policy* (Oxford, 1979), p. 6.
[81] *Ibid.*, pp. 6–9; Pitfield, 'Labour migration and the regional problem', pp. 367–75.
[82] P. Abercrombie, *The Greater London Plan 1944* (London, 1945).

of the main arguments of this chapter, namely, that migration is best understood as a political and cultural phenomenon as well as a facet of demographic and economic systems. This has some important implications for our understanding both of the causes of migration and of the historical experience of migrants in urban Britain. It suggests that this history ought not be understood as a series of inevitable responses, respectively, to the demand for labour and to the capacities of particular groups to adapt. Instead, this essay has argued for the adoption of more interactive and dynamic models of explanation. It has also argued that mobility cohered into a problem of migration as it was interpreted through some of the predominant social and political concerns of the moment, and as it was seen to contribute to them. Migrants repeatedly have been the objects of policy makers' interventions, reformers' Jeremiads and journalists' sensationalism. Successive controversies on migrants and migration allow us to trace and illumine anew the changing formulations of 'the social problem' in urban Britain.

· 7 ·

Pollution in the city

BILL LUCKIN

WE LIVE in an era in which global crisis is permanently, threateningly present. Despite that fact little work has yet been completed within the mainstream of social, economic and urban history on the origins, distribution and impact of environmental pollution in the 'first industrial nation'.[1] Nor have the nature and extent of the dilemma in towns and cities between the mid-nineteenth and mid-twentieth centuries been systematically explored or interpreted. Compared with similar research in North America and, to a lesser extent, France, British environmental history is in this sense underdeveloped and methodologically immature.[2] This is surprising on a number of counts. First, research programmes are frequently influenced and at times determined by pressing contemporary concerns. Secondly, cognate disciplines – and particularly sociology and anthropology – have already begun to throw light on pollution processes as social as well as socially constructed, phenomena.[3] Thirdly,

I would like to thank Anne Hardy, John Hassan, Graham Mooney and Harold Platt for comments and criticisms of earlier drafts of this chapter.

[1] The best existing study is A. S. Wohl, *Endangered Lives* (London, 1983). But see also K.Thomas, *Man and the Natural World* (London, 1983); P. Brimblecombe and C. Pfister, eds., *Silent Countdown: Essays in European Environmental History* (London and Berlin, 1990); and M. Shortland, ed., *Science and Nature* (Stamford in the Vale, 1993). In addition, the writings of Christopher Hamlin, liberally cited below, are seminal. J. A. Hassan, *Prospects for Economic and Environmental History* (Manchester, 1995) outlines the larger historiographical situation.

[2] For North America see M. V. Melosi, ed., *Pollution and Reform in American Cities 1870–1930* (Austin, Tex., 1980); K. E. Bailes, *Environmental History: Critical Issues in Comparative Perspective* (Lanham, 1985); and J. A. Tarr, *The Search for the Ultimate Sink: Urban Pollution in Historical Perspective* (Akron, Ohio, 1996). On France see A. Corbin, *The Foul and the Fragrant*, trans. M. L. Kochan (Leamington Spa, 1986). D. Reid, *Paris Sewers and Sewermen: Realities and Representations* (Cambridge, Mass., 1991); and A. F. Laberge, *Mission and Method: The Early Nineteenth Century French Public Health Movement* (Cambridge, 1992).

[3] M. Douglas, *Purity and Danger* (London, 1966); M. Douglas, 'Environments at risk', in M. Douglas, *Implicit Meanings* (London, 1975), pp. 230–48; and M. Douglas and A. Wildavsky, *Risk and Culture* (Berkeley and London, 1982). See also U. Beck, *The Risk Society: Towards a New Modernity*, trans. M. Ritter (London, 1992); and B. Wynne, *Rationality and Ritual: The Windscale Inquiry and Nuclear Decisions in Britain* (BSHS Monograph, 3, Chalfont St Giles, 1982).

writers in these fields are providing provisional answers to a crucial and essentially historically rooted question: how was it that, in this particular place and
this particular time, this particular environmental dilemma came, finally, to be
intepreted as unendurable?[4]

In what follows the literature will be surveyed in order to illuminate relationships between urban and environmental change during the period under review.
An opening section outlines the social and legal processes and traditions that partially defined urban-based pollution. This is complemented by an overview of
the production, treatment and disposal of human and manufacturing waste, and
the contamination of river and domestic drinking water. A fourth section is
devoted to the construction of a provisional narrative of the beginnings of a
'refuse revolution'. By way of conclusion, an assessment is provided of the
impact of atmospheric pollution and general chronological issues. Although
attention is directed throughout to the fortunes of individual towns and cities,
the approach is also ecological and systemic, emphasising the ways in which individual localities transmitted waste material to others within the urban hierarchy.
An additional and important theme is that relatively small towns frequently triggered regional environmental dilemmas that were disproportionate to their demographic status.

(i) SOCIAL AND LEGAL CONTEXTS

Pollution attributable exclusively to urban-located activities is difficult to
identify. But it undoubtedly afflicted all those places in which demographic
growth during the late eighteenth and early nineteenth centuries was unusually
rapid, in-migration heavy and the poorest members of the community subject
to exceptionally high levels of overcrowding. Manufacturing pollution – both
of air and of water – was also invariably present, though not necessarily as
a result of effluents associated with new and dynamic sectors of the economy;
traditional activities – such as mining, papermaking and dyeing – also radically undermined environmental salubrity. The unplanned proximity of mills,
factories and workshops to domestic dwellings ensured that conditions of
life were always likely to deteriorate from levels that had intermittently threatened to become critical during the early and mid-eighteenth century. But
there was little predictability or homogeneity. Indeed, it is precisely unexpected
variations within and between urban areas which require the close attention
of the environmental historian. In terms of relevant quantitative indicators,
analysis of the level of infant mortality, characterised by George Rosen as a
highly sensitive guide to the quality of environmental and communal life, is

---

[4] Douglas, 'Environments at risk'; Douglas and Wildavsky, *Risk and Culture*; and C. Hamlin,
'Environmental sensibility in Edinburgh, 1839–1840: the fetid irrigation controversy', *JUH*, 20
(1994), 311–39.

indispensable.[5] Thus in later nineteenth- and early twentieth-century London, Sheffield and Bradford there were clear connections between higher than average infant mortality and poorer than average access to environmental and infrastructural provision.[6] Prolonged exposure to an industrialised environment may also in itself have played a role in sustaining levels of infant death greatly above the national average.[7] In terms of cause-specific mortality at all ages, large-scale incidence of cholera, typhoid, dysentery and diarrhoea invariably indicated radical deterioration in the quality of water supplies, while upward seasonal shifts in pneumonia, bronchitis and asthma would in time point to dangerously high levels of atmospheric impurity. In spatial terms, adverse developments in one part of an urban community invariably had dangerous repercussions for the inhabitants of others. Like bacteria and viruses, sulphurous smoke and polluted drinking water were blind to the formal administrative subdivisions of nineteenth- and twentieth-century towns and cities. Pollution generated in a large industrial area flowed outwards to exert far-reaching though non-quantifiable effects on the inhabitants of other towns, suburbia and, increasingly, as time went on, villages and hamlets. Sometimes relatively small towns – St Helens or Widnes in the early years of the alkali industry, Swansea at the beginning of the copper-smelting boom – inflicted disproportionate damage on the regions in which they were located.[8]

In a classic article, Emmanuel Ladurie has argued that the 'microbe' played a key role in the cultural 'unification' of the known world between the fourteenth and seventeenth centuries.[9] The spatial dissemination of urban-generated pollution may have worked in a similar manner, with environmental deterioration

[5] G. Rosen, 'Disease, debility and death', in H. J. Dyos and M. Wolff, eds., *The Victorian City*, vol. II (London, 1973), pp. 650–1. See also P. Townsend, N. Davidson and M. Whitehead, eds., *Inequalities in Health* (Harmondsworth, 1988), pp. 43–5, 228–9 and 274–6.

[6] N. Williams, 'Death in its season: class, environment and the mortality of infants in nineteenth-century Sheffield', *Social History of Medicine*, 5 (1992), 71–94; N. Williams and G. Mooney, 'Infant mortality in an "age of great cities": London and the English provincial cities compared, c. 1840–1910', *Continuity and Change*, 9 (1994), 185–212; and B. Thompson, 'Infant mortality in nineteenth-century Bradford', in R. Woods and J. Woodward, eds., *Urban Disease and Mortality in Nineteenth-Century England* (London, 1984), pp. 120–47.

[7] C. H. Lee, 'Regional inequalities in infant mortality in Britain, 1871–1971: patterns and hypotheses', *Population Studies*, 45 (1991), 55–65; and E. Garrett and A. Reid, '"Satanic mills, pleasant lands": spatial variation in women's work and infant mortality as viewed from the 1911 *Census*', *HR*, 68 (1994), 156–77.

[8] T. C. Barker and J. R. Harris, *A Merseyside Town in the Industrial Revolution* (Liverpool, 1954); A. E. Dingle, '"The monster nuisance of all": landowners, alkali manufacturers and air pollution 1828–1864', *Ec.HR*, 2nd series, 35 (1982), 529–48; and R. Rees, 'The South Wales copper-smoke dispute, 1828–95', *Welsh History Review*, 10 (1981), 480–96.

[9] E. Le Roy Ladurie, 'A concept: the unification of the globe by disease (fourteenth to sixteenth centuries)', in E. Le Roy Ladurie, *The Mind and Method of the Historian*, trans. S. and B. Reynolds (Chicago, 1981), pp. 28–83. See also A. W. Crosby, *Ecological Imperialism: The Biological Expansion of Europe 900–1900* (Cambridge, 1986), ch. 9.

reflecting and defining the increasing interconnectedness and indivisibility of the myriad localities that comprised nineteenth- and twentieth-century Britain. Simultaneously, and paradoxically, however, pollution of air and water reinforced deeply embedded tensions and hostilities *between* town and country.[10] This is best illustrated by what, until the Edwardian period, continued to be the single most significant institutional definer and reflection of environmental conflict and anxiety – the demand, in terms of a common law injunction, that a given action be formally designated a nuisance and steps taken to reduce or stabilise its intensity. The reasons for the longevity of nuisance proceedings – levelled against either an individual or a collective board – may be explained in terms of the weakness of national legislation. Thus progress between the passing of the Rivers Pollution Prevention Act of 1876 and the Rivers (Prevention of Pollution) Act of 1951 should be attributed more to the activities of joint regional river boards, first established in the 1890s, than largely inactive municipalities and sanitary authorities. (A cluster of complementary acts passed between the early 1860s and the later 1880s to protect salmon against over-fishing and polluted river water proved largely ineffective.[11]) For the bulk of the period under review, scientists failed to agree on what constituted a polluted supply of water, or how quantitative chemical standards should be enforced on socially disparate riparian interest groups. For their part, the latter clung tenaciously to customary usage, denying that contaminated water was responsible for the transmission of disease and insisting that any form of control would traumatically undermine regional economic activity, inflicting unemployment and poverty on entire urban communities. When, from the mid-1870s onwards, a legal framework for prosecution was finally created, enforcement lay predominantly in the hands of sanitary authorities, who were themselves frequently guilty of large-scale sewage pollution, as well as being under the influence of powerful cliques of manufacturers. The marginally more active policies followed from the 1890s onwards by the river boards, mainly situated in the northern industrial areas, were based on commitment to the environmental integrity of the watershed, rather than the property rights or interests of individuals or individual urban localities. Stricter control of the pollution of rivers, whether attributable to the disposal of untreated or under-treated sewage or manufacturing effluent, represented, in that sense, a reduction in the power and influence of urban elites in relation to the use of the environment. But it also gave rise to the belief that trade was being made subservient to the rod.

[10] L. Stone, *The Crisis of the Aristrocracy* (Oxford, 1965), pp. 386–96; R. Williams, *The Country and the City* (London, 1973); P. J. Corfield, *The Impact of English Towns 1700–1800* (Oxford, 1982), ch. 5; and Thomas, *Man and the Natural World*, pp. 243–54. For a comparative perspective see the path-breaking W. Cronon, *Nature's Metropolis: Chicago and the Great West* (New York, 1991), ch. 8.
[11] R. M. MacLeod, 'Government and resource conservation: the Salmon Acts Administration, 1860–1886', *Journal of British Studies*, 8 (1968), 114–50. See also P. Bartrip, 'Food for the body and food for the mind: the regulation of freshwater fisheries in the 1870's', *Victorian Studies*, 28 (1985), 285–304.

With only minor, local exceptions, legal action against suspected smoke polluters was even less effective. There may have been extensive propaganda against
noxious vapours and this was reflected in minor victories achieved against the
chemical and related industries under successive and incremental Alkali Acts
from the 1860s onwards.[12] But it was long-term technological change in relation to the production of smokeless fuel immediately before and after the Second
World War, together with a catastrophic environmental and human tragedy – the
Great London Smog in 1952 – which finally precipitated the passing of the Clean
Air Act in 1956.[13] Local research in the field is meagre but only a small number
of centres – Derby, Birmingham, Sheffield, Liverpool, Manchester and London
– framed local acts or by-laws that annually led to the prosecution of more than
a handful of offenders.[14] During the 1850s largely ineffectual regulations were
introduced in the capital through the unexpected intervention of Lord
Palmerston.[15] At the same time by-laws in smoky Bradford proved unenforce-
able:[16] and twenty years later, in Leeds, it was still very nearly impossible to
obtain meaningful prosecutions.[17] The reasons for failure were clear. Even more
comprehensively than in relation to the pollution of rivers, *laissez-faire* arguments
– that any attempt to enforce anti-smoke legislation on to the manufacturing
districts would be accompanied by the closing down of factories – neutralised
reformist agendas. The widely held belief that foggy towns were prosperous, and
that domestic smoke was harmless when compared with a very small number of
noxious manufacturing vapours, further strengthened the non-interventionist
case. To this was added the problem of inspection. The precise origin, it was
argued, of a specific black and sooty emission could only be identified if an
enforcing agency were to employ police, spies or inspectors. Until the early
twentieth century the last of these possibilities – a fully fledged and centralised
anti-smoke bureaucracy – continued to be stridently opposed by businessmen
and *laissez-faire* politicians. 'Parliament', as one commentator has noted, 'passed
laws giving local authorities the power to act; the local authorities, forced to confront the polluters at close quarters in the councils and courts, wavered and
passed the responsibility back to the central government. In the end, little abate-

---

[12] R. M. MacLeod, 'The Alkali Acts administration, 1863–84: the emergence of the civil scientist',
Victorian Studies, 9 (1965), 85–112.
[13] H. Heimann, 'Effects of air pollution on human health', in *Air Pollution* (World Health
Organisation Monograph, 46, Geneva, 1961), pp. 172–6; and W. P. D. Logan, 'Mortality in the
London fog accident, 1952', *The Lancet*, 1 (1953), 336–8.
[14] R. Hawes, 'The municipal regulation of smoke pollution in Liverpool, 1853–1866', *Environment
and History*, 4 (1998), 75–90. See also C. Bowler and P. Brimblecombe, 'The difficulties of abating
smoke in late Victorian York', *Atmospheric Environment*, 24B (1990), 49–55.
[15] E. Ashby and M. Anderson, *The Politics of Clean Air* (Oxford, 1981), pp. 16–17.
[16] A. Elliott, 'Municipal government in Bradford in the mid-nineteenth century', in D. Fraser, ed.,
Municipal Reform and the Industrial City (Leicester, 1982), pp. 123–4.
[17] B. Barber, 'Municipal government in Leeds, 1835–1914', in Fraser, ed., *Municipal Reform*, pp.
75–6.

ment was achieved.'[18] These, then, were the legal and social contexts within which, between the mid-nineteenth and earlier twentieth centuries, farmers continued to seek injunctions against manufacturers for polluting river water that ran through their fields and landowners sued manufacturers for damage inflicted on crops, gardens and what would later come to be known as 'amenity'. In more complex variants of the same scenario, sanitary authorities took action against other sanitary authorities, for failing to cleanse or deodorise sewage which, when it flowed downstream, made life unendurable for those forced to live too close to river banks. At a bizarre extreme, as in Birmingham during the 1870s, a landowner obtained an interim order against that municipality as a result of the latter's seeming *success* in meeting the conditions of an earlier restraint.[19] Until the very end of the nineteenth century, therefore, the socially constructed and inherently pre-industrial and anti-collectivist mechanism of the nuisance continued to a significant degree substantively to define pollution and pollutant. But it also increased rather than diminished conflict between interest groups, holding different views about the uses of nature. The concept of the nuisance – finally – directs historical attention to the role played throughout the period by displacement, or the manner in which a state of affairs deemed unendurable in one centre might be transposed in a subtly different form to another locality, geographically distant from it.

Such quasi-solutions could drag an agency responsible for an original improvement into extended conflict with another public body or bodies. The environmental history of the Thames and the London region illustrates the point. Following the crisis on the river in 1858 – the year of the so-called 'Great Stink'[20] – the Metropolitan Board of Works constructed an intercepting sewage system for the capital which deposited semi-deodorised effluent at downriver outlets at Crossness and Barking. From the late 1860s on, the inhabitants of the latter community became convinced that they were being poisoned by sewage vapour. These, and similar, complaints during the next twenty years further weakened an already insecure relationship between the Metropolitan Board and another body, the Thames Conservancy Board, which held formal responsibility for the state of the river between Staines and the sea. In this instance, as in many others, displacement destroyed cooperation between agencies responsible for the smooth running of local self-government in Victorian and Edwardian Britain, redoubled tensions between town, country and suburbia and laid bare

---

[18] C. Flick, 'The movement for smoke abatement in nineteenth-century Britain', *Technology and Culture*, 21 (1980), 50.

[19] C. Hamlin, 'Providence and putrefaction: Victorian sanitarians and the natural theology of health and disease', *Victorian Studies*, 28 (1984–5), 393. See also J. F. Brenner, 'Nuisance law and the industrial revolution', *Journal of Legal Studies*, 3 (1974), 403–33.

[20] T. F. Glick, 'Science, technology and the urban environment: the Great Stink of 1858', in L. J. Bilsky, ed., *Historical Ecology* (Port Washington, 1980), pp. 122–39; and B. Luckin, *Pollution and Control* (Bristol, 1986), pp. 17–20.

in the starkest possible detail the full potential volatility of the politics of pollution. It also juxtaposed the static, locality-based characteristics of existing methods for the prevention of environmental deterioration against the dynamic and ever-shifting realities of pollution in an industrialising society.

(ii) CLEANSING THE TOWNS

Nothing, except perhaps political dissidence or ingratitude on the part of the working classes, was more loathsome to the Victorian and Edwardian social elites than sewage.[21] This detestation of matter out of place, together with the near-collapse of traditional, semi-voluntary and contract-based methods of disposal, went hand-in-hand during the 1840s and earlier 1850s with widespread fear of potential urban implosion. Within less than a generation, however, the panic-motivated reformist programme, associated with the Chadwickian sanitary idea, and predicated on a vision of synchronised interaction between public water supply and sewage disposal systems, would be subjected to intense criticism.[22] Rivers that had scarcely been able to sustain salmon at the beginning of the century were, by the 1860s, being compared to open sewers. Only a minority of medical men and epidemiologists were yet fully converted to the germ theory of disease. But the unbearable stench of ever larger numbers of the nation's watercourses convinced contemporaries that it was unlikely that there were no connections at all between river pollution and devastating epidemics of cholera, typhoid and diarrhoea. The geographical spread of the water closet, which would have continued to play a central role in Chadwick's flawed system for the repurification of great towns and cities, has frequently been held responsible for this first national crisis of the rivers. But recent research points to different and more complex sets of chronologies and explanations. Topographical conditions, interacting with divergent accounts of the seemingly indefinitely flexible miasmatic theory of disease, legitimated the adoption of a bewildering range of environmental solutions. In addition, institutional and economic constraints dictated that nearly every urban centre between the late nineteenth and earlier twentieth centuries was characterised by subtly different relationships between water supply, sewage disposal and preferred domestic sanitary technology. Focusing on the last of these variables, Anthony Wohl has identified 'three stages. The first

---

[21] Douglas, *Purity and Danger*; C. Hamlin, 'Edward Frankland's career as London's official water analyst 1865–1876: the context of "previous sewage contamination"', *Bulletin of the History of Medicine*, 56 (1982), 56–76; Hamlin, 'Providence and putrefaction'; and R. L. Schoenwald, 'Training urban man', in Dyos and Wolff, eds., *Victorian City*, vol. II, pp. 669–92.

[22] R. A. Lewis, *Edwin Chadwick and the Public Health Movement 1832–1854* (London, 1952), ch. 2; C. Hamlin, 'Edwin Chadwick and the engineers, 1842–1854: systems and anti-systems in the pipe-and-brick sewers war', *Technology and Culture*, 33 (1992), 680–709; and G. Davison, 'The city as a natural system: theories of urban society in early nineteenth-century Britain', in D. Fraser and A. Sutcliffe, eds., *The Pursuit of Urban History* (London, 1983), pp. 349–70.

was the drainage of cesspools, making them smaller, water-tight and air-tight and thus self-contained. The second step was to introduce a system of dry conservancy into the homes of the poor. Only after the water was laid on, could the w.c., the third step, be adopted.'[23] Yet, as Arthur Redford has pointed out, 'in Manchester as late as 1911, less than half of the houses had water sanitation': the remainder of the population was forced to rely on a complex mix of methods and sub-methods – pail closets, ash-boxes, midden privies and wet and dry middens.[24] Individual towns and cities, then, followed different and asymmetrical paths towards relative environmental salubrity. A crucial relationship, and one that had been insistently underscored by the Chadwickians, was between the construction of a large-scale sewage system and the installation of a city-wide supply of water. A close fit between the two encouraged the adoption of policies predicated on the introduction of water-operated sanitary appliances: lack of synchronisation led to the coexistence of the kinds of wet and dry methods that have already been mentioned. As early as 1859 Glasgow gained access to an excellent water supply piped down from Loch Katrine. But opinion within the city remained divided on medical grounds about the most desirable form of sanitary technology. In addition, timidity about the financial implications of investing in major public works delayed the construction of a sewage system. The problem was only finally resolved in 1888 when the company selected to build the city's underground railway also agreed to 'undertake a . . . remodelling of the sewage system at their [own] expense'.[25] In this case, incompatibility between urban networked systems continued for nearly thirty years. In neighbouring Edinburgh, by contrast, the implementation of a programme of environmental reform had to await the emergence of a consensus in relation to the filth-impregnated meadows into which the city had traditionally drained its untreated sewage. In the event, indecision reigned supreme, until the final completion of the city's sewage system in the aftermath of the First World War.[26] In Belfast, the disposal question remained unsettled for nearly a quarter of a century. An initial proposal to invest in an intervening sewage system was accepted in 1887 and the project itself completed seven years later. But, in the absence of a natural drop, and of a strong ebb tide, Belfast Lough rapidly became foully

[23] Wohl, *Endangered Lives*, p. 95. See also M. J. Daunton, *House and Home in the Victorian City* (London, 1983), p. 248.
[24] A. Redford and I. S. Russell, *The History of Local Government in Manchester*, vol. III: *The Last Half Century* (London, 1940), p. 128. See also A. Wilson, 'Technology and municipal decision-making: sanitary systems in Manchester, 1868–1910' (PhD thesis, University of Manchester, 1990).
[25] O. Checkland and M. Lamb, eds., *Health Care as Social History* (Aberdeen, 1982), p. 6; and R. A. Cage, 'Health in Glasgow', in Cage, ed., *The Working-Class in Glasgow*, p. 68.
[26] P. J. Smith, 'The foul burns of Edinburgh: public health attitudes and environmental change', *Scottish Geographical Magazine*, 91 (1975), 25–37; and P. J. Smith, 'The legislated control of river pollution in Victorian Scotland', *Scottish Geographical Magazine*, 98 (1982), 66–76. See also Hamlin, 'Environmental sensibility'.

polluted. Typhoid, transmitted mainly via contaminated shellfish, intermittently raged through the city, to the extent that an official report concluded in 1906 that, in terms of the dreaded 'autumn fever', 'no other city or town of the United Kingdom equals or approaches it'.[27] Conditions, programmes and policies in Swansea were different again. Deep drainage of the town had been started as early as 1857. But construction was exceptionally slow, with the project failing to keep pace with an explosive rate of urban expansion. Between 1867 and 1889, an area of no fewer than 5,000 acres (2,025 ha), 'much of it innocent of sanitation', became the responsibility of the medical officer and his staff. Only in the early twentieth century would Swansea's disposal system move towards completion.[28] In Leeds interactions between social, political and technological processes from the 1840s right up until the early twentieth century were so labyrinthine as to defy meaningful paraphrase.[29]

In these, and numerous other urban locations between the mid-nineteenth and early twentieth centuries, methods of sewage disposal may be revealingly characterised in terms of the social construction of technology, involving systemic and sub-systemic interactions between human and non-human actors.[30] A sanitary engineer might conceive of an ideal blueprint for the disposal of human waste in a given urban environment, but only rarely would such a plan fully cohere with existing provision of a public water supply. Nor did medically authenticated legitimation of a particular form − or mix − of sanitary technologies necessarily coincide with the engineering view of the best and most hygienic method for the disposal of town waste. In that sense, the very idea of completion might remain indefinitely problematic. An intercepting sewage system could be formally and triumphantly inaugurated, yet large sections of an urban community − and particularly working-class areas − remain ill-equipped, in terms of domestic appliances, plumbing and architectural arrangements, to be able to capitalise upon it. Rapid rates of demographic growth frequently generated additional problems in relation to disposal systems and the sub-systems that they comprised. At the political level, an initial decision to reform techniques of dealing with an intolerable waste problem might coexist with and itself further stimulate the radicalisation of traditional municipal values. But full realisation of real and social costs, as well as the bewildering technicalities, associated with the

[27] I. Budge and C. O'Leary, *Belfast* (London, 1973), pp. 110–11. On similar conditions in urban Ireland see J. V. O'Brien, *'Dear Dirty Dublin'* (Berkeley, 1982), pp. 18–19.
[28] G. Roberts, *Aspects of Welsh History* (Cardiff, 1969), pp. 145–55.
[29] Barber, 'Municipal government', pp. 67–70; and B. J. Barber, 'Aspects of municipal government, 1835–1914', in D. Fraser, ed., *A History of Modern Leeds* (Manchester, 1980), pp. 301–26.
[30] W. E. Bijker, T. P. Hughes and T. J. Pinch, eds., *The Social Construction of Technological Systems* (Cambridge, Mass., 1987); W. E. Bijker and J. Law, eds., *Shaping Technology/Building Society* (Cambridge, Mass., 1992); and L. Winner, 'Upon opening the black box and finding it empty: social constructivism and the philosophy of technology', *Science, Technology and Human Values*, 18 (1993), 362–78.

building of a comprehensive system might later lead to a cooling of activist ardour. Sometimes, as Christopher Hamlin has shown in relation to smaller towns, a community might be paralysed by the prospect of 'large sanitary works'.[31] Environmental and technical dilemmas were only rarely exclusively environmentally or technically solved: and success or failure might depend, in the final analysis, on the quality of relationship between locality and centre. If, during the second half of the nineteenth century, interactions between water supply, sewage disposal and domestic sanitary technologies were numerous and unpredictable, the development of sewage treatment was no less complex. Chadwickian-cum-Benthamite commitment to the profitable agricultural rein-vestment of town waste remained hypnotically attractive until the later nine-teenth century. The reasons were clear. Economy-minded municipalities deplored every form of needless waste; folk memory evoked comforting images of nightstallmen removing potentially valuable excreta from town centres to verdant meadows; and a minority of towns had indeed successfully invested in progressive techniques of sewage farming. But, in larger towns, exclusively agri-cultural modes of disposal had long lacked credibility, with contractors having to be paid rather than paying to remove ever larger and unsaleable volumes of human waste from cesspools, middens and pits.[32] By the later nineteenth century municipalities were increasingly aware that an injunction might at any moment demand a more efficient form of treatment than could be provided by agricultu-ral irrigation or any other known technique. (Disillusion had already developed in relation to the plethora of patent chemical deodorisers – many of them crank-ish and counter-productive – that had come on to the market during the 1860s.[33]) In the 1890s expert attention turned towards biological – or bacterial – filter-bed treatment; and, within another generation, what seemed to be an even more effective aerobic process, making use of activated sludge, had been adopted in a number of towns.[34] In the longer term, however, neither the improved filter-bed, nor the activated sludge procedure, achieved technical hegemony in the quest for a means of repurifying sewage, which would approximate to an 'artificial intensification and acceleration of the ordinary aerobic processes of natural purification that go on in rivers polluted by limited amounts of organic wastes'.[35]

---

[31] C. Hamlin, 'Muddling in bumbledom: on the enormity of large sanitary improvements in four British towns, 1855–1885', *Victorian Studies*, 33 (1988–9), 55–83.

[32] N. Goddard, '"A mine of wealth": the Victorians and the agricultural value of sewage', *Journal of Historical Geography*, 22 (1996), 274–90; and J. Sheail, 'Town wastes, agricultural sustainability and Victorian sewage', *UH*, 23 (1996), 189–210.

[33] PP 1870 XL, Second Report of the Rivers Pollution Commissioners: The A.B.C. Process of Treating Sewage, p. 449 *passim*.

[34] F. E. Bruce, 'Water supply and waste disposal', in T. I. Williams, ed., *A History of Technology*, vol. VII: *The Twentieth Century c. 1900 to c. 1950* (Oxford, 1958), pp. 1382–98. See also C. Hamlin, 'William Dibdin and the idea of biological sewage treatment', *Technology and Culture*, 29 (1988), 189–218.

[35] Ministry of Housing and Local Government, *Taken for Granted: Report of the Working Party on Sewage Disposal* (London, HMSO, 1970), p. 7.

Landlocked Birmingham, whose drainage and pollution problems have already been touched upon, deployed the full available range of sewage treatment techniques between the mid-nineteenth and mid-twentieth centuries. Following the initial installation of sedimentation plant in the 1850s, by the 1870s the city was experimenting with lime precipitation. But volumes of sewage continued to rise and the council was next advised by experts to invest in 2,500 acres (1,013 ha) for the purpose of agricultural irrigation. Initially unwilling to become involved in so large an outlay, the council had nevertheless, under repeated threat of legal action, purchased 1,500 acres (608 ha) by the later nineteenth century.

Thereafter land irrigation rapidly began to be replaced by bacterial beds. During the interwar years, Birmingham, like other large centres, embraced the activated sludge procedure, only to shift back, during the 1950s, towards a mixed regime, dependent on activated sludge and alternating double filtration beds.[36] The problem might now seem to have been technologically solved: but the city was still confronted by a serious displacement dilemma in relation to the disposal of sludge. According to traditional agricultural criteria, the rule of thumb had been that 10 acres (4 ha) were required to cleanse the sewage of an urban population of a thousand. The comparable figure for single filtration was 1 acre (0.4 ha); for alternating double filtration, two-thirds of an acre (0.3 ha); and for activated sludge, half an acre (0.2 ha).[37] During the early nineteenth century, it had been assumed that town waste could be fed directly on to the land as a means of simultaneously cleansing urban areas and boosting agricultural production. The processes – economic, technological and cultural – whereby the concept of town waste had become separated from that of an idealised agriculture had been long and confused. The uneven development of technologies for sewage treatment – culminating in the bacterial and aerobic revolution between 1890 and 1920 – redefined the ways in which sanitary engineers and public health activists conceived of relationships between technology and nature. Displacement continued throughout to be a dominant problem associated with environmental quality in urban and immediately extra-urban locations, but, precisely because they sought to mimic nature, the new aerobic techniques both redefined displacement and naturalised technological systems.

(iii) RIVERS AND WATER SUPPLIES

It is no easy task to integrate this account of sewage disposal and treatment with a narrative of changing levels of river pollution between the mid-nineteenth and mid-twentieth centuries. But the emerging consensus is that, in terms of pollution attributable to human waste, increasingly efficient disposal techniques led

---

[36] H. S. Tinker, 'The problem', in Institution of Civil Engineers, *Advances in Sewage Treatment* (London, 1973), pp. 3–4. See also J. Sheail, 'Sewering the English suburbs: an inter-war perspective', *Journal of Historical Geography*, 19 (1993), 433–47; and J. Sheail, 'Taken for granted: the interwar West Middlesex Drainage Scheme', *LJ*, 18 (1993), 143–56.   [37] Tinker, 'Problem', p. 5.

to a slow though regionally uneven recovery. Focusing on a single, though in many respects untypical, river – the Thames – one commentator has identified a period of deterioration between 1800 and 1850; slow and chequered improvement between 1850 and 1900; renewed decline between 1900 and 1950; and decisive renewal in the years after 1950.[38] It should, however, be borne in mind that there were no major surveys of Britain's waterways between 1915 – the year of the final report of an epic Royal Commission on Sewage Disposal, set up in 1902 – and the end of the Second World War. But an investigation undertaken by the Trent Fishery Board in 1936 stated that, out of 550 miles (885 km) of river, nearly 'a quarter were lethal to all animal and plant life'.[39] This may have been predominantly attributable to the ever-increasing volume, as well as growing chemical complexity, of manufacturing effluent – in 1937 local authorities were finally required to allow such waste directly into their sewers.[40] In the early 1950s a more optimistic report stated that grossly polluted stretches of non-tidal rivers had been reduced.[41] By that date, also, fish and other forms of sensitive aquatic life not seen in the Thames since the pre-crisis days of the 1820s finally began to return to their ancient haunts.[42] Yet, even following the passing of the Rivers (Prevention of Pollution) Act of 1951, it proved difficult to move swiftly against local authorities, still reliant on antiquated methods of sewage disposal, or manufacturers ignorant or dismissive of best existing environmental practice. Any progressivist temptation to associate the post-war quasi-nationalisation of water with more coherent and comprehensive anti-pollution measures must therefore be resisted.[43] Towards the end of the 1950s the scourge of poliomyelitis directed the glare of publicity on to seaside resorts which, since the 1870s, had sought to deal with massively increased volumes of sewage during the summer season, by building ever longer and larger outlet pipes. Astonishingly, along a coastal strip 150 miles (241 km) in length between Liverpool and Barrow-in-Furness, a 'minimum of 200,000 gallons of crude sewage was discharged per mile daily'.[44] The historical moment, therefore, at which it had finally become technologically and epidemiologically imperative to repair or replace Victorian seaside sewage systems coincided with the first environmental 'crisis of the beaches'. The state of the rivers would continue to attract official and lay attention, but by the 1960s the ever-sensitive weathervane of environmental anxiety had swung towards the displacement of raw sewage and sludge into seas and oceans.

[38] L. B. Wood, *The Restoration of the Tidal Thames* (Bristol, 1982).

[39] B. W. Clapp, *An Environmental History of Britain since the Industrial Revolution* (London, 1994), p. 89.

[40] J. Sheail, 'Public interest and self-interest: the disposal of trade effluent in inter-war Britain', *Twentieth Century British History*, 4 (1993), 149–70. [41] Clapp, *Environmental History*, p. 89.

[42] A. Wheeler, *The Tidal Thames* (London, 1979), ch. 4.

[43] J. A. Hassan, 'The water industry, 1900–1951: a failure of public policy?', in R. Millward and J. Singleton, eds., *The Political Economy of Nationalisation, 1920–1950* (Cambridge, 1995), pp. 189–211. [44] J. A. Hassan, *Environmental and Economic History* (Manchester, 1995), p. 9.

The polio scare of the late 1950s was all the more shocking since water as a free or unusually cheap semi-public good had long been disassociated from death and disease. At the beginning of the period, there had been heavy reliance on informal sources – springs, wells and streams; indeed, some individuals claimed to prefer the taste of such supplies to those provided by the private and municipal concerns.[45] By the mid-nineteenth century, however, and more intensively during the final thirty years of the century, there was large-scale investment in public water supply systems.[46] But in terms of availability, reliability and salubrity there continued to be large differentials. (The two variables – quality and quantity – were closely linked: the smaller the amount of available domestic water, the more likely that it would be used in ways that increased rather than reduced the spread of infection.) Thus in Edinburgh in 1872 less than half the houses below a value of £5 a year had access to water.[47] In Dundee, during the 1860s, supplies continued to be derived from wells 'or from barrels on carts sold at 1/2d or 1d a bucket'.[48] And in Merthyr – the most polluted town in Britain? – there was an all-out water war. For more than ten years, from mid-century on, the iron masters – coordinated by the Guests and the Crawshays – had claimed the foully contaminated Taff as their own for manufacturing purposes, while simultaneously seeking to convince the rest of the community that, as controllers of the local Board of Health, big employers should be empowered to establish a private water company. The plan was eventually stymied by parliamentary agents who reminded the iron masters that no government had yet 'granted rating powers to be used for guaranteeing profit to a commercial company'. Meanwhile, very large numbers of working-class inhabitants in Merthyr were forced to obtain their water from pools, ponds and ditches.[49] London, which depended until 1903 on private companies rather than a single, metropolitan concern, demonstrated wide disparities. Thus, as late as the 1890s, 31 per cent of all inhabitants in the capital lacked access to a permanent supply, a figure that rose to approximately one half in working-class districts to the north and east.[50]

---

[45] M. Sigsworth and M. Worboys, 'The public's view of public health in mid-Victorian Britain', *UH*, 21 (1994), 243–4.

[46] J. A. Hassan, 'The growth and impact of the British water industry in the nineteenth century', *Ec.HR*, 2nd series, 38 (1985), 531–47.   [47] Wohl, *Endangered Lives*, p. 62.

[48] I. H. Adams, *The Making of Urban Scotland* (London, 1978), p. 136.

[49] R. K. J. Grant, 'Merthyr Tydfil in the mid-nineteenth century: the struggle for public health', *Welsh History Review*, 14 (1989), 574–94. See also G. Best, *Mid-Victorian Britain 1851–75* (London, 1971), pp. 45–6.

[50] B. Luckin, 'Evaluating the sanitary revolution: typhus and typhoid in London, 1851–1900', in Woods and Woodward, eds., *Urban Disease*, pp. 111–12. But see also A. Hardy, 'Urban famine or urban crisis? Typhus in the Victorian city', *Medical History*, 32 (1988), 419 n. 133; A. Hardy, 'Water and the search for public health in London in the eighteenth and nineteenth centuries', *Medical History*, 28 (1984), 250–84; and A. Hardy, 'Parish pump to private pipes: London's water supply in the nineteenth century', in W. F. Bynum and R. Porter, eds., *Living and Dying in London*, *Medical History* (Supplement, 1991), pp. 76–93.

In terms of safety, it was only during the final thirty years of the century that in the capital and elsewhere a majority of companies began to deliver a moderately reliable supply; crucial technical improvements included the construction of adequate reservoir storage capacity, more carefully selected sources of raw water and closely controlled rates of slow sand filtration. During the transitional period between 1850 and 1870, when a public supply finally replaced informal sources, it was widely and correctly believed that companies had intermittently pumped sewage-tainted water directly into the homes of their consumers. Patterns of cholera mortality retrospectively confirmed such a view, as well as the contention that it was improvements in waterworks technology, combined with increased hygienic awareness, that had played a major role in saving Britain from the epidemiological disaster that struck Hamburg in 1892. During the final thirty years of the century, typhoid, rather than cholera, emerged as a key indicator of the extent to which a given supply might be unsafe or a water company guilty of technical ineptitude.[51] As typhoid declined, so public confidence in water as a routinely reliable commodity increased. But still there were avoidable tragedies. Even after the introduction of chlorination during the First World War, there continued to be small-scale, water-transmitted outbreaks of the infection; and as late as 1937, Croydon, a pioneer of progressive sewage farming, was stricken by an epidemic traced back to faecally contaminated supplies.[52] Smaller, non-industrial towns in the South may have delayed[53] but, by the end of the period, the great majority of urban areas enjoyed a cheap, plentiful and salubrious supply of water. Poliomyelitis may have briefly and frighteningly reactivated fears of large-scale water-transmitted infection but it relatively rapidly yielded to medical and epidemiological delimitation. The purification of polluted supplies of drinking water had finally ensured that both the external environment and the internal micro-environment had been rendered massively more congenial, in particular, to the well-being of the most vulnerable age groups – infants, children and the elderly.

(iv) A REFUSE REVOLUTION?

Changes in services for household waste also raised standards and expectations. At the beginning of the period, domestic and other refuse was either piled at a distance from dwellings or deposited in dustholes before being removed, more or less efficiently, by contractors. (The evidence frequently fails to discriminate between domestic refuse, street sweepings and sewage.) In Stirling in the late eighteenth and early nineteenth centuries, collection had been in the hands

[51] N. M. Blake, *Water for the Cities: A History of the Urban Water Supply Problem in the United States* (New York, 1956), p. 264.
[52] J. Stevenson, *British Society 1914–45* (Harmondsworth, 1984), p. 210.
[53] P. J. Waller, *Town, City and Nation* (Oxford, 1983), pp. 301–2.

of contractors. But carting waste away from the town centre proved to be an expensive item in relation to the operation as a whole. Consequently, those who had tendered cheaply and persuasively soon began to indulge in false economies. In the early 1840s, therefore, the council decided to sack the contractors and employ direct labour. But it offered exceptionally low wages and the job continued to be badly and sloppily done. In desperation contractors were recalled.[54] The years between the late 1840s and the 1880s are a dark age in the social history of cleansing and scavenging but the consolidating Public Health Act of 1875 allowed local authorities to cart away domestic refuse, and following further legislation in 1907 to do the same for trade waste. Between 1880 and 1914 urban Britain may have gone through a refuse revolution. (There continued, however, to be strong though inexplicable resistance to the fixed, French dustbin.[55]) Services were believed to be more efficient in Scotland and the North than in London, where several boroughs during the interwar period continued to rely on slapdash and unhygienic contractors.[56] In this field, at least, municipal socialism was far from triumphant. As patterns of production, energy use and consumption shifted and diversified, so, also, did the structure of household waste and the contents of the typical urban dustbin. Dust itself had accounted for no less than 80 per cent of the total in one London borough in the 1890s[57] and, in 1895, an authority on the subject insisted that 'nothing is to go into the dustbin except dust, ashes and paper'.[58] By 1950, dust had been almost wholly replaced by paper, board, putrescibles and plastics.[59] Destructors and incinerators were adopted in many towns from the Edwardian period onwards, not least in the hope that large enough quantities of heat would be generated to produce cheap supplies of public service electricity.[60] In the longer term, however, burgeoning volumes – and categories – of household refuse necessitated widespread use of landfill techniques. By the 1960s, over 90 per cent of the waste collected by all local authorities – urban and rural – was being dealt with in this way. Soon, however, yet further displacement problems, related to a chronic shortage of extra-urban land space, persuaded policy makers to reconsider the advantages of selective incineration.[61] (Twenty years later excessive emission of dioxins would again cast doubt on the desirability of the procedure.)

[54] F. McKichan, 'A burgh's response to the problems of urban growth: Stirling, 1780–1880', *SHR*, 57 (1978), 68–86. See also G. Kearns, 'Cholera, nuisances and environmental management in Islington, 1830–1855', in Bynum and Porter, eds., *Living and Dying*, pp. 76–93.

[55] A. Hardy, *The Epidemic Streets* (Oxford, 1993), p. 189 n. 173.

[56] F. Flintoff and R. Millard, *Public Cleansing* (London, 1969), pp. 1–2. See also W. A. Robson, *The Government and Misgovernment of London* (London, 1939), pp. 201–12.

[57] M. Gandy, *Recycling and the Politics of Urban Waste* (London, 1994), p. 42. See also the same author's *Waste and Recycling* (Aldershot, 1993).   [58] A. Briggs, *Victorians Things* (London, 1988), p. 27.

[59] Gandy, *Waste and Recycling*, p. 42.   [60] *Ibid.*, p. 40.

[61] Department of the Environment, *Refuse Disposal: Report of the Working Party on Refuse Disposal* (London, HMSO, 1971), pp. 8–9.

(v) CONCEPTUALISING THE SMOKE PROBLEM

The campaign to combat the gross deterioration of river and drinking water, coordinated by the Rivers Pollution Commissioners under the leadership of the distinguished chemist, Edward Frankland, had been mobilised in the 1860s and 1870s. Urban-based anti-smoke movements are less amenable to precise chronological definition. Concern over stench, dust and soot had first revealed itself in medieval London. In the late seventeenth century, John Evelyn presented the monarch with what would now be termed an environmental manifesto to combat atmospheric pollution. Besides transmitting a subtle ideological subtext, Evelyn's much reprinted and cited pamphlet, *Fumifugium*, established itself as a canonical document in relation to every subsequent attempt to reduce atmospheric pollution in London and elsewhere.[62] Eighteenth-century attitudes towards, as well as preventive action against, smoke remain obscure but London probably experienced a heavily soot-laden fog about once every four years during the period as a whole;[63] and poets, satirists and playwrights declaimed insistently against the atmospheric filth of the ever-expanding city – its foul trades, odours and vaporous fogs. Such discourses would stabilise an enduring cultural pattern. Domestic smoke and soot were acceptable and might even be physiologically beneficial. Specified manufacturing vapours and steam engine soot, by contrast, would need to be curbed. In the early nineteenth century, metropolitan reformers confronted this steam engine problem and the extent to which new methods of production, as well as old and filthy trades, now endangered architecture, plant life and health. Compared with cities like Manchester, Salford and Glasgow, however, the capital still suffered only minor damage from the atmospheric by-products of manufacturing processes. In the industrial districts flakey soot floated down in huge quantities on to gardens, allotments and newly washed clothes, encouraging the establishment in Manchester of the first authentic anti-smoke pressure group. London's famous fogs, meanwhile, were visibly and permanently transforming themselves into an ominous dirty yellow. Yet official eyes were still directed obsessively downwards, intent on finding solutions to the twin and environmentally related threats of cholera and unprecedentedly contaminated streets, courts and alleys.

The Chadwickian sanitarians – not least Neil Arnott, inventor of a stove that was claimed to reduce expenditure on domestic fuel and warm rooms more efficiently – were not, however, indifferent to the problem. Developing a line of argument which would, in one or another form, be sustained until the end of the century, they insisted that solar light was an essential precondition for healthy urban existence. If it were absent, or restricted, disease and, more specifically,

[62] M. Jenner, 'The politics of London air: John Evelyn's *Fumifugium* and the Restoration', *HJ*, 38 (1995), 535–51.   [63] Clapp, *Environmental History*, p. 43.

222

fever would flourish. Such an epidemiological calamity would lead to reduction in earnings and added expense for medical assistance – cumulative costs that would be further increased by 'money that the benevolent [must] subscribe to fever hospitals and other institutions'.[64] By the 1850s Chadwick himself was developing a more sophisticated variant of this kind of cost-benefit analysis and claimed that the capital's perennial winter and spring fogs involved £5m a year in extra washing bills, or between a twelfth or thirteenth of a typical middle-class income.[65] When such debilitating meteorological episodes dramatically increased in frequency and intensity – peaking in London between the 1870s and the 1890s – similar exercises in the evaluation of environmental damage would be undertaken and given wide publicity.

The displacement effects of late nineteenth-century smoke fog, mainly attributable to the consumption of ever-increasing quantities of domestic coal, were probably less severe than those associated with a sewage-polluted river, transmitting cholera or typhoid bacteria from one urban centre to another geographically distant from it. But no such optimism was justified in relation to the appallingly damaging fall-out, and venomous riverside waste-heaps, associated with the alkali industry, centred on St Helens, Widnes, Tyneside and Glasgow.[66] In 1862, frustrated by a string of failed legal suits and restraints against the manufacturing interest, the largest landowner in the region, Lord Derby, coordinated a packed select committee. With remarkable rapidity, he gained the support of both houses for a system of inspection that encouraged less environmentally harmful, as well as more economic, methods of production. Angus Smith, the first chief inspector (who would also later oversee the implementation of the half-hearted Rivers Pollution Prevention Act of 1876), and his successor, Alfred Fletcher, opted for a collaborative rather than confrontational relationship with the manufacturing interest. In a classic account of the Alkali Inspectorate, Roy MacLeod has discerned a six-phase progression from 'experimentation in methods and administration' during the 1860s to mature consolidation in the 1890s and the first decade of the twentieth century.[67] At the same time, however, the new bureaucracy, centred on London, Liverpool, Newcastle, Manchester and Glasgow, became aware of severe structural and operational limitations. As soon as one vapour had been evaluated and partially controlled, another, the product of the ever-growing complexity of the late nineteenth-century economy, became equally threatening. Debilitating, also, was the veto which successive Alkali Acts placed on investigation of and action against the environmentally harmful consumption of domestic fuel. Smith and Fletcher were

---

[64] PP 1844 XVII, First Report of the Commissioners for Inquiring into the State of Large Towns and Populous Districts, p. 43.
[65] N. Arnott, 'On a new smoke consuming and fuel-saving fire place', *Journal of the Society of Arts*, 1–2 (1852–4), 428–35. Comment by Edwin Chadwick, *ibid.*, 435.
[66] MacLeod, 'Alkali Acts', *passim.*   [67] *Ibid.*, 86.

anxious to transpose an increasingly coherent and practical body of chemical and meteorological knowledge on to the domestic smoke problem. By the late nineteenth and early twentieth centuries medical men were devoting increasing attention to the connections between adverse atmospheric conditions and the incidence of pneumonia, bronchitis and asthma;[68] and the damage done to children by an inadequate supply of sunlight and the associated scourge of rickets.[69] At an extreme, social theorists and reformers constructed deeply pessimistic linkages between perpetual fog, degenerationist and social Darwinistic anxiety, and a generalised crisis of the city.[70]

Such agendas appeared to confirm entropic obsessions, associated, on the one hand, with debates surrounding the Second Law of Thermodynamics and, on the other, with the conclusions of W. S. Jevons' disturbing *The Coal Question*, first published in 1866.[71] Environmental concern now combined with and reinforced communal disquiet over resource depletion and the sustainability of urban and, indeed, every other form of advanced civilisation. Precipitated by an unprecedentedly lavish use of domestic coal, the smoke fog crisis had triggered a national debate on the possibility of absolute energy depletion. A major priority was to find ways of luring the ordinary domestic consumer away from the blazing, open hearth, and to persuade him to invest in stoves and modified grates which burnt smokeless rather than traditional, smoky coal. But the major reformist body in the field in the 1880s – the National Smoke Abatement Institution – brought to its task many of the economic and social assumptions of the aristocratic and upper middle-class elite. It underestimated costs of conversion in relation to net disposable income, the extent to which permanent access to the 'cheerful hearth' confirmed upward social mobility and familial solidarity and the amount of extra housework that would need to be expended on laying and stoking a modern grate. A similar, though less socially exclusive, pressure group, the Manchester and Salford Noxious Vapours Abatement Association, campaigned against the continuing though typologically distinctive forms of smoke pollution which continued to bedevil the northern industrial regions.[72] An anti-smoke organisation also established itself in Leeds. 'In our own inspections for three weeks', an activist there reported in 1906, 'out of 79

---

[68] 'Advantages of the fog', *The Lancet*, 1 (1892), 1433; and H. C. Bartlett, 'Some of the present aspects of practical sanitation', *Transactions of the Sanitary Institute of Great Britain*, 6 (1884–5), 44–5.

[69] A. Hardy, 'Rickets and the rest: childcare, diet and the infectious children's diseases', *Social History of Medicine*, 5 (1992), 389–412.

[70] The literature on this theme is now large but a comprehensive bibliography is contained in D. Pick, *Faces of Degeneration* (Cambridge, 1989). See also the classic formulations in G. Stedman Jones, *Outcast London* (Oxford, 1971), pp. 127–9, 149–51 and 286–7.

[71] W. S. Jevons, *The Coal Question* (London, 1866); P. Brantlinger, ed., *Energy and Entropy* (Bloomington, Ind., 1989); and Briggs, *Victorian Things*, pp. 298–308.

[72] S. Mosley, 'The Manchester and Salford Noxious Vapour Abatement Association, 1876–1895' (MA thesis, Lancaster University, 1994).

boiler chimneys 51 emitted black, opaque smoke for over ten minutes in the hour. Yet the convictions for smoke nuisance were ludicrously few: in one year, there was only one, and the average is three per annum, with a fine of 10s. each.'[73]

By the earlier twentieth century, then, remarkably little had been done to reduce the regular and debilitating incidence of smoke fog in either London or the great manufacturing centres. Fortuitously, however, the Edwardian era witnessed what is perhaps most accurately described as an autonomous meteorological improvement.[74] But relief was short-lived. As the First World War drew to a close, the capital was again shrouded in impenetrable fog during February, 1918. Nor was there any radical improvement during the interwar years. Foggy episodes were shorter than they had been between 1870 and 1900, and fog-related deaths from bronchitis, pneumonia and asthma seemingly less numerous. But on four occasions during the 1920s, and four more in the 1930s, London was paralysed.[75] Whether a similar pattern was reproduced in the urban North of England, and in industrial Scotland and Wales, is unclear. Prolonged depression certainly seems likely, in itself, to have produced precisely those relatively smoke-free skies that had earlier been feared and decried as symbols of communal unemployment and poverty. But, for those in work, coal was plentiful and cheap and the attractions of a roaring, and smoky, hearth no less seductive. Observers travelling through and reporting on the state of industrial Britain during the 1930s still frequently referred to ubiquitous smoke and fog; and so, also, did pressure groups campaigning for tighter legislative control.[76] Progressives might sing the praises of clean electricity, but working-class sectors of British cities were still heavily dependent on coal for the purpose of domestic heating.

In the immediate aftermath of the Second World War, the capital experienced yet another severe fog cycle with excess deaths reportedly rising by 800 between 27 November and the beginning of December 1948, and, astonishingly, by no fewer than 4,000 during the terrible darkness that descended on the city between

---

[73] J. B. Cohen, 'A record of the work of the Leeds Smoke Abatement Society', *Journal of the Royal Sanitary Institute*, 27 (1906), 71–3. For a revealing North American comparison see H. L. Platt, 'Invisible gases: smoke, gender, and the redefinition of environmental policy in Chicago, 1900–1920', *Planning Perspectives*, 10 (1995), 67–97.

[74] H. T. Bernstein, 'The mysterious disappearance of Edwardian London fog', *LJ*, 2 (1975), 189–206.

[75] W. A. L. Marshall, *A Century of London Weather* (London, 1952), pp. 42–53; J. H. Brazell, *London Weather* (London, 1968); and T. J. Chandler, *The Climate of London* (London, 1965), ch. 12.

[76] On Manchester, in particular, see J. B. Priestley, *English Journey* (Harmondsworth, 1987. Reprint), pp. 237–48. On twentieth-century pressure group activity see E. Ashby and M. Anderson, 'Studies in the politics of environmental protection: the historical roots of the British Clean Air Act, 1956. II. The ripening of public opinion, 1898–1952', *Interdisciplinary Science Reviews*, 2 (1977), 190–206. Issues of representation and reform during this period are confronted by T. Boon in 'The smoke menace: cinema, sponsorship and the social relations of science in 1937', in Shortland, ed., *Science and Nature*, pp. 57–87.

5 December and 8 December 1952.[77] These post-war smogs almost certainly contained life-damaging elements not present during comparable episodes in mid- and late Victorian Britain: medical scientists and epidemiologists in the 1950s were in possession of knowledge that had not been available to those who had sought to investigate and understand the great smoke fogs of the earlier period. In that sense, the death-toll attributable to urban atmospheric pollution over the previous hundred years had almost certainly been higher than was implied by contemporary statistical estimates. Finally, in 1956 the Clean Air Act entered the statute book. Before the legislation became fully operational nineteen local authorities had established smokeless zones, and forty more had obtained local acts to control smoke from industrial chimneys.[78] Belatedly, 150 years of anti-smoke propaganda had begun to do its work.

(vi) CHRONOLOGIES

Goaded on by the lash of moralised sanitary ideology, the sewering and cleansing of towns and cities that had started during the 1840s would in time stabilise and then dramatically transform the urban environment during the late nineteenth and early twentieth centuries. Yet the measures directed towards that goal – the disposal and treatment of sewage, provision of a genuinely public supply of water, street cleaning and systematic removal of household refuse – gave rise to unprecedentedly grave displacement problems in a society whose systems of local self-government were incapable of reacting rapidly to socially and epidemiologically debilitating pollution of air and water. Reformist activity between the 1860s and 1890s was, therefore, simultaneously devoted to the construction of social infrastructure, and the amelioration of some at least of the evils inflicted on rivers by the cleansing of the cities in the 1840s and 1850s. In terms of sewage disposal, large-scale systems were easier to design than build or – problematic term – complete. Continuingly rapid demographic expansion, administrative restructuring, lack of technological know-how, the vicissitudes of municipal politics – each or all of these ensured that comprehensive systems could take anything up to a generation and a half to achieve. A network of public water supply systems, without which the draining of urban areas would not have been possible, was, on the other hand, more rapidly and – in social and political terms – less problematically installed. (The repeated reactivation of the London water question between 1870 and 1900, involving acrimonious debate between rival supporters of private and metropolitan control, may have been the exception that proved the rule.) Laggards there may have been but, between 1870 and 1914, the great majority of towns and cities gained access to water supplies that could be described, in quantitative terms, as 'adequate'. But safety, reliability and equal-

---

[77] Heimann, 'Effects of air pollution'; and Logan, 'Mortality'.
[78] E. H. Blake and W. R. Jenkins, *Drainage and Sanitation*, 11th edn (London, 1956), p. 479.

ity of access were less easily obtained and it was only in the interwar period that urban communities finally came to be exempt from occasional, and sometimes serious, outbreaks of water-transmitted infection. New forms of waterworks technologies and procedures for the treatment, rather than the deodorisation, of sewage were crucial to this transformation. The bootstrap empiricism that had informed techniques of water purification during the early and mid-nineteenth century, had, by the 1890s, been refined and systematised, in the light of what was now known about biological processes underlying slow sand filtration. As for sewage treatment, aerobic methods gradually replaced traditional procedures associated with agriculture and agricultural irrigation. As commitment to the commonsensical necessity of returning waste to the fields weakened, so new techniques – as well as, to a certain extent, the nature in which they were situated – were imaginatively and scientifically reconceptualised: fertilisation was replaced by systems that imitated what really occurs when streams and rivers become moderately, though not foully, polluted. Precisely what to do with residual sludge remained – and still remains – a troubling dilemma.

These changes proceeded in a social and political framework in which national legislation, repeatedly undermined by powerful manufacturing interests, remained weak and imprecise. (Water-transmitted industrial effluent proved exceptionally difficult to identify and prosecute.) From the 1890s onwards regional river boards extended their administrative control. But compared with the Alkali Inspectorate, they lacked the power to take action against clearly specified and legislatively outlawed pollutants. Despite major successes, the Alkali Inspectorate itself continued, as we have seen, to be debarred from intervening in cases traceable to the unacceptably smoky consumption of domestic fuel. This cultural sanctity of the hearth was reinforced by the fact that epidemiological data on the incidence of pneumonia, bronchitis and asthma remained ambiguous when compared with similar bodies of knowledge, widely available from the 1870s onwards, on water-transmitted cholera and typhoid. There are also grounds for believing that atmospheric pollution attributable to domestic smoke could only be vigorously prosecuted once both the water and noxious vapour problems had been identified and partially resolved. Successful environmental intervention may, in that sense, have depended – to borrow Mary Douglas and Aaron Wildavsky's phrase – on the 'selection' of a single, and no more than a single, environmental threat at a given historical juncture. Even when scientific and administrative scrutiny was brought intensively to bear on the domestic fuel problem, the diagnosis of coal smoke as an unquestionably noxious residue was only haltingly and unwillingly accepted. There was a significant shift in municipal opinion during the Edwardian period – years that were characterised, paradoxically, by an improvement in urban atmospheric conditions – and even more decisive change between 1918 and 1939. But it was only following the traumatic events in the capital in 1952 that the state initiated far-reaching legislative action. Britain's still smoky towns and cities during the early 1950s may be categorised as intermediate between the blatantly polluted urban environments of the mid-Victorian period, and the invisibly threatened conurbations of our own times. When, in the early 1960s, the Clean Air Act became fully operational, many places were visually and aesthetically transformed. Yet within less than a generation, collective environmental *angst* would be reactivated. Trepidation, this time, was grounded less in the collective conviction that foul air and water would once again drag urban Britain down into squalor and decimating infectious disease, than that new and, to laypeople, bewilderingly complex chemical pollutants – the products of ever more energy-intensive patterns of production, transportation and consumption – would threaten the sustainability of late twentieth-century urban, and, indeed, global life. Similarities – as well as subtle differences – with earlier waves of environmental concern, themselves rooted in and magnified by fear of entropy and the potential collapse of advanced civilisation, would soon become too striking to be ignored.

In conclusion, this overview may be seen as partially substantiating Jeffrey Williamson's important argument that Britain significantly underinvested in 'city social overhead' during the earlier years of industrialisation. However, as has been emphasised throughout, technical incompetence and the vagaries of local politics invariably played as important a role in inhibiting effective environmental intervention as the immaturity and rigidity of national capital markets.[79] In that sense, however brilliantly elaborated it may be, cliometric counterfactualism is no substitute for fully contextualised accounts of the environmental histories of individual towns and cities.

---

[79] J. G. Williamson, 'Did England's cities grow too fast during the Industrial Revolution?', in P. Higonnet, D. S. Landes and H. Rosovsky, eds., *Favorites of Fortune: Technology, Growth and Economic Development since the Industrial Revolution* (Cambridge, Mass., 1991), pp. 390–1. See also J. G. Williamson, *Coping with City Growth during the British Industrial Revolution* (Cambridge, 1990), and particularly chs. 8–10.

From Shillibeer to Buchanan: transport and the urban environment

JOHN ARMSTRONG

THIS CHAPTER looks at the interaction between changes in methods of transport and the growth of the urban environment. It takes essentially a functional approach, explaining in what ways developments in transport enabled towns and cities to grow in size, scale and function and hence the roles which transport systems played in these urban centres. In addition it looks at transport as a network of which cities were the nodal points and where the lines were often symbolic as well as physical boundaries. Finally it examines the growth of transport facilities as specific loci within the city.

(i) THE COMPACT CITY

In early Victorian Britain most towns and cities were small by subsequent standards, although to contemporaries they seemed gross and overblown. London was out of all proportion to the rest of the country with its population in 1851 of 2.7 million[1] and its geographical extent, including both the City and West End, of about 20 square miles (51.8 square km).[2] Most towns were small in size, for instance Manchester in the 1840s was only about 1 mile square (2.59 square km) with a population of 300,000[3] and other urban centres were rarely much larger. The most common method of moving about these cities was by foot. Pedestrians dominated the traffic, not just walking to work, but carrying baskets or packs of goods, pushing barrows and hand carts and leading donkeys, horse-drawn carts and waggons.[4] Most people lived close to their places of occupation. For the working classes this was partly a function of low disposable incomes,

---

[1] B. R. Mitchell and P. Deane, *Abstract of British Historical Statistics* (Cambridge, 1962), p. 19.
[2] T. C. Barker and M. Robbins, *A History of London Transport*, vol. 1: *The Nineteenth Century* (London, 1963), pp. xxviii–xxix.   [3] Mitchell and Deane, *Abstract*, p. 24.
[4] Contemplation of some of Gustav Doré's prints of the 1870s bears this out. Daunton has characterised this 'a walking city': M. J. Daunton, *Coal Metropolis* (Leicester, 1977), p. 127.

providing no surplus to pay for the cost of fares to travel to work, partly a result of the long hours expected of them leaving no time to spare on regular journeys and partly the convenience of being within earshot of the factory hooter or sight of the factory clock. As late as 1897 a questionnaire of 160,000 trade unionists resident in south London disclosed that well over three-quarters used no public transport for journeys to and from work.[5] In addition, the casual nature of much employment, with the need to arrive early to obtain a job and perhaps the requirement to return in the afternoon if unsuccessful in the morning, militated against moving far from the workplace.[6]

On the supply side, the economics of intra-urban transport were of the high cost, high fare variety which effectively excluded the working classes from horse buses, hackney carriages and cabs. George Shillibeer, the pioneer of omnibuses in London, charged 1s. 6d. for the journey from Paddington to the Bank in 1829,[7] and this at a time when average male wages were less than £1 per week. The ordinary worker could not afford such forms of transport, except on extraordinary occasions. The costs of the horse bus were high because they were limited in size, twelve to twenty passengers being the maximum,[8] and because the cost of feeding the horses was so large. John Tilling estimated each beast ate twenty pounds of corn per day plus ten pounds of chaff and cost around 10s. per week to feed.[9] Horses were also expensive, £30 to £40 each, and had a working life limited to five or six years, after which they were fit only for the knacker's yard.[10] Each omnibus required more than one team of horses as they needed periods of rest through the day, so that each bus employed about a dozen animals in all and cost about £500 a year for animal feed alone.[11] Such conveyances proceeded at little more than walking pace so that they saved exertion rather than time and often began running too late for the early-starting workman. As a result Theo Barker has suggested most Victorian intra-urban journeys were by foot: 'Victorian towns were predominantly places for walking, not for riding, for legs not for wheels.'[12] The upper classes could afford their own carriages and the professional might take a cab or hackney, but as Michael Barke has shown for

[5] H. J. Dyos, 'Workmen's fares in south London, 1860–1914', *Journal of Transport History*, 1 (1953), 12.
[6] Dyos estimated that in the 1860s there were about 680,000 casual labourers in London, alone: H. J. Dyos, 'Railways and housing in Victorian London, *Journal of Transport History*, 2 (1955), 15.
[7] Barker and Robbins, *London Transport*, I, pp. 20–2; A. Major, 'Shillibeer and his London omnibus', *Transport History*, 10 (1979), 67–9.
[8] A. D. Ochojna, 'The influence of local and national politics on the development of urban passenger transport in Britain, 1850–1900', *Journal of Transport History*, new series, 4 (1978), 126.
[9] J. Tilling, *Kings of the Highway* (London, 1957), p. 80.
[10] *Ibid.*, pp. 63 and 81; Ochojna, 'The influence', 127.
[11] Barker and Robbins, *London Transport*, I, p. 39.
[12] T. C. Barker, 'Urban transport', in M. J. Freeman and D. H. Aldcroft, eds., *Transport in Victorian Britain* (Manchester, 1988), p. 135.

Newcastle, before 1870 even the middle classes normally lived above or near to their shop, counting house or office so that wheeled travel was unnecessary.[13] He found that in 1850 40 per cent of the middle classes lived over their workplace and the average journey to work was about half a mile (0.8 km), only ten minutes' walk. By 1870 a little over 30 per cent combined their residence and their workplace and the average distance had doubled to a mile, say between fifteen and twenty minutes' walk. The significant changes occurred in the next two decades, for by 1896 only 16 per cent were living above the shop and the average trip to work had become nearly 2 miles (3.2 km) – rather far to walk. Barke's findings are confirmed by Jane Springett and Martin Daunton. Springett found in Huddersfield that in 1864 about half of the middle class lived more than 1 mile (1.6 km) from their workplace, but by 1881 this had risen to nearly two-thirds.[14] In Cardiff Daunton found 86 per cent of the members of the Chamber of Commerce lived within the city in 1875, 58 per cent in 1891 and only 41 per cent in 1911,[15] thus demonstrating a similar trend of middle-class individuals moving out of the city, though perhaps at a slower rate. The working classes were least able to afford long journeys to work, and most likely to live near their workplace and walk to work. Alan Dingsdale has shown that in mid-century Halifax nearly 40 per cent of carpet workers lived within a quarter of a mile of their workplace. David Green, examining London tailoring artisans, found that in the period 1857 to 1877 their average distance to work was about one and a half miles (2.4 km).[16] Both studies showed that distance to work increased over time. Of Dingsdale's carpet workers only about a quarter lived within a quarter of a mile of their workplace in 1892 and the average journey to work of Green's tailors rose to 2.8 miles (4.5 km) in the 1890s. The use of public transport had increased. In addition, the early railways did not encourage short-distance commuting by the masses, preferring to be seen as interurban. They rarely provided early or third class trains, let alone special workmen's fares, and made their first stops too far outside the urban centres. Even then the fare of a penny per mile put it out of the reach of regular commuting by workers.

The necessity for the vast majority of people to move about the towns on foot was not without some advantages. It may have encouraged social interaction and social cohesion. Pedestrians could talk to the people they met regularly on their route, exchange gossip or news, inquire after mutual acquaintances and friends,

[13] M. Barke, 'The middle-class journey to work in Newcastle upon Tyne, 1850–1913', *Journal of Transport History*, 3rd series, 12 (1991), 107–34.

[14] J. Springett, 'Land development and house building in Huddersfield, 1770–1911', in M. Doughty, ed., *Building the Industrial City* (Leicester, 1986), p. 42.   [15] Daunton, *Coal Metropolis*, p. 138.

[16] A. Dingsdale, 'Yorkshire mill town: a study of the spatial patterns and processes of urban industrial growth and the evolution of Halifax, 1801–1901' (PhD thesis, University of Leeds, 1974); D. R. Green, 'Distance to work in Victorian London: a case study of Henry Poole, bespoke tailors', *Business History*, 30 (1988), 179–94.

and hence establish personal contact and understanding. A great deal of social life took place on the streets of the towns and the slow speed of pedestrian movement and the lack of barriers to communication encouraged this.[17]

(ii) EXTERNAL LINKAGES

Transport developments played two different functional roles in facilitating the growth and maintenance of urban centres: the internal and external needs. The former role was to provide intra-urban transport to allow cheaper and faster travel within towns; the latter was to link different towns together and also connect them to the rural areas. It is to the latter role that we now turn.

Towns could not exist in isolation. They depended on the more rural areas and also other urban centres. Two of the key functions of towns were concentration and specialisation. Simply by virtue of being large agglomerations of population they needed to import huge supplies of food to sustain this population.[18] Transport played a crucial role in this, whether it was the coaster and railway competing to bring beef from Aberdeen,[19] fish brought by train from Yorkshire ports, such as Grimsby, Scarborough and Hull, to the inland towns, such as Leeds and Manchester, and to the London market,[20] the coaster carrying grain from East Anglia to London and exotic imports from London to Hull, or the canal bringing potatoes, carrots, onions and turnips to Manchester from the fertile loams around Warrington and Altrincham.[21] Roger Scola studied the food supply of Manchester in the Victorian period and demonstrated the multiplicity of components of this flow, as to both commodities and means of transport. In order to maintain its population and allow it to increase the town had to receive a growing quantity and variety of raw and processed foodstuffs. Janet Blackman, examining the food supply of Sheffield, stressed the importance of the railway in providing fast transport for perishable produce from more distant sources.[22] Thus steam railways and steamboats played an increasing part in food supply and innovated where needed, for example, in providing special fast trains to move perishable commodities, and later refrigerated trucks to move liquid milk.[23]

[17] Jane Jacobs, *The Death and Life of Great American Cities* (London, 1962), pp. 56–8.
[18] J. Simmons, *The Railway in Town and Country, 1830–1914* (Newton Abbot, 1986), pp. 45–52; T. R. Gourvish, 'Railways 1830–70: the formative years', in Freeman and Aldcroft, eds., *Transport*, pp. 77–8.
[19] G. Channon, 'The Aberdeenshire beef trade with London: a study in steamship and railway competition, 1850–69', *Transport History*, 2 (1969), 1–24.
[20] R. Robinson, 'The evolution of railway fish traffic policies, 1840–66', *Journal of Transport History*, 7 (1986), 38–42.   [21] R. Scola, *Feeding the Victorian City* (Manchester, 1992).
[22] J. Blackman, 'The food supply of an industrial town: a study of Sheffield's public markets, 1780–1900', *Business History*, 5 (1963), 83–97.
[23] P. J. Atkins, 'The growth of London's railway milk trade, c. 1845–1914', *Journal of Transport History*, new series, 4 (1978), 208–26; R. Barker, 'The Metropolitan Railway and the making of Neasden', *Transport History*, 12 (1981), 40.

However, growth in urban centres did not depend solely on an adequate food supply. If the growing population was to be housed and employed then the physical infrastructure needed to be expanded. This involved the movement of large quantities of basic building materials such as bricks, slates, timber, stone, sand, lime, etc. Some were manufactured locally. Where suitable clay deposits were easily available the builder might make the bricks just ahead of the frontier of construction, utilising the excavations to provide cellars or basements to the properties.[24] However, some of these raw materials were found only in specific geographical locations, such as Welsh slate or Portland stone. These being bulky, low value commodities they were often moved to the towns as far as possible by the cheapest method, viz, water, that is coaster or canal,[25] and where bricks were 'imported' as distinct from being locally burnt they too moved by canal barge or coastal ship,[26] until the advent of the fletton industry which used the railway for access to the London and Home Counties market.

The urban centres also needed to bring in vast quantities of coal to warm their citizens in winter, provide power for their steam engines and illuminate their houses and streets. Some cities were built on or very close to coal measures, such as Newcastle-upon-Tyne, Liverpool and Glasgow, but some other major cities needed to bring their fuel long distances. The most glaring example is London which brought most of its coal 200 or 300 miles (362 or 483 km) as much was coming from the North-East and South Wales.[27] The quantities involved were large. In 1850 about 3.6 million tons came into London, by 1870 this had risen to 6.8, by 1900 it was 15.7 and by 1911 it was over 17 million tons.[28] That such large quantities could be moved over such long distances and still be sold at a reasonable price was in part a result of cheap transport via the steam collier and the railway. These two modes competed fiercely for the coal traffic, eventually reaching a rough implicit division, in which the railways concentrated on coal suitable for domestic heating which was retailed in a multitude of locations in relatively small lots, and the coaster reigned supreme for industrial users who needed huge cargoes at a few places, such as gas works, power stations and riverside factories which employed coal for raising steam.[29]

However, the flow of goods was not all one way. The towns and cities of the later nineteenth century created large quantities of waste products which needed

---

[24] M. Jahn, 'Suburban development in outer west London, 1850–1900', in F. M. L. Thompson, ed., *The Rise of Suburbia* (Leicester, 1982), p. 109.

[25] J. Lindsay, *A History of the North Wales Slate Industry* (Newton Abbot, 1974), pp. 188–94.

[26] J. Armstrong and D. M. Fowler, 'The coastal trade of Connah's Quay in the early twentieth century: a preliminary investigation', *Flintshire Historical Society Journal*, 34 (1996), 122–5; A. Cordell and L. Williams, *The Past Glory of Milton Creek* (Gillingham, 1985), pp. 17–21; H. Benham, *Down Tops'l* (London, 1951), pp. 139–41.   [27] Simmons, *Railway in Town*, pp. 41–5.

[28] Mitchell and Deane, *Abstract*, p. 113; *Coal Merchant and Shipper*, 26 (1913), 111.

[29] J. Armstrong, 'Late nineteenth-century freight rates revisited: some evidence from the British coastal coal trade', *International Journal of Maritime History*, 6 (1994), 68–78.

removing from the urban environment. Hence alongside the inward networks there was also an outward flow, though of a less valuable and more noxious type. At the simplest level the human and animal excrement needed to be removed at least until mains drainage made the former less visible. Both waste products had value as fertilisers and were often processed locally initially. Agar Town in north London was on the edge of the built-up area in the early nineteenth century and was where rubbish sorters, knackers' yards, bone boilers and tallow chandlers congregated to carry out their smelly trades.[30] This was increasingly unacceptable and the waste products had to be removed from the towns before processing. Thus sailing barges bringing grain and hay from East Anglia into London often took street scourings and night soil back to fertilise the farms.[31] Similarly, the canal barges bringing vegetables into Manchester took the contents of its privies back to fertilise the loamy southern plains of Lancashire and Cheshire.[32] Ash was a by-product of the immense quantities of coal burnt in domestic grates and their relative inefficiency meant that it contained significant amounts of combustible material. Hence it was sought by brickmakers to mix with the clay and reduce their need for more expensive small coal.[33] As a result small coasters and canal barges carried this waste product out to Essex, Kent and Middlesex from central London to provide the brickmakers with a cheap fuel. In these ways transport from the city was crucial in preventing the urban centres from becoming more unhealthy than they were and may be seen as having contributed to the reduction in the death rate in the later nineteenth and twentieth centuries. Without such a rubbish removal system health considerations might have placed a limit on town size.

One aspect of industrialisation and urbanisation was growing specialisation of production in larger scale factories thus extracting economies of scale and lower unit costs. This brought about urban centres as houses and other social infrastructure clustered around the factory, e.g. Port Sunlight on the Wirral and Bournville on the south-western edge of Birmingham.[34] Such large-scale units of production depended on the efficiency of the transport systems both to bring in their raw materials and to distribute their finished goods. Most factories were engaged in the transformation of bulky inputs, such as tallow, alkali and various vegetable oils in the case of Lever, or cocoa beans, milk and sugar in Cadbury's operations, into higher-value finished goods or components. Thus regular reliable transport was required to keep an even flow of raw materials, for substantial losses resulted from any interruption to the production lines. Also, as these

[30] J. T. Coppock and H. C. Prince, *Greater London* (London, 1964), p. 127.
[31] Benham, *Down Tops'l*, pp. 111 and 126.   [32] Scola, *Feeding*.
[33] P. Malcolmson, 'Getting a living in the slums of Victorian Kensington', *LJ*, 1 (1975), 37.
[34] D. J. Jeremy, 'The enlightened paternalist in action: William Hesketh Lever at Port Sunlight', *Business History*, 33 (1991), 58–81; C. Wilson, *The History of Unilever*, vol. 1 (London, 1954), ch. 10; I. A. Williams, *The Firm of Cadbury* (London, 1931), pp. 54–100.

firms shifted from serving a local market to servicing a national and then international market, based on their cost and quality advantage, reinforced by heavy advertising of branded products, so their reliance on transport networks increased. Thus the ability of railway, coaster and canal to bring in raw materials and distribute branded products was crucial to industrialisation and urbanisation. These large-scale firms used cheap transport to penetrate distant markets, ending local high cost monopolies and creating a more national market of relatively homogeneous tastes. The interurban exchange of goods grew in scale and scope and relied on the improved speed and frequency of the transport systems. Nor should the movement of passengers between towns be ignored. The growth of trade created a rise in the number of contacts and meetings between businessmen and hence in the number of journeys between towns. These the railway facilitated by virtue of its speedy, reliable and comfortable service. It also gave birth to intertown travel for pleasure and leisure, allowing comparisons to be made between towns within the UK, and hence the beginnings of a move towards conformity to a national pattern, more evident in the early twentieth century when the same multiple shops with company-specific styles could be seen in most high streets. The growth of firms dedicated to organising trips between towns, such as Thomas Cook, facilitated mass movement. As early as the 1840s Cook was arranging excursions from one town to another by railway.[35] This gave rise to a new profession, the travel agent, which was of increasing importance in the later twentieth century.

(iii) INTRA-URBAN TRANSPORT

In addition to linking towns to each other, and to the rural areas which provided raw materials and raw foodstuffs for the urban centres, the other contribution of transport to Victorian cities was in making it easier for people and goods to travel within towns. As we have already seen, in the early decades of Victoria's reign the majority of people moved by foot and this continued to be the case in most provincial towns and cities until the last quarter of the nineteenth century. London was always different because of its huge size compared to other cities in terms both of population and built-up area. As a result it often led in the search for improved methods of urban transport because its population was more far flung than that of any other British city.

While the horse remained the power source passenger transport was likely to be both expensive and relatively slow. As previously explained, the horse was costly to feed and had a short working life. If it was made to work above a walk the former increased and the latter decreased, thus raising costs. As a result even

---

[35] D. A. Reid, 'The "iron roads" and "the happiness of the working classes": the early development and social significance of the railway excursion', *Journal of Transport History*, 3rd series, 17 (1996), 58; P. Brendon, *Thomas Cook* (London, 1991).

just before the First World War Maud Pember Reeves reported a fish fryer living in Kennington who walked every day to Finsbury Park and a bottle washer who walked to and from work daily in the north of London.[36] They were not unusual. The first important technical change in surface transport continued to rely on the horse but eased its burden by putting the bus on rails and calling it a tram. The effect was to double the burden the horse could draw,[37] so that trams carried up to forty seated passengers.[38] This was much in excess of the horse omnibus and thus reduced the operating cost per passenger. Of course, the capital costs of installing track were high and needed approval from the local authority, some of which were resistant to the disruption. The first commercial tram in Britain was opened in Liverpool docks in 1859 and was pioneered by W. J. Curtis and William Busby.[39] In 1860 Curtis laid his first line in London, along the Liverpool Road in Islington. However, horse trams were still expensive, costing 2d. per mile[40] and thus available for the middle class on a regular basis or as a novelty, rather than daily commuting, for workers. There was also much initial opposition to them, not merely from bus proprietors, but from other road users because in some cases the rail was raised above the surface of the road and caused an obstruction. It was the adoption of the flush rail which made the tramway acceptable.

There is much controversy over the effects of the 1870 Tramways Act. It was intended to simplify the procedure for obtaining permission for tramways by allowing the Board of Trade to authorise them by certificates which would not need parliamentary approval but merely be laid on the table of the two Houses of Parliament.[41] This procedure would have overridden any objections by local authorities. However, the 1870 act did not turn out as intended as a result of parliamentary complications. It continued to allow local authorities to prevent a scheme going ahead, and frontagers (property holders on the route) could also stop the tramway, if enough of them objected.[42] This was reinforced by the 1872 act.[43] Thus, this legislation made it more difficult to obtain approval rather than easing it. As Charles Harvey and Jon Press say, 'Tramway promotion was time-consuming and costly . . . regulation seriously handicapped the growth of urban transport.'[44]

[36] M. Pember Reeves, *Round About a Pound a Week* (London, 1913), pp. 40 and 198.
[37] Ochojna, 'The influence', 127.
[38] Tilling, *Kings*, p. 79; R. J. Buckley, *A History of Tramways from Horse to Rapid Transit* (Newton Abbot, 1975), pp. 7–8.
[39] C. E. Lee, 'The English street tramways of George Francis Train', *The Journal of Transport History*, I (1953), 20–7 and 97–108, which comprehensively demolishes Train's claims to have pioneered horse trams in Britain; Tilling, *Kings*, p. 78; Buckley, *History*, pp. 10–12.
[40] Lee, 'English', 99; Ochojna, 'The influence', 128–9.
[41] Barker and Robbins, *London Transport*, I, p. 191.
[42] *Ibid.*, p. 192; Ochojna, 'The influence', 136–7.
[43] Barker and Robbins, *London Transport*, I, p. 195.
[44] C. E. Harvey and J. Press, 'Sir George White and the urban transport revolution in Bristol 1875–1916', in C. E. Harvey and J. Press, eds., *Studies in the Business History of Bristol* (Bristol, 1988), p. 141.

Yet despite this setback, many historians agree that there was a boom in tramway promotions in the early 1870s. Richard Buckley suggests the act was 'the signal for a wave of promotions and construction'.[45] Harvey and Press state that 'a promotional boom followed' the 1870 act.[46] By 1877 there were forty tramway companies and about 215 miles (346 km) of track laid.[47] By 1890 nearly 1,000 miles (1,609 km) of tramway had been opened in Britain and Michael Thompson estimates the horse population employed in bus and tram haulage was about 280,000.[48] Reconciling these two views is not as difficult as it might seem. Despite the complicated process, the demand for tramways had reached a point where sufficient interests were reconciled to them. At the same time there were enough safeguards built in by the acts – the ability of local authorities to purchase after twenty-one years, the inability to sell concessions – to convince doubters that tramways might be a genuine service to the public rather than a new way of lining the promoters' pockets. This combined with the fact that in Britain 'private transport companies were forbidden to speculate in land or build houses'[49] meant tramway development was slower in Britain than some other countries, because transport promoters were unable to capture the increment in land values brought about by improved transport systems.[50] In comparison, in many other countries, such as America, the extension of transport networks was accompanied by land purchases by the service provider in order to reap the economic rent created by the rise in land values consequent upon the arrival of the tramway. In these cases flat rate fares encouraged travellers to go to the end of the line where the largest developmental gains were likely to be realised by the promoters.

Towards the end of the nineteenth century a number of developments came together to bring about regular use by working people of urban passenger transport. On the demand side average real wages were rising from the 1870s to the turn of the century, providing extra purchasing power for semi-luxuries such as a newspaper, tobacco or tram fares. At the same time working hours were reduced, giving a little more time in which to complete longer journeys to work. On the supply side there was a massive breakthrough with the application of electricity to the tram. Horse traction had placed a severe limit on capacity, cost reduction and speed. The average tramcar employed eleven horses which com-

---

[45] Buckley, *History* p. 12.   [46] Harvey and Press, 'Sir George White', p. 138.
[47] Ochojna, 'The influence', 138.
[48] P. S. Bagwell, *The Transport Revolution since 1770* (London, 1974), pp. 153–5; F. M. L. Thompson, 'Nineteenth-century horse sense', *Ec.HR*, 2nd series, 29 (1976), 80.
[49] R. Dennis, *English Industrial Cities of the Nineteenth Century* (Cambridge, 1984), p. 114.
[50] S. B. Warner, *Streetcar Suburbs: The Process of Growth in Boston, 1870–1900* (Cambridge, Mass., 1962); D. Ward, 'A comparative historical geography of streetcar suburbs in Boston, Massachusetts and Leeds, England, 1850–1920', *Annals of the Association of American Geographers*, 54 (1964), 477–89; G. Lowry, *Street Car Man: Tom Lowry and the Twin City Rapid Transit Company* (Minneapolis, 1979), p. 33. For an excellent summary of this debate see M. J. Daunton, 'Urban Britain', in T. R. Gourvish and A. O'Day, eds., *Later Victorian Britain, 1867–1900* (London, 1988), pp. 40–2.

prised well over half the operating costs of a tramway and the maximum speed was constrained to 6 miles (9.7 km) per hour.[51] In the very last years of the nineteenth century and early years of the twentieth a number of lines were electrified.[52] The 'first electrically operated public tramway using the trolley system in Britain' was that from Roundhay to Sheepscar in Leeds, opened in 1891.[53] The first electric tramway in the London area was that from Shepherds Bush along the Uxbridge Road to Acton and Kew Bridge operated by London United Tramways Ltd and opened in April 1901.[54] The crucial importance of electricity was to reduce the operating costs by about 30 per cent[55] and to increase the speed of the tram. Producing electricity was cheaper than feeding horses, and the electric tramcar carried greater numbers of passengers than the horse-drawn. Increasing the working speed augmented the time saved over walking. The capital costs were high, but the costs of electricity were often quite reasonable because trams provided a daytime demand to complement the normal peak evening and night-time load for lighting streets and later houses. By the turn of the century in Bristol, whereas fares on horse trams had averaged a little over 1d. a mile, those on electric trams were slightly under ¾d. a mile and cheap workman's fares about ⅓d. As a result of this reduction in real costs, the number of journeys per head rose from around eight per annum in the mid-1870s, to fifty-five in the mid-1890s, and over 130 by 1906.[56] By the last years before the First World War most towns and cities had a network of electric tramways easing the burden of getting to and from work for the ordinary people, and they were intensively used by them.

In retrospect the domination of the electric tramway might seem inevitable, but there were experiments with forms of traction other than horse and electricity. Steam was tried on the Clyde and in Wantage in the 1860s, and in the 1880s the North London Tramway system tried it for several years as did the line between Stamford Hill and Edmonton and that between Wortley and Kirkstall in Leeds.[57] However, steam trams did not catch on as they were noisier, dirtier and required a separate large power car which was a less efficient method. Gas trams were tried in Lytham St Anne's and Trafford Park, compressed air in Stratford in east London, and cables were used at Streatham, Highgate Hill and in Edinburgh.[58] However, each of these modes of propulsion was found inferior to electricity, either because of clumsiness of operation, problems of carrying

[51] Buckley, *History*, pp. 22–4.

[52] For example, Glasgow electrified its network from 1901: M. Simpson, 'Urban transport and the development of Glasgow's West End', *Journal of Transport History*, new series, 1 (1972), 151.

[53] G. C. Dickinson, 'The development of suburban road passenger transport in Leeds, 1840–95', *Journal of Transport History*, 4 (1960), 218.

[54] J. H. Price, 'London's first electric tramway', *Journal of Transport History*, 3 (1958), 205.

[55] Ochojna, 'The influence', 144.   [56] Harvey and Press, 'Sir George White', pp. 152–3.

[57] *Ibid.*, p. 141; Dickinson, 'The development', 218; Buckley, *History*, pp. 26–44.

[58] D. L. G. Hunter, 'The Edinburgh cable tramways', *Journal of Transport History*, 1 (1954), 170–84.

fuel or some other complication. In addition, the tramway was not welcomed everywhere. Although some authors have seen the trams as symbolically important, tying the various districts of an urban area together with metal tracks and reducing the difficulty and time required to travel from one neighbourhood to another, they could also be divisive. There was a split almost on class grounds between anti- and pro-tram lobbies. The workers saw them as cheap transit systems allowing them more choice of location and an easier journey to work. Middle-class individuals opposed them for the same reason. Thus Harrow School objected to tramway proposals from 1899 to 1906 on the grounds of noise, indiscipline and objection to the growth of 'small houses', that is working-class housing.[59] Similarly, the university opposed tram tracks in University Avenue, Glasgow, ostensibly because the vibration would upset their delicate instruments, but really because they feared the intrusion of higher density housing.[60] Ealing council resisted the extension into Ealing of the tramline between Shepherds Bush and Acton, opened in 1876. It was essentially on class grounds that it would bring a working-class, jerry-built element into a middle-class neighbourhood.[61] Its opposition was successful until 1901 when London United Tramways extended their line to Southall. Clifton, a middle-class area of Bristol, rejected an extension of the tram network into their area in 1878 and 1880.[62]

Criticism is levelled at Britain for her slow adoption of electrified tramways compared to other countries, especially the United States. This may be part of the search for examples of Britain's relative decline in the late nineteenth century, but, objectively, there is something in the charge. David Ward, comparing Boston, Massachusetts, and Leeds, demonstrated that they were roughly equal sized in terms of population, yet in 1916 Leeds had 114 miles (183 km) of track whereas Boston had over 300 miles (483 km). The former carried about 94 million passengers, the latter more than three times as many.[63] This experience can be generalised. In 1898 the whole of England had 618 miles (994 km) of electric tram tracks whereas Boston alone had 316 miles (508 km).[64] This slow adoption of electric tramways is accepted; the causes are still a subject of debate. Ward stressed that Boston experienced a greater growth of population than Leeds in crucial decades when electrification was possible. Boston began electrification in 1887, whereas Leeds started in 1894. Ward explained this by the characteristics of the two markets. Boston enjoyed a large influx of Maritime Canadians 'who had the means and preference for suburban living' from the late 1880s.[65] This gave a boost to Bostonian tramways. Leeds, on the other hand,

[59] T. May, 'Road passenger transport in Harrow in the nineteenth and early twentieth centuries', *Journal of Transport History*, 1 (1971), 30–3.   [60] Simpson, 'Urban transport', 151.
[61] P. Hounsell, *Ealing and Hanwell Past* (London, 1991), p. 127.
[62] Harvey and Press, 'Sir George White', p. 145.
[63] Ward, 'A comparative historical geography', 477–89.   [64] *Ibid.*, p. 485.   [65] *Ibid.*, pp. 481–6.

experienced emigration in some decades such as 1900–10 and had insufficient population with the means and taste for suburban living, terrace housing at high density being their effective preference, whereas Bostonians preferred semi- or detached houses at lower density.

John McKay agreed that Britain was slow to adopt electrification but blamed it entirely on the 1870 act, already mentioned.[66] It had authorised twenty-one-year leases, after which local authorities were allowed to buy the system at the price of the assets, no consideration being given for goodwill. As there had been a boom in tramway construction in the early 1870s, these leases began expiring in the mid-1890s. Thus the private companies operating the horse-drawn systems were reluctant to electrify their tracks with no guarantee of a lease renewal to allow them to recoup what would be very heavy capital expenditure. Thus McKay suggests electrification had to await municipalisation and was aided by the ability of city corporations to raise large sums at relatively low interest rates. In this view McKay is supported by Vesey Knox writing in 1901.[67] He argued the 1870 act was 'the most disastrous legislative experiment . . . during the last half century'. Being published in the *Economic Journal*, his views must command some respect, but the article is high on assertion and invective and low on evidence. How can these two views be reconciled? Did the legal framework in Britain slow down electrification or was it the different nature of the market in the UK compared to the USA? It is tempting to weld the two together and suggest that lower income levels in Britain, a tradition of living in city centres, and the institutional framework combined to retard electrification. In the USA, however, higher real wages, a more individualistic tradition, and lack of constraining legislation, combined with the ability to garner economic rent by speculating in land purchase and property development to encourage rapid electrification and an extensive rather than an intensive network. What is needed is more research into the circumstances of particular cities, in both Great Britain and the United States, to determine the relative importance of the various factors mentioned above. Alternatively perhaps a cliometrician can devise an economic model to demonstrate that Britain's apparent lag was completely rational and efficient.

In London there were also the underground railways. The size of London's geographic spread and its population go a long way to explaining why London was the first city in the world to have such systems and why few cities followed London's lead and that at some remove in time. The first underground railway, the Metropolitan, built on the cut and cover basis and using steam locomotives, was opened in 1863 from Paddington to Farringdon.[68] The Metropolitan

[66] J. P. McKay, *Tramways and Trolleys* (Princeton, 1976), pp. 168–78.
[67] V. Knox, 'The economic effects of the Tramways Act of 1870', *Economic Journal*, 11 (1901), 492–510.
[68] This paragraph relies on: Barker and Robbins, *London Transport*, 1; T. C. Barker, 'Tube centenary: 100 years of underground electric railways', *LJ*, 15 (1990), 160–3; M. D. Reilly, 'Urban electric railway management and operation in Britain and America, 1900–1914', *UHY* (1989), 22–37.

District Railway soon followed this lead and work on the Inner Circle began. However, steam locomotives meant smoke, soot and black spots and were a limitation to this mode of transport. Two breakthroughs were made in the last decades of the nineteenth century. The first was the discovery that London clay facilitated the driving of deep level tubes built of steel rings bolted together. This had the benefit of avoiding the disruption to buried sewers, gas mains, etc., and minimising subsidence risk to existing properties. The other innovation was the use of electric traction. Initially, the first tube, the City and South London as it became known, intended to use cable traction. However, by 1890 when it opened, the directors had been convinced of the efficiency of electric locomotion. The Joint Select Committee of 1892, as Jack Simmons has pointed out, validated this decision and imposed it on the plethora of schemes which rapidly followed. These lines made up the basic underground system until the 1960s.[69] However, these schemes took some time to move from paper plans to iron reality for they required large amounts of capital which were not easily raised. By about 1907 the vast majority had been constructed. The tubes had a great impact on the capital. From the start the Paddington to Farringdon line offered cheap, early morning workmen's trains and the tubes were required by the LCC to 'furnish an adequate number of cheap and convenient trains'[70] so that mass urban transit in London became a reality before the First World War. In addition, the tube network shrank the size of the city and served as a symbol of the holism of the metropolis, a point we shall return to later. The effect of electrification on the original cut and cover lines, which soon followed suit, was to allow them to improve and expand the service offered, for they were more sales maximisers than profit maximisers and perceived this as a way of combating electric tramway competition.[71] These policies may not have aided shareholder returns but they did facilitate urban development.

The financing of British urban transport improvements was a curious mixture of private and public, domestic and foreign. Given the prevailing government philosophy and the abundance of capital in the first country to industrialise, the railways and canals were virtually wholly privately financed in the UK whereas many other nations relied to a much greater extent on government expertise, finance or land. So it was with horse buses, horse trams and the early cut and cover underground railways. The British government put no money into them; private entrepreneurs found the capital and took the risk, following the tradition established with turnpike roads. However, the 1870 act empowered local authorities to purchase tramcar systems after twenty-one-years' operation in private hands, and many availed themselves of this opportunity. Even earlier some councils, like Bristol, built their own tramways and then hired them out to private operators. In the 1890s there was much municipalisation, so that by

---

[69] J. Simmons, 'The pattern of tube railways in London. A note on the joint select committee of 1892', *Journal of Transport History*, 8 (1966), 234–40. [70] *Ibid.*, 238.
[71] Reilly, 'Urban electric', 23–5.

1905 there were more towns with municipally owned tramways than in private hands.[72]

The logic of municipalisation sprang from a combination of factors. Some local councillors espoused Fabian views on public ownership, some saw the provision of services to ratepayers as a legitimate role of local government.[73] The apparent profitability of tramways encouraged some to believe that any surpluses could be employed to reduce the rate burden, while others saw it as an opportunity to improve the conditions of the employees, and yet others to provide the passengers with a better service. One of the benefits of municipalisation was that when electrification became available in the 1890s the capital expenditure involved was raised more cheaply and easily by local authorities than private companies.

Once having become involved in tram provision, it was logical for councils to provide trolley bus services too, to feed their tramway system, and then later bus services, if for no other reason than to fend off private interlopers. Thus ratepayers' money went into the improvement of local transport. Earlier, local authorities had spent a large portion of their income on maintaining transport provision. For, as Robert Millward and Sally Sheard have shown, throughout the last thirty years before the First World War, local authorities in aggregate spent more on road provision than they did on education, public health or the police. Road building accounted for about 17 per cent of total expenditure.[74] In part this may reflect the expansion in urban areas and the concomitant need for more road infrastructure, but it also suggests intensive use of existing roads so that they required repair, or widening and strengthening. The cycle lobby pressed in this direction, forming the Road Improvement Association in 1886 and the Cyclists' Touring Club, which had a membership of 60,000 in 1899.[75]

Foreign involvement in British urban transport provision is surprising. It might have been anticipated that the 'workshop of the world' which was also the world's capital market would lead rather than follow in urban transit systems. As it was, horse bus operations received a fillip in the mid-1850s when the Compagnie Générale des Omnibus de Londres, established with French capital, endeavoured to monopolise London bus traffic. It met with indifferent success, to the extent that in 1859 it was transformed into a British company.[76] The French seem to have perceived earlier than the British that network industries were most efficient as local monopolies and that competition could lead to a deterioration in services and some public danger.

[72] Harvey and Press, 'Sir George White', p. 153.

[73] J. R. Kellett, 'Municipal socialism, enterprise and trading in the Victorian city', *UHY* (1978), 36–45.

[74] R. Millward and S. Sheard, 'The urban fiscal problem, 1870–1914: government expenditure and finance in England and Wales', *Ec.HR*, 2nd series, 48 (1995), 505–6.

[75] J. B. F. Earle, *Black Top: A History of the British Flexible Roads Industry* (Oxford, 1974), p. 10.

[76] Barker and Robbins, *London Transport*, I, p. 69.

The importance of foreign capital and enterprise reasserted itself in the 1860s when horse tramways began to be constructed. In this case it was Americans, led by G. F. Train, who mounted the incursion. Although his extravagant claims have been largely discounted and his preference for the raised step rail was a mistake, he introduced some American capital into the undertaking.[77] The Americans had already introduced horse trams in Philadelphia and saw no reason why it should not be as successful and profitable in the UK. This lead of the Americans in urban rapid transit systems was further demonstrated in the 1890s when electrification was undertaken, for the method adopted was essentially that introduced in Richmond, Virginia, by F. J. Sprague.[78]

In a similar vein, although the early cut and cover underground lines were entirely British financed, when it came to the true tubes – the deep-level underground railways – American finance and enterprise were crucial to their construction and success.[79] Chief among the financiers was C. T. Yerkes from Chicago. The explanation of American involvement lies essentially in the earlier adoption of electrification for street railways in the USA and the profits to be made from promotion more than operation. It was thought that these profits could be replicated in Britain using similar methods, which were not free from criticism of bribery and corruption. Thus America encountered and solved problems of urban transport a little earlier than Britain, perhaps because her population and economy were growing even faster than Britain's, and then tried to repeat the financial gains by bringing the new technologies to Europe.

(iv) THE SPRAWL TO SUBURBIA

If the late nineteenth century saw the beginnings of mass urban transit allowing the skilled workers to live further away from their workplace, they were only emulating the previous practice of the middle classes. The precise timing depended on the size of the city, but the middle classes began the move out of the city centres to the suburbs. Michael Simpson dates this in Glasgow from the 1850s[80] while Barke suggests the process began in Newcastle in the 1860s.[81] The difference in timing is probably explained by differences in absolute size. There are a number of common causal factors. On the push side the city centres were becoming increasingly noisy, dirty and dangerous. The perception of cities as unhealthy was reinforced by comparative death rates. The growth of horse-drawn traffic added to noise pollution. Horses also soiled the roadway, making work for the 'crossing sweeper'.[82] There were some forces working in the

---

[77] *Ibid.*, pp. 178–84.   [78] Buckley, *History*, pp. 10–12.
[79] T. C. Barker and M. Robbins, *A History of London Transport*, vol. II: *The Twentieth Century to 1970* (London, 1974) pp. 61–84.   [80] Simpson, 'Urban transport', 149.
[81] Barke, 'Middle-class journey'.
[82] Jane Jacobs quotes an excellent description of the noise and mess of horse transport in London in 1890: Jacobs, *Death and Life*, pp. 341–2.

opposite direction. The advent of the electric tram reduced marginally the amount of horse droppings. More important was the introduction of surface dressings. Granite setts were noisy, slippery and difficult to wash down, so they represented a pollution problem. Wood paving was tried but was also criticised for being slippery and because of its porosity it did not improve the insanitary conditions. As a result of the unsatisfactory nature of these road conditions, in 1869 the City of London experimented with compressed mastic asphalt in Threadneedle Street.[83] This had the advantage of reducing noise substantially, as well as providing an impermeable surface which was easy to wash down and so reduced the fly and droppings problem. Despite new road building, traffic jams continued and worsened, so that the *Building News* of 1874 could talk of 'the daily deadlock from forenoon to evening' on London Bridge and its approaches.[84] Crime and civil disturbance seemed to be worse in the cities than the rural areas. Air quality, with domestic coal fires adding to the smoke and specks of steam engine boilers, was poor and in windless conditions could be appalling.[85] In addition, as commercial activities increased the merchants, retailers and offices needed additional space, and hence moved into previously residential districts often bidding up the rents, making it too expensive for domestic use.[86] Thus the urban middle classes looked for more salubrious surroundings and secured them in the suburbs. Here they found cleaner air – especially if they moved westward and hence upwind of the prevailing airstream – more space and perhaps a neat garden, which aped in miniature the upper-class estate, some protection from disease, dirt and crime and a greater degree of privacy. The 'vulnerable' wife and children were placed in safety, leaving the 'stronger' patriarch to do battle daily with the corrupting city. Thus was the Victorian patriarchal family preserved.

The ability of the middle classes to afford both the cost of transport and the extra time taken was important. For the upper middle class initially this might well take the form of a private carriage and hence the construction of a new turnpike road might lead to the building of suburban villas with stabling attached. This was what Simpson found in the West End of Glasgow.[87] Here the construction of the Great Western Road as a turnpike in the early 1840s was ahead of residential development and led to a boom in house building of the substantial sort with stables. This move was emulated at a later date by the lower middle classes. The Highbury New Park estate in north London, developed from the 1850s, was intended for middle-class commuters to the City. It was built in the expectation that residents would use their own carriage or the North London Railway from Canonbury to Fenchurch Street, or from 1865 Broad

[83] Earle, *Black Top*, p. 9.
[84] D. J. Olsen, *The Growth of Victorian London* (London, 1976), pp. 303–6.
[85] H. T. Bernstein, 'The mysterious disappearance of Edwardian London fog', *LJ*, 2 (1975), 189–99.
[86] Dyos, 'Workmen's fares', 4; Ochojna, 'The influence', 132. [87]Simpson, 'Urban transport', 149.

Street, at a first-class fare of 6d.[88] This was obviously aimed at upper-middle-class occupants. As white-collar jobs proliferated with the growth of the service sector, especially central and local government employment, retailing and clerical and administrative posts, so more workers became salaried with a greater security and regularity of payment and status. Thus the Pooters, so scathingly portrayed, were not atypical in their search for material refinement,[89] he using the bus to travel to the City,[90] although their son for a while aspired to a pony and trap.[91] Emulation of the values of their 'social superiors' was a strong spur to moving from the city centres.

Such moves were facilitated by the construction and extension of horse-drawn and electric trams but there is some debate over how far these and other transport systems, such as motor buses in the early twentieth century and the underground railways in London, were causal of urbanisation and how far they were a response to it. H. J. Dyos, for example, in his pioneering study of the development of Victorian Camberwell[92] was unable to be certain of the contribution of transport to the growth of particular neighbourhoods. Although he devotes some space to explaining the development of transport facilities to the area,[93] he has to conclude rather lamely that 'few daily travellers can have been totally indifferent to the length and cost of the journey to work'.[94] Similarly, Thompson's study of Hampstead places no great importance on the development of public transport systems as a causal factor in its growth.[95] To demonstrate that this was not solely a metropolitan feature, Simpson's study of Glasgow's West End can be cited. He states: 'most forms of transport followed rather than led suburban development' and 'in no case did either [tramways and railways] build lines and stations ahead of substantial urban growth, and termini were always located behind the western edge of the development area'.[96] As Donald Olsen said of John Kellett's major study of five cities, 'railway extensions usually followed rather than preceded suburban development, and at best served to reinforce population movements already in progress'.[97] This view can be bolstered by consideration of the motivation of private transport businesses. Such firms wished to provide services only where there was a high probability of a substantial traffic to generate ample revenue and hence profits. This was likely where there was already residential development, while the opposite was true of currently unsettled areas. Even where the tram or tube was operated by a local authority the same rule applied, for the municipalities saw such activities as partly a service to the electorate but also as a contributor of surpluses which kept down the level of the rates and ensured their re-election. Richard Dennis concluded

---

[88] T. Hinchcliffe, 'Highbury New Park: a nineteenth-century middle class suburb', *LJ*, 7 (1981), 29–44.   [89] George and Weedon Grossmith, *The Diary of a Nobody* (London, 1894).
[90] *Ibid.*, p. 36.   [91] *Ibid.*, p. 164.   [92] H. J. Dyos, *Victorian Suburb* (Leicester, 1961).
[93] *Ibid.*, pp. 60–80.   [94] *Ibid.*, p. 63.   [95] F. M. L. Thompson, *Hampstead* (London, 1974).
[96] Simpson, 'Urban transport', 146.   [97] Olsen, *Growth*, p. 294.

that transport extensions were probably not causal, but rather that for the average worker rising expectations of housing, combined with decreasing quantities of suitable residential property in the centre, obliged them to undertake longer journeys to work.[98] In this view transport responded to other moves for a shift to suburbia and then facilitated its furtherance. G. C. Dickinson and C. J. Longley believed that the combination of electrification and municipalisation of the tramways led to 'the breakthrough to cheap popular fares', so that by 1913 1d. fares, affordable by the average workingman, were giving 2 miles (3.2 km) of travel in the larger cities.[99] What is more difficult to estimate is the extent to which the proximity of a tramline led builders to construct housing in the anticipation that the tramway would be extended once the traffic justified it. In some cases the combination of existing forms of transport plus anticipated developments in them was enough to encourage house building. Thus the White Hart Lane estate in north London was built gradually between 1903 and 1915 by the LCC as it was within walking distance of two Great Eastern railway stations offering workmen's fares, there were cheap trams in nearby Tottenham High Road, and a tube was projected – the North-East London Railway.[100] The provision of electric trams also acted as a spur to improving the railway service for commuters, for electric trams were often more frequent and cheaper than the mainline railways. In Newcastle, for example, within a year of the corporation operating electric trams the North-Eastern Railway (NER) lost about 4 million short-distance passenger journeys. As a result the NER began electrification of its suburban lines, especially to the coast at Whitley Bay and Monkseaton, so encouraging the growth of these towns as dormitories for Newcastle.[101]

(v) IMPACT ON SHAPE

As well as having an effect on the size and scale of towns, transport modes had an impact on the shape of urban centres. They did this directly in their demand for space within the urban environment. The building of new roads or the widening and improvement of existing ones required land and usually that meant the demolition of some of the buildings on it. To minimise cost and objections it made sense to drive such 'improvements' through low quality housing where it could be claimed that the road was sweeping away unhygienic slums containing criminals and beggars.[102] Thus Victoria Street, New Oxford Street and

[98] Dennis, *English Industrial Cities*, p. 140.
[99] Kellett, 'Municipal socialism', 36–45; G. C. Dickinson and C. J. Longley, 'The coming of cheap transport – study of tramway fares on municipal systems in British provincial towns, 1900–14', *Transport History*, 6 (1973), 107–27.
[100] R. Thorne, 'The White Hart Lane estate: an LCC venture in suburban development', *LJ*, 12 (1986), 80–8.
[101] K. Hoole, 'Railway electrification on Tyneside, 1902–67', *Transport History*, 2 (1969), 258–63.
[102] Olsen, *Growth*, p. 296.

Regent Street all demolished rookeries and slums.[103] Patricia Malcolmson, examining some notorious areas of west London in the middle of the century, found many occupants had migrated there from the slum clearances accompanying the construction of Drury Lane, Strand and New Oxford Street.[104] A similar effect was felt by the vast amount of railway building. The tracks required a swathe of land and the stations and termini compounded this greed for ground. Michael Robbins has calculated that there were fifteen termini and about 300 mainline stations in London.[105] Dyos, in a pioneering article, claimed there were about seventy railway schemes between 1853 and 1901 which displaced about 76,000 people in London alone.[106] At the same time, he estimated, a further 28,500 people were displaced in London for road improvement and dock extension schemes.[107] Henry Binford in a study of the Charing Cross Railway, shows that this 2 mile (3.2 km) railway required the acquisition of several hundred houses containing between 1,500 and 4,000 people. The estimates of Dyos are probably minimum levels for London. If the rest of the country could be included, the numbers would rise appreciably.

The effect of these clearances is still disputed. The view of the transport firms was that they were helping to clear squalid sinks of iniquity, and that those displaced could move to the healthier suburbs. As Dyos has argued, there is an alternative view.[108] As a result of road and railway construction overcrowding increased in adjoining areas and the lower supply of houses bid up the rents which had to be paid, worsening the situation of the lowest classes. This is to be explained by the large amount of casual labour which militated against workers living far from their place of work, as well as the cost and time involved in commuting.

The impact on the towns was dramatic. Not only did railway companies become among the larger urban landowners, but the railways altered the status and value of the land through which they passed. Land located immediately adjacent to railway viaducts, goods yards and stations was affected by the noise, smoke and traffic congestion so that it was often dominated by less salubrious trades and dwellings. Elsewhere, proximity to a railway station pushed up land values and hence rentals. The railway lines became boundaries, defining neighbourhoods or zones with different social status. The phrase 'to be born on the wrong side of the tracks' came into common usage. François Bédarida, in his study of Poplar, showed how docks, canals and railways cut the area into 'tiny

---

[103] H. J. Dyos, 'Urban transformation: a note on the objects of street improvement in Regency and early Victorian London', *International Review of Social History*, 2 (1957), 262–4.

[104] Malcolmson, 'Getting a living', 31.

[105] M. Robbins, 'London railway stations', *LJ*, 1 (1975), 247.

[106] Dyos, 'Railways and housing', 14.

[107] H. J. Dyos, 'Some social costs of railway building in London', *Journal of Transport History*, new series, 3 (1957), 29.   [108] Dyos, 'Railways and housing', 14–15.

neighbourhood units isolated from each other by these major physical obstacles'.[109] He believed this had the effect of strengthening solidarity within these separate areas so that they became more cohesive and mutually supporting. However, outsiders were objects of suspicion and resentment. The persistence of transport lines as boundaries in this area was shown after 1870 when school board blocks were defined by the lines of the railways and canals. Daunton, looking at Cardiff, found that the Great Western, Taff Vale and Rhymney Railways cut the city up into districts, which were separate in character and some of which, such as Cathays and Splott, were socially cohesive.[110]

New road building had a similar importance. These new wide thoroughfares were lined by the most fashionable shops built in the most splendid architectural style allowing the middle classes to shop and move between home and office or theatres, shops and other fashionable areas. However, behind these grand façades the courts, alleys and tenements often continued to exist so that the new thoroughfares became lines of security for the middle classes allowing them to travel without having their sensibilities affected by the squalid conditions of the majority of the workers. In this way they were encouraged to ignore the social problems which seethed a stone's throw from their secure route. The railways had the opposite effect. By cutting through working-class districts they forced their passengers to contemplate the meanness and squalor. By carrying travellers at roof top level on viaducts they gave them a panoramic view of mean back yards, crowded cottages and squalid settlements. Thus the middle-class traveller – the MP shuttling between his constituency and the Palace of Westminster, the judge out on the circuit, the scholar returning to his university – had to acknowledge the problem and was persuaded of the need for action.[111]

Transport improvements also had an impact on the aesthetics and feel of the city. New roads, as already explained, provided secure access between fashionable parts of the city to the middle class and hence raised status and prestige. The railways were much more visually intrusive with their viaducts, embankments and bridges cutting across the visual landscapes. Some of Gustav Doré's prints demonstrate this clearly with the railway running across the centre of the print, elevated and very evident, like an idol or deity. As Olsen has put it, the new transport systems 'represented the most startling novelties in the [urban] environment. They contributed not only visual shocks but movement, unfamiliar noises and smells, and altered both the pace and rhythm of urban life.'[112] The trams were little less dramatic taking up the middle of the road with their tracks and imposing a discipline on parking habits. This was compounded by electrification when poles and wires, well above eye level and therefore visible

[109] F. Bédarida, 'Urban growth and social structure in nineteenth-century Poplar', *LJ*, 1 (1975), 166.
[110] Daunton, *Coal Metropolis*, pp. 141–2.
[111] J. R. Kellett, *Railways and Victorian Cities* (London, 1979), pp. 337–43.
[112] Olsen, *Growth*, p. 294.

from some distance, festooned the city's main streets. By comparison the tubes, hidden underground, intruded much less.

Transport systems also had an architectural presence in the town. The most grandiose and visual were the railway companies' mainline termini. These were far more than functional. Some, such as Charing Cross, employed the associated hotel as a classical façade to hide the less attractive business end. Others, such as Euston or St Pancras, were ornate, demonstrating the wealth, power and prestige of the railway company.[113] The Doric arch at Euston was particularly symbolic, denoting the victory of the railway company in its struggle over opposition, and the towers on some stations indicated the soaring aspirations of an *arriviste* industry in its search for respect and prestige.[114] As Geoffrey Channon has shown, London termini were not necessarily built for sound economic reasons but for prestige and 'political' purposes.[115] They were often 'monuments to the self confidence, determination and pugnacity of their builders'.[116] As Robbins has reminded us, stations needed to be seen as part of their function of attracting people and goods,[117] but many went well beyond this, building in the currently fashionable architectural style to emphasise the solidity and respectability of the enterprise – gothic and classical – though the latter was much criticised by Pugin and others for putting form above function.[118] Because of their centrality in urban life, they became one of the nodal points of the city, like the town hall, the central library or the cathedral, and as such places for meetings and rendezvous, where a whole gamut of emotions was displayed from joy to sorrow, as partings and reunions occurred.[119] Later, tube stations were often built by fashionable architects, especially those on the outer arms of the Piccadilly and District Railways such as Park Royal and Southgate, both designed by Charles Holden, in a modern style to emphasise the modernity, speed and comfort of the method of transport and to entice passengers.[120] Central bus and coach stations, such as Victoria in London, were also designed to indicate the modernity of the mode of conveyance and so broke from the classical or gothic forms associated with the railway stations, going for the simpler, cleaner aerodynamic lines that were mirrored in the buses and coaches which plied from there.

Thus in a number of periods the buildings of transport systems acted to impress, entice and act as metaphors of the companies that created them. They

---

[113] *Ibid.*, p. 92.

[114] J. Richards and J. M. MacKenzie, *The Railway Station* (Oxford, 1986), pp. 23–4.

[115] G. Channon, 'A nineteenth-century investment decision: the Midland Railway's London extension', *Ec.HR*, 25 (1972), 448–70.   [116] Olsen, *Growth*, p. 93.

[117] Robbins, 'London railway', 241.

[118] E. Jones, *Industrial Architecture in Britain, 1750–1939* (London, 1985), pp. 112–14.

[119] Richards and MacKenzie, *Railway Station*, pp. 6–7; G. Biddle and J. Spence, *The British Railway Station* (Newton Abbot, 1977).

[120] G. Weightman and S. Humphries, *The Making of Modern London 1914–1939* (London, 1984), pp. 70–2 and 91.

could also be seen as symbols. The mainline railway stations were symbols of escape from the crowded smoky urban centres to the seaside or the cleaner country.[121] Later, the underground employed leading designers to create posters which talked of parks, riversides, woods and hills as 'London's lungs' and by extension the tube lines which conveyed one there were symbols of escape to these rural idylls. The logo, approved by Frank Pick for the underground, installed on the inside and outside of stations, on posters and maps, became very well recognised and acted to symbolise the unity of the Greater London area, eventually extending well beyond the LCC area and breaking down some of the concept of London as a collection of villages, stressing the tube as a shrinker of distances and a method of linking and integrating the various districts. Transport nodes also acted as loci of attention. They were places to meet friends, to dawdle or to drink while waiting for a train or bus. Thus around these focal points grew up ancillary services such as the railway station bookstall and buffet. If people were congregating and waiting at these locations it provided an opportunity to sell them a good or a service. The placing of a bus or train stop encouraged the appearance of shops or kiosks selling newspapers, sweets and tobacco. Tube stations were often the centre of a block of shops, or were the site of a pitch for flower sellers, shoe repairers or dry cleaners. The large flow of travellers through these loci acted as magnets to other small retailers anxious to provide goods or services to this passing trade. Thus nodes on the transport network became important points for social and commercial interaction. Coach and bus stations served similar roles between the wars. As Frank Pick explained, when advising the Soviets on the construction of the Moscow metro system, the stations should be centres 'at which other public services might be rendered – post offices, telephones, police call boxes, and public lavatories at surface level'.[122]

Nor should transport systems be ignored as employers of labour within urban centres. By the end of the nineteenth century a large number of workers were directly employed as carters, tram drivers, railwaymen, etc. Bédarida found over 30 per cent of the working population of Poplar were directly engaged in the transport industries in 1851 and although this had dropped by 1901 it was still over a quarter.[123] Malcolmson, examining the slums of Victorian Kensington, stressed the employment created by public transport businesses such as the London General Omnibus Company which built a stable and smithy in Goreham Place in 1882 and the Central London Railway which opened a goods yard nearby. Barker hinted at the scale of employment created by the Metropolitan Railway and the Great Central Railway when they built engine sheds, repair works and associated sidings at Neasden and then built several

[121] Olsen, *Growth*, pp. 86 and 313; Simmons, *Railway in Town*, pp. 236–9 and 245–68.
[122] M. Robbins, 'London Underground and Moscow Metro', *Journal of Transport History*, 3rd series, 18 (1997), 49.   [123] Bédarida, 'Urban growth', 171.

hundred workmen's cottages for their employees.[124] This was carried to its extreme when transport firms created new towns which grew up around work-shops or railway nodal points, such as Crewe, Swindon, Wolverton or Doncaster.[125] Here the size, scale and shape of the town was determined by the transport undertaking so that rows of similar terraced houses dominated some to give a solidly working-class look and feel. Swindon, for example, was developed by the Great Western Railway as an 'engine establishment' from 1841 when its population was about 2,000. By 1900 it was around 40,000 largely as a result of the expansion of railway employment. Despite vigorous house building, demand always exceeded supply, resulting in severe overcrowding, high death rates and lagging provision of public amenities.[126] Similarly dock companies could dominate port cities, as Sarah Palmer shows (see Chapter 4).

(vi) INTERWAR ARTERIAL ROADS AND RIBBON DEVELOPMENT

The interwar years saw a building boom on an unprecedented scale.[127] Something in the region of 220,000 houses were built on average every year between 1920 and 1939.[128] Although a little of this took place within the exist-ing cities, for example slum clearance and renewal, most perforce had to be outside on green-field sites thus extending the sprawl and scale of urban centres. This centrifugal tendency was aggravated by the continued voracity of com-merce for city-centre office locations. The flight to suburbia discussed in a pre-vious section continued and was speeded up. These estates were not built solely for private ownership. Local authorities played a much greater part: about 35 per cent of all new houses were built for them and hence popularly dubbed 'council houses'.[129] For instance the Watling estate, between Edgware and Mill Hill, was built between 1924 and the 1930s for the LCC. As most of the residents – 18,000 by 1930 – depended on jobs in the centre of town, they needed a frequent, cheap and rapid means of returning there. This was provided by the Cricklewood to Edgware tram, and the Hampstead to Edgware tube where Hendon Station was

[124] Malcolmson, 'Getting a living', 39; Barker, 'The Metropolitan', 38–56.
[125] Simmons, *Railway in Town*, pp. 171–95; D. K. Drummond, *Crewe: Railway Town, Company and People 1840–1914* (Aldershot, 1995); P. S. Bagwell, *Doncaster* (Doncaster, 1991); W. H. Chaloner, *The Social and Economic Development of Crewe, 1780–1923* (Manchester, 1950); B. J. Turton, 'The railway towns of southern England', *Transport History*, 2 (1969), 105–35; R. Barker, 'The concept of the railway town and the growth of Darlington, 1801–1911: a note', *Transport History*, 3 (1970), 283–92.
[126] K. Hudson, 'The early years of the railway community in Swindon', *Transport History*, 1 (1968), 130–52.
[127] H. W. Richardson and D. H. Aldcroft, *Building in the British Economy between the Wars* (London, 1968). [128] Mitchell and Dean, *Abstract*, p. 239.
[129] M. J. Daunton, ed., *Councillors and Tenants* (Leicester, 1984).

opened in 1923 and Burnt Oak in 1924.[130] In addition some firms continued to build homes for their workers such as the Great Western estate in North Acton and the Guinness Company on Park Royal.[131] The causes of the exodus from the city centre to the outskirts were similar to those of the late nineteenth and early twentieth centuries: living standards were rising to the extent that artisans could contemplate buying a cottage in the suburbs on a mortgage from a building society, the cities were perceived as crowded and unclean, whereas the suburbs appeared spacious, salubrious and safe.

Transport facilities, whether built ahead of development or following it, were a crucial factor and the baton of front runner moved away from the rail and tramway to motor vehicles. The first motor bus service to operate in the UK was in Edinburgh in 1898. The first in London was in 1899 between Charing Cross and Victoria.[132] Tillings, who had been major operators of horse buses and trams, bought their first motor bus in 1902. Progress was slow initially as reliability was not high, whereas costs were, but by 1910 there were more motor buses than horse buses in London.[133] Bristol Corporation bought Thornycroft buses in 1905, essentially to feed into tram routes.[134] The advantage of the motor bus over the horse bus was its greater power and therefore speed and acceleration and its lower running costs once technical progress had been made on tyres, fuel consumption, etc.[135] Compared to the tram the motor bus was more flexible and incurred much lower capital costs. For a while a hybrid between the tram and motor bus flourished. This was the trolley bus, combining the smoothness and lack of emissions of the tram with quieter operation than it or the motor bus. The first in Great Britain were introduced in 1911 in Leeds, Bradford and Aberdare.[136] They were less capital intensive than electric tramways and were often operated in areas at the end of the tram tracks where traffic was insufficient to justify extending the trams. Thus new, faster, cheaper forms of mass travel appeared on the streets of the cities allowing the workers to live further from their workplace. The interwar period was one of cheap fares, as Dickinson and Longley have demonstrated for Leeds,[137] but this relied heavily on cheap tram fares, perhaps because insufficient charge was made by municipalities for depreciation, rather than on buses. Features which improved operating costs were the

[130] R. Durant, *Watling: A Survey of Social Life on a New Housing Estate* (London, 1939).
[131] *VCH*, Middlesex, VII, pp. 13–14 and 173–4.
[132] Tilling, *Kings*, p. 89; J. Hibbs, *The Bus and Coach Industry* (London, 1975), p. 28.
[133] Hibbs, *The Bus*, pp. 28–9.   [134] Harvey and Press, 'Sir George White', p. 152.
[135] T. C. Barker and D. Gerhold, *The Rise and Rise of Road Transport, 1700–1990* (London, 1993), pp. 89–91.
[136] D. G. Tucker, 'The trolleybus proposal at Stroud, Glos. in 1903: the Stroud District and Cheltenham Tramways Bill', *Journal of Transport History*, 6 (1977), 40.
[137] G. C. Dickinson and C. J. Longley, 'Twopence to the terminus? A study of tram and bus fares in Leeds during the interwar period', *Journal of Transport History*, 3rd series, 7 (1986), 45–60.

use of double decker buses to increase revenue and diesel fuel to reduce costs, so that by 1932 bus costs were lower than trams.[138]

There was also a new competitor beginning to emerge to cheap public transport, namely private transport. For the middle classes the appearance of the cheap motor car, such as the Austin Seven or Morris Eight, costing about £100 new and much less second hand,[139] brought private transport within reach. Sales reps, factory managers, professionals and shop owners could aspire to commute by car. These remained too expensive for the ordinary workers[140] but they could afford bicycles, perhaps bought on hire purchase, and often covered significant mileage on them pedalling to work. By the interwar period a bicycle could be purchased for about £5, roughly two weeks' wages, and many were bought for commuting to work. For instance, in 1938 a standing conference on regional planning estimated that over one fifth of all workers on the Park Royal industrial estate arrived by bicycle.[141] This amounted to 6,500 each morning and each evening. The cheap bicycle was a great liberator of working-class youth. For the slightly better off and more daring there was the motor cycle, possibly with a sidecar, which was cheaper to purchase and operate than a car. 1929 saw the peak year ever in Britain for motorcycle registrations at nearly 750,000;[142] thereafter they declined as affluence led some to small cars and unemployment reduced demand at the other end. The growth of arterial roads, dual carriageways and bypasses was both effect of the growing number of motor vehicles and further encouragement.[143] The ability to commute longer distance freed the worker from locational tyranny and also provided the possibility of escape from the town to the country or the seaside at the weekend. The growing mobility also encouraged new shapes and styles within the towns in the form of garish petrol stations and garages,[144] and on the outskirts, large road houses which catered for those who drove and drank and ate. In addition, many of the houses built in the 1930s on the more affluent estates were equipped with their own garage – a nursery

---

[138] *Ibid.*, 54–5

[139] R. J. Wyatt, *The Austin Seven: The Motor for the Million, 1922–1939* (Newton Abbot, 1972); R. A. Church and M. Miller, 'The big three: competition, management and marketing in the British motor industry, 1922–1939', in B. E. Supple, ed., *Essays in British Business History* (Oxford, 1977), pp. 163–86.

[140] S. Bowden and P. Turner, 'Some cross section evidence on the determinants of the diffusion of car ownership in the interwar UK economy', *Business History*, 35 (1993), 55–69.

[141] PRO, HLG 52/746, report of 18 November 1938; *Acton Gazette*, 18 October 1935.

[142] Mitchell and Deane, *Abstract*, p. 230; S. Koerner, 'The British motor-cycle industry during the 1930s', *Journal of Transport History*, 16 (1995), 55–76.

[143] Bagwell, *Transport Revolution*, pp. 270–7; H. J. Dyos and D. H. Aldcroft, *British Transport* (Leicester, 1969), pp. 366–71.

[144] R. Brown, 'Cultivating a "green" image: oil companies and outdoor publicity in Britain and Europe, 1920–1936', *Journal of European Economic History*, 22 (1993), 347–65; D. F. Dixon, 'Petrol distribution in the UK, 1900–1950', *Business History*, 6 (1963), 7–8.

for the baby Austin replacing the more conventional offspring. The motor vehicle also dictated the shape of the town as housing often clung to the sides of main roads leaving towns – the new arterials and bypasses – as this provided a route back to the centre for the commuter. Hence the ribbon development which Priestley commented upon in his English journey of 1933,[145] and which caused town planners some concern.

The growth of motor transport, combined with rising costs in the city centres, led firms which needed more space to move to the outskirts themselves, either to industrial estates or to line the highways. They could employ road transport to carry their goods back into the city centre or to nearby docks or railway goods yards. Where their deliveries were too scattered or they did not run to their own van or lorry, firms like Pickfords or Carter Paterson were available, now using motor vans rather than horse-drawn vehicles and offering a variety of qualities of services.[146] Thus cheaper rents and rates more than offset any extra costs of distribution. In similar vein their workforce could be drawn from the surrounding suburbs, or use bus, bicycle, tram or motor bike to reach the new location. Employers often lobbied for improved public transport provision to the estates or along the roads and were generally successful, though a problem was already beginning to be evident in the 'rush hour' or peak demand, as noted by the Barlow Commission.[147] To meet the demand for public transport in the early morning to go to work and then again in the late afternoon to return home required many more vehicles than were needed in the rest of the day. Hence transport undertakings had excess capacity which made these services uneconomic. Another problem with motor transport was the rising number of accidents and the injuries and deaths which resulted. By 1929 there were over 1,300 fatalities and 55,000 injuries in the LCC area alone.[148] This and the growing congestion caused by the vast increase in motor vehicles led to government action which had an impact on the appearance of towns, in the form of street furniture. To control and channel traffic various devices were introduced, such as traffic lights, zebra crossings with Belisha beacons, signs and bollards. Another downside of motor traffic was the competition between bus operators which could take the form of sharp practices such as running just ahead of a competitor to cream off its passengers, not stopping to let passengers alight, racing, etc.[149] These dangers became so acute that in 1924 London was dealt with in a separate act and the rest of the country in 1930. So regulation and quantity licensing

[145] J. B. Priestley, *English Journey* (London, 1934), p. 22.

[146] G. L. Turnbull, *Traffic and Transport* (London, 1979), pp. 151–3.

[147] W. Ashworth, *The Genesis of Modern British Town Planning* (London, 1954), p. 217.

[148] Weightman and Humphries, *Making 1914–1939*, p. 96.

[149] R. Graves and A. Hodge, *The Long Weekend* (Harmondsworth, 1971), p. 180; J. Hibbs, 'The London independent bus operators, 1922–34', *Transport History*, 5 (1972), 274–83.

were introduced[150] and the London Passenger Transport Board was established in 1933 to coordinate and control London's passenger traffic of all modes.

Thus the interwar period saw the amplification of previous trends. The growth of city size continued as suburbs spread ever wider, supported by both public and private transport. The motor vehicle had already started its rise to dominance and gave warning of its need for wider and straighter roads as well as its danger in terms of accidents, congestion and pollution. It also had its impact on the look of the city as street furniture and garages proliferated. Although undoubtedly a facilitator and liberator in this period, perhaps because ownership was so limited, motor traffic served notice of its future ability to strangle the city.

(vii) THE DOMINANCE OF THE MOTOR VEHICLE

The dominant theme of the years since the Second World War in intra-urban transport must be the growth of road traffic, especially the private motor car, causing the demise of the tram, trolley bus and horse-drawn vehicles. The same theme applies to interurban passenger transport, with the long-distance coach increasingly gaining market share along with the private car at the expense of the train. The number of motor cars registered rose four and a half times between 1948 and 1965 with powered two wheelers increasing fourfold between 1948 and 1960.[151] At one level this symbolised greater mobility and freedom of movement for many both within and between urban centres. As a result of rising real wages, the desire for a more rural life style and the ability to afford greater transport costs, the emptying of city centres as residential locations speeded up. The scale of towns increased as yet more acres of houses with garages and associated drives and roads spread around the outskirts of existing cities and new towns were designated. With the real cost of cars falling as to both purchase and running, thanks partly to a very active second-hand market and readily available consumer credit, the motor vehicle played an ever larger role in life styles.

Public transport reached its apogee in the late 1940s while petrol rationing, austerity and the export drive kept the home market starved of private vehicles. In 1950 it was estimated that three-quarters of all passenger miles were performed by rail and public road transport.[152] In the 1950s and 1960s this began to be eroded as petrol rationing ended in 1952 and the skilled working classes became able to enter car ownership. The effects were liberating in that workers could choose from a wider range of residential possibilities and at weekends or

---

[150] C. Mulley, 'The background to bus regulation in the 1930 Road Traffic Act: economic, political and personal influences in the 1920s', *Journal of Transport History*, 3rd series, 4 (1983), 1–19.

[151] B. R. Mitchell and H. G. Jones, *Second Abstract of British Historical Statistics* (Cambridge, 1971), p. 106.

[152] Derek H. Aldcroft, *British Transport since 1914: An Economic History* (Newton Abbot, 1975), p. 165.

evenings could leave the urban areas to visit seaside resorts or country beauty spots, becoming independent of public transport and taking with them their own picnics, folding chairs, kettles and other paraphernalia. In this way they became liberated from the towns but also isolated from the new locations. The rise of private transport aggravated problems already beginning to be apparent in the interwar period. The most pressing was that the towns which had developed in the era of horse transport were not suitable for motor vehicles. This was particularly true of city-centre streets, especially when motorists assumed unrestricted and often anti-social parking. This clogged the traffic arteries and so reduced average speeds. The response was to introduce parking restrictions which made the high street less attractive as a shopping centre and began the move to out of town shopping centres or 'malls' which aggravated the decay of city centres. In addition, the sheer volume of traffic contributed to the arterial sclerosis so that roads were widened, and underpasses, flyovers and roundabouts built. They began to change the shape of towns, rather like the railways earlier, needing land which often necessitated the demolition of houses and cut up neighbourhoods. As traffic accidents rose (there were about 4,500 fatalities in road accidents in 1948 and nearly 8,000 in 1964)[153] further measures were taken to control traffic – with more traffic lights, one-way streets and crossings – and also to separate it from the foot traffic. Hence some sections of town were made into pedestrian precincts and the motor vehicle excluded from these areas. The concern over pollution in which motor fumes mingled with the emissions from coal fires to create a killing mixture of 'smog' also encouraged pedestrianisation and, more effectively, clean air legislation. It also speeded the move to the suburbs and encouraged the construction of bypasses to take through traffic around those towns which were mere staging posts on main routes.

Another effect of the growth of traffic levels and with it the associated dangers to pedestrians was to remove the streets from children as informal playgrounds. Increasingly, hopscotch, football or cricket, skipping and marbles had to take place in designated areas such as parks or playgrounds rather than in the street. This broke up the spontaneous play and interaction of the children, requiring it to be more planned and formalised. This form of alienation also began to extend to the adult population as streets became less congenial locations to gossip and exchange news. In addition, as people used their own private transport for commuting and leisure trips they had less opportunity for friendly interaction as they were isolated in their mobile steel box. Thus the ability to pass the time of day and socialise was much reduced. Indeed, the car was often claimed to promote antagonisms rather than amities. So concerned were the government and various pressure groups about the role of the motor car in the city that a study group was set up under Colin Buchanan at the Ministry of Transport. The report, pub-

[153] W. Plowden, *The Motor Car and Politics 1896–1970* (London, 1971), p. 483.

lished in 1963,[154] became famous and much read and quoted but surprisingly little acted upon. His analysis of the growth of the problem was widely accepted but his remedies were seen as expensive by a fag-end Conservative government and too minimalist in support of public transport by the incoming Labour administration. In retrospect, some of his ideas seemed impractical, such as vertical separating of traffic types, and the density of road construction advocated was expensive and environmentally unfriendly. What was important and lasting was that it carried the debate about the role of the motor vehicle in the city to a higher level of analysis and demonstrated the great complexity of the problem. That issue continued to provoke much discussion and remained unresolved over the next few decades.

[154] C. Buchanan, *Traffic in Towns* (London, 1963).

PART II

Governance

· 9 ·

Central government and the towns

JOHN DAVIS

(i) THE MUNICIPAL CITY

I N 1890 Sidney Webb offered an imaginary but by no means fanciful parable of urban life. He described the movements of 'the Individualist Town Councillor' who

> will walk along the municipal pavement, lit by municipal gas and cleansed by municipal brooms with municipal water, and seeing by the municipal clock in the municipal market that he is too early to meet his children coming from the municipal school hard by the county lunatic asylum and municipal hospital, will use the national telegraph system to tell them not to walk through the municipal park but to come by the municipal tramway, to meet him in the municipal reading room, by the municipal art gallery, museum and library, where he intends to consult some of the national publications in order to prepare his next speech in the municipal town-hall, in favour of the nationalization of the canals and the increase of the government control over the railway system. 'Socialism, sir,' he will say, 'don't waste the time of a practical man by your fantastic absurdities. Self-help, sir, individual self-help, that's what's made our city what it is.'[1]

A century later water and gas would be in private hands, the hospital would be managed by an unaccountable trust and the school might have opted out of local authority control. Progress would have seen off the trams, but the buses that replaced them would have been privatised and deregulated. The municipal brooms would have been put out to tender and the surviving local authority services would probably be strictly cash-limited. The 'Individualist Town Councillor' would know to watch his step on the municipal pavement and not to rely upon the town hall clock.

Whilst it is possible that a city large enough to have indulged itself in this degree of municipal provision by 1890 might have developed a prestige transport

---

[1] S. Webb, *Socialism in England* (London, 1890), pp. 116–17.

project like the Newcastle Metro or the Manchester Metrolink in recent years, it is impossible to deny the recent evaporation of Webb's ideal of comprehensive municipal provision. Nor can it easily be denied that much of the responsibility for this is down to Whitehall's suspicion of local pluralism and local authority initiative over the last twenty years. Those critical of modern centralism join a lengthy tradition running back through local government analysts like Webb's intellectual heir W. A. Robson to Joshua Toulmin Smith virtually at the start of our period.[2] Much of their work is simplistic and verging on the polemical. Reaction to it from the 1960s onwards took the form of a subtler appreciation of the ambiguities within British administration and the practical limits to its apparent centralisation.[3] Still more recently the restraints placed upon local government during the Thatcher and Major years have once again underlined the pronounced central bias within a system characterised by the dependence of virtually all municipal action upon statutory sanction, by central government's veto powers over local borrowing and some other local authority actions, by the weakness of the local taxation system in its successive forms and by local authorities' consequent dependence upon central government grants. What is noteworthy about Webb's example, though, is how many of the local powers that he cites – and others gained later – had been removed from municipal control by 1950, when this volume ends. Gas, water and electricity were nationalised before they were privatised. Local authorities lost their hospitals to the National Health Service and their long-established poor law powers in stages to the Unemployment Assistance Board and the National Assistance Board. Much of the damage was done by a post-war Labour government which broadly shared Webb's vision of comprehensive public provision of social services and which was not moved by any hostility towards local authorities. Whatever is true of the Thatcher/Major years, it would be inaccurate to ascribe the erosion before 1950 of the Victorian tradition of urban municipal enterprise to any central hostility to its aspirations or even to central suspicion of local authorities themselves. The truth is more complex.

(ii) THE VICTORIAN SYSTEM

What Webb was describing was the local manifestation of a process of government growth – in public health, welfare, education, local transport, etc. – in response to the effects of industrialisation and urbanisation. This process had a national as well as a local dimension. Ambitious as Webb's local agencies were, they were not entirely autonomous. At the very least they could do nothing that

---

[2] W. A. Robson, *The Development of Local Government*, 3rd edn (London, 1954), pp. 36–42.

[3] E.g. G. W. Jones, ed., *New Approaches to the Study of Central-Local Government Relationships* (Farnborough, 1980); R. A. W. Rhodes, *Control and Power in Central-Local Government Relationships* (Farnborough, 1981).

was not prescribed or allowed by statute law – the doctrine of *ultra vires* – while in respect of some services they acted as little more than executors of policies composed by central government and endorsed by parliament. No local operation could be undertaken without regard to the central state, defined to include both parliament and central government.

What impressed Josef Redlich, describing English local government to German readers at the turn of the century,[4] was not, therefore, the lack of central supervision but the absence of any legal hierarchy of authorities.[5] Where most British commentators, then and since, have seen *ultra vires* principally as a constraint upon local authorities, Redlich stressed the equality of central and local authorities before the law. To modern eyes his view appears rather quaint and over-theoretical, underplaying the ability of a government with a working majority to get its way even in the Victorian parliament, but Redlich does provide a valuable reminder of the extent to which Victorian government depended upon negotiation rather than decree to implement its wishes in the localities. These constitutional limitations were reinforced by a general political presumption in favour of restricting the power of central government, evident less in the familiar Victorian commitment to *laissez-faire* – usually subject to qualification in respect of the social services – than in the view voiced by Joshua Toulmin Smith and other defenders of local democracy that central *dirigisme* was un-English (normally meaning French) and represented a threat to Saxon liberties. Mid-Victorian governments themselves saw the political case for decentralisation: 'it is evidently wise' Sir Charles Wood assured Lord John Russell in 1850 'to put as little on the Government whose overthrow causes a revolution as you can and to have as much as you can on the local bodies which may be overthrown a dozen times and nobody be the worse'.[6] Such an attitude was feasible in an age when central rate support was minimal and when national governments ran little risk of being held to account for the failings of local authorities. It ensured that in the nineteenth century the lion's share of governmental expansion was effected by and through local bodies.

The principal difficulty was the functional one that no uniform network of local authorities existed to receive devolved powers. In the shire counties of England and Wales, admittedly, a more or less uniform network of justices of the peace existed, with various local administrative powers – over police, highways, asylums, etc. – but the JPs were not elected and mid-Victorian governments felt reticent about extending their powers, and particularly about extending the powers of these rural grandees over the towns. Urban communities were entitled to seek incorporation on the standardised terms of the 1835 Municipal Corporations Act, one of the attractions of which was exemption from the

---

[4] References are to the English edition, translated by Francis Hirst, which appeared as J. Redlich and F. W. Hirst, *Local Government in England*, 2 vols. (London, 1903).   [5] *Ibid.*, II, p. 246.
[6] Quoted by P. J. Waller, *Town, City and Nation* (Oxford, 1983), pp. 244–5.

county rate, but this was an optional procedure and dependent upon privy council approval. Not all towns were municipal boroughs, but those that were varied enormously in size. Consequently, national legislation for most of the nineteenth century could not necessarily be devolved upon municipal boroughs, in the way that it would be entrusted to county boroughs after 1888. Instead, legislation designed to tackle particular social needs spawned various *ad hoc* local authorities: guardian boards under the 1834 Poor Law Amendment Act (in Scotland parish boards of management under legislation of 1845), school boards under the 1870 Education Act (1872 in Scotland). To complicate matters further, the 1848 Public Health Act allowed communities to petition for the formation of a local board of health, though boroughs already incorporated could also adopt the act. Scotland saw the progressive extension of the right to adopt the general municipal powers – including sanitary powers – previously conferred upon individual towns by local Police Acts, to royal burghs in 1833, burghs of barony in 1847, places with 1,200 inhabitants in 1857 and with 700 inhabitants in 1862.[7] Most of these *ad hoc* local bodies had *ad hoc* central authorities to watch over them: the Poor Law Board in England and Wales (the Board of Supervision in Scotland), the Education Board in England and Wales and the Scottish Education Department in Scotland and, initially, the General Board of Health in England and Wales. Some established departments also supervised specific local authority functions, most obviously the Home Office in its regulation of police forces and the Board of Trade in authorising municipal gas, water, lighting and tramway operations.[8]

To recite this catalogue (which would be still more complex if extended to cover county administration, particularly in Scotland) is to advertise the danger inherent in any generalisation about Victorian central–local relations. Different departments, different local authorities, different types of local authority differed in their attitudes and priorities. The Scottish system differed from the English one. Some patterns none the less stand out. First it is clear that though bound by statute, Victorian local authorities enjoyed in practice considerable freedom to indulge in municipal experiments, as Webb's fable shows. Much was achieved, as John Prest has recently shown, by means of private local acts, particularly after procedure was made cheaper and easier by the Clauses Consolidation Acts of the 1840s,[9] but central government also actively encouraged local enterprise by promoting permissive acts, notably the housing legislation of 1875 and the two measures emanating from the Board of Trade which allowed municipalities to buy up private tramways (1870) and electricity undertakings (1882 and 1888) on

---

[7] G. S. Pryde, *Central and Local Government in Scotland since 1707* (Historical Association Pamphlet no. 45, London, 1960), p. 15; cf. the useful historical survey of central administration 'Scottish administration' compiled in the Scottish Office in 1943: Scottish Record Office, HH 36/18.

[8] Redlich and Hirst, *Local Government*, II, pp. 312–13.

[9] J. Prest, *Liberty and Locality* (Oxford, 1990).

terms so advantageous that they were held to have discouraged private investment.[10] The modern observer is struck by how little concern is expressed by the
central state, at least until the 1890s, at the rapid expansion of the local sphere.
It is true that parliament, at the behest of some public utility companies, included
in the 1872 Borough Funds Act a clause making municipal promotion of private
bills dependent upon the prior approval of a meeting of owners and ratepayers
– an irksome constraint but one which did not greatly inhibit local enterprise.[11]
It is also true that the Treasury worried that the growth of local borrowing might
imperil national credit. This was why the Local Government Board (LGB) was
empowered to approve local authority loans,[12] but this power was clearly not used
so stringently as to choke off local borrowing, which increased almost fivefold in
the last quarter of the century.[13] It is also clear that central government was not
especially anxious to goad local bodies into developing prestige projects like street
improvements, town halls or public libraries, or into municipalising public utility
services which would otherwise be provided privately. 'Gas and water socialism'
was still considered a local option, as it would not be after 1945.

What was not considered optional was the maintenance of minimum standards in those services which had been the subject of national legislation, and in
which wide variations in the quality of local services were intrinsically undesirable. This was where central–local friction was most likely to arise in the
Victorian period. The potential for conflict was accentuated by the functional
division of the central agencies: the *ad hoc* central agencies were, of course, particularly preoccupied with the quality of local provision of their particular services, but the Home Office was no more likely to look benignly upon an
inefficient borough police force. National legislation concerning education, sanitation or police had been passed because wide local disparities in these services
were considered intolerable. Though the 1848 Public Health Act was so framed
as to encourage local initiative, and spawned a variety of local authorities, its core
principle – that there was 'no prescriptive right to be dirty'[14] – applied to all of
them. Whatever the educative value of local self-government, the authorities
themselves accepted that 'a town cannot be allowed to learn by experience the

---

[10] H. Finer, *Municipal Trading* (London, 1941), pp. 56–7, 125–8.
[11] For this episode see the memorandum in PRO HO45/9302/11111 (3 and 52), also C. Bellamy,
Administering Central–Local Relations, 1871–1919 (Manchester, 1988), p. 200. The act was 35 & 36
Vict. c. 91.
[12] Redlich and Hirst, *Local Government*, II, pp. 298–9; Bellamy, *Administering Central–Local Relations*,
p. 79.
[13] Total local authority indebtedness (England and Wales) rose from £84.2 million in 1873–4 to
£393.9 million in 1903–4. Within this total town council indebtedness rose much more rapidly,
from £28.9m to £210.8m: PP 1904–5 LXVII, *Return Showing the Total Amount of the
Outstanding Balances of the Loans of Local Authorities*. LGB approval was not necessary for loans
raised under the provisions of private acts.
[14] PP 1868–9 XXXII, *First Report of the Royal Sanitary Commission*, Q4788 (E. H. Pember).

results of pleuro-pneumonia or smallpox',[15] and contagious disease had no respect for local authority boundaries, as Victorian sanitary reformers never tired of pointing out. Likewise the public elementary education system had been created in 1870 to fill gaps in the voluntary network; once created, the greater financial strength of the board schools underlined the deficiencies of the voluntary schools, leading to their transfer to a form of local authority control in 1902.

The aim of central government in the Victorian period was not so much to bully local authorities into conforming with centrally prescribed policies as to ensure the observance of minimum standards in what were seen as national services at a time of otherwise undirected municipal expansion. This might involve the coercion of penny-pinching authorities, but over the course of the century 'bumbledom' became less of a menace. By 1903 Redlich believed that a recalcitrant police committee was less likely than an apathetic Home Office.[16] The main problems were less obvious: that an authority exercising public health powers under a local act might consider them discretionary – 'powers to be used or laid aside at the pleasure of the Authority on whose petition they were granted rather than . . . accompanied by a duty to put them in force'[17] – or that the expense of prestige projects might lead an authority to skimp on basic services.[18]

Whatever shortcomings they uncovered, central agencies had to be aware that the local bodies concerned were almost always elective, deriving a legitimacy from their election that could not be claimed by a quango like the Poor Law Board. This consideration worked to discredit the model of central control prescribed by Edwin Chadwick for the Poor Law Board (PLB) and later the General Board of Health. Founded on Benthamite suspicion of the motives and competence of local government, the 1834 poor law system rested upon a statutory code of 'astonishing definiteness',[19] augmented by similarly minute central Orders and enforced by an active inspectorate. Redlich believed that their awareness of the Board's powers induced local guardians to seek its advice and follow it rather than risk provoking peremptory ordinances,[20] though one suspects that the relative absence of central–local conflict in nineteenth-century poor law administration owed something to shared attitudes at both levels. The Local Government Board, successor to the PLB, found much local support for its crusade against outdoor relief in 1879,[21] while both central and local agencies followed public opinion in humanising the poor law from the 1890s.

---

[15] E. Jenks, 'Central and local government (concluding article)', *Local Government Review*, 3 (Feb. 1911), 159. [16] Redlich and Hirst, *Local Government*, II, p. 309.

[17] PP 1871 xxxv, Second Report of the Sanitary Commission, p. 42.

[18] R. G. Hetherington, the inspector appointed by the Local Government Board to review the Leeds and Bradford extension applications in 1920, considered that 'Bradford had devoted more attention to the more showy elements of City administration while Leeds had struck deeper at the root causes of unsatisfactory conditions': report in PRO HLG 43/580.

[19] Redlich and Hirst, *Local Government*, II, p. 251. [20] *Ibid.*, p. 260.

[21] K. Williams, *From Pauperism to Poverty* (London, 1981), pp. 96–100.

Attempts to implement the Chadwickian model in public health administration would, though, produce a local furore and an eventual central climb-down that had lasting effects. The General Board of Health, created by the 1848 Public Health Act, arrived as a prescriptive and rather bossy central body in an area where central coercion was probably less necessary than the sanitary lobby claimed. Several towns had secured sanitary powers by private act before 1848, while rate-payers in around 700 towns and districts would petition under the 1848 and successor acts to establish local Boards of Health by 1871.[22] They may have been induced to do so by knowledge of the reserve powers possessed by the General Board,[23] but it is significant that in Scotland, spared the General Board of Health,[24] local voluntarism worked in much the same way, inducing communities to adopt the general municipal powers conferred by the Police Acts under the general statutes of 1850 and 1862. The prospect of 'sewage boiling up from inadequate sewers'[25] usually provided incentive enough to adopt the acts and the rating powers that came with them. In any event the General Board had few admirers in a parliament already sensitive to state *dirigisme* and it was blown away in 1854.[26]

The lessons of this episode proved enduring. Central government conspicuously avoided entanglement in the education question once the 1870 act had regulated the terms of sectarian conflict. The Education Department was capable of enormously fastidious regulation of such uncontentious issues as classroom dimensions and even the colour of the ink used by examiners,[27] but steered clear of disputes with school boards over sectarian questions, potentially more explosive even than public health. It was happy that the electoral system for school boards ensured the local representation of religious minorities, shifting 'the conflict from Whitehall to the various board offices throughout the country', and its spokesmen before the Cross Commission in 1887 called for further devolution.[28] As a result it was largely reactive in its dealings with local authorities,[29] a feature considered a weakness by educational reformers at the turn of the century.

---

[22] PP 1868–9 XXXII, First Report of the Royal Sanitary Commission, Q7805 (Trench). It should be admitted that some parishes adopted these powers 'although they had no intention in fact of ever building a sewer or providing a drain', in order to protect themselves from amalgamation by the county justices into highway districts under the 1862 Highways Act: V. D. Lipman, *Local Government Areas, 1834–1945* (Oxford, 1949), pp. 57–8.

[23] To impose the act in areas where the death rate exceeded twenty-three per thousand: 11 & 12 Vict. c. 63, s. 8.

[24] Scotland had no central health authority before the establishment of the Local Government Board for Scotland in 1894.

[25] F. McKichan, 'A burgh's response to the problems of urban growth: Stirling, 1780–1880', *SHR*, 57 (1978), 82.

[26] S. E. Finer, *The Life and Times of Sir Edwin Chadwick* (London, 1952), pp. 460–73.

[27] G. Sutherland, *Policy-Making in Elementary Education, 1870–1895* (Oxford, 1973), p. 47. The Education Department was replaced by the Board of Education in 1899.

[28] E. Lyulph Stanley, quoted *ibid.*, p. 93.   [29] *Ibid.*, p. 3.

This combination of detailed intrusiveness and strategic weakness was still more characteristic of the Local Government Board, created in 1871. The LGB represented the first attempt to rationalise central administration of local government – the first step away from ad hockery – by combining poor law and public health supervision in one department. In theory it did so by extending the poor law system to public health, turning the poor law inspectors into general inspectors, and the creation of the LGB was shortly followed by the overhaul of sanitary law to reach a state of 'formal perfection'[30] in the Public Health Act of 1875. But the 1871 Royal Sanitary Commission, whose report provided the blueprint for the LGB, had steered well clear of 'the rock on which the General Board of Health was wrecked'.[31] The purpose of the reform was 'not to centralize administration, but on the contrary to set local life in motion', recognising that there were 'limits to the power of any Central Authority to remedy the evils produced by local inefficiency'.[32] The central body should exercise default powers only when an authority showed persistent neglect, and then through financial penalties, in the hope that the ratepayers would be induced to elect more diligent representatives in future.[33] In practice limited docking of grants-in-aid would mean little to the larger boroughs.[34] Much the same applied to the poor law, where the LGB 'was rarely a force for change in the late nineteenth century',[35] applying the elaborate poor law code in detail, but only rarely offering strategic direction to the local bodies.

There thus emerged that hybrid form of central control that characterised the late nineteenth century: highly detailed statutory codes applied with a light hand. Operating a mountain of statutes and empowered to issue provisional orders in several areas, the Local Government Board's ability actually to get things done remained limited. The danger that its processes would become congested by detail, dismissed by the Sanitary Commission in 1871,[36] had become real enough to warrant a departmental inquiry by 1898.[37] By the 1920s, when the assistant secretary of the LGB's successor, the Ministry of Health, defended his department's right to oversee local regulation of such details as pleasure boat charges and hackney carriage fares before the Royal Commission on Local Government,[38] such fussiness had become part of office culture, but its real value

[30] Redlich and Hirst, *Local Government*, II, p. 250.
[31] PP 1871 xxxv, Second Report of the Sanitary Commission, pp. 41–2.　[32] *Ibid.*, pp. 37, 77.
[33] *Ibid.*, pp. 60, 43.　[34] Redlich and Hirst, *Local Government*, II, p. 142.
[35] M. A. Crowther, *The Workhouse System, 1834–1929* (London, 1981), p. 80.
[36] 'This is rather a question of the extent of staff than of principle': PP 1871 xxxv, Second Report of the Sanitary Commission, p. 60.
[37] PP 1898 XL, First and Second Reports of the Local Government Board Inquiry Committee; Bellamy, *Administering Central–Local Relations*, pp. 139–40.
[38] Evidence of I. G. Gibbon, assistant secretary to the Ministry of Health, before the Royal Commission on Local Government, minutes of evidence, part I, 13 Apr. 1923, Q. 1519.

remains unclear. It is hard to doubt that such preoccupations limited the LGB's ability to act in a strategic manner. Even its more meaningful powers – the right to audit local authority accounts (excepting municipal corporations, whose auditors were popularly elected), to approve by-laws and to sanction local authority loans – were reactive rather than directive. 'The Local Government Board is emphatically not a motor engine', Redlich observed, contrasting it with what he believed to be the business-like operations of English provincial corporations.[39]

Not the least of its problems was that of having to deal directly with an enormous number of local authorities. The Royal Sanitary Commission had considered witness suggestions that intermediate bodies be created at county level to relieve the Board of much administrative detail, but had determined that 'direct communication between the Central and Local Authorities will keep up systematic administration better than an Intermediate central power in every county'.[40] The creation of the county councils in 1888 was in part an acknowledgement that this view had been misguided. Many motives lay behind the decision of Lord Salisbury's Conservative administration to democratise county government – most obviously the need to prove to the party's new Whig allies that Conservatives could pass reformist legislation and the need to legitimise the intended increases in rate support for rural ratepayers[41] – but it is clear that once the decision had been taken to proceed with county legislation, the Salisbury government wished to create county authorities which could act as the primary units of local government. C. T. Ritchie, the responsible minister as president of the Local Government Board, envisaged the county council as 'a great engine of reform'.[42] It was intended both to take up some of the direct administrative duties of central government departments and to oversee the performance of secondary authorities within its area.

The bill as introduced would have created a uniform two-tier system across England and Wales, broken only by the ten largest provincial towns and cities, whose borough councils were given full county powers in their own right and classified as 'county boroughs'. It made administrative sense but was weakened by two political flaws. In the first place it was too large to pass intact in one session. By the 1880s central government no longer faced a bloc of unpredictable independent backbenchers, but the urgency of the parliamentary process still gave considerable blocking power to opponents of specific provisions in a large bill. Central government was probably less beholden to parliament than Redlich's analysis implied, but it still faced substantial parliamentary obstacles to any major structural reform of local government. In the event it proved necessary to jettison

---

[39] Redlich and Hirst, *Local Government*, II, pp. 300, 298.
[40] PP 1871 xxxv, Second Report of the Sanitary Commission, p. 60.
[41] J. P. D. Dunbabin, 'The politics of the establishment of county councils', *HJ*, 6 (1963), 228.
[42] Quoted by Lipman, *Local Government Areas*, p. 153.

proposals for second-tier district councils and the projected devolution of powers from central departments.[43]

The second flaw lay in its *insouciant* disregard of tension between urban and rural communities.[44] The distinction between urban and rural local authorities had been evident in law and practice since the reform of municipal corporations in 1835; the Boundary Commission appointed after the Municipal Corporations Act stressed the need separately to delineate town and country,[45] and much Victorian political rhetoric was devoted to emphasising the social and political differences between them. Strong as the administrative case was for creating a supervisory tier at county level, as proposed in 1888 it implied an unwelcome degree of shire interference in urban affairs. This is shown most clearly by the ill-fated devolution proposals. Although many of the powers concerned were trivial – reminders of how bureaucratic the Victorian minimal state could be[46] – others touched the central pillars of urban municipal enterprise. The counties would have acquired from the Board of Trade regulatory powers under the gas and waterworks legislation, the Tramways Act and the Electric Lighting Act, and from the Local Government Board powers under the Baths and Washhouses Act and the (Torrens) Artizans' Dwellings Act, along with default powers over sanitary authorities.[47] Even when the devolution schedule was dropped, the counties retained some default powers, along with the power to lend to second-tier authorities and to approve boundary changes. Above all the boroughs – excepting the ten projected county boroughs – would remain subject to the county rate. None of this was very tactful. The sharp separation of urban and rural authorities was probably undesirable in any case, but if it was necessary to pick sides it would have made more sense to link the larger towns to their rural hinterlands than to force them back into their historic counties. This was, though, a Tory measure designed to relieve rural ratepayers, and it would have been inconsistent to subject large numbers of them to the higher rating levels of the towns. The result was an inelegant scramble by borough MPs to secure county borough status for their towns as the bill passed through the

[43] All that remained of the devolution proposals was an indeterminate and discretionary power for the LGB to transfer functions from itself and other government departments to the counties and county boroughs by Provisional Order. This power was apparently never used, remaining 'no more than a theoretical acknowledgment by Parliament that central control over local government stands in need of decentralisation' – Redlich and Hirst, *Local Government*, II, pp. 72–3.

[44] Douglas Ashford speaks not of *insouciance* but of a more culpable concern 'with projecting the dogma of town versus country into the twentieth century [rather] than with strengthening local democracy', D. E. Ashford, *British Dogmatism and French Pragmatism* (London, 1982), p. 3.

[45] Lipman, *Local Government Areas*, pp. 32–3.

[46] E.g. 'power to appoint officer to determine the question as to sufficiency of bridge to sustain locomotive' under the 1862 Locomotive Act, and 'power to revoke sanction by sanitary authority of use of steam whistle or steam trumpet in a manufactory' under the 1872 Factories (Steam Whistles) Act, both powers enjoyed by the LGB: PP 1888 IV, Local Government (England and Wales) Bill, First Schedule. [47] *Ibid.*

Commons, which ended with sixty-one towns and cities being lifted out of the county network.[48]

The consequences of these parliamentary retreats would be enormous. In the first place the LGB was denied the chance to lighten its load.[49] Secondly, the act introduced a form of apartheid into urban government, by which the boroughs satisfying the 50,000 qualifying population requirement for county borough status (along with a clutch of cathedral cities given this status for elusive historical reasons) retained full powers of self-government, while other municipal boroughs were subject to their county councils. Thirdly, the local government map was frozen in a rather anomalous state. The piecemeal admission of towns to the county borough schedule during the Commons committee stage meant that a county borough was inevitably defined by its existing municipal boundaries (often set down in the 1830s) regardless of the town's connections with its rural hinterland and its potential for future expansion. The problems thus created would bedevil twentieth-century attempts to widen the scope of local government, and did much to make the expansion of the central state probable.

In retrospect this was important because 1888 represented the last occasion on which central government actively pursued decentralisation for its own sake. The idea that decentralisation could provide a hedge against radical statism had appealed to many of those on the Liberal right who had defected from the Gladstonian party in the mid-1880s.[50] It became one of Salisbury's hobby-horses.[51] The financial settlement which accompanied the act was intended to give the local authorities an independent source of income – in the form of a share of the revenue from excise licences and probate duties – which was relatively safe from parliamentary erosion.[52] Subsequently, though, although the central state did much to empower local government, its purpose was generally to enlist local bodies to implement central policies. The democratisation of national politics drew central government to concern itself more with social policy, which generally required detailed administration at the local level. The resource disparities within Ritchie's first tier necessitated increasing levels of central subsidy to get the work done. The choice between public services and economy in administration became prominent in both national and local politics, encouraging the use of national party labels in local politics. The party politicisation of local government gave, in turn, an extra edge to central–local relations.

---

[48] Waller, *Town*, p. 246; for more details of the 'scramble' see Lipman, *Local Government Areas*, pp. 147–50.

[49] Though Redlich suggested in 1903 that 'the transference of even the smallest power to a County Council is regarded with the utmost jealousy, however overloaded the central department may be', Redlich and Hirst, *Local Government*, i, p. 202.

[50] See, e.g., Goschen's Edinburgh address of 1883 on 'Laissez faire and government interference' cited in T. A. Jenkins, *Gladstone, Whiggery and the Liberal Party, 1874–1886* (Oxford, 1988), p. 175.

[51] R. A. Shannon, *The Age of Salisbury, 1881–1902* (London, 1996), p. 161.

[52] G. C. Baugh, 'Government grants in aid of the rates in England and Wales, 1889–1990', *Bull. IHR*, 65 (1992), 218.

For all the book's progressive tone, the municipal nirvana represented in Webb's *Socialism in England* is best seen as the high point of Victorian local autonomy. His imaginary local authority was clearly well resourced, but local autonomy implied varying levels of provision overall. For many small or medium-sized authorities the financial and legal obstacles to effective sanitary provision were enormous,[53] and could not be diminished merely by central chivying. Another influential book published in 1890, Sir John Simon's *English Sanitary Institutions*, illuminated the considerable shortcomings in public health administration half a century after Chadwick's *Sanitary Report*, providing telling evidence of the failure to guarantee minimum standards in basic services.[54] Twentieth-century governments would be less tolerant of local underperformance. Moreover, their definition of an acceptable minimum would tend to rise, as would the number of services to which it was applied. Under these circumstances the protection of local autonomy would become more difficult.

(iii) LOCAL GOVERNMENT AND 'NATIONAL EFFICIENCY'

The weaknesses of the first tier did not deter governments after 1888 from conferring powers and duties upon it,[55] and the financial autonomy envisaged in 1888 was undermined almost from the start by the proliferation of new percentage grants intended to encourage the adoption of permissive powers.[56] It was probably only the unambitious attitude of the Salisbury governments towards domestic policy which concealed the shortcomings of the 1888 system in its first decade. The Conservatives were, though, moved by an ideological eagerness to confer education powers upon the counties and county boroughs, in order to legitimise rate subsidies for the voluntary elementary schools and to prevent the further aggrandisement of the school boards, many of which had been colonised, in the Tory view, by nonconformist educational faddists. The counties and county boroughs became recipients of the 'whisky money' which they were empowered to spend on technical education.[57] In 1897 they were authorised to

---

[53] C. Hamlin, 'Muddling in bumbledom: on the enormity of large sanitary improvements in four British towns, 1855–1885', *Victorian Studies*, 3 (1988–9), 55–83.

[54] Sir J. Simon, *English Sanitary Institutions, Reviewed in their Course of Development, and in Some of their Political and Social Relations* (London, 1890), pp. 390–2, 396–401, 406–8, etc., though Simon did acknowledge signs of recent improvement.

[55] Parliament conferred twenty new powers upon the first tier in the ten years after the 1888 act, but virtually all were adoptive. The most substantial related to intermediate education, technical instruction, the housing of the working classes, isolation hospitals (county councils only) and small holdings: from Statement III with the LGB's memorandum to the Royal Commission on Local Taxation, PP 1898 XLII, pp. 66–88.   [56] Baugh, 'Government grants in aid of the rates', 219.

[57] By 1902, sixty-one out of sixty-four county boroughs had done so, according to Gorst (speech at Bradford, April 1902, *School Board Chronicle*, 3 May 1902). For the 'whisky money' and its application see E. P. Hennock, 'Technological education in England, 1850–1926: the uses of a German model', *History of Education*, 19 (1990), 299–331.

assume control of all secondary education in their areas, to the chagrin of the school boards.[58] In 1902 the school boards were abolished and the counties and county boroughs assumed responsibility for both the former board schools and the voluntary schools in their areas. The disappearance of the school boards ended one of the most important experiments in urban municipal enterprise, and the new responsibility for the voluntary schools burdened urban authorities with a substantial obligation.

For the towns these developments epitomised the turn-of-the-century move from local voluntarism to national obligations. Elementary education was not, of course, a new local authority function when the county boroughs acquired it in 1902, but it was already the fastest growing item of unremunerative expenditure in the local budget,[59] and the new responsibility for the financially straitened voluntary sector increased the burden.[60] It may have deterred further investment in secondary education, in the form of the higher grade schools, which many of the larger urban school boards had developed, in response to demands from lower-middle- and working-class parents, since the first experiment in Leeds in 1872.[61]

The Conservative education ministers had been set on abolishing the School Boards since their return to office in 1895,[62] but the fact that the reform was eventually delayed until 1902 meant that it was passed in the astringent climate of national introspection generated by military embarrassment in the Boer War. Education and health – both key local authority services – were central concerns of the 'national efficiency' movement prominent in Edwardian politics. In many ways these years formed a pivotal period in the development of central–local relations – years in which the local authorities experienced an intense fiscal crisis while coming under growing public pressure to improve their performance. H. A. Tennant's demand, in the course of the debate over school medical inspection in 1906, that 'we ought not to allow the local authorities to differ from the nation in a matter in regard to which the nation has already decided'[63] was a sign of the times – of a much diminished public tolerance of local diversity. So was Lloyd George's pillorying in the Commons of allegedly negligent sanitary authorities during the 1911 debate over national health insurance (in order to

---

[58] By Clause VII of the Directory of the Department of Science and Art: N. D. Daglish, 'Sir John Gorst as educational innovator, a reappraisal', *History of Education*, 21 (1992), 268.

[59] Bellamy, *Administering Central–Local Relations*, p. 64.

[60] Particularly in towns like Stockport where the strength of Catholic voluntarism had obviated the need to establish a school board: Waller, *Town*, p. 111.

[61] N. D. Daglish, 'The politics of educational change, the case of the English higher grade schools', *Journal of Educational Administration and History*, 19 (1987), 36–50; R. Barker, *Education and Politics, 1900–1951: A Study of the Labour Party* (Oxford, 1972), p. 14.

[62] According to Gorst, *School Board Chronicle*, 3 May 1902.

[63] Quoted by N. D. Daglish, 'Robert Morant's hidden agenda? The origins of the medical treatment of schoolchildren', *History of Education*, 19 (1990), 146.

justify making them liable for any insurance committee costs attributable to sanitary default).[64] So was the creation of a new, centralised, health establishment in Scotland in the form of the separate Scottish Insurance Commission under the 1911 act.[65]

National insurance, like most of the other Liberal welfare reforms of 1905–14, virtually by-passed local government: as in 1945–51 a major expansion of the state's welfare role was achieved without the aid of local authorities.[66] The reason was clear enough: the education burden coming on top of the explosion of local debt in the late nineteenth century had left local authorities wary of new duties. From 1902, when *The Times* launched an influential assault on municipal socialism, ratepayer politics began to concern itself more with reducing the rate burden than with improving local services. Several 'profligate' authorities paid the price in the borough elections of November 1906, as did, most conspicuously, the Progressive (i.e. radical Liberal) London County Council in March 1907. In these years urban authorities became increasingly anxious to secure a reform of the local tax system that would ease their fiscal problems. Witnesses before the 1900 Royal Commission on Local Taxation and the departmental Kempe Committee which reported on the same subject in 1914 called for a wide definition of services which could be considered 'national' rather than 'local' in nature, with the implication that such services should be funded, totally or partially, by the centre.[67] The only major change, however, in the midst of this theorising was a negative one: the conversion of the 1888 assigned revenues into a Treasury grant, frozen at its 1908–9 level, in 1911. This was nothing less, as Bernard Mallet claimed, than 'a complete abandonment of the theory and practice of assigned revenues'.[68] Lloyd George, of course, envisaged a local tax on site values in the 1914 budget, though with a national site valuation still far from completion he was forced to fall back upon a conventional central subsidy, which was then defeated by his own backbenchers.[69]

[64] Hansard, Parliamentary Debates, Fifth Series (Commons) 30, cols. 1841–51. For the local authority response see 'The chancellor answered', *Municipal Journal*, 18 Nov. 1911, and, for the aggrieved reaction in one of the towns named, *Harrogate Advertiser*, 11 Nov., 18 Nov. 1911.

[65] I. Levitt, *Poverty and Welfare in Scotland, 1890–1948* (Edinburgh, 1988), pp. 51–2.

[66] J. Harris, 'The transition to high politics in English social policy, 1880–1914', in M. Bentley and J. Stevenson, eds., *High and Low Politics in Modern Britain* (Oxford, 1983), pp. 60–1, 76.

[67] The Royal Commission's Final Report (PP 1901 XXIV, pp. 431–2) distinguished between 'services which are preponderantly National in character and generally onerous to the ratepayers and services which are preponderantly Local in character and confer upon the ratepayers a direct and peculiar benefit more or less commensurate with the burden'. The Kempe Committee considered that these words had 'given rise to considerable confusion of thought in regard to the proper amount of assistance to be given by the State to local authorities': PP 1914 XL, Final Report of the Departmental Committee on Local Taxation, England and Wales, p. 557.

[68] B. Mallet, *British Budgets, 1887–8 to 1912–13* (London, 1913), p. 286; Baugh, 'Government grants in aid of the rates', 218–19.

[69] For this fiasco see A. Offer, *Property and Politics, 1870–1914* (Cambridge, 1981), pp. 392–400.

In the absence of any progress in this direction the local authority lobby became notably more resistant to new duties which they considered intrinsically 'national'. The case of national insurance is instructive. Both parts of the 1911 National Insurance Act, covering health and unemployment insurance, had some bearing on existing local authority services. The quangos devised in 1911 would later become the thin end of a wedge which would prise the poor law from local control in 1934 and 1948. The response of the Association of Municipal Corporations (AMC), representing urban authorities south of the border, was, however, to distance local government from 'a scheme which is admittedly and indeed necessarily a national scheme' and to attack those sections of the bill which did entail local liability.[70] The issue of principle raised by the innovation of a centralised and unelected bureaucracy in the welfare sphere went unraised. In effect the AMC was renouncing the sort of social municipalism pioneered by the LCC Progressives in the 1890s. As central government found itself being pushed into social politics by electoral pressure and party competition, local goverment distanced itself from the early welfare state.

(iv) BOROUGH EXTENSION

The First World War enhanced the problems faced by local authorities. In the first place the destruction of the Liberals as a party of government removed the only party seriously interested in reforming the rating system. At the same time wartime politics intensified the national efficiency ethos of the pre-war years, which evolved into the reconstruction drive of 1917–18. Local government was expected to play its part in building a land fit for heroes to live in but, inevitably, it was given little say in its tasks. Where pre-war legislation had generally been permissive, post-war measures were more likely to be mandatory. Christopher Addison's 1919 Housing Act caught the mood. Counties and county boroughs were, in contrast to earlier housing legislation, *obliged* to submit rehousing schemes to the LGB – or to the new Ministry of Health, which replaced the LGB during 1919 – in return for 100 per cent funding above the yield of a penny rate. Another innovation was the proposal for a set of regional commissioners charged with implementing the act. They would, Addison explained, 'have real powers, and every effort would be made to get the scheme through as quickly as possible';[71] their duties were likely to include castigating

---

[70] Most notably the provision that sanitary authorities share liability for shortfalls in the funds of local insurance committees where these could be attributed to above-average sickness rates, and contribute to the cost of investigations into higher than normal incidence of sickness. See the report of the AMC's Law Committee on the 1911 bill and related material in AMC minutes, 1911, PRO 30/72/41.

[71] Report of conference between the LGB and local government associations, *Municipal Journal*, 14 Feb. 1919.

local authority laggards. Less ostentatiously, these years saw a number of fresh health powers conferred upon the counties and county boroughs.[72] As with housing, new duties were sweetened by new subsidies, in these cases grants of 50 per cent or 75 per cent of expenditure incurred.

The response of urban authorities to these new burdens was to intensify attempts to improve their position within the 1888 system. Towns which were not county boroughs sought county borough status, while the county boroughs themselves sought to extend their boundaries, to absorb suburban areas beyond their original limits. Between 1889 and 1922, when the Royal Commission on Local Government was established, twenty-three new county boroughs were created,[73] while 182 existing county boroughs drew up proposals for boundary extension. These proposals laid bare the tension between town and country which had always been inherent in the 1888 system. Rapidly growing towns which had not gained county borough status in 1888 resented becoming the milch cows of their counties. County boroughs believed that their suburbs had become free riders, making use of borough services without paying the borough rate.[74] County councils resisted the loss of their most lucrative rateable property. Ritchie's deference to historic shire areas in 1888 had indeed left many of the smaller counties highly vulnerable to urban secession: the 1913 applications from Luton, Bedford and Cambridge for county borough status, for example, would virtually have obliterated Bedfordshire and Cambridgeshire.[75]

The defeat of these proposals indicated an increasingly determined county resistance to borough aggrandisement before the First World War, which also succeeded in containing the extent (though not the number) of borough extensions.[76] The most conspicuous extension, the addition of 30,000 acres to Birmingham in 1911, proved to be easily the largest scheme to win approval after the turn of the century.[77] After the war the stakes were raised by heavier

[72] Under the 1918 Maternity and Child Welfare Act, the 1920 Blind Persons Act and the 1921 Public Health Act. The last two were mandatory, as was the 1916 legislation requiring counties and county boroughs to provide treatment for venereal disease: J. P. Bradbury, 'The 1929 Local Government Act, the formulation and implementation of the poor law (health care) and exchequer grant reforms for England and Wales (outside London)' (PhD thesis, University of Bristol, 1990), pp. 7–12.

[73] The mergers of Hanley with Stoke-on-Trent and Plymouth with Devonport reduced the net increase to twenty-one: Lipman, *Local Government Areas*, p. 170.

[74] E.g. in Bradford, where the local inquiry into the 1920 extension proposal heard that 'the inhabitants of the surrounding districts use the Museums and Art Gallery, Public Parks and Recreation Grounds, Public Libraries, Markets and Baths, established by the Corporation', but could not be taxed by it, Corporation of Bradford, Representation to the Minister of Health as to the Proposed Alteration of the Boundary of the City, 1920, PRO HLG 43/581, p. 66.

[75] Lipman, *Local Government Areas*, pp. 174–7.　　[76] *Ibid.*, pp. 178ff.

[77] The Swansea extension of 1918 was the only other extension above 10,000 acres: *ibid.*, p. 179. For the Birmingham scheme see A. Briggs, *History of Birmingham*, vol. II: *Borough and City, 1865–1938* (Oxford, 1952), pp. 135–63, and 'Valeat Quantum', 'The Birmingham city extension scheme', *Local Government Review*, I (1910), 177–9.

statutory duties, by greater ratepayer militancy and, after 1920, by the slump. Borough authorities concerned themselves not only with the adequacy of their tax base but also with the broader relationship between local government and the local economy. In the crowded West Riding of Yorkshire the proposal of Sheffield in 1919 to 'swallow' Rotherham in adding 107,000 acres to its area caused Leeds to fear that its neighbour would become 'the metropolis of the West Riding . . . by reason of its greater unity' unless Leeds also sought to expand.[78] The simultaneous extension proposals from Leeds and Bradford in 1920, involving a thinly veiled carve-up by the two cities of the urban authorities lying between them in what was essentially a conurbation, discredited the whole anarchic process.[79]

County opinion became steadily more splenetic in its opposition to borough extension,[80] with the vocal support of shire backbenchers in the Commons. County insecurity was increased by the fear that central government, in the form of the Local Government Board and its successor, the Ministry of Health, really sided with the towns. This was technically true in that virtually all the proposals for new county boroughs and more than half those for borough extensions were promoted by provisional order under the aegis of the central department.[81] The Ministry of Health came under particular fire for sending helpful instructions on extension procedure 'like Christmas cards' to each county borough towards the end of the calendar year, without telling county councils 'how to defend their hearths and homes'.[82] Whatever its sympathies, the Ministry found itself deprived of its already limited power to direct the process when the Royal Commission on Local Government was appointed in 1923.

The main purpose of the Commission, whose lengthy deliberations were otherwise ignored by the Baldwin government,[83] was to put the lid on this freelance revision of the 1888 map. This it did quite effectively. Legislation of 1926, based upon the Commission's first report, stipulated that new county borough proposals could no longer be promoted by provisional order but only by the more expensive and vulnerable process of local act, and only Doncaster gained county borough status between 1926 and the Second World War.[84] Borough extension was not halted – indeed, the aggregate area transferred each year from counties to boroughs was larger after 1926 than before – but the changes were largely marginal readjustments, 'essentially local and even opportunist',[85] rather than major

---

[78] Alderman C. H. Wilson, Leeds city council, quoted in *Municipal Journal*, 8 Aug. 1919. Sheffield was eventually granted only a 6,686 acre extension: Lipman, *Local Government Areas*, p. 179.

[79] 'Disruption of local government', *Municipal Journal*, 15 Oct. 1920.

[80] The aged Lord Rosebery, for example, attributed Edinburgh's proposal to absorb Leith and Musselburgh to an 'unbridled and Prussian desire for domination', *Municipal Journal*, 23 Jan. 1920.

[81] Lipman, *Local Government Areas*, p. 170.

[82] Royal Commission on Local Government, minutes of evidence, part I, 13 Apr. 1923, Qq. 2093, 2108 (from Pritchard and Adkins).　　[83] Bradbury, '1929 Local Government Act', p. 47.

[84] Lipman, *Local Government Areas*, pp. 184–6.　　[85] *Ibid.*, p. 187.

schemes for urban expansion. The other substantial initiative emanating from the Commission, the county review, allowed county councils to overhaul second-tier areas, without jeopardy to the county boroughs. These cumbersome investigations had revised the boundaries of some 1300 non-county boroughs and urban and rural district councils by 1938,[86] but like the limited borough extensions of the 1930s they could not address the fundamental problem of the urban–rural divide. There was, therefore, very little to show for the towns' efforts to improve their position within the 1888 system, but the unedifying scrummage after 1919 would have a lasting effect in Whitehall, implanting the view of local authorities as jealous fiefdoms more concerned with their boundaries and rate bases than with the public good.

(v) THE 1929 LOCAL GOVERNMENT ACT AND CENTRAL–LOCAL RELATIONS IN THE 1930S

The Ministry of Health recognised that to broach boundary revision was to open a can of worms. It therefore moved cautiously with respect to the two related local government questions which it had, in large part, been created to solve: the reform of the poor law and the overhaul of public medical services. Both were assumed to be best handled at the county/county borough level because the extreme fragmentation of poor law and sanitary areas was seen as part of the problem; indeed, the county councils had been given new public health powers after 1918 even though they were not sanitary authorities.[87] Observing the local authority civil war in the early 1920s, the Ministry decided at an early stage that reorganisation of the first tier was not an option.[88] With boundary revision impossible and local taxation reform off the agenda, it was clear that adequate local performance would depend upon continuing high levels of central subsidy. The choice between percentage grants and block grants for this purpose was a technical one, but one which encapsulated important questions of principle. Percentage grants provided an incentive to local action and even, in some circumstances, a precondition of it – Sir Ernest Simon, in his 1926 account of Manchester City Council 'from within', pointed out that the six major extensions of municipal activity adopted since he joined the Council's service in 1912 had all been lubricated by grants-in-aid: 'no other new work of importance has

[86] *Ibid.*, p. 200. The Kent county review, which 'extended over 36 days, was attended by most of the leaders of the Parliamentary Bar and must have cost the ratepayers many thousands of pounds. The printed volumes of evidence covered over 2,900 pages': memorandum by the Minister of Health on local government reform, 14 July 1943, in the papers of the War Cabinet's Committee on Reconstruction Problems, PRO CAB 117/218.

[87] Evidence of I. G. Gibbon, assistant secretary to the Ministry of Health, before the Royal Commission on Local Government, minutes of evidence, part I, 13 Apr. 1923, memorandum, para. 164, p. 74.   [88] Bradbury, '1929 Local Government Act', p. 113.

been taken up'.[89] The Ministry believed that percentage grants had produced a high level of service where they had been applied in recent public health legislation, but they tended, unless the percentage was very high, to favour wealthier authorities which could afford their share of the expenditure.[90] Above all they left central government at the mercy of local decisions. The Geddes Committee saw the percentage grant system as a 'money-spinning device', and Lord Salisbury considered it 'death to economy'.[91] Block grants had the advantage of putting a ceiling on central liabilities, with the added benefit that an overall block grant could be distributed in a redistributionary way to aid poorer authorities. The impact of the slump after 1920 tilted the balance in favour of the block grant. Severe and highly localised unemployment accentuated the problems faced by poor authorities, while central government became more eager to cap its rate support.

Thus Neville Chamberlain's Local Government Act of 1929 transferred poor law powers from the Boards of Guardians, which were abolished, to the county councils and county boroughs, and introduced a block grant in place of the cluster of central grants which had grown up since the 1840s. On the surface, therefore, it followed the earlier Conservative measures of 1888 and 1902 in treating the counties as the principal multi-purpose local government units, but it would prove to be the last major attempt to do so. Deterred by the difficulties of local finance and the ineluctable problem of local authority areas, central government found itself nationalising services or devolving them to quangos. The London Passenger Transport Board, created in 1933, assumed responsibility for the LCC's tramways. In 1934 the creation of the Unemployment Assistance Board relieved local authorities of responsibility for maintaining the able-bodied unemployed. The Trunk Roads Act of 1936 transferred power over main roads not to a quango but directly to the Minister of Transport.

One advantage of these *ad hoc* arrangements rapidly became clear: once nationalised a service could be organised without reference to the local authority map. This usually implied the creation of large regional units with a view to economies of scale. This had first become evident in the 1920s. Seven regional electricity boards followed the creation of the Central Electricity Board in 1926, while in 1928 the Board of Education established the first of five regional councils for technical education.[92] The Ministry of Health reorganised its medical staff in regional groups in the 1930s, and just before the outbreak of war its

---

[89] E. D. Simon, *A City Council from Within* (London, 1926), pp. 123, 121.
[90] Memorandum of 30 Jan. 1925 in the file 'Control of Local Authorities by Government Departments', PRO T/161/248/S.26701.
[91] Quoted by Bradbury, '1929 Local Government Act', pp. 161, 190.
[92] H. Finer, *English Local Government* (London, 1933), pp. 149–50; 'Regionalism, digest of evidence given at an enquiry held by the solicitor general, Part II – reorganization of local government areas' (June 1941), p. 31, PRO CAB117/219.

housing advisory committee was contemplating the creation of regional housing authorities to deal with the problem of out-county estates.[93] Management of trunk roads was regionalised after 1936. The special areas legislation designed to relieve unemployment blackspots might be seen as a form of selective regionalism, as might John Gilmour's reorganisation of central government in Scotland in 1939.[94] 'The history of local government over the last 40 years', Brian Smith wrote in 1965, 'is characterised by not only the loss of municipal enterprises but also by a corresponding regionalisation of those enterprises on an *ad hoc* basis'.[95] The pattern would be repeated after the war with the creation of the National Health Service.

The idea of reorganising the whole local government system on a regional basis became modish in public administration circles in the 1930s. In 1934 the Special Investigator for Tyneside drew attention to the fragmented nature of the region's local government, which he considered a deterrent to investment. The government's apparently disproportionate response of a Royal Commission might suggest some interest in encouraging amalgamations, and the Commission's Majority Report duly proposed a regional authority which would swallow up Northumberland County Council and leave the area's county boroughs, including Newcastle itself, with 'the small change of local government'.[96] Having alienated both city and county authorities, the Ministry distanced itself rapidly from the majority proposals. Its public preference was for the Minority Report of Charles Roberts, recommending what amounted to the expansion of Newcastle, though the minister, Kingsley Wood, insisted upon the unlikely consent of its neighbours.[97] Regionalism tended likewise to be translated into borough extension by the larger provincial cities. The setting up of the Tyneside Commission led to proposals for regional authorities in Manchester, Merseyside and the Potteries.[98] In Liverpool it was urged that fear of the city's aggrandisement had diminished 'because the economic slump has taught us that as a community our interests are identical', and the response of Birkenhead and Wallasey suggested that a degree of local coordination, at least, was feasible.[99] Wood indicated that

---

[93] 'Regionalism, digest of evidence given at an enquiry held by the solicitor general, Part I – devolution of functions' (Apr. 1941), p. 11; *ibid.*, 'Part II – reorganization of local government areas', p. 27.

[94] J. Mitchell, 'The Gilmour Report on Scottish central administration', *Juridical Review* (Edinburgh, 1989), 173–88, though the 1939 reorganisation did not involve any change to service areas.

[95] B. C. Smith, *Regionalism in England. 2. Its Nature and Purpose, 1909–1965* (London, 1965), p. 64.

[96] George Chrystal, of the Ministry of Health, quoted by J. R. Owen, 'Defending the county? The reorganisation of local government in England and Wales, 1935–1950' (PhD thesis, University of Bristol, 1990), p. 85. The second chapter of this thesis, pp. 56–115, provides an excellent account of the Tyneside Commission.

[97] Owen, 'Defending the county?', p. 92. 'At present there is not the faintest sign of agreement among the numerous councils concerned' – *Newcastle Journal*, 16 Dec.1937.

[98] J. Cliff in *Municipal Journal and Public Works Engineer*, 9 Sept. 1938.

[99] *Liverpool Post and Mercury*, 5 Apr. 1934 (editorial), 7 May 1934.

local government reorganisation for the distressed areas alone would be considered when the special areas legislation came up for review in 1939,[100] but the Newcastle precedent was hardly promising, and government had not ventured any further down the thorny path of boundary review before war broke out.

Without any structural change, central government became more cautious about imposing further duties upon local authorities in the 1930s. After the flurry of social measures which had followed the First World War, there were only two significant extensions of local health responsibility in the thirties[101] and no major education act. Local authorities found their previously ambitious role in public housing largely confined to slum clearance – 'the most difficult, least prestigious and least profitable part of the market' – by the legislation of 1933 and 1935.[102] There is little evidence, though, that local authorities were anxious to return to centre-stage. The local dignitaries who comprised the Ray Committee on local expenditure, set up after the 1931 financial crisis, showed an indecent enthusiasm for the task of retrenchment, anxious only that their efforts should not be negated by new statutory duties. 'It is indeed a wonderful experience – or, rather, it would be – to find that those departments which by percentage grants and other "inducements", have been increasing local expenditure and State grants, must now slumber, and refrain from the pursuit of the ideal', wrote the AMC's house journal.[103] Representing the whole range of municipal authorities – non-county as well as county boroughs – the AMC was bound to seek to preserve the Victorian tradition of voluntarism, by which ambitious authorities were left free to construct their aerodromes and abbatoirs and open municipal savings banks,[104] or seek powers to trade in milk, coal and bread,[105] as long as no further mandatory duties were imposed upon authorities unwilling to bear them.

This was in itself defensible, but two of its consequences were harder to justify. In the first place the AMC worked strenuously – and successfully – to water down the redistributive effects of the 1929 block grant arrangements, frustrating one of the act's purposes in the interests of the wealthier authorities.[106] Secondly,

---

[100] *Newcastle Journal*, 22 Oct. 1937.

[101] The 1936 Midwives Act and the 1939 Cancer Act: Bradbury, '1929 Local Government Act', p. 64. [102] J. A. Yelling, *Slums and Redevelopment* (London, 1992), pp. 87–93, 102–6.

[103] 'Local government finance. Report of the Committee on Local Expenditure', *Municipal Review*, Dec. 1932.

[104] 'Municipal aerodromes', *Municipal Review*, July 1930 (Bristol, Ipswich, Nottingham, Portsmouth and Doncaster); Liverpool opened England's largest municipal abbatoir in Sept. 1931, *ibid.*, Oct. 1931; Sir Percival Bower, 'Birmingham Municipal Bank', *ibid.*, Mar. 1930. Five other authorities put proposals for municipal banks to parliament between 1920 and 1927, though all were rejected or withdrawn. The LCC and the city councils of Manchester, Liverpool, Nottingham, Dundee and Aberdeen also considered the question before a parliamentary committee recommended that no further applications be approved: PP 1928 XI. Report of the Committee on Municipal Savings Banks, pp. 736, 740–4. [105] As proposed by a bill of 1930: Finer, *Municipal Trading*, pp. 63–4.

[106] Until 1937 only 25 per cent of the block grant was available for redistribution: Bradbury, '1929 Local Government Act', p. 240.

it appears that, as the Ministry of Health had feared, the replacement of percentage health grants by the block grant in 1929 removed the incentive built into the old system and encouraged some authorities to skimp on public health provision. The Ministry's health surveys in the early 1930s found almost a third of county boroughs to be seriously deficient.[107] Recent quantitative research suggests that expenditure levels owed more to the political complexion of the council than to its rate base.[108]

(vi) WAR AND REFORM

By 1939, then, the image presented by local government was unedifying. Local authorities were resistant to any significant boundary reform, wary of new powers unless they were optional and often negligent in their use of the powers that they did possess. It is unsurprising, then, that when the austerity atmosphere of the 1930s gave way to the reformist climate of wartime, with its calls for innovation in post-war social policy, ministers were tempted to by-pass local government altogether rather than find themselves drawn into more futile disputes over areas and rate support. The Churchill coalition government approached the question of local government reform without enthusiasm, and largely because commitments to health and welfare reform made the issue impossible to ignore. The Ministry of Health still hoped that five or ten years' experience of the new services would point to regionalism as 'the logical outcome', but the ten regional commissioners appointed to coordinate emergency services during the war had a difficult relationship with the local authorities. The Ministry eventually acknowledged that a regional reorganisation had 'apparently no supporters in local government circles'.[109] What the local authorities did want was unclear. The AMC's 1942 proposal effectively to cover the country with county boroughs was particularly speculative, and Henry Willinck, the Minister of Health, may have been right to conclude two years later that it had been conceived 'somewhat lightheartedly and partly . . . as a protest at the reopening of the subject'.[110] The Association's later and more plausible demand for another Royal Commission had little appeal, however. Interwar experience had convinced Whitehall that local authorities would in practice prove completely intractable in the face of structural reform: 'if they are to be shifted they must either be taken by surprise, or a powerful assault is

---

[107] *Ibid.*, pp. 310, 300; in Scotland attention was focused upon the inadequacy of hospital provision: Levitt, *Poverty and Welfare in Scotland*, pp. 162–9.

[108] M. Powell, 'Did politics matter? Municipal public health expenditure in the 1930s', *UH*, 22 (1995), 360–79.

[109] Reconstruction Committee: 'Memorandum on local government reform by the Minister of Health', 15 July 1944, in PRO PREM/4/88/3.

[110] *Ibid.* For the AMC's proposal see AMC minutes, 23 July 1942, and *Municipal Review*, Aug. 1942, 129–34.

needed to dislodge them from their positions'.[111] Ministers were sceptical of the suggestion that structural reform must precede any change in local authority powers, particularly in view of local authorities' previous resistance to such reform. Willinck's predecessor Ernest Brown had seen this suggestion as a blocking manoeuvre, akin to the argument that the implementation of the Beveridge Report should await the achievement of full employment.[112] In the event the Ministry of Health produced the 1945 White Paper on 'Local Government in England and Wales during the Period of Reconstruction' in order to deflect demands for a Royal Commission.[113] There would be no Royal Commission, only a Boundary Commission, whose ultimately fruitless sessions would stretch almost to the end of the decade, while the simultaneous reconstruction of Britain's welfare services made their deliberations otiose. When the Commission was wound up in 1949, having changed not one boundary,[114] local authorities had already seen their public utility services, their hospitals and what remained of their poor law powers nationalised.

(vii) CONCLUSION: CENTRAL GOVERNMENT AND THE TOWNS

The reaction against utilitarianism in the 1840s cast a long shadow. The defeat of Benthamism in the public health debates of mid-century established principles which would soon become axiomatic. Without paid agents in the localities, it had always been clear that Britain's central government would depend upon local authorities to implement any extension of governmental power: 'so completely is self-government the habit and quality of Englishmen that the country would resent any Central Authority undertaking the duties of the local executive'.[115] It had always been clear that government growth could only be effected through constitutionally independent local bodies; the question was how far those bodies could be directed or coerced. The poor law system, the greatest triumph of the utilitarians, remained highly prescriptive, but the defeat of Benthamism over public health would prove more significant because the sanitary authorities evolved into multi-purpose authorities while the poor law authorities remained *ad hoc* bodies. The two cardinal principles held by the opponents of utilitarianism – that executive power should be devolved as far as possible and that local authority areas should be defined by historical tradition

---

[111] 'Regional devolution by the central government and relationship with local authorities' (Sheepshanks memorandum), 7 Apr. 1943, Scottish Record Office, HH/36/18.

[112] War Cabinet, Committee on Reconstruction Problems, 'Memorandum by the Minister of Health on local government reform, 14 July 1943', PRO CAB/117/218.

[113] Owen, 'Defending the county?', p. 186.

[114] C. J. Pearce, *The Machinery of Change in Local Government, 1888–1974* (London, 1980), p. 70. For the recommendations in the Commission's first two reports see Lipman, *Local Government Areas*, pp. 476–84.   [115] PP 1871 xxxv, Second Report of the Sanitary Commission, pp. 41–2.

rather than by the requirements of administrative rationalism – established the nature of local authorities in the Victorian state.

Victorian local authorities were thus expected both to speak for their communities and to act for them, to be representative and executive bodies at the same time. The characteristic Victorian argument was that significant executive powers were necessary to attract 'the best men' into local government service. By the end of the century this elitist aim had been augmented by the hope on the municipal left – Webb's ideal of 1890 – that local government could bring about the democratic control of public services. The essential flaw in the Victorian conception of local government – that the executive ideal implied large service areas and substantial local administration, while representative aspirations required small areas and minimal bureaucracy – remained concealed by the voluntaristic nature of the nineteenth-century system. The scope for local initiative in the Victorian municipal code was enormous. 'Food, shelter, education, work, leisure, wholesome amusement, a living wage, security against poverty, provision for old age, and all other necessities can be made certain for all by use of existing powers', claimed a writer in 1900, going on to argue that a town council could constitute itself a friendly society executive, or become a cooperative society, a life assurance society or a loan society,[116] but relatively few local powers were mandatory. There was little to restrain an ambitious authority but equally little to chastise a sluggish one: tolerance of service disparities was built into the Victorian system. These disparities were accentuated by the inadequacies of first-tier reform in 1888. The Tories' deference to existing boundaries left the county map largely untouched. Their deference to their rural supporters dissuaded them from any attempt to link town and country. Their preference for gentry government prompted their attempt to make the shire counties the principal local authorities, which was then thwarted in the Commons by the piecemeal creation of county boroughs.

The result was a system ill equipped to handle the government growth of the twentieth century, as national politicians interested themselves in the social politics that had previously been a local preserve, and the state and the public became less tolerant of local shortcomings. The growing burden of mandatory powers accentuated rate disparities between individual authorities and, in general, between urban and rural bodies. Highly rated county boroughs sought to absorb the suburbs beyond their boundaries, while the neighbouring county authorities sought just as eagerly to retain them. Small boroughs resisted amalgamation with larger ones and steered clear even of cooperation in joint committees for fear of inviting amalgamations.[117] The term 'buffer states', applied to the communities lying between Leeds and Bradford in the 1920 amalgamation

---

[116] H. B. S., 'What an urban councillor might do', *Municipal Reformer and Local Government News*, Feb. 1900.   [117] Lipman, *Local Government Areas*, p. 181.

proposals, was an appropriate metaphor of war.[118] Local authorities presented an unedifying image in the 1930s. Consumed by particularistic squabbles over boundaries, hostile to new powers, increasingly parsimonious in the exercise of the powers they did possess, resistant to the equalisation proposed in 1929 and to regional reconstruction which might have strengthened the system, they appeared beyond reform.

It was thus unsurprising that Sidney Webb's heirs abandoned his faith in local government as the agents for the socialisation of Britain. In 1890 Webb had seen the steady growth of municipal enterprise – 168 towns with municipal gas, 31 with municipal trams, etc. – as evidence of the progressive displacement of capitalism by social collectivism.[119] By the 1940s, though, two-thirds of Britain still depended upon private companies for gas, and while 'excellent hospitals have been provided by some of the larger local authorities . . . the country relies largely on the voluntary hospitals'.[120] The AMC's Special Conference on Local Government in 1946 heard many Labour councillors argue that 'local government has failed to meet up to the ordinary economic needs of the masses of the people'.[121] A Southampton councillor claimed that 'the war has advanced local government twenty years and local government is not ready to accept it'. A Poplar delegate reminded her audience that 'Poplar people went to prison over the Poor Law and we were very glad to get rid of the Poor Law to a central authority. The people have been very much better served because there was much more money in the pool.'[122]

That their views were broadly shared by the Minister of Health, Aneurin Bevan, is suggested by Bevan's impatience with the Boundary Commission and his eventual proposal, in October 1949, for a complete overhaul of local government. Bevan envisaged abandoning the very premises of the Victorian system. He proposed a network of 238 all-purpose authorities, two-thirds of them with populations of 150,000 or fewer. Their boundaries were drawn so as to ensure that the majority of the population lived within 10 miles (16 km) – and almost nobody more than 20 miles (32 km) – from the administrative centre, and to combine urban and rural districts.[123] The representative ideal was paramount: 'to

[118] See, e.g., the report on the Bradford proposals by R. G. Hetherington in PRO HLG/43/580.
[119] Webb, *Socialism in England*, p. 102.
[120] C. E. P. Stott, 'The gas industry in relation to local authorities', appendix to Report of AMC Special Conference on Local Government, 25/6 Sept. 1946, p. 30, in AMC minutes, 1946; 'Regionalism, digest of evidence given at an enquiry held by the solicitor general, Part II – reorganization of local government areas', p. 23.
[121] Report of AMC Special Conference on Local Government, 25/6 Sept. 1946, p. 20, AMC minutes, 1946. Quotation from Jack Braddock of Liverpool.
[122] Report of AMC Special Conference on Local Government, 25/6 Sept. 1946, pp. 18–19, 23, in AMC minutes, 1946.
[123] Cabinet Committee on Local Government, 'Organisation of all-purpose authorities in England and Wales. Memorandum by the Minister of Health, 14 October, 1949', PRO CAB/134/470.

revive and maintain local government as a form of government which is truly local, which is near to the people and in which they will take an interest'. The new bodies' powers were made contingent upon this aim. Powers would be tailored to areas, and 'if a particular service requires that these units should everywhere be made larger, it must be because that service is fundamentally not of a kind which can properly be run by elected local government bodies'.[124]

It is not difficult to envisage the obstacles which Bevan's proposals would have encountered, but in the event they were shelved with the approach of the 1950 general election. As a result the 1888 system survived for another quarter century. Local authorities became, increasingly, agents of the central welfare state, their incapacity offset by central subsidies which covered over 60 per cent of local expenditure by the 1970s. This state of affairs had not, in the main, been produced by central malevolence towards local pluralism, but it did leave local authorities vulnerable to attack in the 1980s from a national government critical of the welfare state, committed to the reduction of public expenditure and disposed to see local government as a sinister interest. Ironically, it had been the Conservatives in local government, inclined to associate Attleeian socialism with an intrusive Whitehall bureaucracy, who had predicted this danger in the 1940s. Aware of the growing legislative habit of conferring open-ended powers upon ministers,[125] the Tory councillors at the AMC's 1946 conference reminded their audience that the war had been fought for the values of democracy and pluralism. The warning voiced by a non-county borough delegate at the AMC's 1946 conference was typical: 'One of the speakers has just said that we could not have government without local authorities . . . You have only to look around the world today and find that efforts are being made to govern countries without local authorities, and we want to avoid that by all means in this country.'[126] The speaker was Alderman Roberts, mayor of Grantham.[127]

---

[124] *Ibid.*, paras. 3, 11; Owen, 'Defending the county?,' pp. 223–4.

[125] E.g. the broad definition of the ministers' powers in the 1944 Education Act (s. 1(1)) and the 1945 Water Act (s. 1) and, later, the ascription to the home secretary of an unspecified duty of 'general guidance' of local authorities under the 1948 Children's Act: 'it was thought desirable (by someone) to emphasise the subordinate position which local children authorities were expected to adopt' – J. A. G. Griffith, *Central Departments and Local Authorities* (London, 1966), pp. 50–1.

[126] Report of AMC Special Conference on Local Government, 25/6 Sept. 1946, p. 14, in AMC minutes, 1946.

[127] Alderman Roberts' daughter Margaret would marry Denis Thatcher in 1951.

1 Doré's portrayal of the traffic on Ludgate Hill captured and exaggerated the
congestion and blocked circulation of mid-Victorian London. From G. Doré
and B. Jerrold, *London: A Pilgrimage* (London, 1872).

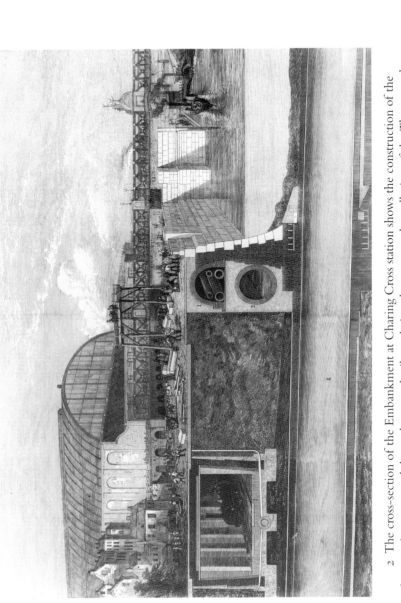

2 The cross-section of the Embankment at Charing Cross station shows the construction of the intercepting sewer and the underground railway designed to prevent the pollution of the Thames and to create better communication. From *Illustrated London News*, 22 June 1867.

3 W. P. Frith, *The Railway Station, 1863*, depicts Brunel's Paddington station, the terminus of the Great Western Railway. The painting indicates the fascination with the bustle of the concourse, with its social narratives of partings and meetings.

4 'Smoke the unnecessary evil': these photographs of Sheffield in 1945
contrast a working day and holiday. They capture an image of industrialising
Britain, of chimneys, pollution and an oppressive urban environment, to be
swept away by post–war planning. From Sheffield Town Planning Authority,
*Sheffield Replanned: A Report Setting out the Problems in Replanning the City and
the Proposals of the Sheffield Town Planning Committee* (Sheffield, 1945).

5 Market Street, Manchester, c. 1895. The traffic including horse trams, cabs and delivery vans.

6 Market place, Marlborough, Wiltshire: a small market town, photographed in the early 1950s.

7 Belvoir Road, Coalville, Leicestershire c. 1900: a small Midland industrial town, showing the main shopping street.

8 The clock tower and campanile dominates Town Square, at the centre of Stevenage, which was designated as the first new town in 1946 by Lewis Silkin, the Minister of Town and Country Planning, whose portrait is seen on the tower. The sculpture, 'Joy-ride' by Franta Belsky, was commissioned by the Stevenage Development Corporation to symbolise the new town and the arrival of a new generation.

9 Donaldson's Hospital, Edinburgh: a Renaissance palace celebrating merchant wealth and philanthropy.

10 Woodhouse Mechanics Institute and Temperance Hall, Leeds: a simple, chapel-like building dedicated to self-improvement. Samuel Smiles delivered his lectures on 'self-help' to the organisation in the 1840s.

11 Nineteenth-century court housing in central Liverpool, photographed in 1920, showing the congestion and lack of through ventilation.

12 By-law housing in Cardiff, built in the late nineteenth century, for unskilled workers (below) and the lower middle class (above), shows the more open layout.

13 Typical Edinburgh tenements, built in the 1860s: a dense, high–rise form of residence which was unusual in England.

PEABODY-SQUARE, WESTMINSTER, FOR THE DWELLINGS OF THE POOR.

14 Peabody Square, James Street, Westminster: a block of flats built by the Peabody Trust on land cleared of slums. The architectural form arose from the high price of land, and was not popular. From *Illustrated London News*, 27 March 1869.

15 Suburban council housing, built under the 1919 act, Curtis Road, Liverpool, 1920 shows the adoption of low-density suburban forms.

16 Council flats built under the 1930 act, St Andrew's Gardens, Liverpool, 1935 for slum clearance in the inner city.

17 Middle-class housing in Camberwell: (a) Dagmar Road, 'a new and most respectable house, with bay windows rising from the half sunk basement to the second storey'.

17 (*cont.*) (b) De Crespigny Park, 'unattached, double-fronted . . . a flight of steps to stucco pillars at the entrance' (G. Gissing, *In the Year of the Jubilee* (London, 1894)).

18 Southgate station on the Piccadilly line, designed by Charles Holden *c.*
1933: the station served a prosperous suburb in north London.

19 Large-scale construction of speculative houses by T. F. Nash Ltd in 1932.
The firm owned a farm of 250 acres near Rayner's Lane station on the
Metropolitan Line. From A. A. Jackson, *Semi-Detached London* (London, 1973).

THE WAY WE LIVE NOW

1. **The redevelopment problem.**
Endless rows of grimy houses: no gardens,
no parks, no community buildings, no hope.

2. **Slum clearance.** This was a beginning:
the people who lived here moved to the
pre-war housing estates.

3. **The housing estates** were an improvement: but the people live on main traffic
routes, noisy, a danger to their children:
they have no meeting places, no community
life.

4. **Wythenshawe.** A later development.
The main road by-passes the town; trees
are preserved, schools set in ample playing-
fields; but there is still no provision for
community life, for full living. We can do
still better than this.

Plate 2

20 'The Way We Live Now': this diagram portrays post–Second World War
perceptions of the development of cities. Wythenshawe was the largest
interwar council estate in Manchester; what was now needed was a sense of
community and neighbourhood, of socially balanced communities with
industry as well as housing. From *City of Manchester Plan, 1945.*

21 Stevenage, a post-war new town, gave these ambitions physical expression.

NEW BUILDINGS OF THE CITY OFFICES COMPANY, LOMBARD-STREET.

22 An early speculative office block: the City Offices Co., on the corner of Gracechurch Street and Lombard Street, in the City of London. From *Illustrated London News*, 1 August 1868.

SLOUGH ESTATES LIMITED.
(Interior of Standard Factory.)

23 Slough Estates Ltd: the trading estate in the late 1920s, showing standard factory units leased to firms.

24 Parks Committee visit to Philips Park, Manchester, 1913, from Hazel
Conway, *People's Parks: The Design and Development of Victorian Parks in Britain*
(Cambridge, 1991).

Western Lawns, Eastbourne

25 Western Lawns, Eastbourne, c. 1900. Eastbourne was the 'queen of resorts', built on the estate of the dukes of

BY Night as well as Day Selfridge's will be a centre of attraction. Contrary to the usual custom after closing time, our windows will not be obscured by blinds, but brilliantly lit up every Evening until Midnight.

These twenty-one windows, twelve of which are fronted with the largest sheets ot plate glass in the world, will be frequently re-dressed, and will present a constant pageant of prevailing Fashion. We hope by beautiful setting and study of harmonious colouring to give pleasure to the artistic sense of every passer-by, and to make the "Window Shows at Selfridge's in Oxford Street" worth a considerable detour to see.

26 Selfridge's store on Oxford Street in 1909. The advertisement indicates the colonisation of the night by new technology. Advertising for the store announced that 'this house is dedicated to Woman's Service first of all', with 'unaccustomed and luxurious appointments' to make shopping pleasurable. It also offered a 'home-like lounge for smoking, and gentlemen are invited to use it as they would their club'.

27 An alternative vision of consumption: the Birmingham Co-operative
Society: (a) central premises, *c.* 1916; (b) Branch 43, Park Road, Aston Cross,
c. 1930.

· I O ·

The changing functions of urban government:
councillors, officials and pressure groups

BARRY M. DOYLE

MUNICIPAL BOUNDARIES – legal, administrative and physical – have never been simple or fixed, shifting as the local and central polity responded to the changing economic, social and demographic imperatives of the developing urban form. Thus, between 1830 and 1950 urban governance in Britain was transformed from a system of locally initiated, semi-private structures with very limited powers and scant state or democratic supervision, through an era of proliferating single purpose boards, to the powerful, unified and democratically elected bodies which reshaped the urban environment in the early twentieth century. In the course of this transformation, local government took on a bewildering array of powers; raised, borrowed and spent thousands of millions of pounds; and ultimately employed an army of almost 1 million workers. Furthermore, this revolution was almost entirely the result of local initiative, for whilst all local government powers had to be sanctioned by parliament, the central state imposed few obligations on the municipalities. In these circumstances service provision varied over time and place, with many similar authorities playing very different roles in terms of utility provision, sanitary improvement, slum clearance, housing, recreation facilities, poor relief benefits or hospital management. This patchiness is usually attributed to the inadequacies of local politicians who, despite the urgings of enlightened central bureaucrats or passionate local socialists, skimped on expenditure in order to ease the rates bill. However, this view has come under increasing scrutiny with revisionists emphasising how much, not how little, was done, given the unequal distribution of resources across the country and the often unhelpful and centralising tendencies of the national state.

Thus, to understand the development of local government in this period, it is vital to understand local governors – both elected and administrative – how their powers and composition changed over time, the framework within which they operated and the pressures they faced from beyond the council chamber. The object of this chapter, therefore, is to sketch out the structure of local government – its changing form, expanding competence and variable financial regime – and to relate this to the development of a cadre of professional municipal officials, the changing social and political profile of the borough council and the relations of both these groups with the extensive range of pressure groups and voluntary organisations operating in the urban sphere in the course of this period. Though urban governance for most of the nineteenth century was a patchwork of often competing boards, commissions, private companies and voluntary providers, this chapter will concentrate on the activities of the borough councils which for most of the period were the dominant bodies in local politics.

(i) FORM, FUNCTION AND FINANCE

Prior to 1835, urban government was in the hands of unreformed corporations, the traditional rural institutions of parish, vestry and county bench, and an array of improvement commissions created to execute local improvement acts. In terms of the competence of urban governance, the Municipal Corporations Act of 1835 was largely symbolic, most of the challenges of urbanisation being met by a range of elected single purpose authorities for poor relief, burial, health, highways and schools, with rate levying powers and overlapping functions, authority and boundaries. Although towns like Liverpool utilised local acts to consolidate control of many of these functions in the hands of the council,[1] in general it was, as Lord Goschen noted, a chaotic system.[2] The situation was even worse in London, where the Corporation (excluded from the 1835 act) refused to exercise its rights beyond the square mile. Responsibility for good government rested with some 300 local commissioners and vestries and the Metropolitan Police until the establishment in 1855 of the indirectly elected Metropolitan Board of Works, charged with improving the capital's infrastructure, and the London School Board in 1870. In addition, across Britain local authorities entered into joint ventures to run capital projects, especially docks, ports and harbours, and acquired powers to regulate various private activities for social or public health reasons.[3]

The single purpose system came under attack from the early 1870s, culminating in the Local Government Act of 1888 which created new multi-purpose authorities with clearly delineated powers, most major towns becoming autonomous county boroughs, whilst London was unified through the London County Council. A structured system of government for the non-borough areas

[1] D. Fraser, *Power and Authority in the Victorian City* (Oxford, 1979), p. 30.
[2] P. Waller, *Town, City and Nation* (Oxford, 1983), p. 265.
[3] J. Kellett, 'The "commune" in London: trepidation about the LCC', *History Today*, 33 (May 1983), 7; M. Falkus, 'The development of municipal trading in the nineteenth century', *Business History*, 19 (1977).

288

followed in 1894, with a second tier for London in 1899 when twenty-eight metropolitan boroughs were created. Yet these reforms did not necessarily lead to a rational system, especially in areas such as Lancashire, which remained a hotchpotch of incomplete and competing fiefdoms. Furthermore, the new system left education and poor relief outside the control of the multi-purpose authorities, the former passing to the counties in 1902, whilst the latter had to await the Local Government Act of 1929, which heralded the apotheosis of autonomous, multi-purpose local government.[4] The enormous changes which occurred in urban government as a result of the post-war reforms were not reflected in the shape of local governance, with little interest shown in either elected regional authorities, or bodies to manage the substantial conurbations in industrial areas.

Municipal power expanded enormously, but unevenly, between 1830 and 1940 as the responsibility for seeking, adopting and executing power usually remained with the locality through one of four routes: general obligatory legislation; local improvement acts; adoption of permissive sections of national legislation; and, later, Local Government Board orders. Obligatory powers, most accompanied by the carrot of central subsidy and the stick of inspection, increased markedly from the 1880s, culminating after 1945 as nationalised services delivered by regional boards replaced 'municipal socialism' in many areas of service provision.[5] Yet despite this 'the large majority of municipal powers in 1900 were still the result of local initiative',[6] giving urban governors considerable discretion over which services they provided. Local improvement acts, simplified by general clauses acts, were employed for a wide range of purposes, often conferring novel rights to provide services, control nuisances or execute extensive capital projects. But this route was not always taken as it was expensive, time-consuming and hazardous as parliamentary committees could be tough on bills which set uncomfortable precedents or offended powerful local interests.[7] Those lacking the power or political will to innovate could draw on a growing range of adoptive powers or Local Government Board Orders, which sanctioned loans, capital projects or permissive services via a local inquiry. For most of the period, therefore, the central state was a facilitator, creating the conditions under which municipalities operated, extending cash or credit, but rarely

---

[4] There are many accounts of the structural changes in local government including above, pp. 261–86; Waller, *Town*, ch. 6; B. Keith-Lucas, *English Local Government in the Nineteenth and Twentieth Centuries* (London, 1977).

[5] For a summary of the legislation affecting local government in 1948 see 'Local government in 1948: review of the chief events of the year', in *The Municipal Yearbook and Public Utilities Manual, 1949* (London, 1949), p. xliii.

[6] J. Garrard, 'Local power in Britain at the end of the nineteenth century', *University of Salford Occasional Papers in Politics and Contemporary History*, 29 (n.d. [1992]), 2.

[7] *Ibid.*, 3; J. R. Kellett, 'Municipal socialism, enterprise and trading in the Victorian city', *UHY* (1978), 43–4.

compelling action. Local authorities utilised these powers to extend services and regulation in five main areas: public safety, environmental control, the welfare of children, culture, recreation and leisure, and commercial services. Furthermore, the importance of each of these areas changed over time as local government moved from policing the people and their environment towards providing general services for the whole community.

Public safety, the driving force in early local government, included all means designed to protect the individual, especially the middle-class ratepayer, from the dangers inherent in the urban environment. Policing was central to the 'reform period', with the Metropolitan Police Act of 1829 and the New Poor Law of 1834 followed by the Municipal Corporation Act of 1835 which required borough councils to establish watch committees and police forces. The County and Borough Police Act of 1856, made policing compulsory, instituting a process of centralisation through inspection sweetened by state funding.[8] Concern with policing was prompted by a desire to control the chaotic urban environment and elevate, socially and morally, the new town dwellers. Thus boroughs charged their police with 'the monitoring and suppression of popular activities and recreations considered conducive to immorality, disorder, or crime',[9] many urban authorities utilising local acts to suppress or control animal fighting, indecency, brothels, dancing and gambling.[10] The later nineteenth century saw a shift in emphasis from the general policing of working-class activities to a concerted assault on clearly identified deviant groups – prostitutes, drunkards, habitual criminals – whilst after 1900 they acquired extensive new powers and responsibilities with the advent of the motor car. Yet despite these changes the policeman's main duties remained ensuring an orderly urban environment and policing the morals and pastimes of the working class.[11]

From the early 1840s public safety increasingly included public health, a significant minority of local authorities seeking powers to control housing, sanitation and improve public cleanliness. Although the Public Health Act of 1848 helped to create a compulsory structure, sanitary improvement was often determined by older methods, including the common law[12] and local acts, whilst the system as a whole left too much to local initiative and too many places excluded – in particular London and Scotland. However, universality and compulsion were extended by a series of acts between 1866 and 1875 which imposed sanitary inspectors and a uniform system of sanitary districts. Early hospital provision

[8] D. Taylor, *The New Police in Nineteenth-Century England* (Manchester, 1997), p. 32; C. Elmsley, *The English Police*, 2nd edn (London, 1996).

[9] R. D. Storch, 'The policeman as domestic missionary: urban discipline and popular culture in northern England, 1850–80', in R. J. Morris and R. Rodger, eds., *The Victorian City* (Harlow, 1993), p. 286. [10] *Ibid*.; Keith-Lucas, *English Local Government*, p. 15.

[11] J. White, 'Police and people in London in the 1930s', *Oral History*, 11 (1983).

[12] C. Hamlin, 'Muddling in bumbledom: on the enormity of large sanitary improvements in four British towns, 1855–1885', *Victorian Studies*, 33 (1988–9), 63.

– poor law infirmaries, asylums for pauper lunatics and fever and isolation hospitals[13] – was also part of the wider municipal policing function, providing protection to the community not the individual, by segregating those who posed a moral, social or physical threat. However, the meaning of public health changed after 1900, with a greater emphasis on education and prevention. Medical Officers of Health (MOHs) began to tackle infant mortality and TB, Huddersfield opening a milk depot for poor mothers as early as 1903, whilst eugenic concerns following the First World War prompted the establishment of clinics for mother and infant welfare and venereal diseases.[14] The right to provide acute general hospitals was extended to the municipalities in 1929, when control of the poor law medical facilities was transferred to Public Assistance Committees. Municipal medicine flourished in the London area and the North-West, but facilities varied greatly as some authorities placed stress on providing services for mothers and children, rather than general hospitals.[15]

Overlapping with the concern for public safety was the need to provide and maintain a satisfactory urban infrastructure. Public health related amenities, such as cemeteries, sewers and drains, were a major element in municipal expenditure, as was the provision of water, with the vast majority of urban water supplied by municipalities by 1900.[16] Many councils promoted major capital projects, coastal towns redeveloping their ports and harbours, whilst resorts like Brighton built sea defences, promenades and pleasure grounds. Developments in transport prompted spectacular interventions, like Manchester's controlling interest in the Manchester Ship Canal, whilst motor cars created novel problems with traffic flow and parking, necessitating a different approach to road building. From the mid-nineteenth century, through by-laws and general legislation, councils were able to regulate and demolish housing, facilitating major slum clearance projects which saw insanitary dwellings replaced by impressive commercial or civic buildings reflecting the power and prestige of the locality.[17] However, housing and slum clearance legislation from 1890 onwards provided a framework for municipal intervention in the housing market, making many interwar local authorities the main residential developer in their area. Councils erected almost 1.1 million

[13] V. Berridge, 'Health and medicine', in F. M. L. Thompson, ed., *The Cambridge Social History of Britain, 1750–1950*, vol. III: *Social Agencies and Institutions* (Cambridge, 1990), p. 209; S. Cherry, *Medical Services and the Hospitals in Britain, 1860–1939* (Cambridge, 1996).

[14] H. Jones, *Health and Society in Twentieth-Century Britain* (London, 1994), chs. 2 and 4; H. Marland, 'A pioneer in infant welfare: the Huddersfield scheme, 1903–1920', *Social History of Medicine*, 6 (1993), 25–50.

[15] Cherry, *Medical Services*, table 4.1, p. 46; M. Powell, 'Did politics matter? Municipal public health in the 1930s', *UH*, 22 (1995), 360–79; M. Powell, 'An expanding service: municipal acute medicine in the 1930s', *Twentieth Century British History*, 8 (1997), 334–57.

[16] R. Millward and S. Sheard, 'The urban fiscal problem, 1870–1914: government expenditure and finances in England', *Ec.HR*, 2nd series, 48 (1995), 506; Waller, *Town*, p. 302.

[17] A. Mayne, *The Imagined Slum* (Leicester, 1993); H. Carter and C. R. Lewis, *An Urban Geography of England and Wales in the Nineteenth Century* (London, 1990), pp. 199–200.

new homes by 1939, creating a new style of residential development as well as massively increasing the estates and debts of the average municipality.[18] As postwar legislation removed many services from the hands of town hall, reshaping the urban environment became the key interest of municipal politicians and professionals.

Education also began as a form of policing but gradually developed into a general service by the 1950s. The Education Act of 1870, which empowered locally elected school boards to provide elementary schools, signalled the start of compulsory state funded education, but it was the Education Act of 1902 which, by transferring responsibility to the county boroughs and county councils, made education the central plank in local authority provision in the twentieth century. In addition to compulsory elementary education, the new Local Education Authorities (LEAs) could supply or support other forms of schooling, furnish meals for the necessitous and arrange medical services, gradually developing a secondary sector, including grammar schools and modern schools, to teach both academic and technical and practical subjects. Furthermore, from the later nineteenth century, councils began providing technical education aimed at improving the skills base of the local workforce, often working with employers to develop relevant day release classes, as occurred in the Norwich footwear industry.[19] The Education Act of 1944 replaced elementary education, with general primary and selective, tripartite secondary schooling, a system which appeared to signal the culmination of the process of providing education for all.[20]

Prior to their involvement in formal education, local authorities had begun to provide rational recreations, including parks, museums and libraries facilitated by permissive legislation of the 1840s and 1850s. Although few boroughs made use of the legislation, the majority of ratepayers being of the opinion that funding the leisure or improvement of the poor was not their business, the legislation did acknowledge that 'the provision of cheap, improving leisure-time facilities should be a public municipal affair'. Furthermore, a number of local authorities did act to open museums (Norwich, 1856), libraries (Manchester and Liverpool, 1850) and swimming baths and lay out urban parks such as those in Birmingham and Bristol, which reflected civic pride and provided amenities for rational recreation.[21] But municipalities soon diversified into entertainment, especially in the Edwardian period,[22] and sporting facilities, with substantial growth in the provision of football and cricket pitches and the operation of com-

[18] J. Burnett, *A Social History of Housing, 1815–1985*, 2nd edn (London, 1986), ch. 8.
[19] B. M. Doyle, 'Modernity or morality? George White, Liberalism and the nonconformist conscience in Edwardian England', *Historical Research*, 71 (1998), 329–30.
[20] E. Royle, *Modern Britain: A Social History, 1750–1985* (London, 1987), pp. 352–67.
[21] *Ibid.*, pp. 250–1.
[22] R. Roberts, 'The corporation as impresario: the municipal provision of entertainment in Victorian and Edwardian Bournemouth', in J. K. Walton and J. Walvin, eds., *Leisure in Britain, 1780–1939* (Manchester, 1983), pp. 139–40.

mercial venues, like Doncaster racecourse. The interwar period saw the 'far greater municipalization of leisure', the Physical Training and Recreation Act of 1937 advancing local authorities almost £1 million for sporting facilities, whilst the development of municipal parks was accompanied by an ideological shift towards user-friendly spaces with pitches, gardens and boating lakes. Provision for middle-class activities like tennis and golf multiplied,[23] as did libraries and their use, whilst services for children expanded, including summer camps and playgrounds in parks. This increasing municipal involvement in fun was most obvious in seaside towns, but it reflected a general trend away from improving rational recreation for the working-class adult, towards leisure facilities for all members of the community irrespective of age or class.

The scale of municipal involvement in commercial activities between 1830 and 1950 was quite extraordinary, facilitated by a group of general acts and a huge raft of local initiatives. Councils were active in the development and provision of utilities and transport – gas, electricity, trams, buses, ferries – as well as the regulation of these services in private hands, with most large towns controlling at least one by 1914; the provision of markets and possession of certain traditional privileges and enterprises – such as Colchester's oyster fishery – and the operation of other enterprises which were certainly not necessities, including municipal banks and civic restaurants. Most of these concerns were profitable, yet the willingness to embark on municipal trading ventures varied greatly across the country, determined by the need to bolster weak rate income, the balance of costs versus perceived income, the social and political complexion of the council, local boosterism and the willingness of parliament to sanction novel trading ventures.[24]

This expansion in services produced a remarkable rise in local authority expenditure, which increased thirtyfold in eighty years, from £27m in 1870, to £960m in 1947–8. As the major concerns of urban government changed, so did the distribution of costs, away from basic 'policing' towards public health, education and trading services, the proportion taken by poor relief falling from 12–13 per cent prior to the First World War to a mere 3 per cent in the later 1940s. On the other hand, there was a dramatic growth in the outlay on housing between the wars, to around 5 per cent of all spending in 1947–8, whilst public health service costs rose rapidly in the 1890s and 1900s, and again after 1930.[25] Education costs increased fortyfold between the early 1890s and the late 1940s, but the greatest area of expenditure in the high period of local government was

---

[23] S. G. Jones, *Workers at Play* (London, 1986), pp. 91–5.

[24] Falkus, 'Development of municipal trading'; Kellett, 'Municipal socialism'; E. P. Hennock, 'Finance and politics in urban local government in England, 1835–1900', *HJ*, 6 (1963), 212–25; W. H. Fraser, 'Municipal socialism and social policy', in Morris and Rodger, eds., *Victorian City*, pp. 258–80.

[25] Millward and Sheard, 'Urban fiscal problem', 504–6; Powell, 'Expanding service', 341.

trading services, which expanded from 12 per cent of all outgoings in 1892–3 to 22 per cent in 1947–8, largely due to the development of tramways and electricity supply. Yet there were clearly great variations in the scale of expenditure and the spending priorities of differing authorities. In the second half of the nineteenth century boroughs like Birmingham and Glasgow invested heavily in utilities, capital projects and social amenities, as did new towns like Middlesbrough, whilst older cities like Norwich proved very reluctant to spend before the end of the century. In the first half of the twentieth century variation continued, with small county boroughs like West Hartlepool spending very little on either health care or housing between the wars, whilst similar sized boroughs like Wakefield concentrated their health spending on infectious diseases. Most of the major cities spent heavily on the new social services, especially Liverpool, Birmingham and Glasgow – though both Manchester and Birmingham did attempt to introduce a form of 'rationing' in the mid-1920s.[26]

Paying for this expansion was a perennial problem for local governors who by the 1880s could draw on four sources for finance: rates, central government grants, income from estates, dues and services, and loans. Up to the late 1920s rates, a locally levied tax on occupiers of land and buildings, remained the most important source, revenue growing fourfold between the early 1840s and 1900, whilst the average rate in the pound – the proportion of rateable value actually paid by the occupier – almost doubled between 1885 and 1910,[27] with similar increases after 1914. As rates were regressive and inflexible, bearing little relation to ability to pay, especially for small businesses, there were frequent calls for economy, forcing local and national politicians to seek alternative sources of finance. Yet central government did little beyond rationalising assessment, collection and valuation and derating industrial and freight transport property by 75 per cent in 1930, a reluctance Philip Waller attributes to the Treasury's preference for grant-in-aid over flexible and buoyant forms of local income.[28]

Initial government grants were targeted at rural areas but from the 1850s percentage grants multiplied as government accepted the national character of many of the new compulsory obligations of local authorities, state support rising from less than £1m in 1868, to £20.9m in 1910.[29] Assigned revenues were introduced in 1888 to replace annually voted grants, but the inflexible distribution system devised in 1888 and the almost immediate proliferation of new percentage grants for education, housing and health led to their decline. They were replaced in

---

[26] *Twenty-Eighth Annual Report of the Local Government Board, 1898–99* (London, HMSO, 1899), pp. 654–5; *Whittaker's Almanac 1951* (London, 1951), p. 591; Fraser, *Power and Authority*; Briggs, *Victorian Cities*; E. Watson, 'The municipal activity of an English city', *Political Science Quarterly* (1901), 262–82; Fraser, 'Municipal socialism'; Powell, 'Did politics matter?', 372–4; J. L. Marshall, 'The pattern of housebuilding in the inter-war period in England and Wales', *Scottish Journal of Political Economy*, 15 (1968). [27] Waller, *Town*, p. 257. [28] *Ibid.*, p. 263.
[29] G. C. Baugh, 'Government grants in aid of the rates in England and Wales, 1889–1990', *Bull. IHR*, 65 (1992), 216–17; Waller, *Town*, p. 264.

1929 by 'block grants', which provided the first attempt to utilise a resources and needs formula in grant aid, a problem finally tackled successfully in 1948.[30] Yet it was only with the reforms of 1948 that government grants became more important than the rates, and for most of the period they remained less significant than either other sources of income or loans.

Revenue from sources other than the rates took a variety of forms. Ownership of extensive estates, markets or docks could be crucial, Edwardian Manchester receiving £15,000 from markets, whilst Doncaster's estate income ensured no rates were levied at all.[31] Conversely, those with limited estates, such as Birmingham and Middlesbrough, looked to municipal trading for the money to improve their towns – Birmingham's gasworks contributing £25,00–30,000 annually, enough to pay for a municipal art gallery and ensure the completion of substantial urban improvements without raising the rates.[32] Profits from trading services and other sources were even more significant in the interwar period, contributing £2m to relieve rates in the late 1930s. But much of this benefit was lost after 1945 when nationalisation of gas and electricity forced greater dependence on grants and loans. Throughout the nineteenth century municipalities borrowed extensively to fund infrastructural improvements, including reservoirs, harbours, roads, schools and sewerage, as well as the establishment of utilities. Loans became less important after about 1905, as the need to undertake large-scale capital projects diminished, and from then on the emphasis was on funding house building, which accounted for around half of the interwar debt increase. By the late 1890s urban authorities had amassed outstanding debts of £240m – 50 per cent more than current rateable value – with the burden increasing sixfold to stand at almost £1,500m by 1936–7, leaving a substantial legacy in terms of debt charges, equivalent to over 20 per cent of expenditure throughout the first half of the twentieth century.

(ii) THE MUNICIPAL OFFICER

Local government growth was accompanied by the expansion and consolidation of an elite of municipal officials, many with the status and power of their political masters. Very few positions in this municipal bureaucracy were compulsory, though by the 1870s urban authorities were obliged to appoint a medical officer of health, surveyor, inspector of nuisances, town clerk and treasurer. Beyond this, they had considerable discretion over whom to appoint, under what conditions and qualifications and for what salary. There was no general system of appointment or clear promotion routes, whilst beyond teaching and medical appointments, specific qualifications were rare, with leadership skills acquired on the job.

---

[30] Baugh, 'Government grants in aid of the rates', 220.   [31] Waller, *Town*, p. 256.
[32] Hennock, 'Finance and politics', 221–2.

Salaries were also *ad hoc*. Town clerks in larger boroughs earned between £1,000–2,000, though Glasgow's Sir James Marwick received £3,500 in the 1890s. The salaries of other officials were meagre in comparison, county borough surveyors, engineers and accountants earning between £400 and £1,000, whilst many small towns paid their officials little more than an honorarium.[33] Furthermore, most senior posts remained part time until the twentieth century, for though larger towns were employing full-time town clerks from the 1840s, full-time medical officers of health remained much less common (slightly over one third by 1920) with many officials continuing in private practice or occupying a number of municipal offices. As a result, the development of a municipal professional ethos owed much to the consolidation of organisations like the Institution of Municipal Engineers, which provided a sense of identity and legitimacy in the form of examinations and qualifications and widened the horizons of municipal officials, 95 per cent of whom were locally recruited.[34]

The nature of officials' political relationships changed as they became more professional, mobile and autonomous. Prior to the Municipal Corporation Act, the office of town clerk was usually controlled by the Tories, but after 1835 'there was an exhilarating effusion of party appointments when municipal reform transferred power from one elite to another'.[35] The revival of urban Toryism in the 1840s led to some redressing of the balance, and by the second half of the nineteenth century most senior appointments reflected the politics of the incumbent party. Political alliances between officials and councillors were strengthened by a shared social profile. Prior to 1914 most senior officials were local men or long-term migrants, with strong business and professional involvement in the locality. Intermarriage between the political and administrative elite was not uncommon, whilst social connections, like the Masonic links between councillors and officials in Norwich and Wolverhampton, were widespread. Though occasionally, as with Herbert Morrison's tenure as leader of the London County Council, such interactions could be banned, overall relationships between council members and officials were remarkably close, especially in smaller communities with compact elites.[36]

---

[33] Waller, *Town*, p. 286; B. Keith-Lucas and P. G. Richards, *A History of Local Government in the Twentieth Century* (London, 1976), p. 103; I. Maver, 'The role and influence of Glasgow's municipal managers, 1890s–1930s', unpublished paper, *Urban History Group Annual Meeting* (Leeds, 1998); G. W. Jones, *Borough Politics: A Study of the Wolverhampton Borough Council, 1888–1964* (London, 1969), pp. 268–82.

[34] J. Garrard, 'Bureaucrats rather than bureaucracies: the power of municipal professionals, 1835–1914', in *Occasional Papers in Politics and Contemporary History*, 33 (University of Salford, 1993), pp. 18–20. *Municipal Yearbook, 1949*, pp. 1027–47, for a list of professional organisations.

[35] D. Fraser, *Urban Politics in Victorian England* (Leicester, 1976), pp. 145–7.

[36] Garrard, 'Bureaucrats rather than bureaucracies', 23–4; B. M. Doyle, 'The structure of elite power in the early twentieth-century city: Norwich, 1900–1935', *UH*, 24 (1997), 187; Jones, *Borough Politics*, pp. 135–7; J. Gyford, *Local Politics in Britain*, 2nd edn (London, 1984), p. 31, n. 4.

As local government became too complex for councillors to master, the town clerk, and subsequently the treasurer, became *de facto* chief officers, acquiring considerable power over other departments and the direction of policy. Administrative control of the council, the power to define its legal competence and shape local acts, combined with frequent longevity in office made the town clerk 'the most stable and permanent element in English municipal government . . . the living embodiment of the local traditions of government'.[37] Pivotal figures, some masterminded substantial municipal projects requiring great skill, vision and determination, occasionally against the wishes of the council, though some were uninterested in the progress of their locality. Most, however, were competent administrators, running efficient organisations without making too many waves, an approach which became more common in the 1920s as clerks struggled to cope with the huge increase in council business.

The omnipotence of the town clerk was weakened as the expansion of local government after 1890 privileged those with particular expertise like James Dalrymple, manager of the 4,400 strong trams department in Edwardian Glasgow. The technical complexity of departments like gas and electricity contributed to the growing autonomy of chief officers, for though responsible to a committee, most councillors had neither the time nor the inclination to master the intricacies of the service. As a result many departments were left to the 'experts', with scrutiny retained over salaries and staffing whilst most major capital projects were adopted on the advice of the chief officer. As a result, public officials had a considerable say in policy as well as administration. During the nineteenth century men like Joseph Heron of Manchester and Samuel Johnson of Nottingham acted as members of the councils as opposed to its employees, rebuking or challenging councillors in the chamber, whilst Horatio Brevitt of Wolverhampton characterised himself as a public official, not a 'servant' of the council, with the independence to decide which orders to carry out.[38] Other officers adopted positions which came close to opposition, especially health officials like M'Gonigle in interwar Stockton-on-Tees, who became enmeshed in intense political controversies. This problem arose partly from the absence of an unequivocal chief executive or a class of generalist administrators. Glasgow's attempt to appoint a non-lawyer as town clerk in 1905 was blocked by the Scottish legal fraternity, but by the 1920s pressure was mounting for municipal administrators on the civil service model, with E. D. Simon and others questioning the need for expert departmental heads when most of the job was routine administration.[39] Furthermore, from 1900, rising rates and expenditure and increasingly powerful labour movements, especially after 1918, exposed local

[37] J. Redlich and F. W. Hirst, *Local Government in England*, vol. 1 (London, 1903), pp. 312–13.
[38] Jones, *Borough Politics*, p. 270.
[39] Maver, 'Glasgow's municipal managers'; E. D. Simon, *A City Council from Within* (London, 1926), pp. 130–50; H. Finer, *English Local Government* (London, 1933), pp. 231 and 260–3.

officials to intense political scrutiny. Accusations of corruption and evidence of a scandalous lack of administrative control, weakened the power of men like Brevitt and Dalrymple and in some authorities the treasurer, through the finance committee, acquired overall supervision of council affairs. In addition, the position of town clerks and utility managers was challenged in the twenties by the emergence of new officials who were beginning to consolidate their local power and national prestige in areas like housing, education and planning.[40] Thus by the 1930s the power of municipal managers had spread and weakened as greater scrutiny and complexity ensured that one individual could no longer 'boss' a town, whilst the personal autonomy given to managers of some large departments was eroded by accusations of corruption and increasing political interference.

(iii) THE CHANGING BOROUGH COUNCILLOR

This political interference was possible because ultimately the municipal officials were responsible to their elected masters, the borough councillors. Before 1835 most boroughs were in the hands of self-selecting Anglican Tories, though in some cases they had adapted to incorporate new social actors. In Leeds and Liverpool, therefore, reform replaced a Tory Anglican elite of merchants and manufacturers with a Liberal nonconformist elite of merchants and manufacturers, but in Exeter change was more apparent, with lawyers, retailers and 'the trade' ousting the traditional medical and commercial men.[41] In unincorporated towns experience varied, Manchester witnessing 'a blatant struggle for local power between rival groups of similar social status within the upper ranks of the middle class',[42] while in Birmingham, where the un-elected Improvement Commission was representative of the city's elite, the new council was more obviously *arriviste*, dominated by small business until after the Commission was wound up in 1851. However, strict property qualifications for candidates ensured that for the rest of the century change in the council chamber involved little more than the reallocation of places between those incorporated in 1835.

The main change up to 1914 was the declining dominance of substantial manufacturers and merchants and their replacement by small producers, retailers and the drink trade. In Leeds, the social composition of the corporation changed markedly in the mid-nineteenth century as *petit bourgeois* elements triumphed to such an extent that by the 1870s there were no professionals on the council at all. Middlesbrough's iron-masters, who dominated early municipal government, receded from ten council members in the 1870s to just one in 1912, whilst the

---

[40] Jones, *Borough Politics*, pp. 279–80.
[41] E. P. Hennock, 'The social compositions of borough councils in two large cities, 1835–1914', and R. Newton, 'Society and politics in Exeter, 1837–1914', in H. J. Dyos, ed., *The Study of Urban History* (London, 1968), pp. 310–11 and 330–1; Fraser, *Urban Politics*, pp. 129–30.
[42] Fraser, *Urban Politics*, p. 119.

predominance of 'large' merchants and manufacturers fell from around half of the councils of Bolton, Salford, Blackburn, Rochdale, Bristol and Leicester in the 1860s and 1870s to a quarter or less by 1910.[43] Though there was a commensurate rise to prominence for the shopkeeper in most towns, especially during the late 1880s and 1890s, the political balance between large and small business was complex. In Cardiff and Exeter, 'large business' was never important on the council, and council social structure changed little before the end of the century, whilst in Birmingham and Leeds, the mid- to late nineteenth century saw a revival of the political position of prominent businessmen.[44] Of equal importance, however, was the massive growth in the recruitment of professionals to borough councils between 1870 and 1914, as in Leeds, Leicester, Bristol, Cardiff, Birmingham and Wolverhampton where their proportion of council members increased from between 0 per cent and 15 per cent to around a quarter. Furthermore, other social groups did begin to break through after 1890, the transfer of education in 1902 and the opening of borough councils to women candidates (in 1907) resulting in the cooption of 2,000 women and the election of around fifty female councillors by 1914. Working men councillors were rare before the end of the 1890s, but by 1900 many towns had a handful of mostly union men, associated with the Liberal or Conservative parties.[45] This changed in the early Edwardian period as Labour made noteworthy gains, especially in east and south London, West Yorkshire and Scotland, and though this rise was piecemeal and erratic, Keith Laybourn has estimated that there were around 500 Labour borough councillors (out of 8,000) by 1914.[46]

The years following the First World War witnessed a major transformation in the composition of elected representatives. As Labour broke through, the number of working-class representatives grew substantially, whilst there was a sharp fall in the participation of professionals from the early 1920s and economic

---

[43] Hennock, 'Compositions of borough councils', p. 333; A. Briggs, *Victorian Cities* (London, 1963), p. 258; J. Garrard, 'Urban elites, 1850–1914: the rule and decline of a new squirearchy?', *Albion*, 27 (1995), 603; H. E. Meller, *Leisure and the Changing City, 1870–1914* (London, 1976), p. 87; P. Jones, 'The recruitment of office holders in Leicester, 1861–1931', *Transactions Leicestershire Archaeological and Historical Society*, 58 (1981/2), 73–4; W. Miller, 'Politics in the Scottish city, 1832–1982', in G. Gordon, ed., *Perspectives of the Scottish City* (Aberdeen, 1985), p. 192.

[44] M. J. Daunton, *Coal Metropolis* (Leicester, 1977), pp. 151–9; Newton, 'Exeter', pp. 309–13; Hennock, 'Compositions of borough councils', pp. 323–6 and 335.

[45] Jones, 'Office holders', 73–4; Meller, *Leisure and the Changing City*, p. 87; Daunton, *Coal Metropolis*, pp. 152–3; Hennock, 'Compositions of borough councils', p. 321; Jones, *Borough Politics*, p. 369; P. Hollis, 'Women in council: separate spheres, public space', in J. Rendall, ed., *Equal or Different?* (Oxford, 1987), pp. 210–11 esp. n. 37.

[46] C. Cook, 'Labour and the downfall of the Liberal party, 1906–1914', in A. Sked and C. Cook, eds., *Crisis and Controversy* (London, 1976), pp. 38–65; Miller, 'Politics in the Scottish city', p. 191; G. L. Bernstein, 'Liberalism and the progressive alliance in the constituencies, 1900–1914: three case studies', *HJ*, 26 (1983), 618–40; K. Laybourn, 'The rise of Labour and the decline of Liberalism: the state of the debate', *History*, 80 (1995), 214.

leaders from around 1930, leading to greater influence for small businessmen, shopkeepers and increasingly women and middle-ranking white-collar workers.[47] But it was the immediate aftermath of the Second World War which signalled the real break with the Victorian council, as Labour swept to power across the country, ousting hundreds of old-style councillors. The municipal governors of the 1950s were much more likely to be workers, non-proprietorial managers, women and the retired than professionals or owner-managers, with shopkeepers alone providing continuity with the Victorian council chamber.

Few historians have questioned the causes of the changing status of municipal government, most accepting that economic and social leaders withdrew voluntarily from municipal government, choosing instead to live semi-detached lives in outer suburbs where they might mix socially and politically with the county elite. Withdrawal is usually seen as the result of changes in the structure of the firm, a desire to separate themselves socially and physically from the cities they helped to form, movement on to a regional or national political and economic stage, and/or as a reaction to challenges to their 'natural' authority by lower social groups.[48] In many cases, especially amongst second-generation urban economic leaders like the Reading Palmers, or the Middlesbrough ironmasters, withdrawal was voluntary,[49] but for many it was not. For the absence of members of certain groups on the council did not mean they were not trying to get there, a point noted by Derek Fraser in relation to the large number of unsuccessful professional candidates for Leeds town council in the 1870s.[50] Problems also arise with the classification of individuals, especially when distinguishing between large and small employers, and in assigning individuals with multiple interests to a single category. Thus the tendency to lump all retailers together as a single *petit bourgeois* group creates problems understanding the structure and nature of local politics, for changes in retailing, especially the department store and the multiple chain, produced shopkeepers of immense political, economic and social power. Although a good many shopkeepers were of limited economic means, they were balanced by men like Duckworth in Rochdale, or the Chamberlins who, in addition to owning a Norwich department store, ran a clothing firm and held directorships of major London stores.

This also helps to illustrate a third significant caveat to discussions of the

---

[47] Jones, 'Office holders', pp. 73–4; Jones, *Borough Politics*, p. 369.

[48] See for example R. H. Trainor, 'Urban elites in Victorian Britain', *UHY* (1985), 1–17; Garrard, 'Urban elites'; P. Joyce, *Work, Society and Politics* (Brighton, 1980); M. Savage, *The Dynamics of Working-Class Politics* (Cambridge, 1987). For the contrary position see Doyle, 'Structure of elite power'.

[49] S. Yeo, *Religion and Voluntary Organisations in Crisis, 1890–1914* (London, 1976); Briggs, *Victorian Cities*, pp. 257–9; B. M. Doyle, 'Urban Liberalism and the "Lost Generation": politics and middle class culture in Norwich, 1900–1935', *HJ*, 38 (1995), 633.

[50] Fraser, *Urban Politics*, p. 131. See also Doyle, 'Structure of elite power', 195–6.

changing social status of council members, the problem of assigning individuals, especially lawyers or accountants, to a single category. Sir A. K. Rollitt of Hull, a lawyer and shipowner, managed to combine vice-presidency of the Law Society with presidency of the Associated Chambers of Commerce of the UK and the Municipal Corporations Association, whilst younger members of the Bristol Frys and Norwich Jewsons diversified into the professions yet continued to hold significant business interests within the family firm and beyond.[51] Thus, to see the decline of manufacturers and merchants as necessarily leading to the decline of large-scale business *interests* on the council is overly pessimistic. In fact this process frequently reflected the greater diversity of the local economy, as large-scale retailing and an increasing number and diversity of professionals emerged to service the needs of maturing urban environments, with the latter often serving a pivotal role between manufacturing, commerce and retailing. Even the appearance of women and managers did not necessarily herald the end of social leadership on the council, as many female councillors were from prominent families – such as the Norwich Colmans – whilst many local managers had considerable power at least until the Second World War.

(iv) POLITICS AND PARTY

Corporation reform injected party politics into municipal elections from the very start,[52] although until at least the 1890s party programmes were rare and party discipline in the council chamber almost non-existent. This first round of elections, fought between Liberal reformist candidates and old corporation Tories, resulted in a Liberal landslide, with forty-plus majorities in Leeds, Liverpool and Leicester. The old guard was even ousted in Exeter and Colchester, though Nottingham, with a pre-reform Whig elite, produced a much closer contest, whilst Tories in Bristol actually held on to control. Liberals continued to perform well in newly incorporated boroughs, but elsewhere the Conservatives fought back, recovering control of Exeter, Colchester and Liverpool and making impressive gains in Leeds and Nottingham.[53] By the later 1840s, however, municipal politics in most places had settled into inactive one party rule, and as party conflict eased, the number of contested elections declined so that by the 1850s party battles were rare, with council composition

[51] E. H. H. Green, *The Crisis of Conservatism: The Politics, Economics and Ideology of the British Conservative Party, 1880–1914* (pb. edn, London, 1996), p. 105; Meller, *Leisure and the Changing City*, pp. 91–2; Doyle, 'Urban Liberalism', 625–6.

[52] J. A. Phillips, 'Unintended consequences: parliamentary blueprints in the hands of provincial builders', in D. Dean and C. Jones, eds., *Parliament and Locality 1660–1939* (Edinburgh, 1998), pp. 92–105.

[53] Fraser, *Urban Politics*, pp. 124–5, 137 and 143; Fraser, *Power and Authority*, pp. 114, 123–4, 134; Newton, 'Exeter', p. 302; D. Cannadine, 'The transformation of civic ritual in modern Britain: the Colchester oyster feast', *P&P*, 94 (1982), 110.

and policy most likely to change as a result of internal party divisions, as in Birmingham in the 1850s.[54]

Urban politics was revived from the late 1860s by the extension of the franchise, secret ballot and development of local political organisations. Incumbents, whether Tories in Liverpool and Cardiff, Liberals in Leeds or economists in Birmingham, faced concerted assaults from the opposition, leading to new administrations in Cardiff and Birmingham.[55] But from the late 1880s, the cultural politics of 1835 came under pressure from class and ideology as the Liberal Unionist split, the creation of the county boroughs and the formation of the Independent Labour party (ILP) in 1893 transformed urban politics. In particular, the ILP saw control of the town hall as the best way to improve the lives of working-class people through a programme of municipal socialism, and as a building block for victory in national politics. Candidates began to appear in places like Leeds in 1894–5, but although they secured some seats in Bradford, Bristol and Glasgow and control of West Ham in 1898, in most cases, including the LCC, the ILP breakthrough had to await the new century.[56]

Labour weakness on the LCC was accounted for, in part, by the unique nature of London politics, where the Progressives, encompassing 'all shades of Liberal, from staid Liberal Unionist to Fabian "permeator"' faced the conservative Moderates for control of the new body. The Progressives developed a fairly coherent policy of municipal socialism, making them a truly municipal party able to secure substantial majorities at most of the elections between 1889 and 1904.[57] But in 1907 the Moderates captured the LCC in a remarkable turnaround,[58] presaging a fundamental shift in urban leadership as the Liberal hegemony was destroyed all across Britain. Following the 1902 Education Act the Liberals had captured control of places like Sheffield and Exeter,[59] but this was municipal Liberalism's swansong as a growing Labour challenge and an impressive Conservative recovery in 1907–9 saw them routed in Leeds, Sheffield, Bradford and Nottingham. And despite a fightback between 1910 and 1912 municipal Liberalism suffered further severe losses to left and right in November

---

[54] Fraser, *Urban Politics*, p. 146; Miller, 'Politics in the Scottish city', p. 191; Hennock, 'Compositions of borough councils', 322–3.

[55] Daunton, *Coal Metropolis*, p. 167; Hennock, 'Compositions of borough councils', pp. 323–4; Fraser, *Urban Politics*, pp. 125 and 137.

[56] T. Woodhouse, 'The working class', in D. Fraser, ed., *A History of Modern Leeds* (Manchester, 1980), p. 360; Meller, *Leisure and the Changing City*, p. 86; Miller, 'Politics in the Scottish city', p. 191; Cook, 'Downfall', p. 60.

[57] K. Young, *Local Politics and the Rise of Party* (Leicester, 1975), p. 39; Redlich and Hirst, *English Local Government*, I, p. 267; S. Pennybacker, '"The millennium by return of post": reconsidering London progressivism, 1889–1907', in D. Feldman and G. Stedman Jones, eds., *Metropolis London* (London, 1989), pp. 129–62.   [58] Young, *Rise of Party*, p. 94.

[59] H. Mathers, 'The city of Sheffield, 1893–1926', in C. Binfield *et al.*, eds., *The History of the City of Sheffield, 1843–1993*, vol. I (Sheffield, 1993), p. 79; Newton, 'Exeter', p. 303.

1913.[60] Considerable disagreement surrounds the meaning of these results, Labour optimists pointing to the growing number of Labour councillors especially the impressive performance of 1913, and the development of anti-socialist pacts in places like Bradford, as evidence of Liberal collapse.[61] However, others, whilst accepting Labour advances in Leeds or Bradford, emphasise their weak performance in cities like Birmingham, Sheffield and Liverpool, and the limited scope of most anti-socialist pacts.[62] In fact, the real beneficiary of Liberal weakness in the Edwardian period was the Conservative party which, by a combination of skilful propaganda, protest votes and anti-Tory division, captured the lion's share of borough government for the first time since the 1830s.[63]

The election of 1919, however, did herald a major transformation in municipal politics, as Liberal disarray and a proliferation of candidates, including ratepayers and ex-servicemen, helped Labour record massive gains, some in the most improbable of places. In the metropolitan boroughs, Labour's tally of councillors grew twelvefold to 573, the party taking control of twelve boroughs overnight as Municipal Reform and Progressive representation almost halved.[64] In the provinces Labour advance was equally impressive, consolidating their position in Bradford and Leeds, recording remarkable gains in previously barren territory, such as Tory Birmingham (nineteen gains) and Liverpool (eleven), and winning their first ever representation in places like Dudley and Cardiff.[65] The response to Labour's breakthrough was a wave of anti-socialist agreements, including new parties as in Sheffield and Edinburgh, and a complete end to hostilities between the older parties in many other places. These agreements stemmed the Labour flood in 1920 and pushed the socialists back in 1922, especially in the big cities, like Liverpool and London, where their metropolitan borough representation was halved in 1922. Labour's only success was in Glasgow in 1920, when a municipal general election saw them win 40 per cent

---

[60] Cook, 'Downfall'.

[61] R. McKibbin, *The Evolution of the Labour Party, 1910–24* (Oxford, 1974), esp. p. 85; M. G. Sheppard and J. L. Halstead, 'Labour's municipal election performance in provincial England and Wales, 1901–13', *Bulletin of the Society for the Study of Labour History*, 39 (1979), 39–62; Laybourn, 'State of the debate', 214 and 220; K. Laybourn and J. Reynolds, *Liberalism and the Rise of Labour, 1890–1918* (London, 1984), pp. 150–1.

[62] Cook, 'Downfall', p. 62; Bernstein, 'Liberalism and the progressive alliance', 638–40; D. Tanner, 'Elections, statistics, and the rise of the Labour party, 1906–1931', *HJ*, 34 (1991), 893–908; T. Adams, 'Labour and the First World War: economy, politics and the erosion of local peculiarity?', *Journal of Regional and Local Studies*, 10 (1990), 26; B. M. Doyle, 'A conflict of interests? The local and national dimensions of middle class Liberalism, 1900–1935', in Dean and Jones, eds., *Parliament and Locality*, esp. pp. 136–7.

[63] Young, *Rise of Party*, pp. 104–12; J. Lawrence, 'Class and gender in the making of urban Toryism, 1880–1914', *English Historical Review*, 108 (1993), 629–52.

[64] Young, *Rise of Party*, p. 119; C. Cook, *The Age of Alignment* (London and Basingstoke, 1975), p. 74; Adams, 'Labour and the First World War', 24.

[65] Cook, *Alignment*, p. 51; Daunton, *Coal Metropolis*, p. 228.

of the seats.[66] Furthermore, despite some organisational benefits from anti-socialist arrangements, Liberal representation also declined consistently in the mid-1920s, as poor leadership, financial weakness and a range of polarising tendencies weakened local parties.

The general strike and its aftermath had a deep effect on Liberal and Labour municipal fortunes, the 1926 borough elections heralding the start of a period of sustained Labour growth which saw them capture their first provincial borough, Sheffield.[67] Yet despite this substantial advance Labour was still a long way from municipal dominance in 1927. Of the 53 boroughs with more than 75,000 inhabitants, Labour held 1,005 of the 3,202 seats (31.4 per cent), the Conservatives 1,194 (37.3 per cent), coalitions and Independents 421 (13.2 per cent), and the Liberals a sizeable 582 (18.2 per cent). Though severely weakened, Liberals were still first or second in eighteen of the largest councils in England and Wales, remaining particularly strong in the boroughs of the North-East. However, as a result of more than one hundred gains a year between 1926 and 1929, Labour consolidated their position, capturing fifteen of the eighty major boroughs, including Leeds, Bradford, Hull, Stoke and Derby, though they continued to struggle in Birmingham and Liverpool and towns like Leicester, Manchester and Newcastle where Liberalism endured.[68]

Labour experience in the 1930s was equally erratic, polling badly in 1930–1 when as a result of the economic crisis, government unpopularity and anti-socialist fightbacks they lost hundreds of seats and most of their councils. Full recovery in London and the provinces came in 1933 and 1934, which saw the party recapture authorities lost in 1930–1, and make new gains, including Willesden, Norwich, Glasgow and the prize of the LCC. But Labour remained inconsistent, faltering somewhat from 1935 onwards, especially in the larger urban areas like Leeds and Hull and remaining very weak in Liverpool and Birmingham.[69] Anti-socialist resilience was based on greatly strengthened municipal alliances, including a proliferation of merged parties, whilst independent municipal Liberalism collapsed as the middle class rallied to the anti-socialist cause, Liberal candidatures slipping to fewer than 140 of almost 2,500 nominees in 1938. Liberal decline was matched by a growth of Independents and 'Others', whose candidate percentage increased from 15.3 in 1930 to 25.4 in 1934, and settled around 23 per cent in the later 1930s.[70] As a result of these trends, a form of two party voting emerged in most areas, as provincial England saw the eclipse

---

[66] Cook, *Alignment*, p. 76; Miller, 'Politics in the Scottish city', p. 198.

[67] Mathers, 'City of Sheffield'; M. Meadowcroft, 'The years of political transition, 1914–39', in Fraser, ed., *Leeds*, pp. 424–5; Miller, 'Politics in the Scottish city', p. 198.

[68] Cook, *Alignment*, pp. 68–70; C. Cook, 'Liberals, Labour and local elections', in G. Peele and C. Cook, eds., *The Politics of Reappraisal, 1918–39* (London, 1975), pp. 168–71.

[69] Young, *Rise of Party*, pp. 141–2, 158, 160, 224–5 and 264–5; Cook, 'Liberals, Labour and local elections', pp. 172–6; P. J. Waller, *Democracy and Sectarianism* (Liverpool, 1981), pp. 341–3.

[70] Cook, 'Liberals, Labour and local elections', p. 177.

of Liberalism and the dominance of straight socialist/anti-socialist contests. Thus, by the outbreak of the Second World War, Labour was the main party of the left in municipal politics, securing enough councillors to control or dominate about twenty of the largest authorities. Yet ironically, Labour's importation of national party politics into local elections created an avowedly non-party response on the right, with middle-class municipal politics less governed by the demands of national parties than at any time before or since.

The war ensured a further change in the structure and development of municipal politics, confirming Labour's dominant position in urban government and accelerating the trend towards the nationalisation of local politics. The municipal elections of 1945 saw a Labour landslide unlike anything since 1835, the socialists gaining around 1,000 seats, almost wiping out the Liberals in the process. In addition to winning 23 of the 28 metropolitan boroughs, Labour captured 61 of 143 provincial borough councils, doing particularly well in industrial towns and outer London boroughs, whilst anti-socialists – with the exception of Conservative control in Liverpool and Birmingham – were restricted to forty or so suburban and coastal towns.[71] Following further successes in 1946, including the routing of the beleaguered Conservatives in the LCC elections, Labour could boast a majority of the members of the 83 county boroughs. The Conservatives responded by setting up a Local Government Division whilst the diminishing need to court Liberal voters encouraged them to intervene directly in local politics, and enforce Conservative identification, if not discipline, at election times. Between 1947 and 1951 the Conservatives pushed Labour back as a combination of better organisation, government unpopularity and increased turnout led to substantial gains, so that by November 1949 'almost the whole of the Labour victories of 1945 were wiped out'.[72] Labour had built their progress in urban politics, and to a great extent their victory in 1945, on their belief in municipal socialism, yet the actions of the party in power nationally severely weakened Labour's unique municipal position and, in tandem with Conservative reinvigoration, produced widespread defeat at the end of the period.

Although Labour had built their success, to some extent at least, on a coherent policy of municipal socialism, for most of the period middle-class politicians eschewed programmatic politics, continuously asserting that politics had no place in the council chamber. Throughout the nineteenth century candidates in municipal elections fought under party labels, but usually as individuals, whose qualifications for office were based on their experience as businessmen, their past record, their strong local ties or their bland assertions that they would deliver economy with efficiency. Where divisions of policy did emerge they

[71] Young, *Rise of Party*, p. 197; *Times*, 2 Nov. 1945, p. 8.
[72] J. Maud and S. E. Finer, *Local Government in England and Wales*, rev. 2nd edn (London, 1964), pp. 82–4.

were invariably between economists and spenders; the former usually associated with *petit bourgeois* elements, whilst the latter were often drawn from the ranks of big business and the professions.[73] This situation did begin to change with the appearance of Labour candidates from the mid-1890s. In some places Liberals responded by producing their own 'municipal programmes' and occasionally changing their names to Progressives[74] but this was short-lived, most being abandoned after 1906. From this point the Conservatives launched an onslaught in municipal politics based upon a strong anti-socialist agenda which increasingly drew in the Liberals.[75] Although cultural divisions between Liberal and Conservative remained strong before 1914, and whilst there is extensive evidence of continuing bitter conflict between the two parties in middle-class areas, in terms of municipal ideology the gap between the two had narrowed to almost nothing in the face of the Labour alternative.[76] In these conditions middle-class politicians drew closer together, reasserting their commitment to non-party municipal politics, especially following the Labour breakthrough of 1919. Yet within the council chamber the anti-socialism of election time could be severely tested, especially by sections of the Liberal party who showed a consistent tendency to vote with Labour on many 'big government' issues. As the Conservatives came increasingly under the control of small businessmen and Labour demanded intervention and expenditure, a new division emerged on spending issues in which it was often possible to find larger manufacturers and professionals maintaining their faith in a more expansive form of local government, often siding with Labour.[77] Thus, though the change to generalised services was in part a response to the expansion of the franchise and the rise of Labour, a substantial Labour presence was not required to ensure such services, and in many places, not least Birmingham and Liverpool, the shift to general services predated any substantial Labour breakthrough. In fact, the acquisition of trading services and the aggrandisement of the local environment was invariably the product of a business view of municipal administration rather than any form of municipal socialism.

Furthermore, when assessing the link between service provision and politics, it is important to note the limitations of Labour's municipal advance in the period 1900–50, not least the party's inability to stamp its authority on the major conurbations. At no time during the interwar period, and not even in 1945, did Labour win control of Birmingham, Liverpool, Edinburgh, Manchester or Newcastle-upon-Tyne. Their position in Leeds and Bradford was shaky for most of the interwar period, whilst substantial Midland towns like Leicester,

---

[73] Hennock, 'Finance and politics'; M. J. Daunton, 'Urban Britain', in T. R. Gourvish and A. O'Day, eds., *Later Victorian Britain, 1867–1900* (Basingstoke, 1988), pp. 44–6.

[74] Bernstein, 'Liberalism and the progressive alliance'.   [75] Lawrence, 'Class and gender'.

[76] Doyle, 'Conflict of interests?', p. 133; Cook, 'Downfall'.

[77] Doyle, 'Structure of elite power', 197–8.

Nottingham and Cardiff did not fall to them until 1945.[78] As a result, places like Norwich, Lincoln or Willesden were much more 'solid Labour' than Leeds or Bradford, whilst enduring Liberal strength and a rejuvenated Conservatism ensured that big city politics was not a Labour monopoly.

(V) INTEREST GROUPS: PRESSURE, PROVISION AND POLITICS

The enduring absence of party discipline from municipal government for most of the period was partly a result of the importance of pressure groups who were intimately bound up with the whole fabric of city politics. In a system of voluntary government, voluntary bodies provided both a complementary and a competitive element. In the nineteenth century the boundaries between the local state, the voluntary sector and the market were blurred if not invisible. Each element encroached on the other, each assisted the other in an effort to provide a complete service. As the period progressed, the local authority took over more responsibility for the provision of services from commercial and voluntary providers, yet right through to the Second World War it was still apparent that the efficient provision of a whole range of services, from education to town planning, depended on tripartite partnerships between public, private and voluntary bodies. This system was underpinned by the interconnected nature of urban elites, whether middle class or working class, whose common membership of the organs of local government and the pressure groups and voluntary associations of their class ensured a continuity and community of interests in the overall sphere of urban governance.[79] Certainly the broad range of influences of the middle class on the one hand and labour on the other were often in conflict, if not antithetical, between 1900 and 1945, but dissent was incorporated largely within the bounds of 'party' as each camp remained able and willing to represent a broad range of interests rather than simply promote a party line.

Prior to corporation reform, local government itself was the result of pressure group activity, and even after 1835 the absence of any clear indication of what the corporations were supposed to *do* left enormous space for influence and pressure. Although landowners and employers continued to command immense power and authority for most of the period,[80] it was the various business, labour, religious, moral, recreational and planning organisations which wielded the greatest influence and shaped the form of municipal provision for most of the period. The interests of property were served by business, property owners' and

---

[78] Cook, 'Liberals, Labour and local elections', p. 171 and *passim*.
[79] Garrard, 'Urban elites'; Trainor, 'Urban elites'; Jones, *Borough Politics*, pp. 129–48; M. Savage, 'Urban history and social class: two paradigms', *UH*, 20 (1993), 72–6.
[80] Garrard, 'Urban elites', 598; D. Cannadine, ed., *Patricians, Power and Politics in Nineteenth-Century Towns* (Leicester, 1982).

ratepayers' associations, which flourished in the period of substantial local government expansion between 1880 and 1935, often sharing common memberships and aims. Strongest when threatened by novel forms of competition from state or working class, they aimed to restrain local authority expenditure, and to use the local state to restrict its own powers and those of competitors, tenants, consumers and employees. In addition to urging economy and demanding inquiries into expenditure, they could also be effective in halting or limiting the expansion of local authority powers through the use of local polls.[81]

Landlords, who owned 90 per cent of all housing in 1914 and were thus the main source of council income, formed a vocal and well-organised pressure group, which often worked together with ratepayers' associations, whilst business organisations were slower to develop, becoming more stable and permanent in the last quarter of the nineteenth century. Originally Liberal or Radical – ratepayers in particular, playing on working-class resentment of the aggrandisement of the environment for the benefit of the middle classes – they were usually associated with the economist party (though their prominence in such movements may have been exaggerated).[82] They shifted to the right and became more active in the 1880s and 1890s as expenditure rose and tenants and councils placed increasing burdens on their members' often precarious financial situation. However, whilst the landlords' crisis of the Edwardian period[83] led to a marked decline in the influence of property owners, the rising rate bill, reduction in business representation on the council and growth of owner-occupation raised the profile of building societies, chambers of commerce and ratepayers' associations between the wars. Building societies and business organisations entered local politics after 1918 either by developing close links with middle-class parties, or by intervening directly in local politics, but state control of the building process, industrial derating and Labour's municipal dominance after 1940 forced them to employ more conventional forms of influence, many ending direct links with council members.[84] Ratepayers also benefited briefly from the substantial disaffection among the growing ranks of lower-middle-class owner-occupiers, but their influence peaked in the early 1930s, declining with rating reform, increasing Labour success and the decision of the National Union of Ratepayers' Associations to go independent in 1937.[85]

Whilst business and property dominated the nineteenth-century town, in the twentieth century this role was increasingly occupied by labour whose main

---

[81] For two such polls in Norwich see Doyle, 'Structure of elite power', 196–7.

[82] Hennock, 'Finance and politics', 217; F. Carr, 'Municipal socialism: Labour's rise to power' in B. Lancaster and T. Mason, eds., *Life and Labour in a Twentieth-Century City* (Coventry, 1986), pp. 172–5. For the contrary position see Daunton, *Coal Metropolis*, ch. 9.

[83] A. Offer, *Property and Politics, 1870–1914* (Cambridge, 1981); D. Englander, *Landlord and Tenant in Urban Britain, 1838–1918* (Oxford, 1983).

[84] Carr, 'Municipal socialism', p. 174; Jones, *Borough Politics*, pp. 130–4; Doyle, 'Structure of elite power', 188–91.   [85] Young, *Rise of Party*, pp. 152–69.

pressure groups – trade unions, cooperative societies and tenants' associations – with their interlocking memberships mirrored those of the middle class. From the mid-nineteenth century, working-class groups, often assisted by middle-class sympathisers, struggled to defend their rights in the face of local state encroachment, especially improvement schemes, subsequently pressuring councils to improve employment conditions, demanding union rates and minimum standards for council employees and those working on council contracts. Assisted by the growth of a unionised municipal workforce, fair wages clauses were widely adopted by 1914, although these could prove difficult to police, especially in councils without Labour majorities.[86] Labour pressure was also felt in housing, working-class politicians often in alliance with tenants' associations, demanding cheap fares, slum clearance, rent restrictions and limitations on eviction. Tenants' associations, particularly prominent in London and Glasgow, were radicalised during the Great War, leading to rent strikes in Glasgow and other areas, whilst municipal tenants' associations developed close links with the Labour party.[87] Municipal associations demanded improved facilities for the new estates, ensured adequate repairs, fought rent rises, enforced compliance with the estates' strict codes of conduct and opposed the rehousing of slum clearance families on their estates. Although these associations remained important after 1940, they were increasingly distant from the Labour parties that controlled the council. Similarly, the Co-operative movement became directly involved in politics between 1900 and 1940, pressuring councils on conventional trading issues such as shop hours and food quality, and more radical concerns driven by a commitment to socialism in consumption. From 1919 the Co-op supported candidates in municipal elections, these sympathetic councillors proving vital in the contest for retailing sites on the new council estates, and though the political impact of the Co-op declined after the Second World War, controversy could still occur as late as the 1950s.[88]

The influence of organised religion was felt most strongly in education, morality and, to a lesser extent, social reform. Sectarianism was initially kept from the borough council by school boards where elections were fought on religious lines with denominational activists keen to ensure equal treatment and root out ritualism. However, with the Education Act of 1902 nonconformist 'passive resistance' organisations were formed, dedicated to the non-payment of the portion of the rates destined for Anglican schools, and when the non-payment campaign fizzled out after 1906,[89] the religious issue switched to the treatment of Catholic schools, dominating local politics in Liverpool and Glasgow. Catholic leaders campaigned for improved provision and resourcing of

---

[86] *Labour Year Book* (London, 1916), pp. 633–5; Jones, *Borough Politics*, p. 292.
[87] Englander, *Landlord and Tenant*, parts 2 and 3.
[88] Adams, 'Labour and the First World War', 31–2; Jones, *Borough Politics*, pp. 134–5.
[89] D. Bebbington, *The Nonconformist Conscience: Chapel and Politics, 1870–1914* (London, 1982).

their schools, urging support for sympathetic candidates – Labour in Glasgow, Irish Nationalists in Liverpool until the 1920s – whilst militant Protestants responded with their own parties in Liverpool, Glasgow and Edinburgh. Balancing these competing interests was extremely difficult for local officials and politicians as evidenced by Labour's inability to overcome sectarianism in Liverpool until after 1945.[90]

Religion's hold over public morality and leisure activities was equally enduring. From early in the period, evangelical pressure groups lobbied local watch committees and chief constables, who often shared similar views on drink, public morality and leisure pursuits.[91] Temperance groups – often opposed by equally well-organised associations of brewers and licensed victuallers – urged strict application of drink laws, sabbatarians prevented the liberalising of park and museum opening hours, purity and vigilance bodies attempted to regulate sexuality, prostitution and the content of entertainments whilst others campaigned against gambling. The parliamentary success of evangelical morality between 1880 and 1914 produced new laws controlling drinking, prostitution, gambling and sexual behaviour, creating tensions between public moralists and the police who often found the laws difficult or distasteful to enforce.[92] Morality groups began to lose their power after 1918, though their impact could still be felt in areas like gambling and the Sunday opening of cinemas, whilst Catholics became more active in social issues, especially birth control. Religious groups also campaigned on social issues, especially housing, poverty and unemployment, with Protestant ministers leading many local charities. Clergymen were particularly prominent in the Charity Organisation Society (COS), with many COS principles and personnel migrating to the Edwardian Guild of Help, a movement dedicated to developing 'both a civic consciousness and a new type of partnership with public bodies'.[93] Intensely local, Guilds of Help worked with the municipalities to provide relief rather than charity, often operating as a council auxiliary, as with school meals in Bradford.[94] Religious activism in social affairs diminished between the wars, though it continued to assist the long-term unemployed, providing drop-in centres and lobbying the council to secure public works.

---

[90] T. Gallagher, 'Protestant extremism in urban Scotland 1930–9', *SHR*, 64 (1985); Waller, *Democracy and Sectarianism*, esp. pp. 200–6 and 339–44.

[91] For close links between the chief constable in Leeds and various temperance and morality groups see Storch, 'Domestic missionary', p. 287.

[92] A. Davies, *Leisure, Gender and Poverty* (Buckingham, 1992), pp. 142–67; M. Clapson, 'Playing the system: the world of organised street betting in Manchester, Salford and Bolton, *c.* 1880 to 1939', in A. Davies and S. Fielding, eds., *Workers' Worlds* (Manchester, 1992), esp. pp. 166–7; S. Petrow, *Policing Morals* (Oxford, 1994), for problems with policing these activities in the capital; D. W. Gutzke, *Protecting the Pub: Brewers and Publicans against Temperance* (Woodbridge, 1989).

[93] K. Laybourn, 'The Guild of Help and the changing face of Edwardian philanthropy', *UH*, 20 (1993), 60.   [94] *Ibid.*, 58 and 51.

Closely connected with the work of the churches was the vast array of voluntary initiatives, some providing services in alliance with the local state.
Philanthropic individuals bequeathed millions of pounds in cash and property to
local governments, especially in the fields of recreation and culture, often
making a difference to the ability or willingness of councils to provide a service.
Thus, Andrew Carnegie ensured the opening of public libraries across the
country, local benefactors in Bristol donated a museum, art gallery and improved
library, whilst elsewhere the rich presented parks and gardens not always welcomed by economy conscious local councillors.[95] The growth of sporting and
leisure associations stimulated local authority provision of swimming pools and
football pitches, whilst groups like the Parks and Open Spaces Society pressed
councils to acquire and make use of various types of land. But sport and leisure
could also be sites of conflict as evidenced by the opposition to the LCC's ambition to build on Hackney Marshes in the 1930s.[96] A mixed economy of provision was also apparent in the fields of education, child care and health. Many
educational services, such as continuation classes and careers advice, were delivered by council/voluntary partnerships, while voluntary initiatives like the
'Children's Care Committee' supervised physically weak children and managed
the supply of meals.[97] The National Society for the Prevention of Cruelty to
Children (NSPCC) and the National Children's Homes worked with local
authorities to protect and give refuge to neglected children, and in health provision, charities assisted medical officers of health with health visiting, the care
of unmarried mothers and the provision of milk. This merging of state and philanthropic services gathered pace after 1900, remaining a major feature of the personal social services.

Planning provides a further example of the merger between public and voluntary activities. The Garden City Association, which brought together a diverse
band of enthusiastic amateurs and secured some success with the permissive 1909
Town Planning Act, developed a more professional image after 1910 through
their journal and university courses.[98] Yet planning in the interwar period was
still a partnership, with women's groups helping to shape the new estates, whilst
social welfare bodies, like the Coventry City Guild, set up committees, conducted surveys and lobbied local government.[99] Yet the zeal of local authorities
to modernise their localities, often under the influence of professional planners,
led to conflict and the development of environmental pressure groups such as

[95] Meller, *Leisure and the Changing City*, pp. 65–71; Garrard, 'Urban elites', 596.

[96] Jones, *Workers at Play*, p. 97.   [97] *Labour Year Book* (1916), p. 577.

[98] H. E. Meller, *Towns, Plans and Society in Modern Britain* (Cambridge, 1997), p. 36; H. E. Meller,
'Urban renewal and citizenship: the quality of life in British cities, 1890–1990', *UH*, 22 (1995),
63–84.

[99] A. Hughes and K. Hunt, 'A culture transformed? Women's lives in Wythenshawe in the 1930s',
in Davies and Fielding, eds., *Workers' Worlds*, pp. 78–83; N. Tiratsoo, *Reconstruction, Affluence and
Labour Politics* (London, 1990), p. 7, n. 11.

the Georgian Society, which sought to humanise the modernisation process. After 1945, however, 'Pride in one's city and citizenship was measured . . . not by the actions of volunteers and private philanthropists, but by the actions of professionals and local government administrators empowered by the new legislation to redevelop city centres.'[100] In such an environment pressure became negative, expressed as opposition to further development or complaint about bad design and inadequate amenities.

The 'nationalisation' of local politics after 1945, combined with the capture of the councils by Labour and the immense restructuring of local government functions and powers between 1945 and 1950, which 'based . . . welfare socialism on the bureaucracy of the national and local state, rather than upon the labour movement or the wider range of working-class organisations',[101] alienated many of the interests which had flourished in nineteenth- and early twentieth-century urban governance. Enthusiastic middle-class amateurs were no longer required, businessmen and property owners looked outwards to the corporatist state, or inwards to an economistic Conservative party, whilst the infrastructure of local socialism – Co-op, friendly society – began to break up under the dual pressure of affluence and state welfare. As a result, when pressure groups began to reappear in local politics in the later 1960s – anti-dampness campaigners, environmental protesters – they were single issue movements, largely unconnected with the structures of 'politics'.[102]

(vi) CONCLUSION

Between 1830 and 1950 the functions, structure and politics of local government changed dramatically as municipal service provision became both more extensive and more inclusive. In the early nineteenth century a limited middle-class electorate had demanded the policing of the urban environment and its inhabitants for their own protection. However, as the electorate grew and towns became more complex and mature, so the emphasis shifted to the delivery of more inclusive services such as education, leisure and housing, whilst the rising cost of infrastructure modernisation and more and better services forced localities to seek alternative sources of finance and develop a bureaucracy to deliver these services efficiently. As a result, councils expanded into trading, borrowing heavily to cover set up costs, central government increased its financial input through grants and subsidised loans, whilst municipal officials consolidated their power, as the increasing size and complexity of local government overwhelmed the amateur councillor. Yet up to 1914 the management of the urban environment remained the privilege of the middle class through their control of the

[100] Meller, 'Urban renewal', 76–7.
[101] R. J. Morris, 'Clubs, societies and associations', in Thompson, ed., *Cambridge Social History*, III, p. 442. [102] *Ibid.*; Gyford, *Local Politics*, p. 83.

council, the bureaucracy and most of the pressure groups. This situation did change after the First World War as the Labour party made headway in council elections, working-class pressure groups asserted their power, municipal professionals became more autonomous and mobile, certain sections of the middle class withdrew from their controlling interest in the city and increasingly large-scale businesses provided services independently which had previously been the province of the municipality. But we must be wary of overestimating the extent of these developments, for up to 1945 the middle class remained largely in control of urban government, whilst Labour's rise to power, though spectacular, was by no means complete. Certainly Labour played a significant part in encouraging the further diversification of local government into housing and health, but in most cases, and especially in the big cities, the bulk of the new services were sanctioned and delivered by non-socialist administrations.

Furthermore, Labour's final capture of municipal government in 1945 was something of a Pyrrhic victory as the party's term in office nationally marked the passing of local autonomy. The nationalisation of gas, electricity and hospitals, a raft of prescriptive legislation in areas like health, child care and planning, and the shifting emphasis of financing away from rates and trading incomes to government grants undermined the financial independence of the municipalities and placed them much more firmly under central government control. This process of centralisation is usually seen as part of a drive to provide uniform, efficient services, something the local state was felt to have signally failed to do in the interwar period. Yet whilst the municipalities may have failed in certain areas to live up to the expectations of the post-war welfare state, it is clear from this survey that they did achieve an enormous amount in one hundred years, very often shaping local services to local needs in a way the central state could never manage. Nor was this transformation the prerogative of any one type of place: social group or political party, small and large towns, workers, *petite bourgeoisie* and big business, Liberal, Conservative and Labour shared in a process which at times was near universal. This was possible because local government was a partnership between the municipality, the private sector and voluntary providers working together to meet the needs of the local community. Politicians, officials and pressure groups frequently shared membership and common values and whilst the balance of power and the nature of alliances shifted over time, ultimately this was a community response which owed little to party ideology or external intervention.

The political economy of urban utilities

ROBERT MILLWARD

(i) AN OVERALL PERSPECTIVE: FROM INVIOLATE PROPERTY TO NATIONALISATION

T HE GROWTH of the urban infrastructure was the most dynamic element in the British economy from the 1870s to the 1930s. Even if one ignores housing, the investment in public health, local transport, policing, water, electricity and gas was accounting, by the early 1900s, for one quarter of all capital formation in Britain and the local government component of that was nearly as large as the annual investment by the whole of manufacturing industry. The mushrooming of electricity systems, waterworks, tramways, harbours and gasworks was a key element, and the interplay between their economic development and the interests of parliament and town councils is the subject of this chapter. Superficially it appears to be about ideology, and municipal socialism in particular. In practice this had a limited role. Certainly there were fears about the growth of government. In 1900 Lord Avebury listed his objections to municipal trading as:

1) The enormous increase in debt . . . ;
2) The check to industrial progress;
3) The demand on the time of municipal councillors . . . ;
4) The undesirability of involving Governments and Municipalities . . . in labour questions;
5) The fact that the interference with natural laws . . . [defeats] . . . the very object aimed at;
6) The risk, not to say, certainty of loss.[1]

American observers, afraid of the social consequences of the congestion and corruption in their immigrant-swollen cities, were fascinated by British municipal

---

[1] See pp. 28–9 of Lord Avebury, 'Municipal trading', *Contemporary Review*, 78 (1900), 28–37.

enterprises. The vaunted civic pride in Glasgow and Birmingham added another ingredient to the debate.[2] Academics were drawn in such a way that we find the British economic historian Percy Ashley writing about municipal trading in the 1900 issue of the American *Quarterly Journal of Economics* and H. G. Gibbons given room in the 1901 issue of the Chicago-based *Journal of Political Economy* to describe 'The opposition to municipal socialism in England'.[3]

But municipal enterprise is only part of the story. There was a huge private sector, including, in 1900, 632 joint stock companies supplying electricity or gas or tramway services under private acts of parliament. It is also a story of great differences. Not every town was like Birmingham in viewing water supply as a health issue and gas a business venture. Scotland forbade any use of trading profits for financing public health, roads or other urban improvement schemes. There were many towns in England and Wales which 'stayed private'. All of which is relevant to the four issues covered in this chapter. The first is to locate the development of utilities within the framework of the urban economic problems of the period – problems of overcrowded living and working conditions yet significant increases in real incomes for much of the population. The causes of municipalisation is the second main theme. It has to deal with the penchant for many of the burgeoning new industrial boroughs like Oldham and West Bromwich to expropriate private companies or initiate new municipal enterprise; to explain the delay in the emergence of integrated systems in London, in the form of London County Council Tramways and the Metropolitan Water Board, until the turn of the century; to explain why Liverpool gas, Newcastle electricity, Sunderland trams, to name but a few, stayed private. The third issue is economic performance. Any attempt to evaluate the effect on performance of the organisation and ownership of utilities requires something more than, for example, simply examining the situation before and after the Glasgow Tramways and Omnibus Company was taken over, if only because economic and technological conditions were changing rapidly at the time. Similarly, comparisons between different institutional arrangements coexisting at the same time – the Gas, Light and Coke Co. Ltd versus Leeds Corporation Gas – need to allow for the differing economic circumstances in London and Leeds. Evaluating performance requires also some estimate of how the urban infrastructure developed over time and here electricity proves to be a useful case study. Finally, into the 1930s and 1940s, we ask what were the forces on the 'road to nationalisation'. The term itself needs unpacking; many sectors – like manufacturing and water supply – were not nationalised and, for those that were, a distinct organisational form was taken – the public corporation.

---

[2] B. Aspinall, 'Glasgow trams and American politics, 1894–1914', *SHR*, 56 (1976).

[3] P. C. Ashley, 'Municipal trading in Great Britain', *Quarterly Journal of Economics*, 15 (1900), 458–64; H. J. Gibbons, 'The opposition to municipal socialism in England', *Journal of Political Economy*, 9 (1901).

Whether or not the services supplied were 'useful', from which the term utilities presumably originated, their development over the 100 years from 1850 is, railways aside, very much an urban story. The main reason for this is that the early technologies of generating stations, water systems, tramways and gas works were best suited to spatially limited groups of high density populations. In this respect the new local governments, established in the fifty years or so after the 1835 Municipal Corporations Act to cope with the rapidly burgeoning towns of the Midlands and the North, were especially suited to develop urban utilities. For much of the second half of the nineteenth century municipal boroughs like Wolverhampton, Rochdale and Brighton could make provision for local undertakings without worrying unduly about any unexploited benefits from links with neighbouring towns. The political tensions associated with such links did not emerge in urban areas until the early twentieth century when a more regional focus for utilities became necessary – electricity grids and water basin development being the classic examples. This shift to a regional focus was one of the first steps in undermining the influence of local governments in the provision of utilities. The difficulties of making the transition were indeed a key ingredient in the push to nationalisation in the decades after 1920. In the nineteenth century, the problems were more in rural areas where gas, electricity and tramway services were left largely to private companies sprawling over huge local government areas.[4]

There were two major surges of activity. The first was the rapid growth of new water and gas systems from the 1850s to the 1870s. The annual investment of some £5 million looks fairly small in comparison to what came later, as Table 11.1 shows, but it represented a very high growth rate of the capital stock. It was closely associated with the growth of industrial towns and especially those granted borough status. Over 100 towns were incorporated as new municipal boroughs in England and Wales between 1837 and the Local Government Act of 1888, with Davenport, Bolton, Manchester and Birmingham at the beginning and the likes of Hyde, Okehampton and Llanfyllin in the last few years.[5] Then came 'electrification' at the very end of the century with annual investment of £8 million in tramways, electric lighting and power undertakings alone. By 1900 there were 1,135 separate statutory private and municipal undertakings in electricity, tramways and gas and probably close to a further 1,000 in water supply. Municipal debt in England and Wales was £95 million in 1875 but had reached £262 million in 1898, leaving Lord Avebury to palpitate on 'how enormous our local indebtedness will become if some check is not put to the present

[4] R. Millward and S. Sheard, 'The urban fiscal problem, 1870–1914: government expenditure and finances in England and Wales', *Ec.HR*, 48 (1995), 501–35.

[5] Census Office, *Censuses of the Population of England and Wales, Summary Tables: 1851, 1861, 1871, 1881, 1891, 1911, 1921*, PP 1852–3 LXXXV, 1862 LI, 1873 LXXII, 1881 XLVI, 1890/1, XLIV, 1901 XL, 1911 LXXI, 1921 XL; Registrar General, *Return of Towns and Boroughs*, PP 1852/3 LXXVII and 1866 LX.

tendency!'.[6] There was a further surge in the interwar period but this was not an urban phenomenon but rather one associated with regional infrastructure development in electricity and eventually with the establishment of the national grid by the Central Electricity Board.

The first surge took place in the mid-nineteenth century in a regulatory regime which parliament had established in the 1840s, partly in response to the fact that the typical provincial town by then was often served by only one utility – the Chester Gaslight Co., the Hartlepool Water Co. – and when there was more than one, as in London, the companies each kept, by agreement, to its own district; the town was 'districted'. However, the legislation was typical of the mid-century in that the combination of a *laissez-faire* parliament and strong local interests, in the form of Highway Surveyors, Sewage Boards, Poor Law Commissioners and the like, were enough to ensure that the regulations were permissive rather than mandatory. The weakness of the regulatory regime was one of the factors behind the drive to municipalisation in the forty years up to the First World War. After the war, growing tensions emerged between urban and regional interests. The parliamentary scrutiny and regulation which followed was itself a central ingredient in the push to nationalisation in the 1940s. Overall, the 100 years from 1840 witnessed a remarkable transformation. In the mid-nineteenth century 'property' was inviolate. Even in 1900 when municipal enterprise was well established, it could be philosophically accommodated as local self-help and the 'changes occurred with very little conscious attempt to expand or transform or exalt the functions of the state'.[7] But by the 1940s the die was cast; one half of all capital formation in Britain was undertaken by the public sector and two-fifths of that was in the new nationalised industries.

(ii) A QUESTION OF PROPERTY: TOWN LIGHTING AND URBAN WATER SUPPLIES IN THE MID-NINETEENTH CENTURY

A 'very extraordinary interference with property' was how Edward Baines, member of parliament, characterised regulation of the railways and this was typical of mid-century parliamentary attitudes to government involvement with industry.[8] How then did government, central or local, ever get involved with utilities? The standard response is that *laissez-faire* and competition existed uneasily in the provision of services like electricity, gas, trams and water, let alone railways. That is, over certain defined areas – routes or districts – natural monopoly conditions existed. Because of the indivisibilities of the investment, it was cheaper for one undertaking to supply services than two or more since the latter

---

[6] Avebury, 'Municipal trading', 29; Ashley, 'Municipal trading', 36.
[7] J. Harris, *Private Lives and Public Spirit: Britain 1870–1914* (London, 1991), p. 216.
[8] J. Clapham, *The Economic History of Britain*, vol. 1 (Cambridge, 1964), p. 306.

Table 11.1 *Investment in the UK: selected sectors 1851–1938 (annual average gross fixed capital formation in £ million at 1900 prices)*

	Water	Gas	Elect.	Road pass. trans.[a]	Docks[b]	Total	Share UK inv.
1851–60	1.7	1.3	—	—	1.7	4.7	7.8%
1861–70	1.8	1.5	—	—	2.0	5.3	6.3%
1871–80	2.8	1.4	—	0.5	2.4	7.1	6.1%
1881–90	2.3	1.5	0.3	0.7	2.6	7.4	7.5%
1891–1900	3.7	2.7	2.4	1.3	2.2	12.3	7.9%
1901–10	4.7	3.2	4.7	4.7	3.4	20.7	10.4%
1911–20	1.7	1.4	5.2	1.1	1.7	11.1	6.9%
1921–5[c]	6.9		10.5[d]	8.5	2.2	28.1	14.3%
1926–30[c]	8.0		18.8[d]	8.9	3.4	39.1	15.3%
1931–5[c]	8.6		22.0[d]	5.1	2.5	38.2	14.4%
1936–8[c]	11.8		24.5[d]	10.1	2.7	49.1	14.5%

[a]Before 1921 this covers trams only. Thereafter it includes buses, cars and other road passenger transport.

[b]Before 1921 this covers docks, piers and quays, etc. From 1921 it includes canals and from 1936 air transport.

[c]All the data from 1921 onwards exclude S. Ireland and are calculated by applying the price indexes for (a) fuel and light, (b) transport and communication, (c) capital goods, in table 62 of Feinstein, *National Income* (see *Sources*, below), to his figures in table 42 on capital formation at current prices in respectively (a) gas, water and electricity, (b) road passenger transport and docks, (c) the UK.

[d]After 1920 electricity includes investment in regional grids and, from 1926, the Central Electricity Board.

Sources: C. H. Feinstein and S. Pollard, *Studies in Capital Formation in the U.K. 1790–1920* (Oxford, 1988), tables 13.1, 13.2, 13.3, 15.9, 15.11; C. H. Feinstein, *National Income, Expenditure and Output of the United Kingdom 1855–65* (Cambridge, 1972), tables 41 and 62.

would involve duplication of mains, track and related networks, quite apart from any savings that arose from concentrating production itself in large electricity generating plants or gas works. Since there were few substitutes for these services ('necessities') the potential for monopoly profits was large. Other basic economic problems were present – spillover effects in health from poor water supplies or leaky gas mains or unsafe trams. But the natural monopoly argument threads through all narratives of the development of utilities in the nineteenth century and is usually accompanied by the prediction that competition either leads to duplicate facilities, high costs, low profits and poor service or it leads to monopoly. 'In the 1830s and 1840s it was common for the mains of three or four . . . [gas] . . . companies to run down the same street in the West End.'[9] David Chatterton, Malcolm Falkus and William Robson argued that, when this led eventually to the elimination of competition, a change in public opinion occurred and promoted the growth of parliamentary involvement in these sectors.[10] Derek Matthews demurred, suggesting that parliament always had the power to regulate and became more active from the middle of the century because by then gas prices had fallen sufficiently to allow gas lighting in middle-class homes – as well as in the houses and factories of the highest income groups.[11] This new vociferous middle-class customer clamoured for control of prices especially when their decline slowed from mid-century. If true, that incentive always probably existed for water customers from the beginning of the century. The evidence is patchy but it appears that the average costs and prices of, for example the London water companies, rose by about 30 per cent in the period 1820 to 1900 when most other prices in Britain were falling.[12]

In fact there are good reasons for thinking that whilst the underlying economics of utilities are such that *laissez-faire* is often not consistent with the public interest, this still left a wide range of possible reactions and collective interventions. Whereas in France, Prussia and Belgium network systems like the railways were planned, in Britain the outcome was more the result of a battle of property interests.[13] The manufacturers of gas and the waterworks entrepreneurs wanted no truck with government. Nor was the weight of opinion in parlia-

[9] See p. 39 of D. Matthews, 'Rogues, speculators and competing monopolies: the early London gas companies, 1812–1860', *London Journal*, 2 (1985), 39–50.

[10] D. A. Chatterton, 'State control of public utilities in the nineteenth century: the London gas industry', *Business History*, 14 (1972), 166–78; M. Falkus, 'The development of municipal trading in the nineteenth century', *Business History*, 19 (1977), 134–61; W. A. Robson, 'The public utility services', in H. J. Laski, W. I. Jennings and W. A. Robson, eds., *A Century of Municipal Progress: The Last One Hundred Years* (London, 1935), pp. 299–331.

[11] D. Matthews, 'Laissez-faire and the London gas industry in the nineteenth century: another look', *Ec.HR*, 2nd series, 39 (1986), 244–63.

[12] See later discussion of water and also J. Cavalcanti, 'Economic aspects of the provision and development of water supply in nineteenth century Britain' (PhD Thesis, Manchester University, 1991).   [13] F. Dobbin, *Forging Industrial Policy* (Cambridge, 1994).

ment in favour of intervention. Deputations to protect the interests of property argued successfully 'that nothing which British governments had ever done or left undone made it likely they would prove good managers; that centralisation was un-English', a sentiment echoed one year later in 1845 by the *Economist*.[14] Why then did government get involved? Fundamentally, there were two reasons. The first was that the huge capital requirements of these enterprises meant that local sources of finance would not be enough. 'Blind capital' would be attracted only if there were limited liability and, since that was regarded as a great privilege, there would have to be a parliamentary act with appropriate scrutiny of the financial soundness of the company. The investment expansion recorded in Table 11.1 was therefore largely financed by borrowing approved under the relevant parliamentary act. Both private and municipal undertakings came to issue their own stock quoted on the London and provincial stock exchanges. There is no doubt that the whole process favoured the large companies and municipalities – only they could deal with the administrative costs of securing stock issues and parliamentary bills. Indeed, over the whole range of urban developments, including investment in the sanitary infrastructure, it was the large local authorities like Leeds and Glasgow which flourished since the finance available from other sources, such as the Public Works Loan Board, involved high interest charges and short repayment periods.[15] The second reason why governments were drawn into the operations of utilities relates to the question of rights of way. Land had to be dug up for mains and leased or purchased for tramways and railway track. Local authorities sometimes had sufficient powers of approval but in the early years of the century this was less likely and the central government was drawn in. By an act of parliament, an undertaking was permitted to lay mains and supply gas and water. Exclusive franchises were never awarded but whoever was first in the field clearly had some advantages. In recognition of this parliament imposed ceilings on tariffs, in line with previous practice for canals.

That was the limit of government involvement in the early days of the nineteenth century. The consumer interest was to be protected by the encouragement of competition. For example, in the first decade of the century in London, there were three water companies but, as the 1821 Select Committee on the Supply of Water to the Metropolis reported, subsequently the 'East London, West Middlesex and Grand Junction Company were formed under . . . several Acts of Parliament . . . The principle of the Acts under which these companies were instituted was to encourage competition.'[16] By the middle of the century, however, London was fairly well 'districted' by the water and gas companies,

[14] As quoted in Clapham, *Economic History*, pp. 414, 422.
[15] J. F. Wilson, S. Sheard and R. Millward, 'Trends in local authority loan expenditure in England and Wales, 1870–1914', *University of Manchester Working Papers in Economic and Social History*, 22 (1993). [16] Select Committee on the Supply of Water to the Metropolis, *Report*, May (1821).

whilst in the provinces it was unusual for there to be more than one company serving a town.

Thus the mid-century stance of government was broadly determined by its interest in 'property'. It was this rather than planning which determined the route system for railways and the form of the controls on gas and water. The latter took basically two forms. First was the control on prices and dividends. It seems doubtful, despite the claims of Chatterton and Matthews, that there was any significant shift in parliament's attitude in the middle of the century.[17] There were certainly lots of complaints about services and many were authoritative. The 1842 Chadwick Report, the two reports of the Commissioners on the State of Large Towns in 1844 and 1845 and the report in 1847 of the Surveying Officers, Arthur Johnes and Samuel Clegg, contained blistering critiques of the market structure of these industries.[18] Moreover the 1847 Gasworks and Waterworks Clauses Act spelled out maximum prices and a 10 per cent limit on dividends. However, this was very much a tidying up operation setting out what should appear in the acts for individual towns and undertakings. The sheer numbers of applications coming forward during the mid-century Victorian economic boom are sufficient explanation. Again, the data are patchy for the early years of the century but it seems that whilst there were only ten municipal corporations in England and Wales operating their own water system in 1845, there were already sixty-seven joint stock companies.[19] In the next ten years the number of municipal systems quadrupled and increased by a further 50 per cent in the subsequent ten years reaching sixty-one in 1865 by which time there were 147 joint stock water companies.[20] In any case the legislation, as is well documented, had no teeth. It only applied to new undertakings, there was no inspectorate, complaints had to be taken up at the Quarter Sessions and the gas companies in particular were adept at 'watering' the capital base in various ways to produce nominally lower rates of profit.[21] Meanwhile, the whole of the unfettered gas sector was expanding at an astonishing rate. There were already 145 undertakings in Britain in 1851 and this figure rose to 330 by 1871. Some of the increase represented an absorption of the small non-statutory companies but

---

[17] Chatterton, 'State control of public utilities'; Matthews, 'Laissez-faire'.

[18] E. Chadwick, *Report on the Sanitary Conditions of the Labouring Population of Great Britain: 1842*, ed. M. W. Flinn (Edinburgh, 1965); Commissioners on the State of Large Towns and Populous Districts, *First Report 1844, Second Report 1845*; Johnes and Clegg, *Observations or General Report on the Existing System of Lighting Towns with Gas, by Messrs. Johnes and Clegg, Surveying Officers*, PP 1847 XXII.

[19] Falkus, 'Development of municipal trading'; A. L. Dakyns, 'The water supply of English towns in 1846', *Manchester School*, 2 (1931), 18–26.

[20] H. Finer, *Municipal Trading* (London, 1941), p. 41.

[21] See pp. 109–15 of R. Millward, 'The emergence of gas and water monopolies in nineteenth-century Britain: contested markets and public control', in J. Foreman-Peck, ed., *New Perspectives on the Late Victorian Economy* (Cambridge, 1991), pp. 96–124.

even their numbers have been estimated to have risen from 486 in 1851 to 764 in 1873.[22]

The second arm of government control related to what we might call supply conditions, which for water supply was probably even more important than the structure of the market. Many of these matters are covered in a separate chapter of this volume (see Chapter 7) but for our purposes it is important to note that the mid-century legislation was as fatally flawed as that related to tariffs. Whilst there were safety and health issues associated with leaky gas mains, the main environmental issue surrounded the cleanliness of the water supply and it was this which was at the heart of the 1840s health reports mentioned above. The 1848 Public Health Act gave local authorities powers to facilitate an improvement in the quality of supply but they were not mandatory. It was compulsory to establish a Local Board of Health only when mortality exceeded 23 per 1,000; otherwise it depended on whether at least 10 per cent of ratepayers petitioned for one. The Local Boards had enabling powers to secure adequate water supplies, to erect free public cisterns and pumps and to establish their own waterworks but none of this was mandatory and in the case of waterworks required the agreement of the local water company. Progress towards clean water supplies at constant high pressure was slow. Even the laws which specified that the companies should supply fire plugs were weak because they failed to specify the minimum distance between the plugs. In 1871 the Royal Sanitary Commission noted in its report that promoters of water bills were still being allowed to escape the obligation to provide a constant high pressure supply.[23]

As a result when local authorities and parliament were faced, from the late 1860s onwards, with the prospect of new utilities in tramways and then electricity supply, the tide had swung towards including public interest clauses in the legislation. Of course 'property' was still a strong vested interest and the secretary of the Board of Trade felt that whilst local authorities were the best bodies to construct and develop the tramlines, given their disruptive nature in Britain's winding narrow streets, the lines should be leased out to company operators. The 1870 Tramways Act did limit local authorities in this way and the private companies were actually allowed to build track as well as operate services and without any ceiling on dividends. But the legislation did very clearly recognise a public interest. Frontagers, the local road authority and the local council all had rights to be consulted and their interests recognised in the process of parliamentary approval. Maximum fares and workmen's concessions were introduced and local authorities could pass by-laws on speed and frequency. The revolutionary change was to grant powers to local authorities under the act to purchase the

[22] Table 1 of R. Millward and R. Ward, 'From private to public ownership of gas undertakings in England and Wales, 1851–1947: chronology, incidence and causes', *Business History*, 35 (1993), 1–21.   [23] Royal Sanitary Commission, *Report* (London, 1871), p. 42.

track and company after twenty-one years. A similar purchase clause was put into the 1882 Electric Lighting Act which also set maximum tariffs for electricity supply and gave local authorities a clear mandate to set up plant. The gate to municipalisation of electricity and trams was open and the weak regulatory regime for gas and water in the 1840–70 period was a contributory element. But very many other factors were involved as we shall now see.

(iii) SOCIALISM OR CAPITALISM? THE RISE OF MUNICIPAL ENTERPRISE

The huge expansion of municipal water systems and gas works in the latter part of the nineteenth century together with their promotion by the Webbs and the Fabians prompted many observers to characterise the rise of municipal trading as 'gas and water socialism'. It was a useful characterisation for opponents. 'Private capital not only complained of government regulation, but also the stimulus given municipal socialism by the [1882 Electric Lighting] Act.'[24] Lord Avebury complained of the 'the new school of "Progressives" . . . [who] seem to consider that we might place over any municipal buildings the motto which Huc saw over a Chinese shop, "All sorts of business transacted here with unfailing success"'.[25]

Both John Kellett and Derek Fraser have shown that municipal socialism as an ideology was very much a phenomenon of the early decades of the twentieth century and of debates about London government in particular.[26] It is true, as Table 11.2 shows, that there was a massive spurt in municipal activity at this time. The metropolitan boroughs were established under the 1894 Local Government Act and many subsequently took to generating electricity. From 1895 to 1900 the number of statutory electricity undertakings in Britain shot up from 91 to 229 of which 71 per cent were owned by local government. The tramways spurt followed in the next five years; already 213 undertakings in 1900 but 311 by 1905 of which one half were municipally owned. But municipalisation was clearly not just a London matter and actually started a good half century earlier. The most dramatic growth in statutory water undertakings was from about 1845 to the early 1870s by which time there were 250 systems run by local government. For gas the most rapid growth was from the 1850s to the 1880s during which period the share of the municipals grew from 13 per cent to 39 per cent, remaining at roughly that level right through to the 1940s – though the initial spurt was most noticeable in Scotland and the share of municipal undertakings in England and

---

[24] See p. 35 of T. P. Hughes, 'British electrical industry lag: 1882–1888', *Technology and Culture*, 3 (1962), 27–44.   [25] Avebury, 'Municipal trading', 25.

[26] J. R. Kellett, 'Municipal socialism, enterprise and trading in the Victorian city', *UHY* (1978), 36–45; W. H. Fraser, 'Municipal socialism and social policy', in R. J. Morris and R. Rodger, eds., *The Victorian City* (London, 1993).

Wales continued to rise in a fairly smooth fashion through to the 1930s. Hence, well before the term municipal socialism was seriously bandied around, a huge part of the shift to public ownership had taken place. In any case, as we shall see, the political hue of town councils dominated by businessmen and ratepayers can hardly be called socialist.

In accounting for the rise in municipal trading many writers have relied on the monopoly argument discussed earlier. The American observers put this at the front of their explanations. 'All services . . . which are in the nature of monopolies should by preference be in the hands of the Municipalities', said the editor of *Traction and Transmission* in 1901 adding that 'private companies cannot be trusted to exercise the powers of monopoly with discretion'.[27] A modern writer on trams said a key element was 'the economic argument. Tramways were the monopoly of a public necessity.'[28] The large team of American civic officials and academics who visited Britain in the early 1900s subscribed to the view that 'there is a desire to keep the city from being mulcted by a private company'.[29] In the authoritative surveys of municipal enterprise by British academics, the monopoly issue was central.[30] Of course, other factors were often thrown in – safety, the disruption of streets by the laying of mains and track. In fact some of the lists become quite bewildering. The *Birmingham Daily Post* in 1872 claimed to be capturing a popular mood in discerning

> a general feeling that for the purposes of preventing the creation of a new monopoly in private hands, to ensure the control of the streets, and then to promote the public convenience, and also to limit as far as possible, injurious competition with Corporation gas lighting, the supply of electric light ought to be in the hands of the local governing authority.[31]

There are problems of both theory and practice in this line of argument. If the sources of concern were the prices and profits of a private company operating in a natural monopoly setting then one solution would have been to regulate those prices and profits. In other words most of the above arguments might explain the desire for *public control* but not necessarily the desire for *public ownership*. Moreover, how is one to account for the behaviour of those town councils who allowed private companies to continue – not simply the likes of Eastbourne, Oxford and York but also industrial and commercial centres like Liverpool, Sheffield and Newcastle did not municipalise operations in some of the utility areas? There is also a North/South divide in some industries. 'Geographically,

---

[27] Editor, *Traction and Transmission*, 1 (1901), 294.
[28] J. P. MacKay, *Tramways and Trolleys* (Princeton, 1976), p. 172.
[29] National Civic Federation, *Municipal and Private Ownership of Public Utilities* (New York, 1907), p. 186.
[30] Falkus, 'Development of municipal trading',145–6; Robson, 'Public utility services', pp. 309–10.
[31] Quoted on p. 19 of Lewis Jones, 'The municipalities and the electricity supplies industry in Birmingham', *West Midlands Studies*, 13 (1980), 19–26.

Table 11.2 *Number of statutory local utility undertakings in the UK 1845–1956[a]*

	Electricity		Trams		Gas		Water		
	PR	LG	PR	LG	PR	LG	PR	Munic[b]	LG
1845	—	—	—	—	n/a	n/a	67[c]	10	n/a
1851	—	—	—	—	125	20	n/a	n/a	n/a
1855	—	—	—	—	136	31	n/a	39	n/a
1865	—	—	—	—	176	59	147[c]	61	n/a
1871	—	—	n/a	n/a	255	75	n/a	n/a	250[d]
1875	n/a	n/a	37[e]	7[e]	269[f]	103[f]	n/a	127	n/a
1879	n/a	n/a	51	9	n/a	n/a	n/a	n/a	n/a
1885	n/a	n/a	129	27	364	160	n/a	195	n/a
1890	n/a	n/a	127	29	416	178	n/a	n/a	n/a
1895	52	39	116	38	492	203	n/a	237	n/a
1900	65	164	114	99	453	240	n/a	n/a	n/a
1905	n/a	n/a	136	175	482	270	n/a	306	n/a
1914	n/a	n/a	108	171	519	312	200	326	820[d]
1926[g]	233	360	71	170	463	321	n/a	n/a	n/a
1934[g]	n/a	n/a	n/a	n/a	412	314	173	n/a	878
1938[g]	208	373	n/a	n/a	405	298	n/a	n/a	n/a
1946[g]	191	374	n/a	n/a	409	271	n/a	n/a	n/a
1956[g]	—	—	—	—	—	—	90	n/a	925

[a]PR is the private sector. LG are local authorities, including all joint boards. The data for trams refer to the ownership of track; for electricity, to undertakings supplying electricity for light or power. Company data generally refer to financial years ending in the years quoted; for local authorities the financial years often end in the following spring.

[b]Undertakings owned by the corporations of municipal boroughs.

c England and Wales only.

d Data probably exclude S. Ireland.

e Data refer to 1876.

f Data refer to 1874.

g Excludes S. Ireland.

Sources: official: Board of Trade, *Annual Returns of All Authorised Gas Undertakings* (1851 onwards); Board of Trade, *Annual Returns of Street and Road Tramways and Light Railways* (1877 onwards), PP 1902 XCIII; Board of Trade, *Return Relating to Authorised Electricity Supply Undertakings in the U.K. Belonging to Local Authorities and Companies for the Year 1900*, PP 1928/9 XXX; Balfour Committee on Industry and Trade, *Further Factors in Industrial and Commercial Efficiency*; Ministry of Fuel and Power, *Engineering and Financial Statistics of All Authorised Undertakings 1946/7*, Electricity Supply Act (41–211–0–47) (London, 1948). Secondary sources: A. L. Dakyns, 'The water supply of English towns in 1846', *Manchester School*, 2 (1931), 18–26; M. E. Falkus, 'The development of municipal trading in the nineteenth century', *Business History*, 19 (1977), 134–61; J. Foreman-Peck and R. Millward, *Public and Private Ownership of British Industry 1820–1990* (Oxford, 1994), chs. 2, 4, 5, 6, 8; E. L. Garcke, *Manual of Electrical Undertakings and Directory of Officials*, vol. i: 1896 (London, 1896); J. A. Hassan, 'The water industry 1900–1951: a failure of public policy?', in R. Millward and J. Singleton, eds., *The Political Economy of Nationalisation in Britain 1920–1950* (Cambridge, 1995), pp. 189–211; W. A. Robson, 'The public utility services', in H. J. Laski, W. I. Jennings and W. A. Robson, eds., *A Century of Municipal Progress: The Last 100 Years* (London, 1935).

most municipal gasworks were located in the industrial midlands, the north and
Scotland, though', said Matthews 'why some councils decided to take over their
gas works whilst others did not is not immediately obvious and the answer must
await more detailed investigation.'[32] How finally are we to account for the
differences across industries – by the 1930s about two-fifths of gasworks were
municipally owned but it was nearer to two-thirds for electricity and four-fifths
in water supply?

Two groups had a powerful interest in these decisions. One group was manufacturers and other businessmen; the other was ratepayers. The idea that many
councillors were strongly motivated by civic pride is a recurring theme in the
literature and often adduced as a reason for municipalisation – in order to ensure
high standards of service. Robert Crawford LLD, ex-councillor, member for ten
years of the Committee on Street Railways, ex-burgh magistrate, deputy lieutenant of the court of the city of Glasgow etc., etc., claimed in 1906 that there
was

> a large infusion among citizens of every class of the civic spirit. There is civic pride
> in civic enterprise and institutions . . .The secret of success . . . lies deeper than
> the mere machinery and must be sought for mainly in the honesty, uprightness,
> capacity, self-sacrifice and patriotism of the men chosen by an intelligent commu-
> nity and entrusted with this great communal duty.[33]

But the businessmen and ratepayers had some very specific economic interests. Linda Jones has estimated that 55 per cent of Birmingham councillors in
the period 1860–91 were businessmen.[34] The fortunes of their factories were
often contingent on good local water and transport and if that required municipal operations, so be it. To take one example of business influence, Wakefield
council wished to avoid some of the health problems in taking their water supply
from the local polluted rivers by drawing on the good clean water in deep local
wells. This option was eventually dropped because the water was hard and therefore unsuitable for use in textile mills whose owners were well represented on
the council.[35] In all towns businessmen had a vested interest in a good water
supply for fire fighting and the American literature shows that fire insurance premiums were noticeably less in towns with good water systems.[36]

[32] Matthews, 'Laissez-faire', 261.
[33] See pp. 3 and 5 of R. Crawford, 'Glasgow's experience with municipal ownership and operation', *Annals of the American Academy of Political and Social Science*, 27 (1906), 1–19.
[34] See p. 24 of L. Jones, 'Public pursuit of private profit: liberal businessmen and municipal politics in Birmingham, 1845–1900', *Business History*, 25 (1983), 24–59.
[35] C. Hamlin, 'Muddling in bumbledom: on the enormity of large sanitary improvements in four British towns, 1855–1885', *Victorian Studies*, 33 (1988–9), 57–81.
[36] L. Anderson, 'Hard choices: supplying water to New England Towns', *Journal of Interdisciplinary History*, 15 (1984), 211–34.

The other group, sometimes overlapping with businessmen, were ratepayers. The last quarter of the century saw town councils in the rapidly expanding industrial boroughs faced with immense financial burdens as they struggled to overcome the terrible living and working conditions which industrialisation had brought. All were investing heavily in water supply, sewerage systems and roads and also had responsibility for the growing bill for policing and education. A commonly quoted index is that, in the last quarter of the century, population in Britain rose by 37 per cent, rateable values by 61 per cent and rates by 141 per cent.[37] Any device which could lower the burden on ratepayers would find ready ears. Fraser suggests that rates were paid by the landlord in England and Wales but by the tenant in Scotland, one outcome of which was that in Scotland municipalities never aimed at using trading surpluses to ease the rates burden.[38] The story in England and Wales was quite the reverse, as we shall see, since setting fares and tariffs for electricity, gas and trams at levels sufficient to generate profits which could finance urban improvements was a way of taxing non-ratepayers, and indeed non-residents, who used the service.

The case of water supply is probably different from that of electricity, gas and trams and nearer to the way councils organised and financed other services like paving, refuse collection, sanitation, bathhouses and cemeteries. The 1875 Public Health Act *required* local authorities to ensure that adequate water supplies existed. Table 11.3 shows the average levels of local authority trading profits each year for a sample of thirty-six towns. The water undertakings made large operating surpluses but (as the 1904–13 data show) these were usually not enough to meet loan charges and so water undertakings generally made a financial loss. If the object was to generate profits, the achievements were poor. More likely the aim was to expand supplies of clean water for residents, as the 1875 act required, and to develop soft water and a firefighting capability for factory owners. Why, though, was water municipalised? In some respects the issue is more difficult to pin down than the cases of electricity, gas and trams where the large set of private operators continued to flourish and provide a benchmark for comparison. Most of the water undertakings became municipal and fully absorbed into local government by virtue of water charges for domestic consumption being levied as a rate – a tax on the rateable value of property like the rest of local taxation.

Some of the explanations in the literature for this shift are not convincing. John Hassan and, much earlier, Albert Shaw and Douglas Knoop, argued that the large-scale schemes for taking water supplies to the large urban conurbations involved levels of finance and a degree of planning beyond the scope of private

[37] Millward and Sheard, 'Urban fiscal problem', 515–17; M. J. Daunton, 'Urban Britain', in T. R. Gourvish and A. O. Day, eds., *Later Victorian Britain, 1867–1900* (London, 1988), pp. 37–67.
[38] Fraser, 'Municipal socialism', p. 278.

Table 11.3 *Average annual gross trading profits per town council 1871–1913 (sample of 36 towns: £000)*

Profits	1871–5	1876–80	1881–5	1886–90	1891–5
Water	n/a	10.91[a]	14.08	17.14	18.76
Gas	n/a	3.94	7.07	12.97	8.35
Markets	n/a	3.36[b]	3.16	2.68	3.03
Estates	n/a	6.32	8.74	9.67	11.85
Total profits	12.23[c]	24.29	33.03	38.57	42.01

	1896–1900	1901–3	1904–10	1911–13
Water				
Profits	20.28	21.35	28.36	32.53
Loan charges	n/a	n/a	31.34[d]	31.88
Gas				
Profits	10.69	12.24	14.71	15.54
Loan charges	n/a	n/a	11.26[d]	12.38
Electricity				
Profits	0.75	8.58	16.99	20.16
Loan charges	n/a	n/a	15.44	19.05
Trams				
Profits	0.71	12.14	18.03	18.20
Loan charges	n/a	n/a	14.10	15.73
Market profits	3.15	3.32	3.04	4.05
Cemetery profits	−0.04	−1.65	0.02	0.76
Harbour profits	−0.25	0.27	0.97	3.44
Estates profits	14.62	15.12	15.50	17.08
Total profits	49.96	71.35	100.03[e]	113.85[e]
Loan charges	n/a	n/a	73.72	88.86
Transfers (net)	n/a	n/a	n/a	15.84
Balance	n/a	n/a	16.39	5.20

[a]Excludes Leicester 1876, 1877, 1878.
[b]Excludes Gt Torrington 1876.
[c]Includes only some of the years for some of the towns.
[d]Excludes Sunderland 1906.
[e]Excludes Thetford 1908–12.
Sources and definitions: The source is Local Government Board, *Annual Local Taxation Returns* 1871–1913. See below for details of the sample towns. Entries are unweighted averages of the 36 towns and therefore columns do not necessarily add up. Profits data are gross trading profits. Profits of electricity, trams, cemeteries and harbours were non-existent or zero before 1896. Loan charges include interest; relevant aggregate data for both these items are not available for the years before 1904. Data refer to the financial years of town councils ending in the year quoted.

Table 11.3 (*cont.*)

The sample of 36 towns: the location of each of the sample of 36 towns and their status in 1913 are as follows.

	North	*Midlands & Wales*	*South*
County boroughs	Blackpool	Bristol	Hastings
	Bradford	Hanley	Norwich
	Leeds	Leicester	Plymouth
	Liverpool	Lincoln	Southampton
	Manchester	Northampton	
	St Helens	Nottingham	
	Sunderland	Oxford	
	Preston	Swansea	
	York	Wolverhampton	
Boroughs	Carlisle	Carmarthen	Gt Torrington
	Doncaster	Louth	Kingston
	Richmond	Luton	Marlborough
		Wrexham	Ramsgate
			Shaftesbury
			Thetford
Urban district councils			Tottenham

enterprise.[39] The investment requirements of the Rivington Pike scheme for Liverpool in the 1840s and the later one for Vyrnwy in Wales, the Loch Katrine project for Glasgow in the 1850s and the Thirlmere and Longdendale schemes for Manchester in the 1870s and 1880s were certainly substantial. But private enterprise had laid a route network for railways in the 1830s and 1840s equivalent to our modern motorway network and the later work on lines linking the outer reaches of Wales and Scotland involved even more costly outlays on bridges, viaducts and tunnels. Rather, one might point to the institutional difficulties in the way of companies earning sufficient profit to expand supplies at a rate demanded by town councils.

That is, water supply is obviously dependent on natural resources and hence, like agriculture, is liable to diminishing returns. Unless significant technical progress in storage and delivery takes place, expansion will lead to rising costs. Clearly this happened in the nineteenth century as the demands from rapid urban population growth and industrialisation exhausted the more obvious local

---

[39] J. A. Hassan, 'The growth and impact of the British water industry in the nineteenth century', *Ec.HR*, 2nd series, 38 (1985), 531–47; A. Shaw, 'Glasgow: a municipal study', *Century*, 39 (1890), 721–36; D. Knoop, *Principles and Methods of Municipal Trading* (London, 1912).

supplies and towns had to look further afield. Data on the cost of water are actually quite meagre but Jose Cavalcanti's recent work on supplies to London suggests that costs per gallon did rise. The annual supply of all the London water companies came to 8,947 million gallons in 1820 and rose to 73,766 million by 1900. His estimates of the companies' total annual costs are £103,000 in 1820 and £1,223,000 in 1900, implying that the costs per thousand gallons rose by 30 per cent from 3d. to 4d.[40] Relative to the prices of all other goods and services, most of which were falling, the real cost of water may have risen by about 50 per cent in the nineteenth century. For the companies to make a normal rate of return, water charges would have had to rise accordingly and large numbers of customers captured in order to exploit the economies of scale and contiguity central to keeping costs per unit down. This is where the maximum prices specified in the legislation did appear to bite. A contemporary authority, Arthur Silverthorne, suggested the maxima allowed in the 1847 Clauses Act were never high enough for the companies and so they, instead, engaged in protracted legal battles over the valuation of property to which the water rate was applied.[41] Most business customers were metered; for example, another contemporary reported that in a sample of twenty-nine undertakings all 'trade' customers were supplied by meter.[42] Many councils dominated by manufacturers had meter schedules which were very generous as was the 'compensation' water allowed to factories operating near rivers and reservoirs subject to development in water schemes. None of this meant profit for the water companies. Similarly, it was important for the companies to capture large numbers of customers given the 'lumpiness' of the investment required in water resource development. Ideally such customers should be geographically concentrated in order to take advantage of the economies of contiguity inherent in distribution networks. A major problem which the companies therefore faced was that for constant high pressure supply to be introduced – which all parliamentary reports were promoting – it was essential for customers themselves to invest in pipes, sinks and drains in their own homes. A great deal of uncertainty therefore surrounded the operation of companies dealing on a one to one basis with households, some of whom would be reluctant to make the necessary investments. A great attraction of municipal operation was that it involved the finance of water services to households by rates, the tax on rateable values. By such a uniform levy, councils automatically enrolled all ratepayers on to the water undertakings' books.[43]

For electricity, trams and gas different issues were involved. One was the desire to curb the excess profits that would arise when private enterprise were left to

[40] Cavalcanti, *Economic Aspects*, tables 4.3, 4.10, 4.12, 5.7.
[41] A. Silverthorne, *London and Provincial Water Supplies* (London, 1884), pp. 10, 12, 38.
[42] See pp. 66–7 of W. Sherratt, 'Water supply to large towns', *Journal of the Manchester Geographical Society*, 4 (1888), 58–71.
[43] Royal Commission on Water Supply, *Report of the Commissioners* (1869), pp. 246–8.

operate services which were natural monopolies. On the face of it this could be done by controlling fares and tariffs and by taxing profits. Such local taxes and controls were often not available to local authorities in Britain, unlike Germany.[44] This helps to explain municipalisation in Scotland where in addition the companies were cheap to buy out since the law never gave them the right to operate in perpetuity, as in England and Wales. For the latter, our thesis is that a driving force behind municipalisation was the desire of local councils to get their hands on the surpluses of these trading enterprises and use them to 'relieve the rates'. This was Joseph Chamberlain's dictum. Unless a council had substantial property income ('estates'), essential town improvements would be deferred unless some revenue other than rates was found.[45] But if it was paramount why did York, Bournemouth, Salisbury and many others refrain from extensive municipal trading? Why did Liverpool, Bristol and Hull allow private gas companies to flourish? Why was there the North/South dichotomy reported by Matthews?[46]

It is important to recognise that in the early years of the century, the owners of the private companies – gas only at that stage of course – were often major local ratepayers. Together with bankers, lawyers and other professionals, they would form the local body of improvement commissioners or councillors.[47] By the late nineteenth century they were a much more dispersed group as capital came from various sources and the local ratepayers were as likely to be dominated by shopkeepers.[48] Many of the growing industrial towns of the Midlands and the North faced a substantial fiscal problem emanating from the rising demands for expenditures on public health, roads, policing, poor relief, education and other services. The local authorities had little room for manoeuvre since they had no powers to raise income taxes or levy duties on commodities or profits or land. Some grants and assigned revenues emerged from central government in the last decades of the century[49] but, in general, little was done to alleviate the widely differing circumstances of the local authorities. The ratepayers staged revolts but also, as Peter Hennock noted, they looked for alternative revenue sources. The ports of Liverpool, Swansea, Bristol, Hull, Yarmouth and

[44] J. C. Brown, 'Coping with crisis: the diffusion of water works in the late nineteenth century German towns', *Journal of Economic History*, 48 (1988), 307–18.

[45] Fraser, 'Municipal socialism', p. 262; P. J. Waller, *Town, City and Nation* (Oxford, 1983), p. 304.

[46] Matthews, 'Laissez-faire'.

[47] For Preston see B. W. Awty, 'The introduction of gas lighting to Preston', *Transactions of the History Society of Lancashire and Cheshire*, 125 (1975); for Chester see J. F. Wilson, 'Competition in the early gas industry: the case of Chester Gas Light Company 1817–1856', *Transactions of the Antiquarian Society of Lancashire and Cheshire*, 86 (1990), 87–110.

[48] E. P. Hennock, *Fit and Proper Persons* (London, 1973); J. Garrard, *Leadership and Power in Victorian Industrial Towns, 1830–80* (Manchester, 1983).

[49] G. C. Baugh, 'Government grants in aid of the rates in England and Wales, 1889–1990', *Bull. IHR*, 65 (1992), 215–37.

Southampton all had substantial income from dockside property.[50] Hence the reason why none of these ports municipalised the local gasworks in the nineteenth century. It can be seen in Table 11.3 that estate income like this was the major source of trading income for the sample of thirty-six towns. Leeds, Manchester and Birmingham, however, did not have large estates and looked elsewhere. Their ratepayers were no longer dominated by the owners of local factories and utilities. The water supply undertakings were out of the question for the reason given before. Indeed, water supply in Manchester and Leeds was openly cross-subsidised from gas profits.[51] Thus receipts from markets and gas undertakings were a useful supplement to estates in the early years whilst electricity and trams were even more attractive because the purchase clauses in the 1870 and 1882 acts meant their acquisition prices would be less than for the gas companies who had unentailed property rights. Mr E. Garcke, that great student of electricity supply developments, managing director of the British Electric Traction Company and champion of the private sector, demonstrated to the Select Committee on Municipal Trading (1903) that most municipal undertakings were being run with a view to profit, and, therefore, he was opposed to the majority of them.[52] By that stage trading profits after deducting loan charges, for the sample towns recorded in Table 11.3, averaged £25,000 per town, of which £15,000 came from estates. This was a sizeable income and enough to finance the whole of the annual labour, maintenance and capital charges of public health and police.[53]

Of course, towns with a good rates base like Bournemouth and Eastbourne would not be under the same pressure to get their hands on trading profits even though their populations were growing. Their 'urban' problems were also nothing like those of Darlington and West Bromwich and the other industrial boroughs of the North and Midlands – hence the North/South divide in the incidence of municipalisation. For a town like Chichester or Chester or Norwich, with a stagnant or only slowly growing population, the pressures were even less. Some governmental units were not well suited to provide a home for utilities. London was the classic case. The formation of metropolitan undertakings was almost impossible as long as the motley collection of vestries, drainage boards and road authorities persisted. Only when London government was centralised by the 1894 Local Government Act was it possible to set in train the establishment of London County Council Tramways and the Metropolitan Water Board. Another kind of difficulty faced the councils of small towns who could ill afford the administrative costs of mounting a parliamentary bill needed for municipalisation. Small towns

---

[50] E. P. Hennock, 'Finance and politics in urban local government in England, 1835–1900', *HJ*, 6 (1963), 212–25. [51] *Ibid.*, 222.
[52] Joint Select Committee of the House of Lords and the House of Commons, *Report on Municipal Trading*, PP 1900 VII and 1903 VII; Garcke's evidence is quoted in Gibbons, 'Opposition to municipal socialism', 254. [53] Millward and Sheard, 'Urban fiscal problem', 508.

in rural areas were the least likely candidates since utilities thrived most economically in high density conditions and sufficiently large catchment areas would in any case straddle several local government boundaries. Joint municipal concerns did emerge but it was more common to leave trams to the private sector and gas supplies were met by companies like East Kent Gas and South Staffordshire Gas.[54]

(iv) ECONOMIC PERFORMANCE

Given the concern about rising municipal debt, about the problems of coping in both America and Britain with the difficult living and working conditions which nineteenth-century urbanisation had brought and given present day interest in privatisation and public ownership, there are surprisingly few quantitative estimates of the performance of the urban infrastructure industries. In the 1890s and early 1900s there was a lot of good knockabout debate on the merits of private and municipal enterprise. In America the *Street Railway Journal* and *Traction and Transmission* hosted articles over the whole range of municipal activities. Much of these took the form of looking at the fares and tariffs levied by samples of undertakings and recording whose were lowest. Alternatively, the unit costs of production and supply were calculated in order to gauge the efficiency of operations. This drew in such worthies as the Director of the Eleventh US census, special commissioner to Cuba, etc., etc., who felt that 'with the exception of two or three exceptionally well managed municipal gas plants, the British Corporation plants are neither so well nor so economically managed as the private plants, nor do they serve the public so advantageously'.[55] This brought replies from the likes of Mr R. Donald who pointed out that Mr Porter's sources were invariably champions of the private sector like the attorney for the private companies on the first electric power bill, Mr Garcke, whom we have met already, a committee of the London Chamber of Commerce and an officer of the London Gas, Light and Coke Company, 'one of the most hated monopolies in the Metropolis'.[56] Donald then went on to show that the accounts of the electricity, tramways and gas undertakings revealed that fares, tariffs and costs were lower in the municipal sector. The trouble was that none of these writers was looking at what affected costs and prices apart from ownership: the cost of coal, the location of the plants, the scale of output. Similarly, Milo Maltbie's claim, that owing 'to the cheapness of price and better service under municipal operations, a larger number of the poorer classes used gas'[57] ignores the fact that

---

[54] L. Bussel, 'Privatisation: tramways: a guide to policy', *Public Enterprise*, 32 (1988).

[55] See p. 111 of R. P. Porter, 'The failure of municipal ownership in England', *Street Railway Journal*, 20 (1902), 109–14, 216–20.

[56] See p. 31 of R. Donald, 'Success of municipal ownership in Great Britain', *Street Railway Journal*, 21 (1903), 30–4 and 72–6.

[57] See p. 559 of M. R. Maltbie, 'Gas lighting in Great Britain, *Municipal Affairs*, 4 (1900), 538–73.

municipal gas plants were, as we noted earlier, located mainly in the North and Midlands with the private companies in the South so that they faced different market and cost conditions. Only if one had satisfactorily allowed for these conditions could conclusions about the role of ownership be drawn.

Similar dangers lie in the strong claim made by some historians, as well as contemporaries, about the cost and quality of services before and after municipalisation. We might expect Mr Crawford, Glasgow councillor (see above), to wax eloquent on the newly municipalised gas works. Under the two private companies, tariffs had been 'too high, quality bad, service faulty' whilst after municipalisation in 1869 'there is no complaint on the part of any sector of the public'.[58] But we also find Mr A. Shaw writing a piece in the learned journal *Century* suggesting that the town had been 'wretchedly supplied with unwholesome water at high rates by private companies' but after these companies had been bought out in the 1850s the municipal exploitation of Loch Katrine brought to the city 'a magnificent and inexhaustible supply of mountain water . . . [and] the city has been able easily to make the works pay'.[59] Finally, William Smart of Glasgow University can be found explaining in the *Quarterly Journal of Economics* of 1895 how, as a result of the municipalisation of the tramways in 1894, fares were reduced, wages increased and the tramcars better fitted whilst the employees had shorter hours and better uniforms![60] The before and after comparisons also do not control for what else was going on. The 1890s and early 1900s in particular were periods of great technical change in electricity supply and tramways and in addition the institutional constraints on the private companies need specifying.

Contemporary evidence on this dimension of performance was therefore contradictory and inconclusive. Subsequently, interest in statistical comparisons seems to have waned and Herman Finer, in his authoritative 1941 study of municipal trading, avoided 'comparisons of the success of municipal and private enterprises . . . for the reason that they are practically impossible', resting his case on Pigou's dictum 'that attempts to conduct a comparison by reference to statistics are foredoomed to failure'.[61] Recently, interest has revived and the broad message from studies of gas and electricity supply in this period is that there is not much to choose between municipal and private enterprise. The important issue is the basis of comparison. For example, given that both forms of ownership existed in this period (contrast the nationalised industries in post-1945 Britain) we can compare towns served by municipal undertakings with towns served by private companies. In addition, data are usually available on the cost of fuel, wage rates and the scale of operations. Table 11.4 displays figures for gas supply in 1898 in thirty-five towns spread fairly evenly across Scotland, England and Wales and including London and Dublin. London has an advantage in its population density, generally a favourable factor for the costs of operation, but

[58] Crawford, 'Glasgow's experience', 10–11.   [59] Shaw, 'Glasgow', 735.

[60] See p. 190 of W. Smart, 'Glasgow and its municipal industries', *Quarterly Journal of Economics*, 9 (1985), 188–94.   [61] Finer, *Municipal Trading*, p. 35.

Table 11.4 *Gas costs and prices in Britain in 1898 (sample of 35 towns)*

	Municipal	London	Provincial private
Cost per million cubic feet in £	1,465	1,700	1,609
Population density (inhabitants per acre)	20.5	60.6	19.5
Wage rates in shillings per week[a]	33.6	38.0	36.4
Price of coal in £ per ton	0.49	0.56	0.65
Price of capital (% interest rate on loans)	3.4	4.11	4.0
Technology of plant (age in years)	21	33	26

[a]Engineering turners, whose wages were highly correlated with gasworkers' wages. See the source for details

Source: R. Millward and R. Ward, 'The costs of public and private gas enterprises in late nineteenth-century Britain', *Oxford Economic Papers*, 39 (1987), table 2 and annex 1.

Sample of towns and undertakings

Private	*Municipal*
Alliance & Dublin Consumers Gas Co.	Blackburn Corporation
Barnet District Gas & Water Co.	Bolton Corporation
Brighton & Hove General Gas Co.	Bradford Corporation
Brentford Gas Co.	Carlisle Corporation
Bristol Gas Co.	Darwen Corporation
Bromley Gas Consumers Gas Co.	Dundee Gas Commissioners
Commercial Gas Co.	Dunfermline Corporation
District Gas Co.	Edinburgh and Leith Corporation
Croydon Commerical Gas & Coke Co.	Glasgow Corporation
Crystal Palace	Lancaster Corporation
Gas Light & Coke Co.	Manchester Corporation
Harrow & Stanmore Gas Co.	Nottingham Corporation
Hastings & St Leonards Gas Co.	Oldham Corporation
Newcastle-upon-Tyne & Gateshead Co.	Salford Corporation
Sheffield United Gas Light Co.	Stafford Corporation
South Metropolitan Gas Co.	Stoke-on-Trent Corporation
Tottenham & Edmonton Gas Light Co.	West Bromwich Corporation
	Widnes Corporation
	Wigan Corporation

the average cost of supply was actually lowest in the provincial municipal undertakings – £1,465 per million cubic feet of gas. One reason for this was the technology of plants which were of a more modern vintage in the municipal undertakings. However, choice of plant in the provincial and London private companies had to take into account the cost of finance which, as Table 11.4 records, was higher than in the municipal plants as were wage rates and coal prices. Overall, this study suggests that, allowing for such factors, there is no statistically significant difference in the cost of supply as between the private and public undertakings.

Did the utilities (whether private or municipal) raise the efficiency of the urban economy? Better quality and cheaper urban transport, gas, electricity and water could lower the costs of factories and property owners in urban areas, raise the productivity of their own machinery, buildings and equipment and lower insurance risks and therefore premiums (for example fire insurance premiums via better water supplies for fire fighting). Few studies in Britain have tackled these issues head on. What is clear is that the ability to lower the costs of local businesses and residents is very much a function of the productivity of the urban utilities themselves and there is some evidence that this was not only high but showed a faster growth than other sectors of the British economy. There is an interesting contrast with the USA, blessed as that country was with abundant natural resources. The opening of the American West, the development of water resources, railways, minerals and the prairies have been shown to be an integral element in the faster growth of living standards there than in Britain.[62] Productivity in the manufacturing sector of the USA was well above that in Britain but the size of the gap did not change over the next 100 years so it was the role of sectors other than manufacturing which explains overall differences in economic growth. No direct comparison of the infrastructure in USA and Britain, nor indeed Germany, has yet been done. What we do know is that productivity growth in transport and communications (mainly railways and shipping) in Britain from the 1850s to the 1930s was generally less than in manufacturing and than the UK average. For the local utilities the picture is rather different. Electricity, water and gas seem, by these standards, to have performed rather well. They were growing very rapidly, output for example at about 5 per cent per annum. Table 11.5 shows that the resources used were growing less rapidly and hence the conventional measure of productivity shows an impressive increase, of the order of three times the UK average. Capital per unit of labour (a simple measure of 'mechanisation') was growing at only 0.3 per cent up to the First World War, so much of the high productivity growth of 1.6 per cent must have been due to technical, managerial and organisational advances in operations – to which local government regulation must be given some credit. It is in the interwar period with the expansion of electricity transmission grids that pure investment plays a much stronger role.

What did this all mean for the finances of these undertakings? Comprehensive data for all undertakings are limited in their breakdown of financial detail though a picture for all the local authority sector is available and is probably indicative of trends in the private sector. The financial outcomes

[62] G. Wright,. 'The origins of American industrial success, 1879–1940', *American Economic Review*, 80 (1990), 651–68; S. N. Broadberry, 'Comparative productivity in British and American manufacturing during the nineteenth century', *Explorations in Economic History*, 31 (1994).

Table 11.5 *Output, resources and productivity growth in gas, electricity and water in Britain 1856–1951 (annual % growth rates)*

	1856–1873	1873–1913	1924–37	1937–51
Output	5.5	5.1	5.8	4.2
Labour	4.7	3.3	3.1	1.4
Capital	4.9	3.6	4.8	0.9
Total factor productivity				
Gas, electricity and water	0.6	1.6	1.8	3.1
UK	0.6	0.5	0.7	1.1

Source: R. C. O. Matthews, C. H. Feinstein and J. C. Odling-Smee, *British Economic Growth 1856–1973* (Oxford, 1982), table 8.3.

reported in Table 11.6 are a mirror image of the objectives of the municipalities discussed earlier. These sectors are very capital intensive. In water supply and trams, operating costs account for only about one half of total outlays with capital charges taking the rest. Though operating costs account for a much larger share in electricity and gas, this is because they use a lot of coal so that their capital–labour ratios are probably similar to water and trams. Over the whole period, gas and trams made the largest *net* profits (aside from estate property, cf above) – about 5 per cent of turnover – with electricity slightly lower. The big difference is with water supply and Table 11.6 shows that for all sample years for which full data are available, the receipts from water charges were never enough to cover operating costs and loan charges. There is some tendency in all sectors for profit rates to decline after the First World War which is partly a reflection of the problems of coping with the shift to a less urban, more regional dimension to operations, a quite decisive factor in eroding the influence of local authorities and other local power groups.

(v) THE EROSION OF LOCAL CONTROL

The urban utilities had flourished during the nineteenth century as long as the technology for water supply, gas and electricity plants and tramways was efficient over areas corresponding roughly to the size of the average provincial town. Economies of scale were substantial and favoured Glasgow, Leeds, Manchester and Birmingham over Dundee, Swansea and Oxford. But all reasonable sized towns could expect to enjoy efficient operations and with little need to worry about having to cooperate with neighbouring towns. All that changed in the twentieth century as regional and national technologies emerged and became an important element in denuding local authorities of influence. We start with a

Table 11.6 *Financial performance of trading activities of all local authorities in Britain 1883–1948 (£ million)*

	Water	Gas	Electricity	Transport	Docks, piers, etc.	Total
1883[a]						
Oper. costs	0.8	2.6	n/a	n/a	1.1	n/a
Gr. profit	0.8	0.6	n/a	n/a	n/a	n/a
Revenue	1.6	3.2	n/a	n/a	n/a	n/a
1894						
Oper. costs	1.1[a]	4.6	0.1[b]	0.1[a]	1.8	7.7[c]
Gr. profit	1.7[a]	1.4	n/a	0.1[a]	n/a	n/a
Revenue	2.8[a]	6.0	n/a	0.2[a]	n/a	n/a
1903						
T. costs	5.4	8.4	2.2	4.1	4.4	24.5
Net profit	−0.4	0.6	0	0.5	n/a	0.7[d]
Revenue	5.0	9.0	2.2	4.6	n/a	25.2[d]
1908						
T. costs	9.1	9.2	3.9	8.2	5.3	35.7
Net profit	−0.4	0.5	0.1	0.9	n/a	1.1[d]
Revenue	8.7	9.7	4.0	9.1	n/a	36.8[d]
1913						
T. costs	10.1	10.1	5.4	10.6	9.7	45.9
Net profit	−0.6	0.8	0.1	0.6	−0.3[e]	0.6[e]
Revenue	9.5	10.9	5.5	11.2	9.4[e]	46.5[e]
1922						
T. costs	18.4	26.8	19.8	27.9	18.4	111.3
Net profit	−3.8	−1.0	0.3	−0.6	−0.2[e]	−5.3[e]
Revenue	14.6	25.8	20.1	27.3	18.2[e]	106.0[e]
1928						
T. costs	19.8	22.0	26.9	29.1	17.0	114.8
Net profit	−0.6	2.1	2.6	0.1	−0.8[e]	3.4[e]
Revenue	19.2	24.1	29.5	29.2	16.2[e]	118.2[e]
1938						
T. costs	24.9	22.6	56.9	29.3	16.1	149.8
Net profit	−1.1[a]	0.1	−0.1	0.6	−0.4[e]	−0.9[f]
Revenue	23.8[a]	22.7	56.8	29.9	15.7[e]	148.9[f]
1948						
T. costs	35.4	51.5	126.0	52.9	25.6	291.4
Net profit	−1.9[a]	0	−3.6	0.2	0.5[e]	−4.8[f]
Revenue	33.5[a]	51.5	122.4	53.1	26.1[e]	286.6[f]

[a]Excludes Scotland. For water revenue 1938 and 1948 it is the net profit element only in receipts which are not covered.

Table 11.6 (*cont.*)

b Excludes England and Wales.
c Excludes water supply and transport in Scotland and electricity in England and Wales.
d Excludes net profits of docks.
e Excludes net profit of docks in Scotland.
f Excludes net profits of water supply and docks in Scotland.
Definitions: revenue includes all receipts, grants, tolls and fees. Oper. costs comprise annual labour, fuel, maintenance and other operating costs. T. costs comprise operating costs plus annual loan charges. Gr. profit is revenue less operating costs as defined above. Net profit is revenue less total costs as defined above. Before 1903 the cost figures for England and Wales in our source exclude loan charges as do the data for Scotland before 1893. The post-1902 data do not identify loan charges separately. The coverage of the cost data for England and Wales changes in 1929 but this has a very small quantitative impact. See Mitchell, *British Historical Statistics*, p. 618 n. 1.
Source: B. R. Mitchell, *British Historical Statistics* (Cambridge, 1988), pp. 609–29.

brief case study of electricity to illustrate the issues and then go on to show how the problems of transition for all utilities were, from the early 1920s, a key element in the pressures for nationalisation.

The early years of electricity supply involved a dimension of economic performance which we have not so far touched on. Was long-term development stultified by either regulation or municipalisation? 'Notwithstanding that our countrymen have been among the first in inventive genius in electrical science', said the British Institution of Electrical Engineers in 1902, 'its development in the United Kingdom is in a backward condition'.[63] For contemporaries like V. Knox, writing in the *Economic Journal* and Mr E. Garcke again, as well as Ian Byatt (current British regulator of water) in his early scholarly days, the legislation for tramways and electricity inhibited development, especially that of the private companies.[64]

Does the evidence bear that out? Early ventures in electricity were of course speculative and so much so as to prompt the *Birmingham Gazette* to suggest that an experiment in electric lighting 'is good enough, perhaps, for speculative investment of private capital, but not good enough to justify the risking of public funds'.[65] The Electric Lighting Act, as we have seen, gave powers to local authorities to take over private companies after twenty-one years. The editor of the American *Municipal Journal* noted that though there were many complaints that this restricted the horizons of private companies, local authorities also had to write off the capital of their undertakings over twenty-five years.[66] In any case the purchase clauses never applied to the power companies and for lighting it

---

[63] Hughes, 'British electrical industry', 38.
[64] V. Knox, 'The economic effects of the Tramways Act of 1870', *Economic Journal*, 11 (1901), 492–510; E. L. Garcke, *Manual of Electrical Undertakings and Directory of Officials*, vol. 1: *1896* (London, 1896); I. C. R. Byatt, *The British Electrical Industry, 1815–1914* (Oxford, 1978).
[65] Jones, 'Municipalities', 21.   [66] Writing in *Traction and Transmission*, 1 (1901), 247.

was extended to forty-two years by an act of 1888. It did not stop a flurry of private companies being set up, some with cables laid on streets or slung over wooden poles. The USA was progressing more quickly than Britain where in 1890 sales were still small and most generating stations had less than 0.1 megawatt capacity.[67] The USA did not, however, have the same British advantages in gas and steam power. The latter was important in manufacturing and transport, and, for lighting, electricity prices could not compete with gas until about 1910.[68] The town clerk of Birmingham was sufficiently confident to be able to report to the Gas Committee in 1882 that 'it may . . . be the wiser course to permit speculators to experiment at their own risk'.[69]

A related source of concern was trams, 90 per cent of which had been electrified in the USA as early as 1890. The investment needed for electricity may have appeared a risky proposition in Britain in the 1890s when the twenty-one-year clauses on the undertakings established in the 1870s were coming to an end. The lag with the USA only lasted a short time because the municipalities took the initiative. Some had stepped in where private development had not been forthcoming – hilly Halifax and Huddersfield, for example. By 1896 the municipalities had been given general permission by parliament to operate trams as well as lay track, and electric mileage rose from 45 in 1895 to 2,195 in 1905/6 by which time 90 per cent of Britain's trams were electric.[70]

Where the local authorities proved a real stumbling block was in the struggle to shift from an urban to regional focus in the production of electricity. The development of high pressure speed turbines meant unit generating costs were lower in larger stations. In addition, developments in the scientific understanding of electrical current allowed supply to be transformed by stations. Interconnection of areas by grids would therefore allow more use of large generating plants and the elimination of idle capacity. Calls for greater coordination between urban areas were being made in the early 1900s and, immediately after the First World War, there was much agitation for the establishment of district boards. Following the Williamson Committee Report of 1918,[71] the only gain was the establishment of a body, the electricity commissioners, to promote technical development. Another government committee was established in 1925 and reported in strong terms on the relatively high cost and low consumption of electricity in Britain, the proliferation of small plants and the need for interconnection.[72] The

[67] L. Hannah, *Electricity before Nationalisation* (London, 1979), p. 12.
[68] Byatt, *British Electrical Industry*, p. 23; J. F. Wilson, 'Competition between electricity and gas in Britain, 1880–1980', International Economic History Association, Pre-Conference on the Development of Electrical Energy (Paris, 1993), pp. 2–3.   [69] Jones, 'Municipalities', 19.
[70] Hannah, *Electricity before Nationalisation*, pp. 15–16.
[71] Williamson Committee, *Report of the Committee Appointed by the Board of Trade to Consider the Question of Electric Power Supply* (1918).
[72] Weir Committee, *Report of the Committee Appointed by the Board of Trade to Review the National Problem of the Supply of Electricity Energy* (1926).

solution, ingenious said Leslie Hannah[73] in the light of fears of nationalisation, was to set up the Central Electricity Board (CEB). Its basic functions were to construct a national grid, close down small stations and standardise electricity frequencies. But it was the institutional arrangement which was truly innovative. Certain stations were to be 'selected'. The CEB would buy electricity from them, transmit and then resell leaving the job of retailing to the companies and local authority undertakings. It bestowed the honour of being selected rather generously in order to oil the process of transition and the work of James Foreman-Peck and Michael Waterson suggests that the best practice local authority and private generating plants were equally efficient (though with a longish 'tail' of unselected municipal plants) which also would have facilitated a smooth transition.[74] The managers of the CEB were not appointed by the Treasury and all capital was raised on the stock market without a Treasury guarantee. It was this which allayed the fears, even though the reality was that it was a publicly owned enterprise since none of the stock was equity. On the face of it the Board was a success. The grid networks were set up first on a regional basis with the Board's first chairman, Andrew Duncan, experimenting in his home territory in Scotland and the national grid completed in 1933. Capital formation each year averaged £20 million (see Table 11.1). The number of consumers shot up from 1 million in 1920 to 9.3 million in 1938/9. With production in non-selected stations dwindling, the thermal efficiency gap with the USA eliminated, the system load factor raised from 25 per cent in 1926 to 37 per cent by 1939 and the Battersea 105 megawatt station the largest in Europe, complaints were few.

The huge number of electricity undertakings still in existence in the 1930s – cf. 581 in Table 11.2 above – constituted the remnants of the 'urban' dimension, mainly involved in retail distribution, many with only a small turnover. In 1934 over 400 undertakings accounted for less than 10 per cent of sales, distribution costs were high and the multiplicity of boundaries prevented efficient development of networks. The trouble was that local authorities accounted for 60 per cent of the undertakings and they were particularly stubborn. Not for them to give up empires and profits. Joint electricity authorities had emerged but the experience was not encouraging and Herbert Morrison did not see them as the way forward.[75] Civic pride and political rivalries permeated the system. The member of parliament for Ashton-under-Lyme observed in 1937 that the local council would rather its electricity undertaking be taken over by a new public board than see it fall into the hands of Oldham borough, the neighbouring authority. Later, when nationalisation loomed, many municipalities were

---

[73] L. Hannah, 'A pioneer of public enterprise: the Central Electricity Generating Board and the National Grid', in B. Supple, ed., *Essays in British Business History* (Oxford, 1977).
[74] J. M. Foreman-Peck and M. Waterson, 'The comparative efficiency of public and private enterprise in Britain: electricity generation between the world wars', *Economic Journal*, 95, Supplement (1985).   [75] Hannah, *Electricity before Nationalisation*, pp. 331–2.

appalled at the prospect that the loss of their undertakings was to be treated simply as a book-keeping entry within the public sector accounts and hence they would receive as compensation simply the amount of their *net* outstanding debt.[76]

(vi) NATIONALISATION AND URBAN INTERESTS

How and why was the erosion of local interests linked to the later nationalisation of gas, electricity and transport in the 1940s? The starting point in unravelling this story is the interwar period and the motley collection of undertakings recorded in Table 11.2. What to do, for example, with all those small undertakings at the end of the national electricity grid network? The McGowan Committee (1936) identified economies which could be realised in marketing and finance from grouping into larger units and from the standardisation of voltages.[77] In so far as the economies of scale were at a regional (or sub-national) level the question was how regional business organisations would emerge. The Committee proposed that they should be developed from existing undertakings but recognised that legislation and compulsory powers would be necessary. Precisely how this would work out was not clear. Herbert Morrison had seen the solution in regional boards publicly owned on CEB lines. This got support from some civil servants, from the Conservative Minister of Fuel in 1942 and by Liberal Gwillam Lloyd George as Minister in 1943. Many professionals saw it as inescapable. Even E. H. E. Woodward, general engineer and manager of the North Eastern Electricity Supply Company who wanted larger business units, saw ownership as irrelevant and advocated public boards.[78] In the event the legislation of 1947 created twelve such regional distribution boards for England and Wales and two for south Scotland to set alongside the North of Scotland Hydro-Electric Board which had been established in 1943.

A similar issue arose in the case of gas with the simplification that before the advent of natural gas in the 1970s there were no major economies of scale in production or distribution. But there were unexploited economies of scale perceived in marketing and finance. A respected view was the Heyworth Report of 1945 which stressed the need for the development of gas appliances, marketing gas in rural areas, developing new uses of gas and expanding research, all of which it saw as requiring regional units of business organisation.[79] The peak number of undertakings had been 519 for the statutory companies in 1914 and 321 for the municipal enterprises in 1926. But on the eve of nationalisation these numbers were only 20 per cent lower, as may be seen in Table 11.2. Moreover,

[76] *Ibid.*, pp. 331–2.
[77] McGowan Report, *Report of the Committee on Electricity Distribution*, Ministry of Transport (1936).
[78] Hannah, *Electricity before Nationalisation*, ch. 10.
[79] Heyworth Report, *Report of the Committee of Inquiry into the Gas Industry 1945*, Cmd 6699 (1945).

the distribution of undertakings was, like electricity, highly skewed. As the Heyworth Committee pointed out there were only sixty-five undertakings in 1944 producing more than 5 million therms per annum but they accounted for 70 per cent of total sales; even some of the large private companies were holding companies which the Committee felt had made only modest improvements in efficiency because they always needed the consent of the subsidiaries. As for the local authority sector, the municipal boundaries were not always optimal for production and distribution, even in the absence of major economies in these functions, and joint boards had not proved successful. The Heyworth Committee makes an interesting contrast ten years on from the McGowan Committee rejecting the latter's idea of grouping round existing undertakings. Heyworth went unambiguously for regional public boards and this was taken up in the 1948 act which established twelve Area Boards producing and selling gas and reporting separately to parliament.

Thus in both electricity and gas the 'public board' element arose in part from the problems associated with a 'natural' or 'voluntary' emergence of larger units of business organisation. The nationalisation programme grafted on to this set of boards, certain institutions, objectives and obligations which cannot be rationalised simply by the pressure to exploit economies of scale.[80] To this matter we shall turn shortly. In the meantime it should be noticed that the complex mixture of private and public interests which constituted, in gas and electricity, obstacles to the formation of bigger units, was repeated in an even stronger form in water supply. In 1914 there were 820 local authority undertakings, some 200 statutory companies and 1,339 non-statutory companies though the local authorities accounted for 80 per cent of the industry's net output. Apart from the sheer number of undertakings and the entrenched position of local authorities there were other interested parties. After the First World War the Ministry of Health was given the responsibility for the planning and conservation of water resources. Other Ministries had an interest including the Board of Trade whose Water Power Resources Committee suggested in 1919 that the wider development of water power schemes was held back by the multiplicity of interests involved.[81] Both Ministries advocated a central water authority. But Catchment Boards and Fishery Boards were also able to make their presence felt through the Ministry of Agriculture and Fisheries. The Federation of British Industries had its own Riparian Owners' Committee which was active on the question of the release of 'compensation water' from reservoirs. As John Sheail has shown, the requisite planning of water use and resource development therefore faced considerable

---

[80] M. Chick, 'Competition, competitiveness and nationalisation', in G. Jones and M. W. Kirby, ed., *Competitiveness and the State: Government and Industry in Twentieth Century Britain* (Manchester, 1991).
[81] J. A. Hassan, 'The water industry, 1900–1951: a failure of public policy?', in R. Millward and J. Singleton, eds., *The Political Economy of Nationalisation in Britain 1920–1950* (Cambridge, 1995).

obstacles.[82] In 1934 the Committee on Scottish Health Services recorded hundreds of separate undertakings working independently to serve their own areas. In England and Wales a White Paper was drafted to confer on the Minister of Health the role of a central coordinating authority empowered to regulate the acquisition of water rights, create joint boards and revise the areas of supply and distribution. The White Paper never materialised in the 1930s though a Central Advisory Water Committee was established in 1937.[83]

Thus the broad stance of governments in the interwar years was to achieve reorganisation through voluntary amalgamation. This was largely unsuccessful so that by the 1940s investigative bodies like the Heyworth Committee were openly espousing public ownership. It is important to note that support for public boards did not just come from the Labour party. In the depressed economic conditions of the interwar period the Conservative party could not reject public ownership out of hand especially given their role in the creation of bodies like the Central Electricity Board and the London Passenger Transport Board. The 'étatist' wing of the party was barely distinguishable on many issues from the Morrisonian wing of the Labour party and in 1938 Harold Macmillan described Labour's programme for the nationalisation of the Bank of England, coal mining, power, land and transport as mild compared with his own plan.[84] The Conservatives' Industrial Charter of 1947 opposed nationalisation and direct planning in principle but fudged privatisation outside one or two small sectors in road and air transport, claiming that privatising the large public corporations would be too disruptive. Moreover, a large body of professional opinion, including the investigative bodies mentioned already, were by the late 1930s and 1940s canvassing a more interventionist government stance in industrial matters.

Indeed, industrial policy involving mere arms-length regulation had been discredited by the 1940s. The coal owners' image had been dented as early as the 1920s.[85] During the Second World War their 'solution' for the industry was a Central Board comprising representatives of the management and owners but no miners or customers and yet supposedly acting as trustees for the industry in dealings with parliament.[86] Similar 'corporatist' solutions forwarded by the Joint Committee of Electricity Supply Associations and, for airlines, by the various shipping and railway undertakings with shares in airline companies were not well received.[87]

---

[82] J. Sheail, 'Planning, water supplies and ministerial power in inter-war Britain', *Public Administration*, 61 (1983), 386–95.   [83] Hassan, 'Water industry'.

[84] See ch. 2 of Millward and Singleton, eds., *Political Economy of Nationalisation*.

[85] B. Supple, '"No bloody revolutions but for obstinate reactions"?: British coal owners in their context 1919–1920', in D. Coleman and P. Mathias, eds., *Enterprise and History: Essays in Honour of Charles Wilson* (Cambridge, 1984).

[86] M. W. Kirby, *The British Coal Mining Industry 1870–1946* (London, 1977), p. 194.

[87] Hannah, *Electricity before Nationalisation*, p. 342; see also p. 2 of P. Lyth, 'A multiplicity of instruments: the 1946 decision to create a separate British European airline and its effects on airline productivity', *Journal of Transport History*, 11 (1990), 1–17.

For the Labour government of 1945–51, taking the *infrastructure* into public ownership had two clear merits. It provided the opportunity for exploiting the scale economies which many observers claimed existed: in the distribution networks and in the marketing and finance of electricity and gas; in the generation of electricity supply, high tension transmission already being in public ownership; in the merger of local water undertakings, drainage authorities and sewage works into integrated river basin systems; in railway scale economies not yet realised by the four companies. Secondly, it offered the prospect of eliminating the excess profits which were available for the private undertakings with *de facto* monopolies 'in the field' or which would have been available if private firms had been amalgamated into new large business units. Of course, public ownership was not theoretically needed to achieve this since there was always the option of arms-length regulation. It was the perceived failure of interwar regulation in airlines, gas and water supply, retail electricity supply and railways which enhanced the case for an alternative form of industrial intervention. The litany of failed regulation is to be found in the stream of government inquiries: the 1931 Boscawen Report on transport, the 1936 McGowan Report on electricity, the 1930s reports of the Joint Committee on Water Resources and Supplies, the 1938 Cadman Report on civil aviation, the 1945 Reid Report on coal and the Heyworth Report on gas.[88] This is then sufficient to explain the emergence in the 1940s of the publicly owned Area Gas and Electricity Boards, the Railway Executive, British Overseas Airways Corporation, British European Airways Corporation and the concentration of generation and transmission in the new British Electricity Authority.

The priorities of the Labour government were of course determined by the severity of the problems they faced and the ease with which they could be resolved. This is particularly germane to understanding inaction in the whole field of water resource development which remained very much a local affair and in urban areas therefore the municipal borough still dominated matters. Arguments for nationalisation had been advanced since the turn of the century. A plan for nationalisation was adopted in 1948 by the Cabinet's Industries for Nationalisation Sub-Committee but was buried under other events. There were three underlying elements in this outcome. First was the absence of any chronic supply crisis: demand was growing at 1.6 per cent per annum 1900–50, much less than subsequently and less, so far as we can gather, than in the nineteenth century.[89] Although the physical infrastructure of land drainage and sewage works was neglected there was nothing like the collapse of underground networks which occurred later. At the same time the range of interested parties in the industry and the range of interested government departments were much

---

[88] Boscawen Report, *Royal Commission on Transport, Final Report, with Additional Recommendations*, Cmd 3751 (1931); Cadman Report, *Report of the Committee of Inquiry into Civil Aviation*, Cmd 5685 (1938); Reid Report, *Report of the Technical Advisory Committee on Coal Mining*, Cmd 6610 (1945); McGowan, *Report*; Heyworth, *Report*.   [89] Hassan, 'Water industry'.

larger than in gas and electricity. The suppliers of services included private water companies, local authority water supply undertakings, drainage authorities, local authority sewage authorities and river conservancy bodies. Property rights in land and water were held by all the above institutions together with riparian interests, landowners and industrialists. Within Whitehall they had a fertile field for lobbying amongst the various government departments involved: Ministry of Health, Board of Trade, Ministry of Agriculture and Fisheries, Department of Scientific and Industrial Research. The hurdles to be surmounted in any reorganisation of the industry were formidable. As Table 11.2 shows, there were still 925 separate local authority undertakings in 1956 and the development of river basin management and national coordination had to await an act of 1973.

For the sectors which were, in the 1940s, transferred out of private and municipal ownership, there remains to explain the institutional arrangements which emerged. In particular why was urban government replaced not only, and sometimes not at all, by regional bodies but by national boards? The answer lies in the form of economic planning adopted by the Labour government. Planning embraced relationships between industries and this explains why, from 1931, it was 'transport' rather than 'railways' which appeared in the list of industries to be nationalised and why, in 1947, the railways were but one of five Executives under the control of the British Transport Commission. This umbrella organisation, as well as the British Electricity Authority, the British Gas Council and the National Coal Board were also vehicles for the reconstruction of the economy. Each had to draw up programmes for investment in physical capital and training for staff and workers and was answerable to the Minister of the sponsoring government departments. This was certainly consistent with earlier Labour party ideas on public boards being subject to the control of a National Investment Board though the effectiveness of this linkage has been disputed.[90] Thirdly, though perhaps most elusive of all, was the idea that nationalised industries would provide common services, that is rail services, gas and electricity supply throughout the country at uniform charges. Fraser and Martin Chick have argued that this originated in municipal provision of the 'necessities' of life.[91] By the interwar period gas, electricity and water were established items of consumer budgets and probably with low price elasticities of demand. Chick has identified a growing conviction in some quarters that electricity was not a luxury for higher income groups. The musings of the War Cabinet Sub-Committee on the future of electricity supply included the argument that 'the Public have increasingly come to regard electricity as a necessity and not a mere luxury and

[90] See p. 217 of G. N. Ostergaard, 'Labour and the development of the public corporation', *Manchester School*, 22 (1954), 192–226; A. Cairncross, *Years of Recovery: British Economic Policy 1945–51* (London, 1985), p. 484.
[91] Fraser, 'Municipal socialism'; M. Chick, 'The political economy of nationalisation: electricity supply', in Millward and Singleton, eds., *Political Economy of Nationalisation*, pp. 257–74.

it should be regarded from the same point of view as sewerage or water', a position perfectly in line with Morrison's ideas about uniform prices for electricity.[92] Providing services in this way clearly meant ignoring the costs of supply to different parts of the country and accorded with a one-nation approach to economic issues.

Hence the Nationalisation Acts of 1945–8 had two central features. First was that the new corporations were to serve the public interest and so a public purpose was written into the acts and embraced the provision of common services and the development of investment programmes. Thus the British Electricity Authority was required 'to develop and maintain an efficient, coordinated and economical system of electricity supply . . ., the Electricity Boards [to] secure . . . the development, extension to rural areas and cheapening of supplies of electricity'.[93]

Consonant with these aims was the constitution of the Boards whose members were to be as disinterested as the corporation's objectives. Such had been the philosophy behind the CEB. Similarly, the new corporations were not to pursue profit. Finance was to come from fixed interest stock – either the industry's own or government bonds – and any surpluses actually earned were required by the statutes to be devoted to the public purpose, that is reinvested in the industry. The investment programmes were not simply a commercial matter and had to be approved by the relevant Minister of the sponsoring department.

Moreover, the new undertakings were expected to be commercially orientated, innovative and enterprising. Thus, like the CEB and the London Passenger Transport Board, they were to have their own corporate legal status free from Treasury supervision, able to appoint their own employees and to be sued in the courts. The injunction to provide 'cheap and efficiently supplied services' in the Electricity Act recurs in all the statutes and has to be seen in conjunction with another injunction, variously worded, along the lines of 'revenues shall not be less than sufficient for meeting all outgoings properly chargeable, on an average of good and bad years'. Vague though this wording might be for accountants, it was roundly interpreted to have the straightforward interpretation of breaking even taking one year with another, and was much more easily monitored than the even vaguer public purposes. Financial deficits were a consequence and this distinguishing feature of the post-war nationalised sector contrasts strongly with the experiences of the local utilities with which we started this story.

[92] Chick, 'Political economy', p. 270.
[93] Section 1(1) and 1(6) of Electricity Act 1947 (10 and 11, Geo. 6), *Public General Acts and the Church Assembly Measures of 1947: Vol. II* (HMSO, 1947).

· 1 2 ·

The provision of social services

MARGUERITE DUPREE

(i) INTRODUCTION

ISTORIANS OF the provision of social services in Britain since the mid-nineteenth century no longer focus their accounts around an irreversible linear view of the 'rise of the welfare state' or the steady growth of collective and, especially, central government provision for social welfare which culminated in the legislation of the Labour government of the later 1940s.[1] Instead, they emphasise the importance of other agencies in addition to the state in the provision of welfare. There has been a 'mixed economy of welfare' in which a variety of suppliers, or alternative sources of assistance, may be involved in the provision of individual welfare in addition to those designated by statute. The state was only one element, and, for much of the nineteenth and early twentieth centuries, arguably not the most important element. Especially significant was voluntarism or voluntary activity arising from 'individual choice in individual, self-governing ways', which recent analysts, following and modifying Richard Titmuss in his influential 1955 lecture on 'The social division of welfare', subdivide into voluntary, commercial and informal 'sectors'.[2] In Victorian Britain the expenditure and personnel of voluntarism far exceeded that of the central and local state, while that of the local state of poor law

---

[1] P. Thane, 'Historiography of the British welfare state', *Social History Society Newsletter*, 15 (1990), 12–15; A. Digby, *British Welfare Policy* (London, 1989); G. B. A. M. Finlayson, *Citizen, State and Social Welfare in Britain 1830–1990* (Oxford, 1994); M. J. Daunton, 'Payment and participation: welfare and state formation in Britain 1900–1951', *P&P*, 150 (1996), 169–216; M. J. Daunton, 'Introduction', in *Charity, Self-Interest and Welfare in the English Past* (London, 1996), pp. 1–22; P. Johnson, 'Risk, redistribution and social welfare in Britain from the poor law to Beveridge', in Daunton, ed., *Charity, Self-Interest and Welfare*, pp. 225–48.

[2] Finlayson, *Citizen, State and Social Welfare*, pp. 6–7; G. B. A. M. Finlayson, 'A moving frontier: voluntarism and the state in British social welfare 1911–1949', *Twentieth Century British History*, 1 (1990), pp. 183–4; Digby, *British Welfare Policy*, pp. 85–99; R. M. Titmuss, 'The social division of welfare', in R. M. Titmuss, *Essays on 'The Welfare State'* (London, 1958), pp. 351.

guardians and local authorities exceeded that of the central.[3] The history of the provision of social welfare since the mid-nineteenth century is one, in part, of the changes and continuities within the different sectors. It is also concerned with the shifting boundaries or the 'moving frontier' within this mixed economy of welfare – sometimes, as in the case of voluntary hospitals, directly from voluntarist activity to statutory agencies, but most often a continuous if varied interrelationship between voluntarism and the state, which itself had constantly shifting boundaries within the local state between the poor law and local authorities and, as John Davis shows in his chapter (see above, pp. 261–86), between local and central government.

The recent studies of social welfare provision emphasise the changing balance within the mixed economy of welfare at the national level and are based on a wide range of heterogeneous examples. Were there urban aspects to the provision of social welfare? If we accept Philip Abrams' critique of urban history and his suggestion that historians who want to study welfare provision should do just that and not confuse the issue by the 're-ification of the city',[4] then there is no reason to go further. Yet, without treating the city as if it were an actor or searching for 'the urban variable' as part of an explanation, it is useful to examine the provision of social welfare in towns and cities for a number of reasons.

First, in the nineteenth century especially, 'new forms of charity have generally been forged in urban settings'.[5] As R. J. Morris argues, size, density and complexity are the defining characteristics of towns and cities, and they intensify 'externalities' for which the power structures of urban places devise responses. Externalities arise when effects on production and welfare are outside the market and go wholly or partially unpriced, bringing a need for non-market interventions, including the provision of social welfare, which became more pressing as towns grew in size. While there is an emphasis in the historical literature on the low demand for fixed capital in British industry, this approach misses the high demand for capital in the urban infrastructure. This high demand was not only for drains and water, as Robert Millward describes in his chapter (see above, pp. 315–49), but also for social welfare in forms such as hospitals, workhouses and schools, which would have benefited the poor and given a reasonable return but which was not met because of free rider problems and difficulties of urban finance, particularly a narrow local tax base.[6] Yet, the cities saw a wide

---

[3] Daunton, 'Payment and participation', 171.

[4] R. J. Morris, 'Externalities, the market, power structure and the urban agenda', *UHY*, 17 (1990), 101; P. Abrams, 'Towns and economic growth: some theories and problems', in P. Abrams and E. A. Wrigley, eds., *Towns and Societies* (London, 1978).

[5] Jonathan Barry and Colin Jones, 'Introduction', in Jonathan Barry and Colin Jones, eds., *Medicine and Charity before the Welfare State* (London, 1991), p. 11.

[6] J. G. Williamson, *Coping with City Growth during the British Industrial Revolution* (Cambridge, 1990), pp. 267–305; N. F. R. Crafts, 'Some dimensions of the "quality of life" during the British Industrial Revolution', *Ec.HR*, 2nd series, 50 (1997), 633–4.

variety of experiments, innovations and initiatives designed to control and influence the incidence of externalities, some of which were through central or local government agencies, such as the poor law, others by voluntary societies, such as hospitals and children's homes, and others by informal social structures, such as family and kin, neighbourhoods or ethnic groups. 'The nineteenth-century city became a vast laboratory which tested the effectiveness of market mechanisms to the limit and then tested the operation of other ways of producing and delivering goods and services.'[7]

A second reason to examine the provision of social welfare in towns and cities is the different circumstances of urban and rural workers. Rural workers, for example, received payments in kind to an extent that disappeared for urban workers; the nature of rural credit differed in important respects from that which was available to town dwellers; and there were marked differences between rural and urban labour markets.[8]

Third, even though the proportion of the population of Britain living in towns and cities increased during the first half of the period of this chapter, reaching nearly 80 per cent by 1911, urban history even in the second half of the period is not the history of the nation writ large. Philip Waller pointed out the paradox that as the proportion of the population living in towns and cities rose, the value of the diminishing rural portion of the population was enhanced, and 'the nation's governing voice was not a city echo'. While 'the completeness of the urbanisation of society [meant that] almost everything that went on in towns affected society at large, . . . towns were subject to limitation and direction by national authorities' in which rural aristocratic elements and other interests were disproportionately paramount.[9]

Fourth, and finally, at the same time that it is important to recognise similar characteristics among urban areas and identify distinct phases in urban history, it is important to recognise variations between types of towns and cities within different periods and between England and Wales on the one hand and Scotland on the other. 'It is an essential part of the urban historian's task to demonstrate that urban functions and dysfunctions, the urban experience and the urban influence, were very variable.'[10] Victorian towns, in particular, enjoyed much discretion by deciding whether to adopt 'permissive' national statutes. The result was considerable variation in policy.[11] Voluntarism and local government were still important in the provision of social welfare in the interwar years. The Victorian practice of allowing local authorities to decide whether or not to take up government subsidies persisted; local authorities kept their responsibility for many services, took care of all not covered by national insurance and were

[7] Morris, 'Externalities', 106–7.
[8] J. Treble, *Urban Poverty in Britain 1830–1914* (London, 1979), p. 5.
[9] P. J. Waller, *Town, City and Nation* (Oxford, 1983), p. 23.   [10] Waller, *Town*, p. viii.
[11] R. H. Trainor, *Black Country Elites* (Oxford, 1993), p. 16.

responsible for the bulk of investment of public funds. The depression put a heavy burden on local as well as national finances, and that burden varied according to the economic, social and political structure of urban areas.[12] To take just one feature, local variations in services depending on political decisions made at a local level could affect infant mortality.[13]

The variety of cities is matched by the range and fragmentation of social services whose aim is to support 'the material welfare of the people, either through the maintenance of incomes or provision of services'.[14] There is no generally accepted view of what services should be included under the general heading of social welfare, though there is agreement that their aim is the 'enhancement of the personal welfare of individual citizens'[15] or 'collective responsibility for individual contingencies'.[16] Some analysts include areas such as education, housing or workmen's compensation, and others do not.[17] This chapter will concentrate on the provision of urban social services concerning poverty and health, especially 'critical life situations' associated with unemployment, low wages, life-cycle stages (young married couples, the elderly, etc.), illness and death. 'Impersonal environmental services such as public sanitation, street lighting, housing and town planning'[18] and moral and cultural services such as education will be excluded.

Thus, this chapter focuses on the continuities and changes in the provision of social services with regard to poverty and health. It explores alternative sources of assistance and their interrelationships in the mixed economy of welfare, examining to what extent these changed during the period and paying particular attention to whether there were distinctive urban aspects and to variations among urban areas.

(ii) VOLUNTARISM, LOCAL AUTHORITIES, THE POOR LAW AND THE LOCALITY 1840–1880

Self-maintenance and family maintenance were the aims of the provision of welfare in Britain throughout the century from 1850, whatever the balance of

---

[12] M. A. Crowther, *British Social Policy 1914–1939* (Basingstoke, 1988), pp. 16–17.

[13] L. Marks, *Metropolitan Maternity* (Amsterdam and Atlanta, 1996); E. P. Peretz, 'The costs of modern motherhood to low income families in interwar Britain', in V. Fildes, L. Marks and H. Marland, eds., *Women and Children First: International Maternal Welfare 1870–1945* (London, 1992), pp. 257–80; and E. P. Peretz, 'Infant welfare between the wars', in R. C. Whiting, ed., *Oxford* (Manchester, 1993), pp. 131–45.   [14] Crowther, *British Social Policy*, p. 9.

[15] PEP, *Report on the British Social Services: A Survey of the Existing Public Social Services in Great Britain with Proposals for Future Development* (London, 1937), p. 10.

[16] Digby, *British Welfare Policy*, p. 7.

[17] For example, Crowther, *British Social Policy*, includes housing but not education, while PEP, *Report on the British Social Services*, p. 10, includes education but not housing.

[18] PEP, *Report on the British Social Services*, p. 10.

the welfare mix.[19] Self-reliant, provident behaviour, 'help from within', was the secure basis on which individuals could make arrangements for their own welfare.[20] In the mid–nineteenth century voluntarism, directed toward encouraging and sustaining independence and self-maintenance, was the logical outcome of *laissez-faire* ideology, not its opposite, and it dominated the welfare mix.[21] Its continuing presence and vitality was a major feature throughout the century, even as its limitations became increasingly apparent and the central state's role in provision grew to emerge as the dominant partner in the mix after 1948. Yet, the dominance of voluntarism in the mid–nineteenth century was not a by-product but an integral part of the contemporary concept of the 'minimal', 'enabling' central state in which a high level of discretion and initiative was delegated to local government within the framework of national law and supervised by the central authority. A vast network of voluntary organisations, together with elected local officials, superintended, financed and initiated, within limits established by law, most welfare services.[22]

In short, social welfare provision in the mid–nineteenth century was locally financed and locally administered and thus highly variable, even more so in Scotland than in England, as will be seen below. As R. J. Morris argues in his chapter in this volume, the growth of a range of voluntary associations was important in creating the stability of British society in the growing towns of industrialising Britain as voluntarism became municipal and increasingly mutually interdependent with the local state of local government and the poor law. First in the larger incorporated industrial cities such as Birmingham, Sheffield and Leeds and after 1860 in middle-size industrial towns such as those in the Black Country the common assumptions helped to forge a middle-class identity, while in older cities with a legacy of institutions, such as Bristol with its endowed charities, there were bitter divides within the elite.[23] This predominance of voluntarism and local government in the provision of social welfare in general had the confidence of contemporaries that it could cope with the problems of urbanisation and urban poverty: low wages and irregular demand for labour; personal circumstances which few families could provide against such as sickness, handicap, injury, widowhood, old age, large numbers of children, rapid immigration and high incidences of disease. It also encouraged and made possible the wide range and influence of women

---

[19] J. Lewis, 'Family provision of health and welfare in the mixed economy of care in the late nineteenth and twentieth centuries', *Social History of Medicine*, 8 (1995), 3.

[20] Finlayson, *Citizen, State and Social Welfare*, p. 21.   [21] *Ibid.*, p. 72.

[22] P. Thane, 'Women in the British Labour party and the construction of state welfare 1906–1939', in S. Koven and S. Michel, eds., *Mothers of a New World* (London and New York, 1993), pp. 357–8.

[23] Below, pp. 395–426; D. Smith, *Conflict and Compromise* (London, 1982); Trainor, *Black Country Elites*; M. Gorsky, *Patterns of Philanthropy* (Woodbridge, 1999).

in voluntary organisations and their influence in local government, allied to their role of informal providers.[24]

As indicated above, historians have divided voluntarism into several sectors: informal, voluntary and commercial. The informal sector included the provision of welfare within kinship networks and neighbourhoods. The aim of the voluntary sector was to benefit the community without financial gain to itself. It included both self-help or mutual aid, whose object was the well-being of the individual or group choosing to take part in it. Voluntarism also included charity (the advancement of the interests of others, rather than of self) and philanthropy (upper- or middle-class concern, often generalised or institutionalised, for those who occupied a lower station in life) whose aim was to promote the interests of others. Finally, the commercial sector included welfare initiatives for profit, such as insurance companies or private medical practice.[25]

The continuing importance of family and kin as sources of assistance in the face of the potential disruption of urbanisation and industrialisation is one of the striking features of the mid-nineteenth century. Family and kin were not demoted to a subsidiary role in the provision of welfare; nor was it a 'golden age of family responsibility'. Families often provided assistance with finding a job or accommodation for members migrating to cities and, depending on the housing supply, they huddled together at times of unemployment. Also, at different stages in the life cycle families were particularly important in providing assistance with accommodation. For young men in urban areas in the mid-nineteenth century, for example, the age at leaving home was higher than in rural areas or in earlier periods. Again, depending on the housing supply, newly married couples frequently co-resided with parents, and sometimes where mothers worked outside the home there was a co-residing grandmother or other relative to provide child care. At the same time considerable numbers of children without their parents resided with grandparents.[26]

In the mid-nineteenth century the reliance on families for the provision of social welfare may have been even greater in urban industrial towns than rural areas and small towns. Irish immigrants to London and Lancashire towns were noted especially for their assistance to relatives.[27] This may in part have been due to the limits that the laws of settlement and the local control of poor relief placed on the entitlement to relief. Irish migrants could legally reside where they wished in Britain, and English law required short-term relief to be given where an appli-

---

[24] Lewis, 'Family provision of health and welfare', 1–16; J. Lewis, 'Gender, the family and women's agency in the building of "welfare states": the British case', *Soc.Hist.*, 19 (1994), 37–55; Thane, 'Women in the British Labour party', p. 358.

[25] These definitions follow Finlayson, *Citizen, State and Social Welfare*, pp. 6–8, 46.

[26] M. Dupree, *Family Structure in the Staffordshire Potteries, 1840–1880* (Oxford, 1995); M. Anderson, *Family Structure in Nineteenth-Century Lancashire* (Cambridge 1971).

[27] L. H. Lees, *Exiles of Erin* (Manchester, 1979), p. 124; J. Denvir, *The Irish in Britain* (London, 1892), p. 426.

cant applied. But, if applicants accepted relief they could be removed to their place of settlement, i.e. Ireland in the case of the Irish-born, unless they rented property with a rateable value of £10 a year (or 4s. per week) for at least a year, or after 1846, as will be seen below, resided in the parish long enough to become 'irremovable'. The extent of the problem of relief for the Irish differed from place to place, as a large number of Irish poor had settled into a relatively small number of British towns. London and Liverpool, in particular, exported Irish paupers at a high rate in the 1850s. Yet, the cost of removal was high and local officials had discretion over the provision of relief. In six county towns the Irish-born made up a small proportion of the population and an even smaller proportion of the paupers on relief lists – slightly over 7 per cent of the population and 6 per cent of those on the relief list in York; virtually no paupers were sent back, and those whose settlements were examined were given relief. The number of Irish deported dropped overall in the 1860s and access to poor relief eased.[28]

Doubt remains about the relative importance for the aged poor of the role of the family in relation to collective poor relief. In England the poor law statute of 1601, which remained in force until 1948, specified that certain relatives – the father and grandfather, mother and grandmother and children – were liable if they were 'of sufficient ability' to relieve and maintain 'every old, blind, lame and impotent person or other poor person not able to work'. The statute was rarely enforced and court decisions in the seventeenth and eighteenth centuries narrowed its interpretation; local poor law officials saw no reason to pursue poor men for payments they could not afford. Children were expected to provide support, but only if they could afford it without impoverishing themselves or their children. Family support and poor relief were not alternatives but shifting components in the bundle of support that maintained the elderly. The poor law was a residual provider of relief in most cases; its relief was intended to encourage family support by supplementing the little that families could afford to give. While the poor law made an important contribution to the incomes of the aged poor, it was not dominant; families generally contributed more, though not necessarily in cash or even co-residence.[29]

There were significant local variations in the mix of the components of support for the elderly. In northern industrial towns such as the Potteries or Preston families were a particularly significant source of support. Over 80 per cent of those age sixty-five and over lived with family or kin, and roughly 60 per cent lived with one or more children. This pattern contrasts with the picture of relatively little sharing with children which appears to have been the case in rural areas and small towns 'where time after time, for place after place, the percentage of elderly who lived with a child were found not to be above 40 per cent,

[28] L. H. Lees, *The Solidarities of Strangers* (Cambridge, 1998), pp. 218–27.
[29] P. Thane, 'Old people and their families in the English past', in Daunton, ed., *Charity, Self-Interest and Welfare* (London, 1996), pp. 117–23, 143.

with a few more per cent living with some other kin, especially grandchildren, nieces or brothers or sisters'.[30] Thus, the collectivity, particularly the poor law, played a more central role in rural areas and small towns. In industrial towns such as the Potteries the importance of family and kin may in part have been due to the combination of relatively little need with a relatively large capacity for family care. In the Potteries in 1861 there were only 727 people age seventy-five and over out of a population of over 100,000. Moreover, it was more likely that an elderly person age seventy-five or over would have a female carer available than in England in the twentieth century. In the Potteries in 1861 the ratio of women age fifty to fifty-nine (those most likely to assume caring roles) to persons age seventy-five and over in the population was 5:1, compared with ratios for England of 3:1 in 1901, 1:1 in 1976 and less than 1:1 in 1986.[31] Throughout the country the elderly in workhouses tended to be those without relatives.

While family and relatives tended to provide assistance for more important and more long-term difficulties, for mundane day-to-day problems and urgent crises proximity could be more important than kinship as the framework for negotiating assistance:[32] many nineteenth-century commentators remarked on the prevalence of the assistance of the poor to the poor. In the Potteries, for example, Emily Rowley sent the ten-year-old girl living with her to buy potatoes for herself and her next-door neighbour; and Mary Ann Culverhouse knocked on the wall to summon the next-door neighbour when her mother collapsed and died from the shock of finding that Mary Ann had given birth. The neighbourhood beerhouse could also serve as a focus for the provision of general assistance for neighbours. In the Potteries in 1880 there were 1,200 beerhouses patronised by both men and women, who could be 'an open-hearted and open-handed lot; ever ready to help the suffering in any form – sickness, distress, or whatever it was. A subscription list was always open for cases of urgent necessity . . . for we knew all calls for assistance were deserving ones.'[33]

While the continuing importance of family, kin and neighbours as sources of assistance should not be underestimated, the growth of the voluntary sector and its relationships with the informal and the statutory provision of welfare are distinctive features of urbanisation in Britain and reflect its variety. A vast expansion of mutual aid and philanthropic activity in the face of the economic and demographic hazards characterised the provision of social welfare in mid-nineteenth-century cities. Yet, their extent and the form they took varied between England and Scotland and among cities, and were related to the economic, social and political structure of urban areas as much as to the hazards faced.

---

[30] D. Thomson, 'Welfare and the historians', in L. Bonfield, R. Smith and K. Wrightson, eds., *The World We Have Gained* (Oxford, 1986), p. 364.

[31] For the figures from 1901 to 1986 see M. Bulmer, *The Social Basis of Community Care* (London, 1987), p. 2.   [32] Dupree, *Family Structure*, pp. 278, 327, 344.

[33] J. Finney, *Sixty Years' Recollections of an Etruscan* (Stoke-on-Trent, 1903), p. 36.

Mutual aid, or help from within a group of like-minded people, was widely practised over a wide range of working-class activity in towns and cities. Among the working class it originated as a barrier against poverty and as a route to self-help and some degree of financial security and personal welfare. Not thrust upon them by other groups, it involved a collective strength absent from the middle-class pursuit of self-help by individual enterprise.

Particularly prominent were friendly societies. They provided a means of insuring against illness, old age and death, with weekly allowances when ill, funeral payment to widows and medical attendance received in return for weekly contributions, often made at convivial meetings in public houses. There was a substantial number of local societies in the early nineteenth century (9,600 in 1803), but the key feature between 1825 and 1875 was the growth of affiliated orders of local societies, providing greater financial stability and viability. By 1872 there were about 1.2 million members of friendly societies in Britain, mostly in urban areas, such as those in Lancashire where relatively high wages allowed workers to afford contributions. While both of the main affiliated orders originated in south-east Lancashire, the Oddfellows were strongest in the industrial North, and the Ancient Order of Foresters, with flexible rates of contribution and benefit, attracted members in lower wage areas in southern England.[34]

Trade unions also provided collective self-help with pay for strikes, sickness and unemployment for about 500,000 members in 1872. After 1850 major national unions, notably the Amalgamated Society of Engineers and the Amalgamated Society of Carpenters and Joiners, developed among skilled artisans, similar to the affiliated orders of friendly societies but including relief for the unemployed. Yet, regional autonomy survived in the non-tramping trades and trade union societies grew in the coalfields throughout the country and in the three main centres of unionism in the earlier nineteenth century: London with societies in a wide range of occupations, particularly artisan and riverside trades; the Lancashire cotton industry; and the sailors and shipwrights in the north-eastern coal trade.[35] The pattern of union membership with its access to unemployment pay could reflect the local economy where there was a marked cyclical pattern as in shipbuilding. Similarly, the Co-operative movement, with between 300,000 and 400,000 members in 1872, was especially successful in medium-size towns in the textile districts (the biggest societies were in Halifax, Leeds, Bury and Rochdale), the mining villages of North-East England and the shoe and hosiery districts of the East Midlands where there were relatively stable earnings; they were less successful both in large centres, especially London and Birmingham where small workshop employment predominated, and in low-paid

---

[34] Finlayson, *Citizen, State and Social Welfare*, pp. 24–8; M. Purvis, 'Popular institutions', in J. Langton and R. J. Morris, eds., *Atlas of Industrialising Britain, 1780–1914* (London, 1986), pp. 194–5.
[35] Finlayson, *Citizen, State and Social Welfare*, p. 29; H. Southall, 'Unionisation', in Langton and Morris, eds., *Atlas*, pp. 189–92.

agricultural areas. The Co-ops covered a variety of provident activity, providing a system of automatic accumulation or self-imposed forced savings through the dividend that could be drawn on in times of need. Regional variations of dividends and prices existed. They were highest in Scotland and the North of England where Co-operative societies dominated the grocery trade in many towns and villages and could set the market price; in the South, especially in London, the Co-ops faced stiff competition from other retailers. In addition, the Co-ops were a major provider of costless credit for the well-to-do artisans in periods of irregular income.[36] In addition, there were specialised groups such as burial societies and penny banks, especially popular in cities among those with lower incomes. Burial societies had 1.4 million members in 1872 and Glasgow had 213 penny banks and 60,000 depositors in 1861.[37] Mutual aid organisations were particularly important in the provision of medical care. In Huddersfield and Wakefield, and elsewhere, these affected far more people than were hospital in-patients.[38]

With relative economic prosperity in the 1850s and 1860s active participation in such societies by skilled artisans became a sign of respectability. Although the assumptions and practices within the societies were egalitarian they led paradoxically to inegalitarian results emphasising differences between the skilled and unskilled within the working class. Nevertheless, the pride in working-class mutuality and meeting in public houses meant that the convergence of mutual aid and the values of middle-class individualistic self-help was never complete.

The philanthropic activity and paternalism in mid-nineteenth-century cities offered help from without even though it involved interference in the market economy, at the same time as those involved in these activities constantly preached the virtues of provident behaviour. Church activities, for example, included 'philanthropy which probably did more for the poor, and more humanely, than the poor law'.[39] The paternalism of individual employers was a notable feature, particularly in the cotton and woollen towns in Lancashire and Yorkshire with Titus Salt's Saltaire only one of the most prominent manifestations.[40] But paternalism, even combined with the benefactions of individuals and other traditional forms of charity – including endowed trusts, almsgiving and casual visiting – clearly grew inadequate to meet the growing demands in expanding towns. Increasingly voluntary societies, financed by subscriptions and

[36] Finlayson, *Citizen, State and Social Welfare*, pp. 29–30; M. Purvis, 'Popular institutions', in Langton and Morris, eds., *Atlas*, pp. 194–6; P. Johnson, *Saving and Spending* (Oxford, 1985), pp. 130, 140–1.

[37] Finlayson, *Citizen, State and Social Welfare*, pp. 31, 34.

[38] H. Marland, *Medicine and Society in Wakefield and Huddersfield, 1780–1870* (Cambridge, 1987).

[39] J. Cox, *The English Churches in a Secular Society* (New York and Oxford, 1982), ch. 3; H. McLeod, 'New perspectives on Victorian working class religion: the oral evidence', *Oral History*, 14 (1986), 35.

[40] P. Joyce, *Work, Society and Politics: The Culture of the Factory in Later Victorian England* (Brighton, 1980); J. Reynolds, *The Great Paternalist* (London, 1983).

governed by committees, developed which intervened in the relationship between benefactors and the needy and called on the support of the public at large. Town-based benevolent societies were one example, and a city such as Manchester developed a variety of such organisations to make voluntary provision for the poor.[41]

A prominent example of philanthropic activity, and often a source of civic pride, were the voluntary hospitals whose number grew rapidly in the mid-nineteenth century. Between 1861 and 1891 charitably financed general hospitals increased from 130 to 385, with an additional rise in the number of specialist voluntary hospitals.[42] Despite the overall increase there was considerable variation in the provision of voluntary hospitals among urban areas – variations related not to perceived medical needs but to the economic, social and political structures of towns. It is worth exploring two examples of this general feature of urban social provision in some detail.

In her comparison of medical provision in Huddersfield and Wakefield in the mid-nineteenth century, Hilary Marland points out that in the former town charitable provision developed early. A charitable dispensary was established in 1814; a purpose-built infirmary followed in 1831 which admitted workers on the borderline of pauperism, thereby reducing poor rates. Huddersfield was a fast-growing textile town with a population increase that made charitable provision all the more necessary; there was money from the expanding industry available to fund charitable provision; and the town's merchant-manufacturers were able to provide wealth and leadership. In contrast, in Wakefield the committee of the dispensary was reluctant to admit paupers and a purpose-built infirmary was not opened until 1879. Wakefield was a traditional market and service centre, with a slow rate of population growth and retarded industrial development, leaving less money available to fund charitable enterprises, less incentive to provide large-scale medical relief and a lack of strong leadership to direct fund raising or policy making. The small scale of medical charities forced the Wakefield Guardians to provide medical relief, and a higher proportion of the Wakefield population received medical treatment via the poor law than in Huddersfield.[43]

In Lancashire too in the thirty years between 1857 and 1887 new or larger voluntary hospitals were built in all the major towns, not because of changes in medicine or perceived medical need, but because the economic and social climate changed in ways that made these institutions attractive to a range of political views. What was gained were medium-size urban hospitals which provided not so much medical care (already available via friendly societies) as nursing and healthy surroundings. With the cotton famine over, charity funds were available.

---

[41] Finlayson, *Citizen, State and Social Welfare*, pp. 59–61; A. J. Kidd and K. W. Roberts, eds., *City, Class and Culture* (Manchester, 1985).

[42] F. K. Prochaska, *Philanthropy and the Hospitals of London* (Oxford, 1992), p. 5.

[43] Marland, *Medicine and Society*, pp. 92–3.

In Wigan and Oldham, for example, mill owners used infirmaries to establish a public presence and begin to rival local gentry. Infirmaries were established especially where large employers dominated as in Rochdale, Bolton and Bury and where the Conservative party was strong. At the same time Liberals and nonconformists saw hospitals as not corrupting like other charity. Also workpeople's contributions in Preston and Blackburn were significant in supporting the building of infirmaries.[44] Voluntary hospitals could also be contested sites within cities. Medical staff clashed with lay governors over issues such as the length of stay of patients. As workingmen's contributions became increasingly important in the finances of many hospitals, they demanded representation on the boards of governors.[45]

In the nineteenth century three notable innovations in the organisation of voluntary societies became prominent which were geared to urban problems: branch societies, district visiting and agencies for the coordination of charities and the dissemination of practical information.[46]

Like friendly societies in the mid-nineteenth century, voluntary organisations, such as the Charity Organisation Society or the National Society for the Prevention of Cruelty to Children, developed branch societies in cities throughout the country.

District visiting 'represented the charitable world's most significant contribution to relieving the nation's perennial ills, especially in their urban manifestation'.[47] The rationale behind visiting was that those who could not provide for themselves could only be helped by the agency of another human being. The visiting societies existed primarily in cities and were usually organised around parishes, bringing the 'face-to-face charity of the country village to city slums'. Earlier in the nineteenth century the Glasgow clergyman Thomas Chalmers articulated and implemented visiting among the poor in St John's Parish: 'each applicant for relief was treated on his merits, closely scrutinised by responsible neighbours and after all possibilities of family support were exhausted, aided from voluntary funds. Chalmers believed that the best system of relief was voluntary, mutual aid within the local community: family responsibility and personal independence were the pillars of a Christian society.'[48] Chalmers' views were highly influential. Another notable experiment in visiting was the Ranyard Mission in London, initiated as a response to the problems of urban life, whose visitors, 'Bible women', were working-class women drawn from the

[44] J. V. Pickstone, *Medicine and Industrial Society* (Manchester, 1985), pp. 138, 144.
[45] B. Abel-Smith, *The Hospitals 1800–1948* (London, 1964); K. Waddington, *Charity and the London Hospitals, 1850–1898* (Woodbridge, 2000).
[46] Prochaska, *Philanthropy*, p. 4; Frank Prochaska, *The Voluntary Impulse: Philanthropy in Modern Britain* (London, 1988), pp. 43–52.   [47] Prochaska, *The Voluntary Impulse*, p. 43.
[48] M. A. Crowther, 'Poverty, health and welfare', in W. H. Fraser and R. J. Morris, eds., *People and Society in Scotland*, vol. II: *1830–1914* (Edinburgh, 1990), p. 266.

neighbourhood but supervised and paid by middle-class superintendents from outside the district.

The proliferation of voluntary societies and charitable organisations, combined with their independence and lack of coordination, led both to fears of duplication and indiscriminate, overlapping relief and to the emergence of organisations for the coordination of charitable relief, particularly the Liverpool Central Relief Society established in 1863 and the COS established in 1869. These coordinating societies utilised visitors to disseminate practical information and distinguish the deserving from the undeserving poor. Most of the coordinating charities dealt with poor relief, promoting self-help schemes, providing information, attacking malpractices (particularly indiscriminate almsgiving) and seeking coordination between charities and poor law officials. They attempted to apply ideas from social science to parish administration to encourage more sophisticated approaches to welfare provision. By the mid-nineteenth century in England a division of responsibilities emerged in the wake of the 1834 poor law Amendment Act with charity intended to assist the 'deserving' who could be aided by preventive or remedial action, while the poor law was to deal with the 'undeserving' in workhouses where hard conditions were imposed on the able-bodied.

The relationship between charity and the poor law, however, was never this neat, varying considerably over time and place. For example, in the early 1860s in the face of massive, long-term urban industrial poverty in Lancashire during the Cotton Famine – when thousands were out of work or on short time through no fault of their own and the income of shopkeepers and landlords dropped – many guardians and charitable workers refused to hold to the strict enforcement of the poor law. 'Guardians proved active and flexible enough to cope with thousands of extra applicants.' Charitable efforts were coordinated by a Central Relief Committee. Collecting money, deciding how it was to be spent and financing local efforts that functioned alongside the poor laws, it 'supplemented rather than supplanted, the official machinery'. Yet, 'only by redefining the labor test and by encouraging public employment could work be made a requirement of relief to the unemployed. Only by massive, voluntary efforts could industrial poverty be dampened during a depression.'[49]

Furthermore, London remained problematical. In the later 1860s when pauperism declined in the rest of the country and both skilled and unskilled workers found their real incomes and standards of living rising, there was no decrease of pauperism in the capital. A host of social commentators warned of the 'demoralisation' of the poor in the metropolis, initiated by the operation of public and private charity and the segregation of the rich and poor. The number and extent of charities in London were thought to have increased to an unprecedented

[49] Lees, *Solidarities*, pp. 235–7.

extent. At the end of the 1860s it was estimated that over £2 million was annually spent on legal relief and over £7 million on private charity. The large and increasing flow of charity from the West End to the East End of London in the 1860s was thought to result from the absence of direct economic links between rich and poor, the disproportionate weight of members of the older professions in the London population and the geographical gulf between rich and poor. By the 1850s this social divide had widened with the exodus of the wealthy and upset the 'balance' between charity and the poor law which could only work when rich and poor were roughly balanced in each district. As a result the poorest districts had the highest rates and the lowest benefits, while the charge in the rich districts was nominal and the relief generous. As discussed further below, legislation in 1867 which increased the size of the responsible units helped to meet this aspect of the problem. In 1871 the central poor law authorities, responding to the problems of London, attempted to restrict outrelief and with the assistance of the COS eliminate the mix of charity and poor relief that undermined the distinction between the deserving and undeserving poor.[50]

In Scotland philanthropic organisations for the relief of the poor flourished – dispensaries, orphanages, district nursing, institutions for the handicapped and the convalescent, model lodging houses, homes for fallen women. Although the financial outlay of Scottish charity cannot be estimated it was particularly important for the provision of social welfare, as poor relief was the responsibility of local kirk sessions until the Poor Law Amendment (Scotland) Act of 1845, and, unlike England, the able-bodied were not entitled to relief under the poor law even after 1845.[51] Voluntary hospital provision for the sick poor in Scotland was particularly prominent. Edinburgh, Glasgow and Aberdeen had their great Royal Infirmaries, founded in the eighteenth century but rebuilt and extended in the nineteenth. Urban expansion in the nineteenth century led to further efforts, with new voluntary hospitals such as the Western Infirmary in Glasgow opened in 1874. The large voluntary hospitals were supported not only by middle-class charity but increasingly by mutual aid with donations by workmen, organised within their workplace, to secure admission for themselves. Specialist voluntary hospitals also developed in the major cities, and most burghs had substantial general hospitals supported by charity.[52]

In the commercial sector, where considerations of profit predominate in the provision of welfare, both large companies and individual enterprises provided social welfare in Victorian towns and cities. Industrial insurance companies such as the Royal Liver or the Prudential emerged during the mid-nineteenth century, financing funerals and death benefits from small premiums paid weekly to house-to-house collectors, thereby providing mutual aid without

---

[50] G. Stedman Jones, *Outcast London* (Oxford, 1971), pp. 239–44, 249.
[51] Crowther, 'Poverty, health and welfare', p. 286; O. Checkland, *Philanthropy in Victorian Scotland* (Edinburgh, 1983).   [52] Crowther, 'Poverty, health and welfare', pp. 276, 286.

participation but for profit. The 'man from the Pru' became part of urban, working-class neighbourhoods. Also, as urban neighbourhoods developed the number of pawn shops kept pace, providing weekly sums integral to the economy of many families. Pawnbroking differed between small towns and large cities; in the former a pawnbroker could exert pressure on customers to redeem parcels, while in larger cities, such as Leeds, with many pawnbrokers, any pressure to redeem goods would merely drive customers to a competitor.[53] For those who could afford it, orthodox and unorthodox medical practitioners provided medical care. In Huddersfield, Wakefield and elsewhere self-medication – with patent medicines whose sale made fortunes for still familiar names such as Boot, Wellcome, Holloway and Beecham – was the source of much health care. [54]

During the mid-nineteenth century voluntarism, with its three sectors, often overlapping, provided a considerable network of welfare. Despite its variety, there were several pervasive characteristics. Voluntarism depended on personal initiative with individuals making active contributions to their own welfare; it featured strong attachments to separate societies, valuing independence and often resistant to affiliation; it was prone to overlap, competition, lack of uniformity and inconsistency; and it was designed to instil habits of self-reliance and sobriety in an urban setting, encouraging and sustaining independence and self-maintenance.

The statutory sector was broadly complementary to voluntarism with much legislation designed to enable and reinforce voluntarist practice. It remained small: a minimal, localised state set the framework within which individual effort and voluntary and local initiative could go forward. At the same time it also adopted a paternalist, protective role, providing safeguards through factory legislation for those who could not indulge in such pursuits and remained vulnerable.[55]

Free trade policies promoted commercial prosperity and economic growth enabling the urban able-bodied poor in theory to provide their own welfare by mutual aid or self-help, while the permissive public health acts attempted to enable cities and towns to remove other hindrances – dirt and disease – to the urban population. At the same time, legislation attempted to encourage the activities of mutual aid and voluntary societies. Although the friendly societies were ambivalent about any interference with their independence, the Friendly Society Acts were intended to assist the societies to work efficiently and effectively, avoiding bankruptcy and fraud. They embodied the absence of central compulsion and discretion left to individual initiative which matched the emphasis on participation and freedom of action so characteristic of voluntarism.[56]

---

[53] Finlayson, *Citizen, State and Social Welfare*, pp. 64–6; M. Tebbutt, *Making Ends Meet* (Leicester, 1983), pp. 2–3; D. Vincent, *Poor Citizens: The State and the Poor in Twentieth-Century Britain* (London, 1991), pp. 11–13.

[54] Marland, *Medicine and Society*, pp. 214–51; A. Digby, *Making a Medical Living* (Cambridge, 1995).

[55] Finlayson, *Citizen, State and Social Welfare*, p. 91. [56] *Ibid.*, p. 88.

In England the 1834 Poor Law Amendment Act, too, was intended to reduce rates and increase self-help and mutual aid by removing the collective, local assistance for the able-bodied which was deemed to undermine self-reliance. The legislation may have encouraged the increase in the number of friendly societies established after 1834. Yet, the Royal Commission on the Poor Laws and the New Poor Law in England were primarily concerned with rural problems and expenditure: urban parishes were comparatively well run and efficient. Nevertheless, in the following years controversies in urban unions forced adjustments by the 1860s that helped to make urban unions viable.[57]

The anti-poor law movement and widespread northern urban opposition emerged in the later 1830s when the new central authority created by the 1834 act sent its assistants to create the new unions of parishes under elected Boards of Guardians who would carry out the requirements of the 1834 act. Urban parishes, wanting to give outrelief to the able-bodied unemployed in periods of trade depression, feared that, with their powers diluted in wider unions, a rigid policy would be imposed on them, allowing relief for able-bodied men only in the workhouse. The Poor Law Commissioners were forced to compromise, and issued unions with a labour test order requiring some form of task work to test the genuine need of able-bodied applicants. This was less costly than workhouse provision and provided the flexibility required in urban areas to deal with periods of 'exceptional distress'.[58]

Rating and settlement were equally important issues in the 1830s and 1840s and led to reforms in the 1860s that made the poor law more suited to urban conditions. The 1834 act made no changes to the existing system of finance: as the parish rather than the union remained the basic unit, parishes with the highest relief paid most into the union's common fund. This 'narrow, local fiscal base limited scope for spreading risk between rich and poor areas'.[59] At the same time there were only minor changes in settlement so that entitlement, while ultimately inclusive, was geographically limited. Rural parishes of settlement were responsible for their migrants to urban areas until 1846 when Peel, to soften the blow of the repeal of the Corn Laws on the landed interest, introduced the concept of irremovability after continuous residence of five years. The cost of the irremovable poor was placed on the union common fund instead of the parish of residence, spreading the burden of relief and paving the way for the union to take more of the financial responsibility from individual parishes.

But, the boundaries of unions rarely corresponded with the boundaries of other administrative units of an urban area. In unions with an urban core and rural parishes, the latter resented having to share, through their contribution to the common fund, the new relief burdens of the urban cores; some rural parishes broke away into separate rural unions, 'sharpening the distinction between

---

[57] M. E. Rose, 'Introduction', in M. E. Rose, ed., *The Poor and the City* (Leicester, 1985), pp. 4–5.
[58] Rose, 'Introduction', p. 6.   [59] Daunton, 'Introduction', p. 8.

the urban poor law and its rural counterpart' and inadvertently creating homo-geneous urban unions.[60] Legislation in 1861 changed the basis for assessing parish contributions from relief expenditure to rateable value and in 1862 the union became responsible for the assessment of property to the poor rate. Finally, the Union Chargeability Act of 1865 established the union as the sole local author-ity in poor law matters as it abolished separate parish expenditure so the whole cost of relief fell on union funds, and the union rather than the parish became the unit of settlement in which individuals resident for one year became irre-movable.

Severe financial inequalities between unions in the larger towns and cities remained, and issues of economy continued to preoccupy the meetings of many Boards of Guardians. Nevertheless, the reforms of the 1860s made the poor law more suitable to urban conditions and provided a financial basis for the Goschen Minute of 1869 which attempted to eliminate outdoor relief from competition with voluntary provision and gave a boost to the COS and its efforts to cooper-ate with the poor law to coordinate relief. Paradoxically, relief policy did not reflect economic conditions: in the 1870s when real incomes were rising the policy was to restrict outdoor relief. The extent to which cooperation between the COS and poor law guardians occurred varied greatly within London and among urban unions in the North and Scotland. Most of the poor law unions in the largest cities – London, Liverpool, Manchester and Birmingham – and in some medium-size towns – Preston, Salford, Reading and Oxford – reduced the proportion of paupers on outdoor relief to below 30 per cent of the total number of paupers. Indoor relief was 'an urban strategy used extensively only in the largest cities'.[61]

In Scotland with some of the worst urban and rural poverty in the country, the poor law differed significantly from that in England.[62] The old poor law based on voluntary giving by the kirk session was not reformed until 1845 when, in contrast to England, reform was designed to increase rather than restrict relief. Overseen by a Board of Supervision in Edinburgh, the 1845 poor law compelled parish boards to raise money to relieve the poor, though they could choose whether to levy compulsory rates. The 1845 act, however, gave no right of relief to the able-bodied, did not require parishes to build poor houses, though some larger towns did within the limits of their finances, and was administered in small parishes which encouraged parsimony. 'At all times the Scottish system relied less on indoor relief than the English';[63] it was less expensive to give small amounts of outdoor relief, and the able-bodied had no right to relief so indoor relief was not a test. In Scotland there were 886 separate parish administrations containing less than 15 per cent of the British population while there were only

---

[60] Rose, 'Introduction', p. 9.   [61] Lees, *Solidarities*, p. 265.
[62] This account of the Scottish poor law relies on Crowther, 'Poverty, health and welfare', pp. 265–89.   [63] *Ibid.*, p. 275.

slightly over 600 poor law unions in England and Wales; also, in Scotland there was extreme variation in the size of parishes, from 28 acres (11.5 ha) to 267,047 acres (108,154 ha) and from 98 to over 500,000 inhabitants.[64]

The Scottish poor law compounded the problems of urban poverty even more than the English.[65] The Poor Law Act of 1845 increased the residence qualification for settlement from three to five years; unaffected by the Union Chargeability Act of 1865 in England and Wales, it was not reduced to three years until 1898. The small size of Scottish parishes made acquisition of settlement more difficult and sharing the burden of relief across boundaries more difficult. As a result charity had to fill many of the gaps.

(iii) CHALLENGES, CHANGES AND CONTINUITIES 1880–1914

From the 1880s, while urbanisation continued until nearly four-fifths of the British population lived in cities and towns on the eve of the First World War, a series of economic, social, political and intellectual challenges cast doubt on whether voluntarism and the complementary, minimal, localised state could and should cope with the burden of poverty. In general the provision of social welfare requires a greater degree of uniformity and higher level of minimum provision than do public utilities and it became steadily clearer that local government, both municipal and under the poor law, like voluntary provision, worked against universally adequate provision. Moreover, the local rate base even when augmented by income from municipal enterprise was not sufficient to avoid an urban financial crisis at the turn of the century.[66] New forms of voluntary and statutory provision and a new balance of the 'mixed economy' emerged which, nevertheless, displayed many continuities with earlier theory and practice.[67] At the same time, the reform of the income tax gave a more buoyant central tax system compared to local rates and municipal enterprise.[68]

Late nineteenth-century social investigations, most notably Charles Booth's study of London and Seebohm Rowntree's study of the outwardly prosperous cathedral town of York,[69] revealed 25–30 per cent of the inhabitants of cities and towns in the UK were below the poverty line, without the income to meet a minimum standard of physical efficiency. At the same time only 2–3 per cent of the population of England and Wales and a slightly lower proportion in Scotland were in receipt of poor relief. In 1901 Rowntree illuminated a way of life strikingly independent of the regulations and officers of national or local bureaucracies, with the poor in the city finding other ways of alleviating their

---

[64] *Ibid.*, pp. 271–2, 274.   [65] *Ibid.*, p. 279.   [66] See above, pp. 294–5, 329.
[67] Finlayson, *Citizen, State and Social Welfare*, p. 106.
[68] Daunton, 'Payment and participation', 173–7.
[69] Charles Booth, *Life and Labour of the People in London*, 17 vols., 3rd edn (London, 1902–3); B. Seebohm Rowntree, *Poverty: A Study in Town Life* (London, 1901).

poverty, informally and through mutual aid and the voluntary and the commercial sectors. With the welfare legislation of the 1906 Liberal government, 'the strategies of the poor and state began to impinge on each other in ever more complex ways',[70] with voluntarism, too, changing yet remaining very much in evidence.

The informal provision of welfare continued to be pervasive. For households in towns and cities, especially, there were opportunities for mothers to take on part-time employment in their homes, taking in sewing, laundry or lodgers, and a chance of finding some means of children's employment for contributing to family income and alleviating a family's troubles. 'In terms of the flow of cash into the home, supplementary earnings were of far greater significance to the poor than all forms of welfare combined.'[71] Whether in paid employment or not, 'women managing poor households created structures of mutual assistance with other women within a short walk which supplied by far the most dependable and effective material and emotional support available to them outside their own family'.[72] These networks took different forms in different types of urban communities. For example, Elizabeth Roberts found that in Preston, but not in Barrow or Lancaster, women paid relatives to look after children. Compared with Barrow and Lancaster, in Preston there was relatively little migration, families were more likely to have extended kin living nearby and wives were full-time textile workers. Only in Preston did she find evidence of paying relatives for services; it was an integral part of the very closely knit family relationships in the town where there was an expectation of sharing income beyond the nuclear family to the kinship group. 'Paying for services was the most obvious way of sharing income, and moreover only appears to have taken place when those providing the services had a smaller income than those paying for it.'[73]

Sometimes those providing support were kin as in the case of the Lambeth fish fryer who lost his job

> owing to the business being sold and the new owner bringing in his own fryer. The man had been getting 26s a week, and owed nothing. His wife's brothers and parents, who lived near by, combined to feed three of the four children; a certain amount of coal was sent in; the rent was allowed to stand over by a sympathetic landlady to whom the woman had been kind in her confinement.[74]

But often it was neighbours brought together not by affection or calculation but united by 'a kind of mutual respect in the face of trouble'.[75] They could serve as a defence against outside intervention as much as an alternative source of assistance, and solidarity was often riven by tensions.[76] For example, rented accommodation facilitated mobility which constantly threatened structures of shared

---

[70] Vincent, *Poor Citizens*, p. 5.   [71] *Ibid.*, pp. 19–20.   [72] *Ibid.*, p. 13.
[73] E. Roberts, *A Woman's Place* (Oxford, 1984), p. 180.
[74] M. Pember Reeves, *Round About a Pound a Week* (London, 1913), p. 40.   [75] *Ibid.*, p. 40.
[76] E. Ross, 'Survival networks – women's neighbourhood sharing in London before World War I', *History Workshop*, 15 (1983), 4–27.

knowledge on which neighbourhood assistance was based. Yet, towns also favoured networks of informal mutual assistance which once in place could serve as an incentive to residential stability.[77] Still, the resources for neighbourhood assistance, so important in the short term, were limited. Relatives and neighbours supported the Lambeth fish fryer and his family for nine weeks until he obtained another position; 'a magistrate calculated that neighbours, together with local sources of credit, could sustain a deserted mother and her children for about two weeks'.[78]

Mutual aid was thriving in the form of stocking clubs (for children's winter stockings), crockery clubs and Christmas dinner clubs involving a weekly payment of 3d. or 4d. until the object had been attained.[79] Friendly societies, however, experienced financial difficulties. Sales of sickness insurance were declining as the less well-off third of the working class could not afford the weekly subscriptions; there was competition for members; and the proportion of ageing members increased. By the 1890s James Riley argues that friendly societies 'lost their nerve'. Members began to yield to advice and direction they had formerly resisted and there was less enthusiasm for the social aspects of the movement.[80] Although the friendly societies provided medical care for members under their control, only a portion of working-class men and very few women benefited.

Community-based charities continued to be important and some new philanthropic endeavours began such as Barnardos, the Salvation Army and the settlement house movement. Overall the contributions of charity to relief exceeded that of outrelief under the poor law, but their proportions in the mix varied considerably among cities and towns, even among those with similar overall levels of spending as indicated in the rough estimates in Table 12.1. In 1905–8 Bristol and Birmingham, with relatively high overall levels, had quite different proportions for charity and the poor law, with the poor law accounting for 23 per cent of relief in Bristol and only 4 per cent in Birmingham. Similarly, at relatively low levels of overall spending, Sunderland relied heavily on the Poor Law (41 per cent) and Exeter relatively little (6 per cent). In general, charities relying on voluntary contributions provided more relief than endowed charities, but some older cities, such as Norwich, relied more heavily on endowed charity, while newer cities, such as Leeds and Birmingham, relied more on voluntary contributions.

Yet, overall the limitations of philanthropy became apparent during the later nineteenth century. Demand increased faster than the incessant, competitive search for funds could supply it, and doubts emerged about the effectiveness and

[77] Pember Reeves, *Round About a Pound a Week*, pp. 39–41.
[78] *Ibid.*, p. 40; Vincent, *Poor Citizens*, p. 15.
[79] Pember Reeves, *Round About a Pound a Week*, p. 72.
[80] C. Riley, *Sick Not Dead* (Baltimore and London, 1997), pp. 120–2.

Table 12.1 *The mix of charity and outdoor poor relief in certain English towns c. 1905–1908: percentage of total annual expenditure on relief*

	Endowed charities (%)	Voluntary charities (%)	Poor law outrelief (%)	Total (£)
Bristol	9	68	23	191,663
Birmingham	7	89	4	187,274
Leeds	4	81	15	102,591
Newcastle-upon-Tyne	9	75	16	99,330
Sheffield	15	63	22	82,032
Leicester	15	46	39	79,614
Norwich	22	55	24	66,167
Sunderland	2	57	41	56,214
Exeter	7	87	6	53,338

These estimates are derived from the Royal Commission on the Poor Laws and Relief of Distress which compiled a 'relief budget' for 'a few typical cities, towns and villages'. The figures are for the total annual income for the endowed and voluntary charities, and for the total annual expenditure on outrelief. The Royal Commission assumed that all the charities' annual income was expended on relief.

Sources: for Birmingham, Leicester, Leeds and Sunderland PP 1910 (Cd 5078), Royal Commission on the Poor Laws, Appendix vol. XXVI, pp. 42–53. For Newcastle-upon-Tyne, Sheffield, Norwich, Bristol and Exeter: for charities *ibid.*, p. 41; and for annual expenditure on outrelief PP1907 (321), Annual Local Tax Returns 1905–6, pt I, pp. 42–77.

adequacy of social welfare provision based on the voluntary sector. Despite the efforts of the COS to coordinate and to categorise by casework, the disjointed and disorganised nature of charitable effort persisted. As mentioned above, some towns and large cities – particularly some parts of London such as Marylebone, Kensington, St George's in the East, Stepney, Whitechapel, Paddington, Camberwell and Islington – applied COS principles, to the extent that outdoor relief was nearly abolished, yet others did not.

The North-East of England illustrates the variations among similar urban areas and the local influences leading to such differences. Facing unemployment that was urban, industrial and temporary in the North-East were a number of active COS branches, yet they did not cover the entire urban North-East and achieved mixed results in terms of both casework and cooperation with poor law authorities.[81] In West Hartlepool where there was exceptionally close cooperation

[81] Keith Gregson, 'Poor law and organised charity: the relief of exceptional distress in North-East England, 1870–1914', in Rose, ed., *The Poor and the City* (Leicester, 1985), pp. 94–131.

between the COS and the guardians, there was a continuous link between the two with cross-membership between the Board of Guardians and the committee of the society and close contact between the poor law officers and the COS. The clerk and one of the two relieving officers were long-time members of the COS. West Hartlepool joined Kendal, Norwich, Oxford, Whitechapel and Marylebone, in having a close relationship between the COS and the poor law, but stood in stark contrast to the neighbouring union centred on Stockton where there was little organised charity even in periods of exceptional need and little cooperation between organised charity and the poor law. In Darlington there was much charitable activity, but despite the pressure of a COS branch, it cherished its independence, was not afraid to be called indiscriminate, and clashed with the poor law. The North-East as a whole featured 'all shades of activity from an almost total lack of charitable effort and cooperation with the poor law through cooperation to a cooperation verging on integration'.[82]

Not only did the COS fail to achieve cooperation through overlapping membership with the poor law guardians in most unions, but in major cities such as Manchester and Bradford church and missionary societies, expanding their efforts in the later nineteenth century, remained aloof from the COS in order to apply their own, far wider criteria to determine who was deserving of relief. In some cases they became an alternative to the poor law. Yet, church-initiated efforts to coordinate the work of charities, criticised by the COS for indiscriminate giving which undermined the responsibilities of families, failed because of denominational rivalries.[83]

The culmination of the search for a solution to social problems by means of charity organisation were the guilds of help and the councils of social welfare which grew up in the Edwardian period in an attempt to coordinate the provision of welfare at the town level. These new forms of charity organisation and personal service societies drew on civic consciousness and the failure of the COS both to coordinate local charity and to determine the 'helpable', and by 1919 they developed into the National Council of Social Services.[84]

The first Guild of Help was launched in Bradford in September 1904; by 1911 there were seventy such bodies mainly located in the North of England where the COS was weakest. The guilds were influenced by the German Elberfeld system where all relief was administered by the municipality on a district basis with no full-time officials: the work was undertaken by unpaid helpers appointed

---

[82] *Ibid.*, p. 122.
[83] A. Kidd, 'Charity organisation and the unemployed in Manchester, *c.* 1870–1914', *Soc.Hist.*, 9 (1984), 58–9; M. Cahill and T. Jowitt, 'The new philanthropy: the emergence of the Bradford City Guild of Help', *Journal of Social Policy*, 9 (1980), 364; J. Lewis, 'The boundary between voluntary and statutory social service in the later nineteenth and early twentieth centuries', *HJ*, 39 (1996), 163.
[84] A. Olechnowicz, *Working-Class Housing in England between the Wars* (Oxford, 1997), esp. ch. 5.

to visit and assist those in need, combining the functions of a relieving officer and a COS visitor. The guilds emphasised the importance of friendly visiting in order to foster a sense of civic responsibility for poverty. As city-wide attempts to help the poor through voluntary service, these guilds differed from the COS in three ways. The guilds recruited helpers from the whole populations, claiming that 50 per cent were working class though recent studies show the Bradford, Halifax, Bolton and Poole guilds were mainly middle class. Also, any citizen could be helped; the guilds refused to draw a boundary line between poor law and charity clients, insisting that no one was 'unhelpable'. In addition, they were prepared to cooperate with new state legislation and the new organisations it created. The name was chosen to avoid class, political and religious distinctions. Its strategy, however, was to coopt churches into its work, and it succeeded because its emphasis on visiting and refusal to grant direct relief appealed to charity organisations such as the District Provident Society (DPS) in Manchester while it adopted the less exclusive approach of mission workers. The Reading guild's central board of management had representatives from forty-five groups, linking charitable and religious work in the town,[85] and many visitors for the guilds had been visitors for church and mission charities. The Manchester guild developed in 1907 after traditional relief measures proved inadequate in the face of unemployment in 1903–5 when poor law funds could not be used to subsidise relief work, forcing the municipal authority to do so in a time of financial crisis. The chairman was the lord mayor, but it involved no local authority expenditure. It was a surrogate for municipal action.

The councils of social welfare, in contrast to the guilds' emphasis on personal social work, put more emphasis on securing cooperation within a district, through joint machinery, unlike the COS which advocated only common membership with the guardians. In Hampstead, for example, the council had representatives from the COS, the local authority and the guardians, who referred all cases to the council, which cooperated with local authorities in the provision of infant and maternal welfare centres.[86] Thus, at a time when the nature of state provision was changing, the COS was becoming increasingly isolated by insisting on maintaining its firm commitment to separate spheres for voluntary agencies and the state with a small sphere for a deterrent state relief system based on distinguishing between the 'deserving' and 'undeserving'. The guilds and councils differed in the extent to which they were prepared for voluntary activity to be tied to the state by joint machinery or financial aid. However, they were similar in welcoming the state's becoming the provider of first resort and voluntary agencies playing a complementary role, after a renegotiation of the division of labour between state and voluntary activity so it was task-based and not

[85] S. Yeo, *Religion and Voluntary Organisations in Crisis, 1890–1914* (London, 1976), p. 219.
[86] Lewis, 'Boundary', 168.

client-based. 'The voluntary agencies would provide friendly visiting and co-ordinate charitable and state efforts . . . while the state provided a national minimum level of service and relief.'[87]

From the 1880s voluntary hospitals, both general and specialist, grew in numbers. In Glasgow, for example, the Royal Infirmary was joined by two other general infirmaries and a host of specialist hospitals. Infirmaries also developed societies attached to them such as the Bradford Royal Infirmary where a Samaritan Society was founded by doctors' wives to assist with clothing and food for outpatients. Provident dispensaries appeared in many cities. In Manchester, for example, the Provident Dispensaries Association attempted to promote thrift and grew up under the auspices of the DPS. The latter investigated applicants conducting 1,000 investigations in 1866 and 45,000 in 1886, but the proportion of applicants rejected dropped from 42 per cent to 11 per cent and the provident feature faded. 'In the later 19th century more charitable giving was made to medical charities than any other form of voluntary relief.'[88] Yet, the competition among voluntary societies led to falling subscriptions. For example, the Bradford Royal Infirmary needed to launch a £50,000 appeal in 1902. Others increasingly depended on small workplace subscriptions. By 1900 the financial position of many of Manchester's medical charities was precarious.[89]

While community-based charity and philanthropy continued to be important, in response to criticisms that charities were too small in scale to be effective, large charitable trusts and foundations emerged after 1900 following the American model. Allowed to deal with a wide range of issues, they were bigger, more centralised and male dominated, in contrast to the more local, single-issue charities with self-governing branches in which women tended to play major roles.[90]

While the mutual aid and philanthropic provision of welfare experienced difficulties in the late nineteenth and early twentieth centuries, the commercial sector flourished. Pawn shops were a prominent feature of urban neighbourhoods and a significant part of the financial strategy of many working-class families. The Edwardian period was the 'golden age of pawnbroking': 'not before or since were there so many shops in so many neighbourhoods prepared to issue tickets on so wide a range of goods'.[91] Burial insurance was a staple in budgets of the poorest families.[92] Industrial insurance companies and collecting friendly societies expanded rapidly, faster than the mutual aid friendly societies based on the more prosperous sections of the working class. By 1914 door-to-door collectors handled 46 million policies a year,[93] and after a fierce

[87] *Ibid.*, 176.   [88] Kidd, 'Charity Organisation', 50.
[89] Cahill and Jowitt, 'New philanthropy', 371; Kidd, 'Charity organisation', 54.
[90] Prochaska, *Voluntary Impulse*, p. 77.   [91] Vincent, *Poor Citizens*, p. 12.
[92] Pember Reeves, *Round About a Pound a Week*, pp. 66, 73–4.   [93] Vincent, *Poor Citizens*, p. 17.

battle they had secured a place as a partner of the state in the new organisation of welfare provision brought in by the National Insurance Act of 1911. The private market continued to provide health care for the better off, while prosperous working people relied on patent medicines, and voluntary provision through friendly societies, dispensaries or voluntary hospitals and the poorest depended on the poor law.

The proportion of GNP devoted to the social services doubled between 1890 and 1914 and much of the increase was in new forms in the statutory sector. Yet, it tended to bypass the local provision by the poor law and the increasingly financially beleaguered municipal authorities. Increasingly, both seemed to be ill-suited to provide the uniformity required of the provision of social welfare.

Despite the adjustments to urban conditions resulting from legal and administrative changes in the poor law in England and Wales in the 1860s, the poor law declined in importance in social policy as the rural population fell after 1870. The stricter application of the workhouse test after the Goschen Minute deterred the able-bodied and filled the workhouses with children, the chronic sick and elderly for whom 'less eligibility' was inappropriate. As the sums spent on outdoor relief fell, those on indoor relief rose and the general workhouse gave way to separate, more specialised institutions for children, and to poor law hospitals for the sick, though this process took place more slowly in Scotland. The Goschen Minute envisaged a system in which the poor law guardians and charitable organisations could between them tackle all aspects of poverty. But, by the mid-1880s the Chamberlain Circular appealed to town councils to provide work for the unemployed to keep them from having to apply for poor relief. No clear role for the poor law emerged in the 1880s and 1890s despite the intense debate on urban poverty.

Increasing unemployment in the early 1900s and the failure of joint distress committees of guardians, town councillors and representatives of charitable organisations to cope adequately with its relief highlighted the failure of Boards of Guardians in their approach to urban, industrial distress. From 1894 any rate-payer could vote or stand for election as a guardian, and before and after the First World War Poplar was only one of a number of urban unions to adopt generous relief policies and raise fears that guardians were subject to working-class pressure and could no longer be trusted. This trend played into the hands of Neville Chamberlain who imposed tighter financial controls from the centre and then abolished the Boards of Guardians in the Local Government Act of 1929.[94]

This, however, was after another Royal Commission had been set up in 1905 to investigate the shortcomings of the poor law system. This time, in contrast to 1834, urban problems were at the centre of the agenda. Both the majority and minority final reports agreed to abolish the Boards of Guardians and transfer

---

[94] *Ibid.*, pp. 25, 59–61; Crowther, *British Social Policy*, pp. 48–9.

their responsibilities to town and county councils. However, the divided proposals and the alternative welfare plans of the Liberal government left the poor law in place in 1909 and the First World War solved the problem of unemployment in the short run.[95]

In other spheres too the poor law's position in social welfare provision was weakened as town councils took over an increasingly overlapping range of functions, especially in the field of child welfare and health services. The absorption of educational responsibilities by local authorities in 1902 paved the way for local authority administration of the 1906 Education Act permitting local authorities (and in 1914 making it compulsory for them) to supply school meals financed by rates supplemented by charities. Though subject to a means test to determine the deserving which led to inconsistencies as in the experiences of south London families visited by Pember Reeves, free or subsidised school meals, bypassing the poor law, directly contributed to the well-being of poor families.[96]

Municipal provision for health care also expanded. Municipal hospitals, which previously tended to be set up *ad hoc* for fever epidemics, became permanent infectious disease hospitals. Concern about high infant mortality and the health of children led to the establishment in some cities of infant welfare centres and health visitors under the auspices of local authorities or in conjunction with voluntary societies. In 1918 the Maternity and Child Welfare Act compelled local authorities to set up committees on maternity and child welfare and enabled them to support ante-natal and child welfare clinics.

Yet, the Edwardian urban financial crisis and the increasing priority for uniformity of provision and minimum standards in social welfare meant that significant parts of the welfare legislation of the 1906 Liberal government bypassed local authorities creating non-elected boards, without protest.[97] At the same time this increased role of central government affected the control of entitlement. As central government took increasing responsibility for social welfare provision, it redrew the boundaries of welfare entitlement making them symmetrical with those of the economy and national state, encouraging uniformity in practices that had differed substantially throughout the country. Entitlement, which had been a local problem determined by the parish or poor law union through its policies of settlement and removal, had been associated with free entry to the country. Now it came to be determined by the boundaries of the national state and controlled by national legislation which restricted the entry of certain groups, as the Aliens Act of 1905 restricted Jewish immigration, or specified whether immigrants were eligible for welfare payments.[98]

From the 1880s surveys such as Booth's of London made it apparent that urban

---

[95] Rose, 'Introduction', pp. 12–13.

[96] Vincent, *Poor Citizens*, p. 44; J. R. Hay, *Origins of Liberal Welfare Reforms 1906–1914*, 2nd edn (Basingstoke, 1983), pp. 43–4; Pember Reeves, *Round About a Pound a Week*, pp. 205–6.

[97] Above, p. 274. [98] Above, p. 200; Lees, *Solidarities*, p. 351.

poverty was especially severe among the old and it was virtually impossible to save enough for old age out of weekly income. Neither friendly societies nor charity were providing sufficient protection for men and virtually none at all for women who formed the greater proportion of the elderly. It was acknowledged that the poor elderly should no longer be expected to care for themselves and hence the deterrent poor law was not an appropriate means of assistance. Non-contributory, non-pauperising, old-age pensions under the 1908 Pensions Act were financed out of general taxation and paid at post offices to men and women aged seventy and over with an annual income less than £31 10s. The benefits were not universal; until 1919 there were clauses requiring suitable behaviour, and the amount (raised to 10s. in 1919) was only enough to supplement living expenses. Nevertheless, the benefits of 1s.–5s. were significant in encouraging, rather than undermining, family care.[99] The National Insurance legislation of 1911 was also significant in bypassing local authorities and the poor law, in drawing on funding from national rather than local taxation, and in its compulsory contributions. Local authority resources were inversely related to the extent of unemployment in their areas, so a national measure in the context of the labour market was the only solution.

It is important not to overestimate the extent to which the 1911 act – and early twentieth-century social legislation more generally – marked a break from previous state provision. The ideology and implementation of state provision retained strong traces of voluntarism, participation, self-help and deterrence. The introduction of unemployment and health insurance in 1911 continued much of the pattern set by the 1834 poor law which limited coverage.[100] Where the Elizabethan Poor Law was universal and comprehensive, covering the entire population for the life-cycle risks of old age, widows, orphans, to which everyone was liable, the New Poor Law tended to focus on a despised minority, and was exclusive, leaving the better-off middle classes and working classes to their own resources. It was also gender-specific, as work came to be seen as the responsibility of the individual and ideals of domesticity restricted women's work to the home; it introduced punitive treatment of men to force them into the labour force, and small pensions for widows and children. The Edwardian social legislation reinforced the restrictive pattern of the New Poor Law by limiting access to unemployment and sickness insurance to specified limits of income and occupations. It was a move toward 'an exclusive risk

[99] M. Anderson, 'The impact on the family relationships of the elderly of changes since Victorian times in governmental income-maintenance provision', in E. Shanas and M. B. Sussman, eds., *Family, Bureaucracy and the Elderly* (Durham, N. C., 1977), pp. 36–59.

[100] The following view of Edwardian social legislation in a longer perspective draws on Daunton, 'Payment and participation', esp. 180–1; Lees, *Solidarities*, pp. 349–52; P. Johnson, 'Risk, redistribution and social welfare in Britain from the poor law to Beveridge', in Daunton, ed., *Charity, Self-Interest and Welfare* (London, 1996), esp. pp. 245–6.

pool, contractual entitlement and a self-financing system of intra-personal redistribution'.[101]

Financed by contributions by employees, employers and the state, payment of contributions under the 1911 National Insurance Act did not give employees a right to benefit, but it did provide an automatic method of discrimination and was relatively inexpensive for the state. The unemployment insurance side of the legislation was limited from the outset to provide insurance to cover cyclical unemployment in a narrow range of industries which responded to depression by lay-offs rather than short-time working. Benefits were kept low, lasting up to fifteen weeks, to avoid encouraging unemployment. Health insurance covered all employees but not their dependants, providing treatment by general practitioners, though not hospital care. Although contributions were compulsory, the legislation worked through agencies in the voluntary and commercial sectors – mutual aid friendly societies, the collecting friendly societies and industrial insurance companies – which collected contributions amidst conflict with each other and the government. The result was a loss of control of medical treatment as appointed insurance committees took over control from the friendly societies.

By 1938 national health insurance only covered 42 per cent of the population. The social assurance and social assistance system introduced by the Labour government after 1945 was a return to the universal and comprehensive policy of the Elizabethan poor law.

(iv) WARS, UNEMPLOYMENT AND THE WELFARE STATE

In the face of two wars separated by mass unemployment, between 1914 and 1948 the national government substantially increased the amount it spent on social welfare, augmenting but increasingly bypassing the provision of local authorities. The abolition of the Boards of Poor Law Guardians and the local authority absorption of the administration of the poor law in 1929 were at once a culmination of the municipalisation of social welfare provision and a reduction in democratic accountability and participation in relief administration. Yet, increasing provision by central government did not bring uniformity. Mass unemployment – due to the drop in world demand for exports which hit Britain's staple industries such as cotton textiles, iron and steel, and shipbuilding in the Midlands and North especially hard – varied across the country leaving the south of England relatively unscathed. Variation among urban areas remained a key feature of social welfare provision. The informal and voluntary sectors changed but remained significant in the mix of providers of social welfare. Despite the increase in public welfare, it was not sufficient to displace voluntarism and in many urban areas they were increasingly intertwined.

---

[101] Johnson, 'Risk, redistribution and social welfare', p. 246.

Persistent mass unemployment, never dropping below 1 million and reaching a peak of well over 3 million in 1932, was a new phenomenon during the period. Nevertheless, surveys of urban poverty in the 1920s and 1930s reveal a fall in primary poverty since the turn of the century.[102] Rising real wages during war and during the interwar years for those in work meant that the market reduced the problem of low pay, the principal cause of poverty before the First World War. The long fall in prices from 1920 also meant that it was easier for the unemployed to survive on relief payments. Simultaneously, working-class families grew smaller in size as the birth rate fell. In the late nineteenth century 70 per cent of couples gave birth to four or more children, while in the 1920s 70 per cent of couples gave birth to fewer than four children more of whom survived, leading to a smaller, more predictable and affordable family size.[103] In addition, the fall in adult death rates meant that a smaller proportion of marriages were broken by death within their first twenty years. Yet, mass unemployment forced many of the skilled working class whose self-respect was based on independence to rely on statutory relief, and families and neighbourhoods, the main agents of the informal sector, had more contact with the state as family incomes which previously had no public assistance came to incorporate some state benefits.

The basic techniques of survival and informal assistance changed little for those subjected to the shortcomings of the labour market in urban neighbourhoods. Families have 'always been the main providers of welfare', especially women in families performing unpaid work caring for young, old and husbands, stretching inadequate incomes by methods including short changing their own diet and health care.[104] Although there was a shift in the balance of the mixed economy of welfare towards statutory provision there is no evidence that the government took over the role of the family. Instead, the family's contribution to the health and welfare of its members was considered crucial by not only the voluntary sector, but also local and national governments: 'a large part of their action was directed towards eliciting the kind of behaviour from adult members of poor families that would secure their self-maintenance and the health and welfare of their children'.[105]

Compared with the period before the First World War, the receipt of public money during the interwar years was commonplace among the urban poor and working-class communities. Yet it was inadequate, and the first response of

---

[102] A. L. Bowley and A. R. Burnett-Hurst, *Livelihood and Poverty* (London, 1915), and A. L. Bowley and M. Hogg, *Has Poverty Diminished?* (London, 1925); Rowntree, *Poverty*, and B. S. Rowntree, *Poverty and Progress* (London, 1941); Rowntree's summaries of his findings are conveniently presented in R. Pope, A. Pratt and B. Hoyle, *Social Welfare in Britain 1885–1985* (London, 1986), pp. 82–90.   [103] Vincent, *Poor Citizens*, pp. 81–2.

[104] Lewis, 'Gender', 38; J. Lewis, 'Agents of health care: the relationship between family, professionals and the state in the mixed economy of welfare in twentieth-century Britain', in J. Woodward and R. Jutte, eds., *Coping with Sickness* (Sheffield, 1996), p. 166.

[105] Lewis, 'Agents of health care', p. 166; Lewis, 'Family provision of health and welfare', 3–5.

families threatened with destitution was to send out members to earn whatever they could through casual employment, cleaning windows, gardening, portering, taking in washing, mending and lodgers.[106] Both benefits and family enterprise were required just to survive and reach the minimum subsistence level, and some forms of deprivation in some urban places were more affected than others, depending on the local administration and level of benefit, local population structure and local labour market. In York in 1936, for example, relief payments provided 80 per cent of the income of the unemployed and 66 per cent of the income of the elderly.[107] Evidence from the New Survey of London in 1929–30 suggests that benefits accounted for 44 per cent of pensioners' incomes while 35 per cent came from employment.[108] As in earlier periods, relatively little income came from family members outside households, and adults including the elderly tended to head their own households and co-reside only with closest kin if at all. In London in 1929–30 less than 2 per cent of the income of pensioners came from other family members, and 30 per cent of the elderly lived alone, 32 per cent co-resided with their children and most of the rest lived with their spouse.[109] Yet, relatives who lived outside the household provided a great deal of informal care and support, making up the difference between income from benefit and employment on one hand, and subsistence on the other, through indirect transfers in kind, e.g. care and general assistance and, especially for the elderly, provision of meals.[110]

Legally in England under the poor law from 1601 to 1948, as mentioned above, an extended family of three generations as well as husband and wife were responsible for the maintenance of each other apart from grandchildren who were not responsible for grandparents. In Scotland, where the right to parish relief was less, three generations were mutually responsible with further responsibility for siblings and in-laws. In 1948 throughout the country responsibility was reduced to husband and wife and to parents for children less than sixteen years old. During the interwar years state relief for the unemployed tended to be outside the poor law, and during the 1930s legislation did not define the household or family, making it possible for administrators to extend the number of relatives who were liable for the support of applicants through the household means test, as households, particularly in areas of housing shortage, might well include relatives who would not be legally liable under the poor law. A survey of five towns showed that the number of members of households who were not classified as liable relatives in the poor law definition varied from 45 per 100 families in Reading to 16 per 100 families in Huddersfield. Rather than standardising benefits this exacerbated local variation, penalising stable families who stayed

---

[106] Vincent, *Poor Citizens*, p. 89.   [107] *Ibid.*, p. 72.
[108] Chris Gordon, *The Myth of Family Care? The Elderly in the 1930s*, The Welfare State Programme, London School of Economics, Discussion Paper 29 (London, 1988), p. 59.   [109] *Ibid.*, pp. 45–6.
[110] *Ibid.*, p. 53.

together in areas of housing shortage, making the able-bodied more dependent on the family, and shifting the burden of unemployment from the state on to the family.[111] The household means tests (by 1939 there were at least eighteen separate means tests imposed by central and local government) also undermined the basis of working-class strategies for survival in another way. Where maximising the earning potential of subordinate family members through part-time or casual work had been the most effective defence against hardship, it became a major threat to receipt of assistance.[112]

Similarly, the informal assistance within urban neighbourhoods based on long, shared experience of hardship and struggle continued, with children cared for if their mother were ill or temporary accommodation provided if made homeless. Yet, the ambiguities and tensions of neighbourhood structures of mutual assistance also continued with warmth and generosity compromised by jealousy and conflict exacerbated by the increasing scope and bureaucratisation of relief. More households were affected, and private, often anonymous information from neighbours, rather than the investigations of inspectors, was the major source of information to authorities regarding alleged transgressions of relief regulations. At the same time the building of council estates was beginning to break up informal networks in inner-city neighbourhoods, leaving nuclear families more dependent on their own resources.[113]

The First World War led to a shortage of personnel for staff and collectors for friendly societies and industrial insurance companies. Yet problems of lapses in contributions were overcome and the approved societies, both friendly societies and industrial insurance companies associated with the national health insurance system, emerged from the war with greater strength than expected.[114] Employment and wages during the war kept contributions high; sickness claims on the domestic front fell; and 'actuarial deaths' (contributors such as women engaged in war work whom the societies lost track of) increased, leaving most societies with substantial reserves at the end of the war.

Nevertheless, between 1916 and 1921 there was a sharp decline in the proportion of working-class assets held in friendly societies, as they did not share in the rise of savings in the last two years of the war and the post-war boom.[115] Membership of the ordinary and affiliated orders had been stagnant in the Edwardian period, rising temporarily after the 1911 National Insurance Act attracted extra private business to the societies; yet, they did not expand membership during the interwar years and had an ageing membership. At the same time not even the long-established affiliated orders could maintain the traditions

---

[111] M. A. Crowther, 'Family responsibility and state responsibility in Britain before the welfare state', *HJ*, 25 (1982), 132–3, 144–5.   [112] Vincent, *Poor Citizens*, pp. 77–8.

[113] *Ibid.*, pp. 82–6; Olechnowicz, *Working-Class Housing in England Between the Wars*, chs. 3 and 6 and *passim*.   [114] Finlayson, *Citizen, State and Social Welfare*, pp. 205–7.

[115] Johnson, *Saving and Spending*, p. 207.

of 'mutuality and fellowship that had been the hallmark of friendly societies in Victorian Britain'.[116] Trade union membership fell rapidly between 1926 and 1931 due to unemployment. Their ability to pay unemployment benefit on top of state relief appears to have been reduced; saving for old age through unions may have declined. Yet, generalisations about the welfare policies of trade unions are 'sure to be misleading, because rates of contribution and benefit varied enormously between industrial sectors, with the established craft unions in printing, engineering, and building levying high membership fees but offering generous welfare benefits'.[117]

More impersonal forms of saving, however, grew during the interwar years. Centralised societies, such as the Hearts of Oak, and deposit societies, such as the National Deposit Friendly Society, which involved no mutuality, grew substantially. The latter, operating by post from an office in central London, increased its membership from less than 50,000 in 1899 to 1.2 million in 1933.[118]

In addition, contributory schemes for hospital care without sickness benefit which had begun in the later nineteenth century expanded rapidly during the interwar years. The absence of the state benefit covering hospital care except for sanatorium care for tuberculosis; the increasing efficacy and costs of hospital treatments for all classes; and the failure of income to match expenditure which led voluntary hospitals, in England, though far less in Scotland, to introduce systems of partial payment – all encouraged the growth of hospital contributory schemes. In London the Hospital Savings Association grew from 62,000 to 1.9 million contributors in 1938. It offered hospital care without means testing or other payment for 3d. per week per family, though it was extended as a privilege rather than a right to avoid contractual liability.[119] In northern industrial cities and Scotland, voluntary contributory schemes organised at the workplace which collected small weekly sums from workers and in exchange gave 'lines' to contributors for hospital care for themselves and dependants also grew during the interwar years, though as emerges below these could be a mixed blessing to hospitals.

The continued vitality of philanthropy and charity is a significant feature of the provision of welfare in this period. Both the First and Second World Wars provided a focus for much voluntary giving and effort, ranging from the Soldiers' and Sailors' Family Association providing for the immediate financial needs of the relatives of servicemen during the First World War and the formation of the British Legion in 1922 to meet the needs of returning servicemen, to the Society of Friends War Relief Committee and the Young Women's Christian Association (YWCA) and Young Men's Christian Association (YMCA) meeting civilian needs in bombed cities during the Second World War. Between the wars mass

---

[116] *Ibid.*, p. 68. See also Riley, *Sick Not Dead*, pp. 41–3, 122.
[117] Johnson, *Saving and Spending*, p. 78; Finlayson, *Citizen, State and Social Welfare*, p. 212.
[118] Johnson, *Saving and Spending*, p. 68; Finlayson, *Citizen, State and Social Welfare*, p. 213.
[119] Johnson, *Saving and Spending*, p. 72.

unemployment gave a new lease of life to middle-class philanthropy which had run into crisis before 1914. The increase in state social services did not lead to a decrease in the amount given in charity. The total 'real income' of charities was roughly constant 1911–41. The distribution of contributions to different types of charities changed little, though the relative importance of income from charitable contributions declined while that from interest and payments by or for persons to whom services were rendered increased.[120] Also, international events elicited new developments in response, such as the Jewish Refugees Committee.

At the same time, many voluntary organisations were changing toward greater integration, often on a civic or local basis. The National Council of Social Services, set up in 1919 to preserve the tradition of voluntary service initiated before the war by the Guilds of Help, worked to reduce overlapping and duplication among voluntary organisations in towns and cities, promoted cooperation with the developing statutory services and, among other things, formed a New Estates Community Committee which tried to establish community centres and associations on the new housing estates of the interwar years.[121] Voluntary organisations increasingly adopted a not altogether new attitude of cooperation with local authorities, labelled the 'new philanthropy';[122] at the same time, the state provision of unemployment relief released voluntary effort in other directions, especially of churches, previously devoted to material relief.[123] This led to a complex mix of sources of finance and control for many organisations providing urban social welfare. This was characteristic of the period in which a range of views of the provision of welfare jostled with each other, from a form of voluntary philanthropy in which the national state had no proper role, to a vision in which only the state must provide. Illustrating this heterogeneity were the 1,500 occupational centres for the unemployed financed jointly by churches, companies, national and local authorities with salaried officials coordinating the voluntary service. The future Mrs Richard Titmuss, for example, worked for the Fulham Fellowship for the Unemployed, initiated in the early 1930s by the minister of the West Kensington Congregational Church explicitly to ameliorate the difficulties of the urban unemployed who did not have the activities of the countryside, 'gardening or poaching' to 'keep himself fit'. The minister first opened his church premises and then six other clubs for unemployed men and one for women over thirty offering them somewhere to go and activities to keep them busy and fit, ranging from boot and furniture repair, sewing, handicrafts, sports and cooking to language lessons, drama and shorthand for blackcoated workers.

---

[120] Constance Braithwaite, *The Voluntary Citizen: An Inquiry into the Place of Philanthropy in the Community* (London, 1938), pp. 109–10.

[121] Olechnowicz, *Working-Class Housing in England Between the Wars*, esp. ch. 5.

[122] Elizabeth Macadam, *The New Philanthropy: A Study of the Relations Between the Statutory and Voluntary Social Services* (London, 1934); Prochaska, *The Voluntary Impulse*; summarised in Finlayson, 'Moving frontier', pp. 202–3.   [123] Vincent, *Poor Citizens*, p. 86.

From 1932 to 1940 the Fulham clubs were financed partially from the London branch of the National Council for Social Services and from the Mayor of Fulham's appeal and resulting Unemployment Scheme; premises were provided free by the London County Council and a local business guaranteed running expenses. Although the new Labour council in the mid-1930s opposed voluntary help on the grounds that it was the role of the state to provide assistance, the mayor did not withdraw support until 1937 when he argued that the establishment by the national government of the Unemployment Assistance Board relieved the borough from the need to provide help for able-bodied, unemployed men, even though the Fulham Fellowship did not see its work as 'assistance work, it is social and personal . . . bringing men and women together that is of very real benefit'.[124]

The voluntary provision of urban medical services, notably district nursing and voluntary hospitals, illustrates two characteristics of voluntary provision in the interwar years: the increasing proportion of finance from the state or municipality for services rendered on its behalf; and attempts to coordinate provision. An urban innovation beginning in Liverpool in 1859, voluntary associations employing nurses for a salary to do visiting nursing in people's homes were all located in urban areas until the late 1880s. By 1935 they covered 95 per cent of the population of England and Wales. In both large cities and small towns, from Birmingham to Banbury, charity went further in the 1930s than the 1890s. It provided only one third of the cost rather than the whole cost; it made up the difference between the cost of the service and the amount which those benefiting could afford to pay from their own resources, from mutual insurance or from public authorities on their behalf. At the same time, charity changed from provision for the poor by the well-to-do to contributions by house-to-house collection among all classes, contributory schemes for the better off, increasingly important public grants and service to all.[125] Rising population and boundary extensions in Birmingham gave impetus to negotiations among the existing associations which led to the amalgamation of six societies covering different parts of the city into a single city-wide association (City of Birmingham District Nursing Association). Yet, the difficulties of coordination among fiercely independent voluntary associations were apparent as several other societies joined only later and three remained outside entirely.[126]

The financial difficulties of voluntary hospitals, apparent before 1914, mounted thereafter as equipment became increasingly expensive, and demand and specialisation grew. Like the district nursing associations voluntary hospitals – apart from cottage hospitals – were essentially urban institutions, though

---

[124] Ann Oakley, *Man and Wife – Richard and Kay Titmuss: My Parents' Early Years* (London, 1996), pp. 36–40, 54–5. See also R. H. C. Hayburn, 'The voluntary occupational centre movement 1932–39', *Journal of Contemporary History*, 6 (1971), 156–71, and Pilgrim Trust, *Men without Work* (Cambridge, 1938). [125] Braithwaite, *Voluntary Citizen*, p. 311. [126] *Ibid.*, pp. 211–13.

usually with rural catchment areas. During the interwar years, in contrast to the late nineteenth century, their sources of finance diversified from legacies and subscriptions to include state support and increasingly contributory schemes and pay beds, especially in England, which made their services available to the better off. The voluntary hospitals were highly dependent on local economic prosperity and were especially vulnerable to the effects of the depression in what became Special Areas in the 1930s. In Newcastle, for example, the habit of firms making large donations, once interrupted, was not resumed on the same scale, and hospitals which had developed workplace-based contributory schemes were vulnerable to the fate of large employers. Provision was highly variable across the country, from large prestigious teaching hospitals to struggling general hospitals. Unlike district nursing associations, voluntary hospitals required finance for non-recurrent capital expenditure, traditionally provided through fundraising campaigns, legacies and large donations. Given prevailing levels of poverty in many industrial towns such as Sunderland, it was impossible to raise capital through charitable appeals, asking local people to provide the money. The financial difficulties of voluntary hospitals led to attempts to coordinate them and develop uniform standards. Before the First World War the King's Fund attempted to facilitate coordination of the London hospitals, and nationally voluntary hospitals associated both to lobby the government for aid (receiving £1 million from the government immediately after the First World War) and, paradoxically, at the same time to preserve their independence. With the 1929 Local Government Act it became government policy to encourage the coordination of municipal and voluntary hospital services, though their only means was loan sanction for local authority capital projects and it had little impact. The Special Area Commissioners, however, had more success. Without powers to intervene in the location of industry, they devoted much of their financial assistance to easing social conditions including capital grants to voluntary hospitals to meet approximately 80 per cent of the cost. These required government representation on the hospital boards of governors for accountability, and the Commissioners and Ministry of Health used the grants to promote coordination of services and to constrain competition and duplication with other hospital services in an otherwise largely unplanned system of urban welfare provision.[127] During the Second World War the government's Emergency Medical Service coordinated hospital services, including voluntary hospitals, and after the war, despite their strong desire to retain their separate identity, their proven inability to provide adequate, universal, comprehensive care led to their forced absorption into the National Health Service (NHS).[128]

[127] John Mohan, 'Neglected roots of regionalism? The commissioners for the Special Areas and grants to hospital services in the 1930s', *Social History of Medicine*, 10 (1997), 243–62; S. Cherry, *Medical Services and the Hospitals in Britain, 1860–1939* (Cambridge, 1996), pp. 54–74.
[128] Finlayson, 'Moving frontier', 198–9.

Pawnbroking, as we saw above, was a quintessentially urban means of bridging the gap between income and expenditure with pawn shops, yielding a gross profit of 4–6 per cent on turnover, concentrated in city-centre areas of densely packed working-class housing. Although the absence of pawnbrokers on new housing estates did not stop the habit of pawning, after 1914 the number of brokers and the amount of business declined despite the problems of unemployment and short-time working. They suffered from the new competition of banks and building societies offering immediate liquidity, from the rapid growth of hire-purchase schemes overcoming the need to pawn in order to purchase new articles, and from the growth of public pensions and unemployment relief.[129]

At the same time that the mutual aid friendly societies were declining after 1918, the industrial life assurance companies expanded among the working class, as endowment policies designed to give an annuity at a certain age grew dramatically in popularity, replacing 'whole life' policies that yielded a lump sum at death. This change in the type of industrial assurance purchased reflected the decline in infant mortality and increased adult longevity. Thus, there was a change in the pattern, similar across urban areas, of widespread burial club membership and more restricted friendly society membership, to one of endowment policies from industrial life assurance companies after 1918 providing contractual saving for private old-age provision.[130] The income of industrial assurance companies increased from £25.3 million in 1919 to £59.8 million in 1939 and 'practically every family, even the very poorest', from York to Bristol had taken out industrial life policies.[131]

Unlike unemployment insurance administered by civil servants, an alternate channel for the provision of social welfare existed for health insurance with commercial insurance and friendly societies receiving a subsidy from public funds for providing their members with access to basic medical care from general practitioners and with sickness benefit. This partnership of the approved societies with the state attracted criticism from historians and contemporaries throughout the interwar years. As mentioned above, the approved societies, particularly the large, commercial insurance companies, accumulated substantial reserves during the First World War which they maintained afterwards and were reluctant, for reasons of business competition, to pool with smaller societies or raise benefits. Yet, as Noelle Whiteside argues, these reserves were not sufficient to extend health insurance to dependants even though societies agreed about the desirability of extending the scope of the scheme, and the societies saved the government money by absorbing the administrative overheads.[132] The Beveridge Report echoed the criticisms that benefits varied among societies and were not

---

[129] Johnson, *Saving and Spending*, pp. 170–4; Tebbutt, *Making Ends Meet*, esp. ch. 6.

[130] Johnson, *Saving and Spending*, pp. 41, 59, 207, 209.   [131] Finlayson, 'Moving frontier', 194.

[132] N. Whiteside, 'Private agencies for public purposes: some new perspectives on policy making in health insurance between the wars', *Journal of Social Policy*, 12 (1983), 165–93; Finlayson, *Citizen, State and Social Welfare*, p. 269.

universal in coverage; it called for 'a single Approved Society for the nation', i.e. the national state. In 1946 the Labour government dissolved the partnership begun in 1911 between the government, on the one hand, and the commercial companies and the waning mutual aid friendly societies, on the other, and made national insurance solely the responsibility of the state.[133]

Central government expenditure on social services rose fivefold between 1918 and 1938 from £114 million to £596 million, underpinned by the ability of income tax to 'command consent' and increase revenue in contrast to other European countries.[134] The major increase took place within the first four years when expenditure rose from £114 million in 1918 to £490 in 1921, due largely to new emergency commitments to unemployment relief. Once the initial commitments were made, changing levels of unemployment accounted for much of the subsequent fluctuations in expenditure.

Between 1918 and 1921 the British government inadvertently both undertook the substantial and irreversible extension of state expenditure and prevented the poor law from resuming its pre-war role as the principal source of relief for those unable to support themselves. During the war families of servicemen received assistance, protecting them from the poor law, in the form of separation allowances which, unlike the insurance system, provided benefits for wives and children. As soldiers returned at the end of the war it was impossible to withdraw this form of assistance, and the government introduced the 'out-of-work donation' for ex-servicemen and then civilians which provided non-contributory, non–poor law support for the unemployed and maintenance for their families. Although the scheme was temporary, its commitments were permanent; failure to maintain existing commitments might well have provoked revolution. Unemployment insurance introduced in 1911 to a few trades was extended, as had long been intended, in 1920 to the rest of the working class (except agricultural workers and servants). Introduced in 1911 to cope with short-term cyclical unemployment, however, the insurance scheme of 1920 was inadequate to cope with the downturn of the economy in the autumn of 1920 and the start of long-term mass unemployment. The insurance scheme was bankrupt by July 1921, but the commitments forced the government to provide 'uncovenanted benefits' to those faced with the poor law when their fifteen weeks of entitlement expired and to supply benefits for dependants.[135] Although the level of benefit was cut by 10 per cent under the 'Geddes axe', reinstated by the Labour government in 1924 and cut again in 1931, this acceptance of responsibility for unemployed workers and their dependants was a major concession. Yet, rather than the lynchpin of a new system of welfare provision, unemployment relief undermined other innovations particularly in housing, health and education.

[133] Finlayson, 'Moving frontier', 198; Finlayson, *Citizen, State and Social Welfare*, pp. 269–70.
[134] Daunton, 'Payment and participation', 178–9.   [135] Vincent, *Poor Citizens*, p. 54.

After the major increase in central government expenditure on unemployment relief between 1918 and 1921, the cuts in provision to prevent further growth coincided with restrictions that arose from the old concern for indiscriminate relief and from ambiguities surrounding insurance contributions and restricted entitlements. As mentioned above, there was an increasing proportion of families whose income was augmented by relief payments and associated intervention with multiple means tests separating the poor from relief. Forty insurance acts passed between 1920 and 1934 attempted to reconcile the ambiguities of

> benefit generated by membership of a scheme with support justified by membership of society; benefit designed for the breadwinner with support given to all his dependants; benefit guaranteed by contribution with support conditional on behaviour; benefit intended for occasional loss of work with support required for long-term unemployment and benefit funded by actuarial practice with support financed by Treasury subsidy.[136]

Around the attempts to meet the crisis of unemployment a new pattern of local government emerged during the interwar years which still left much local variation, if not discretion to local authorities. The new pattern emphasised both the difficulties central government and local authorities had in achieving the greater degree of uniformity and the higher minimum standards that came to be demanded for the provision of social welfare. This pattern also featured the trade-off between local accountability, on the one hand, and the uniformity achievable through central government finance and administration, on the other.

Although local government expenditure was restricted by the limits of the rate and municipal trading basis of local government finance (as John Davis describes in Chapter 9), it maintained a constant 40 per cent of the increased government expenditure on social services during the interwar years. The period was marked both by the declining importance of rate income for local authorities and by the growing importance of central government grants which accounted for 30 per cent of income in 1920 and 44 per cent in 1938.[137] An increasing proportion of the grants were not allocated to specific purposes. If central government subsidised rates from taxation, some of the national income could be distributed from richer to poorer parts of the country; yet, at the same time central government could demand more control over local policy and restrict local initiatives.

This increasing central government contribution to local government finances, together with local variations in the operation of the poor law, led to Chamberlain's Local Government Act of 1929 and the abolition of the Poor Law Guardians, though not the poor law. The area and population covered by the

---

[136] *Ibid.*, p. 69.
[137] A. Peacock and J. Wiseman, *The Growth of Public Expenditure in the United Kingdom* (London, 1961), pp. 100, 101, 103, 117.

individual local authorities that distributed poor relief were small, particularly in Scotland where they were single parishes in contrast to the clusters of parishes or unions in England and Wales. After 1918 the demand that the central government should equalise the burden of unemployment across the country led to a series of battles in mining communities in North-East England and South Wales and most prominently in the London borough of Poplar. In the face of low pay and casual employment, rather than structural unemployment, the Poplar guardians refused to operate the strict means tests of the poor law. They argued that relief should be paid according to need at a level equivalent to wages rather than below, and they argued they should not pay high rates to cope with the area's social problems when wealthy areas had few paupers and low rates. The Poplar guardians went to jail over their demand for subsidies from the wealthier parishes of London. The government responded by a further redistribution of funds among London parishes and allowed the guardians to arrange Exchequer loans, but several authorities fell into even worse debt while ignoring relief scales. In the mid-1920s Chamberlain brought in several acts to curtail expenditure, culminating in the acts which abolished the guardians and shifted their duties to the committees of enlarged local authorities. The local authority Public Assistance Committees would be able to provide more expensive and wide-ranging services, but the votes of the poor would have far less weight in the larger authority committees, making it more difficult to exert pressure to ignore relief scales.

Thus, with the absorption of the administration of the poor law by local authorities in 1929, and subsequently with the Treasury taking first financial responsibility and then in 1934 administrative responsibility for unemployment relief, there was a marked loss of local accountability for relief functions. But, as L. J. Sharpe and Kenneth Newton suggest, the alleged 'loss' may have enhanced the capacity of local government to act in other areas, as structural unemployment meant that those local authorities with the highest unemployment were those whose capacity to meet the increase in relief payments was weakest. Shifting responsibility to the authority with responsibility for the whole of the national economy during the 1930s and more emphatically after the Beveridge Report and National Insurance Act of 1947, they argue, was a vital gain for local authorities.[138]

A similar argument can be made for the provision of health services, particularly hospital services. Local government was dominant in provision of health services in the interwar years, particularly in England after the 1929 Local Government Act shifted the administration of poor law health services to local authorities, and planners assumed that local government would provide health services in the future. The London County Council in the 1930s was 'arguably

---

[138] L. J. Sharpe and K. Newton, *Does Politics Matter? The Determinants of Public Policy* (Oxford, 1984), p. 36.

the largest hospital authority in the world, rivalling in size the entire voluntary sector of England and Wales'.[139] Yet, local government was not well equipped for provision of health services, because both the local government areas and local government finance were inadequate. There was much discussion by Fabians and geographers of a new pattern based on the regionalisation of local government and the prime example of the inefficiency of the existing system was health. It was these services, particularly the general and specialist hospital services, which were seen to gain most from reorganisation along regional lines; regionalisation would bring substantial economies of scale, more uniform standards and better career structures for staff. Hospital services especially required an area larger than existing local authority areas.

The difficulties in the 1930s of providing coherent, uniform hospital services with local authorities leading the way in cooperation with voluntary hospitals can be illustrated by the differing problems the Scottish Office had in implementing the Local Government Act in three different urban areas. In Glasgow it was difficult to convert the existing poor law institutions into general hospitals under the control of the local medical officer of health as poor law recipients, usually elderly, chronically ill patients still required accommodation, though only intermittent medical attendance and not continuous skilled nursing care. Implementation required funding for extra accommodation and a reorganised GP service so there could be both an extension of surgical facilities and more specialised assistance for the elderly, the chronically sick and children.[140] In Lanarkshire it was difficult to obtain local authority cooperation. The act resulted in seven authorities – one county council and six burghs – each with its own provision for infectious diseases, TB, child welfare and poor relief. Together with twenty voluntary hospitals the county had forty separate bodies providing institutional care. Because hospitals were seen to need elaborate equipment and specialisation, the Scottish Office argued that the local authorities on their own could not provide the necessary services; cooperation was essential and it would not allow any of the existing authorities to develop by themselves. Although the county and other burghs agreed to participate in a new, large county hospital, the burgh of Motherwell refused, wanting to build a new block for the sick poor at its poor house. Despite the 'bait'of a Special Areas grant, agreement was never reached.[141] In Greenock, with its damp climate and northerly exposure contributing to 'perhaps the worst record of public health in Scotland', it was impossible to secure the agreement of the local voluntary hospital, afraid of a possible rival, for a new local authority hospital for the non-pauper chronically ill.[142]

Ideas in favour of the regionalisation of local government were widely diffused by 1939. If local government must be reorganised on a regional basis,

[139] C. Webster, *The Health Services since the War*, vol. 1 (London, 1988), p. 6.
[140] I. Levitt, *Poverty and Welfare in Scotland 1890–1948* (Edinburgh, 1988), pp. 162–4.
[141] *Ibid.*, pp. 162–5. [142] *Ibid.*, pp. 165–9.

and health services organised along local government lines, then health services should be organised on regional lines. This vision of the future was opposed by the medical profession and local government associations which fought to maintain the status quo. By 1945 the *Economist* argued that health costs were the highest expenses for local government after education. It was beyond the capacity of the existing local government structure to administer health and particularly hospital services successfully and it might lead to the collapse of all local government services, particularly education and housing in which local variation was more acceptable. Thus, it would be better to surrender one sphere, the health services, relieving local government of the cost and fund it from the Treasury, than surrender in all. Aneurin Bevan adopted such a scheme, seeing it as politically acceptable to doctors and the local authorities association and as having the greatest chance of success, though he viewed it as an interim, temporary arrangement, undesirable in the long term due to its lack of democratic accountability, but acceptable in the short term until there was local government reform and the NHS could come back to local government.[143]

There was still a vital place for local authorities and voluntary organisations in the provision and organisation of services connected with social welfare, despite the transfer from local to national government of assistance by cash payments in the interwar years, and even after 1948 and the creation of the NHS with its tripartite structure of regional hospital boards, local authority services and general practitioner services. Equally, from the perspective of urban history an essential point is that variations in the complex mix of agencies mattered in terms of life and death, particularly in the interwar years, as the provision of maternal and infant welfare services illustrates.

National legislation relating to maternal and infant welfare services between 1902 and 1936 included the Maternal and Child Welfare Act of 1918 which enabled local councils and voluntary institutions to apply for grants of up to 50 per cent of expenditure on services including infant welfare clinics, paid midwives, health visitors, day nurseries, milk and food for needy mothers and infants. Provision was not mandatory and was highly dependent on local interpretation and policy making, as well as on local socio-economic circumstances. Maternal and infant welfare services were more comprehensive in London than elsewhere. (79 per cent of London boroughs put in half or more of the services, compared with 72 per cent of county boroughs and 47 per cent of county councils.) But, within London provision was highly variable reflecting diversity of socio-economic conditions among boroughs and the autonomy of local authorities. Lara Marks has shown that there was not always a direct relationship between social deprivation and mortality patterns. For example, Stepney was

---

[143] C. Webster, 'Regionalisation of local government and the origins of the NHS', paper given to the Symposium on the National Health Service: Its Past, Present and Future, Wellcome Institute for the History of Medicine, 3 July 1998.

one of the poorest boroughs with a great deal of casual labour and high population density, but it had lower rates of maternal mortality than Woolwich, a less densely populated district predominantly of skilled artisans, or the more prosperous boroughs of Hampstead and Kensington, due in part to the relatively good maternity care available through the large number of teaching hospitals in Stepney. Moreover, the richer borough of Kensington had higher infant mortality rates than the poorer Woolwich. Stepney and Woolwich, which had more local authority funds committed to maternal and infant welfare services, had a greater reduction in their infant mortality rates than Hampstead or Kensington which were politically more conservative, providing fewer municipal services and relying more on the voluntary sector. Yet, it was not a straightforward issue of local authority versus voluntary provision. Many of the interwar schemes stemmed from previous voluntary initiatives, sometimes in collaboration with local authorities. Voluntary organisations, often supported by government grants, continued to play an essential role in the provision of maternal and child welfare into the interwar years; the extent depended on the precedent for such work in each individual borough and was shaped by their political outlook. Municipal provision appeared earliest in Woolwich which had few middle-class residents and a strong Labour council, while council initiatives were less important in Stepney which had a weak Labour party but many voluntary agencies before the First World War, particularly organisations of Catholic and Jewish immigrants as well as teaching hospitals. Rather than disappearing in the 1920s with the rise of the Labour party in Stepney, these voluntary organisations were incorporated into municipal provision. In Kensington and Hampstead voluntary organisations based on their large upper and middle classes dominated maternal and infant welfare services, with the local council of the National Council for Social Welfare in Hampstead promoting effort and initiating cooperation between voluntary and state activity.[144]

Variations in levels of provision – and complex mixtures of voluntary and local authority services – existed in urban areas outside London as well as within the metropolis. Elizabeth Peretz found that local attitudes influenced provision in Merthyr Tydfil and Oxford as well as in Tottenham. Tottenham, which escaped the worst of the depression, had a strong Co-operative Labour presence and a dwindling charitable middle class throughout the interwar period. Its services were a source of civic pride, offering the widest range, the most generous scales and free access to some services. Merthyr Tydfil was Labour-dominated, yet in comparison to Tottenham it had a restricted maternity and child welfare service, though as a depressed area it attracted some charitable help. The relatively poor

[144] Marks, *Metropolitan Maternity*, pp. 3–7, 151–60, 171; L. Marks, 'Mothers, babies and hospitals: "The London" and the provision of maternity care in east London 1870–1939', in V. Fildes, L. Marks and H. Marland, eds., *Women and Children First: International Maternal and Infant Welfare 1870–1945* (London and New York, 1992), pp. 48–73.

service was partly attributable to the lack of money within the council. It had difficulties raising rates, other expenses were high and so there was not enough money even to match the national grants. Moreover, the councillors wanted more money given to families so they could buy the goods and services they wanted rather than being reliant on a variety of means-tested, narrowly pre-scribed goods and services. Maternal and child welfare was seen to be the patron-ising domain of the Liberals and Conservatives in the area and was scorned by wives who were proud of their households and maternal ability. Oxford also had few services and most were organised by charitable groups 'under the licence' of the local authority; there was little take up of the few free services. It was pros-perous enough to have provided full services and to have encouraged poorer mothers to claim what they needed for free. Yet, the councillors, most of whom were Conservatives or Liberals who also sat on the committees of voluntary organisations in the city, regarded local authority services 'as the expensive option, to be used only when voluntary organisations had failed', and they were concerned not to undermine self-help, debating in 1933 whether mothers should pay to attend infant welfare clinics so they would appreciate them more.[145]

(v) CONCLUSION

A changing balance among the sectors of the mixed economy of welfare char-acterised the provision of social welfare in urban Britain during the period between 1840 and 1950, both overall and within towns and cities. In general, in the mid-nineteenth century, after the New Poor Law of 1834 restricted the uni-versal and comprehensive provision of the Elizabethan poor law for poverty and health care, voluntarism, combined with local authority provision (both munic-ipal and the poor law) provided for the social welfare needs of the inhabitants of Britain's towns and cities. In the late nineteenth and early twentieth centuries financial crises for both the voluntary sector and local government, together with a growing conviction that they and the poor law neither could nor should provide sufficiently for their needs in an increasingly urban society, led to a growing reliance on national finance and administration, contractual entitlement and further narrowing of the risk pool. Sometimes these changes were in con-junction with, but often they bypassed, local authorities and voluntarism. Poverty and health were seen to require more uniform provision and higher minimum standards than other services. As Pat Thane argues, voluntarism and local authority provision were an integral part of the 'minimal', 'enabling' central state in the mid-nineteenth century, allowing the central government to con-

---

[145] E. Peretz, 'The costs of modern motherhood to low income families in interwar Britain', in Fildes, Marks and Marland, eds., *Women and Children First*, pp. 268–77; Peretz, 'Infant welfare'.

centrate on the diplomatic and supervisory functions it performed well. The shift (especially after 1946) to national government finance and administration for universal provision of minimum standards of relief from poverty and of medical care in hospitals and by general practitioners left local government to concentrate on education, housing and other functions that appeared at the time better suited to the structure of local authorities. Crucial to this shift, as Martin Daunton argues, was the ability of the national government to increase revenue through income tax. The changing balance was an uneven process, far from inevitable, fraught with tensions and conflicts, marked by collaboration, changes in the sectors and losses as well as gains. The poor law guardians, for example, increasingly marginalised in the provision of urban social welfare, gave way in 1929 to large local government committees and eventually the central government at the cost of a loss of local, democratic accountability and opportunities for local influence on the levels and conditions of relief payments.[146] Similarly, the decline of friendly societies is linked to a loss of local influence over individual health care, though their coverage was far from universal. The national insurance legislation of 1911 created a partnership between the central government and commercial insurance companies which was dissolved by the national insurance legislation of 1946 with each going a separate way. Meanwhile, the central government absorbed, under the appointed, nationally financed regional hospital boards of the NHS, the voluntary and local authority hospitals which ran in parallel and often in competition in the 1930s.[147]

Yet, even after 1946 at the height of central government provision of social services for the relief of poverty and medical care, voluntarism and local authorities were not a by-product but an integral part of the contemporary concept of the welfare state.[148] Since then the balance has changed: rather than coming under local government, the NHS and the provision of health care became further removed from local government by the abolition of the medical officers of health in 1974, and from the 1980s there has been growing emphasis on the provision of social welfare by the voluntary and commercial sectors. Nevertheless, within these overall changes in the balance of the welfare mix, variations in the source and, to some extent, in the level of provision among individual urban areas remain. Different locations within the urban hierarchy can make a difference. Urban history still matters, even in the provision of those social welfare services, earliest and least controversially transferred to central government.

[146] Vincent, *Poor Citizens*, pp. 61–2; Daunton, 'Payment and participation', 172–81.

[147] Finlayson, 'Moving frontier'; C. Webster, 'Labour and the origins of the National Health Service', in N. Rupke, ed., *Science, Politics and the Public Good: Essays in Honour of Margaret Gowing* (London and Basingstoke, 1988), pp. 184–202.

[148] W. Beveridge, *Voluntary Action: A Report on Methods of Social Advance* (London, 1948); Finlayson, *Citizen, State and Social Welfare*, pp. 288–93.

13

Structure, culture and society in British towns

R. J. MORRIS

A T THE start of the period covered by this volume, two men wrote about social relationships in British towns in very different ways. Thomas Chalmers was a Scottish minister of religion.[1] He spent much energy trying to reconcile political economy and evangelical religion. In 1821, he wrote:

> In a provincial capital, the great mass of the population are retained in kindly and immediate dependence on the wealthy residents of the place. It is the resort of annuitants, and landed proprietors, and members of the law, and other learned professions, who give impulse to a great amount of domestic industry, by their expenditure; and, on inquiry into the sources of maintenance and employment for the labouring classes there, it will be found they are chiefly engaged in the immediate service of ministering to the wants and luxuries of the higher classes in the city. This brings the two extreme orders of society into that sort of relationship which is highly favourable to the general blandness and tranquillity of the whole population. In a manufacturing town on the other hand, the poor and the wealthy stand more disjointed from each other. It is true they often meet, but they meet more on an arena of contest, than on a field where the patronage and custom of the one party are met by the gratitude and good will of the other. When a rich customer calls a workman into his presence, for the purpose of giving him some employment connected with his own personal accommodation, the general feeling of the later must be altogether different from what it would be, were he called into the presence of a trading capitalist, for the purpose of cheapening his work, and being dismissed for another, should there not be an agreement in their terms.[2]

His own experience was in Edinburgh and Glasgow but equally he saw a contrast between places like Oxford and Bath on the one hand and manufacturing

---

[1] Rev. William Hanna, *Memoirs of Thomas Chalmers, D.D. LL.D.*, 2 vols. (Edinburgh, 1854); Stewart J. Brown, *Thomas Chalmers and the Godly Commonwealth in Scotland* (Oxford, 1982); Stewart J. Brown and Michael Fry, eds., *Scotland in the Age of the Disruption* (Edinburgh, 1993).

[2] T. Chalmers, *The Christian and Civic Economy of Large Towns*, vol. 1 (Edinburgh, 1821–6), pp. 27–9.

cities like Leeds and Manchester on the other. For Chalmers, towns with different economic and social structures produced very different sorts of social relationships. In other words, specific economic structures, market relationships as well as relationships of production, provided the explanation or at least created conditions for different cultural outcomes. Chalmers' work was driven by anxiety over religious observance, pauperism and disorder. He saw the town as a place of problems created by these new conditions but problems for which thinking and moral men could provide solutions.

Robert Vaughan was very different, a dissenting minister from the West of England, an intellectual of the Congregational Union. In *The Age of Great Cities*, published in 1843, he defended cities as places of freedom and progress, part of 'the struggle between the feudal and the civic'.[3] He had very clear ideas as to why this should be so. He regarded the spread of knowledge as crucial for freedom. Cities were part of this as they provided conditions for the creation of an active press and publication by 'large sales and small profits'.[4] Art and science flourished in the cities because they were places of 'ceaseless action . . . [and] . . . accumulation' which provided resources for 'minds capable of excelling in abstract studies'. He recognised that the 'more constant and more varied association into which men are brought by means of great cities tends necessarily to impart greater knowledge, acuteness and power to the mind than . . . a rural parish'.[5] The urban labour market was another source of freedom as 'the poor are little dependent on the rich, the employed are little dependent on their employers'.[6] It was not just that Vaughan was more optimistic than Chalmers about urban life, but his whole structure of argument differed. Vaughan looked to something which a later generation of sociologists would call an 'urban way of life' and derived from this a whole set of social relationships.[7] Urban in the generic sense created the conditions for freedom, choice, wealth and progress. Although he recognised class conflict and the inequalities of wealth, Vaughan's ideal was a society of rational, knowledgeable individuals not a society of hierarchies. The inequalities of feudalism and class would be reduced by the working of the intelligence and association of the city. The urban created relationships now identified with modernity.[8]

These two attempts to explain and understand what was happening in British towns contained elements of a wider and continuing debate on the nature and relationship of social structure and culture in British towns. Although definitions

---

[3] Robert Vaughan, *The Age of Great Cities* (London, 1843), p. 2.   [4] *Ibid.*, p. 82.   [5] *Ibid.*, p. 146.
[6] *Ibid.*, p. 300.
[7] Louis Wirth, 'Urbanism as a way of life', in Louis Wirth, *On Cities and Social Life*, ed. Albert J. Reiss, jr. (Chicago, 1964).
[8] M. Savage and A. Warde, *Urban Sociology, Capitalism and Modernity* (Basingstoke, 1993); Gunther Barth, *City People: The Rise of Modern City Culture in Nineteenth Century America* (Oxford, 1980); M. Berman, *All That Is Solid Melts into Air* (New York, 1982).

are contested they must be attempted. Social structures are perceived regularities of social behaviour and characteristics identified by relevant social actors or by the observer analyst. These structures are orderly, patterned and persistent. Those selected for comment and analysis are those judged to be important in the explanation of action, experience and change.[9] In the European literature of the last two hundred years, structures involved in the material relationships of production have been given especial attention but attention has rapidly extended to relationships of reproduction and association such as gender, family and the urban. The identification of social structures is important because of their place in explanation.[10] Few studies consider that historical actions and change were determined by key structures but many do see structure as one of several influences. Indeed, the influence of structure in these accounts may go beyond the meanings attributed to them and work in ways not perceived by historical actors.[11] One theoretical extreme questions the knowability of social structure. After all, the evidence from which such structures were deduced were themselves cultural products, but the task of inferring structures remains a matter of self-conscious historical and analytical judgement. Perhaps most common is the view that structure, especially those related to material production, set broad limits within which human agency could act and react.[12]

In explanations of the nature of experience in British towns, human agency operated not just to produce specific actions but in the creation of culture. That culture may be defined as the series of meanings which human beings attributed to actions, objects, to other people over the whole range of practice from religion to politics, production and consumption.[13] Cultural resources guide action by providing boundaries, legitimacy and motivations as well as by opening up possibilities. Causal relationships are contested. A simplistic and rarely presented view might consider culture as a product of structure, especially economic structure. More common is the view that culture is influenced by structure. Thus the wage labour of large factories makes class-conscious politics possible but was in no way a sufficient 'cause'. The perspective which regards culture as an autonomous element in any historical situation is especially important for urban historians as urban cultures not only build upon the resources inherited from their own past but also import and select cultural elements from

[9] Joseph Melling and Jonathan Barry, eds., *Culture in History: Production, Consumption and Values in Historical Perspective* (Exeter, 1992); Peter L. Berger and Thomas Luckmann, *The Social Construction of Reality* (London, 1971); John Rex, *Key Problems in Sociological Theory* (London, 1961).

[10] Melling and Barry, *Culture in History*, especially introduction and essays by Stephen Mennell and Iain Hampsher Monk, pp. 3–74.

[11] A. Giddens, *The Constitution of Society* (Cambridge, 1984), pp. 25–8, 177–81.

[12] Raymond Williams, *Problems in Materialism and Culture* (London, 1980), pp. 31–49

[13] Clifford Geertz, 'Religion as a cultural system', in Michael Banton, ed., *Anthropological Approaches to the Study of Religion* (London, 1966), pp. 1–46; M. Douglas and B. Isherwood, *The World of Goods* (London, 1979).

national and international culture. Mendelssohn's Elijah came to the Birmingham Music Festival in 1846 because the middle-class elite of that city wanted to take part in the broad stream of European culture not because of the small workshop nature of production or even the rapidly changing nature of the market in that city.[14]

Within the debate remains an interest in long-term social processes. Did the spread and intensification of capitalist relationships create certain types of conflict and social identity? Is there a long-term process of 'civilisation' in which perhaps towns and cities are implicated? Do the social and cultural processes of modernity exist in which the accumulation of wealth and knowledge leads to a rational individualistic society? How far do traditions of law, market relationships and certain types of institutional practice produce a 'civil society'?[15]

This debate over structure and culture matters for several reasons. Culture includes the many processes that give meanings. These meanings have agency. They promote individual actions. They are the basis on which identities are created and mobilised. The attention given to structure derives from the feeling that it matters if a town depends on wage labour working in large units of production, rather than casual labour on uncertain and low wages. This attention derived from the belief that social relationships were influenced by the fact that a town derived its income from the pensions and rentier incomes of retired males or unmarried females rather than from an elite of merchants and manufacturers employing wage labour. These structures were related to different social situations.

Under the conditions of industrial capitalism selling to 'distant markets' the city, the town, the urban place was the site where the processes that link culture and structure were interacting in the clearest and strongest ways. In a true sense the city was the frontier of capitalism and modernity. Capitalism, that is a system of social and economic relationships defined by private ownership, the search for profits and a cash economy, was linked to modernity, a system defined by the accumulation of knowledge, rationality and the division of public and private in human actions and feelings. The city itself was one product of this interaction. The city was both a structure and a cultural product.[16] Once created in both its material and cultural sense, the city became an object of contest within the middle class, between classes and between self-aware interest groups

---

[14] R. J. Morris, 'Middle-class culture, 1700–1914', in D. Fraser, ed., *A History of Modern Leeds* (Manchester, 1980).

[15] Norbert Elias, *The Civilizing Process* (Oxford, 1994), originally published 1939; J. A. Hall, ed., *Civil Society* (Cambridge, 1995); Robert D. Putnam, *Making Democracy Work* (Princeton, 1993); Savage and Warde, *Urban Sociology*.

[16] R. J. Morris, 'The middle class and British towns and cities of the Industrial Revolution, 1780–1870', in D. Fraser and A. Sutcliffe, eds., *The Pursuit of Urban History* (London, 1983), pp. 286–305.

around which other identities and realised structures were formed. In the minds of those involved the town itself became an 'actor'. It was reified and people reacted to the relationships of the towns and the perceived realities of social structure.[17]

The interest in the relationship between urban culture and the economic and social structure of British towns was and is part of a wider inquiry into the nature of the British response to industrial change. It was part of a desire to understand the long-term stability of British society coupled with the persistence of class-based conflicts of industrial and urban change.[18] Before going further, a warning. This section is not just about what happened in British towns and cities, it is about a debate, an argument, a search for understandings. Because of this the section must be read at two levels. It is about the social processes and experiences of these towns and cities. It is about what actually happened. It is also an account of the way in which historians and contemporaries have tried to understand what was happening. Before the mid-1970s, historians gave central place to the politics, and to the relationships, consciousness and culture of social class. From the late 70s, this emphasis was being supplemented by the identities and struc-tures of gender and those of nationalism, religion and ethnicity. At the same time there was a growing awareness of the independent generation of culture and its powerful agency in the direction of human conduct. This was accompanied by a less intense debate which questioned the clarity and validity of the urban–rural dichotomy, the integrity of the urban place and even any concept of the urban itself. History as always is not just an account of the past, it is an account of the relationship between past and present .

The reluctance of historians to debate the nature of the city or of the urban as a social structure or as an aspect of culture poses considerable problems for an inquiry into the relationship between culture and structure in the towns and cities of Britain. The definition of the urban as a form of human association and settlement with the properties of size, density and variety is incomplete but density, especially transactional density, and variety though not 'causes' of an 'urban way of life' are crucial parameters in urban experience and identities. The urban place was also a focus for power, a 'fort', a 'market' and a 'temple'.[19] In the nineteenth-century town, the market and its institutions were increasingly diffuse and pervasive. The castle and the city walls had been replaced by the town

---

[17] This is in part a response to the warning and challenge of Philip Abrams, 'Towns and economic growth: some theories and problems', in P. Abrams and E. A. Wrigley, eds., *Towns in Societies* (Cambridge, 1978), and R. E. Pahl, *Whose City?* (London, 1970), pp. 183–212.

[18] R. J. Morris, *Class and Class Consciousness in the Industrial Revolution, 1780–1850* (London, 1979); M. Savage and A. Miles, *The Remaking of the British Working Class, 1840–1940* (London, 1994).

[19] Wirth, 'Urbanism as a way of life'; Max Weber, *The City*, trans. and ed. Don Martindale and Gertrud Neuwirth (New York, 1958); Paul Wheatley, 'What the greatness of a city is said to be', *Pacific Viewpoint*, 4 (1963), 163–89.

hall and the local government rate demand. The 'temple' no longer had the mystic of the priest king, but municipal ceremonies, foundation myths and sport were some of the ways in which the urban places of industrial Britain inspired loyalty and gave meaning to citizens' lives.

The Lancashire mill towns were not representative British towns but to historians and contemporaries they represented the leading edge of the fundamental impact of industrial change.[20] The cotton-spinning town of Oldham in Lancashire has become a 'type site'. In mid-century, the social relationships of Oldham were dominated by a wage relationship in which 12,000 wage-earning families sold their labour to seventy families which gained income from the ownership of capital in the cotton-spinning, coal-mining and hatting industries.[21] The outcome was an aggressive radical culture which gained control of key agencies of local government, the vestry, police and poor law and guided a series of main force confrontations, notably in the general strikes of 1834 and 1842. This culture was informed by an experience of economic change in which wages had fallen, income was disrupted by massive fluctuations in demand and technological change seemed to bring increased inequality and loss of control for working people. The political debates of this period blamed the 'oppressive conduct of capitalists' and their 'misapplication of machinery' and identified change in the overall system of economic and political arrangements as a solution.[22] In the 1830s, Manchester, influenced by the large units of production of the cotton industry, had been unable to sustain a coherent campaign in favour of parliamentary reform whilst Birmingham, dominated by small workshop production, generated the Birmingham Political Union which became a model for working-class and middle-class cooperation.[23] A generation later the casual labour market of east London produced a political culture with little formal organisation but outbreaks of violence which spread to Trafalgar Square and the West End in 1885 and 1886. This brought a broadly based philanthropic response from the middle classes of the capital.[24] Bath fitted the consumer society which Chalmers identified as the basis of kindly relationships. In fact the outcome in the 1840s was an active radical political culture with clear demands for political change widening the franchise and introducing the secret ballot. Other areas dominated by skilled labour, notably Edinburgh and parts of south London, were the base for an assertive radical culture of the skilled male labour force but a

[20] Friedrich Engels, *The Condition of the Working Class in England*, trans. and ed. W. O. Henderson and W. H. Chaloner (Oxford, 1958); Sir George Head, *Home Tour through the Manufacturing Districts of England in the Summer of 1835* (London, 1836).
[21] J. Foster, 'Nineteenth-century towns – a class dimension', in H. J. Dyos, ed., *The Study of Urban History* (London, 1968), pp. 281–300.
[22] J. Foster, *Class Struggle and the Industrial Revolution* (London, 1974), pp. 115–17.
[23] A. Briggs, *Victorian Cities* (London, 1963), pp. 89–93; Asa Briggs, 'The background of the parliamentary reform movement in three English cities (1830–2)', *Cambridge Historical Journal*, 10 (1950–2), 293–317.   [24] G. Stedman Jones, *Outcast London* (Oxford, 1971), pp. 290–6.

culture which was prepared to bargain with the agencies of middle-class and elite power.[25]

Further inquiry added increasing layers of complexity to the initial account. The nature of local leadership was crucial. The Birmingham banker, Thomas Attwood, was influential in the creation of the consensus which was the basis of the Birmingham Political Union and in sustaining this consensus through several conflict-ridden years. Equally, elements of recent history and historical memory were important. In Manchester memories of Peterloo were a major barrier to cooperation. In 1819, a radical demonstration had been violently broken up by volunteer yeomanry closely identified with the local middle classes. A comparison of Oldham with other Lancashire mill towns reduced the importance of the large technologically advanced factory as a basis for explanation. In 1841, the number of workers per firm in the cotton textile industry of Oldham was 79, well below Blackburn (281), Manchester (264) and Ashton (241).[26] In Birmingham any consensus relationship derived from the experience of small workshops rapidly deteriorated in the 1830s and 1840s under the impact of competition from a very few large units and the control of the market by merchants.[27] Manchester was as much a place of warehouses, banks and shops as it was of factories. Factories were only one aspect of the economic power of a middle-class elite of substantial employers, merchants and professionals. They were linked to the urban by the local land and labour markets, by an increasingly complex infrastructure and by an increasingly focused urban government.[28] At the start of this period, the middle classes of Leeds and Glasgow included substantial numbers of commercial and professional people. West Bromwich, Bilston and Wolverhampton were similar. All included large numbers of tradesmen and shopkeepers.[29]

In Oldham, the middling classes of shopkeepers and small masters, often subjected to threats of exclusive dealing in elections, featured in the analysis as

[25] R. S. Neale, *Class and Ideology in the Nineteenth Century* (London, 1972), pp. 41–74; R. S. Neale, *Bath, 1680–1850. A Social History. Or, A Valley of Pleasure, Yet a Sink of Iniquity* (London, 1981); G. Crossick, *An Artisan Elite in Victorian Society* (London, 1978); R. Q. Gray, *The Labour Aristocracy in Victorian Edinburgh* (Oxford, 1976).

[26] D. S. Gadian, 'Class consciousness in Oldham and other North-West industrial towns, 1830–1850', *HJ*, 21 (1978), 163–6.

[27] C. Behagg, *Politics and Production in the Early Nineteenth Century* (London, 1990).

[28] V. A. C. Gatrell, 'Incorporation and the pursuit of Liberal hegemony in Manchester, 1790–1839', in D. Fraser, ed., *Municipal Reform and the Industrial City* (Leicester, 1982); Simon Gunn, 'The Manchester middle class, 1850–1880' (PhD thesis, University of Manchester, 1992).

[29] R. J. Morris, *Class, Sect and Party* (Manchester, 1990); Stana Nenadic, 'The structure, values and influence of the Scottish urban middle class: Glasgow, 1800–1870' (PhD thesis, University of Glasgow, 1986); S. Nenadic, 'The Victorian middle classes', in W. H. Fraser and I. Maver, eds., *Glasgow*, vol. II: *1830–1912* (Manchester, 1996), pp. 265–99; R. H. Trainor, 'Authority and social structure in an industrial area: a study of three Black Country towns, 1840–1890' (DPhil thesis, University of Oxford, 1981); R. H. Trainor, *Black Country Elites* (Oxford, 1993). These measures were based upon the analysis of trades directories and parliamentary poll books.

Figure 13.1 'Middle-class' occupational structure of five British towns 1832–1834
Sources: as in n. 29.

objects of contests between working-class and middle-class elite organisation. In fact, these middling groups were the creative leadership of local radicalism in places as varied as Oldham, Bath and Gateshead.[30] There was no simple relationship of economic structure and outcome in terms of conflict and class. Ashton and Blackburn were both dominated by large firms but Blackburn was a peaceful place with a working class apathetic to class action, whilst in Ashton militant Chartists faced a pro-New Poor Law Board of Guardians. Oldham was a place of class cooperation radicals whilst nearby Rochdale experienced a more liberal basis for such cooperation. The nature and response of middle-class leadership was an important element in explaining differences. In Stockport, effective repression, especially in the use of blacklists of strikers, was used. Finally, both radicals and middle-class leaders were influenced by recent local history and memory. Oldham had a radical tradition drawn from the 1790s whilst the successful patronage and manipulation of local culture by Blackburn mill owners through schools, libraries, reading rooms and Mechanics Institutions was based upon a coherent response to late eighteenth-century experience of rioting and mill burning.[31] The relationship between the economic and social structures of an urban place and political and cultural outcomes was complex.

This account of structures derived from production must be supplemented by those of reproduction, notably gender, as well as those 'imagined' but very real and powerful identities of ethnicity and sectarianism.[32]

[30] Neale, *Class and Ideology*, pp. 15–61; T. J. Nossiter, *Influence, Opinion and Political Idioms in Reformed England* (Brighton, 1975).
[31] D. S. Gadian, 'Class formation and class action in North-West industrial towns, 1830–1850', in R. J. Morris, ed., *Class, Power and Social Structure in British Nineteenth-Century Towns* (Leicester, 1986), pp. 23–58.
[32] Benedict Anderson, *Imagined Communities: Reflections on the Origin and Spread of Nationalism* (London, 1983); Ernest Gellner, *Nations and Nationalism* (London, 1983).

The early nineteenth century saw a substantial renegotiation of the subordinations of gender around a culture of domesticity. This culture was initially an expression of the ambitions of the middle classes to assert difference but by mid-century was a formidable influence on all social classes.[33] The making and impact of this culture was closely related to the situations, structures and networks of urbanism. It was fuelled by a variety of cultural products which relied upon the interactions and markets of the town. Print culture was vital, through newspapers, periodicals, household and etiquette manuals as well as novels. The lecture and the sermon from the threatening warmth of the evangelical to the cold rationality of the unitarian served urban audiences.[34] It was not just as Vaughan had predicted that the massing of people in the urban place created a viable market and a critical mass for the exchange of ideas but that the modern capitalist city was an environment in which the individual became both spectator and actor. The meetings of the voluntary societies, charities, missionary societies, literary associations first excluded women and then reincorporated them in subordinate, often passive roles. By the late nineteenth century a deep sense of physical and moral insecurity derived from the anonymity of the city expressed itself in a highly gendered form. The brutal Jack the Ripper murders of several women in the 'East End' of London in 1888 were horrific enough but their impact lay in the manner in which they were magnified by all aspects of urban media from a newspaper press feeding on mass literacy to the ballad sheet and popular theatre.[35] The most important location for the urban learning of domesticity and gender were the shopping streets, especially that high point of development the department store. It was not just a matter of following fashion or exchanging gossip in the tea shops and restaurants. Shops and department stores were places were women and men learnt the new domestic technologies, Kendrick's coffee grinder, Ransome's lawn mower, or the new enclosed stoves. At one level shopping was an aspect of the market economy, but by the end of the century it was an intensely gendered ceremony which dominated key parts of the central business district. In Edinburgh, the elaborate architectural decoration of Messrs Jenner's new department store on Princes' Street included a number of female statues 'giving symbolic expression to the fact that women have made the business concern a success'.[36]

The most important spatial expression of the culture of domesticity was the middle-class residential suburb. A number of prosperous urban dwellers had always lived in a scattering of villas around the edges of the great towns. These had grown in number in the later eighteenth and early nineteenth centuries. In

---

[33] L. Davidoff and C. Hall, *Family Fortunes* (London, 1987).

[34] J. Seed, 'Theologies of power: unitarianism and the social relations of religious discourse, 1800–1850', in Morris, ed., *Class, Power and Social Structure*, pp. 108–56

[35] J. R. Walkowitz, *City of Dreadful Delight* (London and Chicago, 1992).

[36] John Reid, *The New Illustrated Guide to Edinburgh* (Edinburgh, c. 1900), p. 89.

the walking city the inhabitants were limited to those who could afford their own transport. Many partially retired from business would ride into the counting house two or three days a week. Between 1750 and 1850 a series of west ends and new towns served those seeking socially exclusive residential locations. The horse omnibus from the 1840s, the suburban railway in the 1880s (dates were earlier in London) and the horse-drawn (1870s) and electric tram (1890s) enabled the full development of the middle-class residential suburb.[37] Nowhere was the interaction of urban structure and culture more clearly demonstrated than in such suburbs. They were the perfect outcome of the cultural ambitions for middle-class domesticity, privacy, the separation of home and work, the combination of rural tree-lined romanticism with the best features of urban civilisation, the clear and respectable separation of gender roles, the controlled display of consumer achievement and the discreet leisure of church, chapel and tennis club. At the same time, this achievement depended upon the market-driven income structure of the urban place. Property developers experienced considerable tension between cultural pressures and the profit-seeking, effective demand-responding imperatives of the apparently impersonal forces of the capitalist market. In Edgbaston, one of the most firmly controlled suburban places in Britain, estate managers stopped the building of a chimney for some unfortunate resident's glass house but in the end they had to admit artisan house building at the edge of their property as the expansion of Birmingham reordered the patterns of price and demand upon the landscape.[38] By 1900 the suburb not only sustained the culture of domesticity but acted as a major spatial restriction frustrating and limiting social action and imagination. In 1909, H. G. Wells followed the thoughts of his fictional Ann Veronica,

> She walked down the station approach, past the neat unobtrusive offices of the coal merchant and the house agent . . . Morningside Park was a suburb that had not altogether, as people say, come off . . . her eyes wandered to where the new red and white villas peeped among the trees . . . 'Ye gods!' she said at last. 'What a place! Stuffy isn't the word for it . . .'.[39]

With an Irish-born population of between 5 per cent to 10 per cent in most major British cities as well as important sectarian divisions amongst Protestants, the impact of ethnic and sectarian relationships in British cities has been underestimated. Liverpool was an urban economy dominated by casual and unskilled labour, with no leavening of industrial and skilled labour as in east London. A liberal patrician elite, like the Gregs and the Rathbones, offered a philanthropic balm to social relationships but without the coherence or authority of east

[37] A. D. Ochojna, 'The influence of local and national politics on the development of urban passenger transport in Britain, 1850–1900', *Journal of Transport History*, new series, 4 (1978), and above, pp. 229–57.
[38] D. Cannadine, *Lords and Landlords* (Leicester, 1980), pp. 21–225.
[39] H. G. Wells, *Ann Veronica* (Harmondsworth, 1968), pp. 10–11.

London.[40] Liverpool, controlled by a Tory Anglican elite, came as near as any British city to a 'boss' system of client populist politics. The Conservative Working Men's Associations (CWMAs) tied the ward parties to the Orange Order and other Protestant organisations. The system thrived in a labour market in which jobs depended upon personal links, the clerk seeking a 'situation' or the dock workers at the daily hiring,[41] and where ethnic identities had their own labour market niches, the Irish in the docks, the Welsh in the warehouses and the Protestant English amongst the carters and corporation workers.

The potential for such ethnic and sectarian politics in Glasgow was considerable. In the last half of the century 25 per cent of adults were Irish born and 30 per cent came from the Highlands. Despite the presence of evangelical Protestant preachers and an Orange Order dominant in nearby single-industry towns, Glasgow followed a liberal then labour path of class bargaining and class conflict for several reasons. One key to this was the nature of the male labour force. The 70 per cent who were skilled had a strong sense of collective identity in defence of workplace autonomy when faced with the fluctuations of the international market for engineering and shipbuilding. Insecurity meant there was little spatial segregation in housing. The squalid housing conditions of Glasgow and Irish and Highland memories created a strong shared collective 'interest' against the landlords which found a ready response in the liberal elites' hostility to the aristocracy. The institutional infrastructure of the Glasgow working class was very different from that in Liverpool. Friendly societies, trades unions, cooperatives as well as nonconformist Presbyterian chapels were joined in the 1890s by ILP branches and a Trades Council. All these were on offer in Liverpool but little regarded by those who preferred the CWMA, Tontines or the ethnic specificity of Welsh chapels and the Ancient Order of Hibernians. The strikes of 1909 to 1912 in Liverpool saw frequent violence which spilled over into sectarian house-wrecking and demonstrations. In Glasgow, working-class action on rents, wages and working practices was more disciplined. The 'Red Clyde' was feared in London not because it was violent but because it was organised.[42]

Close examination of urban labour forces indicated that very few were likely to experience their situation as a coherent 'interest' in conflict with their employers. Although different urban labour markets could be classified as factory work, casual labour or workshop employment, there was little homogeneity of

[40] M. Simey, *Charity Rediscovered* (Liverpool, 1951; repr., Liverpool, 1992); J. Smith, 'Class, skill and sectarianism in Glasgow and Liverpool, 1880–1914', in Morris, ed., *Class, Power and Social Structure*, pp. 157–205.

[41] P. J. Waller, *Democracy and Sectarianism* (Liverpool, 1981); G. L. Anderson, *Victorian Clerks* (Manchester, 1976); D. Lockwood, *The Blackcoated Worker* (London, 1958).

[42] Smith, 'Class, skill and sectarianism'; Alan McKinlay and R. J. Morris, eds., *The ILP on Clydeside, 1893–1932: From Foundation to Disintegration* (Manchester, 1991); William Kenefick and Arthur McIvor, eds., *Roots of Red Clydeside, 1910–1914* (Edinburgh, 1996); and see above, p. 197, and below, p. 442.

experience. The factory labour force was divided by hierarchies of gender, skill and age. In many occupations the relationship of labour and capital were mediated by jobbing labour and subcontracting.[43] The potential which the labour–capital relationship might have for conflict and radical political challenge was often mediated by a variety of paternalist employer strategies which, though based on older traditions of social relationships, were strategies which were renewed and thrived in urban environments.

Metaphors of family and community shaped relationships right across the manufacturing districts. The mills of Messrs Lawrence in Chorley were decorated when their son came of age in 1899. Many mills and workplaces organised trips and feasts. Owners sponsored schools, reading rooms and mechanics institutions providing land, buildings and finance.[44] Paternalism marked out territories within the urban place as in the spectacular factory 'villages' like that of Titus Salt on the edge of Bradford or the two simple pillars which marked the industrial suburb of Prinlaws in the burgh of Leslie in Fife. Such paternalism survived into the twentieth century. In Glasgow, engineering employers like Beardmore sustained their authority by direct involvement in the work and drinking culture of the firm. In these firms the wage relationship was a personal as much as a market one. The flax-spinning firm of John Fergus and Son in Fife must have been typical of many in which the 'maister' walked around the firm stuffing five pound notes in the pockets of his employees as the end of year bonus. Housing was important. In Prinlaws, those who occupied the houses of John Fergus were expected to send their daughters to work in the mill or lose their house. In Saltaire no washing was to hang out on Sundays. Paternalism was a hard assertion of authority. Some of the most bitter industrial conflicts of the century arose from the breakdown of such strategies.[45] It was a bargain which ensured the stability of an often low-paid labour force and should not be confused with benevolence.[46]

The paternalism of the mill town was not some deviation or manipulation of the class outcomes of the capitalist relationships of labour and capital but found a ready response in the 'populist' perceptions of social reality which pervaded the culture of these towns and which ran alongside and interacted with class perceptions. Broadsheet ballads, dialect poetry, popular theatre, often through the melodrama of good and evil, and, by the end of century, the seaside postcard

[43] R. Samuel, 'The workshop of the world: steam power and hand technology in mid-Victorian Britain', *History Workshop Journal*, 3 (1977), 6–72; P. Joyce, *Work, Society and Politics* (Brighton, 1980); P. Joyce, 'Work', in F. M. L. Thompson, ed., *The Cambridge Social History of Britain 1750–1950*, vol. II: *People and their Environment* (Cambridge, 1990), pp. 157–93.
[44] Joyce, *Work, Society and Politics*, pp. 134–57.
[45] H. I. Dutton and J. E. King, *Ten Per Cent and No Surrender* (Cambridge, 1981); Robert Duncan, *Steelopolis: The Making of Motherwell, c. 1750–1939* (Motherwell, 1991).
[46] R. J. Morris and J. Smyth, 'Paternalism as an employer strategy, 1800–1960', in J. Rubery and F. Wilkinson, eds., *Employer Strategy and the Labour Market* (Oxford, 1994), pp. 195–225.

were some of the media for this culture. A virtuous people faced those in authority with deep distrust and a contempt for 'putting on airs'. At the same time this
critique recognised the true gentleman and the fair employer.[47] In this context,
John Fielden, employer of thousands and radical leader in Oldham, was no
paradox but a capitalist acting out the popular model.[48] Class was not an inevitable expression of the antagonism of labour and capital but rather a sense of 'us'
and 'them' centred on an assertion of the dignity of work and a pride in our own
folk. Trades union banners carried not just portraits of labour leaders but details
of the tools and products of labour – looms, ships, railway locomotives, printed
books.[49]

For the urbanist this presents two dimensions of analysis. Many of these cultural products were place specific – the mill, the trade, the processional route,
the holiday week for sending postcards. Regional identities, often expressed in
language, bound groups of towns together – Lancashire was gradely, Tyneside
canny and the Lowland Scots couthy. At the same time the media and much of
the content were part of an urban national network. Print was an urban media.
True it was not excluded from the countryside but the urban place and the urban
network was the focus of production, consumption and distribution. The
Northern Star, *Chambers Edinburgh Journal* and later *Reynolds News* were urban
products that spread along the networks of road and rail. The travelling theatre,
the political orator on the stump, the traditions of banners, meetings and marches
were all urban. The railway with its point delivery system more than road and
canal made the urban the contact point between local and national culture. The
increasing concentration of population, as Vaughan predicted, created the
market and the audience for such products.

The notion of towns as an arena of class conflict driven by the confrontations
of wage labour and capital was at best only a partial account, even for a town
dominated by factories and other relatively large units of production. The social
and political relationships of British towns and cities in this period were subject
to a much more complex set of influences which included the opportunities,
problems and limitations set by the economic relationships of production and
reproduction, the nature of local leadership amongst elite and other social
groups, the legacy of past history and historical memory and the identities of
gender, ethnicity and religion. Each town was part of a national and sometimes
international network. Cultural products and structural effects were rarely
derived from a specific place but were influential because of the interaction of
the town with the rest of the network. This network brought not just newspapers, periodicals, new novels, sheet music, travelling lecturers, politics and

<hr>

[47] P. Joyce, *Visions of the People* (Cambridge, 1991).
[48] Stewart Angas Weaver, *John Fielden and the Politics of Popular Radicalism, 1832–1847* (Oxford, 1987).
[49] R. Hoggart, *The Uses of Literacy* (London, 1957); John Gorman, *Banner Bright:An Illustrated History of the Trade Union Banners* (London, 1973).

plays but also the glazed pipes for the sewage system, the rails which linked the suburb to the centre, the steel frame for the piano at the music festival and the dozens of products which filled the department store. The urban nature of the town, the influence of the transactional density, the variety of experience and choice, the town as a focus of power in terms of the market, the state and the production of culture directs attention to the Vaughan as well as the Chalmers form of inquiry.

Whatever the complexities of urban social behaviour, the language of urban social description in the period went back again and again to a language of class. Such language was there in Chalmers' work as well as in the account of Manchester written by one of his pupils, James Kay.[50] This language was often mingled with that of 'the people' and of 'the poor'. Alexander Brown, a Glasgow letter press printer, produced his *Midnight Scenes and Social Photographs* in 1858:

> the public, the middle and higher classes of society, the poor, the occupants of the low closes and wynds, an immense concourse of men, women and children, their pestilential dwellings, virtuous and vicious, the lower classes, smart little factory girls, the lowest lodging houses for travellers and others, beggars, the Christian community, the people, the poor . . . their dirty pestilential dwellings, evangelical protestants, the merchant, the industrious mechanic, idle workmen, the lower orders, respectably dressed people, a crowd of low people, this social volcano, this lowest class of people.[51]

This was a language of class, poverty and threat which linked the lowest status groups with specific areas of the great cities, reinforcing this link by statistical and cartographic presentations. In Andrew Mearns' account of London in the early 1880s, 'the poor and outcaste classes of society' were distanced from the potential actors, 'the Christian people'.[52] The real change, seen most clearly in the work of Booth and Rowntree, was the greater attention paid to the relationships of reproduction in the household. Lady Bell's account of the iron workers of Middlesbrough started with a clear recognition of the complex class basis of production: a thousand working men's homes; lady visitors; the relations between capital and labour, between employers and employed; these workmen, their conditions, mental, moral and physical; employers; professional men; tradesmen; arms of powerful men; the ironworkers; the working men. It was also a language of the dissonance between production and reproduction. It was a language of household budgets, of women as good or bad managers, of drink and gambling as the difference between order and disaster in the working-class

[50] J. P. Kay, *The Moral and Physical Condition of the Working Classes Employed in the Cotton Manufacture in Manchester* (Manchester, 1832; repr., Didsbury, 1969).
[51] 'Shadow' (Alexander Brown), *Midnight Scenes and Social Photographs* (Glasgow, 1858; repr., Glasgow, 1976), with an introduction by John McCaffrey.
[52] A. Mearns, *The Bitter Cry of Outcast London* (London, 1883; new edn, ed. A. S. Wohl, Leicester, 1970).

home.[53] Sir William Collins, the lord provost who had promoted the Glasgow City Improvement Scheme which provided houses 'for the working classes', was keenly aware of the manner in which class structure, urban space and the household labour market related to each other. Men preferred to live centrally so that their household had access to the more varied labour market of the city. They might travel to the shipyards but wanted their wives and daughters to be able to work in the city when the fluctuating labour markets of Clydebank and Partick put them out of work.

Witnesses separated the working classes from a lower social stratum. This was not simply a matter of Irish influence, 'they are very destructive', but a broader cultural influence which the policy makers sought to combat 'The wife of a working man living up a common stair among miscellaneous neighbours, not probably all of good character may be subjected to bad influences' (James Gowans, chairman of the dean of guild court in Edinburgh).[54] This complex language of class was the language of urban problem solving and policy making for the urban elites and middle classes. The languages of gender, ethnicity and religion, often embedded in these accounts, tended to be languages of prescription and moral assertion. When the middle-class elite and their intellectual allies tried to understand the urban places in which they lived and worked it was this language of class to which they turned.[55]

The world of Oldham, Liverpool, Glasgow and the rest was not just a world of class, of conflict, of consciousness and ideology, it was also a world of meetings, debates, of motions proposed and voted upon, of petitions and public subscriptions, of voting and elections. It was a world of continual contest over the use, accumulation and control of the material resources of the town. In many contests, legitimacy was increasingly allocated to rule-based decision making in courts, societies, partnerships and above all in representative institutions. Increasing authority was attributed to public argument based upon evidence and reasoning. Legitimacy went with representative power which was only indirectly related to any notion of democracy. The key figures were members, citizens, inhabitants. In the abstract the definition of such groups lacked any precision, but in practice definition was usually clear and rule-based, the payment of a subscription, the ownership of property and increasingly residence within a spatially defined area, the town. This process was not just a matter of municipal councils and their growing number of subcommittees. The identity of organised social life with the urban place was also linked to the increasing density of voluntary associations. This accelerated and became more public in the middle years of the nineteenth century. A wide range of institutions, from charitable societies like

---

[53] F. Bell, *At the Works* (London, 1907); E. J. Yeo, *The Contest for Social Science* (London, 1996), pp. 223–8.
[54] PP, 1884–85, xxxi, Royal Commission on the Housing of the Working Classes, Qqs. 19,339 and 18,841. [55] A. Lees, *Cities Perceived* (Manchester, 1985); Yeo, *The Contest for Social Science*.

the Stranger's Friend Benevolent Societies, cultural societies like the Literary and Philosophical Societies and economic interest groups like the Chambers of Commerce and the Licensed Victuallers Societies all saw the town as the focus for their activities.

The urban place in Britain was the site for the creation, extension and con-solidation of a civil society. This was a long process with origins in the seven-teenth century. Civil society involved the increasing range of social activity which was free of the prescriptive relationships of family or of the state – free of the tyranny of cousins and the tyranny of the state.[56] The creation of civil society was a process and many of its achievements were imperfect. The decision to join or form a political party in a pluralistic society based upon the rule of law was open to an increasing number of people, but for many their Whig or Tory iden-tity was still prescribed by family or religion. The increasing dominance of the market economy and the spread of associational culture also increased choice. Central to these processes were many of the issues of class relationships. Civil society involved processes of bargaining between 'interests'. The notion of 'interests' economic or cultural must be at the heart of any relationship between structure and culture. Civil society allowed plurality in the conflicts and bargain-ing which took place. Conflict was not just a matter of class but a matter of status, occupation, religion, ethnicity and gender. The growth of civil society in British towns allowed the negotiation of such conflicts as an increasingly rule-based process in which the process itself became a touchstone of the legitimacy and general acceptance of any resolution reached. It was a process which allowed dominance without homogeneity.

The British town proved an ideal site for creating the social processes and rela-tionships vital to civil society. This development was not restricted to the nine-teenth century but was one which had origins in the seventeenth century. A tentative, fourfold, overlapping periodisation indicates the dominant sets of rela-tionships in urban culture, structure and action. The late seventeenth-century settlement established a variety of corporatist urban structures, many of which survived into the 1840s. These institutions were structured by limited forms of representation and rule-based forms of debate and decision taking. Some form of chairman, convener, mayor or sovereign was appointed, often in rotation or by vote, and always with specific and circumscribed authority. Motions were debated and voted upon. Decisions were recorded in minutes. Between about 1780 and 1860 voluntaristic and *ad hoc* agencies dominated. Schools, hospitals, libraries, gardening clubs were directed by voluntary societies which held public meetings, published accounts and offered membership to all who would pay sub-scriptions. Water, gas, even cemeteries were provided by joint-stock companies which followed the same type of public form. Paving, lighting, police and the

---

[56] E. Gellner, *Conditions of Liberty* (London, 1994); Hall, ed., *Civil Society*.

care of the poor were provided by a variety of disparate tax-collecting agencies with legal powers and specific spatial references usually to the urban place.[57] Somewhere around 1860 the emphasis changed to the municipal, a representative corporate structure which dominated urban culture. The twentieth century saw the slow disintegration of the urban place as structure as a result of the impact of processes which made the urban culture itself universal.

The extension and organisation of the non-prescriptive aspects of urban life enabled people to use the structures of civil society, the market, the voluntary society, the open and representative institutions of local government to make choices. Hence the complexity of any explanation of urban social behaviour and culture. It also helps explain many features of that complexity. The nineteenth-century British city was a middle-class place in terms of culture, government, property ownership and social authority. Within the middle classes the merchants and professional men tended to find it easier to gain influence in government and the voluntary sector. The merchants were used to the bargaining and rule-based activity of the partnership and contract whilst the professional groups were skilled in the rule-based corporate guarding of their income as well as the application of science or rule-based systems of knowledge and expertise. The manufacturers used to the direct authority of capital over labour had to learn other ways.[58] There was considerable evidence of aristocratic influence but this was only obtained through the institutionalised, rule-based, social and political processes of civil society. In Scotland, the attempts of the duke of Buccleuch to sustain his authority in Hawick by the older methods of direction and client politics were a messy failure. In Edinburgh where he operated by quiet influence, notably as patron in many voluntary societies, he was able to take a quiet share in the culture and authority of that city.[59] By the 1850s and 1860s, many groups of skilled male wage earners had learnt the rules and procedures of civil society and were able to claim a small part in the exercise of legitimate authority at the urban level. Their trade societies and educational traditions were an ideal base from which to debate the motion in the informed and argued manner required by civil society. Those elements of the population who took direct action through riots, crowds or violent strikes could be controlled by military action or the new police. Those who played by the 'rules' were much harder to dominate. Many other 'interests' were formed. Small property owners, especially shopkeepers, organised to defend themselves against increased local taxation. By the 1890s,

[57] R. J. Morris, 'Clubs, societies and associations', in F. M. L. Thompson, ed., *The Cambridge Social History of Britain, 1750–1950*, vol. III: *Social Agencies and Institutions* (Cambridge, 1990), pp. 395–444.
[58] Morris, 'The middle class and British towns and cities'; Trainor, *Black Country Elites*; J. Garrard, *Leadership and Power in Victorian Industrial Towns 1830–80* (Manchester, 1983); E. P. Hennock, *Fit and Proper Persons* (London, 1973).
[59] R. J. Morris, 'Urbanisation and Scotland', in W. H. Fraser and R. J. Morris, eds., *People and Society in Scotland*, vol. II: *1830–1914* (Edinburgh, 1990), pp. 73–102.

'labour' saw the municipal as the arena for asserting their interest through fair labour clauses and the amelioration of the poor laws.

Some towns were better than others at creating an expanding and stable civil society. Medium-sized towns which had no tradition of coherent local government or a weak structure of mediating voluntary organisations were especially vulnerable to breakdowns of law and order. This usually meant industrial towns with an experience of rapid growth in the early nineteenth century but no tradition of incorporation. Other places had a weak professional and mercantile middle class to sustain a mediating and leadership role.[60] This role was often expressed through organisations like the mechanics institution or local hospital. Breakdown was not just a matter of riot and crime but might involve the inability to counter epidemic disease because of poor organisation. Birmingham despite its late incorporation still had a rich array of institutions such as the grammar school, a number of dynamic nonconformist elite congregations and later the university. This was associated with a strong civic culture. Sheffield on the other hand had a strong neighbourhood culture with very little respect for town wide institutions and hence was unable to generate a strong civic culture. Later in the century the growth of retail cooperative societies and associated social and political activities drew working people into a stable relationship with civil society, which had a strong regional concentration in the northern industrial areas.[61] The voluntary societies produced and sustained a strong identity built around the urban place. Most took the name of the town itself and sought membership from the town. Thus the basis of stability and social mediation was identified with the specific urban place.

As the power of the urban identity gathered pace it reproduced itself, through another generation of cultural products such as municipal parks, statues and football clubs all of which created, asserted and recreated urban character. The second half of the nineteenth century saw the creation of a powerful municipal culture. By the end of the nineteenth century in Britain, the word 'municipal' was closely associated with notions of local pride, of improvement and of achievement. This was physically embodied in town halls, gas works, clean water, improved housing, libraries and museums – it was closely allied with local school boards and poor law authorities, with their school buildings and hospitals. When overseas visitors came to Britain, they came to the best governed cities in the world, whether that was Glasgow or Birmingham.[62] Municipal corporations had been associated with exclusion and corruption before the 1830s and then with middle-class squabbles over spending.[63] Somewhere around 1860,

[60] L. H. Lees, 'The study of social conflict in English industrial towns, *UHY* (1980), 34–43.
[61] D. Smith, *Conflict and Compromise* (London, 1982); Martin Purvis, 'Popular institutions', in J. Langton and R. J. Morris, eds., *Atlas of Industrialising Britain, 1780–1914* (London, 1986).
[62] B. Aspinwall, *Portable Utopia* (Aberdeen, 1984,) p. 177 and appendix A.
[63] Fraser, ed., *Municipal Reform.*

there was a change of mood, a change in both the quality and quantity of municipal activity. In 1859 Glasgow opened the new Loch Katrine water supply. The
importance of this move was indicated by the presence of Queen Victoria to
turn the taps. In 1866, the Glasgow City Improvement Act provided authority
to clear and remodel 88 acres (35.6 ha) in the centre of Glasgow. By 1902 the
city owned 2,488 houses.[64] Birmingham was late entering this phase of municipalism, but the results were spectacular. In 1873, the gas works were bought by
the corporation and water a year later. By 1875, adequate national legislation was
available and there was no need for the expense of a specific local act. Outcomes
and motives were mixed. The Birmingham clearance scheme was announced
'without any thought of profit, and with the one desire to advance health and
morality'. The plan was to buy 93 acres (37.7 ha) running through some of the
worst 'back slums' of Birmingham and 'run a great street as broad as a Parisian
boulevard from the middle of New Street to Aston Road'. Communication and
retailing were as important as sanitation. Joseph Chamberlain freely admitted the
'twofold aspect of the scheme'.[65]

Municipal corporations entered a phase of service provision and the accumulation of major blocks of urban capital. Activity included parks, libraries, slaughter houses, lighting, roads and police but in terms of income flow gas, water and
tramways dominated.[66] By 1900, the municipal corporation was a major business enterprise with the ratepayer as property taxpayer and consumer. Municipal
activities were a mixture of social engineering and the manipulation of economic externalities. This switch of focus in urban culture was related to several
factors. The dissenting and evangelical members of the middle classes were no
longer outsiders in the local power structure. The energy they had channelled
into voluntary activities was now diverted towards the municipal and local state.
Their schemes gained authority from cultural representations of the town developed over the previous twenty years, notably maps, surveys and statistical reports.
Men like R. W. Dale in Birmingham preached, 'the town was a solemn organism through which should flow, and in which should be shaped all the highest,
loftiest and truest ends of man's moral nature'.[67] By the 1880s, this moral agency
had extended to a commitment amongst many middle-class activists to 'civilisation'.[68] Although they never matched the big spenders of gas, water and sewers,

[64] C. M. Allen, 'The genesis of British urban redevelopment with special reference to Glasgow',
Ec.HR, 2nd series, 18 (1965), 598–613; J. Graham Kerr, ed., *Glasgow: Sketches by Various Authors*,
British Association for the Advancement of Science, Glasgow Meeting, 1928 (Glasgow, 1928); T.
Hart, 'Urban growth and municipal government: Glasgow in a comparative context, 1846–1914',
in A. Slaven and D. H. Aldcroft, eds., *Business, Banking and Urban History* (Edinburgh, 1982), pp.
193–219.   [65] A. Mayne, *The Imagined Slum* (Leicester, 1993), pp. 57–63.
[66] W. H. Fraser, 'Municipal socialism and social policy', in R. J. Morris and R. Rodger, eds., *The
Victorian City* (London, 1993); J. R. Kellett, 'Municipal socialism, enterprise and trading in the
Victorian city', *UHY* (1978), 36–45.   [67] Hennock, *Fit and Proper Persons*, p. 75.
[68] H. E. Meller, *Leisure and the Changing City, 1870–1914* (London, 1976).

the parks, libraries and art galleries built in the later part of the century were a very visible outcome of the municipal state. This growth in municipal activity was associated with the creation of a municipal culture. It was powerful enough for men like Joseph Chamberlain and William Chambers to stake the reputation and leisure of a successful capitalist upon their association with that culture; 'if a man has leisure, and wants occupation, his taste must be difficult indeed if he cannot find some congenial employment in connection with the multifarious duties of the Town Council of Birmingham'.[69]

By 1900, municipal Britain was represented by a series of major and minor monuments, each of which had a half-understood iconography. Leeds Town Hall, conceived and built in the 1850s, was not just an assertive rival to nearby Bradford's St George's Hall. There were classical echoes of power and citizenship. Birmingham had a forum and Liverpool its acropolis. Other places looked to Florence and Flanders. Halifax had a mixture of Renaissance palace and medieval cathedral. These historical references all entailed success in trade, independence in citizenship and claims to recognition for taste and artistic creativity. Lions were everywhere. Foundation myths as powerful as anything found in the ancient world were created, reproduced and celebrated.[70] When City Square was laid out in Leeds in the 1890s it was peopled by the Black Prince, Joseph Priestley and several naked ladies, all in a stone which was rapidly covered in soot from the smoke of local prosperity, a subtle mixture of local historical mythology and claims for classical taste.[71] Middlesbrough, of recent origin, had to be satisfied with statues of its founding capitalists, ironmasters, Bolkow and Vaughan. St Andrews in Fife mixed crow stepped gables with Flemish elements combining a Scottish statement with a reference to the municipal glories of Flanders. In Dunfermline, the new corporation buildings of 1875–9 mixed Scottish Baronial and French Gothic quietly asserting a mythic Scottish past and claims for European importance. There was a statue of Robbie Burns inside.[72] Ceremony was as important as stone in this culture. When the prince of Wales opened Middlesbrough Town Hall in 1889, he was presented with a key of gold and Cleveland steel representing local produce as well as the money its production would make. A wide range of social groups were incorporated in social ritual as well as political negotiation. When the foundation stone of Glasgow municipal buildings was laid in 1883, the ceremony was a municipal sacrament. The procession not only included all elements of authority but also represented the trades

---

[69] Quoted by B. I. Coleman, *The Idea of the City in Nineteenth-Century Britain* (London, 1973), p. 161. [70] Joseph Rykwert, *The Idea of a Town* (Princeton, 1988).

[71] Asa Briggs, 'Leeds, a study in civic pride', in Briggs, *Victorian Cities*, pp. 139–83; Fraser, ed., *Leeds*, p. 110; Derek Linstrum, *West Yorkshire: Architects and Architecture* (London, 1978).

[72] John Gifford, *The Buildings of Scotland: Fife* (London, 1988), and Glen L. Pride, *The Kingdom of Fife: An Illustrated Architectural Guide* (Edinburgh, 1990). My thanks to Helen Morris for help with this section.

of Glasgow. It was an assertion of Glasgow. The mottoes represented that populist brand of universality which was so important in working-class culture, both in England and Scotland; 'May the tree of liberty flourish around the globe, and every human being partake of its fruits'; 'Trust and try.' The metal workers carried a working model of the riveters at work. Amongst the corporation trades people were the gas works employees with model of a gas works, bronzed furnace rakes and gilded repairing lances. Their banner recommended 'light, truth, purity, heat and power'. The cleansing department had a water butt inscribed 'down with the dust'. The sanitary department proclaimed 'testing your drains saves sorrow, fever and pains'.[73] By the 1890s this municipal culture had drawn in the aristocracy as patrons, whilst the new associations of the working classes saw gaining municipal power as a major objective.

Both the historical literature and contemporary reflection provided much less guidance on the relationships of urban structure and cultures after 1920. This was the result of a variety of processes which reduced the specific nature of the links between culture, structure and the urban place. These processes worked in a number of ways. They increased the universality of many cultural influences. They also worked to destroy the coherence and integrity of the specific urban place both as a structure and as a cultural entity.

Between 1850 and 1920, the membership of urban economic, social, political and cultural elites was overlapping, closely integrated and identified with place. J. H. Chance the West Bromwich glassmaker was typical of many who were active in local government, in voluntary and charitable activity as well as being major local employers and owners of capital. In many Lancashire towns, leading manufacturers were regarded as natural leaders of local government.[74] Change was slow and uneven but there were three elements. The coming of universal suffrage between 1918 and 1928 enabled the Labour party to gain power in several towns challenging an older elite and creating a new concentration of power which had no relationship to the ownership and control of local capital. In the Scottish steelmaking town of Motherwell, David Colville, leading industrialist, and John Craig, one of his employees, were members of parliament and leaders of the YMCA and Temperance movements. In the 1920s, they were replaced as a political elite by the Labour party which used the poor law, an agency of the local state to support the dependants of strikers during the mining disputes of 1921 and 1926.[75] In Ashington, in the Northumberland coalfield, the power of the duke of Portland was reduced by the mutualist agencies of the local Co-operative Society in the organisation of retailing and leisure.[76] The

---

[73] *Description of Ceremonial on the Occasion of Laying the Foundation Stone of the Municipal Buildings in George Square Glasgow, 6th October 1883* (Glasgow, 1885), pp. 39–40.

[74] Trainor, *Black Country Elites*, p. 102; Garrard, *Leadership and Power*, p. 24.

[75] Duncan, *Steelopolis*, p. 173.

[76] Mike Kirkup, *The Biggest Mining Village in the World: A Social History of Ashington* (Morpeth, 1993).

authority of many professional groups employed by local government grew slowly and became decisive in the 1950s when the town clerk, the health professionals like the medical officer of health and above all the borough planning officer and the borough architect were career professionals whose point of reference was their own professional organisation rather than the local political elites who employed them.

The most important change was in the structure of the ownership of local capital. In the Scottish county of Fife, the town of Kirkcaldy was dominated by the linoleum making firm of Nairn's. The family lived in or near the town. Their influence like the smell of their production process pervaded the town. The cottage hospital was financed in 1874 whilst the museum and public library were memorials to a son killed in the 1914–18 war.[77] On a larger scale, Benwell, a western industrial suburb of Newcastle-upon-Tyne, was dominated by the great engineering firms. The families of Armstrong, Stephenson, Hawthorne and Joicey were linked through marriage and business transactions. They provided MPs and mayors. They financed schools, hospitals and churches. They were a visible presence in Newcastle.[78] The change was cumulative. By the 1890s, many of these families relied on national organisation for their power. The challenge of the engineering trades unions in the 1890s was met by the Engineering Employers Federation (1895). In 1927, the Armstrong Company was forced to amalgamate with its rival Vickers to avoid bankruptcy. In 1947, coal nationalisation accelerated the loss of the control of local capital by local families. In Kirkcaldy, Sir Michael Nairn found he could no longer treat the local hospital as a personal benevolent interest when he tried to order the relaying of faulty linoleum. The hospital had recently been transferred to the National Health Service. Locally owned and controlled companies found themselves increasingly alongside incomers. In the 1950s, the local companies in the Fife town were now compared with incomers like De La Rue. In the Clyde shipbuilding towns, US management styles increased the turmoil of local labour relations.[79] This was not just a matter of wage rates and differentials but of small things such as setting aside a room for workpeople to eat their midday 'piece'. Loss of local control accelerated in the late 1950s. Many family firms, which survived the 1930s paying low or no dividends to family shareholders, because they offered employment to other family members, were closed or taken over.[80] Families which once owned this local capital had acquired widespread national and international assets and power. Some retained a local interest in financial services, property devel-

---

[77] Morris and Smyth, 'Paternalism as an employer strategy'.

[78] Benwell Community Project, *The Final Report No. 6. The Making of a Ruling Class* (Newcastle-upon-Tyne, 1978).

[79] John Foster and Charles Woolfson, *The Politics of the UCS Work-In* (London, 1986), pp. 23–165.

[80] Robin Mackie, 'The survival and decline of locally based and family firms in the Kirkcaldy area, c. 1900–1960' (PhD thesis, University of Edinburgh, 1995).

opment and in local politics, tending to favour non-elective positions such as the new town corporations. Urban economic structure was now based upon the multi-national and multi-locational firm. Headquarters, located in a metropolitan centre like London, took the authority which once belonged to the resident of the 'maister's' house. Many towns were dominated by branch plants, some 'footloose', others more dependent on local skills.[81] Between 1920 and the 1960s, the major owners of capital had detached themselves from the specific urban place so that control was now mediated through a variety of institutional forms based upon the state, the market and bureaucracy.

A powerful municipal culture, the integration of local political, economic and social elites and the local identity and ownership of capital were key features of late nineteenth- and early twentieth-century towns in Britain, but during the 1920s and 1930s key institutional structures which had supported all this began to be diminished, undermined and replaced. The poor law which had been the basis of local power and decision making for three centuries was replaced by national agencies in 1911 and 1929. In Poplar and West Ham, control of the local elective Board of Guardians was a major target for the local Labour party, as a means of increasing the welfare of the unemployed. Poplar's efforts were illegal and councillors were imprisoned.[82] West Ham was defeated by the refusal of the Local Government Board to make loans and by the realisation that a spatially limited agency could do little to counter the effects of international economic factors which produced the spatially specific and uneven outcome of unemployment. At the same time, the local elective body was vulnerable to local demonstrations, pickets and demonstrations. In West Ham, the Guardians were howled down at public meetings.[83] In 1930, all this was replaced by the Public Assistance Committees which were controlled from London and had no powers of local discretion. The process was completed in 1947, when the National Health Service took over poor law and voluntary hospitals. Very often there was no direct demolition of a municipal/urban place structure but as new technologies began to deliver the sort of services which had once been urban-based, new national rather than urban agencies were formed often as much for political as for technological reasons. Gas and water had been at the centre of municipal culture. Electricity rapidly became part of a national grid despite formal ownership by local agencies.[84] Newspapers, often two or three per town, had been a key aspect of urban identity. The new medium of radio was carefully fashioned as a national identity. Lord Reith the first governor general of the British

---

[81] D. Massey, *Spatial Divisions of Labour* (London, 1984).

[82] Gillian Rose, 'Locality, politics and culture: Poplar in the 1920s', *Environment and Planning D: Society and Space*, 6 (1988), 151–68.   [83] John Marriot, *The Culture of Labourism* (Edinburgh, 1991).

[84] *PEP Report on the Supply of Electricity in Great Britain* (London, 1936), pp. 9–33; *Report of the Committee of Inquiry into the Electrical Supply Industry* (the Herbert Report), Cmnd 9672 (London, HMSO, 1956).

Broadcasting Corporation (BBC) believed that strong central direction would enlarge cultural interests and help overcome social divisions. The result was the dominance of a London-centred middle-class elite culture.[85] Universities in their modern form played a major and complex part in the reproduction of British culture. Owen's College in Manchester and the Yorkshire College at Leeds were products of local initiatives, sponsored by local groups of businessmen, with local economic interests in mind. Lancashire chemicals and Yorkshire textiles both stood to gain from the work of their local colleges. Local identity was rapidly disciplined by two factors, the financial power of the University Grants Committee and the desire of all institutions to participate in an active and resourceful international scientific and humanistic culture.[86] The Labour movement changed in the same way, based upon local organisation, the Co-op, the ILP branch, the socialist Sunday School and the Woodcraft Folk it was rapidly restructured as a national movement with powerful centralising ambitions. In St Helens 'the men at that time became labour people through reading books and papers . . . the party nationally used to send them out'.[87]

At the same time the urban places were changing their social identity. During the nineteenth century, British towns were middle class. Municipal heroes like Joseph Chamberlain and William Chambers were from the middle-class elite. In map, newspaper and directory towns were presented as creations of their middle-class elite. By the mid-twentieth century middle-class identity had retreated to the suburbs. For the working classes the journey was in the opposite direction. The late nineteenth-century working classes operated around the neighbourhood.[88] The poor were a product of the slum.[89] During the 1920s and 1930s, the identity of the town became a working-class one. This move can be seen in urban politics, in urban leisure identities and in the cultural products and experiences of the towns. This reflected the slow change in the relationship between capital, labour and the specific urban place. During the nineteenth century, urban capital mobility was limited. Transaction costs were high because of the wide range of location specific externalities for the owners of local capital. The owner merchant-manufacturer benefited from local reputation in terms of credit. Each industry was surrounded by its supporting services. There was a

---

[85] Asa Briggs, *The Golden Age of Wireless*, vol. II of *The History of the Broadcasting in the United Kingdom* (Oxford, 1965), pp. 7 and 38–41; John Whale, *The Politics of the Media* (London, 1977); Raymond Williams, *Television, Technology and Cultural Form* (London, 1974).

[86] R. H. Kargon, *Science in Victorian Manchester* (Manchester, 1977), pp. 153–213; P. H. J. H. Gosden and A. J. Taylor, eds., *Studies in the History of a University, to Commemorate the Centenary of the University of Leeds, 1874–1974* (Leeds, 1975), pp. 1–42.

[87] Charles Forman, *Industrial Town* (London, 1979), p. 178.

[88] G. Stedman Jones, 'Working-class culture and working-class politics in London, 1870–1900: notes on the remaking of a working class', *Soc. Hist.*, 7 (1974); E. Ross, 'Survival networks – women's neighbourhood sharing in London before World War I', *History Workshop*, 15 (1983), 4–27.

[89] Mayne, *The Imagined Slum*.

network of credit based upon family, friends and even religious congregation. The cost of leaving those multi-dimensional but coherent elites was high. In many cases a skill-specific labour force tied businesses to a particular location. By the mid-twentieth century capital became more 'footloose' and was embedded in national and international organisation.[90] The influence of structural change on labour mobility was different. In the nineteenth century transaction costs were low. Labour had few possessions to carry. There was some loss of poor law rights but this was reduced in the 1840s. Those with highly paid skills were prepared to move considerable distances, as were Irish and Highland migrants. Wage earners developed a facility for what would now be called community development. Women worked by way of neighbourhood, whilst men devised institutional supports in trades unions and friendly societies. In the twentieth century transaction costs for labour grew. As the availability of local authority housing increased, then the length of residence was related to 'points' in the queue for such high quality housing. As the expansion of employment slowed in many urban areas, the importance of family and friends to 'speak for' a job applicant became increasingly important.[91]

In the 1920s and 1930s, urban politics became identified with the working class, or at least with the working-class party. There was no simple basis to this identity. The labour politics of Poplar in east London were driven by the morality and mutuality of its neighbourhood communities as well as the melodrama of the public meeting and street demonstration.[92] In nearby West Ham, dominated by Labour from 1919 to 1975, the working-class population was more organised. An industrially weak union movement around the railway and gas works saw politics as an alternative means to achieve their aims. The Co-op, especially the Women's Co-operative Guild was an important means of educating and drawing people into politics. Stratford Co-op was also used to organise food supplies during strike action. The unevenness of local Labour political power was an expression not only of 'interests' but also of 'capacities' and 'alternatives'. In places like Middlesbrough the Liberal party proved able to accommodate the ambitions of a mainly skilled organised working class. By 1927, Labour-controlled local authorities included West Ham, St Helens, Wigan, Merthyr Tydfil, Smethwick, Birkenhead and Sheffield, the only large-sized town. In Sheffield the 'success' of labour was related to the weakness of local municipal traditions and the incoherence of the urban elite.[93] It was not until the 1930s that labour administrations gained power in major centres like Leeds and Glasgow.

The impact of these changes appeared in a series of articles on major provincial cities which appeared in *Picture Post* in the late 1930s. This was a self-conscious

[90] Massey, *Spatial Divisions*.

[91] M. Young and P. Willmott, *Family and Kinship in East London* (London, 1957); P. Willmott and M. Young, *Family and Class in a London Suburb* (London, 1960).

[92] Gillian Rose, 'Poplar in the 1920s', 151–68.   [93] Smith, *Conflict and Compromise*.

middle-class informed radical paper with a forceful London-based perspective. Its reporters and camera men were both disturbed and filled with wonder at what they saw. In Glasgow, they met a 'veteran socialist' P. J. Dollan and saw a labour city which had made progress 'with slum clearance and re-housing . . . [and the] free distribution of milk to schoolchildren'.[94] On the Tyne, they were troubled by 'one class towns'; 'what can you do to build up a properly balanced local government in a place like Jarrow, when more than half the working population were out of work for years and the middle class does not exist'.[95] In many towns, working-class neighbourhoods came to represent the town. In Newcastle, the 'Scotswood Road' was a symbol of Newcastle and the Tyne, in part because of the regional national anthem, the Blaydon Races, and in part because it was the basis of a powerful working-class culture. In Glasgow, the Gorbals played the same role.[96]

The complex relationship of working-class identity with the urban place was not just a matter of politics but was expressed and experienced through professional sport. Professional sport was one of the most distinctive products of the industrial towns. The new codes which the gentlemen evangelicals brought to the boys clubs of the 1860s were rapidly appropriated. This development reflected many defining aspects of the urban. The new codes involved a disciplined rule-based contest on the spatially bounded area of the pitch, a perfect response to the scarcity of space and complexity of the urban. They were played before growing crowds of paying spectators recruited from a massed population which was just beginning to experience a little surplus time and income for leisure. The multiplication of teams allowed these urban populations to make choices of identities and loyalties. Such sport was market-based, rule-based and bounded. It was urban but the actions and cultures produced a web of identities and relationships which went well beyond sport.

When Newcastle United won the English Football Association Cup in 1910, 1924 and 1932, they exposed the dynamic relationships of class, city and region in the first half of the twentieth century. The nature of the team, the newspaper press and local government gave the town and the municipality a central place. The triumphant return of the team to Central Station and the pre-match dinner involved mayor, sheriff, town clerk, councillors, MPs and the Tramways Band. Emphasis was placed on social unity. Supporters were greeted by a director of the London and North-Eastern Railway (LNER) at King's Cross. There was still some coherence between local people and local capital. When the winning goal was scored in 1932, 'men who had never met before shook hands, Byker and Jesmond, Scotswood and Gosforth had forgotten all social barriers'.[97] This was during a decade of bitter trades union conflict especially in the locally important mining industry.

[94] *Picture Post*, 1 Apr. 1939.   [95] *Ibid.*, 3 Dec. 1938
[96] A. McArthur and H. Kingsley Long, *No Mean City* (London, 1956); A. Desmond Walton (compiler) *Old Scotswood Road* (Newcastle, 1997).   [97] *Sunday Sun*, 24 Apr. 1932.

The experience of 'the match' placed Newcastle in a hierarchy of village, small town and wider region. Many of the players came from the villages and small towns around Newcastle. Jack Allen who scored the goal in 1932 came from Newburn, a small village long ago overtaken by the expansion of Newcastle. His mother went to see the match but his dad was doing the delivery rounds from the shop. As he did so people kept coming out of their houses to tell him the news from the 'wireless'. The new technology made this a shared event for the whole of Tyneside. In 1924 the crowds had gathered around the newspaper offices to hear the results coming over the telegraph.[98] Ashington continued to provided players like Jackie Milburn into the 1950s but by the 1960s the Charlton brothers went to Leeds and Manchester to play their football. The national and later international market destroyed the coherence of the local and the urban.

The central event was the 'invasion' of London, a class event and a centre periphery event. The 'cloth caps' took over London. The cloth cap was a powerful image of the working class and the North. When *Picture Post* went to Wigan, the dominant photograph was of two men standing at the bar in cloth caps drinking their beer from a glass without a handle. There was no need for a caption.[99] The notion of the 'invasion' of London by the North was one which went back at least as far as the Great Exhibition.[100] It was based upon the railway network. The railway made the trip to the final a major collective experience in a way which the dominant road system of the late twentieth century does not. This was an important provincial metropolitan relationship embedded in the structure of an urban hierarchy dominated by London but in which Newcastle was a powerful independent and self-confident part. London was a dynamic and exciting source of cultural energy. There was a mixture of naive wonder and self-confidence in taking over the metropolis. In 1924, the crowds were 'admiring the wonderful electric signs'.[101] They were equally pleased with the statue put up in Trafalgar Square (the Newcastle captain was called Jimmy Nelson). At the same time the Tynesiders were sure that they could teach London a thing or two about friendliness and enjoying themselves.

The manner in which urban culture represented urban experience led to a number of newspaper cartoons which appeared in the 1950s reflecting 1930s boyhood experience. Andy Capp first appeared in the *Daily Mirror* in 1954. He was so named because he wore a cap and was one (at least to his wife). His creator Reg Smyth claimed that 'the workshy little fellow who bullied his wife and liked his beer . . . [was] . . . just like they are in Hartlepool'.[102] Maybe that was true but the workshy bit was a charivari inversion of the skilled heavy industry wage earners' need to control the pace of labour and the ill-treated wife reflected the power relationships of an economy in which high paid male manual labour

[98] *Ibid.*   [99] *Picture Post*, 11 Nov. 1939.

[100] Tommy Tredllehoyle, *Trip to Lunnan* (Manchester, 1851).

[101] *Newcastle Daily Journal*, 26 Apr. 1924.   [102] *Northern Journal*, 16 Nov. 1977.

dominated. It was quite different from the Broons, a Dundee-based cartoon in which a large turbulent family maintained a contested gender balance, reflecting a local economy dominated by female factory work. Glasgow took a different approach. Lobey Dosser, the Calton Cowboy, rode the Wild West with a Glasgow accent.[103] It could only have been the product of many boyhood hours in cinemas showing film after film from Hollywood. The universal experience of the cinema was turned into a very specific local experience just as a hundred years before the middle-class elite of the great cities had appropriated the music of Europe to create their own specific urban traditions such as the Hallé Orchestra. This tension between the international product, often of US origin, and the local and specific was a major feature of urban culture after the 1920s.

After 1920, the language of urban social description and the conditions under which that language was generated changed in ways which reflected changes in urban structures and institutions. The main architects of these descriptions were no longer clergyman and doctors deeply embedded in the local elite, but were more likely to be academics and planners whose points of reference were national and even international peer groups. The Social Survey of Merseyside carried out by D. Caradog Jones and his assistants from the School of Social Sciences in Liverpool University was characteristic of a number of surveys of poverty which included that by Herbert Tout on Bristol and the New Survey of London. Explanation and understanding was sought in class terms but there was little evidence of the sense of conflict evident in mid-nineteenth-century studies nor even the 'threat' which remained in later studies. Class was expressed in terms of consumption through a concept of poverty and through housing conditions. The middle class, excluded from the survey, ate more meat and fresh vegetables than the working class and regarded the bath as a 'necessity' not a luxury.[104] There was little effort in Britain to study 'an urban way of life' although much attention was given to the relationship between urban and rural. Social structure and the city were related in both academic and popular work through area and place as the unit of study and description. In Liverpool and Birkenhead 'mostly working class property [had] sunk into slums' which were quite different from 'rows of villas and new housing estates, together with superior middle class suburbs'.[105] *Picture Post* in its accounts of provincial cities used the association with instinctive skill; 'the snack bar of the Grand Hotel . . . fashionable Birmingham . . . , the Casino Dance Rooms . . . not quite so fashionable Birmingham, Hockley way . . . skilled craftsmen . . . , aristocratic Edgbaston . . . , Handsworth . . . dull respectability'.[106] By the 1950s, the understanding and identification of the relationships of social structure to the urban

[103] Actually Bud Neill learnt his culture from the cinema in the Troon Playhouse; Ranald MacColl, *Lobey's the Wee Boy: Five Lobey Dosser Adventures by Bud Neill* (Glasgow, *c.* 1985).
[104] D. C. Jones, ed., *Merseyside*, vol. 1 (Liverpool, 1934), pp. 102 and 115.   [105] *Ibid.*, I, p. 57.
[106] *Picture Post*, 21 Jan. 1939

entered a new phase in which the specificity of the urban place declined. Bethnal Green was the place to find the working-class family and examine the relationship between the working-class family and space/place. Understanding was based upon the 'traditional urban space' of densely packed housing with a stable, interrelated population. This was contrasted with the new spaces of the municipal housing estate and middle-class villa development.[107] Banbury in Oxfordshire was an ideal place to contrast the status-related behaviour of a traditional elite with that of the more privatised and conflicting values of the in-migrant sections of the population. The account retained much of the specificity of Banbury but the author admitted it was exceptional that 'an area can be isolated for study in so closely integrated a country as Great Britain'.[108] In the 1960s, Luton was simply a place in which the affluent workers could be studied. Little reference was made to the specific nature of the place. The study was part of a national debate about the manner in which well-paid wage earners acquired middle-class values.[109] In Britain a society of urban places had completed its transformation into an urban society.

Between 1840 and 1950 the urban place changed from an entity which could be experienced as a unit to one which could be conceived as a unity before finally becoming the environment which encompassed experiences and communities. The 'knowable community' began in the coffee house or market place in which walking and talking made possible the concept of an urban place.[110] By the 1840s, the urban place was incorporated in the meeting, the organisation that carried the name of the town and above all the municipal, the agent of local government. This was 'knowable' through the media of print. Newspapers were identified with the particular urban place. They created a basis of common knowledge for drawing room and neighbourhood. The printed report and the poster supplemented this knowledge. Philanthropy and voluntary action were important but by the 1870s it was the municipal, its buildings, actions and public figures like the mayor who were the known community for each urban place. Politicians and philanthropists who were often also owners of local capital and leading professional people were public figures who inhabited reports and platforms to the common knowledge of the urban population. It was this coherence which fragmented in the twentieth century. Known communities were national, specialised or neighbourhood.

Nowhere was this change clearer than in the novels produced at the start and end of the period. Charles Dickens was a man who made sense of London. His novels display anger and alienation. The uncaring detachment of governors and profit takers was often represented by urban description like that of Tom All

---

[107] Young and Willmott, *Family and Kinship in East London*.
[108] M. Stacey, *Tradition and Change* (London, 1960), p. vi.
[109] John Goldthorpe, David Lockwood, Frank Bechhofer and Jennifer Platt, *The Affluent Worker*, 3 vols. (Cambridge, 1968).   [110] Richard Sennett, *The Fall of Public Man* (New York, 1977).

Alone's in *Bleak House*, and the isolation and bewilderment of much urban experience by incidents like Florence Dombey's journey through London but the characteristic structure of a Dickens novel draws everything together. The novels begin by outlining groups of characters who are isolated from each other whilst the story proceeds by showing the often hidden links between each group. The dishonesty and greed of the financier brings ruin to the hard-working artisan in *Little Dorrit* and the distress of Joe, the street sweeper, brings sickness and disfigurement to the middle-class heroine of *Bleak House*. Whatever grief and disorientation intervenes, the novels of Dickens, like those of Mrs Gaskell for the industrial towns, always restore order.[111] There was no such outcome for the poets and novelist of the 1940s and 1950s. T. S. Eliot in the 'Wasteland' never resolved his alienation. Rose Macaulay in *The World my Wilderness* retained the bombed ruins of the late 1940s city as the place of urban children. By the late 1950s, the fictions of the city were more aggressive and confident but the urban place was a backdrop within which the characters had their experience. In *Room at the Top* and *Saturday Night and Sunday Morning* or even *A Kind of Loving,* Joe Lampton, Arthur Seaton and the rest are wrapped around by Nottingham or Warlay and can only resolve the tensions of the novel by distancing themselves from their urban place.[112]

The search for a clear relationship between key structural features such as the large unit of production and political cultures such as the aggressive sometimes violent challenges to existing forms of authority was a search which tempted both the contemporaries and historians of the middle years of the nineteenth century. The industrial towns, the rapid growth of the regional centres like Manchester and Leeds as well as the power and growth of London demanded attention. The factory, the foundry, the railway network which linked all to London were spectacular and new. The perfecting of market relationships, the spread of new forms of political knowledge and ambition and the prominence of wage labour relationships made an uneven impact and explanations seemed to be possible on a town-by-town basis. The project was the more tempting as each town was separate and discreet in its geography, its forms of government and in its elites and organisations. No simple generalisations emerged for several reasons. Each urban place experienced massive inequalities but in different ways which varied from the wage relationships of the factory, the dissatisfaction with prices paid to outworkers to the tensions of the grain market. Distribution and production were tied together by the economic structure of the market, by forces which the radicals often called 'competition'. The manner in which each place resolved the tensions created by such inequalities was not influenced by

[111] Kathleen Tillotson, *The Novels of the Eighteen-Forties* (Oxford, 1954); R. Williams, *The Country and the City* (London, 1973), pp. 176–220.
[112] John Braine, *Room at the Top* (London, 1957); Alan Sillitoe, *Saturday Night and Sunday Morning* (London, 1958); Stan Barstow, *A Kind of Loving* (London, 1960).

simple economic structures such as the size of the units of production or the proportion of wage labourers. Each town was affected by its own political history
and tradition, by the leadership of the radicals who challenged established structures of power or by the skill and values of elites who sought to conciliate or
suppress by a variety of voluntary, ideological and main-force-based means. Nor
can explanation remain focused on the urban place itself. Each place was part of
a wider network. This provided access to a variety of ideas, people, forms of
organisation and products which flowed along such networks. The visiting lecturer, the radical periodical or the fashion and consumer goods which raised
ambitions all made their impact and can probably be traced to the railway station
not the local economic or social structure.

A close examination of the evidence showed that the urban nature of place
was important in two respects. First, this provided an increasing experience of
size and density, and variety. Density was not simply a matter of people per acre
but a transactional density and a density of flows of people, goods and information. The urban place was one of ever increasing choices. It was this if nothing
else which made any simple relationship between structures and cultures unlikely
if not impossible. Secondly, the urban place was a focus of power and institutional resources. The dominant agencies of local government, the local media,
the institutions of education, culture and philanthropy and the elite belonged to
the town. This produced three overlapping phases in the relationships of culture
and structure. The first saw a rapid expansion of 'civil society'. The towns
created and developed a wide range of organisational resources. These were
dominated by principles of representation and debate. These organisations
offered people a choice of identities, politics and association. But most important experience of such organisation enabled people in the towns to negotiate
and persuade. Such negotiations might address economic inequalities or religious differences. Cultural and political outcomes depended as much on variations in cultural and institutional resources as upon the balance of economic
interests. Birmingham, rich in institutional resources, produced a powerful
municipal culture very different from fragmented Sheffield, although both had
economic structures which depended upon small workshops and a small number
of major capitalist employers. The dominance of this municipal culture from the
1870s marked the second phase. Identity and pride were based upon the achievements of a local government led by selected members of the local economic and
professional elite. By the 1920s, populations turned naturally to municipal
government to secure their living standards and much of their leisure. In St
Helens 'men from the town hall would pump gas into the place to kill infection'.[113] The 1920s and 1930s saw the beginnings of the collapse of this close
relationship between the urban place, civil society and the municipal. The towns

---

[113] Forman, *Industrial Town*, p. 150.

were abandoned by their elite. The middle class withdrew into their suburbs. The working-class claim to the town was expressed in many ways from labour politics to football teams. Elites were now organised around national and specialist groups. Even the labour movement provided a means of taking part in national events and organisations. The general strike or the National Health Service ignored and overlay the specific nature of the urban. These were only some of the forces which led to the fragmentation of the specific urban place. By the 1960s the urban places of Britain had become an urban society.

PART III

Construction

14

Patterns on the ground: urban form, residential structure and the social construction of space

COLIN G. POOLEY

(i) INTRODUCTION

IT CAN be suggested that the analysis of space is particularly relevant to large urban areas. There is general acknowledgement in much sociological and geographical literature that the processes of modernisation and urbanisation have both changed the ways in which spaces are used and created feelings of placelessness in urban areas.[1] Whilst reviewing studies of the cultural meaning of space, R. Rotenberg suggests that 'urban agglomeration invites special treatments of space',[2] whilst M. La Gory and J. Pipkin develop a more extended argument supporting the significance of space for urban areas:

> Spatial structure is particularly important to the city, for urban society is composed of diverse groups living close to one another. The city is a compact community. Land is relatively scarce; thus the urban space is necessarily highly organized and segregated. Space is a major social force literally shaping the lives of those within the urban container. We make the city, but once created it remakes us. The buildings we occupy and the neighborhoods we reside in restrict our activities. The buildings and neighborhoods not only limit our social participation but also influence what we think and feel about others who share our city.[3]

Although this argument is directed mainly at studies of the contemporary American city, its sentiments can equally easily be applied to British cities in the nineteenth and twentieth centuries. In focusing on the 'socio-spatial dialectic'[4]

---

[1] E. Relph, *Place and Placelessness* (London, 1976); D. Harvey, *The Condition of Postmodernity* (Oxford, 1989); D. Massey, *Space, Place and Gender* (Cambridge, 1994); D. Harvey, *Justice, Nature and the Geography of Difference* (Oxford and Cambridge, Mass., 1996).

[2] R. Rotenberg and G. McDonogh, eds., *The Cultural Meaning of Urban Space* (Westport, Conn., 1993), p. xii.

[3] M. La Gory and J. Pipkin, *Urban Social Space* (Belmont, Calif.,1981), p. 3.

[4] E. Soja, 'The socio-spatial dialectic', *Annals of the Association of American Geographers*, 70 (1980), 207–25; See also M. Dear and J. Wolch, 'How territory shapes social life', in J. Wolch and M. Dear, eds., *The Power of Geography* (Boston, 1989), pp. 3–18.

this chapter essentially attempts to examine the ways in which people made urban spaces and, in turn, were influenced by the spaces in which they lived and worked. The main focus of the chapter is on residential space, but more limited reference is also made to spaces through which people passed, or in which they spent varied periods of time for work, consumption, leisure or social activities. Following discussion of some theoretical considerations, the chapter outlines national trends from the 1840s to the 1950s before illustrating these themes through specific case studies drawn from provincial towns for which relevant data exist. The built form of urban areas, especially housing, is related to the social construction and meanings ascribed to spaces inhabited by urban populations. A detailed consideration of London is presented above in Chapter 3.

(ii) CONCEPTS OF SPATIAL STRUCTURE

Urban spaces are almost always contested in terms of their production, use and meaning. The city, past and present, has been created from debates over the production and design of space, structured by competition for space by urban populations and viewed through the varied meanings that urban inhabitants ascribe to both public and private spaces.[5] Although, traditionally, urban residential space has received most attention, and was arguably the space in which many people spent most of their time, attention has also recently been focused on the contestation of other public and private spaces including streets, parks, squares, shops and workplaces in cities in many parts of the world.[6] Moreover, representations and meanings of space, both residential and non-residential, are fundamentally structured by class, ethnicity and gender.[7] The same space may be viewed and used in contrasting ways by different urban residents. This section outlines some of the more influential approaches to the study of urban spatial structure and highlights some issues of particular relevance to the study of British cities from the mid-nineteenth century.

[5] P. Howell, 'Public space and the public sphere: political theory and the historical geography of modernity', *Environment and Planning D: Society and Space*, 11 (1993), 303–22; A. Madanipour, 'Urban design and dilemmas of space', *Environment and Planning D: Society and Space*, 14 (1996), 253–78; A. Madanipour, *Design of Urban Space* (Chichester, 1996).

[6] M. Harrison, 'Symbolism, ritualism and the location of crowds in early-nineteenth century English towns', in D. Cosgrove and S. Daniels, eds., *The Iconography of Landscape* (Cambridge, 1988), pp. 194–213; J. Lawrence, 'Geographical space, social space and the realm of the department store', *UH*, 19 (1992), 64–83; P. Goheen, 'The ritual of the street in mid-nineteenth century Toronto', *Environment and Planning D: Society and Space*, 11 (1993), 127–45; P. Goheen, 'Negotiating access to public space in mid-nineteenth century Toronto', *Journal of Historical Geography*, 20 (1994), 430–49; A. Brown-May, 'A charitable indulgence: street stalls and the transformation of public space in Melbourne, c 1850–1920', *UH*, 23 (1996), 48–71.

[7] G. Pratt and S. Hanson, 'Gender, class and space', *Environment and Planning D: Society and Space*, 6 (1988), 15–35; M. Huxley and H. Winchester, 'Residential differentiation and social reproduction: the inter-relations of class, gender and space', *Environment and Planning D: Society and Space*, 9 (1991), 233–40.

Early ecological work focused on the ways in which distinctive groups of the population associated themselves with particular areas of the city, and developed biological analogies of the way in which urban society functioned. These were based on 'natural' processes of competition and dominance through which urban society was divided into separate biotic and cultural levels, with the spatial order of the city primarily resulting from competition at the biotic level.[8] Although such deterministic arguments have been rejected by most authors, the broad principles have been influential in much later work. Thus much of the debate about the nature and extent of residential segregation in nineteenth-century towns, and the degree of 'modernity' achieved by such cities, draws its inspiration from the Chicago School of urban ecology.[9]

Criticism of ecological approaches has led researchers to embrace a wider range of social theory in the examination of social and spatial structure. In the 1960s behavioural approaches were common, based on analysis of the decision-making process in residential location but, given the difficulty of researching decisions in the past, such models have been applied only to a limited extent in historical studies.[10] Much more influential has been the development of Marxian analysis, not least because of the obvious relevance of the writings of Marx and Engels to the process of urbanisation and the development of a class-based urban society.

Application of Marxian analysis to the study of spatial structure starts from the assumption that one of the main functions of the city is to meet the needs of capitalism. This can be achieved through a number of processes.[11] First, the segregated industrial city is structured in such a way that it facilitates the circulation and accumulation of capital through the reduction of production and exchange costs for entrepreneurs. Second, the spatial structure of the city encourages the reproduction of established relationships between labour and capital. The

[8] G.Theodorson, ed., *Studies in Human Ecology* (New York, 1961); P. Knox, *Urban Social Geography*, 3rd edn (Harlow, 1995), pp. 157–76; D. W. G. Timms, *The Urban Mosaic* (London, 1971); R. Park and E. Burgess, eds., *The City* (Chicago, 1967); R. Sennett, ed., *Classic Essays on the Culture of Cities* (New York, 1969).

[9] D. Ward, 'Victorian cities: how modern?', *Journal of Historical Geography*, 1 (1975), 135–52; D. Ward, 'Environs and neighbours in the "Two Nations": residential differentiation in mid-nineteenth century Leeds', *Journal of Historical Geography*, 6 (1980), 133–62; J. H. Johnson and C. G. Pooley, eds., *The Structure of Nineteenth-Century Cities* (London, 1982), pp. 195–298; R. Dennis, *English Industrial Cities of the Nineteenth Century* (Cambridge, 1984), pp. 200–49.

[10] J. Wolpert, 'Behavioural aspects of the decision to migrate', *Papers and Proceedings of the Regional Science Association*, 15 (1965), 159–69; L. Brown and E. Moore, 'The intra-urban migration process: a perspective', *Geografiska Annaler*, 52B (1970), 1–13; R. Golledge, 'A behavioural view of mobility and migration research', *Professional Geographer*, 31 (1980), 14–21; C. G. Pooley, 'Choice and constraint in the nineteenth-century city: a basis for residential differentiation', in Johnson and Pooley, eds., *The Structure*, pp. 199–234.

[11] D. Harvey, 'Class structure in a capitalist society and the theory of residential differentiation', in R. Peel *et al.*, eds., *Processes in Physical and Human Geography* (London, 1975), pp. 354–72; D. Harvey, *The Urbanization of Capital* (Oxford, 1985); D. Harvey, *Consiousness and the Urban Experience* (Oxford, 1985); I. Katznelson, *Marxism and the City* (Oxford, 1992).

segregation of working-class neighbourhoods and the mobility constraints placed on the poor, which affect all aspects of their daily life, are factors which perpetuate capitalist structures in the relationship between classes. Third, the city encapsulates many of the contradictions of a capitalist society as urban areas undergo change and groups with different stakes in the capitalist system compete with each other for urban space and resources. Thus in conflicts over city-centre redevelopment, small business men and women often lose out to larger enterprises. Fourth, the city is the major arena in which the state acts as a legitimating agent to support capitalist structures and diffuse discontent through schemes such as social housing and welfare payments. The ways in which these are allocated frequently lead to further segregation between groups and can have long-term effects on the spatial structure of the city. Marxian analysis has been extensively criticised for its determinism, but the application of Marxian social theory can still provide a powerful and relevant framework for historical research on urban social and spatial structures.

More recently developed post-structural or post-modern approaches to the study of urban spatial structure have often attempted to retain some elements of Marxian analysis, but have combined this with a stronger element of human agency. Central to much of this analysis is the concept of power: urban space is a resource which is contested and control over space conveys advantages to some and disbenefits to others. Structuration theory attempts to combine the analysis of structure and human agency and, as such, it is well suited to the analysis of urban spatial structure.[12] In this context, structuration theory argues that urban space is produced by human actors who operate within the constraints imposed by societal structures. The key focus of action is the intersection of structure and agency, often mediated through institutional structures where, through everyday social practices, people both adapt to the constraints of structures and, in some cases, influence and change structures over time. Some of these processes can be clearly illustrated through a study of the struggle for control over public space in the West End of London as residents sought to reinforce the exclusivity of their residential environment and associated public spaces. Peter Atkins argues that

> the West End was a gilded cage of privilege, the limits of which were constituted not only in the informal and subtle manipulation of the 'quality' of its residential neighbourhoods and communities, but also more crudely through the blockading of streets to keep out undesirables and to restrict or ban access to traffic. In the second half of the nineteenth century there was a shift in public opinion about the balance between public and private rights in the street, symbolic of the wider

[12] A. Giddens, *The Constitution of Society* (Cambridge, 1984). See also N. Gregson, 'Structuration theory: some thoughts on the possibilities of empirical research', *Environment and Planning D: Society and Space*, 5 (1987), 73–91; C. Bryant and D. Jary, eds., *Giddens' Theory of Structuration* (London, 1991); A. Pred, *Making Histories and Constructing Human Geographies* (Boulder, 1990); D. Gregory, *Regional Transformation and Industrial Revolution* (London, 1982).

changes in society which gradually eroded elite power. The eventual freeing of the streets in the 1890s marked the conclusion of a period of struggle and debate about the penetration of privatized space by the public realm, the balance having shifted from the exclusive to the inclusive.[13]

Structuration theory has been criticised for its relative neglect of unforeseen, unintended and unconscious actions, and for its failure to embrace issues of ethnicity and gender,[14] but in its focus on the socio-spatial dialectic of the relationship between people and places it can clearly highlight the processes through which spaces were contested between individuals, vested interests and institutions.

Structuration theory draws heavily on the notion of time-geography developed by Torsten Hagerstrand.[15] His basic model examines the constraints of space and time on individual social practices, and may be used to illustrate the ways in which groups of people facing similar constraints can be thrown together in their time-space activities, thus creating distinctive patterns of social activity and forming the basis of everyday social segregation. These ideas have been elaborated by David Harvey in his 'grid of spatial practices'[16] which links social and cultural theories in the context of space and time. According to Paul Knox, this framework provides 'one way of accommodating a broader, richer array of issues in addressing the ways in which places are constructed and experienced as material artefacts, how they are represented, and how they become used as symbolic spaces in contemporary culture'.[17] Harvey's work thus links the concepts of space and time developed in social theory, to contemporary cultural theory and, whilst retaining some elements of Marxian analysis, demonstrates the ways in which social geography has embraced cultural studies. Analyses of the ways in which urban space were contested also draw heavily on the work of Henri Lefebvre who identified three dimensions of space – mental, physical and social – which he argued should create a unity in the production of the urban environment. He identified three key elements: spatial practice, or the ways in which space is organised and used; representations of space, conceived mainly by architects, planners and those in control of urban environments; and representational space, or the images and meanings associated with space by those

---

[13] P. J. Atkins, 'How the West End was won: the struggle to remove street barriers in Victorian London', *Journal of Historical Geography*, 19 (1993), 266.

[14] Gregson, 'Structuration theory'; Bryant and Jary, *Giddens' Theory*; N. Thrift, 'The arts of living, the beauty of the dead: anxieties of being in the work of Anthony Giddens', *Progress in Human Geography*, 17 (1993), 111–21.

[15] T. Hagerstrand, 'What about people in Regional Science?', *Papers and Proceedings of the Regional Science Association*, 24 (1970), 7–21; T. Hagerstrand, 'Survival and arena: on the life history of individuals in relation to their geographic environment', in T. Carlstein, D. Parkes and N. Thrift, eds., *Timing Space and Spacing Time* (London, 1978), pp. 122–45. On time see B. Adams, *Timewatch* (London, 1995); B. Adams, *Time and Social Theory* (London, 1990).

[16] Harvey, *The Condition*, pp. 211–25.

[17] P. Knox, *Urban Social Geography*, 3rd edn (Harlow, 1995), p. 222.

who use it.[18] Such varied concepts of space are clearly identifiable in the contestation of residential and public space outlined in the study of the West End cited above.

Recent work on the cultural meaning of space, which can be extended to studies of the past as easily as it can be applied to the present, draws on a wide range of cultural theory. The work of Pierre Bourdieu has been especially influential, particularly his concept of 'habitus' which focuses on the construction of meaning in everyday lifeworlds.[19] Whilst 'habitus' is related to objective criteria such as class, gender and ethnicity, it is additionally and crucially a 'distinctive set of values, cognitive structures and orienting practices: a collective perceptual and evaluative schema that derives from its members' everyday experience and operates at a subconscious level, through commonplace daily practices, dress codes, use of language, comportment and patterns of material consumption'.[20] For the study of urban spatial structure, the extent to which those concepts which create 'habitus' have spatial meaning and expression is critical, though the discovery of everyday cultural values in the past is not without difficulty. In present-day studies cultural expression is often associated with patterns of consumption: where you shop, the things you buy and the way you furnish your home are expressions of cultural identity. Patterns of consumption are also inherently spatial as the settings in which consumption takes place are infused with signs and symbols which generate cultural meaning.[21] The same arguments can be applied to past society, although the nature and diversity of cultural expression in urban space may have been rather different.

For most people their home is the single most important expression of position in society, containing and expressing many layers of cultural and social meaning. The built environment is also central to an understanding of the spatial structure of cities, and hence the study of residential space, and the ways in which housing takes on social and cultural identity, is particularly fruitful. At the urban scale community formation and social interaction are affected by the activities of architects, designers, developers and planners who impose their views of the ways in which urban space should be organised, but may not have taken into account the needs of residents. The design of public urban space is also in the hands of a few with power and, as with much Victorian city-centre redevelop-

---

[18] H. Lefebvre, *The Production of Space* (Oxford, 1991). See also Madanipour, 'Urban design and dilemmas of space', 342.

[19] P. Bourdieu, *Distinctions*, trans. R. Nice (London, 1984). See also P. Shurmer-Smith and K. Hannam, *Worlds of Desire, Realms of Power* (London, 1994); R. Shields, *Places on the Margin* (London, 1991); D. Sibley, *Geographies of Exclusion* (London, 1995); C. Philo, ed., *New Words, New Worlds* (Lampeter, 1991). [20] Knox, *Urban Social Geography*, p. 224.

[21] G. Pratt, 'The house as an expression of social worlds', in J. Duncan, ed., *Housing and Identity* (London, 1981), pp. 135–80; D. Rose, 'Rethinking gentrification', *Environment and Planning D: Society and Space*, 2 (1984), 47–74; D. Ley, 'Styles of the times: liberal and neo-conservative landscapes in inner Vancouver, 1968–1986', *Journal of Historical Geography*, 13 (1987), 40–56; S. Lash and J. Urry, *Economies of Signs and Space* (London, 1994).

ment, may symbolise the wealth and achievements of a small elite group. But the ways in which such spaces are used can be structured by the views and experiences of many ordinary citizens: at the micro-scale, perceptions of different types of housing form, patterns of occupancy and household structures affect the cultural and social meanings that individuals attach to particular spaces.[22]

Space and its cultural associations are clearly differentiated commodities, and not all groups have equal access to the most desirable spaces or find that the existing urban structure serves them well. The development of feminist social and cultural theory has focused attention particularly on gender issues in the use and organisation of space: many of the spaces that women use most are constructed by and controlled by men.[23] However, women are not the only groups that may be marginalised in the urban structure: the poor, the aged, children, the disabled and ethnic minorities amongst others may find that the urban spatial structure in which they live does not suit their needs. Awareness of urban space, the ways in which it is used, and the meanings that it holds are also differentiated by such factors as gender, age, ethnicity, class and disability. Typically, women and small children may spend most time in and around the home, thus the quality and convenience of the residential environment has particular salience for these groups, and their wider perception of urban spatial structure will be constrained by limited mobility. Space is not a static commodity. Although locations are fixed, the uses and meanings attached to particular places change over time. Thus suburban expansion, offering improved living conditions to some, may have totally destroyed the homes of residents in a small village engulfed by that expansion. The restructuring of urban space also varied between different categories of town. Urban size, the nature of the economy and topographic features may all have influenced the changing spatial form of towns at the local level. The analysis of urban spatial structure to be developed in the remainder of this chapter draws on some of the social and cultural theories outlined above, but focuses particularly on the residential environment, and on ways in which the experience and meaning of space was differentiated in the past.

(iii) THE CHANGING STRUCTURE OF BRITISH TOWNS

This section describes and explains some of the principal changes in urban form from the 1840s to the 1950s, focusing on the implications of these shifts for the

[22] D. Appleyard, 'The environment as a social symbol', *Journal of the American Planning Association*, 45 (1979), 143–53; A. Buttimer, 'Social space and the planning of residential areas', in A. Buttimer and D. Seaman, eds., *The Human Experience of Space and Place* (London, 1980), pp. 21–54; R. Shields, 'Social spatialization and the built environment: the West Edmonton Mall', *Environment and Planning D: Society and Space*, 7 (1989), 147–64; M. J. Daunton, *House and Home in the Victorian City* (London, 1983).

[23] S. Bowlby, ed., 'Women and the environment', *Built Environment*, 10 (1984); Pratt and Hanson, 'Gender, class and space'; L. McDowell, 'Space, place and gender relations. Parts 1 and 2', *Progress in Human Geography*, 17 (1993), 157–79, 305–18.

lives of urban residents. This will be achieved by addressing three related questions. First, what were the main changes in urban form? Second, were there measurable alterations in levels of residential segregation? Third, did the significance and meanings attached to urban space by city residents change?

With relatively few exceptions, the main dimensions of Britain's urban hierarchy, and the associated characteristics of urban form, were established by the 1840s.[24] London was already a sprawling metropolis of over 1.8 million people in 1841, and provincial cities such as Liverpool, Manchester, Birmingham and Glasgow each had well-established urban structures with populations in excess of 180,000.[25] Exceptions were the newly emerging urban centres: industrial towns such as Barrow (which grew from a hamlet of around 200 people in 1841 to a town of 51,712 population in 1891); resorts such as Blackpool (1,304 (including visitors) in 1841 and 23,846 in 1891); or expanding residential suburbs, especially around London, which grew rapidly in the twentieth century (for instance Chingford (Essex) grew from 2,731 in 1891 to 48,355 in 1951, and Hornchurch (Essex) from 3,841 in 1891 to 104,092 in 1951).[26] The fact that the majority of Britain's urban settlements were well established by the mid-nineteenth century meant that changes in urban form were created either through industrial or suburban expansion or through the restructuring of existing space. This was especially important in that such processes also led to the restructuring of urban communities and to changes in the everyday lives of urban dwellers.

Although in some respects all locations are unique, every British town was affected by some of the same processes which restructured urban form from the mid-nineteenth century. Demographic change was crucial to the restructuring of most urban centres. Voluntary out-migration, declining fertility and an ageing population were already apparent in many inner-urban areas, though such demographic processes were differentiated by city size, with large urban areas losing most population from their inner districts from the 1850s, and many small towns retaining their central communities. However, by the twentieth century almost all towns experienced central decline and suburban expansion as those able to move voluntarily took advantage of improved suburban living conditions. Demographic change was exacerbated by the processes of commercial and

[24] C. M. Law, 'The growth of urban population in England and Wales, 1801–1911', *Transactions of the Institute of British Geographers*, 41 (1967), 125–43; B. T. Robson, *Urban Growth* (London, 1973); G. E. Cherry, *Cities and Plans* (London, 1988); T. Slater, ed., *The Built Form of Western Cities* (Leicester, 1990); J. W. R. Whitehand, *The Making of the Urban Landscape* (Oxford, 1992).

[25] On London see D. J. Olsen, *The Growth of Victorian London* (London, 1976); K. Young and P. Garside, *Metropolitan London* (London, 1982); H. Clout and P. Wood,, eds., *London* (Harlow, 1986). On provincial cities see for example Dennis, *English Industrial Cities*; A. Briggs, *Victorian Cities* (London, 1963); G. Gordon, ed., *Regional Cities in the UK, 1890–1980* (London, 1986).

[26] J. D. Marshall, *Furness and the Industrial Revolution* (Barrow-in-Furness, 1958); J. K. Walton, *The English Seaside Resort* (Leicester, 1983); A. A. Jackson, *Semi-Detached London* (London, 1973); F. M. L. Thompson, ed., *The Rise of Suburbia* (Leicester, 1982).

industrial development which particularly affected older residential neighbour-hoods from the mid-nineteenth century. Large cities and smaller expanding towns faced pressures for commercial redevelopment in the central business district and for an expanded range of civic buildings and associated services. Such activity disrupted existing inner-urban communities and forced up land values, thus pushing out residential development. Central areas of commercial cities such as Manchester were also affected by the expansion of warehouses and offices, whilst residential communities adjacent to canal or dock-side industry were affected by the mid-Victorian rebuilding and expansion of many industrial premises.[27] Although the extent to which towns were affected by such processes varied with urban size (larger settlements in most cases feeling the greatest effects) and with local and national economic conditions – for instance, northern industrial towns underwent substantial restructuring in the second half of the nineteenth century but moved into a period of relative recession in the twentieth century as the focus of economic activity shifted to southern and Midland England[28] – all settlements experienced some of the same processes of urban change.

Technological change also affected the form of cities from the 1840s. All towns depend for their economic livelihood on the ability to move goods and people around, but the ways in which such movement took place fundamentally influenced the structure of cities. Until the late nineteenth century most people walked to work, constrained by the cost and availability of transport. Thus residential areas were tied quite closely to industrial and commercial districts. Gradually, development of the horse-drawn omnibus (from the 1840s), trams from the 1870s and, especially in London, suburban rail connections allowed larger numbers of people to live further from their workplace. The provision of infrastructure associated with transport innovations also changed the city. Tramlines were laid on widened streets, railway companies acquired large areas of land for sidings and engine sheds, and competed with other uses for prestigious central sites for mainline stations. Such development often threatened central residential areas and forced residents to move elsewhere. In the twentieth century the increased use of personal transport, the bicycle, motorcycle and car, further reduced constraints on where people could live and influenced the

---

[27] H. B. Rodgers, 'The suburban growth of Victorian Manchester', *Transactions of the Manchester Geographical Society*, 58 (1961–2), 1–12; R. Varley, 'Land use analysis in the city centre with special reference to Manchester' (MA thesis, University of Wales, 1968). More generally see Jackson, *Semi-Detached London*; Thompson, *Rise of Suburbia*; R. Lawton and C. G. Pooley, 'The social geography of nineteenth-century cities: a review', in D. Denecke and G. Shaw, eds., *Urban Historical Geography* (Cambridge,1988), pp. 159–74.

[28] J. Langton and R. J. Morris, eds., *Atlas of Industrialising Britain, 1780–1914* (London, 1986); C. H. Lee, 'Regional growth and structural change in Victorian Britain', *Ec.HR*, 2nd series, 34 (1981), 438–52; M. Jones, 'The economic history of the regional problem in Britain, 1920–1938', *Journal of Historical Geography*, 10 (1984), 385–95.

design of new residential suburbs and the redevelopment of older urban areas.[29] Motorised transport demanded wider streets. From the 1930s junctions were redesigned with traffic lights to accommodate increased traffic volumes, houses were increasingly built with garages and urban streets had to accommodate increased numbers of parked and moving vehicles. By the 1950s the volume of motorised traffic in cities was fundamentally affecting the quality of life of many urban residents.[30]

In parallel with the above processes, the changing aspirations of individuals and families were also affecting the form of cities. Particularly from the 1920s, families were expecting and demanding improved housing in suburban residential environments. Those aspiring to new life styles fuelled the residential expansion of the interwar period, and encouraged the relative neglect of inner-urban communities and the expansion of suburbs through both private and local authority housing schemes. Planned intervention in the urban environment also caused further dislocation in inner-city areas. Although slum clearance was minimal and piecemeal in most towns in the nineteenth century, from the 1890s many towns embarked on a more vigorous programme of slum clearance (especially effective from the 1930s), which destroyed many inner-urban communities and fundamentally changed the structure of urban areas.[31]

Whilst urban form clearly changed from the mid-nineteenth century, there is more debate about the extent to which levels of residential segregation increased over the same period. A simplistic view of the British city undergoing a transition from a largely unsegregated pre-industrial form to a highly segregated 'modern' state is clearly inappropriate.[32] There is need to consider not only the varied processes producing segregation, but the different scales at which segregation occurred and the meanings attached to segregated space.

In his study of mid-Victorian Leeds, David Ward emphasised the extent to which many areas of the city contained residents drawn from a range of social groups.[33] Although the extremes of rich and poor were segregated, in many neighbourhoods there was a clear mixing of the population. Ward argued that it was only in the late nineteenth century that the development of improved urban

---

[29] D. Cannadine and D. Reeder, eds., *Exploring the Urban Past* (Cambridge, 1982), pp. 87–118; H. J. Dyos and D. Aldcroft,. *British Transport* (Leicester, 1969); D. H. Aldcroft and M. J. Freeman, eds., *Transport in the Industrial Revolution* (Manchester, 1983); J. R. Kellett, *The Impact of Railways on Victorian Cities* (London, 1969); W. H. Bett and J. C. Gillham, *Great British Tramway Networks* (London, 1967).

[30] R. Tolley, *Calming Traffic in Residential Areas* (Tregaron, 1989); M. Hillman, J. Adams and J. Whitelegg, *One False Move* (London, 1990).

[31] Young and Garside, *Metropolitan London*; A. Ravetz, *Model Estate* (London, 1974); M. Young and P. Willmott, *Family and Kinship in East London* (London, 1957); J. A. Yelling, *Slums and Redevelopment* (London, 1992).

[32] Timms, *Urban Mosaic*. See also the discussion in Dennis, *English Industrial Cities*, pp. 200–49, and Johnson and Pooley, eds., *The Structure*, pp. 195–298.

[33] Ward, 'Victorian cities'; Ward, 'Environs and neighbours'.

transport systems enabled a 'modern' segregated city to emerge. However, other studies have come to rather different conclusions. In Liverpool, a high degree of segregation between socio-economic and migrant groups has been demonstrated from the mid-nineteenth century and, at a smaller scale, studies of Wolverhampton, Cardiff, Merthyr Tydfil and Plymouth amongst others have suggested varying degrees of segregation from the 1850s.[34] It can be suggested that all these studies seek too rigidly to fit British urban structure into an inappropriate ecological framework of transition towards a 'modern' urban structure derived from the work of the Chicago School in the 1920s, but collectively they do demonstrate the complexity of urban residential segregation.

Much of the difference between Ward and other researchers can be accounted for by differences in the methods and categories used in different studies, and there is little evidence that there were any real differences in the levels of segregation experienced in the major British cities.[35] In the mid-nineteenth century, all towns demonstrated some differentiation between social and ethnic groups with, not surprisingly, the most noticeable segregation in larger cities. However, in all towns, and most markedly in smaller places, there was still a good deal of residential intermixing of the population in particular localities. As the nineteenth century progressed the processes outlined above, which shaped and changed urban form, also affected levels of segregation. Gradually more people could afford to live further from their workplaces, restructuring of the economy changed the location of industry, and increased personal mobility and a more differentiated housing market widened residential choice. For many, however, constraints were as significant as choice of residential location. Power to acquire access to desirable urban residential space was crucial, and those caught up in slum clearance schemes in the 1890s or 1930s had little residential choice. Thus the development of substantial local authority housing estates around towns heightened levels of segregation and, in some cases, led to physical barriers between private and corporation housing developments despite their close proximity. At the same time inner-city communities became increasingly neglected and marginalised, leading to high levels of segregation between the old, the poor and recent immigrants who mainly lived in inner-urban areas and the majority of the suburbanising population.[36]

---

[34] R. Lawton and C. G. Pooley, *The Social Geography of Merseyside in the Nineteenth Century* (Final Report to the SSRC, 1976); M. Shaw, 'The ecology of social change: Wolverhampton, 1851–1871', *Transactions of the Institute of British Geographers*, new series, (1977), 332–48; H. Carter and S. Wheatley, *Merthyr Tydfil in 1851* (Cardiff, 1982); C. R. Lewis, 'A stage in the development of an industrial town: a case study of Cardiff, 1845–1875', *Transactions of the Institute of British Geographers*, new series (1979), 129–52; M. Brayshay and V. Pointon, 'Migration and the social geography of mid-nineteenth century Plymouth', *The Devon Historian*, 28 (1984), 3–14.

[35] C. Pooley, 'Residential differentiation in Victorian cities: a reassessment', *Transactions of the Institute of British Geographers*, new series, 9 (1984), 131–44.

[36] Demonstrated by a wide range of inner area studies in the 1970s. For example HMSO, *Change and Decay* (London, 1977). See also A. Coleman, *Utopia on Trial* (London, 1985).

The pattern and process of intra-urban residential mobility is crucial to under-standing changing levels of residential segregation, but few studies have charted individual residential mobility from the 1840s to the 1950s. In his study of Leicester, Roger Pritchard demonstrates the way in which levels of mobility increased from the late nineteenth century into the twentieth century, and studies focused solely on nineteenth-century residential mobility have clearly shown the way in which most people moved frequently within local communities. Longer-distance moves were most often undertaken by those with higher incomes, and the effect of this residential movement within urban areas was to sustain working-class communities but gradually to increase levels of segregation between groups as those on higher incomes distanced themselves from the least attractive neighbourhoods.[37]

It should also be noted that, even in localities which appeared to be relatively mixed in residential terms, neighbours from different social strata did not neces-sarily interact with each other. High-class districts always contained a large service class designed to serve the rich, but the relationship between these neigh-bours was formal and instrumental. Despite living close together they were not part of the same community. Similarly, in other neighbourhoods, the fact that people lived close together did not mean that they interacted with each other. For instance, they could be segregated in time and space through the rhythms of their everyday lives.[38] Thus in late nineteenth-century suburbs, although clerks and skilled factory workers on similar incomes may have lived close to each other, the location of their workplaces and their hours of employment could mean that they rarely met on the street. The development process also increased social seg-regation as high-status areas inevitably attracted appropriate shops, cafés and other facilities which attracted their patrons from particular ranks of society. This is clearly demonstrated by Donald Olsen in the context of Victorian London who cites the *Builder* of 1867 on the development of the Grosvenor estate:

> In the first instance mansions are built for the ultra wealthy; a smaller class of house, equal as to taste and locality, is provided for those equal in degree, though not in requirements; first-class shops are brought into the district to provide for them; their dependants are provided for, and a bank established; the result promising to be an ornament to the Metropolis.[39]

Thus, residential exclusiveness was extended to other spheres as shops, parks, res-taurants and meeting places associated with particular residential developments perpetuated segregation on a day-to-day basis.

---

[37] R. M. Pritchard, *Housing and the Spatial Structure of the City* (Cambridge, 1976); R. Dennis, 'Intercensal mobility in a Victorian city', *Transactions of the Institute of British Geographers*, new series, 2 (1977), 349–63; C. G. Pooley, 'Residential mobility in the Victorian city', *Transactions of the Institute of British Geographers*, new series, 4 (1979), 258–77.

[38] E. P. Thompson, 'Time, work discipline and industrial capitalism', *P&P*, 37 (1967), 56–97.

[39] Olsen, *Growth*, p. 146.

Social segregation also occurred by age, gender and ethnicity. The old and infirm may have been housebound and thus effectively segregated from the community in which they resided. Men and women may have rarely met outside the home because of their different activity patterns, women on suburban estates often experiencing isolation and loneliness. Migrant groups such as the Irish or Jews may have distanced themselves from neighbours because of fear of violence or a desire to retain a distinct cultural identity. Such processes of social interaction are hard to determine precisely in the past because they mostly left no permanent record, but oral studies of twentieth-century communities have suggested such patterns, and there are a small number of studies which attempt to reconstruct nineteenth-century communities from a variety of sources.[40] Diaries and life histories can sometimes give insights into the ways in which different family members utilised the community and spaces in which they lived. For instance the life history of Benjamin Shaw, who lived in Preston (Lancs.) in the early nineteenth century, indicates how his wife (Betty) 'Kept company with the lowest & poorest of the neighbours, & hearing their tales of distress, was often imposed on to help them', whereas Ben who was bent on self-improvement objected to close association with the neighbours and did not wish his wife to learn their 'bad practises'.[41] Use of local spaces and interaction with neighbours were clearly gendered in the Shaw household.

Whereas everyday social interaction was rarely recorded, unusual events such as demonstrations, riots and other occasions which caused large crowds to gather were reported in the local press and by contemporary commentators.[42] It is usually argued that urban space became more exclusive and privatised during the nineteenth century. Processes of suburbanisation, changes in transport, improved policing and surveillance all enabled at least some individuals to enjoy greater amounts of personal and private space, and to avoid the noise, crowds and potential dangers of the public urban sphere. As Mark Harrison notes, there was 'a sharp discontinuity between the city as an open stage for the enactment of civic mystery and dispute, and the city as a controlled set of enclosed spheres in which other than officially institutionalised mass activity was incomprehensible and alarming'.[43]

There was never, however, a smooth transition from a chaotic early nineteenth-century city to a more controlled and regulated twentieth-century urban

[40] J. White, *Rothschild Buildings* (London, 1980); J. White, *The Worst Street in North London* (London, 1986); R. Dennis and S. Daniels, 'Community and the social geography of Victorian cities', *UHY* (1981), 7–23; G. Kearns and C. W. J. Withers, eds., *Urbanising Britain* (Cambridge, 1991).
[41] Cited in S. D'Cruze, 'Care, diligence and "Usfull Pride" [*sic*]: gender, industrialisation and the domestic economy, *c.* 1770 to *c.* 1840', *Women's History Review*, 3 (1994), 327.
[42] G. Rudé, *The Crowd in History* (London, 1981); G. Stedman Jones, *Outcast London* (Oxford, 1971); M. Harrison, *Crowds and History* (Cambridge, 1988).
[43] Harrison, 'Symbolism, ritualism and the location of crowds', p. 195.

environment. Events such as strikes, political demonstrations and even mass leisure activities such as football matches could transform normally peaceful streets and alter the popular perception of particular urban spaces. This was particularly true of cities such as Liverpool in which there was a strong tradition of sectarian division. The first decade of the twentieth century saw heightened sectarian tension between the Roman Catholic and Protestant communities in Liverpool, prompting the chief constable to comment in 1905: 'The long continuation of this unfortunate state of affairs has caused a setback to that improvement in the peace and order of the streets . . . not only through the disturbances themselves, but also through the danger which it has attached to otherwise harmless street processions and demonstrations.'[44] Thus, a climate of sectarian clashes changed the popular perception of routine processions and parades, and created particular problems for the policing of the streets. During 1909 there were especially severe sectarian clashes, with a total of 201 incidents of riot reported by the police.[45] The following year the chief constable noted the effect such disturbances had on the social geography of the city, affecting both everyday interaction on the streets and residential segregation:

> During a period of peace from faction . . . there is more or less interchange, and it is difficult to say definitely that the people in this street are Protestants, in that Roman Catholics, but as soon as the disturbances break out the trek from each side to the other begins . . . and a wavy line of demarcation shows itself, becoming more and more definite as the disturbances continue.[46]

Thus, the residential structure of the city was affected by levels of conflict between groups and the interaction of communities on the streets. Locations perceived to be safe during periods of sectarian peace became no-go areas as tension rose. This process has, of course, been particularly evident in Belfast,[47] and the Liverpool chief constable regularly compared the situation on Merseyside to that in Northern Ireland.

It seems obvious that, as the built form of the city changed and associated levels of residential segregation increased, so the meanings attached to urban space also altered. For those people trapped in inner-city districts which became caught in a spiral of decline, perceptions of urban space must have changed dramatically from the mid-nineteenth century. Despite high-density living and acute poverty, it is usually assumed that Victorian working-class communities

[44] L. Dunning, *Report on the Police Establishment and the State of Crime* (Liverpool, 1905), p. 32.
[45] L. Dunning, *Report on the Police Establishment and the State of Crime* (Liverpool, 1909). See also E. Midwinter, 'The sectarian troubles and the Police Inquiry of 1909–10', in E. Midwinter, *Old Liverpool* (Newton Abbot, 1971), pp. 172–87.
[46] L. Dunning, *Report on the Police Establishment and the State of Crime* (Liverpool, 1910), p. 41.
[47] A. Hepburn, 'The Catholic community of Belfast, 1850–1940', in M. Engman *et al.*, eds., *Ethnic Identity in Urban Europe* (Aldershot and New York, 1992), pp. 39–70; F. Boal, 'Territoriality and class: a study of two residential areas in Belfast', *Irish Geography*, 6 (1971), 229–48; P. Doherty, 'Ethnic segregation levels in the Belfast urban area', *Area*, 21 (1989), 151–9.

were close knit and vibrant areas in which people had a strong sense of place identity. This comes through strongly in Robert Roberts' description of inner-city Salford at the turn of the century.[48] Housing conditions may have been poor, and poverty in some cases severe, but such working-class communities provided security, friendship and gave real meaning to people's lives. Even in the 1930s Walter Greenwood's fictitious account of a similar area stresses that although such areas were under increasing pressure from redevelopment and economic restructuring the sense of community survived.[49] However, since the Second World War such areas have experienced increased community disintegration, and by the 1950s many inner-urban residents instead of identifying strongly with their local community have felt increasingly trapped, marginalised and threatened by a neighbourhood which had changed dramatically. A locality which offered security to a young man in the 1920s may well have appeared threatening and alien to the same man forty years later. What once was an attractive environment is now a marginal space within a changed urban form.

The breakup of inner-city communities is the most dramatic example of areas in which place identity and the meanings attached to space have changed over time, but there are other locations in which similar processes have occurred. For those who aspired to suburban living in the 1930s, the new environment offered many benefits. However, there were also disadvantages. For some the increased costs of housing and commuting to work were more than they could afford and they became victims of suburban poverty. Many women, unable to gain work in the 1920s, found suburban life styles tedious and lonely as they missed the close-knit community of inner-city areas. Thus the aspirations and expectations of suburban living were not always borne out in reality, and initial delight with a particular environment could turn to concern and alienation as circumstances changed.[50]

The meanings attached to space have also been influenced by other changes taking place in society. As Peter Willmott and Michael Young have shown in their classic studies, the dominance of the nuclear family and the transference of social life from the wider community based on the street or public house to the home and the radio/television have also led to a changed perception of place. Whereas in the past the street was a locale for socialising, in the later twentieth century it has increasingly become at best an instrument for movement in and out of communities, and at worst a perceived threat due to high levels of traffic or fear of crime.[51] Place also means less in the twentieth century as personal

[48] R. Roberts, *The Classic Slum* (Manchester, 1971).
[49] W. Greenwood, *Love on the Dole* (London, 1933).
[50] Jackson, *Semi-Detached London*; Pilgrim Trust, *Men without Work* (Cambridge, 1938).
[51] Young and Willmott, *Family and Kinship*; M. Young and P. Willmott, *The Symmetrical Family* (London, 1973); M. J. Daunton, 'Public place and private space: the Victorian city and the working-class household', in D. Fraser and A. Sutcliffe, eds., *The Pursuit of Urban History* (London, 1983), pp. 212–33; S. Smith, *Crime, Space and Society* (Cambridge, 1986). See also R. Sindall, *Street Violence in the Nineteenth Century* (Leicester, 1990).

mobility has increased and time–space compression has taken place. Not only can people travel further, more quickly and easily, but increasingly they are able to control the environment in which they travel. In terms of place identity there is a world of difference between travelling on public transport and travelling by car. Until at least the 1940s most people travelled to work, school or recreation on foot or by public transport. They thus occupied public spaces and could have easily developed a strong sense of place identity for the localities through which they passed. Greater use of the private car from the mid-twentieth century has meant that people have been increasingly cut off from places through which they pass. Inside the car it is possible to create an artificial personal environment devoid of any affiliation with the surrounding townscape. With more home-based activities, and less need to interact with neighbours and surroundings, it can be suggested that people have created their own artificial 'habitus', distinct from the local community and almost devoid of place identity. As most people spend a large part of their lives in and around the home, and residential development has had a major impact on British urban areas, the following sections focus particularly on housing market changes since the 1840s, and examine the relationship between the provision of housing, access to housing and the use made of residential space.

(iv) THE CHANGING NATURE OF PRIVATE RESIDENTIAL SPACE

The private housing market underwent fundamental change in the century after 1840, producing alterations in housing tenure, quality, access and form. These features both reflected broader changes in the nature of society and economy and, in turn, created new ideals and aspirations which had wide-ranging implications.

In the nineteenth century most urban residents rented a house or rooms from a private landlord. Only the very rich could afford to purchase a house outright, and a small but increasing number of skilled working-class and middle-class households built and purchased their housing through the use of terminating building societies. By the late nineteenth century home ownership had attained levels of 15–20 per cent in more affluent industrial areas with stable employment (especially South Wales, east Lancashire, West Yorkshire and North-East England), but nationally no more than 10 per cent of households were owner-occupiers. Most families rented their housing and most landlords owned relatively small numbers of properties. The twentieth century saw a fundamental change in the tenure structure of cities as the ideology of home ownership became dominant and renting from a private landlord became an increasingly marginalised tenure used only by those on low incomes or seeking temporary accommodation. By 1961, 41 per cent of households in Britain were owner-occupiers (Table

Table 14.1 *Housing tenure in Britain, 1914–1961 (%)*

Year	Owner-occupied	Public rented	Private rented	Other tenures[a]
1914	10.0	1.0	80.0	9.0
1938	25.0	10.0	56.0	9.0
1951	29.0	18.0	45.0	8.0
1961	41.0	26.0	27.0	6.0

All figures before 1961 are estimates.
[a]Includes housing occupied by virtue of employment and rented from Housing Associations.
Sources: various, including M. Boddy, *The Building Societies* (London, 1980), p. 154; Census of England and Wales and Census of Scotland, 1961. See also C. Pooley, ed., *Housing strategies in Europe* (Leicester, 1992), p. 84.

14.1) and the substantial but declining numbers of households in privately rented housing were significantly disadvantaged. In Scotland rates of owner-occupancy were lower, but the same trends are observable.[52]

Six main factors explain the rise of home ownership and the decline of private renting in the twentieth century.[53] First, rising real incomes gave families a wider choice and made it possible for at least some working-class households to commit themselves to mortgage repayments. Second, a decline in the cost of ownership made renting less attractive as house construction costs fell and loan interest rates remained low. Third, building societies were becoming larger and adopted a deliberate policy of lending to individuals who were purchasing for owner-occupancy as opposed to lending mainly to landlords who purchased several houses, as had been the case in the nineteenth century. Fourth, changing aspirations within society created an environment in which families perceived home ownership to be preferable to renting. Fifth, landlords increasingly saw

---

[52] J. Burnett, *A Social History of Housing, 1815–1985*, 2nd edn (London, 1986); E. Gauldie, *Cruel Habitations* (London, 1973); S. D. Chapman, ed., *The History of Working-Class Housing* (Newton Abbot, 1971); P. H. J. H. Gosden, *Self Help* (London, 1973); S. Price, *Building Societies* (London, 1958); E. J. Cleary, *The Building Society Movement* (London, 1965); M. Boddy, *The Building Societies* (London, 1980); J. Springett, 'Building development on the Ramsden estate, Huddersfield', *Journal of Historical Geography*, 8 (1982), 129–44; Daunton, *House and Home*; H. J. Dyos, *Victorian Suburb* (Leicester, 1961); P. Aspinall, 'The internal structure of the housebuilding industry in nineteenth-century cities', in Johnson and Pooley, eds., *The Structure*, pp. 75–106; M. Doughty, ed., *Building the Industrial City* (Leicester, 1986); R. Rodger, ed., *Scottish Housing in the Twentieth Century* (Leicester, 1989).

[53] See C. Pooley, ed., *Housing Strategies in Europe* (Leicester, 1992), pp. 83–7; M. J. Daunton, *A Property-Owning Democracy?* (London, 1987); S. Merrett, *Owner-Occupation in Britain* (London, 1982).

renting as a poor investment as the political influence they had in the nineteenth century was eroded by extension of the franchise, and the imposition of rent controls in 1915 at least temporarily restricted landlords' incomes. Sixth, the activities of local authorities in slum clearance physically removed substantial numbers of rented houses in the twentieth century, whilst private rebuilding was almost entirely for owner-occupancy.

For individual families access to owner-occupied housing could be achieved through two separate routes. In the early 1920s, when there was relatively little new building in the private sector, many families who aspired to home owner-ship simply bought the house which they had previously rented (from 1914 to 1939 over 1 million rented houses were sold to owner-occupiers), but from the mid-1920s when private house construction expanded, the main route to home ownership was by purchasing a new house in the suburbs. This process was par-ticularly marked in the more prosperous towns of southern and Midland England. In northern cities hit by recession in the interwar period the expan-sion of home ownership was rather slower. Whichever route was taken, owner-occupancy usually provided better quality housing than was available in the privately rented sector. Existing property bought by sitting tenants consisted mostly of newer and larger rented housing in the inner suburbs, whilst newly built housing was almost always semi-detached and suburban. These new private estates had a considerable impact on the form of most towns as low-density development often extended beyond existing city limits whilst slum clearance sites in town centres could remain undeveloped for several years due to lack of interest by builders and developers who preferred to build in more lucrative sub-urban locations. In Scotland, traditional tenement building styles continued to be important, and a substantial proportion of new developments in cities like Glasgow and Edinburgh were in the form of suburban tenements for skilled working-class and middle-class families.[54]

Although owner-occupancy expanded rapidly in the twentieth century, and ideologically it became the dominant tenure, access to home ownership was not available to all. The main source of finance for house purchase was a loan from a building society. Although such societies had declared aims of helping ordi-nary working people to improve their housing, and were driven by large capital reserves and low interest rates to expand the range of clients to whom they lent, home ownership was restricted to those on regular incomes who could afford to move to suburban locations some distance from their place of work. Thus loans made by the Manchester and Hull branches of the Bradford Building Society in the 1930s were predominantly to those in trade, clerical work and public or professional employment. Some skilled workers in manufacturing industry

---

[54] C. G. Pooley and M. Harmer, *Property Ownership in Britain, 1850–1965* (Cambridge, 1999); M. Yeadall, 'Building Societies in the West Riding of Yorkshire and their Contribution to Housing Provision in the Nineteenth Century', in Doughty, ed., *Building the Industrial City*; Rodger, ed., *Scottish Housing*.

gained mortgages but very few with unskilled or semi-skilled occupations.[55] The benefits of expanding home ownership were not shared equally in the twentieth century.

The impact of these changes in the housing market on people's lives and the ways in which residential space was used in urban areas can be illustrated through a series of case studies of specific types of housing. This will take the form of a life cycle analysis, showing how changes in society and economy interacted with the everyday decisions of urban dwellers to structure the ways in which properties were habited during the life of particular types of housing. Four housing forms are chosen for analysis: small terrace housing built in the 1820s, an inner-city tenement block built in the 1880s, better quality terrace housing built in the first decade of the twentieth century, and suburban semi-detached housing built in the early 1930s.

Almost every town in England and Wales experienced rapid population growth in the early nineteenth century. Whilst some of this population crowded into rooms in existing properties which filtered down from the departing middle classes, there was also an expansion of new purpose-built terrace housing. Typically constructed in narrow streets close to areas of industrial employment, in northern towns in particular such housing could also be of very high density laid out in courts, sometimes back-to-back and often with a separately habited cellar. In Liverpool in 1851 such housing in a dockside area of Scotland ward was occupied by mainly unskilled and semi-skilled families,[56] many of whom lived in only one or two rooms with communal water, cooking and sanitary facilities (Figure 14.1). Space was acutely restricted in such housing and many members of the family were forced to live much of their lives in the yard or on the street. Limited residential space meant that public areas including common stairs, yards and back streets effectively became an extension of private space, with consequent implications both for community solidarity and neighbourhood squabbles. The implications of high-density living for social order were highlighted by the chief constable of Liverpool in 1903 who, commenting on a decline in violent brawls, stated: 'To the demolition of the old back to back courts may be ascribed no small part of the improvement in this matter. The enclosed courts gave two quarrelsome people no chance of getting away from each other, but only gave them a fighting ground out of sight of the constable on the beat.'[57] Whilst most men were out of the house at work for long periods, the restricted living space would have been felt especially acutely by women and children. Conditions and contemporary attitudes (in the 1860s) are summed up by the comments of journalist Hugh Shimmin on a court in Thomas Street:

[55] Pooley and Harmer, *Property Ownership*.
[56] I. Taylor, 'The court and cellar dwelling: the eighteenth-century origin of the Liverpool slum', *Transactions of the Historical Society of Lancashire and Cheshire*, 122 (1970), 67–90; Pooley, 'Choice and constraint'.
[57] L. Dunning, *Report on the Police Establishment and the State of Crime* (Liverpool, 1903), p. 15.

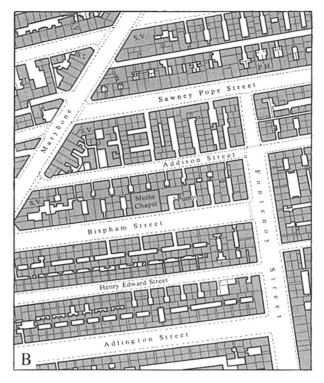

Figure 14.1 Back-to-back and court housing in Liverpool, built 1805–1815 (1848)
Source: J. A. Patmore and A. Hodgkiss, eds., *Merseyside in Maps*
(London, 1970), p. 18.

In the back part of this house . . . there is a dwelling worthy of particular attention. It is the home of a father, mother and five children. The rooms they occupy
are immediately over a stable and midden, and the privy, which is used in common,
is under the stairs. The entrance of the house is up a dark, crooked flight of stairs.
You cannot walk straight going up, the ceiling is so low, and, when you gain the
first landing the stench from below is stifling . . . The husband is in constant
employment, and was said to be very steady, but how he could reconcile himself
to look daily upon the amicable union of filth and laziness which his house exhibited was a puzzle. The convenience of this home to his labour was given as the
reason for remaining in such a doghole . . . The woman was sallow, but lively, and,
although her children had weak eyes and a sickly look, were streaked with dirt,
and gnawed at junks of bread whilst staring at us, the mother said they never
seemed to ail much.[58]

[58] H. Shimmin, *The Courts and Alleys of Liverpool* (Liverpool, 1864), pp. 11–12.

By the 1890s such housing was still occupied by poor families, though at slightly lower densities as voluntary out-migration and limited public health interventions removed some people from inner-city areas. Such housing was increasingly perceived as a public health problem as city authorities adopted a more interventionist approach to slum housing.[59]

Although housing conditions were poor for the families that lived in such districts, there would have been a strong sense of community and employment ties meant that many families that might have afforded better housing were unable to move away. Although in some towns early nineteenth-century housing was demolished in the 1890s, more typically such property survived until large-scale slum clearance schemes of the 1930s. Living conditions were often little better than the mid-nineteenth century, as recalled by a respondent eventually rehoused in the 1920s:

> We lived with my mother when we were first married. It was a little two-bed-roomed terraced house and there was my mother, aunt and cousin in one bedroom and me, my husband and the baby in the other. It was an old house, very cold and damp and it didn't have any conveniences at all. No water at all in the house. I don't know how we did it, but we had to do the washing outside.[60]

In Liverpool and other cities, a series of inner-area clearance schemes swept away slum housing and, although most families were rehoused in new corporation housing on or near the same site, traditional communities were often destroyed. Although the new schemes were welcomed by some, the disruption to established patterns of life was felt acutely by many of those dispossessed from the slums. For financial and other reasons some families chose to move into poor-quality privately rented housing elsewhere rather than live in new corporation housing schemes (see below). As one disillusioned tenant stated: 'The Corporation thought they were giving the likes of us the world, getting us out of the slums, but they didn't care that none of us could afford the bloody houses. They dumped us out here and then forgot about us.'[61]

In a Scottish city such as Glasgow similar processes were evident, but the housing form was different and, if anything, both housing conditions and poverty were worse than in English towns. All towns in Britain experienced an expansion of new private building in the 1880s. Whilst in England and Wales this mostly took the form of terrace housing, in Glasgow tenement blocks close to the city centre were the norm (Figure 14.2). In the 1890s a typical Glasgow tenement was occupied at very high density by a mixture of skilled and unskilled

[59] Yelling, *Slums and Redevelopment*; P. J. Waller, *Democracy and Sectarianism* (Liverpool, 1981).
[60] M. McKenna, 'The suburbanisation of the working-class population of Liverpool between the wars', *Soc. Hist.*, 16 (1991), 179.
[61] *Ibid.*, 185. See also D. C. Jones, ed., *Merseyside* (Liverpool, 1934); C. G. Pooley and S. Irish, 'Access to housing on Merseyside', *Transactions of the Institute of British Geographers*, new series, 12 (1987), 177–90.

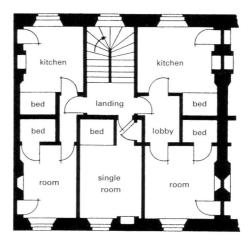

Figure 14.2 Floor plan of a typical late nineteenth-century working-class
tenement in Glasgow (internal stair, no internal sanitation)
Source: R. Rodger, 'Scotland', in C. Pooley, ed., *Housing Strategies in Europe
1880–1930* (Leicester, 1992).

working-class families. The main difference from England was the very high
level of occupancy, albeit in rather larger rooms. Perhaps eight people would
share one or two rooms for eating, sleeping and everyday living with bed spaces
curtained off from the main room to provide limited privacy. Such housing conditions fundamentally affected social interaction and use of space. Privacy was
limited and many activities would take place outside the home. With such overcrowded conditions and a lack of basic facilities cleanliness and tidiness were
difficult, and inquiries at the turn of the century demonstrated the extent to
which Scottish housing conditions affected the health of the population.[62] J. B.
Russell wrote in 1888:

> Glasgow stands alone with the highest death-rate, the highest number of persons
> per room, the highest proportion of her population occupying one-apartment
> houses, and the lowest occupying houses of five apartments and upwards . . . These
> facts prove beyond a doubt that the predominant factor in the health of cities is
> the proportion of house space to inhabitant . . . It is those small houses which give
> . . . the striking characteristics of an enormous proportion of deaths in childhood,
> and of deaths from diseases of the lungs at all ages. Their exhausted air and poor
> and perverse feeding fill our Streets with bandy-legged children.[63]

[62] Rodger, *Scottish Housing*; A. Gibb, *Glasgow* (London, 1983); R. A. Cage, ed., *The Working Class
in Glasgow, 1750–1914* (London, 1987), esp. chs. 2 and 3; A. K. Chalmers, *The Health of Glasgow,
1818–1925: An Outline* (Glasgow, 1930); A. MacGregor, *Public Health of Glasgow, 1905–46*
(Edinburgh, 1967).   [63] Quoted in Gibb, *Glasgow*, p. 136.

By the first decade of the twentieth century housing conditions in Glasgow tenements had become a major local political and social issue, with rent strikes by tenants and local women protesting vigorously about the conditions in which they had to spend most of their lives. However, things changed only slowly. Although there was some slum clearance in the 1930s, by the 1950s many such tenements were still standing, usually occupied by an increasingly marginalised population of transients, the very poor and young single people (including students) seeking temporary accommodation.[64]

At the end of the nineteenth century many towns expanded with rows of brick-built terrace housing providing much better accommodation than their mid-nineteenth-century counterparts. Providing increased space, privacy and sanitary amenities such houses were almost exclusively in single-family occupancy and attracted mainly skilled working-class and lower-middle-class households. Particularly in the more prosperous economies of southern towns such as Reading, Hastings or Bristol such properties were typically bought by sitting tenants in the 1920s. Clearly these were households that were satisfied with their housing conditions, they had sufficient space and facilities to maintain their desired life style, and they chose to take advantage of the attractions of home ownership with the minimum disruption to their everyday life.[65] However, by the 1950s such properties had become less attractive. Areas that had been outer suburbs in 1910 were now close to decaying inner-city districts, and many families left for better quality suburban housing. Those left behind were often the elderly and the very poor whilst low-income families, transient populations and recent immigrants (especially from New Commonwealth countries) took the place of those leaving. The nature of the community fundamentally changed and many families were alienated from an environment in which they had grown up. In the 1960s such property was either demolished to make way for new housing schemes or, if it survived, rehabilitated under inner-city improvement schemes of the 1970s.

Upwardly mobile families who, in the 1930s, frequently moved into new, low-density, suburban owner-occupied housing were also drawn predominantly from skilled manual and non-manual households (Table 14.2). For some this was their first experience of home ownership, but others moved from owner-occupied terrace housing they had bought earlier in the century. Cardiff is typical of a medium-sized town which developed substantial peripheral estates of privately owned housing in areas such as Whitchurch and Llandaff from the late 1920s. Families moving into such housing were almost always skilled workers, who

[64] J. Melling, *Rent Strikes* (Edinburgh, 1983); U. Wannop, 'Glasgow/Clydeside: a century of metropolitan evolution', in Gordon, ed., *Regional Cities*, pp. 83–98; S. Checkland, *The Upas Tree* (Glasgow, 1981).

[65] M. Swenarton and S. Taylor, 'The scale and nature of the growth of owner-occupation in Britain between the wars', *Ec.HR*, 2nd series, 38 (1985), 373–92; Pooley and Irish, 'Access to housing'.

Table 14.2 *Socio-economic group of mortgage clients in three northern towns in the 1930s (%)*

Socio-economic group	Hull 1928–38	Bradford 1935	Manchester 1929–38
Professional	1.5	4.2	3.8
Intermediate/managerial	19.3	18.8	21.5
Skilled non-manual	39.6	35.4	43.1
Skilled manual	35.5	34.4	26.9
Semi-skilled	1.5	5.2	3.1
Unskilled	2.5	2.1	1.5
Total with occupation	197	96	130

Sources: mortgage ledgers of Bradford Equitable Building Society and directories of Hull, Bradford and Manchester.

gained a mortgage of around £450 to enable them to purchase the property. Whilst such housing provided both good-quality accommodation and ample space for daily life, it could also lead to isolation on new estates as those moving in had few friends and were distant from places of work and recreation. The space afforded by new suburban housing allowed a more home-based life style, but to some extent this was also forced on families by the lack of alternatives within the new communities. Arguably this problem was much graver in large cities, where distances were greater, than in small towns where it was easy to travel from the suburbs to the city centre.

The links between housing change, the built form of cities, the use of space and broader societal processes are complex. Whilst predominance of the privatised nuclear family was in part produced by changes in levels of fertility, family aspirations, employment opportunities, mobility and the availability of home-based entertainment, it can be argued that the development of specific housing forms not only accommodated such changes but also encouraged them. A house which provided separate rooms for each child, in which functions of eating, sleeping and socialising were separated into distinct spaces, and in which families were cut off from neighbours by gardens and private drives encouraged people to become more inward looking and less involved with the local community. The dominant ethos of owner-occupancy also encouraged increased pride in the home, leading to more time spent on home improvements, decorating, gardening and other home-based activities.

The rise of owner-occupancy is also linked to the type of liberal democratic capitalist society that has developed in Britain in the twentieth century. All political parties have to some degree maintained a commitment to owner-occupancy since the 1920s, with widespread ownership seen, especially in the interwar period, as a way not only of distributing wealth more evenly but also of ensuring mass commitment to a capitalist society. Although home ownership has brought benefits to many in terms of improved housing, it has not been without drawbacks. Due to the dependence on large mortgage debts, ownership of property has not necessarily brought with it power and control over residential space. During the interwar recession mortgage debt became an impossible burden for some, who were forced back into the declining privately rented sector, whilst others who bought older inner-city property have seen their neighbourhood change around them in a way which they could not influence. For some the attractions of owner-occupancy turned sour, a trend which has continued into the 1980s and 1990s as negative equity caused by falling property prices has trapped many families in houses they wish to leave.[66] For such home owners the flexibility of the nineteenth-century rented property market could hold some attractions.

(v) THE CHANGING NATURE OF PUBLIC RESIDENTIAL SPACE

Whilst the private housing market was transformed from the 1840s to the 1950s from renting to ownership, the public housing market grew from nothing to account for almost one third of the housing stock of Great Britain. Public housing was especially important in Scotland and in most large urban areas: by the 1950s renting from the local authority was the single most important tenure in some British cities. Although the framework for public intervention in housing has been established through national legislation, before the First World War local by-laws and interpretation of national legislation were of most importance. Even in the twentieth century there were significant variations between places in the ways in which local authority housing was provided.[67]

In the mid-nineteenth century public intervention in housing was both limited and, for most people, politically unacceptable. Until the 1860s state intervention consisted of control and regulation of private property through limited building regulations, controls on occupancy levels, or slum clearance of severely sub-standard dwellings. All rebuilding was left to the private sector. The first council housing built for families (as opposed to corporation-built lodging houses) was begun under local legislation in Liverpool in the 1860s and

[66] Daunton, *Property-Owning Democracy?*; R. Forrest, A. Murie and P. Williams, *Home Ownership* (London, 1990); P. Saunders, *A Nation of Home Owners* (London, 1990); V. Karn, J. Kemeny and P. Williams, *Home Ownership in the Inner City* (Aldershot, 1986); R. Forrest and A. Murie, 'Home ownership in recession', *Housing Studies*, 9 (1994), 55–74.
[67] S. Merrett, *State Housing in Britain* (London, 1979); D. Niven, *The Development of Housing in Scotland* (London, 1979); Rodger, *Scottish Housing*.

completed under the Artizans' and Labourers' Dwellings Act (1868) in 1869.[68] From the 1870s to the First World War many large cities and a few smaller towns provided some local authority housing, but the amount was tiny in relation to the size of the housing problem faced in industrial towns.

Motives for the provision of social housing by local corporations in the nineteenth century were complex and variable.[69] They combined self-interest, spurred on by fear of disease and working-class revolution, with genuine concern for living conditions experienced by the poor (expressed most clearly by local campaigners with first-hand experience of urban slum conditions), and political expediency. Since the cost of all schemes had to be borne by ratepayers, and many ratepayers were also slum landlords who stood to lose by slum clearance schemes, objections to reform were considerable. However, by the 1880s there was grudging acceptance that the private market was failing to provide adequately for low-income families and that, for a variety of reasons, there should be some (preferably temporary) intervention by the state. Following the First World War the scope and nature of social housing provision by local authorities changed radically with national legislation from 1919 requiring local authorities to survey housing need and provide council housing with most of the cost provided through national taxation. Whereas prior to 1919 most municipalities had demolished more houses than they built, and thus exacerbated the housing crisis for the poor, after 1919 the scale of house construction increased dramatically (Table 14.3).[70]

Explanation of increased state involvement in housing provision is complex and, in detail, beyond the scope of this chapter. Although the First World War acted as a catalyst, concern about urban housing conditions was of much longer standing. Decline in the privately rented sector, temporary collapse of the private building industry and genuine concern about working-class protest over housing conditions all contributed to the decision by Lloyd George's Liberal government to pass new national housing legislation in 1919. Whereas in the nineteenth century the small amount of council housing constructed was designed for the very poor who were dispossessed from slum clearance schemes, after 1919 the focus shifted to general-needs provision, designed to meet the housing requirements of a much broader spectrum of the working classes. This continued, with changes in the quantity, quality and financing of schemes until 1930 when new legislation again focused attention on slum clearance and rebuilding in urban

---

[68] C. G. Pooley and S. Irish, *The Development of Corporation Housing In Liverpool 1869–1945* (Lancaster, 1984); C. G. Pooley, 'Housing for the poorest poor: slum clearance and rehousing in Liverpool, 1890–1918', *Journal of Historical Geography*, 11 (1985), 70–88.

[69] S. Lowe and D. Hughes, eds., *A New Century of Social Housing* (Leicester, 1991); Pooley, ed., *Housing Strategies*, pp. 87–93; M. J. Daunton, ed., *Councillors and Tenants* (Leicester, 1984).

[70] M. Swenarton, *Homes Fit for Heroes* (London, 1981); Daunton, ed., *Councillors and Tenants*; J. A. Yelling, *Slums and Slum Clearance in Victorian London* (London, 1986); Yelling, *Slums and Redevelopment*.

Table 14.3 *Slum clearance and rebuilding in Liverpool 1876–1940*

Years	Total houses demolished	Total houses erected	% of houses erected built by corporation[a]
1876–80	1,130	11,567	0.0
1881–5	3,099	6,704	4.0
1886–90	1,844	3,176	0.0
1891–5	4,276	1,787	5.7
1896–1900	3,975	8,683	0.5
1901–5	2,813	10,837	12.4
1906–10	2,496	10,504	4.3
1911–15	2,024	4,212	11.3
1916–20	439	496	62.9
1921–5	496	8,122	73.3
1926–30	890	20,337	68.1
1931–5	1,213	19,805	43.1
1936–40	4,561	16,249	56.6

[a]Includes houses erected by Liverpool corporation outside the city boundary.
Sources: Annual Reports of the Medical Officer of Health (Liverpool).

areas. Following the Second World War, when housing conditions had been exacerbated by the wartime cessation of house construction and by the effects of bomb damage, attention again shifted to general-needs housing with both Labour and Conservative governments committed to a high output of dwellings in both the private and public sectors in the 1940s and 1950s.

Council housing in Britain has taken a variety of forms. Before the First World War most corporation schemes for social housing were tenement blocks on central sites close to the main centres of industrial employment. Only in London, where central land values were prohibitive, did early schemes take the form of lower-density suburban building. Although some tenement blocks were large, and somewhat bleak and overpowering, others were smaller and had more subtle design features. Under the legislation of 1919 corporations were required to build at low density on suburban sites. Most properties were good-quality three-bedroom semi-detached or terrace houses, though the space and amenities provided were gradually reduced during the 1920s as subsequent legislation reduced costs. From 1930, although some general-needs provision continued, most housing was provided for slum clearance tenants. This either took the form of relatively small and cheaply built suburban housing, often inconveniently located away from transport routes and amenities, or of forbidding five-storey tenement blocks built on clearance sites in the city centre. These had the attraction of proximity to central sites of employment, and of retaining links to a local community, but high-density living in flats with some communal facilities did not suit all tenants. Following the Second World War both general-needs housing and slum clearance schemes were continued from the 1940s, with large-scale suburban estates and inner-city high-rise blocks developed in subsequent years. Cumulatively, this building activity had a massive effect on the form of cities, transforming central areas through slum clearance and redevelopment and contributing to suburban sprawl through the development of peripheral estates.[71]

Although in theory social housing was provided for those in most housing need, who were not adequately catered for in the private housing market, in practice this was not always the case. In the late nineteenth century, ratepayers were persuaded to underwrite housing schemes on the assumption that they would be self-funding. In many cases schemes were eventually a charge on the rates, but in theory at least rent income was supposed to cover loan charges and maintenance costs. This meant that councils had effectively to operate as private landlords and ensure that rental income was secure. Thus in Liverpool, for instance, although tenants dispossessed from slum housing were accommodated, the manager of Artizans' Dwellings selected those tenants who had the most secure employment and who conformed to corporation ideals of good tenants. Others were left to crowd elsewhere in the privately rented housing stock, and anyone who failed to pay rent was quickly evicted. The same principles continued after 1919. General-needs housing was not meant to provide accommodation for the poor, but to house the deserving working class who were forced into sub-standard rooms by the post-war housing crisis. In theory, the poor would be helped by vacated property filtering down to those in most need. Housing linked to slum clearance schemes in the 1930s was less selective, and councils were obliged to provide some housing for all dispossessed tenants who wanted such accommodation, but there is evidence that those who were considered the greatest risk were put in older Artizans' Dwellings, rather than new flats and houses, and others excluded themselves from council schemes on the grounds of cost. Access to most public housing schemes was thus restricted in some way, with those most disadvantaged being thrown back on the declining privately rented sector.[72]

The effects of these developments on tenants, and the ways in which new housing schemes affected communities and changed the everyday use of space,

---

[71] Pooley, 'Housing for the poorest poor'; J. Melling, *Housing, Social Policy and the State* (London, 1980); Yelling, *Slums and Slum Clearance*; Yelling, *Slums and Redevelopment*; Young and Garside, *Metropolitan London*; Swenarton, *Homes Fit for Heroes*; Daunton, ed., *Councillors and Tenants*; Pooley and Irish, *The Development of Corporation Housing*; A. Sutcliffe, *Multi-Story Living* (London, 1974); Merrett, *State Housing*; P. Balchin, *Housing Policy* (London, 1985).

[72] Pooley and Irish, *The Development of Corporation Housing*; Pooley, 'Housing for the poorest poor'; Pooley and Irish, 'Access to housing'; C. G. Pooley and S. Irish, 'Housing and health in Liverpool, 1870–1940', *Transactions of the Historic Society of Lancashire and Cheshire*, 143 (1994), 193–219.

can be illustrated through three case studies which examine the life cycle of different types of social housing. These examples are drawn from corporation housing built under local schemes from the 1890s, good-quality suburban housing built under the Addison Act of 1919, and inner-city tenements built in the 1930s. All three case studies are drawn from Liverpool which had a more vigorous programme of public housing than many cities and for which detailed information exists.

Liverpool corporation built a total of 2,895 dwellings under local schemes before 1919. Gildarts Gardens, begun in 1897 and completed in a series of stages by 1904, was among the larger schemes, eventually providing 229 flats of various sizes. As with other such schemes the blocks were built on land close to the dockside and city centre, which had been cleared of slum housing, and following the corporation's policy of restricting dwellings to those dispossessed almost all the initial tenants came from surrounding streets (Figure 14.3a). In 1905 rents for rooms in these dwellings ranged from 1s. 6d. (7.5p) for a one-room flat on the third floor to 5s. 6d. (27.5p) for four rooms on the ground floor. Household heads worked predominantly as dock labourers, general labourers, seamen and carters in 1904, but there was a vacancy rate of over 20 per cent in every year from 1903 to 1909 and in some years the corporation was losing as much as a quarter of rental income through empty flats and irrecoverable arrears. The policy of selecting only 'a better class of dispossessed' for the dwellings meant that they were very hard to fill and that, although most tenants had unskilled and casual work, they were not drawn from the most needy members of society.[73]

Most families moving into the dwellings previously lived in one or two rooms in the private sector and, although corporation tenements were new, in many respects they offered a similar living environment. They were criticised at the time for a lack of amenities (many were built cheaply with shared facilities and no hot water supply) and due to the relatively high rents many families occupied only one or two rooms. Between 1907 and 1915 overcrowding in corporation property was a frequently reported problem.[74] Levels of crowding, use of space and links to the local community would thus have changed little for most tenants of the new dwellings. Whilst some families settled and remained in corporation dwellings for many years, the high vacancy rate reflected not only the difficulty that the corporation had in finding tenants, but also the fact that many left quickly due to high rents and an oppressive management regime imposed by the corporation. Such families were forced back into private rooms in the inner city. In the 1920s and 1930s, as new corporation housing became available, many families requested transfers out of old dwellings to new council flats and houses (Table 14.4). A block such as Gildarts Gardens thus rapidly became marginalised

---

[73] Liverpool Council Proceedings (1904–5), p. 426; Annual Reports of the Manager of Artizans' and Labourers' Dwellings (Liverpool); Annual Report of the Medical Officer of Health (Liverpool, 1906–7), p. 2103.

[74] Annual Reports of the Medical Officer of Health (Liverpool, 1907–15).

Figure 14.3 Origins of tenants moving to new local authority housing in
Liverpool
(a) Gildarts Gardens (built 1897–1904)

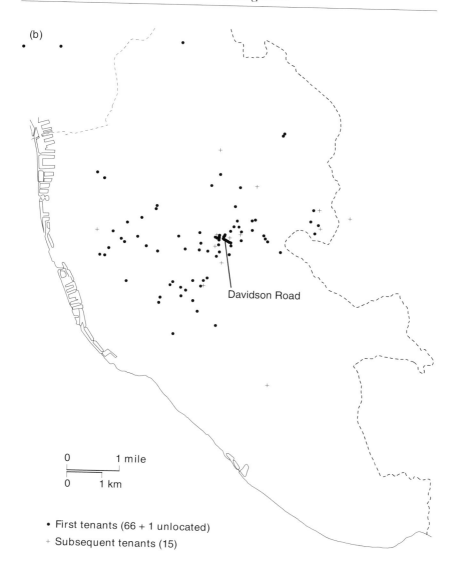

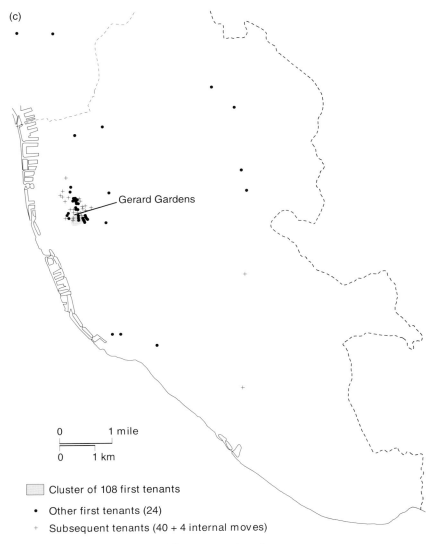

(c)

Gerard Gardens

0   1 mile
0   1 km

▨ Cluster of 108 first tenants
•   Other first tenants (24)
+   Subsequent tenants (40 + 4 internal moves)

Figure 14.3 (cont.)
(c) Gerard Gardens, 1930 act (tenements)
Source: C. G. Pooley and S. Irish, The Development of Corporation Housing in
Liverpool, 1869–1945 (Lancaster, 1984).

Table 14.4 *Characteristics of tenants of selected Liverpool corporation estates c. 1890–1945*

	Pre-1919 housing[a]	Suburban 5-room 1919 act[a]	Suburban 4-room 1924 act[a]	Inner-city tenement 1930 act[a]
A. Household characteristics				
Mean household size	3.7	4.1	4.6	5.5
% household heads (hh) female	27.0	11.8	9.4	13.6
% hh in non-manual work	2.5	30.8	8.0	0.8
% hh in skilled manual work	14.3	54.2	40.9	7.0
% hh in semi-skilled work	22.5	8.9	16.2	29.5
% hh in unskilled work	56.0	5.6	32.8	61.2
% hh employed on docks	32.0	4.0	11.0	20.0
% hh employed in commerce	1.0	11.0	3.0	0.0
% hh employed by corporation	4.9	17.0	16.4	8.0
Mean household income (pw)	£2.09	£4.60	£3.27	£2.56
B. Characteristics of corporation house				
Mean weekly rent	28.9p	89.2p	58.8p	39.9p
Mean number of rooms	2.7	5.0	4.0	3.8
Mean length of occupancy	12.7 yrs	18.1 yrs	19.7 yrs	14.4 yrs
C. Characteristics of previous house				
Mean weekly rent	28.4p	73.5p	52.9p	23.5p
Mean number of rooms	2.1	5.4	4.3	2.3
Mean length of occupancy	7.8 yrs	3.1 yrs	2.9 yrs	12.8 yrs
% moving due to demolition	23.2	0.0	1.7	75.6
% moving due to transfers[b]	24.1	18.2	23.1	18.2
Sample size (households)	556	473	1414	176

[a] Pre-1919 properties in eleven different inner-city locations; 1919 act houses on the Lark Hill estate; 1924 act houses on the Norris Green estate; 1930 act tenement: Gerard Gardens.

[b] % of households moving from one corporation property to another through transfers or exchanges.

Sources: Liverpool corporation housing records. Data relate to all tenancies starting prior to 1945. Household details are characteristics at the start of the tenancy.

in the city's housing system, containing those who could not move to better accommodation, and used as a dumping ground by the corporation for tenants that it had to house but did not want to put in newer property. Thus as the environment of the inner city spiralled into decline, so too the community in a block such as Gildarts Gardens disintegrated, and many of those left behind must have felt increasing alienation from the locality in which they had spent most of their lives.

The development of suburban council estates made a massive impact on Liverpool's urban structure with 32,820 houses built in the suburbs 1919 to 1945. The Larkhill estate was one of the larger developments with 2,310 houses erected by 1945, the majority consisting of larger parlour houses built under the Addison Act of 1919. Rents for these houses of three bedrooms and two living rooms were around 16s. (80p) per week inclusive of rates in the period 1925 to 1930, an outlay which was above most rents in the private sector and comparable with the cost of mortgage repayments on a similar property. Not surprisingly, most tenants were in skilled non-manual or manual occupations and had previously lived in good-quality housing elsewhere in the city. Whereas the mean number of rooms in the previous residence of all tenants of pre-1919 corporation properties up to 1945 was only 2.1, for tenants of parlour houses on the Larkhill estate it was 5.4 (Table 14.4). Suburban corporation tenants were both self-selected (in terms of their perceived ability to pay high rents and commuting costs to city-centre places of work), and selected by the corporation in terms of their ability to pay and suitability as tenants.[75] It might, therefore, be suggested that such families would have had little difficulty adjusting to life in the suburbs, but this was not always the case. Relocation to suburban corporation property usually meant leaving behind friends and relatives in other parts of the city and, as most tenants in suburban streets were drawn from a large number of previous locations, it was difficult to reconstruct communities in the suburbs (Figure 14.3b). For some, the increased space of a large house and garden posed difficulties ranging from simple lack of furniture, to disorientation and isolation in an environment which was perceived as unfriendly and, at least initially, lacked transport and amenities. A tenant on the Norris Green estate in Liverpool recalled: 'You see there wasn't any doctors, clinics or anything at first so it means that you had to travel for everything, but the problem was there wasn't any trams to take you. It got a lot of people down and they didn't stick it.'[76]

There were many complaints about the levels of social and other facilities on the new suburban estates. Although land was laid aside on all estates for the provision of shops, schools and churches, development of these facilities usually lagged behind houses. For instance, in 1941, residents on the Speke estate com-

[75] Liverpool Housing Committee Minutes; Pooley and Irish, *The Development of Corporation Housing*; Pooley and Irish, 'Access to housing'. [76] McKenna, 'The suburbanisation', 187.

plained that, although they had lived there for two years or more, only three small shops had been provided. Similarly, on the Sparrow Hall estate there were bitter complaints in 1940 that no Roman Catholic school had been built despite the fact that the population rehoused from the inner city was almost entirely Catholic. Recreational and leisure facilities were particularly slow to develop on all estates, with public houses banned from many estates in the 1920s and 1930s on moral grounds, and few community centres, clubs or other facilities despite energetic lobbying from local councillors and tenants' associations. Thus in 1937 a report highlighted the lack of facilities for young people on suburban council estates, estimating that the Walton Clubmoor estate contained 1800 residents aged ten to eighteen years who had nothing to do except attend church activities or cinemas. It was argued that provision of a youth social centre was urgently needed to prevent the estate becoming a 'breeding ground for social discontent'.[77] These examples show clearly the ways in which private and public space continued to be linked, with lack of amenities creating the potential for social tension within the new communities. The increased cost and lack of facilities were too much for some families and they returned to inner suburban housing, but the majority of tenants did settle quite quickly on an estate such as Larkhill, surviving the recession years, and eventually creating new stable communities. Of those who did not leave quickly, most remained in the same house for a long time, and in the period after 1945 the good-quality estates built under the 1919 act were by far the most attractive corporation stock in most cities with tenancies often passed from parents to children. In contrast, suburban estates built under slum clearance schemes in the 1930s took much longer to stabilise.

Under the Greenwood Act of 1930 Liverpool corporation built 3,727 units in flats, mostly in the city centre. Gerard Gardens, containing 312 units built 1936–9 on land made available through slum clearance in the north-central part of the city, was typical. As with the early Artizans' Dwellings most tenants came from the surrounding streets (Figure 14.3c) and there was thus some chance that local communities would survive the dislocation of slum clearance and rebuilding. The corporation had an obligation to offer housing to all those dispossessed through slum clearance and the occupational profile of tenants in Gerard Gardens was quite different from that of the Larkhill estate. Over 90 per cent of household heads were in semi-skilled or unskilled work, their mean income was less than half that of suburban tenants, 75.6 per cent moved due to the demolition of their previous homes and, on average, they had lived previously in only 2.3 rooms. Although rents were mostly higher than in previously occupied privately rented housing, ranging from 3s. 7d. (18p) for a bed-living room to 10s. 6d. (52.5p) for a five-bedroom flat, they were much lower than in the suburbs (Table 14.4).[78]

[77] Pooley and Irish, *The Development of Corporation Housing*, pp. 102–3. [78] *Ibid.*

The experience of families entering dwellings such as Gerard Gardens was quite variable. Some settled quickly and were able to retain community links to familiar places and people. However, others found the blocks of flats unfriendly in comparison with life in a terrace street and had difficulty adjusting to life on the fifth floor. The blocks were built without lifts and for women with small children the flats were not always convenient. The fact that rents were mostly higher than had previously been paid in the private sector meant that many families took the smallest space possible, thus as families grew there was an acute problem of overcrowding in some corporation properties. Thus the problems associated with negotiating privacy in the restricted space of privately rented rooms were transferred to the new corporation flats. Although well built in comparison with many private properties, blocks such as Gerard Gardens rapidly attained a bad reputation in the post-war period.[79] In part associated with the declining fortunes of the inner-city district in which they were situated, this was exacerbated by the wartime expedient of using vacant corporation properties to house families made homeless through bomb damage. Many of these families came from good-quality privately rented and owner-occupied housing, and disliked and resented life in the corporation blocks. Although most moved out as soon as circumstances allowed, their complaints added to the declining reputation of inner-city tenements. By the 1950s they were perceived as residual housing for the very poor and the aged trapped in the inner city, and by the 1970s most had fallen into a state of disrepair. Gerard Gardens has been demolished, but some similar blocks have been refurbished and sold into the private sector in the 1980s.

The development of public intervention in housing thus affected the form of cities, the lives of tenants and the ways in which people used the urban space in which they lived. There are also links to wider society. Most significantly, public housing provision has been one of the most obvious expressions of expanding welfare provision from the early twentieth century. This can be viewed in a number of ways. In Marxian terminology this is an expression of the contradictions of capitalism, as the state is forced to cover the imperfections of the private market but does so in such a way that most public housing is perceived as inferior and thus marginalised and stigmatised. For others, however, intervention has been seen as a symbol of the growing dependency culture of the twentieth century, where an increasing proportion of the population have come to rely on the state for housing, health and welfare needs. This view gained ascendancy in the 1980s and has led to the widespread sale of council property into the private sector. However, for many individuals corporation involvement in housing has much less complex implications. Despite its imperfections, council housing has

[79] Liverpool Council of Social Service, *Wartime Bulletin of Information Vol 3, No. 67* (10 November 1942).

464

provided improved housing for many and, particularly in the case of suburban estates, has continued to provide valued homes well into the late twentieth century.[80]

Examination of the links between the built form of cities and the social construction of space in the past is not easy. Although reconstruction of the ways in which urban structure changed over time is relatively straightforward, there is little direct evidence as to how people used the spaces in which they lived, worked or undertook social engagements. The extent to which changes in urban structure altered people's lives is often little more than conjecture. Much more research is needed on the links between residential spatial structure and social and cultural identity.

---

[80] K. Bassett and J. R. Short, *Housing and Residential Structure* (London, 1980), pp. 159–232; D. Harvey, 'The political economy of urbanization in advanced capitalist societies: the case of the U.S.', in G. Gappert and H. Rose, eds., *The Social Economy of Cities* (Beverley Hills, Calif., 1975), pp. 119–64; P. Minford, M. Peel and P. Ashton, *The Housing Morass* (London, 1987); H. Dean and P. Taylor-Gooby, *Dependency Culture* (New York and London, 1992); R. Forrest and A. Murie, *Selling the Welfare State* (London, 1988); M. Kleinmann, 'Large scale transfers of council housing to new landlords. Is British social housing becoming more European?', *Housing Studies*, 8 (1993), 163–78.

· 15 ·

Land, property and planning

J. A. YELLING

THE CHAPTER proceeds from two beginnings, one dealing with the overall shape and form of cities, and the other with property development. These are then brought together through a study of late Victorian and Edwardian land reform, which had important implications both for control of urban development through town planning and for property relations. Conditions in the interwar period are next discussed, and the chapter concludes with a short account of the climactic period of planning during the Second World War. While this reflected new concerns of the 1930s, as well as those of the war itself, it also brought to maturity conceptions of town planning and property relations which had their origins in the nineteenth century. In turn, these conceptions helped shape the context within which modern historical research on urban form and landed estates began after the war.

(i) URBAN GROWTH AND FORM

It is only relatively recently that more sophisticated attempts have been made to estimate the extent of urban land. Robin Best calculated from development plans that c. 1950 about 1.8m acres (729,000 ha) of England and Wales lay in 'core' urban settlements of over 10,000 population. Even on the widest definition, including most forms of development, urban land use accounted for only 3.6m acres (145,800 ha) or 9.7 per cent of the whole area, and the comparative figure in Scotland was 2.5 per cent. Best felt that 'the tendency to exaggerate the sprawl of urban areas is rife, and probably reflects the inherent dislike and even fear of urbanisation which is felt by many people in this country'.[1] *Outrage*, the blast against 'subtopia' published in 1955, warned that 'if what is called development is allowed to multiply at the present rate, then by the end of the century, Great

[1] R. H. Best, *Land Use and Living Space* (London, 1981), p. xv.

Britain will consist of isolated oases of preserved monuments in a desert of wire, concrete roads, cosy plots and bungalows'. It went on to attack the 'suburban ethos' as drifting 'like a gaseous pink marshmallow over the whole social scene'.[2]

Best was able to take his calculations back to 1900, when his estimate of urban development in England and Wales, in the wide sense, was 2m acres (810,000 ha), plus 170,000 (68,850 ha) in Scotland. During the first half of the twentieth century, therefore, the extent of urban land by this measure had increased by 80 per cent.[3] Generally, the census statistics on the extent of urban land are of little value, since administrative areas defined as urban contained large amounts of agricultural land. However, exceptional statistics for 1911, which allow such land to be deducted, suggest an urban acreage by this measure of 1.25m acres (506,250 ha) in England and Wales or 3.3 per cent of the whole area.[4] Further back it is not possible to go, but urban populations were growing fast in the late nineteenth century, and between 1841 and 1911 80 per cent of net additional dwellings were located in the urban areas as defined by the census. In the face of such growth the predominant reactions to prevalent urban form at the end of the nineteenth century were very different from those expressed by *Outrage*, but equally intense and wide-ranging. For Leo Chiozza Money 'almost the entire area of the United Kingdom is sparsely populated. It is an empty country dotted with small crowded spots called towns.'[5] In the view of contemporaries, urbanisation was often associated with the depopulation of the countryside, and the problems of congestion in large cities: problems that included slums, overcrowding, the physical and moral health of the people and even political stability.

Public debate about trends in urbanisation and urban form has a long history and has often taken polemical forms. From the end of the nineteenth century, however, it took on a new significance in connection with the early origins of modern town planning. In the official sense, this began tentatively within a small-scale suburban framework, but it was promoted by concerns that were much larger than those of the local environment. It was certainly connected to most of the issues mentioned at the end of the last paragraph and indeed drawn into contemporary politics through the 'land question', then at the height of its importance. Ways in which such politics was linked to town planning will be discussed in a later section, but it is important to bear in mind at the outset that control of land and land uses involves deep cultural and social values, not just matters of technical significance and detailed regulation. The concerns that built around urban concentration and later around urban dispersal were linked in this sense, that both tendencies were thought to be detrimental to existing categories of urban and rural, and to associated ways of life, and hence needed to be controlled.

[2] I. Nairn, *Outrage* (London, 1955), pp. 365–6.
[3] R. H. Best, *The Major Land Uses of Great Britain* (Wye, 1959), pp. 61–80.
[4] PP 1913 IV, local taxation return for 1911–12.
[5] L. Chiozza Money, *Riches and Poverty* (London, 1911), p. 87.

Processes of urbanisation also involved major shifts of economic value. Victorian and Edwardian statisticians attempted to measure these using the values of land and property that were calculated for the purpose of levying rates and taxes. In 1850–1 land had been assessed at £42.8m in England and Wales and houses at £39.4m. By 1900–1 the figures were respectively £37.2m and £157.1m, reflecting urbanisation and agricultural depression.[6] The figure for houses included both buildings and the land beneath them, but Sidney Webb pioneered attempts to calculate this land value separately, as site rent.[7] More recent figures by Colin Clark suggest that such site rent in England and Wales rose from £6m in 1845, or 1.8 per cent of estimated national income, to £59.2m in 1893, by which time it comfortably exceeded the value of agricultural land and reached a maximum of 5.1 per cent of national income.[8] Residential site rents largely fell on the relatively small areas which were urban. They reached their maximum when the debate on urban dispersal began to develop. Equally, the later loosening of cities was accompanied by a reduction in the relative weight of urban land costs, which continued until at least the early 1950s.

Early industrial development promoted urbanisation at many scattered points as well as in larger centres. Conurbations grew up, of which the Black Country was a type example, formed by industrial concentration but composed of many varied settlements, and with no clear separation of rural and urban. By contrast, urbanisation in the late nineteenth century focused more on existing centres, leading to the growth of major cities, but those cities were themselves less concentrated in form. Infilling, previously an important process, was becoming less intense, while suburbs were being formed at lower densities. The process of suburbanisation created an outward moving zone of maximum growth and conversion of land, but the transformation of city centres into specialised commercial, cultural and administrative areas was the crucial process which provided a continued focus for the city. Generally, this focus remained sufficiently strong in the early twentieth century for cities still to be thought of in traditional terms, despite much lower densities of outer growth and growing concern for the urbanisation of the countryside at or beyond their fringe (Map 15.1). As a result, cities such as Birmingham can be depicted in a familiar way as consisting of a central core surrounded by additive rings of development whose increasing width reflects successively lower densities. This of course varies regionally and locally, according to the development history of cities, so that for Glasgow, for example, such a pattern of spatial expansion is less pronounced.

---

[6] Sir J. Stamp, *British Incomes and Property* (London, 1922), pp. 49–51.
[7] PP 1890 XVIII, Committee on Town Holdings, appendix 1, p. 341.
[8] C. Clark, 'Land taxation: lessons from international experience', in Acton Society Trust, P. Hall, ed., *Land Values* (London, 1965), pp. 126–46; figures for Scotland 1875–1914 are given in R. Rodger, 'Rents and ground rents: housing and the land market in nineteenth century Britain', in J. Johnston and C. G. Pooley, eds., *The Structure of Nineteenth-Century Cities* (London, 1982), pp. 39–74.

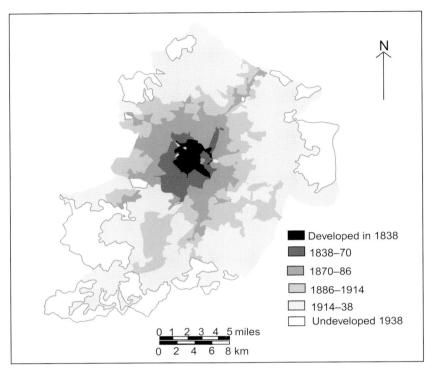

N
↑

Developed in 1838
1838–70
1870–86
1886–1914
1914–38
Undeveloped 1938

0 1 2 3 4 5 miles
0 2 4 6 8 km

Map 15.1 The built-up area of Birmingham 1838–1938
Source: redrawn from R. F. Broaderwick, 'An investigation into the location of
institutional land uses in Birmingham' (PhD thesis, University of Birmingham,
1981), fig. 3.1, p. 53.

At the beginning of the twentieth century writers such as Charles Booth
(1902), and R. M. Hurd (1903) in the United States, claimed to have uncovered
the laws and principles governing the growth of large cities.[9] Cities were evidently complex, but none the less large-scale generalisations could be made
about the zoning of land uses and values and their change through time. In their
work, the focus is no longer on a simple contrast between urban and rural.
Instead, there is a transition from the central business district through congested
working-class areas to low-density middle-class areas on the fringe. Correspondingly, land values descended sharply from a peak in the central business district,
and then continued to decline outwards. As Booth observed, there was an apparent paradox in that poorer populations (and with them most urban 'problems')
were located on the higher-value land. Social status and respectability increased
outwards or, as Avner Offer put it more recently, there was a 'moral gradient'

[9] C. Booth, *Life and Labour of the People in London*, vol. XVII (London, 1902), pp. 189–208; R. M.
Hurd, *Principles of City Land Values* (New York, 1903).

which rose from the city centre out into the untouched countryside, inversely to the land rent gradient.[10]

Booth, like many contemporaries, was deeply concerned with the problem of urban congestion, but by 1902 he took an optimistic view of the future. Congestion, he thought, was a historical feature which failed to reflect the current technical advances in communications. He based this view on his studies of London's expansion, and hence believed that decongestion was already under-way, but that it should also be accelerated, for example through the planned use of municipal tramways. Booth emphasised the reciprocal nature of urban development. Growth pulses transmitted from the centre encouraged outward expansion. Equally, outer development had effects which worked back into the centre. It was this latter process which gave rise to his optimism over congestion.

Booth was largely concerned with long-term developments, and paid little attention to another major feature of Victorian urban development, a pattern of booms and slumps resulting from long cyclical movements in constructional activity of some fourteen to twenty-one years duration. Particularly marked was the long upswing in British building from the mid-1860s to a peak in the mid-1870s, and another boom developing to a peak around the turn of the century. The 1880s and the period 1905–14 were periods of lower activity, although with much local and regional variation.[11] Subsequent study of these patterns has shown that the mechanisms that linked different forms of development were more complex than Booth imagined, but they have not contradicted his general point about reciprocity. It seems likely that the various sectors of building – such as industrial, commercial or residential – were essentially linked together in one overall cycle, although with an uneven process of growth and decline, creating leads and lags appropriate to each sector.[12] Moreover, in the case of London (where exceptionally the cycle has been studied in relation to a city rather than a region) conclusions have been reached similar to those of Booth. The building cycle was linked to major transport innovations, the (re)development of the commercial core occurring together with the growth of suburban transport and building.[13] One exception is that public and institutional building involving more extensive land uses may show some counter-cyclical tendencies, or at least be relatively more significant in periods of low activity.[14]

---

[10] A. Offer, *Property and Politics, 1870–1914* (Cambridge, 1981), p. 329.

[11] J. P. Lewis, *Building Cycles and Britain's Growth* (London, 1965); S. B. Saul, 'House-building in England 1890–1914', *Ec.HR*, 2nd series, 15 (1962), 119–37; R. Rodger, 'Scottish urban house-building 1870–1914' (PhD thesis, University of Edinburgh, 1975).

[12] M. Gottlieb, *Long Swings in Urban Development* (New York, 1976), p. 80. Rodger, 'Scottish urban housebuilding', pp. 67–78.

[13] Lewis, *Building Cycles*, pp. 129–39; K. C. Grytzell, *County of London Population Changes 1801–1901* (Lund Studies in Geography, Series B 33, 1969).

[14] J. W. R. Whitehand, *The Changing Face of Cities* (Oxford, 1987), pp. 11–59; R. Rodger, 'The building cycle and the urban fringe in Victorian cities: a comment', *Journal of Historical Geography*, 4 (1978), 72–7.

Britain's industrial regions and cities developed around notoriously distinct economies in the nineteenth century. In most cases various forms of industry, rather than commerce, were the primary motor of local economic development, and naturally the secular growth pattern of each industrial area impacted on its associated urbanisation. The local business cycle affected building development, but such pulses in growth were transmitted into a long building cycle through complex interactions within a chain of development agencies. In the large and volatile house-building sector rising wage rates generated by industrial growth increased effective demand for building, but also increased the costs. Initially, rent rises could be easily absorbed and profitability increased, drawing new house-builders into an expanding cycle of activity. Eventually, however, profitability was reduced as lower sectors of the market had to be tapped and rent increases could no longer be passed on. Vacancies began to rise, but high levels of activity frequently continued for some time. This might be attributed to mistaken expectations, but also land was in the development 'pipeline' and small builders were unable to wait. The subsequent building slump was then much affected by the degree of 'overhang' from the previous boom. Landlords tended to resist downward pressure on rents, so probably helping to extend the period of low activity.

Much interest attaches to the Edwardian building slump which was both severe and prolonged. Various cyclical factors were probably at work. The previous boom had contributed a large 'overhang' particularly in London. Soon after the slump began, there was a downturn in the economic cycle in 1907–10, and afterwards political uncertainties at home and abroad helped to prolong the slump. There is also, however, much interest in the possibility that secular trends were at work.[15] The increasing cost of new buildings relative to incomes in the late nineteenth century, itself partly the product of increased public regulation, served to dampen effective demand. Increasing rates within urban areas had a similar effect, whilst also reducing landlord profitability. More widely, the whole economy was now mature, and awaiting fresh developments while, as argued above, urbanisation itself was entering a new stage. It is not just knowledge that 1914 was to come which provides the sense that this was a period of difficult structural transition.

Work which brings together analysis of building cycle mechanisms with study of how change was transmitted through the urban spatial structure is urgently needed. It should help to clarify both the manner in which urban form developed in the late nineteenth century and how it was constrained by current political economy. For it remains the case that there was a prolonged downturn in activity in the period before 1914 when technological solutions to urban expansion seemed available, and widespread overcrowding and sharing of houses

---

[15] Cyclical and secular trends are discussed in Offer, *Property and Politics*; Rodger, 'Rents and ground rents', pp. 67–9; M. J. Daunton, *House and Home in the Victorian City* (London, 1983), pp. 201–33.

remained. Contemporary politics excluded any direct attack on the problem. Shifts within the burden of taxation were debated – from local rates to national taxes, and within rates from buildings to land. They could at best have provided partial solutions, and were never put to the test. Much the same is true of other remedies, such as those suggested by Booth. However, some of these were later to have an effect on urban form through their influence on nascent town planning. Essentially they involved an emphasis on decentralisation and low-density living environments, contrasted with congestion, and a special focus on control of land and land values.

(ii) PROPERTY DEVELOPMENT

Property is involved in urbanisation in two obvious ways. The passage from rural to urban land uses takes place within a framework of ownership which has its own effects on development outcomes. These have been the subject of an important historical debate. Secondly, urban development produced changes in property ownership brought about in part by the requirements of the processes involved and the demands of the users. In relation to housing, 'the market in land, and hence the market in housing was really a market in property rights . . . The effect of housebuilding was to create new property rights and interests out of existing ones.' This was specially significant since land tenure was given primacy in English law, and was 'deeply embodied in the social and political institutions of Victorian society'.[16] In this section these two aspects will be treated successively. Finally, a theme of the last section will be recalled: while changes at the urban fringe must retain attention, they should be conceived of as part of a series of changes which involved the existing built-up area.

Writing in the early 1960s, Donald Olsen called his study of the Bedford and Foundling Hospital estates *Town Planning in London in the Eighteenth and Nineteenth Centuries*.[17] At its outset the architecture of these estates tended to be viewed as standing apart from that of ordinary commercial building and, if not directly attributable to aristocratic tastes, as John Summerson[18] had suggested, then at least the ability of such estates to organise a planned and coherent development seemed a plausible explanation of their particularity. These estates were not only large and compact, but also developed on a leasehold system – that is the land was not sold outright to builders or developers, but both land and buildings reverted to the estate at the end of the lease. This not only provided a mechanism of control through covenants in the leases, but also seemed to provide the incentives for larger and longer-term objectives to be promoted over short-term rewards. Outside such estates of exemplary development, the rest of late

[16] J. Springett, 'Land development and house-building in Huddersfield 1770–1911', in M. Doughty, ed., *Building the Industrial City* (Leicester, 1986), p. 26.
[17] D. J. Olsen, *Town Planning in London* (New Haven, 1964; 2nd edn, London, 1982).
[18] J. Summerson, *Georgian London* (London, 1962).

eighteenth- and early nineteenth-century cities seemed to stand in stark contrast: densely and often irregularly built, lacking in open space, with little coordination of land uses. The worst parts, built with a mixture of courts, back to
backs and non-residential uses, seemed often to reflect a fragmentation of property. Particular parcels, often of small extent, became units of urban development, their size and shape carrying forward elements of the pre-urban cadaster
into a chaotic new townscape.[19]

Olsen's link between the management of landed estates and the development
of town planning was certainly a correct one. For although town planning had
many points of origin, the careful regulation of space through the social grada-
tion of residence and ordered disposition of land uses, which became established
as good practice on these estates, also passed into planning doctrine. Moreover,
the subsequent development of Olsen's studies, reinforced by other scholars, paralleled the changing prestige of town planning between the 1960s and the
1980s.[20] The extent to which it was possible, or even desirable, for a single large
authority to exercise control over land was put into doubt, the piecemeal and
informal became more fashionable, and above all the market was resurrected as
a reputable institution and consumer demand established as the vital factor determining outcomes. Locally, the extent to which landed estates could produce
exemplary development was seen to depend on the position in the market that
particular projects could command. Nationally, Martin Daunton showed that
variations in wage levels were a key factor in understanding regional variations
in building standards.[21]

As the mechanisms of development were studied more carefully it became
evident that a chain of agencies and multitude of hands contributed to the building of Victorian cities.[22] In this schema the case in which the landowner acted
also as developer and tightly controlled the supply chain was only one possibility. More usually, there were separate developers and builders, and an important
ingredient in the success of such agencies was to sense what the market would
stand in particular localities and at particular times. The development role was
especially important since the layout and physical preparation of land for building necessarily involved an orientation towards a particular market. Moreover,
there was in this process the possibility of transcending the limitations of separate landownership. New building regulations had their effects in the late
Victorian period, and may also have been a factor that encouraged the greater
use of specialist developers. In any event, the polar cases of organised coherent

---

[19] M. J. Mortimore, 'Landownership and urban growth in Bradford and its environs in the West
Riding conurbation, 1850–1950', *Transactions of the Institute of British Geographers*, 46 (1969),
105–18.

[20] D. Cannadine, *Lords and Landlords* (Leicester 1980); F. M. L. Thompson, *Hampstead* (London,
1974).   [21] Daunton, *House and Home*, pp. 60–88.

[22] H. J. Dyos, *Victorian Suburb* (Leicester, 1961); D. Cannadine and D. Reeder, eds., *Exploring the
Urban Past* (Cambridge, 1982), pp. 154–90.

development through a large landed estate and undesirable irregularity elsewhere became less prominent.

In north Leeds agricultural estate owners rarely engaged in building estate development after 1870, and even before this date the prevalence of freehold tenure meant that land was often sold for development.[23] Several large estates made attempts to let land on other tenures, but competition from rival developers meant that prospective purchasers were usually able to insist on freehold tenure. Similarly, the Ramsden estate in Huddersfield, despite its large size and strategic position in the town, was unable to impose 99 year leases in the 1860s and had to adopt 999 year leases instead.[24] By contrast, there was always a ready market for freehold land even in towns dominated by leasehold tenure. It would appear therefore that leasehold tenure needed to be established under conditions in which competition from freehold could be controlled. This was most likely to be the case early in urban development, and the notable contrasts between major English cities in the nature of their tenure were clearly evident in the late eighteenth and early nineteenth centuries.[25] In Scotland, certainly, a distinctive tenure, the feuing system, was already established which contrasted with the English types. Richard Rodger's attempt to link this feature to the particular form and density of Scottish towns constitutes perhaps the most notable attempt in recent literature to preserve a strong role for supply factors in the complex interaction of causes affecting urban development.[26]

Despite the fact that, according to Jane Springett, the Ramsden estate was 'brought to heel' by the *petite bourgeoisie* in the 1860s, it none the less had a discernible impact on the town through the controls exerted over the development of the estate. The result was that a lesser proportion of lower-class property was built, but to some extent at least at the expense of higher rents and greater crowding of dwellings than in neighbouring towns. Elsewhere, too, large estates were frequently associated, other things being equal, with higher-value residential property, while the reverse was true on fragmented lands. Even in the East End of London large estates such as the Mercers were able to some extent to shape their own market.[27] They were able to do so because of the quality of the initial building, and because of the controls that were exercised over tenancy and land use. Clearly, controlled development could not transcend the larger effects of class or income, and beyond a certain point insistence on high-quality building led to rents which suppressed demand and resulted in housing problems

[23] C. Treen, 'The process of suburban development in north Leeds 1870–1914', in F. M. L. Thompson, ed., *The Rise of Suburbia* (Leicester 1982), pp. 157–210.
[24] Springett, 'Land development', p. 27.
[25] C. W. Chalklin, *The Provincial Towns of Georgian England* (London, 1974); C. W. Chalklin, 'Urban housing estates in the eighteenth century', *Urban Studies*, 5 (1968), 67–85.
[26] Rodger, 'Rents and ground rents', pp. 53–5.
[27] M. Paton, 'Corporate East End landlords: the example of the London Hospital and the Mercers Company', *LJ*, 18 (1993), 113–28.

emerging in other ways. None the less, it remained the case that, other things being equal, higher-quality residence was associated with a more controlled environment. Also, since it is generally accepted that the imposition of greater controls over development and land use was usually not immediately advantageous to the landowner, something should still be retained of the notion of long-term versus short-term advantage and of the importance of non-economic motives in development.

It must always be borne in mind that conditions at the edge of towns were always very variable both in terms of landownership and in terms of physical disposition, layout and land uses. None the less, as a general rule the trend was towards division from larger physical units towards smaller plots, and correspondingly towards increasing fragmentation of property. C. Treen's list of major developers operating in north Leeds 1871–1914 involved purchases of up to 89 acres (36 ha), but the largest landowners sold more than twice as much land, and in the case of the Brown estate received a gross income of £207,000.[28] Real estate subdivision was, however, more profitable than building itself, which was subject to intense competition. The presence of a large number of small units with low capital in the building industry meant that there was a high demand for small lots, which when professional services and physical site preparation were added produced very high costs. The Brown estate trustees, selling freehold plots directly to builders, achieved average prices over the period 1883–1902 of £992 per acre. Estates which sold land for subdivision to developers in the same period achieved rather less than half this price. On the other hand, land with only agricultural value was currently selling for only £70–£80 per acre. Land could be sold more quickly to developers, with fewer costs to bear, and without engaging in all the minutiae and risks of estate development. The passage of land from landowner to developer to builder would thus seem to involve a progressive decline in profit made, particularly when related to the risk and effort involved.

Similarly, it is generally agreed that the ownership of house property was relatively fragmented and involved the employment of petty capital. Owners of good-class residential property had less trouble, but relatively low rewards, whereas towards the bottom end of the market profitability was potentially much higher but at higher risk and requiring personal involvement.[29] To that extent the owners of large-scale capital may be seen as subcontracting the less profitable activities. However, a more positive view might emphasise the advantages gained in property development and property ownership from local knowledge and local connections. Indeed, local influence has been seen as central to the condition of the *petite bourgeoisie*, and hence small-scale property ownership as a factor closely related to the fortunes of this class. Such consid-

---

[28] Treen, 'Suburban development', pp. 202–4.   [29] Daunton, *House and Home*, pp. 91–127.

erations also direct attention to the manner in which the leasehold system served to perpetuate large-scale interests in residential property. For while ratebooks provide a list of property owners which is useful in many respects, they also tend to mask financial realities in towns where leasehold prevailed. Well in advance of the date at which property was due to revert to the estate, the financial balance began to tilt towards the ground landlord. The realisable value of the ground rents came increasingly to reflect the reversionary value, while the interest of the leaseholder was correspondingly diminished. As Christopher Chalklin put it, 'the value of the leasehold urban estate formed in the eighteenth century only became outstanding two or three generations later when the building leases expired'.[30] By the late nineteenth century such estates would be at or near the reversionary date. Undoubtedly, some large gains were made at this point. However, the extent to which monetary expectations were realised once more underlined the way in which the fortunes of landed estates were subject to market and other factors over which only limited control could be exerted. Indeed, the argument concerning the position of landed estates on the reversion of urban properties tends, not unnaturally, to mirror that concerning their role in initial development.

One advantage claimed for landed estates was that 'a freeholder of an individual building could at best try to adapt it to the changing character of the neighbourhood. A large landowner could change the character of the neighbourhood itself.'[31] The renewal of the Grosvenor estate in Mayfair was a model of the kind of change which such property could bring about. Partial redevelopment, segregation of land uses, release of land to model dwellings companies, all required control over a substantial area, and an ability to absorb short-term loss of income.[32] Mere mention of the word Mayfair, however, highlights the extent to which the decisions were necessarily affected by location and market potential. While what happened to landed estates on reversion has been subject to fewer studies than their original development, it seems that in most cases it made economic sense to postpone major decisions, and relet on higher repairing leases. Rising costs promoted the development of cheaper land on the outskirts, but at the same time selective out-movement reduced the extent to which it was profitable to invest in inner-urban property. This developing geography was, of course, attributable to many factors, but it should not be excluded that conditions under which property was supplied affected it at the margins. Landed estates fostered a taste for residential areas which were socially graded and strictly controlled in terms of their land use, but in turn such conditions were more easily supplied in development than in redevelopment or renewal.

[30] Chalklin, 'Urban housing estates', 73.   [31] Olsen, *Town Planning*, p. 160.
[32] M. J. Hazelton-Swales, 'Urban aristocrats: the Grosvenors and the development of Belgravia and Pimlico in the nineteenth century' (PhD thesis, University of London, 1981); PP 1887 XIII, Committee on Town Holdings, pp. 323ff.

(iii) LAND REFORM AND URBAN DEVELOPMENT

During the late Victorian and Edwardian period economic change and electoral pressures for social reform brought to prominence unorthodox doctrines associated with the land question, the tariff question, socialism and national efficiency. Both of the main political parties were brought into crisis by attempts to accommodate these new tendencies with more traditional elements of their programmes.[33] It was a variable and incomplete process, and outcomes in terms of urban development did not have widespread effects before 1914. Such a context is, however, essential to understanding the nature of particular results that were to have greater future application. It is generally accepted that 1890–1914 was the formative period of modern British town planning, and henceforth the control of land, and of land uses and land values, became of heightened significance.[34] Equally, this was a crux period in the field of housing policies. The period immediately before the First World War was the first in which the main political parties could be said to have distinctive housing programmes, and henceforth electoral outcomes would have a more direct impact on urban development.[35] Most of the doctrines mentioned above had some impact on housing and town planning. Land reform was, however, a dominant feature in this field in the sense that it not only drew on its own body of principles, but was the means by which other purposes could be realised and their values absorbed. It had undoubted links with many of the novelties of the period: the garden suburbs at Bournville, Hampstead and elsewhere, the first garden city at Letchworth, suburban council estates and town planning legislation.

The existence of landed estates and of the leasehold system was crucial to the way in which the land question was conceived. It epitomised, in the view of reformers, the control that landownership gave over those who lived on the land, as well as a division between the productive use of land and the 'unearned increment' arising from its ownership. There were, however, divisions within reformist ranks not only over the degree but also the manner in which large concentrations of property should be broken down. Some types of land reform were aimed specifically at the special legislation that governed such estates, as in the debate over the Settled Land Act (1882) or leasehold

[33] Offer, *Property and Politics*; H. Emy, *Liberals, Radicals and Social Politics 1892–1914* (Cambridge, 1973); E. H. H. Green, *The Crisis of Conservatism: The Politics, Economics and Ideology of the British Conservative Party 1880–1914* (London, 1995).

[34] W. Ashworth, *The Genesis of Modern British Town Planning* (London, 1954); G. Cherry, *The Evolution of British Town Planning* (Leighton Buzzard, 1974); A. Sutcliffe, *Towards the Planned City* (Oxford, 1981); S. V. Ward, *Planning and Urban Change* (London, 1994).

[35] J. A. Yelling, *Slums and Slum Clearance in Victorian London* (London, 1986), pp. 64–9.

enfranchisement.[36] Various versions of land taxation formed a second and predominant thrust of attack. The other major strand, equally old, involved some form of collective landownership. As reflected in the Land Nationalisation Society (LNS), this took the view that 'the evil of the system is not that land is held in great estates, but that it is treated as private property at all'.[37] All the same, the LNS case was clearly related to the landed estate system since their model of reform was essentially based on a ground landlord–tenant relationship in which collective control replaced the private owner. The force of these divisions is shown by LNS support of the decision of some Liberal MPs to oppose the Leasehold Enfranchisement Bill of 1891. However, the existence of different strands of opinion also widened the participation in land reform. After all, some inherent contradiction between support for landed estates and for owner-occupation was not seen as a weakness in the Conservative 'ramparts of property' strategy.[38]

Land reformers found that emphasis on the maldistribution of property was not enough to give them political impetus. Their doctrines also had to be linked to contemporary preoccupations and observable evils. They achieved a degree of success, and an essential unity of purpose, by promoting a key image of the period – the congested city contrasted with the depopulating countryside. A wide range of land reform elements could be drawn into this debate. Economically, urban congestion was directly linked to high land values, to the concept of urban site rent as 'unearned increment' and to the idea that urban property owners were currently sheltering under a form of monopolistic protection. Politically, the extremes of urban congestion and rural emptiness could be seen to reflect the land nationalisers' emphasis on the control that landowners exercised over their land and the conflict of interest with the tenants that inevitably arose. It was an image that would carry a powerful mixture of conservative and radical implications, and link with other rising concerns of the period, such as the debate on 'national efficiency'.[39]

I have argued previously that a key factor in the emergence of this focus was the failure of land reformers to make progress by directly imposing the costs of urban improvement on landowners.[40] In the 1890s, the Progressives on the

---

[36] D. Reeder, 'The politics of urban leasehold in late Victorian England', *International Review of Social History*, 6 (1961), 413–30; R. Douglas, *Land, People and Politics* (London, 1976); H. J. Perkin, 'Land reform and class conflict in Victorian Britain', in J. Butt and I. Clark, eds., *The Victorians and Social Protest* (Newton Abbott, 1973); S. Ward, 'Land reform in England, 1880–1914' (PhD thesis, University of Reading, 1976).

[37] J. Hyder, *The Case for Land Nationalisation* (London, 1913), p. 221.

[38] Offer, *Property and Politics*, p. 156.

[39] P. L. Garside, '"Unhealthy areas", town planning and eugenics in the slums 1890–1914', *Planning Perspectives*, 3 (1988), 24–46; W. Voigt, 'The garden city as an eugenic utopia', *Planning Perspectives*, 4 (1989), 295–312.   [40] Yelling, *Slums and Slum Clearance*, pp. 65–7.

London County Council had raised the compensation and betterment issue in its special form in relation to street improvement and slum clearance.[41] It was argued that these public activities were carried out at great loss to the ratepayer, because of the high cost of compensation for the necessary purchase of the property, but that such improvements also brought betterment of property values which largely escaped local taxation. If the costs of such schemes could not be reduced by new legislation, then a lateral shift on to cheaper land in the suburbs became a way in which the landlords could be outflanked, and existing site rents brought down through a large increase in housing supply. This could accommodate Fabian interest in municipal administration and William Thompson's scheme for the organised dispersal of the population through municipal land and building. Equally, site value rating could arguably achieve this end without public expense, essentially by taxing undeveloped land and by reinforcing market pressures to move from expensive to cheaper sites. Cheap land, the reduction of costs, the powerful effects of competition, all connected to traditional liberal values, and the significance given to them helps explain the way in which Ebenezer Howard and Thompson discussed the potential impact of their schemes on existing cities in terms of the purely beneficial effects that would arise from major reductions in rents and property values.[42]

Howard's 'peaceful path to real reform' is, however, most closely related to the strand of thinking represented by the land nationalisers (Figure 15.1). This was particularly concerned with the social organism, and became linked to the nascent town planning movement through the view that 'the community as a whole, that is to say the actual occupiers of the land in their collective capacity, shall decide the uses to which land shall be put'.[43] Robert Beevers claims that 'the Garden City Association was initially founded around a nucleus of members of the Land Nationalisation Society'. This was equally true of the National Housing Reform Council, which played a large part in the origins of the 1909 Housing and Town Planning Act.[44] Control over land was seen to be the factor that would release all kinds of benefits – escape from overcrowding, greater aesthetic beauty, more sense of community. However, there were also elements of the programme that drew the movement closer to the great estates and to the traditional proponents of paternalism. The LNS secretary, Joseph Hyder, wrote: 'We have always been told by the champions of private property in land that

[41] H. R. Parker, 'The history of compensation and betterment since 1900', in Acton Society Trust, *Land Values*, pp. 53–72.
[42] E. Howard, *Tomorrow* (London, 1898), p. 44; W. Thompson, 'The powers of local authorities', in *The House Famine and How to Relieve It* (Fabian Tracts 101, 1900), p. 25.
[43] Hyder, *Land Nationalisation*, p. 221.
[44] R. Beevers, *The Garden City Utopia* (London, 1988), p. 72; J. A. Yelling, 'Planning and the land question', *Planning History*, 16 (1994), 4–9.

Figure 15.1 Draft diagram for Ebenezer Howard, *Tomorrow*
Source: Hertfordshire Archives and Local Studies.

great estates are better managed than small ones, and there is much truth in the contention . . . the good of the estate as a whole is more likely to be kept in mind when it is under one ownership.'[45] The LNS was therefore to accept property fragmentation as a key cause of slums, and in the practical advance of town planning this emphasis became still more apparent. Features of land use control on large well-managed private estates were accepted as good planning practice, and when town planning was officially introduced in 1909 as a limited measure of suburban land regulation, planning schemes came into being most easily around the core of a large estate.

[45] Hyder, *Land Nationalisation*, p. 321.

New ways of thinking about 'community' were a feature of the new liberalism, designed to mitigate the social effects of economic individualism while preserving individual enterprise. Community was given a territorial focus, and often tied to projects of land reform. Thus in Howard's model garden city a better environment and provision of amenities was to be merely one product of a web of individual and collective activities and voluntary associations which would bind the community together. These varied enterprises were to be founded on community ownership of the land and the revenues which arose from it. The great difficulty lay, however, in the initial purchase of this land, for the use of private trustees as at Letchworth had obvious disadvantages. At first, there were some signs that municipal landownership might be promoted for the purpose. In Unionist Birmingham, John Nettlefold, inspired by the example of Germany, proposed that 'a Corporation cannot own too much land', and saw this as a basis for creating 'a healthy happy community' in which private persons and public utility societies would erect houses within the framework of a planning scheme.[46] However, community landownership was never able to perform this mediating role as the key point on which municipal activity should focus. Opposition to any extension of municipal landownership was strongly entrenched as Aldridge, Nettlefold and Thompson found when they tried to link it to town planning in preparation of the 1909 act.[47] On the other hand, municipal housing had already become an important factor. It raised problems of an altogether different order, for it shifted the nature of municipal control from relationships between landlords and ground landlords to relationships between landlord and tenant. This issue increasingly became a point of divergence around which political programmes were built.

In her account of the development of Huddersfield, Springett presents the incorporation of the town as a triumph for the bourgeoisie, and for local property interests in particular.[48] It was they who henceforth controlled the council and, for instance, approved building regulations that were less stringent than those that the Ramsden estate had attempted to impose. While such conflictual relations within the world of property may not have been the norm, this situation does capture the sense in which the nineteenth-century growth in property ownership should naturally be reflected in the composition of local councils. At the end of the period electoral developments seemed to threaten this relationship, and the activities of local councils became increasingly a focus of resentment among property owners. According to authors such as David McCrone and Brian Elliot this reflected not only the potential damage to material interests but also the loss of social status and control which even small property

---

[46] G. Cherry, *Birmingham* (Chichester, 1994), p. 104.
[47] A. Sutcliffe, 'Britain's first town planning act: a review of the 1909 achievement', *Town Planning Review*, 59 (1988), 289–303.   [48] Springett, 'Land development', p. 52.

owners possessed vis-à-vis their tenants.[49] In this changing situation not only were property interests thrown closer together, but in many ways the owners of large estates were better placed than their smaller counterparts. They were able to connect with some of the new developments and to attempt to mould them in directions favourable to their interests. Smaller owners and their organisations, however, found little in the way of strategy except a dogged emphasis on *laissez-faire* and the traditional virtues of political economy. While this was perfectly capable of winning battles it seemed to run against the tide of opinion in all political parties that new electorates would require new ways forward.

A final point to consider is how the political developments in this period affected the perception of supply and demand factors in urban development, and hence the debate that was considered in the last section. They undoubtedly did tend to suppress the significance of demand factors and to elevate land reform, however essential, to an importance in economic, social and political life that it could not sustain. The reasons for this were, however, deep-seated and like the reform movements themselves strongly rooted in Victorian thought and practice. In the first place the significance given to land partly reflected the remarkably strong defence that had been built up against income transfers. Given increased electoral pressures for social reform an indirect route through land was all the more tempting because other possibilities seemed to be more effectively blocked. In the second place, the apparent inviolability of the economic system through the period, coupled with the importance given to paternalism, meant that there was a strong tendency to put the blame for observed defects on particular agents or agencies. Good property tended to be associated with good management and poor property with bad without sufficient attention to the different markets that were served. With the indirect method now favoured in housing and town planning, new forms stood to benefit from the contrast that would be made with the older property and older property relationships in the existing part of cities. Not surprisingly, when the Unionists first breached the political taboo on housing subsidies in 1911, one main purpose was to deflect municipal enterprise back to the oldest and poorest properties by resurrecting slum clearance.[50]

To conclude, by 1914 a series of important new developments had occurred. There was now a practical political debate which brought into question not just particular patches of property, but the whole pattern of urban development. Strong connections had been made in this debate between urban form and land values. Increased attention was given to municipal activity in the field of land

---

[49] D. McCrone and B. Elliot, 'The decline of landlordism: property rights and relationships in Edinburgh', in R. Rodger, ed., *Scottish Housing in the Twentieth Century* (Leicester, 1989), pp. 214–35; for tensions between landlord and tenant see D. Englander, *Landlord and Tenant in Urban Britain, 1838–1918* (Oxford, 1983); Daunton, *House and Home*, pp. 222–3, sees private landlords as falling between the interests of the main political parties.

[50] Yelling, *Slums and Slum Clearance*, p. 69.

and housing, offering a potential new agency for development. Balanced against this was the strength of established positions. Most of the new forms had required the impetus of the building boom of the turn of the century to bring them into being. With the onset of slump they were cut back much like ordinary development. The decline of property values prior to the First World War may have been due in part to political fears, but it was not the product of the kind of scenario envisaged in housing and town planning reform.

(iv) INTERWAR BRITAIN

In 1932 Thomas Sharp attacked the way in which 'town extensions sprawl out in sloppy diffuseness all over the countryside'. Instead of the urbanity of the past there were now 'little dwellings crouching separately under trees' which were 'mean and contemptible'. He had little doubt that the responsibility for this disaster lay with Ebenezer Howard and other social reformers, so that 'since the war open development has been sacrosanct'. The sloppy thinking of sociologists was, however, only part of a wider change in social relations, for Sharp believed that 'democracy is at present reducing the English countryside from the beauty which it attained under aristocracy'. A new kind of town planning was necessary because 'the only way we are likely to attain any beautiful civic expression is by stringent but enlightened control from authority'.[51]

Such observations show one way in which changes in the perception of town and country were linked to political and socio-economic developments, in this case those resulting immediately from the war. One important source of Sharp's anguish was the Housing and Town Planning Act (1919) and the 'homes for heroes' housing programme which it implemented. Through Raymond Unwin's influence on the Tudor Walters Report the standards laid down in the act were directly related to the pre-war models of town planning, as at Hampstead and Letchworth, and made to symbolise the idea of a new beginning.[52] Lower densities, combined with a government pledge to build in much larger quantities, entailed a major expansion of urban development, as well as greater public expenditure and higher taxation. At the same time, the *Estates Gazette* had talked of a 'revolution in landholding' and claimed that by the end of 1921 one quarter of England had changed hands.[53] The apparent, and rather exaggerated, demise of the great estate, and the loss of control which it represented, certainly influenced many planners through the period, including I. G. Gibbon and Patrick Abercrombie.[54] It greatly added to fears of the spread of

[51] T. Sharp, *Town and Countryside* (London, 1932), pp. 149, 163, 218, 220.
[52] M. Swenarton, *Homes Fit for Heroes* (London, 1981).
[53] F. M. L. Thompson, *English Landed Society in the Nineteenth Century* (London, 1963), pp. 332–3.
[54] I. G. Gibbon, *Problems of Town and Country Planning* (London, 1937); on Abercrombie see J. Sheail, *Rural Conservation in Inter-War Britain* (Oxford, 1981), p. 21.

urban influences into the countryside. It was also in the 1930s that Summerson began his urban estate studies that were subsequently to influence historical work. Planning moved more decisively away from any connection with the more individualistic versions of land reform, such as leasehold reform or site value rating, and became more definitely an alliance against *laissez-faire*.

There was, however, another and predominant way in which events moved forward from 1919, centred on the role of government in housing and town planning. Although the 'homes for heroes' programme came to an end in 1921, demonstrating the power of contrary forces, its continuing effects were seen in the revival of municipal house building in the 1920s and the continuation, albeit in modified form, of new housing and planning standards. However, those standards were forced down, and planners increasingly found it desirable to talk of 'practical' rather than 'visionary' planning. Property owners kept up a barrage of opposition to the 'confiscation' of property under the new slum clearance compensation provisions of 1919, and similar sentiments were much to the fore in the events that led up to the 1932 Town Planning Act.[55] In this kind of debate there was no doubt that housing and town planning reformers were for the 'new' rather than the 'old', and Unwin was a leader of opposition to the government's withdrawal from general social housing in 1933. In this he was joined by Maynard Keynes, personifying the way in which traditional planning was now able to link with new concerns.[56]

The manner in which economic developments of the early 1970s corresponded with a distinct change in the politics of housing and town planning has concentrated attention on the way in which the two were previously linked. In this sense there is both an economics and politics of 'mass' production and consumption, and although it is not possible to identify any single point in time at which such features began, both were certainly in process of formation in inter-war Britain. Arguably, the new style of suburban housing became at that time an item of mass production and consumption alongside such linked items as domestic appliances and the transport that made suburbanisation possible. Politics affected this at various levels. The whole idea of 'mass' production and consumption may be affected by the politics and social expectations current in developed countries at this time. The variable forms of 'mass' production and consumption were affected by political traditions and different economic histories. Two obvious features in Britain are divisions over public and private ownership and the marked regional impact of the new consumer industries. Again, politics may be concerned with the management of factors of production, such as land, so that mass production can take place, and with the regulation of the effects of mass consumption, such as urban sprawl or traffic.

[55] P. Garside, 'Town planning in London 1930–1961: a study of pressures, interests and influences affecting the formation of policy' (PhD thesis, University of London, 1979).
[56] J. A. Yelling, *Slums and Redevelopment* (London, 1992), pp. 89, 95–6.

Parry Lewis and Harry Richardson, working in the 1960s, argued that after 1914 building cycles could not be recognised and analysed in the traditional way.[57] In part this was due to such forms of government intervention as rent control and subsidised housing. It was accepted that earlier mechanisms at work in building cycles were still relevant, notably in the private building boom of the 1930s. Land values thus rose at that time, although not beyond levels previously reached *c.* 1900. However, a main point, in Richardson's view, was that housing output exceeded the previous highest level in every year after 1924, and that there was therefore no slump. It carried the implication that governments were now expected to regulate affairs so that this did not occur. Events since the 1960s have, by contrast, encouraged the view that the factors shaping building cycles were still in place, and that it was a combination of fortuitous circumstances that produced the long boom. As with the pre-1914 slump, war intervened before the argument could be decisively settled. Still, government intervention undoubtedly had important effects on urban development at all levels. Regionally, Ward summarised state urban expenditure as concentrated on '"middle Britain" i.e. the most favoured parts of outer Britain and the more peripheral parts of inner Britain'.[58]

Politically, the overall responsibility of the national government for housing did become established *de facto* in the interwar period, and was only seriously questioned in limited periods of economic crisis. This was to have major effects on housing tenure. The management of the post-war housing crisis through rent control meant that until the end of the 1930s the private landlord ceased to be a major agent in new build, and private renting became increasingly associated with older properties. After the end of 'homes for heroes' Conservative governments continued to allow an expansion of suburban council housing in the 1920s because the housing shortage had to be overcome before rent control could be dispensed with. However, they also took steps to promote owner-occupation. While this tenure was not yet associated with substantial fiscal advantages, by the mid-1930s new building society procedures (coupled with changes in supply) had brought it within reach of most families with stable and relatively high incomes. Indeed, it became associated with middle-class social status – something not generally true of the limited owner-occupation prior to 1914.[59] In the 1930s, when council housing was redirected to slum clearance, owner-occupied houses accounted for the great bulk of suburban expansion in all those cities with reasonably flourishing economies.

The clearest link between mass production and mass consumption lies through economies of scale, which found their easiest expression in suburban

---

[57] Lewis, *Building Cycles*, p. 232; H. W. Richardson and D. H. Aldcroft, *Building in the British Economy Between the Wars* (London, 1968), p. 213.

[58] S. V. Ward, *The Geography of Inter-War Britain* (London, 1988), p. 171.

[59] M. J. Daunton, *A Property-Owning Democracy?* (London, 1987), pp. 72–4.

growth. The presence of a new scale in urban development was marked most obviously in council building and landholding. Thus in Birmingham 'by the end of the 1930s vast municipal estates ringed the city periphery in the north east and south, no less than fifteen individual estates each having more than 1,000 houses'.[60] Such scale was related to economies of production and management, although there may also be other explanations. Housing functions could be more easily discharged through a small number of large peripheral holdings, particularly in view of the sharp divide which was established in the public mind between public and and private. However, there were some comparable developments in the private sector during the building boom of the 1930s. M. C. Carr, summarising the results of his study of the London borough of Bexley, says:

> The large uniform lower middle class estate was developed wherever the large-scale speculative private builder could find the size of site which gave him the most efficient use of the scale advantage he had over the smaller builder. Smaller plots were developed by the smaller builder with better housing . . . Consequently available large sites . . . whatever their location were developed in the 1930s with lower middle class housing.[61]

These remarks revive claims made in respect of Victorian building, only in reverse form. Undoubtedly, they need to be similarly qualified, as previously discussed. Moreover, Carr himself refers to exceptions in which on large estates with suitable status characteristics and building restrictions better-class housing resulted. Older features of landed estate development could therefore persist, but effects were now much reduced. Socio-economic changes, combined with continued legal revision in the Law of Property Act 1925, meant that leasehold development was now rarer. This was, however, a period in which large-scale regional builders emerged, particularly in outer London. New Ideal Homesteads Ltd, which had originated in Bexley, claimed to have been erecting 10,000 houses in 1933. Costain in 1935 had an estate at Elm Park (Essex) planned for 7,500 houses, and had developed three estates of over 1,000 houses in the London area.[62] It had now also become widespread practice for builders to be their own developers, so providing a more direct relationship with the market. Michael Ball describes this as part of a new structure of housing provision, the origins of which were highly dependent on the contingent factors of this period. Such a structure linked methods of production and consumption, but *inter alia*

---

[60] Cherry, *Birmingham*, p. 144; for London examples of public and private suburbia see A. A. Jackson, *Semi-Detached London* (London, 1973).

[61] M. C. Carr, 'The development and character of a metropolitan suburb: Bexley, Kent', in Thompson, ed., *Rise of Suburbia*, p. 254.

[62] J. D. Bundock, 'Speculative housebuilding and some aspects of the activities of the speculative housebuilder within the Greater London outer suburban area 1919–39' (MPhil thesis, University of Kent, 1974), pp. 274ff.

'builders could gain economies by combining the spheres of land development and housebuilding. Independent land developers consequently were squeezed out.'[63] Builders therefore provided a new means of injecting large-scale capital into the development process.

None the less, it would be wrong to give the impression that suburban development was now a highly ordered process. The building industry still remained considerably fragmented, and the contingencies of property continued to affect development patterns. Town planning did not directly contribute to these developments through any compulsory powers of land assembly. It did, however, involve separation of land uses through 'character' zoning and establish densities which tended to demarcate one type of residential development from another. Arguably, these features helped in the definition of distinctive suburban environments which could be promoted as an advance over existing forms. However, it has been generally agreed that formal town plans had only a limited impact, since they usually followed existing development, and were frequently modified in detailed application. Under the Housing and Town Planning Act (1919) planning remained the responsibility of local authorities rather than county councils[64] and governed only areas of potential development. The act also gave powers for joint plans covering wider districts, which were usually advisory and often preceded the preparation of formal local plans, as in most of outer London, Manchester, Sheffield and other areas. By the early 1930s a considerable number of local plans were at the stage when interim powers could be utilised. What was revealed by developments at this time was therefore not just an absence of town planning, but a more complex situation involving inherent problems.

These became more apparent when planning was extended to built-up areas after 1932. In the County of London, for instance, draft proposals for the first urban scheme included height restrictions, developed from previous building regulations, but no density or land use zones or public road proposals.[65] These were not included because of the compensation implications, which were on an even greater scale than in suburban localities. Suburban plans had at least the protection of a clause which enabled densities to be controlled without compensation, although development itself could not be prevented. Struggles over compensation and betterment in the 1932 act had not, however, produced any satisfactory solution for urban areas. Consequently, practical results in both urban and suburban areas seemed often to come from more direct action by local authorities. The purchase of open space, although sometimes initially inspired by local planning surveys, was a notable example. Inside cities, slum clearance and redevelopment areas were formulated by local authority housing depart-

[63] M. Ball, *Housing Policy and Economic Power* (London, 1983), p. 29.
[64] Except within the area of the London County Council.
[65] I. G. Gibbon, *History of the London County Council 1889–1939* (London, 1939), p. 536; Garside, 'Town planning'.

ments outside the framework of town planning, although they had a much greater impact than the nascent town plans.[66]

The high cost of potential compensation which deterred planning, and the difficulties in collecting betterment highlighted in the struggle over the 1932 Town Planning Act, produced more interest in resolving the matter within uniform landownership. Gibbon, whose work is an essential guide to the pre-occupations of the period, defined planning as laying down 'such provisions for the use of land as would be made by a person of enlightened and public spirit if he owned all the land'.[67] He was especially concerned with the 'multiplicity of separate ownerships' which existed in cities, and which in his view made it impossible to plan them to best advantage. He hoped to resolve this by means of schemes for pooling individual interests, which would allow the benefit of unprofitable land uses, such as open space, to be captured by other development within the same landownership. These arguments once again connected planning with landed estates, and also with the growing interest in redevelopment during the late 1930s. The literature, and official reports such as that of the Moyne Committee, continued to associate slums and other problems with fragmented ownership.[68] However, despite some breakup of urban estates, in many towns the inner areas were precisely those where building leases were now terminating. Yet the advantages of large estates as units of renewal failed to make their mark because of the larger pattern of social and economic change.

The immediate effect of the financial crisis of 1931 was to bring about a reverse for housing and planning schemes, and at one time to threaten a real return to pre-war conditions. In the longer run, however, it produced a new set of concerns which strengthened the economic aspects of housing and town planning.[69] Strong disparities in regional growth connected the outward spread of London not to sloppy social thinking, but to the depressed regions of the North. Similarly, interest in the economic aspects of urban 'obsolescence' kindled by the Housing Act 1935 caused the question to be increasingly debated in terms of large-scale contrasts thrown up by new growth. The economic aspect was strengthened by the support which Keynes gave to housing programmes, redevelopment schemes and town planning. The compensation and betterment problem also linked to an important principle of Keynes, namely the 'fallacy of composition' whereby what was economic for the collectivity was not necessarily economic at the individual level. While new economic thinking and schemes of the 'middle way' did not prevail over older traditions, they did at least weaken resistance to planning on the grounds that it was hopelessly uneconomic.

[66] M. Miller, 'The elusive green background: Raymond Unwin and the Greater London Regional Plan', *Planning Perspectives*, 4 (1989), 15–44; Yelling, *Slums and Redevelopment*, pp. 164–70.
[67] Gibbon, *History of the London County Council*, p. 13.
[68] *Report of the Departmental Committee on Housing (Moyne)*, Cmnd 4397 (London, 1933).
[69] The argument in the rest of this section draws on Yelling, *Slums and Redevelopment*, pp. 171–7.

By the end of the 1930s, therefore, planning had recovered effective large-scale strategic arguments. However, it had not recovered the exceptional unity of purpose that had marked its formative phase before 1914. It was no longer possible to present outward movement as an unequivocal benefit, and the result was a distinct split within the professions concerned with urban development. 'Mainstream' planners, including Unwin and Abercrombie, sought to reshape traditional policies by lifting planning to a new regional scale, and by using open space to limit continous sprawl and to shape distinct communities against a green background. This group continued to emphasise urban congestion for which the remedy was outward movement. Another group, however, particularly strong among architects and local authority officials like Herbert Manzoni in Birmingham, saw obsolescence as the key problem for which the solution was a more efficient land use which reflected the economic value of the land.

With economic depression, rent control and intense competition from suburban development, obsolescence of inner-city property was seen to extend well beyond that taken in contemporary slum clearance. Obsolescence was accepted as an economic, not just a physical, process, while new forms of architecture offered the prospect of redevelopment at high density which would bring the value of buildings back into line with that of the land. This was very different from the decentralisation, low densities and lower land values traditionally advocated by planning supporters, although it placed equal emphasis on new forms. While the Barlow Report leant in favour of the mainstream approach, other contemporary writings increasingly reflected the new enthusiasm for large-scale urban redevelopment.[70] At the outset of the war there was little consensus either on this issue or on the overall scope for planning.

(v) WARTIME PLANS

As in the First World War housing and town planning came to the fore after 1939 as a focus for a programme of reconstruction and reconciliation. Commonly, town planning is seen as occupying the role that the government housing programme provided in the earlier conflict. Certainly, there is some justification for this, because reconciliation had always been a major theme of town planning and because the term 'planning' contained an essential reference to the role of public policy in leading the nation's affairs, and this was at the heart of new reforms. It remained true, however, that the most popular form of town planning lay in the improvement of housing conditions. Beveridge called for a 'revolution in housing standards' as a means of reducing 'the greatest inequality between different sectors of the community'. At the same time, he introduced Keynesian

---

[70] *Report of the Royal Commission on the Distribution of the Industrial Population (Barlow)*, Cmnd 6153 (London, 1940).

themes by enlisting increased housing expenditure as 'the most immediate contribution that can be made towards winning full employment by the radical route of social demand'. This would involve 'substituting a vast orderly programme of expansion for the distinctive meaningless fluctuations of the past'.[71] As is well known such ideas were contested even during the war, but they did shift policy to some extent.

It was in this context that the Uthwatt Committee on Compensation and Betterment produced a document which seemed possibly about to alter the whole future of property relations.[72] Yet in another way the Committee's purpose was a more limited one – to carry into policy a scheme for the nationalisation of development rights on undeveloped land that had been put to the Barlow Committee by Sir Arthur Robinson. State permission would now be necessary for development. Its refusal would entail no compensation, and if granted the state would tax away most of the development gain. Urban land was treated separately in the Report, but eventually similar controls were established for major land use change, when attempts to collect betterment within the same land use were abandoned. Still, the 1947 Town Planning Act did redirect betterment arising from 'planning gain' into the public purse, and appeared to release planning from some of its financial shackles. Equally radical was the Uthwatt Report's support for a leasehold system based on public ownership of land. It recommended that all development pass through a central planning agency which should only lease land, and that no private freehold should be created in redevelopment areas. Freehold owner-occupation, linchpin of the property strategy of Britain's dominant political party, was to be frozen out of all new development.

Whereas green belts and new towns were to become the best-known features to result from wartime planning, the greater innovatory challenges lay within the city itself. Redevelopment was a policy which directly linked Beveridge's aims of improved housing and increased employment through construction, since projection of future population suggested that replacement would soon become the most important element of building. The City of Manchester Plan (1945) envisaged that 'in 25 years from now about one half of the houses in the city may have been swept away and replaced'.[73] Typically, it placed this action within a zonal framework in which Zone B, next to the city centre, was 'chiefly the most urgent inner redevelopment areas and approximately bounded by the intermediate ring road, the most important zone from a planning point of view'. Survey reports suggested that 93 per cent of households in Zone B wished to leave their present house, and only 17 per cent of these wished to remain in the

---

[71] W. Beveridge, 'Introduction', in J. Madge, ed., *The Rehousing of Britain* (London, 1945), p. 5.
[72] Ministry of Works and Planning, *Interim and Final Reports of the Expert Committee on Compensation and Betterment (Uthwatt)*, Cmnd 6386 (London, 1942).
[73] R. Nicholas, *City of Manchester Plan* (London, 1945), p. 14.

zone.[74] The Plan had less to say about the city centre but war damage, affecting many major British cities, provided a new arena for public policy which considerably aided planning's claim to be central to economic as well as social and aesthetic life.[75]

The concept of large-scale redevelopment arose from concerns of the 1930s, but the treatment of both redevelopment and city centres also linked back to the longer planning tradition. Aided by the fortuitous manner in which the Barlow Report fed immediately into policy formation at the beginning of the war, 'mainstream' planning ideas were carried forward by the Reith Ministry, the Dudley Report and the London Plans.[76] John Forshaw and Abercrombie's plan for the County of London (1943) thus envisaged much lower densities of redevelopment than had been current before the war, and a wider variety of land uses within a framework of communities and neighbourhoods. Mixed development, later to take on quite different connotations, was originally conceived in order to allow the house back into redevelopment alongside the flat.[77] These trends were not always supported by those that had been at the forefront of pre-war redevelopment. They met with various degrees of resistance in places like Birmingham, Liverpool and Glasgow, presaging later conflicts between 'housers' and 'planners'.[78] However, in the short run they prevailed everywhere to some extent, partly because of the recognised popularity of the house among working-class populations.

Although land concerns re-emerged in the 1960s, again in a context of planning, the Second World War was probably the closest occasion on which land came to occupying a central role in public policy as the point around which tensions between public and private could be resolved. Cheap land, freed from the economic pressures and spatial constraints of unfettered private ownership, could it was argued allow a greater variety of land uses and townscapes, and provide a basis for drawing communities together and expressing their needs in planned developments. This failed to come about, as it had in the past, because such policies simply lacked the strength to become a focus of solid public support. Moreover, while in the face of future uncertainties they had some attraction for both of the main political parties, they were the primary focus for neither. Far from land becoming a point around which public and private could be drawn

---

[74] *Ibid.*, pp. 18–21, 211.

[75] N. Tiratsoo, *Reconstruction, Affluence and Labour Politics* (London, 1990); J. Hasegawa, *Replanning the Blitzed City Centre* (Milton Keynes, 1992).

[76] J. B. Cullingworth, *Environmental Planning 1939–1969*, vol. I: *Reconstruction and Land Use Planning 1939–1947* (London, 1975); Ministry of Health, *Design of Dwellings* (Dudley Report) (London, 1944); J. H. Forshaw and P. Abercrombie, *The County of London Plan* (London, 1943); P. Abercrombie, *The Greater London Plan 1944* (London, 1945).

[77] J. A. Yelling, 'Expensive land, subsidies, and mixed development in London, 1943–56', *Planning Perspectives*, 9 (1994), 139–52.

[78] M. Glendinning and S. Muthesius, *Tower Block* (New Haven and London, 1994).

together, in key areas of post-war development they were still kept rigidly apart, notably in housing where the renewed growth of owner-occupation and council provision continued a major tenure change with important implications for the division of the 'unearned increment'. Community planning faded into the background. A decade after the war, land values were rising rapidly, and were soon to reach unprecedented heights which some were to ascribe to the unintended effects of planning itself.[79]

This is not to deny that town planning was placed in a quite different position after the war, and that the 1947 act allowed public policy to play a much greater role than had been the case in pre-war plans. Moreover, many aspects of policy, such as green belts, new and expanded towns, redevelopment and road plans, were clearly promoted by wartime planning, and came to a demise together in the 1970s along with Keynesian economic management. Despite that, what happened later even in these areas was not a coming to fruition of wartime intentions. Nor can this simply be ascribed to the Conservative governments from 1951 and the ending of the tax on development gain. The continuance of a Labour government would probably have seen a closer realisation of the plans, but many significant changes had already occurred, as John Cullingworth's official history shows.[80] To take only a few examples, collection of betterment within urban land uses had been abandoned, as had a central planning agency, and housing subsidies were kept outside the framework of planning. Post-war economic and political pressures soon produced a 'return to reality' which limited more radical movement from pre-war positions, while the impact of the planning tradition derived from the formative period before 1914 was further attenuated.[81]

[79] P. Hall *et al.*, *The Containment of Urban England*, 2 vols. (London, 1973).
[80] Cullingworth, *Environmental Planning*.
[81] N. Bullock, 'Ideas, priorities and harsh realities: reconstruction and the LCC, 1945–51', *Planning Perspectives*, 9 (1994), 87–101; Tiratsoo, *Reconstruction*; Yelling, 'Expensive land'.

· 16 ·

The evolution of Britain's urban built environment

PETER SCOTT

(i) INTRODUCTION

URING THE Industrial Revolution much manufacturing, office and retail activity was conducted in buildings which were partly occupied for residential purposes, and had often been originally built as dwelling houses. Shopkeepers lived above their shops, offices were located in the homes of professional men and warehouses formed part of merchants' residences. However, during the nineteenth century a long-run trend towards increasing functional and geographical specialisation of non-residential property emerged, and accelerated during the twentieth century, creating the functionally segregated built environments of modern urban centres. Offices became concentrated in office districts in the heart of cities, in close proximity to central shopping areas, while urban residential populations became increasingly decentralised and industrial districts coalesced on the fringes of towns and cities, alongside major transport routes. This chapter examines the evolution of commercial and industrial premises from around 1840 to the 1950s, together with associated changes in the property investment and development sectors and the building industry.

(ii) THE VICTORIAN BUILT ENVIRONMENT

The 'traditional' landowners (principally the aristocracy, crown and Church, and educational, social and charitable institutions such as Oxford and Cambridge colleges, public schools, London livery companies and hospitals), which had dominated the urban property market during previous centuries, remained central players during the Victorian period. Their policies towards urban property underwent only minor adaption from the pattern which had emerged by the end of the eighteenth century, involving the development of urban landholdings, when opportunity arose, preferably by granting building leases.

Estate development policy aimed to let land on 99 year building leases, including restrictive covenants designed to prevent alterations which would mar the estate's building plan.[1] Builders, however, generally preferred freehold tenure, and while large estates often had sufficient market power to impose 99 year leases, competition from freehold land sometimes forced landlords either to sell land outright or to offer 999 year leases. Martin Daunton's examination of prevailing tenure in twenty-six towns and cities in England and Wales during the 1830s and 1840s revealed thirteen instances where freeholds were prevalent, while short leases dominated in five cases, long leases in five, a combination of both in one case and chief rents (which were similar to feu duties) in two.[2] The feu was the dominant form of tenure in Scotland. The original owner or 'superior' would grant land to a 'vassal' in return for a fixed annual 'feu duty'. There were (until 1874) also often 'fines' when the land passed from one vassal to a successor.

The perpetual nature of the feu, unlike the leasehold system operative elsewhere in Britain, gave the original landowner no interest in any capital appreciation of the land. Together with the lack of any lump sum available for reinvestment (unlike freehold sales), this made Scottish landowners more cautious in disposing of land than their English counterparts, until it had reached its maximum development value. This increased prices for development land and, together with high building costs (partly arising from stringent building regulations), resulted in Scottish urban centres being developed at substantially higher densities than English cities.[3]

Landlords would often invest substantial sums in the laying-out of roads and the provision of other amenities on estates before granting building leases, thus making them more attractive to speculative developers. Other ways in which landlords might indirectly contribute to, or reduce, the cost of speculative development included granting peppercorn or reduced rents for the first several years of leases, and, as Donald Olsen has noted, failing to impose or enforce stringent covenants regarding building standards.[4] Initiating estate development sometimes also entailed providing loans to builders.

Urban estate development generally proved a profitable activity for aristocratic and other traditional landowners, income generated usually exceeding the returns on investment in their agricultural estates by a considerable margin.[5] However, their influence as active agents of development was limited by the fact that they seldom engaged in major purchases or sales of land, except to consolidate existing holdings. Capital was usually tied up in current landed estates, the

---

[1] D. J. Olsen, *The Growth of Victorian London* (London, 1976), p. 127.

[2] M. J. Daunton, *House and Home in the Victorian City* (London, 1983), p. 75.

[3] *Ibid.*, pp. 68–71.   [4] Olsen, *Growth*, pp. 156–7.

[5] H. J. Dyos, *Victorian Suburb* (Leicester, 1961), p. 88; D. Cannadine, *Lords and Landlords* (Leicester, 1980), p. 222.

sale of which was often prohibited by elaborate statutes or settlements. In addition to these legal restrictions, non-monetary factors such as tradition, prestige and political power appear to have deterred landowners from switching assets. However, as the nineteenth century progressed other institutions, with a more purely commercial attitude towards property, gradually grew in importance as agents of urban development.

This process accelerated from the 1850s. The second half of the century witnessed a substantial rise in the income of Britain's growing middle class, and the consequent growth of middle-class savings. Such savings might be invested directly in property, or indirectly via a property-orientated institutional investment market. Solicitors often invested clients' funds in mortgages (partly to secure the legal work associated with property development). The nineteenth century also witnessed a trend towards significant property market activity by the financial institutions. Insurance companies were active in the market throughout the century, via mortgage lending. Loans were initially secured mainly on agricultural land, though substantial lending for house building took place from the 1850s, as transport improvements opened up new areas to residential development. Such lending was concentrated in large schemes, involving middle-class or 'superior' working-class dwellings.

Insurance companies also contributed to the development process by lending to ground landlords,[6] and even occasionally undertook investment in building estates directly, either voluntarily or (more commonly) as a result of mortgage default by the original developer. Building societies made extensive loans to finance development projects. Like the insurance companies, they were occasionally forced to take over these developments, though the 1874 Building Societies Act prevented them holding on to such property.[7]

Another growing source of property development finance was the stockmarket. The late nineteenth century saw the formation of a substantial number of companies whose purpose was the development and ownership of property, as shown in Table 16.1. The ownership, maintenance and development of property by limited liability companies offered investors the possibility of acquiring a stake in the property sector without the need to commit substantial funds or deal with management and maintenance. The timing of the sector's emergence was connected with legislative changes during the 1850s and 1860s which facilitated limited liability incorporation, together with the accelerating pace of urban development during this period.

Residential property was dominated by small-scale, predominantly lower-middle-class, investors, reflecting their 'local economic concerns, their narrowness of horizon and quest for security'.[8] Analysis by Daunton of assets passing at

[6] Olsen, *Growth*, p. 157.
[7] D. Cannadine and D. Reeder, eds., *Exploring the Urban Past* (Cambridge, 1982), p. 168.
[8] M. J. Daunton, *A Property-Owning Democracy?* (London, 1987), p. 34.

Table 16.1 *New public property companies 1845–1938*

	Total	Annual average
1845–9	1	0.2
1850–9	2	0.2
1860–9	7	0.7
1870–9	7	0.7
1880–9	14	1.4
1890–1902	20	1.5
1903–13	9	0.8
1914–32	26	1.4
1933–8	40	6.7

Source: Thomas Skinner & Co., *Skinner's Property Share Annual 1950–51* (London, 1950).

death in the United Kingdom indicated that house and business property formed over a quarter of gross capital for people leaving less than £5,000, while for those leaving £10,000–£20,000 it amounted to 14 per cent, declining further for higher wealth groups.[9] The avoidance of residential property by wealthy investors may reflect superior returns on alternative investments which were found inaccessible by those of moderate income, or the ability of small capitalists to reduce costs by undertaking management personally.

A further factor behind the growth of the property investment market was the development of market intermediaries and a market press. The 1850s saw the establishment of a number of journals covering property transactions, most importantly the *Estates Gazette* (1858). The development of a property press provided a vital source of information in a market lacking any centralised market place.[10] There was an attempt to set up such a market, with the establishment of the Estates Exchange in 1857, though this did not progress beyond the maintenance of registers recording property transactions.[11]

On the 'demand-side', substantial finance was required by both builders and developers seeking to make a speculative profit by purchasing land considered 'ripe' for development. Developers might let or resell land to builders (sometimes supplying them with capital) or develop at least part of it directly – the functions of the financier, landowner and speculative builder often overlapped in an industry characterised by relative ease of entry and financial realities which often required extreme flexibility of function.[12]

[9] Daunton, *House and Home*, p. 103.
[10] F. M. L. Thompson, 'The land market in the nineteenth century', in W. E. Michinton, ed., *Essays in Agrarian History*, vol. II (Newton Abbot, 1968), p. 40.   [11] *Ibid.*, p. 40.
[12] Cannadine and Reeder, *Exploring*, pp. 157–8.

The builders themselves ranged from master builders employing large numbers of men on a permanent and semi-permanent basis, other large-scale builders who were much more reliant on subcontracting for their labour, to a great number of small-scale speculative builders who accounted for the bulk of residential property development. In 1872 the mean builder in London had only 5.4 houses under construction, while three-quarters of firms were working on 6 or fewer; only 0.1 per cent were building over 60 houses, representing a mere 2.4 per cent of total housing construction. However, concentration increased markedly during the next thirty years; by 1899 the mean London builder worked on 11.6 houses and those building over 60 houses accounted for 2.7 per cent of firms and 29.9 per cent of construction.[13] Speculative builders proved notoriously unsuccessful in recognising the early signs of downturns in the housing market, the result being a highly cyclical industry with periodic phases of substantial oversupply and building bankruptcies.[14] However, the building industry experienced rapid long-term growth during this period, employment rising from 390,000 in 1851 to 953,000 in 1901.[15]

Institutional buildings, and some commercial premises, were developed via contracting rather than speculative activity. The growth of projects related to railway development and public works during the mid- and late nineteenth century led to a substantial expansion of the contracting industry. Firms operating in this sector tended to be larger, and more stable, than their speculative counterparts. Some major contractors, such as Glasgow-based Hugh Kennedy, combined contracting with speculative property development and investment. Rents from developed properties provided a regular source of income, which was a valuable asset given the cash-flow problems which occasionally arose in contracting.[16]

One of the main ways in which contractors could undercut their rivals was by attempting to force down labour costs through lower wages or increased hours. Such activity produced considerable opposition from workers in the skilled building trades, characterised by strong craft traditions that helped foster a collective ethos. Attempts to address the ensuing problem of hostile industrial relations culminated in the establishment of a formal system of collective bargaining – including conciliation and arbitration procedures – during the last decades of the nineteenth century, which provided workers with some measure of protection against the 'cut-throat' competition which the tendering system would otherwise have produced.[17]

The nineteenth-century growth of the property investment, development and

---

[13] Daunton, *Property-Owning Democracy?*, p. 102. [14] *Ibid.*, p. 15.
[15] M. Bowley, *The British Building Industry* (Cambridge, 1966), p. 326.
[16] N. J. Morgan, 'Hugh Kennedy', in A. Slaven and S. Checkland, eds., *Dictionary of Scottish Business Biography 1860–1960*, vol. II (Aberdeen, 1990), pp. 141–3.
[17] R. Price, *Masters, Unions and Men* (Cambridge, 1980).

building sectors took place alongside a transformation in the character of urban centres, residential property being squeezed out by commercial buildings. The City of London had begun to lose its population during the first decade of the nineteenth century; by the third quarter of the century population declines were also being experienced in the central wards of Liverpool and Birmingham as offices, shops, factories and warehouses displaced housing.[18] During the last two decades of the century a number of great provincial cities acquired central 'layouts', further accelerating this trend.[19]

The growth of 'central business districts' within cities was closely linked to the development of functionally and geographically specialised commercial buildings, particularly offices and warehouses. Until the nineteenth century the office functions of business were dealt with in coffee-houses, counting houses and the homes of merchants, specialist office buildings being rare.[20] However, as the complexity of administration increased more and more businessmen found it necessary to establish a formal office. As Jon Lawrence has noted, 'The growth of paper documentation, the need to be personally contactable, and the need to be near to public sources of commercial information such as the Post Office, reading rooms and coffee houses, made it increasingly essential to maintain a formal office at no great distance from the key centres of commercial activity.'[21]

Until the 1830s office development usually involved the adaptation of existing premises, so that their previously residential upper floors could be let for commercial use,[22] although some large companies, in sectors such as banking and insurance, did erect purpose-built offices.[23] London's first known speculative office block was built in Clements Lane, in around 1823, though the number of speculative office developments only became at all significant in the 1840s,[24] gathering pace during the mid-Victorian period. The pattern of City office development was mirrored by that of other major commercial centres. For example during the early nineteenth century the growing demand for offices in Liverpool's central commercial district was met largely through the conversion of private houses and other buildings, the first purpose-built office blocks appearing in the 1830s and 1840s.[25] R. A. Varley's study of Manchester's Central Business District suggests that the segregation of land use into definable areas was under way by the 1820s, with the emergence of a visible office district in the vicinity of

[18] A. Briggs, *Victorian Cities* (London, 1963), p. 26.   [19] *Ibid.*, p. 26.
[20] P. Cowen *et al.*, *The Office* (London, 1969), p. 25.
[21] J. Lawrence, 'From counting house to office: the transformation of London's central financial district, 1693–1871' (unpublished paper, 1994), p. 15.   [22] *Ibid.*, p. 14.
[23] P. W. Daniels, *Office Location* (London, 1975), p. 17.
[24] Edward L'Anson, 'Some notice of office buildings in the City of London', *Royal Institute of British Architects, Transactions* (1864), 25–6.
[25] D. K. Stenhouse, 'Liverpool's office district, 1875–1905', *Historical Society of Lancashire and Cheshire*, 133 (1984), 72.

the Royal Exchange.[26] Manchester's warehouses had already begun to occupy a defined area, the nucleus of a warehouse district having emerged by 1800.[27]

By the 1860s office development in London had become 'so considerable that almost all the eligible sites in the City have been converted to this purpose'.[28] The diminishing supply of suitable sites led to rising land values. This stimulated the establishment of a number of publicly quoted property companies specialising in the development and ownership of City office property, such as City Offices Co. Ltd and the City of London Real Property Co. Ltd, both established in 1864. These operated alongside smaller property companies established by groups of businessmen to develop specific sites, often partially for their own use, such as Gresham Chambers Co. Ltd.[29]

The rapid growth in office employment continued during the late nineteenth century. Clerical employment in England and Wales rose from 1.0 per cent of the labour force in 1851 to 3.9 per cent in 1901,[30] facilitated by advances in communications and other office technology, such as the spread of the telegraph and postal services and the invention of the telephone, typewriter, arithmometer and stencil duplicator. The growth of office centres was matched by an expansion in the office functions of industrial concerns, with office premises usually attached to their factories.

The late nineteenth century witnessed a substantial increase in the size of office blocks, largely as the result of technological innovation – the spread of the hydraulic lift. Hydraulic lifts became common in City offices after 1882, when the London Hydraulic Power Co. started operation.[31] Lifts made upper floors attractive to commercial tenants for the first time, starting a 'vertical transport revolution,' which provided a powerful impetus to the continued expansion of the City when the supply of non-office buildings for redevelopment began to run short.[32] The lift opened up the possibility of much taller buildings, made technologically possible by the development of steel-framed construction techniques in America during the late nineteenth century. According to Marion Bowley, Britain's first steel-framed building was London's Ritz Hotel, built in 1904.[33] Reinforced concrete also began to be adopted by the British building industry from around the turn of the century; like structural steel its introduction, and subsequent development, lagged behind that in other countries.[34] While the 1894 London Building Act and other by-laws are often cited as the cause of the slow adoption of these technologies, Bowley argues that conservatism on the part of

[26] R. A. Varley, 'Land-use analysis in the city-centre, with special reference to Manchester' (MA thesis, University of Wales, 1968), p. 89.   [27] *Ibid.*, pp. 84–5.
[28] L'Anson, 'Some notice', 26.   [29] Lawrence, 'From counting house', p. 24.
[30] Daniels, *Office Location*, p. 33.
[31] R. Turvey, 'London lifts and hydraulic power', *Transactions of the Newcomen Society*, 65 (1993–4), 147.   [32] R. Turvey, 'City of London office rents: 1864–1914' (unpublished paper, 1994), p. 4.
[33] Bowley, *British Building Industry*, p. 12.   [34] *Ibid.*, pp. 15–27.

the architectural and other building-designing professions constituted a more fundamental barrier.[35] Bowley's study also highlights the organisation of the building industry – particularly the separation of the design of buildings and their construction – as a major factor inhibiting cost-reducing technical changes which would benefit builders but provided fewer incentives for independent designers.

Another important growth area for specialist commercial buildings was retailing. Evidence suggests that the number of 'fixed' shops in Britain was already experiencing rapid growth by the end of the eighteenth century.[36] However, it was not until the second half of the nineteenth century that an industry which had hitherto been dominated by single units, managed by their owners and employing, at most, a handful of people, was to see the rise of giant, nationally based enterprises, a few of which would, by 1900, rank alongside Britain's largest companies.

While some locally based multiple retailers did develop during the first half of the nineteenth century there is very little evidence of multiples operating in more than one urban centre.[37] W. H. Smith began to develop their network of railway station book stalls during the late 1840s, and other multiples, such as J. Menzies and the Singer Manufacturing Company, had appeared by the 1850s, though the number of multiple traders only became substantial from the 1870s. Footwear was one of the first trades in which multiple retailers established a substantial presence, though from the early 1880s the number of branches of footwear multiples was overtaken by those in the food industry.[38] Important factors behind the emergence of the food multiples – in common with their non-food counterparts – were rising real living standards, the growing urbanisation of Britain's population and improvements in transport and communications.

However, food multiples enjoyed specific advantages, due to the boom in cheap imported foodstuffs from the 1870s. They typically adopted a retailing strategy based around selling a very limited range of goods at cut prices; for example the most successful retailer of this type, Thomas Lipton, initially concentrated on selling ham, butter and eggs. Booming world production, and the impact of technology on long-distance transport (including chilled and refrigerated shipping) led to rapid price falls for these commodities during the late nineteenth century, and similarly dramatic consumption increases. Traditional suppliers, such as the producer-retailers who resisted the introduction of imported meat and therefore could not match the price cuts, left the market

---

[35] *Ibid.*, pp. 7–35.
[36] M. J. Winstanley, 'Concentration and competition in the retail sector, *c.* 1800–1990', in M. W. Kirby and M. B. Rose, eds., *Business Enterprise in Modern Britain* (London, 1994), p. 241.
[37] G. Shaw, 'The evolution and impact of large-scale retailing in Britain', in J. Benson and G. Shaw, eds., *The Evolution of Retail Systems, c. 1800–1914* (Leicester, 1992), p. 139.
[38] J. B. Jefferys, *Retail Trading in Britain, 1850–1950* (Cambridge, 1954), p. 23.

open to the new multiples.[39] The cut-price strategies adopted by these retailers (and other multiples, selling cheap factory-made goods such as footwear and clothing) required a high turnover in order to generate a profit. Thus the early multiples concentrated their stores in the main thoroughfares of towns, or in other areas with substantial pedestrian flow. This led to the growing concentration of retail activity in 'High Street' centres, a trend which was to continue, and accelerate, over the next seventy years.

Developments in land transport also played an important role in concentrating retail activity into 'shopping centre' districts. Railways exerted a considerable influence on the internal structure of central retail areas from the 1840s. In addition to increasing the general accessibility of High Streets, they encouraged the growth of retail centres via two additional mechanisms. First, they forced up land values, by differentiating site accessibility, and by their own considerable use of urban land. Secondly, they placed a physical constraint on the expansion of many city centres, the railway lines acting as boundaries.[40] The development of urban tramways from the 1880s also influenced retail location, both central and suburban shopping areas coalescing along their lines.

Another consequence of the multiples' strategy of high turnover and low profit margins was a growth in typical shop size. Expenditure on retail outlets rose; prestige fascias were used to give each multiple chain its own defined 'corporate style', while plate glass windows, extensive lighting and marble or polished hardwood counter tops gave stores an attractive, clean, appearance which acted as a powerful advertisement. For example, Boots had a general policy of acquiring premises which would make attractive shop sites and rebuilding, or at least extensively refitting, them, with the aim of creating 'a spectacular new shop whose size and layout eclipsed all other chemists' shops and, where possible, all other retail businesses in the locality'.[41] This considerable advertising expenditure embodied in their stores' appearance was matched by extensive local press, and other, advertising, to bring the prices of their 'bargain' lines to the attention of the shopping public.

As the multiples grew they diversified into other economic activities. Some acted as wholesalers for rurally based retailers. A number, such as Boots, Burton and Lipton, also integrated backwards into manufacturing or primary production. By 1914 Britain had a very substantial large-scale retailing sector; sixteen multiples had over 200 branches each, seven of which had over 500 branches.[42] Almost all the largest multiples had become public companies by 1914, some ranking alongside Britain's largest firms.

[39] G. Shaw, 'Changes in consumer demand and food supply in nineteenth-century British cities', *Journal of Historical Geography*, 11 (1985).
[40] G. Shaw, 'The European scene: Britain and Germany', in Benson and Shaw, eds., *Evolution of Retail Systems*, p. 22.   [41] S. Chapman, *Jesse Boot of Boots the Chemists* (London, 1973), p. 86.
[42] Jefferys, *Retail Trading*, p. 25.

In addition to the beginnings of a 'multiple revolution', two other important forms of large-scale retailing emerged during the mid-late nineteenth century, further intensifying the trend towards functional and geographical specialisation of retail outlets. The Co-operative movement experienced meteoric growth during the second half of the nineteenth century and the Edwardian period, its retail turnover rising from £2.5 million in 1863 to £88 million in 1914. Meanwhile its (almost exclusively working-class) membership had increased nearly sixfold over the thirty-five years to 1914, to over 3 million.[43] Based on a structure of autonomous local Retail Societies, associated with each other through the Co-operative Union and the two Co-operative Wholesale Societies (English and Scottish), the Co-op's influence was strongest in the North and in Scotland. Their trade concentrated on foodstuffs and other household items in mass demand.

Attempts at retail cooperation can be traced back to the eighteenth century, the number of Co-operative Societies becoming substantial during the 1820s.[44] However, few Co-operatives were of long duration prior to the 1840s, their subsequent success being largely based on the trading methods popularised by the Rochdale Pioneers during the mid-nineteenth century. These included the distribution of any surplus as 'dividends' to members, in proportion to their purchases. Most Retail Societies had only a handful of branches, functioning as small multiples but benefiting from the greater cost advantages accruing from centralisation of purchasing via the Wholesale Societies. Average shop size was fairly large by contemporary standards, the Co-op's policy being to avoid minor shopping areas.

Department stores represented an attempt at increased scale primarily via expansion in the size of individual stores. Their origins have been traced to a number of 'monster shops' which had emerged in London and other large cities by the 1820s (mainly confined to the drapery trades), or to even earlier antecedents.[45] By the middle of the century the largest London-based monster shops had several hundred employees, while a handful had developed into department stores in the modern sense of the term, with four or more departments selling different classes of goods.[46] During the third quarter of the nineteenth century the number of department stores grew substantially, mainly due to established drapery and clothing shops adding further departments.

The rise of the department store was intimately linked with the emergence of modern consumerism in Britain, a phenomenon which has been dated (con-

[43] *Ibid.*, p. 16.
[44] M. Purvis, 'Co-operative retailing in Britain', in Benson and Shaw, eds., *Evolution of Retail Systems*, p. 110.
[45] Shaw, 'Evolution', p. 138; P. Glennie, 'Consumption, consumerism and urban form: historical perspectives,' *Urban Studies*, 35 (1998), 936.   [46] Shaw, 'Evolution', pp. 138–40.

troversially) to the 1880s.[47] Its emergence at this time was a function of sharply rising living standards and the appearance of mass-produced consumer durables such as factory-made furniture, sales of which were boosted by the growth of hire-purchase facilities. While department stores had originally emphasised low prices, by the 1890s they competed mainly in terms of their range of goods, quality of service and amenities. People were able to see and inspect a vast selection of new products, attractively displayed in elegant surroundings. In addition, they could enjoy facilities such as tea rooms and restaurants, hairdressing salons, rest and club rooms, toilet and washing facilities,[48] the department store constituting an important leisure outlet in its own right.

During the last quarter of the nineteenth century and the years before 1914 there was a substantial growth in department store retailing in large urban centres. Store size grew, culminating with the construction of Gordon Selfridge's massive Oxford Street store, from 1909. Comprehensive store redevelopment or construction represented the last phase of pre-war department store growth; prior to 1890 most department stores expanded via successive extensions, either amalgamating or rebuilding adjoining properties.[49]

Industrial property experienced a slower trend towards functional and, especially, geographical specialisation (within particular urban centres) than was the case with offices and shops. As late as the mid-nineteenth century a very wide variety of goods were still produced in shops and workrooms rather than factories. However, during the second half of the century factory production expanded to include most areas of manufacturing, due to advances in mechanisation (accelerated by the development of cheap steel) and improvements in transport and communications. Before 1850 many market towns had few firms employing a dozen or more people; twenty years later there were frequently several firms employing hundreds in multi-storey, steam-powered, factories.[50] New and small manufacturers were often able to rent space in such factories. The practice of renting 'room and power' or 'space and turning' was common in the North and Midlands from the eighteenth century, being especially important in the textile industry. In some trades and parts of the country it flourished up to the First World War.[51]

The period between 1880 and the First World War saw the zenith of the multi-storey factory. During this period steel-framed factories of four, five or

[47] Shaw, 'The European scene', p. 29. Some commentators have argued that a 'consumer revolution' could be identified in Britain as early as the late eighteenth century; see N. McKendrick, 'The consumer revolution in eighteenth-century England', in N. McKendrick, J. Brewer and J. H. Plumb, eds., *The Birth of a Consumer Society: The Commercialisation of Eighteenth-Century England* (London, 1982).   [48] Winstanley, 'Concentration and competition', p. 243.
[49] Shaw, 'Evolution', pp. 143–9.
[50] B. Trinder, *The Making of the Industrial Landscape* (London, 1982), p. 215.
[51] D. A. Farnie, *The English Cotton Industry and the World Market, 1815–1896* (Oxford, 1979), p. 291.

even six stories were erected in Lancashire (preceding the adoption of steel-framed technology in British office buildings).[52] Steel frames allowed not only larger buildings, but also more generous fenestration, increasing the amount of light available for their workforce. However, the advent of the internal combustion engine was soon to make the multi-storey factory obsolete, as is discussed below.

During the nineteenth century factory development occurred on a largely unplanned basis, where access to power, raw materials, or transport favoured location. Sites adjacent to railways, canals, docks or rivers did sometimes develop as almost exclusively industrial areas, especially at points where rail and water networks intersected, but grew in an unplanned, evolutionary manner. The need for factories to be close to their workforce severely limited the segregation of industrial and residential areas, though transport improvements towards the end of the century facilitated separation.

In addition to the development of distinct office, shop and industrial building forms, purpose-built premises connected with catering and entertainment had also begun to appear in significant numbers during the nineteenth century. Specially designed gentlemen's clubs were developed from around 1815, while the coming of the railways led to the construction of purpose-built hotels from the 1850s.[53] The development of restaurant chains was initiated around the 1860s, roughly concurrent with the emergence of the property company sector (both stimulated by legislation to facilitate limited liability incorporation).[54] There was also a considerable expansion in the number of institutional buildings during the nineteenth century, such as hospitals, workhouses, town halls and prisons. Over the century to 1914 the diversity and specialisation of Britain's urban built environment had increased enormously, though the pace of change was to accelerate further after the First World War.

(iii) THE BRITISH COMMERCIAL PROPERTY SECTOR BETWEEN THE WARS

The interwar period saw important changes in the character of Britain's commercial property sector. The development of motorised transport encouraged both an intensification of specialisation within urban centres and the suburbanisation of residential and industrial buildings. High street areas became dominated by large-scale retailers, industrial estates mushroomed around the fringes of the London conurbation and a truly nationally based commercial property market emerged.

[52] Trinder, *The Making*, p. 205.
[53] Robert Thorne, 'Places of refreshment in the nineteenth-century city', in A. D. King, ed., *Buildings and Society* (London, 1980), p. 232.   [54] *Ibid.*, p. 239.

Table 16.2 *The distribution of national retail sales 1900–1939*

Type of retailer	Proportion of total sales (%)				
	1900	1910	1920	1930	1939
Co-operatives	6.0–7.0	7.0–8.0	7.5–9.0	8.5–10.0	10.0–11.5
Department stores	1.0–2.0	1.5–3.0	3.0–4.0	3.5–5.0	4.5–5.5
Multiples[a]	3.0–4.5	6.0–7.5	7.0–10.0	12.0–14.0	18.0–19.5
Other[b]	86.5–90.0	81.5–85.5	77.0–82.5	71.0–76.0	63.5–67.5

[a]Multiples with ten or more branches.
[b]The 'Other' category is a residual, the difference between estimates for the defined categories and the total volume of retail trade.
Source: J. B. Jefferys, *Retail Trading in Britain, 1850–1950* (Cambridge, 1954), p. 73.

The pace of change in the property market was set by the multiple retailers. They represented the most rapidly expanding sector of retailing, while other large-scale retailers also gained market share at the expense of independent local traders, as illustrated in Table 16.2. The reasons behind the multiples' rapid growth mainly represented the continuation of trends which had become apparent before 1914 – rising living standards, economies of scale with regard to the expansion of average shop size and scale economies from operating a large branch network, particularly in purchasing, transport and advertising. Motor transport – the car for the middle classes and the motor bus for the working classes – provided a further boost to their growth, by increasing the accessibility of town centres. Property-related financial innovation also facilitated expansion, as is discussed below.

This period saw a change in the character of the multiples. While the early food and footwear chains had sold only a very limited range of goods, emphasising cut prices, the range of stock carried by the interwar multiples increased substantially, while the price gap between them and other retailers narrowed. This was influenced, to some extent, by the spread of resale price maintenance (RPM). Originating in the 1890s, RPM agreements controlled the prices of almost 30 per cent of goods purchased by consumers in 1938.[55] RPM slowed the process of growth in average shop size, as large-scale retailers, unable to undercut independent traders on price, were forced to compete in terms of convenience by increasing their branch network. For some goods, such as chocolate and

---

[55] *Report of the Committee on Resale Price Maintenance* (Cmd 7696, 1949), p. 1, cited in J. B. Cullingworth, *Town and Country Planning in Britain*, 10th edn (London, 1988), p. 54; Winstanley, 'Concentration and competition', p. 252.

tobacco, manufacturers imposed RPM as a conscious attempt to maintain a large number of outlets (an important element of their marketing strategy) by assuring retailers' margins.[56]

One of the main avenues of interwar expansion for the multiples was the variety store, Woolworth's and Marks and Spencer being the outstanding examples. Variety stores were characterised by large premises (sometimes covering several floors), a wide variety of goods, clearly marked low prices and a low level of service, anticipating the growth of self-service retailing after 1945. Like the department stores, the variety chains placed a large range of products before the customer, allowing them to be inspected without any obligation to purchase. They thus contributed to the growth of the more relaxed, leisure-orientated, form of shopping that had been pioneered by the department store.

Accounting for a negligible proportion of the multiples' turnover in 1920, the variety stores' share grew to almost 20 per cent by 1938.[57] This was partly the result of a 'democratisation' of shopping, which allowed their cheap manufactured consumer goods to appeal to a wide range of consumers. As P. R. Chappell of W. H. Smith's Advertising Department stated, 'This is an age of cheapness and all classes – even the Queen herself – have patronised Woolworths.'[58] This 'democratisation' was partly the result of the influence of the cinema and other developments in mass media and entertainment, together with rising living standards for those in work.

The variety chains grew both by extending the number of their branches and by substantially expanding average store size; by 1938 the average employment per variety store branch was over seven times the average for all other multiples.[59] This trend towards increasing average store size was also true, to a lesser extent, for other multiples during this period. The rising cost of developing their ever-growing premises, together with increasing competition for 'prime' locations, led to a switch from renting to ownership as the dominant form of shop tenure among the multiples. This further increased the costs of store acquisition, though the multiples soon evolved methods of financing both store costs, and their general expansion, by capitalising on the value of their premises.

During the 1920s this was achieved by using premises as collateral for mortgages or overdrafts. However, the maximum sum that could be raised by this means was generally restricted to two-thirds of a property's value, limiting the long-term growth which could be generated via such finance.[60] During the 1930s a number of major retailers made use of a financing technique which realised the full purchase and development cost of stores, the sale and leaseback. This

[56] H. Mercer, *Constructing a Competitive Order: The Hidden History of British Antitrust Policies* (Cambridge, 1995), p. 21.   [57] Jefferys, *Retail Trading*, p. 70.
[58] C. Wilson, *First with the News* (London, 1985), p. 326.   [59] Jefferys, *Retail Trading*, p. 63.
[60] See P. Scott, 'Learning to multiply: the property market and the growth of multiple retailing in Britain, 1919–1939', *Business History*, 36 (1994), 1–28.

involved the sale of stores to long-term investors, such as insurance companies, who would simultaneously grant the vendor a long (99 or 999 year) lease on the property, at a rent typically yielding between 4 and 5 per cent of the sum raised by the sale. Stores were sold at a price calculated to cover their full purchase, development and fitting costs, repaying the retailer's entire outlay on each property and allowing expansion to be almost entirely financed using this technique.[61]

Some multiples preferred to rent, rather than buy, premises when they located in suburban centres. However, they still obtained considerable financial advantages over small-scale retailers. To ensure the success of new suburban shopping parades developers found it necessary to attract a well-known multiple which would take the best located store. In return for locating there, and thus increasing the desirability of the remaining shops, and the overall value of the development, expanding retailers such as Woolworth's and Tesco were able to secure substantial concessions from the developer, such as a very low initial rent, a five-year rent-free period, or free shop-fittings.[62]

During the interwar years the expansion of the Co-operative Societies continued, membership rising from 4.5 million in 1920 to 8.5 million in 1939.[63] The Co-ops extended their territorial range into the Midlands and South, where they had hitherto been only patchily represented. They also partially reversed their policy of operating only from large shops, to meet the demands of consumers who were now making more frequent grocery purchases. Meanwhile, the potential for scale economies was increased by the amalgamation of Co-operative Societies. The challenge of expanded size was met by organisational improvements, involving the introduction of techniques developed by the multiples.[64] However, the Co-ops proved relatively unsuccessful in expanding into non-food retailing. Their local structure prevented the establishment of nationally based specialist Co-operative societies dealing in non-food trades, such as footwear, severely limiting the potential for scale economies. Meanwhile, they experienced difficulties with regard to price-maintained lines, due to a boycott by suppliers who claimed that the dividend constituted a breach of RPM.

The number of department stores in Britain increased from about 175–225 stores in 1914 to about 475–525 in 1938.[65] There was no significant increase in the size of new department stores compared with their Edwardian counterparts, though there were substantial improvements in layout, including the more widespread use of lifts and escalators. A series of amalgamations led to the sector being dominated by four large groups (Debenhams, United Drapery Stores, Great Northern & Southern Stores and the John Lewis Partnership), but amalgamation did not lead to rationalisation in areas such as purchasing, sales or pricing policy.[66] Fierce competition from the multiples limited the further growth of the

---

[61] See *ibid*.   [62] O. Marriott, *The Property Boom* (London, 1967), p. 18.
[63] Jefferys, *Retail Trading*, p. 55.   [64] *Ibid*., p. 56.   [65] *Ibid*., p. 59.   [66] *Ibid*., p. 60.

department store sector, while the growing democratisation of shopping, referred to above, reduced its largely 'middle-class' appeal.

By 1939 large-scale retailers accounted for 33–6 per cent of retail sales.[67] However, their influence on town-centre High Street trading was much greater; by the end of the 1930s there were very few good High Street shopping pitches which were not occupied by multiple retailers, department stores or Co-ops.[68] The battle for the High Street was entering a new phase, in which acquiring attractive sites would usually involve purchasing from other large-scale concerns rather than drawing on the pool of premises occupied by local traders. The independent trader had become increasingly confined to niche lines offering few scale economies such as fish and fruit and vegetables, together with the corner shop convenience trade. The influence of the corner shop was, to some extent, strengthened by the trend towards consumers making smaller, more frequent, purchases of provisions, and the growth of RPM, which reduced the multiples' price advantage.

In addition to the further development of central High Street shopping areas, the interwar years witnessed a transformation in the character of local retail centres. Prior to the First World War isolated shops sprang up all over residential areas, usually involving the conversion of private dwellings. However, during the interwar years developers built small parades of half a dozen or so purpose-built shops to serve their new residential estates, while discouraging the conversion of houses. These parades, one serving each estate, almost certainly lacked the scale economies achieved by larger, suburban, shopping centres. Their development reflected attempts by estate developers to capitalise on the often lucrative retail business created by their residential estates, at a time when local authority powers to enforce a more efficient pattern of shop provision were extremely limited.[69] However, a substantial number of larger suburban shopping centres did also emerge, often along major arterial roads.

Multiple retailers also constituted major agents of development. In addition to often developing their own stores, some multiples undertook more comprehensive projects. For example Sainsbury's built a number of suburban shopping parades under the auspices of its development company, Cheyne Investments Ltd.[70] A similar strategy was adopted by Burton, though rather than developing shopping parades the company concentrated on large, consolidated, High Street sites. These would be extensively redeveloped, the resulting block frequently including additional shops on either side of the Burton's store, and a first-floor billiard hall. Specialist shop developers, such as Edward Lotery and George Cross, provided another important source of retail provision, building shopping parades alongside new arterial roads and suburban housing estates.

[67] *Ibid.*, p. 74.   [68] *Ibid.*, p. 90.   [69] W. Burns, *British Shopping Centres* (London, 1959), p. 25.
[70] B. Williams, *The Best Butter in the World: A History of Sainsbury's* (London, 1994), p. 78.

The nation-wide activities of the major multiples led to a demand for property market intermediaries with a similar national coverage. A group of specialist commercial estate agents, based around Maddox Street in the West End of London, emerged to serve this market, providing a range of services for both retailers and other players in the commercial property market. They grew to constitute both important repositories of nation-wide property market information (regarding prevailing rents, available properties, planning regulations, etc.) and vital intermediaries between property occupiers, developers, long-term investors and speculators.[71]

Commercial estate agents were particularly important in facilitating the insurance company sector's growing participation in the property investment market. Insurance companies provided much of the capital for commercial property development during this period, especially in the 1930s, when cheap money led them to turn to property in search of satisfactory yields. For example, during the 1935 financial year the Prudential invested over £3.5 million in property, achieving a yield of 5.25 per cent, at a time when gilts were yielding only 2.9 per cent.[72] Money flowed from the insurance companies to property developers and retailers via both mortgages and, from the 1930s, sale and leaseback deals.

Cheap money also encouraged a substantial expansion of the property company sector, as is shown in Table 16.1. Property company capital issues rose from an average of only 1.9 per cent of all new company issues from 1930–1 to 6.9 per cent from 1933–5.[73] Cheap money allowed property companies to achieve high dividends by adopting a highly geared capital structure. For example, if a property company's assets yielded 5 per cent on costs, and three-quarters of that cost was raised via 5 per cent debentures, the yield on the company's ordinary shares (comprising the remaining 25 per cent of its capital) would also amount to 5 per cent. However, if, as a result of cheap money, the property company was able to replace its fixed interest securities by new debentures yielding 3.75 per cent, the same 5 per cent earnings from the property portfolio would now produce an ordinary share dividend of 8.75 per cent.

This considerable flow of stockmarket and institutional funds to the commercial property sector, driven by cheap money, contributed to a construction boom which (together with the much more important boom in residential building) assisted Britain's recovery from depression during the 1930s. Over the interwar period as a whole the building and contracting industries experienced substantial growth, their employment rising from 514,390 in 1924 to 609,410 in 1930 and 746,260 in 1935.[74] Small concerns experienced particularly rapid expansion; firms employing ten or fewer people accounted for 18.53 per cent of sectoral

---

[71] P. Scott, *Property Masters* (London, 1996), pp. 39–47.   [72] *Ibid.*, p. 72.
[73] E. Nevin, *The Mechanism of Cheap Money* (Cardiff, 1955), p. 280.
[74] P. E. Hart, *Studies in Profit, Business Saving and Investment in the United Kingdom 1920– 1962*, vol. I (London, 1965), p. 95.

employment in 1924; by 1935 this had increased to 32.69 per cent.[75] As in the Victorian period, capital was relatively easily available for even small-scale speculative builders, via the use of property assets as collateral for loans from building societies, insurance companies, banks and solicitors.[76]

While retailing experienced a considerable boom, there was relatively little interwar office development. This period saw considerable improvements in office design, made possible by the belated use of steel-framed construction. By freeing external walls of their load-bearing function, steel frames led to a new architectural style, marked by regular fenestration, enhanced daylight and flexible internal planning.[77] However, the demand for new office space proved insufficient to generate a substantial volume of speculative development, the few really large speculative office blocks, such as London's first 'skyscraper', Bush House, often proving slow to let.[78] Only about 20 per cent of the City's 1900 office stock had been replaced by 1939.[79]

Manufacturing companies continued to locate their administrative headquarters together with their main factories, ICI and Unilever being exceptional in opting for a City headquarters. However, many manufacturing companies, especially those supplying the 'new' consumer goods industries, chose to locate their head offices (together with their main manufacturing facilities) in the London region, usually along London's arterial road network. A prime example of such development was Brentford's 'Golden Mile', where a number of major companies, such as Firestone, Curry's, and Smith's Crisps, built factories facing the new Great West Road.

Such factories were fronted with prestigious office buildings, designed by leading architects such as Wallis, Gilbert & Partners. The characteristic features of their 'Jazz' or 'Art Deco' style fronts were broad, two-storey, buildings with a central stair tower, forming a framed façade which was often embellished using chromium, coloured tiling, stained glass and relief-moulded concrete. These buildings acted as substantial advertisements and combined the advantages of prominent location, proximity to the manufacturing workforce and easy access to central London.

The advent of the automobile had changed both the location and design of factories. Its production typified the 'new' assembly process industries that flourished during the interwar years, involving a multitude of components, each of which had to be added in an ordered sequence. This required production to flow smoothly across a horizontal factory floor, necessitating large, single-storey, 'shed' factories. The modern shed factory was born in the home of production-line technology, Detroit, developed by architects such as Albert Kahn. Reinforced

---

[75] *Ibid.*, p. 95.

[76] British Library of Political and Economic Science Archive, Andrews-Brunner papers, Box 352, note of Oxford Economists' Research Group meeting with Sir Malcolm McAlpine and Mr Bennett, 28 May 1937.   [77] S. J. Murphy, *Continuity and Change* (London, 1984), p. 66.

[78] Marriott, *Property Boom*, pp. 20–1.   [79] Cowen *et al.*, *The Office*, p. 157.

concrete floors provided adequate load-bearing, steel skeletons allowed large roof-spans with the minimum of internal supports, and north-light or single-span roofing contained windows arranged so as to let in natural daylight, while sheltering the factory floor from the wide variations in temperature and lighting arising from direct sunlight.[80] Even a well-fenestrated multi-storey factory could not provide good access to natural daylight above a width of about 60 feet (18.29 m).[81] The new factories were economical and simple to build, adaptable and easily capable of extension, facilitated rapid construction and incurred low maintenance costs.[82] Both steel and reinforced concrete were used to achieve these ends.

The switch from steam to electricity as the main power source for industry provided a further impetus to the transition from multi-storey to single-storey factories. Electricity did not require transmission from one central point, therefore removing the need to arrange production three-dimensionally around the steam engine. It also freed the location of industry from power constraints, especially with the development of the national grid following the 1926 Electricity (Supply) Act.[83] Electrically powered factories opened up new possibilities of smoke-free 'clean' industry, which could be located close to housing without the pollution which was characteristic of nineteenth-century industrial districts.

Meanwhile, the years after the First World War saw a dramatic rise in the proportion of industrial merchandise carried by road rather than rail, a trend which was of particular importance for cargo which had a high value in relation to its bulk. The development of good medium- and long-distance arterial roads did not keep pace with the growth of motor freight traffic and the new industries found themselves competing for relatively scarce factory sites which, ideally, would provide good access to a major road, together with rail facilities.

At the same time that this transition in the physical determinants of industrial location was taking place there was also a revolution in ideas regarding industrial planning. The 'industrial estate' originated with the development, from 1897, of Trafford Park – a 1,200 acre (486 ha) site adjacent to the Manchester Ship Canal. Its development as an area exclusively for industrial use, managed by a company which provided utilities and transport infrastructure, served as the prototype industrial estate, inspiring the development of other large estates such as Slough, Park Royal and Team Valley.

Meanwhile another 'blueprint' for industrial estate development was being pioneered by the garden city movement. Britain's first Garden City, Letchworth (1903), was developed as a planned community, with industry zoned into a single industrial estate within convenient travelling distance of its inhabitants. Letchworth, and Britain's second Garden City, Welwyn (1920), proved successful in attracting industry, especially firms in high value-added sectors, which required skilled labour, paid high wages and found the planned industrial and

[80] J. Marshall, *The History of the Great West Road* (Hounslow, 1995), p. 56.   [81] *Ibid.*, p. 56.
[82] *Ibid.*, p. 56.   [83] S. V. Ward, *The Geography of Inter-War Britain* (London, 1988), p. 119.

residential environments of the garden cities attractive. The garden city concept inspired the development of other planned communities, with industry zoned on estates, by the Corporations of Manchester and Liverpool, and influenced similar, smaller-scale, projects by private developers such as John Laing & Sons and the Thames Land Co.[84]

Following the end of the First World War a large number of modern single-storey factories built for the war effort became available for civilian use. Some of these, typically on the edges of the London conurbation in areas such as Park Royal, Slough and Hendon, stimulated the development of further factories, often available for renting, forming the nuclei of industrial estates. At a time when finance for growing industrial enterprises in the new industries was not readily provided by the City, renting factories on industrial estates, which avoided sinking capital in factory premises and might thus reduce total start-up costs for a small manufacturer by 50 per cent or more, appeared extremely attractive. By 1939 there were at least sixty-five industrial estates in Britain, employing around 285,000 people.[85] About 70 per cent of workers on industrial estates were located in the South-East, many in estates along London's arterial roads, illustrated in Figure 16.1. Estate occupants were typically inner-London firms which had decentralised in order to obtain larger, more modern premises, that were better situated (particularly with regard to road transport). A similar trend of outward industrial migration occurred in the Birmingham conurbation, though this was almost entirely based around ribbon development rather than industrial estates.[86]

A lack of modern factory premises, built for renting, compounded the problems that Britain's traditional industrial areas faced in attracting new industry as a result of their relatively poor road transport networks, depressed local economies and remoteness from Britain's largest and most prosperous centre, London. Declining textile areas benefited from vacant factory space; for example twenty-six of the twenty-eight new firms established in Long Eaton between 1928 and 1950 occupied former lace mills.[87] However, industrial areas dominated by steel, coal or shipbuilding could offer no such facilities, while former textile factories proved less attractive than modern factory premises. The government was eventually persuaded, reluctantly, to remedy the lack of appropriate factory infrastructure in the depressed areas via a very limited programme of government-financed industrial estate development (together with other measures of assistance) during the mid-late 1930s, as discussed in Chapter 18.

[84] P. Scott, 'Planning for profit: the Garden City concept and private sector industrial estate development during the inter-war years,' *Planning History*, 16 (1994), 9–15.
[85] P. Scott, 'Industrial estates and British industrial development: 1897–1939', *Business History*, 43 (forthcoming).
[86] Nuffield College, Oxford, Archive, Nuffield College Social Reconstruction Survey Papers, C1/5, 'West Midlands Regional Report (Part A)' (October 1941). See also below, pp. 581–2.
[87] J. M. Hunter, 'Factors affecting the location and growth of industry in Greater Nottinghamshire', *East Midland Geographer*, 3 (1964), 341.

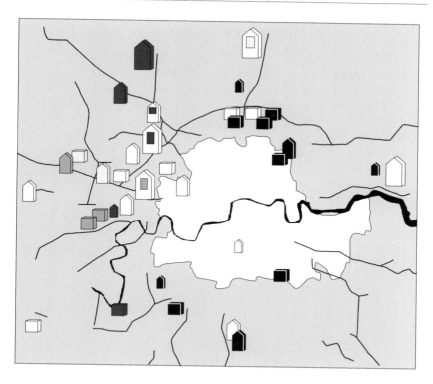

Developer	Commercial Structures Ltd	John Laing & Son Ltd	Allnatt Ltd	Percy Bilton Ltd	Others
>100 acres					
20–100 acres					
<20 acres					
Unknown acreage					

Estates involving more than one developer are indicated by a combined symbol e.g.: Commercial Structures Ltd with others

Figure 16.1 Industrial estates and arterial roads in Greater London *c.* 1938
Note: this map omits one estate for which insufficient information is available regarding location and uses one symbol for directly contiguous estates.
Source: P. Scott, 'Industrial estates and British industrial development, 1897–1939', *Business History*, 43 (forthcoming).

(iv) WAR AND RECONSTRUCTION

The onset of the Second World War led to a virtual halt in property market activity and a severe fall in commercial property values, particularly in London. Property speculators and developers were only saved from widespread bankruptcies by a voluntary moratorium on loans on the part of insurance companies, building societies and other lenders, though in a few cases insurance companies did foreclose on mortgages. However, despite extreme political and economic uncertainty, together with the physical danger to property from bomb damage, a number of far-sighted entrepreneurs began to purchase property during the war. The rationale behind such investment was simple; if the Allies were victorious property values would appreciate substantially, while if the Germans invaded Britain it would be of little importance where they had invested their money.[88] Speculators and developers also invested in bomb-damaged sites; bombing cleared large central areas which, if consolidated into single plots, might eventually be used to develop substantial buildings.

Following Labour's 1945 election victory the property sector, like many other areas of the economy, experienced a level of government intervention that was unprecedented in peacetime. Building licences severely restricted the volume of commercial property development, in order to direct scarce building materials to priority sectors. The 1947 Town and Country Planning Act provided the framework for more permanent post-war town planning controls, bringing almost all development under government control by making it subject to planning permission. Development rights and the development value of land were effectively nationalised by the act, leaving landowners with their existing (1947) use rights and land values.[89] Compensation for the loss of development rights was to be paid from a national fund, while developers had to pay a levy amounting to 100 per cent of any increase in land values resulting from new development.

The imposition of a 100 per cent tax on property development removed any incentive to develop property. A system of building licences, capital issues controls and other regulations, together with an acute shortage of building materials, placed further obstacles in the path of the developer, with the result that there was little development of new commercial property during 1945–51 outside a few narrow areas. Most commercial property development that did occur was permitted by government according to one of three criteria. Properties which might collapse, or otherwise endanger the public, if they did not receive attention were given top priority. 'Dangerous structure notices' were issued, enabling the owner to obtain a building licence.[90] Firms which were involved in eco-

[88] Marriott, *Property Boom*, p. 45. [89] Cullingworth, *Town and Country*, p. 16.
[90] J. Rose, *The Dynamics of Urban Property Development* (London, 1985), p. 150. There is evidence that this legislation was often abused in practice, via the granting of licences for structurally sound buildings.

nomic activity considered essential to Britain's post-war recovery, such as manufacturers producing goods for export, were also given high priority for essential redevelopment work. Finally, there was a considerable demand for new
property for the government's own use. Developers built offices for government
occupation under 'lessor schemes', licences being granted in return for the
developer's agreement to let the building to the government at a pre-determined
rent.

Meanwhile, the supply of commercial property had been substantially
reduced by the war; bombing had damaged or destroyed 75,000 shops, 42,000
commercial properties and 25,000 factories.[91] This damage was concentrated in
London and a number of ports and important industrial centres, such as Bristol,
Hull, Portsmouth and Coventry. Within London the worst hit area was the City,
with a third of buildings totally destroyed. Furthermore, requisitioning led to
many commercial enterprises losing the use of their premises for some time after
the war. Given the shortage of commercial premises arising from these conditions, property values inevitably soared, stimulating an investment boom on the
part of institutional and private investors. There was also a boom in corporate
property investment; many of Britain's largest property companies, such as Land
Securities, MEPC and Hammersons, were founded during the years 1944–54.

Rising property values also played an important part in the hostile takeover
boom of the early–mid-1950s. Corporate raiders such as Charles Clore, Isaac
Wolfson and Hugh Fraser found that they could use the sale and leaseback mechanism to acquire entire companies in property-rich sectors such as property,
retailing and hotels, with undervalued property assets (their balance sheet values
typically being based on purchase costs minus depreciation). In an era when high
corporate taxation depressed dividends (and, therefore, share values) it was often
possible to acquire such companies for less money than could subsequently be
raised from the sale of their properties to an insurance company, simultaneously
leasing them back for 999 years to preserve the company's value as a going
concern.

The election of a Conservative government in 1951 led to a substantial water-
ing-down of Labour's town planning legislation. The Town and Country
Planning Act of 1953 removed the 100 per cent development levy introduced
by the 1947 act and in November 1954 the other major impediment to property
development, building licences, was abolished, following several years of their
gradual relaxation. Meanwhile, building materials shortages, which would have
restricted development even in the absence of controls, had substantially eased.

The newly deregulated commercial property sector faced very buoyant
demand. In addition to pent-up demand arising from the lack of new development during the previous fifteen years, the service sector was experiencing rapid

---

[91] B. P. Whitehouse, *Partners in Property* (London, 1964), p. 13.

expansion, growing by 24.2 per cent in terms of real GDP from 1955 to 1964. The result was an unprecedented development boom. During 1955 to 1964 the value of commercial construction averaged £1,847 million in real (1980) prices, compared to an average of only £90 million during the previous nine years.[92] During the 1950s property development was probably the most prosperous sector of the British economy. Marriott estimated that no fewer than 110 people became millionaires between 1945 and 1965 as a result of their activities in this sector, most of whom started their careers without any capital 'beyond the odd hundred pounds'.[93] These included many of the most prominent entrepreneurs of the era, such as Charles Clore, Jack Cotton and Harold Samuel. Conversely, there were very few examples of business failures in the property sector during this period, in contrast to its experience during the 1970s and 1980s.

The boom was based on institutional finance and individual talent; as the property entrepreneurs usually had little initial capital they relied on the financial institutions to fund their operations. The property boom years saw a substantial rise in the level of both direct institutional investment in property and the provision of development finance.[94] A very substantial volume of institutional funds was also channelled to the property company sector via mortgage finance and institutional purchases of property company shares. By the mid-1950s some astute institutional investors were reacting to accelerating inflation by searching for ways to conduct property investment and development finance so as to obtain a share of the future capital appreciation of the assets in which they invested. This led to a number of innovations, the most important of which was the rent review.

Rent review clauses, introduced around 1955, provided for upward only revisions in rents to market levels, at regular intervals specified within leases. Reviews were first introduced only at relatively long intervals, typically every thirty-three years, leaving the property developer with most of the 'equity' of the property assets concerned. Over the years 1954–64 rents for vacant city offices increased at an average compound rate of approximately 8 per cent per annum,[95] while, as a result of rents being fixed for long periods within leases, the capital return on investment property averaged only 1.4 per cent.[96] However, a gradual reduction in the interval between rent reviews over the following decades was to transform property from a fixed-interest security to an equity investment. A similar transformation occurred in the property development finance market; from the late 1950s a substantial number of institutional investors abandoned their previous policy of providing fixed interest mortgage finance in favour of packages which

---

[92] Sources: 1948–54, M.C. Fleming, 'Construction and the related professions', in W. F. Maunder, ed., *Reviews of United Kingdom Statistical Sources*, vol. XII (Oxford, 1980); 1955–64, CSO, *Annual Abstract of Statistics* (various issues). As the figures for 1954 and 1955 are based on different (government) sources there may be some degree of distortion, though this is not likely to be great.

[93] Marriott, *Property Boom*, p. 2.   [94] Scott, *Property Masters*, pp. 252–3.

[95] Rose, *Dynamics*, p. 154.   [96] Scott, *Property Masters*, p. 282.

offered them an equity stake in the property companies whose activities they funded.

While the property boom massively increased the scale and prosperity of the British property development industry it did little to enhance the developer's public image. Property developers regularly exploited various flaws and loopholes in the post-war planning controls, undertaking development which was against the spirit, but not the letter, of the legislation. Another source of bad publicity concerned the demolition of historic buildings to make way for new office blocks. The 1950s saw a substantial increase in public concern regarding the loss of Britain's building heritage, a large number of notable buildings being replaced by what were widely regarded as some of the ugliest buildings ever seen in Britain's cities. The developer's image was also tarnished by a small number of cases of straightforward corruption, though scandals involving prominent figures in the industry were relatively few, certainly far fewer than were produced by the financial services boom of the 1980s.

The 1950s property boom, like all development booms, contained the seeds of its own destruction. By the early 1960s City office floor space was expanding at such a rate that significant oversupply was inevitable within a few years, reducing rents and leading to a downturn in development activity. In the event this was not allowed to take place, due to the introduction of the Brown Ban[97] on office development in and around London, by the 1964 Labour government. This marked the end of the 'golden age' of the British property development industry, subsequent booms (in the early 1970s and mid-late 1980s) being followed by severe crashes within a few years.

The 1950s was a period of unprecedented prosperity for the building industry, demonstrated by both rising employment (1,220,600 in 1954, compared with 757,200 in 1935), and increased industrial concentration. Firms employing over ten people accounted for 80.7 per cent of building employment in 1954 compared to 66.3 per cent in 1935; the respective figures for firms employing 500 or more were 23.4 per cent and 11.4 per cent.[98] Full employment contributed to rising building costs, but also served to stimulate innovation and efficiency improvements, since it was no longer possible to hire labour on a casual basis and lay it off during breaks in the work schedule.[99]

The post-war years saw substantial further growth of the office sector; office work expanded from 6 per cent of total employment before the war to 16 per cent in 1951, reflecting the growth of government, the tertiary sector and administrative jobs within manufacturing.[100] Following the lifting of building licence controls in November 1954 the City, and other major office centres, entered a phase of unprecedented growth. In addition to the office requirements

[97] 'Full stop for London offices', *Economist*, 230 (7 Nov. 1964), pp. 616–17.
[98] Bowley, *British Building Industry*, pp. 425–6.   [99] *Ibid.*, pp. 408–12.
[100] D. Cadman and A. Catalano, *Property Development in the UK* (Reading, 1983), p. 4.

of the City's traditional business occupants, many of the country's largest industrial companies sought prestige headquarters at the heart of Britain's capital,
divorcing their administrative centres from their factory premises.

The City's attractions as a headquarters location included its large number of
business and financial service firms, enabling companies to buy in these services
rather than providing them internally. The growing internationalisation of
British industry was a further factor leading to the concentration of head offices
in London, due to the greater need for international connections and associated
services. The post-war merger movement also increased the number of head
offices in London, given the strong relationship between company size and the
geographical separation of head office and manufacturing activities. Despite fears
of congestion in the City, decentralisation had already begun during the 1950s
(largely in response to soaring City office costs), becoming apparent by the end
of the decade. However, decentralisation did not progress far beyond the edges
of the conurbation, building in the London region accounting for an estimated
80 per cent of all new office floor space in England and Wales over 1945–62.[101]

Skyscapers of over twelve floors were still exceptional during the 1950s. Offices
in smaller towns were generally of one to five storeys, while even in larger urban
centres office blocks were generally only five to twelve storeys high. Offices were
generally designed along functional lines, to minimise costs and maximise floor
space within 'plot ratio' and other planning restrictions. They were produced economically (by the standards of the contemporary construction industry), but were
generally lacking both in aesthetic appeal and in such practical considerations as
quality, durability and amenities. As Jack Rose, one of the most active office developers during this period, recalled, 'In essence, the standard of building conformed
to the sellers' market.'[102] There were, however, a few more prestigious and innovative developments. For example, Fountain House in Fenchurch Street, built
during 1954–7, introduced the New York style of setting a tower at one end of a
low-built podium and was also one of the first British offices to use curtain walls.
This construction technique – which was later to become associated with lower-
quality developments – involved hanging external walls (usually made predominantly from glass) from the concrete floors like curtains.

During the immediate post-war years austerity, tight government controls and
restrictions on new property development had drastically limited competition
and change in the retail sector. However, by the 1950s the rising volume of retail
trade was producing pressure for further change; by the end of 1954 the value of
GDP accounted for by the distributive trades had increased by more than one
third, in real terms, compared to 1938. Further pressure for retail development
arose from the trend towards self-service retailing. This was pioneered by the

---

[101] S. Taylor, 'A study of post-war office developments', *Journal of the Town Planning Institute*, 52
(1966), 55.   [102] Rose, *Dynamics*, p. 153.

Co-operative movement, which opened Britain's first self-service grocery store, in Portsmouth, in 1947.[103]

During the late 1940s the Ministry of Food had taken steps to encourage self-service retailing, offering a hundred special building licences to retailers prepared to experiment with self-service conversion and share their experiences with other interested parties.[104] However, despite a positive response to this initiative it was not until the mid-1950s that the removal of building restrictions allowed the number of self-service stores to become substantial. By the middle of 1957 there were at least 80 supermarkets in Britain; five and a half years later their numbers had increased more than tenfold to about 1,000.[105] Serving a population that was still not largely car-borne, early supermarkets were generally restricted to units of under 10,000 sq. ft (929 sq. m), in central locations. Nevertheless, their development called for a substantial increase in average store floor space, while many non-food multiples also wished to develop significantly larger premises. The demand for major shopping centre developments was therefore considerable; by 1963 seventy large-scale central area shopping schemes were awaiting ministerial approval.[106]

Major 1950s shopping developments were often based on fully or partly pedestrianised precincts, pioneered in American suburban centres prior to the Second World War. However, by the end of the decade the first schemes for covered shopping centres (also inspired by American developments) were being considered, such as the Elephant and Castle Centre in London, and Birmingham's Bull Ring Centre. By 1960, therefore, the stage was set for further substantial changes in both the scale and form of central area shopping development.

During the 1940s and 1950s factory design remained broadly along 1930s lines, though materials shortages led to the demise of the elaborate façades which fronted many interwar factories. Factory location was subject to unprecedented control, via location of industry legislation designed to direct industry towards the regionally assisted Development Areas. Building licences, supplemented in 1947 by Industrial Development Certificates, prevented industrialists from building or extending factory premises of over 5,000 sq. ft (464 sq. m) without government approval. Meanwhile, the government undertook extensive factory building in the Development Areas during the immediate post-war period, much of which was located on industrial estates developed (or converted from wartime Royal Ordnance Factories) by government-financed companies.

The 1951 Conservative government drastically reduced the volume of government factory construction in the Development Areas and permitted more industrial development in the prosperous Midlands and South-East (trends

[103] H. Mason, 'The twentieth-century economy', in B. Stapleton and J. H. Thomas, eds., *The Portsmouth Region* (London, 1989), p. 175.   [104] Williams, *Best Butter*, pp. 126–7.
[105] W. G. McClelland, *Studies in Retailing* (Oxford, 1963), p. 19.
[106] Cadman and Catalano, *Property Development*, p. 5.

which were already visible during Labour's final years in office). Low unemployment in Britain's formerly depressed regions reduced political pressures for an active regional policy, while government intervention in the location of industry was seen as being in conflict with the government's national economic policy framework and its non-interventionist economic philosophy.[107] This downgrading of regional policy was partially reversed at the end of the decade, due to a renewed rise in regional unemployment which was to prove a long-term feature of the British economy.

Substantial government-sponsored factory development did occur during the 1950s under another initiative, New Town development. The Labour government had initiated fourteen New Towns between 1946 and 1950 as part of its comprehensive town planning framework; eight were located on the fringes of the London region, to decentralise the metropolis's population, together with six provincial New Towns. While the provincial New Towns were mainly connected with existing or planned industry, the London New Towns required the creation of an almost entirely new industrial base. Little development took place during Labour's time in office, due to legal problems and materials shortages. However, the Conservatives substantially accelerated the New Towns programme, as New Town housing development constituted a convenient means of fulfilling part of their pledge to build 300,000 new homes. During the 1950s London New Town factory construction (undertaken by the government-financed New Town Development Corporations on one or more industrial estates within each town) substantially exceeded government-sponsored factory development in Britain's declining regions.[108]

Meanwhile, the development of private sector industrial estates was largely suppressed by the continuing need for Industrial Development Certificates, which prevented the speculative development of factory premises. By failing actively to plan industrial development so as to protect Britain's declining regions, or abolish Industrial Development Certificates and leave firms to locate where they chose, government location of industry policy during the 1950s achieved neither the potential benefits of planning nor *laissez-faire*. Furthermore, the London New Towns programme directed the lion's share of government-sponsored industrial development to the already prosperous London region.

(V) CONCLUSION

By the 1950s retailing and office functions had become concentrated in particular districts within central urban areas, while manufacturing had moved out to

---

[107] P. Scott, 'The worst of both worlds: British regional policy, 1951–1964', *Business History*, 38 (1996), 41–64.

[108] P. Scott, 'Dispersion versus decentralisation: British location of industry policies and regional development 1945–1960', *Economy and Society*, 26 (1997), 579–98.

zones on the fringes of towns and cities. Economic and technological developments had exerted a powerful impetus to the process of functional and geographical concentration of non-residential property, town planning legislation (which was largely ineffective in its zoning powers prior to 1945) merely formalising trends towards geographical specialisation which had been gathering pace for many decades. This geographical and functional specialisation reached its zenith during the 1950s and 1960s. Thereafter, it has been increasingly reversed by economic, social and technological developments which have led to the decentralisation of some office and retailing activities to edge-of-town and out-of-town locations, while more recently the information technology revolution has raised the possibility of the home once again becoming a significant location for some of the activities currently undertaken in specialist commercial buildings.

The planners and the public

ABIGAIL BEACH AND NICK TIRATSOO

IN THE current literature, it is often asserted that the planning system which emerged in mid-twentieth-century Britain was remarkably and regrettably undemocratic. Planners had long wished to impose their own idiosyncratic ideas and now found themselves legally entitled to do so. Ordinary people's wishes were ignored, as common sense was jettisoned in favour of dogma. The schemes that resulted won plaudits in professional competitions but were rarely liked by the public. In the long term, some believe, this 'reform from above' actually exacerbated the urban decay and social deprivation it set out to alleviate. Many would no doubt instinctively sympathise with Lady Thatcher's robust declaration at the 1987 Conservative Conference that planners were culpable: they had 'cut the heart out of our cities'.[1]

In the following chapter, we scrutinise some of the basic historical components of this pervasive view and show that they are far too simplistic. Town planners in Britain had always meditated on the question of public participation, even if their solutions were sometimes vague or actually ambiguous. Moreover, the planning system created by Labour after the Second World War was relatively open and allowed – often encouraged – involvement from ordinary citizens. Planners and planned, it is true, did not always coexist happily under the new legislation, but this was not because the former simply ignored the latter. To understand the problems that developed means, in our view, admitting into the analysis factors that are frequently ignored, particularly the question of finance, the local government milieu in which planning occurred and the precise configuration of real (as opposed to assumed) popular thinking about the urban environment at this time.

The town planning movement which coalesced in Britain at the end of the nineteenth century was an eclectic mix of influences and interests. It contained

The authors would like to thank Martin Daunton, Steven Fielding, Junichi Hasegawa and Tatsuya Tsubaki for help and advice in their research for this chapter.

[1] M. Thatcher, *Speeches to the Conservative Party Conference 1975–1988* (London, 1989), p. 128.

elements of the technical and professional disciplines of architecture, surveying and sanitary inspection, and drew intellectual support from the developing academic fields of geography, geology, sociology and social psychology. It was informed by the pragmatic experience of late Victorian and Edwardian environmental reform and, simultaneously, by the philosophies of social conservatism, liberal progressivism and utopian socialism.[2] It was the preserve of the visionary and the technician and was both liberating and highly prescriptive. The precise sources of inspiration and impetus are still unclear, and it is not the purpose of this chapter to explore them in any depth. Nevertheless, it is important to note the composite nature of the discipline during its formative years: an understanding of the often contradictory messages informing the planning process may help to explain the at times problematic relationship which emerged between the practitioners of planning and the public.

During the first half of the twentieth century, public participation in the planning process was advocated by a number of social commentators, a few politicians and, most consistently, by leading planning experts, but this professed ideal was complicated by a concurrent emphasis on the edifying nature of good planning. Participatory citizens, supportive of cohesive and dynamic communities, were sought but, it was widely felt, first required instruction and tangible examples. This prescriptive accent reflected both the nature of the developing town planning movement and the intellectual environment into which it was received. In the early twentieth century, a keen interest in the relationship between the physical environment and social organisation developed among middle-class professionals and policy makers. A language of social improvement emerged that was an amalgam of Darwinian and Larmarckian theories of evolution, the social philosophy of Herbert Spencer, the radical reformism of Robert Owen and John Stuart Mill, and the pragmatic experience of half a century of public health policy.[3] The notion of town planning was part of this rhetoric. Drawing support and personnel from an assortment of progressive groups and from a preventive health lobby which had long advocated the social importance of environmental improvements, as well as financial backing from prominent politicians and businessmen with an affinity for the notion of regeneration (for national efficiency, if not ethical or spiritual reasons), a town planning movement began to press the case for housing and land-use reform.[4] At the centre of their advocacy lay the

---

[2] P. Hall, *Cities of Tomorrow* (Oxford, 1988).

[3] D. Porter, '"Enemies of the race": biologism, environmentalism and public health in Edwardian England', *Victorian Studies*, 34 (1991), 158–78; J. Harris, *Private Lives, Public Spirit: Britain, 1870–1914* (Harmondsworth, 1994 edn), pp. 242–5.

[4] On 'national efficiency' see G. Searle, *The Quest for National Efficiency: A Study in British Politics and Political Thought, 1899–1914* (Oxford, 1971). The Birmingham housing reform advocate, J. S. Nettlefold, part of Joseph Chamberlain's network, cited national efficiency as one of the factors motivating his call for housing reform. See J. S. Nettlefold, *A Housing Policy* (Birmingham, 1905), and *Practical Town Planning* (London, 1914).

relationship between the built environment and the community. Good town planning, in conjunction with other ameliorative reforms, could favourably influence not just the health but the spirit of the nation.

The beneficial, indeed edifying, influence of a good physical environment had emerged as a strong theme in a number of late Victorian housing and social reform experiments. Tangible examples of this pragmatic 'idealism', for instance, were seen in the settlement house movement, and perhaps most notably in Canon Samuel Barnett's project at Toynbee Hall in the East End of London,[5] and in the housing refurbishment and management schemes of Octavia Hill which had been supported (financially and morally) by John Ruskin from the 1870s.[6] Urban improvement, as espoused by Barnett and Hill, was a social as well as a physical activity which, crucially, hinged on the development of positive relationships between individual citizens and their environment. Hill's housing reform efforts, for example, focused on her tenants rather than on the actual fabric of the buildings she took over. Through personal intervention and door-to-door contact by Hill and her team of women housing workers, tenants were encouraged, through a combination of incentives and penalties, to assume responsibility for the maintenance and improvement of their own homes. As Helen Meller has recently argued, for Hill, 'urban renewal took place around a healthy community', the development of which was first and foremost 'a matter of personal caring'.[7] Canon Barnett's work in Whitechapel, centred on the university settlement at Toynbee Hall, similarly invested in personal relationships, and the mutual learning which could arise from a closer interaction of wealthy and poor, of the cultured and the unrefined.[8] Both projects were clearly restricted by the numbers of people who could be reached in this way. Nevertheless, significant elements of their message, if not their methods, were taken up by the emerging town planning movement which, composed largely of a mixture of idealist (often idiosyncratic) reformers and, from the 1910s onwards, technical experts eager to carve out a professional identity for themselves, contained a distinctly didactic message.

The work of Raymond Unwin, planner and architect, along with his cousin Barry Parker, on the first Garden City at Letchworth between 1904 and 1906

---

[5] H. O. Barnett, *Canon Barnett: His Life, Work and Friends* (London, 1921 edn); A. Briggs and A. Macartney, *Toynbee Hall: The First Hundred Years* (London, 1984).

[6] O. Hill, *Homes of the London Poor* (London, 1875; repr. 1970); O. Hill, *House Property and its Management* (London, 1901); O. Hill, 'Management of homes for the poor', in her *Letters to my Fellow Workers* (published privately, 1898–9). See also A. Power, 'The development of unpopular housing estates and attempted remedies, 1895–1984' (PhD thesis, University of London, 1985), pp. 20–32.

[7] H. E. Meller, 'Urban renewal and citizenship: the quality of life in British cities, 1890–1990', *UH*, 22 (1995), 68.

[8] *Ibid.*, 68–9; Barnett, *Canon Barnett*; Briggs and Macartney, *Toynbee Hall*. See also S. A. and H. O. Barnett, *Towards Social Reform* (London, 1909).

(and also on much of Hampstead Garden Suburb, the co-partnership housing development initiated by Henrietta Barnett, wife of Canon Barnett), illustrates the ambiguities which this didacticism brought to the developing relationship between the planner and the planned. Unwin's work was deeply influenced by his political views. He was a socialist in the mould of Edward Carpenter and William Morris who believed that social progress was obtainable through the substitution of the values of community and human dignity for class antagonism. Influenced by Morris and also by John Ruskin in his early years, Unwin shared their conviction that beauty could be found in all aspects of daily life and should be positively cultivated by, and for, all.[9] He also took from them, and from the wider 'Arts and Crafts' fraternity, the belief that form should reflect function.[10] Town and housing design offered him a medium through which to explore these conjunctions between art, life and morality. In Unwin's view, a reciprocal and interactive relationship existed between the built environment and the community. Social coherence, for instance, could be encouraged through the visual coherence of a place, and a sense of community enhanced by the 'aesthetic control' of building materials, housing design and layout.[11] This conception of town planning, however, contained an equivocal message about the role of the ordinary citizen in the planning process. If a town's design and architecture was to reflect, and indeed shape, the spirit and the purpose of 'the individual lives lived within' it, then who was to decide or interpret what that spirit and purposes should be?[12] Barry Parker and Raymond Unwin both considered town planning (or 'civic art' as they had originally called it) a 'democratic art', believing that the public should participate in the plan-making process. The role of the architect-planner was to give physical shape to the needs and aspirations of a community.[13] This commitment to democratic planning, however, was underwritten by a belief that ultimate responsibility must lie with the architect. As the 'disinterested mentors' of the citizens of 'England's emerging democracy', architects would teach the people, 'through the experience of living within healthy, liberating environments', the 'difference between good architecture and bad', helping them to develop 'a worthy moral aesthetic of their own'.[14]

The inherent tension between these two aspects of Unwin and Parker's planning philosophy can be seen in their rejection of the parlour in cottages designed

[9] S. Meacham, 'Raymond Unwin, 1863–1940: designing for democracy in Edwardian England', in S. Pedersen and P. Mandler, eds., *After the Victorians* (London, 1994), pp. 79–83.
[10] C. F. A. Voysey, C. R. Ashbee, W. R. Lethaby, M. H. Baillie Scott and many other designers and architects contemporary to them all carried references to Morris in their work.
[11] R. Unwin and B. Parker, *The Art of Building a Home* (London, 1901), pp. 107–8.
[12] Meacham, 'Raymond Unwin', p. 84.
[13] M.G. Day, 'The contribution of Sir Raymond Unwin and R. Barry Parker to the development of site planning theory and practice c. 1890–1918', in A. Sutcliffe, ed., *British Town Planning* (Leicester, 1981), p. 157.   [14] Meacham, 'Raymond Unwin', p. 84.

for Letchworth Garden City. The separate parlour was, in their view, a waste of valuable space in the crowded working-class home and a misguided 'craving for bourgeois respectability' which should have no place in a modern democracy. A single, large day-room, they suggested, better reflected the needs and living arrangements of the worker's family. Yet, to those with few resources to spare, the parlour 'though perhaps irrational, embodied, in an important, tangible form a family's ability to afford something beyond the minimum'.[15] As the first issue of the *Garden City* journal put it, workmen and their wives 'like the parlour and they mean to have it'.[16] Unwin's cottages may have been 'good enough as scenery' but 'they were not designed to suit the needs or prejudices of the London workman' who was coming to live and work there.[17]

A comparable tension can be seen in the work of the Scottish planner, Patrick Geddes.[18] Geddes was an idiosyncratic participant in the emerging field of town planning, but his ideas on urban regeneration, or 'civics' as he termed it, similarly inferred an ambiguous relationship between the planners and the planned. His thinking on civics contained a vigorous conception of citizenship, extending beyond a shared knowledge of place, to entail a certain progressive dynamism. As R. J. Halliday puts it, in Geddesian civics 'the precondition of citizenship was not just social awareness, but also the drastic and planned improvement of both natural and urban environment'.[19] As a cog instrumental in driving the whole machine, the citizen of Geddes' prescription was to be an active participant in the regenerative process. The citizens he saw in early twentieth-century Edinburgh, however, displayed a marked apathy and a lack of care or knowledge about their place. Nevertheless, Geddes was optimistic that this could be reversed and, indeed, saw evidence of the beginnings of change in the growing interest in civic societies and associations. Education, in his view, was the key to unlocking this potential citizenship. A crucial part of the educational experience would be the survey – to collect, marshal and exhibit data on all aspects of life in the city and region. The sheer physical task of this work, it was argued, would equip the citizens engaged on the project with a better understanding of the present and future needs of their place.[20] Children, in particular, were targeted as the future citizens of the renascent town. Yet, education at a higher level also had a role to play in Geddes' scheme. The university, in particular, was regarded as an ideal focus for a regenerating city. In Edinburgh's case, the university, set in the midst of the old town, could help the city 'become, once again, an "Athens of the North", as it had been in the late eighteenth

---

[15] *Ibid.*, p. 86.   [16] *The Garden City*, 1 Oct. 1906, not paginated, quoted in *ibid.*, p. 94.
[17] D. B. Cockerall, 'A workshop in London and in Letchworth', *The City*, 1 Feb. 1909, 35, quoted in *ibid.*, p. 94.   [18] H. E. Meller, *Patrick Geddes* (London, 1990), p. 35, quoted in *ibid.*, p. 94.
[19] R. J. Halliday, 'The sociological movement, the sociological society and the genesis of academic sociology in Britain', *Sociological Review*, new series, 16 (1968), 393.
[20] H. Meller, ed., *The Ideal City* (Leicester, 1979), p. 29.

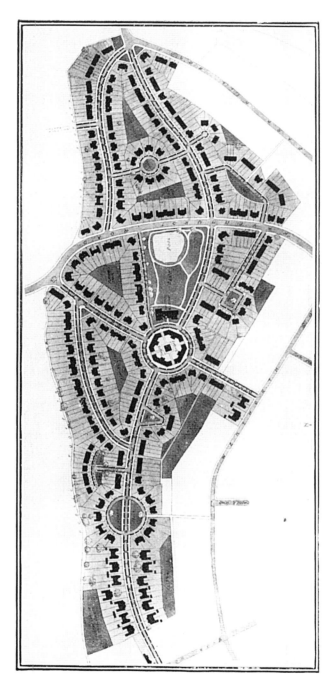

Figure 17.1 Plans comparing the layout of the estate built by Harborne Tenants Ltd in Birmingham at ten houses per acre with hypothetical by-law layout at forty houses per acre
Site plan of Harborne tenants showing ten houses per acre

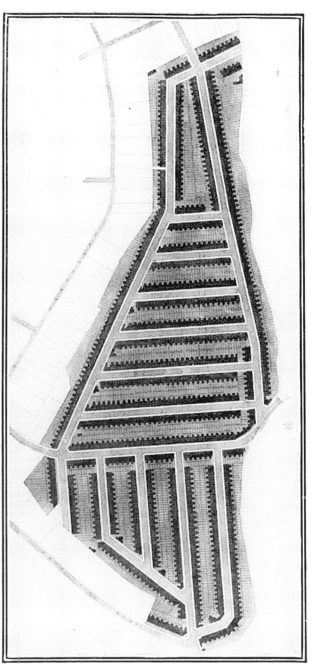

Figure 17.1 (*cont.*) Ordinary type of site plan showing forty houses per acre
Source: L. P. Abercrombie, 'Modern town planning in England: a comparative review of
"garden city" schemes in England, Part II', *Town Planning Review*, 1 (1910–11), plate 42.

century'.[21] Geddes' project, therefore, exhibited a tension between the ideal of the participatory citizen and direction from an elite body. He, typically, had a term for this dualism, calling it 'aristo-democracy'.[22] The problem with a latent citizenship was that it required some precipitating factor; if this was to be education, then who was to be the educator? Geddes spoke in terms of both self-education by experience but also of the guiding light of the university and those, like Geddes himself, who had already made the transition.

The tension between the aristocratic and the democratic was never fully resolved by Geddes, nor, indeed, by Raymond Unwin.[23] Such dualism was not uncommon in early twentieth-century social thought, and, in articulating it, Geddes and Unwin were, as Standish Meacham has put it, 'men of their time and of their class, preaching along with other men and women to settlement house audiences, in Fabian Society lectures, to University Extension and Workers' Educational Association students a particular brand of high-minded culture which they believed would bring about the enlightenment of individuals and the creation of a right-minded democratic society'.[24] It was, moreover, a durable legacy of the early planning movement. Later town planners, such as Frederic Osborn, secretary of the Town and Country Planning Association during the 1930s, felt the potential contradiction just as keenly. Like Geddes before him, Osborn seems to have been torn by his eagerness to involve the public in town planning issues, and his awareness of the complexity and what he regarded as the novelty of his subject. Frederic Osborn recognised that the public had a right to express their preferences on the issue, and, indeed, welcomed this form of decentralisation of initiative. For instance, he criticised the 'Bloomsbury' view of planning held by certain architects and aesthetes who dismissed the Garden Cities of Letchworth and Welwyn, which Osborn saw as 'the practical exposition of the people's wants', as naive and gauche.[25] Yet, it is common to find amongst Osborn's correspondence an exasperation with the public. Writing to Sir Montague Barlow on the proposals of the Uthwatt Committee on compensation and betterment, he bemoaned the handicap imposed on the Town and Country Planning Association 'by the inability even of the select public to understand the issues . . . It really is too new a topic for the phase it has reached. Gradually the powers are being built up, but it needs a much clearer and stronger public opinion to get them used rightly.'[26] This knowledge gap between

[21] Meller, 'Urban renewal and citizenship', 70.
[22] P. Geddes, *Dramatisations of History* (Bombay, 1923), p. 174.
[23] Meacham, 'Raymond Unwin', p. 84.   [24] *Ibid.*, pp. 84–5.
[25] Frederic Osborn Archive, Welwyn Garden City, B.119, letter from F. J. Osborn to C. B. Purdom, 2 June 1944.
[26] Frederic Osborn Archive, B.14, letter from F. J. Osborn to Sir Montague Barlow, 11 July 1944. Ministry of Works and Planning, *Interim and Final Reports of the Expert Committee on Compensation and Betterment (Uthwatt)*, Cmds 6291 and 6386 (London, 1940–1).

themselves, a highly trained minority, and the public, the bewildered lay majority, continued to frustrate planners and architects into the post-war period.

If the intellectual basis of town planning in the early twentieth century implied
an ambivalent relationship between the planners and the public, the wider experience of town planning practice imposed further limitations on both the advocacy and the achievement of a broad-based public involvement in the planning
process. From the very beginning the town planning movement was susceptible
to countervailing pressures, particularly from its financial and business backers.
Ebenezer Howard's vision of a new 'Garden City', a self-contained entity
offering inhabitants a home, work and community amenities, was based on the
traditional symbol of community: the common entitlement to the land. Land
reform was, in Howard's view, 'the foundation on which all other reforms must
be built'.[27] Drawing heavily on the ideas of Henry George, an American advocate of land reform whose criticism of landlordism was beginning to find favour
among British radical liberals, Howard envisaged his garden city as a vehicle for
returning to the community the 'unearned increment' in value which hitherto
fell to landlords in the form of rent.[28] As well as providing the financial basis for
the new city, this measure would, Howard argued, bring a qualitative social,
indeed, spiritual benefit, unifying the residents through a common interest.[29]
Moreover, by giving residents a voice over land use, collective tenure was a mechanism of empowerment, offering protection from abuse by those with money.[30]

This model for the 'progressive reconstruction of capitalist society into an
infinity of co-operative commonwealths' was to be given tangible form in the
first garden city at Letchworth. However, fundamental components of the plan
were frustrated by commercial realism and the need for pragmatism.[31] Howard's
'Georgite' position on rent, for instance, was substantially altered in its translation into practice. The major objective of securing the increment in rent of
enhanced land value was not realised in Howard's lifetime and only partially
afterwards. Commercial pragmatism diluted the ideal: leases of 999 years carrying only nominal ground rents had to be granted to industrialists in order to
induce them to bring their enterprises to the town, and rents of housing plots
could not be revised for 100 years. Howard's ideal of tenant self-government was
similarly compromised. This had been a key part of Raymond Unwin's agenda
for the garden city – a part of his commitment to a diminution of 'class' distinctions. Yet, as Meacham has noted, Letchworth's governmental structure 'did little

---

[27] R. Beevers, *Garden Cities and New Towns* (London, 1990), p. 26; Hall, *Cities of Tomorrow*, p. 87.
See also E. Howard, *Garden Cities of Tomorrow* (London, 1902).

[28] For a discussion of the ideas of Henry George and the politics of the land question see A. Offer,
Property and Politics, 1870–1914 (Cambridge, 1981).

[29] D. MacFadyen, ed., *Sir Ebenezer Howard and the Garden City Movement* (Manchester, 1933), p. 64.

[30] E. Howard, 'The land question at Letchworth, II', *The City*, 1 (1909), 183–4.

[31] *Ibid.*, 178. See also E. Howard, 'Our first Garden City', *St George's Magazine* (July 1904), 182.

to promote democratic participation across class lines' and 'the constantly intrusive presence of the Company in the affairs and decision-making of the community cast a paternalistic pall over the enterprise'.[32]

A comparable tension also emerged at Hampstead Garden Suburb and in other communities built on the co-partnership model during this period.[33] The planners' rhetoric stressed the social value of mixed neighbourhoods, but a conception of 'equality' was noticeably absent. Instead, the dominant sentiments were 'fraternity', 'community' and 'fellowship'.[34] The actual involvement of tenants in the running of the estates varied widely and, in the cases of the flagship Ealing and Hampstead Tenants' Societies, was very quickly diminished. The Ealing society, whose initial management committee consisted of eleven members, seven of whom were tenants, 'had inherited the Tenant Co-partners' rule of one person one vote'. However, this policy was changed between 1907 and 1908: the new constitution allowed voting by proxy and, crucially, awarded 'an additional vote for every set of ten shares held'.[35] Interestingly, both at Ealing and at Hampstead Garden Suburb, associations of tenants were formed in the aftermath of this change 'to advocate the return to those principles of true co-partnership in housing, the wilful or careless neglect of which has been the fruitful cause of much discontent among the Hampstead Tenant Shareholders, and others'.[36] Other societies maintained a degree of tenant involvement at the level of the management committee beyond the First World War, but it is clear that pressure from commercial interests strained the relationship between non-tenant members and tenants at various points during their history.[37]

At a time when the questions of landownership and taxation had become highly politicised, co-partnership housing and site planning tended to be seen as a less controversial substitute for more elemental reform. In a similar way, the 1909 Housing and Town Planning Act, while it reflected the contemporary resonance of the garden city idea, clearly stopped short of the movement's ideals. Under its provisions, local authorities were permitted to prepare town planning schemes for land which was about to be developed or which 'appeared likely to be used for building purposes', giving them power to control standards of layout and impose conditions of development.[38] Existing built-up areas were unaffected. Moreover, the municipalities were not given powers to acquire land compulsorily for future town extension as many reformers, such as J. S.

[32] Meacham, 'Raymond Unwin', p. 95.
[33] J. Birchall, 'Co-partnership housing and the garden city movement', *Planning Perspectives*, 10 (1995), 329–58; K. J. Skilleter, 'The role of public utility societies in early British town planning and housing reform, 1901–1936', *Planning Perspectives*, 8 (1993), 125–65; M. Miller and A. Gray, *Hampstead Garden Suburb* (Chichester, 1992).   [34] Birchall, 'Co-partnership housing', 346.
[35] *Ibid.*, 349.   [36] Quoted in Skilleter, 'The role of public utility societies', 145.
[37] Birchall, 'Co-partnership housing', 350–2.
[38] S. M. Gaskell, '"The suburb salubrious": town planning in practice', in Sutcliffe, ed., *British Town Planning*, pp. 19, 41.

Nettlefold and T. C. Horsfall, had urged.[39] As a result, planning was limited in practice to suburban extension, and not the novel development envisaged by Ebenezer Howard, and 'as time passed, most observers came to agree that the intricacies of the Act, which were designed mainly to protect private property, were a serious obstacle' to imaginative and community-orientated town planning.[40]

However, the dilution of the garden city model and the concurrent dwindling of the co-partnership housing movement did not dissolve the town planning movement's exploration of the connection between tenure and citizen empowerment, for many planners and politicians now transferred their hopes to the local authority, as the locus of community democracy. Labour and Fabian socialist reformers, whose numbers were beginning to swell the borough councils of London and some other large urban centres, particularly supported the elected local authority as the prime medium for a democratic housing and planning policy. Raymond Unwin, himself a Fabian socialist, was in the forefront of this shift, diverting his energies into the development of council housing during and after the First World War. Yet, the interwar local government framework brought its own constraints upon the development of a wide public involvement in the planning process, not least of which was the failure to develop a comprehensive framework for compensation and betterment.

Since the late Victorian and Edwardian periods, the problems of local government finance, and the rating system in particular, had developed into an issue of huge political importance.[41] From 1918 this was exacerbated by the rising social demands placed upon local authorities and, as the post-war boom disintegrated into slump and cutbacks, many found it increasingly difficult to meet the demands made upon them. While social reconstruction, and particularly housing and unemployment relief, remained at the forefront of political debate, ratepayers' associations and pressure from conservative municipal reform groupings seemingly put a ceiling on the raising of revenue from the traditional rates.[42] The local execution of town planning schemes was severely limited by this pressure. While decentralisation of the working population into garden cities had retained the imagination of the planners, and had gained the support of the Labour party, both at national and local levels, the structure of local government

[39] G. E. Cherry, *Cities and Plans* (London, 1988), p. 71; Nettlefold, *Housing Policy*; T. C. Horsfall, *The Improvement of the Dwellings and Surroundings of the People: The Example of Germany* (Manchester, 1904).

[40] A. Sutcliffe, *Towards the Planned City* (Oxford, 1981), pp. 82, 84–6; Gaskell, '"The suburb salubrious"', 41.

[41] J. Harris, 'The transition to high politics in English social policy, 1880–1914', in M. Bentley and J. Stevenson, eds., *High and Low Politics in Modern Britain* (Oxford, 1983), pp. 73–6; Offer, *Property and Politics*.

[42] J. E. Cronin, *The Politics of State Expansion: War, State and Society in Twentieth Century Britain* (New York, 1991), p. 94.

finance acted as a strong barrier to its practical implementation. Locating industrial and retail activity within the city centre was a profitable strategy for local
authorities in terms of the collection of rates for its coffers. Suburban housing
development had brought similar benefits but with the greater restrictions of the
1935 Ribbon Development Act this was an increasingly closed option. By way
of contrast, the building of out-county housing estates or satellite town developments would diminish the authorities' rateable value. For many local authorities, therefore, the development of an innovative plan for decentralisation was,
virtually, financial folly. The issue was further compounded by the failure of
planning legislation to address successfully the problem of compensation and
betterment. The 1909 act had skirted around this issue, largely under pressure
from property interests, and while the 1932 Town Planning Act included provisions for the recovery of betterment from owners whose property increased in
value as a result of a town planning scheme, it lacked strength to ensure implementation and was rarely effective. The result, Lewis Silkin, Labour's town planning spokesman, argued in 1943, was 'the prevention of really bold and
imaginative schemes' with local authorities tending 'to take the line of least resistance and to prepare schemes which involve the minimum risk of compensation, generally based on the existing uses of land'.[43]

Yet, while elements of the intellectual and political climate inhibited the artic-
ulation and development of a broadly participatory town planning process
during the interwar years, town planning thought undoubtedly retained an
interest in the potential social value of community-oriented planning. Much
town planning literature, for instance, continued to be informed by a rhetoric
of social integration and cooperation which stressed the importance of a vigorous and participatory community life. This approach to town planning and
housing policy, indeed, seemed even more imperative in the light of the perceived social and economic trends of the period, and in response to the specific
experiences of building during these years. The *New Survey of London Life and
Labour*, produced by Herbert Llewellyn Smith and his team of researchers from
1928, for example, assembled evidence of the continued segregation of the social
classes in London. While the middle classes were increasingly located in the burgeoning suburbs, the whole of London's inner east was conversely characterised
by a high concentration of working-class families.[44] It was, moreover, a situation
which found echoes in other major urban locations, particularly in the Distressed
Areas, such as the north-east conurbation. Concern for the implications of this
unbalanced social structure was one of the ways in which the question of community continued to be examined in the interwar period. The development of
large, out-of-town housing estates, built primarily to resettle the slum-bound

---

[43] L. Silkin, *The Nation's Land* (London, 1943), p. 9.
[44] H. Llewellyn Smith, ed., *New Survey of London Life and Labour* (London, 1930–5); J. A. Yelling, *Slums and Redevelopment* (London, 1992), p. 177.

working classes, occasioned widespread criticism. The huge Dagenham and Becontree estate on the east London and Essex border, for example, became an emblem among planners and sociologists, representing the problems that could result from a social housing policy which, however well meaning, failed to confront the complexities of building for a new community.[45] Social integration, it was quickly realised, required more than the building of new self-contained settlements. Several points were highlighted.

One area of interwar town planning thought which addressed the question of the relationship between the built environment and the developing community, as noted above, focused on the social mix of the community. During this period, indeed, a balanced mix between the social classes became, for many planners and social commentators, the defining characteristic of good town planning. At the centre of their criticism lay the policy of rehousing the working population in out-county housing estates. Instead of building stable and integrated communities, local authorities had created new zones of exclusion. Looking back from 1950, L. E. White felt that the one-income estate had become 'the true habitat for a rootless generation'.[46] Yet, while this remained a popular view among planners and politicians, informing new towns and housing policy into the post-war period, a number of commentators preferred to stress the advantages of social homogeneity, often advocating the redevelopment of inner-city areas as an alternative policy.[47] This, they argued, was more in line with residents' wishes. While the physical infrastructure of many inner-city areas was admittedly deplorable, residents found compensation in a positive social life and network. Mrs Bentwick's study of Bermondsey for the London County Council noted that although people liked cottage homes in preference to flats, they nevertheless preferred flats in Bermondsey to cottages elsewhere. 'One reason for the happy atmosphere of the Borough', she argued, 'is the fact that 95 per cent of its population is working class. It is the mixed boroughs like Kensington and Wandsworth which lack this extreme civic pride and consciousness and sense of unity.'[48] At the heart of both viewpoints lay a belief that good town planning required a positive interaction between the planners and the public which they served. Yet, neither had developed a coherent argument on how this might realistically be achieved.

A number of commentaries on town planning in the interwar years, however, did stress the importance of understanding both the existing life and the future hopes of incoming residents. For example, in their evaluation of the housing and planning policy of the corporation of Bristol, Rosamund Jevons and John Madge

---

[45] For the development of Dagenham and Becontree, see A. Olechnowicz, *Working-Class Housing in England Between the Wars* (Oxford, 1997).
[46] L. E. White, *Community or Chaos?* (London, 1950), p. 13.
[47] Yelling, *Slums and Redevelopment*, pp. 177–82.
[48] Greater London Record Office, AR/TP/1/56. Report on Bermondsey, 3 May 1941, quoted in Yelling, *Slums and Redevelopment*, p. 181.

noted the failure of many planners fully to 'appreciate the implications of living in central areas' before building the new estates on the outskirts of the city:

> A knowledge of the institutions upon which urban populations rely for amuse-
> ments, for convenience and in time of need, is of primary importance as a guide
> to the amenities required in new neighbourhoods. This knowledge gives an insight
> into the nature of an environment which appeals to the tastes and imagination of
> town people; it is up to the planners to retain the advantages of this environment
> and at the same time to eliminate its faults. Prejudice against urbanism as such is
> not an attitude calculated to lead to organic planning.[49]

Nevertheless, while Jevons and Madge seem to have recognised the importance of prior and on-going consultation between planners and residents, they, like many other commentators, did not press this argument to its logical conclusion: the best means to achieve such a confluence of aims in practice, for instance, were barely articulated.

A more developed sense of the interaction between the emerging commu-
nity and the built environment perhaps surfaced in the continuing interest in the social function of communal buildings and institutions. Throughout the 1930s the New Estates Community Committee of the voluntary organisation the National Council of Social Services (NCSS) pressed the case for community associations and community centres.[50] These local groups and buildings, it argued, could play a crucial role in breaking down the barriers of isolation which, it was felt, were an all too common feature of the new housing estates. The lack of an established tradition of community activity within the new estates was problematic, but also provided a positive opportunity and a challenge 'to those who live there to build up a community life that is something different from the life of the old towns'. The absence of vested interests and competing organisations, indeed, could be valuable, creating 'greater opportunity for self-
development' and providing 'a clear field on which to plan what the citizens themselves desire to realise'.[51] Yet, as Jevons and Madge noted, the resident pop-
ulation needed to develop its own sense of the value of these institutions and buildings if a genuine sense of community was to develop. While the local authority had responsibility for providing communal buildings, the balance of evidence from Bristol, they suggested, was 'against continued municipal control'. Instead, the local community should be encouraged to take over their

[49] R. Jevons and J. Madge, *Housing Estates* (Bristol, 1946), p. 85.

[50] The New Estates Community Committee of the NCSS was established in 1928. It was representative of the NCSS, the British Association of Residential Settlements and the Educational
Settlements' Association. It was chaired by Ernest Barker, theorist and writer on English political
thought (and the first Professor of Political Science at Cambridge) and an active advocate of community regeneration. On the National Council of Social Service see M. Brasnett, *Voluntary Social
Action: A History of the National Council of Social Service, 1919–69* (London, 1969). See also R. Clarke,
ed., *Enterprising Neighbours: The Development of the Community Association Movement in Britain*
(London, 1990). On Barker, see J. Stapleton, *Englishness and the Study of Politics* (Cambridge, 1994).

[51] Anon., 'Community work in the new housing estates', *Social Service Review*, 11 (1930), 93.

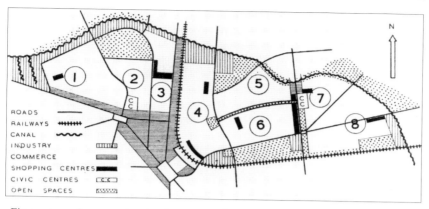

Figure 17.2 Suggested redevelopment of an area of 980 acres in East London
'As the key plan and axonometric view show, the area comprises the two
communities of Shoreditch and Bethnal Green, which are built up of three and
five neighbourhood units respectively; each unit has its own local shopping and
community centre. The populations of the units vary between 6,900 and
10,800 and are housed at a net density of 136 persons to the acre. New open
space is shown provided to bring the standard up to 4 acres per 1,000 persons.
To achieve this layout, decentralisation of a proportion of the 1938 population
will be necessary. 126 acres of new open space are shown in the scheme,
which, together with the existing 30 acres and an allowance of 134 acres of the
adjoining open spaces (Victoria Park and proposed new parks) give a total of
290 acres. The axonometric view shows the character of development at the
136 density and the proportion of flats and houses that it is possible to provide.
The proposals embody the character and vitality of a new East End.'
Source: County of London Plan, 1943.

management as soon as possible: 'People dislike to think that some paternal
outside authority is trying to teach them how to be pally when mutual help is a
virtue which they were practising generations before new estates were planned.
In the long run, inhabitants alone can build up their own community life.'[52] The
integrative role and democratic potential of community-run institutions continued to interest planners after the Second World War. Not only did the NCSS
maintain its sponsorship of the Community Association and Centre movement
into the post-war period, but neighbourhood plans, for both new and existing
towns, often incorporated designs for locally managed communal buildings and
projects, such as community, arts and health centres. The Second World War and
the need for large-scale reconstruction of the urban environment, indeed, forced
planners and politicians to address the nature of their relationship with the public
under whom they served more thoroughly than ever before.

[52] Jevons and Madge, *Housing Estates*, p. 93.

539

RECONSTRUCTION OF AN AREA IN
SHOREDITCH AND BETHNAL GREEN

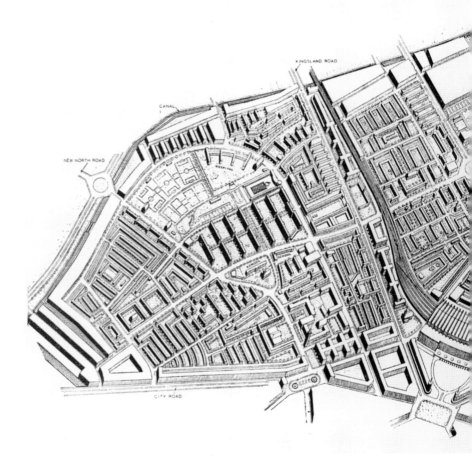

Figure 17.2 (cont.)

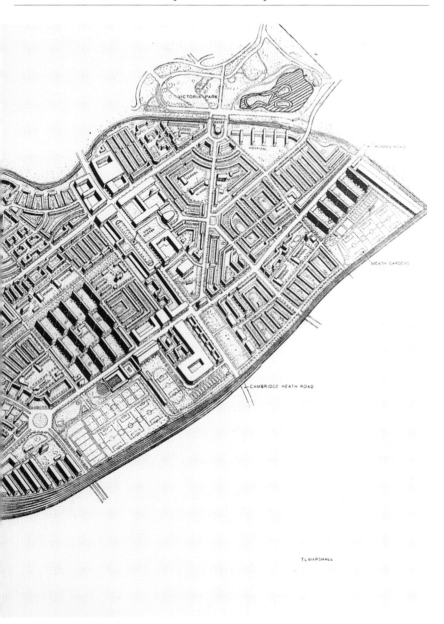

Labour's victory in the 1945 general election certainly promised a new dawn for town planning. The party had long-standing links with the planning movement and shared many of its broad goals. Labour believed that British cities were technically dysfunctional. Many suffered from congestion and were poorly zoned. Most, too, had failed their working-class populations, as the numerous slum districts graphically demonstrated. More fundamentally, the pattern of urban living seemed to discourage community and good fellowship, ideals that were at the very heart of Labour's socialism.[53] Aneurin Bevan, Minister of Health in the new government, denounced the social segregation that was apparent in cities and argued that people must be brought together. There was great merit, he believed, in the old village pattern, where 'the doctor could reside benignly with his patient in the same street'.[54] In this view, there was no better way of reintegrating citizens than involving them in decision making about their own localities.

During the next few years, Labour did much to act upon such ideas. The central piece of fresh legislation was the 1947 Town and Country Planning Act. This rationalised the number of planning authorities, devolving responsibility on to county boroughs or county councils, and instructed the new bodies to prepare development plans for their localities. It also introduced complex procedures for dealing with compensation and betterment, allowing national resources to be used as necessary in the solution of local ownership problems.

This legislation clearly meant that civil servants, councillors and professional planners would play new and enhanced roles, but it also allowed for a considerable measure of public input. Planning authorities were instructed to consult as widely as possible when constructing their plans. Moreover, ordinary citizens had the right to challenge the final recommendations, through an appeals procedure before an inspector at a public hearing. The objective was to strike a balance between the requirement for technical expertise in planning and the interests of the individual.

Other policies reinforced the drive towards community and participation. Labour was formally committed to building new housing estates as neighbourhood units on the lines advocated by Sir Charles Reilly, Lever Professor of Design at Liverpool University, since it was believed that these would promote social intercourse and intelligent debate (in Reilly's words, 'the advantages of a residential university').[55] It also wanted to bridge the gap between those in town halls and their constituents. A Consultative Committee on Publicity for Local Government was created in 1946 to review procedures and make recommendations. The central overall aim, as the leader of Coventry's authority explained at the end of the war, was to perfect 'a new democratic technique' which would

[53] S. Fielding *et al.*, *'England Arise!' The Labour Party and Popular Politics in 1940s Britain* (Manchester, 1995).   [54] Quoted in *Architects' Journal*, 24 June 1948.   [55] *Tribune*, 16 Feb. 1945.

Table 17.1 *Appeals under the 1947 Town and Country Planning Act 1947–1950*

	1947	1948	1949	1950
Cases disposed of	2,481	2,750	4,237	3,797
Appeals allowed	417	424	768	995
Appeals dismissed	920	831	1,169	1,271
Appeals withdrawn	1,144	1,495	2,300	1,531

Source: Cmd 8204, Ministry of Local Government and Planning, Town and Country Planning 1943–51 (April 1951), p. 179.

'make the citizen conscious of the vital part, the living part he [*sic*] has to play ... in a real democracy'.[56]

What did these various measures achieve? The 1947 act's financial measures remained controversial but its appeals procedure proved something of a success. The Ministry responsible, it was noted, seemed to be making a real effort at openness. An American academic visitor reported: 'Inspectors . . . permit gratuitous expressions of opinion. Objections to evidence on technical grounds are rather unpopular. Letters and petitions are admitted without formal identification and substantial latitude is permitted in cross-examination. Expenses of hearing are nominal, making redress practically available to all.'[57] Furthermore, it was obvious that complaints were receiving a fair hearing. As Table 17.1 illustrates, successful appeals always made up at least 30 per cent of the cases adjudicated upon.

On the other hand, progress elsewhere was far less marked. Few councils were able even to envisage building neighbourhood units because of the stringent financial controls which were imposed on them by Whitehall, especially after 1947. Nor did the drive for local publicity gain any great momentum. Some councils opened information offices, while others held planning or reconstruction exhibitions, but they were in a minority. Many felt nothing new was required. One town clerk told the Consultative Committee 'that news travelled so fast in his area that there was little need of any channel of communication with the public'.[58] Most worrying for Labour, finally, was the widely shared perception that few members of the public were becoming in any way 'planning minded'. As the prominent London School of Economics (LSE) political scientist W. A. Robson argued in 1952, planning seemed to have become becalmed

---

[56] *Coventry Evening Telegraph*, 12 June 1945.
[57] R. Vance Presthus, 'British town and country planning: local participation', *American Political Science Review*, 155 (1951), 765–6.
[58] H. J. Boyden, *Councils and their Public* (London, 1961), p. 2.

at what he called 'the Third Programme stage of evolution', with just a few hundred thousand of Britain's 40 million inhabitants interested.[59]

What explains this relative failure? Obviously, part of the apathy, even hostility, can be discounted to the very specific circumstances of launching a new regulatory system. Contemporaries recognised this, with the journal *Planning*, for example, observing in 1950: 'it is largely the negative aspect of town and country planning – the limitation of immediate individual freedom for the ultimate common good – which is obvious at the moment, while it is too early as yet to point to widespread positive results'.[60] On the other hand, this was certainly not the whole explanation. There were problems with the way planning was being implemented at local level and a deeper set of antagonisms apparent amongst the public. Each of these factors will now be examined in turn.

Self-styled or qualified planning officers and consultants – figures like Max Lock in Middlesbrough – were generally very keen to involve the public but this did not mean that they necessarily had any clear method for turning their wishes into reality. It was generally agreed that planning should start with research. The planner needed to know how people lived and what they wanted in the future. However, obtaining such information was often difficult. Few local authorities had the resources to finance their own research departments or surveys. One inquiry in 1953 noted:

> The London County Council has the largest local planning organisation in England. More than 260 persons were employed in June 1952. Twenty-four persons were on the 'research' staff. Almost all these persons gathered facts for information purposes or current administrative assignments. The chief of research was trained as a surveyor. The research staff comprised surveyors, geographers, architects, one or two statisticians, and perhaps a sociologist. There were no economists on the staff.[61]

Nor were data necessarily available elsewhere. The government's Social Survey provided some useful snap-shots of living patterns but departmental research facilities were generally small and overstretched. Academic sociologists sometimes worked on similar problems but rarely seemed to answer the kind of questions that planners generated.

This information gap was itself a formidable problem but planners then had the further difficulty of trying to decide how popular participation should actually be organised. One view was that they should simply explain their recommendations in as clear a way as possible and leave it at that. Most, however, believed that the public should be given some kind of veto. Nevertheless, there was no consensus about what this meant in practice. Plans normally contained

---

[59] W. A. Robson, 'Town planning as a problem of government', *Journal of the Town Planning Institute*, 38 (1952), 219.   [60] *Planning*, 8 Aug. 1950.

[61] L. Rodwin, 'The achilles heel of British town planning', *Town Planning Review*, 24 (1953), 23.

technicalities and so there was some anxiety that the untutored mind would not really comprehend important, perhaps fundamental, details. Planners and Labour politicians also worried that any consultation process might be subverted by vested interests – for example, organised groups of property owners who were known to be against the whole idea of planning.

Matters became even more complicated when planners took their ideas out into the wider local authority milieu. Fellow professionals – civil engineers, surveyors and architects – rarely displayed any great desire to let the public scrutinise their work. Most believed that they followed a purely technical vocation. Others admitted a sociological dimension but did not agree that the public were ready to play any active role in decision making. At a women's housing and planning conference in 1942, members of the panel were asked: '"Should people get what they want or what they ought to want?"' Judith Ledeboer, the first woman architect at the Ministry of Health, was quite clear in her answer: 'architects should stick to the good and the simple in housing designs. If they do this and people learn to relate what they want with what is good we shall arrive at good architecture.'[62] Four years later, a brains trust of eminent architects brought together by *Building* magazine displayed even more uncompromising attitudes. A question about what the public wished for in architecture elicited the following replies:

> Mr. Morgan: I suppose, as with everything that succeeds and which is fine, if you give them the right stuff as regards form and design in the long run they will come to appreciate it.
>
> Mr. Bossom: The public generally have no knowledge of what they want . . .
>
> Mr. Lutyens: The public are generally only concerned with their own house. It is questionable if they have any views at all.[63]

In these circumstances, relationships between planners and their colleagues could easily be tense. Donald Gilson, overseeing Coventry's reconstruction, found himself constantly at loggerheads with the local chief engineer. Other planning consultants felt that they had been discriminated against and their work undermined, simply because of professional jealousies.[64]

Politicians operating in local government were rarely very interested in responding to these complaints. A few Labour authorities were keen to introduce real public participation in planning, but many councillors felt uneasy about the whole matter. Both the style and the substance of town hall politics encouraged caution. It was generally believed, to begin with, that the public already had plenty of levers with which to influence council policy. Individuals or deputations could present their cases by lobbying. Pressure might be exerted through the press. Finally, of course, there was the ultimate sanction of elections: voters

---

[62] *Women's Housing and Planning Conference – 28th May, 1942* (London, 1942), p. 3.
[63] Anon., 'Dinner for six', *Building*, 21 (1946), 101.
[64] A. Ling, 'Plans – problems of realisation', *Journal of the Town Planning Institute*, 32 (1946), 34.

could simply remove individuals who failed to please them. Given these safe-guards, it was concluded, the sensible option was to let councillors get on with their business without subjecting them to further complications like public consultation. This was all the more so because many held relevant qualifications and had, anyway, to respect the long-standing procedures and customs of local government life. Of course, there were those who asserted that these arguments meant that councils could easily become unhealthily opaque, but this was not a charge which worried the majority. Confidentiality was seen as a positive virtue in many circumstances because it ensured fair play. Anyone with nefarious purposes who abused their position would soon be tripped up by the time-honoured checks and balances of public life.

The particular configuration of political issues which concerned councillors in the late 1940s reinforced these gut feelings against the principle of extended participation. The received wisdom was that local administrators stood or fell on their ability to deliver a fairly restricted number of services in the cheapest possible way. Most of those involved in campaigning believed that the public were particularly sensitive to variations in rate levels. However, everyone knew that, in the post-war situation, council finances were more strained than ever. German bombing had left many areas with diminished rateable values but large and urgent housing problems. The political parties might quarrel about abstract issues, but few councillors believed they had much real room for manoeuvre. The priorities, especially in urban areas, must necessarily be housing and the quick restoration of commercial activity. Again, therefore, the underlying logic discouraged new forms in planning. Experimenting with participation might delay rebuilding and end up costing a great deal of money. The better option was to proceed with the least possible consultation that Westminster would allow and deal with any public criticism later.

The second major problem for planners during these years was public opinion. A few organised pressure groups supported the new regulatory system, but most people felt it to be either irrelevant or in some way irritating. The great popular desire was for housing and a quiet life. Only a tiny minority was excited by the prospect of participating in their communities. These points can be illustrated by looking at popular attitudes to planning during the war and in the first years of peace.

Public interest in planning was at a peak in the dark days of 1940 and 1941. The destruction wrought by German bombers encouraged much excited talk about how Britain could be rebuilt after the war and there was a steady stream of cheap pamphlets which outlined the options. Nevertheless, this mood did not last. Looking back on 1942, the *Architects' Journal* columnist 'Astragal' recognised that enthusiasms were waning. In the heady days of the blitz, the public might have wanted a new beginning but now their aspirations tended towards the mundane:

A vague nostalgia for the suburban plot, a persistent aversion to blocks of flats, and a mild anger at the quality of the buildings which during the previous years had tumbled nightly about the people's ears, were the only active sentiments which occasionally, like barnacled but faintly remembered monsters of the deep, broke surface in the placid pool of public opinion.[65]

As planners recognised, an alarming gap could therefore be seen opening up between themselves and the ordinary citizen.[66]

During the next three years, a series of surveys did much to illuminate how popular preferences were evolving. For most ordinary people, it seemed, the central point of interest was the home. The war had been immensely destructive and disruptive of family life and now the general desire was to recreate what had been lost. Indeed, for many, the ideal of the home became a kind of grail, the only possible way to rediscover emotional and psychological security. When asked about the significance of home, therefore, people often lapsed into semi-mystical reverie. Questioned during an inquiry on the subject, one woman commented: 'Home means a place to go to when in trouble. A place where bygone days were happiest . . . A place to glorify when away and rely on always.'[67]

This enthusiasm, even obsession, coloured views about wider town planning issues. In describing their priorities, the great majority insisted on the fundamental importance of privacy and seclusion. Mass-Observation's major survey *People's Homes* reported: 'The "own front door" which can be shut, figures largely in people's ideas about the home. A garden that is overlooked, windows into which neighbours can see, balconies visible from the road . . . are all deplored. But above all, people dislike sharing a house with another family or even with one person, as many have to do.'[68] In practical terms, such feelings translated into a general preference for suburban living. Typically, a Women's Advisory Housing Council inquiry of 1943, based on 2,000 questionnaires, found that only 17 per cent of respondents wanted to live in a city or big urban area, while 30 per cent nominated the country and 52 per cent a suburb or small town.[69]

Compared to this clear choice, popular thinking about other planning issues tended to be vague or even contradictory. The authors of *People's Homes* felt that 'interest in community as a whole' was 'almost completely lacking among the housewives they met with' and this conclusion was repeated in several other surveys.[70] Perhaps the only strong trend that could be discerned was (once again) the widespread dislike of sharing. Thus, Townswomen's Guilds declared by a big

[65] *Architects' Journal*, 21 Jan. 1943.   [66] Editorial comment in *Architectural Design*, 13 (1943), 178.
[67] Mass-Observation, 'Some psychological factors in home building', *Town and Country Planning*, 11 (1943), 8–9.   [68] Mass-Observation, *People's Homes* (London, 1943), p. xix.
[69] Anon., 'The Englishwoman's castle', *Town and Country Planning*, 11 (1943), 106.
[70] Mass-Observation, *People's Homes*, p. xxii, and, for example, B. S. Townroe, 'What Do the Services Think?', *Architectural Design*, 12 (1942), 202.

majority against communal laundries; indeed nearly every answer in their inquiry 'showed strong feeling – such as "Emphatically, no" and "we prefer to wash our dirty linen in private"'.[71] Similarly, when another sample of women were asked about what amenities they wanted within a mile or two of their homes, most opted for practical facilities (a maternity and child welfare clinic, a health centre) while far fewer seemed to care about such things as neighbourhood laundries and restaurants. As this investigation readily indicated, the desire was for a situation which would allow the individual family to cope independently.[72]

Labour's victory in 1945 gave some grounds for believing that the public's enthusiasm for democratic planning might still be rekindled. Exhibitions on reconstruction schemes and the design of homes proved popular and a number of local authorities, as we have seen, launched initiatives aimed at encouraging participation. However, it was not long before this was revealed as something of a false dawn. For ordinary people, the central concern still remained housing. To the civilian's discontent with the billeting and forced sharing of wartime was now added the returning serviceman's desire to restart family life in reasonable surroundings. Those with money sought to buy any accommodation available, but, for the great majority, the only option was the council. Departments dealing with housing found themselves besieged, having to open at all hours of the day. Other parts of the local authority machine were also affected. Sudbury in Suffolk had appointed a planning officer in 1944 and given him a lock-up shop in one of the main streets to use as a drawing office and information centre. This was an imaginative move but it, too, became entangled in the housing crisis. As a later report remarked: 'It was rather sad, though perhaps not surprising, that many came to the Planning Centre hoping to be helped to find living accommodation.'[73]

Alongside this focus on housing, observers noted a widespread backlash against the enforced community of the wartime years. Good neighbouring had allegedly increased during the blitz but after 1945 older patterns quickly reasserted themselves. Geoffrey Gorer, analysing 11,000 questionnaires sent to a popular newspaper in the early 1950s, commented: 'The typical relationship of the English to their neighbours can best be described as distant cordiality. Some two-thirds know most of their neighbours well enough to speak to; but not one in 20 know them well enough to drop in on without an invitation.'[74] Similar trends were remarked upon in relation to a wide range of organisations across civil society. John Hawgood, Professor of Modern History and Government at Birmingham University, judged that, as things stood, the majority wanted only limited engagement in formal groupings:

[71] Anon., 'Townswomen's views on post-war homes', *Townswoman*, 10 (1943), 138.
[72] Anon., 'Englishwoman's castle', 106.
[73] K. Jeremiah, *A Full Life in the Country* (Sudbury, 1949), p. 14.
[74] G. Gorer, *Exploring English Character* (London, 1955), p. 52.

Evidence for this is to be found in the small attendances at public meetings (except in the heat of national elections), and at general meetings of co-operative and friendly societies and other associations. Effective voting power . . . is too often left in the hands of a caucus, changing little in personnel from year to year. Alternatively, everything is happily left to the officials of the organisation . . . The attitude of the average ordinary member is that he is 'too busy' or that it would be 'a waste of time' to participate more actively.[75]

These choices and dispositions inevitably coloured how people felt about planners and planning. One common view was that planners were standing in the way of new housing. A report on London described this kind of logic: 'Why don't they build some dwellings on that bomb-site? The town planning say its to be open space. What's the use of open space? Isn't there the doorstep and the street? What we want is homes.'[76] Elsewhere, planners were lumped together with 'humourless high brows, intent on such alien activities as "social engineering", or, in plain English, "pushing people around"'.[77] By the early 1950s, a BBC Home Service play could present planners as almost entirely isolated, and the town planning world as populated only by eccentrics and those on the make. George Scott-Moncrieff's plot follows the fortunes of a planner in a small Scottish town. He organises an exhibition to publicise his ideas and attracts the local 'interested' public:

> There is the lady who invites him to address the local Art Circle – which turns out to consist of her two sisters and herself; there is the local landowner, who says the model of the community centre looks like a carbuncle; there is Councillor Gillies, who owns property in the town centre and is only concerned with the basis of compensation, and there is Baillie Bonnyrig, who is concerned only with his own prestige. No one – except the government official – is interested in the plan itself.[78]

In conclusion, it is apparent that the story we have told in the preceding paragraphs points to rather different lessons from those advanced in many other accounts. Examined in the abstract, planners and the system they helped shape were not perfectly democratic. Indeed, Silkin himself was quite clear that the 1947 act's stipulations were by no means wholly satisfactory on this score.[79] Nevertheless, when full context is readmitted back into the picture, it is really rather remarkable that things had even progressed this far. The problem for those who favoured planning was that they were forced to introduce changes in very difficult circumstances. Finance was tight and many local authorities unamenable. Most pertinently, active and participating citizens were vastly outnumbered by a majority who thought little of planning or planners. Those involved at a

[75] J. A. Hawgood, *The Citizen and Government* (London, 1947), p. 13.
[76] E. E. Pepler, 'London housing and planning', *Town and Country Planning*, 19 (1951),157.
[77] J. Gloag, 'Planning and ordinary people', *Town and Country Planning*, 20 (1952), 509.
[78] Reported in *Journal of the Town Planning Institute*, 39 (1953), 33.
[79] L. Silkin, 'Planning and the public', *Journal of the Town Planning Institute*, 39 (1953), 26–33.

professional level may be criticised for not having developed more definite strategies in the interwar period, but it is equally true that nobody could have foreseen the very real obstacles to democratic planning which so quickly revealed themselves after Germany had been defeated. Significantly, even today, the relationship between planners and planned often remains fraught, and this despite several large-scale inquiries on consultation and participation, as well as the expenditure of much money on planning propaganda and education.[80]

[80] The recent Local Government Commission apparently spent nearly £15m trying to coax opinions from the public, but only persuaded one in fifteen households to answer its questions in writing. See *Independent*, 16 Dec. 1996.

· PART IV ·

Getting and spending

· 18 ·

Industrialisation and the city economy

DAVID REEDER AND RICHARD RODGER

A T ITS simplest, entirely new factory towns were created by industrialisation. This subspecies of the industrial city was the result of evolving
technological developments and changing advantages associated with
different industrial locations. New Lanark, Styal, Middlesbrough, Clydebank
and Slough shared this lineage, as did many factory villages, some of which
enjoyed only the briefest of expansionary phases before stagnation set in and
obscurity beckoned. All were essentially the product of industrialisation, dependent upon the rhythms established by the industries themselves. Yet the drama
of such industrial transformations distracts from a fuller understanding of the
complexity of the relationship between industry and the city. Urbanisation and
industrialisation were interwoven processes driving economic change during the
nineteenth century and the British industrial city in the modern period was a
complex and evolving genus. It was both influenced by the fortunes of the major
growth industries in the national economy – coal, textiles, iron and steel, shipbuilding – and also itself contributed to economic growth. Even by mid-century
a wide array of other industries had been established within the towns as had
service industries and distributive functions to support urban growth.[1]

While the trajectory of the growth in the established industrial and market
centres undoubtedly was influenced by technological development and a
common reservoir of commercial knowledge, the precise path of urban expansion depended to a considerable extent on the resources, facilities, expertise and
personal networks created within such towns and cities. Indeed, the defence of

The collection and analysis of census data for this chapter was made possible by a grant from the
Nuffield Foundation and carried out by Amanda Mason, Daisy Powell and Kirsty Turner, formerly
of the Centre for Urban History at Leicester University, to whom we are grateful. We should also
like to thank the editor of the volume for helpful comments and suggestions on an earlier draft.
[1] Barrie Trinder, 'Industrialising towns 1700–1840', in Peter Clark, ed., *The Cambridge Urban History
of Britain*, vol. II: *1540–1840* (Cambridge, 2000), pp. 805–29.

local autonomy and opposition to centralisation in the nineteenth century was in part an attempt to maintain those distinctive urban features that contributed to the prosperity of local inhabitants. This perspective on the internal dynamics of the industrial city challenges the view, characteristic of a post-1960s phase of industrialisation, that cities are at best an irrelevance and at worst a hindrance to economic development. This was certainly not the case in the heyday of the industrial city. Then the different factor endowments of highly individual towns contributed a powerful supply side explanation for the specific character of industrialisation in a given urban locus and these distinctive characteristics in turn redefined relationships both within and between regional economic systems bound together by a network of external economies.[2] However, the urban context of regional economic development is a neglected subject and on the externalities which this context offered to firms are frequently taken for granted.

Conventional accounts of economic change have not only tended to reinforce the stereotypical view of the industrial city; they have also given the impression that it was a dependent variable whose fortunes were prey to powerful economic forces over which they had no control. If, therefore, one aim of this chapter is to survey the impact of industrialisation on the modern city economy, and on the city itself, to an extent, another aim is to highlight the ways in which the industrial city operated to promote and retain business. The question then to consider is whether this role was maintained or undermined during the course of the twentieth century.

(i) THE URBAN DIMENSION TO INDUSTRIALISATION

Towns and cities were the information superhighways of the nineteenth century. The coffee-houses, clubs and pubs to be found in urban locations offered information about local trading conditions, investment and work opportunities, where labour might be hired and supplies obtained. Not to be in touch incurred a risk for business and from the second quarter of the nineteenth century the proliferation of trade directories, masonic lodges and trade associations was indicative of a demand for business news. Information concerning risk and uncertainty, key variables in business survival, could be evaluated more fully where bankers, insurance agents, brokers, merchants and distributors coexisted in close proximity. Just how significant knowledge-based human capital is to the process of industrial development has been underlined in a recent econometric study whose authors demonstrate that as represented by professional groups, it exerted a systematic influence on the long-run growth of British cities from

---

[2] See, for example, the work of P. Hudson, 'Capital and credit in the West Riding wool textile industry c. 1750–1850', in P. Hudson, ed., *Regions and Industries* (Cambridge, 1989), pp. 69–102. For the origins of regional economies see Clark, ed., *Cambridge Urban History of Britain*, II.

1861.[3] As they provocatively assert: 'The talk of the bourgeoisie, not the smoke of the factory, was the defining characteristic of the modern city economy' – an interesting reversal of the conventional view of the role of the city in the growth of commerce and the professions. However, there were more direct and informal ways of acquiring the knowledge necessary to assessing the credentials and trustworthiness of business contacts, and to monitoring quality and ensuring supplies – all of which were imperative to success in the volatile business environment of the Victorian city.

This volatility was a particular feature of urban economies dependent on the operations of small firms. Predictably, one man firms and family enterprises tended to cluster in retail and building – sectors that served a predominantly local market – but they were also to be found in the manufacturing sectors of the urban economy with national and even international markets. A striking feature of the economies of Scottish towns in the mid-Victorian decades and after was the existence of both concentration and fragmentation in business organisation with 1 per cent of firms in 1851 employing over a quarter of the total workforce, whilst 90 per cent of firms employed fewer than twenty workers apiece.[4] There is no reason for thinking that this pattern was not replicated in England and Wales, as the county-based evidence on employment sizes indirectly suggests. Even in the North-West region, where small firms were relatively less well represented, the Manchester factory system of the 1850s had a dualistic character 'which was dominated by a small number of large-scale firms overlooking a thick undergrowth of very small scale enterprises'.[5] One reason for the number of small firms in manufacturing was that traditional techniques and labour-intensive production methods enabled workshop-based, handicraft production to coexist with more technically advanced and larger scale activity for much longer than a simple chronology of scientific inventions.[6] In this highly competitive world of small producer capitalism, personal reputation and a first-hand knowledge were at a premium.

Crucial to the strategies of small and medium-sized firms seeking to achieve stability or growth was a private world of social networks established, for example, through church and chapel, or by means of personal and kinship ties, or through overlapping leisure and cultural pursuits. Chapel-going in

[3] C. J. Simon and C. Nardinelli, 'The talk of the town: human capital, information, and the growth of English cities, 1861–1961', *Explorations in Economic History*, 33 (1996), 384–413.
[4] R. Rodger, 'Concentration and fragmentation: capital, labor, and the structure of mid-Victorian Scottish industry', *JUH*, 14 (1988), 185–90; P. Johnson, 'Economic development and industrial dynamism in Victorian London', *LJ*, 21 (1996), 30.
[5] R. Lloyd-Jones and M. J. Lewis, *Manchester and the Age of the Factory* (Manchester, 1988), p. 33.
[6] M. Berg, 'Technological change in Birmingham and Sheffield in the eighteenth century', in P. Clark and P. Corfield, eds., *Industry and Urbanisation in Eighteenth Century England* (Leicester, 1994), pp. 20–32; R. Samuel, 'The workshop of the world: steam power and hand technology in mid-Victorian Britain', *History Workshop Journal*, 3 (1977), 6–72.

nonconformist business communities, to highlight one element in this, was not only important in shaping the outlook of the *parvenu* industrial entrepreneur, but in factory towns relatively devoid of family connections, involvement in the chapel played a 'large, sometimes overwhelming part in the establishment of business reputations'.[7] Recent work on the operations of small firms has emphasised the importance of family to business survival, whether in terms of family partnerships – important to those industrial sectors with a need for relatively high levels of fixed capital – or in terms of a multitude of small individual enterprises which relied on their families to provide capital, labour and premises. Indeed, the survival of any city business beyond the life span of the founder depended to a considerable extent on the ability and willingness of family members to become involved. Families were of importance also in the formation of locally based networks of trust; and in several of the manufacturing trades, informal networks, external to the firm but internal to local communities, were reinforced by geographical concentrations into particular districts or localities.[8] Early access to local information networks was one of the external economies that Alfred Marshall thought significant enough to substitute for the internal economies of large-scale production in what he called the 'industrial districts'.[9]

The development of a more formal institutional framework to help provide a measure of control in an uncertain world complemented but never replaced these informal links. The Chamber of Commerce was perhaps the most important of these institutions, formed in the major towns and cities from the eighteenth century, mainly by leading employers but seeking to represent the interests of the business community as a whole, a responsibility which in Scottish burghs was discharged by the guildry – members of the general business community – who elected representatives directly to key council committees. In the second half of the nineteenth century, associations of specific producers – iron and coal masters, employers in engineering, cotton manufacturing and

[7] T. Koditschek, *Class Formation and Urban Industrial Society* (Cambridge, 1990), p. 266.
[8] S. Nenadic, 'The small family firm in Victorian Britain', *Business History*, 35 (1993), 86–114; S. Nenadic, *et al.*, 'Record-linkage and the small family firm: Edinburgh 1861–91', *Bulletin of the John Rylands Library*, 74 (1992), 169–93; S. Nenadic, 'The life-cycle of firms in late nineteenth-century Britain', in P. Joubert and M. Moss, eds., *The Birth and Death of Companies* (Carnforth and Park Ridge, N. J., 1990); and S. Nenadic, 'The Victorian middle classes', in W. H. Fraser and I. Maver, eds., *Glasgow*, vol. II: *1830 to 1912* (Manchester, 1996), esp. pp. 280–83. See also G. Jones and M. B. Rose, 'Family capitalism', *Business History*, 35 (1993), 1–16; M. B. Rose, 'Beyond Buddenbrooks: the family firm and the management of succession in nineteenth-century Britain', in J. Brown and M. B. Rose, eds., *Entrepreneurship, Networks, and Modern Business* (Manchester, 1993), pp. 127–43; and R. Church, 'The family firm in industrial capitalism: international perspectives on hypotheses and history', *Business History*, 35 (1993), 17–43.
[9] Marshall, *Principles*, Bk 4, ch. 4, quoted by W. Lazonick in B. Elbaum and W. Lazonick, *The Decline of the British Economy* (Oxford, 1986).

shipbuilding – consolidated their mutual interests into loose federations, forfeit-
ing a measure of independence principally in the quest for a more concerted
approach to wage negotiations.[10] In such cases, mutual gain outweighed individual autonomy in the search for industrial expansion, and in other respects,
too, industrialists acknowledged that they needed to concede a degree of independence for the advantages conveyed by provincial stock and commodity
exchanges, banks and new forms of company organisation fostered by legislation governing joint-stock companies (1844) and limited liability (1862). Even
at the more modest level of the small producer and distributor, a network of
city-based Trade Protection Societies developed in the second half of the nineteenth century to inform members of those debtors against whom they had
taken action through the courts on their behalf to recover debts.[11] Only where
sufficient numbers of industrialists or members of employers' organisations
existed could the advantages and the overheads associated with formal cooperation outweigh the costs. It was the larger towns and cities, therefore, which
were the forcing house for institutional development, as they were for informal
contacts, and in conveying this advantage, the improved information networks
which developed themselves reinforced the position of the larger urban and
regional centres.

In contrast to such forces for more concerted institutional development, the
financing of industry is worth further comment since it illustrates the parallel
development of relative autonomy in the provision of credit and capital prior to
the twentieth century.[12] In the mid-Victorian decades banking was conducted
locally and on a relatively small scale by private and joint-stock banks whose
business was heavily dependent on the economy of the immediate vicinity. In
many urban localities in the northern and Midland industrial regions, interrela-
tions between banking and industry were close: businessmen were influential
participants in the work of local banks, and, as directors, able to offer their personal knowledge of the credentials of applicants for overdrafts, a common source
of business capital. This was, however, a system under pressure as structural and
institutional changes in banking began to undermine these local links which
became increasingly mediated through people and institutions based in or connected with regional capitals. However, financial historians have argued that in
the later nineteenth century there were other sources of funds available locally

---

[10] See, for example, J. McKenna and R. Rodger, 'Control by coercion: employers' associations and
the establishment of industrial order in the building industry of England and Wales 1860–1914',
Business History Review, 59 (1985), 203–31.

[11] N. Wood, 'Debt, credit and business strategy: the law and the local economy, 1850–1900' (PhD
thesis, University of Leicester, 1999).

[12] For a review of the sustained importance of local capital supplies see R. Burt, 'Segmented capital
markets and patterns of investment in late Victorian Britain: some evidence from the non-ferrous
mining industry', *Ec.HR*, 2nd series, 51 (1998), 709–33.

to British businessmen, many of them small specialist producers, and the enduring nature of locally funded firms cannot be stressed enough.[13]

An evolving apparatus of commercial and financial institutions was complemented by the provision of private and public infrastructural support. Businessmen, including industrialists, were like other middle-class investors active in the market for railway stock, and the railway companies' sidings, engine sheds and operating facilities occupied some 5 to 9 per cent of the urban area of the larger British cities.[14] In contrast to these private initiatives, albeit with very public results in terms of the zoning of cities and the development of transport corridors through them, a public contribution to industrial development was also forthcoming. Through the town council and its committees, new roads and sewers were laid out, streets straightened and widened to facilitate commerce and insanitary areas prejudicial to business interests cleared; gas and water undertakings were increasingly taken into the public domain, and in the later part of the century technical schools and colleges were built, franchises for trams and power generation granted, and licences of various sorts approved.

In varying degrees, each of these municipal strategies provided infrastructural support for business activities financed overwhelmingly by a system of local taxation whose incidence fell almost exclusively upon residential rather than business interests. However, municipal relations with business were not always harmonious. In many towns and cities there was a tension between a wish to attract business and a perceived need to mitigate through by-laws and other regulations the diseconomies caused by industrialisation from smoke emissions and water pollutants. Concern for environmental standards was used to legitimate official interventions which, though designed to contain industrial contamination, could also be to the advantage of industrial and business interests.[15] The provincial cities, and the burgeoning administration they required, offered a way forward by which business interests might hope to shape their own future while displaying civic involvement. Whilst this remained the case, as it was for most of the century, the business elite represented an important constituency in council

---

[13] We have drawn mainly on M. Collins, *Banks and Industrial Finance in Britain, 1800–1939* (Basingstoke, 1991), and P. L. Cottrell, *Industrial Finance 1830–1914* (London, 1980). The few local studies include M. Collins and P. Hudson, 'Provincial bank lending: Yorkshire and Merseyside 1820–1860', *Bulletin of Economic Research*, 31 (1979), and L. Newton, 'Regional bank–industry relations during the mid-nineteenth century: links between bankers and manufacturing in Sheffield, *c.* 1850 to *c.* 1885', *Business History*, 38 (1996), 65–83. F. Capie and M. Collins, 'Industrial lending by English commercial banks 1860s–1914. Why did banks refuse loans?', *Business History*, 38 (1996), 1–25, show that banks did approve lending to industrialists but only after very careful thought.

[14] J. R. Kellett, *The Impact of Railways on Victorian Cities* (London, 1969), p. 290.

[15] For the Manchester experience, R. H. Kargon, *Science in Victorian Manchester* (Manchester, 1977), pp. 117–34. More generally see B. W. Clapp, *An Environmental History of Britain since the Industrial Revolution* (London, 1994).

chambers throughout the United Kingdom, even if the extent of their representation and commitment to developing municipal services varied as between different towns and cities.

These externalities apart, perhaps the most obvious advantage which towns and cities offered manufacturers was an almost infinite supply of labour. Although urban population growth rates in the established industrial regions may have peaked in the 1840s, the impact of net natural increase as well as of continuing urban immigration (proportionately less significant in the later decades of the century) ensured that until the 1880s at least the population growth of most industrial towns and cities was sustained. An accumulating reservoir of labour, particularly amongst the unskilled and semi-skilled, exerted downward pressures on wages and thus reduced manufacturers' labour costs. Furthermore, with social welfare costs absorbed in varying degrees by charity and poor law guardians, fluctuations in output and pressure on profitability could be met by forcing adjustments on to labour, specifically through lower wages and bouts of unemployment. British industrialists' preference for an essentially labour-intensive mode of production was consistent with this continuing supply of low-skilled, low-wage labour, and, it has been argued, was a rational business strategy, at least at the plant if not at a national level, which contrasted markedly with the high-technology innovation and investment approaches adopted by German and American industrialists from the 1870s.[16]

That said, some manufacturing employers acknowledged the importance of their relationships with workforces and local communities. By the 1860s this was reflected in the strategy of factory paternalism, of particular significance in the smaller textile towns, where it was based on the cultivation of personal relationships between the business-owning family and the families of the workforce.[17] Elsewhere, the existence of a dominant employer had far-reaching consequences for local communities taken to an extreme in factory districts such as Ackroyden, Saltaire, Port Sunlight and Bournville where relatively enlightened entrepreneurs, often Quakers, accepted responsibility for infrastructural provision and social facilities. Even where this kind of paternalism was not practised, a factory owner with a dominant position in a town was able to exert controls over the housing and living conditions of the families he employed, as in Clydebank, or in various colliery districts, where supervisors and foremen have been likened to 'non-commissioned officers' able to exercise considerable

---

[16] For the argument about rationality, see D. N. McCloskey and L. G. Sandberg, 'From damnation to redemption: judgements on the late-Victorian entrepreneur', *Explorations in Economic History*, 9 (1971), 90–108; for an extensive bibliography on British business see P. L. Payne, *British Entrepreneurship in the Nineteenth Century* (Basingstoke, 1974).

[17] P. Joyce, *Work, Politics and Society* (Brighton, 1980); H. F. Gospel, *Markets, Firms, and the Management of Labour in Modern Britain* (Cambridge, 1992), pp. 25–8.

influence over their workforce and families by favours concerning the availability of work and housing accommodation.[18]

In manufacturing industry generally, recruitment of labour was usually *ad hoc* and often based on family contacts. Where the local economy was not firing on all cylinders, these informal contacts were all the more important, with foremen able to dispense considerable patronage through the allocation of a limited amount of work. Wage bargaining was also locally based although from the 1870s subject less to plant level negotiations and increasingly to more formal negotiations between employers' associations and city-wide branches of trade unions. These changed institutional arrangements were complemented from 1896 in certain industries by compulsory conciliation and arbitration procedures, though to begin with such arrangements were usually locally based too, 'covering a town or district which suited a situation where labour and product markets were still often local in scope'.[19]

Finally, it is worth noting how the operations of craft-based industries, particularly the metalworking industries, were closely linked into the labour resources of local communities. Small firms producing a wide range of differentiated products benefited from the traditions of skill in localised manufacturing districts in which knowledge of materials and methods was transmitted across the generations by parental example and in locally based apprenticeship systems. This practical, low-cost approach to training and recruitment had come to be supplemented by the end of the century with the evening classes of the city technical colleges and the quasi-vocational and more practical studies of higher grade schools.[20]

To summarise, towns and cities offered the advantages of concentration to industry as expressed through a supportive network of institutional structures which added a measure of social stability as well as of economic stability under conditions of rapid change. The economic advantages of concentration were associated with reduced costs of production, giving a commercial edge in an

[18] J. Melling, '"Non-commissioned officers": British employers and their supervisory workers, 1880–1920', *Soc. Hist.* 5 (1980), 183–221; K. Burgess, 'Authority relations and the division of labour in British industry, with special reference to Clydeside 1860–1930', *Soc. Hist.*, 11 (1986), 211–33. For historical commentaries on labour strategies and the management of labour more generally, see H. F. Gospel and C. R. Littler, eds., *Managerial Strategies and Industrial Relations* (London, 1983) and Gospel, *Markets*, p. 7, notes that 'there was insufficient organisational ability in most British firms to develop and administer strong internal systems of labour management'.

[19] Gospel, *Markets*, p. 33. Note also the importance of familial and community checks in monitoring apprenticeship in the shipyard trades: A. McKinley, 'A certain short-sightedness: metal working, innovation, and apprenticeship 1897–1939', in H. F. Gospel, ed., *Industrial Training and Technological Innovation* (London, 1991), p. 102.

[20] For recent commentaries on apprenticeship as a form of industrial training see C. More, *Skill and the English Working Class, 1870–1914* (London, 1980), and B. Elbaum, 'The persistence of apprenticeship in Britain and its decline in the United States', in Gospel, ed., *Industrial Training*, pp. 194–212. See below, pp. 586–9, for the development of scientific and technical education.

increasingly well-informed market. The urban dimension through formal markets and informal networks offered opportunities to producers to secure credit, screen sharp practices, regulate quality of workmanship, control access to suppliers and customers, enforce contracts and thereby to delimit the scale of risk. In the language of the business historian, cities offered externalities which helped minimise transaction costs. New factors affecting this process were transport changes and the further development of communications with the invention of the telegraph and telephone. These developments, particularly rapid after 1900, exposed producers to greater competition and narrower margins by shrinking distance and time, thereby putting a further premium on commercial information and institutional control.

(ii) TRAJECTORIES OF URBAN-INDUSTRIAL DEVELOPMENT

The linkages between industrialisation, the growth of employment opportunities and the fortunes of British towns and cities are both obvious but yet difficult to disentangle, given the considerable variation in the trajectories and resulting profiles of urban-industrial development. One approach emphasises the importance of regional specialisation in a periodisation which uses the Kondratief long waves as an heuristic device to identify phases of development.[21] Thus the period from the 1840s to the 1880s can be depicted as an extended 'Industrial Revolution' phase in which urban growth was concentrated on towns and cities in established textile, mining and metalworking regions, and from the 1860s was a notable feature also of those regions whose economies were being transformed by the application of new engineering techniques, development of steel, expansion of chemicals, the growth of railway terminals and locomotive construction.

On Tyneside, Teesside and Clydeside, the interdependency of a group of leading sector industries – coal, iron and steel, engineering and shipbuilding – was the driving force in economic growth benefiting older established industrial centres such as Newcastle as well as bringing new centres of mushrooming population into being, such as Middlesbrough or Barrow-in-Furness, to take an example from the North-West industrial region. Developments in the iron and steel industry were pivotal and because iron bars, pipes and tubes, sheet steel and plates were essential intermediate products for railway, marine, civil and related areas of heavy engineering, then for reasons of convenience and transport costs, the location of firms in these specialist areas was almost invariably near the point of production. As a general rule, the ratio of value to volume in iron and steel was low and so transport costs ruled out moving such heavy and bulky goods far

[21] G. Shaw, 'Industrialisation, urban growth and the city economy', in R. Lawton, ed., *The Rise and Fall of Great Cities* (London, 1989), pp. 55–79.

from the blast furnace or coal pit, a circumstance which contrasted strongly with consumer goods industries where high value added was not overturned by long-distance transport costs. South Wales was the exception, failing to develop its coal- and iron-producing capabilities into this kind of interlinked regional economy, with adverse consequences for the nineteenth-century growth of Cardiff, the coal metropolis of the west, but a city with a negligible manufacturing base. Old industrial cities, outside of the dynamic regions, were unable to sustain momentum, as in the case of Norwich, whose successor industries to the defunct textiles were insufficiently important to arrest this city's slide down the urban rankings from fourteenth to thirty-second place between 1851 and 1951.[22] Regional economic development set the parameters for the economic growth of particular towns and cities, although in Scotland there were always pockets of industrial nonconformity in which regional influences were minimal. There were also English county towns, such as Ipswich, which developed a manufacturing basis dependent on a mainly agricultural region.

In the phase after the 1880s to the First World War, the links between industrialisation and urban growth were affected not only by a more complex pattern of regional trends but also by an altogether wider economic base to urbanisation with the expansion of commercial services and service-oriented industries. During this phase urban growth was itself a potent influence in generating new employment opportunities especially in food processing, retailing, the building industry and transport, with multiplier effects which may have had as much or more importance than the direct contribution of manufacturing employment for which the larger industrial towns and cities were noted. The growth of demand for services and consumer-oriented industries gave competitive advantages to towns within the metropolitan orbit resulting in the beginnings of a migrational shift from older areas of traditional manufacturing to London and the South-East.[23]

Prior to the First World War the experiences of the established industrial regions became more variable. Some regions – the Black Country for example – went through a transitional phase in the later nineteenth century. The Lancashire cotton region was beginning to suffer from competitive pressures on

[22] For Teesside and Tyneside, see N. McCord, *North East England* (London, 1979), esp. Part 2 1850–1920, and I. Bullock, 'The origins of economic growth on Teesside, 1851–1881', *NHist.*, 9 (1974), 79–95; for Clydeside, A. Slaven, *The Economic Development of the West of Scotland 1750–1960* (London, 1975); for Merseyside, see S. Marriner, *A Social and Economic History of Merseyside* (London, 1982); for South Wales, see M. J. Daunton, *Coal Metropolis* (Leicester, 1977), pp. 37–54. The reference to Norwich comes from Clark and Corfield, eds., *Industry and Urbanisation*, p. ix.

[23] C. H. Lee, 'Regional growth and structural change in Victorian Britain', *Ec.HR*, 2nd series, 34 (1981), 450–1 and C. H. Lee, 'Regional structure and change', in J. Langton and R. J. Morris, eds., *Atlas of Industrialising Britain, 1780–1914* (London, 1986), pp. 30, 140–3; and C. H. Lee, 'The service sector, regional specialisation and economic growth in the Victorian economy', *Journal of Historical Geography*, 10 (1984), 149–53.

its chief export, whilst other regions, such as Tyneside, were still rapidly expanding production and urban populations. But if stability of employment is taken into account, it can be argued that the most important contrast emerging before the end of the nineteenth century was that between the industrial North (including industrial Scotland) and a broadly defined southern region, especially outside London, whose superiority in terms of higher levels of employment was structural in nature.[24] A significant element in the structural advantage of the Kentish region prior to 1914 was 'the existence of small scale, often traditional forms of manufacture, of the kind that abounded in Kent'[25] and which helped to make the Kentish towns, outside of the Thames-side industrial belt, less vulnerable to cyclical influences.

During the 1920s regional experiences tended to polarise in terms of wage rates and unemployment levels, as the Barlow Report on the distribution of industrial population was to make clear in making a distinction between the declining outer regions of industrial Britain, affected by structural and cyclical unemployment in export-oriented staple industries, and the more prosperous regions, which included parts of the Midlands, the metropolitan region and the South-East.[26] Contrasting regional fortunes lay behind the somewhat jaundiced comparison that J. B. Priestley made in his *English Journey* between the sooty and ugly environment of the mill and foundry towns of an old industrial England 'no longer added to' and 'with no new life poured in' and the consumerism and modernity of a new urban England 'of arterial and by-pass roads, of filling stations and factories that look like exhibition buildings'.[27] The continued advances of electric power generation contributed to this new industrial geography by reducing the former dependence on coal supplies. A liberating development, it enabled the service-oriented industries of towns and cities on the edges of metropolitan areas to gain competitive advantage as new growth centres.

Whilst regional trends provide a discursive framework for interpreting the differing experiences of industrial towns and cities, the regional effect cannot be statistically demonstrated and needs to be complemented by an approach that concentrates more on the changing mix of economic activities in particular industrial centres. It was never the case that all towns in a region had similar growth rates, since their experience varied according to the composition of declining and expanding industries within them.[28] Thus different towns in the Black Country were affected to differing degrees by the crisis which the district

---

[24] H. R. Southall, 'The origins of the depressed areas: unemployment, growth and regional economic structure before 1914', *Ec.HR*, 2nd series, 41 (1988), 236–58.

[25] A. Armstrong, ed., *The Economy of Kent 1640–1914* (Maidstone, 1995), p. 268.

[26] Royal Commission on the Distribution of the Industrial Population, Report, Cmd 6153 (1940). See also J. P. Fogarty, *Prospects of the Industrial Areas of Great Britain* (London, 1945), pp. 1–33.

[27] J. B. Priestley, *English Journey* (New York, 1934), pp. 398–9.

[28] B. T. Robson, *Urban Growth* (London, 1973), pp. 111–27. See also the discussion by R. Dennis, *English Industrial Cities of the Nineteenth Century* (Cambridge, 1984), pp. 41–7.

as a whole went through in the later nineteenth century. In the cotton district of Lancashire, the town of Preston was exceptional in being able to recover from economic decline in the later nineteenth century to diversify away from reliance on an export-oriented staple and benefit from its growing importance as a regional service centre. Even in regions which suffered from very heavy unemployment in the interwar years, the individual characteristics of towns mediated the impact of depression. So also in the more prosperous regions of the South and South-East, there was no uniform pattern of urbanisation.[29]

Few, if any, urban locations were dominated exclusively by a single industrial activity, depending more typically on a variable mix of economic interests. It was the mix of these interests – manufacturing industry as contrasted with commercial activities, several complementary industries or a single sector, dominated by skill in contrast with unskilled and irregular employment opportunities, males as opposed to female-dominated workplaces – which perhaps more than anything else imprinted towns and cities with different social structures and characteristics. Without wishing to be unduly deterministic, urban social and political fingerprinting resulted in no small measure from the employment characteristics within the city boundaries.

The most obvious general comparison to make perhaps is that between highly specialised industrial towns and cities and those with a greater variety of industries and of economic functions. Some locations were entirely dominated by a single industry – for example, Ebbw Vale, Middlesbrough and Motherwell where steel works predominated, or shipbuilding centres, such as Jarrow and Birkenhead, or the engineering towns of Crewe, Coventry and Derby. In these and other towns concentration was reinforced when the leading industry was in the hands of one or two large organisations, such as Pilkington's at St Helens, the railway works in Derby, the two large firms (after 1914) of Dorman Long and Bolckow Vaughan in Middlesbrough, the Thames-side naval dockyard towns and those with ordnance factories which were so heavily reliant on government contracts. Such highly specialised towns, with their large proletarian workforces, had a very different character from cities with an extensive middle class, but they also differed from each other and from exclusively textile centres in relation to the nature of the production process, extent of female employment and levels of skill in the workforce. Particular values were dominant, as in the case of Dundee where the jute industry relied heavily on single girls who had migrated from particular counties in Ireland, and, as with textile towns gener-

[29] On Teesside, Middlesbrough and Stockton had very high rates of unemployment but the depression affected Darlington – an older market town as well as a heavy engineering centre – less severely and for a shorter period. See K. Nicholas, *The Social Effects of Unemployment on Teesside, 1919–39* (Manchester, 1986), pp. 24–42. For a comparison between the Black Country towns, see R. H. Trainor, *Black Country Elites* (Oxford, 1993), pp. 25–32. On Preston, see M. Savage, *The Dynamics of Working-Class Politics* (Cambridge, 1987), pp. 64–70, 95–9.

ally, the gender balance, marriage prospects, mortality and fertility rates of the town were affected accordingly, as were the songs, stories and leisure time pursuits.[30] More importantly from the perspective of this chapter, a highly specialised town concentrated on one or two industries was likely to experience very rapid growth whilst market conditions were favourable but was, by the same token, all the more vulnerable to cyclical downswings and secular decline in the dominant industry or industries.

On the other hand, most larger cities and especially the regional centres, by the nature of their size and functionality, offered just such complementarity. This was their comparative advantage. Together with the industrial sector with which they were often first identified larger cities offered finance, markets, a multiplicity of specialist suppliers, education, justice and administration. In this respect there was a qualitative difference between the regional city and even the larger of the factory towns. In particular, the presence of an educated middle class, often employed in commercial and legal activities, meant income levels largely insulated from the vagaries of the trade cycle. Consequently, middle-class patterns of consumption offered employment stability for domestic servants and gardeners, printers, stationers, engravers, coachbuilders and instrument makers, as well as providing a measure of predictability for clothiers, butchers, spirit dealers and numerous building tradesmen concerned with the repair and maintenance of suburban houses. Perhaps nowhere in Britain was this more highly developed than in Edinburgh, the epitome of the diversified economy, where an unusually high proportion of professional employment produced an equally heavy concentration of specialist craftsmen, clerks and domestic servants who were themselves thereby shielded from the vagaries of the trade cycle.[31] Lower down the urban hierarchy, a similar point can be made about county towns, as we have seen, whose particular specialisms were balanced by a greater range of manufacturing and service employment than in the specialised industrial centres.

(iii) URBAN EMPLOYMENT STRUCTURES: AN OVERVIEW

In a more systematic way the diversity in the employment structures of urban Britain and the main trends in employment as between the three census dates of 1851, 1911 and 1951 are presented in Tables 18.1–4. These summary tables are

---

[30] It was not simply the dominance of one industry that brought economic difficulties for Dundee but the gender composition of the labour force reflecting a heavy reliance on female labour and lack of opportunities for male employment; see J. Butt, 'The changing character of urban employment 1901–1981', in G. Gordon, ed., *Perspectives of the Scottish City* (Aberdeen, 1985), p. 216.

[31] For further detail on Edinburgh, see R. Rodger, 'Employment, wages and poverty in the Scottish cities, 1841–1914', in Gordon, ed., *Perspectives*, p. 39. Rodger and Butt provide a systematic comparative study of the employment structures of four Scottish cities 1841 to 1981 in this volume, and Rodger's chapter is reprinted in R. J. Morris and R. Rodger eds., *The Victorian City* (London, 1993), pp. 73–113.

Table 18.1 *Percentage of workforce in manufacturing industry 1861–1951*

Males

City	1861	rank	1911	rank	1951	rank
Coventry	73.4	1	65.9	1	74.6	1
Stockport	73.1	2	54.9	9	55.2	7
Preston	71.7	3	58.6	2	45.9	14
Sheffield	70.2	4	58.4	3	60.1	5
Birmingham	68.4	5	57.5	4	64.0	2
Dundee	67.4	7	57.5	5	49.1	9
Northampton	67.4	6	56.7	6	48.6	10
Leicester	65.2	8	53.6	10	53.9	8
Leeds	61.6	9	52.4	11	48.0	12
Wolverhampton	61.3	10	55.6	8	61.1	4
Derby	58.7	11	49.5	12	61.9	3
Manchester	57.9	12	40.6	17	41.0	17
Glasgow	56.4	13	45.0	14	45.6	15
Newcastle-upon-Tyne	52.4	14	44.8	15	40.4	18
Bristol	49.3	15	36.1	19	34.5	20
Reading	47.4	16	40.4	18	32.8	23
Ipswich	44.4	17	42.2	16	42.8	16
Cardiff	40.2	18	28.2	22	36.8	19
Oxford	39.8	19	24.1	23	47.5	13
Edinburgh	39.0	21	29.0	21	33.7	21
Liverpool	39.0	20	31.1	20	33.3	22
Maidstone	29.0	22	n/a	n/a	26.1	24
St Helens	n/a	n/a	45.4	13	56.6	6
Middlesbrough	n/a	n/a	55.7	7	48.5	11
GB	39.0		33.1		38.2	

Females

City	1861	rank	1911	rank	1951	rank
Dundee	84.7	1	72.9	2	55.1	11
Preston	83.2	2	79.6	1	58.0	7
Stockport	80.2	3	72.9	3	62.5	3
Coventry	76.4	4	52.9	9	63.7	2
Leicester	68.9	5	68.2	4	67.0	1
Glasgow	67.1	6	41.5	12	42.1	16
Northampton	66.9	7	60.3	5	57.2	8
Derby	65.1	8	50.4	10	50.5	13
Manchester	64.8	9	53.5	8	52.8	12
Leeds	63.0	10	60.3	6	58.8	5
Birmingham	54.1	11	57.5	7	60.6	4
Sheffield	41.9	12	41.1	13	56.1	10
Ipswich	41.0	13	34.3	17	40.3	17
Bristol	40.8	14	42.3	11	37.5	18
Cardiff	40.2	15	28.2	20	36.8	19
Wolverhampton	38.1	16	41.1	14	57.0	9
Liverpool	36.5	17	36.3	15	44.7	14
Newcastle-upon-Tyne	35.9	18	28.3	18	35.3	20
Edinburgh	30.7	19	21.3	23	30.2	22
Reading	30.1	20	34.1	18	34.5	21
Oxford	29.0	21	24.5	21	26.9	23
Maidstone	27.0	22	n/a	n/a	25.9	24
St Helens	n/a	n/a	36.2	16	58.2	6
Middlesbrough	n/a	n/a	23.0	22	42.6	15
GB	43.0		39.5		46.3	

calculated from census occupational data for twenty-four towns and cities chosen to represent specialised industrial centres, regional and port cities and smaller county towns with manufacturing interests.[32]

An industrial city might be defined in terms of an employment structure with more than half of the male population engaged in manufacturing industry. On that criterion, fourteen towns and cities in the sample (Table 18.1) made the grade in 1861 of which ten had more than 60 per cent so employed. However, this seems too narrow a definition since it would exclude cities such as Bristol and Newcastle whose manufacturing components for male occupations were not much more than a third in 1911 and 1951 but still above that for Great Britain as a whole. Moreover, account needs to be taken of female employment: the importance of domestic service to women evidently reduces the proportions engaged in female manufacturing employment in 1861 but the tables clearly show how in the textile and clothing towns especially female participation in manufacturing reinforced the manufacturing bias of their urban economies at that date and continued to make a significant contribution to industrial employment thereafter.

Comparing 1911 with 1861 in Table 18.2 shows that in all cases manufacturing employment was a smaller proportion of employment structures in the later year. This is elaborated upon in Table 18.3 to show the changing pattern of employment categories. By 1911 the category of transport services had taken over from building and construction as the leading non-manufacturing employment category in our select list of towns and cities. Amongst manufacturing employment, category X (metals and engineering, but also including shipbuilding) was more strongly represented in 1911 whilst the categories of textile manufacture and clothing were less well represented as leading categories of male employment, although still amongst the principal female employments along with the food and drink trades. In the case of females, the decline in domestic service after 1861 was compensated to an extent by growth in the categories of commercial and service employment, but the most significant increases in the proportions employed were still to be found in those occupational categories, mainly textiles and clothing, that had been dominant in 1861. On the other hand, in respect of male employment the problems affecting cotton textiles in the later nineteenth century were largely responsible for the declining ratios of the male workforce employed in manufacturing in the case of Stockport and Manchester and this would have been a more pronounced feature presumably if other more specialised textile centres had been included.

[32] The data upon which the occupational tables are based are taken from the published censuses for 1861, 1911 and 1951. From occupational categories identified in 1911, adjustments have been made in those for 1861 and 1951 to render them as consistent as is possible, though it is recognised that this has limitations because of the definitional changes and different systems of classification used by the census authorities. For further details contact Richard Rodger or David Reeder.

Table 18.2 *Ratio of manufacturing to service employment: selected towns and cities 1861–1951*

	Males				Females		
	1861	1911	1951		1861	1911	1951
Coventry	4.8	3.0	4.7	Dundee	6.0	2.9	1.4
Stockport	4.6	1.7	1.8	Preston	5.3	4.1	1.5
Preston	4.4	2.0	1.1	Stockport	4.2	2.9	1.9
Sheffield	4.2	2.1	2.2	Coventry	3.4	1.2	1.9
Northampton	3.7	1.8	1.4	Leicester	2.3	2.4	2.3
Dundee	3.4	1.8	1.4	Glasgow	2.2	0.8	0.8
Birmingham	3.4	1.8	2.5	Northampton	2.1	1.7	1.5
Leeds	3.4	1.6	1.3	Derby	2.0	1.1	1.1
Wolverhampton	3.1	1.6	2.3	Manchester	1.9	1.2	1.2
Leicester	3.1	1.6	1.7	Leeds	1.9	1.7	1.6
Derby	2.5	1.3	2.3	Birmingham	1.3	1.5	1.7
Manchester	2.0	0.9	0.9	Cardiff	0.9	0.5	0.8
Glasgow	2.0	1.1	1.1	Sheffield	0.8	0.7	1.4
Newcastle-upon-Tyne	1.7	1.2	0.9	Ipswich	0.7	0.5	0.7
Reading	1.6	1.0	0.6	Bristol	0.7	0.8	0.7
Bristol	1.5	0.8	0.8	Wolverhampton	0.7	0.7	1.4
Ipswich	1.4	1.0	1.1	Liverpool	0.6	0.6	0.9
Oxford	1.0	0.4	1.3	Newcastle-upon-Tyne	0.6	0.4	0.6
Edinburgh	1.0	0.6	0.7	Edinburgh	0.5	0.3	0.5
Cardiff	0.9	0.5	0.8	Maidstone	0.5	n/a	0.4
Liverpool	0.8	0.5	0.6	Reading	0.5	0.6	0.6
Maidstone	0.8	n/a	0.5	Oxford	0.4	0.3	0.4
St Helens	n/a	2.6	2.5	St Helens	n/a	0.6	1.5
Middlesbrough	n/a	1.6	1.2	Middlesbrough	n/a	0.3	0.8
GB	1.3	0.7	0.8	GB	1.0	0.7	0.9

A ratio of 1.0 indicates that the numbers employed in manufacturing employment and service employment (professional, office, commercial, distributive and domestic employment, or 'non-industrial' in the appendix) were the same. Thus, in Dundee, for example, manufacturing employment in 1861 was six times greater than employment in the broadly defined service sector.

It is not easy to assess the degree of specialisation characteristic of urban economies in a systematic comparative way since the industrial categories used in the published census tables frequently included a range of different trades. This is the case, for example, with Birmingham – 'a city of a thousand trades' – many of which were included within the all-encompassing category of metals and engineering. Whilst leading sectors were important they can have a misleading

Table 18.3 *The concentration of employment: occupation distribution according to the two largest employment categories 1861–1951*

Census category	Occupation	1861 Males	1861 Females	1911 Males	1911 Females	1951 Males	1951 Females
III	Professional					2	7
IV	Domestic		20		20		
VI	Transport	4		16		10	
VII	Agriculture	2					
IX	Mines, quarrying	1		1		1	
X	Engineering, metals	13		16	2	19	4
XI	Precious metal	1					
XII	Building	6	1	1			
XIV	Bricks, glass, pottery			1			
XVIII	Textiles	9	8	3	6	3	5
XIX	Clothing	4	15	2	14	2	4
XX	Food, drink and tobacco			1	1		4
XXII	General manufacturing	3					
XXIII	Dealing	1		5	3	10	23

This table shows, for example, that in nine towns and cities textiles, census category XVIII, was one of the two largest areas of male employment, and in eight towns and cities this was the case for female employment in 1861.

impression and attribute an undue importance to a single sector, understating the contribution of a range of local industries which, though individually small, make for a more or less variegated city economy than an association with one or two products would imply.[33] What Table 18.4 offers, therefore, is only a very crude indicator and one that can be interpreted from two points of view. Looking at the situation in 1911, it is possible to point to some highly concentrated local economies – for example, Middlesbrough and Coventry – yet, on the other hand, from our select list, eighteen out of the twenty-three towns and cities in 1911 had less than half of their male workforce employed in the two leading employment categories. Edinburgh, as already indicated, had the most diversified employment structure with a greater ratio of the male workforce employed in professional, government and commercial services and in the service industries. As expected, the regional centres and port cities were more diversified than specialist industrial centres but they also differed in the degree to which this was so. Regional cities such as Leeds, Birmingham and Manchester

[33] M. Hewitt, *The Emergence of Stability in the Industrial City* (Aldershot, 1996), pp. 23–67, and Butt, 'The changing character of urban employment', pp. 221–2, make this point for regional centres such as Manchester and Glasgow.

Table 18.4 *Index of concentration: proportion of males and females employed in the largest single occupational category 1861–1951*

	Males			Females		
	1861 (%)	1911 (%)	1951 (%)	1861 (%)	1911 (%)	1951 (%)
Sheffield	49	45	53	41	33	36
Stockport	45	21	28	69	49	24
Northampton	44	39	23	62	55	38
Preston	41	26	24	73	69	30
Wolverhampton	39	42	45	46	32	37
Birmingham	33	37	49	32	27	35
Coventry	32	52	66	65	22	41
Leicester	32	25	22	48	33	32
Cardiff	30	30	24	55	39	23
Liverpool	29	33	26	49	34	19
Dundee	26	28	19	37	49	31
Leeds	22	21	23	38	35	32
Newcastle-upon-Tyne	20	29	28	49	39	25
Manchester	19	18	17	42	27	21
Derby	17	31	41	43	25	18
Glasgow	17	24	28	36	21	23
Reading	15	18	17	58	37	23
Maidstone	13	n/a	15	49	n/a	21
Bristol	13	18	15	47	30	20
Edinburgh	13	15	14	52	39	20
Oxford	12	15	41	60	53	31
Ipswich	8	13	16	47	41	23
St Helens	n/a	29	42	n/a	32	30
Middlesbrough	n/a	43	40	n/a	43	26
GB	24	13	20	37	35	12

Though this table shows that, for example, 41 per cent of male employment in Preston in 1861 was in a single sector, it does not follow (and was not the case) that the figures for subsequent dates refer to the same sector, but simply that this was the largest concentration of employment in any census category.

were characterised by fairly diverse occupational structures in that all three possessed substantial manufacturing bases, and had, in addition, a developing range of service industries. In Manchester, a city which had developed significant commercial and distributive functions, manufacturing constituted a relatively smaller element in the economy compared to other regional centres. There were also contrasts between the regional cities and the port cities, the figures for the latter reflecting how their economies were shaped by and dependent on transport, commercial and port activities. Amongst the leading categories of male employment in these port cities was category X which included shipbuilding as well as metals and engineering, and also category VI – transport services, although for females the most important categories, apart from domestic service, were dress, footwear and clothing – and the category of food, drink and tobacco. It is also worth noting more generally the employment effect of transport on a variety of urban locations, and how in particular the growth in the numbers employed in transport made the economies of Cardiff and Derby considerably more concentrated in 1911 than in 1861.

Finally, a broad comparison of the 1911 with the 1951 data can be made, although it is worth noting that this is a problematic exercise because of inconsistencies in the occupational categories in the census. There is no reason to doubt, however, the very variable picture which the tables suggest with regard to changes in the degree of dependency on a manufacturing base of these towns and cities. Many reached or passed a peak of industrialisation with the proportions in manufacturing male employment either little changed since 1911 or in decline: thus the economies of Wolverhampton, Dundee, Northampton, Middlesbrough and Preston all seem to have become less dependent on their staple manufacturing industries. By contrast, other towns and cities became more concentrated in terms of their reliance on a single industrial sector – Oxford notably, but also Coventry, Birmingham, Derby and St Helens strengthened their manufacturing base in terms of male employment. A degree of polarisation emerged, therefore, in the first half of the twentieth century such that by 1951 there were no towns and cities in the selection provided in Table 18.4 where the concentration on a single occupational category was in the 30–40 per cent range.

The importance of the engineering sector to an increasing number of towns and cities, as shown in Table 18.3, was a contributory factor in the adaptation of older manufacturing interests as well as the growth of new industries during the interwar years. The way that women were absorbed into previously male-dominated industrial employment in Coventry and Birmingham was an indication of this flexibility in working practices. Both Reading and Maidstone were undoubtedly affected by new industrialisation in the interwar years and after, though this was complemented by the growth of service employment. Indeed, trends in these towns in relation to the growth of commercial and professional employment in this forty-year period, 1911–51, were indicative of the greater frequency of non-manufacturing employment generally (other than transport service) in the table of leading employment categories – the category of dealers in both male and female employment structures and the category of professional and subordinate services for females. At the same time the growth of the service sector, important though it was, had yet to transform the character of the leading industrial centres of the country, many of which had become increasingly dependent on employment in the category of light engineering.

(iv) INDUSTRIAL DIVERSIFICATION AND THE IMPACT OF THE NEW INDUSTRIES

Whereas some urban locations hardly changed the balance of their occupational structures, or experienced only a modest degree of diversification, others were able to adapt to changing market conditions by extending the range of their manufacturing base. A number of cities replaced faltering or decaying industrial sectors (or particular industries within the census categories) with new infusions (see Tables 18.1–4). Diversification can be regarded as a consequence either of an organic process of growth which derived from the demands placed on the economy by the growth of urban populations or of the increasingly complex and specialist needs of dominant sector industries. Diversification within a particular industrial sector, however, was another possibility and one not without risk to the city since it could lead to an over-reliance on a single sector and a vulnerability to structural changes within it. The growth of nineteenth-century Nottingham exemplifies the self-renewing process associated with diversification, triggered by the multiplier effects of the introduction of lace and hosiery to the town. Building construction, textile machinery firms and tertiary activity, especially in retailing, helped to sustain a buoyant economy attractive to new industries such as Raleigh in bicycles and Player's in tobacco.[34] What this model does not explain is why some towns and cities were more successful than others in attracting capital and enterprise into new industrial developments.

As the earlier discussion of regional disparities suggests, part of the answer lies in the extent to which resources of labour and capital were locked into the low-growth industries of the twentieth century. The economic history of Glasgow, for example, is a telling commentary on the inability of a once great commercial and industrial centre to attract sufficient new industry significantly to arrest a long-drawn-out syndrome of manufacturing decline which set in after the First World War. Whilst Glasgow's late nineteenth-century industrial structure was more diversified than is implied by its dominant image as a centre of heavy industry, the fate of shipbuilding and heavy engineering during the interwar years determined the fortunes of associated trades, and led to depression in the regional economy. In consequence, Glasgow 'was unable to make the consumer leap into the next stage of urban industrial growth' and eventually entered a period of contraction in which all the factors that had combined so successfully in the growth phase were reversed.[35]

---

[34] R. A. Church, *Economic and Social Change in a Midland Town* (London, 1966); J. Beckett, ed., *A Centenary History of Nottingham* (Manchester, 1997).

[35] S. Checkland, *The Upas Tree* (Glasgow, 1981); U. Wannop, 'Glasgow/Clydeside: a century of metropolitan evolution', in G. Gordon, ed., *Regional Cities in the UK, 1890–1980* (London 1986), pp. 83–98; J. Butt, 'The industries of Glasgow', in Fraser and Maver, eds., *Glasgow*, II, pp. 96–140.

Conversely, a city with a range of different industries serving different markets was more likely to sustain long-term evolutionary growth. The case has been made by the business historians of Bristol, a city with a somewhat chequered economic history during the nineteenth century. During the first half of the century several traditional Bristol industries lost their competitive edge vis-à-vis the major industrial districts and eventually disappeared; but over the second half of the century, other industries in and around the city – notably the consumer goods industries of chocolate, cocoa and tobacco – showed considerable resilience. The point is that none of the contracting industries had a sufficiently large stake in the urban economy to induce a spiral of economic decline. Bristol, unlike Glasgow, was able to generate or attract sufficient new industry both to take up the slack and to create further employment opportunities: in construction, urban transport services, locomotive manufacturing, transport engineering, the motor vehicle and aircraft industries, the latter expanding greatly in the 1930s. The adaptability of its manufacturing economy, along with its role as a consumption centre for a large urban cluster, lay behind the Bristol story of 'gradual if rather unexciting economic growth in the late Victorian period and beyond'.[36]

The city of Leeds offers a further example of an evolutionary economy based partly on its functions as a regional centre but also on the flexible nature of its industrial structure. Always more than a textile centre, the growth of engineering, expansion of printing and the establishment of the clothing trades by Jewish immigrants provided the dynamic for economic growth in the late nineteenth and early twentieth centuries. This diversification more than made good the loss of employment from the secular decline of the woollen industry and other sunset trades during the interwar years. The secret of the Leeds economy lay in the strength of industrial linkages as well as the persistence of localised concentrations of ancillary trades, and the flexibility of production methods in the clothing trade with its subcontracting workshops. On the other hand, the continuing success of these traditional industries meant that the new growth sectors of the interwar economy were underrepresented and this was eventually to bring increasing rigidities.[37]

---

[36] K. Morgan, 'The economic development of Bristol, 1700–1850', in M. Dresser and P. Ollerenshaw, eds., *The Making of Modern Bristol* (Tiverton, 1996), p. 69. According to P. Ollerenshaw and P. Wardley, 'Economic growth and the business community in Bristol since 1840', in Dresser and Ollerenshaw, eds., *The Making*, p. 124, Bristol displayed a pattern of 'undramatic but sustained economic growth, rising incomes, industrial innovation and structural change over the long run'. See also C. E. Harvey and J. Press, 'Industrial change and economic life in Bristol since 1800', in C. E. Harvey and J. Press, eds., *Studies in the Business History of Bristol* (Bristol, 1988), pp. 1–32.

[37] This account is derived from S. Caunce and K. Honeyman, 'Introduction: the city of Leeds and its business 1893–1993', in J. Chartres and K. Honeyman, eds., *Leeds City Business 1893–1993* (Leeds, 1993), pp. 1–23.

The development of the 'new' industry growth sectors – chemicals, new synthetic materials, motor vehicles and electrical engineering – was crucial to urban regeneration and had begun to revive the economies of a number of cities, especially in the Midlands, before they became conspicuous in the national output figures.[38] This was dramatically so in regard to Coventry, a city whose economic and demographic fortunes, previously in decline for thirty years following the collapse and attrition of silk weaving and watchmaking, were transformed in the twentieth century. An influx of new entrepreneurial energy, technical skills and capital pulled the city out of stagnation, creating a new kind of factory boom town whose growth was carried forward by a flood of migrants, representing 45 per cent of its population increase in the interwar years. The location of bicycle and motor car production in the city was the prime factor although Coventry also benefited from the arrival of other major manufacturing activities in artificial textiles, ordnance work and electrical equipment. How can this influx of new industry be explained? There were no special inducements and Coventry had a relatively low municipal profile, but it had the advantages of good communications, an abundant supply of appropriate labour, including female labour (for Courtauld's), and available and cheap workshop and factory space. Moreover, once industrial restructuring began it developed a momentum of its own, propelled by linkages across and within different parts of the engineering sector, particularly in the demand for motor car components. The engineering industries in Coventry benefited also from the rearmament drive in the late 1930s and during the war itself. In this context of rapid expansion local employers adopted various strategies to overcome labour supply problems, including support for institutionalised technical education through probationer-apprenticeship schemes and day release classes.[39]

Coventry offers an insight into a more abrupt process of industrial change. The development of new industry in this city had a more conspicuous impact than in such mature industrial centres as Birmingham which still retained a great variety of trades. Even the comparable, if fortuitous, development of a motor car industry in the suburb of Cowley in Oxford generated fewer linkages in a city where the academic industry still remained such an important influence.[40]

---

[38] For an overview of the debate on new growth industries in the interwar economy, see D. H. Aldcroft and H. W. Richardson, *The British Economy 1870–1939* (London, 1969); for differing interpretations of interwar growth, see D. H. Aldcroft and P. S. Fearon, *Economic Growth in Twentieth Century Britain* (London, 1969).

[39] See D. W. Thoms and T. Donnelly, 'Coventry's industrial economy, 1880–1980', and B. Lancaster and T. Mason, 'Society and politics in twentieth century Coventry', in B. Lancaster and T. Mason, eds., *Life and Labour in a Twentieth Century City* (Coventry, 1986), pp. 11–56 and 342–69. Also D. Thoms, 'Technical education and the transformation of Coventry's industrial economy, 1900–1939', in P. Summerfield and E. J. Evans, eds., *Technical Education and the State since 1850* (Manchester, 1990), pp. 37–54.

[40] The most recent account is in R. C. Whiting, ed. *Oxford Studies in the History of a University Town since 1800* (Manchester, 1993).

Coventry's diversification had resulted in a concentrated economy, however, and the extent of its dependence on the motor car industry was eventually to pose the most serious threat to its future prosperity.[41]

The growth industries of the interwar years not only regenerated the economies of older industrial cities but helped to revive the fortunes of middle-rank county towns, particularly in the Home Counties. These towns benefited from their proximity to London as well as the success of specialist consumer-based industries. In Reading (biscuit making), Luton and Oxford (new centres of motor manufacturing) and Maidstone (food processing and engineering) new sectors were superimposed on more established industries, also based on consumption, such as brewing and printing.[42] Many towns in the orbit of London owed their success to a more variegated industrial development, as with the towns of Hertfordshire such as Watford and Slough. These Hertfordshire towns exemplify the way that prosperous mixed light industries were attracted to the South-East by efficient communications and distribution networks, as well as by cheap sites and the availability of new factory buildings.[43]

An industrial Arcadia emerged along the new arterial roads in Leeds, Birmingham, Manchester and in Greater London, as industrial estates sprouted widely spaced factories on green-field sites. It was a development which engulfed older villages and also affected small market towns.[44] In Hertfordshire a mixture of town planning idealism and entrepreneurial acumen brought into being new communities. Like the industrial cities of the Midlands, these were boom towns with very high rates of immigration. But whereas the older cities contributed in larger measure to remaking their own economies from existing infrastructural resources and services, the new towns and industrial districts drew heavily on inward investment as well as labour and were dependent also on private capital for the provision of services. There was a similarity in that respect between the factory villages and new company towns of the nineteenth century (Middlesbrough, in its early stages, and Crewe) and the industrial trading estates and interwar planned towns.

The development of Slough illustrates the mechanisms of change.[45] A small country town in the late nineteenth century, the beginnings of Slough's industrial development was already in evidence along the Bath Road prior to the First World War. It was accelerated by the formation of a large industrial estate of 600

---

[41] As Fogarty, prophetically warned, *Prospects*, p. 353.

[42] P. Clark and L. Murfin, *The History of Maidstone* (Stroud, 1995), p. 251, state that Maidstone 'with its thriving industries, shops and services . . . moved into the top flight of expanding towns in the south east'.   [43] Fogarty, *Prospects*, pp. 392–5.

[44] The phenomenon of arterial industrial development was also reproduced in older industrial centres. See M. Bateman, 'Leeds: a study in regional supremacy', in Gordon, ed., *Regional Cities*, p. 106, who discusses the role of the Leeds ring road and arterial routes and notes that they were 'modelled on the example of Liverpool'.

[45] The principal sources are J. Hunter, *The Story of Slough* (Newbury, 1983), pp. 68–82, and M. Cassell, *Long Lease!* (London, 1991).

acres to capitalise on a demand for low rented factory accommodation. The site
– a government repair depot during the First World War – was bought out by
entrepreneurs involved in the motor repair business. They had the foresight to
convert the trading company into an estates company in 1926, initially to provide
factories for firms – mostly those requiring extensive space – willing to move
there, but from 1928 adopted a policy of building 'off the peg' adaptable units
aimed at light industry. Companies were attracted by good communications and
as a result of the investment of the Slough Estates Company in roads and factory
units and in centralised services such as power, light, steam and water, as well as
gas distribution, and in the building of railway lines and loading facilities. This
initial outlay was supplemented by overseas inward investment encouraged by a
government scheme for Imperial Preference which enabled Slough to advertise
itself as a gateway to British Empire markets for foreign companies. One
hundred companies housed in seventy-two premises had located in Slough by
1933. Many were household names – Black and Decker, Horlicks, Aspro and
Weston's biscuits – as well as companies specialising in light engineering and new
fabrics and materials like rayon and bakelite. The majority of these firms were
relatively small local concerns which rapidly developed national markets.[46] Such
a remarkably rapid development meant that Slough in effect became a new
twentieth-century style of company town, though no responsibility was assumed
by employers for housing the workforce. Nor was there much in the way of
social facilities until the building of a community centre with support from
leading tenants. Since the factory premises were 'de-rated' or exempt from local
taxes, the local authority considered that for its part it was exempted from
making contributions to amenities on the estate.

In the 1920s and 1930s Slough must have seemed like a frontier town.
Encouraged by payments under the Industrial Transference Scheme labour
migrated to such nodes of economic development and capital was also attracted
from other parts of the country and from abroad. Much the same could be said
of Letchworth and Welwyn during the interwar years. The first of the garden
cities, they were creations of private enterprise and as such speculative and
under-capitalised until industrial development paid off in substantial increases in
rental value and an expanded local tax base.[47] From the outset and with inadequate financial resources, Garden City Companies created new towns with
limited infrastructural provisions. Services had to be provided *de novo* and these
towns soon acquired the reputation of being 'do-it-yourself' communities. In
contrast to the older centres, they had neither civic traditions nor local resources
of capital and labour.

---

[46] For another industrial estate development with several developers but a similar mix of industries
see J. Armstrong, 'The development of the Park Royal industrial estate in the inter-war period',
LJ, 21 (1996), 64–77.
[47] F. J. Osborn and A. Whittick, *New Towns* (London, 1977), pp. 18–19, 25.

The composition of local industry was crucial to the trajectory of growth, both for firms and for towns, too. This 'path-dependency', to use the term applied to explain Britain's national economic performance, identifies Britain as having a high proportion of its output in products which had low growth potential in the early twentieth century and in the interwar years.[48] The high wage-cost-price structure and overvalued pound did few favours to British manufacturers in the interwar years, but more serious was this overdependence on stagnant or declining economic sectors. By contrast, towns and cities with diversified production structures gained because they were less exposed to risk and business failure. Industrial diversity was also a critical ingredient in the responsiveness of towns to technological change, especially if the engineering sector was of a broad-based and adaptable mechanical engineering and tool-making variety rather than marine, railway, civil, agricultural or other specialist subspecies of engineering.[49] Like a skittle, the broader based the industrial structure the less likely was it to be knocked over when recession approached. Under these circumstances — less exposure to cyclical and secular decline and better prospects for industrial regeneration — then levels of consumption locally remained robust for goods and services. It was not just that diversified towns had high propensities to consume — the inhabitants of Merthyr and Jarrow had that too because they had no opportunity to save — but that the purchasing power locally was sustainable despite the ravages of the depression elsewhere.

(V) STRUCTURAL CHANGE AND THE INDUSTRIAL CITY

The rise of the new towns and industrial districts was one of the factors affecting the relationships between urban and manufacturing interests in the twentieth century. These relationships were also affected by structural changes within manufacturing industry as well as by more wide-ranging changes in the conditions influencing the development of city institutions and services. The remaining sections summarise the general trends whilst stressing the variability of their impact on the experience of different towns and cities in what is very much an underresearched topic.

How important, then, was the changing scale and nature of production to relationships between urban and manufacturing interests? According to one school of thought a series of technological and organisational developments in the leading industries of the late nineteenth and early to mid-twentieth centuries — continuing mechanisation of processes, transformation of workshop-based to

[48] S. N. Broadberry, *The Productivity Race* (Cambridge, 1997); R. C. O. Matthews, 'Some aspects of post-war growth in the British economy in relation to historical experience', *Transactions of the Manchester Statistical Society* (1964) tables 5, 6.

[49] S. B. Saul, 'The market and the development of the mechanical engineering industries in Britain, 1860–1914', *Ec.HR*, 2nd series, 20 (1967), 111.

factory-based methods increasingly geared to mass production, growth in the scale of production, and new forms of business organisation – provided the momentum for the economies of industrial cities.[50] The growth in the scale of units was characteristic of the iron and steel industry, armaments, shipbuilding and certain branches of textiles whilst mergers took place in the 1880s in soap and chemicals, brewing, tobacco and food processing as part of international business trends on a scale sufficient in more recent times to have referred the amalgamations to the Monopolies and Mergers Commission.[51] Prior to the First World War, however, mergers were limited in extent and did not much affect corporate structures in Britain overall. Even amongst merged concerns the holding form of company organisation enabled local firms to retain a degree of autonomy, a characteristic which diverged strongly from the cartels and corporate structures which had developed in Germany and the USA between 1890 and 1914. Many large firms remained family owned and managed, and the family interest continued to be strong in those firms which adopted limited liability. This was the case amongst the Oldham limiteds, quoted public companies such as Crawford, Dowry, Haugh, New Hay, Moorfield and Werneth, in the years *c.* 1880–1914, though they were out-performed in terms of profitability and growth by private companies – Fielden Bros., Horrockses, Osborne, Tootals.[52] Neither private nor public firms used bank borrowing to fund capacity extensions in the Lancashire textile industry, preferring stock options and appeals to existing investors to finance expansion in what represented 'urban estates' or personal capitalism rather than organisational units with fully fledged managerial hierarchies.

Complementing this emphasis on the durable role of family firms and local capital supplies as the main dynamic of urban growth is an explanation that stresses the contribution of small firms and flexible modes of production connected to the traditional organisation of craft-based workshops and associated forms of outwork. Recent studies have led to new claims for the importance of small producer capitalists in generating technical change and economic growth.[53] At the same time the growth of large firms itself created further opportunities for small-scale operations by generating new demands for bespoke machines, tools, components, materials. In Bradford the large combined worsted mills

[50] See, for example, A. D. Chandler Jr., *Scale and Scope* (Cambridge, Mass., 1990).

[51] P. L. Payne, 'The emergence of the large scale company in Great Britain, 1870–1914', *Ec.HR*, 2nd series, 20 (1967), 519–42; M. A. Utton, 'Some features of the early merger movements in British manufacturing industry', *Business History*, 14 (1972), 51–60; L. Hannah, 'Mergers in manufacturing industry, 1880–1919', *Oxford Economic Papers*, 26 (1974), 1–20.

[52] S. Toms, 'Windows of opportunity in the textile industry: the business strategy of Lancashire entrepreneurs, 1880–1914', *Business History*, 40 (1998), 3.

[53] See the examples in C. Sabel and J. Zeitlin, 'Historical alternatives to mass production: politics, markets and technology in nineteenth-century industrialisation', *P&P*, 108 (1985), 133–76; Rodger, 'Concentration and fragmentation'; Johnson, 'Economic development'.

coexisted with small-scale engineering enterprises, in Newcastle small-scale suppliers to the large Tyneside shipyards sprang up, whilst in Birmingham and
throughout the Black Country during the early twentieth century long-
established small-scale iron and metal firms turned to making components for
the motor car industry.[54]

Thus in many of the older industrial cities – the metalworking centres especially – a dualistic economy, already in evidence by the 1860s, was reinforced.
This is best exemplified by Sheffield, a city in which small-scale production as
represented initially by the 'little maisters' of the cutlery industry played an innovative part in the city's transition to steel production.[55] Yet the expansion of steelmaking was also associated with a degree of concentration in crucible steel
production and a spectacular growth of large firms in the making of heavy steel
goods, notably armaments. In Sheffield, large and even giant firms coexisted
with many small firms in what can be represented as two business systems,
differently organised and spatially differentiated. Many of the larger works gravitated to green-field sites in the east end districts of Attercliffe and Brightside to
form, in effect, new industrial fiefdoms. In contrast, the centre of Sheffield presented a very different picture of business organisation with its 'outworkers,
teams, merchants and manufacturers drawn together by a complex of interdependence of skills and products'.[56]

The minute subdivisions in Sheffield's economy encouraged product differentiation, whilst an outwork and rentier system facilitated quick responses to
changes in design and fashion. This was complemented by a marketing strategy
based on an establishment of brand names and capitalising on the city's reputation for quality – a reputation its leading manufacturers sought to maintain by

[54] Fogarty, *Prospects*, pp. 339–53; G. C. Allen, *The Industrial Development of Birmingham and the Black Country, 1860–1927* (London, 1929; repr., 1966), pp. 291 *et seq.*

[55] The statistical analysis of Sheffield firms has been undertaken by R. Lloyd-Jones and M. J. Lewis, most recently in their chapter, 'Business structure and political economy in Sheffield: the metal trades 1880–1920s', in C. J. Binfield *et al.*, eds., *The History of the City of Sheffield, 1843–1993*, vol. II (Sheffield, 1993), pp. 211–33. The authors point out that the persistence of the small private firm had to do with its role as a vehicle for family control, but in Sheffield constraints on growth were reinforced by an extensive outwork system.

[56] S. Taylor, 'The industrial structure of the Sheffield cutlery trades, 1870–1914', in Binfield *et al.*, eds., *History of the City of Sheffield*, p. 203, quoting R. J. Islip, 'A future for the past in Sheffield?', *Yorkshire Architect* (May/June 1978). Taylor argues for the rationality of the complicated structure of the cutlery industry in which factory, worshop and outwork, mechanised and hand production, coexisted. For the crucible steel production industry, see G. Tweedale, 'The business and technol-ogy of Sheffield steelmaking', in Binfield *et al.*, eds., *History of the City of Sheffield*, p. 149, drawing on J. G. Timmins, 'Concentration and integration in the Sheffield crucible steel industry', *Business History*, 24 (1982), 61–78. For a pioneering study of the process of industrial location in the steel industry, see R. T. Simmons, 'Steam, steel and Lizzie the Elephant – the steel industry, transport technology and urban development in Sheffield, 1809–1914' (PhD thesis, University of Leicester, 1995). For similarities and contrasts between the Sheffield and Birmingham city economies and their social implications, D. Smith, *Conflict and Compromise* (London, 1982).

endowing Firth College in order to train metallurgists. Sheffield continued, therefore, to provide an environment in which small firms in the various branches of the metal trades could survive and flourish.[57] Detailed analysis has shown that until 1921, and despite wartime mergers, the iron and steel trades in Sheffield went against the national and international trend by continuing to register an increase in the proportion of small firms.[58] Yet this highly specialised manufacturing economy served the city less well in the difficult 1920s, a decade which exposed structural weaknesses. In circumstances where the cutlery industry was faced with tariff barriers and the competitive pressure of low-quality steel, a multiplicity of small firms, once a strength, became a weakness. The market no longer functioned efficiently: too many firms produced too many product lines. The competitive edge was surrendered to those producers capable of greater standardisation, whether in Britain or abroad. In these changed conditions, flexibility gave way to conservatism amongst the small family-based units, reinforced by the power of craft-based trade unions. The cooperative dynamic which Marshall had regarded as essential to the success of small producer capitalism in the industrial districts was lacking, if, indeed, it had ever existed. In consequence, Sheffield businessmen were unable to present a united front on important political issues and the attachment to trademarks and industrial secrets inhibited them from working together.[59]

Elsewhere, large- and small-scale units of production sought from different perspectives to contain costs of production in the difficult national and international circumstances which Britain faced in the 1920s. The concentration of production, reinforced in the 1930s by rationalisation schemes funded by the government and the Bank of England to cocoon capacity in textiles and shipbuilding, was intended to generate economies of scale in an effort to withstand the assault on profits and to avoid bankruptcy in the context of an international depression. But increased scale was also associated with logistical difficulties. For example, in the 1920s, non-traditional building methods employed by larger firms using poured concrete and shuttered construction techniques encountered supply difficulties, inconsistent quality control and organisational difficulties in coordinating the different stages of building.[60] In parallel, this enabled smaller

<hr/>

[57] Tweedale, 'Sheffield steelmaking', p. 174.

[58] The detailed analysis referred to is by Lloyd-Jones and Lewis, 'Business structure', in Binfield *et al.*, eds., *History of the City of Sheffield*, pp. 211–33. The general account is G. Tweedale, *Steel City* (Oxford, 1995). See also G. Tweedale, 'The business and technology of Sheffield steelmaking', in Binfield *et al.*, eds., *History of the City of Sheffield*, pp. 142–93.

[59] The problems of the interwar period are discussed by all the business historians previously cited in Binfield *et al.*, eds., *History of the City of Sheffield*, and by S. Pollard in his chapter on 'Labour', pp. 260–78. See also A. White, '"We never know what price we are going to have till we get to the warehouse": nineteenth century Sheffield and the industrial district debate', *Soc. Hist.*, 22 (1997), 307–17.

[60] S. Marriner, 'Cash and concrete. Liquidity problems in the mass production of "homes for heroes"', *Business History*, 18 (1976), 52–89; F. Wellings, *A History of Marley* (Abington, 1994).

builders to fill orders using locally produced materials from known suppliers. Grates, keys, plumbing and gas fitments, electric cables and switches were examples of products which sustained small-scale suppliers locally.

In addition, the wider adoption and distribution of electrical power through the development of the national grid enabled production and the point of distribution to be increasingly detached. Light industrial and finishing processes facilitated product differentiation to take place at a distance from the factory gate. Though a considerable volume of freight was still carried on the railways, the interwar years witnessed an increase in the number of vans and lorries operating within towns, and this improved business flexibility and nurtured small business endeavours. On the back of changes in transport developments and distributed energy sources, a vigorous counter-culture of successful small business was sustained in interwar Britain, arresting what seemed, at least in the long-term national picture, an inexorable trend towards larger scale of production, to such an extent that between 1935 and the census of production in 1951 'the level of industrial concentration advanced imperceptibly, and may actually have diminished'.[61]

Nevertheless, growth in the scale and complexity of industry had a visible impact on the appearance of the British industrial city in that textile and steel mills, shipbuilding yards and, later, automobile plants required sites, buildings and workforces on a scale not encountered before. By the early twentieth century industrial and commercial property had become a significant part of the urban real estate market. Rising rentals forced more specialised land use within cities as users sought to evaluate how important city-centre access was to their business activities and in many cities, not only in Sheffield, the rents and congestion of the central areas and the need for space led to peripheral industrial development. In Birmingham, for example, many of the growth industries of the late nineteenth century had moved to the middle ring whilst the newest and largest factories of the twentieth century were to be found on the outskirts of the city: the Austin Motor Works at Longbridge was particularly extensive covering 100 acres (40.5 ha) by 1922 and employing 20,000 workers on the eve of the Second World War.[62] In other cities the development of trading estates to attract migrant capital and the strategic requirements of wartime industrial sites and 'ghost factories' accelerated this tendency to peripheral development. Lubricated by increased private road transport and changed residential patterns,

[61] G. A. Phillips and R. T. Maddock, *The Growth of the British Economy 1918–1968* (London, 1973), p. 80. A new phase of mergers, acquisitions and the establishment of subsidiaries set in after 1950.
[62] A. Sutcliffe and R. Smith, *History of Birmingham*, vol. III: *Birmingham 1939–1970* (Birmingham, 1974), pp. 157–8. See also M. J. Wise and P. O'N. Thorpe, 'The growth of Birmingham 1800–1950', in R. H. Kinvig, J. G. Smith and M. J. Wise, eds., *Birmingham and its Regional Setting: A Scientific Survey* (Birmingham, 1950), esp. pp. 222–8. For the scale of Austin's plant see R. A. Church, *Herbert Austin* (London, 1979), pp. 48, 149, and more generally on the relationship of the car industry to Birmingham, pp. 42–56 and 89–110.

the centrifugal forces of the twentieth-century city replaced its earlier centripetal role. These forces substantially shaped the requirements of industrial location whether in the Manchester or Birmingham city region or on Merseyside. Extensive peripheral estates with road and rail links and industrial services attracted the new growth industries as well as encouraging existing local industry to relocate on more spacious sites close to suburban housing.[63]

This did not necessarily mean the demise of the older inner-city economy. Indeed, the almost infinite capacity of small-scale firms to rediscover a market niche was testimony to the constantly mutating nature of the urban economy. In compact industrial cities such as Leicester there was, even after 1945, a heavy concentration of industrial premises. Hosiery factories and light engineering firms, for example, remained prominent in and around the central area despite some peripheral development, mainly of large-scale firms, in new industries such as electrical engineering.[64] In other industrial cities the older districts of small-scale operators and workshop concerns were still in existence through the interwar years and after the Second World War. Birmingham's industrial prosperity in the twentieth century continued to depend very much on the adaptability of small firms typical of the city's central area to the pattern of growth and decay. As M. P. Fogarty noted in 1945, the successful continuance of this process, and the fact that the supply of new firms did not fail, was largely due to 'the environment – to the proximity of large number of small firms with their associated force of skilled labour and their ancillary services'.[65] Conditions in Birmingham, he further pointed out, were similar in many respects to those of east London. In 1948 P. Sargant Florence, the Birmingham economist, was still able to argue that industrial districts in central areas reproduced in many respects the major advantages of a large-scale plant in the form of the physical juxtaposition of consecutive processes and auxiliary services, and in 1953 he coined the phrase 'industrial swarming' to explain how Birmingham still functioned as a local economic unit.[66] Clearly, the external economies so important to the foundation of Birmingham's international reputation were robust contributors to the recreation of its business identity in the mid-twentieth century.

One aspect of this urban context of importance to the small-scale suppliers of the automobile assembly plants in Birmingham and Coventry was business networking. For example, for the majority of small-scale, owner-managed or family firms supplying components to the automobile assembly plants in Birmingham and Coventry throughout the interwar years, direct personal contacts were

[63] See also above, pp. 575–6.
[64] C. Harrison and D. Reeder, 'The local economy', in D. Nash and D. Reeder, eds., *Leicester in the Twentieth Century* (Stroud, 1993), pp. 59–61. [65] Fogarty, *Prospects*, p. 351.
[66] P. Sargant Florence, *Investment, Location and Size of Plant* (Cambridge, 1948; new edn, 1974), p. 74; P. Sargant Florence, *The Logic of British and American Industry* (London, 1953, 2nd edn, 1961), pp. 86–92.

essential to obtain business: directors and managers participated in such local business networks as those formed in the recreational institutions scattered across the Coventry region, notably the Coventry and County Club, the 'unofficial headquarters' of the Coventry motor industry.[67]

These continuities apart, due weight must be given to the ramifications of changes in corporate organisation during and after the First World War with a new wave of defensive mergers in the 1920s. These changes had implications not only for urban land use but also for the life of the city more generally and on its government in particular. Until the First World War there was still a structural basis for the government of cities: family firms were still dominant and multi-plant concerns rare. Hence, efficiency depended on investment in local infra-structures from which family firms derived external economies in a symbiotic relationship between business interests and urban governance. Wage negotiations and industrial disputes, too, continued to be conducted mostly at a regional or district level and the formal conduct of industrial relations through conciliation and arbitration discussions had a firm local focus, as in the Lancashire mill towns. There is a strong argument, however, that the position changed remarkably quickly after 1914.[68] Labour relations became a matter for national settlements and industries were involved in negotiating with the government during the war for access to materials or the terms of the Excess Profits Duty. The centralisa-tion of banking and monetary policy through the Bank of England was, to some extent, at the expense of the autonomy of industrial regions as deflationary mea-sures to buttress the exchange rate undermined local authority expenditure in a *de facto* early version of rate-capping.[69] Many family firms foundered in the difficult circumstances of post-war Britain; others converted into joint-stock companies or were swallowed by larger businesses. Collectively, these develop-ments forced a deepening fracture both between ownership and control and between local business loyalties and board room priorities detached by non-local balance sheets and stock market prices.

This is a crucial matter for understanding the way that cities functioned in the interwar years and beyond, if, as has been claimed, the old representatives of family capitalism who had previously been so important to funding and running urban associations were being replaced by more impersonal boards of directors and salaried managers with control located distantly in a London head office. The larger firms tended to outgrow their local origins as they spread their oper-ations to other parts of industry and overseas. The formation of multi-branch

[67] B. Beaven, 'Re-constructing the business community: the small firm in the Coventry motor industry, 1896–1939', *Business Archives*, 72 (1996), 15–29. We are grateful to Lucy Newton for drawing this paper to our attention.
[68] M. J. Daunton, 'Payment and participation: welfare and state formation in Britain 1900–1951', *P&P*, 150 (1996), 169–216.
[69] J. Foreman-Peck, 'Industry and industrial organisation in the inter-war years', in R. Floud and D. McCloskey, eds., *The Economic History of Britain since 1700* , 2nd edn (Cambridge, 1994), vol. II, pp. 392–3, drawing on W. A. Thomas, *The Provincial Stock Exchanges* (London, 1973).

firms such as ICI in 1926 or at a more modest scale of operations, Marley tiles, and the adoption of Fordist attitudes and work practices also loosened local ties as corporate structures, targets and attitudes infiltrated British board rooms. In the competition for shrinking markets in the depressed 1920s national advertising campaigns necessarily had to be homogenised and could no longer appeal to local loyalties. When local firms ceased to be independent businesses but just one of many production units in a national or international combine, they tended to be run by on-site managers who were subject to decisions taken from a distance. The movement of company headquarters to London further accelerated this tendency. In addition, it is possible to discern a partial movement towards the internalisation of suppliers, and of such functions as industrial training and research amongst the larger and more integrated companies.[70]

But the extent to which these trends resulted in what has been called the decomposition of local capital is more arguable. Take, for example, the following description of the movements of company headquarters by a financial historian:

> By 1930 28 out of the top 50 companies by capital and by 1935 15 out of the top 50 companies by employment had London offices and they were responsible for 32 per cent of capital and 39 per cent of the total labour force. There had been a noticeable increase over the previous thirty years both in the importance of large scale companies in manufacturing and in control from London. ICI in chemicals, Vickers in engineering, Richard Thomas in coal-mining . . . were some of the best known examples. Yet despite this shift to London of head offices, this still left the majority of manufacturing companies being run from other British cities, with Manchester, Glasgow and Birmingham being noticeable industrial centres. At the same time, there were numerous other industrial companies, many of which remained privately owned, that continued to be run from the location of their production, whether this was in the older northern towns or the new urban centres growing up around London.[71]

At a smaller scale of operations the adaptation of small businesses, with their dynastic ability to survive and grow, frequently provided a degree of continuity and leadership within towns and cities all over Britain and was an especially influential factor in towns in which family-run firms still set the tone of social

---

[70] Gospel, *Markets*, p. 10 and Part 2, argues that in the course of the twentieth century there has been a growing tendency on the part of British firms to internalise labour activities and to develop stronger internal arrangements. However, he is at pains to point out that this development of strategies of internalisation has been slow and uneven. According to D. M. Ross, 'For many large firms, sub-contracting has replaced internalisation as the most efficient and attractive way of conducting aspects of the business.' See D. M. Ross, 'The unsatisfied fringe in Britain, 1930s–1980s', *Business History*, 38 (1996), 11–26, making reference to the work of G. Bannock on small firms in modern economic history. More generally, see L. Hannah, *The Rise of the Corporate Economy* (London, 1983), and L. Hannah, 'Visible and invisible hands in Great Britain', in A. D. Chandler and H. Daems, eds., *Managerial Hierarchies* (Cambridge, Mass., 1980).

[71] R. C. Michie, 'London and the process of economic growth since 1750', *LJ*, 22 (1997), 63–90.

life during the interwar years and possibly into the 1960s. This was the case, for example, in Leicester and Northampton where durable business interests were reformulated through successive generations and business dynasties remained prominent as political and social leaders. In Leicester, a town of many small fortunes, leading businessmen continued to act as senior aldermen during the interwar years and contributed to charitable activities and civic bequests.[72] In Northampton, business families continued to demonstrate a form of town patriotism in which promotion of the town became an aspect of business strategy and a response to the increasingly cut-throat competition in the footwear industry.[73]

(vi) INDUSTRIALISTS AND CIVIC INITIATIVES

If, in some cities, civic culture was still viable during the interwar years, in others it was an ideology under siege. In the larger cities, one force amongst several weakening the older ideals of social citizenship was associated with the development of corporate forms of organisation where the consequent changes in managerial structures were associated with a renewed surge of suburbanisation, ever more distant from the city centre.[74] At the same time, the extension of central government powers and financing during the interwar years tended to reinforce the trend towards metropolitan centralisation. It lay behind the view, expressed by Herbert Read and J. B. Priestley amongst others, that the independent civic culture of the north was in danger of being eclipsed with the erosion of provincial autonomy.[75]

It was also the case that the old allegiances were especially hard to maintain in those industrialised towns and cities faced with difficult economic circumstances. Remaking these cities politically carried an agenda that threatened to impose extra financial burdens on local industry. In any case, the costs and burdens of unemployment on populous urban areas during the 1920s were made considerably worse by the nature of poor law funding. Rates levied on local industries and residential interests took little account of the ability to pay and so towns and cities with high unemployment often suffered punitive local taxation which resulted in increased burdens for those industries remaining in the locality,

---

[72] Leicester was characteristically a city of small family firms: see Nash and Reeder, *Leicester*, pp. 54, 93–4.

[73] The argument about Northampton is drawn from M. Dickie, 'Town patriotism and the rise of labour in Northampton' (PhD thesis, University of Warwick, 1987). See also C. Brown, *Northampton, 1835–1985* (Chichester, 1990), pp. 79, 138–9, 156.

[74] H. E. Meller, 'Urban renewal and citizenship: the quality of life in British cities, 1890–1990', *UH*, 22 (1995), 63–84, and *Towns, Plans and Societies in Modern Britain* (Cambridge, 1998). For the argument that the centrifugal force in urbanisation has weakened the concepts of public service and citizenship in Scotland, see R. Rodger, 'Urbanisation in twentieth-century Scotland', in T. M. Devine and R. J. Finlay, eds., *Scotland in the Twentieth Century* (Edinburgh, 1996), pp. 122–52.

[75] M. Slater, 'Making it new: visual modernism and the "myth of the north" in inter-war England', *Journal of British Studies*, 37 (1998), 436.

paradoxically encouraging them to move elsewhere or increasing the likelihood of their bankruptcy. Consequently, the rating system further ratcheted up the local taxes payable by firms who could not move to other urban or green-field areas. This vicious circle was not tackled until 1929 when the de-rating proposals of the Local Government Act relieved local industry of rates. In turn, this arrangement undermined the buoyancy of local government finance, even in the more prosperous industrial regions, and adversely affected the capacity of local government to maintain and add to the services and institutional support crucial to the survival of small-producer capitalism and to flexible production. Indeed, increasing rigidities were introduced into existing local infrastructures, for example, in transport systems limited to existing administrative boundaries and in a deficiency of housing provisions in thriving industrial towns such as Slough.

Such trends, and their implications for the externalities offered to local businesses, can be exemplified with a summary account of the changes affecting that complex of formal and informal institutions which carried scientific and technological information in the industrial cities. A vigorous wave of educational foundations in the later nineteenth century diversified and extended the informal and philanthropic societies and institutions already in being. In the 1870s and 1880s, individual and mostly well-established local businessmen, acting in conjunction with Mechanics Institutes, had provided substantial personal donations to organise and finance new technical institutes and higher level colleges – the embryonic civic universities – in an effort to expand the skills and research base available to them, and this process gained a renewed momentum in the 1890s when towns and cities reformed or built new institutions with finance from government and municipal rates. By then, a number of cities had higher technical institutions and some had university departments geared to local industries. As the principal of Huddersfield Technical School commented in his annual report for 1904: 'The right policy for Huddersfield . . . like Bradford, [is] to concentrate on developing those technical departments which could help the trade and add to the wealth of the community.'[76]

Although the demand for full-time degree courses and graduates in scientific and technological subjects was slow to develop in the later nineteenth century, links were forged between professional scientists, mainly chemists, prominent members of local scientific elites and leading businessmen in the major indus-

[76] Cited by J. O'Connell, 'From Mechanics' Institute to Polytechnic: further and higher education 1841–1970', in E. A. Haigh, ed., *Huddersfield* (Huddersfield, 1992), pp. 577–8. The Technical Instruction Acts 1889 and 1891 empowered municipalities to levy a rate in aid of technical instruction, and the Local Taxation Act made a fund available (the so-called whisky money) on which municipalities could draw to cross-subsidise technical education. For one assessment of the impact of these measures, see G. W. Roderick and M. D. Stephens, *Education and Industry in the Nineteenth Century* (London, 1978), pp. 72–9. For a more upbeat assessment see E. P. Hennock, 'Technical education in England 1850–1926: the uses of a German model', *History of Education*, 19 (1990), pp. 299–332.

trial cities such as Liverpool, Manchester and Glasgow. In some instances, the initiative came from businessmen, as in the case of Henry Simon, an ex-German *émigré* who marked a successful business career in his adopted city with financial support to several cultural institutions and the endowment of a physics laboratory at Manchester Owens College in 1898 to be orientated towards local industry on the European Polytechnic model.[77] Elsewhere, the initiative was dependent on the efforts of individual scientists who built up alliances with local business and provided consultancy and other research services, as in the case of Henry Roscoe, chemist, and Hans Reynold, engineer, at Manchester.[78] The institutional cement binding the representatives of these groups was provided by the local branches of professional societies such as the Society of the Chemical Industry and the Society of Engineers and Metallurgists. The formation of a Department of Industrial Chemistry at Liverpool in 1925 was a late manifestation of this local conjunction of scientists and industrialists.[79] However, trends in corporate organisation previously mentioned, along with the growth in central funding for industrial and scientific research and the status ambitions of the provincial universities, all contributed to weakening these alliances. Individual business endowments still continued as in the case of the Leicester businessmen who founded the University College in 1927, or of Jesse Boot, who refounded University College in Nottingham in 1928.[80] Otherwise, the general trend was for the local connections between business and higher education, especially scientific education, to become less significant both to the larger companies and to university scientists themselves.

By contrast, the importance of technical education in the local economy was enhanced as the former dominance of Britain's major industrial interests came under ever greater foreign competition after 1870, and as wartime casualties and post-war labour shortages encouraged mechanisation and the further

---

[77] B. Simon, *Henry Simon of Manchester: In Search of a Grandfather, Henry Simon (1835–99)* (Leicester, 1997).

[78] For critical assessments of the impact of these local initiatives on the supply of scientific manpower, See Roderick and Stephens, *Education and Industry*, pp. 96–109, and, more recently, A. Guagnini, 'The fashioning of higher technical education in Britain: the case of Manchester, 1851–1914', in Gospel, ed., *Industrial Training*, pp. 69–92. See also M. Sanderson, *The Universities and British Industry 1850–1970* (London, 1972); M. Sanderson, 'The professor as industrial consultant: Oliver Arnold and the British steel industry, 1900–1914', *Ec.HR*, 2nd series, 31 (1978), 585–600; G. Tweedale, 'Science, innovation and the "rule of thumb": the development of British metallurgy to 1945', in J. Liebenau, ed., *The Challenge of New Technology* (Aldershot, 1988), pp. 58–82; J. Butt, *John Anderson's Legacy: The University of Strathclyde and its Antecedents 1796–1996* (East Linton, 1996), shows the wide-ranging interconnections between science, industry, and academic research. See also D. Edgerton, *Science, Technology and British Industrial 'Decline', 1870–1970* (Cambridge, 1996), for an overview.

[79] S. M. Horrocks, 'Academic and scientific elites in Liverpool in the late 19th and 20th centuries' (paper presented to the Centre for Urban History seminar, 1995). We are grateful to Sally Horrocks for this information and other references.

[80] B. Burch, *The University of Leicester: A History 1921–96* (Leicester, 1996).

substitution of unskilled and semi-skilled labour for former skilled workers, so bringing the apprenticeship system under further pressure.[81] At the national level, the question of industry's relations with technical education was a recurring theme of government reports in the 1920s, and by the 1930s there was some evidence that new demands were being made on the colleges. A continuing shortage of skilled labour together with the need for new skills lay behind the growth of day release studies from the 1930s to the 1950s, and, in some localities, the growing involvement of local industrialists as members of boards of governors. More by default than intent, perhaps, city technical colleges with feeder technical schools began to assume a more central position in the local economy during the 1930s. The expansion of City and Guilds of London Institute qualifications, the inception in 1921–2 of National Certificates and Diplomas (precursors of HNC and HND qualifications) and the development of local courses concerned with accounting, typing and secretarial practice provided an opportunity for the colleges to take a more prominent role in the development of traditional skills, albeit still largely supplementary to practical training, as well as introducing more systematic training in design, office and technical skills. The work of the technical colleges was especially important to local economies with skill shortages. But again, constraints on local government finances and the variability in municipal responses meant that improvements in the supply of technical education were very patchy over the country as a whole and the colleges continued to cater mainly for part-time students. These deficiencies should not lead us to underplay the potential which the city had from the 1930s for reconfiguring the nature of the labour supply, of reinventing a role which it had in the earliest stages of industrialisation.[82] It can be argued that this was a factor in helping to reinvigorate the industrial sector in the 1930s, as in Northampton, where businessmen and councillors together sought to improve the quality of technical education courses with a new Technical College and Junior Technical School opened in 1931.[83] National policy initiatives which fostered light industry on new industrial estates, New Towns and Special Development Areas were

[81] For the importance of human investment to British manufacturing performance see Broadberry, *The Productivity Race*.

[82] D. Reeder, 'A recurring debate. Education and industry', in G. Bernbaum, ed., *Schooling in Decline* (London, 1979), esp. pp. 126–30. For the growth in demand for technical education in the 1930s, see the work of D. W. Thoms, 'Technical education and the labour supply in England between the wars', *The Vocational Aspect of Education*, 27 (1976), 73–84, and 'Market forces and recruitment to technical education: the example of the junior technical schools', *History of Education*, 10 (1981), 125–32. The most recent study of technical schools is M. Sanderson, *The Missing Stratum: Technical School Education in England 1900–1990s* (London, 1994). For deficiencies in the number and condition of the Technical Colleges and the 'drive' to improve these, see B. Bailey, 'The development of technical education, 1934–39', *History of Education*, 16 (1987), 49–66.

[83] Dickie, 'Town patriotism'; Brown, *Northampton*, pp. 79, 138–9, 156.

also dependent upon the availability of transferable skills, and in some measure the city colleges and technical institutes contributed to this.

More 'dirigiste' central government policies towards industrial location developed from the late 1920s. They took a variety of forms: fiscal measures as in the altered basis of rating in the Local Government Act of 1929 designed to encourage relocation in depressed regions, limited public works projects, schemes encouraged by the Treasury which aimed to retire excess productive capacity in the staple industries in the 1930s, and incentives to labour to relocate in areas with employment growth prospects. The Special Areas (Development and Improvement) Act of 1934 carried further the regional approach to industrial relocation reinforced after the Second World War by controls on industrial building in towns and cities with relatively full employment, and by the 1950s the earlier strategy of promoting new industrial estates was overtaken by overspill policies and the formation of New Towns.[84]

The growth of state intervention has to be regarded as a factor in weakening local autonomy, but towns and cities were not themselves neutral in this process of industrial relocation, often participating in promotional activities and consciously building an image to attract and retain industry. This was easier to do in the more prosperous cities of the interwar years which could capitalise on a reputation for prosperity and exploit images of inventiveness and modernity. Yet it was also attempted in places that had to overcome more negative images. In periods of economic decline, promotional activity tended to reach a peak, albeit with a shift in emphasis towards more practical issues such as the provision of information on sites and infrastructure. The problem in the declining economic regions, however, was that civic leaders lacked the vision to work towards promoting a regional approach. Local rivalries and petty wrangling inhibited regional collaboration as in the North-East where the difficulties experienced in forming the North-East Development Board were put down to a lack of the spirit of cooperation among the thirteen Tyneside authorities. Such negative parochial attitudes have to be set against the positive initiatives that were taken.[85]

Towns seeking to diversify were to the fore in forming municipal committees, as in Northampton; elsewhere in the Midlands, growing concern in Derby about its overreliance on railway engineering led to the formation of an economic regeneration committee. More imaginatively, perhaps, the energetic secretary of

---

[84] M. Keating, *The City That Refused to Die* (Aberdeen, 1988), pp. 18–21, 24–8, 114; J. B. Cullingworth, *Problems of an Urban Society* (London, 1973), vol. I, pp. 89, 121–3. For a review of the issues, see R. H. Best, *Land for New Towns* (London, 1964). P. Dunleavy, *The Politics of Mass Housing in Britain 1945–1975: A Study of Corporate Power and Professional Influence in the Welfare State* (Oxford, 1981), esp. chs. 3–4, provides a contrasting view of how high rise housing underpinned existing industrial and commercial interests.

[85] H. Loebl, *Government Factories and the Origins of British Regional Policy, 1934–1948* (London, 1948), pp. 33–6.

the Tyneside Development Board, Stanley Holmes, travelled abroad to encourage industrialists threatened by the darkening political climate of continental Europe in the 1930s to relocate in or around Newcastle.[86] Most promotional activity about a town or city took the form of publicity and information, or of large scale events such as the great North-East Coast exhibition in Newcastle in 1929, or the provision of land and buildings.[87] The outstanding example of municipal initiatives to diversify a declining manufacturing economy was provided by the Manchester corporation with the building of the Ship Canal in the 1880s and the promotion thereafter of the first and still the largest industrial estate at Trafford Park, which at its peak was the locus of 55,000 jobs on its 7 square kilometre site (700 ha) site.[88] On Merseyside, included in the Board of Trade surveys of the depressed regions in 1932 but not designated as a Special Area, Liverpool took powers under the Liverpool Corporation Act, 1936, to develop industrial estates at Speke, Aintree and Fazakerley, and at Kirkby after the Second World War.[89] Municipal initiatives, supplemented by road and rail links, were sufficient to encourage Dunlop's to move from their cramped Walton site to Speke rather than to relocate at Fort Dunlop, Birmingham, and it was new factory units built on municipally acquired land for sale or lease on favourable terms which attracted newcomers in pharmaceuticals and food processing to Liverpool in preference to other locations.

In post-1945 Britain, Keynesian macro-economic policy assumed that demand management could provide a framework which would counter the cyclical excesses experienced between the wars. New prospects for full employment and a comprehensive social welfare system were developed at a centralised level, and nationalisation and regional planning initiatives appeared to sound the death knell for the urban dimension. Yet, on economic as well as administrative matters, the tension between local self-determination and national policy objectives was nothing new. In addition to governmental attempts to influence the location of industry, the Bank of England had directed interest rate policy and influenced the parameters of money supply for almost a century before it obtained central bank status in 1948. During that period and beyond, local finance and personal contacts, so evident in the instances noted earlier, remained

[86] M. Barker, 'Newcastle/Tyneside 1890–1980', in Gordon, ed., *Regional Cities*, pp. 129–30.
[87] For examples, see M. Barker and K. Harrop, 'Selling the industrial town: identity, image and illusion', in J. R. Gold and S. V. Ward, eds., *Place Promotion* (Chichester, 1994) esp. pp. 94 *et seq.*; S. V. Ward, 'Local industrial promotion and development policies', *Local Economy*, 5 (1990), 100–18; M. Bonsall, 'Local government initiatives in urban regeneration 1906–1932', *Planning History*, 10 (1988), 7–11.
[88] For the development of Trafford Park, see D. A. Farnie, *The Manchester Ship Canal and the Rise of the Port of Manchester, 1894–1975* (Manchester, 1980), ch. 6.
[89] R. H. Lister, 'Regional policies and industrial development on Merseyside, 1930–60', in B. L. Anderson and P. J. Storey, eds., *Commerce, Industry and Transport* (Liverpool, 1983), pp. 147–86; R. Lawton and C. M. Cunningham, eds., *Merseyside* (Liverpool, 1970).

critical to a multiplicity of small businesses: credit availability rather than cost was a more pertinent business influence for such firms than marginal interest rate adjustments. Localism remained powerful, too, even in the fashionable face of post-war regional planning since it was the cities that were obliged under the Town and Country Planning Act, 1947, to draw up proposals for their own futures. Pressures for central area redevelopment may have threatened some of the old local economies, but as an icon of post-war redevelopment and modernism, regional planning yielded to locally determined solutions. Nor was the Board of Trade in a sufficiently strong position to override local industrialists in the administration of the Distribution of Industry Act. In the late 1940s and early 1950s, new industrial building in the Development Areas fell to one third of that in the immediate post-war years 1945–7, and in what has been described as only a 'nominally coercive regional policy', local factors such as the existence of local markets and available skilled labour remained uppermost in the choice of industrial location by firms.[90] Conversely, as a Board of Trade survey demonstrated, the duplication of management structures associated with remote sites, excessive transport costs and the distance from supply networks – the diseconomies of distance from established urban infrastructures – deterred businesses from moving to Development Areas.

Most importantly, though, the political complexion of the urban areas assumed an increasingly Labour hue in the twentieth century. Indeed, it has been argued that one of the most important functions of the city was as a catalyst in the transformation of national politics, providing launch pads for generations of socialist and Labour politicians.[91] 'Red Clydeside' presented such radical socialist ideas in the burghs of the west of Scotland in their most potent form in the decades on either side of the First World War, but the emergence of a shop stewards' movement between the wars and industrial tensions after 1945, as captured, for example, in the image of 'Working for Ford', indicate from the point of view of labour the inseparable relationship between industry and city.[92] Bossism and machine politics were less prevalent than in Kansas City or Mayor Daly's Chicago, but in Bessy Braddock's Liverpool or political fiefdoms elsewhere in urban Britain, the city provided an inescapable framework for local business, just as the dominant employers and small-scale producers provided the context for the local political climate. Relationships between central and local interests, like those between business and civic interests, had undoubtedly changed in character over

---

[90] S. Rosevear, 'Balancing business and the regions: British distribution of industry policy and the Board of Trade, 1945–1951', *Business History*, 40 (1998), 77–99; G. McCrone, *Regional Policy in Britain* (London, 1969), p. 112.

[91] Savage, *The Dynamics*; M. Savage, 'Urban history and social class: two paradigms', *UH*, 20 (1993), 61–77.

[92] H. Beynon, *Working for Ford* (Harmondsworth, 1984). See also T. Lane and K. Roberts, *Strike at Pilkingtons* (London, 1971).

the course of the century to 1961. In addition, the extended parameters of the business environment may have diminished the central role of the city as an information and networking system designed to cushion risk and promote business opportunities. But this role had not been eclipsed, nor was it likely to be, given the persistence of dualistic features in local economies, many of which still bristled with many small local firms. What cannot be done, at this juncture, due to a dearth of research, is to specify the precise ways in which this role was maintained in the declining years of the industrial city. There is no reason, however, to doubt the capacity of the British industrial city to reinvent itself as it had already once done during the first half of the twentieth century.

· 19 ·

The urban labour market

DAVID GILBERT AND HUMPHREY SOUTHALL

OWNS ARE often presented as market centres, but mainly as places for the buying and selling of goods, or for financial transactions. However, the role of towns, and particularly of large towns, is closely connected to the operation of markets for labour. In this chapter, labour is defined in a specific way. Traditionally, the realm of labour has been defined both narrowly, in that 'labour' has been equated with the working class, and often with male manual workers, but also broadly, in that labour history concerns itself with working life as a whole, and with associated leisure activities. Here the concern is with markets for labour, which means a very specific aspect of people's lives: the processes through which individuals acquired an occupation, with its associated status and skills, and acquired particular jobs; or looked at the other way, how employers acquired a workforce and filled particular positions. These processes had not only economic significance, influencing the development of civil society in many towns. They shaped people's lives, the communal life of individual towns and the ways in which towns were connected into an urban system.

'Labour' is a particularly complex commodity: a labour supply is not manufactured but bred, and takes years to mature; a labour supply can only be hired, never bought, and once hired must still be encouraged or coerced to undertake useful work. It is incredibly differentiated, and this differentiation grows as an economy develops. All these characteristics interact to create large externalities, meaning non-price mechanisms through which one economic actor affects another, and the economics of towns and cities are all about externalities. Many externalities associated with towns are strongly negative, such as congestion, pollution and epidemic disease, but labour markets also create large positive

We must thank Ian Gregory for assistance in preparing the maps, and the various researchers who provided the data on which they are based; this work forms part of a major project to construct a historical Geographical Information System for Britain to which many funding bodies have contributed.

externalities, often justifying urban locations despite the many drawbacks. A fundamental reason why labour markets create large externalities is that employers, with the obvious exception of formal slavery, cannot *own* their workforces and therefore cannot rely on benefiting from what they invest in their workforce. In the development of labour markets in Britain, two general strategies were available, with very different implications for the urban system.[1]

First, the employer could rely on an external labour market to supply the necessary skills, and accept that this might mean paying workers a premium for the training they had in some sense funded for themselves. Such rich external labour markets were concentrated in major urban centres, or sometimes specialised agglomerations such as the Staffordshire Potteries, and there was a further premium to be paid for congestion. Reliance on external labour markets gave employers no particular stake in individual workers, and the notion of a career had limited meaning: instead, workers' earning capacity was regularly assessed over their lifespan by the market, and while initially it tended to rise as they gained experience and contacts, in the longer term it fell through worsening fitness and health, and increasingly obsolete skills.

Secondly, employers could seek to internalise the labour market and create their own workforce. This was more easily achieved where skills were specific to the particular firm, but then the employer had to fund all training; where the workplace was isolated, in which case the employer often had to provide housing and amenities; or where the enterprise was large, so that employees could be motivated by the prospect of progression up an elaborate hierarchy. As enterprises became larger and more complex, understanding of how the organisation operated became a significant skill in its own right.

In reality, these two models blended and the costs of creating a workforce rarely fell entirely on the employer or entirely on the workers. The state also came to take on a growing share of these costs. However, in any given period different sectors of the labour market can be placed somewhere between these extremes: in the 1860s, both casual labourers and artisans had regularly to look for work while clerks, factory workers and miners in some coalfields often had long associations with particular workplaces; similarly in 1950s Britain there were still casualised dockers and a large apprenticeship system alongside armies of 'company men' working towards a gold watch. Further, over the hundred years or so with which we are concerned, men's work at least saw a growing internalisation of labour markets and the emergence of the 'modern career', in which employment within a single organisation was seen as ideally a lifetime commitment with steady earnings growth terminating with retirement at a fixed

[1] These basic labour market concepts are discussed in many texts on labour economics, such as J. T. Addison and W. S. Siebert, *The Market for Labor: An Analytical Treatment* (Santa Monica, 1979), but for their application to the study of towns and cities see also A. J. Scott, *Metropolis: From the Division of Labour to Urban Form* (Berkeley, 1988).

age. Of course, the growing numbers of women in waged work were excluded from these norms. Indeed, it can be argued that the development of this modern career pattern depended on this restriction of women to short careers before marriage and a subsequent marginal position in the labour market as part timers, very poorly paid outworkers and unpaid domestic workers.[2]

Our main concern here is with entry into the labour market and subsequent career paths, and their consequences for individual towns and the urban system. There are, however, other dimensions of the operation of labour markets which had a direct influence on the nature of towns and cities. One example is the way that attempts to regulate prices and wages influenced the development of urban institutions; until the late nineteenth century most employers' organisations were restricted to a single town or district. Some urban institutions were straightfor-wardly economic such as the boards of conciliation and arbitration which spread across the country in the 1860s and 1870s.[3] But the development of other kinds of urban institution was often shaped by strategies which were developed to reg-ulate labour markets. As we argue later, the provision of local social infrastruc-ture by 'paternalist' employers often made good economic sense in specialised industrial communities, while in larger towns there were often close links between the networks established in employers' organisations and those of local government. Similarly, the influence of organised labour spread beyond the industrial relations system into the provision of social institutions and the involvement in urban government.

In what follows, we examine several of the most important sectors of the labour market, following the paths taken by individuals over their lives. We sketch out the development of each of these sectors, developing an account of the changing nature of life-paths and career structures, and their implications for the developing urban system. Three dangers with this approach need to be noted. First, our sectors cannot be exhaustive. Three other groups which played a notable role in shaping the urban system were workers in retailing, workers in public utilities and the non-casual sectors of transport, notably the railways. Secondly, our sectors of the labour market should not be confused with indus-trial sectors. Very similar practices characterised artisan employment in strikingly different nineteenth-century industries, such as engineering, building and print-ing, while their employer's business was a near-irrelevance to the twentieth-century office worker. Thirdly, any discussion of the labour market must speak of 'skill', but all notions of 'skilled' and 'un-skilled' workers, or even more or less skill, are determined as much by social attitudes as by levels of technology or

---

[2] A. Miles, *Social Mobility in Nineteenth- and Early Twentieth-Century England* (Basingstoke, 1999), ch. 6.

[3] S. Webb and B. Webb, *The History of Trade Unionism* (London, 1894), pp. 322–7; H. A. Clegg, A. Fox and A. F. Thompson, *A History of British Trade Unions since 1889*, vol. 1: *1889–1910* (Oxford, 1964), pp. 24–5.

expertise. The bricklayer's skill lies in the speed and quality of the resulting construction while his hod carrier's skill lies in carrying heavy loads over his shoulder for hour after hour and year after year; but only the former was classed as 'skilled' by society, and this was reflected in earnings. Similarly, women have almost always been denied the title of 'skilled worker', despite the obvious technical difficulty of tasks such as short-hand typing. The final section of the chapter examines the interactions between these labour market processes and the form of the urban system, concentrating on spatial divisions of labour and the ways in which economic fluctuations altered the relationships between different sectors of the labour market and transformed the geography of towns and cities.

(i) THE CASUAL TRADES

Labour markets in their most visible and least structured form were to be found in the stereotypical casual trades of Victorian Britain: men presenting themselves in hiring halls or at the dock gates for hire by the day, and being selected mainly on the basis of physical strength, not skill. Elements in this stereotype are misleading, in particular the association between casual labour and the docks, particularly the London docks. Dock labour must be discussed, both because of the abundant evidence provided by contemporary social surveys and because of its association with a particular type of town, but this section also investigates the less well-defined informal sector and 'boy labour'.

Some aspects of dock work were far from unskilled, and two groups in particular had many of the characteristics of artisans, including their well-developed trade unions: the lightermen, who often owned their own boats; and the stevedores, responsible for arranging the cargo within ships' holds and therefore for ensuring the balance and stability of the vessel. Further, moving heavy cargo certainly demanded physical strength but it also required a particular kind of skill, knowing how repeatedly to lift and move heavy objects without straining muscles. In consequence, there were significant groups within the dock labour force who had relatively steady employment based on relationships with particular employers. Tom Mann suggested in 1893 that 10 to 20 per cent of the labour force earned 30s. per week or more, and this fraction probably rose during the 1890s and 1900s as many employers instituted a system of 'permanent' and 'preference' men.[4]

The real locus of casual labour was not *in* the docks but at the dock gates and in the streets beyond. The numbers daily seeking work were most visible to middle-class observers in London's East India Dock Road, or at the hiring stands along the dock wall in Liverpool, because there was always *some* chance of finding work on the basis of strength alone. The comings and goings of ships

---

[4] G. Phillips and N. Whiteside, *Casual Labour* (Oxford, 1985), pp. 25–8.

coupled with the near impossibility of six full days a week at such physically demanding work meant that foremen relatively often had to hire beyond their circle of 'pals', and then all was confusion and luck played a role. One foreman in the 1900s described the experience of taking-on: 'a great roar went up from hundreds of throats calling my name . . . A great mass of faces and hands . . . appeared before me, fighting and struggling, so much so, that it was difficult to detect which face the hand belonged to.'[5] However, this very public hiring process was unusual. The army of casual workers employed in other parts of the transport sector, as porters, messengers and so on, were hired in their ones and twos, and not necessarily for the day. A whole series of factors explained the existence and size of this part of the labour market.

First, the seasonality of demand for labour was clearly a factor in casualisation, especially in the docks: in London, timber from the Baltic arrived mainly in the autumn and was absent in the ice-bound spring;[6] in Liverpool, cotton was a key commodity and most came in between October and May.[7] Outside the docks, winter weather and limited daylight had an obvious impact on building and affected many other sectors, much work being done outdoors and artificial lighting being ineffective. Another source of seasonality in London was increased demand during the fashionable 'season' between April and July, while in Warwick in 1907 a compositor, Paul Evett, noted: 'Several other fresh compositors started work soon after I arrived. They were of the travelling fraternity, who had learnt by experience where seasonal work was to be found, and here they knew that the Autumn County Voters' Lists were to be printed; also the Warwickshire County Directory.'[8] In an economy where such small-scale fluctuations mattered, transitory employment was endemic and many workers organised their lives around it through 'dove-tailing': gas workers such as Will Thorne moving to the Bedfordshire brickfields in summer;[9] building workers going to the docks in winter, and so on.[10]

Secondly, as discussed in the conclusion, deep recessions every eight to ten years were almost as regular a feature of the Victorian economy as was seasonality. Here a whole locality and, increasingly, the whole nation was affected equally and there was limited scope for 'dovetailing'. However, many workers had secondary occupations, less lucrative, they could fall back on; and in the process they might push other workers out. Hence, musical instrument makers became cabinet makers, and cabinet makers became carpenters. Those at the

---

[5] Charity Organisation Society, Special Committee on Unskilled Labour (1908), Qq. 697; as cited by D. W. Gray, 'Entry to the metropolitan labour market in Victorian and Edwardian Britain' (PhD thesis, Queen Mary College, University of London, 1992), p. 148.

[6] G. Stedman Jones, *Outcast London* (Oxford, 1971), p. 36.

[7] E. Taplin, *The Dockers' Union: A Study of the National Union of Dock Labourers 1889–1922* (Leicester, 1985), p. 14.

[8] P. Evett, 'My life in and out of print' (typescript, Brunel University Library, 1951), p. 5.

[9] W. Thorne, *My Life's Battles* (London, 1925), p. 36.   [10] Stedman Jones, *Outcast London*, p. 40

bottom of the chain could seek work at the dock gates, if they were strong enough, or be forced into street trading or criminality. In such an unstable economy, with such a limited safety net for the unemployed, it was inevitable that large numbers of people would move between occupations rather than simply accept unemployment. One measure of the privileged status of the better paid among the artisans, such as the engineers, is that they could afford to pay themselves sufficiently generous welfare benefits through their unions that they could afford to *be* unemployed; most workers had to find some source of income, however inadequate.

Thirdly, although the economy as a whole was growing some groups experienced severe long-run decline. In London, substantial numbers of casual workers had begun as silk weavers and, later, as shipbuilders.[11] Across the country, agricultural depression in the 1870s and 1880s forced large numbers of labourers off the land, with few skills. One indicator of the linkage between urban and rural unskilled labour markets comes from industrial organising: in the early 1890s the dockers' unions worked to establish agricultural unions in Lincolnshire and Oxfordshire, 'for they and the agricultural labourer were continually competing with one another. It was easy for the town labourers to frustrate a strike in the country, and for the countrymen to frustrate another in the town.'[12]

Finally, in most families living standards depended heavily on how many worked, and particularly on how many children were in waged work while still young enough to be living at home: we lack large-scale surveys of earnings in nineteenth-century towns, but in interwar London the earnings of household heads peaked at age thirty-five, but those of households as a whole peaked when their heads were aged fifty-five, mainly because of the additional earnings of other household members;[13] analysing several hundred autobiographies, Andy Miles concludes that until the late nineteenth century 'the overriding force behind movement into the labour market was the demand of the family economy'.[14] In consequence, only well-paid artisans could invest heavily in their children through training and apprenticeship; in textile and mining towns there was work for adolescents in the mills and pits; but in the great cities and particularly in London large numbers of children crowded into the so-called 'Boy Labour' occupations. This happened to Walter Southgate: despite an excellent school record and the offer of a seven-year apprenticeship which would have developed his interest in art and drawing, his father was unwilling to keep him

---

[11] *Ibid.*, pp. 100–6.
[12] W. Hasbach, *A History of the English Agricultural Labourer* (London, 1908), pp. 301–2.
[13] D. Baines and P. Johnson, 'Did they jump or were they pushed? The exit of older men from the London labour market, 1929–31', *Journal of Economic History*, 59 (1999), 949–71. For more limited nineteenth-century evidence see, for example, the discussion of household budgets in J. Foster, *Class Struggle and the Industrial Revolution* (London, 1974), pp. 91–9.
[14] Miles, *Social Mobility*, p. 119.

Table 19.1 *Occupations of children on leaving school in London and in large urban manufacturing districts in England and Wales in the 1890s*

Occupation	London (%)	Manufacturing districts (%)
Building trades	3.1	4.1
Woodworking	3.5	1.2
Metals, engineering and shipbuilding	3.7	8.5
Mining and quarrying	—	3.3
Textiles	0.2	12.6
Clothing	2.6	3.4
Printing and allied trades	4.4	1.8
Clerical	8.0	11.8
In shops	13.9	12.7
Transport	39.9	21.8
Newsboys and street vendors	3.7	3.1
Domestic service	1.2	0.4
Miscellaneous	9.2	11.1
No reported occupation	6.3	4.4

Source: Report on the Number of Children Attending Elementary Schools Who Are Known to be Working for Wages, with the Different Classes of Employment into Which the Boys and Girls Attending Elementary Schools in England and Wales Went on Leaving Schools during Each Complete Year, PP 1899 LXXV.2. Figures are percentages of the total number of responses: 25,768 for London, 48,093 for the manufacturing districts.

so long: 'There was now nothing for it but to take the first situation, pot luck, that offered itself. It might be as a messenger boy, a van boy, a shop boy or any other dead-end job. The main consideration was that I had to bring a little cash into the home each week to feed myself.'[15] As Table 19.1 shows, very large numbers of London school-leavers in the 1890s went into 'transport', covering running messages, acting as a van driver's assistant, and so on. This was a problem in itself as such jobs were insecure with a high turnover of workers, most van boys being hired by the day. However, the larger problem was that they seldom led into adult jobs, the Post Office, for example, employing hundreds of telegraph boys but dismissing almost all at age sixteen. As a result, large numbers of workers found themselves entering adulthood with no real skills and little option but to seek work as general labourers.

The 1870 Education Act established a network of school boards funded from

[15] W. Southgate, *That's the Way it Was: A Working-Class Autobiography 1890–1950* (London, 1982); as cited by Gray, 'Entry to the metropolitan labour market', p. 283. The treatment here of boy labour as a whole is largely based on Gray's work.

rates and taxes, and gave boards the power to make education between five and ten compulsory. The 1880 act removed the boards' discretion, and the 1891 act introduced free education; the 1918 act ended local exemptions, and established a national minimum leaving age of fourteen.[16] Unlike earlier legislation limiting children's involvement in particular types of workplace, compulsory attendance was enforceable through both registers in schools and checking school-age children on the streets. The London School Board appointed attendance officers for each division of the city soon after its creation in 1870. Initially, magistrates were sympathetic to poor parents dependent on their children's earnings, but by 1900 90 per cent of the 28,836 summonses led to convictions, and attendance at board schools rose from 66 per cent in 1870 to 88 per cent in 1904, although work by children outside school hours remained a concern.[17] This is one of the clearest instances of successful state intervention into labour markets; for example, an estimated 80,000 juveniles were removed from the London labour market in 1899 just by raising the minimum age at which exemption from compulsory schooling could be granted from eleven to twelve.

What were the consequences of casualism for urban society? Arguably, the most important consequence was simply the poverty that went with it. The squalor and congestion of so much of the Victorian city was not due, ultimately, to a failure of government or the housing market, but to the inhabitants' lack of resources, and this was due not simply to low wages but to the intermittent nature of so much of their income. For most working-class households, once again excluding artisans, having multiple earners was essential, as in the complex economies of the great cities there was a good chance that at least one of them would find work.

Beyond this, the key consequence of the casual labour market was that individuals and households had to organise their lives so as routinely to find work, and routinely to survive without it; and this led to an intense localism. We tend to explain the compact nature of the nineteenth-century city by poor transport prior to the railways but in Dickens' London, it was perfectly possible for Wemmick, Jaggers' clerk in *Great Expectations*, to work in the City and *walk* home to the then-greenery of Walworth; for Wemmick, already, 'the office is one thing, and private life is another'.[18] What prevented such a separation for the poor, and kept them penned into crowded slums, was not lack of transport but poverty and insecurity: a family that must often depend on the generosity of others cannot afford to live among strangers. Highly localised contact networks were crucial to survival: for the worker, contacts with foremen and sources of information about vacancies, rarely formally advertised; for the housewife, shop-

16 Gray, 'Entry to the metropolitan labour market', pp. 204–7.
17 *Final Report of the London School Board, 1870–1901*, pp. 199–203 (as cited by Gray, 'Entry to the metropolitan labour market', pp. 231–6).
18 C. Dickens, *Great Expectations*, ed. M. Cardwell (Clarendon Dickens edn, Oxford, 1983), p. 208.

keepers who will provide goods on unsecured credit and neighbours who will lend a cup of sugar.

Social reformers of the late nineteenth century saw casualisation as the root of most of the evils of 'Outcast London', and in the twentieth century a series of legal measures sought to 'decasualise' the docks, despite significant opposition from the dockers themselves. In practice, the state sought to create a clear divide between registered dockers, who were then to be guaranteed employment, and the casual tail. However, in practice the mechanisation of cargo handling and eventually containerisation drastically changed the nature of dock work, employers seeking a more permanent and skilled but far smaller workforce.[19]

A whole series of social changes, many of them based on legislation, reduced casual labour in the wider economy. First, the most marginal workers were removed through compulsory education and state pensions, both changes with vast but little appreciated consequences for the labour market. Whether or not compulsory school attendance did much for skill levels among the urban poor, it eliminated much of the 'boy labour' problem at a stroke. Similarly, the most infrequently employed had tended to be the most elderly, and the introduction of comprehensive state pensions and an increasingly universal male retirement age of sixty-five removed this stratum; state disability benefits had a similar effect.

Secondly, the operation of the National Insurance system, introduced in 1911 but only becoming comprehensive in the 1920s, served to regulate many aspects of the labour market and in particular promoted a clearer distinction between the employed and the unemployed: rules requiring everyone to pay into the fund but denying benefits to those unemployed for less than four consecutive days penalised both casual and short-time working. Many other changes in employment and tax law made the labour market either less flexible or more secure, according to viewpoint, and casual workers had either to transform themselves into self-employed freelancers or to operate on or beyond the margins of the law.

Thirdly, employers arguably found a greater need for a stable workforce. Firms were becoming larger and more complex, making it harder for casual workers to be slotted in and made productive in a short time. More and more roles were hard or impossible to monitor, and the easiest way to create trustworthy employees was through rewarding loyalty, impossible with casuals; interestingly, recent technological changes have simplified surveillance and may promote a return to casualisation. Lastly, the growth of the service sector meant that many employees were the public face of an organisation, dealing with customers, and again it was hard to employ casuals in such a role. This list excludes rising skill levels in a crude sense, as nineteenth-century skilled artisans were often no more permanently linked to an employer than the unskilled labourer, and it is to them that we now turn.

---

[19] Phillips and Whiteside, *Casual Labour*, pp. 261–8.

(ii) SKILLED ARTISANS

The artisan trades sought to identify themselves by an emphasis on formal training: it was only possible to become a millwright or a stonemason by serving an apprenticeship. These rules had originally been enforced by the guild system, but by the early nineteenth century the traditional guilds had either disappeared or become organisations solely for employers, as with the livery companies of the City of London. The earliest trade unions appeared in the artisan trades and presented themselves as successors to the journeymen's organisations that had existed within the old guilds. In practice, their memberships were relatively small: in 1871 an estimated 15 per cent of stonemasons, 11 to 12 per cent of carpenters and joiners, under 10 per cent of plasterers.[20] What mattered far more was the extent to which most trained men and many of the employers took certain principles for granted.

The most basic principle was a clear divide between the skilled and the unskilled: becoming 'skilled' required training during adolescence, and access to the latter depended heavily on family resources and contacts; but the use of family contacts did not necessarily mean boys following their father's trade, and even then the 'inheritance' of skill was not necessarily achieved through a formal apprenticeship. Our knowledge of these processes is inevitably partial but, for example, 50 per cent of all working-class autobiographers obtained their first jobs through their fathers, and another 22 per cent through broader family networks.[21] However, in interwar London precise occupational continuity between fathers and sons was far lower than this suggests: only 7.6 per cent of sons interviewed by the New Survey of London had exactly the same occupation as their father, and 20.4 per cent were in the same broad occupational order. These figures may of course reflect a long-run decline in occupational continuity, which is often assumed but for which there is limited evidence, or the peculiar diversity of the London labour market.[22]

Nineteenth-century artisans certainly placed great emphasis on obtaining 'places' for their sons, and such sponsorship often served as a substitute for formal apprenticeships. George Howell suggested in the 1870s that under 10 per cent of union members had served a formal apprenticeship, which required an indenture of five or seven years to be completed by age twenty-one.[23] For example, the Liverpool Typographic Society's rules of 1816 defined a journeyman as 'a person who has served seven years in the business of a Printer or the eldest son

[20] R. Price, *Masters, Unions and Men* (Cambridge, 1980), p. 62.
[21] Miles, *Social Mobility*, pp. 120–1.
[22] D. E. Baines and P. Johnson, 'In search of the "traditional" working class: social mobility and occupational continuity in inter-war London', *Ec.HR*, 2nd series, 52 (1999), 692–713.
[23] G. Howell, 'Trade unions, apprentices and technical education', *Contemporary Review*, 30 (1877), 854.

of a Printer and brought up to that business',[24] and even in 1867 one of the main complaints of the workers at a Lincoln engineering firm was that it employed 'strange boys instead of the workmen's sons'.[25] Artisans could enforce such rules and preferences first because hiring decisions were made by foremen who had come up through the trade and would only hire 'time-served' men, and secondly because training was carried out 'on the job' by the most experienced hands and they could refuse to train 'strange boys'. Many unions also sought to limit the total number of apprentices in a given shop.

These limitations on entry had various consequences. First and most obviously, for most of the nineteenth century artisans were able to maintain large pay differentials relative to the unskilled. In the early 1870s farm labourers were struggling to raise weekly wages from as little as 11s. or 12s. per week,[26] but carpenters and joiners in towns such as Northampton and Cardiff earnt 27s. or 30s.[27] In 1889, the dockers fought for their 'tanner', meaning 6d. per hour, but the 'standard rate' for London engineers was 38s. per week. Without progressive taxation these differentials were reflected in living standards so that an established artisan could hope to employ a servant girl. Secondly, apprenticeships whether formal or informal meant low wages during adolescence and only relatively well-off households could afford to forgo the higher earnings of dead-end 'boy labour' jobs. Coupled with the preferential hiring of artisans' sons, this made artisan trades self-reproducing – although statistical evidence from the census and marriage registers suggests that while artisans' sons were generally in an artisan occupation of some kind inheritance of a specific craft was far from the norm.

A third consequence was that the exclusivity of artisans *within* a working-class community, often reflected in superior housing and sometimes by geographical segregation, was matched by a geographically wider inclusivity. Artisans were forced to move between towns by the very specialisation of their occupations, by the operation of limits on apprenticeship and by custom, and this promoted links between their communities and the development of national organisations. Most artisan trades were scattered around the country in small groups, so if one employer was laying men off there would be few local alternatives; as early as 1794 the Liverpool Society of 'Carpenters' was encouraging jobless members to look elsewhere:

> That if any member . . . shall happen to be discharged from his place of work upon honourable terms and cannot get employment . . . at his own art trade or business within the Corporation of Liverpool for the space of one month such

[24] PRO, FS1/302, Lancaster 1273: Liverpool Typographic Society, *Rules* (1816), rule 3.
[25] Modern Records Centre, Warwick, MSS 259/1/1/18, minute of 9 Apr. 1867.
[26] A. Armstrong, *Farmworkers: A Social and Economic History 1770–1980* (London, 1988), pp. 118–33.
[27] Board of Trade Labour Department, 'Rates of wages and hours of labour in various industries in the United Kingdom for a series of years' (unpublished, 1908).

member shall be allowed . . . the sum of half a guinea to enable him to go to the next . . . place where the said trade of shipwrighting is carried out in order to get work.[28]

London was the exception to this, and there unemployed men were being paid benefit, rather than being forced to move away, as early as 1798.[29] Secondly, many crafts limited the number of apprentices who could be employed by a single master and this forced the larger employers, often in the larger towns, to import journeymen.[30] Lastly, and perhaps in order to ensure that individual artisans possessed broadly based skills and avoided dependence on individual masters, artisan culture valued and encouraged mobility. As one young engineer, Thomas Wood of Keighley, put it:

> I thought I was deficient in my trade, though I learned all I could learn there. But I heard about new tools, new machines, and new ways of working. I could never hope to see them in our shop, and if I was to learn, and improve, I would do so now before I either married or thought of it. So one Friday in the summer of 1845 I left my old master for good and ever.[31]

Thomas Wright commented that 'the majority of [the tramps in a London club house] are generally young fellows who have come up from provincial towns on completing their apprenticeship'.[32]

Artisan unions developed a network of 'houses of call', public houses associated with their trades and sometimes named after them, such as the *Carpenters' Arms*, where travelling members could find both information about available jobs and assistance if no work was to be had. Such networks supported remarkably high levels of mobility even before the railways, when most travelling was on foot. Very detailed records survive for one particular 'tramping' union, the Steam Engine Makers' Society: between 1835 and 1846, on average 13 per cent of the membership left their branch for another town each year, rising slightly in the early phases of the 1842 depression, and over 7 per cent crossed a county boundary or went abroad. Of the 896 members who belonged for six years or more over this period, 49 per cent made no moves, 15 per cent moved from one town to another within a county at least once, 30 per cent changed counties and 6 per cent went abroad. Payments of 'travelling benefit' were concentrated into recession years; during the worst, 1841/2, 19 per cent of the membership received at least one travelling payment; the average distance covered, chiefly by

---

[28] PRO, FS1/251, Lancaster 343; rules approved 16 Dec. 1794.
[29] PRO, FS1/408B, Middlesex 216: 'Articles of agreement of a friendly society of tin plate workers . . . instituted January 1st, 1798'.
[30] A. E. Musson, *The Typographical Association: Origins and History up to 1949* (Oxford, 1954), pp. 178–88.   [31] T. Wood, 'Autobiography', *Keighley News* (Keighley, 1956), 7 Apr. 1956, p. 7.
[32] T. Wright, *The Great Unwashed, by the Journeyman Engineer* (London, 1868), p. 161.

walking, by these 227 men was 334 miles (537 km), with 127 travelling over 200 miles (322 km) and 6 over 1,000 (1,609 km).[33]

Mobility assisted mobility: because they were mobile as a group, artisans were likely to find relatives and friends as they moved around the country. Take the example of Robert Gammage, later a leading Chartist but in the spring of 1839 just an unemployed coachmaker aged nineteen and barely out of his apprenticeship. Leaving Northampton, he visited Newport Pagnell and stayed at his union's clubhouse; Huntingdon, at a friend's mother's; Hertford, with friends; Hatfield, to see a cousin he had not seen since childhood. In London he first stayed at the clubhouse but then lodged for six weeks with his uncle and aunt. In Maidstone he had another friend from Northampton and in Balcombe, north of Brighton, he had a half-sister.[34]

Such a contact network affects both the labour market and society. While unemployed casual labourers depended on a highly localised survival network and were at a great disadvantage seeking work in another part of the same town, men such as Gammage could circulate around a genuinely national labour market confident of a friendly welcome. Further, this system of circulation and that labour market gave artisans a contact network which was the foundation for first their trade unions and other mutual organisations, and then the political movements in which they played a central role, most obviously Chartism[35] but also the new popular Liberalism of the 1870s and 1880s.[36] New ideas circulated rapidly via this network: Gammage's travels saw him subscribing to the Chartist *Northern Star* while living in Tory Dorset, and lending it to his friends;[37] on a larger scale, in Kentish London it was the artisans of Woolwich Arsenal and Dockyard who founded Arsenal football team, the Woolwich Building Society and the Royal Arsenal Co-operative Society.[38]

In mid-nineteenth-century Britain, artisans were a class apart if only because of their higher incomes. During the twentieth century, their privileged position was eroded, but at very different speeds in different sectors. Engineers had formed the vanguard of many working-class movements but the development of machine tools in the 1890s, the increasing role of the state in technical

[33] H. R. Southall, 'The tramping artisan revisits: labour mobility and economic distress in early Victorian England', *Ec.HR*, 2nd series, 44 (1991), 272–96.
[34] W. H. Maehl, ed., *Robert Gammage: Reminiscences of a Chartist* (Manchester, 1983), pp. 48–9. For further discussion of 'tramping' autobiographies, see H. R. Southall, 'Mobility, the artisan community, and popular politics in early nineteenth century England', in G. Kearns and C. W. J. Withers, eds., *Urbanising Britain* (Cambridge, 1991), pp. 103–30.
[35] D. Thompson, *The Chartists: Popular Politics in the Industrial Revolution* (Aldershot, 1984), pp. 152–66.
[36] E. Biagini, *Liberty, Retrenchment and Reform: Popular Liberalism in the Age of Gladstone, 1860–1880* (Cambridge, 1992), ch. 6.   [37] Maehl, ed., *Robert Gammage*, p. 49.
[38] G. Crossick, *An Artisan Elite in Victorian Society: Kentish London 1840–1889* (London, 1978).

education and the growing role of professionally trained engineers reduced the craft's control of the industry's technological base. A new class of semi-skilled machinists with firm-specific skills grew rapidly and the Amalgamated Society of Engineers, then the largest national union in the country, was defeated in the 1897–8 lock-out by a new national employers' organisation. The notion of craft privileges lingered on into the demarcation disputes which plagued the motor industry in the 1950s and 1960s, but the notion of the engineer as an *independent* craftsman, carrying his own tools and moving easily from one employer to the next, had long been lost. However, craft traditions in printing lasted far longer, surviving the transition from hand typesetting to compositing machines and only truly being defeated in the Wapping dispute of the 1980s. In building, a tradition of independent craftsmen and self-employed gangs moving between sites survives to the present.

(iii) FACTORY WORKERS

Both artisans and the labouring poor were to be found in cities from the earliest times, but the factory worker was almost by definition a creation of the Industrial Revolution; for by some definitions the very essence of that revolution was the replacement of outwork, often spread across rural districts, by closely supervised work in the employer's building, using the employer's tools.[39] The new factories meant working not simply in close proximity to others, but to a regular rhythm often determined by others; directly by an overseer or indirectly by the speed of machinery: much of the skill lay not in the individual task but in this learnt ability to synchronise. Therefore, such work often required a new workforce. Further, many early factories were in relatively remote locations, sited to take advantage of raw materials or water power, and therefore the employer had to assume responsibility for housing and even shopping facilities. Where such factory communities were small they really lie outside the scope of this book, but many new communities created by single factories were urban in both character and size, while the switch to steam power permitted firms to cluster together.

It has long been known that the expansion of the population of industrial Lancashire and Yorkshire was mainly the result of higher birth rates, not in-migration: the availability of industrial work meant that couples no longer needed to acquire land before marrying, so industrial communities had lower average ages of marriage.[40] Studies of mid-nineteenth-century industrial towns

---

[39] S. Marglin, 'What do bosses do? The origins and functions of hierarchy in capitalist production', in A. Gorz, ed., *The Division of Labour* (Hassocks, 1976), pp. 13–54.

[40] For an overview, see R. Lawton, 'Population and society 1730–1914', ch. 11 in R. A. Dodgshon and R. E. Butlin, eds., *An Historical Geography of England and Wales*, 2nd edn (London, 1990), pp. 285–321. For a case study comparing industrial and non-industrial communities, see D. Levine, *Family Formation in an Age of Nascent Capitalism* (New York, 1977).

Table 19.2 *Mean distance (miles) from place of birth, by occupational group: all males,*
aged fifteen and over, in 1851

Casual trades			
General labourers	18.4	Railway navvies	45.0
Artisans			
Plasterers	35.0	Shipwrights	28.3
Tailors	34.4	Wheelwrights	18.9
Cabinet makers	34.2	Bricklayers	17.7
Printers	32.9	Stonemasons	15.6
Carpenters and joiners	28.7	Blacksmiths	13.5
Factory workers			
Iron manufacture	13.6	Cutlery and scissor mfr.	10.3
Cotton and cotton goods	8.8		
Miners			
Coal miners	22.7		
Professional and clerical			
Clergymen	62.2	Doctors and surgeons	48.2
Schoolmasters	52.4	Commercial clerks	18.7
Agricultural			
Farmers	16.0	Farm labourers and servants	11.9
All occupied males	21.9		

Source: computed from Michael Anderson's sample from the 1851 census. For more
details see H. R. Southall, 'The tramping artisan revisits: labour mobility and economic
distress in early Victorian England', *Ec.HR*, 2nd series, 44 (1991), 272–96 (291–4).

show surprisingly limited migration fields. For example, of Preston's population
in 1851, 48 per cent had been born within the town and another 21 per cent
within 10 miles (16 km); only 17 per cent came from over 30 miles (48 km)
away.[41] In Oldham, another cotton town, 61 per cent of 1851 household heads
were born within 3 miles (4.8 km) and only 12 per cent more than 20 miles (32
km) away, compared to 29 per cent and 20 per cent respectively for more traditional Northampton.[42] Data on occupation-specific mobility is scarcer, but Table
19.2 presents figures computed from Anderson's large sample from the 1851
census: workers in cotton textiles, the archetypal factory occupation, lived a
lower average distance from their birthplace than any other group listed.

Where both the labourer's lack of skill and the artisan's consecration of skill

[41] M. Anderson, *Family Structure in Nineteenth-Century Lancashire* (Cambridge, 1971), pp. 34–41.
[42] Foster, *Class Struggle*, p. 77.

placed them in geographically broad labour markets, the factory worker's skills were firm or locality specific, necessitating a far stronger bond between individual and workplace. The extreme examples of company towns are well known, such as New Lanark and Saltaire: the employer consciously creating a complete community with housing, shops, schools and churches as a free-standing settlement. However, much larger towns were less formally structured as a series of communities each centred on a mill. Patrick Joyce comments:

> The pattern established in the cities by mid-century – rigid zonal segregation by class . . . – was not repeated in the factory towns . . . Bradford is perhaps the best place to consider developments first, being the largest of the factory towns rather than the smallest of the industrial cities . . . Until very late in the [nineteenth] century the factory town was in fact more a congeries of settlements than an entity in its own right. The life of the leading Bradford employers was led within the confines of Thornton, Great Horton or Manningham, residential continuity being reflected in an intense and personal involvement in the life of the township.[43]

Sometimes that involvement reflected religious or social beliefs, or was motivated by a quest for political power. However, much supposedly 'paternalist' behaviour can be understood in conventional economic terms. The workers and the community depended on the mill, but the mill would be unable to operate without its workforce and township, hence the employer had to sustain both. This led naturally to a concern with infrastructure, education and health, but also to a need to sustain the workforce during recessions. While having multiple earners in the same household was a risk-spreading strategy among casual workers in the great cities, in mid-nineteenth-century cotton towns whole families were employed in the same mill. Where labourers and artisans were laid off and had to rely on their own resources, the textile industry in particular operated a short-time system, whereby the whole workforce worked short hours for reduced pay. In the worst recessions, there was little work in the mills to be shared out and the workforce was maintained through work creation schemes, sometimes building follies, but mainly digging sewers and paving streets, funded by employers or, during the 1860s cotton famine, loans from central government to local authorities.[44] By the turn of the century, work in the Lancashire mills was increasingly women's work, their husbands working in other sectors such as engineering.[45]

---

[43] P. Joyce, *Work, Society and Politics* (London, 1980), pp. 25–6. For more detailed discussion of Bradford, and the role of manufacturers in providing water supplies and fire brigades, see T. Koditschek, *Class Formation and Urban Industrial Society* (Cambridge, 1990), pp. 105–15.

[44] M. E. Rose, 'Rochdale man and the Stalybridge riot: the relief and control of the unemployed during the Lancashire cotton famine', in A. P. Donajgrodzki, ed., *Social Control in Nineteenth Century Britain* (London, 1977), pp. 185–206; N. Longmate, *The Hungry Mills* (London, 1978), pp. 282–3.

[45] M. Savage, 'Labour market structure in Preston, 1880–1940', in M. Savage, *The Dynamics of Working-Class Politics* (Cambridge, 1987), pp. 64–100.

After 1914, some industries such as textiles experienced sustained decline and employers were less concerned to retain their workforces; for example, employment in cotton textiles fell from 600,000 in 1920 to 350,000 in 1939. The new National Insurance system catered primarily for workers who were either in full-time employment or unemployed, and industries which had relied on short-time tended to be penalised. Even so, the practice remained widespread, particularly in those industries dominated by women workers effectively excluded from the Insurance system: in 1930 there was extensive short-time working in carpet making, boots and shoes, clothing and wool textiles, involving up to 50 per cent of all workers.[46] Stagnant or declining demand for labour meant that employers need be less concerned with housing provision, while the expansion of local government enabled employers to reduce their role in the community.

While the fragmented textile industry declined, other factory industries changed scale through both the emergence of multi-site firms and the expansion of individual sites. The most extreme example of the latter was Woolwich Arsenal, which at its peak during the First World War employed 74,467. That involved the Ministry of Munitions in a linked housing scheme, the Well Hall estate designed as a planning showpiece and erected in under a year.[47] In a marked change of scale from the pre-war industry, the largest individual inter-war plants were created by the motor industry, Ford employing 25,000 at Dagenham.[48] Here, however, the company no longer needed to take responsibility for housing its workforce, the nearby Becontree estate having already been developed by the London County Council. Similarly, the Austin plants in Birmingham were able to draw workers from across the city: by 1937, only 10 per cent were walking to work, 25 per cent using buses, 14 per cent each by car and bicycle and 9 per cent by train.[49]

Other new consumer goods industries clustered together on industrial estates, such as Slough and Park Royal, both based on former munitions plants and each employing about 30,000 workers. Here individual firm sizes were relatively small; in 1952, the Park Royal area contained 305 firms, only five employing over 1,000. With less specialised needs than the older factory industries of the North, and able to draw on a metropolitan labour supply made increasingly mobile by the bus and the private car, such firms had no need to dominate their local labour markets. Assembly line production of new consumer durables and packaged foods, such as Heinz at Hayes and Mars at Slough, was increasingly seen as women's work. Slough's population growth from 20,285 in 1921 to

[46] N. Whiteside, *Bad Times* (London, 1991), pp. 78–9.

[47] M. Miller, 'Raymond Unwin', in G. E. Cherry, ed., *Pioneers in British Planning* (London, 1981), pp. 77–102.

[48] S. B. Saul, 'The motor industry in Britain to 1914', *Business History*, 5 (1962), 22–44.

[49] West Midland Group, *Conurbation* (London, 1948); cited by D. Smith, '"Not getting on, just getting by": changing prospects in south Birmingham', ch. 7 in P. Cooke, ed., *Localities: The Changing Face of Urban Britain* (London, 1989), p. 238.

52,590 in 1939 was obviously linked to the success of the trading estate but involved the employers' visible hand far less than had Bradford's growth a century earlier.[50]

If the employers' hand was less visible in shaping individual cities, the emergence of multi-site enterprises meant that employment practices began to shape the urban system as a whole. A first major wave of mergers peaking in 1898 saw major consolidations in textiles with the Calico Printers' Association, for example, merging forty-five firms in 1899, and the creation of other major firms such as Imperial Tobacco and Associated British Portland Cement. However, many of these mergers were essentially defensive, with unwieldy central management (the Calico Printers had eighty-four directors) and the constituent companies retaining much independence. The interwar period saw not only another wave of mergers but more professional and centralised corporate management. This made possible both the spiralist managerial careers discussed in the later section on white-collar workers and the development of a spatial division of labour not only within firms and sectors but also between towns.[51]

The urban economy of nineteenth-century Britain, and particularly of the factory industries, was based on a very fine division of labour in terms of products based partly on natural resources and partly on historical accident, so we have the Staffordshire Potteries, the cotton district of the North-West and so on. Such specialisation declined during the twentieth century both through the decline of manufacturing as a whole and, arguably, through manufacturing's lesser need for very distinctive trades: workers at Park Royal could far more easily switch between products than nineteenth-century textile workers. However, the new multi-site enterprises progressively removed functions such as marketing, research and development, and high-level management away from the original manufacturing sites, centralised them and, generally, located them in the South-East. One consequence was a new class division between regions, the middle classes being concentrated in the South-East as shown in Map 19.4.[52] A second was the development of local cultures in the old industrial areas in which production workers had very little prospect of a developing career, and where communities relied on employment being provided by large outside firms; for example, during the 1960s, only 37 per cent of new industrial employment in west central Scotland was created by indigenous firms, 33 per cent by firms from the rest of the UK and 30 per cent by overseas firms.[53] In more recent decades, as small firms gained renewed importance as generators of

[50] P. Hall, *The Industries of London since 1861* (London, 1962), pp. 121–39; J. T. Coppock and H. C. Prince, eds., *Greater London* (London, 1964), esp. chs. 1 and 9.

[51] L. Hannah, *The Rise of the Corporate Economy* (London, 1976), pp. 23, 83.

[52] C. E. Heim, 'Industrial organisation and regional development in inter-war Britain', *Journal of Economic History*, 43 (1983), 931–52; D. Massey, *Spatial Divisions of Labour* (London, 1984), esp. ch. 4.

[53] J. R. Firn, 'External control and regional development: the case of Scotland', *Environment and Planning A*, 7 (1975), 393–414.

employment, these areas were again handicapped by an apparent lack of entre-preneurship.[54]

(iv) MINERS

Coal mining's place in Britain's industrial and urban landscapes is often consid-ered separately from other industries. Accounts of mining communities in the nineteenth and early twentieth centuries commonly emphasise the importance of relatively closed local societies with a stable workforce and population, depending on natural increase and local migration for recruitment.[55] Sociological models of the mining community as an 'isolated mass' drew upon earlier charac-terisations of the apartness of mining people and places.[56] Travel literature from the early eighteenth century onwards treated British mining districts as distinc-tive and disturbing, populated by 'dark, demonic' figures.[57] By the time of the Second World War Bernard Newman was still writing of miners as isolated, strange and different: 'Miners are a tribe apart from the rest of the population. In this lies the foundation of their tragedy. Their villages are occupied only by miners, save for the few local tradesmen . . . The community feels itself socially ostracized, a race apart.'[58] Career structures in mining were never as apparent or developed as those in craft industries and white-collar work, but many hundreds of thousands of men spent their working lives within the industry, often at a single pit, particularly during the late nineteenth and early twentieth centuries.

However, by no means all miners lived and worked in 'typical' pit commu-nities, and there was more interdependence between mining and other labour markets than is often acknowledged. Single-industry villages were most common in those coalfields which expanded rapidly during the nineteenth century, particularly South Wales, the North-East, Lanarkshire and South Yorkshire. Even in these areas there were often close connections with other labour markets. For example, there were wide variations in South Wales, by 1911 the largest British coalfield. Mining dominated the urban labour market in the Rhondda and the other central valleys, but in towns like Ebbw Vale, Tredegar, Merthyr and Pontypool miners lived alongside substantial numbers of iron and steel workers, and in the Swansea valley and Llanelli districts there was some interchange between the mines and the tinplate and copper industries.[59] In the

---

[54] D. Keeble, 'Small firms, new firms, and uneven regional development in the United Kingdom', *Area*, 22 (1990), 234–45.

[55] A. K. Cairncross, *Home and Foreign Investment* (Cambridge, 1953), pp. 70–2.

[56] C. Kerr and A. Siegal, 'The interindustry propensity to strike – an international comparison', in A. Kornhauser, R. Dubin, and A. M. Ross, *Industrial Conflict* (New York, 1954), pp. 189–212.

[57] R. Williams, *Notes on the Underground: An Essay on Technology, Society, and the Imagination* (Cambridge, Mass., 1990), p. 66. [58] B. Newman, *British Journey* (London, 1946), p. 213.

[59] C. Williams, '"The hope of the British proletariat": the South Wales miners, 1910–1947', in A. Campbell, N. Fishman and D. Howell, eds., *Miners, Unions and Politics 1910–47* (Aldershot, 1996), p. 133.

western anthracite section of the coalfield some miners were still working small-holdings and living in rural cottages as late as the interwar period. In some other coalfields miners were much more integrated into local industrial labour markets. Mining in Lancashire took place around large urban areas marked by occupational diversity, and many colliers had their first taste of work in the local cotton mills rather than down the pit.[60]

Coalfield labour markets tended to be marked by extreme gender divisions. The employment of women underground was outlawed in 1842, and female surface workers, concentrated in the south Staffordshire and west Lancashire coalfields, made up a tiny proportion of the late Victorian mining workforce. In Lancashire and the East Midlands mining took place in regional labour markets where there were significant employment prospects for women, but this was not the case in most of the main export coalfields. Many women in these areas entered into marriage and out of waged employment at an early age but there was also a consistent movement of young women out of the coalfields into other labour markets, particularly into domestic service in London and other major cities as discussed below. The mining areas continued to export young women during the interwar and post-war periods, but by this time factory work in the new consumer industries was becoming increasingly important.

Migration into mining areas was a highly significant feature of the developing urban geography of Victorian Britain. Employment in coal mining increased from about 40,000 at the time of the first census in 1801, to about 215,000 in 1850, over a million by the outbreak of the First World War, and a peak of about one and a quarter million in 1920. Before 1850 recruitment into the new mining areas came from surrounding agricultural districts, and there was relatively little interregional migration within the industry. Mining was an important point of entry into the industrial labour force for rural workers, and in the long term played an important role in urbanising British society. The coalfield areas also grew because of high internal rates of natural increase in the coalfield communities. There were a few exceptions to these generalisations. There were small inter-coalfield flows of experienced hewers, particularly when new pits were opened, and inter-coalfield migration as a whole became more important towards the end of the nineteenth century. There were significant numbers of Irish miners in some coalfields, notably in Scotland and parts of South Wales, and the collapse of the Cornish copper industry in the 1860s also provided a new source of colliery labour.[61]

During the expansion of the mining industry, employers adopted various

[60] T. Griffiths, 'Work, class and community: social identities and political change in the Lancashire coalfield, 1910–1939', in A. Campbell, N. Fishman and D. Howell, eds., *Miners, Unions and Politics 1910–47* (Aldershot, 1996), p. 199.
[61] R. Church with A. Hall and J. Kanefsky, *The History of the British Coal Industry*, vol. III: *1830–1913: Victorian Pre-eminence* (Oxford, 1986), p. 192.

strategies to recruit and retain a stable workforce. In the early nineteenth century bonding contracts had guaranteed minimum earnings and regular employment. Ironically, the annual bonding system used in the North-East encouraged local migration as many miners sought improved contracts each year: 'many thousands of families would change districts annually, and in April and May the whole mining districts were alive from side to centre with loaded vehicles from big wagons to "cuddy" carts'.[62] It became more difficult to maintain bonding arrangements as mining companies became more vulnerable to discontinuities in demand associated with the trade cycle.[63]

After 1850 less direct strategies became more important in recruitment and retention. Small and relatively isolated settlements provided environments in which companies could exert close control over the mining population. In some places this worked through a broad paternalism, with the company involved in all aspects of local associational culture. This was eroded both by changes in the organisation of companies, which tended to become larger and more removed from local society, and by the development of autonomous working-class organisations in many mining villages. Communal welfare facilities such as halls and sports grounds were increasingly provided by the union rather than the company, although there were wide variations between the coalfields. None the less model village developments by mining companies in new twentieth-century coalfields still attempted to recreate older patterns of deference and company control.[64] The most consistent form of company influence involved housing. Tenure systems varied widely between mining districts. Many miners rented their houses, often directly or indirectly from the colliery company. The North-East was distinctive for the number of tied houses, while South Wales and parts of the Scottish coalfields had traditions of owner-occupation. None the less, most colliery companies agreed that 'where houses are provided, it is the means of ensuring a steady class of workmen and regularity of work'.[65]

The need to sustain a stable workforce was also reflected in the main expression of economic distress in British coalfields before 1914. Images of hard times in the coalfields are dominated by the queues and soup kitchens of the interwar slump, yet long-term unemployment was not an important feature of the nineteenth-century mining industry. The main responses to cyclical changes in demand were short-time working and variations in the length of the working week. Underemployment rather than unemployment helped to maintain a core

---

[62] E. A. Rymer, 'The martyrdom of the mine, or, a 60 years' struggle for life', ed. R. G. Neville, *History Workshop*, 1 (1976), 8.   [63] Church *et al.*, *Victorian Pre-eminence*, pp. 236–7.

[64] See R. Waller's discussion of social and labour relations in the new Dukeries coalfield of Nottinghamshire in *The Dukeries Transformed* (Oxford, 1983).

[65] Company secretary of Carlton Main colliery, Yorkshire, 1878. Quoted in Church *et al.*, *Victorian Pre-eminence*, p. 278. See also M. J. Daunton, 'Miners' houses: South Wales and the Great Northern coalfield, 1880–1914', *International Review of Social History*, 25 (1980), pp. 143–75.

workforce. Underemployment remained an important strategy into the interwar period, particularly in the Midlands coalfields.[66] However, in most of the export coalfields full redundancy had become the dominant labour market response to the slump. The coal industry was hit early and long-term unemployment, conventionally defined as continuous unemployment for more than a year, remained a serious problem in the industry throughout the 1930s. The Pilgrim Trust's *Men Without Work* report suggested that long-term unemployment in 1929 was 'mainly a localized abnormality of coal-mining districts dependent on mines abandoned or permanently closed'.[67] While other industrial groups also suffered severe long-term unemployment in the 1930s, miners remained the largest single occupational group among the long-term unemployed; by 1936, 12 per cent of coal miners had been unemployed for more than a year.[68]

The changing nature of economic distress in the coal industry had important ramifications for other labour markets. The sheer size of the mining workforce meant that the flows of labour into and out of the industry were among the most significant influences on patterns of internal migration.[69] Mining employment declined significantly from the mid-1920s with almost half a million men leaving the industry between 1924 and 1934. Employment declined less dramatically in the late 1930s and 1940s. Miners have had a reputation for geographic and occupational immobility, but the exodus from the declining export coalfields was substantial. Although there was government encouragement through the industrial transference scheme, most of this migration was voluntary. Migrants tended to be younger and more economically active than the general coalfield populations, and their loss significantly altered the age structures of coalfield settlements. Between them the South Wales and Northumberland–Durham coalfields are estimated to have lost 638,000 people between 1921 and 1936.[70] Some miners moved to pits in Nottinghamshire, South Yorkshire and Kent, but there was also considerable migration into the new industries of Greater London and the South-East of England. Migrating miners played a major part in industrial and urban restructuring.

(V) DOMESTIC SERVICE

The largest urban labour market for women was in domestic service. Through the nineteenth century service became increasingly dominated by women

---

[66] C. P. Griffin, '"Three days down the pit and three days play": underemployment in the East Midlands coalfields between the wars', *International Review of Social History*, 38 (1993), 321–43.

[67] Pilgrim Trust, *Men without Work* (Cambridge, 1938), p. 6.   [68] *Ibid.*, p. 18.

[69] D. Friedlander and R. J. Roshier, 'A study of internal migration in England and Wales: Part 1', *Population Studies*, 19 (1966), 265.

[70] B. Supple, *The History of the British Coal Industry*, vol. IV: *1913–1946: The Political Economy of Decline* (Oxford, 1987), p. 490.

workers. At the beginning of the century there were around eight women servants for every male servant; by the end of the century the ratio was over twenty
to one. However, the absolute numbers of men in domestic service did not
decline significantly, and men's privileged position in service was reinforced.
Within residential service butlers were usually paid more than cooks or house-
keepers, and coachmen, grooms and footmen more than even the most experienced of housemaids.[71] Live-in maids and non-residential workers in domestic
service were invariably women, and usually very poorly paid. The gendered
nature of this labour market makes it hard to estimate its size. The closeness
between paid service and those tasks traditionally defined as women's unpaid
domestic labour meant that this work was often regarded as marginal to conventional waged labour markets. The categories used in the decennial census
changed frequently, and both householders and enumerators often failed to distinguish between unwaged housework and waged domestic service. A substantial proportion of those recorded by the census as domestic servants in the census
were related to the head of household.[72] There were similar problems distinguishing domestic servants from nurses and those employed in laundry work. It
is also likely that part-time work undertaken by married women was substantially underenumerated.[73] None the less it is possible to use census returns to give
some very general indications of the changing size of the market for domestic
servants. There were around 1.2 million domestic servants recorded in the 1851
census. This increased to over 2 million in the last three decades of the nineteenth century.[74] The numbers employed in domestic service declined slightly
during the Edwardian period, and more rapidly after the First World War.
However, even as late as 1951 1.8 million workers were recorded as domestic servants, of whom 1.3 million were women.

The broad categories of the census obscured wide variations in the nature of
jobs and career patterns. The most common popular image of domestic service
has been of the retinues of servants retained in country houses or large town
houses. Employment 'below stairs' in a 'big house' was marked by fine distinctions between the various jobs but was generally relatively secure, and for some
could mean a lifetime's work in service. However, most domestic servants worked
outside of these more formal employment structures. The commonest form of
domestic servant was probably the young unmarried 'maid of all work' from a
rural or industrial area living and working single-handedly in a middle-class

[71] See P. Horn, ed., *The Rise and Fall of the Victorian Servant* (Dublin, 1975), pp. 184–8.
[72] E. Higgs, *Domestic Servants and Households in Rochdale* (New York, 1986).
[73] E. Roberts, *Women's Work, 1840–1940* (Basingstoke, 1988), p. 18.
[74] Census returns indicate an absolute decline in the number of servants from 1871, but this is likely
to have been an effect of more careful distinctions being made between paid service and unpaid
domestic labour. See E. Higgs, 'Domestics servants and households in Victorian England', *Soc.
Hist.*, 8 (1983), 201–10.

home.[75] This form of domestic service normally ended on marriage and the formation of an independent household. By contrast other forms of domestic service such as charring and laundry work were usually restricted to older married or widowed women.

There were various ways of 'getting a place' in service. By the middle of the nineteenth century annual hiring or so-called 'Mop' fairs were falling into disrepute, and young women and men seeking positions increasingly used informal networks of neighbours and family or relied upon the help of local clergy and gentry. Urban tradesmen often acted as unofficial registry offices for servants and by the end of the nineteenth century advertising for positions in newspapers became more common.[76] Many young women worked their way through a series of positions, taking them away from their immediate areas into service in cities and towns. There were limited opportunities for domestic service in most parts of the country, even in working-class districts of British cities where poorly paid part-time cleaning and washing jobs were to be found. At the very bottom end of the market, Victorian artisans and shopkeepers could employ domestic servants taken from workhouses or charitable institutions for as little as £3 a year, about a third of the wages paid to the most junior maids in the large households, or even in some areas without wages in return for board.[77]

The interactions between domestic service and other labour markets were important in shaping the urban geography of Britain. Although all major towns and cities had significant demand for servants, London was by far the most important single labour market. Within London there was a strikingly polarised geography of female domestic service, as shown in Map 19.1. The enormous numbers of female domestic servants in some districts affected the overall gender balance: in 1861, Kensington Registration District had twice as many women as men in the age group twenty to twenty-four, and Hampstead three times as many.[78] Plotting similar information for 1911 shows little change, and brings out the scale of social disparities within London: Hampstead had 737 domestic servants per thousand households, the highest rate in the country, while Bethnal Green had thirty-five, the lowest in the country apart from six small Urban Districts in Lancashire.[79]

Domestic service played a significant and underrecognised role in rural–urban migration, and in-migration between British urban areas. A high proportion of

---

[75] E. Higgs, 'Domestic service and household production', in A.V. John, ed., *Unequal Opportunities* (Oxford, 1986), pp. 125–50. [76] Horn, ed., *Rise and Fall*, pp. 37–8.

[77] F. K. Prochaska, 'Female philanthropy and domestic service in Victorian England' *Bull. IHR*, 54 (1981), 79–85.

[78] Data from table 2 'Ages of males and females' in the divisional tables in *Census of England and Wales 1861*, vol. II: *Ages, Civil Condition, Occupations, and Birth-Places of the People*, PP 1863 LIII, parts 1 and 2.

[79] Data from table 15(B) 'Grouped occupations of females aged ten years and upwards', in *Census of England and Wales 1911*, vol. X: *Occupations and Industries*, part 1, PP 1913 LXXVIII, pp. 424–61.

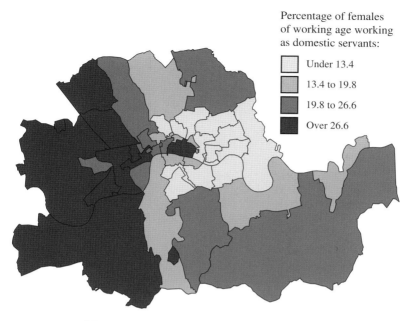

Percentage of females
of working age working
as domestic servants:

Under 13.4

13.4 to 19.8

19.8 to 26.6

Over 26.6

Map 19.1 Domestic servants in London 1861
Source: 1861 census (data transcribed and provided by David Allan Gatley).

young women entering service came either from agricultural districts or from areas of heavy industry where women had few employment opportunities. Women's entry into domestic service was often a consequence of a lack of alternative employment possibilities. In the cotton- and textile-producing districts of northern England women were likely to choose factory work as an alternative to domestic service. In these areas domestic service acted as a labour market which could absorb young women in times of economic distress. Women factory workers were poorly organised and thus largely excluded from trade union unemployment relief before the First World War, and payments to women were restricted under the state insurance schemes. The most familiar story of migration during the interwar depression concerns the northern unemployed moving south into the new factories in London and the South-East, but the established paths into service provided young women entering the labour market with an alternative southerly escape route from hard times.

Employment prospects for women outside of domestic service were primarily limited by the sex-typing of occupations. A number of factors caused the long slow decline in employment in domestic service through most of the twentieth century including changes in the nature of middle-class households and the mechanisation of housework, but the most significant was the growth of alternative employment opportunities for young women. At the end of the nineteenth century rural depopulation had more or less drained one of the largest pools of female labour without relatively attractive alternative employment prospects. The First World War pushed many women into jobs traditionally defined as male, and the number of women employed in domestic service dropped from 1.65 million in 1914 to 1.25 million in 1918.[80] The backlash against women workers in many industries which followed the war forced many women back into domestic service, but the rise of new kinds of 'women's work' on factory production lines, in consumer industries and in clerical work continued to erode the supply of servants. These new occupations were concentrated in the parts of the country where domestic service was most important.

(vi) WHITE-COLLAR WORK

The expansion of white-collar work, particularly during the twentieth century, made a very direct and obvious mark on the physical landscape of British towns and cities. Whole central districts were turned over to office buildings and to servicing the needs of the new legions of office workers. But the expansion of white-collar work had other influences on the development of the British urban system. White-collar work, with the security that came from regular salaried income, produced new possibilities and expectations for millions of households: it was a major influence on the growth of suburbia, it introduced new working roles for women and new forms of gender-segregation in urban labour markets and it led to new forms of career patterns and spatial movement through the urban system.

To some extent both the growth and the changing gender relations of office work can be gauged by census records of the number of clerical workers (see Table 19.3) In 1851 fewer than one worker in a hundred was a clerk, and to all intents and purposes all clerks were men. A hundred years later, one in ten workers was employed in clerical work, and a clear majority of clerical workers were women. However, as with many other forms of work, general census categories obscure social, organisational and technical changes in the nature of white-collar work . By the mid-twentieth century what the census enumerated as clerical work was but part of a larger labour market for white-collar workers. For example, those classified as managers increased from around 3 per cent of the workforce in the late Victorian economy to 4.5 per cent by 1951, yet managerial work had shifted away from supervision of industrial production towards the administration of people or products.[81] Similarly, the nature and status of professional work had broadened. Although the elites of medicine, the law and the higher echelons of the civil service remained relatively closed and

[80] J. Bourke, *Working-Class Cultures in Britain 1890–1960* (London, 1994), p. 103.
[81] M. Savage *et al.*, *Property, Bureaucracy and Culture* (London, 1992), pp. 49–50.

Table 19.3 *Growth and feminisation of clerical work*
1851–1981

Year	Clerks as percentage of total labour force	Female clerks as percentage of all clerks
1851	0.8	0.1
1901	4.0	13.4
1951	10.5	59.6
1981	16.9	74.4

Source: D. Lockwood, *The Blackcoated Worker*, 2nd edn (Oxford, 1989), p. 222.

self-recruiting, by the interwar period significant numbers were employed in lower status professions, notably in school teaching and welfare services.

Mid-Victorian clerks were employed in a variety of organisations. The majority of clerks worked in the 'counting houses' of commercial and industrial companies.[82] Offices tended to be small: in 1871 Benjamin Orchard estimated that the average size of commercial offices in Liverpool was just four clerks, and many smaller firms employed a solitary book-keeper.[83] The largest employers were local and central government, banks, insurance companies and railway companies, and it was within these corporate organisations that new white-collar roles and career structures started to develop. By the late nineteenth century commercial firms were also centralising and expanding, and the labour market for white-collar work was dividing into two distinct sections. For some clerical workers, the increasing size and scale of businesses and organisations brought the chance of a career with considerable prospects for upward mobility. However, many men in lower grades of clerical work faced increasing competition for their jobs from foreign and women workers.

Organisational career structures developed earliest in the banking industry. Unlike many commercial firms apprenticeship as a clerk in a bank usually guaranteed a secure post and a foot on the career ladder. Most large or medium-sized banks had a structure of branches, and a good ratio of managers to ordinary clerical workers. This meant both that there were good prospects for upward mobility through the organisation, and that geographical mobility and career mobility were closely linked. The career of William Smalley, first a clerk then manager in the North and South Wales Bank, was not untypical. After joining the bank as a clerk in 1851 he moved between posts in Mold, Liverpool, Holywell and Oswestry before being appointed manager in Llanidloes in 1862. He then moved back to the bank's head office in Liverpool, and on to another manager's post at

---

[82] See D. Lockwood, *The Blackcoated Worker*, 2nd edn (Oxford, 1989); G. Anderson, *Victorian Clerks* (Manchester, 1976).   [83] B. G. Orchard, *The Clerks of Liverpool* (Liverpool, 1871), p. 7.

Rhayader, before finally settling at the Rhyl branch in 1865.[84] During the late nineteenth and early twentieth centuries amalgamations and takeovers created a banking industry which was national rather than regional in scale, and which was increasingly centralised in London, with concomitant consequences for career paths.[85]

Organisational career structures were rather different for managers in manufacturing industry. The single firm career was equally important: the Acton Society Trust's 1956 survey of forty-four of the largest manufacturing companies in Britain found that 63 per cent of managers had either worked exclusively in one company, or had joined their present company before the age of twenty-five.[86] However, this did not imply that managers in manufacturing were as geographically mobile as their counterparts in financial services. Britain retained many relatively small family-controlled firms, and larger manufacturing companies were slow to develop the kind of integrated organisational structures which were common in the United States. Where large British companies had been formed through merger, the management structures and practices of the original companies were often retained under a small central holding company. Managers in manufacturing were therefore among the least geographically mobile of the emerging twentieth-century middle class.

The state's increasing involvement in health, law and education meant that organisational career paths became more important for the professions during the first half of the twentieth century. However, for many professionals career progression remained one of changing jobs within an occupation rather than promotion in a single organisation. Professionals were the first major occupational group to establish career patterns in which occupational advancement worked through criteria which were not spatially fixed, and where the relationship of the individual to town or region became more or less contingent.[87] The career paths of many nineteenth-century clerics, lawyers and doctors prefigured the kind of simultaneous spatial and social mobility associated with the 'spiralism' of many mid- and late twentieth-century careers.[88] This is not to say that the distribution of professionals across the country was either even or random. Professional networks and formal organisations were usually urban and increasingly based in London. The professions established a pattern of living which provided a model for the new aspirational middle classes. London and the South-East was reinforced as the most prestigious region, particular suburbs and districts of major towns and cities were marked as socially desirable, and the kind

[84] G. L. Anderson, *Victorian Clerks* (Manchester, 1976), p. 22.
[85] M. Savage, 'Career mobility and class formation: British banking workers and the lower middle classes', in A. G. Miles and D. Vincent, eds., *Building European Society* (Manchester, 1993), p. 200.
[86] Acton Society Trust, *Management Succession* (London, 1956), cited in Savage *et al.*, *Property, Bureaucracy and Culture*, pp. 50–1.   [87] Savage *et al.*, *Property, Bureaucracy and Culture*, pp. 49–50.
[88] W. Watson, 'Social mobility and social class in industrial societies', in M. Glucksman and E. Devons, eds., *Closed Systems and Open Minds* (Edinburgh, 1964), pp. 129–57.

of privatised domestic life associated with an un-rooted career became an established middle-class norm.

Alongside these developments were other changes in the white-collar labour market which had quite different implications for social and geographical mobility. Indeed, it can be argued that the development of the middle-class career structure, whether organisational or occupational, depended upon the simultaneous growth in the number of low-paid and low-status clerical workers, who were locally based and had very limited career prospects. As early as the 1870s, English clerks were concerned that they were being undercut by German and Scottish clerks who 'swarm to England and France in thousands, accepting duties at any salary they are offered'.[89] However, the growth of female employment was a far more lasting and significant change in the white-collar labour market. The Post Office Savings Bank and the new telegraph services were early employers of female clerks in the 1880s, followed by larger commercial firms, insurance firms and the banks. Certain new clerical skills, notably shorthand and typing, came to be defined as women's work.[90] The First World War saw a major expansion in the number of women clerks, and unlike in engineering and factory work, this was a permanent change in the labour market.

In the early expansion of women's clerical work, women were seen as a direct challenge to the position of male clerks.[91] However, this effect was concentrated at the bottom of the clerical labour market, and by the 1920s job opportunities and career structures for men and women were becoming increasingly differentiated. In the banks, for example, women were given a special, separate grade within the organisation, while male clerical work became increasingly managerial with clear opportunities for promotion and mobility.[92] The lack of career prospects for women white-collar workers was reinforced by social and in some occupations legal constraints on work after marriage. In the Civil Service the marriage bar was removed only as late as 1946, and the ban was actively supported by many single women workers who saw married women as competition for their position. This marked gendering of white-collar work had very direct consequences for the nature of cities. The growth of a relatively privileged male white-collar salariat was a key influence on the growth of suburbia, particularly between the wars. A form of domestic life in which male commuting and female housework became established norms was related to social and cultural expectations, but also to the very different labour market opportunities for middle-class married men and women. London was the paramount centre for female clerical work, and the city saw the development of a new geography of independent young female households, concentrated in the inner west London suburbs.

[89] C. E. Parsons, *Clerks: Their Position and Advancement* (London, 1876), p. 16.
[90] Roberts, *Women's Work*, p. 38.
[91] M. Zimmeck, 'Jobs for the girls: the expansion of clerical work for women 1850–1914', in John, ed., *Unequal Opportunities*, pp. 153–77.   [92] Savage, 'Career, mobility', p. 197.

(vii) CONCLUSION: LABOUR MARKETS AND THE URBAN SYSTEM

The central concern of this chapter has been how labour markets shaped the lives of individual people and, indirectly, the form of individual towns: the casual workers, confined to particular quarters by their dependence on information networks for finding work; the artisans with their movements from town to town and their 'houses of call' serving as informal labour markets; domestic servants, so numerous in some parts of cities as to create otherwise inexplicable demographic structures; the role of employers in building new communities to house their workers. This conclusion shifts focus to the urban system as a whole and explores the complex divisions of labour which characterised both nineteenth- and twentieth-century Britain.

Traditionally, regional geographers have argued that the Industrial Revolution meant an end to the distinctive local cultures of pre-industrial times: people no longer wore characteristic local clothing but cloth from Lancashire and shoes from Northamptonshire. Similarly, traditional housing styles using local materials were replaced by standard styles using bricks from Bedfordshire and slates from North Wales. In 1983, John Langton argued that the Industrial Revolution had actually increased regional diversity, pointing out that precisely this homogenisation of consumption required specialisation in production, in how people and communities earned their living: Lancashire *became* the 'cotton districts', Llanberis and Blaenau Ffestiniog almost synonymous with slate.[93]

This argument can easily be taken too far: while mining and weaving were highly localised, artisans tended to be found in every town, and as we have seen were highly mobile between them; while a town might be unable to change its specialisation, people could and did make large career changes; and London was always a vast exception. Map 19.2 draws on two census reports, eighty years apart, which provide comparable occupational statistics for individual towns.[94] The upper pair of maps classify the urban workforce of each county into three broad categories: those where service sector employment was greater than all in

[93] J. Langton, 'The Industrial Revolution and the regional geography of England', *Transactions of the Institute of British Geographers*, 9 (1984), 145–67.

[94] Such an analysis, completely excluding rural populations, is possible for relatively few censuses. The 1841 census tabulated occupations by county and selected towns, sometimes using boroughs and sometimes *ad hoc* assemblies of parishes, whereas later nineteenth-century censuses used Registration Districts which combined towns with their hinterlands. 1841 was the first census systematically to gather occupational data and, because it reported them in almost raw form, it is possible here to assign them to the 1921 occupational classification. The 1921 census was the first to report occupations for all individual local government districts, so here the county figures summarise those for all individual County and Municipal Boroughs, Urban Districts, and for Scotland Cities and Large Burghs. The 1921 data for England and Wales consequently include figures for smaller towns relative to Scotland, and to 1841. Here, and in Maps 19.3 and 19.4, the small number of Scottish towns in the data necessitates merging counties into five broader regions.

manufacturing; those others where the old staple industries employed more than light manufacturing; and those where light industrial employment exceeded the staple industries.[95] The lower pair of maps use the same data to measure the *degree* of occupational specialisation in each locality: towns with low index values had a broadly based employment structure, while high values indicate a reliance on one or two sectors.[96]

Urban specialisations in 1921 were much as we would expect, showing a clear polarisation between the manufacturing districts of the North and of South Wales, and the remainder of the country dominated by the service sector; only a relatively small area in the South-East Midlands was dominated by light industry.[97] The 1841 map differs significantly, revealing a pre-railway and partially pre-factory occupational geography: most of the heavy industry of the North-East of England had still to develop, while much of the textile industry was still based in small towns away from the coalfields, in Wiltshire and North Wales. However, the domination of the South-East by services was already established.

We tend to assume that towns specialised by product, and hence in terms of manufacturing, but the lower pair of maps and especially that for 1841 partly reflect specialisation within services. Berkshire was the second most specialised 1841 county based entirely on figures for Reading, half the workforce being classed as 'Commercial, financial and insurance'. While Wiltshire's specialisation was primarily into textiles, occupying 55 per cent of workers in Trowbridge, towns in Berkshire and Somerset were again specialised into services: retailing in Reading, and the various luxury trades of Bath, where 39 per cent of workers were in domestic service. Cheltenham and Brighton had the same percentage, while 51 per cent of all workers in Leamington Spa were in domestic service. Manufacturing specialisations also emerge, such as the Staffordshire Potteries with 61 per cent of Burslem's workers, 53 per cent of Stoke's and 34 per cent of Hanley's in the sector: no other town had over 10 per cent. The two towns most dominated by mining were Aberystruth (42 per cent) and Bedwellty (38 per cent), both in Monmouthshire. Lancashire was not among the most specialised counties because of the diverse economies of Liverpool and Manchester, but

[95] This classification was developed by Eilidh Garrett and Alice Reid of the ESRC Cambridge Group. Of the thirty-two available categories, categories I and II are grouped as agricultural (defined as dominant in 1841 in three counties where the only data concern a single small town: Dolgellau, New Radnor and Buckingham); III (mining), V (brick making), VII (most metal workers) and XII (textiles) as 'Staple'; VI, VIII, IX, X, XI, XIII through XX, XXIX and XXX as 'Light'; XXI through XXVIII as 'Services'; and XXXI and XXXII as discarded residual categories.

[96] The method is taken from R. C. Tress, 'Unemployment and the diversification of industry', *Manchester School*, 9 (1938), 140–52; Tress himself was able to compute his index for only a small number of towns. Our county index values are averages of index values computed for individual towns, weighted by total numbers employed, so a county consisting of towns with diverse but extreme specialisms will have a high index value.

[97] The growth of services pre-1914 is emphasised by C. H. Lee, 'Regional growth and structural change in Victorian Britain', *Ec.HR*, 2nd series, 34 (1981), 438–52.

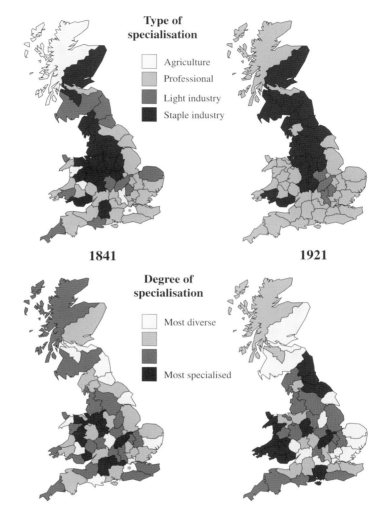

Map 19.2 Urban occupational specialisations 1841 and 1921, by type and by degree

Source: 1841 and 1921 census occupational tables.

many other towns were dominated by textiles; for example, 63 per cent of Blackburn's workers were in the sector. Such extreme concentrations of the workforce into a single sector limited available services, and the lives of the inhabitants. Unsurprisingly, dominant sectors were generally smaller by 1921, so only 41 per cent of Blackburn's workers, and 14 per cent of Trowbridge's, were in textiles in 1921; only 36 per cent of Stoke's in pottery; only 22 per cent of Bath's in domestic service; and so on.

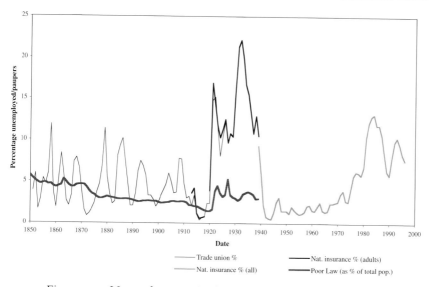

Figure 19.1 Unemployment in the United Kingdom 1851–1996
Sources: trade unions pre-1881: B. R. Mitchell, and P. Deane, *Abstract of British Historical Statistics* (Cambridge, 1962), p. 64; trade unions 1881–1926: Department of Employment and Productivity, *British Labour Statistics: Historical Abstract 1886–1968* (London, 1971), p. 305; 1913–39: *British Labour Statistics*, table 160 (data exclude juveniles and persons insured under the agricultural scheme); 1939–47: *British Labour Statistics*, table 161 (data include juveniles and persons insured under the agricultural scheme); 1948–68: *British Labour Statistics*, table 165; post-1968 data taken from various issues of the *British Labour Statistics Yearbook*, *Social Trends* and the *Employment Gazette*.

One consequence of such specialisation, especially when into one of the traditional staple industries, dependent on investment and overseas demand, was vulnerability to cyclical fluctuation. As A. C. Pigou put it in 1913: 'A nation which concentrates its forces upon the manufacture of the instruments of industry courts thereby a relatively heavy burden of unemployment.'[98] He was commenting on Britain as a whole, but this was even more true of individual regions and towns. Figure 19.1 plots national unemployment rates, variously measured, from 1851 to the present.[99] The period covered saw such changes to the labour market that simplistic comparisons of levels must be avoided, but four distinct regimes of unemployment can be identified: from 1850 to 1914, an almost regular cycle of eight to ten years; sustained high unemployment in the interwar

[98] A. C. Pigou, *Unemployment* (London, 1913), p. 112.
[99] The large problems of measurement and interpretation are discussed in H. R. Southall, 'Working with historical statistics on poverty and economic distress', in D. F. L. Dorling and S. N. Simpson, eds., *Statistics in Society: The Arithmetic of Politics* (London, 1999), pp. 350–8.

(a) 1871-1910   **(b) 1931**

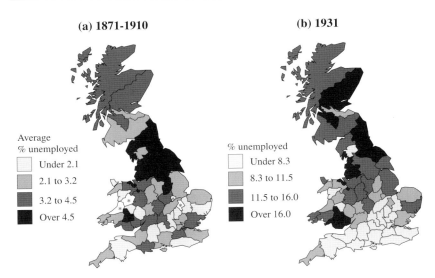

Map 19.3 Urban unemployment rates 1871–1910 and 1931
Sources: (a) Amalgamated Society of Engineers, *Monthly Reports*, and
Amalgamated Society of Carpenters and Joiners, *Monthly Reports*, January and
July only; (b) 1931 census reports, *Occupational Tables*, combining tables 16 and
17; Scottish data from 1931 census reports, vol. 3, *Occupations and Industries*,
table 2.

period; the post-Second World War boom; and higher unemployment again
since the 1970s.

Many have asserted that pre-1914 unemployment was concentrated in the
South.[100] Map 19.3(a) shows long-run average unemployment among members
of the two largest artisan unions between 1871 and 1910, these rates being dominated by the impact of cyclical recessions. Rates were clearly higher in the
factory districts.[101] Although these data concern only artisan unionists, other evidence such as the marriage rate suggests that major recessions had a drastic
impact on all parts of the labour market, through short-time and pay cuts as well
as lay-offs; for example, total numbers of marriages in Bolton doubled between
1842 and 1845 as the economy recovered, while those where the groom was an
engineer trebled and even middle-class marriages increased by two-thirds. Much
of our knowledge of nineteenth-century towns comes from the census, but from
1851 onwards it was *always* carried out during an upturn in the cycle. How

100 H. R. Southall, 'The origins of the depressed areas: unemployment, growth and regional economic structure in Britain before 1914', *Ec.HR*, 2nd series, 41 (1988), 236–58
101 Computed using the January and July returns from all British branches of both unions, but engineers, and carpenters and joiners were inherently urban.

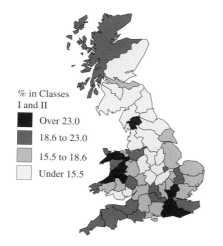

% in Classes
I and II

■ Over 23.0

▓ 18.6 to 23.0

▒ 15.5 to 18.6

□ Under 15.5

Map 19.4 Distribution of the urban middle class 1951
Sources: data for England and Wales from 1951 census, *County Reports*
(London, 1956), table 27; Scottish data from 1951 census reports, vol. 4,
Occupations and Industries (Edinburgh, 1956), table 10.

different a picture would we obtain from a recession year census? 'Dovetailing',
discussed above, would change the occupational structure; many artisan household heads would be on the road or even abroad, looking for work; many houses
stood empty, young couples moving in with relatives to save rent.[102]

Map 19.3(b) shows urban unemployment during the interwar Depression; the
use of census data enables us to cover all towns, and only towns, but the county
aggregates conceal many extremes: for example, 52 per cent in Port Glasgow and
49 per cent in Jarrow, but only 17 per cent in both Paisley and Durham City.
However, the regional divide was marked and consistent: only one tiny town in
the entire South-East outside London, Wivenhoe in Essex, had a rate over 15
per cent. A final contrast is with the 1951 census, where the national rate had
fallen from 12 per cent to 2 per cent, and the highest rates were mostly seaside
resorts, the census falling outside the holiday season.

By then, however, another division of labour between towns was influencing
prosperity: as discussed in the sections on factory and white-collar workers,
between centres of command and control, and hence white-collar jobs, and
older industrial towns, still reliant on manufacturing but now stripped of their
entrepreneurs and most of their managers. Map 19.4 shows middle-class occupations, excluding clerical workers, and hence high earners. High rates in

[102] H. R. Southall and D. Gilbert, 'A good time to wed? Marriage and economic distress in England
and Wales, 1839–1914', *Ec.HR*, 2nd series, 49 (1996), 35–57.

627

Westmorland and rural Wales concern very small urban populations, and without these a very clear North–South divide emerges. A more extreme divide existed for 'managers', about 6 per cent of the 1951 workforce in the Home Counties and 10 per cent in communities such as Purley and Esher, but about 2.5 per cent in Durham and Monmouthshire, and little over 1 per cent in some mining towns.[103] This was the legacy of industrialisation in much of urban Britain at the end of our period: communities with full employment but dependent on a narrow economic base and often on one or two large employers controlled from outside; and as a result of that base and pattern of control, having a narrow social base as well.

[103] Computed from tables 20 and 21 in *Census 1951 England and Wales: Occupational Tables* (London, 1956; transcription supplied by Daniel Dorling) and table 6 in *Census 1951 Scotland*, vol. IV: *Occupations and Industries* (Edinburgh, 1956).

20

Urban fertility and mortality patterns

SIMON SZRETER AND ANNE HARDY

(i) INTRODUCTION

DURING THE decades of the 1870s and 1880s, urban – and with it national – mortality, fertility and nuptiality patterns all appear to have almost simultaneously begun to enter a new era.[1] For the first time large industrial cities were proving themselves capable of combining high rates of expansion with improving (albeit very gradually before the twentieth century) mortality conditions for the majority of the urban working population. Secondly, marital fertility was apparently coming under tight control. Whereas previously fertility had been regulated in British society primarily through a set of institutional arrangements governing young adults' expectations of the appropriate economic circumstances under which marriage could be undertaken, now there were increasingly systematic attempts to control the chances of conception after marriage, as well.[2] There was also an increase in the rate of overseas migration (mainly from Britain's cities) during this period, the other principal component in the demographic equation, though this was never as influential a factor as in Ireland's demographic history.[3] Thus, the demographic

---

[1] For accessible introductions, see N. Tranter, *Population and Society 1750–1940: Contrasts in Population Growth* (London, 1985); and M. Anderson, ed., *British Population History* (Cambridge, 1996).

[2] E. A. Wrigley and R. S. Schofield, *Population History of England* (London, 1981), chs. 10–11. For a recent review of developments in this field and interesting additional insights into the nature of institutional controls on marriage in early modern Britain, see S. Hindle, 'The problem of pauper marriage in seventeenth-century England', *Transactions Royal Historical Society*, 6th series, 8 (1998), 71–89.

[3] The emigration rate was running at about 2.5 persons per thousand over the two decades before 1870 and rose to about 4.5 per thousand over the next four decades (during which period there was also a somewhat off-setting inflow from Eastern Europe), thereafter falling back to about 2.5 per thousand in the 1920s. These rates of emigration were dwarfed by Ireland's, which were as high as 14 per thousand in the 1850s, 1860s and 1880s. Scottish emigration rates ran at about 5 per thousand throughout the second half of the nineteenth century, but then increased to approximately 10 per thousand during the period 1900–30, when they exceeded Irish rates. D. E. Baines, *Emigration from Europe 1815–1930* (London, 1991), Table 3; and see also D. E. Baines, *Migration in a Mature Economy* (Cambridge, 1985).

history of urban Britain during the period 1840–1950 is particularly dominated by the dramatic changes in mortality and fertility occurring during the central decades of that period, *c.* 1870–1930, which will therefore constitute the primary focus of attention in this chapter.

These developments had many long-term implications for the social character and needs of Britain's cities. In the earlier nineteenth-century decades the proliferation of hordes of infants, children, youths and young men and women on the unpaved and unlit streets of the smoky, industrial 'frontier' towns was undoubtedly something which endowed them with a novel and threatening character, compared with the more familiar complexion of life in the older and slower-growing southern county, market and cathedral towns, including even London. The full cultural and political sociological implications of this novel age structure still remain to be explored by historians. But it can be safely asserted that the relentless youthfulness was caused by the combination of the new cities' expansion through substantial in-migration of young adults, the relatively high fertility of their inhabitants and the fact that they were expanding so fast in proportionate terms each decade (so that the relatively small cohorts of oldest residents were proportionately swamped by the much larger and ever-expanding successive cohorts of younger newcomers). The subsequent fall in fertility (initially partially offset by the dramatic improvements in infant survivorship achieved 1900–30) and the attenuated flow of migration from the de-populated countryside combined to produce a marked slow-down in the rate of growth of most cities from the beginning of the twentieth century. These were the principal demographic forces resulting in the twentieth-century 'ageing' of Britain's great industrial centres, whereby the world's new, vigorous shock cities of the mid-nineteenth century have matured to become the country's familiar 'senior citizens' in an architectural, residential and sociological sense, reflecting the relative 'greying' of their residents through an evening up of the balance of middle-aged and senior citizens relative to the young.

Historians and social scientists have long been attracted to the idea that these important demographic movements – the apparently almost simultaneous downturn in the mortality and fertility indices – must in some way be causally related to each other. This is the suspicion lying behind the long-influential notion that a 'demographic transition' necessarily results from the kind of sustained economic growth involved in industrialisation and the concomitant rise of a 'modern' urban society.[4] However, attempts to verify empirically a direct relationship between mortality and fertility change in this period in Britain,

---

[4] For the most influential formulation of the theory of demographic transition, see F. W. Notestein, 'Population – the long view', in T. W. Schultz, ed., *Food for the World* (Chicago, 1945), pp. 36–57; and for a critical history of the idea, see S. Szreter, 'The idea of demographic transition and the study of fertility change: a critical intellectual history', *Population and Development Review*, 19 (1993), 659–701.

including careful efforts to distinguish infant from child and other forms of mortality, have only resulted in negative or contradictory statistical findings.[5] In this chapter, therefore, separate treatments of the history of changing urban mortality and fertility have been offered, reflecting the two distinct bodies of historiography.

(ii) URBAN MORTALITY PATTERNS

Two principal features dominate urban mortality patterns in the period 1840 to 1950: initially high death rates (extremely high in many industrial towns), which began to decline from about 1870; and a gradual shift in the main causes of death from infectious to chronic and degenerative diseases.[6] The high death rate/high infectious disease rate regime, especially marked in the second and third quarters of the nineteenth century, was the result of unregulated industrial and urban growth, which reduced many residential areas in towns and cities across Britain to squalid, stinking dormitories. Whereas eighteenth-century citizens had often made successful efforts to clean up their towns and stave off the ravages of infectious disease, such efforts seem to have been insufficiently maintained during the first half of the nineteenth century.[7] By 1840, urban Britain was highly insanitary, as Edwin Chadwick's great Sanitary Report of 1842 graphically documented and as the ensuing Health of Towns Commission confirmed.[8]

These urban environments formed a perfect breeding ground for endemic infectious diseases, as well as for that terrifying visitor, cholera. Badly ventilated and overcrowded houses, where families too often lived each to a room, with as many families in the house as there were rooms, encouraged the spread of diseases transmitted by droplet infection and close contact: whooping cough, measles, scarlet fever, smallpox and tuberculosis. Thousands of children died

---

[5] M. Kabir, 'Multivariate study of reduction in child mortality in England and Wales as a factor influencing the fall in fertility' (PhD thesis, University of London, 1979); R. Woods, P. A. Watterson and J. H. Woodward, 'The causes of rapid infant mortality decline in England and Wales, 1861–1921', *Population Studies*, Part I, 42 (1988), 343–66, part II, 43 (1989), 113–32.

[6] For important recent historical epidemiological studies, see A. Mercer, *Disease, Mortality and Population* (Leicester, 1990); R. Woods and N. Shelton, *An Atlas of Victorian Mortality* (Liverpool, 1997); J. Vogele, *Urban Mortality Change in England and Germany, 1870–1913* (Liverpool, 1998); A. Cliff, P. Haggett and M. Smallman-Raynor, *Deciphering Global Epidemics. Analytical Approaches to the Disease Records of World Cities, 1888–1912* (Cambridge, 1998); R. Woods, *The Demography of Victorian England and Wales* (Cambridge, 2000).

[7] For eighteenth-century reforms and renovations see C. W. Chalklin, *The Provincial Towns of Georgian England* (London, 1974); P. J. Corfield, *The Impact of English Towns 1700–1800* (Oxford, 1982), ch. 7; James Riley, *The Eighteenth-Century Campaign to Avoid Disease* (London and Basingstoke, 1985); P. Borsay, *The English Urban Renaissance: Culture and Society in the Provincial Town, 1660–1770* (Oxford, 1989); Roy Porter, 'Cleaning up the Great Wen', in W. F. Bynum and R. S. Porter, eds., *Living and Dying in London, Medical History* (Supplement, 1991).

[8] M. W. Flinn, ed., *Report on the Sanitary Condition of the Labouring Classes of Great Britain* (Edinburgh, 1965).

every year from secondary respiratory infections following on measles and whooping cough, because these diseases were considered as a child's rite of passage, and sufferers not put to bed and nursed, but allowed to run the streets as usual.[9] Outbreaks of typhus, which is spread in the faeces of the human body louse, characterised times of economic depression, when families tried to economise on rent by doubling up in already inadequate accommodation.[10] Toilet facilities were too often neglected and frequently completely insufficient for the number of people using them, resulting in endemic gastro-intestinal infections, of which typhoid and diarrhoea were the most fatal. Typhoid, indeed, flourished as urban water supplies deteriorated in quality – as raw sewage entered rivers and streams from which domestic water supplies were drawn in ever increasing quantities, and as pressures on urban land led to wells and cess pits being sunk too close together, so that leakage and soakage from one to the other was commonplace.[11] Festering deposits of domestic refuse and stable manure – the latter a massive problem in a horse-drawn society – constituted regular health hazards which local government struggled to contain into the early twentieth century. In particular, they formed splendid breeding grounds for flies which swarmed in their millions in Victorian cities in the summer months, and were heavily implicated as the vehicle of transmission for infant diarrhoea, which killed thousands of babies between July and October every year.[12]

As a group, the infectious diseases were responsible for some 40 per cent of all urban deaths around 1840, but by 1900 their mortality had fallen to less than 20 per cent. Typhus and smallpox had virtually vanished from the mortality tables; typhoid and tuberculosis were greatly reduced and still falling; scarlet fever had markedly reduced in virulence. Deaths from whooping cough had begun to decline, and even measles, diphtheria and diarrhoea were showing signs of diminishing fatality. While some of these decreased fatalities can be explained by improved water supplies (typhoid, cholera), or rising standards of personal hygiene and housing (typhus), or autonomous decreases in virulence (scarlet fever), the overall reduction in deaths from this group of diseases has been the

[9] A. Hardy, *The Epidemic Streets* (Oxford, 1993), chs. 1, 2; A. Hardy, *Health and Medicine in Britain since 1860* (Basingstoke, forthcoming).

[10] See A. Hardy, 'Urban famine or urban crisis? Typhus in the Victorian city', in R. J. Morris and R. Rodger, eds., *The Victorian City* (London, 1993).

[11] A. Hardy, 'Parish pump to private pipes: London's water supply in the nineteenth century', in Bynum and Porter, eds., *Living and Dying*.

[12] For the most convincing demonstration of the significance of flies in producing infant diarrhoea, see the outstanding article by Ian Buchanan: 'Infant feeding, sanitation and diarrhoea in colliery communities, 1880–1911', in D. J. Oddy and D. Miller, eds., *Diet and Health in Modern Britain* (London, 1985), 148–77. See also Nigel Morgan, 'Infant mortality, flies and horses in later nineteenth century or early twentieth century towns: a case study of Preston', *Continuity and Change* (forthcoming).

subject of a major historical debate, centring on Thomas McKeown's contention that improved nutrition leading to enhanced resistance was primarily responsible for their decline. McKeown acknowledged only a secondary contribution for public health measures, but others have given much greater weight to social intervention.[13]

In his concern to de-mythologise the achievements of medical science, McKeown placed primary emphasis on the importance of economic growth as his preferred alternative explanation for rising standards of health in the population. Primarily, he envisaged this occurring through increased real wages facilitating improved *per capita* nutritional intake. However, it has recently been argued that a diametrically opposite interpretation of the relationship between economic growth, urbanisation and health seems more consistent with the evidence of Britain's economic and demographic history.[14] When the health of the industrial urban workforce is measured either through life tables or by the record of children's height attainments, there are unequivocal signs of serious deterioration during precisely the period of most pronounced *per capita* economic growth and rising real wages: the second and third quarters of the nineteenth century. This deterioration was not truly repaired until the last quarter of the century, or even later where infants are concerned.[15]

The sanitation, hygiene, crowding and poverty diseases were undoubtedly both the chief killers and the principal causes of feeble growth among the survivors: generations of children whose metabolisms were chronically starved of

[13] The principal statement by Thomas McKeown was *The Modern Rise of Population* (London, 1976). The opposing case was made in S. Szreter, 'The importance of social intervention in Britain's mortality decline, c. 1850–1914: a reinterpretation of the role of public health', *Social History of Medicine*, 1 (1988), 1–37; and the ensuing debate: S. Guha, 'The importance of social intervention in England's mortality decline: the evidence reviewed', *Social History of Medicine*, 7 (1994), 89–113; S. Szreter 'Mortality in England in the eighteenth and nineteenth centuries: a reply to Sumit Guha', *Social History of Medicine*, 7 (1994), 269–82. Important historical studies documenting the nature of public health work and preventive medicine in Britain's nineteenth-century cities have included R. Lambert, *Sir John Simon 1816–1904 and English Social Administration* (London, 1963); F. B. Smith, *The People's Health, 1830–1910* (London, 1979); A. S. Wohl, *Endangered Lives* (London, 1983); Hardy, *Epidemic Streets*; J. M. Eyler, *Sir Arthur Newsholme and State Medicine, 1885–1935* (Cambridge, 1997).

[14] S. Szreter, 'Economic growth, disruption, deprivation, disease and death: on the importance of the politics of public health for development', *Population and Development Review*, 23 (1997), 693–728.

[15] S. Szreter and G. Mooney, 'Urbanisation, mortality and the standard of living debate: new estimates of the expectation of life at birth in nineteenth-century British cities', *Ec.HR*, 2nd series, 51 (1998), 84–112; for evidence on heights, see R. Floud, K. Wachter and A. Gregory, *Height, Health and History* (Cambridge, 1990). Note that the most recent research indicates more modest gains in national average real wages during the second quarter of the nineteenth century than previously suggested (though whatever gains there were would have been proportionately greatest among urban industrial, rather than rural workers): C. Feinstein, 'Pessimism perpetuated: real wages and the standard of living in Britain during and after the Industrial Revolution' *Journal of Economic History*, 58 (1998), 625–58.

energy for growth by the necessity of repeatedly waging battles against infectious diseases, often simultaneously sapped of strength because of bouts of diarrhoea in early childhood and heavy work regimes for older children.[16] Why should health have deteriorated so markedly at this particular point in time in Britain's industrial cities? Given that British towns and cities, including even the megalopolis of London, did seem to have been capable of combining both great size and rapid demographic expansion with the preservation or even enhancement of health, both during 'the long eighteenth century' (before the 1820s) and, again, from the 1870s onwards, there is no compelling logic behind the argument that it was simply the rapidity of urban growth or the size or density of settlement *per se* which can be held responsible for a deterioration at this point in time. It has consequently been argued, quite to the contrary of the McKeown thesis, that it was rapid economic growth itself which caused the health problems, by setting in train 'the four Ds' of disruption, deprivation, disease and death.[17]

According to this interpretation, economic growth entailed environmental disruption in Britain's expanding industrial cities, which critically required mechanisms of collective action to solve expensive problems relatively rapidly, in order to avoid undesirable health implications. However, the ideological, administrative, social and political disruption, which was itself integral to the kind of rapid economic growth which Britain was experiencing at this time, produced, instead, for two generations, a political and administrative stalemate where the health investments required by Britain's new towns were concerned. Neither old wealth and patrician authority, which had managed urban growth successfully in the eighteenth century, nor the proliferating factions of new men of commercial means and their various denominational allies could enforce any solution upon each other. *Laissez-faire* and the ratepayers' freedom from local taxes were all that such communities of mutually suspicious factions could agree upon. Furthermore, this principle of 'do-nothingism' was successfully carried from the local into the national political arena under the banner of 'local self-government', with Joshua Toulmin Smith's popular revolt in the early 1850s against Chadwick's attempt to impose from the centre a solution to the towns' health problems.[18] In consequence, in the harsh and deteriorating conditions of ever more densely packed industrial towns, deprivation followed for those

---

[16] On the 'insult accumulation' borne by urban children, who, faced with infant diarrhoea and respiratory dangers, were also subjected in their second year of life to biannual waves of whooping cough and measles, followed up in their third and fourth years by the depredations of scarlet fever and diphtheria, see R. Woods and N. Shelton, *An Atlas of Victorian Mortality*, ch. 8.

[17] Szreter, 'Economic growth'.

[18] J. Prest, *Liberty and Locality* (Oxford, 1990); for the most recent of a sequence of distinguished studies of Edwin Chadwick, see C. Hamlin, *Public Health and Social Justice in the Age of Chadwick* (Cambridge, 1998).

without voice and entitlement, notably, rural in-migrants and the Irish, women and children, and property-less males lacking skills in regular demand. The rough justice of industrial towns chronically lacking infrastructure investment ensured that the third 'D', disease, afflicted all; but death itself undoubtedly fell unequally – mainly upon the poor, rather than upon those few who could afford to escape to the genteel, residential suburb which each city acquired during this period, usually on its upwind, western side.[19]

By placing most weight on the changing political sociology of the nation and its industrial towns as the key to explaining their mortality history, this interpretation can comprehend the apparent anomalies of London's and Bristol's relative salubrity (because in both cases there were substantial incumbent patrician elites where the interests and beliefs of landlords, merchants and men of business had had much more time to come to some understanding and mutual accommodation, not to say intermarriage, to facilitate collective action), and also the fact that the crisis was apparently shared by all fast-growing industrial towns in the second quarter of the century, almost regardless of their size.[20] It can also explain the timing of environmental investments and associated mortality improvements when they eventually belatedly arrived, from the 1870s onwards in the largest industrial cities and somewhat later in smaller centres. For this was the point at which there emerged a bold and imaginative new 'urban patrician' class able to overcome the mid-century stalemate of ratepayer factionalism.

Paradigmatically personified in Joseph Chamberlain, elected mayor of Birmingham for an unprecedented three consecutive terms 1872–5, such leading local men of ambition and civic pride now found themselves able to enlist the political support of a newly enfranchised, non-property-owning working-class electorate (the 'compound' voter) to push through a series of ambitious and expensive measures, despite the continuing concerns of economising ratepayers, the petty bourgeoisie.[21] This ushered in the era of collective, municipal activism known as the 'civic gospel', representing a long-overdue moral crusade to attack the structural causes of urban disamenity. In order to placate the very real concerns of the ratepayers the movement was also necessarily accompanied by

[19] H. J. Dyos and D. A. Reeder, 'Slums and suburbs', in H. J. Dyos and M. Wolff, eds., *The Victorian City* (London, 1973), vol. I, pp. 359–86; R. Dennis, *English Industrial Cities of the Nineteenth Century* (Cambridge, 1984), esp. chs. 3–8.
[20] W. A. Armstrong, 'The trend of mortality in Carlisle between the 1780s and 1840s: a demographic contribution to the standard of living debate', *Ec.HR*, 2nd series, 34 (1981); P. Huck, 'Infant mortality and living standards of English workers during the Industrial Revolution', *Journal of Economic History*, 55 (1995), 528–50.
[21] On Chamberlain and Birmingham's civic gospel, see E. P. Hennock, *Fit and Proper Persons* (London, 1973); P. T. Marsh, *Joseph Chamberlain: Entrepreneur in Politics* (London, 1994), chs. 2–4. On the timing of the expansion of the working-class borough vote, principally 1869–84, see J. Davis and D. Tanner, 'The borough franchise after 1867', *HR*, 69 (1996), 306–27.

significant fiscal innovations: the indirect taxation of 'gas and water socialism' plus the use of massive long-term loans secured on the rates for the major capital projects, such as domiciliary water supply and mains sewering.[22] With the national electorate similarly broadened in a sequence of steps during the last third of the nineteenth century, the leaders of the national parties also found it increasingly in their interests to be seen to be sponsoring social, housing and public health legislation which could be plausibly presented as being in the interests of the respectable working man and his family, even if the interests of the slum dweller remained as yet beyond the pale of political calculation. In consequence, the period 1865–1914 can be characterised by a rising and cumulative momentum, albeit in fits and starts, with uneven geographical enthusiasm and certainly never with the active enthusiasm of the ratepayers, of social legislation and local initiatives and of preventive and public health activism interacting at both local government and national political level. This culminated in the wide-ranging set of social and health measures implemented between 1908 and 1914 by the New Liberal administration in Westminster.

Through this long, protracted set of contingent political developments, the disruption, deprivation, disease and death which proliferated in Britain's shock cities of the 1830s and 1840s was finally addressed. Eventually, this was achieved to such effect that by 1911 it is clear that the big industrial cities had pulled themselves round to equal London in salubrity, and thereafter they ran with London in an upper division of healthy urban areas.[23] Towns with populations of 10,000–100,000 seem to have been much slower to improve, beginning to make significant inroads into their death rates only in the interwar period.[24] By 1950, however, a marked levelling out in urban mortality rates generally had been achieved, with urban Britain, perhaps for the first time, almost as healthy as its rural counterpart.

Integral to this reduction in urban mortality, in epidemiological terms, was the displacement of the acute infectious diseases as leading causes of death, and the emergence of chronic and degenerative disease to prominence in their

[22] On the financial importance of these fiscal innovations for municipal finance, see R. Millward and S. Sheard, 'The urban fiscal problem, 1870–1914: government expenditure and finance in England and Wales', *Ec.HR*, 2nd series, 48 (1995), 501–35; and on some of their origins in Chamberlain's business acumen, see Marsh, *Chamberlain*, chs. 3–4. Of course, as Avner Offer has shown, the urban rate burden on property did subsequently rise substantially but these devices crucially bought time before the burdens became obvious: A Offer, *Property and Politics, 1870–1914* (Cambridge 1981), esp. Parts III and IV.
[23] Crude death rates for Birmingham, for example, fell below the national average from 1921, for Sheffield from 1922.
[24] This is broadly consistent with Millward and Sheard's thesis that, independent of the issue of political will, there was also a hierarchy of borrowing powers among Britain's towns, such that the largest had access to the cheapest loans and therefore tended to undertake expensive improvements and services earlier: Millward and Sheard, 'Urban fiscal problem'.

stead.[25] In this transition, changing patterns of urban mortality played a critical part.[26] Measles was especially deadly in urban areas: in 1881–90, the twenty-eight great towns averaged 628 measles deaths per million population compared to 496 in the fifty large towns. Between 1871 and 1890, Lancashire (the most highly urbanised county in Britain), London and (oddly) Monmouthshire in that order, registered the greatest number of deaths from the disease, whether accounted by total population or by that under the age of five years.[27] Within towns and cities, however, levels often varied with locality: in Birmingham, for example, which had a clearly zoned social geography, death rates from both measles and whooping cough being highest in the poor inner-city wards, lower in the middle band, and lowest of all in the well-to-do suburbs of the city's outer ring, in a pattern which held good until the Second World War.[28] From the late 1880s, diphtheria was principally a killer only in towns, while scarlet fever and whooping cough followed similar patterns. Tuberculosis, however, had both a very varied regional pattern, and a more muted tendency to be more fatal in urban areas.[29]

For the most part, death rates from the infectious diseases of childhood manifested a clear pattern of increase from South to North across the country as a whole.[30] In this they were similar to infant and maternal mortality, and to a number of other diseases, which repeated the classic pattern of the North/South divide, apparently already well established by 1840.[31] Infant mortality, another standard predictor of social and sanitary conditions,[32] was well known to be much higher in towns than in rural areas, as well as being higher north of a line drawn from the Wash to the Bristol Channel, and especially in Wales.[33] Even within the urban hierarchy, unexpected variations in infant mortality were to be found between different types of town: Leicester and Preston, for example, were

---

[25] This has been a general pattern in the developed world: A. R. Omran, 'The epidemiological transition: a theory of the epidemiology of population change', *Millbank Memorial Fund Quarterly*, 49 (1971), 516; S. Kunitz, 'Speculations on the European mortality decline', *Ec.HR*, 2nd series, 36 (1983), 349–64.   [26] See Hardy, *Epidemic streets*, chs. 1, 2.

[27] Supplement to the Registrar General's 55th Annual Report, PP 1895 XXIII part 1, p. xlviii.

[28] MOAR, Birmingham, 1901–39.

[29] Gillian Cronje, 'Tuberculosis and mortality decline in England and Wales, 1851–1910', in Robert Woods and John Woodward, eds., *Urban Disease and Mortality in Nineteenth-Century England* (London, 1984); and see below, n. 89.   [30] RGSR, 1931, pp. 38–9.

[31] Suggestive research is presented in Paul Huck, 'Infant mortality in nine industrial parishes in northern England, 1813–1836', *Population Studies*, 48 (1994), 512–26. See also S. Szreter and E. Garrett, 'Reproduction, compositional demography and economic growth; family planning in England long before the fertility decline', *Population and Development Review*, 26 (2000), 45–80.

[32] See G. Mooney, 'Did London pass the "sanitary test"? Seasonal infant mortality in London, 1870–1914', *Journal of Historical Geography*, 20 (1994), 158–74.

[33] Supplement to the Registrar General's 75th Annual Report, PP 1914–16 VIII, p. xxxviii.

neither in the first rank of English cities, but together they topped the infant mortality league in the years up to 1910.[34]

The nature of local circumstances determining levels of infant mortality undoubtedly varied: unhygienic conditions, maternal health and employment, and nutrition, as well as wider environmental influences such as topography and the weather, all played a part. It is well known that national levels of infant mortality did not begin to fall until 1901, although a trend decline beneath the peaks of epidemic diarrhoea has been detected from the 1870s.[35] When the levels did begin to fall, they did so with a remarkable degree of uniformity in different areas, so that indefinable national and even international factors seem to have been at work. Local studies may in future be more suggestive of causes than national patterns. East London's Jewish community achieved infant mortality levels well below those for the rest of London by 1895, and ahead of the national decline, since Jewish domestic practices involved high standards of care and hygiene.[36] A recent study of four London boroughs has shown that poor social and economic conditions were a primary determinant of high infant mortality, and that the pace and degree of infant mortality decline after 1901 varied depending on both local social and economic conditions and on medical and welfare provision.[37]

The three principal causes of infant mortality before 1914 were diarrhoea and gastro-enteritis, bronchitis and pneumonia, and prematurity. While prematurity proved harder to shift, levels of both diarrhoea and respiratory disease fell in the early decades of the twentieth century: diarrhoea rates nationally had halved their 1896–1900 levels by 1921–5, respiratory disease had similarly fallen by 1931–5.[38] In the same period, urban/rural differences narrowed, but did not disappear (Table 20.1). Diarrhoea and respiratory disease were largely urban diseases for infants, as was transmitted syphilis, whereas prematurity was scarcely influenced by urbanisation at all.[39] While immaturity remained an important contributor to neonatal deaths (first four weeks of life) throughout the period, being mentioned on some 50 per cent of neonatal death certificates as late as 1950, the 'density' differences shown by the categories used in Table 20.1 in the breakdown of neonatal mortality were significant.[40]

From at least 1880, London had particularly low rates of neonatal death, only bettered by the county boroughs and small towns of southern England, and this was a characteristic it shared with some other cities, notably Liverpool. On the first day of life, indeed, there was little density distinction in the level of infant deaths, but after the first day excess mortality in the towns was rapidly established

[34] N. Williams and G. Mooney, 'Infant mortality in "an age of great cities"', *Continuity and Change*, 9 (1994), 191–6.   [35] Woods, Watterson and Woodward, 'Rapid infant mortality decline'.

[36] L. Marks, *Model Mothers* (Oxford, 1994), p. 49.

[37] L. Marks, *Metropolitan Maternity* (Amsterdam and Atlanta, 1996), chs. 3, 5.

[38] RGSR, 1948–9, p. 33.   [39] *Ibid.*, 1923, pp. 21, 30.   [40] *Ibid.*, 1950, p. 4.

Table 20.1 *Average infant mortality rates per 1,000 births 1911–1945*

	England and Wales	London	County boroughs	Urban districts	Rural districts
1911–14	110	108	125	107	90
1931–5	62	63	71	60	55
1943–5	47	48	54	46	41

Source: RGSR, 1948–9, p. 36.

and continued through the first year of life. None the less, the excess mortality of the North/South divide was greater than that of the county boroughs over the rural districts, and was strongly marked on the first day of life. The northern excess was both greater and more uniform than the urban, testifying to the importance of factors other than those predicted by town life *per se*, in particular the degree of industrial activity, and the nature and extent of sanitary provision.[41] It was a distribution maintained throughout the period.[42]

Refinements in qualitative and quantitative analysis of evidence relating to infant mortality – and other mortalities – seem likely to enhance understanding of these patterns. Recent research indicates that the nature of individual urban economies was a key factor determining levels of infant mortality, rather than size or density. Infant and other death rates were highest in industrialised towns, while both suburban areas and non-industrial towns were far healthier. Whereas infant mortality rates remained notoriously high in Leicester in the later nineteenth century, for example, rates in Blaby, immediately south of the city, declined. In the market town of Banbury, similarly, infant mortality fell more or less continuously between 1850 and 1900.[43] Thus a growing literature points to industrial cities rather than cities *per se* as being associated with high mortalities.[44]

In sharp contrast to declining levels of infant mortality after 1901, levels of maternal deaths did not change for the better until 1937, and indeed rose for a

[41] E. Garrett, A. Reid, K. Schurer and S. Szreter, *Changing Family Size in England and Wales: Place, Class and Demography in England and Wales, 1891–1911* (Cambridge, forthcoming); John M. Eyler, *Sir Arthur Newsholme and State Medicine, 1880–1935* (Cambridge, 1997), pp. 297–310.

[42] RGSR, 1923, pp. 12–14; 1946, p. 24.

[43] N. Williams and C. Galley, 'Urban–rural differentials in infant mortality in Victorian England', *Population Studies*, 49 (1995), 407.

[44] Besides the article cited in the previous footnote, see P. Watterson, 'The role of the environment in the decline of infant mortality: an analysis of the 1911 census of England and Wales', *Journal of Biosocial Science*, 18 (1986), 457–70; Woods, Watterson and Woodward, 'Rapid infant mortality decline', Part I, 343–66; *ibid.*, Part II, 113–32; N. Williams, 'Death in its season: class, environment and the mortality of infants in nineteenth-century Sheffield', *Social History of Medicine*, 5 (1992), 71–94; Williams and Mooney, 'Infant mortality', 185–212; Garrett, Reid, Schurer and Szreter, *Population Change in Context*, chs. 4 and 6.

time.[45] As with infant deaths, there was a pronounced North/South divide in their distribution. John Tatham noted the regional divide for the decade 1881–90, recording that all the fourteen counties with rates in excess of the national average of 4.73 per 1,000 births lay north of a line drawn from the Humber to the Severn, while every one of the twenty-eight counties south-east of the line had below average rates.[46] This distribution had, however, little to do with urbanisation.[47] Indeed, the large cities, which possessed organised maternity services and relatively effective obstetric care tended to have lower rates of mortality than other urban areas, in a pattern that remained broadly consistent between the 1880s and the 1930s.[48] London, for example, in the years 1891–1910, consistently had the lowest death rates from causes other than puerperal sepsis, and in the twentieth century remained well ahead of other urban areas in its favourable maternal death rates.[49] The aggregate experience of a city could, however, mask significant local variations: in early twentieth-century London, marked differences in levels of maternal mortality between boroughs reflected variations in the local provision of maternity care.[50] Although maternal death rates plummeted following the introduction of the sulphonamide drugs in 1936, and again following that of penicillin, differential rates between the different density categories remained, reflecting the greater accessibility of treatment in urban areas.[51] Meanwhile, the extension of blood transfusion techniques after 1940 reduced the dangers of shock and haemorrhage in childbirth, and contributed to further lowering of maternal death rates. By 1950, maternal mortality rates in rural areas were more than twice those of London (Table 20.2).

It was not until after the First World War that the changing age structure of Britain's urban population began to direct concern towards mortality patterns among the old. In 1911, the over seventies constituted under 3 per cent of the population of England and Wales, by 1921 they had reached 3.4 per cent and by 1931, 4.3 per cent. Partly as a reflection of the growing importance of these deaths, certification of deaths in old age began to become more precise, so that the number of deaths certified simply as from 'old age' was greatly reduced. Deaths attributed to bronchitis in this age group also fell; in partial compensation the attributions to heart disease and cancer rose.[52] The implications of this

---

[45] For the changing pattern of maternal mortality see Irvine Loudon, *Death in Childbirth* (Oxford, 1992), chs. 14, 15.

[46] Supplement to the Registrar General's 55th Annual Report, PP 1895 xxiiii part i, p. lii. For the regional variations see also Loudon, *Death in Childbirth*, pp. 251–3.

[47] Supplement to the Registrar General's 75th Annual Report, PP 1914–16 viii, pp. xci–xciii.

[48] Loudon, *Death in Childbirth*, p. 252.

[49] Supplement to the Registrar General's 75th Annual Report, PP 1914–16 viii, p. cciii.

[50] Marks, *Metropolitan Maternity*, chs. 3, 6.

[51] RGSR, 1947, p. 221. For the impact of the sulphonamides see Irvine Loudon, 'Puerperal fever, the streptococcus and the sulphonamides 1911–1945', *British Medical Journal*, 2 (1987), 485–9.

[52] *Ibid.*, 1935, pp. 41–2.

Table 20.2 *Maternal mortality per 1,000 live births according to urban density*
1921–1949

	London	County boroughs	Urban districts	Rural districts	England and Wales
1921–5					
Sepsis	1.36	1.61	1.29	1.25	1.40
Other causes	1.63	2.42	2.69	2.84	2.50
Total	2.99	4.03	3.98	4.09	3.90
1931–5					
Sepsis	1.50	1.69	1.77	1.82	1.76
Other causes	1.66	1.94	2.48	3.01	2.54
Total	3.16	3.63	4.25	4.83	4.30
1948–9					
Total[a]	0.48	0.92	1.07	1.23	0.99

[a]Deaths per 1,000 live and still births.
Source: RGSR, 1921–39.

changing age structure for urban mortality patterns with respect to cause of death are still obscure; as the medical officer for Birmingham noted in 1931, it was difficult to know how much the apparent increases in heart disease and cancer were due to better diagnosis and how much to the increase in the numbers of elderly people.[53] Differing age structures in different types of town, and within towns, also existed. Two of the great cities, for example, Glasgow and Birmingham, the one noted for poverty and deprivation, the other for relative prosperity and with a reputation for healthiness, both contained below average populations of the elderly between 1901 and 1951 (Table 20.3). This may have been a common feature of great city populations (Table 20.4). Furthermore, there were significant differences in survival rates between the poorer and wealthier quarters of Birmingham: in 1931, 34.7 per cent of deaths in the inner wards occurred at ages over sixty-five; in the more salubrious outer suburbs, the percentage was 41.8.[54]

Occupational structure was another factor which helped to differentiate the mortality experiences of individual towns and cities, and the local effects of occupation and industrial environment were very various. During the course of the nineteenth century, legislation went some way to reducing the prevalence of some of the worst industrial diseases, such as Sheffield knife grinders' lung, or the phossy jaw endured by girls working in the match industry.[55] But other

[53] MOAR, Birmingham, 1931, p. 13.   [54] *Ibid.*, p. 12.   [55] See Wohl, *Endangered Lives*, ch. 10.

Table 20.3 *Populations aged over sixty-five, percentage of total population, Birmingham, Glasgow and England and Wales 1901–1951*

	1901	1921	1931	1951
Birmingham	3.3	4.7	—	9.2
Glasgow	3.1	—	5.6	8.6
England and Wales	4.7	6.1	7.4	10.9

Sources: MOAR, Birmingham and Glasgow.

industrial factors continued to affect urban mortality patterns, notably, for example, the pall of smoke from industry and from domestic fires which over-hung the northern industrial towns, and which was associated with excess rates of respiratory illness, and with endemic rickets among poorly nourished small children.[56] In Oldham, for example, it was estimated that 960 tons of soot were deposited per square mile within the city area in the year 1914–15, with conse-quences for the health and welfare of local people.[57] Such environmental con-sequences were at least in part responsible for the generally high levels of mortality in mining communities, even if not among working miners them-selves.[58] Working conditions in factories were a further consideration, not just for the textile towns of the North, but in other industries. The boot and shoe factories of Leicester and Northampton, for example, were known to contrib-ute to increased rates of respiratory tuberculosis in those towns.[59]

A wide variety of factors thus contributed to the construction both of a town's individual mortality experience and to its placing within any general patterns of urban mortality. A comparison of the mortality patterns of four county boroughs (Bolton, Northampton, Reading and Warrington) in the years 1911–13 illus-trated the complexity of the determinants of mortality levels in these compar-ably sized towns. There was, for example, no close relationship between mortality and real wage levels: Reading, with 23 per cent of working-class fam-ilies in poverty had less mortality at every age of life than the other three towns, whose poverty ratings stood at 8 per cent (Bolton and Northampton) and 13 per cent (Warrington). The two northern towns had the worst mortalities overall, with little to chose between them, and also had the most overcrowded dwell-ings. Yet overcrowding was by no means the principal determinant of mortality

---

[56] Domestic smoke was a far from inconsiderable factor in nineteenth-century air pollution. It was, for example, very largely the cause of the notorious London fogs of the period. For its connec-tion with rickets see A. Hardy, 'Rickets and the rest: childcare, diet and the infectious children's diseases', *Social History of Medicine*, 5 (1992), 389–412.

[57] Leonard Hill and Argyll Campbell, *Health and Environment* (London, 1931), pp. 2, 71–5.

[58] Supplement to the Registrar General's 75th Annual Report, PP 1914–16 VIII, p. xxxii.

[59] Major Greenwood, 'The influence of industrial employment on general health', *British Medical Journal*, 1 (1922), 753.

Table 20.4 *Estimated mean populations aged over sixty-five in selected cities 1921–1930, percentage of total population*

Greater London	6.5	Stoke	4.3
Bethnal Green	3.3	Swansea	5.2
Bolton	5.6	York	6.6

Source: RGSR, 1931, table 4.

by the 1910s. Housing conditions in Northampton, where 8.7 per cent of working-class houses were overcrowded, were considerably better than those of Reading (13.5 per cent overcrowded), yet it was only in the age group twenty-five to forty-five that Northampton's death rates approached parity with those of Reading.[60] Bolton and Warrington, like the rest of the North-West, suffered high death rates from pneumonia. Their death rates from respiratory tuberculosis, however, were on a par with those of Reading at ages up to twenty-five; it was only at ages forty-five to sixty-five that their tuberculosis rates became markedly worse than those of the other two towns. Taken in all, this interurban comparison did not reveal, in its author's words, 'some one industrial factor in the northern towns which destroys life'.[61]

Against this background, it is unsurprising that relatively little is known of the impact of war and economic depression in the twentieth century on specifically urban mortality patterns. Once again, historical studies have tended to focus on overall experience at the national levels with selected local examples, and detailed studies of the local and comparative impact of these events remain a future research undertaking.[62] The likelihood is that war, especially the First World War when food rationing was in its infancy, had some differential impact on local civilian death rates depending on the age structure of the local population and the type of employment available in different urban areas, yet evidence on this subject needs to be treated with caution. The issue of the increased death rates for respiratory tuberculosis during the First World War, for example, which has provoked controversy over the respective roles of housing and nutrition in its genesis, may yet prove to be more complex when investigated at local level, or within the general pattern of urban mortality experience.[63] In Glasgow, for instance, tuberculosis death rates continued to fall during the First World War from a relative peak in 1915, while in Scotland as a whole rates remained raised

---

[60] *Ibid.*, p. 711.   [61] *Ibid.*, p. 712.

[62] In the current literature see J. M. Winter, *The Great War and the British People* (London and Basingstoke, 1986); Linda Bryder, 'The First World War: healthy or hungry?', *History Workshop Journal*, 24 (1987), 141–57; H. Jones, *Health and Society in Twentieth-Century Britain* (London, 1994); and references cited below in nn. 61 and 66.   [63] See Bryder, 'First World War'.

for the duration of the war. The city suffered a relatively much greater and more sustained rise in tuberculosis rates during the Second World War, which lasted from 1940 through to 1948. In 1950, tuberculosis notification rates in Glasgow were still 48 per cent above their pre-war average.[64] In Birmingham, the tuberculosis death rates remained in line with pre-war figures during the First World War, rising a little in 1917, and only markedly in 1918, the year of the Spanish influenza. But both Birmingham and Glasgow, like Scotland and England and Wales, experienced a sharp fall in registered tuberculosis deaths in 1919.[65] During the Second World War, Birmingham's tuberculosis experience was again not fully consistent with the national pattern. The city's tuberculosis death rate stood at 71–2 per 100,000 population between 1934 and 1938, but rates rose to 77 in 1939, 1940 and 1942, with a peak of 81 in 1941, before resuming the decline at pre-war level in 1943. In neither war, therefore, did these two sample cities' respective experiences with tuberculosis meet the norm as set by national figures (that is, increases in the death rate between 1914 and 1916, and in the first years, 1940–2, of the Second World War).[66]

Urban mortality experience during the post-war depression and in the 1930s is likely to have been equally various and dependent on local circumstances. If tuberculosis rates are taken as some index of social well-being, it may be possible to compare the effects of depression on different cities. Glasgow's tuberculosis rates, for example, fell after the First World War until 1926, and thereafter fluctuated at around 80 per 100,000 before rising sharply to over 100 in 1940. In Birmingham, where a mixed industrial economy protected the city from the worst of the Depression, the rates remained relatively stable between 1919 and 1933, falling sharply in 1934.[67] In these years, moreover, death rates in the poorest wards moved much closer to the average of the city as a whole, although serious differences between them remained.[68]

In fact, discrepancies in urban experience in the interwar period generated heated debates among contemporaries, and have subsequently exercised historians, on issues of poverty, housing and ill-health.[69] Infant mortality continued to vary considerably between towns and within them, while reductions in

---

[64] MOAR, Glasgow, 1950, p. 9. For Glasgow's tuberculosis experience, see Neil McFarlane, 'Hospitals, housing and tuberculosis in Glasgow, 1911–51', *Social History of Medicine*, 2 (1989), 59–85.

[65] The influenza epidemic is undoubtedly a complicating factor in the picture; government disability allowance policies in wartime may also have been influential: see MOAR, Northampton, 1924, p. 28. On government policy, see S. M. Tomkins, 'The failure of expertise: public health policy in Britain during the 1918–19 influenza epidemic', *Social History of Medicine*, 5 (1992), 435–54. [66] Winter, *The Great War*, p. 139. [67] MOAR, Birmingham, 1950, p. 24.

[68] *Ibid.*, 1931, p. 11.

[69] See Charles Webster, 'Healthy or hungry thirties?', *History Workshop Journal*, 13 (1982), 110–29; Charles Webster, 'Health, welfare and unemployment during the Depression', *P&P*, 109 (1985), 204–30; John Stevenson and Chris Cook, *Britain in the Depression*, 2nd edn (London and New York, 1994), ch. 3.

tuberculosis mortality were smaller in depressed areas of the country than in the more prosperous areas; in 1931–5, for example, the tuberculosis death rate for women aged fifteen to thirty-five was more than twice as high as the national average in Gateshead, South Shields and Merthyr Tydfil.[70] By 1950, these cities still had among the highest tuberculosis death rates in the country for both men and women, although Bootle, Lancashire, retained a historic pre-eminence in the tuberculosis league, with death rates in 1950 of 942 per million living for men and 721 for women compared with its nearest rivals, Tynemouth (916 for males) and Merthyr (625 for females).[71]

Tuberculosis remained a problem in several urban areas into the 1950s, notably in the Tyneside and Merseyside conurbations, in Walsall, West Bromwich and Smethwick in the Black Country of the West Midlands, and in all urban areas of Wales.[72] While housing problems, poverty and employment are all likely to have played a part in determining relative prevalence, other factors could be considered. For some years after the end of the war, rising numbers of tuberculosis deaths among elderly men in Greater London caused concern. Among contemporary explanations offered were that these men had borne the stress of two world wars, and that the reactivation of early infection was critical in killing them. In 1947, their death rate was especially striking – and the Registrar General speculated that it had been brought about by the stress of life in the underground bomb shelters during the war. Death rates from tuberculosis among women by contrast, maintained a steady decrease between 1931 and 1947.[73]

One notable change in urban mortality patterns which was of less demographic than social consequence was the altering distribution of place of death within urban areas: between 1840 and 1950, people increasingly died not at home, but in institutions. During the nineteenth century old people especially, but after *c.* 1870 also young children, increasingly began to die in hospital. The introduction of the New Poor Law in 1834, with its 'less eligibility' principle, followed by the disassociation of the poor law infirmaries from the workhouses in 1867, meant that growing numbers of the elderly and chronic sick poor resorted to the infirmaries as debility and poverty overtook them. Meanwhile, the introduction of isolation hospitals for infectious disease cases after 1870 meant that more children died away from home. In London as a whole, 16 per cent of deaths occurred in institutions in 1861, but this had reached nearly 30 per cent by 1901. In the different registration districts, increases might be even more striking: the proportion of institutional deaths rose from 19 to 63 per cent in the Strand district between 1861 and 1901, while in the City it rose from 23 to 66 per cent.[74] This pattern replicated itself in provincial towns and cities,

---

[70] Stevenson and Cook, *Depression*, pp. 51, 55.   [71] RGSR, 1951, p. 121.   [72] *Ibid.*
[73] *Ibid.*, 1948–9, p. 97.   [74] Williams and Mooney, 'Infant mortality', 188–9.

although the greater level of hospital provision in the latter probably accelerated local trends. In Northampton, deaths in institutions rose from 30 per cent of all deaths in the 1920s to nearly 50 per cent by 1939; in Birmingham they were 40 per cent in 1925, but over 50 per cent by the mid-1930s.[75]

The rising proportion of elderly people in the population, and to a much lesser degree rising accident rates with the increasing popularity of the motor car, contributed substantially to this trend, especially as death rates for the infectious diseases of childhood declined. In mid-1920s Birmingham, for example, 23 per cent of all deaths occurred in poor law institutions, a mere 2.8 per cent in 'publicly provided Fever Hospitals, etc.'.[76] The transfer of many poor law infirmaries into the municipal sector following the Local Government Act 1929 accelerated this trend. City public health departments increasingly used the municipal hospitals as a care facility for elderly people: after the transfer of the hospitals to the National Health Service in 1948, medical officers complained about the growing difficulty of obtaining hospital admission for chronic elderly patients.[77] The pressures, however, remained. With post-war housing shortages and a growing reluctance among families to care for elderly relatives within their own homes, institutional care met a persistent social problem.[78]

By the interwar period, significant changes in the pattern of causes of death were also emerging. The reduction in importance of the acute infections as causes of death, together with the ageing of the population, began to tilt the balance of causation towards long-term and degenerative diseases. The detailed geography of this newly emerging shift in the pattern of death remains obscure, but it seems likely that it began in the countryside, where life expectancies had long been higher. Many aspects of this transition are complicated by problems of diagnosis and changing medical fashion. For instance, the rise in deaths from late-onset diabetes which began in the later nineteenth century in part reflected a new medical awareness of the condition, while the fact that the disease appeared to be more frequent in towns could be a result of that awareness.[79] None the less, it is significant that death rates from late-onset diabetes fell during the First World War, and rose again after 1918: the condition is associated with obesity and a sedentary life style, and rising incidence indicates growing levels of consumption which were temporarily suspended by the relative deprivation of the war years.[80] The regional and density variations in this pattern are unclear.

The distribution of cancer deaths is more readily accessible, since medical

[75] See MOAR.   [76] MOAR, Birmingham, 1925, p. 20.   [77] *Ibid.*, Glasgow, 1951, p. 10.
[78] *Ibid.*, Birmingham, 1948–9, p. 14. For the changing balance of emphasis on family and community care see J. Lewis, 'Family provision of health and welfare in the mixed economy of care in the late nineteenth and twentieth centuries', *Social History of Medicine*, 8 (1995), 1–16.
[79] Supplement to the Registrar General's 65th Annual Report, PP 1905 XVIII, p. cii. See also Anne Hardy, 'Death is the cure of all diseases: using the General Register Office Cause of Death statistics for 1837–1920', *Social History of Medicine*, 7 (1994), 485–6.   [80] RGSR, 1931, p. 70.

observers soon suspected environmental influences operating on that distribution. Stomach cancer, for example, was by the 1940s seen to be heavily influenced by environmental factors, operating especially in the northern industrial towns, and producing wide differences between rates in different towns. Between 1921 and 1939, Bootle, Birkenhead, Oldham and Swansea were among the top eight county boroughs for stomach cancer among both men and women (crude mortality rate (CMR) averages between 20 and 40 per cent), while Bournemouth, Canterbury and Burton-on-Trent had among the lowest rates for both men and women in a group of eleven low-rate towns (CMR ranging from 25 to 45 per cent below the mean).[81] Cancer of the uterus, meanwhile (like breast cancer known to be correlated with fat consumption), showed marked disparities between density groups at ages forty-five to sixty-four: in 1947 the rates stood at 455 per million for the county boroughs, 400 for the urban districts, 338 for Greater London and 321 in the rural districts.[82] Death rates for the respiratory cancers showed an even clearer link to urban density for both sexes between 1940 and 1949, from a maximum in Greater London to a minimum in the rural districts, though always greatly higher for men.[83]

While the increase of deaths from respiratory cancer in the twentieth century was recognised to be real, rising absolute mortalities from peptic ulcer, coronary heart disease, arterio-sclerosis and cancer generally reflected the shifting age structure of the urban population.[84] In 1950, the medical officer for Birmingham noted that if corrected for age, female cancer mortality in the city had fallen in the twentieth century, and the rise in male deaths was only small. Only the 'undue' rises in the cancers of the lung and prostate stood out as separable from improvements in diagnosis.[85]

Between 1840 and 1950 Britain experienced an epidemiological transition from a high-mortality regime dominated by infant death and infectious disease to a low-mortality one, where older adult and chronic disease predominated. However, the timing of the transition may well have been rather uneven. As described above the most recent research confirms contemporaries' perceptions of a severe deterioration in industrial towns and cities in the 1830s and 1840s. Thereafter, William Farr recorded some improvement in crude mortality rates in the later 1850s in many towns.[86] However, the new life tables constructed for the largest British cities demonstrate that although the 1850s may have brought alleviation of the atrocious levels of mortality prevailing in the 1830s and 1840s, there was no further improvement between the 1850s and 1860s. It was only thereafter, during the last three decades of the century, that increases in life expectancy at birth of between two and eight years were finally registered in all

[81] *Ibid.*, 1947, p. 169.   [82] *Ibid.*   [83] *Ibid.*, 1948–9, p. 160.   [84] *Ibid.*, p. 158.
[85] MOAR, Birmingham, 1950, p. 43.
[86] Supplement to the Registrar General's 25th Annual report, PP 1865 XIII, pp. 28–33.

Table 20.5 *Expectation of life at birth in selected
cities in England and Wales 1861–1901*

Cities	1861–70	1891–1901
London	38	44
Manchester	31	38
Liverpool	30	38
Birmingham	37	42
Bristol	40	47
Salford	35	37
Hull	38	44
Portsmouth	42	46
Bolton	37	42
Brighton	41	47
Sunderland	39	41
Cardiff	41	45
Norwich	40	47
Preston	35	39

Source: illustrative selection from S. Szreter and G.
Mooney, 'Urbanisation, mortality and the standard of
living debate: new estimates of the expectation of life
at birth in nineteenth-century British cities', *Ec.HR*,
2nd series, 51 (1998), tables 1, 8.

the large cities, taking them into historic new territory, above forty years in
several places (Table 20.5).[87]

A 1930 survey of mortality patterns in William Farr's healthy (rural) districts
between 1851 and 1925 identified the periods of greatest improvement in mortality for both the healthy districts and for England and Wales as a whole as the
years 1881–90 and 1901–25.[88] Investigations by Thomas McKeown and his colleagues also indicated the eighth decade of the nineteenth century and the first
two decades of the twentieth as periods of considerable significance for mortality in England and Wales.[89] Studies of the experiences of individual cities tend
to confirm this picture for the nineteenth century.[90]

[87] See Szreter and Mooney, 'Urbanisation'.
[88] E. Lewis-Faning, 'A survey of the mortality of Dr Farr's 63 healthy districts of England and Wales
during the period 1851 to 1925', *Journal of Hygiene*, 30 (1930), 152.
[89] T. McKeown and R. G. Record, 'Reasons for the decline of mortality in England and Wales
during the nineteenth century', *Population Studies*, 16 (1962), 117–18; T. McKeown, R. G.
Record and R. D. Turner, 'An interpretation of the decline of mortality in England and Wales
during the twentieth century', *Population Studies*, 29 (1975), 392–3.
[90] See, for example, Barbara Thompson, 'Infant mortality in nineteenth-century Bradford', in Woods
and Woodward, eds., *Urban Disease*, p. 136; Robert Woods, 'Mortality and sanitary conditions in
late nineteenth-century Birmingham', in Woods and Woodward, eds., *Urban Disease*, p. 185.

The detailed timing and cause of death geography of Britain's changing urban mortality patterns in the crucial century between 1840 and 1950 is only now beginning to be researched.[91] Nevertheless, a pattern of significant variations in urban mortality experience is clearly visible beneath the national picture which does not support either McKeown's nutritional hypothesis or the more general assumption that economic growth straightforwardly leads to improved health.[92] Recent research points to the significance of both public health interventions and local patterns of self-help and welfare provision in determining such local variations.[93] The research projects currently nearing completion will extend our understanding of the processes at work in Britain's epidemiological transition, but the agenda on the importance of social intervention and political will in activating Britain's mortality decline remains open for further exploration.[94]

(iii) FERTILITY AND NUPTIALITY

In addressing the history of urban fertility in the period 1840–1950, the predominant feature was the pronounced secular decline in marital fertility which all sections of British society, rich and poor, Anglican and nonconformist, Welsh, English, Scots and Irish, experienced at some point after the 1860s.[95] Illegitimate

---

[91] Woods and Shelton, *An Atlas of Victorian Mortality.*

[92] McKeown's argument would predict that the urban workers with their higher real wages and greater access to a more varied food supply should have been leading a decline in mortality from the mid-nineteenth century at the latest. This was not the case, however. As Szreter, 'Social intervention', 11–14, pointed out, McKeown's thesis was particularly dependent on the decline in TB as providing the principal evidence in favour of the thesis that nutritional improvements due to rising living standards were the primary source of health improvements in the nineteenth century. It is therefore significant that Woods and Shelton have concluded from their recent exploration of the detailed geography of pulmonary tuberculosis that it no longer makes sense to see improvements in living standards as a major candidate in accounting for the decline in TB because they could find no sensible pattern in the geography of its relative incidence in Britain's 600 or so registration districts throughout each decade of the second half of the nineteenth century, in terms of an urban–rural, wealthy–poor differential: Woods and Shelton, *An Atlas of Victorian Mortality,* ch. 8, esp. p. 114.

[93] See Hardy, *Epidemic Streets;* Eyler, *Sir Arthur Newsholme;* Marks, *Metropolitan Maternity;* James C. Riley, *Sick Not Dead* (Baltimore and London, 1997).

[94] Szreter, 'Social intervention'; Hardy, *Epidemic Streets;* C. Nathanson, 'Disease prevention as social change: toward a theory of public health', *Population and Development Review,* 22 (1996), 609–37; Szreter, 'Economic growth'. Current research projects are moving this agenda forward, as described in Bill Luckin and Graham Mooney, 'Urban history and historical epidemiology: the case of London, 1860–1920', *UH,* 24 (1997), 37–55; Millward and Sheard, 'Urban fiscal problem', 501–35; F. Bell and R. Millward, 'Public health expenditures and mortality in England and Wales, 1870–1914' *Continuity and Change* 13 (1998), 1–29.

[95] For England and Wales the principal source is: census of 1911, vol. XIII, *Fertility of Marriage Report (FMR), Part 1,* Cd 8678 PP 1917–18 XXXV; *Fertility of Marriage Report, Part 2,* Cd 8491, was published separately (not as a Parliamentary Paper) by HMSO in 1923. See also *Census of Scotland 1911,* vol. III, Section F (PP 1914 XLIV); *Census of Ireland 1911,* General Report, section XIV (PP 1912–13 CXVIII). There are indications of slightly lower marital fertility already in the 1860s and perhaps the 1850s among some sections of urban society, such as certain professionals and those

fertility also fell dramatically at the same time. However, contrary to popular pre-conceptions, even in London illegitimacy does not seem to have played a particularly central or leading role in the history of specifically urban fertility during the period 1840–1950. In an international, comparative perspective illegitimate fertility was generally remarkably low throughout the British Isles, including Ireland.[96] It was only relatively high (for Britain) in exclusively rural areas: the counties of East Anglia, the Welsh borders, Yorkshire (but not the West Riding) and, especially, in the north-east and south-west Scottish counties (i.e. excluding Glasgow and Edinburgh).[97]

As officially stated in the Report of the Royal Commission on Population of 1944–9, it has always been acknowledged that the rapidly falling birth rate must have been in some sense associated with the expansion of urban society, if for no better reason than that the well-established demographic findings from official sources show that agricultural labourers, as a category of the workforce, along with the most rural of counties, continued to exhibit relatively high fertility rates in Edwardian England and Wales even into the interwar years.[98] Nevertheless, compared with the virtually obsessive attention that has been devoted over many decades to debating the meaning of putative social class differentials in fertility change, there has been remarkably little systematic research aimed at elucidating whether towns and cities may have exhibited distinct fertility regimes.[99] However, both of the two most recent research studies of falling fertility in England and Wales have concluded by pointing towards the probable significance of an individual urban community's socio-economic, political and cultural character and history as a major and distinctive influence.[100] But neither these two, nor any other study of England and Wales, has had access to a sufficient quantity of high-quality data on the individual families living in different towns to be able to pursue these hypotheses with definitive rigour. It seems unlikely that this will be possible before the year 2012, when all the

---

Footnote 95 (cont.)

of private means and in the mill towns of the textiles industry: *FMR, Pt 2*, pp. cxi–cxiii; J. A. Banks, *Victorian Values, Secularism and the Size of Families* (London, 1981), p. 40. There are also signs that some southern rural populations may have controlled fertility when times were hard after the enactment of the New Poor Law in 1834: B. Reay, 'Before the transition: fertility in English villages 1800–1880', *Continuity and Change*, 9 (1994), 91–120.

[96] E. Shorter, J. Knodel and E. van de Walle, 'The decline of non-marital fertility in Europe, 1880–1940', *Population Studies*, 25 (1971), 375–93.

[97] M. S. Teitelbaum, *The British Fertility Decline: Demographic Transition in the Crucible of the Industrial Revolution* (Princeton, 1984) p. 151, table 6.10a; M. Flinn *et al.*, *Scottish Population History from the 17th Century to the 1930s* (Cambridge, 1977), pp. 349–67.

[98] *Report of the Royal Commission on Population*, Cmd 7695 (PP 1948–9 XIX), para. 96.

[99] For an extended critique of the intellectually impoverishing limitations of the class-differential model of fertility decline, see S. Szreter, *Fertility, Class and Gender in Britain, 1860–1940* (Cambridge, 1996), *passim*.

[100] *Ibid.*, pp. 546–58; Garrett, Reid, Schurer and Szreter, *Changing Family Size*, chs. 4–7.

original detailed evidence from the 1911 fertility census of Great Britain will finally become publicly available for academic research.

Nevertheless, there is a certain amount of relevant detailed information currently available on the differential fertility and nuptiality characteristics of towns in England and Wales during this period of falling fertility. This comes from a large table compiled by T. H. C. Stevenson, the General Register Office's (GRO) chief medical statistician who was the moving force behind the 1911 census's fertility inquiry. This table shows the average number of children ever born and surviving to all married couples, where the wife was still under age forty-five in 1911, in each county borough and each urban district in England and Wales, including London's boroughs.[101] Table 20.6 is derived from this source and is therefore able to give a range of fertility, nuptiality and related indices for the principal, distinct, self-governing urban communities of England and Wales as they existed in 1911, listed in order by their respective regions and counties.[102]

The first and most obvious point to emerge from this tabulation is that the evidence flatly contradicts any strong or simple version of the hypothesis that 'urbanisation' was the primary cause of falling or low fertility, in the sense that there is no direct correlation between the size of a town or urban district in 1911 and the relative marital fertility level. Thus, although it is true that in general rural areas remained with higher marital fertility for longer than most urban areas, Table 20.6 indicates that a considerable number of urban communities exhibited fertility levels as high as or higher than the rural sections of many counties. This was notably true of towns in the North-East (Gateshead, South Shields, Sunderland, West Hartlepool, Newcastle, Middlesbrough), in Lancashire (St Helens, Warrington, Wigan), in the Black Country (West Bromwich, Walsall, Dudley, Wolverhampton) and in South Wales (Merthyr Tydfil, Aberdare, Rhondda). These were all primarily involved in the iron and steel, metalworking, heavy engineering or shipbuilding, and coal-mining industries. Thus, although fertility reduction tended to occur earliest in some urban communities, there remained in 1911 enormous variation between different towns in their fertility and nuptiality behaviour. The specific economic and industrial character of an urban community seems to have had quite a powerful influence, at least in discriminating between these high-fertility towns and the rest, regardless of size or regional, cultural considerations. Hence, the above examples and hence, also, the fact that Barnsley, the coal-mining centre of West Yorkshire, was the only urban centre east of the Pennines with very high fertility in 1911.

---

[101] *FMR, Pt 2*, table 44, pp. 172–216, 'England and Wales – Marriages where the wife not attained the age of 45 years at census – Married couples, children born, and children dead, classified by area of enumeration, duration of marriage, and age of wife at marriage'.

[102] These data are derived from a database constructed by Garrett, Reid, Schurer and Szreter, *Changing Family Size*. We wish to record our thanks to Eilidh Garrett for providing the tabulations presented here in Table 20.5.

Table 20.6 *Urban nuptiality and marital fertility in England and Wales 1871–1911*

Census division	Place	Pop. 1911	Standardised fertility	Mar. duration 5–9 years									
				Mar.	Celib.	N 20–4	Av. par. 20–4	N 25–9	Av. par. 25–9	25–9 per 100 20–4	25–9 par./ 20–4 par.	Sex ratio 20–39
												4.52
				ENGLAND AND WALES								
	Great towns		4.52									
	Other urban areas		4.44									
	Rural areas		4.67									
	ENGLAND		4.49									
	WALES		5.00									
London	LONDON	4,521,685	4.39	33.5	18.8	60,994	2.40	35,035	1.92	57	0.80	84
South-East	READING	75,198	4.06	41.0	15.8	998	2.25	751	1.91	75	0.85	91
	BOURNEMOUTH	78,674	3.59	42.1	34.7	786	2.11	653	1.79	83	0.85	54
	PORTSMOUTH	231,141	3.94	36.7	15.1	3,010	2.14	1,817	1.84	60	0.86	108
	SOUTHAMPTON	119,012	4.13	33.8	13.9	1,508	2.29	911	1.84	60	0.80	91
	CANTERBURY	24,626	4.28	36.6	19.0	279	2.34	181	1.96	65	0.84	91
	GILLINGHAM	52,252	3.67	35.8	7.3	711	2.07	441	1.82	62	0.88	148
	CROYDON	169,551	4.10	41.1	21.0	2,416	2.23	1,846	1.89	76	0.85	77
	WIMBLEDON	54,966	3.97	42.1	22.7	711	2.19	612	1.76	86	0.81	68
	BRIGHTON	131,237	3.97	37.8	24.4	1,545	2.19	1,035	1.75	67	0.80	73
	EASTBOURNE	52,542	3.62	41.7	32.7	556	2.07	417	1.80	75	0.87	59
	HASTINGS	61,145	3.86	38.6	33.9	554	2.23	438	1.79	79	0.80	62
South-West	EXETER	48,664	4.05	40.9	19.7	578	2.35	400	1.69	69	0.72	79
	PLYMOUTH	112,030	4.00	33.8	16.7	1,437	2.11	802	1.79	56	0.85	82
	BATH CITY	50,721	3.84	41	32.6	496	2.33	396	1.71	80	0.73	63

Region	Place	(1)	(2)	(3)	(4)	(5)	(6)	(7)	(8)	(9)	(10)	(11)
	(row cut off at top)					732	2.18	594	1.94	81	0.89	103
South Midlands	ACTON	57,497	4.29	40.3	17.9	914	2.29	603	1.82	66	0.80	83
	EALING	61,222	3.84	46.9	28.0	852	2.14	766	1.84	90	0.86	64
	EDMONTON	64,797	5.04	28.8	7.6	976	2.61	501	2.14	51	0.82	94
	ENFIELD	56,338	4.44	34.0	11.9	771	2.45	535	2.10	69	0.86	90
	HORNSEY	84,592	3.33	46.0	25.4	910	1.98	931	1.71	102	0.86	67
	TOTTENHAM	137,418	4.49	35.0	11.2	2,207	2.38	1,344	1.96	61	0.82	91
	WILLESDEN	154,214	4.19	40.2	15.8	2,375	2.30	1,795	1.86	76	0.81	84
	NORTHAMPTON	90,064	4.03	34.3	14.1	1,209	2.17	788	1.68	65	0.78	88
	OXFORD CITY	53,048	4.09	45.6	27.3	598	2.27	493	1.89	82	0.83	73
East Anglia	EAST HAM	133,487	4.49	33.9	7.2	2,061	2.40	1,333	2.00	65	0.84	90
	ILFORD	78,188	3.77	42.2	17.5	1,115	2.18	1,021	1.76	92	0.81	79
	LEYTON	124,735	4.28	38.9	13.1	1,947	2.30	1,324	1.96	68	0.85	86
	SOUTHEND ON SEA	62,713	3.54	35.5	22.1	876	2.09	602	1.72	69	0.82	71
	WALTHAMSTOW	124,580	4.57	32.0	7.9	1,992	2.46	1,179	2.16	59	0.88	91
	WEST HAM	289,030	5.09	27.5	7.6	4,368	2.63	1,988	2.23	46	0.85	94
	YARMOUTH	55,905	4.55	31.4	17.7	667	2.48	384	2.06	58	0.83	77
	NORWICH CITY	121,478	4.63	32.7	17.7	1,629	2.51	915	1.93	56	0.77	81
	IPSWICH	73,932	4.47	37.2	17.8	1,018	2.43	659	1.88	65	0.77	88
West Midlands	BRISTOL	357,048	4.31	35.3	16.7	4,777	2.32	3,038	1.90	64	0.82	78
	GLOUCESTER CITY	50,035	4.38	34.3	14.6	637	2.44	400	1.88	63	0.77	86
	BURTON-ON-TRENT	48,266	4.33	37.4	10.2	661	2.38	464	1.80	70	0.75	101
	SMETHWICK	70,694	4.65	31.7	8.5	1,109	2.44	630	1.97	57	0.81	95
	STOKE-ON-TRENT	234,534	5.04	26.7	8.6	3,771	2.73	1,652	2.10	44	0.77	94
	WALSALL	92,115	4.94	28.1	9.8	1,377	2.67	654	2.09	47	0.78	93
	WEST BROMWICH	68,332	5.14	28.9	10.1	1,085	2.66	494	2.10	46	0.79	100
	WOLVERHAMPTON	95,328	4.69	33.6	12.2	1,337	2.50	784	2.07	59	0.83	94
	BIRMINGHAM CITY	525,833	4.62	30.4	12.1	8,133	2.50	4,149	2.02	51	0.81	90
	COVENTRY CITY	106,349	4.03	33.4	11.2	1,967	2.20	1,038	1.91	53	0.87	114
	DUDLEY	51,079	5.13	23.2	8.5	777	2.64	349	2.17	45	0.82	96
	WORCESTER CITY	47,982	4.20	36.3	16.4	633	2.41	383	1.91	61	0.79	81

Table 20.6 (cont.)

Census division	Place	Pop. 1911	Standardised fertility	Standardised Mar.	Standardised Celib.	N 20-4	Av. par. 20-4	N 25-9	Mar. duration 5-9 years Av. par. 25-9	25-9 per 100 20-4	25-9 par./20-4 par.	Sex ratio 20-39
North Midlands	DERBY	123,410	4.06	32.6	12.5	1,861	2.30	1,085	1.88	58	0.82	91
	LEICESTER CITY	227,222	4.19	34.1	14.3	3,345	2.27	2,024	1.74	61	0.77	81
	GRIMSBY	74,659	4.28	30.6	8.8	1,047	2.27	507	1.89	48	0.84	103
	LINCOLN CITY	57,285	3.74	37.0	14.5	868	2.17	525	1.83	60	0.84	102
	NOTTINGHAM CITY	259,904	4.19	31.3	15.8	3,922	2.32	1,974	1.80	50	0.78	81
Yorkshire	YORK CITY	82,282	4.42	37.7	16.1	1,033	2.38	762	1.98	74	0.83	95
	HULL	277,991	4.58	28.3	10.9	3,970	2.49	1,943	2.07	49	0.83	93
	MIDDLESBROUGH	104,767	4.94	29.1	8.3	1,626	2.66	827	2.18	51	0.82	108
	BARNSLEY	50,614	5.00	28.7	11.7	832	2.63	373	2.15	45	0.82	104
	BRADFORD CITY	288,458	3.66	39.3	17.1	3,952	1.97	2,999	1.58	76	0.80	83
	DEWSBURY	53,351	3.89	38.0	15.0	710	2.18	550	1.64	77	0.75	88
	HALIFAX	101,553	3.62	41.5	18.3	1,219	2.04	1,075	1.57	88	0.77	80
	HUDDERSFIELD	107,821	3.83	45.5	17.6	1,417	2.17	1,282	1.65	90	0.76	85
	LEEDS	445,550	4.28	34.9	12.8	6,266	2.30	4,012	1.83	64	0.79	86
	ROTHERHAM	62,483	4.65	27.3	8.1	1,022	2.52	463	1.95	45	0.78	111
	SHEFFIELD	454,632	4.39	28.3	10.3	7,551	2.43	3,655	1.90	48	0.78	98
	WAKEFIELD	51,511	4.28	34.4	13.8	725	2.29	449	1.86	62	0.81	103
Lancashire–Cheshire	BIRKENHEAD	130,794	4.91	34.5	16.6	1,681	2.73	1,058	2.22	63	0.81	92
	CHESTER	39,028	4.68	33.6	18.6	487	2.55	287	2.08	59	0.82	87
	STOCKPORT	108,682	4.38	37.5	15.7	1,619	2.16	1,116	1.82	69	0.84	86
	WALLASEY	78,504	4.11	41.5	19.6	1,008	2.31	799	1.89	79	0.82	74
	BARROW-IN-FURNESS	63,770	4.65	34.3	6.6	976	2.43	591	2.01	61	0.83	114

	Col1	Col2	Col3	Col4	Col5	Col6	Col7	Col8	Col9	Col10	Col11
BLACKBURN	133,052	4.14	38.5	17.4	1,932	2.23	1,290	1.73	67	0.78	81
BLACKPOOL	58,371	3.59	35.6	24.0	697	2.12	473	1.73	68	0.82	70
BOLTON	180,851	4.50	39.3	15.5	2,370	2.34	1,812	1.86	76	0.80	84
BOOTLE	69,876	5.02	30.1	9.5	846	2.74	485	2.37	57	0.87	93
BURNLEY	106,322	4.15	33.0	13.2	1,706	2.21	942	1.65	55	0.75	85
BURY	58,648	3.85	41.1	19.7	799	2.07	636	1.59	80	0.77	87
LIVERPOOL CITY	746,421	5.05	31.4	14.1	9,551	2.76	5,411	2.26	57	0.82	87
MANCHESTER CITY	714,333	4.49	35.4	14.6	10,619	2.39	6,633	1.92	62	0.80	90
OLDHAM	147,483	4.08	35.8	13.8	2,226	2.09	1,408	1.68	63	0.80	91
PRESTON	117,088	4.79	38.1	18.6	1,555	2.51	1,077	2.05	69	0.82	81
ROCHDALE	91,428	3.90	39.3	17.0	1,384	2.03	979	1.64	71	0.81	86
SALFORD	231,357	4.73	33.7	12.8	3,603	2.52	2,027	1.98	56	0.79	92
SOUTHPORT	51,643	3.80	43.0	33.5	512	2.08	467	1.71	91	0.82	60
ST HELENS	96,551	5.60	25.5	8.7	1,442	2.88	608	2.31	42	0.80	116
WARRINGTON	72,166	5.11	26.4	8.8	1,096	2.68	495	2.24	45	0.84	104
WIGAN	89,152	5.53	29.7	12.4	1,290	2.77	622	2.32	48	0.84	95
North											
DARLINGTON	55,631	4.42	35.5	13.8	841	2.46	499	2.01	59	0.82	90
GATESHEAD	116,917	5.12	27.6	9.8	1,657	2.75	1,657	2.75	100	1.00	97
SOUTH SHIELDS	108,647	5.04	23.2	8.0	1,433	2.68	590	2.18	41	0.81	92
STOCKTON ON TEES	52,154	4.90	31.3	8.8	761	2.65	399	2.25	52	0.85	100
SUNDERLAND	151,159	5.15	26.8	10.8	2,124	2.72	975	2.29	46	0.84	87
WEST HARTLEPOOL	63,923	5.10	28.9	6.8	904	2.69	460	2.11	51	0.78	94
NEWCASTLE-UPON-TYNE	266,603	4.81	30.8	11.7	3,570	2.62	2,019	2.09	57	0.80	94
TYNEMOUTH	58,816		29.6	12.2	770	2.74	387	2.25	50	0.82	91
Wales											
ABERDARE	50,830	5.05	27.7	6.5	776	2.61	366	2.38	47	0.91	117
CARDIFF CITY	182,259	4.47	31.4	9.1	2,418	2.42	1,307	2.06	54	0.85	95
MERTHYR TYDFIL	80,990	5.22	27.4	7.5	1,194	2.74	569	2.25	48	0.82	124
RHONDDA	152,781	5.32	26.6	2.9	2,446	2.75	1,026	2.40	42	0.87	139
SWANSEA	114,663	4.77	33.3	11.3	1,702	2.54	900	2.03	53	0.80	106
NEWPORT	83,691	4.78	32.5	9.4	1,177	2.56	649	2.07	55	0.81	103

Table 20.6 (*cont.*)

Explanatory notes

1. In Table 20.6 the name of each town is listed in order according to region and county. Its name is followed by its population size in 1911.

2. The column headed 'Standardised fertility' gives for each town a single, comparable measure of the marital fertility (the average number of live births experienced) of a single *birth cohort* of women, originally born between 1871 and 1880, who were living in each town at the 1911 census (the figure is truly comparable across towns because it has been standardised for the differing proportions of women in each town who married at each of three different ages: 15–19, 20–4, 25–9).

3. For this same birth cohort of women, born 1871–80 and marrying under age 30, the next column, 'Mar.', gives the percentage who married at age 25–9: a measure of the tendency to postpone marriage among this cohort. The adjacent column 'Celib.' gives a further measure of marriage postponement: the percentage of women never married in 1911 at age 45–9.

4. The six columns grouped together under the sub-heading 'Mar. duration 5–9 years' give fertility information for a further, distinct *marriage cohort*: those women married between 1901 and 1905. The first two columns give the number of women married at age 20–4 (N 20–4) and their average fertility after just 7.5 years of marriage (Av. par. 20–4). The second two columns give the same information for those women married at age 25–9. The fifth column gives the number marrying at 25–9 expressed as a percentage of the number marrying at 20–4, showing the extent to which marriage was delayed above age 24 in each town among this second, Edwardian marriage cohort.

5. The last of these six columns expresses the fertility (average parity) of the later-marrying couples (female age at marriage 25–9) as a percentage (a decimal fraction) of the younger-marrying (age 20–4). Wherever this produces a value below 0.95 in the column '25–9 par./20–4 par.', this indicates that births over the first 7.5 years of marriage were being restricted to an even greater extent by those marrying relatively late (above 25 years old) than by those marrying younger (under age 25).

6. The final column of Table 20.6 gives the sex ratio in 1911 of persons aged 20–39 years in each town. This gives a measure of the relative gendering of the labour market in each town.

Source: FMR, Pt 2, table 44.

These high-fertility towns were those in which the principal employment opportunities were confined to a particular set of industries where an almost exclusively male workforce had been established during the course of the nineteenth century (often the result of a three-way process of male negotiation – between the representatives of labour, employers and the state).[103] There was very little for young women of the proletarian class to do in these communities, either to support themselves or to contribute to their parents' budget. Consequently, they either married relatively young, with financial dependence on an earning husband being their principal alternative to dependence on their father and brothers, or they left for work elsewhere. This is reflected in Table 20.6 both in the relatively young female marriage age indices of these towns (typically less than 60 marriages at age twenty-five to twenty-nine per 100 marriages at age twenty to twenty-four) and in the unusually male sex ratios.[104] The sex imbalance towards males was also the product of the reciprocal effect of an influx of young men looking for the work that was available. For those women who did not choose to leave these communities, marriage and childrearing was the principal role available.

With mothering such an important source of social identity to women in these towns, it is less surprising that there would be little initiative towards its restraint. In these kinds of towns fertility did not begin to fall until proletarian parents, particularly fathers, had been gradually forced into a re-evaluation of the economic and emotional 'costs' of childrearing during the period 1870–1930. This occurred as a result of the ever-increasing determination on the part of the philanthropic middle-class urban missionary, charity workers and the state to impose upon the working classes an ever-accumulating burden of duties and obligations in respect of childrearing.[105] This included compulsory but paid-for (until the mid-1890s) schooling; and the range of measures implemented by the gathering momentum of the successive infant, child and, ultimately, maternal welfare movements across this period, culminating in the first decade of the new century when preoccupations with 'National Efficiency' came to the fore.[106]

---

[103] S. Walby, *Patriarchy at Work* (Cambridge, 1986), ch. 5; E. Jordan, 'The exclusion of women from industry in nineteenth-century Britain', *Comparative Studies in Society and History*, 31 (1989), 273–96.

[104] Note that because of the higher mortality of males the average sex ratio at these ages was somewhat below 100; hence towns with ratios of about 95 and above, although not reflecting an absolute imbalance in favour of males, indicate a relative male surplus.

[105] For full details, see Szreter, *Fertility, Class and Gender*, pp. 513–25. For relevant evidence, see G. K. Behlmer, *Child Abuse and Moral Reform in England 1870–1908* (Stanford, 1908); R. Cooter, ed., *In the Name of the Child* (London, 1992); H. Hendrick, *Child Welfare* (London, 1994); G. K. Behlmer, *Friends of the Family* (Stanford, 1998).

[106] J. S. Hurt, *Elementary Schooling and the Working Classes, 1860–1918* (London, 1979); J. Donzelot, *The Policing of Families* (New York 1979); J. Lewis, *The Politics of Motherhood* (London, 1980); D. Dwork, *War is Good for Babies and Other Young Children* (London, 1987).

Fatherhood and masculinity remain a drastically underresearched topic especially for the nineteenth century. Its history is at present mainly traceable as the reciprocal reflection of the better documented social and legal history of mothering and motherhood. On the Victorian middle classes, a certain amount of work has identified considerable strains and stresses in this period, one which witnessed both the erection at mid-century of the reviled statutory monuments to the infamous 'double standard' of sexual morality, in the form of the 1857 Matrimonial Clauses Act and the 1864–6 Contagious Diseases Acts, but also their subsequent effective repeal in the 1880s.[107] For the working classes direct accounts of fatherhood remain anecdotal or indirect and there has been little attempt to provide a systematic account, still less an account which would distinguish the kinds of regional and industrial variations in fathering which are implied by the great local differences in fertility and nuptiality which are known to have existed.[108] Along with this goes a similar absence of systematic study of regional and local patterns of courtship, although, once again, the demographic record indicates that much local diversity will be found.[109]

The reciprocal to the high fertility of the mining, heavy engineering, iron and steel towns can be found in many – though not quite all – of the low-fertility mill towns, either side of the Pennines in the Lancashire cotton and the West Yorkshire wool and worsted industries. They all exhibit, in the 'Mar.' column of Table 20.6, a significantly higher ratio of later female marriages (60–90 marriages at age twenty-five to twenty-nine per 100 marriages at age twenty to twenty-four) along with a strongly female sex ratio (final column, Table 20.6). Exceptionally low fertility is recorded among three of the four large Yorkshire wool towns: Halifax, Huddersfield and Bradford, with the fourth, the shoddy town of Dewsbury, not far behind. There is an evident contrast with the other, higher-fertility Yorkshire towns a few miles to the south, in the region where steel, engineering and coal were more significant industries (Wakefield,

---

[107] D. Roberts, 'The paterfamilias of the Victorian governing classes', in A. S. Wohl, ed., *The Victorian Family* (London, 1978), pp. 59–81; J. Tosh, 'Domesticity and manliness in the Victorian middle class: the family of Edward White Benson', in M. Roper and J. Tosh, eds., *Manful Assertions* (London, 1991), pp. 44–73; A. James Hammerton, *Cruelty and Companionship: Conflict in Nineteenth-Century Married Life* (London, 1992); J. Tosh, *A Man's Place* (New Haven, 1999).

[108] For some relevant material, see: N. Tomes, '"A torrent of abuse": crimes of violence between working-class men and women in London 1840–1875', *Journal of Social History*, 11 (1978), 328–45; J. R. Gillis, *For Better, for Worse: British Marriages, 1600 to the Present* (Oxford, 1985); L. Segal, 'Look back in anger: men in the fifties', in R. Chapman and J. Rutherford, eds., *Male Order: Unwrapping Masculinity* (London, 1988), pp. 69–96; and J. R. Gillis, *A World of their Own Making: A History of Myth and Ritual in Family Life* (Oxford, 1996), ch. 9.

[109] For some limited ethnographic observation on plebeian courtship in Edwardian Middlesbrough, see F. Bell, *At the Works* (London, 1907), pp. 178–81; on Lancashire see E. Roberts, *A Woman's Place* (Oxford, 1984), pp. 72–80; and A. Davies, *Leisure, Gender and Poverty* (Buckingham, 1992), chs. 4–5. See also S. Humphries, *A Secret World of Sex: Forbidden Fruit: The British Experience 1900–50* (London, 1988), chs. 3–4, 7.

Rotherham, Sheffield and especially Barnsley). In Lancashire, although also generally exhibiting relatively low fertility, the textile towns present a slightly more varied picture, with only Bury and Rochdale recording as low fertility as that found in the principal mill towns of the West Riding. Indeed, Preston's fertility – uniquely for a textile community – was much closer to that of the Yorkshire engineering and iron and steel towns mentioned above; and was actually higher than Barrow-in-Furness, the Lancashire shipbuilding centre.[110]

The only important exceptions to the analysis presented so far are found in the three Mersey and Wirral communities of Bootle, Birkenhead and Liverpool (the nation's second largest nineteenth-century city until it was surpassed by Glasgow in 1871). These three all exhibit very high fertility although they were not communities particularly dominated by mining or heavy industry. They demonstrate the capacity for a particular category of cultural or 'ethnic' influence, in the form of the substantial Irish Roman Catholic presence, also to have a highly significant influence upon the fertility characteristics of large urban communities.

It is, of course, no surprise that the human activity of genesis should have been profoundly influenced by people's religious beliefs and practices and this is a general finding which has been replicated by studies of falling fertility in many other countries, from the earliest work by W. H. Beveridge onwards.[111] As Michael Mason's fascinating study has carefully documented, the beginning of the period under consideration here – the 1840s – was the tail end of an era of several decades of quite widespread experimentation in gender and sexual roles and reproductive practices within British society. Much of this was mediated through the teachings and practices of the large number of religious and freethinking sects proliferating at that time, embracing a range of reproductive ideologies from consensual unions and 'free love' through to millenarian abstinence.[112] But by the last quarter of the nineteenth century, there seems to have

---

[110] On the reasons for Preston's unusually high fertility for a textile town, see Szreter, *Fertility, Class and Gender*, pp. 511–12. The analysis there is derived from the superb, detailed monograph on Preston's social and labour history in this period by Mike Savage, *The Dynamics of Working-Class Politics* (Cambridge, 1987).

[111] W. H. Beveridge, 'The fall of fertility among the European races', *Economica*, 5 (1925), 10–27. For a more recent reprise of this theme in the context, again, of a European survey, see R. Lesthaeghe and C. Wilson, 'Modes of production, secularisation and the pace of the fertility decline in Western Europe, 1870–1930', ch. 6 in A. J. Coale and S. C. Watkins, eds., *The Decline of Fertility in Europe* (Princeton, 1986), pp. 261–92. See also J. Simons, 'Reproductive behaviour as religious practice', in C. Hohn and R. Mackensen, eds., *Determinants of Fertility Trends: Theories Re-Examined* (Liège, 1980), pp. 131–45. By far the most rigorous and extensive examination of the relationship between religious belief and fertility change in Britain is to be found in Banks, *Victorian Values*.

[112] M. Mason, *The Making of Victorian Sexual Attitudes* (Oxford, 1994); and on the gender and reproductive ideology and practices of the most important of these various experimental groups, the Owenite socialists, see Barbara Taylor, *Eve and the New Jerusalem: Socialism and Feminism in the Nineteenth Century* (London, 1983).

been a relative lack of marked differentiation between Protestant denominations in England and Wales on matters of sexuality and reproduction.[113]

However, it is evident, as the Mersey–Wirral cities illustrate, that religious affiliation continued to exert very substantial influence upon fertility behaviour where distinctions of both faith and ethnic identity were involved. The refugee Jewish community of east London certainly brought with it a highly distinctive family life and hygienic code of childrearing, which included both relatively high fertility and the achievement of very high survivorship rates in one of the country's harshest urban areas (there were also, of course, more modest Jewish trading communities of older settlement in Manchester, Leeds and Liverpool).[114]

The religious influence was clearly every bit as important, and on a much larger demographic scale, where Ireland was concerned. However, there were, of course, other very significant historical considerations, too. In particular, Ireland's high rates of migration and also her much delayed marriage patterns were both quite distinctive, the grim sequelae of the terrible famine. Nevertheless, once married, Irish rates of childbearing were relatively unrestrained until the interwar years and therefore much higher than in the rest of Great Britain in 1911. The religious influence is evident in the principal exceptions to this, in that lower fertility was already apparent before the Great War in the Protestant enclaves in Dublin, and in the three most urbanised Ulster counties, those containing and bordering Belfast (counties Antrim, Armagh and Down).[115] However, with the evidence that is currently available, it is impossible in Ireland to disentangle the urban from the religious influence, in bringing about relatively low fertility in these places.

This combined religious and ethnic influence is also evident in the case of the Scottish nation, in that this distinctive Protestant population of Presbyterians was one which experienced a somewhat different and later fall in fertility than that

---

[113] Although this remains a relatively unexplored subject from a demographic point of view. The most probable candidate for such an association on a significant scale in the late nineteenth century were the Secularists, a substantially urban movement which most closely represented the continuation of the Owenite inheritance. But it seems to have been as much associated with low-fertility textile towns, notably in the West Riding and in Lancashire, as with the high-fertility coal and heavy engineering communities of the North-East, or with, say, London, Leicester or Northampton, places noted neither for particularly low nor particularly high fertility. See E. Royle, *Radicals, Secularists and Republicans: Popular Freethought in Britain, 1866–1914* (Manchester, 1980), ch. 5; and Banks, *Victorian Values*, chs. 3–4. On freethinkers see also S. Budd, 'The loss of faith: reasons for unbelief among members of the secular movement in England, 1850–1950', *P&P*, 36 (1967), 106–25; and her *Varieties of Unbelief: Atheists and Agnostics in English Society, 1850–1960* (London, 1977).

[114] On the Jewish family and working life in the East End, see Marks, *Model Mothers*; D. Feldman, *Englishmen and Jews* (London, 1994).

[115] C. O'Gráda, *Ireland Before and After the Famine: Explorations in Economic History, 1800–1925* (Manchester, 1988), Appendix 7, pp. 168–9; and see C. O'Gráda, *Ireland: A New Economic History 1780–1939* (Oxford, 1994), pp. 218–24, which reports research showing differentially low fertility in the comfortable, middle-class Protestant Dublin suburb of Rathgar.

south of the border. Furthermore, the Scottish propensity to marry, although not as low as the Irish, was generally somewhat lower than that of the English and Welsh indicating an even more tightly restrained culture of sexual abstinence among the young.[116] The most detailed data currently available, an analysis of marital fertility and nuptiality patterns for Scottish parishes during the period 1881–1911, show a complex and predominantly regional set of demographic regimes in Scotland, rather than a simple urban–rural differential.[117] Certainly, marital fertility in 1901 was relatively low in the city of Edinburgh, in the more comfortable suburban parishes of Glasgow, in Dundee and in the relatively urban county of Fife (lying between Edinburgh and Dundee and containing Dunfermline). But fertility was equally low in the very rural south-eastern borders area (excluding the mining district of East Lothian) and also across a north-central Highland swathe stretching from Arran to Rannoch Moor.[118] Scottish urban sex ratios during the nineteenth century varied in similar fashion to those of England and Wales, with female imbalances in most towns and strongest in the textile areas of Angus (Forfar), especially in 'Jute-town' (Dundee); while in the heavy industry Lowlands, including Glasgow, there was a relative (though not absolute) male imbalance, particularly due to Irish male in-migration to the coalfields.[119]

Scottish towns, therefore, like those of England and Wales, also exhibited substantial variations in their demography in a way that was related to their varying industrial and social structure. It is also the case that Lowland Scotland, embracing the principal urban populations, exhibited the characteristic 'English' demographic pattern of a culture of sexual restraint during the period of fertility decline. Unlike most other European populations, the initial decades during which fertility within marriage fell were also characterised by an increasing reluctance to undertake marriage.[120]

As a result of the predominant influence of economic function and industrial character, quite extreme local geographical variations in urban fertility can be discerned in England and Wales from Table 20.6. The contrast between Barnsley and Huddersfield, just 15 miles (24 km) apart in South Yorkshire, was replicated on a similar scale over the same short distance between Wigan and Bury in south Lancashire. In England's other two largest conurbations, the London metropolis and the West Midlands, extreme geographical variation in fertility between districts sitting cheek by jowl was also visible. The light industry centre of

---

[116] Flinn *et al.*, *Scottish Population History*, pp. 335–48.

[117] M. Anderson and D. J. Morse, 'High fertility, high emigration, low nuptiality: adjustment processes in Scotland's demographic experience, 1861–1914', Parts I and II, *Population Studies*, 47 (1993), 5–25 and 319–43.   [118] *Ibid.*, 16–21.

[119] Flinn *et al.*, *Scottish Population History*, pp. 317–20.

[120] S. Szreter, 'Falling fertilities and changing sexualities in Europe since *c.* 1850: a comparative survey of national demographic patterns', in L. A. Hall, F. Eder and G. Heckma, eds., *Sexual Cultures in Europe*, vol. II: *Studies in Sexuality* (Manchester, 1999), pp. 159–94.

Coventry was only about 15 miles (24 km) from West Bromwich, a classic Black Country centre of heavy industry; and low fertility Hornsey in north London was only about 5 miles (8 km) from high-fertility Edmonton. In London's case, of course, these were differences due to the influences of social class relations, producing large-scale residential segregation between rich and poor, or 'sub-urbanisation' as H. J. Dyos and David Reeder defined it, rather than the more purely industrial distinctions which lay behind the wide variations in commu-nity fertility found in Lancashire, West Yorkshire and the West Midlands.[121]

A general reason for the relative absence of visibility of class differentials in that part of the data in Table 20.6 which is drawn from the towns in the North and the Midlands was the much slighter presence there of several important sec-tions of the upper and middle classes. Outside the metropolis and the Home Counties, there was a much thinner spread of those of private means, the pro-fessional, administrative, commercial and financial elite and the army of domes-tic servants, household suppliers and supporting, lower-middle-class, clerical employees who worked and served alongside the diverse members of this upper middle class. This was not simply a case of an arithmetic absence of the metro-politan-style upper and middle class. There were also significant cultural impli-cations for the social tone of the northern and Midland industrial, urban communities and for the manner in which their political and social relations were conducted.[122] It was a smaller and differently formed middle class in most north-ern and Midland towns, composed much more of industrial employers and suc-cessful shopkeepers, often themselves nonconformist and risen from the local community within living memory. Of course, affluent suburbs inhabited by a professional and commercial elite like Sketty or Singleton Park in Swansea, Edgbaston or Handsworth in Birmingham, or Hallam in Sheffield, certainly contained localised residential concentrations of a more exclusive middle class, as did select districts of all other major cities, such as Manchester, Liverpool/ Birkenhead, Leeds, Bradford and Newcastle/Gateshead. But these were rela-tively small enclaves by comparison with the widespread presence of this class in the imperial capital and the Home Counties. In the northern and Midland cities they were rather dwarfed by the enormous proletarian populations which the relatively labour-intensive industrial processes of Britain's world-serving staple industries had called into existence.

London was not the only urban centre in the South with a distinctive genteel tone. This was also true of many southern market, cathedral, county or resort towns, such as Bath, Oxford, Reading, Exeter, Bournemouth, Eastbourne or Brighton, and the growing residential communities of the early stockbroker belt,

---

[121] Dyos and Reeder, 'Slums and suburbs'.
[122] L. H. Lees, 'The study of social conflict in English industrial towns', *UHY* (1980), 34–43; R. J. Morris, 'Voluntary societies and British urban elites, 1780–1850: an analysis', *Historical Journal*, 26 (1983), 95–118; S. J. D. Green, 'In search of bourgeois civilisation: institutions and ideals in nineteenth-century Britain', *NHist.*, 28 (1992), 228–47.

which came to ring London during the period 1890–1930, such as Wimbledon, Pinner and 'urban Surrey'. Here fertility was in general significantly lower than in the majority of northern towns (except, of course, those involved in textiles manufacture). A recent study has shown that, just as all the inhabitants of mill towns appear to have participated in the relatively low fertility of those directly working in the textiles industry, so, too, in these southern, more genteel towns and suburbs, even the wives of the proletarians who lived there seem to have married somewhat later and exhibited lower fertility than the wives of the same occupational categories of workers in northern and Midland industrial towns.[123]

While it seems plausible to presume that this partly reflects some form of mimesis by the southern serving and labouring class of their social superiors, this does not seem likely to be the whole story in an age where open, public discussion of matters of sexuality and reproduction across the class divide was almost unheard of and was vigorously pursued in law when attempted, until Marie Stopes' successful publication in 1918 of the nation's first user-friendly marital sex manual, *Married Love*.[124] It seems equally probable that this was also an example of differences between the North and the South in terms of gendered labour market opportunities affecting parental roles and perceptions of the relative costs of childrearing.[125] With their consumer goods, distribution, clerical and domestic service industries, the much more middle-class southern towns provided a relatively wide range of employments for female proletarians, indicated by their more female sex ratios in Table 20.6. Levels of remuneration were modest in absolute terms but were relatively favourable because of the relatively low wage levels of many male working-class occupations in the South, at least until the interwar period when new industries, such as motor cars, aviation, radio and electronics, light industry and consumer durables increasingly tended to prefer location in the South and Midlands, away from the heartlands of organised labour and near the capital city, as the largest centre of dependable demand in an economy experiencing unemployment elsewhere.[126] Before that, factory industry in the South was more or less confined to agricultural machinery making and food-processing plants; and trade union activity was a rarity. A small town like Banbury was famous far and wide in the mid-nineteenth century as 'the Manchester of the South' because of its unusual radical politics, something which would have been quite unremarkable further north. In these rather different circumstances in the southern market towns and growing commuter suburbs, where there was more female access to a range of independent sources

---

[123] Garrett, Reid, Shurer and Szreter, *Population Change in Context*, chs. 4–5.

[124] M. Stopes, *Married Love: A New Contribution to the Solution of Sex Difficulties* (London, 1918).

[125] See Szreter, *Fertility, Class and Gender*, ch. 9, on perceived relative childrearing costs.

[126] E. H. Hunt, *Regional Wage Variations in Britain, 1850–1914* (Oxford, 1973). On the interwar economy, see the illuminating case study of the Slough trading estate by Mike Savage: 'Trade unionism, sex segregation, and the state: women's employment in "new" industries in inter-war Britain', *Soc. Hist.*, 13 (1988), 209–29; and more generally see S. Glynn and A. Booth, *Modern Britain: An Economic and Social History* (London, 1996), chs. 2, 4.

of livelihood, young women from the poorer classes were able to marry some-what later, were more likely to be able to continue to earn after marriage and were more likely to need to do so because of their husbands' relatively meagre incomes. All of these were practices associated with lower marital fertility.

It was, therefore, probably the varying labour market conditions and their implications in structuring proletarian gendered work and familial roles and parents' perceived relative costs of childrearing which primarily produced the marked regional patterns of urban fertility differential, between heavy and light industry, textiles and non-textiles towns in the North and the Midlands; and between the North and Midlands, on the one hand, and the South and South-East on the other hand. Thus, no towns in the South of England – not even the largest and most commercial ones, such as Norwich, Bristol or Southampton – exhibited fertility levels as high as the heavy industry and mining towns of the North and the Midlands. But on the other hand only a handful of resort and London dormitory towns in the South (Eastbourne, Gillingham, Bournemouth, Southend) recorded fertility levels as low as the principal wool towns of West Yorkshire. Furthermore, as Blackpool in Lancashire shows, the 'resort effect' on fertility was not confined to the south of the country, suggesting that it had more to do with the concentration of female employment opportunities, as in the tex-tiles towns, than the presence of genteel patrons.

However, the case of the six towns of the Potteries (amalgamated as the borough of Stoke-on-Trent in 1910) shows that high levels of female employ-ment did not invariably result in later marriage and low fertility. In this case detailed research has shown that family working practices in the Potteries' numerous bottle kilns were typically sufficiently flexible and near to home as to enable mothers, with the assistance of siblings, neighbours and a relatively plen-tiful supply of local relations, to combine work with effective domestic supervi-sion, in a manner that was closer to home-working than to the practices of large, shift-working textile factories.[127] The net result, therefore, was that the perceived relative opportunity costs of childrearing (in terms of a trade-off against the mother's capacity to undertake gainful employment) were not so obvious in the six towns of the Potteries as in the mill towns.

In general, the Lancashire textiles industry's historic combination of relatively weak male unions (except certain branches of mule spinning), which had failed to exclude women and children from the factory workforce, resulted in low male wages, relatively high female earning capacity and so a powerful incentive on married couples not to produce so many young children so fast as to overstrain the cheaper and more informal childminding arrangements which were available (grandparents and other kin, neighbours and the community's elder daughters)

---

[127] See Szreter, *Fertility, Class and Gender*, pp. 497–9; the three most important studies of work and family in the potteries are J. Sarsby, *Missuses and Mouldrunners: An Oral History of Women Pottery-Workers at Work and at Home* (Milton Keynes, 1988); R. Whipp, *Patterns of Labour* (London, 1990); and M. Dupree, *Family Structure in the Staffordshire Potteries, 1840–1880* (Oxford, 1995).

and so precipitate a wife's need to leave the factory before the eldest children could begin to earn their keep.[128] As mentioned above, in most Lancashire mill towns even though the capacity for women to offer labour in this way was primarily confined to the textiles industry, it was a sufficiently important component of the local labour market that the options which it provided seem to have had a more general cultural and demographic effect, resulting in later marriage and lower fertility than in other proletarian towns as a general feature of these communities.[129]

It seems that the relationship between female employment and low fertility must have operated in a somewhat different way in the woollens industry, since there was remarkably little *married* female employment there, by comparison with the Lancashire mill towns. However, there was a great deal of *unmarried* female participation; and women postponed marriage even later in the West Yorkshire wool towns than in Lancashire and seem to have restrained their fertility, after marriage, to an even greater extent than in Lancashire. The general implication seems to be that in both West Yorkshire and Lancashire textiles towns the community of women tended to achieve a high degree of sexual bargaining power, apparently sufficiently acknowledged by their menfolk that family formation and the process of childrearing occurred more on their terms and on a basis of marked moderation by comparison with most other industrial communities.

The proximate explanation for the unusually pronounced fertility-restraining practices of the West Yorkshire towns may lie in their particularly assiduous application of the practices required by the traditional British culture of sexual abstinence. It has recently been argued that the long-standing mystery of the methods actually used by married couples, particularly proletarians, to control births throughout the period of falling fertility in Britain principally involved attempted abstinence, before the use of condoms became aesthetically and morally more acceptable, as well as affordable in the 1930s.[130] One of the

---

[128] M. Anderson, 'Household structure and the Industrial Revolution: mid-nineteenth century Preston in comparative perspective', in P. Laslett and R. Wall, eds., *Household and Family in Past Time* (Cambridge, 1972), pp. 215–35; see also R. Burr Litchfield, 'The family and the mill: cotton mill work, family work patterns and fertility in mid-Victorian Stockport', in Wohl, ed., *The Victorian Family* (1978), pp. 180–96; and E. Garrett, 'The trials of labour: motherhood versus employment in a nineteenth-century textile centre', *Continuity and Change*, 5 (1990), 121–54.

[129] T. H. C. Stevenson specifically tested for this in the original official analysis of the 1911 census data: *FMR, Pt 2*, p. cxvii.

[130] Szreter, *Fertility, Class and Gender*, ch. 8. From the beginning of the 1930s onwards appliance methods of contraception assumed a more acceptable form, price and availability. The key technical development was the latex process of rubber manufacture perfected for mass production in 1929. See J. Peel, 'The manufacture and retailing of contraceptives in England', *Population Studies*, 17 (1963), 113–25. It also happened that in the following year three principal official institutions of relevance, the BMA, the Anglican Church and the Ministry of Health, all reversed their long-standing formal prohibition on such forms of contraception, recognising its legitimacy in certain circumstances. See R. A. Soloway, *Birth Control and the Population Question in England 1877–1930* (Chapel Hill, 1982), chs. 11–14.

principal forms of evidence in favour of this thesis was the finding that within each of 200 occupational subdivisions of the nation distinguished in the official tabulations from the 1911 census, those who restrained fertility the most during the first five to ten years of their marriage were also those who had postponed marriage the most. In other words, those sections of the population wishing to avoid large families began by delaying their marriages to the greatest extent; and thereafter they produced a pattern of relatively infrequent births from the beginning of their marriages onwards. It was argued that these patterns are consistent with a popular culture lacking any widespread knowledge of a secure form of birth control and therefore resorting to the extension of the traditional British practices of delayed marriage, pre-marital sexual abstinence and additionally – the new feature of this period – systematic *post-marital* attempted abstinence (reduced coital frequency in marriage). As the figures in Table 20.6 in the columns headed '25–9 per 100 20–4' and '25–9 par./20–4 par.' show, the West Yorkshire wool towns exhibit among the strongest indices of this form of behaviour: the combination of late marriage and the particularly marked restraint of births from early in marriage among those marrying late. It may well be, therefore, that the culture of sexual abstinence was stronger in these West Yorkshire textile communities than anywhere else among the working classes. The possible local cultural reasons for this remain an open hypothesis for future research to evaluate.

By the end of the period under review here, children had everywhere in society come to be viewed by parents as a major responsibility and investment of time, energy and financial resources: Viviana Zelizer's 'priceless children'.[131] Once the bottom fell out of the international coal market in the 1920s and mining communities had suffered their first serious wage cuts and unemployment in living memory, even these redoubts and cherished symbols of working-class virility and fertility had rapidly become communities of small families of just two or three children.[132]

Indeed, by mid-century urban Britain appeared to be exhibiting a greater degree of socio-demographic uniformity than ever before, in terms of both its mortality and its fertility patterns. Furthermore, as F. M. L. Thompson has noted, by 1950 'urban' Britain embraced most of British society, in both cultural and residential terms.[133] Even if, as many have argued, this nation of gardeners, fishermen, ramblers and *The Archers* has always remained 'rural' in its emotional disposition, what was true of urban-dwelling Britain by the mid-

[131] V. A. Zelizer, *Pricing the Priceless Child: The Changing Social Value of Children* (New York, 1985).
[132] On birth control practices in interwar South Wales, see the important new oral history research by Kate Fisher: 'An oral history of birth control practice c. 1925–50. A study of Oxford and South Wales' (DPhil thesis, University of Oxford, 1997).
[133] F. M. L. Thompson, 'Town and city', in F. M. L. Thompson, ed., *Cambridge Social History of Britain, 1750–1950*, vol. I: *Regions and Communities* (Cambridge, 1990), p. 2.

twentieth century was generally true of the British.[134] Michael Anderson has written of the emergence of a single 'modern' family life cycle in this post-industrial, mid-twentieth-century urban society, entailed by a much greater certainty and predictability of the *rites de passage*: the unlikelihood of premature death; the small variation in the number of children born; the consequent small and uniform kinship group; the ubiquity of a period of relatively comfortable retirement.[135]

In all this the social and demographic consequences of the welfare state of course loom large. Steps were taken by the New Liberal administration at the end of the first decade of the twentieth century to ensure the family-supporting income of the nation's male breadwinners against loss through accident, illness or cyclical trade depression. This was ambitiously reconceived during the Second World War as a general social security system providing a range of services, free at point of use, direct to all members of the population, although retaining the notion of a contributory insurance principle. However, these measures were premised on a particular conception of the family and on a highly gendered model of the respective responsibilities of husbands for income earning and of mothers for child care, which reflected the assumptions of the middle-class male and female policy makers (such as Eleanor Rathbone) who campaigned for and implemented the central measures of the welfare state.[136]

But it seems as significant to emphasise the continuation of considerable variety in family forms even during the mid-century decades of the twentieth century; and also to acknowledge the further change and diversity that has occurred since the consolidation of the welfare state in the 'post-war settlement', partly in spite of and partly because of the form of social security support which it has offered. The pioneering urban anthropology of Norman Dennis, Fernando Henriques and Clifford Slaughter, Michael Young and Peter Willmott, and Elizabeth Bott during the 1950s, along with the early social surveys of marriage and sexual practices by John England, Eustace Chesser and Geoffrey Gorer found evidence of profound differences in family life and intimate relationships between different sections of society.[137] It was found that

---

[134] Ralf Dahrendorf, *On Britain* (London, 1982); Patrick Wright, *On Living in an Old Country: The National Past in Contemporary Britain* (London, 1985).

[135] M. Anderson, 'The emergence of the modern life cycle in Britain', *Soc. Hist.*, 10 (1985), 69–87; see also P. Thane, *Old Age in England: Past Experience, Present Issues* (Oxford, 2000), chs. 14 and 20.

[136] J. Macnicol, 'Family allowances and less eligibility', in P. Thane, ed., *The Origins of British Social Policy* (London, 1978), 173–202; Lewis, *Politics of Motherhood*; S. Koven and S. Michel, 'Womanly duties, maternalist policies and the origins of welfare states in France, Germany, Great Britain and the United States, 1880–1920', *American Historical Review*, 95 (1990), 1076–108; S. Pedersen, *Family, Dependence and the Origins of the Welfare State* (Cambridge, 1993).

[137] N. Dennis, F. Henriques, and C. Slaughter, *Coal is Our Life* (London, 1956); M. Young and P. Willmott, *Family and Kinship in East London* (London, 1957); E. Bott, *Family and Social Network*

families in the traditional working-class areas of the North and the East Midlands where the long-declining staple industries still predominated, tended to live in more gendered communities, where husband and wife each had a separate network of same-sex close friends, including the same-sex members of their own respective families. This was also true of London's indigenous working class of the East End and other, old-established plebeian communities in the South. Despite having this in common, all these communities also differed culturally, as most obviously demonstrated by the profound regional and local variations of popular accent and even dialect which still persist to this day. By contrast the middle classes were found by these studies to exhibit a quite different and relatively uniform pattern of a closer conjugal relationship between husband and wife, sharing a similar set of friends of both sexes while living relatively independently of their respective parents, indeed often living in different parts of the country because of the geographical mobility required to pursue professional and managerial careers. The aspirant lower middle class and the more affluent working class provided further variants between these two poles. They typically lived in the distinct parts of the country that had seen the rising prosperity of new industries from the interwar years onwards: the West Midlands centre of automobile, metal alloy and general transport engineering, and the great swathe of consumer durable, light industry and communications services companies, much of which grew outwards in an arc from the North Circular road in the buoyant London-centred economy of the South-East.

Furthermore, belying this appearance of mid-century stability and uniformity, even during the 1940s and 1950s there was also a wider and more general sexual revolution brewing beneath the surface of British society. It exploded in the public arena as Flower Power in the late 1960s; but such an acute vital statistician as John Hajnal had long before noticed its herald sign as a new downward movement in the age at marriage from the late 1930s onwards.[138] This marked the beginnings of the end of the culture of abstinence; and of the centuries-old late marriage pattern, which Hajnal, himself, was the first to document.[139] In

Footnote 137 *(cont.)*

(London, 1957; 2nd edn, 1971); L. R. England, 'Little Kinsey: an outline of sex attitudes in Britain', *Public Opinion Quarterly*, 13 (1949), 587–600; E. Chesser, *The Sexual, Marital and Family Relationships of the English Woman* (London, 1956); G. Gorer, *Exploring English Character* (London, 1955); G. Gorer, *Sex and Marriage in England Today* (London, 1971). Note that more recent sociological research has argued, in critique of Bott's 'joint' versus 'segregated' typology, that there is significantly more complexity and variation to be found in marital relationships than this dichotomy implies: S. Edgell, *Middle-Class Couples: A Study of Segregation, Domination and Inequality in Marriage* (London, 1980); J. Atkinson, 'Gender roles in marriage and the family. A critique and some proposals', *Journal of Family Issues*, 8 (1987), 5–41.

[138] J. Hajnal, 'Age at marriage and proportions marrying', *Population Studies*, 7 (1953–4), 111–36.

[139] J. Hajnal, 'European marriage patterns in perspective', in D. V. Glass and D. E. C. Eversley, eds., *Population in History: Essays in Historical Demography* (London, 1965), pp. 101–43.

due course there has been such a downgrading of this long-standing British cultural practice, whereby the intention to marry was viewed as the gatekeeper of active sexuality, that typical age of female sexual initiation is now almost below the legal limit for marriage; while the state's need to recognise fiscally the status of 'cohabiting' couples as equivalent to marriages signifies how common it has become as a context for raising children.[140]

Meanwhile, the enormous rise in single parenting, especially single mothers, whether voluntary or through desertion or separation, alongside the complex family forms and sibling relationships created by remarriages, in addition to the diversity of family forms among Britain's new immigrant groups of the mid-twentieth century, are all factors which continue to create an enormous range of variability in family sizes and structures.[141] Although the fertility of individual women themselves may vary much less than in the past (in that, since the 1940s, the vast majority of women in the population have only experienced between zero and four births, whereas a century earlier one in six women were experiencing ten or more confinements), there is now as great a variety of family forms extant as ever.

The decades of the 1940s and 1950s, therefore, were no more than a temporary moment of relative uniformity in the nation's urban fertility and nuptiality patterns. This illusion was created by the fact that one set of dramatic changes, a long-term revolution in the perceived relative costs of childrearing, had spent itself as a force for secular fertility change; while its corollary and historical successor as a major dynamic for further socio-demographic and nuptiality change, the assertion of sexual autonomy on the part of this more highly valued younger generation in the context of a society guaranteeing a degree of minimal social security, was about to break upon the nation's cultural institutions with its full force. That this had not already become more widely manifest following the apparent thawing out of upper-middle-class sexual sensibilities in the 1920s was due to an unusual succession of subsequent sweeping historical events. The 1930s Depression, the Second World War, and the succeeding Cold War era of austerity, rationing and National Service, conspired to maintain for a further generation within popular culture a powerful set of countervailing values of parsimony, self-sacrifice, national insecurity, self-discipline and submission to traditional authority. As a result, attachment to the historic culture of late marriage and sexual abstinence was retained in this highly urban society for a further generation after the initial acceptance of contraceptive technology, until

---

[140] K. Wellings, J. Field, M. Johnson and J. Wadsworth, *Sexual Behaviour in Britain: The National Survey of Sexual Attitudes and Lifestyles* (Harmondsworth, 1994), pp. 37–9.

[141] K. Kiernan, H. Land and J. Lewis, *Lone Motherhood in Twentieth-Century Britain: From Footnote to Front Page* (Oxford, 1998); I. Diamond and S. Clarke, 'Demographic patterns among Britain's ethnic groups', in H. Joshi, ed., *The Changing Population of Britain* (Oxford, 1989), pp. 177–98.

the liberalisation of public conventions and codes of sexual morality in the course of the late 1950s and 1960s.[142]

(iv) CONCLUSIONS

The period 1840–1950 certainly witnessed great transformations in urban mortality, fertility and nuptiality. The dramatic downward falls in national aggregate levels of both mortality and fertility *c.* 1870–1930 have always attracted much attention; but these developments need to be seen as phases within a significantly more complex series of other highly significant demographic transformations both before and after. For instance, Britain's new industrial cities were already exhibiting great demographic novelty in the period 1750–1840 if the important issues raised by Allan Sharlin prove to be at least partially correct, as appears to be likely.[143]

Sharlin addressed the observation, since time immemorial, that urban settlement had always functioned as a great demographic maw, devouring the flower of the countryside's youth like a Minotaur's labyrinth.[144] Sharlin argued that we need to recognise that early modern cities' chronic thirst for in-migrants was due not only to the migrants' high mortality, but also to their low fertility, due to the constrained marriage options which in-migrants frequently faced in an environment of unavoidably high living costs and relative scarcity of high-premium skills, a hypothesis that has now received some empirical support.[145] In the light of this perspective it could be said that the new kind of urban system thrown up in Britain by the industrial mechanisation of productive processes was already exhibiting novel demographic features during the late eighteenth and early nineteenth centuries because it was characterised by relatively high and rising nuptiality and fertility among its in-migrants.

However, there may have been little new in this period in Britain's industrial

---

[142] On the wider ideological and cultural forces of liberalisation in the post-war decades, see J. Lewis and K. Kiernan, 'The boundaries between marriage, non-marriage, and parenthood: changes in behaviour and policy in postwar Britain', *Journal of Family History*, 21 (1996), 372–87; and for a study subscribing to a similar chronology through analysis of a very different genre of literature, the rise of soft-porn magazines, see Marcus Collins, 'The pornography of permissiveness: men's sexuality and women's emancipation in mid-twentieth-century Britain', *History Workshop Journal*, 46 (1998), 55–76.

[143] A. Sharlin, 'Natural decrease in early modern cities: a reconsideration', *P&P*, 79 (1978), 126–38.

[144] For an influential estimate of this effect in relation to London, see E. A. Wrigley, 'A simple model of London's importance in the changing British society and economy, 1650–1750', *P&P*, 37 (1967), 44–70.

[145] K. Lynch, 'The European marriage pattern in the cities: variations on a theme by Hajnal', *Journal of Family History*, 16 (1991), 79–96; J. de Vries, *European Urbanisation 1500–1800* (London, 1984), p. 190; C. Galley, 'A model of early modern urban demography', *Ec.HR*, 48 (1995), 448–69; S. King, 'Dying with style: infant death and its context in a rural township 1650–1830', *Social History of Medicine*, 10 (1997), 3–24.

cities with respect to the other side of the demographic equation, mortality. The beginning of the period reviewed here, the 1830s and 1840s may well have been the worst ever decades for life expectancy since the Black Death in the history of those parishes which were now experiencing industrialisation, whether they were a Glasgow or a Manchester, a Walsall or a Carlisle. These industrial settlements were teeming with young adults and their young broods, something never seen on this scale before in Britain's towns. But they were also overcrowded and insanitary, and succumbing to wave after wave of decimating diseases of filth and infection, the old story of high urban mortality.

In the face of this withering firepower there is clear evidence, in the national aggregate demographic record, that the apparently ever-increasing inclination of proletarians to marry each other at ever younger ages from 1750 until 1825 shuddered to a standstill and even went into retreat during the second quarter of the nineteenth century, when average age at marriage rapidly rose back to what it had been in the mid-eighteenth century. Almost certainly the insecurity of the trade cycle in this period, in the context of a central state dramatically reducing the social security and welfare provisions of the Old Poor Law, also contributed significantly to the marked flight from marriage during these two decades. Thus, when the subsequent sustained mid-Victorian revival of trading prosperity arrived, along with the cheaper food and therefore rising real wages for the urban workforce which the repeal of the corn laws was popularly believed to guarantee, proletarian marriage surged once again for a further quarter-century and, with it, the nation's and the cities' fertility.

Although there was some alleviation during the third quarter of the nineteenth century of the atrocious levels of urban mortality found in the industrial towns in the catastrophic second quarter, substantial and absolute improvements, above the levels of life expectancy found in the few towns for which we have reliable records for the last quarter of the eighteenth or first quarter of the nineteenth century, did not occur until the very last quarter of the nineteenth century. The urban mortality rates of elder children and young adults began to edge downward during the last three decades of the century, while those of infants did not decisively fall until the first three decades of the twentieth century, when they did improve remarkably quickly. Only at this point, with the eradication of most sanitation-related and infectious disease coming to be appreciated as a realistic aspiration, was it finally becoming apparent to contemporary medical and public opinion that preventive public health infrastructure, increasingly accurately guided by medical science, had succeeded in finding a safe way through the Minotaur's labyrinth, inaugurating an entirely new era in the relationship between high density urban settlement, health and mortality.

By contrast with this story of urban mortality finally emerging into a new era by the mid-twentieth century, from the perspective of the Sharlin thesis and *la longue durée* the twentieth century has, in a sense, seen the fertility of urban society return to the customary pattern of restraint of past millennia, after a relatively brief period of excess and carefree abandon during the later eighteenth and the nineteenth centuries. This may seem a perversely paradoxical conclusion to draw in the face of over half a century of demographers' hailing the 'modern' fertility decline as *La révolution démographique*.[146] There has undoubtedly been a transformation, since the 1870s, in the degree of precise control over the timing and number of children born to urban-dwelling women and men; and in the social universality of the extent to which this control is exerted. But the historical record does seem to show that urban populations before the modern era were not especially fertile in the aggregate. Of course, this was partly the result of the involuntary winnowing of high infant and child mortality, and partly due to institutional limitation on access to marriage for important subsections of the population such as poor in-migrants and those apprenticed to trades. But it was also partly due to the same set of status and aspirational reasons which prevail among today's urban dwellers, acutely conscious of the trade-off between the need and desire to accumulate security and status-conferring material and cultural capital and the divinely ordained or natural imperative to burden themselves with 'hostages to fortune'.[147] This was how the highly urban, as well as urbane, Sir Francis Bacon presented the key considerations involved in contemplating marriage and its issue, over two and a half centuries before 'modern', post-industrial, urban society's 'révolution démographique'.

---

[146] A. Landry, *La révolution démographique* (Paris, 1934).

[147] This phrase is drawn from one of *The Essays*, Francis Bacon's famous aphoristic *Counsells, Civill and Morall*, three editions of which were published in his lifetime between 1597 and 1625. It is cited in Banks, *Victorian Values*, p. 47.

21

The middle class

RICHARD TRAINOR

(i) THE ISSUES

IN RECENT years historians have begun to put flesh on the bones of the modern British middle class.[1] Given the rapidly increasing proportion of the population living in urban (including suburban) rather than rural areas, much of this work has dealt with towns, cities and urban regions.[2] These studies have identified the substantial economic, social and political resources that the middle class marshalled in urban Britain. Indeed, writing with reference to the period 1780–1870, R. J. Morris has argued that British towns were 'substantially the creation of their middle class, and in turn provided the theatre within which that middle class sought, extended, expressed and defended its power'.[3] Thus no survey of urban Britain would be complete without an analysis of the middle class. Equally, no analysis of the middle class can avoid sustained attention to the 'urban variable'. As Mike Savage has suggested, analysis of place is central to the investigation of class formation, a concept which in turn provides a useful way

---

I wish to acknowledge the highly skilled research assistance of Dr Mark Freeman in the preparation of this chapter.

[1] For a recent survey of the literature see A. Kidd and D. Nicholls, eds., *The Making of the British Middle Class?* (Stroud, 1998), introduction.

[2] For example H. Berghoff, 'British businessmen as wealth-holders 1870–1914', *Business History*, 23 (1991), 222–40; J. Field, 'Wealth, styles of life and social tone amongst Portsmouth's middle class, 1800–75', in R. J. Morris, ed., *Class, Power and Social Structure in British Nineteenth-Century Towns* (Leicester, 1986), pp. 67–106; A. C. Howe, *The Cotton Masters 1830–1860* (Oxford, 1984); T. Koditschek, *Class Formation and Urban Industrial Society* (Cambridge, 1990); R. J. Morris, *Class, Sect and Party* (Manchester, 1990); N. J. Morgan and R. H. Trainor, 'The dominant classes', in W. H. Fraser and R. J. Morris, eds., *People and Society in Scotland*, vol. II: *1830–1914* (Edinburgh, 1990), pp. 103–37; S. Nenadic, 'The Victorian middle classes', in W. H. Fraser and I. Maver, eds., *Glasgow*, vol. II: *1830 to 1912* (Manchester, 1996), pp. 265–99; R. H. Trainor; *Black Country Elites* (Oxford, 1993).

[3] R. J. Morris, 'The middle class and British towns and cities of the Industrial Revolution, 1780–1870', in D. Fraser and A. Sutcliffe, eds., *The Pursuit of Urban History* (London, 1983), p. 287.

of avoiding both the solely structural, and the solely cultural, approaches to the vexed but crucial subject of class.[4]

Yet this chapter cannot be a straightforward survey. For a start, rather than assume the impact of the middle class on urban Britain, it is necessary to demonstrate how far and how this influence was sustained – in relation both to the surprisingly influential aristocracy and to the increasingly well-organised working class.[5] This demands particular care because historical research on the middle class has concentrated on the period prior to 1900, after which significant changes occurred – notably accelerating suburbanisation – in the structure and nature of urbanisation. Moreover, the chapter must deal not only with issues of social structure, broadly defined, but also with the roles played by middle-class individuals and groups in the broader economic, social and political life of urban Britain.[6] To a significant extent, therefore, this must be a study of elites as well as of class.[7]

Before going further it is appropriate to define 'class' in general and 'middle class' in particular. In this study, a class is a group which shares a similar economic situation, level of prestige and eligibility for key positions: it is not assumed that such a group thinks alike or acts coherently.[8] This chapter approaches the middle class broadly, including all employers, all non-manual employees and all (apart from the landed aristocracy and gentry) people supported by independent income. As this middle class encompassed very considerable contrasts in resources, the study often subdivides the group into upper, middle and lower strata; this tripartite division – similar to that adopted in the 1860s by R. D. Baxter and echoed by many other contemporary commentators – avoids the inordinately diverse lower stratum of twofold division schemes.[9] Other sorts of subdivision – by occupational group, and by religious and political affiliation, for example – are also adopted. In our own time, admittedly, 'middle class' has

---

[4] M. Savage, 'Urban history and social class: two paradigms', *UH*, 20 (1993), 61, 69. For a measured defence of class analysis see Kidd and Nicholls, *Making*, introduction, pp. xvi–xxiii.

[5] Savage, 'Urban history', pp. 71–2; M. Savage, *The Dynamics of Working-Class Politics* (Cambridge, 1987); D. Cannadine, *Lords and Landlords* (Leicester, 1980).

[6] However, there is less coverage here of economic and cultural issues because of the chapters in this volume by Reeder and Rodger, and by Morris, respectively.

[7] To avoid repetition with the chapter on urban government the emphasis here falls on middle-class elites as a whole and, more particularly, on their involvements in secular and religious voluntary societies. Elites are primarily defined as those who held leadership positions in the major institutions. For an explanation of this approach – which does not take for granted either the agendas of these institutions or the influence of their leaders – see Trainor, *Black Country Elites*, pp. 18–21.

[8] For a detailed explanation of this approach see *ibid.*, pp. 16–17. Cf. John Scott, *Stratification and Power: Structures of Class, Status and Command* (Cambridge, 1996).

[9] R. D. Baxter, *National Income: The UK* (London, 1868), p. 35, who identifies the divisions with income ranges: up to £300, £300–£1,000 and (subdivided at £5,000) £1,000+. For a multidimensional approach adapted to regional variations, see Trainor, *Black Country Elites*, pp. 387–9.

become a rather vague and contested term.[10] Also, in the Victorian period as now, such a term was at least as much a cultural construct as a neutral tool of social classification. Yet in the early nineteenth century, 'contemporaries were quite clear . . . what it meant . . . to speak of working-class and middle class'.[11] The term broadened during the Victorian period to cover the range of occupations intended here. During the first half of the twentieth century and beyond, its meaning – both in popular and in scholarly discourse – remained stable and, for most observers, unproblematical.[12]

In dealing with the urban middle class since the mid-nineteenth century the chapter has to cope with the conflicting views of historians, many of whom – with important exceptions relating to the early Victorian decades and, throughout the period, to London – have tended during the last twenty-five years to emphasise division and weakness rather than coherence and strength. There is general agreement that, between the late eighteenth century and about 1870, the middle class developed rapidly within, and exercised considerable influence over, British towns, especially in provincial industrial areas. This was the middle class which played important roles in the repeal of the corn laws, the reform of municipal corporations and the rise of a network of thriving urban institutions with prominent roles for prosperous businessmen.[13] Yet some historians believe that, even in this part of the period and in the local arena, the influence of middle-class leaders was limited by internal divisions, the impact of landed elites and the intractability of the working class.[14] From this point of view, on the national stage middle-class impact was even more constrained – not only by the persisting power of traditional governing elites but also by a deep division between the provincial urban middle class, on the one hand, and its relatively larger, better-off equivalent in London and environs, on the other.[15] There is

---

[10] For a scholarly attempt to unravel these complexities, see T. Butler and M. Savage, eds., *Social Change and the Middle Classes* (London, 1995).

[11] E. Royle, *Modern Britain: A Social History 1750–1997* (London, 1997), p. 106. For the process by which the term 'middle class' was constructed see D. Wahrman, *Imagining the Middle Class: The Political Representation of Class in Britain, c. 1780–1840* (Cambridge, 1995).

[12] Trainor, *Black Country Elites*, pp. 54–62. Cf. R. Lewis and A. Maude, *The English Middle Classes* (London, 1949); I. Bradley, *The English Middle Classes are Alive and Kicking* (London, 1982).

[13] See, for example, the works cited in n. 2 above; D. Fraser, *Urban Politics in Victorian England* (Leicester, 1976); D. Fraser, ed., *Municipal Reform and the Industrial City* (Leicester, 1982).

[14] See in particular J. A. Garrard, *Leadership and Power in Victorian Industrial Towns 1830–80* (Manchester, 1983); F. M. L. Thompson, 'Social control in Victorian Britain', *Ec.HR*, 2nd series, 34 (1981), 189–208.

[15] The most influential works are those of W. D. Rubinstein, particularly: 'The Victorian middle classes: wealth, occupation, and geography', *Ec.HR*, 2nd series, 30 (1977), 602–23; 'Wealth, elites and the class structure of modern Britain', *P&P*, 76 (1977), 99–126; *Men of Property* (London, 1981); *Elites and the Wealthy in Modern British History* (Brighton, 1987). Cf. also M. J. Wiener, *English Culture and the Decline of the Industrial Spirit* (London, 1981).

even more support from historians for the view that, from the late nineteenth century, urban provincial middle-class elites (within which participation by the wealthy was already falling) faced increasing incursions in the local arena from central government and an insurgent working class. Moreover, during the same period the national position of the provincial urban middle class – more dependent on industry and less closely tied to finance, commerce, land and the professions than was its metropolitan equivalent[16] – may have declined even more rapidly. Especially after 1918, as British industry lost momentum (especially in the North and in Scotland), and as London and its dynamic suburbs appeared increasingly dominant in the nation's political, economic, social and cultural life, provincial towns and cities evidently lost many of their middle-class inhabitants, especially from the upper strata. In many localities, it would seem, lower-middle-class worthies and the representatives of organised labour subsequently battled for the scraps of a once vibrant urban culture. By the 1940s, apparently, with the partial exception of London, Britain's towns and cities were bereft of effective middle-class influence, except in narrowly economic terms.[17]

Some studies have cast doubt, for the pre-1914 period, on the proposition that a professionally, financially and commercially focused middle class centred in the South-East of England overshadowed an industrially centred middle class based in the Midlands, the North and Scotland.[18] But this is still contested terrain.[19] Given the attention devoted to these issues during the last quarter century, there is need for an analysis of the middle class between the mid-nineteenth and the

[16] See, for example, C. H. Lee, 'The service sector, regional specialisation and economic growth in the Victorian economy', *Journal of Historical Geography*, 10 (1984), 139–55; G. Ingham, *Capitalism Divided?* (Basingstoke, 1984). On persisting divisions between professionals and others in the middle class, see M. Savage *et al.*, *Property, Bureaucracy and Culture* (London, 1992), pp. 44–5 and *passim*.

[17] For these arguments see, for example, H. J. Dyos, 'Greater and Greater London: notes on metropolis and provinces in the nineteenth and twentieth centuries', in J. S. Bromley and E. H. Kossman, eds., *Britain and the Netherlands*, vol. IV: *Metropolis, Dominion and Province* (The Hague, 1971), pp. 89–112; A. A. Jackson, *The Middle Classes, 1900–1950* (Nairn, 1991), pp. 31, 105, 239–40, 244; P. L. Garside, 'London and the Home Counties', in F. M. L. Thompson, ed., *The Cambridge Social History of Britain, 1750–1950*, vol. I, *Regions and Communities*, pp. 494, 496–7, 504, 531–3; B. Robson, 'Coming full circle: London versus the rest, 1890–1980', in G. Gordon, ed., *Regional Cities in the UK, 1890–1980* (London, 1986), pp. 217–21; W. D. Rubinstein, 'Britain's elites in the interwar period, 1918–1939', in Kidd and Nicholls, eds., *Making*, pp. 186–202.

[18] See, for example, Berghoff, 'Regional variations in provincial business biography: the case of Birmingham, Bristol and Manchester, 1870–1914', *Business History*, 37 (1995), 64–85; M. J. Daunton, 'Gentlemanly capitalism and British industry 1820–1914', *P&P*, 122 (1989), 119–58; S. Gunn, 'The failure of the Victorian middle class: a critique', in J. Woolf and J. Seed, eds., *The Culture of Capital* (Manchester, 1988), pp. 17–43; R. H. Trainor, 'Urban elites in Victorian Britain', *UHY* (1985), 1–17; R. H. Trainor, 'The elite' (hereafter referred to as 'Glasgow's elite'), in Fraser and Maver, eds., *Glasgow*, II, pp. 227–64.

[19] For a sophisticated restatement of the 'overshadowing' thesis see F. M. L. Thompson, 'Town and city', in Thompson, ed., *Cambridge Social History*, I, 65–73.

mid-twentieth centuries which analyses the differences – and similarities – between the roles it played in various types of towns and cities.[20]

(ii) SIZE, OCCUPATIONAL STRUCTURE AND INTERNAL STRATIFICATION

The first stage in this process is to examine the relative size, the occupational structure and the internal stratification of the urban middle class, paying particular attention to variations between the urban provinces and the urban South-East. Analysis of occupational patterns significantly and increasingly qualifies, though it does not eliminate, the impression of London's superior position within the later nineteenth- and early twentieth-century middle class. More positively, in combination with various types of qualitative evidence the occupational data demonstrate the existence of a diverse and increasingly numerous middle class in the urban provinces, especially but not only in key regional centres such as Birmingham, Leeds, Manchester and Glasgow.

While occupation is an imperfect proxy for class it provides the single best clue to overall social position, not least because it is closely associated with prestige.[21] Thus, significant differences in average earnings correspond to the various 'occupational classes' based on the census. Also, by the 1950s a town's occupationally derived social class composition correlated closely with many of its other social characteristics.[22] Still, it is difficult to infer social stratification from occupational groups in the published census. The socially heterogeneous categories changed between censuses, and only from 1911 did they even attempt to map social inequality. Similarly, only in the twentieth century do the figures for the proportion of *females* employed in middle-class occupations become at all meaningful. There is also a distortion caused by the fact that the census groups which are very largely middle class tend to be white collar, thereby excluding owners of workshops and small factories.[23] None the less, these problems do not have a consistent bias, with regard either to the overall size of the middle class or to its regional distribution. Also, when used cautiously – for example, by restricting intercensal comparisons to periods when there *was* much consistency of classification[24]

---

[20] In doing so the chapter will pay less attention to country and market towns, and to London, because of the chapters in this volume devoted to these subjects.

[21] W. A. Armstrong, 'The use of information about occupation', in E. A. Wrigley, ed., *Nineteenth-Century Society* (Cambridge, 1972), pp. 202–3 and *passim*.

[22] G. Routh, *Occupation and Pay in Great Britain 1906–60* (Cambridge, 1965), pp. 103–8; C. A. Moser and W. Scott, *British Towns* (Edinburgh, 1961), pp. 33, 52–5, 77–9.

[23] D. C. Marsh, *The Changing Social Structure of England and Wales 1871–1961* (London, 1965 edn), pp. 125, 130; R. Lawton, 'Census data for urban areas', in R. Lawton, ed., *The Census and Social Structure* (London, 1978), pp. 82–145. Cf. E. Higgs, *A Clearer Sense of the Census* (London, c. 1996).

[24] Cf. Marsh, *Social Structure*, p. 130; Armstrong, 'Use of information', p. 194.

– such information can provide useful albeit rough indicators of social structure. These measures are especially helpful for the twentieth century, for which more socially precise information derived from the manuscript census is, with rare exceptions, not yet available.

It is appropriate to examine first the *occupation orders* – i.e. the simple aggregations of occupational groups – keeping in mind the consensus that the middle-class proportion of the *total* population expanded gradually but steadily during the period 1850–1950, especially in lower-middle-class occupations, rising from perhaps a sixth to about a quarter.[25] We should also be aware that estimates based on the proportion of the adult male population possessing the borough parliamentary franchise between 1832 and 1867 suggest that the middle class constituted a significant minority in all types of town but that the proportion varied widely, from as low as 10 per cent in industrial areas to more than 25 per cent in cathedral and county towns.[26]

In 1851 – using the four categories most likely to contain middle-class individuals[27] – London led all the boroughs (except Portsmouth) in England and Wales with 8.63 per cent of its occupied males. At the other extreme, predictably, were industrial towns such as Oldham (2.22 per cent) and Merthyr Tydfil (1.48 per cent). Yet relatively high results, while found in south-eastern citadels such as Cambridge (7.28 per cent) and Chichester (6.59 per cent), were not confined to that region, as the cathedral city examples of Exeter (7.45 per cent), Lincoln (6.04 per cent), and Durham (6.45 per cent) indicate. More surprisingly, given the bias of these measures against areas with large amounts of industrial enterprise, there were significant figures for Liverpool (6.68 per cent), Manchester and Salford (6.15 per cent), Newcastle-upon-Tyne (5.27 per cent), Nottingham (4.35 per cent) and Birmingham (4.37 per cent). Similar interurban patterns emerge from another early Victorian measure: the number of income taxpayers (at a time when vulnerability to income tax roughly coincided with middle-class status) in 1860. Even allowing for likely biases toward the metropolis in the collection of income tax (see below, p. 689), London's figure of 36.56 per cent confirms its position as the mid-nineteenth century urban locality with

---

[25] G. Best, *Mid-Victorian Britain 1851–75*, rev. edn (St Albans, 1973), pp. 101–2; A. L. Bowley, *Wages and Income in the United Kingdom since 1860* (Cambridge, 1937), pp. 127–36; C. Erickson, *British Industrialists* (Cambridge, 1959), pp. 233–5; Royle, *Modern Britain*, pp. 88–90, drawing on J. A. Banks, 'The social structure of nineteenth century England as seen through the census', in Lawton, ed., *Census*, pp. 194, 197; J. Burnett, *A Social History of Housing, 1815–1985*, 2nd edn (London, 1986), p. 95.

[26] Morris, 'The middle class and British towns and cities', pp. 287–8. Cf. Trainor, *Black Country Elites*, p. 63.

[27] I = General and Local Government; III = Learned Professions (and their immediate subordinates); IV=Literature, Fine Arts and the Sciences; VII = Buyers, Lenders etc. of Money, Houses and Goods. Even taken together, these categories significantly understate middle-class numbers by missing, for example, managers and clerks employed in industry.

the greatest proportion of middle-class males. However, while cathedral, county and market towns come next in the pecking order – Gloucester has 21.55 per cent, Buckingham 30.50 per cent and Banbury 20.35 per cent, for example – major provincial cities such as Bristol (19.51 per cent), Liverpool (17.33 per cent), Manchester (15.32 per cent) and Birmingham (14.22 per cent) also have substantial proportions. As in the census, it is the overwhelmingly industrial towns (Blackburn at 7.83 per cent and Leicester at 6.07 per cent, for example), which come last – and even there a far from negligible proportion and number of middle-class individuals are indicated.[28]

Similar results emerge from analyses of occupation orders I (Government), III (Professions and their Subordinates) and V (Commercial and Clerical) from the censuses of 1881 to 1911 inclusive. Many south-eastern towns had clear leads over their counterparts drawn from other regions. Thus London and Croydon (11.35 per cent and 10.97 per cent in 1881, respectively) – joined by Middlesex (at 19.03 per cent) in 1911 – had the largest proportions, and industrial towns such as Burnley and Walsall (both at 3.16 per cent in 1881; 6.37 per cent and 6.72 per cent respectively in 1911) had among the lowest. Yet each of these lists also shows the major provincial English cities to have had substantial proportions of their male workforces in these key middle-class categories. Manchester and Liverpool, for example, already at 8 per cent in 1881, moved up in 1891 to 10.5 per cent, to the range 10–12 per cent in 1901 and to 12–13 per cent in 1911. These results, reflecting the very considerable white-collar presence in the industries as well as the commercial trades of these cities, indicate that in the provinces significant middle-class percentages were not confined either to the more genteel cities like Bristol (7.68 per cent in 1881, 12.70 per cent in 1911) and Norwich (6.02 per cent in 1881, 10.94 per cent in 1911) or to county towns such as Bath and York (12.60 per cent and 10.15 per cent respectively in 1911). It is also worth noting the high ratings for Midland and northern towns like Birkenhead and Southport (12.11 per cent and 15.88 per cent respectively in 1911) which had substantial middle-class *suburban* populations. Scottish towns, too, scored well on such measures.[29]

Occupation orders, analysed by conurbation, from the 1921 and 1951 censuses, produce similar conclusions. In 1921, for example, Greater London easily led the male figures for commercial, professional and clerical occupations (Figure 21.1). Yet in none of the key provincial urban areas were the individual or combined totals for these categories less than substantial. The results for 1951 are

---

[28] See W. D. Rubinstein, 'The size and distribution of the English middle classes in 1860', *HR*, 61 (1988), 65–89, with conclusions differing in emphasis to the interpretation offered here.

[29] Morgan and Trainor, 'Dominant classes', pp. 105–8, give even higher figures for Scotland, having taken detailed middle-class dealing and industrial occupations out of other orders. A number of cities absorbed previously separate middle-class areas in the thirty years prior to 1914, as Birmingham did Handsworth and Glasgow did Hillhead.

comparable, though Figure 21.2 shows little London advantage in *female* middle-class employment, and Figure 21.3 suggests some contraction of London's male middle-class advantage compared to thirty years before – perhaps because in an increasingly white-collar and professional society older occupational contrasts between the Metropolis and the provinces had begun to fade.

Even greater parity between London and provincial cities emerges when the focus shifts (in Figure 21.4) to the *socio-economic groups* of the 1951 census, a measure of households rather than of individual salary earners, and one which includes many of the managers, employers and shopkeepers missed by the occupation orders' emphasis on white-collar groups. London's lead remained substantial, but the major English provincial conurbations, and Central Clydeside, showed significant middle-class proportions as well. An even flatter set of overall comparisons emerges in Figure 21.5 which depicts the Registrar General's troublesome *five-class* scheme. This measure supports the case for the significant size of the provincial middle class but to a misleadingly great degree due to the notoriously bloated class III, which includes a significant proportion of manual workers.[30] More indicative are statistics (not given here) concerning the proportions of the occupied workforce in middle-class *status aggregates* such as employers and managers: these too indicate less of a lead for London than do the pre-1951 figures for occupation orders.

What these various measures suggest, then, is that significant and rising proportions of the workforces, and thus of the total populations, of major provincial urban areas – and even of many individual provincial towns – were middle class. Also, the gap between the relative sizes of the provincial and metropolitan middle classes, which may have been diminishing as early as the turn of the century, was contracting by the early 1950s.

Given London's huge size compared to other British cities, in terms of *absolute* numbers of middle-class inhabitants the capital was even more firmly in the lead. But in this respect, too, provincial strength was considerable. Thus Glasgow, for example, had over 11,000 men and women in commercial occupations in 1881. Manchester had more than 3,000 and Birmingham more than 2,000 accountants in 1901, when Glasgow and Edinburgh combined had just short of a thousand physicians, surgeons and general practitioners and more than 16,000 clerks. By 1951 the provincial numbers in such occupations were much greater. South-east Lancashire then boasted more than 125,000 clerks and typists, while Bristol had more than 25,000.[31] Provincial cities and towns shared in the rise in

---

[30] See Armstrong, 'Use of information', p. 204; and A. M. Carr-Saunders *et al.*, *Survey of Social Conditions in England and Wales* . . . (Oxford, 1958), pp. 116–17. Concentrating on the proportions of classes I and II shows a significant, but not massive, lead for London – a conclusion supported, for the South-East as a whole, by Moser and Scott's analysis of English and Welsh towns with at least 50,000 inhabitants (*British Towns*, Map 1).

[31] Published census; Morgan and Trainor, 'Dominant classes', pp. 107–11.

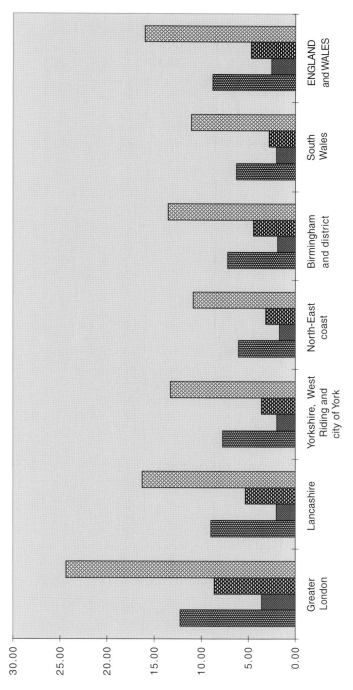

Figure 21.1 Occupation Orders XXIII, XXV and XXVIII, males aged twelve and over, as percentage of total occupied, in six mainly urban areas of England and Wales, plus England and Wales as a whole, 1921

XXIII = commerce, finance and insurance (excluding clerks)

XXV = professional occupations (excluding clerks)

XXVIII = clerks, typists, etc.

Source: census for 1921.

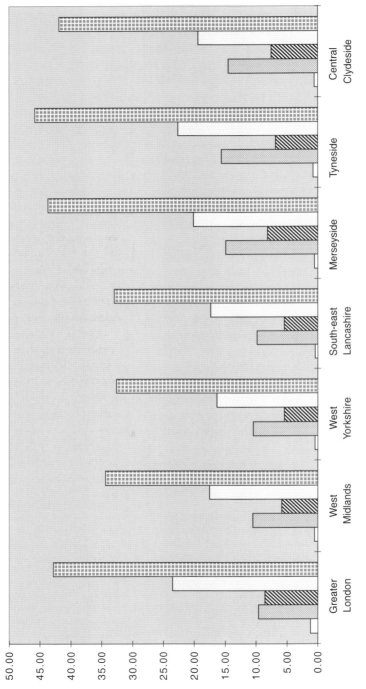

Figure 21.2 Occupation Orders XVI, XVIII, XIX and XXIII, females aged fifteen and over, as percentage of total occupied, in conurbations, 1951

XVI = administrators, directors, managers (not elsewhere specified)

XVIII = commercial, finance and insurance occupations (excluding clerical staff)

XIX = professional and technical occupations (excluding clerical staff)

XXIII = clerks, typists, etc.

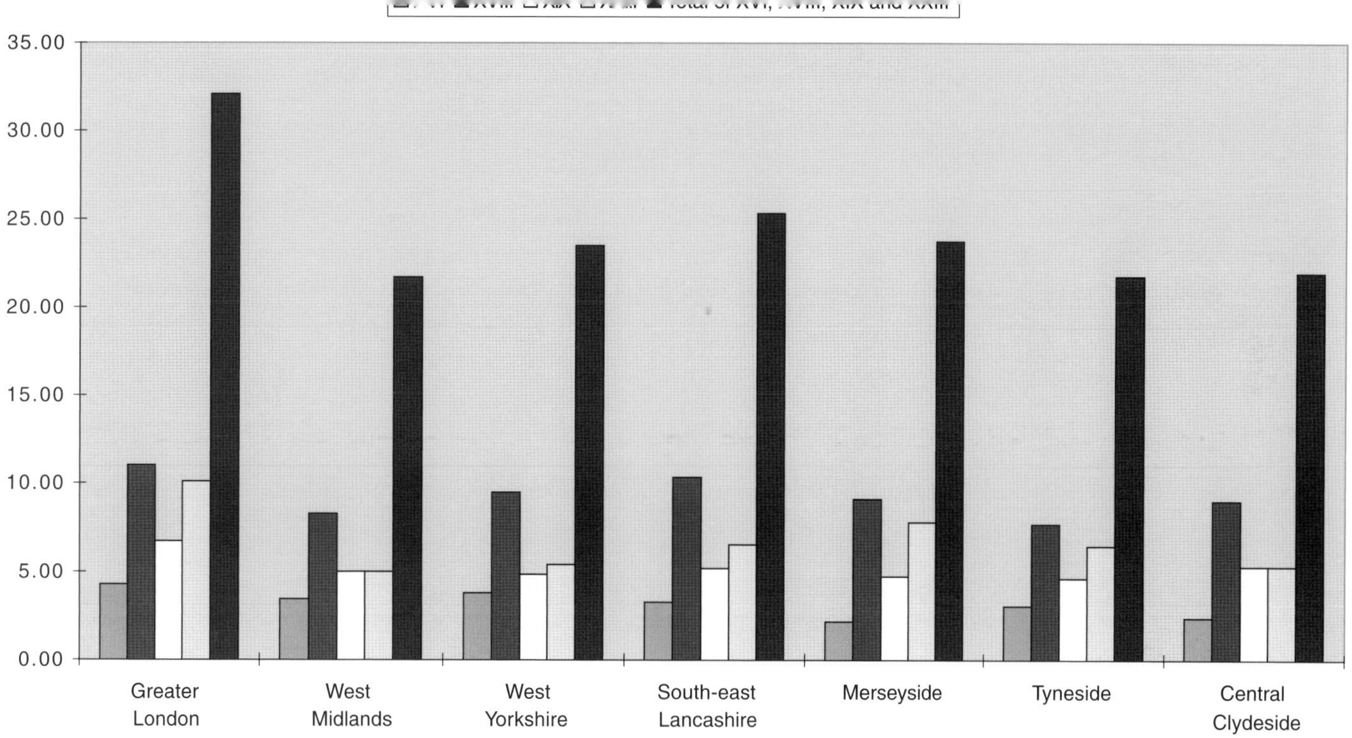

Figure 21.3 Occupation Orders XVI, XVIII, XIX and XXIII, males aged fifteen and over, as percentage of total occupied, in conurbations, 1951

XVI = administrators, directors, managers (not elsewhere specified)

XVIII = commercial, finance and insurance occupations (excluding clerical staff)

XIX = professional and technical occupations (excluding clerical staff)

XXIII = clerks, typists, etc.

Source: census for 1951.

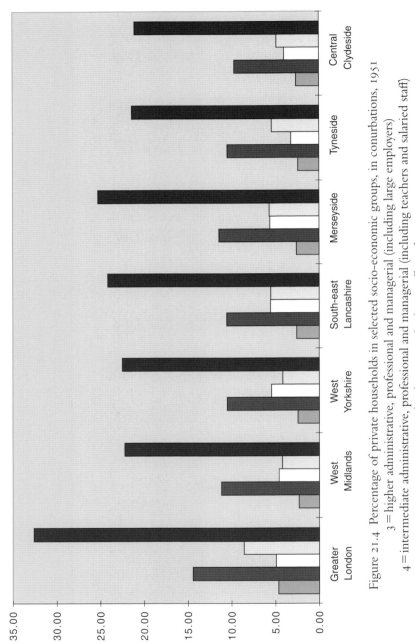

Figure 21.4 Percentage of private households in selected socio-economic groups, in conurbations, 1951
3 = higher administrative, professional and managerial (including large employers)
4 = intermediate administrative, professional and managerial (including teachers and salaried staff)
5 = shopkeepers and other small employers
6 = clerical workers

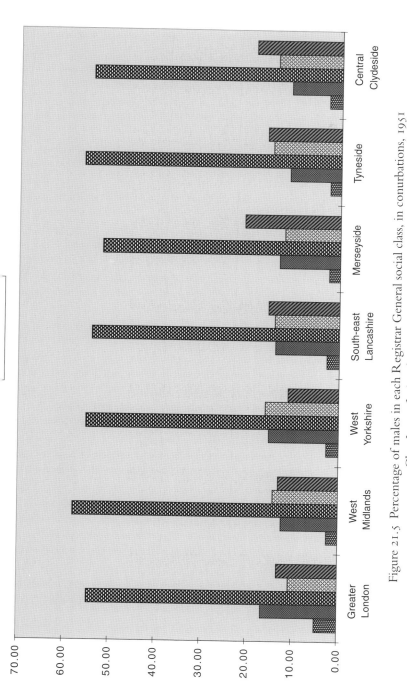

Figure 21.5 Percentage of males in each Registrar General social class, in conurbations, 1951

Class I = professional and analogous occupations

Class II = intermediate occupations (e.g. many shopkeepers)

Class III = skilled occupations (including foremen and most clerks)

Class IV = partly skilled occupations

Class V = unskilled occupations

Source: census for 1951.

clerical employment – evident from the late nineteenth century, and accelerating from the First World War – which (along with a corresponding decline in the number of employers) was the most striking change in the internal occupational composition of the middle class. Thus the provincial urban middle class was numerous and was drawn from a variety of occupations outside as well as within industry, just as the London (and broader south-eastern) urban middle class included many members who drew their livings from industry as well as from commerce and dealing.

This judgement is confirmed by a variety of impressionistic information, for the twentieth as for the nineteenth century. Thus from the 1820s all provincial cities – and, by the 1870s, all substantial provincial towns – participated significantly in middle-class suburbanisation, often initially within city boundaries.[32] Also, while nothing elsewhere could rival Oxford Street's shops, provincial cities boasted the substantial department stores which depended to a significant degree on middle-class customers, especially women.[33]

Clearly the proportion of the population which was middle class affected the social atmosphere of a town or city. Arguably, the social relations of towns with relatively small middle classes might have been especially stark, featuring a 'naked battle between capital and labour, with the proviso that labour often genuinely deferred to capital'.[34] Yet the existence of a middle class even of 10 per cent of the population of a later nineteenth-century industrial town could mean a much more complex pattern of social relations – especially if that middle class included a series of gradations between the very rich and those not much better-off than the skilled working class – than in those early industrial localities where large industrialists faced a large working population with few intermediaries.[35]

The internal stratification of the middle class, therefore, shaped the lives of middle-class urban dwellers and influenced the impact that the middle class had on Britain's towns and cities more generally. There were enormous differences in resources – and in life style (see pp. 691–8 below) – between: the upper middle class of large industrialists and other leading business and professional people; the middle middle class of middling manufacturers, managers and substantial dealers and professionals; and the lower middle class of white-collar employees and small (but employing) retailers and craftsmen. In the Black Country, for example, the middle class stretched from the Bilston steelmaster Sir Alfred Hickman (who left £1 million at his death in 1910) through solid professional people like the West Bromwich surveyor Thomas Rollason (£19,099 in 1903) to individuals of modest means such as the Dudley grocer Robert Preece (£1,498 in 1893).[36] The

---

[32] See, for instance, F. M. L. Thompson, ed., *The Rise of Suburbia* (Leicester, 1982), 'Introduction', p. 6.   [33] Jackson, *Middle Classes*, pp. 247, 253.

[34] Rubinstein, 'English middle classes in 1860', p. 80.

[35] Cf. Trainor, *Black Country Elites*, pp. 69–70, 90–2; D. C. Howell and C. Baber, 'Wales', in Thompson, ed., *Cambridge Social History*, I, p. 317.

[36] Somerset House, printed probate calendars.

urban, like the national, middle class was shaped like a pyramid: the lower middle class was always by far the most numerous of the three categories; this predominance probably increased as the numbers of white-collar employees swelled from 1870 faster than numbers declined within the *petite bourgeoisie* of small masters and dealers.[37] Yet, even with adverse changes in income tax from 1914, the upper middle class stayed well off – and numerous in absolute terms – right down to 1939.[38] Meanwhile, the situation of the lower middle class remained perilous: even in the interwar years ordinary doctors' bills threatened family solvency in the household of the future historian J. F. C. Harrison, for example.[39]

Such vast differences in wealth and income contributed to feelings of superiority and resentment among the various strata of the middle class. Hence, for example, the 'ratepayers' movements' of the early and mid-Victorian years in which the lower middle class (often in alliance with working-class ratepayers who, like themselves, bore disproportionate rate burdens) often opposed the improvements backed by the 'solid' middle class, that is its upper and middle strata.[40] Likewise, even a young man from a comfortable middle-class home, the future historian Richard Cobb, resented deeply the condescension of his better-off cousins from Sevenoaks.[41] These contrasts in resources and attitudes among social strata partly coincided with differences among the major *occupational* groups within the urban middle class. Retailers, craftsmen and all but the top white-collar employees were especially suspect, while there were hints of tensions between industrialists, on the one hand, and professionals and the commercial/financial sector, on the other.[42] Thus, with regard to occupational groups as well as social strata, the urban middle class would appear, in F. M. L. Thompson's words, fragmented into 'layer upon layer of subclasses, keenly aware of their subtle grades of distinction'.[43]

Yet, other resource-related factors bound together the three major social strata, and the various occupational groups, of the urban middle class. All but its lowest fringe had advantages over the majority of the population both in overall material resources and in terms of mortality and morbidity. The great bulk of the group also had significant stakes in the middle-class version of 'respectability' and participated in the middle-class income and property cycles linked to

[37] For the survival of the latter see G. J. Crossick and H.-G. Haupt, *The Petite Bourgeoisie in Europe 1780–1914* (London, 1995), pp. 126, 218–19.
[38] Rubinstein, 'Britain's elites in the interwar period', pp. 190–1.
[39] J. F. C. Harrison, *Scholarship Boy: A Personal History of the Mid-Twentieth Century* (London, 1995), p. 18.
[40] On these movements see E. P. Hennock, 'Finance and politics in urban local government in England, 1835–1900', *HJ*, 6 (1963), 212–25; Trainor, *Black Country Elites*, pp. 254–6.
[41] R. Cobb, *Still Life: Sketches from a Tunbridge Wells Childhood* (London, 1992), pp. 121–2.
[42] Trainor, *Black Country Elites*, pp. 81–6; H. J. Perkin, *The Origins of Modern English Society 1780–1880* (London, 1969), ch. 10.
[43] F. M. L. Thompson, *The Rise of Respectable Society* (London, 1988), p. 173.

stages of life.[44] In addition, few middle-class people were complacent regarding these advantages. Rising standards of prestigious consumption strained family budgets. Also, while economic vulnerability was most typical of the lower middle class, fear of downward mobility affected most of the group, notably during and immediately after nineteenth-century slumps and in the 1930s.[45] As working-class organisations such as trades unions and trades councils began to make a significant impact on urban as on national life from the late nineteenth century, resource patterns encouraged greater identification with the broader middle class even amongst the especially marginal *petite bourgeoisie*. Likewise, with regard to occupational distinctions, as the period progressed the more substantial shop-keepers, craftsmen and white-collar workers increasingly saw themselves, and were regarded, as members of the 'solid' middle class. Thus at the start of the twentieth century a prosperous Bolton wholesale and retail ironmonger and general dealer lived near some mill owners and socialised both with doctors and solicitors.[46] With respect to tensions between industrialists and professionals, these were not typical of provincial cities and towns such as Leeds, Salford or West Bromwich, in part because there was no sense of 'pan-professional identity', in part because the working lives of many urban professionals and businessmen were closely intertwined.[47] With regard to industrialists and the commercial/financial sector, while in London the externally orientated City elite had limited dealings with manufacturers, in provincial cities the two sectors were tightly linked. As a manufacturer from the Chamberlain/Kenrick clan commented, there was no condescension to manufacturers in Birmingham.[48] Even in London, residence and social mixing correlated more with social stratum than with occupation.[49]

There remains the possibility that the pattern of social stratification within the

[44] R. J. Morris, 'The middle class and the property cycle during the Industrial Revolution', in T. C. Smout, ed., *The Search for Wealth and Stability* (London, 1979), pp. 91–113; Burnett, *Housing*, pp. 185–6; V. Berridge, 'Health and medicine', in F. M. L. Thompson, ed., *The Cambridge Social History of Britain, 1750–1950*, vol. III: *Social Agencies and Institutions* (Cambridge, 1990), p. 231.

[45] J. Banks and O. Banks, *Prosperity and Parenthood* (London, 1954); Nenadic, 'Victorian middle classes', *passim*.

[46] G. Crossick, 'Urban society and the petty bourgeoisie in nineteenth-century Britain', in Fraser and Sutcliffe, eds., *Pursuit*, pp. 307–26; Trainor, *Black Country Elites*, pp. 59–62; father of Bernard Thornley, ESRC Qualidata Centre, University of Essex: Family Life and Work Archive, QD1/FLWE/33 (hereafter cited as QD1 etc.).

[47] J. Garrard and V. Parrott, 'Craft, professional and middle-class identity: solicitors and gas engineers, *c*. 1850–1914', in Kidd and Nicholls, eds., *Making*, pp. 148–68; Morris, *Class, Sect and Party*, p. 325; Trainor, *Black Country Elites*, p. 84. For a partial exception see D. Smith, *Conflict and Compromise* (London, 1982), pp. 105, 113. Relations may have become more difficult during the twentieth century as the relative standing of managers rose (cf. P. Thompson, *The Edwardians* (London, 1975), p. 299; H. J. Perkin, *The Rise of Professional Society: England since 1880* (London, 1989)).

[48] Michael Hope, QD1/FLWE/MUC/2 C707/473/1–4; Berghoff, 'Regional variations', p. 73.

[49] This is implicit in the analysis of upper-class, upper-middle-class and lower-middle-class districts of London in H. McLeod, *Class and Religion in the Late Victorian City* (London, 1974).

middle class differed radically between London and the provinces, making the two groups almost incomparable, with implications for the ability of the provincial middle class to function not only outside their regions but perhaps inside them as well. Evidence from the size of fortunes left at death and from income tax assessments suggests that London enjoyed disproportionate shares of top fortunes and incomes.[50] It seems natural that so large and long-established a metropolis, which was also the capital, should contain large numbers – perhaps the majority – of the most important members of Britain's professional, commercial and (with the shift to London of company headquarters after the First World War) even industrial communities.

Yet possible biases in favour of London in probate and income tax material suggest caution. Also, a study of the wealth left at death by key businessmen throughout England and Wales suggests that neither London, nor the non-industrial occupational groups clustered there, were especially likely to generate wealth.[51] Likewise, analysis of a key taxation return from 1880 in terms of amounts assessed per capita suggests that provincial cities were comparable to London as a whole (though not to the City in isolation), albeit industrial towns, like some county towns and ports, lagged well behind both (see Table 21.1). Moreover, data for the Victorian period on Birmingham, Bristol, Manchester, the Black Country, Glasgow and other Scottish cities indicate significant numbers both of large fortunes and of high incomes. The middle classes of these urban places, therefore, included individuals able to deal on terms of equality with London's wealthy elite and with great potential for influence within their own towns and cities.[52] Differential economic development in favour of the South-East in the first half of the twentieth century may have increased the advantages of the metropolis with respect to its absolute number, and proportion, of the upper middle and middle middle classes.[53] But even in the depths of the Depression of the 1930s J. B. Priestley noted many comfortable homes, hotels and clubs in the cities and suburbs of the North.[54] Also, the fact that in

---

[50] W. D. Rubinstein, 'British millionaires, 1809–1949', *Bull. IHR*, 47 (1974), 202–23; Rubinstein, 'Victorian middle classes'; Rubinstein, *Elites and the Wealthy*.

[51] T. Nicholas, 'Wealthmaking in nineteenth- and early twentieth-century Britain; industry v. commerce and finance', *Business History*, 41 (1999), 16–36. On sources see, for example, M. Jubb, 'Income, class and the taxman: a note on the distribution of wealth in nineteenth century Britain', *HR*, 60 (1987), 117–24; M. S. Moss, 'William Todd Lithgow: founder of a fortune', *SHR*, 62 (1983), 47–72; Trainor, *Black Country Elites*, pp. 64–5, 69.

[52] Trainor, *Black Country Elites*, pp. 65–8; Berghoff, 'Businessmen'.

[53] Thus Rubinstein finds (*Elites and the Wealthy*, pp. 89–111) that, while provincial counties such as Yorkshire and Lancashire increased their total tax yields in relation to London and the Home Counties during the mid-nineteenth century, thereafter (until the disappearance, from the inter-war period, of regionally based tax statistics) the South-East increased its significant residual lead. Cf. Jackson, *Middle Classes*, ch. 2, *passim*.

[54] See, for example, J. B. Priestley, *English Journey* (London, 1934), pp. 158, 302, 304, 312.

Table 21.1 *Amounts assessed to income tax, in pounds per head of population, for selected parliamentary boroughs 1880*

City of London	816.15	Norwich	8.23
Derby	46.42	Leeds	8.02
Westminster	45.00	Hull	7.54
London with City	25.39	Leicester	7.43
Manchester	24.94	Coventry	7.41
Edinburgh	21.06	Northampton	7.32
Liverpool	19.94	Oxford	7.30
Darlington	16.76	Bath	7.15
Glasgow	16.70	Sheffield	7.10
Cardiff	15.16	Stoke-on-Trent	7.05
Inverness	14.57	Ipswich	7.03
London without City	13.80	Bedford	6.76
Newcastle-upon-Tyne	12.74	Wolverhampton	6.46
Reading	11.87	Bolton	6.43
Salisbury	11.27	Winchester	6.42
Bristol	11.19	Colchester	6.28
Lincoln	11.05	Berwick-upon-Tweed	6.22
Wakefield	10.82	Stockport	6.21
Worcester	10.79	Preston	5.98
Bradford	10.64	Cheltenham	5.92
Nottingham	10.34	Dudley	5.64
Birmingham	10.02	Plymouth	5.32
Middlesbrough	9.50	Oldham	5.24
Halifax	9.29	Salford	4.87
Aberdeen	9.28	Walsall	4.69
Greenock	9.25	Portsmouth	4.19
Brighton	9.01	Wednesbury	4.02
Southampton	8.91	Blackburn	3.81
Chester	8.89	Port Glasgow	3.62
Exeter	8.82	Merthyr Tydfil	3.11
Huddersfield	8.65	South Shields	2.53
Dundee	8.44		

London with city = Chelsea, Finsbury, Greenwich, Hackney, Lambeth, London (City), Marylebone, Southwark, Tower Hamlets, Westminster.
Population figures are for 1881.
Assessment is for schedule D.
Source: PP1882 LII (149).

1951 London's advantage (see Figure 21.4) in socio-economic group 3 – the higher administrative, professional and managerial category – was not especially large in comparison to the provinces suggests that major provincial urban areas contained many members both of the upper middle class and of the middle middle class. This impression is further confirmed by returning (in Figure 21.5) to the five-class data, in which the capital and other parts of the South-east had only moderate leads in class I. Thus, while outnumbered by their south-eastern counterparts, the better-off provincial members of the middle class formed a substantial proportion both of the provincial middle class as a whole and of the upper ranks of the British middle class more generally.

(iii) LIFE STYLE AND IDENTITY

What was the social environment of this socially, occupationally and geograph-ically diverse urban middle class? During working hours, there were consider-able differences between the activities of a substantial businessman, a professional person, a shopkeeper and a white-collar employee. Industrialists and merchants had considerable autonomy: in the 1880s the father of the Glaswegian J. J. Bell, for example, worked hard in his city-centre office but on a pattern of his own choosing before returning to his suburban home for dinner.[55] Professionals might be more driven by clients but also had significant control over their working conditions and hours. By contrast, even those retailers and publicans who employed staff were under pressure to remain at their shops for many of the long hours during which they opened, especially prior to 1914.[56] White-collar workers usually had considerably less control than any of these 'independent' groups over either the structure or the pace of the working day. Thus the Glasgow clerk Robert Ferguson, who entered the workforce in a printing firm just before the First World War, had to heed the office manager, 'a pretty tough guy, you had to be on your toes all the time'. Similarly, clerks had to take much more care of their appearance than did skilled workers who sometimes earned as much or even more. Ferguson differed from his siblings in manual occupa-tions because 'I was very conceited . . . with dress, I had to be. I had to shave every morning of life, before I went to work.' He had to give up boxing because 'If you get marked – it looks terrible the next day.' Yet Ferguson profited from other distinctions from manual workers. During fifty-two years of work with

---

[55] J. J. Bell, *I Remember* (Edinburgh, 1932), pp. 27–38. For a general discussion of hours of work see H. Cunningham, 'Leisure and culture', in F. M. L. Thompson, ed., *The Cambridge Social History of Britain, 1750–1950*, vol. II: *People and their Environment* (Cambridge, 1990), pp. 286–7.

[56] Yet resulting strains on family life might be eased if the employer lived either 'over the shop' or (in small or medium-sized towns) close enough so that, as with Arnold Bennett's 'Edwin Clayhanger' in the Potteries, it was possible to return home for meals even after a separate resi-dence had been acquired – *Clayhanger* (Harmondsworth, 1973).

the same firm, he 'never started before nine o'clock' and enjoyed clean working conditions, security and fringe benefits: 'I'm the staff you see. And I go about with my bowler hat on from morning 'til stopping time. My pay was . . . very regular. Holidays were paid . . . too . . . [for] staff . . . But [not] the workers.'[57] As white-collar workers began to constitute a larger proportion of the middle class, Ferguson's work experience became increasingly typical, as much in its highly structured, often limited career pattern as in its separation from manual workers.[58]

In terms of housing, as of work, the various strata of the middle class differed significantly; a highly varied supply of urban dwellings catered to their contrast-ing demands.[59] In England before 1914 the typical lower-middle-class family lived in a terrace house, while its middle-middle-class counterpart usually had a 'semi'. Upper-middle-class families favoured detached houses.[60] The latter were often located in the suburbs which the upper stratum had pioneered, either in an urban enclave such as Birmingham's Edgbaston or in a cosy area outside the city boundary such as Glasgow's Bearsden. There was a huge contrast between the modest house of the famous fictional clerk 'Mr Pooter' with his single servant, and the huge, well-staffed piles inhabited by the Chamberlains and Kenricks.[61] Also, while the distances involved were smaller in provincial cities than in London, in large towns there was considerable residential segregation within the middle class by the late nineteenth century. Thus, 'If London had its Dulwich, Richmond and Edgware, the same single class exclusiveness was to be found in Bristol's Clifton, Cotham and Redland, Nottingham's Wollaton, West

[57] QD1/FLWE/260, pp. 58, 36, 12, 17–18.

[58] For the general pattern, which as in Ferguson's case often persisted well into the post-1945 period, see D. Lockwood, *The Blackcoated Worker* (London, 1958). For the increasing limitations to the prospects of urban clerks, see G. L. Anderson, *Victorian Clerks* (Manchester, 1976); and G. L. Anderson, 'The social economy of late Victorian clerks', in G. Crossick, ed., *The Lower Middle Class in Britain, 1870–1914* (London, 1977), pp. 113–33. On career patterns, see K. Stovel, M. Savage and P. Bearman, 'Ascription into achievement: models of career systems at Lloyds Bank, 1890–1970', *American Journal of Sociology*, 102 (1996), 358–99; M. Savage, 'Discipline, surveillance and the "career": employment on the Great Western Railway, 1833–1914', in A. McKinlay and K. Starkey, eds., *Foucault, Management and Organization Theory* (London, 1998), pp. 65–92. For the complex way in which social mobility affected the urban middle class see A. Miles, *Social Mobility in Nineteenth- and Early Twentieth-Century England* (Basingstoke, 1999).

[59] M. A. Simpson and T. H. Lloyd, eds., *Middle Class Housing in Britain* (Newton Abbot, 1977), 'Introduction', p. 10.

[60] Thompson, *Rise of Respectable Society*, p. 174. There were, of course, significant regional varia-tions (M. J. Daunton, 'Housing', in Thompson, ed., *Cambridge Social History*, II, p. 214), not least with regard to Scotland, where many middle-class families lived in tenement flats, some of which were large and opulent.

[61] G. Grossmith and W. Grossmith, *Diary of a Nobody* (Bristol, 1892); Cannadine, *Lords and Landlords*. For the early process of suburbanisation see Thompson, *Rise of Suburbia*, p. 12; for the significance of servant-keeping to the nineteenth-century middle class, see L. Davidoff, 'The family in Britain', in Thompson, ed., *Cambridge Social History*, II, p. 81; and Thompson, *Rise of Respectable Society*, pp. 175–6.

Bridgeford [*sic*] and Mapperley Park, or Manchester's Alderley Edge and Wilmslow.'[62] Variations in housing, then, not only 'mirrored' social distinctions within the middle class but also 'helped to define and reinforce them'.[63]

None the less, aspects of urban middle-class housing also drew the strata together, albeit in ways which differed from region to region. Throughout the middle class, by the beginning of our period, there was a strong desire for domesticity, comfort and privacy. Within the home this meant – allowing for huge contrasts in scale and quality – elaborate decoration and furnishings. As the American visitor Ralph Waldo Emerson noticed, 'If [an Englishman] . . . is in [the] middle condition, he spares no expense on his house . . . it is wainscoted, carved, curtained, hung with pictures and filled with good furniture.'[64] Middle-class homes also emphasised clear categorisation of rooms, isolating families from their servants.[65] In terms of location, the middle class favoured distinct separation from working-class houses, significant distancing from their own place of work and (money permitting) a low-density neighbourhood. Thus, aided by transport innovations, even the lower middle class increasingly suburbanised, especially from the 1880s.[66] In terms of location, if not scale, of housing they then resembled the vast majority of their middle-class betters: even in Lancashire, Yorkshire and the Home Counties only a small minority of the upper middle class ventured farther into the countryside than the urban fringe.[67]

The residential changes which affected the urban middle class during the period 1918–50 – increased ownership, the diffusion of the 'semi' and accelerated suburbanisation – reinforced these common features. In contrast to the pre-1914 tradition of middle-class renting, between the world wars 'owner-occupation developed as the typical middle-class tenure', covering just over half the group by 1939. The proportion was especially high in those towns, largely found in the South-East, with especially large middle-class populations.[68] As a result, 'much of the middle middle and some of the lower middle class' could become property owners.[69] Builders catered for this swollen demand particularly through 'semis'. Well-adapted to the modest means of the new owners, these houses represented a 'change of both lifestyle and status' for families like the

---

[62] Burnett, *Housing*, p. 106, pp. 189–90 (quote); Thompson, *Rise of Suburbia*, p. 8. Cf. R. Dennis, *English Industrial Cities of the Nineteenth Century* (Cambridge, 1984), chs. 3, 7 and 8; C. Pooley, 'Residential differentiation in Victorian cities: a reassessment', *Transactions of the Institute of British Geographers*, new series, 9 (1984), 131–44.   [63] Thompson, *Rise of Respectable Society*, p. 174.

[64] R. W. Emerson, *English Traits* (London, 1913), p. 106, quoted by Burnett, *Housing*, p. 109.

[65] Daunton, 'Housing', p. 211; Burnett, *Housing*, p. 102; R. G. Rodger, *Housing in Urban Britain 1780–1914* (Cambridge, 1995), p. 41.

[66] Thompson, *Rise of Suburbia*, pp. 17, 20.

[67] R. H. Trainor, 'The gentrification of Victorian and Edwardian industrialists', in A. L. Beier, D. Cannadine and J. M. Rosenheim, eds., *The First Modern Society* (Cambridge, 1989), pp. 167–97.

[68] Daunton, 'Housing', p. 218; M. Swenarton and S. Taylor, 'The scale and nature of the growth of owner-occupation in Britain between the wars', *Ec.HR*, 2nd series, 38 (1985), 388–91; Burnett, *Housing*, p. 97.   [69] R. McKibbin, *Classes and Cultures* (Oxford, 1998), p. 73.

Harrisons of Leicester, who had previously lived in a cramped terrace house: 'A bathroom and indoor lavatory, a front door that no longer opened directly onto the street, a garden with a lawn and flower beds – these were things which transformed the quality of family life.'[70] The Harrisons' existence was more securely middle class than before, even if it still lacked the servant-keeping which continued to assist many middle-middle- and most upper-middle-class urban households down to 1939.[71] The Harrisons continued to live in Leicester, but by the outbreak of war a significantly increased percentage of the urban middle class resided outside city boundaries. Upwardly mobile business families such as the Vaughans abandoned a middle-class quarter of Brixton for New Malden to the south-west, just as (less often but still frequently) their northern counterparts did for places such as the Wirral.[72] Yet living even farther afield – in villages and the countryside – was still a minority persuasion, even for Londoners and Lancastrians.[73] Thus, as substantial numbers of middle-class people (especially from the middle and lower strata) still lived in or adjacent to towns and cities in the 1920s and 1930s, the middle-class 'withdrawal' from urbanity – though it had important consequences, notably by reducing the fiscal resources for solving social problems within towns and cities – also had distinct limits.[74]

The more general life style of the urban middle class paralleled its housing patterns in following a pattern of diversity within an increasingly common pattern. Certainly there were major contrasts. The upper middle class, in both London and the provinces, indulged in formal visiting cards and frequently promoted 'high culture' in their town or city. While some of these families hunted, more typical were the millowning Cloughs of Keighley, who abstained from such pursuits but employed a large household staff, had formal visiting days, attended concerts in Leeds and Bradford, enjoyed a month's holiday and took their paternalistic responsibilities toward the millworkers seriously.[75] Middle-middle-class

[70] Harrison, *Scholarship Boy*, pp. 46, 50.
[71] On servants, see McKibbin, *Classes and Cultures*, p. 61; Burnett, *Housing*, p. 258; Cobb, *Still Life*, pp. 8, 64.
[72] P. Vaughan, *Something in Linoleum: A Thirties Education* (London, 1994); Priestley, *English Journey*, p. 237. For the north–south contrast, see McKibbin, *Classes and Cultures*, p. 74; for the participation in early twentieth-century suburbanisation of the provinces even in the North and Scotland see: Jackson, *Middle Classes*, pp. 30, 46; Swenarton and Taylor, 'Owner-occupation', 390; A. O'Carroll, 'Tenements to bungalows: class and the growth of home ownership before "World War II"', *UH*, 24 (1997), 221–41.
[73] Priestley, *English Journey*, pp. 178, 180, 183; Thompson, ed., *Cambridge Social History*, I, pp. 73–4.
[74] See, for example, Priestley, *English Journey*, pp. 30, 359, which concentrates on the outflow of members of the upper middle class but notes that 'professional' and 'clerking' groups remained (p. 196). Cf. B. M. Doyle, 'The structure of elite power in the early twentieth-century city: Norwich, 1900–1935', *UH*, 24 (1997), 179–99. For an example of fiscal difficulties, see D. J. Rowe, 'The North-East', in Thompson, ed., *Cambridge Social History*, I, p. 463.
[75] QD1/FLWE/282. Cf. Davidoff, 'The family in Britain', p. 100; R. J. Morris, 'Middle-class culture, 1700–1914', in Fraser, ed., *A History of Modern Leeds* (Manchester, 1980), pp. 200–22; Trainor, 'Gentrification'. For studies demonstrating the internal social integration of the upper middle class, see Howe, *Cotton Masters*, and Koditschek, *Class Formation*.

families like the ironmongering Thornleys of Bolton were more focused, as were counterparts in London, on their immediate locality. There was culture aplenty but mainly in the form of shelves lined with books. The paterfamilias had limited leisure and short holidays; his wife had only limited domestic help. Socialising was less formal than in the Clough household.[76] More confined still – to particular neighbourhoods – was the life style of the lower middle class. For example, the publican father (1860–1900) of Robert Ferguson, having worked very long hours through the week, devoted his Sundays to a nap and a walk, though he was an active Freemason.[77]

Yet many aspects of differing life style – notably those entailed by the distinctions between suburb and town, seaside and inland location and London and the provinces – cut across these contrasts among social strata. An especially important source of division, especially in the Victorian decades, was the drink question. Yet there was much peaceful coexistence, on this issue as on related partisan and sectarian differences. While marriages tended to take place within denominations, there was much social mixing across religious lines, notably by the Kenricks of West Bromwich. Such rapprochement drew on the increasing availability of 'neutral' leisure institutions such as art galleries, the Volunteers and golf clubs.[78] More fundamentally, most middle-class urban dwellers shared an emphasis on family-centred relaxation at home. Thus John Clough's mill-owner father served wine at home but avoided pubs and clubs; Michael Hope's mother never dined out except with relatives; Bernard Thornley's parents entertained friends at home for meals; and the Balcombe family (gramophone manufacturers of Stoke Newington and Brighton) held tea parties at their house every Sunday night.[79] Therefore, while some people in middle-class occupations – notably in the dealing and craft trades – were 'drawn . . . through work and residence, towards a working-class way of life', there was increasing participation, even by the *petite bourgeoisie*, in a more general middle-class life style.[80]

Central to life style, yet with ramifications well beyond, was the role of women. Again there were important contrasts among the various strata. Upper-middle-class women such as Mrs Hope of Edgbaston had the leisure for an elaborate social round; wives such as Mrs Thornley sometimes had tasks in the shop as well as more intensive chores at home; mothers such as Mrs Harrison spent a

---

[76] QD1/FLWE/33. Cf. McLeod, *Class and Religion*, p. 148.   [77] QD1/FLWE/260.

[78] Thompson, *Rise of Respectable Society*, pp. 308, 319; B. Harrison, *Drink and the Victorians* (London, 1971); Trainor, *Black Country Elites*, p. 73; P. Joyce, *Work, Society and Politics: The Culture of the Factory in Later Victorian England* (Brighton, 1980), pp. 18, 22.

[79] On general patterns, McLeod, *Class and Religion*, pp. 133–6. Examples drawn from Essex Archive (see references above and, for Balcombe, QD1/FLWE/MUC 2059).

[80] Thompson, *Edwardians*, p. 115; G. Crossick, 'The petite bourgeoisie in nineteenth-century Britain: the urban and liberal case', in G. Crossick and H.-G. Haupt, eds., *Shopkeepers and Master Artisans in Nineteenth Century Europe* (London, 1984), pp. 67, 84–8. For the reflection in lifestyle of increasingly strong middle-class identity, see Trainor, *Black Country Elites*, pp. 75–9.

great deal of their time on housework.[81] Yet important aspects of women's lives were characteristic of virtually the entire urban middle class. In particular, the concept of 'separate spheres' had wide implications, although it was imperfectly realised (especially in the lower middle class) and came under increasing attack at the end of the nineteenth century. While at first restricting the public activities of middle-class women to auxiliary roles, this pattern gave females special responsibility for home and family – not only for supervising servants and the care of children (significant tasks given the large size of households) but also for the family's social activities and reputation.[82] In these ways women had an important impact not only on individual families but on the urban middle class more generally.

Nevertheless, the roles played by urban middle-class women were more diverse even before, and especially after, the First World War. Many middle-class households were headed by women, notably the widow of a London architect who had to give up 'all the frills' but maintained a highly respectable life style and sent her daughter to a prestigious school.[83] By the early years of the twentieth century the public roles available to women were beginning to widen, and routine white-collar jobs (and, in restricted sectors and numbers, professional posts) were becoming available. Also, women could resort to respectable tea rooms in cities such as Birmingham or, if they were well off, to women's lunch societies such as the Three Counties Club.[84] The interwar period saw an extension of these trends without dramatic change. By the 1930s 'respectable' women could visit wine bars with male escorts. More conventionally, but reflecting a diversification of the middle-class wife's pivotal social role (and, perhaps, falling middle-class fertility), the spouse of an important businessman in the West Riding, while doing much of the housework, would 'probably keep herself smart and pretty and reasonably well-informed and be ready to join her husband at cards or golf or whatever pastime he favours'.[85]

The integration of life style across the middle class, to which women contributed significantly, progressed during the interwar years, assisted in particular by the decreasing formality of socialising. Social life in the middle class remained

---

[81] Cf. P. Branca, *Silent Sisterhood* (London, 1975), and, on the masculine dimension, J. Tosh, *A Man's Place* (New Haven, 1999), and articles on 'Masculinity and the lower middle class', in *Journal of British Studies*, 38 (1999), by P. Bailey, A. J. Hammerton, C. P. Hosgood and F. Mort.

[82] QD1/FLWE/MUC/2 C707/473/1–4; QD1/FLWE/33; L. Davidoff and C. Hall, 'The architecture of public and private life: English middle-class society in a provincial town 1780–1850', in Fraser and Sutcliffe, eds., *Pursuit*, pp. 327, 340, 344; L. Davidoff and C. Hall, *Family Fortunes* (London, 1987), *passim*; L. Davidoff et al., *The Family Story* (London, 1999), pp. 25–9, 123–7.

[83] QD1/FLWE/MUC/2 C707/460/1–2, 5; Nenadic, 'Victorian middle classes', pp. 269–71.

[84] P. Hollis, *Ladies Elect* (Oxford, 1987); Michael Hope, QD1/FLWE/MUC/2 C707/473/1–4.

[85] Priestley, *English Journey*, pp. 13, 164. On the complex question of fertility see above, pp. 649–70, and M. Anderson, 'The social implications of demographic change', in Thompson, ed., *Cambridge Social History*, II, pp. 42, 44, 45. For the restricted social lives of many interwar middle-class suburban women see Davidoff et al., *Family Story*, p. 200.

much more based on formal associations than in the skilled working class, as the emphasis on church and tennis clubs in J. F. C. Harrison's boyhood indicates. Yet Michael Hope's mother neither made nor returned 'calls' after 1914; it became increasingly acceptable to entertain visitors in family rooms; and for suburbanites such as the Vaughans regular outings to the local cinema, grill room and theatre overshadowed special excursions to the West End. Also, car ownership extended. Still, for most white-collar workers improvements in public transport were more important; with exceptions mainly in the religious sphere (see below, p. 706), it remained true that 'the upper and lower middle classes would never meet in leisure'.[86]

To what extent did they meet at school and university? In England the educational paths taken by the upper middle class diverged greatly from other parts of the group. By the late nineteenth century the urban upper middle class frequently sent their sons, though less often their daughters, away to prep school and public school. From this group were drawn many of the relatively few pre-1914 middle-class graduates of English universities, as in John Clough's path from Tonbridge to Cambridge. Also, even without university, public school ties conferred privileged access not only to employment in the City but also to managerial posts in the increasing number of public companies. Meanwhile, the children of the lower middle class overwhelmingly attended day schools. This basic duality persisted into the interwar period, with a marked social gap persisting even between high-flying urban grammar schools and minor public schools.[87]

Yet the disintegrative effects of these patterns are easily exaggerated. In Scotland, public schools were much less important than in England, and there was broad middle-class access to prestigious day schools (and universities).[88] Also, in some English cities, notably Birmingham, the proportion of boys going to public school was low. There many well-off children attended highly rated day schools, supplementing the middle-middle-class as well as lower-middle-class youngsters who mixed in such institutions throughout England.

[86] Cunningham, 'Leisure and culture', p. 298. Cf. McKibbin, *Classes and Cultures*, p. 87; Vaughan, *Linoleum*, pp. 77–8; QD1/FLWE/MUC/2 C707-473/1–4; S. O'Connell, 'Taste, status and middle class motoring in interwar Britain', in D. Thoms *et al.*, eds., *The Motor Car and Popular Culture in the Twentieth Century* (Aldershot, 1998), p. 188, modified by Harrison, *Scholarship Boy*, pp. 59, 62, and Burnett, *Housing*, pp. 251–2, 260.
[87] Davidoff, 'The family in Britain', pp. 79, 101; G. Sutherland, 'Education', in Thompson, ed., *Cambridge Social History*, III, pp. 148–9; McKibbin, *Classes and Cultures*, pp. 72–3; Vaughan, *Linoleum*, p. 184; S. Fletcher, *Feminists and Bureaucrats* (Cambridge, 1980); J. M. Quail, 'From personal patronage to public school privilege: social closure in the recruitment of managers in the United Kingdom from the late nineteenth century to 1930', in Kidd and Nicholls, eds., *Making*, pp. 169–85; and P. Thompson, 'Snatching defeat from the jaws of victory: the last post of the old City financial elite, 1945–95', in *ibid.*, pp. 228–46.
[88] R. D. Anderson, *Education and Opportunity in Victorian Scotland: Schools and Universities* (Oxford, 1983; repr., Edinburgh, 1989), and R. D. Anderson, 'Secondary schools and Scottish society in the nineteenth century', *P&P*, 109 (1985).

University, in turn, was of relatively small career importance for the urban middle class, at least until after 1914. Most fundamentally, before 1944 access to secondary schooling of *any* kind – which in turn was crucial for much desirable middle-class employment – was highly skewed in favour of children from middle-class homes. By the interwar years, even if day schools like those attended by Paul Vaughan and J. F. C. Harrison could not match the aura of the public schools, increasingly they compensated through marked success in getting students into university, including Oxbridge which 'admitted [them] to the ranks of the privileged'.[89]

As many aspects of the social environment indicate, there were important differences not only of status but also of life chances within the urban middle class. Michael Hope felt the superiority of the Kenrick side of his family to his father's relatives, who were middling manufacturers; Robert Ferguson saw his father as only on the fringe of 'business people', who lived in 'posh house[s] on the outskirts'.[90] But there were important elements of common feeling within the middle class. In a largely middle-class environment such as Tunbridge Wells there was 'emphatic and utterly confident speech – a communication between equals'.[91] Even in Bolton, 'people [who] were doing the same sort of thing' – that is, those in the same 'financial circumstances' – 'tended to clique together to some extent'.[92] Also, there remained a clear sense of difference, even for some of the wealthiest members of the middle class, from the true upper class. As John Clough put it, his family 'talked another language' from the gentry.[93] More importantly, for all but the lowest fringe, by the interwar years there was a growing unity around middle-class occupations, in part stimulated by the organised working class, in part encouraged by the increase of the white-collar element at the expense of the *petite bourgeoisie*. Thus the Bolton mill welfare manager Nellie Trainor, the daughter of an overlooker, both in her childhood and as an adult felt clear superiority even to skilled manual workers.[94] By the 1930s this increasingly strong and broad urban middle-class identity was reflected in widespread support for the established churches and, in particular, for the Conservatives (see below, p. 712). Even a relatively humble member of the middle class such as Ferguson could comment sympathetically that 'If you've got

[89] Harrison, *Scholarship Boy*, pp. 54, 65 (quote); Vaughan, *Linoleum*, p. 96 and *passim*; Sutherland, 'Education', p. 162; H. Berghoff, 'Public schools and the decline of the British economy 1870–1914', *P&P*, 129 (1990), 156, 164; Berghoff, 'Regional variations', 67; P. Searby, 'The schooling of Kipps: the education of lower middle class boys in England, 1860–1918', in P. Searby, ed., *Educating the Victorian Middle Class* (Leicester, 1982), p. 117; Trainor, *Black Country Elites*, pp. 77–9.   [90] QD1/FLWE/260, 42, 40.   [91] Cobb, *Still Life*, p. 17.   [92] QD1/FLWE/33, 32.
[93] QD1/FLWE/282, 54. For a generally sceptical view of urban middle-class cultural independence see Thompson, ed., *Cambridge Social History*, I, pp. 42, 44.
[94] McKibbin, *Classes and Cultures*, pp. 70, 96ff, 102–3; QD1/FLWE/152, 41–2. A similar case of clear middle-class identity following marginal social origins was that of Mr Adams, a pottery manager (QD1/FLWE/24 in North Staffordshire).

your own premises you don't vote Labour'; 'it's a matter of the working man against the capitalist'.[95]

(iv) THE MIDDLE–CLASS ROLE IN URBAN ELITES

Public involvements by the urban middle class had significant consequences both for the middle class itself and for urban society more generally. Resources, life style and identity gave the middle class as a whole significant advantages in urban public life. The latter, in turn, also reflected the distinctive roles of the various social strata within the middle class.

Middle-class interventions in public affairs varied not only over time (see below, pp. 701–3, 710–13) but also among different types of urban settlement. Neighbouring landed elites were particularly influential in market towns such as Victorian Peterborough,[96] while in London the wealthiest individuals usually concerned themselves more with institutions in the City than with the public life of the localities where they resided. Similarly, while industrialists played particularly significant roles in the public affairs of small- and medium-sized industrial towns, the top leaders of provincial capitals such as Glasgow, Manchester and Bristol inevitably had more diverse occupations. Equally, the leaders of the larger cities were, at least in the mid-nineteenth century, of higher average social standing than the elites of medium or small towns. Likewise, patterns of leadership differed among, and within, major social arenas such as local government and voluntary societies (see below, pp. 704–10).[97] Yet, the general pattern of middle-class involvement, especially before 1914 – and even more so prior to about 1890 – was one of social, partisan and religious diversity balanced by particularly important roles for the well-to-do.

From the perspective of the turn of the twenty-first century the most surprising aspect of this pattern is that so many prosperous individuals were willing to serve in prominent public positions. A crucial factor was the prominence of the urban arena in a society where, before the 1920s, communication was primarily local. The urban scene, meanwhile, featured the huge range of institutions – and positions of leadership – which British towns and cities had spawned from the 1780s: municipal corporations, boards of poor law guardians, health commissioners, school boards and panels of borough JPs; Mechanics Institutes, reform societies and voluntary hospitals; churches, chapels, synagogues and their

[95] QD1/FLWE/260, 28, 29. These comments were made well after 1945 but evidently refer to views Ferguson frequently encountered throughout his adult life. For similar attitudes in the interwar period see Vaughan, *Linoleum*, p. 29.

[96] P. Jones, 'Perspective, sources and methodology in a comparative study of the middle class in nineteenth-century Leicester and Peterborough', *UHY* (1987), 22–32.

[97] As recent analysts of 'civil society' have emphasised, attention should not be confined to statutory institutions (see 'Special issue: civil society in Britain', *UH*, 25 (1998)).

affiliated social and cultural organisations; associations and clubs attached to political parties; Chambers of Commerce and trade.[98] Partly in consequence, especially at the start of the period local institutions had considerable discretion, which was only partially lost to Whitehall and other London-based bodies before 1914.[99] Thus service in these institutions often brought prominence and prestige both within the local middle class and, to a lesser but significant extent, throughout local populations. Indeed, it was difficult to win renown in towns and cities before the First World War without at least a modicum of conspicuous public involvement in one of the many types of activity available – or, at a minimum, a reputation for large-scale generosity to public causes.[100] Such participation also provided leaders with the opportunity to enhance their influence on issues such as: the level of municipal rates; the programmes of literary and philosophical societies; the admission policies of voluntary hospitals; the theological tone and social outreach of churches and chapels; the vigour and content of local and parliamentary election campaigns; and the strategies of employers' organisations. As these decisions had implications for local prosperity, social stability, public welfare, cultural dynamism and spiritual vitality as well as for the fortunes of individuals and firms, public affairs appealed to the altruistic as well as to the selfish impulses of the middle class.[101]

Victorian and Edwardian urban public life, therefore, mobilised a significant minority of middle-class men[102] and, increasingly, women into its leadership roles. In a self-consciously idealistic society lofty motives appealed across middle-class strata and occupations. Meanwhile, more practical considerations[103] – including possession of enough property to meet formal qualifications and the availability of spare time and money – determined the extent and nature of the role played by particular groups. Upper-middle-class businessmen sought confirmation of their respected place in the community. Sometimes (like their colleagues in the upper class who ventured into towns) they preferred honorary roles, especially in the voluntary sector, to positions which entailed direct managerial responsibility. Yet, particularly when their own economic interests were local,[104] the wealthy often wished to be directly involved in major practical

[98] See, for example, Trainor, *Black Country Elites*, pp. 93–4; Trainor, 'Glasgow's elite', pp. 231–2.
[99] See above, pp. 261–86 for the evolution of such controls in local government.
[100] See, for instance, the obscurity suffered by Bennett's 'Osmond Orgreave' because of his aloofness from such activities – *These Twain* (Harmondsworth, 1975), p. 159.
[101] On the question of motives, see Trainor, *Black Country Elites*, pp. 103–11.
[102] In Black Country towns between 7 per cent and 18 per cent served during a given subperiod (Trainor, *Black Country Elites*, pp. 94–6).
[103] Many of these factors gave the middle class in general an advantage over the working class in terms of access to elite posts.
[104] Absence of local interests could lead to aloofness from many aspects of public life, as Cardiff and (in a much more complex way) London demonstrate. See M. J. Daunton, *Coal Metropolis* (Leicester, 1977), pp. 150, 157; Reeder, 'Perspectives on London administrative history', in D. Owen, *The Government of Victorian London, 1855–1889* (Cambridge, Mass., and London, 1982), p. 350.

decisions. For less well-off members of the urban middle class, elite service could bring prominence and respect. Thus in Bolton the people who mattered were 'civic leaders, the clergy, doctors, leading industrialists, employers'.[105] For the main leadership posts such factors operated most effectively, notably in London, on the middle middle class – especially professionals – who could more realistically aspire to fame than all but the most energetic and charismatic members of the lower middle class. The latter, also, had to cope with the consensus, particularly strong in the mid-nineteenth century, that wealth and social standing were required for public service.[106]

Yet urban elites were more diverse from the start of the period than this pattern suggests – and they became more so, particularly from the late nineteenth century. From the outset there was much greater social variety in *auxiliary* roles such as Sunday school teacher, election volunteer and charity fund-raising committee member. Mainstream elite posts increasingly shared this variety. Due partly to agitation from below, partly to more flexible recruitment mechanisms, partly to a broadening concept of the prerequisites for leadership, the lower middle class – and, to a limited extent, representatives of manual workers – gained significant shares of elite posts from the last third of the nineteenth century.[107] This increasing diversity reinforced the legitimacy of the elites, especially in the eyes of middle-class populations (increasingly composed of the lower middle class) which still had most effective access to these positions. Yet, the bulk of principal leadership posts usually remained in the hands of the upper-middle and middle-middle strata. The effectiveness of leadership from this 'solid' middle class was reinforced by considerable 'overlapping' of leaders from different spheres, especially by those higher in the social hierarchy, many of whom also had family or business links to each other.[108] Admittedly, as the glamour of the new institutions diminished, as public affairs became less deferential and as some wealthy citizens turned their attention to the suburbs and the countryside, active participation by the upper middle class (and especially by the wealthiest) declined. However, this was a gradual and limited trend, so that down to the 1890s and, to a lesser extent, down to 1914 the elites of most medium and large towns retained a number of wealthy individuals. Likewise, in Birmingham,

[105] Bernard Thornley, QD1/FLWE/33, 33.
[106] McLeod, *Class and Religion*, p. 148; E. P. Hennock, *Fit and Proper Persons* (London, 1973), p. 308; Trainor, *Black Country Elites*, pp. 102–3; J. A. Garrard, 'The history of local political power: some suggestions for analysis', *Political Studies*, 25 (1977), 254–7. For the importance of the role played by humble activists see Garrard, *Leadership and Power*.
[107] For mid-century aspects of sharing with groups outside the solid middle class, see Koditschek, *Class Formation*, 'Epilogue'; and Morris, *Class, Sect and Party*, p. 330.
[108] Trainor, 'Urban elites', p. 8; Trainor, *Black Country Elites*, pp. 119–26, 377; D. Fraser, *Power and Authority in the Victorian City* (Oxford, 1979), p. 102; R. Q. Gray, *The Labour Aristocracy in Victorian Edinburgh* (Oxford, 1976), pp. 141–2; P. Hills, 'Division and cohesion in the nineteenth-century middle class: the case of Ipswich 1830–1870', *UHY* (1987), 43–4; Hollis, *Ladies Elect*, p. 20; H. E. Meller, *Leisure and the Changing City, 1870–1914* (London, 1976), p. 241.

Richard Trainor

Bristol and Manchester a high proportion of well-off businessmen remained involved in local public life.[109]

A few examples of energetic, wide-ranging civic involvement by late Victorian and Edwardian businessmen illustrate the persisting contribution of the well-to-do to urban public life. Reuben Farley, a West Bromwich ironfounder, was a leading figure in local civic life from the 1840s until his death in 1898. Farley was vice-chairman of the guardians, chairman of the commissioners, a member of the school board and five times mayor. In voluntary activities he played important roles in the building society, Mechanics Institute, hospital (where he was on the board for thirty years, seventeen as vice-chairman) and Institute, and lesser parts in the choral society, football team, horticultural society, temperance movement, Volunteers and YMCA. Moreover, Farley helped knit together local government and philanthropy by obtaining and supplying benefactions for the town, and by supporting the municipalisation of the Institute. Accumulating £200,000 during his lifetime, Farley continued to live in West Bromwich, where he served as the leading civic collaborator of the town's absentee aristocrats, the earls of Dartmouth. Throughout his public life, Farley promoted a progressive paternalism, stressing the need for property to fulfil its duties as well as to enjoy its rights, especially in the increasingly tense social atmosphere of the late nineteenth century. A similar example from a large city is Glasgow's Sir James Bell, baronet (who left £291,000 in 1929), a steamship owner with major railway and banking interests, who served as lord provost in the 1890s (giving 10,000 of the poor dinner to mark the marriage of the duke of York) and Glasgow's first lord lieutenant, while also finding time to look after his yacht and his country estate. A parallel case from the same city was the progressively minded baronet Sir William Bilsland, a well-off Glasgow baker, whose service as lord provost in the early years of the twentieth century capped many years of hard work on the Council where he vigorously promoted art galleries and sanitation improvements.[110]

Still, social diversity meant that urban elites could benefit from a variety of leadership styles. Increasingly, there was an efficient division of labour between the generous and ceremonial roles of the wealthiest businessmen, on the one hand, and the more detailed, energetic involvement of lesser but still substantial middle-class citizens, on the other.[111] Especially in middle-sized towns like those in the Black Country, urban elites also avoided the extremes both of unhealthy

[109] Trainor, 'Urban elites', 5; Trainor, 'Glasgow's elite', pp. 239–46; Trainor, *Black Country Elites*, pp. 96–112; E. S. Griffiths, *The Modern Development of City Government in the United Kingdom and the United States* (London, 1927), vol. I, pp. 186–7; Meller, *Leisure and the Changing City*, p. 87; D. Cannadine, 'The transformation of civic ritual in modern Britain: the Colchester oyster feast', *P&P*, 94 (1982), 115; R. A. Church, *Economic and Social Change in a Midland Town* (London, 1966), pp. 370–3; Hennock, *Fit and Proper Persons*, p. 227; A. J. Kidd, 'Charity organisation and the unemployed in Manchester c. 1870–1914', *Soc. Hist.*, 9 (1984), 9; S. Yeo, *Religion and Voluntary Organisations in Crisis, 1890–1914* (London, 1976), pp. 227–8, 300; Berghoff, 'Regional variations', 68, 72–3. [110] Trainor, *Black Country Elites*, pp. 125, 354–5; Trainor, 'Glasgow's elite', p. 255.
[111] Trainor, 'Glasgow's elite', p. 255; Trainor, *Black Country Elites*, pp. 110–11, 360.

702

dependence on a small number of individuals and of leadership so diffused that elites were depersonalised and robbed of glamour.[112]

A trend toward diversity also applied to the partisan and religious affiliations of the leaders of civic institutions. In early nineteenth-century towns near or actual monopolies, often of Tory Anglicans, frequently prevailed. Subsequent reforms often merely substituted a Liberal nonconformist predominance. Yet by the later Victorian years there was a tendency for both major political factions, and both major religious blocs, to win significant proportions of elite posts. Such diversity did much to reinforce the legitimacy of the elites as in most towns each faction claimed a significant share of the middle-class population, the source of the vast majority of elite members.[113] By the end of the nineteenth century even previously shunned factions such as the Primitive Methodists and Catholics gained minor shares of representation, thereby boosting the popularity of local leaders with the population more generally.[114]

Diversity had its price. Quite apart from the battles with working-class representatives that increasingly preoccupied town councils and voluntary hospitals from the closing years of the nineteenth century, variety among middle-class leaders at first contributed to squabbling within elite institutions, notably on issues related to rates, drink, religion in schools and the selection of presiding officers. Yet, while there were periodic revivals of acrimony, in general it faded from public affairs in places as varied as Bristol, Colchester, Exeter, Ipswich and textile Lancashire. The attainment of significant shares of posts in itself took some of the force out of factionalism, as did the shared experience of running voluntary and statutory institutions. Harmony was furthered, and symbolised, by ever more inclusive civic rituals – notably when the foundations of new buildings were laid, as in Glasgow in 1883 – which attracted representatives from all the main institutions as well as large, socially mixed crowds. Local middle-class leaders seized these opportunities to emphasise the civic contribution of the various religions and political parties; to a lesser extent they also recognised the claims of various occupational and social groups, thereby helping to ease the more intractable social tensions which underlay public life in towns and cities.[115]

---

[112] Trainor, 'Urban elites', 10; Trainor, *Black Country Elites*, pp. 364–5. For the contrasting situation in cities see: Meller, *Leisure and the Changing City*, pp. 90–4; G. Stedman Jones, *Outcast London* (Oxford, 1971), pp. 14, 251–2; N. Evans, 'The first charity in Wales', *Welsh History Review*, 12 (1985), 341–2.

[113] Berghoff, 'Businessmen'; Berghoff, 'Regional variations', pp. 78–9; Howe, *Cotton Masters*, p. 61; Rubinstein, *Men of Property*, ch. 5; Trainor, *Black Country Elites*, pp. 112–16, 177–81, 210.

[114] On this paragraph generally see Trainor, 'Urban elites', p. 7; Trainor, *Black Country Elites*, pp. 112–19; Fraser, *Urban Politics*.

[115] Trainor, 'Urban elites', 7–8; Trainor, 'Glasgow's elite', pp. 242–4, 246–50; Trainor, *Black Country Elites*, pp. 255–64, 320–4, 358–9, 377; Meller, *Leisure and the Changing City*, pp. 77–9, 84, 122; Cannadine, 'Transformation', 116; R. Newton, *Victorian Exeter, 1837–1914* (Leicester, 1968), pp. 102–6, 183–4, 213–38; Hills, 'Division and cohesion', 44–9; Garrard, *Leadership and Power*, p. 107. Cf. S. Gunn, 'Ritual and civic culture in the English industrial city, *c.* 1835–1914', in R. J. Morris and R. H. Trainor, eds., *Urban Governance* (Aldershot, 2000).

Ritual is futile if its symbols contradict public perceptions. The increasing vogue for civic ceremonial reflected, in part, compromises that upper-middle-class and middle-middle-class leaders made with lower-middle-class and working-class interests (and with partisan and religious minorities) on issues ranging from gas rates to hospital admission tickets to pub licensing. Yet, while generalisation is difficult,[116] evidently well-off leaders usually retained consider-able influence. Their plans for new hospitals and sewers, for example, often were adopted, and the greatly expanded public and private services they provided reached large numbers of inhabitants, including many within the middle class itself. Also, while the urban leaders of the Edwardian period had to take into account a much wider range of interests than their early Victorian predecessors, the civic decisions even of the often tense 1900s commanded much wider legit-imacy than had those of the tumultuous 1840s.[117]

(v) MIDDLE-CLASS INVOLVEMENT IN THE MAJOR SPHERES OF URBAN PUBLIC LIFE

A survey of the various arenas of urban elite activity confirms these broad patterns of middle-class public involvement. In the economic sphere, while the rising numbers of middle-class rentiers were detached, top industrialists and merchants were especially influential in bodies such as Chambers of Commerce and employ-ers' organisations. Also, prosperous doctors, lawyers and (increasingly) members of the 'new professions' asserted themselves through local and regional profes-sional organisations which protected standards while providing social activities and professional development. Yet the resilient category of family manufacturing firms retained considerable influence, retailers were able to make their mark through Chambers of Trade, and even humble occupations such as commercial travellers had organised pressure groups by the end of the nineteenth century. By that time, too, broad middle-class opinion had become a constraint on the actions of the largest employers, notably during strikes in industrial towns.[118] In any case, such employers increasingly used conciliation boards and collective bargaining to complement a modified 'paternalistic' approach to their own workforces.[119]

---

[116] For an emphasis on the limits to elite influence, see Garrard, *Leadership and Power*, which con-centrates on the especially contested sphere of local government. A more positive assessment, albeit complicated by an argument for the decline of 'urban squires', is in his 'Urban elites, 1850–1914: the rule and decline of a new squirearchy?', *Albion* 27 (1995), 583–621, e.g. 609.

[117] On this paragraph generally, see Trainor, 'Urban elites', 9–11; Trainor, *Black Country Elites*, pp. 354–62.

[118] J. Harris, *Private Lives, Public Spirit: Britain 1870–1914* (London, 1994), p. 106; Trainor, *Black Country Elites*, pp. 161–2; M. W. Kirby and M. B. Rose, eds., *Business Enterprise in Modern Britain from the Eighteenth to the Twentieth Century* (London, 1994).

[119] Cf. P. Joyce, 'Work', in Thompson, ed., *Cambridge Social History*, II; Trainor, *Black Country Elites*, pp. 139–66.

Local government, meanwhile, provided many in the lower ranks of the middle class with leadership posts in institutions such as Boards of Guardians and school boards, even while the solid middle class retained (admittedly with increasing difficulty) control of councils themselves in the face of the house ownership and rates crisis of the turn of the twentieth century. This was an especially contentious area of elite activity – especially in protecting 'law and order' and dispensing poor relief – but also one which allowed middle-class activists particular prominence and (subject to the attentions of Whitehall) influence.[120]

The vast, heterogeneous array of voluntary societies did not depend on compulsory rates and was largely free of central government interference. In further contrast to local government leadership, its positions did not carry the same symbolic weight for jealous partisans and sectarians, and its elections were seldom raucous. Thus the voluntary sector was less crisis-prone than local government. Also, while it provided outlets for large numbers of middle-class activists (including women) of varying degrees of social substance, it allowed their social superiors comparatively tranquil roles in major institutions. Occasionally there were disputes, as in the battle between the 'struggling middle class' and the 'upper middle class' at Dudley Grammar School, but these tended to be transient.[121] Voluntary societies, therefore, provided the solid middle class with an ideal medium for exercising leadership without partisan, religious and – to a significant extent – social tensions. In addition, in London and in the provinces voluntary societies were important sources of status for middle-class individuals as well as being major outlets for middle-class leisure. Conspicuous philanthropic service brought significant prestige, especially with the rank and file of the urban middle class, many of whom were involved in local voluntary societies as members and subscribers.[122] Admittedly, in towns such as Reading some wealthy leaders withdrew before 1914 from philanthropy, which also suffered inroads by the state. Yet in most respects urban charity flourished down to the First World War, aided by innovations such as the Guilds of Help.[123]

---

[120] Crossick and Haupt, *Petite Bourgeoisie*, pp. 128, 131; Trainor, *Black Country Elites*, pp. 235–45. On the crisis, see Daunton, 'Housing', pp. 225–7; A. Offer, *Property and Politics, 1870–1914* (Cambridge, 1981); R. Millward and S. Sheard, 'The urban fiscal problem, 1870–1914: government expenditure and finances in England and Wales', *Ec.HR*, 2nd series, 48 (1995), 501–35. For full treatment of urban government, see above, pp. 298–301 and Trainor, *Black Country Elites*, ch. 6.

[121] *Dudley Herald*, 9 Aug. 1873, quoted by J. G. Worpell, 'The endowed school in society' (CNAA PhD thesis, 1981), p. 98.

[122] R. J. Morris, 'Voluntary societies and British urban elites, 1780–1850: an analysis', *HJ*, 26 (1983), 95–118; Morris, *Class, Sect and Party*; R. J. Morris, 'Clubs, societies and associations', in Thompson, ed., *Cambridge Social History*, III, p. 409; McLeod, *Class and Religion*, pp. 134–5; P. Shapely, 'Charity, status and leadership: charitable service and the Manchester man', *Journal of Social History*, 32 (1998), 151–77.

[123] Yeo, *Religion and Voluntary Organisations*, pp. 103, 227–8, 296, 300; Garrard, 'Urban elites'; Doyle, 'Structure of elite power', 192–4, and sources cited there. Also relevant to this paragraph is Trainor, *Black Country Elites*, pp. 312–27.

A strong rival to the voluntary sphere in terms of importance to the urban middle class was religion. Especially at the start of the period, middle-class religious attendance, though generally lower than within the upper class, exceeded (especially in the upper middle class) that of the working class. Quite apart from concern for personal salvation and the close link between religion and better-off Victorians' approach to social issues, the urban middle class had strong practical incentives to take religion seriously. As the daughter of a London architect put it, 'We had quite a lot of amusement out of our church activities'; 'it was part of . . . being . . . respectable and a pillar of the local society'. In turn-of-the-century Glasgow, similarly, middle-class people were expected to be members of a church and felt it 'paid to join'.[124] Even for those middle-class people who did not attend church, decorous behaviour on Sunday was *de rigueur*.[125] In the main denominations, the solid middle class dominated key lay positions such as churchwarden and trustee, but there was scope for activism by the lower middle class, male and female, in other parts of the very complex structures of churches and chapels.[126] Such involvement enhanced the legitimacy of participating members of the middle class, notably West Bromwich ironfounder Charles Bagnall, whose service as a 'regular and laborious Sunday school teacher' was said to be 'far more to his honour' than his social position and his secular public role.[127] Moreover, religion inspired much middle-class involvement in public affairs by lifting people's attention above narrow concerns. During the last quarter of the nineteenth century, religion – notably in the form of the 'civic gospel' of towns such as Birmingham and Wolverhampton – went from being the basis of strife to a support for civic cooperation.[128]

The role played by partisan activity and affiliation in the life of the urban middle class also deserves serious attention.[129] Between 1832 and 1867 the middle class constituted the bulk of the urban electorate, for parliamentary as well as municipal elections.[130] Although this middle-class role as the focus of

[124] Mrs West, QD1/FLWE/MUC/392 C707/392/1–2, 29, 50; Robert Ferguson, QD1/FLWE/ 260, 43.

[125] McLeod, *Class and Religion*, pp. 139–40, confirmed by examples from the Essex Archive.

[126] McLeod, *Class and Religion*, p. 136; J. Obelkevich, 'Religion', in Thompson, ed., *Cambridge Social History*, III, pp. 338–9; C. G. Brown, 'Did urbanisation secularise Britain?', *UHY* (1988), 1–14; J. Seed, 'Theologies of power: Unitarianism and the social relations of religious discourse, 1800–1850', in Morris, ed., *Class, Power and Social Structure*, pp. 142–5; Trainor, *Black Country Elites*, pp. 179–82. [127] *Wolverhampton Chronicle*, 22 Apr. 1857.

[128] S. J. D. Green, 'In search of bourgeois civilisation: institutions and ideals in nineteenth-century Britain', *NHist.*, 28 (1992), 246; Trainor, *Black Country Elites*, pp. 279–80, 358–9. See J. N. Morris, *Religion and Social Change* (Woodbridge, 1992), for the declining importance for middle-class leaders of the churches vis-à-vis municipal affairs and p. 711 below for the fall in middle-class attendances from the late nineteenth century.

[129] For the role of party politics in urban government see above, pp. 301–7.

[130] For particular working-class strength in the electorates for guardians and school boards see Trainor, *Black Country Elites*, pp. 234–8.

urban electoral attention proved transient, the group – particularly in the form of the burgeoning lower middle class – remained a substantial minority of borough and parliamentary electorates, even in industrial towns.[131] Moreover, the middle class assumed key roles in mounting urban election campaigns. As first Liberal and then Unionist organisations became more elaborate from the 1870s, a division of labour evolved in which upper-middle-class worthies (sometimes in collaboration with neighbouring aristocrats and gentry) became officers of local associations, middle-middle-class citizens served on committees, and lower-middle-class (and, increasingly, working-class) individuals acted as foot soldiers and loyal members of party clubs. Also, as in the religious sphere there were active partisan roles for some middle-class women, notably in the Primrose League.[132] Well-off urban businessmen often did much to select candidates for their parties and sometimes stood themselves. During the last third of the nineteenth century some urban middle-class voters evidently shifted toward the Conservatives, particularly in areas with high proportions of middle-class residents. Reinforced by the subdivision of urban constituencies and the Liberal Unionist breakaway from Gladstonianism, this trend resulted in a rising number of middle-class Unionist MPs. Yet many middle-class voters, especially nonconformists, remained Liberals down to 1914, and a significant minority persisted as Liberal party activists as well.[133]

While each sphere of urban public life drew on the middle class in a distinct way, then, there were broad similarities, especially diversity balanced by influential roles for the well-to-do. Appropriately, there was also close collaboration, within particular towns, among the elites of these various arenas, especially the well-off leaders who held major posts in both the local government and the voluntary sectors. A classic case was the Kenrick family, which played key roles in the voluntary associations as well as the Councils of Birmingham and West Bromwich.[134] In some situations, especially when controversial employers simultaneously maintained high profiles in other spheres of urban public life, the interaction among different areas of leadership could be counterproductive. Yet, as the 'civic' emphasis of urban public affairs increasingly rele-

[131] M. Pugh, *The Making of Modern British Politics 1867–1939*, 2nd edn (Oxford, 1993), pp. 90–1.
[132] Trainor, *Black Country Elites*, pp. 203–8. Cf. J. Garrard, 'Parties, members and voters after 1867: a local study', *HJ*, 20 (1977), 145–63.
[133] J. Cornford, 'The transformation of Conservatism in the late nineteenth century', *Victorian Studies*, 7 (1963), 35–66; J. Cornford, 'The parliamentary foundations of the Hotel Cecil', in R. Robson, ed., *Ideas and Institutions of Victorian Britain* (London, 1967), pp. 268–311; Trainor, *Black Country Elites*, p. 210; B. Doyle, 'Urban Liberalism and the "Lost Generation": politics and middle class culture in Norwich, 1900–1935', *HJ*, 38 (1995), 617–34; J. Lawrence, 'Popular politics and the limitations of party: Wolverhampton, 1867–1900', in E. F. Biagini and A. J. Reid, eds., *Currents of Radicalism* (Cambridge, 1991), p. 73; Pugh, *Modern British Politics*, pp. 47–8.
[134] Trainor, *Black Country Elites*, pp. 105, 109, 121, 124, 129; R. A. Church, *Kenricks in Hardware: A Family Business 1791–1966* (Newton Abbot, 1969).

gated the unpleasantness of strikes, prosecutions and 'callovers' of paupers to the margins of public attention, 'overlapping' evidently did more to reinforce the position of middle-class leaders, and of the urban middle class as a whole, than to detract from it.[135] More generally, large employers could have particular impact, even when they were not the wealthiest members of urban elites, because of their perceived economic and social importance.[136]

Of course, middle-class leaders did not operate in a civic vacuum. Urban elites had to cope with a variety of 'outside' interests – notably aristocrats, large firms, neighbouring localities (including, for smaller towns, regional capitals) and central government – each of which limited their autonomy.[137] The extent of these constraints, with the possible exception of Whitehall, varied – generally to the disadvantage of smaller towns. Yet the socially substantial, interconnected nature of most urban elites enabled them to neutralise many of these threats, turning some into civic advantages. Relations with the landed elite, for example, were softened by adapted behaviour on both sides. Except in towns such as Eastbourne where aristocratic property dominated, the peers' interaction with middle-class elites was increasingly on the latter's terms. While the upper class gained support for its urban economic activities – and the occasional parliamentary seat – middle-class leaders even in medium-sized towns secured cash, prestige and, in many cases, land for civic projects.[138] Large firms proved more awkward, especially as increasingly they could close local plants and move elsewhere, but even so local leaders did not always treat them with kid gloves. Similarly, while nearby large cities often overshadowed small and medium-sized towns – as Manchester did Salford – smaller authorities sometimes combined with each other to prevent intimidation, as in the Black Country towns' gas war with Birmingham. Central government was a more formidable adversary, but it supplied local leaders with encouragement, expertise and – increasingly – cash for major projects.[139]

More generally, middle-class leaders helped themselves, and their localities, significantly through external connections. For notables from smaller towns, these links often took the form of involvements at the district or regional level – in mayors' conferences, religious and political coordinating bodies and employers' organisations. As the disparate cases of the West Midlands and west central Scotland demonstrate, the top leaders of lesser towns, like many of their counterparts from regional capitals, also had active ties to London in business, in civic

[135] Trainor, *Black Country Elites*, pp. 366–70.
[136] S. Nenadic, 'Businessmen, the urban middle classes, and the "dominance" of manufacturers in nineteenth-century Britain', *Ec.HR*, 2nd series, 44 (1991), 66–85.
[137] Cf. Garrard, 'Local political power'.
[138] D. Cannadine, ed., *Patricians, Power and Politics in Nineteenth-Century Towns* (Leicester, 1982), including Trainor, 'Peers on an industrial frontier', pp. 69–132; Trainor, 'Gentrification'; Trainor, *Black Country Elites*, pp. 86–9, 104–5.
[139] Trainor, *Black Country Elites*, pp. 252–3, 264–5. Cf. Garrard, *Leadership and Power*.

work, in 'Society' and as MPs.[140] There were also many useful contacts *among* provincial cities, assisted by the especially great physical mobility of the urban middle class.[141] In these contexts the broader geographical scope of upper-middle-class leaders more than compensated their localities for the usually mild effects of 'gentrification'.[142] Even at more modest social levels, public involvements by urban middle-class individuals often drew them, sometimes influentially, into national networks based for example on religious denominations, charities and the emerging profession of local government service.[143] Key provincial urban dwellers may have remained 'semi-detached' from the metropolitan elite even in 1914, but they had behind them influential bodies such as Glasgow's Chamber of Commerce, an important vehicle for regional interests in the thirty years preceding the First World War.[144] Also, effective interventions outside urban regions drew on the decreasing gap, within the upper middle class in particular, between 'the provinces' and 'the metropolis'.[145]

Middle-class urban social strategies, motivated by a mixture of fear and benevolence, tended to focus on the working class.[146] The approach urban middle-class leaders adopted combined elements both of paternalism and of individualism.[147] Two dilemmas presented themselves, between coercion and conciliation, and between direction from above and collaboration. Within a pattern of broadened social provision each was eventually largely resolved in favour of the latter alternative.[148] Did these strategies have much success with the working class? There were many respects in which they did not, as indicated by instrumental working-class attitudes to middle-class projects, and sheer

[140] Trainor, *Black Country Elites*, pp. 126–32, 222–30; Trainor, 'Glasgow's elite', pp. 250–2; and (on the paragraph generally) Trainor, 'Urban elites', 8–9.

[141] Burnett, *Housing*, p. 99. For its increase during the interwar years see McKibbin, *Classes and Cultures*, pp. 81, 93.   [142] Cf. Howe, *Cotton Masters*; Trainor, 'Gentrification'.

[143] R. Gray, 'The platform and the pulpit: cultural networks and civic identities in industrial towns, c. 1850–70', in Kidd and Nicholls, eds., *Making*, pp. 130–47. Cf. Morris, 'Clubs, societies and associations', p. 414; H. L. Malchow, *Gentleman Capitalists* (London, 1991).

[144] E. Gordon and R. Trainor, 'Employers and policymaking: Scotland and Northern Ireland, c. 1880–1939', in S. Connolly *et al.*, eds., *Conflict and Identity* (Preston, 1995), pp. 254–67. On the question of integration, see Berghoff, 'Businessmen', and, more positively, his 'Regional variations'; for a less enthusiastic view of provincial impact in the twentieth century, see D. Read, *The English Provinces c. 1760–1960: A Study in Influence* (London, 1964), ch. 5.

[145] R. H. Trainor, 'Neither metropolitan nor provincial: the interwar middle class', in Kidd and Nicholls, eds., *Making*, pp. 203–13. Cf. McKibbin, *Classes and Cultures*, who argues (pp. 74, 86, 90–1, 101) for persisting North–South tensions and for a shift of the balance of the middle class toward the South but also suggests (pp. 70, 96ff, 102) an increasing unity, based more on occupation than on region.

[146] Cf. V. A. C. Gatrell, 'Crime, authority and the policeman-state', in Thompson, ed., *Cambridge Social History*, III, p. 255.

[147] J. Seed, 'Unitarianism, political economy and the antinomies of liberal culture in Manchester, 1830–50', *Soc. Hist.*, 7 (1982), 1–25; Joyce, 'Work', p. 168.

[148] Trainor, *Black Country Elites*, pp. 132–6.

avoidance of them.[149] Paradoxically, the more coercive strategies of urban middle-class leaders – notably in law enforcement and poor relief – achieved many of their objectives while the relatively positive initiatives – recreational reform and the social outreach of organised religion, for example – had much more mixed results. Still, churches and chapels attracted many to societies if not always to services, and socially progressive policies in both major parties succeeded in mobilising large numbers of working-class electors down to 1914 in a controlled competition compatible with the pursuit of shared social ideals.[150] More generally, urban civic life, by bringing large numbers of working-class people into contact with middle-class leaders in relatively benign modes, may have done much to promote the emergence of 'viable class relations' in Britain's towns and cities.[151]

(vi) PUBLIC LIFE IN THE INTERWAR YEARS

The interwar years – with the increasing geographical mobility of middle-class managers, accelerated suburbanisation, industrial depression and the further rise of Labour – disrupted middle-class urban leadership more than had even the Edwardian period. Yet it is easy to exaggerate the decline in the public role of the middle class which occurred during the 1920s and 1930s. Wealthy businessmen continued to prize service to the community even as their enthusiasm for particular elite roles diminished.[152] Also, some of the middle-class activism which was 'lost' to cities and towns resurfaced in nearby suburbs. Thus, although there was some fall in the social standing of middle-class urban leaders, there was as much a reshaping as a diminution of public involvement by the urban middle class in the interwar years.[153]

---

[149] See in particular Thompson, 'Social control'. With regard to philanthropy, its impact tended to vary with the scale of the resources inherited from the past and the scope of current problems – thus in the late Victorian period Bristol was far better placed in both respects than was Cardiff. See Meller, *Leisure*; N. Evans, 'Urbanisation, elite attitudes and philanthropy: Cardiff, 1850–1914', *International Review of Social History*, 27 (1982), 290–323.

[150] H. McLeod, 'New perspectives on Victorian working class religion . . .', *Oral History*, 14 (1986), 31–49; J. Lawrence, 'Class and gender in the making of urban Toryism, 1880–1914', *English Historical Review*, 108 (1993), 633, 640; Trainor, *Black Country Elites*, pp. 174–84, 192–8, 208–22, 359; H. Perkin, 'The development of modern Glossop', in A. H. Birch, *Small-Town Politics* (Oxford, 1959), p. 26; J. M. Lee, *Social Leaders and Public Persons* (Oxford, 1963), p. 34. For the significant extent to which parties, rather than simply social structures, shape electoral behaviour, see J. Lawrence and M. Taylor, eds., *Party, State and Society: Electoral Behaviour in Britain since 1820* (Aldershot, 1997).

[151] Trainor, *Black Country Elites*, pp. 371–2. Cf. Perkin, *Origins*, ch. 9, *passim*.

[152] M. Dintenfass, 'Coal masters and the culture of the middle class, c. 1890–1950', in Kidd and Nicholls, eds., *Making*, pp. 214–27.

[153] Cf. Rubinstein, 'Britain's elites in the interwar period', whose section (pp. 198–9) on the 'collapse' of the provincial elites notes the reduction in wealthy councillors and the waning of Liberalism and dissent within elites.

This balance between change and stability characterised middle-class involvements in both local government and the voluntary sector. In the former, 'decline' came mainly from the 1930s and even then usually was not drastic. Partly enforced by the rise of Labour, this change shifted the balance of leadership from the upper to the lower echelons of the middle class.[154] In part because of significant continuities in voluntary as well as local government leadership civic pageantry remained strong in many towns, attracting broad public attention to middle-class elites.[155] Yet there was less 'overlapping' than before 1914 between councillors and the leaders of voluntary societies. Also, cracks had begun to emerge in the previous predominance of the well-off middle class in the voluntary sphere.[156] The truly dynamic areas of interwar voluntary activity focused either on social distress – as in prominently-led bodies coordinating local charities – or on entertainment, notably the myriad dramatic societies run by 'small businessmen, teachers, clerks, [and] artisans'.[157]

Likewise, there was change, but not collapse, in middle-class involvement in urban religion and politics. In the former, where a falling-off in middle-class attendance at church and chapel had set in from the late nineteenth century, there was a further interwar decline in middle-class fervour, perhaps especially among upper-middle-class men. John Clough, for example, never attended after the war; he played golf instead, taking advantage of a significant relaxation of taboos concerning Sunday behaviour.[158] In Preston, the elite left church leadership to the lower middle class, which at St Philip's Leicester used church premises every night for 'the various guilds, dramatic society, badminton club, cricket club, cubs, brownies, scouts, guides, whist-drives, dances, bring-and-buys, [and] jumble sales'.[159] In places such as Norwich it was only from the 1930s that such vitality began significantly to drain away, especially from dissent.[160] Yet persisting religious feeling was a two-edged sword: religious affiliation continued to complicate middle-class social life in provincial towns, as did the related issue of drink, though neutral socialising in settings such as Conservative organisations helped to promote collaboration. Likewise, new types of middle-class social

[154] Doyle, 'Structure of elite power'. Cf. Savage, *The Dynamics*; and Savage, 'Urban history'.
[155] Cannadine, 'Transformation', 108; M. Dickie, 'Town patriotism in Northampton, 1918–1939: an invented tradition?', *Midland History*, 17 (1992), 109–17.
[156] Savage, *The Dynamics*; McKibbin, *Classes and Cultures*; M. Stacey, *Tradition and Change* (London, 1960).
[157] Priestley, *English Journey*, pp. 197, 199. For the renewed role of voluntary societies in Lancashire and their survival elsewhere despite crisis, see Savage, *The Dynamics*, p. 184; and Morris, 'Clubs, societies and associations', p. 422.
[158] QD1/FLWE/282. On males generally see Cobb, *Still Life*, p. 70; on the complex process of decline see J. Cox, *The English Churches in a Secular Society* (New York and Oxford, 1982); and S. J. D. Green, *Religion in the Age of Decline* (Cambridge, 1996).
[159] Savage, *The Dynamics*, pp. 118–21; J. F. C. Harrison, *Scholarship Boy*, p. 23.
[160] Doyle, 'Structure of elite power', 191–4; Obelkevich, 'Religion', p. 349; Priestley, *English Journey*, pp. 106–10.

organisation such as Rotary, which drew distinctions on grounds of modern status rather than traditional allegiances, rapidly increased their membership in response to the rootlessness of many middle-class residents.[161] In party politics, after a protracted transition, especially in parliamentary voting and in areas with strong dissenting traditions, the long-standing bifurcation of middle-class political allegiance weakened in response to the rise of organised labour. By the 1930s, although the Conservatives needed significant urban working-class support in order to win elections, they were especially likely to secure urban seats where the middle-class vote was large. The middle class, moreover, became the backbone of the livelier Tory organisations which developed during the interwar years.[162] In politics, as in religion, as consensus replaced traditional middle-class rivalries, some dynamism and inspiration may have been lost to public life.[163] Yet if so this diminution was only a partial falling-off from the very high standards of the pre-1914 period.

(vii) OVERVIEW: THE SECOND WORLD WAR AND BEYOND

The outbreak of the Second World War brought many changes to the urban middle class. While the dramatic uprooting of large numbers proved transient, other novelties – sharp rises in taxation and in fertility and the disappearance of domestic servants, for example – proved both long-lasting and unsettling.[164] Yet on the whole these disruptions tended to accelerate the long-developing integration of the various strata and factions of the urban middle class, which may well have been more of a coherent social entity in the 1950s than before or since.[165] For the most part change in the early post-war period built on forces that had been shaping urban middle-class private and public existence before 1939. As J. F. C. Harrison suggests, 'in the 1950s the pattern of middle-class life

[161] McKibbin, *Classes and Cultures*, pp. 90–1, 96.

[162] *Ibid.*, pp. 57–8, 199, 260–1, 276–7; B. M. Doyle, 'A conflict of interests? The local and national dimensions of middle class Liberalism, 1900–1935', in D. Dean and C. Jones, eds., *Parliament and Locality 1660–1939* (Edinburgh, 1998), pp. 133, 137; Pugh, *Modern British Politics*, p. 243; S. Ball, 'The national and regional party structure', in A. Seldon and Ball, eds., *The Conservative Century* (Oxford, 1994), pp. 264, 293.

[163] Cf. the uneasiness felt by the 'provincial lady' at the assumption, both in Devon and in London, that everyone 'in civilised circles' was Conservative – E. M. Delafield, *The Provincial Lady Goes Further* (London, 1984), p. 213.

[164] For example, the 'baby boom' complicated access to the Butler Act's grammar schools, exacerbating regional anomalies (Sutherland, 'Education', p. 165). Those middle-class families which opted, for these or more snobbish reasons, for prep and boarding schools often faced major financial strains in postwar circumstances; see, for example, R. M. Dashwood, *Provincial Daughter* (New York, 1960), pp. 17, 37, 44.

[165] But the middle class had certainly not become a homogeneous entity, as indicated by the profound differences in life style and cultural orientation even within its upper echelons between, say, Richard Titmuss and Evelyn Waugh: A. Oakley, *Man and Wife – Richard and Kay Titmuss: My Parents' Early Years* (London, 1996); M. Davie, ed., *The Diaries of Evelyn Waugh* (London, 1976).

was still much the same as earlier'.[166] There was little further falling off in church attendance during the decade, for example. Also, while Labour secured unprecedented middle-class support in 1945 in urban areas such as Lewisham, even in that dismal year for Tories two-thirds of middle-class voters stayed loyal. Conservative membership leapt in the 1940s in the face of the perceived acute threat from 'socialism', and middle-class support for the Tories rose significantly in the 1950s.[167] In addition, there was considerable continuity, albeit on the pattern of the 1930s rather than of the pre-1914 period, in middle-class involvement in urban voluntary societies and statutory bodies.[168]

Thus the urban middle class of the 1950s resembled – in many aspects of its social structure, its life style and its mores as well as its public involvements – its interwar counterpart and, in important respects, its Victorian and Edwardian predecessors. In the early 1960s forces which would complicate the coherence of the middle class during the last third of the century – such as the explosive growth in white-collar employment and the blurring of the distinction between middle-class and working-class leisure patterns – were still largely in the future.[169] Also still mostly to come were factors which would propel a significant further slice of the middle class outside towns (and even suburbs) and their public affairs: accelerated outward movement, often into distant rural areas;[170] dramatic deindustrialisation north of Watford during the 1980s; the radical centralisation of government during the same decade; and the sharp decline of Conservatism in many urban areas, especially in Scotland and Wales. In a sense this watershed was symbolically appropriate. For it was only as the widespread urban clearance and redevelopment schemes of the 1960s, 1970s and 1980s destroyed much of the physical legacy of the Victorian city that the social descendants of the nineteenth-century middle class decisively turned their backs on the remnants of the urban communities they had done so much to create.

[166] Harrison, *Scholarship Boy*, p. 188.
[167] Morris, 'Clubs, societies and associations', p. 423; Obelkevich, 'Religion', p. 349; T. Jeffery, 'The suburban nation: politics and class in Lewisham', in D. Feldman and G. Stedman Jones, eds., *Metropolis London* (London, 1989), p. 206; J. Bonham, *The Middle-Class Vote* (London, 1954), p. 168; McKibbin, *Classes and Cultures*, p. 67. For a classic example of the fears aroused in the middle class by the Attlee government, see Lewis and Maude, *English Middle Classes*.
[168] This point is developed in R. Trainor, '"Decline" in British urban governance 1850–2000: a reassessment', in Morris and Trainor, eds., *Urban Governance*.
[169] For the persistence of a broad middle-class self-identification into the 1960s see A. Marwick, *The Sixties* (Oxford, 1998), pp. 277–9; for leisure separation of the classes at mid-century see Stacey, *Tradition and Change*, p. 171.
[170] Thompson, 'Town and city', I, pp. 74–5; Morris, 'Clubs, societies and associations, p. 442.

· 22 ·

Towns and consumerism

JOHN K. WALTON

ERCY REDFERN, the historian of the Co-operative Wholesale Society, published a series of lectures in 1920 on *The Consumers' Place in Society*. This was a tract in praise of consumer democracy and the co-operative commonwealth, stressing that trade union struggles were necessarily sectionalist and the only way to advance and protect the interests of the masses was through the mobilisation of consumers. Redfern began, however, with a lament:

> Libraries of books, publications of a special Ministry of Uses, and many journals would be necessary to deal adequately and continuously with the consumers' problem of organising the world and its resources for the utmost human use and enjoyment. These do not exist. Manchester, for some uncomplimentary reason, is supposed to be the special home of consumers' advocacy. Yet the Manchester Reference Library – an admirable institution – contains sufficient volumes under the title 'Labour' to fill several crowded pages of its great catalogue; whereas a single entry under consumption (amidst two-score devoted to the disease) provides for all the books specifically relating to the consumer.[1]

Until a few years ago that could almost have been said of books on the social history of consumption and consumerism in Britain, as compared with the proliferating historiography of popular politics and the labour movement. Now the wheel is turning with gathering momentum, as the older heavy industries decline into extinction and consumer-related topics are fashionable, while studies of the labour movement are in eclipse. This may be thought a rather present-minded set of preoccupations, but history has always been written thus, and earlier neglect of consumption was undoubtedly misplaced. Not that Redfern, from his almost millenarian and quasi-revolutionary perspective, would necessarily approve of how this trend has worked out. Much recent work on leisure and mass consumption has tended to stress the autonomy and agency

[1] P. Redfern, *The Consumer's Place in Society* (Manchester, 1920), p. 5.

715

of consumers, their ability to create and diversify identities from the goods and life styles which are on offer through the cornucopia of the market place.[2] This approach has emerged in overt or implicit opposition to a historiography emanating from Marx and Engels via Gramsci which has stressed capitalist consumerism as a snare and a distraction, a diversion from serious thought and an offering of baubles to seduce the pliant mind into acquiescence and win assent to the existing economic order. Such assent need not be unconditional, and Gramsci's notion of hegemony entails the idea that attempts to manipulate will be contested, and that consumers will try to exploit what is available within an accepted system on their own terms; but this mode of analysis locates the power and initiative to define commonsense and set priorities firmly in the hands of the capitalist producers in alliance with retailers and the world of advertising and publicity.[3]

Redfern anticipated neither of these historiographical tendencies: he was keen that consumers should be satisfied and obtain value for money, and that their lives should be enhanced by the widening availability of objects of desire, but his was a vision of moral and intellectual improvement through the fairer distribution of goods and opportunities, owing much to John Ruskin's teachings about the responsibility to put nature's bounty to good, sound, lasting use in ways which celebrated the creativity of the craft worker.[4] His was no paean of praise for the imaginative adaptation of whatever mass-produced goods profit seekers might produce and advertisers boost for mass markets, regardless of the conditions under which they might be manufactured or the quality and durability of the goods themselves.[5] He was no celebrant of the fashionable or the ephemeral: at the centre of his concerns was an anxiety that goods should be produced by properly rewarded workpeople in a fulfilling manner, supervised by people who recognised a responsibility to workers and customers alike. Here are his thoughts on the subject, encapsulated:

> All labour and effort, and all material resources, must be consciously devoted to the good of the whole people as consumers; and all owners and business organisers, and all workers, ceasing to be masters and exercisers of absolute rights, must become the agents and stewards of the community, and of the world order of communities. And consumption must be illuminated and uplifted by a religious sense of the meaning and purpose of life; so that the waste and misuse of the stuff of life may be ended, and all material be transformed into happy being, as in the little bodies of the birds exulting in the blue awakening of an April day.[6]

---

[2] G. Cross, *Time and Money* (London, 1993), ch. 7.
[3] P. Bailey, *Leisure and Class in Victorian England*, 2nd edn (London, 1987), pp. 9–11.
[4] J. Desforges, 'Co-operation, labour and consumption in Liverpool, 1890–1914', in B. Lancaster and P. Maguire, eds., *Towards the Co-operative Commonwealth* (Loughborough, 1996), p. 30.
[5] See also T. Billington Greig, *The Consumer in Revolt* (London, n.d., c. 1913).
[6] Redfern, *Consumer's Place*, p. 19.

Even if we leave the little birds to one side, this view of consumerism is a world away from the secular celebrations of department stores and shopping mall culture as cornucopia of opportunity, satisfying legitimate desires for transient enjoyments and butterfly identities, which appear in some of the postmodernist literature.[7] It is a strong version of the 'moral economy' of Co-operation: a particularly overwrought rhetorical summation of the ideology of Co-operative movement activists at the peak of that movement's membership, influence and hopes of remaking the world, though it was, perhaps, a vision hardly shared by the stolid bulk of rank-and-file members whose main concern (it is alleged) was to maximise the dividend on their purchases.[8] It is, however, a point of view on consumerism which was growing in strength and moral authority during the second half of the nineteenth century, and coming to a peak in the interwar years, when the Co-op was truly a mass movement.[9] I have started with Co-operation and its official ideals, indeed, because the movement pioneered many aspects of urban mass consumption, in its own distinctive manner, in the face of fierce opposition from private traders, and its comparatively recent eclipse at the hands of chain stores and multinationals has produced a tendency for history to be written for those who appear to be the winners, leaving this enormous and influential organisation on the sidelines. The Co-op merits more attention than it has received from historians, and we shall return to this theme.[10]

Co-operation in its British retailing incarnation was pre-eminently an urban movement; and whatever forms or aspects of consumerism we choose to emphasise, it was in the towns, where consumers aggregated, debated the quality and desirability of goods, displayed themselves and their possessions in the public arena, articulated their possession of cultural capital and distinguished their life styles from others within shared grammars of consumption, sustained themselves and enjoyed themselves, that consumption and consumerism had their most concentrated and influential being.[11] Urban growth and consumer capitalism went hand in hand. Consumerism shifted from being an elite phenomenon to one accessible to the masses during the 'age of great cities' which was ushered in by the rise of the world economy, the factory system (and its corollary the sweated trades) and the communications revolutions in the middle decades of the nineteenth century, and which provided a favourable environment for mass consumption during the great commodity price fall of the last quarter of the

---

[7] R. Shields, ed., *Lifestyle Shopping* (London, 1992).

[8] P. Gurney, *Co-operative Culture and the Politics of Consumption in England, 1870–1930* (Manchester, 1996), pp. 1, 238 and *passim*; and see also P. Johnson, *Saving and Spending* (Oxford, 1985).

[9] Gurney, *Co-operative Culture*, Part III.

[10] See especially Gurney, *Co-operative Culture*; Lancaster and Maguire, eds., *Co-operative Commonwealth*; *North-West Labour History*, 19 (1994), special issue on the Co-operative movement; S. Yeo, ed., *New Views of Co-operation* (London, 1988).

[11] It is surprising that these relationships, as such, have been so little discussed with reference to the nineteenth and twentieth centuries.

nineteenth century. This was a key transitional period, when new kinds of retail outlet facilitated and encouraged consumer spending at working-class level: the department store in its more democratic incarnations, the 'multiples' of the 'retailing revolution', the penny bazaars in covered markets which brought forth Marks and Spencer, the stained-glass extravaganzas of the new shopping arcades, the central Co-operative 'emporia', and so on.[12] The same period saw the rise of professional sport for working-class audiences, the emergence of the music hall and the popular seaside holiday and the novel availability of cheap convenience foods, along with new opportunities for domestic leisure and the enhancement of home comforts, as cheap by-law and suburban housing and (in some cases) the advent of smaller families reduced pressure on space as well as income.[13]

The developments of these formative years were built on strikingly in the new century, and for those who remained in work the renewed spell of falling prices during the interwar years enabled novel aspirations to be pursued through trading-up to more spacious semi-detached houses, home improvements, domestic electrical goods and the cult of gardening, while dance halls and cinemas became almost universal in the popular entertainment field, and the spread of bicycles, motorcycles and even cars offered widening choices and increased autonomy in the sphere of personal mobility.[14] Some aspects of these developments were socially selective in their impact, requiring significant spare disposable income and a capacity to save and budget; but others, like the cinema, became practically universal.[15] In the post-war years these trends were to be greatly intensified, as the variety of goods and brands on offer and the power and sophistication of advertising and genuinely mass media became greatly enhanced

[12] Bill Lancaster, *The Department Store: A Social History* (Leicester, 1995); Gareth Shaw, 'The evolution and impact of large-scale retailing in Britain', and M. Purvis, 'Co-operative retailing in Britain', in J. Benson and G. Shaw, eds., *The Evolution of Retail Systems, c. 1800–1914* (Leicester, 1992), chs. 7 and 8; Goronwy Rees, *St Michael: A History of Marks and Spencer* (London, 1961); P. Mathias, *Retailing Revolution* (London, 1967).

[13] W. H. Fraser, *The Coming of the Mass Market, 1850–1914* (London, 1981); John Benson, *The Rise of Consumer Society in Britain, 1880–1980* (London, 1994); T. Mason, *Association Football and English Society, 1863–1915* (Brighton, 1980); W. Vamplew, *Pay Up and Play the Game* (Cambridge, 1988); P. Bailey, ed., *Music Hall* (Milton Keynes, 1986); J. S. Bratton, ed., *Music Hall* (Milton Keynes, 1986); J. K. Walton, *The English Seaside Resort* (Leicester, 1983); J. K. Walton, *Fish and Chips and the British Working Class, 1870–1940* (Leicester, 1992).

[14] R. McKibbin, *The Ideologies of Class* (Oxford, 1990), ch. 5; J. Stevenson, *Social Conditions in Britain between the Wars* (London, 1977); N. Gray, *The Worst of Times* (London, 1986); M. Swenarton, *Homes Fit for Heroes* (London, 1981); A. A. Jackson, *Semi-Detached London* (London, 1973); A. Rybaczek, *Homes Fit for Heroes in Inter-War Ashton* (Ashton-under-Lyne, 1995); J. Turnbull, 'Housing tenure and social structure: the impact of inter-war housing change on Carlisle' (PhD thesis, University of Lancaster, 1992); J. Foreman-Peck, S. Bowden and A. McKinlay, *The British Motor Industry* (Manchester, 1995); S. O'Connell, 'The social and cultural impact of the motor car in Britain, 1918–1939' (PhD thesis, University of Warwick, 1996).

[15] J. Richards, *The Age of the Dream Palace* (London, 1984).

when real incomes rose unprecedentedly during the 1950s and 1960s, while the development of age-specific and other niche markets (with the invention of the teenager and the targeting of the child as consumer) complicated the issue further.[16] This chapter traces these processes in all their ramifications, focusing on the relationship between the rise of mass consumption and the urban setting in which its earliest and most developed manifestations took place: a link which has been surprisingly neglected in most of the current literature covering the period from the early nineteenth to the mid-twentieth century.[17]

This neglect is all the more surprising because it is more than thirty years since Tony Wrigley proffered a 'simple model' which connected the migration-fuelled growth of an increasingly large and anonymous London with a transition from tradition to performance as the key element in the acquisition as opposed to the inheritance of status, and an associated inflation of the importance of the presentation of self through dress and the display of possessions in a new urban world of competitive emulation.[18] The burgeoning literature on eighteenth-century consumers and consumerism has built on these ideas and extended their logic into lesser urban centres, most obviously in arguments for a provincial 'urban renaissance' spreading its influence by way of the new resorts and the centres of county administration and society,[19] and in the emphasis placed on the development as consumers of women of the emergent urban middle classes of the eighteenth century, who described their possessions in lovingly elaborate language.[20] This latter approach offers a specifically urban focus on consumption, directed more to the private than the public sphere. The new consumer values which are presented in this literature also left their traces in the probate inventories which listed the possessions of rural dwellers, and through the petty chapmen who hawked ribbons and laces through the countryside; but their motive force was the dynamo of urban gregariousness, which introduced new standards, set new fashions and sent old certainties spinning.[21] Development of these and related ideas in the increasingly urbanised setting of the nineteenth and twentieth centuries needs to be high on the agenda of urban historians. As matters stand, however, the most recent survey of the 'rise of consumer society' in Britain over the century after 1880 uses urban growth as a necessary backcloth to the central theme, and comments that 'it would be almost impossible to overlook the fact

---

[16] J. Obelkevich and P. Catterall, eds., *Understanding Post-War British Society* (London, 1994); but see D. Fowler, *The First Teenagers* (London, 1995), ch. 4, for the interwar development of teenage consumption. [17] Benson, *Consumer Society*, is (literally) a text-book example.
[18] E. A. Wrigley, 'A simple model of London's importance', *P&P*, 37 (1966), 44–70.
[19] P. Borsay, *The English Urban Renaissance* (Oxford, 1989).
[20] L. Weatherill, *Consumer Behaviour and Material Culture in Britain 1660–1760* (London, 1988); L. Davidoff and C. Hall, *Family Fortunes* (London, 1987); A. Vickery, 'Women of the local elite in Lancashire 1760–1820' (PhD thesis, University of London, 1992).
[21] M. Spufford, *The Great Reclothing of Rural England* (London, 1984); B. Lemire, *Fashion's Favourite* (Oxford, 1991).

that retailing, sport and most other consumer services became concentrated overwhelmingly in urban areas', but does not engage with the relationship between towns and consumption/consumerism as a theme or organising principle.[22] This is also true of most of the previous work by historians on related matters.[23] We need more focused work on the dynamic aspects of the interaction between towns and consumption.

For the nineteenth and twentieth centuries, in fact, most of the historical work linking towns and consumption focuses on developments in urban retailing rather than directly on the changing attitudes and expectations of the consumers themselves. The rise of the West End and other London shopping districts, and the emergence of specialised retail nuclei in the provincial towns, constitutes an important theme in this literature.[24] It is also important to be aware of the survival and indeed expansion of retail markets, especially for food, in nineteenth- and twentieth-century industrial towns, as municipal investment brought impressive new premises and regulation safeguarded quality and hygiene.[25] We can also chart the continuing spread of corner shops as well as specialised retail businesses during the second half of the nineteenth century and beyond, as the former colonised new working-class neighbourhoods and the latter extended along the tram routes and congregated in secondary shopping centres in middle-class suburbs as urban sprawl proceeded.[26] The rise of the multiple grocery (with the flagship firm of Lipton particularly well documented) and the department store from the 1870s and 1880s, and the development of chain stores such as Marks and Spencer and Woolworth's from the turn of the century and especially in the interwar years, made their own distinctive impact on patterns of urban retailing provision. So did the spread of the Co-operative movement itself, with its proliferation of societies, branches and later central emporia into new areas from the mid-nineteenth century, and especially during the late Victorian price fall, although the movement was to attain its greatest

[22] Benson, *Consumer Society*, p. 45.

[23] But see H. Cunningham, 'Leisure and culture', in F. M. L. Thompson, ed., *The Cambridge Social History of Britain, 1750–1950*, vol. II: *People and their Environment* (Cambridge, 1990), ch. 6.

[24] G. Shaw and M. T. Wild, 'Retail patterns in the Victorian city', *Transactions of the Institute of British Geographers*, new series, 4 (1979), 278–91; G. Shaw, 'Retail patterns', in J. Langton and R. J. Morris, eds., *Atlas of Industrialising Britain, 1780–1914* (London, 1986), pp. 180–4; Benson and Shaw, eds., *Evolution of Retail Systems*, Part III.

[25] M. Phillips, 'The evolution of markets and shops in Britain', in Benson and Shaw, eds., *Evolution of Retail Systems*; M. J. Winstanley, 'Concentration and competition in the retail sector, c. 1800–1990', in M. W. Kirby and M. B. Rose, eds., *Business Enterprise in Modern Britain* (London, 1994), pp. 240–1; and research in progress by Debbie Hodson towards a Lancaster University PhD thesis on urban markets in nineteenth-century Lancashire.

[26] Winstanley, 'Concentration and competition', p. 251; M. J. Winstanley, ed., *A Traditional Grocer: T. D. Smith's of Lancaster, 1858–1981* (Lancaster, 1991), C. P. Hosgood, 'The "pigmies of commerce" and the working-class community: small shopkeepers in England 1870–1914', *Journal of Social History*, 22 (1989), 439–59.

geographical coverage and social penetration either side of the Second World War.[27] The impact of changing urban population distributions and transport networks on all this provides further grist to the mill of the quantitatively minded historical geographer. But the charting of changing patterns of retail provision is only part of the story.

An understanding of the social history of consumption needs to be based on the manufacturing and marketing of products as well as their direct delivery to consumers. It also needs to embrace not only the purchasing power and desires of the consumers themselves, but also the process of shopping as a cultural activity in its own right, and the question of how objects are treated after the purchase is completed.[28] The motives behind the purchase of goods, and the circumstances under which this takes place, have been the subject of politically charged debate. Adherents of the theory of conspicuous consumption have tended to stress emulation as the motive force for growth in demand for goods which go beyond sustaining a basic standard of living, whether in their function, design or opulence of construction or finish.[29] But this line of approach is based on a historically specific critique of the perceived behaviour of particular aspirant social groups in the United States of the early twentieth century, founded in earlier 'commonsense' social criticism advanced by novelists and journalists, which perhaps transfers uneasily to notions of the rise of 'mass' consumerism; and its psychological assumptions are somewhat reductive. Emulative bases for consumer behaviour have also been associated with notions of a 'trickle-down effect' of prosperity and enjoyment from the wealthy to the poor, which are associated with political positions justifying inequality and regarding the rich as necessary innovators who should be left to get on with the task of creating new needs and demands to which others may aspire.[30]

Marxist approaches, on the other hand, grow out of Marx's concept of commodity fetishism, which sets an aura or halo round goods made for sale, giving them and the relationships which surround them a sacred and unchallengeable status, and thereby, by extension, turning shopping into a sacrament.[31] This is a fertile field for presentations of the manipulation of consumers by capitalist manufacturers and retailers, who pull the heartstrings of desire through advertising and display, and encourage people to focus their attention on gaining access

---

[27] See above, nn. 10 and 12.

[28] B. Fine and E. Leopold, *The World of Consumption* (London, 1993).

[29] T. Veblen, *The Theory of the Leisure Class* (London, 1924); P. Johnson, 'Conspicuous consumption and working-class culture in late Victorian and Edwardian Britain', *TRHS*, 5th series, 38 (1988), 27–42; H. J. Perkin, *The Origins of Modern English Society* (London, 1969), ch. 3.

[30] Fine and Leopold, *World of Consumption*, pp. 138–47; D. Miller, *Material Culture and Mass Consumption* (Oxford, 1987), pp. 147–57, bringing in a useful discussion of Bourdieu; M. Douglas and B. Isherwood, *The World of Goods* (London, 1979), ch. 2.

[31] K. Marx, *Capital*, 12th edn (London, 1908), pp. 41–55; M. Berman, *All That Is Solid Melts into Air* (London, 1983), pp. 87–129.

to a glittering array of (it is assumed) increasingly tawdry and trivial goods rather than on what are seen as the real issues of workplace or political conflict. Workers are thus doubly exploited, as both wage labourers and consumers, in the interests of sustaining profit in an ever-expanding system of manufacture and sale.[32]

Critics of this frame of reference have pointed to patronising aspects of (especially) the cruder ascriptions of 'false consciousness', and these have been even more evident in the work of cultural critics who have associated 'mass consumption' with surface gloss, cheapness and nastiness.[33] A more sophisticated, and highly influential, mode of analysis has been provided by Pierre Bourdieu, who has emphasised the importance of the distinctions engendered between consumer goods and cultural products, through the development of systems of discrimination which place some items and activities above others in an elaborate pecking order. These distinctions are founded in the acquisition of 'cultural capital' through education and socialisation, which generates sets of consumer preferences which are shared across social and occupational groups and whose deeply ingrained assumptions generate evaluations whose exclusions and downgradings, at least, can become almost automatic. Above the level of mass consumption, and displaying contempt for it in most forms, floats a hierarchy of intersecting preferences and expectations, where consumption patterns are fuelled less by crude emulation than by inherited or acquired systems of taste and discrimination. Bourdieu seems both to expose and endorse the system he presents, whose logic seems to detach 'mass' consumerism from these more sophisticated upper layers and intersecting circles, convincingly undermining 'trickle-down' ideas, and whose validity as a basis for critical analysis can be extended from the France of the 1960s in which his fieldwork was based. But we should not neglect the capacity of the lower levels of consumers, excluded from this system by their lack of bourgeois forms of cultural capital, developing their own distinctions and deploying their own forms of cultural capital, displaying agency and choice in a market place whose complexity is traduced by the vocabulary of 'mass' and 'masses'. Indeed, anthropological approaches have stressed the ways in which the consumption of goods and services is central to social interaction, which may entail consumers attaching their own meanings to and deriving their own individual or communal satisfactions from what is on offer. Consumption within the capitalist market place need not be passive, and suppliers of goods and services need to be responsive to demand as well as trying to create and channel it.[34] This is compatible with a Marxian reading of developments, mediated through Gramsci, in which consumers react to and impact

[32] Fine and Leopold, *World of Consumption*, chs. 9–10.
[33] J. Golby and W. Purdue, *The Civilisation of the Crowd* (London, 1984), p. 12.
[34] P. Bourdieu, *Distinction*, trans. R. Nice (London, 1984); Miller, *Material Culture*, ch. 10; Douglas and Isherwood, *World of Goods*, chs. 3–4; Golby and Purdue, *The Civilisation of the Crowd* (London, 1984).

on the nature and circumstances of what is provided for them, while participating in a process which is ultimately orchestrated from without, and not primarily for their own benefit. They are given choices, but not within a framework of their own conscious choosing; and this limits the array of possibilities open to them, although they will not necessarily be aware of this beyond a consciousness of the limitations of their resources in time and money.[35] Such are the debates on consumption in 'industrial society' or 'modernity', which brings us through to the middle decades of the twentieth century. It might be argued that presentations from a 'cultural studies' perspective of the nature of consumption in 'post-industrial' society, the world of the shopping mall and the out-of-town retail complex, of the integration of shopping and leisure on special sites for those who can afford access, lie beyond the scope of a chapter with this time-span, on the assumption that ways of theorising post-industrial societies are not readily applicable to their forebears.[36]

These controversies are based overwhelmingly on activities which went on in urban spaces, although many of the consumers came into town from surrounding areas to participate in the rituals of consumption, and we must not regard town and country as binary opposites or keep them in separate compartments.[37] Towns have been backcloths or bystanders in most of the literature, but some writers have acknowledged the surging excitements of the new environments of urban sociability, the swirling colour and bustle of the public spaces in which consumption flourished and was promoted.[38] The transformation of London's West End from the 1860s and 1870s, with the rise of department stores and fashionable shopping areas, has been mapped with particular attention; and the increasing visibility of women as shoppers in these contested spaces (alongside female service workers and prostitutes, in an environment where perceived ambiguities of status and intent issued forth in frequent sexual harassment) brought colour and conflict, pleasure and peril to such public urban settings.[39] Ladies shopping for pleasure increasingly came in from peripheral suburbia, by omnibus, train or (towards the turn of the century) tram if not by carriage; and the desire to use the expanding purchasing power of middle-class incomes to embellish detached domesticity generated a genre of shopping for fabrics and furniture as well as

[35] See above, n. 3.

[36] T. Richards, *The Commodity Culture of Victorian England* (London, 1991), tries to push notions of the origins of a 'commodity culture' to the Victorian middle classes; but he has to wrench his evidence out of context, misreading his material all too visibly in the process, to present this interesting argument.

[37] P. J. Waller, *Town, City and Nation* (Oxford, 1983); R. E. Pahl, *Divisions of Labour* (London, 1984).

[38] Berman, *All That Is Solid*, Parts III and IV, deals with Paris and St Petersburg in ways which might be transferred to the British setting.

[39] J. R. Walkowitz, *City of Dreadful Delight* (London and Chicago, 1992), ch. 2; P. J. Atkins, 'The spatial configuration of class solidarity in London's West End, 1792–1939', *UHY*, 17 (1990), 36–65.

clothing and personal ornamentation. Refreshments and up-market entertainments followed suit, pulling the sexes together but also allowing women a measure of autonomy in shared pleasures. The changing social geography of the urban middle class transformed parts of the central business district into temples of consumerism, rendered increasingly secure for worshippers at the shrine as they became more socially homogeneous and better policed. This applied to resorts, and to historic cities like Chester, as well as to London, Manchester or Leeds, as the shopping and entertainment catchment areas of the larger and more attractive places widened, while on the fringes of the larger cities the suburbs themselves were generating intermediate shopping centres and department stores of their own.[40] Meanwhile, we still know far too little about the shopping and entertainment options of lower-middle and working-class women outside the home, although music hall's opening out to a wider constituency of broadly defined urban respectability included women within its generous remit, while at the same time offering roles and modes of self-presentation to women as well as men, whether played straight or deployed with irony or self-deprecation.[41] At the bottom of the scale, and well into the interwar years in depressed working-class areas like Salford, many people depended on the corner shop and skilfully managed market trading for the overwhelming bulk of their purchases, and took their entertainment alfresco as they found it in the market place, while what popular consumerism there was found outlets in the 'penny capitalists' who played music or sold licks of ice-cream or other cheap delicacies through the back streets.[42] The later decades of the nineteenth century brought novelties for all, but some were much more mobile and flexible in their pursuit of a widening range of goods and pleasures than others; and here access to the two key resources, time and money, inextricably interlinked, remained crucial to an ability to benefit.[43] But in various ways, across a range of action-spaces, the city itself emerged as an object of consumption and desire, in both the public and the private sphere, for men at almost all social levels and for many middle-class women; and this applied to the most prosaic manufacturing centres as well as to the resorts, opulent suburbs and elite shopping areas which were beginning consciously to market their attributes in late Victorian times. These perceptions of the changing relationships between towns and consumption need further development.

The rise of consumerism as a mass phenomenon, entailing the spread of a general capacity and desire to choose between and enjoy an array of non-essential goods and services, and to pick out more desirable versions of essential

---

[40] C. Young and S. Allen, 'Retail patterns in nineteenth century Chester', *Journal of Regional and Local Studies*, 16 (1996), 1–18; J. Benson and G. Shaw, 'Retail patterns', in Benson and Shaw, eds., *Evolution of Retail Systems*.   [41] Bratton, *Music Hall*.

[42] J. Benson, *The Penny Capitalists* (Dublin, 1983); A. Davies, *Leisure, Gender and Poverty* (Buckingham, 1992); C. Chinn, *They Worked All Their Lives* (Manchester, 1988).

[43] Cross, *Time and Money*.

ones or expand existing notions of what was essential, was an extension of the competitive and hedonistic consumption enjoyed by aristocrats, gentry and the aspiring professional and business 'middling sort', which had been developing in favoured urban settings since at least the later seventeenth century, and spread from the metropolis, the resorts and the county towns into the newly prospering manufacturing and mercantile towns of the late eighteenth and early nineteenth centuries. By the mid-nineteenth century the substantial middle classes were ceasing to live 'over the shop' and moving out in growing numbers to suburbs like Birmingham's Edgbaston and Manchester's Victoria Park, where women devoted themselves to domestic pursuits which included the acquisition, display and care of possessions whose aesthetic and fashionable attributes counted for at least as much as their utility.[44] The myth of the abstemious, accumulative, puritanical master manufacturer was largely just that, and Quaker mill owners accumulated their wine cellars and art collections along with the rest, enjoying to the full the consumer opportunities their enhanced purchasing power provided.[45] But the commercial and professional middle class of London, where the greatest fortunes were concentrated, took the palm.[46] Writing in the 1860s the French academic Hippolyte Taine commented on the eight miles of middle-class housing between London Bridge and Hampton Court, remarking that 'they turn out houses as we turn out Paris fancy-goods' and identifying this phenomenon with the existence of 'an opulent free-spending middle class very different from our own'.[47] Such households needed to acquire the 'paraphernalia of gentility', in J. A. Banks' memorable phrase, to fit in with the consumer conventions of their neighbours and coevals: they needed to employ the almost-statutory three servants, to send their boys to the right schools, to have access to horses and a carriage of appropriate standard, and to lay claim to suitable cultural capital in tangible form through the display of gardens, libraries, solid furniture and pictures.[48] They needed to be able to entertain at an appropriate level, with suitable cuisine, service and utensils for the exchange of hospitality according to rules which could be bent but seldom broken. The voluntary organisations so characteristic of Victorian England (and afterwards), from the Literary and Philosophical Society and the chapel to the Freemasons and Rotary, encouraged social mixing beyond immediate circles of family, neighbours and business associates, enabling identities to be tried out on a wider stage but expanding the opportunities for and potential consequences of conflict and embarrassment.

[44] Davidoff and Hall, *Family Fortunes*; R. J. Morris, *Class, Sect and Party* (Manchester, 1990); M. Spiers, *Victoria Park* (Manchester, 1975); M. Simpson and T. H. Lloyd, eds., *Middle Class Housing in Britain* (Newton Abbot, 1977).
[45] A. C. Howe, *The Cotton Masters 1830–1860* (Oxford, 1984); R. Boyson, *The Ashworth Cotton Enterprise* (Oxford, 1970).   [46] W. D. Rubinstein, *Men of Property* (London, 1981).
[47] H. Taine, *Notes on England*, trans. Edward Hyams (London, 1958), p. 14.
[48] J. A. Banks, *Prosperity and Parenthood* (London, 1954), ch. 6.

These were, above all, urban preoccupations; and for most people they entailed conformity rather than boundary-transgressing cultural innovation.[49]

It is not clear how far the ripples of such comfortable but anxious consumerism reached into the mid-Victorian lower middle and upper working class: the worlds of Charles Pooter and of Thomas Wright's journeyman engineer.[50] Banks focuses mainly on the opulent and comfortable middle class, who set standards which were only attainable in attenuated form for their social inferiors. The first claims on any surplus in the lower reaches of the middle class were often directed towards services rather than goods: domestic labour to free the wife from degrading drudgery, display the household's command over the cheap labour of suitably uniformed others and allow the cultivation of accomplishments and domestic ceremony; laundry to display appropriate crispness and cleanliness according to exacting presentational codes, within the family and before the world; and education to provide the young with the social and commercial skills and cultural repertoire which would sustain the family into the next generation.[51] Even the seaside holiday, which in its respectable family incarnation became a touchstone of status for mid-Victorian urban middle-class families, and multiplied examples of a distinctive kind of consumer-oriented town in the process, entailed expenditure on services (transport and accommodation) at least as much as goods.[52] Among marginal members of the middle class, the prior requirement to hire domestic help – if only a charwoman or maid of all work – ate into disposable income for the recreational shopping and entertainment which towns came to offer. Urban consumerism was driven back into the home, especially as suburbs proliferated on and beyond the fringes of the larger towns and work, public entertainment and specialised shopping all entailed journeys into and back from the town centre.[53] This was partly a life cycle stage, and middle-class bachelors were better customers for urban entertainment, although at a more prosperous level the gentlemen's club offered its own version of serviced quasi-domesticity in homosocial enclaves where men mixed with their peers; but the respectable family set a premium on domesticity, however

[49] V. Mars, 'Ordering dinner' (PhD thesis, University of Leicester, 1997); Douglas and Isherwood, *World of Goods*, ch. 4.

[50] G. Grossmith and W. Grossmith, *The Diary of a Nobody* (Gloucester, 1991 edn); T. Wright, *Some Habits and Customs of the Working Classes* (1867; repr., London, 1967); and T. Wright, *The Great Unwashed* (1868; repr., London, 1968).

[51] P. Horn, ed., *The Rise and Fall of the Victorian Domestic Servant* (Dublin, 1975); P. Malcolmson, *English Laundresses: A Social History 1850–1930* (Urbana, Ill., 1986); J. K. Walton and A. Wilcox, eds., *Low Life and Moral Improvement in Mid-Victorian England: Liverpool through the Journalism of Hugh Shimmin* (Leicester, 1991), ch. 16 ('A bad servant manufactory'); J. R. de S. Honey, *Tom Brown's Universe* (London, 1977).   [52] Walton, *English Seaside Resort*, ch. 2.

[53] H. J. Dyos, *Victorian Suburb* (Leicester, 1961); F. M. L. Thompson, ed., *The Rise of Suburbia* (Leicester, 1982); Jackson, *Semi-Detached London*; G. Stedman Jones, 'Working-class culture and working-class politics in London, 1870–1900: notes on the remaking of a working class', *Journal of Social History*, 7 (1974), 460–509.

rudimentary its claims to domestic comfort might look to a censorious superior gaze.[54] The cheap German piano was becoming an emblematic consumer durable for the urban lower middle class by the mid-Victorian years, but shopping for pleasure rather than to meet narrowly defined necessities was something which emerged at this level only with the late Victorian price fall which also brought the mainstream urban working class into the frame.[55]

The coming of a genuine 'mass market' for most consumer goods and services was an urban phenomenon of the late nineteenth and early twentieth centuries. Periodic surges of inflation in the mid-Victorian years eroded the gains in money wages which were enjoyed in some skilled and supervisory male working-class occupations at this time, and such gains tended to find their way into hedonistic or ritualised masculine consumption on drink and associated pursuits rather than into family budgets and the acquisition of consumer goods.[56] Rising real wages fuelled by the falling prices of basic commodities, on the other hand, tended to spread the benefits through the family as the increased spending power was passed on into the housekeeping budget; and the growing importance of Co-operative dividends in many northern and Midland settings in the late nineteenth century reinforced this trend.[57] Beer consumption *per capita* began to decline from 1876, and the fortnightly sixpences which might be devoted to the concomitant rise of football as a spectator sport did not counterbalance this trend.[58] Convenience foods took pressure off the working-class housewife in the absence of labour-saving housework devices, just as domestic servants reduced the workload of her 'betters'. Fish and chips, the most obvious example, began in the 1870s as (mainly) a late-night treat for men returning from the pub, but was generalising its influence as a regular family meal by Edwardian times.[59] More families began to afford new ready-made clothes (especially for men), substantial furniture and ornaments to gather dust in the front parlour, seaside holidays and associated souvenirs, bicycles (if only second-hand), cheap newspapers and books, even pianos and sheet music: a whole cornucopia of non-essential items, some of which were themselves recent inventions, which reached out to hitherto distant or makeshift realms of fashion, fantasy and frivolity.[60]

For families whose breadwinner remained in work, falling rents and family sizes, together with further declines in basic commodity prices, opened

[54] Taine, *Notes on England*, p. 186; Walton and Wilcox, eds., *Hugh Shimmin*, ch. 6.
[55] C. Ehrlich, *The Piano*, revised edn (Oxford, 1990); Fraser, *Mass Market*; G. Crossick, ed., *The Lower Middle Class in Britain, 1870–1914* (London, 1977).
[56] E. H. Hunt, *Regional Wage Variations in Britain, 1850–1914* (Oxford, 1973); N. Kirk, *The Growth of Working-Class Reformism in Mid-Victorian England* (London, 1985); A. T. McCabe, 'The standard of living on Merseyside, 1850–75', in S. P. Bell, ed., *Victorian Lancashire* (Newton Abbot, 1974).
[57] J. K. Walton, *Lancashire: A Social History 1558–1939* (Manchester, 1987), p. 296.
[58] A. E. Dingle, 'Drink and working-class living standards in Britain, 1870–1914', *Ec.HR*, 2nd series, 25 (1972), 608–22; Mason, *Association Football and English Society*. [59] Walton, *Fish and Chips*.
[60] Fraser, *Mass Market*; A. Briggs, *Victorian Things* (London, 1988).

out purchasing power for new consumer durables in the interwar years. The radio stands out most obviously here alongside the wider dissemination of the bicycle and the development of new personal means of transport, as motor-cycles and cars came within the means of some working-class people in the 1930s; but these innovations were part of a much wider pattern. Municipal housing helped to boost the home-centred culture of the suburbs, extending it to new social groups, and pressure from neighbours and municipal landlords to maintain and make use of gardens boosted demand for tools, seeds and related products.[61] These themes applied more generally and obviously to the middle classes, who jealously guarded the status of their own interwar suburbs and bought into the mythology and conventionalised vocabulary of exposed timber, stained glass, rockeries and garden gnomes.[62]

These comments about the urban working class and the mass market need some qualification. Even in the 1840s some working-class families had the capac-ity to acquire substantial furniture (as in the mahogany sideboards of homes in Manchester's Hulme) which was decorative and satisfying as well as functional; but part of its value lay in its availability for pawning in hard times. It was a solid, dependable way of saving for a rainy day, and could be enjoyed more sensually than money locked away in an untrustworthy bank.[63] Such rationales for pawning were not usually understood by unsympathetic commentators from outside the culture, but they persisted even as savings banks became more reli-able and other ways of providing security became more widespread.[64] This is a reminder that the meanings of consumer goods might extend beyond the more obvious aspects of utility and display. The Sunday suit often had similar func-tions as part of a weekly economic cycle of display, pawning and release which was also a way of coping with inadequate domestic storage space.[65] When the more general transition to the mass market got under way in the late nineteenth century, its impact was geographically and socially skewed. The northern textile towns, especially those of Lancashire with their high family incomes, led the way, along with the artisan and craft workers of London; but some of the most impressive gains in real wages around the turn of the century came in industries such as mining, where there was less scope for augmenting the breadwinner wage and a higher incidence of isolated communities, with fewer shopping or commodified entertainment opportunities.[66] Here, too, housing conditions

[61] McKibbin, *Ideologies of Class*, ch. 5; S. Constantine, 'Amateur gardening and popular recreation in the nineteenth and twentieth centuries', *Journal of Social History*, 14 (1980–1), 387–401; G. L. Murfin, *Popular Leisure in the Lake Counties* (Manchester, 1990).

[62] P. Oliver, I. Davis and I. Bentley, *Dunroamin* (London, 1981).

[63] W. Cooke Taylor, *Notes of a Tour of the Manufacturing Districts of Lancashire* (London, 1842); M. Tebbutt, *Making Ends Meet* (Leicester, 1983).   [64] Johnson, *Saving and Spending*.

[65] Tebbutt, *Making Ends Meet*.

[66] Walton, *Lancashire*, ch. 13; C. Feinstein, 'Variety and volatility: some aspects of the labour market in Britain 1880–1913', in C. Holmes and A. Booth, eds., *Economy and Society: European Industrialisation and Its Social Consequences* (Leicester, 1991), pp. 154–74.

were often particularly poor, and the new influences for mass consumption generally had less scope to operate, encouraging the perpetuation of masculine consumption patterns based on drink and gambling.

Not only were many families banished from their precarious hold on access to consumer goods by trade depressions or labour disputes, illness or injury, when ornaments and emblems of comfort and privacy had to be turned into cash and commercial entertainment became inaccessible; not only did the poverty cycle bite into consumer capacity when children were young; but there were also enduring pools of the poverty of casual labour and the sweated trades, where the struggle for survival left no room for frivolity of any sort, and stale bread and rags were precious resources. Descriptions of domestic interiors during the great trade depression of 1842; or the Cotton Famine of the early 1860s, which pushed so many Lancashire labouring families into temporary but desperate poverty; or of the sufferings of articulate working men like Joseph Gutteridge in the Coventry ribbon trades, tell this sort of story from a perspective of deep but short-term crisis.[67] But the fate of the sweated garment workers described by Henry Mayhew in London's East End, or of Charles Booth's Classes A and B nearly half a century later, or of the casual labourers of mid-Victorian Liverpool as described in a range of poverty surveys, points to the existence of a submerged stratum whose only hope of entry into a realm of consumer choice was through a successful bet or raffle, or through enjoying a weekend binge involving easily cooked chops or steak before starving through the rest of the week, or through putting alcohol and tobacco before more 'rational' and acceptable ways of ekeing out a pittance. The conditions in many houses were not such as to encourage attempts at beautification or enhanced comfort.[68] Where steadily provided domestic garment work was part of a stable family economy and performed by experienced women who knew the value of their skills, matters could be different and houses 'clean and well-furnished', with ornaments and the occasional piano, as Clementina Black's optimistic assessment of Liverpool vestmakers documents for the Edwardian years; but she was only too aware of how exceptional this was.[69]

These comments remain relevant in the interwar years, especially where high levels of unemployment or enduring casualisation prevailed. Thus the social survey of Merseyside which was completed by Liverpool University between 1929 and 1932 found that in a given week 39 per cent of a sample whose income

[67] Joseph Adshead, *Distress in Manchester: Evidence of the State of the Labouring Classes in 1842* (London, 1842); Edwin Waugh, *Home-Life of the Lancashire Factory Folk during the Cotton Famine* (London, 1867); V. Chancellor, *Master and Artisan in Victorian England* (New York, 1969), pp. 177–82.
[68] E. P. Thompson and E. Yeo, *The Unknown Mayhew* (London, 1971); D. Englander and R. O'Day, eds., *Retrieved Riches* (Aldershot, 1995); Walton and Wilcox, eds., *Hugh Shimmin*; J. H. Treble, *Urban Poverty in Britain, 1830–1914* (London, 1979); J. Schmiechen, *Sweated Industries and Sweated Labor: The London Clothing Trades* (Beckenham, 1984).
[69] Clementina Black, ed., *Married Women's Work*, 2nd edn (London, 1983), p. 180.

fell below 80 per cent of an assessed poverty line recorded no expenditure in the 'recreation, tobacco, miscellaneous' category, while 29 per cent spent nothing on clothing (in a social setting where most clothing was paid for by monthly instalments from the 'Scotch draper'), and 95 per cent spent nothing on furniture. At these levels, and above, diet itself was probably insufficient in content if not in quantity. The surveyors commented that some expenditure was certainly omitted, especially casual spending on tit-bits, betting and beer; but this was thought to be more likely to occur at the top end of the income spectrum under discussion. Liverpool's cheaper shopping facilities were making consumer goods and choices more readily available by the 1920s and 1930s, but many were still excluded; and this comment would stand for many ports and older industrial areas.[70] We need to set this evidence against George Orwell's perception that the basic comfort and variety afforded by cheap cinema seats, art silk stockings, fish and chips, cheap cigarettes and other accessible items of basic consumption helped to keep the unemployed and their poverty-stricken neighbours from despair and unrest in the worst years of the 1930s. The world of urban consumerism still excluded many of the poor and immobile in industrial villages, small towns and slums, and it was only in the almost-full employment of the post-war years, and then only when the eventual retreat of rationing opened out alternatives to sport, leisure, alcohol and tobacco, that the outermost circles of deprivation and make-do-and-mend were drawn more fully into the consumer market place.[71]

The urban setting ratcheted up the pressure to present the self and build identities through the market place rather than, or as well as, through domestic crafts and personal skills. In concentrations of population, and especially in resorts, city centres or well-frequented thoroughfares where status was acquired through a shared grammar of self-representation rather than being ascribed through deeper knowledge of an individual's antecedents and social context, purchased goods provided a universal language while the home-made was quaint and marginalised. This did not exclude such hybrid activities as the making up of patterns through knitting or home dressmaking, of course, and additional work could be done on purchased articles to give them an individual, personal touch, following a long tradition of buying buttons or tassels to alter the appearance of a dress which might in itself be a consumer durable and even an heirloom; but this had to take place within shifting consensual idioms of the fashionable and the appropriate (which is not to propose a model for consumer behaviour based solely on emulation or 'trickle-down').[72] Second-hand and out-of-fashion goods took their place in the imposed ordering of the market place, and strategies for making

[70] D. C. Jones, ed., *Merseyside* (Liverpool, 1934), vol. 1, ch. 12.
[71] G. Orwell, *The Road to Wigan Pier* (London, 1937); Obelkevich and Catterall, eds., *Understanding British Society.*   [72] Fine and Leopold, *World of Consumption*, chs. 10 and 11.

the best of one's resources were adopted in the knowledge that they were palliative rather than triumphalist. This helps to explain the unwillingness of dwellers in working-class neighbourhoods to admit visitors from beyond the family into houses which did not display a suitable repertoire of furnishings and ornament, and the imperative to corral visitors into an otherwise unused and highly polished formal sitting room.[73] It was, above all, the town and its combination of goods for sale and inescapable personal display which created, reinforced and extended the tyranny of fashion and the market in ever-extending spirals and concentric ripples.

Urban consumption began with the manufacture of goods. This was increasingly an urban activity, as industry continued the move from the countryside which had begun in earnest in the eighteenth century and was being pushed harder by the mid-nineteenth century, as a result of the economies of scale offered by carboniferous capitalism and the communications revolutions which were based on railways, commuting, newspapers and the telegraph. The consumption of news, as commodity and shared activity, was essential to urban living.[74] The marketing and selling of goods had a much longer pedigree as specialist urban activities, but the new urban shopping spaces of the street lined with plate-glass and display, the arcade, the covered market, the department store and the emporium gave an extra impetus to the town as promoter of consumption. Once the purchasing transaction had been completed, the town offered scope for intensive sociability, in private as well as in public and in intermediate zones regulated by subscription and invitation, and expressed through a variety of dining and other hospitality rituals which promoted both consensual and innovative consumption of goods whose identities were recreated through use and reuse in different contexts.[75] We need now to follow the systems of provision and consumption of goods through the urban setting, beginning with their manufacture.[76]

The women's suffrage campaigner Teresa Billington Greig commented forcefully before the First World War on the artificiality of dividing producer and consumer interests in a society where they were necessarily complementary. Wage labourers in manufacturing and retailing were also consumers, and in the latter role they fell victim to all the price-cutting and adulterating devices at which they connived as producers. Cheap goods and nasty depressed living standards, and the worship of work rather than properly directed, life-enhancing leisure and enjoyment cast a blight over millions of lives. Trade unionists equated

---

[73] R. Roberts, *The Classic Slum* (Manchester, 1971).

[74] A. J. Lee, *The Origins of the Popular Press in Britain 1855–1914* (Beckenham, 1976); Lucy Brown, *Victorian News and Newspapers* (Oxford, 1985); J. Kieve, *The Electric Telegraph: A Social and Economic History* (Newton Abbot, 1973).

[75] Walkowitz, *City of Dreadful Delight*, ch. 2; Morris, *Class, Sect and Party*; Mars, 'Ordering dinner'.

[76] Fine and Leopold, *World of Consumption*, ch. 2.

consumers with the idle rich, and forgot that they too bought in the market place. And the poorest workers got the worst of all worlds, living outside the protection offered by strong trade unions and condemned to buy the worst and cheapest goods. So, Greig argued, if any progress was to be made towards a more just society and better living standards, the interests of producers and consumers must be examined in tandem. Her premises are accepted here.[77]

The exploitation of labour to produce cheap consumer goods was increasingly an urban phenomenon, whether or not it was organised in factories. It was already all too apparent to Mayhew in the mid-nineteenth century, as he investigated the falling living standards of the 'dishonourable' sweated trades in London, where the division of labour and the competitive cutting of piece-rates had driven the makers of a range of commodities, from clothing to furniture to toys, into a subsistence poverty of interminable working hours geared to tyrannical deadlines, and alternating with spells of unemployment according to the season and the fashion.[78] Cheap goods for mass consumption (or to meet orders to tight timetables) presupposed this system of work, which the advent of the sewing machine (for example) left unaffected, although the rise of the ready-made clothing industry from the 1850s was associated with a move to factories in places like Leeds; and it transferred overhead costs such as rent, lighting, heating and even some raw materials to the worker at home. No wonder this was an enduring alternative to the factory, especially where land values were high and the vagaries of fashion fickle. Factory work could generate more substantial and reliable purchasing power (although, for example, cotton in Blackburn was more secure and better paid than jam in London, at least until the 1920s); but either way the production of consumer goods at bare subsistence wages set limits to the extent of a notional 'mass market'. The 'sweated trades' proved even harder to regulate than the factories, and they were still attracting the anguished attention of legislators and social reformers in Edwardian times and beyond.[79] Domestic manufacture organised through warehouses and layers of middlemen outlasted the rural stereotypes of 'proto-industrialisation' and became a central feature of urban labour markets, with the opportunities they provided for generating alternative means of subsistence in the low season, enabling workforces to be kept together by 'dovetailing' and the use of local contacts to find what work there was.[80] Among the results were fashionable items of clothing made under atrociously filthy conditions, where workers had neither time nor resources to look after their surroundings, so that workers' pay was regularly docked when lice were found in the finished goods they submitted to the warehouse.[81]

---

[77] Greig, *Consumer in Revolt*, ch. 2.

[78] Thompson and Yeo, *Unknown Mayhew*; G. Stedman Jones, *Outcast London* (Oxford, 1971).

[79] Schmiechen, *Sweated Industries*; D. Bythell, *The Sweated Trades* (London, 1978); J. Buckman, *Immigrants and the Class Struggle* (Manchester, 1983); Briggs, *Victorian Things*, pp. 283–4.

[80] Stedman Jones, *Outcast London*; E. Ross, *Love and Toil* (New York and Oxford, 1993).

[81] Thompson and Yeo, *Unknown Mayhew*, pp. 252–3.

At the other end of the scale, and seeming to suggest that capitalist consumerism did not necessary presuppose a miserable treadmill of working to survive among those who could not aspire to the more pleasurable round of producing to fund consumer shopping, there were the model factories and communities established by paternalist employers in the new consumer industries of (especially) the later nineteenth century, in textiles, clothing, chocolate, tobacco or soap manufacture. From the better-endowed of the 'industrial colonies' of the early Industrial Revolution, with their baths, libraries, gardens and bedroom inspections as celebrated by social commentators of the 1840s, through more architecturally ambitious mid-Victorian initiatives like Saltaire, to the 'garden cities' in miniature of Port Sunlight or Bournville or New Earswick at and beyond the turn of the century, with their facilities for sport, recreation and 'improvement', the consumption of some producers of consumer goods was channelled in approved directions by conscientious employers.[82] But such places were invariably sited on the urban fringe, at what was intended to be a safe distance from urban fleshpots as well as industrial pollution, and workers were eager to take what they wanted from such arrangements and reject the rest. Paternalist employers were always a conspicuous and well-documented minority, and they seem to have succeeded in socialising only a few of their workpeople into becoming ideal subordinate citizens and 'rational' consumers of homes, gardens and approved culture.[83] Meanwhile, Port Sunlight's W. H. Lever was promoting the quasi-slavery of indentured labour on his palm-oil plantations, aided and abetted by British colonial authorities, and similar arrangements prevailed in cocoa.[84] So the quasi-subsistence economy of producers who could not afford to be consumers was exported rather than abolished, contributing in its turn to the cheapness in Britain of new products for the 'mass' market such as soap and chocolate. This was an inconvenient economic reality which sat uneasily alongside the cosy and comfortable cottage homes, art gallery and community centre of Port Sunlight. In the immediate pre-war years Lever was also waging a legal vendetta against the Co-op to oblige it to stock his products, and his concern for his workers as consumers was not only highly selective, but also very much on his own terms.[85] And when William Morris and his followers in the Arts and Crafts movement made more conscientious efforts to educate workers into making, and consumers into preferring, craftsmanship and fine materials, and goods produced in revitalised rural surroundings, they found themselves priced into the prosperous sectors of the market and confined to making fashion goods

[82] Cooke Taylor, *Notes of a Tour*; J. Reynolds, *The Great Paternalist* (London, 1983); W. Ashworth, *The Genesis of Modern British Town Planning* (London, 1954); S. Pollard, *The Genesis of Modern Management* (Harmondsworth, 1964); G. Darley, *Villages of Vision* (London, 1975).
[83] P. Joyce, *Work, Society and Politics* (Brighton, 1980), challenged by J. King, 'We could eat the police', *Victorian Studies*, 28 (1985), 439–71.
[84] J. Walvin, *Questioning Slavery* (London, 1996), p. 180.
[85] Gurney, *Co-operative Culture*, pp. 204–8.

to put on show the cultural capital of discerning *cognoscenti*.[86] This was to prove an enduring dilemma: to provide consumer goods the mass market could afford, it seemed necessary to exploit the labour of urban toilers in stressful factory settings or insanitary garrets and workshops, to depend on cheap and nasty materials and indeed to push distant plantation workers into a re-creation of slavery.[87] But for those who could afford to enjoy shopping, and who did not need to see whence their purchases came, the towns came to offer a cornucopia of displayed delights.

Over the century after 1850, and especially during the transitional late Victorian years, urban retailing and shopping were transformed. The presentation of goods was particularly important here, as the spread of extensive glass-fronted windows (building on technological innovation in the glass industry) enabled consumer items to be displayed in enticing array, with ticketed prices. The new multiple grocers and tea dealers, with Lipton leading the way from the early 1870s, were important innovators here. Such developments shifted the role of the new town-centre shops visibly from meeting needs to stimulating demand: customers were made aware of a range of possibilities which they might not otherwise have considered, and enabled to consider the financial implications without the potential embarrassment of inquiry.[88] The rise of gas lighting around mid-century boosted this trend in two ways, as retailers anxious to illuminate their premises were among the pioneer private users, while the most important early market for gas companies was the provision of street lighting which made window shopping both safer and more comfortable.[89] Electricity, gathering momentum at the turn of the century, was the next stage; and in these fields the legitimacy of municipal intervention in the market place was widely recognised, as the ratepayers obtained access to a consumer democracy which might (at least in theory) keep prices low and sustain the standards of services on which the consumer provision of private enterprise depended. Much the same applied to urban tramways, which became essential to the articulating of the larger towns as systems of consumption as well as production towards the turn of the century.[90]

But the role of advertising extended far beyond window dressing and street display. Its rapid development through press, poster and stunt was a theme of the mid- and late Victorian years. It was overwhelmingly an urban phenomenon. This was where the posters, exhibitions and other displays were concentrated,

[86] J. Press and C. E. Harvey, *William Morris: Design and Enterprise in Victorian England* (Manchester, 1991); F. MacCarthy, *The Simple Life* (London, 1981).
[87] Schmeichen, *Sweated Industries*, pp. 185–6.
[88] Walkowitz, *City of Dreadful Delight*; M. J. Winstanley, *The Shopkeeper's World 1830–1914* (Manchester, 1983); Lancaster, *Department Store*; Mathias, *Retailing*.
[89] J. F. Wilson, *Lighting the Town* (London, 1991), p. 168.
[90] P. Kinchin, *Tea and Taste* (Wendlebury, 1991), p. 18.

increasingly taking over strategic locations and asserting their messages on vehicles and at transport junctions, and making their own controversial contribution to the changing public aesthetic of the city. This was where the emergent advertising agencies had their offices, and where the newspapers, magazines and mail order catalogues that conveyed the fashions and the prices to the suburbs and the countryside were based. Advertising lived by, and formed part of, the communications revolution of which the towns were the nerve centres.[91] The suggestion that middle-class Britain had become a 'commodity culture' by the late nineteenth century, with advertisers' representations of goods dominating people's perceptions of themselves and their world and infiltrating the language and symbols of communication, is interesting, if based more on assertion than on convincing evidence; but crucial changes were indeed concentrated into these years.[92] Urban Britain, and especially the cities and fashionable shopping centres, was becoming an information system for communicating, manufacturing and extending desires. Here developed both the production and the marketing of collectables for a new breed of collectors, who accumulated Staffordshire figures, Stevengraph silk pictures and bookmarks, or holiday souvenirs emblazoned with seaside scenes or municipal heraldry, classifying, ordering and controlling such possessions and insuring the more expensive ones through the new home contents policies of a burgeoning industry.[93] Possessions to embellish and enjoy were available at all levels in different parts of the town, from the back-street flea market to the second-hand bookstall, the curiosity shop, the specialist shop for those of (perhaps) a musical or horticultural bent, and on a more exalted plane the bespoke tailor, the high-class haberdasher and the department store. And at all levels, not just those of the largest or more specialised establishments, this exuberance of provision multiplied, with or without the direct aid of advertising, throughout the second half of the century. It was at this time, too, that the growing and proliferating resort towns and suburbs began to advertise themselves as places to be consumed in a competitive market place, through poster campaigns and guide-books organised by committees of tradesmen and, when this became legal, by municipal governments.[94]

New places of refreshment for shoppers also proliferated in and around the central retail areas which were cohering in the later nineteenth century. They were particularly necessary as comfortable refuges for women, when attempts to stake out shopping streets as legitimate territory for unaccompanied females led to sexual harassment from men in search of the prostitutes who also frequented such districts, while pubs and chop-houses were unwelcoming and public

---

[91] E. S. Turner, *The Shocking History of Advertising* (London, 1952); Fraser, *Mass Market*, ch. 10.

[92] Richards, *Commodity Culture*.

[93] Briggs, *Victorian Things*, ch. 4; and information from Dr Roger Ryan.

[94] Winstanley, *Shopkeeper's World*; Benson and Shaw, *Evolution of Retail Systems*; Walton, *English Seaside Resort*, ch. 2; J. Urry, *Consuming Places* (London and New York, 1994).

conveniences were in short supply.[95] Tea rooms and department store restaurants provided suitable resting places and havens for relaxed discussion. Not that the former, at least, were necessarily gendered space: men were made as welcome as women in the famous Glasgow tea rooms of the 1880s onwards, where Miss Cranston and her colleagues offered decorous fare in surroundings which might be decorated and furnished to the distinctive designs of Charles Rennie Mackintosh. Lower down the social scale late Victorian London and the larger English cities acquired the less pretentious and more mass-produced delights of the Lyons corner house or the cafés of the Aerated Bread Company, while urban Scotland and Wales learned to love their Italian cafés and ice-cream parlours.[96] Different levels of provision were needed, and customers who were insecure in their manners and social status might be intimidated by imposing floorwalkers in the department stores or genteel waitresses in the cafés or restaurants. As the joys of consumer shopping spread among the urban working class in the new century other hierarchies of provision and perception became apparent. Brown's of Chester, the epitome of the high-class provincial department store with its almost tangible aura of selectness, encountered some difficulties when it tried to extend the social range of its customers in the interwar years, not least from a restaurant manageress who was unwilling to add fish and chips to the menu.[97] Mass-Observation surveys from the early 1960s found that many people preferred not to shop at the store they regarded as having the highest reputation in their town, because it was perceived to be too expensive (customers paid extra for the name), or because it had a reputation for the off-hand treatment of less prosperous customers.[98] This is a reminder of the growing importance of store employees, especially shop assistants, in the creation of a consumer-friendly environment, and of the ways in which working-class retailing employees with genteel pretensions, or subjected to strict disciplines of workplace behaviour, might discourage their peers from deriving full participation in and enjoyment of the cornucopia of consumer choice.

These and other limitations notwithstanding, town and city centres were becoming exciting places in which growing numbers of shoppers could escape from the home and the neighbourhood, fantasise about possible purchases, assess what was on display, weigh up the pros and cons of purchase while being continually intoxicated by the enchantments of new possibilities, take possession of the chosen goods, discuss strategies and purchases with friends in secure, comfortable surroundings and enjoy displaying goods which had already been acquired and could be put on show before the gaze of others.[99] Rationing and

---

[95] Walkowitz, *City of Dreadful Delight*, pp. 50–2.
[96] Kinchin, *Tea and Taste*; C. Hughes, *Lime, Lemon and Sarsparilla:* (Bridgend, 1991); T. Colpi, *The Italian Factor* (Edinburgh, 1991), chs. 2–3.
[97] Lancaster, *Department Store*; Mass-Observation, *Browns and Chester* (London, 1947), pp. 188–217.
[98] L. M. Harris, *Buyer's Market* (London, 1963), ch. 9.
[99] Walkowitz, *City of Dreadful Delight*, pp. 46–50.

privation during and after the two world wars interrupted this process but stoked up an even more ardent desire for a return to what was now normality. The consumer districts of towns appealed to the spirits of emulation and self-expression within the shared overarching idioms of fashion and convention, while the excitement of hunting for the desired goods was compounded by the desire to drive a good bargain. These apparent contradictions, these circles which were squared so readily in daily practice, were founded in values which were every bit as Victorian as twentieth-century: we need to remember that stereotypes of Victorian thrift and caution draw more on propaganda and injunction than lived experience, and that, as Taine had noted in the 1860s, there were plenty of hedonistic middle-class Victorians who spent to the limits of their income.[100] Developments in urban retailing merely enabled them, and their heirs, to indulge these propensities more easily and with an ever-widening range of choice, which extended increasingly, as transport improved, to choosing between rival urban shopping centres as well as within individual ones.[101]

Towns, and especially cities, thus became theatres of conspicuous consumption and display in a public setting open to the gaze of all. Shopping areas were policed with increasing attentiveness, and the more secure they became in terms of marginalising threatening transgressions of class and gender boundaries, the freer the shoppers themselves became to put themselves on show, to flirt and to enjoy the anonymity of the crowded street. Women as well as men could claim the privileges of the *flaneur* of the boulevard, strolling, observing, enjoying their own daring, experiencing the safe excitements and unscripted encounters of urban spaces which were increasingly consecrated to leisure and consumption: the parks and promenades which were proliferating in urban (and not just resort) settings during the second half of the nineteenth century, as well as the shopping streets and arcades.[102] This was, admittedly, a phenomenon of larger cities rather than smaller towns; but even the modest Lancashire cotton and engineering town of Accrington had its turn-of-the-century Avenue Parade, slightly wider than the average street, and with little front gardens to the terrace houses, from which the local petty bourgeoisie could be viewed as they promenaded to a new public open space and viewpoint. By the turn of the century, enclosed leisure spaces beyond the street were increasingly available to women without their respectability being compromised, as the more opulent music halls went up-market and brought in sophisticated systems of programme regulation and internal subdivision of the audience.[103] In the interwar years the cinema and even the dance-hall followed this path, although the latter remained disputed moral territory, providing opportunities for consumers to present themselves via their clothing and accessories in a situation of overt sexual negotiation. But not all

[100] Taine, *Notes on England*, chs. 1–2.
[101] J. Herson, 'Victorian Chester: a city of change and ambiguity', in R. Swift, ed., *Victorian Chester* (Liverpool, 1996), pp. 35–6; Harris, *Buyer's Market*, ch. 8.
[102] Berman, *All That Is Solid*, ch. 3.   [103] See above, n. 41.

commercialised urban leisure spaces promoted consumption by display: the football ground is an obvious example, with its workaday throngs of men in un-ostentatious dress, watching players who also travelled by the same public transport and whose life styles were constrained by a maximum wage.[104] For those who were excluded from such enclosed arenas through limited resources in time or money, or chose to vary their repertoire of social display on a day when other opportunities were limited, the Sunday morning church parade for the affluent and respectable was matched by the Sunday evening 'monkey run' which brought young people into informal contact along an agreed area of street, and enabled mutual inspection to lead to closer contact if initial appearances were promising.[105] Here too, display within a consensual array of conventions was an important element in 'clicking' or finding a partner. Less consumer orientated were the gatherings of young men and youths for gambling and the exchange of ideas on the corners of back streets, which were common in industrial towns by the early twentieth century; but even here conversation might readily turn to clothing or bicycles and the fortunes of professional football teams as well as neighbours and workplace politics.[106]

By the early twentieth century women were increasingly in evidence in public, on pleasure bent, and not necessarily under the visible tutelage of men, whether in the city or at the seaside (where men were often absent during the week, coming to join their holidaymaking families by the 'husband train' or 'husband boat', significantly a popular subject of often racy humour).[107] The dangers and delights of this transition, which began in earnest in the late Victorian years, was accentuated by the First World War, and continued thereafter, have been brilliantly chronicled by Judith Walkowitz.[108] The balance of costs and benefits remains a vexed issue, recalling related arguments about consumerism and class. Should we emphasise the gains to women which accrued from the new opportunities to colonise and penetrate new kinds of urban public space, to make choices and to affirm identities, as shoppers and pleasure-seekers? Or should we bemoan their exploitation as manipulated consumers, prisoners of the pressure to emulate and the demands of a cynically orchestrated fashion cycle? The mid-Victorian fads for crinolines and (more enduringly) corsetry and tight-lacing might seem to favour the second interpretation, although later fashions were to prove less constraining and distorting to the female frame. Significantly, perhaps, the 'second coming' of the crinoline was successfully resisted; but corsetry is more complicated, and we need a better grasp of what

[104] Richards, *Age of the Dream Palace*; L. Oliver, 'Limitation or liberation: a study of women's leisure in Bolton *c.* 1919–1939' (PhD thesis, University of Lancaster, 1996).
[105] S. Humphries, *A Secret World of Sex* (London, 1988), p. 142.
[106] Bill Naughton, *Saintly Billy* (Oxford, 1989), ch. 22; M. Childs, *Labour's Apprentices* (London, 1992), pp. 97–8. [107] Walton, *English Seaside Resort*, pp. 23–4.
[108] Walkowitz, *City of Dreadful Delight*, ch. 2.

these and other items of clothing meant to the wearers.[109] Hannah Cullwick, the domestic servant whose diaries provide such a curious and controversial window on the 1860s and 1870s, is an interesting example of a woman who drank unaccompanied in pubs and made occasional excursions to the theatre or the dance hall, while taking pride in the unfashionable nature of her affectionately described clothing and regarding her deliberately down-at-heel presentation of self as providing a measure of protection against annoyance or molestation.[110] These were unusually teasing ambiguities, but they draw attention to the difficulty of categorising female consumer behaviour in the bipolar terms beloved of so many Victorian commentators; and there remains plenty of room for debate on these issues, especially in the twentieth century. What is clear is that growing numbers of women came to enjoy shopping for its own sake, and that this development, which began in earnest in the eighteenth century, spread and ramified from mid-Victorian times, boosted by the comfortable environments of the department store, the arcade and the carefully policed, specialised shopping street. But to describe shopping and consumerism, as many men were prone to do, as a female phenomenon or even a female malady (a notion expressed by emergent interest in women as shoplifters), is to neglect the attractions of these activities for men, in their own right as well as in the role of companion or appendage to consuming women.[111]

At the top end of the scale, mid-Victorian men were far from being immune to the attractions of shopping selectively for a higher quality of clothing, or tobacco, or wine, or horse; and they often had their say in home decoration and furnishing. The specialist cigar and pipe tobacco shop, for example, became a masculine space, at least on the purchaser's side of the counter, catering to layers of constructed masculine expertise in the symbolic grammar and ascribed attributes of a complex hierarchy of goods. The expanding range of goods and opportunities affected both sexes, despite male rhetoric which consigned shopping mania (like gossip) to a female realm. Too obsessive an interest in personal appearance might compromise manliness and invite mockery, as in the (at best) ambivalent music hall portrayals of the 'swell' and the 'masher'; but the main targets here were those who dressed above their station for effect. Frank Mort's subtle analysis of how Burton the High Street tailors negotiated these contradictions in the 1950s, striving to cultivate a restrained, gentlemanly image while extending the market for their suits down the social scale, and emphasising how

[109] E. Wilson, *Adorned in Dreams* (London, 1985); D. Kunzle, *Fashion and Fetishism* (Totowa, N.J., 1982); M. Valverde, 'The love of finery: fashion and the fallen woman', *Victorian Studies*, 32 (1988–9); C. Finch, 'Hooked and buttoned together', *Victorian Studies*, 34 (1990–1).

[110] L. Stanley, ed., *The Diaries of Hannah Cullwick* (London, 1984), pp. 63, 73, 181.

[111] Lancaster, *Department Store*; E. Showalter, *The Female Malady* (London, 1987); E. S. Abelson, *When Ladies Go A-Thieving: Middle-Class Shoplifters in the Victorian Department Store* (New York, 1989); and see now V. De Grazia and E. Furlough, eds., *The Sex of Things* (New York, 1995).

their tasteful products would appeal to the right sort of woman as well as to male peers and superiors, brings out the constraints which limited and defined a mainstream set of male consumer values throughout the period in this delicate territory, where gender identities were both expressed and potentially compromised though the commercially bounded presentation of self in the urban setting.[112]

By the later nineteenth century, and with increasing impact in the twentieth, more consensually masculine interests were being catered for at the level of (especially) white-collar workers and the skilled working class, with the growing interest in 'hobbies' generating a market for tools, raw materials, blueprints, advice manuals and specialised journals.[113] The spread of allotments, greatly encouraged in wartime, and of council estates encouraged an enthusiasm for gardening which was fed through shopping as well as swapping, and the growth of 'do-it-yourself' activity among domesticated men with shorter working hours developed alongside interest in tinkering with radios, gramophones and (by the interwar years) motor vehicles.[114] Women's consumerism was more resolutely gendered in terms of shopping as an activity in itself, with the department store emerging as a particular female haven; but men's, though differently organised and often differently labelled, became no less pervasive and important.[115]

We must consider age as well as gender. The development of consumer expenditure on upper-class children, to make them objects of display as well as to promote their own enjoyment, was an eighteenth-century theme, which passed down the social scale to generate middle-class demand for elaborate dolls and mechanical toys by the mid-nineteenth century.[116] Children – or at least adolescents – as urban consumers on their own account constitute a later phenomenon, but the assumption that the working-class teenage consumer was a product of novel affluence and high employment levels in the 1950s has been convincingly challenged. Teenage wages in the interwar years were not uniformly 'tipped up' to boost the family budget: they might also fund trips to the cinema and the dance hall, magazines, hobbies and attempts to cultivate the appearance (including sophisticated smoking mannerisms) of the film stars on display.[117] Even this was a matter of emphasis rather than complete novelty: Edwardian lads with wages and few commitments might also be consumers of entertainment, cigarettes and clothing, and the teenage 'scuttlers' of turn-of-the-century Salford had their own distinctive gang uniform involving clogs, heavy

[112] F. Mort, *Cultures of Consumption* (London, 1996), pp. 129–45; M. Hilton, 'Constructing tobacco: perspectives on consumer culture in Britain 1850–1950' (PhD thesis, University of Lancaster, 1996); Childs, *Labour's Apprentices*, pp. 125–6; Bailey, *Music Hall*.

[113] McKibbin, *Ideologies of Class* (Oxford, 1990), ch. 5.

[114] *Ibid.*, pp. 143–6 and *passim*; Constantine, 'Amateur gardening and popular recreation'; D. Crouch and C. Ward, *The Allotment* (London, 1988). [115] Lancaster, *Department Store*.

[116] J. H. Plumb, 'The new world of children in the eighteenth century', *P&P*, 67 (1975), 64–93; Thompson and Yeo, *Unknown Mayhew*, pp. 337–59; K. D. Brown, *The British Toy Business: A History since 1700* (London, 1996). [117] Fowler, *The First Teenagers*, chs. 4–5.

belt and brass buckle. Teenagers had been staple consumers of the music hall and more disreputable urban entertainments, along with 'penny dreadfuls' and delicacies hawked through the streets, for much longer than this, wherever their position in the family economy gave them enough ascendancy to enable them to retain a portion of their wages at a time when they were not shackled by responsibility (a problem which many working-class men evaded anyway).[118] All this responded to essentially urban opportunities in juvenile labour markets and shopping and entertainment provision. Access to the emergent consumer society was determined by the poverty cycle as well as by actual levels of income and access to goods and services, and teenage spending power and subcultures were forces to be reckoned with long before the Second World War.

Critiques of the frivolous and destabilising consumer expenditure of working-class adolescents, often in association with fears of the moral and physical decline of the race in corrupt and debilitating urban surroundings, were much in evidence throughout the period. They formed part of an array of attacks on consumer spending which blamed it for inducing secondary poverty, undermining forethought and thrift, diverting expenditure from the substantial and well-made to the tawdry and meretricious, and (to some critics) distracting from due attention to the higher seriousnesses of religion, labour organisation or politics.[119] As in the influential case of Ruskin, critics of consumer taste (as expressed at levels from the commissioners of civic architecture downwards) equated these temptations with urban life, and anti-consumerism tended also to be anti-urbanism.[120] Such attacks came from within the working class as well as from socially superior proponents of rational recreation and evangelical abstemiousness. Protestant nonconformists and early socialists alike were prominent in challenging the emergent consumer culture of the Lancashire cotton towns by the turn of the century, attacking the general preference for Blackpool, the music hall and commercialised leisure, and the liking for strongly flavoured condiments and shop-produced food, as opposed to healthy outdoor recreations and virtuous plain cooking. Female mill workers were accused of putting the acquisition and flaunting of cheap finery above the accumulation of savings and the cultivation of domestic skills and virtues.[121] This was the first act in what was to be a recurring drama in different parts of Britain.

Nor was criticism confined to working-class consumption, which was assumed to entail culpably living beyond one's means. The mid- and late

---

[118] A. Davies and S. Fielding, eds., *Workers' Worlds* (Manchester, 1992); Childs, *Labour's Apprentices*; Chinn, *They Worked All Their Lives*; Ross, *Love and Toil.*

[119] C. Waters, *British Socialists and the Politics of Popular Culture* (Manchester, 1990); P. Joyce, *Visions of the People* (Cambridge, 1991); D. LeMahieu, *A Culture for Democracy* (Oxford, 1988), discuss these issues.   [120] M. Hardman, *Ruskin and Bradford* (Manchester, 1986).

[121] Harvey Taylor, 'The ideological origins of a British outdoor movement' (PhD thesis, University of Lancaster, 1993); Allen Clarke, *The Effects of the Factory System* (Littleborough, 1985).

Victorian years saw an outpouring of sermons against the worship of money and material goods, exhortations both to thrift and to charity, and urgings of the blessings of simplicity and the gross vulgarity of heavy over-ornamentation. Would-be arbiters of consumer taste wrote household manuals to advocate purity and plainness of line and function. The consumers themselves seem to have taken little notice.[122] Changing fashions owed more to advertisements and personal preferences, mediated through the consensus of a variety of social circles which formed a myriad of niche markets for particular products, as befitted an economy in which true mass production was later in arriving than might be assumed: store inventories and mail-order catalogues were thick with goods in endless variety.[123] Even within this climate, after all, products failed as well as succeeding. Items of consumption were available to ever-widening circles of purchasers, whose numbers were expanded still further by second-hand stalls, bazaars and bring-and-buy sales, but variegation outweighed standardisation even in the interwar years, as the enormous proliferation of models and specifications produced by British car firms bears witness.[124] The masses might be consuming, but to call the outcome mass consumption before, perhaps, the 1950s would be to oversimplify.

Nevertheless, the rise of consumer society, driven by urban forces of manufacture, advertising, retailing, shopping, consumption and personal display, was inexorable. The arguments between thrift and consumer enjoyment were increasingly being resolved in favour of the latter, although house purchase in the long run and holiday or Christmas enjoyment in the short enjoined short-term thrift in the pursuit of deferred gratification. For growing numbers of people, including those who remained in employment during the deflationary interwar years, thrift could coexist with instant enjoyment: both could be afforded. Workers in the Lancashire cotton towns, who had pioneered this happy resolution of domestic economic conflict before the First World War, found it harder to sustain in the bleak years of the 1930s; but the sunrise industries of the South and Midlands were able to take up the running. Here were the best markets for businessmen who followed the advice and statistics deployed in the 'Where to sell' manuals which proliferated in the interwar years.[125] The conflict between maximising free time for uncommodified enjoyment, and maximising income to spend in the consumer market place, was resolved for most people in favour of the latter alternative by the 1930s; and consumerism offered industry

---

[122] Briggs, *Victorian Things*, pp. 32–4.

[123] R. Samuel, 'The workshop of the world: steam power and hand technology in mid-Victorian Britain', *History Workshop Journal*, 3 (1977), 6–72; A. Adburgham, ed., *Victorian Shopping: Harrod's Catalogue 1895* (Newton Abbot, 1972).

[124] O'Connell, 'Social and cultural impact'; R.A. Church, *The Rise and Decline of the British Motor Industry* (London, 1994).

[125] *Sell to Britain through the Daily Mail* (London, 1930, and subsequent edns); G. Harrison and F. C. Mitchell, eds., *The Home Market: A Handbook of Statistics* (London, n.d., *c.* 1939).

the opportunity to deploy the carrot as well as the stick in motivating workforces by offering material rewards for time discipline and productivity.[126] This did not always work, as the enduring preference of miners for St Monday bore witness; and some consumer opportunities, like mid-week football matches, cut into working hours. In the years of rationing during and after the Second World War the desire for consumer goods was put on hold and surplus wages were channelled into services such as professional sport, the cinema and holidaymaking.[127] The balance soon began to change in the 1950s, as the flow of goods began to revive and shopping, advertising and the media began a new round of transformation. Revealingly, perhaps, there was debate over whether hobbies and other outside interests improved or undermined performance at the workplace; but shopping and entertainment posed no such dilemma.[128]

There were downsides to all this, or so cultural critics continued to argue. Working-class communities were disrupted by competitive consumption, as part of a wider pathology of post-war changes involving rehousing and the rise of an assertive youth culture. Consumerism, it was argued, encouraged theft and aggression, and replaced dignity, frugality and stoicism with self-indulgence. Problems of relative affluence, which have persisted into the recent revival of poverty and unemployment, have been highlighted by cultural critics from Richard Hoggart to Jeremy Seabrook, who have in turn been accused of condescension and failure to appreciate the ways in which working-class people remake what is on offer to form satisfying and empowering identities.[129] This goes beyond the remit of this chapter. What is clear, however, is that the ideals of Percy Redfern, with which we began, have been left to languish with the decline of the Co-operative movement. This was at its peak in membership terms on either side of the Second World War, and during the 1950s it pioneered the introduction of supermarkets and took pride in trumpeting its investment in new stores which expressed the favoured architectures of the time.[130] Mass-Observation's Bolton surveys already identified seeds of complacency and rigidity in the late 1930s, however, and the movement failed to recruit a new generation of activists in what seemed the secure environment of the post-war welfare state.[131] By 1963 a new Mass-Observation survey was damning:

---

[126] Cross, *Time and Money*, pp. 162–3.

[127] J. K. Walton, 'The world's first working-class seaside resort? Blackpool revisited, 1840–1974', *Transactions of the Lancashire and Cheshire Antiquarian Society*, 88 (1992), p. 19; N. Fishwick, *English Football and Society, 1910–1950* (Manchester, 1989), p. 52.

[128] McKibbin, *Ideologies of Class*, pp. 148–52.

[129] R. Hoggart, *The Uses of Literacy* (London, 1957); J. Seabrook, *City Close-Up* (London, 1971); and numerous other works by both authors; Cross, *Time and Money*, ch. 8; and from a feminist perspective Beatrix Campbell, *Wigan Pier Revisited: Poverty and Politics in the 80s* (London, 1984), pp. 224–7.

[130] *This Is Progress: A Pictorial Record of Co-operative Store and Shop Development* (Manchester, 1959).

[131] Gurney, *Co-operative Culture*, p. 234.

'Although the co-op had a high rate of custom it had low "prestige" and was least liked of all. Its customers were mainly working class and older people who shopped there partly for financial reasons, partly from habit and partly from a feeling of old loyalties.'[132] This is itself evidence of the rise of the new kind of consumer society, market-led and advertising-fuelled, and unconcerned with the aesthetics and morality of production as ends in themselves, which Redfern had feared and disliked; and this survey offered an early indication of the Co-op's failure to combat or come to terms with the new consumerism. Subsequent developments have consigned advocates of Redfern's and related alternative modes of consumption to an increasingly visible (and urban-centred) role as environmental and 'fair trade' campaigners, to local co-operative campaigns on the LETS (Local Exchange Trading Systems) model, to back-street shops and a minority alternative society; but at the time he wrote this outcome was not inevitable, and the hegemony of the commercial model of consumerism still has its articulate opponents.[133] The history of this contest deserves to be chronicled further.

[132] Harris, *Buyer's Market*, p. 79.
[133] P. Lang, *Lets Work: Rebuilding the Local Economy* (Bristol, 1994).

23

Playing and praying

DOUGLAS A. REID

I N 1854 the Baptist Charles Haddon Spurgeon (1834–92) took a preaching
career of star quality to a wider stage at the Surrey Gardens Music Hall. He
was the most famous of a number of nineteenth-century ministers of religion who were renowned for their almost theatrical style. Another who sought
dramatic means to further the cause of God was William Booth, the Salvationist,
for 'why should the devil have all the best tunes?' Together they illustrate one of
the ways in which, in the nineteenth century, religion increasingly appeared to
flatter the realm of leisure by imitation. In earlier centuries leisure activities had
more often appeared to grow out of the religious sphere. However, in the nineteenth century conflict and competition were more important themes than
cooperation, and the estrangement of leisure and religion was symbolised,
above all, by the temperance movement and Sabbatarianism. Similarities and
differences between the religious and the recreational are numerous, hence –
from Birmingham in 1886 – the observation that Good Friday 'was spent by
the minority in the solemnities of ecclesiastical observance, but by the majority
as an opportunity of pleasurable open-air enjoyment'. In fact, much churchgoing could be defined from a utilitarian point of view as having the essential
social qualities of other leisure-time pursuits, namely their voluntary, non-
remunerative, pleasure-seeking nature. Of course, spiritual edification was the
formal aim of churchgoing, but in the later nineteenth century leisure became
an aid to religious mission. By the mid-twentieth century, though, a diminishing minority attended church regularly, and leisure was often a substitute for
religion. In a world of alienated labour, both manual and clerical, the 'machinery of amusement' seemed to fill the void, even to supply a motive for existence:
Londoners told a 1940s sociologist, 'without pleasure the worker may as well be
dead'. Cinema and sport, and the public house, fulfilled key functions of religion by offering sources of social identification and forms of consolation to the

denizens of great cities. We should note, however, that a diffuse, unaffiliated, religiosity remained widespread.[1]

By the 1870s the urban experience was the majority social experience, and increasingly the typical experience, but there remained immense differences in urban types. Was there a common element – an urban variable – which explains much of the history of leisure and religion in the variety of towns and cities, and, indeed, which differentiates their experience from that of the countryside? How much was unique to the towns, and how much was there continuity between them? These questions, and others about the nature of religion and leisure in the urban experience, are explored below, commencing with an analysis which embodies an important distinction, namely that between the growth of leisure time and leisure activities, and links both to the key question of money.

(i) THE QUEST FOR LEISURE TIME

That very large numbers of the employed population increasingly enjoyed approved leisure was one of the many important innovations of the Victorian period, and the overall increase in their leisure time underlay key leisure innovations like railway excursions and Association football. However, if the essence of leisure is time free from obligation (principally, but not only, the obligation to work), ability to participate in most recreations also required financial resources; thus those who were excluded from the labour market because of unemployment or family responsibilities were severely restricted in their leisure. The unemployed had superabundant time, but, in the absence of cash, this was more often a curse than a blessing, especially in interwar Britain when both leisure and unemployment boomed. Similarly, even though there was an overall rise in living standards, the wide spectrum of wages among the employed, together with the effects of individuals' life cycles, had important implications for access both to free time and to commercialised leisure. A St Helens black-

---

[1] W. Owen Chadwick, *The Victorian Church* (London, 1966–70), vol. II, pp. 291–2; K. S. Inglis, *Churches and the Working Classes in Victorian England* (London, 1963), pp. 65, 186–8, cf. *Oxford Dictionary of Quotations*, revised 4th edn (Oxford, 1996); H. McLeod, *Class and Religion in the Late Victorian City* (London, 1974), p. 162 n. 45; Robert Currie, *Methodism Divided: A Study in the Sociology of Ecumenicalism* (London, 1968), pp. 131–8; Brian Harrison, 'Religion and recreation in nineteenth-century England', *P&P*, 38 (1967), 98–125; J. H. S. Kent, 'The role of religion in the cultural superstructure of the later Victorian city', *TRHS*, 5th series, 23 (1973), 161–4; Hugh McLeod, 'New perspectives on Victorian working-class religion: the oral evidence', *Oral History*, 14 (1986), 36–7; *Birmingham Daily Post*, 24 Apr. 1886; William Pickering, 'Religion – a leisure-time pursuit?', in David Martin, ed., *A Sociological Yearbook of Religion in Britain* (London, 1968), pp. 78–80ff; Henry Durant, *The Problem of Leisure* (London, 1938), pp. 1–26; Ferdynand Zweig, *Labour, Life and Poverty* (London, 1948), p. 43; cf. R. McKibbin, *The Ideologies of Class* (Oxford, 1990), p. 161.

smith, a father of eight, 'never had a holiday in his life', recalled his widow. Even after the trend to smaller families had set in a Mass-Observation survey of 700 London housewives found that they worked an average of fifteen hours a day. Moreover, housewives' spending money came from the household budget, unlike the pocket money husbands took directly from their pay. And women still carried the main domestic burdens even when doing paid work: 'A working man is a man of leisure compared with his working wife', noted Ferdynand Zweig.[2] Nevertheless, when all necessary qualifications are made there was an overall growth of leisure which requires explanation.

In the early nineteenth century leisure was regarded as the mark of the gentleman, and popular leisure as idleness, to be censured and discouraged, especially when it took the form of drunken and intermittent 'Saint Monday' absenteeism. Yet if the 'Industrial Revolution' implied increased labour discipline, its productivity gains created an economic surplus from which a distinctly demarcated popular secular leisure was created. How was this achieved? Among the most important factors were: popular activism in pursuit of reduced working hours; favourable periods in the operations of the labour market which maximised organised workers' opportunities; and the (usually reactive) activities of employers and the state. The improvement in living standards (itself partly explained in the nineteenth century by the growing concentration of population in towns and cities) also assisted, by increasing demand for time for self-fulfilment as well as recuperation. In the twentieth century these trends were carried further in a discontinuous but cumulatively impressive expansion of non-work time, and raising of incomes – together the indispensable conditions for the expansion of recreational activities. Such interrelationships may be inferred from the memoir of a tailor, aged fifty-nine, who was born in the 1890s:

> When I was young there were no sports in our lives. Working hours were long and the men were too tired to play. They had no money. All sports cost money, in the boots you wear out, if nothing else. There were no sports grounds provided by the Councils as there are now. Saturday was a working day and games were not allowed on Sunday. When I was ten I had to help my family by earning 2s. 6d. a

[2] B. S. Rowntree, *Poverty: A Study of Town Life* (London, 1901; London, 1922 edn), pp. 84, 169–71, 322, 330–1, 335; Durant, *The Problem of Leisure*, pp. 98–108; Philip Massey, *Portrait of a Mining Town* (published in London by *Fact*, Nov. 1937), pp. 49–50; Hugh Cunningham, 'Leisure', in John Benson, ed., *The Working Class in England, 1875–1914* (London, 1985), pp. 144–7; A. Davies, *Leisure, Gender and Poverty* (Buckingham, 1992), pp. 55–61; C. Forman, *Industrial Town* (London, 1978), p. 129; Mass-Observation, *Bulletin*, 42 (May/June 1951), 'The housewife's day', pp. 3, 5, 13; F. Zweig, *Women's Life and Labour* (London, 1952), p. 141; see also Ellen Ross, 'Women's neighbourhood sharing', *History Workshop*, 15 (1983), 7; Catriona M. Parratt, 'Little means or time: working-class women and leisure in late Victorian and Edwardian England', *International Journal of the History of Sport*, 15 (1998), 22–53; Melanie Tebbutt, 'Gossip and "women's words"', in A. Davies and S. Fielding, eds., *Workers' Worlds* (Manchester, 1992), p. 54.

week [working with a milkman before and after school, for seven hours a day] . . .
Oh no, there was no sport for us. Life was grim and too serious for that.[3]

His experience was of enormous change in the twentieth century, although, in fact, considerable free time had already come to many others as a corollary of nineteenth-century limitations on the length of the normal working week. Unfortunately, before 1924, all discussions about working hours, and, therefore, potential leisure hours, are hampered by scanty information about the relationship between the 'normal' (nominal) working week and the actual total of hours worked. The 'normal recognised' day or week was agreed by trade unions and employers as the basis for the calculation of standard wages, but it was often extended through systematic overtime, or eroded through short time. Nevertheless, despite lags and setbacks the evidence suggests an intelligible conformability between downward shifts in the 'normal' week and actual hours worked, making the former a useful indicator of trends – for there was a 'demonstration effect' outside trade unionism's ranks.[4]

In the 1830s and 1840s the long but ultimately successful campaign for a ten-hour day by textile factory workers stamped the image of the age as one of unbearably protracted working days, particularly for the women and children who carried out the majority of factory work. However, many artisans in the predominantly male handicraft trades – especially in workshop-led towns and cities like Birmingham and Sheffield – retained freedom to regulate their own hours. Moreover, when pressured by employers into regulated workshops they sought to defend the eighteenth-century artisan ten-hour ideal – the standard adopted by the factory campaign. This was emphasised in 1836 by a long strike by London engineers to secure a sixty-hour normal week. Nevertheless, the success of the Ten Hour movement in achieving a similar total by the Factory Act of 1850 had a larger significance, particularly, as we shall see, regarding its Saturday half-holiday provision.[5]

Despite the 1867 Factory and Workshops Acts, which extended the sixty-hour week beyond the textile industries that were so important to Lancashire

---

[3] Cited in F. Zweig, *The British Worker* (Harmondsworth, 1952), p. 128; cf. London School of Economics, *New Survey of London Life and Labour* (London, 1930–5), vol. XI, pp. 3–5.

[4] Department of Employment and Productivity, *British Labour Statistics: Historical Abstract 1886–1968* (London, 1971), pp. 7–8, 160; Durant, *The Problem of Leisure*, pp. 71–6.

[5] S. Webb and B. Webb, *The History of Trade Unionism*, revised edn (London, 1926), pp. 313–17; D. A. Reid, 'The decline of Saint Monday', *P&P*, 71 (1976), 76–84, 98; Hugh Cunningham, *Leisure in the Industrial Revolution c. 1780–c. 1880* (London, 1980), pp. 141–51; Eric Hopkins, 'Working hours and conditions during the Industrial Revolution: a reappraisal', *Ec.HR*, 2nd series, 35 (1982), 52–66; Mark Harrison, 'The ordering of the urban environment: time, work and the occurrence of crowds, 1790–1835', *P&P*, 110 (1986), 156–60; D. A. Reid, 'Weddings, weekdays, work and leisure in urban England, 1791–1911: the decline of Saint Monday revisited', *P&P*, 153 (1996), 135–63; cf. Hans-Joachim Voth, 'Time and work in eighteenth-century London', *Journal of Economic History*, 58 (1998), 35–7.

and Yorkshire towns, industrial muscle rather than paternalistic legislation was the key to progress. Thus the booming labour market of 1870–2 allowed many unionised workers to break through to a nine-hour day, led by Clydeside and Tyneside engineers, whereas Factory Acts were often evaded and did not grant nine hours until decades later. Where statistics allow systematic comparison between a range of trades in several towns it can be seen that the nine-hour norm had emphatically arrived in the 1870s – Figure 23.1 shows normal hours falling by 4.3 between 1871 and 1880. However, enforced overtime in the 1880s pushed unionists to seek an eight-hour norm, and, in 1889, the gas workers, in the full flush of the 'New Unionism' encouraged by the next boom, reduced their hours from twelve to eight. Conversely, advances towards the eight-hour day in engineering were knocked back during the 1897 lock-out, and Figure 23.1 shows only piecemeal progress below the fifty-four-hour norm in the years down to 1914. Moreover, in the sweated trades, in domestic service, and among shop-workers and transport workers, working hours remained much longer.[6]

The eight-hour day only blossomed after the First World War revealed the futility of overwork for productivity, created international expectations of social improvement, raised wages and empowered trade unionists, who sought a shorter week as a specific against the prospects of post-war unemployment. In 1919–20 it swept the country. By 1920 every London trade surveyed had achieved forty-eight hours or less, and Figure 23.1 depicts an average reduction of 4.3 hours since 1914. Moreover, theses gains were long-lasting: despite some claw-back by employers through overtime working, investigations in 1935 and 1938 showed that actual hours worked did not exceed an average forty-eight.[7]

Thus in 1930, the *New Survey of London Life and Labour* concluded that 'the average London worker' now had 'an extra hour a day to himself' as compared with the 1890s. This masculinist construction of the key change wrought by the Eight Hour movement was less applicable to the increasingly numerous clerks, shop assistants and other 'white blouse' workers – many of whom would also have been amongst those Londoners whose journey to work had been lengthening along with the expansion of the capital ever since the 1880s. Also, there

[6] S. Webb and B. Webb, *Industrial Democracy* (London, 1897), vol. I, pp. 352n, 340, 344–7, 349–50, 352n; Webb and Webb, *History of Trade Unionism*, pp. 384n., 402; Monica Hodgson, 'The working day and the working week in Victorian Britain, 1840–1900' (MPhil thesis, University of London, 1974), pp. 54–84; G. Cross, *A Quest for Time* (London, 1989), pp. 56, 65–6, 74–6, 117, 124; David Russell, 'The pursuit of leisure', in D. G. Wright and J. A. Jowitt, eds., *Victorian Bradford* (Bradford, 1982), pp. 201–2; W. H. Fraser, 'The working class', in W. H. Fraser and Irene Maver, eds., *Glasgow*, vol. II: *1830 to 1912* (Manchester, 1996), pp. 320–1, 331; Department of Employment, *British Labour Statistics*, tables 1–6. It is interesting that Sheffield seems to have had a consistently longer normal week than most, just as its Saint Monday tradition was one of the longest lasting: two facts presumably not unrelated. See also P. Joyce, *Work, Society and Politics* (Brighton, 1980), p. 77.

[7] Cross, *Quest for Time*, esp. pp. 115–17, 130–1, 136–9, 146, 186, 190; Department of Employment, *British Labour Statistics*, table 84; *New Survey of London Life and Labour*, I, pp. 117–18.

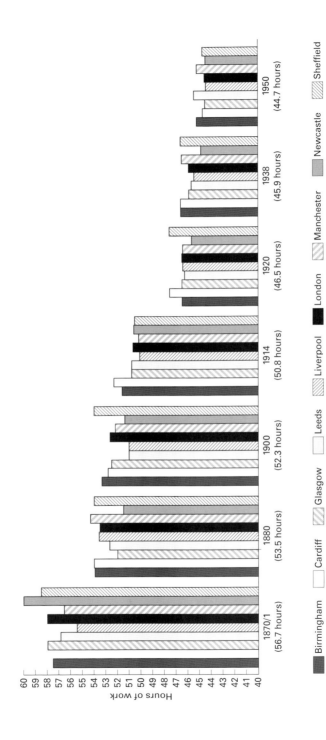

Figure 23.1 Mean 'normal' weekly hours of work 1870–1950 in the building, engineering, footwear, furniture and printing trades in selected towns

Source: drawn from data in Department of Employment and Productivity, *British Labour Statistics: Historical Abstract 1886–1968* (London, 1971), tables 1–6.

were important exemptions for seasonal trades, and increasing shift work meant that many others could not regularly take advantage of the extra hour gained. Thus, despite the reductions in daily working hours emphasised by the *Survey* (and despite the advent of radio entertainment) much leisure in the 1930s in London (and elsewhere) was still focused on the weekend.[8]

The concept of the weekend was pioneered by the middle classes, and encouraged by railway company special tickets – commercial and public offices began closing at Saturday noon from the mid-forties. Thus the 1850 Factory Act's Saturday half-holiday for textile workers represented democratisation (even though it only began at 2 p.m.). Many Ten Hours campaigners hoped that Saturday afternoon recreation would encourage greater Sunday morning church attendance; however, the more obvious results of this block of time were park-cricket, rail and river excursions, brass band contests, Volunteers parading and weddings. In towns like Birmingham and Nottingham, not covered by the act, the half-holiday was granted by employers in (unequal) exchange for the abandonment of Saint Mondays. Perhaps surprisingly, many artisans preferred this, for it legitimated regular leisure time. Yet Saint Monday had been adopted by the new recreations (like railway excursions), and for several decades Mondays and Saturdays complemented each other as popular, especially summer, leisure periods – though Mondays gradually lost ground. The engineers made the 'one o'clock Saturday' part of their Nine Hour campaign, and in 1890 pushed back the starting point to noon. Its practical importance is vividly illustrated by the contrast which obtained between Birmingham and Liverpool (city of dock workers and clerks, unprotected by strong unions or legislation) where its development was delayed to the 1890s. The Birmingham press listed 811 district football teams in 1879–80; in Liverpool there were two. Again, in 1890, Sunderland drapers' assistants 'signalled their half holiday by forming a football club'. That Saturday night had always been sweet to the working and lower middle classes is indicated by popular songs, but perhaps it was even sweeter when the Eight Hour movement confirmed the afternoon preceding it as holiday.[9]

---

[8] *New Survey of London Life and Labour*, I, pp. 19, 116–18, 294; IX, pp. 3–4; Noreen Branson and Margot Heinemann, *Britain in the 1930s* (London, 1971), pp. 92–3, 141; Hilda Jennings and Winifred Gill, *Broadcasting in Everyday Life* ([London], 1939), p. 10.

[9] Jack Simmons, *The Victorian Railway* (London, 1991), pp. 292–4; J. S. Hodgson, 'The movements for shorter hours, 1840–75' (DPhil thesis, University of Oxford, 1940), pp. 213–14; Reid, 'The decline of Saint Monday', 81–4, 87–90, 99–101; D. Russell, *Popular Music in England, 1840–1914* (Manchester, 1987), p. 12; 'Shadow' (Alexander Brown), *Midnight Scenes and Social Photographs*, repr. (Glasgow, 1976), pp. 96–7; John Lowerson, 'Angling', in Tony Mason, ed., *Sport in Britain: A Social History* (Cambridge, 1989), p. 21; D. A. Reid, 'The "iron roads" and "the happiness of the working classes": the early development and social significance of the railway excursion', *Journal of Transport History*, 3rd series, 17 (1996), 57–73; Hugh Cunningham, *The Volunteer Force: A Social and Political History, 1859–1908* (London, 1975), pp. 111–12, 117; P. Mandler, *The Rise and Fall of the Stately Home* (New Haven, 1997), pp. 74, 212; Reid, 'Weddings, weekdays, work and leisure', 147, 150–2; Webb and Webb, *Industrial Democracy*, I, p. 352n.; 'I remember', *Birmingham Gazette*

Sunday mornings were for lie-ins, or church for some (parish constables enforced pub closing during morning service). Some hung around the streets, apparently aimlessly, their children attracting the attention of Sunday School pioneers. A good dinner was an old-established pattern; before late-nineteenth-century housing improvements this required marketing and a trip to the baker's oven. (Work 'remained widespread' in service trades – but also in the iron industry and among the self-employed.) A walk to a pub on the outskirts, or inwards to a central pub, was also common, as was afternoon or evening visiting to family and friends. Baiting, chasing or racing animals, and street-corner gambling, were notoriously popular, but the alternatives were limited by law. Entertainment venues had been forbidden to charge on Sundays since 1780, although the scandalous Sunday press offered vicarious entertainment – the *News of the World* dates from 1843. Organised Sabbatarianism reached its oppressive peak in the mid-1850s, forcing discontinuance of railway excursions, closure of pubs between 3 and 5 p.m. (all day in Scotland), and the withdrawal of bands from parks from London to Liverpool (in Glasgow they were never even permitted). However, the Sunday Trading riots of 1855 prevented legislation against markets. 'Rational Sunday' advocates called for the British Museum to be opened, but unavailingly until 1896 – twenty-four years after Birmingham opened its libraries and art gallery. Railway excursions were reintroduced in the 1870s, by the National Sunday League, but among seaside resorts only Blackpool overcame opposition to paying venues, Winter Garden concerts and Sunday trams, by the 1880s; Bournemouth banned Sunday trains until 1914, and steamers until 1929. The return of music to the parks was mostly delayed until the 1890s; puritanical Cardiff held out until 1913, and throughout Wales pubs had been closed on Sundays from 1881 (stimulating the growth of 'shebeens'). As late as 1901 the LCC banned Sunday football, but just before 1914 it licensed Sunday cinemas (conditional upon charitable donations). The LCC's football ban was modified in 1922; other cities and towns had to wait until the 1940s. However, housing improvements and the wireless enhanced the home as a place of Sunday recreation: by 1939 there were 9 million licence holders. Meanwhile, in 1932 the 'Brighter Sunday' campaign achieved local-option legalisation of cinemas, concerts, debates, galleries, gardens, lectures, museums and zoos – but not dance halls. By 1950 two-thirds of all English cinemas showed films on Sundays, but

---

Footnote 9 (*cont.*)

& *Express*, 27 June 1907; T. Mason, *Association Football and English Society, 1863–1915* (Brighton, 1980), pp. 8 n. 10, 35; *Sunderland Echo*, 4 Feb. 1890, cited in M. Huggins, 'The spread of Association football in North-East England, 1876–90: the pattern of diffusion', *International Journal of the History of Sport*, 6 (1989), 312; Roy Palmer, *A Touch on the Times* (Harmondsworth, 1974), pp. 92–4: 'Stirrings in Sheffield on Saturday night'; Colin M. MacInnes, *Sweet Saturday Night* (London, 1967), p. 106.

for shorter periods, and to lower audiences; only one in twelve Scottish and one in ten Welsh cinemas were open.[10]

Thus the rhythm of popular recreation was determined by developing labour discipline, the Saturday half-holiday, and Sabbatarianism. By 1938, Mass-Observation's study of 'Worktown' (Bolton) found that between Monday and Thursday public leisure was muted. Three-quarters of a sample of families were found at home in midweek, and on Wednesday nights the pubs, like their patrons' pockets, were virtually empty. The billiard halls, central streets, chip shops, cinemas, clubs, dance halls and pubs of Worktown came alive on Fridays, and peaked on Saturdays. 'Of all the things that make life worth living for ordinary Britons' in 1947, Saturday night – with its suspension of normal routines and worries, and pursuit of pleasure – was 'one of the most important', and,

---

[10] Ian Bradley, 'The English Sunday', *History Today*, 22 (1972), 363; John Wigley, *The Rise and Fall of the Victorian Sunday* (Manchester, 1980), pp. 64–73, 82–9, 103–4, 106, 131–4, 147–8; M. Leon Faucher, *Manchester in 1844: Its Present Condition and Future Prospects* (London, 1844; London, 1969), pp. 53–4; Irene Maver, 'Glasgow's public parks and the community, 1850–1914: a case study in Scottish interventionism', *UH*, 25 (1998), 340–1; Brian Harrison, 'The Sunday trading riots of 1855', *HJ*, 8 (1965), 219–45; D. M. Lewis, *Lighten their Darkness* (New York, 1986), pp. 242–3; Peter Stubley, *A House Divided: Evangelicals and the Establishment in Hull 1779–1914* (Hull, 1995), pp. 70–2; B. Harrison, *Drink and the Victorians* (London, 1971), pp. 328–9; Hugh McLeod, 'White collar values and the role of religion', in G. Crossick, ed., *The Lower Middle Class in Britain, 1870–1914* (London, 1977), pp. 64, 71; W. H. Fraser, 'Developments in leisure', in W. H. Fraser and R. J. Morris, eds., *People and Society in Scotland*, vol. II: *1830–1914* (Edinburgh, 1990), p. 241; D. A. Reid, 'Labour, leisure, and politics in Birmingham c. 1800–1875' (PhD thesis, University of Birmingham, 1985), pp. 448–55; Jack Simmons and Gordon Biddle, eds., *The Oxford Companion to British Railway History* (Oxford, 1997), p. 151; Simmons, *Victorian Railway*, pp. 282–4; McLeod, *Class and Religion*, pp. 103, 220–1, 233–9, 267 n. 107; Charles Booth, *Life and Labour of the People in London, Third Series: Religion* (London, 1903), vol. VII, p. 19; J. N. Morris, *Religion and Urban Change* (Woodbridge, 1992), p. 142; Ellen Ross, *Love and Toil* (London, 1993), pp. 87–8; John Lowerson, 'Brothers of the angle: coarse fishing and English working-class culture, 1850–1914', in J. A. Mangan, ed., *Pleasure, Profit, Proselytism: British Culture and Sport at Home and Abroad, 1700–1914* (London, 1988), p. 110; John Lowerson, 'Sport and the Victorian Sunday', *British Journal of Sports History*, 1 (1984), 208–18; S. G. Jones, *Workers at Play* (Manchester, 1986), pp. 191–3; *New Survey of London Life and Labour*, IX, pp. 8, 75–7; J. Briggs, *Sunday Sports in our Public Parks: An Appeal for Fair Play*, 2nd edn (Birmingham, 1920); A. Sutcliffe and R. Smith, *History of Birmingham*, vol. III: *Birmingham 1939–1970* (London, 1974), p. 295; N. Fishwick, *English Football and Society, 1910–1950* (Manchester, 1989), pp. 10, 15; S. G. Jones, 'Working-class sport in Manchester between the wars', in R. Holt, ed., *Sport and the Working Class in Modern Britain* (Manchester, 1990), p. 75; J. K. Walton, 'Municipal government and the holiday industry in Blackpool, 1876–1914', in J. K. Walton and J. Walvin, eds., *Leisure in Britain, 1780–1939* (Manchester, 1983), p. 181; M. J. Daunton, *Coal Metropolis* (Leicester, 1977), pp. 219–21; J. Cox, *The English Churches in a Secular Society* (Oxford, 1982), p. 205; J. Richards, 'The cinema and cinema going in Birmingham in the 1930s', in Walton and Walvin, eds., *Leisure in Britain*, pp. 41–3; S. Rowson, 'A statistical survey of the cinema industry in Great Britain in 1934', *Journal of the Royal Statistical Society*, 99 (1936), 92; H. E. Browning and A. A. Sorrell, 'Cinemas and cinema-going in Great Britain', *Journal of the Royal Statistical Society*, 117 (1954), 147.

despite Sunday's relative liberalisation, 'most people [spent] . . . the entire day either in or around the home'.[11]

In the aftermath of the war, trade unions shaved a further hour off the normal working week by 1950; national industrial bargaining also minimised earlier discrepancies between hours in different cities (Figure 23.1). Economists have stressed fear of unemployment as the key factor interesting trade unions in reductions of hours, and the maintenance or improvement of money incomes as a more powerful influence on their members than dreams of increased leisure. However, this is unconvincing in relation to demand for Saturday half-holidays. Certainly, shorter Saturdays were sometimes 'earned' by rearrangement of working hours on the other days of the week, but the popular insistence on a block of leisure on Saturdays indicates that it was highly valued for its own sake.[12] This point is even clearer regarding the history of annual holidays.

Modern urban holiday-making was established within the annual framework of festivity derived nominally from the ecclesiastical calendar but also from centuries-old 'carnivalesque' traditions marking the turning points of the solar (and hence the agricultural) year. In England Christmas, Easter and Whitsuntide, and fairs and wakes, were the main occasions. Although Calvinism had proscribed the celebration of Christmas in Scotland, Hogmanay soon filled its place in popular esteem. Calvinists also abjured Pentecost, but its English namesake – Whitsuntide – was England's chief holiday, especially in cities like Manchester where there were no wakes. Commerce vied with community: fairs and races abounded; friendly societies feasted and paraded; northern and Midland Sunday Schools promoted highly popular 'Whit Walks' (and Whit 'Sings' in Sheffield parks); brass bands competed; railway excursionists en-trained. Such feasts as Whitsun, and Christmas and New Year's Eve, also tended towards extra-ordinary jollity, bawdiness and aggression as the pubs turned out. But the 'high point of mass drunkenness' in 1930s Bolton was during the main annual holiday in Blackpool. Gregarious – particularly youthful – heavy drinking was characteristic of festival life throughout history; however, it should also be interpreted as a

---

[11] Mass-Observation (ed. Gary Cross), *Worktowners at Blackpool: Mass-Observation and Popular Leisure in the 1930s* (London, 1990), p. 30; Mass-Observation, *The Pub and the People* (London, 1943), p. 112; Mass-Observation, File Report 2467, 'Saturday night', April 1947, *passim* (I should like to acknowledge the permission of the Trustees of the Mass-Observation Archive, University of Sussex to quote from this report); Zweig, *Women's Life and Labour*, p. 148; [Political and Economic Planning], 'Freedom and opportunity', *Planning*, 207, 1 June 1943, 4; Mass-Observation, *Meet Yourself on Sunday* (London, 1949), p. 5.

[12] M. A. Bienefeld, *Working Hours in British Industry: An Economic History* (London, 1972); G. Cross, *Time and Money* (London, 1993), pp. 87–9, 92, 239 nn. 37–42, 241 n. 58; K. Hinrichs, W. Roche and C. Sirianni, eds., *Working Time in Transition: The Political Economy of Working Hours in Industrial Nations* (Philadelphia, 1991), pp. 95–6, 122–4; Jones, *Workers at Play*, p. 15.

reaction to modern urbanism – above all to oppressive discipline and repetitive monotony at work.[13]

The developing holiday patterns of urban regions were differentiated by their economies, by related popular cultures, and by their accessibility to the coast. Where de-centralised (and workshop) production meant slacker industrial discipline, especially in smaller towns working less intensively, economic horizons were relatively low and customary holidays tended to flourish in traditional ways, with neighbourly hospitality, courtship customs and carnivalistic celebrations in streets, pubs and fairgrounds – as at the summer wakes of the Black Country and Potteries, and the parish feasts of the West Riding woollen district. However, despite factory discipline in Lancashire cotton towns, their wakes were stubbornly defended, and employers compelled to accept them – a few days in the 1880s became a week by the 1900s. Moreover, the high family wages of cotton workers channelled through mutual-saving 'going-off clubs' enabled these wakes to be utilised for seaside holidays on nearby coasts, especially at Blackpool, New Brighton and Rhyl. Although the textile towns of the West Riding had the same thrifty traditions as Lancashire they were further from

[13] Peter Burke, *Popular Culture in Early Modern Europe* (London, 1979), pp. 178–204; Christopher A. Whatley, '"The privilege which the rabble have to be riotous": carnivalesque and the monarch's birthday in Scotland, c. 1700–1860', in Ian Blanchard, ed., *Labour and Leisure in Historical Perspective, Thirteenth to Twentieth Centuries* (Stuttgart, 1994), pp. 111–23; M. Macleod Banks, *British Calendar Customs: Scotland* (London, 1939), vol. II, pp. 25–72; Ronald Hutton, *The Stations of the Sun* (Oxford, 1996), pp. 32–3, 121, 277–9ff; Reid, 'Labour, leisure and politics', pp. 70–9, 200; Martin Gorsky, 'Mutual aid and civil society: friendly societies in nineteenth-century Bristol', *UH*, 25 (1998), 306, 314; *City News Notes and Queries* (Manchester, 1879), p. 179; John Bragg, 'Autobiographical notes' [1893], p. 15 (Birmingham Reference Library, 625993); A. J. Ainsworth, 'Religion in the working class community, and the evolution of socialism in late Victorian Lancashire: a case of working class consciousness', *Histoire Sociale*, 10 (1977), 367–8; R. Poole, *Popular Leisure and the Music Hall in Nineteenth-Century Bolton* (Lancaster, 1982), pp. 20, 29; E. Roberts, *A Woman's Place* (Oxford, 1984), p. 161; Davies, *Leisure, Gender and Poverty*, pp. 67, 124–6; Joyce, *Work, Society and Politics*, pp. 249–50; Dave Russell, '"What's wrong with brass bands?" Cultural change and the band movement, 1918–c. 1964', in Trevor Herbert, ed., *Bands: The Brass Band Movement in the 19th and 20th Centuries* (Milton Keynes, 1991), p. 72 n. 62; A. Elton and E. Foster, eds., *Yorkshire Piety and Persuasion: A Social History of Religion from 1600 to 1900* (Leeds, 1985), pp. 62–3; McLeod, 'New perspectives on Victorian working-class religion', 39, 42; R. H. Trainor, *Black Country Elites* (Oxford, 1993), p. 182; C. J. Binfield *et al.*, eds., *The History of the City of Sheffield, 1843–1993* (Sheffield, 1993), vol. II, pp. 416–17, III, p. 69; Steve Fielding, 'The Catholic Whit-Walk in Manchester and Salford 1890–1939', *Manchester Regional History Review*, 1 (1987), 3–10; Alec Greenhalgh, 'Hail Smiling Morn': Whit Friday Brass Band Contests 1884 to 1991* (Oldham, 1992), pp. 11–43, 92; S. J. D. Green, *Religion in the Age of Decline* (Cambridge, 1996), pp. 330–2; Mass-Observation, *The Pub and the People*, pp. 197, 209, 213, 245–8, 248–50; Mass-Observation (ed. Cross), *Worktowners at Blackpool*, pp. 38–40 (cf. pp. 236–8); J. K. Walton, 'The demand for working-class seaside holidays in Victorian England', *Ec.HR*, 34 (1981), 255–6; C. B. Hawkins, *Norwich: A Social Study* (London, 1910), p. 311 (cf. p. 82); D. V. Glass, *The Town and a Changing Civilisation* (London, 1935), pp. 109–10; Robert Sinclair, *Metropolitan Man: The Future of the English* (London, 1937), pp. 95–102, 114–26; Durant, *The Problem of Leisure*, pp. 13–19, 24; cf. McKibbin, *The Ideologies of Class*, pp. 158–9.

the sea, and had lower family incomes, so their mass trek to the coast (especially to Scarborough and Morecambe) lagged about a decade behind Lancashire's. Elsewhere – as on Derby Day – the holiday focus of less-well-off families was on fairs or races. In Glasgow, in the 1830s the July fair was a 'Saturnalia' of circuses, 'free and easies', freak shows, 'penny reels', penny theatres and sundry showmen. From the 1850s it developed as *the* occasion for Glasgow artisans to steam 'doon the watter' to the Clyde coastal resorts, getting 'steaming drunk' in the boats' bars. By 1906 the corporation offered trips to poor mothers and children to ensure that they were not excluded. Meanwhile, poor families from the Black Country towns or London's East End took their children fruit or hop picking to get a rural break.[14]

The 1833 Factory Act stipulated that Good Friday and Christmas Day should be mandatory holidays. In London, however, the vast and growing population of clerks received few holidays: from 1834 even the Bank of England closed for only four working days. The situation was recognised by the 1871 Bank Holiday Act which protected bank clerks' ability to holiday at Christmas, Easter and Whit, and instigated a secular holiday on the first Monday of August. 'Bank Holiday Monday' was an immediate success in London, and in heavily commercial Liverpool businesses followed the Bank's lead; by the later seventies it had achieved much the same impact in more industrial cities where wakes and fairs had been curtailed, like Birmingham and Leeds. Thus the Bank Holiday Act legitimated the notion of uniform popular holidays. By 1901 Seebohm Rowntree noted working men from among the better-off half of the

14 Walton, 'The demand for working-class seaside holidays', 253–9, 262; Alan Kidd, *Manchester* (Keele, 1993), pp. 50–1, 132; Derek Beattie, *Blackburn: The Development of a Lancashire Cotton Town* (Halifax, 1992), pp. 108, 112–15; Paul Wild, 'Leisure in Rochdale', in John Clarke, Chas Critcher and Richard Johnson, eds., *Working-Class Culture: Studies in History and Theory* (London, 1979), p. 146; Mark Judd, '"The oddest combination of town and country": popular culture and the London fairs, 1800–60', and Robert Poole, 'Oldham Wakes', both in Walton and Walvin, eds., *Leisure in Britain*, pp. 11–30, 81, 88–90; Shani D'Cruze, *Crimes of Outrage: Sex, Violence and Victorian Working Women* (London, 1998), pp. 111–36; H. Cunningham, 'The metropolitan fairs: a case study in the social control of leisure', in A. P. Donajgrodzki, ed., *Social Control in Nineteenth Century Britain* (London, 1977), esp. p. 168; H. Cunningham, 'Urban fairs and popular culture in nineteenth-century England', in L. H. van Voss and F. van Holthoon, eds., *Working Class and Popular Culture* (Amsterdam, 1988), pp. 100, 104; D. A. Reid, 'Interpreting the festival calendar: wakes and fairs as carnivals', and J. K. Walton and R. Poole, 'The Lancashire wakes in the nineteenth century', in R. D. Storch, ed., *Popular Culture and Custom in Nineteenth-Century England* (London, 1982), pp. 72–98, 125–53; Hippolyte Taine, *Taine's Notes on England*, ed. Edward Hyams (London, 1995), pp. 32–3; E. King, 'Popular culture in Glasgow', in R. A. Cage, ed., *The Working Class in Glasgow 1750–1914* (London, 1987), pp. 152–5, 157–8, 162, 167–8; Robert Machray, *The Night Side of London* (London, 1902), pp. 281ff; Kathleen Dayus, *Her People* (London, 1982), pp. 98–153, cf. Raphael Samuel, 'Comers and goers', in H. J. Dyos and M. Wolff, eds., *The Victorian City* (London, 1973), vol. I, pp. 137–40.

working-class population of York crowding into Scarborough during the August Bank Holiday week.[15]

In 1911 the Trades Union Congress (TUC) began lobbying for holidays with pay – a benefit which, except in a few progressive firms, had hitherto been a privilege of status of superior salaried clerks. Again, progress followed the First World War. Public opinion sympathised with demands 'for more human conditions', agreeing that 'the working class were entitled to the same sort of leisure as the middle class', and trade unionists pressed their advantages. In 1919 holiday-with-pay agreements benefited about 1 million, and, by 1922, a further half a million non-unionised workers had agreements negotiated through Whitley Councils (established to defuse post-war social unrest). Further progress was halted because of the decline of labour bargaining power wrought by the Slump – Manchester Chamber of Commerce sought the curtailment of Whit walks, and in Blackburn holiday weeks gave way to day-only excursions. But economic recovery allowed the Labour movement to press the issue successfully. The investigative Amulree Committee (1936) proved an important goad to employers. Within a year the number of workers receiving paid holidays had doubled, as employers sought to pre-empt the twelve working days which the TUC advocated – by granting a week. The subsequent Holidays-with-Pay Act (1938) applied only to workers whose conditions were regulated by agencies such as Agricultural Wages Boards. Thus trades unionism benefited urban workers more than government, though, between them, 11 million workers – 60 per cent – received paid holidays by 1939. Bevin's wartime Ministry of Labour pressured employers into universalising one week's holiday, and the buoyant post-war labour market facilitated the achievement of paid Bank Holidays. Research in urban areas in 1947 suggested that whereas before the war two-thirds of the population stayed at home during their holidays, the position was now reversed. Moreover, by 1951 two-thirds of all workers were estimated to receive *two* weeks paid summer holidays – non-statutory for the most part, but well established, as a result of labour market pressures, and because more employers now appreciated the importance of the well-being of labour.[16]

---

[15] J. A. R. Pimlott, *The Englishman's Holiday: A Social History* (London, 1947; Hassocks, 1976), pp. 79–84, 144–9. The 1871 act did not apply in Scotland, but, judging by Dunfermline, the religious fast-days before twice-yearly communions began to perform a similar function as they gave way to the secular – in the form of holidays for railway excursions – during the third quarter of the nineteenth century: Fraser, 'Developments in leisure', pp. 248, 250; *Birmingham Daily Gazette*, 9 June 1875; *Birmingham Daily Post*, 8 Aug. 1876, 7 Aug. 1877, 6 Aug. 1878, 5 Aug. 1879, 26 May 1896; P. Bailey, *Leisure and Class in Victorian England* (London, 1978), p. 12; Walton, 'The demand for working-class seaside holidays', 258–60; Booth, *Life and Labour, Final Volume*, pp. 50–1; Rowntree, *Poverty*, pp. 107–8, 242.

[16] P. J. Waller, *Town, City and Nation* (Oxford, 1983), pp. 140–1; Simmons, *Victorian Railway*, pp. 291–2; Lloyd George cited in Keith Middlemass, *Politics in Industrial Society* (London, 1979),

Douglas A. Reid

(ii) SPACE TO PLAY

Gradually, then, more leisure time was secured, but how did the physical growth of towns affect leisure activities? It is too simple to regard town and country entirely in antithesis, particularly the further back we go, and the further down the scale of size and function from capital to country towns. Even London's popular culture was long reminiscent of rusticity, from the early spring concentration of its fairs, to sports and pastimes such as cock fighting, bullock running, pigeon flying and flower growing; further down the scale working-class Blackburn raced whippets, Norwich workers bred canaries and slum dwellers in York trapped cock-linnets for pub competitions. Yet there is no doubt that increased urbanisation did blight open-air recreations: growing towns meant overbuilding of gardens, crofts and paddocks, enclosure of commons and traffic congestion on bustling streets. Where in Manchester was there for the people to go, asked Leon Faucher in 1844; he saw 'no public promenades, no avenues, no public gardens, and no public common'. By mid-century in Birmingham 'guinea gardens' were sprouting houses. At Coventry and Portsmouth enclosure led directly to the demise of popular sports. It was no accident that cock fighting survived more readily amidst the waste land and rural enclaves of the Black Country than in more densely urban (and numerously policed) Birmingham.[17]

Take the most popular street recreations. Fairs and sports undoubtedly became

Footnote 16 (cont).

p. 143; Forman, *Industrial Town*, p. 94; Beattie, *Blackburn*, p. 160; G. C. Cameron, 'The growth of holidays with pay in Britain', in G. Reid and D. Robertson, eds., *Fringe Benefits, Labour Costs and Social Security* (London, 1965), pp. 277 n. 1, 282–4; Jones, *Workers at Play*, pp. 17–20, 27–33, 77–8; Stephen Jones, 'The Lancashire cotton industry and the development of paid holidays in the nineteen-thirties', *Transactions of the Historical Society of Lancashire and Cheshire*, 135 (1985), 104, 106–7; *Report of the Committee on Holidays With Pay*, Cmd 5724 (1938), pp. 19, 23; Mass-Observation [File Report 2509], *Voluntary Social Service Report no. 1: A Report on Holidays*, August 1947, pp. 1–3; James Walvin, *Leisure and Society* (London, 1978), pp. 80–1, 154.

[17] Judd, '"The oddest combination of town and country"', pp. 11–30; Jim Mott, 'Miners, weavers and pigeon racing', in Michael A. Smith, Stanley Parker and Cyril S. Smith, eds., *Leisure and Society in Britain* (London, 1973), pp. 87–8, cf. 94; *New Survey of London Life and Labour*, IX, pp. 70–1; Van Wilson, *Rich in All but Money: Life in Hungate 1900–1938* (York, 1996), pp. 96–8; Hawkins, *Norwich*, pp. 73, 80, 314–16; Beattie, *Blackburn*, p. 110; R. W. Malcolmson, *Popular Recreations in English Society, 1700–1850* (Cambridge, 1973), pp. 108–9, 141; Anthony Delves, 'Popular recreation and social conflict in Derby, 1800–1850', in Stephen Yeo and Eileen Yeo, eds., *Popular Culture and Class Conflict 1590–1914: Explorations in the History of Labour and Leisure* (Brighton, 1981), p. 100. See also J. L. Hammond and B. Hammond, *The Age of the Chartists, 1832–1854* (London, 1930), pp. 110–19, for the effects of enclosure; Faucher, *Manchester in 1844*, p. 55; *Morning Chronicle*, 27 Jan. 1851; D. A. Reid, 'Beasts and brutes: popular blood sports c. 1780–1860', in Holt, ed., *Sport and the Working Class*, pp. 21–4; for debate about the impact of the new police on leisure, see R. D. Storch, 'The plague of blue locusts. Police reform and popular resistance in northern England, 1840–1857', *International Review of Social History*, 20 (1975); R. D. Storch, 'The policeman as domestic missionary: urban discipline and popular culture in northern England, 1850–1880', *Journal of Social History*, 9 (1976) 481–509; Russell, 'The pursuit of leisure',

758

increasingly more obstructive to the business of towns and more obnoxious to unsympathetic or hostile observers. Sports played *en masse* could damage property, and boisterous throngs of fair-goers intimidated the genteel. The rich, respectable and religious found fault with 'improvident' absences from work, 'debauchery', gambling, intemperance and cruelty. Thus the 1820s saw bullock hunting and fairs repressed in London; in the later 1830s and early 1840s it was the turn of bull running, bull baiting and the occasional fair elsewhere, and in the mid-forties of mass football – 'rude and brutal barbarism' – notably at Derby. It was not accidental that these were also decades of high anxiety about popular radicalism: events from Peterloo to Chartism encouraged a repressive mind-set. 'Fear and disgust' eased by the mid-fifties and mid-sixties; however, the juggernaut of urban modernity continued to roll over originally rural customs and institutions. Central London lost all its fairs, and set-piece street football was abolished even on the capital's periphery. Seemingly symptomatic of this process, white-pinafored milk-maids were displaced from their leading role in the celebration of London's May Day by chimney sweeps, potent symbols of urban dirt. Elsewhere, in the 1860s, 'intensely modern' towns felt they were being 'invaded' by Bohemians and nomads at their fairs. Unsurprisingly, an act of 1871 declared them 'the cause of grievous immorality' in towns, and they were abolished at Blackheath, Charlton and Harrow in 1872, and in a clutch of provincial cities in 1874–8.[18]

Yet more urban fairs survived than were suppressed (the reverse of the situation with street-football). Indeed, Londoners flocking out to Croydon, Barnet and Hampstead made minor fairs major. Moreover, cities grew patchily over the countryside, and private, unlicensed, fairs – with shows and gambling booths –

pp. 205–6; S. J. Davies, 'Classes and the police in Manchester, 1829–1880' in A. J. Kidd and K. W. Roberts, eds., *City, Class and Culture* (Manchester, 1985), pp. 38–40; M. Hewitt, *The Emergence of Stability in the Industrial City* (Aldershot, 1996), pp. 183–4.

[18] Cunningham, 'The metropolitan fairs', pp. 170–2, 180; Cunningham, *Leisure in the Industrial Revolution*, p. 24; Reid 'Interpreting the festival calendar', pp. 133–5, 137, 142, 144; Walton and Poole, 'The Lancashire wakes', pp. 105–6, 117–19; Cunningham, 'Urban fairs', pp. 99–103; D. A. Reid, 'Folk-football, the aristocracy and cultural change: a critique of Dunning and Sheard', *International Journal of the History of Sport*, 5 (1988), 229–31; Malcolmson, *Popular recreations*, pp. 37, 132–3, 141; Steve Poole, '"Till our liberties be secure": popular sovereignty and public space in Bristol, 1780–1850', *UH*, 26 (1999), 48; Brian Harrison and Barrie Trinder, *Drink and Sobriety in an Early Victorian Country Town, Banbury: 1830–1860* (*English Historical Review, Supplement*, 4, London, 1969), p. 6; *Derby Mercury*, 28 Feb. 1844, cited in Delves, 'Popular recreation', p. 107; R. D. Storch, 'The problem of working-class leisure: some roots of middle-class moral reform in the industrial north: 1825–59', in Donajgrodzki, ed., *Social Control*, p. 138; Morris Marples, *A History of Football* (London, 1954), p. 100; Judd, '"The oddest combination of town and country"', p. 26; Roy Judge, *The Jack-in-the-Green* (London, 1979); Charles Phythian-Adams, 'Milk and soot', in D. Fraser and A. Sutcliffe, eds., *The Pursuit of Urban History* (London, 1983), pp. 83–104; *Aris's Birmingham Gazette*, 25 May 1866; Walton, 'The demand for working-class seaside holidays', 259; see also J. N. Morris, 'A disappearing crowd? Collective action in late nineteenth-century Croydon', *SHist.*, 11 (1989), 97–100.

were 'almost incessantly' sprouting up. Even in towns where fairs were formally abolished the shows and crowds very often migrated to private ground, out of reach of their opponents. There was thus continuity as well as change.[19]

What factors helped fairs flourish? Economic arguments were important: livestock dealers valued fairs, as did many municipalities, citing stall rents and crowds of customers for ratepayer publicans and shopkeepers. Furthermore, travelling showmen developed business reputations as their menageries grew larger, and capital investment greater – especially for traction engines to drive ever-more elaborate roundabouts and generate electric light. Fairs became harbingers of modernity: Hull fair had cinematograph tents from 1897, and was called 'Light City' in 1908. Consequently, many towns compromised on fairs' locations: Hull's was moved five times between 1835 and 1888 rather than abolished by the economistic Council – despite a strong nonconformist lobby. By contrast, Birmingham's nonconformist-dominated, but consciously modernising, Council proscribed its fairs. Furthermore, experience taught the police that fairs were not a significant threat to public order, and that many of the objections emanated from middle-class, particularly Quaker, prejudice. By 1885, the home secretary was not prepared to interfere in what he considered 'innocent amusements of the poorer classes'. This toleration – now quite widely shared – represented an important shift from the alarmism of earlier generations. Contrariwise, ordinary people were increasingly able to make their voice effective against undue interference in their recreations at later-nineteenth-century municipal elections in smaller towns, like Walsall, Newcastle-under-Lyme and Canterbury. Numbers counted, and excursionists facilitated flourishing fairs even in some larger cities or on central sites (Glasgow, Hull, Newcastle, Nottingham, Oxford). Blackpool Pleasure Beach was successor to fairs at many Lancashire wakes.[20]

By contrast, folk football was too anarchic, had few business connections and few politically articulate defenders; in Derby in 1833 trade unionists rejected it as an impediment to moral and political progress. It survived only in small towns like Ashbourne (Derbyshire) – after it retreated to their outskirts. Out-of-the-way Workington (Cumberland) proved an exception because its Easter game

[19] F. M. L. Thompson, *Hampstead* (London, 1974), pp. 152, 327; Cunningham, 'The metropolitan fairs', pp. 172, 174–6, 177–8; Select Committee on Public Houses, *Report*, 1852–3 (855), xxxvii, qq. 195–200; *Birmingham Council Proceedings*, 1862–3, p. 55; *Birmingham Morning News*, 11 June 1872.

[20] Cunningham, 'Urban fairs', pp. 99, 101, 103–4; David Braithwaite, *Fairground Architecture* (London, 1968), pp. 19, 105; Vanessa Toulmin, *Randall Williams. King of Showmen: From Ghost Show to Bioscope* (London, 1998), pp. 16–36; Stephen Smith and Kevin Scrivens, *Hull Fair: An Illustrated History* (Cherry Burton, 1991), pp. 7–10; Cunningham, 'The metropolitan fairs', pp. 163, 168, 172–8; Michael E. Ware, *Historic Fairground Scenes* (Ashbourne, 1977), p. 93; Machray, *The Night Side of London*, pp. 125–34; Walton and Poole, 'The Lancashire wakes', p. 116; Poole, 'Oldham Wakes', p. 91; Reid, 'Interpreting the festival calendar', pp. 142, 146; Sally Alexander, *St Giles's Fair, 1830–1914: Popular Culture and the Industrial Revolution in 19th Century Oxford* (Oxford, 1970).

became as much tourist attraction as community celebration, which compensated shopkeepers for the occasional damage – 20,000 railway excursionists arrived in 1930. Guy Fawkes commemorations, on the other hand, enjoyed middle-class patronage until quite late in the century, for reasons of Protestant politics, and thus the popular 'bonfire gangs' who organised events with carnivalesque exuberance often successfully resisted attempts to police them off the thoroughfares. Their celebration of 5 November was strongest in towns with little modern industry and correspondingly closer social relations (southern and Cumbrian towns show this). Nevertheless, cultural and economic modernisation prompted a decreasing middle-class readiness to tolerate their disorderly vigour. Where police action proved ineffective a new solution was developed from the 1870s – subsuming the bonfire gangs within large official masked torchlit parades. Thus social (and political) considerations were as important as restrictions prompted by physical urbanisation.[21]

Nevertheless, despite various restrictions and losses endured by popular culture as towns grew, people made the best of the street space that was available to them, for before the 1950s dangers from vehicular traffic were few outside main thoroughfares, leaving side streets available as key social arenas. In 1849 the streets of Manchester were 'one swarming buzzing mass of people': it could hardly have been otherwise given the huge proportion of the population in major towns which was youthful, and the cramped, garden-less, condition of most housing (until interwar estate developments). Children's street games were seasonal, many representing a remarkable continuity from pre-modern times, ranging from singing and dancing, through scratch football with any object which would roll across cobblestones (and lamp-post cricket), to more boisterous games and tricks against adults. Adolescent boys, in particular, were much criticised for their activities on street corners and waste ground, including gang fighting, foot racing, stone throwing and 'pitch and toss' gambling. On the other hand, the constructive vigour of nineteenth-century street culture was exemplified by the impromptu dancing witnessed in alleys and courts: a barrel organ would strike up a waltz tune, and girls, children and sometimes 'two young men together', soon began 'to foot it merrily' in their clogs. Their elders gossiped on front doorsteps or joined the street corner gamblers. Everywhere streets were enlivened (or made cacophonous, according to taste) by ballad singers and

---

[21] Delves, 'Popular recreation', pp. 104–5; F. P. Magoun, *History of Football from the Beginnings to 1871* (Bochum-Langendreer, 1938), pp. 129, 131, 132–3; Percy M. Young, *A History of British Football* (London, 1969), pp. 7–8; Lyn Murfin, *Popular Leisure in the Lake Counties* (Manchester, 1990), pp. 50–3, 111–117; R. D. Storch, '"Please to remember the fifth of November": conflict, solidarity and public order in southern England, 1815–1900', in Storch, ed., *Popular Culture and Custom*, pp. 73–7, 82, 84–91, 93–4; David Cressy, 'The fifth of November remembered', in Roy Porter, ed., *Myths of the English* (London, 1992), pp. 68–90; Hutton, *Stations of the Sun*, pp. 400–3; Morris, 'A disappearing crowd?', 95–7.

fiddlers – up to about the 1870s – and German and Italian bands thereafter. Remarkably, on Sunday evenings in many cities young men and women effectively took over some of the main streets to promenade – all dressed in their best for these 'monkey parades' – swapping badinage, showing off, 'sky-larking', 'clicking' together. In Newcastle in 1927 'hundreds' danced the Charleston 'on the public highway'. The police periodically arrested youngsters for traffic obstruction, but the custom was well entrenched and flourished until after the Second World War, by which time it seems to have been diminished by Sunday cinema.[22]

The politics of urban blight eventually resulted in one of the most characteristic features of modern townscape – the public park, a form of civic space with very different meanings to the unruly spaces of the street. Concern had been raised in the 1830s on grounds of public health and moral well-being, but action only came in the 1840s, warmed by the thought that parks would encourage the 'kindly intercourse . . . of all classes', and thereby, it was hoped, draw the sting of Chartism. Thus, 'demoralisation, disease and death' in dangerously combustible densely developed east London in 1841 led the government to promise £90,000 for Victoria Park, Bethnal Green. In pointed contrast the rest of the country had to make do with a mere £10,000 – turbulent Manchester was the main beneficiary, in 1846.[23]

---

[22] A. B. Reach, *Manchester and the Textile Districts in 1849*, ed. C. Aspin (Helmshore, 1972), p. 58; Forman, *Industrial Town*, pp. 118–21; Bill Bramwell, 'Public space and local communities: the example of Birmingham, 1840–1880', in G. Kearns and C. W. J. Withers, eds., *Urbanising Britain* (Cambridge, 1991), p. 46; Stephen Constantine, 'Amateur gardening and popular recreation in the 19th and 20th centuries', *Journal of Social History*, 14 (1981), 387–406; S. Martin Gaskell, 'Gardens for the working class: Victorian practical pleasures', *Victorian Studies*, 23 (1980), 479–501; James Walvin, 'Children's pleasures', in Walton and Walvin, eds., *Leisure in Britain*, pp. 231, 234–7; Mason, *Association Football and English Society*, pp. 82–3; D'Cruze, *Crimes of Outrage*, pp. 115–17; S. Humphries, *Hooligans or Rebels?* (Oxford, 1981), chs. 5 and 7; C. E. B. Russell and E. T. Campagnac, 'Poor people's music-halls in Lancashire', *Economic Review* (1900), 305 (for clog dancers); Jones, 'Working-class sport in Manchester', pp. 67–83; James McGurn and Robert Poole, eds., *Tyneside Memories* (York, 1996), pp. 22–3, 70; Richard Middleton, 'Popular music of the lower classes', in Nicholas Temperley, ed., *Music in Britain: The Romantic Age 1800–1914* (London, 1981), pp. 70–3, 79–80; Davies, *Leisure, Gender and Poverty*, pp. 102–8; Roberts, *A Woman's Place*, pp. 71–2, 188; Richards, 'The cinema and cinema going in Birmingham', pp. 42–3; J. Winter, *London's Teeming Streets, 1830–1914* (London, 1993), pp. 68, 188; John Collier and Iain Lang, *Just the Other Day: An Informal History of Great Britain since the War* (London, 1932), p. 173 (for Charleston); Richard Evans and Alison Boyd, *The Use of Leisure in Hull* (Hull, 1933), p. 24; *New Survey of London Life and Labour*, I, p. 46, IX, pp. 71, 77; Mass-Observation (ed. Cross), *Worktowners at Blackpool*, pp. 28, 31–2.

[23] *Aris's Birmingham Gazette*, 25 Jan. 1844; W. H. G. Armytage, 'James Minter Morgan's schemes, 1841–1855', *International Review of Social History*, 3 (1958), 40; R. J. Morris, 'Middle-class culture, 1700–1914', in D. Fraser, ed., *A History of Modern Leeds* (Manchester, 1980), p. 210; J. Reynolds, *The Great Paternalist* (London, 1983), pp. 170, 174, 280; Reid, 'Labour, leisure and politics', pp. 328–9; cf. Thompson, *Hampstead*, pp. 221–2 re Primrose Hill; A. Fein, 'Victoria Park: its origins and history', *East London Papers*, 5 (1962), 73–90.

Public parks were preferred to the earlier 'public walks' in securing urban open space for several reasons: because of the idea (born of the miasmatic theory of disease causation) that it was necessary to create large sanitary 'lungs' to stem the progress of epidemics; because of the realisation of the need for space for the young to run around safely; because of aristocratic example such as Sheffield's Norfolk Park (1841); and because parks so much raised the value of surrounding land that they could act as foci for development and pay for themselves, as Birkenhead showed (1842-7). However, subsequent progress usually came about in spite of small ratepayer-dominated corporations – reluctance to undertake expensive projects left them mainly dependent on benefaction. By contrast, Glasgow and Liverpool (whose large corporate estates lessened the grip of the small ratepayer) provided extensive parks in the 1850s to 1860s – though often with subtle prompting from estate developers. Big cities felt congestion, pollution and population growth all the more, and a new civic religious idealism helped inspire the necessary fiscal generosity – led in Glasgow by Robert Buchanan, in Birmingham by George Dawson and Robert Dale, in Bristol by followers of Matthew Arnold. Furthermore, as towns became cities civic pride burgeoned: in 1878 Leicester rejected the idea of going 'cap in hand' to local landowners to ask for gifts of land, and raised loans instead.[24]

Park creation, then, was part of a process in which municipalities discovered both the desire and the means to act for themselves to civilise their populations; the provision of libraries, art galleries and museums represented a parallel process. The one was ostensibly about public health, the other about education and culture; both can also be seen, however, as attempts to facilitate a predominantly (though not wholly) bourgeois ideal of 'rational recreation', shorn of the temptations and malign consequences they associated with street pastimes. Visitors to parks usually found formally designed landscapes, fenced around with

---

[24] Fein, 'Victoria Park', 73–90; [Anon.],'The lungs of London', *Blackwood's Magazine*, 46 (1839), 227; [Anon.], 'Parks and pleasure grounds', *Westminster Review*, 35 (1841), 422–5, 430n; Sheila Metcalf, 'The idea of a park: the Select Committees and the first public parks', *Journal of Regional and Local Studies*, 4 (1984), 25–8, 30; Hazel Conway, *People's Parks* (Cambridge, 1991), pp. 47–9, 57, 71, 226; C. Stella Davies, *A History of Macclesfield* (Manchester, 1961), pp. 280–2; Reid, 'Labour, leisure and politics', pp. 308–32, 443–8; cf. Hammond and Hammond, *The Age of the Chartists*, p. 346; D. McClellan, *Glasgow's Public Parks* (Glasgow, 1894), pp. 41–5, 71–2, 86–7, 125–7; M. A. Simpson 'The West End of Glasgow, 1830–1914', in M. A. Simpson and T. H. Lloyd, eds., *Middle Class Housing in Britain* (Newton Abbot, 1977), p. 61; Hamish Fraser, 'From civic gospel to municipal socialism', in Derek Fraser, ed., *Cities, Class and Communication: Essays in Honour of Asa Briggs* (Hemel Hempstead, 1990), esp. 61–5; Maver, 'Glasgow's public parks', 323–36; Brian D. White, *A History of the Corporation of Liverpool 1835–1914* (Liverpool, 1951), pp. 84–5; G. F. Chadwick, *The Park and the Town* (London, 1965), p. 89; C. G. Brown, *The Social History of Religion in Scotland since 1730* (London, 1987), p. 132; Russell, 'The pursuit of leisure', pp. 207–8; E. P. Hennock, *Fit and Proper Persons* (London, 1973), p. 212; H. E. Meller, *Leisure and the Changing City, 1870–1914* (London, 1976), pp. 1–18, 89–90, 96–121; Malcolm Elliot, *Victorian Leicester* (Chichester, 1979), p. 155.

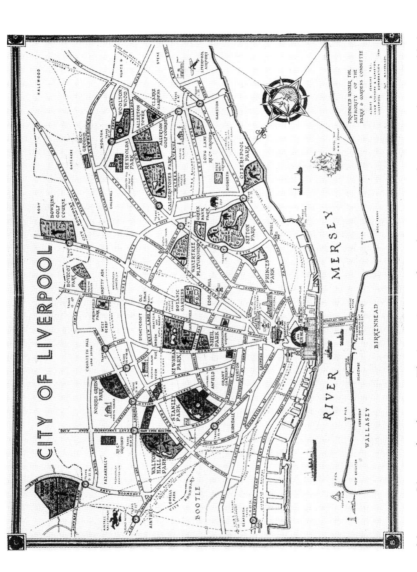

Map 23.1 Liverpool parks 1934. The inner ring was formed 1841–1872, the outer parks were added later.

Source: Hazel Conway, *People's Parks: The Design and Development of Victorian Parks in Britain* (Cambridge 1991) numerous strictly enforced rules, drawing a careful distinction between public parks and unregulated commons (just as public libraries distinguished between the uncontrolled effusions of the market place in print and weightier tomes). This contrast was emphasised in the case of Kennington Common (enclosed and emparked in 1852, four years after it hosted the last great Chartist demonstration) and Mousehold Heath in Norwich (regulated in 1884). Nevertheless, commercial pleasure gardens also found it necessary to deploy policemen to 'ensure respectability and preserve order': an uncivil minority needed restraint to maximise the majority's enjoyment. And there is no doubt that parks were very popular, partly because of the free entertainment provided from their bandstands: one August Sunday in 1857 there were 80,000 visitors to Greenwich Park, 100,000 to Regent's Park and 60,000 to Victoria Park (while 8,000 visited Cremorne Gardens, Chelsea, and 44,000 excursionists left London stations).[25]

Cremorne was one of a number of competitors with Vauxhall Gardens for which nineteenth-century urbanisation created new demand. Admittedly, London's Vauxhall closed in 1859, but though less popular than the free public parks most of the pleasure gardens attracted sufficient custom until the 1870s and 1880s, by which time ground landlords were able to see more profit through their redevelopment. As with fairs, however, the demise of central gardens promoted the careers of some further out – like Riverside Gardens, North Woolwich. Those which survived past 1914-18 had diversified into sporting facilities, and served regional and national rather than simply local publics – principally the Crystal Palace's Sydenham Gardens (1854), and Belle Vue (founded in 1836 to compete with Manchester's Vauxhall).[26]

In big cities the distribution of public parks was usually skewed away from the

---

[25] Thomas Kelly, *A History of Public Libraries in Great Britain, 1845–1966* (London, 1973); Cunningham, *Leisure in the Industrial Revolution*, pp. 105–6, 153–6; Neil McMaster, 'The battle for Mousehold Heath', *P&P*, 127 (1990), 143, 148–53; Russell, 'The pursuit of leisure', p. 208; Reid, 'Labour, leisure and politics', p. 345; 'The London Sunday', quoted from *The Star* in *Birmingham Daily Press*, 19 Aug. 1857, cf. Hewitt, *The Emergence of Stability in the Industrial City*, pp. 163–7; Winter, *London's Teeming Streets*, pp. 170–2, 164–5; Nan H. Dreher, 'The virtuous and the verminous: turn-of-the-century moral panics in London's public parks', *Albion*, 29 (1997), 246–67. For discussion of non-bourgeois 'rational recreation' see Faucher, *Manchester in 1844*, p. 23 n. 8, Reid, 'Labour, leisure and politics', ch. 4; and Martha Vicinus, *The Industrial Muse* (London, 1974), pp. 193–4, 233 n. 11. A technologically sophisticated age should not underestimate the impact of the penny reading, the diorama and the magic lantern.

[26] J. Ewing Ritchie, *The Night Side of London*, 2nd edn, revised (London, 1858), pp. 161–2, 199, 218–26; *A Guide to Belle Vue Gardens* (Manchester, 1869); Kidd, *Manchester*, pp. 52–3, 116–17, 172; Taine, *Notes on England*, pp. 36–7; R. D. Altick, *The Shows of London* (London, 1978), pp. 93–8, 323–5, 456; Reid, 'Labour, leisure and politics', pp. 337–9, 345–50; Warwick Wroth, *The London Pleasure Gardens of the Eighteenth Century* (London, 1896; 1979 reprint), pp. 319–26; Warwick Wroth, *Cremorne and the Later London Gardens* (London, 1907); Mark Girouard, *Victorian Pubs* (London, 1975), p. 15; *VCH*, Hull, I, p. 382; Gregory Anderson and Barbara Ferguson, 'James Reilly. An artisan manufacturer in Victorian Manchester', *Manchester Region History Review*, 8 (1994), 94–5.

most densely populous areas and towards the outskirts, where large blocks of land remained. Admission figures to such parks in Birmingham in the 1870s suggest an annual average of ten visits *per capita*, which has been seen as low (yet this was relatively early, and thirty-four visits *per capita* made to Birmingham's many cinemas in 1950 provide a different perspective). In the 1880s realisation of the problem of location led larger cities to provide local playgrounds for the areas of densest population, though in London's 'central and most congested districts' in the 1930s the street remained the popular and 'often the only playground' for the younger children. Nevertheless, on Bank Holidays Londoners found compensation on trips to Hampstead Heath, Epping Forest and other commons preserved after lengthy struggles.[27]

There were other means of escape from the towns. For men an important way was to join the Volunteer Force (a 'dominantly urban' movement), for their annual camps offered subsidised fellowship and fresh air. Freer spirits went rambling: Glasgow's Saturday-afternooners in 1869, Manchester's YMCA and Sheffield's socialists, in later decades. Cycling was enormously popular in the 1890s, with 300 clubs in London, perhaps mainly lower middle class. More time and higher living standards in the interwar period increased involvement, and in the 1930s old 'rambling' became new youthful 'hiking' – fashionable along with cycling, camping and other manifestations of 'outdoor' feeling: Hull had 400-500 cycling club members in 1933.[28]

However, the unsung (largely male) working-class pastime of coarse fishing facilitated the movement of far larger numbers from cities to rural settings under the aegis of pub-based angling clubs. There were 621 in London by 1900, and – more impressive in *per capita* terms – 100 in Norwich in 1910; Sheffield's had an extraordinary 21,000 members by 1914. In the interwar years the motor charabanc and motor bike and a new trend towards employer sponsorship allowed

---

[27] Reid, 'Labour, leisure and politics', pp. 358–71; Bramwell, 'Public space', pp. 48–53; Browning and Sorrell, 'Cinemas and cinema-going', 139; Trainor, *Black Country Elites*, p. 345; Maver, 'Glasgow's public parks', 339; *New Survey of London Life and Labour*, IX, p. 71; Conway, *People's Parks*, pp. 214–15, 219; Robert Hunter, 'The movements for the inclosure and preservation of open lands', *Journal of the Royal Statistical Society*, 60 (1897), 395–7, 401; Jones, *Workers at Play*, pp. 94, 97; Thompson, *Hampstead*, chs. 4–5; D. Owen, *The Government of Victorian London, 1855–1889* (Cambridge, Mass., and London, 1982), pp. 145–53, 247–9, 251, 358; Anthony Taylor, '"Commons-stealers", "land-grabbers" and "jerry-builders": space, popular radicalism and the politics of public access in London, 1848–1880', *International Review of Social History*, 40 (1995), 383–407.

[28] Cunningham, *The Volunteer Force*, pp. 49, 120–1; King, 'Popular culture in Glasgow', p. 178; Fraser, 'Developments in leisure', pp. 247–8; David Prynn, 'The Clarion Clubs, rambling and the holiday associations in Britain since the 1890s', *Journal of Contemporary History*, 11 (1976), 65–71; Ann Holt, 'Hikers and ramblers: surviving a thirties' fashion', *International Journal of the History of Sport*, 4 (1987), 56–67; David Rubinstein, 'Cycling in the 1890s', *Victorian Studies*, 21 (1977), 48–50, cf. 58–9, 63, 68–71; R. Holt, *Sport and the British* (Oxford, 1989), pp. 196–201; Richard Evans and Alison Boyd, *The Use of Leisure in Hull* (Hull, 1933), p. 15; Jennings and Gill, *Broadcasting in Everyday Life*, pp. 7–8, 10.

angling to maintain its position as one of the chief outdoor activities. The motor charabanc also facilitated excursions to previously untouched beauty spots by a rapidly notorious (because noisy and well-victualled) phenomenon – the 'tripper'. Equally, the massed-ranked chalets of the new holiday camps were rather reminiscent of cities by the sea.[29]

(iii) ENTERTAINING PLEASURES

Drink, however, was 'the shortest cut out of Manchester', or 'out of Whitechapel', or any city. Yet public houses constituted the chief nineteenth-century leisure venue for many other reasons than seeking solace for a desperate or humdrum existence. Alcohol performed numerous functions – commercial, cultural, nutritional and recreational, as well as medical and psychological – and because of this – and because they were free, warm, light and offered company (predominantly but not wholly male before 1914) as well as invigoration and refreshment – public houses were ubiquitous in towns, and their contribution to popular leisure immense. They were centres of sport, news, games, entertainment, debate and culture, for urban landlords were leisure entrepreneurs, as that notable offshoot and ultimate competitor, the music hall, illustrates. Pubs – selling beer and spirits – clustered particularly on transport routes, and on main streets, whereas the 31,000 beerhouses created following the 1830 Beer Act were concentrated in working-class suburbs. By the 1850s in big cities, and even smaller towns like Bolton, many pubs shouted their presence by plate-glass windows, 'flaring gas lights in frosted globes and brightly gilded spirit casks'. Following a frenzy of competition among big brewers in the 1880s and 1890s they reached a lavish climax of engraved glass, mahogany and mosaic as veritable 'palaces' for drinking – feeding on the continuous flow of custom in the big towns, and the free-spending population of the larger ports and resorts.[30]

The architectural flashiness of the city-centre drinking palaces should not blind us to the much more basic beerhouses and pubs – key centres of social life

---

[29] Lowerson, 'Brothers of the angle', p. 109; Lowerson, 'Angling', pp. 19–23; Hawkins, *Norwich*, p. 313; C. E. M. Joad, 'The people's claim', in Clough Williams-Ellis, *Britain and the Beast* (London, 1937), pp. 72–3; Colin Ward and Dennis Hardy, *Goodnight Campers: The History of the British Holiday Camp* (London, 1986).

[30] Joad, 'The people's claim', p. 76; Durant, *The Problem of Leisure*, p. 96; Harrison, *Drink and the Victorians*, pp. 37–63; B. Harrison, 'Pubs', in Dyos and Wolff, eds., *The Victorian City*, I, pp. 169–78; Rudolph Kenna and Anthony Mooney, *People's Palaces: Victorian and Edwardian Pubs of Scotland* (Edinburgh, 1983), pp. 40, 86; Rowntree, *Poverty*, p. 382; G. B. Wilson, *Alcohol and the Nation* (London, 1940), pp. 24–5; Poole, *Popular Leisure and the Music Hall*, p. 41; 'Shadow' (Brown), *Midnight Scenes*, pp. 98–9; Girouard, *Victorian Pubs*, pp. 34, 40–4, 50–9, 75–6, 139, 142, 182–4, 206–7; Joseph Rowntree and Arthur Sherwell, *Temperance Problem and Social Reform*, 5th edn (London, 1899), pp. 83–5; Alan Crawford and Robert Thorne, *Birmingham Pubs 1890–1939* (Birmingham, 1975), [pp. 3–4]; T. R. Gourvish and R. G. Wilson, *The British Brewing Industry 1830–1980* (Cambridge, 1994), pp. 250, 254–66, 268–73, 275–83, 286–9.

in working-class neighbourhoods and smaller towns. Charles Booth drew attention to 'hundreds of respectable public-houses' in London's East End, where, beneath the eye of 'a decent middle-aged woman . . . the whole scene [was] comfortable, quiet, and orderly'. In Edwardian Norwich the public house remained the working man's 'centre of social intercourse', particularly because 'compared with larger cities the Norwich public-house . . . [was] smaller and more home-like'. And in Middlesbrough, the 'ever-present, ever-accessible public-house' was a place of 'society, conviviality, amusement'. Booth believed that pubs played 'a larger part in the lives of the people than clubs or friendly societies, churches or missions, or perhaps than all put together', although after the price rises and shortened hours imposed during 1914–18 the working men's clubs became very much more important. Moreover, on the new interwar estates few pubs were built; brewers offered massive 'Olde English' roadhouses instead.[31]

To the migrant young, however, it was precisely the brilliant lights, the 'buzz' of large town life, which constituted one of its attractions (as well as shorter working hours). In Llewellyn Smith's formulation, London enticed its immigrants through 'the contagion of numbers, the sense of something going on, the theatres and music halls, the brightly-lighted streets and busy crowds – all, in short, that makes the difference between the Mile End fair on a Saturday night, and a dark and muddy country lane, with no glimmer of gas and with nothing to do'. Leisure entrepreneurs knew the value of glitz. Pleasure gardens were famous for their illuminated lanterns and brilliant pyrotechnics; pubs provided dazzling spectacles from the 1820s, as did handsomely appointed music halls from the 1860s; the Savoy Theatre became the first public building in the world lit by electricity in 1881; Italian Renaissance and Baroque style-books were pillaged to create opulent, exotic variety palaces in the decades before 1914. London was the 'Great City of the Midnight Sun / Whose day begins when day is done'. Even in Edwardian Middlesbrough pubs in ill-lit side streets threw out a vividly welcoming 'blaze of light'.[32]

[31] Booth, *Life and Labour of the People in London, First Series: Poverty*, I, pp. 113–14; Hawkins, *Norwich*, p. 312; [Florence] Bell, *At the Works* (London, 1907), p. 188; Bill Bramwell, *Pubs and Localised Communities in Mid-Victorian Birmingham* (Dept of Geography and Earth Science, Queen Mary College, University of London, Occasional Paper no. 22, 1984); John Taylor, *From Self-Help to Glamour: The Workingman's Club, 1860–1972* (Oxford, 1972); Phyllis Willmott, *Growing up in a London Village* (London,1973), pp. 96–9; Laurence Marlow, 'A menace to sobriety? The drink question and the working man's club, c. 1862–1906', in Voss and Holthoon, eds., *Working Class and Popular Culture*, pp. 109–20; Terence Young, *Becontree and Dagenham: A Report Made for the Pilgrim Trust* (London, 1934), pp. 42, 44, 52, 54, 71–2, 81, 190; Mass-Observation, *The Pub and the People*, 202; Crawford and Thorne, *Birmingham Pubs*, pp. [8–12] and plates 9 and 29.
[32] Llewellyn Smith cited in J. A. Banks, 'The contagion of numbers', in Dyos and Wolff, eds., *The Victorian City*, II, pp. 112ff; M. Loane, *From Their Point of View* (London, 1908), ch. 11 ('Why the poor prefer town life'), specifically pp. 249, 254; cf. Standish Meacham, *A Life Apart: The English Working Class 1890–1914* (London, 1977), pp. 41–2; Bell, *At the Works*, pp. 188, 350; *Souvenir: Empire Theatre, Birmingham*, 1912, p. 10; John Earl, 'Building the halls', in P. Bailey, ed., *Music Hall*

As well as migrants the enticements of cities drew in thousands of visitors and tourists. In the 1850s Manchester Whit week closed with 'gaping Saturday' as so many people travelled in from the neighbourhood and 'urged by intense curiosity, insisted on seeing everything in the shop windows and visiting the Exchange and College'. This pattern was repeated in other provincial cities, as railway excursions, and regular services, conveyed people to exhibitions, fairs, museums, music halls, shops, sporting fixtures and theatres. It is significant that music halls emerged more or less contemporaneously in both London and major provincial towns, for their growth was a function of the concentrated market for entertainment presented by all major towns and of the intense competition between beerhouses and other licensed houses following the 1830 Beer Act. The prototype halls were the Grecian Saloon at the Eagle Tavern on London's City Road, and the Star Concert Room at Bolton's Millstone Inn; by the 1840s there were 'announcements of "Free and Easy", and "Free Concert" . . . in every direction'. Significantly, the chain of 'Empire Palaces' that dominated the industry by 1900 was built by H. E. Moss of Greenock, Richard Thornton of South Shields and Oswald Stoll of Liverpool.[33]

Nevertheless, London, with a population of nearly 2 million in 1831 and over 7 million by 1911, undoubtedly took the palm for the concentration and variety of its cultural and entertainment attractions – from the Abbey to the Zoo. Its capacity to draw national audiences via the railway system was demonstrated in 1851 at the Great Exhibition, when as many as a sixth of its 6 million visitors travelled from afar by rail. The Crystal Palace was important in both the metropolitan and the national history of leisure. With its music, ornamental gardens and firework displays it helped to erode the place of Vauxhall, and its numerous contests, festivals and shows drew brass bandsmen, cage-bird fanciers, Co-operators, football fans, Friendly Society members, Handel-lovers, jazz bandsmen,

---

(Milton Keynes, 1986), pp. 27–31; Roger Dixon and Stefan Muthesius, *Victorian Architecture*, 2nd edn (London, 1985), pp. 92–3; Victor Glasstone, *Victorian and Edwardian Theatres* (London, 1975), pp. 90–1, 100–1, 170–1; Charles D. Stuart and A. J. Park, *The Variety Stage* (London, 1895), pp. 190–200; Gavin Weightman, *Bright Lights, Big City* (London, 1992), pp. 40–2; Audrey Field, *Picture Palace: A Social History of the Cinema* (London, 1974), pp. 36, 39; 'Great City', cited in Donald Read, *England 1868–1914: The Age of Urban Democracy* (London, 1979), p. 257.

[33] *Manchester Guardian*, 25 May 1850, cited in Kenneth Allan, 'The recreations and amusements of the industrial working class in the second quarter of the nineteenth century with special reference to Lancashire' (MA thesis, University of Manchester, 1947), p. 172; Wilson, *Alcohol and the Nation*, p. 101. Unlike circuses, theatrical booths or fairground rides, music halls were not regularly translated to rural locations: Clive Barker, 'The Chartists, theatre reform and research', *Theatre Quarterly*, 1 (1971), 3–10; Murfin, *Lake Counties*, pp. 203–4; Stuart and Park, *The Variety Stage*, pp. 13–45; Girouard, *Victorian Pubs*, pp. 36–7; Poole, *Popular Leisure and the Music Hall*, pp. 51–2, 61 n. 3; *Birmingham Journal*, 29 Apr. 1843; Kathleen Barker, 'The performing arts in Newcastle upon Tyne', in Walton and Walvin, eds., *Leisure in Britain*, p. 63; Dagmar Kift, *The Victorian Music Hall* (Cambridge, 1996), pp. 26–7; Russell, 'The pursuit of leisure', pp. 212–13; G. J. Mellor, *The Northern Music Hall* (Newcastle, 1970), pp. 121–56; Andrew Crowhurst, 'Oswald Stoll: a music hall pioneer', *Theatre Notebook*, 49 (1995), 27–49.

Salvationists, Sunday School pupils, Temperance workers, and others, right through until the conflagration of 1936 devoured Paxton's iron and glass masterpiece – although by this time some of its other functions had been usurped by Olympia (1888), Earl's Court (1894) and Wembley (1923).[34]

Tourists and provincial excursionists had also boosted theatre audiences in 1851, though few ventured east to the thriving theatres in Hoxton and Shoreditch, which catered for local workers at one sitting, and later for returning city clerks. Here, and in lesser popular theatres and 'penny gaffs' catering for even the poorest, migrants and settlers found warmth, sociability, entertainment and excitement. As in other cities they cheered Shakespearean ghosts and battles and melodrama – including Boucicault's much-adapted *Poor of Paris, London, Birmingham* etc. However, population movements and the development of music hall and cinema meant that East End theatre was a shadow of its former self by 1914. By contrast, suburban train services in the 1860s and 1870s and the cutting of Shaftesbury Avenue and Charing Cross Road in the 1880s stimulated the 'West End', hosting the genial satires of Gilbert and Sullivan and a new drawing-room drama for the train-borne middle classes. The West End boom resumed after 1918 producing ninety theatres (Manchester had nine, Birmingham, Glasgow and Liverpool six each, and Edinburgh, Leeds, Sheffield, Belfast, Newcastle and Cardiff three apiece).[35]

However, the glamorous 'super-cinemas' of the 1930s ossified theatrical development. Moving pictures had first been seen in music halls (and fairs) in 1896. The cuckoo did not immediately take over the nest, but by 1911-12 London had ninety-four purpose-built cinemas, and 500 altogether. Many were rudimentary 'blood tubs', a few were 'picture palaces' on Oxford Street catering for the 'carriage trade'. Cinema received enormous impetus during 1914–18 and by 1931

---

[34] Altick, *The Shows of London*, pp. 4, 226, 382, 386–7, 505; Simmons, *Victorian Railway*, p. 275; K. Baedeker, *London and its Environs* (London, 1884), pp. 290–6; Chadwick, *The Victorian Church*, II, pp. 392–5; Michael Musgrave, *The Musical Life of the Crystal Palace* (Cambridge, 1995), pp. 17–18, 27–57, 186–9, 194–201, 205–17; Lawrence Magnanie, 'An event in the culture of co-operation: national co-operative festivals at Crystal Palace', in S. Yeo, *New Views of Co-operation* (London, 1988), pp. 174–86; Jones, *Workers at Play*, p. 145; *New Survey of London Life and Labour*, IX, pp. 63, 70–1.

[35] Clive Barker, 'The audiences of the Britannia Theatre, Hoxton', *Theatre Quarterly*, 9, no. 34 (1979), 27–41; Jim Davis, 'The East End', in M. R. Booth and J. H. Kaplan, eds., *The Edwardian Theatre: Essays on Performance and the Stage* (Cambridge, 1996), pp. 201–19; F. Sheppard, *London* (Oxford, 1998), p. 306; *New Survey of London Life and Labour*, XI, pp. 44–7; Michael R. Booth, *English Melodrama* (London, 1965); D. A. Reid, 'Popular theatre in Victorian Birmingham', in David Bradby, Louis James and Bernard Sharratt, eds., *Performance and Politics in Popular Drama* (Cambridge, 1980), pp. 77–85; Jeremy Crump, 'The popular audience for Shakespeare in nineteenth century Leicester', in Richard Foulkes, ed., *Shakespeare and the Victorian Stage* (Cambridge, 1986), pp. 271–82; John Springhall, 'Leisure and Victorian youth: the penny theatre in London 1830–1890', in J. S. Hurt, ed., *Childhood, Youth and Education in the Late Nineteenth Century* (Leicester, 1981); Allardyce Nicoll, *English Drama 1900–1930* (Cambridge, 1973), pp. 19, 47; A. A. Jackson, *The Middle Classes, 1900–1950* (Nairn, 1991), pp. 245–54, 256–9, 260–3, 267.

outnumbered theatre and music hall seats in London by two to one. Continuous strip neon lighting introduced in the 1930s also contributed to the capital's attractions: to contemporaries it imparted a carnival-like air to Piccadilly. Though blacked out in the war, by the later 1940s London had resumed its magnetic role.[36]

(iv) IDENTITIES

Commercial entertainment exemplifies the point that all towns are markets, centres of competition. However, they are also social arenas in which individuals and communities develop their sense of identity. How far was urban identity affected by the development of leisure in nineteenth- and twentieth-century towns and cities?

Take the music halls, whose repertoire consisted of singing, instrumental music, comic patter, clowns, acrobats and dancing, evolving from earlier fare available in streets (especially ballads), bohemian singing saloons, pleasure gardens, circuses and theatres. By the 1860s the first London 'stars' emerged in the shape of the *lion comiques* like George Leybourne – whose regular provincial tours helped to nationalise taste – with his evocation of the insouciant London toff, 'Champagne Charlie', on 'a spree'. The success of 'swell songs' can be seen as an indication of how even the limited leisure time available to young urban lower-class men could be used to construct a liberating alter ego – a fantasy achieved through the surrogate means of wearing a tawdry version of the toff's garb, smoking cheap cigars and empathising with his music hall representation. In fact the 'counterfeit swell' was a recognisable urban type even before the 1860s, as is indicated by a ballad anatomy of the crowds at Birmingham's Vauxhall on Sunday evenings, when entry was free to circumvent the law: they included 'half of the Brummagem people', including soldiers, 'factory lasses', 'young widows', 'old bachelors', courting couples and old marrieds, 'trades and mechanics', 'snobs [cobblers] and tailors', 'naughty boys . . . strutting about . . . smoking cigars', and 'young swells in Paletots white', 'reeling along / Singing "I'm a gent", or some such song'. Leisure was liberating – as a writer in the *Dublin University Magazine* recognised in 1871: 'From being machines, fit only for machine work, or inert quiescence, the masses . . . [were] given the liberty of being men, gentlemen indeed' by their leisure time: experiencing that 'coveted attribute of gentility' – 'the power of being "at large"'. Leisure implied freedom from the restrictions of work (and social obligations), freedom to

---

[36] Robert Graves and Alan Hodge, *The Long Week-end: A Social History of Great Britain, 1918–1939* (London, 1941), pp. 133–4, 380; J. Richards, *The Age of the Dream Palace* (London, 1984), pp. 11–23; Weightman, *Bright Lights, Big City*, pp. 42–3; Rowson, 'A statistical survey of the cinema industry', 71; Seebohm Rowntree and G. R. Lavers, *English Life and Leisure* (London, 1951), p. 403.

dispose of time at will and freedom to role play an alternative existence. Furthermore, male impersonators Nellie Power and Vesta Tilley created 'female swells', partly mocking, partly testifying to the popularity of the male type and partly suggesting possibilities of female freedom. There was much more to the music hall than swell songs, but this stream of urban popular culture enabled the youthful component of the audience the pleasurable fantasy of escaping from the confines of their everyday existence, of being men and women 'of the world', even in unglamorous Carlisle.[37]

By contrast, the group of talented comic performers from poor backgrounds who emerged in the 1880s – Marie Lloyd, Gus Elen, Dan Leno and others – can be interpreted as representing social realism regarding the everyday realities of the hard life lived in London's East End – running the gamut from beer to weddings, constituting a Cockney 'culture of consolation'. However this is not necessarily incompatible with the 'swell' hypothesis, provided that music hall audiences are not perceived as monolithic. It is often assumed (invalidly, as we have seen), that music hall was essentially a London creation, but adopting G. Stedman Jones' view that the truest representatives of East End culture were Dan Leno and Charlie Chaplin, 'little men, perpetually "put upon" . . . products of city life', whose fate depends on luck rather than their own efforts, there seems no reason why such figures should not resonate equally in Liverpool or Glasgow. Similarly, when Gus Elen sang with wry ironic realism that 'You could see to 'Ackney Marshes / If it wasn't for the 'ouses in between' he gave expression to a sense of the boundaries imposed by bricks and mortar which would be appreciated in the inner districts of Hull or Manchester. On the other hand, towns and cities inspired loyalty as well as a desire to escape. 'I belong to Glasgae, dear old Glasgae town', sang Will Fyffe (in the 1920s), and 'on Saturday night Glasgae belongs to me!'. At one level this was merely a comic comment on the numerous Glaswegians who drank too much, but, at another, its chorus gave expression to a basic affection for the city which represented the framework for people's lives.[38]

However, local sentiment regarding cities, and parts of cities, was more

---

[37] P. Bailey, 'Champagne Charlie: performance and ideology in the music hall swell song', in J. S. Bratton, ed., *Music Hall* (Milton Keynes, 1986), pp. 49–69 (68 for Dublin quotation); see also Jane Traies, 'Jones and the working girl: class marginality in music-hall song, 1860–1900', in *ibid.*; *Morning Chronicle* (London), 3 Mar. 1851, for Vauxhall; Peter Davison, *Songs of the British Music Hall* (New York, 1971), pp. 16–19; Martha Vicinus, *The Industrial Muse* (London, 1974), pp. 258–9; Russell, *Popular Music in England*, pp. 87–96, 100; J. R. Walkowitz, *City of Dreadful Delight* (London and Chicago, 1992), pp. 43–6; Kift, *The Victorian Music Hall*, pp. 36–61 esp. 48–52; Murfin, *Lake Counties*, p. 207.
[38] G. Stedman Jones, 'Working-class culture and working-class politics in London, 1870–1900: notes on the remaking of a working class', *Soc. Hist.*, 7 (1974), 496–9; Russell, *Popular Music in England*, pp. 87–96, 100; Walkowitz, *City of Dreadful Delight*, pp. 43–6; Davison, *Songs*, pp. 192–6; MacInnes, *Sweet Saturday Night*, pp. 93–4.

frequently given expression in the context of competitive sport, and especially football (with its rugby variant particularly popular in certain localities, principally due to accidents of provenance rather than to any supposed link between brawn and rugby in heavy-industrial areas). The emergence of mass spectator sports on a national scale was one of the outstanding features of the period since 1850: they were relatively disciplined, time-limited and professionalised phenomena, well suited to the new, ordered, time-constrained, competitive urban environment (variously contrasting with 'folk-football', animal-baiting and cricket, with their rural associations and origins).[39]

A 'football fever' swept over Midland and northern towns in the 1880s. Despite the earlier suppression of set-piece street matches, football was like a subterranean stream, reappearing whenever the crust of repression was weakened – at Owenite galas in the 1840s, on works' trips and in the new parks in the 1850s. In the 1860s and 1870s, however, spontaneous popular enthusiasm was channelled into the new codified games which emerged from the public schools: spreading in the North – in Harrow's 'kicking' version – from Sheffield FC and industrial Turton, near Bolton; and – in Rugby's 'handling' version – from Manchester, Bradford and Leeds. Historians have asserted the missionary zeal of amateur sportsmen to provide the working classes with disciplined, athletic, 'rational recreation' and much has been made of the church affiliations of many clubs. However, hard evidence of footballing parsons is scarce (and even more so of footballing ministers) – though there were certainly cricketing clerics, 'fair play' and obedience to the umpire being considered analogous to Christian ethics and social order. It seems therefore that many church football teams simply represented Bible class and Sunday School friendships developed in sporting directions, some as winter counterparts of cricket teams. Equally the smaller number of work-based football clubs were more often employee rather than employer sponsored. The majority of clubs actually took their provenance from places: public houses, public parks, streets and neighbourhoods – such as Blackburn's Gibraltar Street Rovers, or 'Ardwick' and 'Newton Heath' (later Manchester City and United). This suggests that though football is often considered a 'mass leisure' pursuit much of it reflected existing localised patterns of urban sociability. Even in 1951 when 416 professional clubs attracted nearly a million spectators weekly, another 29,600 clubs involved half a million amateur players.[40]

---

[39] David Russell, '"Sporadic and curious": the emergence of rugby and soccer zones in Yorkshire and Lancashire, c. 1860–1914', *International Journal of the History of Sport*, 5 (1988), esp. 192–201.

[40] H. F. Abell, 'The football fever', *Macmillan's Magazine*, 89 (1903), 276–82; Reid, 'Labour, leisure and politics', pp. 136, 178, 332–3; Percy M. Young, *A History of British Football* (London, 1969), pp. 71, 76–8, 111–12; Mason, *Association Football*, pp. 11–17, 24–34; Gareth Williams, 'Rugby Union', in Mason, ed., *Sport in Britain*, pp. 310–11; Russell, '"Sporadic and curious"', esp. 189–90; Robert W. Lewis, 'The genesis of professional football: Bolton-Blackburn-Darwen, the

Was football's popularity a consequence of the 'dull monotony of life in our large towns' – as was suggested in 1898? Scattered occupational data suggest that football crowds in this period were disproportionally drawn from artisans and white-collar workers, rather than labourers (whose wages still meant life was more about endurance than enjoyment). The excitement of sudden-death cup competitions certainly gave an enormous impetus to the spread of the game. Crowds of four, and even five, figures were soon common, especially after 1883 when Blackburn Olympic showed a northern club could win the FA Cup. However, soccer supporters' enthusiasm also reflected a continuity of function with sporting events in the less-urbanised past, and their communal loyalism sometimes meshed with religious and cultural sectarianism: in Edinburgh and Dundee, and, most notoriously, in Glasgow where the Protestant Rangers versus Catholic Celtic rivalry also incorporated elements of Scottish and Irish nationalism (though Catholic Everton versus Protestant Liverpool represents more myth than substance).[41]

Already by 1880 clubs in large Midland and Lancashire towns were enabled by buoyant gate receipts to pay 'foreign' trainers and players (especially Scotsmen) to enhance competitiveness, with the result that one dominant team usually developed in each area (with more in great cities), and by 1885 the anguished amateurs at the Football Association were forced to accept overt professionalism

Footnote 40 *(cont.)*

centre of innovation 1875–85', *International Journal of the History of Sport*, 14 (1997), 41; A. J. Arnold, 'The belated entry of professional soccer into the West Riding textile district of northern England: commercial imperatives and problems', *International Journal of the History of Sport*, 6 (1989), 320; D. D. Molyneux, 'The development of physical recreation in the Birmingham district from 1871 to 1892' (MA thesis, University of Birmingham, 1957), pp. 39–40, and appendices A and B; Tony Mason, 'The Blues and the Reds', *Transactions of the Historical Society of Lancashire and Cheshire*, 134 (1985), 108, 126 n. 5; M. Huggins, 'The spread of Association football, in North-East England, 1876–90: the pattern of diffusion', *International Journal of the History of Sport*, 6 (1989), 311, 306; Bailey, *Leisure and Class*, p. 139; Keith Sandiford and Wray Vamplew, 'The peculiar economics of English cricket before 1914', *British Journal of Sports History*, 3 (1986), 312–13, 323; R. Holt, 'Working-class football and the city: the problem of continuity', *British Journal of Sports History*, 3 (1986), 5–17; R. Holt, 'Football and the urban way of life in nineteenth-century Britain', in Mangan, ed., *Pleasure, Profit, Proselytism*, pp. 67–85; Cunningham, *Leisure in the Industrial Revolution*, p. 127; [Political and Economic Planning], 'The football industry', *Planning*, 17, 26 (1951), 157, 160, 163.

[41] Ernest Ensor, 'The football madness', *Contemporary Review*, 74 (1898), 752–3; Mason, *Association Football and English Society*, pp. 33–4, 69, 138–9, 143, 150–8; Beattie, *Blackburn*, pp. 120–4; Lincoln Allison, 'Association football and the urban ethos', in J. D. Wirth and R. L. Jones, eds., *Manchester and Sao Paulo* (Stanford, 1978), pp. 216–18; David Russell, *Football and the English: A Social History of Association Football in England, 1863–1995* (Preston, 1997), pp. 12, 23, 56–7; Trainor, *Black Country Elites*, p. 345; Bill Murray, *The Old Firm: Sectarianism, Sport and Society in Scotland* (Edinburgh, 1984), pp. 1–3, 150ff; Mason, 'The Blues and the Reds', 123–6. For earlier parochialism expressed through recreation see Malcolmson, *Popular Recreations*, pp. 82–5; for small town rivalry over wakes and cock fighting and bull baiting see Walton and Poole, 'The Lancashire wakes', p. 107, and Reid, 'Beasts and brutes', pp. 19–21; and over brass-band contests see Russell, *Popular Music in England*, p. 226, cf. p. 245.

Playing and praying

to avoid losing control over the sport. By 1888 the most commercially advanced clubs formed the Football League (Preston, Everton, Burnley, Bolton, Blackburn and Accrington from Lancashire, and the Midlands' Aston Villa, Derby, Notts County, Stoke, West Bromwich Albion, and Wolverhampton Wanderers). Significantly, only two were from towns of less than 80,000 population. The League attracted 600,000 spectators during the first season, and was joined in 1892 by Sheffield's United and Wednesday. The Southern League (1894) also soon attracted very large numbers, especially to London clubs. The Scottish League (1890) sanctioned professionalism in 1893.[42]

Football grounds grew from simple roped-off fields in the 1870s to pitches with grandstands attached in the 1890s as spectator numbers swelled; by 1908–9, 6 million spectators were attracted, giving an average home crowd of 16,000. After 1918 crowds of several tens of thousands became commonplace in the new First and Second Divisions. The roar of the crowd, and its forceful flow through the streets surrounding a stadium, was another characteristic element of the modern townscape – captured artistically by Lowry's *The Football Ground* (1953).[43]

The great bulk of interwar 'shilling supporters' were still adult male working men, though improved living standards increased the proportion of labourers, enhancing football's function as a source of communal identity. There were many others who followed the game as readers of the football 'specials' (established in most towns by the 1890s), and as radio listeners from the 1920s. In large cities the press thus helped in generalising support beyond its traditional territories, as in Birmingham in response to Aston Villa's Cup and League success before 1914 and in the 1930s. Clubs in smaller towns, such as Swindon or Barnsley, were only able to survive the Depression (and the effects of rival attractions such as betting, motorcycles and cinema) by means of community action, such as supporters' club and fund-raising activities. Huge celebrations of cup victories drew upon this shadow support. Brass bands played 'See the conquering hero comes', civic dignitaries mounted receptions and enthusiastic crowds contained significant proportions of normally excluded women, creating an uplifting sense of community, which was then transmitted to the rest of the town by newspaper reports.[44]

[42] Mason, *Association Football and English Society*, pp. 64–78, 143; Russell, *Football and the English*, pp. 22–38; Holt, 'Working class football and the city', 11; Fraser, 'Developments in Leisure', p. 255.
[43] Fraser, 'Developments in leisure', pp. 253, 255; [Political and Economic Planning], 'The football industry', 158, 179; Holt, 'Working-class football and the city', 11; Simon Inglis, *The Football Grounds of England and Wales* (London, 1983); Mason, *Sport in Britain*, pp. 33–7, 48, 152; Russell, *Football and the English*, pp. 30–4, 37–8; Mervyn Levy, *The Paintings of L. S. Lowry* (London, 1975), plate 63, cf. plate 122, *Going to the Match*, 1928.
[44] Mason, *Association Football and English Society*, pp. 158–67, 187–95; Russell, '"Sporadic and curious"', 190, 194–5; Russell, *Football and the English*, pp. 63–5, 99; Jeff Hill, 'Rites of spring: cup finals and community in the North of England', in Jeff Hill and Jack Williams, *Sport and Identity in the North of England* (Keele, 1996), pp. 105, 107; Sutcliffe and Smith, *History of Birmingham*, p. 319; Fishwick, *English Football and Society*, pp. 5–6, 13, 16–17, 42–4, 56–8, 60–1, 66–7.

775

In 1950 football dominated sports' spectatorship: 40 million saw the ninety-two Football League clubs; 25 million watched non-League football and 15 million Scottish League matches. Rugby (8 million) and cricket (5 million) were large also-rans. It is true that gambling opportunities attracted 50 million people (particularly men) to mechanical greyhound racing (established in 1926 at Belle Vue, and at neon-lit tracks in most major towns within a year), and 'hero-worship' attracted 12 million (mainly female) spectators to speedway racing (which was introduced from Australia in 1928). Nevertheless, soccer, had much more social visibility, and it is not too much to say that popular civic identity was more generally created and sustained by the successes of sports teams than by any other factor.[45]

Yet despite football's popularity, in 1950 nearly five times more people went to cinemas than to every other form of taxable entertainment, and spent twice as much there. Cinema appealed to men, women and children – particularly to women. In Salford they especially liked 'the love tales, anything that made you cry'; in the 1930s male working-class Londoners tended to go only when taking a girl out or 'when they have nothing better to do'; the women pursued 'matinée idols' (as did bored lower-middle-class housewives lonely in the new suburbs). Nationally, 19 million people attended cinemas every week by 1939; in 1946, the peak year, attendances numbered more than 31 million, *every week*.[46]

However, cinema attendance was not proportional across the country. In general, the further north a town, the greater the cinema's popularity: thus, in 1950, of forty-nine provincial towns and cities with populations of more than 100,000 the notional 'average person' in Preston, Glasgow, Blackpool, Manchester and Newcastle attended the cinema at least once a week, whereas in Coventry, Luton, Plymouth and Bristol he or she attended only once a fortnight. Despite its large and luxurious cinemas the 'average Londoner' only went once every ten days.[47]

Why was cinema going generally more popular in northern towns? Contemporary commentators stressed that audiences in the 1940s were still preponderantly female, working class and young: factors which surely explain variations in cinema attendance. Thus Coventry and Luton (expanding towns with many male immigrants) had very low male/female ratios, and low cinema attendances. Similarly, working-class towns and cities like Preston, Glasgow and Sunderland

[45] [Political and Economic Planning], 'The football industry', 165, 169–70; Graves and Hodge, *The Long Week-End*, pp. 234–5; *New Survey of London Life and Labour*, IX, pp. 54–5; Mark Clapson, *A Bit of a Flutter: Popular Gambling and English Society, c. 1823–1961* (Manchester, 1992), pp. 141–63; Norman Baker, 'Going to the dogs – hostility to greyhound racing in Britain: puritanism, socialism, and pragmatism', *Journal of Sport History*, 23 (1996), 97–119.

[46] Calculated from Browning and Sorrell, 'Cinemas and cinema-going', 134–5; *New Survey of London Life and Labour*, IX, p. 46; Davies, *Leisure, Gender and Poverty*, pp. 76–7; B. S. Rowntree, *Poverty and Progress: A Second Social Survey of York* (London, 1941), p. 413; Jackson, *Middle Classes*, p. 123. [47] Browning and Sorrell, 'Cinemas and cinema-going', 139–41, 165.

were high on the cinema-going scale, whereas middle-class dormitories like Wallasey and Southend were low. Overcrowded housing surely drove people to the cinema in the twentieth century as to the pub in the nineteenth: hence Glasgow, Dundee and Tyneside's towns went frequently compared with less-crowded Norwich and Northampton. Finally, cinema audiences were predominantly young, and those of them who were still at school could surely afford to go less often. Certainly Bristol, whose citizens had the least propensity to go to the cinema, had more than one third of its over-fifteens in school, and Swansea and Plymouth showed similar contrasts.[48]

The very act of going to city-centre and even town-centre cinemas was a defining element of the urban experience because it was a night 'on the town'. However, Charlie Chaplin aside, the most popular films probably contributed more to the formation of a sense of national than of urban identity. In Bolton in the 1930s these were historical dramas, at one level providing escape from disagreeable social circumstances, but more important in providing role models and gender images of tough guys and womanly women within an increasingly patriotic, democratic, sentimental, public culture. Of course, demographically, by the 1930s the town was the nation.[49]

Critics (often inspired by nonconformity) feared passivity, the end of self-expression and the Americanisation of taste. J. B. Priestley, for instance, depicted cinema going as part of 'the new urban life' of the 1930s 'in which amusement was sold to a "passive drowsy crowd . . . who can do nothing for themselves"'. However, cinema goers were not simply passive spectators, but had pronounced tastes (voting with their feet in favour of entertaining American films vis-à-vis unexciting and stilted British-quota productions). Cinema going in the 1930s was a communal rather than an individualistic experience, through the experience of queuing, community singing and (in South Wales) attending the numerous cinemas established by miners' institutes. Large city cinemas incorporated dance halls and cafés.[50]

Priestley harked back to the lively musical and mutual improvement scene of his Bradford youth, and it is indeed impressive that there were some fifty choirs

---

[48] Kathleen Box, 'The cinema and the public', *The Social Survey*, new series, 106 (1946), 1–2; Richards, *Age of the Dream Palace*, pp. 12–15; for socio-economic differences between towns see C. A. Moser and W. Scott, *British Towns* (Edinburgh, 1961), pp. 104–5ff. Cf. R. McKibbin, *Classes and Cultures* (Oxford, 1998), p. 422.

[49] Jeffrey Richards, 'Cinemagoing in Worktown: regional film audiences in 1930s Britain', *Historical Journal of Film, Radio and Television*, 14 (1994), 154–7; J. Sedgwick, 'Cinema-going preferences in Britain in the 1930s', in Jeffrey Richards, ed., *The Unknown 1930: An Alternative History of the British Cinema, 1929–39* (London, 1998).

[50] Glass, *The Town and a Changing Civilisation*, pp. 111–12, 116; Priestley cited in Stephen Ridgwell, 'South Wales and the cinema in the 1930s', *Welsh History Review*, 17 (1995), 598–611; *New Survey of London Life and Labour*, IX, pp. 11 n. 1, 45; Rowntree and Lavers, *English Life and Leisure*, p. 256; Richards, 'The cinema and cinema-going in Birmingham', 46–7; Richards, *Age of the Dream Palace*, pp. 23–4ff.

and bands extant in Bradford and its environs in 1880–1900, playing Bach to Wagner. Such intense musical culture was widespread throughout the North and in South Wales – and in smaller towns rather than large cities, where occupational communities were stronger, patronage was more accepted and commercial entertainment was less influential. Yet even in London in the 1930s systematic social investigators found evidence that 'the human spirit' craved 'active means of self-expression', through sport, drama, dancing, gardening, flower growing, angling, pigeon fancying – they might also have mentioned knitting, needlework and pub sing-songs. Moreover, the London *Survey* actually found 'a marked increase in the popular appeal of music' since the 1890s, fostered by schools, the new adult education services, youth organisations and workplace and religious bodies, and expressed in bands, choirs and orchestras – with a musical society in 'nearly every suburb'. Nevertheless, parlour musical gatherings were eroded by radio and gramophones, and cinema was quintessentially 'the people's amusement'.[51]

(v) THE LEISURED CLASSES

Although the aristocracy and gentry revelled in country life, landowners were leading figures in early nineteenth-century urban leisure. Nevertheless, this came increasingly under a cloud of evangelical disapproval – directed particularly against theatres, taverns, pleasure gardens, and assemblies – and resulting in legal curbs on cock fighting, gaming and prize fighting. In the same period the middle classes began to seek the best of both town and country, to be domiciled in sylvan suburbs, but within reach of the city for work. Here they built an alternative social life, based on the belief that female virtue was best achieved through domesticity, and on careful association with people of like mind and like status in leisure activities – moulding and reinforcing respectable life styles in intimate arenas such as *soirées* and dinner parties. Yet 'club life', and 'night life', attracted both middle classes and landowners. There was interaction rather than total separation. Thus, cricket, hare coursing, race meetings and riding to hounds drew upon large middle-class segments, as did 'party excursion' to aristocratic seats. Similarly, the London 'Season' – and its focal points such as presentations at Court, the Royal Academy Exhibition, riding on Rotten Row – represented a climax of the hobnobbing, match-making, politicking lives of later nineteenth-century plutocratic 'Society'. Yet many of the houses in Mayfair and Belgravia,

[51] Russell, 'The pursuit of leisure', pp. 216–17; Russell, *Popular Music in England*, pp. 151–2, 162, 165–6, 281 n. 10; Ian Jones, *Brass Bands in York, 1833–1914* (York, 1995); Gareth Williams, *Valleys of Song Music and Society in Wales, 1840–1914* (Cardiff, 1998); *New Survey of London Life and Labour*, IX, pp. 10, 14–16, 47, 62–4; Jones, *Workers at Play*, pp. 63–75, 84, 143–63; Mass-Observation, *The Pub and the People*, pp. 255–62; Evans and Boyd, *The Use of Leisure in Hull*, pp. 17, 20–1; Zweig, *Women's Life and Labour*, p. 143. See also McKibbin, *Ideologies of Class*, pp. 141–8. Note also that library borrowers rose from 9 per cent to 20 per cent of the urban population between 1921 and 1939: Lionel R. McColvin, *The Public Library System of Great Britain* (London, 1942), p. 10.

Kensington and Bayswater were rented for the three to five months of the Season, and during much of that time 'Society' was taking trips out of town to Ascot, Epsom and Henley. Aristocratic and high bourgeois leisure was defined at least as much by country house parties, hunt balls and Cowes Week as it was by metropolitan pleasures (although the decline of the country house after 1918 altered the balance somewhat).[52]

Much middle-class leisure was socially exclusive and 'rational' in aspiration. Restricted-access Botanical Gardens notably exemplified both. They were 'rational' both in an educational or scientific sense, and in the sense of being sedate, refined, ordered, morally safe, in contrast to the sensual gratifications and brutality which were held to characterise both aristocratic and lower-class recreation. This critique was shaped by decades of philosophical distinction between 'rationals' and 'brutes', but most immediately by evangelical concepts of the consequences for personal salvation of 'worldliness', which had come to dominate most religious discourse by the 1830s. Thus evangelicals believed the theatre to be one of the broadest avenues to moral destruction, which, taken in conjunction with the pronounced sensitivity to class characterising these economically disturbed decades, depressed theatrical attendances: the often rowdy and unrestrained behaviour of both gallery 'gods' and 'young bloods' in the boxes was thoroughly distasteful to respectables. Changes in urban topography also played a role as formerly eligible districts began to deteriorate: thus Bristol's Theatre Royal was left behind in King Street when its richer patrons migrated from Queen Square to Clifton. Respectable ladies were loath to risk 'contamination' from 'women of the town', or (in Leicester) to risk being 'jostled by the

[52] F. M. L. Thompson, *English Landed Society in the Nineteenth Century* (London, 1963), pp. 99ff; G. R. Scott, *The History of Cockfighting* (London, 1957), esp. pp. 112–16; John Angell James, *The Christian Father's Present to his Children* (London, 1824; 3rd edn, 1825), pp. 204–6; Ian Bradley, *The Call to Seriousness: The Evangelical Impact on the Victorians* (London, 1976), ch. 5; Roger Munting, *An Economic and Social History of Gambling in Britain and the USA* (Manchester, 1996), pp. 21, 23, 151–2; John Timbs, *Clubs and Club Life in London* (London, 1899), pp. 205–7, 216–17; J. W. Hudson, *The History of Adult Education*, vol. VII (London, 1851), pp. 82–3, 110–24, 162–3; Alan White, 'Class, culture, and control: the Sheffield Athenaeum movement and the middle class', in Janet Wolff and John Seed, *The Culture of Capital* (Manchester, 1988), pp. 104–9, 111 n. 27; S. Nenadic, 'The Victorian middle classes', in Fraser and Maver, eds., *Glasgow*, II, pp. 289–91; A. Briggs, *Victorian Cities* (London, 1963), pp. 179, 256; Joyce, *Work, Society and Politics*, pp. 37–8; Katharine Chorley, *Manchester Made Them* (London, 1950), pp. 23–6, 135–6; Machray, *The Night Side of London*, pp. 161, 171; Walter Besant, *London in the Nineteenth Century* (London, 1912), pp. 260–1, 264; Ralph Nevill, *London Clubs* (London, 1911), pp. 156–7, 207; Ritchie, *Night Side*, pp. 144ff; J. Schlör, *Nights in the Big City* (London, 1998), p. 205; Raymond Carr, *English Foxhunting: A History* (London, 1976); David C. Itzkowitz, *Peculiar Privilege: A Social History of English Foxhunting* (Hassocks, 1977); Beattie, *Blackburn*, pp. 108–9; Mike Huggins, 'Culture, class and respectability: racing and the English middle classes in the nineteenth century', *International Journal of the History of Sport*, 2 (1994), 19–41, esp. 27–8; William Hutton, *History of Birmingham*, new edn (Birmingham, 1835), p. 130, for 'party excursion'; Mandler, *Rise and Fall of the Stately Home*, pp. 72–3, 242ff; L. Davidoff, *The Best Circles* (London, 1973), pp. 65, 86, and plates 15, 16–21; Simpson 'The West End of Glasgow', pp. 53, 81–4; D. Cannadine, *Lords and Landlords* (Leicester, 1980), pp. 211–12ff.

scum that eddies around the entrance of the theatres'. However, theatrical entertainment enjoyed in morally unsullied venues like hotel assembly rooms, temperance halls, town halls, or even the circus, was acceptable. In the upper ranks behaviour was policed by high entrance prices. 'At the opera' – noted a railway manager in 1855 – 'All the men with stiff necks, drawling gentlemanly voices, white kids, and an air which seemed to express their satiated familiarity with the whole thing. The ladies all handsome . . . brilliants, bare necks, and teeth like . . . sunbeam[s].'[53]

If religion enjoined a restricted recreational regime at this stage the ubiquitous churches nevertheless played a significant role in associational life as we shall see; this was especially so for bourgeois women, for whom they provided an important opportunity to transcend the limitations of domesticity via philanthropic and missionary charities, temperance organisations and fund-raising bazaars. For many such women, however, music must have played as important a role – building on the piano's parlour popularity. Music was both enjoyable and 'rational' because it aroused the emotions but not the passions, so women could safely participate and spectate, which they did in large numbers at festivals inherited from the eighteenth century in Birmingham, Leeds and Manchester, and established at Edinburgh in the 1810s, Norwich in the 1820s, Liverpool in the 1830s, Bradford and Leeds (again) in the 1850s, Glasgow in the 1860s and Brighton and Bristol in the 1870s. Metropolitan middle-class enthusiasm had founded the Philharmonic Society in 1813, and the Sacred Harmonic Society, whose annual concerts – seen (not altogether convincingly) as worship rather than entertainment – flourished at the home of the evangelicals, Exeter Hall, from 1834. Some cities had exclusive choirs such as Bristol's Royal Orpheus Glee Society, and private recitals formed a common feature of upper-class social life, but what was most remarkable about choral singing in nineteenth-century towns

[53] Simpson 'The West End of Glasgow', pp. 53–4; J. N. Tarn, 'Sheffield', in Simpson and Lloyd, eds., *Middle Class Housing in Britain*, pp. 177, 186; Bailey, *Leisure and Class*, pp. 35, 41, 55; Cunningham, *Leisure in the Industrial Revolution*, pp. 13, 76, 89–91, 156–7; Reid, 'Labour, leisure and politics', pp. 98–102, 170–4; L. Davidoff and C. Hall, *Family Fortunes* (London, 1987), p. 435; Nenadic, 'Victorian middle classes', pp. 288, 298 n.88; PP 1832 (679) VII, Select Committee on Dramatic Literature, 3–4; Doreen M. Rosman, *Evangelicals and Culture* (London, 1984), pp. 68–80, esp. 75–80; Reid, 'Popular theatre in Victorian Birmingham', pp. 66–7, 70–3, 76–7; Kathleen Barker, *The Theatre Royal Bristol, 1766–1966* (London, 1974), pp. 68, 75–6, 85, 88, 90, 94, 106, 119–20, 123–4, 126–7, 147–8, 155, 165–6; Ritchie, *Night Side*, pp. 174–5; J. C. Trewin, *Mr Macready* (London, 1955), pp. 132, 182; Faucher, *Manchester in 1844*, p. 21 n. 7; Besant, *London in the Nineteenth Century*, pp. 186, 271; Jeremy Crump, 'Patronage, pleasure and profit: a study of the Theatre Royal, Leicester 1847–1900', *Theatre Notebook*, 38 (1984), 84–6; Kathleen Barker, 'Thirty years of struggle. Entertainment in provincial towns between 1840 and 1870', *Theatre Notebook*, 39 (1985), 27–31, 71, 74–5; Michael R. Booth, *Theatre in the Victorian Age* (Cambridge, 1991), pp. 2–3, 17, 22; Jeremy Crump, 'Provincial music hall: promoters and public in Leicester, 1863–1929', in Bailey, ed., *Music Hall*, pp. 55–6; Beattie, *Blackburn*, p. 113; Temperley, *Music in Britain*, pp. 288, 307–10; Jackson, *Middle Classes*, p. 256; Leopold Turner, ed., *Fifty Years on the London & North Western Railway and Other Memoranda in the Life of David Stevenson* (London, 1891), p. 110.

was its widespread nature and social inclusivity. Most towns of over 20,000 population had a choral society by 1850, and 28 per cent of the Glasgow Choral Union were female, and only one third of the Leeds Philharmonic was middle class in the 1890s. Yet, subscription ticket holders made performances by such city choirs into major events in the social calendar of the wealthy. Thus, Manchester's burghers basked in the prestige of Hallé's Orchestra from 1858. The rentier population at spa and seaside resorts also encouraged the growth of numerous concert orchestras in the later nineteenth century – notably Dan Godfrey's Bournemouth Symphony Orchestra (1894). In London there were some attempts to broaden out audiences but George Bernard Shaw noted that 2s. 6d. for a standard concert was 'absolutely prohibitive for four out of five', and the regular Crystal Palace and Queen's Hall concerts were timed to coincide with the Season, ceasing when 'the moneyed classes' left London, recommencing when they returned. However, choral and philharmonic societies in Edgbaston, Dulwich, Ealing and Lewisham exemplify the flourishing of amateur musical societies in select suburbs.[54]

Evangelicals were key supporters of the temperance movement, which, together with greater status consciousness, was a prime factor bringing inns and taverns into disrepute – leading to confident assertions in the 1850s that 'no person above the rank of a labouring man or artisan would venture . . . into a public house'. This considerably oversimplified the situation because it meant 'no person' who could not afford to lose, or was not prepared to risk, a reputation with 'respectable society', and thus, in London, omitted sporting aristocrats, professional 'men about town', Bohemians, Freemasons in pub-based lodges and

[54] Harrison and Trinder, *Drink and Sobriety in an Early Victorian Country Town*, p. 48; G. Best, *Mid-Victorian Britain 1851–75*, rev. edn (St Albans, 1973), pp. 216–17; Frank Prochaska, *Women and Philanthropy in Nineteenth Century England* (Oxford, 1980), pp. 5–11, 47–72, 86–8; L. L. Shiman, '"Changes are dangerous": women and temperance in Victorian England', in Gail Malmgreen, ed., *Religion in the Lives of English Women, 1760–1930* (London, 1986), pp. 193–215; Brown, *Social History of Religion in Scotland*, pp. 141–3; Green, *Religion in the Age of Decline*, pp. 165–76; Davidoff and Hall, *Family Fortunes*, pp. 438–42; Cyril Ehrlich, *Social Emulation and Industrial Progress: The Victorian Piano* (Belfast, 1975); Cyril Ehrlich, *The Piano: A History* (London, 1976); Russell, *Popular Music in England*, pp. 199–200, 216–18; Walter Showell, *Dictionary of Birmingham* (Birmingham, 1885; repr., East Ardsley, 1969), p. 156; Vera Brittain, *Testament of Youth* (London, 1933; repr., London, 1978), pp. 23–5; E. D. Mackerness, *A Social History of English Music* (London, 1964), pp. 111–16, 127, 177, 180–3, 206–7, 230; Percy A. Scholes, *The Mirror of Music, 1844–1944* (London, 1947), pp. 160–6; William Weber, *Music and the Middle Classes* (London, 1975), pp. 100–4, 167; William Weber, 'Artisans in the concert life of mid-nineteenth-century London and Paris', *Journal of Contemporary History*, 13 (1978), 259; Temperley, *Music in Britain*, pp. 15, 115; Briggs, *Victorian Cities*, pp. 170–1, 174, 365; Joyce, *Work, Society and Politics*, p. 38; M. Kennedy, ed., *The Autobiography of Charles Hallé* (London, 1972), pp. 14–15, 122–6; Chorley, *Manchester Made Them*, p. 143; Fraser, 'Developments in leisure', p. 244; Russell, *Popular Music in England*, pp. 67, 199, 201–9; Barker, 'Entertainment in provincial towns', 72–3; Richard Roberts, 'The corporation as impresario: the municipal provision of entertainment in Victorian and Edwardian Bournemouth', in Walton and Walvin, eds., *Leisure in Britain*, pp. 149–50; Musgrave, *Musical Life of the Crystal Palace*, pp. 122–4 (for quotations from Shaw).

a large category of small and large business men who treated 'respectable' tavern 'smoke rooms' as their clubs. The constituency of men able and willing to flout religious and social respectability was joined by provincials taking advantage of the anonymity bestowed by the capital's size. Hence large audiences for *risqué*, well-lubricated entertainment in the Covent Garden area, as at Evans's Song and Supper Rooms, where:

> You find yourself in a room holding perhaps 1,200 gentlemen . . . heavy swells, moustached, and with white kids – officers in the army – scions of noble houses – country gentlemen, and merchants, and lawyers in town on business – literary men, medical students, and old fogies . . . rakes and men about town . . . [And] of course the majority . . . clerks, and commercial gents, and fellows in Government situations.[55]

The London pleasure map stretched westwards from Covent Garden across to Leicester Square and the Haymarket, and incorporated hotels, French restaurants, oyster shops, coffee-houses, Turkish divans and cafés, 'casinos' devoted to drinking and dancing, billiard rooms, gambling dens and brothels. Other cities also developed an unrespectable night life, in defiance of suburban norms and evangelicals' strictures – sometimes exposed in the press as 'fast young Birmingham' or 'The dark side of Glasgow.'[56]

The temporal rhythms of mid-century middle-class leisure are revealing. On Sundays the gay rich went riding on Rotten Row, but wet days were dull, for the zealous churchgoing and quiet seriousness of the pious rich and the respectable middle classes completely set the tone. (French visitors found Edinburgh Sundays even less agreeable.) Suburban religiosity was almost *de rigueur*, although the spirit of 'rational recreation' was honoured there in the breach as well as the observance. 'Very jolly' dances and dinner parties 'went on nearly every night in the week' in Edgbaston's grand houses, and Quadrille Parties at the Assembly Rooms on Wednesday and Friday evenings. Notwithstanding criticism of workers' Saint Mondays, some of these 'principal citizens of Birmingham' met on summer Monday afternoons at the Quoits and Bowls Club for 'a good plain

---

[55] PP 1852 XVII, Report of the Select Committee on Wine Duties, q. 3817; Ritchie, *Night Side*, pp. 15, 87–90, 94, 144ff; Eliezer Edwards, *The Old Taverns of Birmingham: A Series of Familiar Sketches* (Birmingham, 1879); Harrison, *Drink and the Victorians*, pp. 87–112; Harrison, 'Pubs', in Dyos and Wolff, eds., *The Victorian City*, I, pp. 172–4; Girouard, *Victorian Pubs*, pp. 12–13, 15, 45; Fraser, 'Developments in leisure', pp. 239, 241; Ronald Pearsall, *The Worm in the Bud* (Harmondsworth, 1971), pp. 313, 639 n. 8; Michael Mason, *The Making of Victorian Sexuality* (Oxford, 1994), p. 163.

[56] Ritchie, *Night Side*, pp. 59–63, 118, 183–90; Derek Hudson, *Munby: Man of Two Worlds* (London, 1972), pp. 22–3, 155–7; William H. Morton, *Sixty Years Stage Service, Being a Record of the Life of Charles Morton, the Father of the Halls* (London, 1905), p. 59; W. H. Holden, *They Startled Grandfather: Gay Ladies and Merry Mashers of Victorian Times* (London, 1950), pp. 59–110; *Birmingham Daily Mail*, 31 May 1871; *North British Daily Mail*, 27 Dec. 1870, cited in Nenadic 'Victorian middle classes', p. 287 n. 84.

dinner with the best of champagne', followed by sports, or 'a quiet rubber or a game of loo' for cash stakes.[57]

Social dancing was too deeply enjoyable as a physical recreation, too service-able as a courtship ritual, too flexible with regard to venue, to be repressed. Almack's – the leading London assembly – still attracted 'the élite of the land' and 'all the leaders of *bon ton*' in the 1850s. In the 1890s charity balls and 'high class' assemblies were held at leading hotels, while the expanding lower middle class was catered for by 'Teachers' Assemblies', or 'shilling hops' in places like the Kilburn Athenaeum or Holborn Town Hall – some of whom were drawn 'from the big drapery houses of Oxford Street, such as Peter Robinson, Marshall and Snelgrove, Jay's and John Lewis'.[58]

By the 1880s, middle-class women in London were considerably freer to take advantage of city-centre leisure independently (assisted by the development of department stores and restaurants, and their toilet facilities); in Glasgow and Edinburgh tea rooms played a similar role. Late Victorian cities also saw a move-ment for women's clubs, although most were for bridge-playing 'ladies' rather than independent 'women'; by 1899 there were twenty-four in London, two each in Edinburgh and Glasgow, and one each in Bath, Leeds, Liverpool and Manchester. But the First World War halted this trend to separate clubs. A shift in 'Society' from gender segregation and wartime seriousness was seen in the 'night clubs' of the twenties where 'bright young things' could shimmy the night away. In the thirties jazz and cabaret were enjoyed by 'the sort of businessmen who preferred bank-rolls to cheque-books – bookmakers, pools promoters, Soho vice kings, manufacturers from the provinces making whoopee away from their families . . . prostitutes, and . . . adventurers . . . including [military] officers and Colonial officials on leave' – illustrating a basic continuity of city night life across many previous decades.[59]

Meanwhile, as suburbia had expanded in the second half of the nineteenth century so too had the scope of suburban extra-domestic recreation, particu-larly as regards drama and sport. Amateur theatricals constitute an under-explored aspect of suburban social life from the 1870s, really taking off as 'a

---

[57] Wigley, *Rise and Fall of the Victorian Sunday*, pp. 82–3; Taine, *Notes on England*, pp. 10, 283; *Birmingham Journal*, 8 Nov. 1856; quotations from Tom Collins, *School and Sport: Recollections of a Busy Life* (London, 1905), pp. 46, 64. See also discussion of 1851 religious census below.

[58] Francis Rust, *Dance in Society* (London, 1967), chs. 9–13; Holden, *They Startled Grandfather*, pp. 36, 74–9; Chorley, *Manchester Made Them*, p. 145; Winifred Holtby, *The Crowded Street* (London, 1924; London, 1981), pp. 54–5, 92–101; Philip J. S. Richardson, *The Social Dances of the Nineteenth Century in England* (London, 1960), pp. 111, 117–18, 120–1; Machray, *The Night Side of London*, pp. 152–9.

[59] David Rubinstein, *Before the Suffragettes: Women's Emancipation in the 1890s* (Brighton, 1986), pp. 222–6; Jackson, *Middle Classes*, pp. 113, 260; Collier and Lang, *Just the Other Day*, pp. 52–7; Graves and Hodge, *The Long Week-End*, pp. 119–22, 225–7; Robert Murphy, *Smash and Grab: Gangsters in the London Underworld* (London, 1993), pp. 7–9.

sociable entertaining pastime' after the First World War, with over 1,200 amateur groups in Britain by the 1930s (by no means all middle class). However, the most distinctive innovations in middle-class leisure were sporting, especially tennis and golf. Before the 1870s cricket was the most sophisticated suburban sport, providing young commercial and professional men with pleasant summer exercise, and, by association, affirming gentlemanly aspirations. There was little for women but croquet until young suburbans took up the newly invented lawn tennis in the 1870s. It spread rapidly through the medium of the club: one was founded in the very first year of Bedford Park garden suburb, Ealing, in 1879, and Nottingham's exclusive Park estate had virtually no social facilities but tennis courts. Badminton and table tennis also became popular, but lawn tennis took the palm, with affiliated clubs multiplying tenfold by 1930. Tennis appealed to the energetic young; their marriage-broking, status-conscious mothers valued tennis pavilion teas and dances. Golf had some democratic credentials when played on Scottish seaside links, but in club form was a very different phenomenon. Male suburbanites took to the game with alacrity – seeking moderate exercise (especially in middle age) in an associational form which protected or enhanced social status. Thus Glasgow had twenty private golf courses for business types by 1900, compared with two public courses. In England, there were 1,100 courses by 1914, some of them in small country towns and seaside resorts. Stanmore, Middlesex, was typical of the suburban type in requiring two proposers for new members, granting 'Ladies' and some 'artisans' inferior status, and excluding Jews. In industrial towns like Blackburn, with no extensive middle-class suburbs, the golf club (1894), served the whole town, kept exclusive by a limit of seventy members and a 2 guinea annual subscription. Golf and tennis contributed to the liberalisation of the middle-class Sunday; nearly half England's courses were open by 1914, and nearly all by the 1920s (although Calvinist Scotland and nonconformist Wales resisted far longer). Cycling, boating and motoring also played their part.[60]

[60] Jackson, *Middle Classes*, pp. 95–100, 240–4, 275–6, 286, 290; J. L. Garvin, *The Life of Joseph Chamberlain*, 3 vols. (London, 1932–5), pp. 46–8, 74–5; Newspaper Cuttings, Birmingham Drama, 5 vols. (Birmingham Reference Library, 1871–82); A. L. Matthison, *Ladies Long Loved and Other Essays* (London, 1950), pp. 36, 143–6; Cannadine, *Lords and Landlords*, p. 211; Murfin, *Lake Counties*, pp. 188–91; G. W. Bishop, ed., *The Amateur Dramatic Year Book and Community Theatre Handbook* (London, 1929), vol. VII, pp. 87–179; *New Survey of London Life and Labour*, IX, pp. 63–4; Nicholl, *English Drama*, pp. 78–88; cf. Jones, *Workers at Play*, pp. 154–60, and Norman Dennis, F. M. Henriques and C. Slaughter, *Coal is Our Life* (London, 1957), p. 134; John Lowerson, *Sport and the English Middle Classes, 1879–1914* (Manchester, 1993), pp. 97, 105, 110–11, 130–1, 242; Fraser, 'Developments in leisure', p. 257; Helen Walker, 'Lawn tennis', in Mason, ed., *Sport in Britain*, pp. 248–50; Dixon and Muthesius, *Victorian Architecture*, p. 68; K. C. Edwards, 'The Park Estate, Nottingham', in Simpson and Lloyd, *Middle Class Housing in Britain*, pp. 161–2; James Kenward, *The Suburban Child* (Cambridge, 1955), pp. 24–8; Jackson, *The Middle Classes*, pp. 206 (plate 27), 291; Rubinstein, 'Cycling in the 1890s', 48–9, cf. 61–5, 68; Graves and Hodge, *The Long Week-End*, p. 233; John Lowerson, 'Golf and the making of myths', in Grant Jarvie and

London's suburbs were the most enormous and socially differentiated, but their very size and prosperity encouraged an impressive range of activities. Moreover, leisure activities were integral to their interwar extension, as many plots of land were reserved for tennis courts, and even golf courses were constructed, as developers' inducements to house purchasers. Finally, however, as they grew larger it became hard to say exactly when suburbs ceased to function as suburbs and more as towns within the conurbation increasingly attracting commercial leisure facilities: roller skating in the 1870s, theatres and music halls in the 1890s, cinemas in the early 1900s, *palais de danse* in the 1920s, and ice-skating in the thirties. Although the middle-classes included some of the most serious critics of mass leisure, their young were among its enthusiastic aficionados.[61]

(vi) CHALLENGES FOR THE CHURCHES

We turn now from the indirect impact of religious sentiment on urban leisure to the much-debated impact of industrial urbanism upon religious practice. An early and significant religious response to the development of industrial populations may be seen in the voluntary Sunday Schools movement which commenced in Gloucester in 1780 and quickly spread to Manchester and other northern and Midland industrial towns. The schools' aims of teaching factory children to read the Scriptures, and to withdraw them from the temptations of the streets, were buttressed after 1800 by those 'steam engines of the moral world', the religious day schools. The second major response – commencing during the post-Napoleonic War unrest – was 'Church extension'. Parliament acted to remedy the discrepancies between population and Anglican places of worship which were believed to facilitate the flourishing both of Methodism and irreligious popular radicalism. For several decades after 1818 the pillars, spires, towers and high-windowed gables of hundreds of new churches rose into sooty town air, summoning their urban denizens to worship. A similar process occurred in Scotland. Thirdly, and concurrently, there was an attempt to apply

Graham Walker, eds., *Scottish Sport and the Making of the Nation: Ninety Minute Patriots?* (Leicester, 1994), esp. pp. 78–85; R. H. Trainor, 'The elite', in Fraser and Maver, eds., *Glasgow*, II, p. 246; John Guest, *The Best of Betjeman* (Harmondsworth, 1978), pp. 228–30; Lowerson, 'Golf', pp. 189, 205–8; Richard Holt, 'Golf and the English suburb: class and gender in a London club, *c.* 1890–*c.* 1960', *Sports Historian*, 18 (1998), 76–89; Beattie, *Blackburn*, pp. 58–61, 123, 157; Wigley, *Rise and Fall of the Victorian Sunday*, p. 159; Mandler, *Rise and Fall of the Stately Home*, pp. 151, 214, 231–2, 242, 292.

[61] Besant, *London in the Nineteenth Century*, pp. 17, 30, 262–3; Bailey, *Leisure and Class*, p. 156; Penny Summerfield, 'Patriotism and empire. Music-hall entertainment 1870–1914', in John M. Mackenzie, ed., *Imperialism and Popular Culture* (Manchester, 1986), p. 24; Richardson, *The Social Dances*, p. 118; Jackson, *Middle Classes*, pp. 284–5, 317; A. A. Jackson, *Semi-Detached London* (London, 1973), pp. 49–51, 176–80; John Bale, *Sport and Place: A Geography of Sport in England, Scotland and Wales* (London, 1982), pp. 103, 158; Graves and Hodge, *The Long Week-End*, p. 293.

in towns the essentially rural model of pastoral ministry. The most influential theorist of this movement was the Presbyterian Church of Scotland minister, Dr Thomas Chalmers. Whereas the church in the countryside buttressed the social order – using patronage and charity to invoke deference – Chalmers observed in 'every large manufacturing city . . . a mighty unfilled space between the high and the low'. This, he avowed, should be filled with systematic 'ties of kindliness' – district visiting by elders and Sunday School teachers – transferring some of the evangelical energy for foreign missions to heathens in the city of Glasgow itself. Essentially, Chalmers sought to recreate in the manufacturing towns the 'moral regimen' which he felt characterised rural society (and, indeed, smaller provincial towns). Impressed by Chalmers, the evangelical John Bird Sumner (1829–41) set on foot a programme of lay visitations, home instruction and further schooling in Chester diocese (incorporating rapidly urbanising Lancashire), to overcome 'the general state . . . of total apathy' and 'religious destitution'. Conversely, one of the best-known exemplars of a vigorous urban ministry on the rural model was the high churchman, W. F. Hook, of Coventry (1828-37) and Leeds (1837–59), promoting education, sick-dispensing, and self-help institutions, preaching the Gospel, and supporting the Ten Hour movement.[62]

The subdivision of huge parishes was a necessary, though insufficient, step in

[62] A. P. Wadsworth, 'The first Manchester Sunday schools', in M. W. Flinn and T. C. Smout, eds., *Essays in Social History* (Oxford, 1974), pp. 102–5, 108–9; T. W. Laqueur, *Religion and Respectability: Sunday Schools and Working Class Culture 1780–1850* (New Haven, 1976); K. D. M. Snell, 'The Sunday School movement in England and Wales', *P&P*, 164 (1999), 122–68, esp. 139; John Hurt, *Education in Evolution: Church, State, Society and Popular Education 1800–1870* (London, 1971), ch. 1; Michael Sanderson, *Education, Economic Change and Society in England 1780–1870*, 2nd edn (Basingstoke, 1991), pp. 13–14, 19–21; M. H. Port, *Six Hundred New Churches: A Study of the Church Building Commission, 1818–56, and its Church-Building Activities* (London, 1961), pp. 60, 79–81; A. D. Gilbert, *Religion and Society in Industrial England* (London, 1976), p. 130; Dixon and Muthesius, *Victorian Architecture*, ch. 6; Chris Brooks and Andrew Saint, eds., *The Victorian Church: Architecture and Society* (Manchester, 1995), chs. 1, 3 and 4; Brown, *Social History of Religion in Scotland*, pp. 133–4, 141–2; E. P. Hennock, 'The Anglo-Catholics and church extension in Victorian Brighton', in M. J. Kitch, ed., *Studies in Sussex Church History* (London, 1981), pp. 173–88; David E. H. Mole, 'The Victorian town parish: rural vision and urban mission', in D. Baker, ed., *The Church in Town and Countryside* (Oxford, 1979), pp. 361–71; Inglis, *Churches and the Working Classes*, pp. 6–8; Gilbert, *Religion and Society in Industrial England*, p. 130; T. Chalmers, *The Christian and Civic Economy of Large Towns* (Glasgow, 1821-6), cited in B. I. Coleman, *The Idea of the City in Nineteenth-Century Britain* (London, 1973), pp. 35, 42–5; Stewart J. Brown, *Thomas Chalmers and the Godly Commonwealth in Scotland* (Oxford, 1982), pp. 91–151, esp. 101–4; Boyd Hilton, *The Age of Atonement: The Influence of Evangelicalism on Social and Economic Thought, 1795–1865* (Oxford, 1988), pp. 55–70; H. D. Rack, 'Domestic visitation: a chapter in early nineteenth century evangelism', *JEcc.Hist.*, 24 (1973), 359; Robin Gill, *The Myth of the Empty Church* (London, 1993), p. 115; M. Smith, *Religion in Industrial Society* (Oxford, 1994), pp. 100, 103–4ff.; H. W. Dalton, 'Walter Farquhar Hook, Vicar of Leeds: his work for the Church and the town, 1837–1848', *Publications of the Thoresby Society. Miscellany*, 19 (1990), 28–79; Sheridan Gilley, 'Walter Farquhar Hook, vicar of Leeds', in Alastair Mason, ed., *Religion in Leeds* (Stroud, 1994), pp. 50–9; David E. H. Mole 'Challenge to the Church. Birmingham, 1815–65', in Dyos and Wolff, eds., *The Victorian City*, II, pp. 28–9, 170, 276.

this process of Anglican revitalisation. Thus evangelicals also initiated societies of volunteer lay workers, such as the Religious Tract Society, or District Provident Societies. In 1826 in Glasgow, and more generally from 1835, extra-parochial, inter-denominational City Missions were established systematically to encourage Bible reading, and conversion. Thrift, providence, hygiene and self-improvement were taught as necessary preconditions for living a Christian life. The realisation of the depth of popular alienation in the 1830s and 1840s lent urgency to this work, resulting in the employment of professional workers, and attacks on pleasure fairs and Owenite 'Infidels'.[63]

The participation of nonconformists in City Missions illustrates the mitigation but not the elimination of the fierce rivalries between the establishment and dissent. Some Congregationalists and Unitarians developed their own impressive auxiliaries, doing the kind of mission and charity work which characterised the Anglican parochial ideal, as at Carr's Lane in Birmingham. They also addressed the general education of their members through 'mutual improvement societies', and, portentously, in the 1840s the more rationalist denominations like the Unitarians established explicitly recreational offshoots, planting seeds which were to flourish dramatically in the second half of the century. The way had been shown by the Sunday Schools through their Whit Walks, anniversary festivals and railway excursions (from the very inception of the Liverpool to Manchester line in 1830). But it was in the 1840s that chess, singing classes, musical entertainments, tea parties, excursions, even dances, were developed for adult members, to meet a desire for social fellowship and as a counterforce to commercial entertainment, and to 'moralise' the working people it was hoped to evangelise. A readiness to embrace recreation for religious purposes was limited at this stage by the continuing influence of puritanism, but it was also reflected in the foundation of Bands of Hope, providing rational recreation for children as a prophylaxis against intemperance, and the YMCA, directed at the salvation of young shopworkers. The specialised nature of both organisations reflected the increasing complexity of urban society.[64]

How effective were these decades' work in dealing with religious 'destitution'? The unique official census of religious attendance in 1851 offered little

---

[63] Lewis, *Lighten their Darkness*, pp. 4, 34–6, 56, 60, 63–78, 169–75; E. R. Wickham, *Church and People in an Industrial City* (London, 1957), p. 156; Geoffrey Robson, 'The failures of success: working class evangelists in early Victorian Birmingham', in D. Baker, ed., *Religious Motivation* (Studies in Church History, 15, Oxford, 1978), pp. 381–91; Brown, *Social History of Religion in Scotland*, pp. 17, 32, 143–5, 153; Edward Royle, *The Victorian Church in York* (York, 1983), pp. 35–9.

[64] *VCH*, Warwickshire, VII; W. B. Stephens, ed., *The City of Birmingham* (London, 1964), p. 420; cf. Cox, *The English Churches in a Secular Society*, pp. 53–4; Reid, 'Labour, leisure and politics', pp. 123–4; Barry Haynes, *Working Class Life in Victorian Leicester* (Leicester, 1991); D. A. Reid, 'Religion, recreation and the working class: Birmingham 1844–1885', *Bulletin of the Society for the Study of Labour History*, 51 (1986), 9; Lilian L. Shiman, 'The Band of Hope movement: respectable recreation for working-class children', *Victorian Studies*, 18 (1973), 49–74; C. J. Binfield, *George Williams and the YMCA* (London, 1973), chs. 5–8.

encouragement. Depending on interpretation, it suggests that between 40 and 50 per cent of the British population were in church on census Sunday. Today this would be remarkable, but most agreed with census commissioner Horace Mann that it signified an 'alarming' and 'sadly formidable' proportion of the population were 'habitual neglecters' of public worship. As the middle classes were 'distinguished' by their devotions, and the upper classes ranked regular church attendance as 'amongst the recognized proprieties of life', most of the missing, Mann opined, belonged to 'the labouring myriads' or 'artizans', who comprised an 'absolutely insignificant' portion of the congregation, 'especially in cities and large towns'. What were the causes? 'Social distinctions', as manifested particularly in pew rents, made it difficult to overcome the already profound gulf separating 'the workman from his master'. Similarly, differences in social 'station and pursuits' led to cynicism regarding the clergy. Even more profoundly, the 'social burdens' of 'the poor', particularly 'the vice and filth which riot in their crowded dwellings', denied opportunities for religious reflection: 'the masses of our working population . . . the skilled and unskilled labourer alike . . . hosts of minor shopkeepers and Sunday traders . . . and . . . miserable denizens of courts and crowded alleys' were 'engrossed by the demands, the trials or the pleasures of the passing hour, and ignorant or careless of a future'. However, although this led to 'a genuine repugnance to religion itself', there remained 'that vague sense of some tremendous want, and aspirings after some indefinite advancement' which offered an opportunity to a more 'aggressive' missionary activity by the churches. Mann cited the 'zeal and perseverance' of Methodists and Mormons and street preaching. Hence there were solutions which went beyond the obvious one of removing pew rents. 'Ragged Churches' and mission halls could be built where there would be 'a total absence of all class distinctions', lay preachers could be used to confound suspicion of clergy motives, the religious contribution to charity could be more overt and, above all, measures taken to improve housing. All these would be more sensible than construction work, for, already, 'teeming populations often . . . surround[ed] half empty churches'.[65]

How valid was Mann's characterisation of the cities as black holes for the churches? Post-war scholars were in no doubt. E. R. Wickham's study of Sheffield claimed that alienation of the urban working-class population from the

[65] W. S. F. Pickering, 'The 1851 census – a useless experiment?', *British Journal of Sociology*, 18 (1967), 392, 394; David M. Thompson, 'The religious census of 1851', in Richard Lawton, ed., *The Census and Social Structure: An Interpretative Guide to Nineteenth Century Censuses for England and Wales* (London, 1978), p. 244; Michael R. Watts, ed., *Religion in Victorian Nottinghamshire: The Religious Census of 1851*, 2 vols. (Nottingham, 1988), vol. I, p. xiv; for the most recent guide to the literature on 1851 see Clive D. Field, 'The 1851 religious census of Great Britain: a bibliographical guide for local and regional historians', *The Local Historian*, 27 (1997), 194–217; PP 1852–3 LXXXIX, Census 1851, Religious Worship [England & Wales], pp. clviii–clxii. For recent questioning of the effectiveness of home missions see M. Hewitt, 'The travails of domestic visiting: Manchester, 1830–70', *HR*, 71 (1998), 205–6, 217.

churches existed 'from the time of their very emergence in the new towns'. The 'index of attendance' devised by K. S. Inglis stood at 71 for small towns and rural areas as compared with only 50 for 'large towns', and Inglis followed Mann in arguing that 'the absent millions lived in large . . . industrial towns'. Subsequently, Harold Perkin concluded that 'the larger the town the smaller the proportion of the population attending any place of worship; and . . . the larger the town, with the exception of London, the smaller the proportion of Anglican to all attenders'. Like Chalmers, Perkin related working-class indifference to the decline of social dependency in towns, and he believed migrants drifted from rural Anglicanism to nonconformity in small towns, and to indifference in cities. This historiographical trend was reinforced by A. D. Gilbert's work which emphasised a deep link between urbanisation and 'institutional secularisation'.[66]

However, this consensus was challenged in the 1970s, and much subsequent work has followed a revisionist line, doubting whether the influence of urbanisation on religion was so sweeping as had been assumed. Hugh McLeod utilised the 1851 and subsequent unofficial newspaper censuses from the 1880s to argue the primacy of regional and status-system distinctions over simple rural/urban distinctions. Scepticism about urbanisation's effects was stated most trenchantly by Callum Brown in 1988, who utilised regression analysis to suggest that there was 'no statistically significant relationship between churchgoing rate and population size or growth for towns or cities' in England and Wales in 1851. Nor, he argued, was population size of statistical significance for Scottish attendance. Similarly, K. D. M. Snell's investigation of the North Midland figures for 1851 found only small, rather unconvincing, correlations between urbanisation, industrialisation and low overall religious attendance.[67]

Yet, in 1992, Steve Bruce fundamentally questioned the statistical validity of Brown's case – explaining that the divergence of his regressions from Brown's was a consequence of the application of more reliable procedures and, particularly, of Brown's failure to allow for the distortion caused by the unique case of London. Bruce argues that his results essentially reaffirm the message given by the work of Wickham and Inglis. Thus, Brown's statistical case must currently be regarded as 'not proven'. However, this critique of the statistical basis of

---

[66] Wickham, *Church and People in an Industrial City*, pp. 14, 45–8, 177–8; Inglis, *Churches and the Working Classes*, pp. 275–82ff; Harold Perkin, *The Origins of Modern English Society, 1780–1880* (London, 1969), pp. 200, 202; Gilbert, *Religion and Society in Industrial England*, pp. viii, 113; see also K. S. Inglis, 'Patterns of religious worship in 1851', *JEcc.Hist.*, 2 (1960), 82; Pickering, 'The 1851 census – a useless experiment?', 402–3; Chadwick, *The Victorian Church*, II, p. 219; R. B. Currie, A. D. Gilbert, and Lee Horsley, *Churches and Church-Goers: Patterns of Church Growth in the British Isles since 1700* (Oxford, 1977), pp. 99ff.

[67] H. McLeod, 'Class, community and region: the religious geography of nineteenth-century England' in M. Hill, ed., *A Sociological Yearbook of Religion in Britain* (London, 1973), pp. 30, 32–41, 51–3, 66 n. 44; C. G. Brown, 'Did urbanisation secularise Britain?', *UHY* (1988), 6–8; K. D. M. Snell, *Church and Chapel in the North Midlands* (Leicester, 1991), pp. 2, 25–7.

revisionism has yet to be widely appreciated. Partly, no doubt, this is because work on regional sources has continued to show support for the revisionist case. Thus Robin Gill used Episcopal Visitation Returns to show that churchgoing in twelve large towns – including seven cotton factory towns – even grew during 1821-51, the fastest period of urban growth. And Mark Smith's study of the classic industrialising district of Oldham and Saddleworth showed that the efforts of a vigorous evangelical clergy bore fruit in an impressive 45 per cent of the eligible population attending church in 1851.[68]

All in all it is too sweeping to characterise cities and large towns as essentially hostile to religion; regional and class analysis offers a more convincing explanation of the relationship between urbanisation and churchgoing in Britain in the nineteenth century. In 1851, attendances were highest in England south of the line from the Severn to the Wash, which were also the areas of greatest Anglican strength, where squire and parson joined hand in hand to try to dominate the mental, as well as the material, universe of the farm labourer. Within these areas, with the important exception of London, towns and cities generally had higher rates than the average for all cities: some were high-status cathedral cities, health resorts and county towns like Bath, Gloucester and Hastings (with many inhabitants concerned about the 'proprieties of life') but they also included Plymouth and Bristol. This once again suggests the importance of continuities between country and city. Deriving initially from the high proportion of immigrants who made up burgeoning urban populations, such continuities are also illustrated by urban superstitions and rituals matching those found in the countryside, and important to some popular religiosity in London even in the 1930s. Conversely, church attendance was generally weakest in the numerous industrial towns and townships situated in the large upland parishes of the Midlands and North, and lacking the social compulsions associated with southern landed estates. Thus the towns of lowest attendance were low-status industrial towns such as Birmingham, the Potteries and Sheffield; and most towns in Lancashire, the West Riding and the mining towns of the North-East were well below their regional averages. Nevertheless, some, like the Black Country towns and the Welsh industrial towns of Wrexham and Llanelli stood well above them – local factors, such as evangelistic blitzes on the exploited workforces of the Black Country, could affect regional patterns.[69]

[68] Steve Bruce, 'Pluralism and religious vitality', in S. Bruce, ed., *Religion and Modernisation* (Oxford, 1992), pp. 184–5; Gill, *The Myth of the Empty Church*, pp. 95, 100–1, 188, 298; Smith, *Religion in Industrial Society*, pp. 252–3, 269.

[69] McLeod, 'Class, community and region', pp. 31–43; cf. John D. Gay, *The Geography of Religion in England* (London, 1971), pp. 57–63; Paul S. Ell and T. R. Slater, 'The religious census of 1851: a computer-mapped survey of the Church of England', *Journal of Historical Geography*, 20 (1994), 44–61; C. G. Brown, 'The mechanism of religious growth in urban societies. British cities since the eighteenth century', in H. McLeod, ed., *European Religion in the Age of Great Cities* (London, 1995), pp. 254–7; Sarah Williams, 'Urban popular religion and the rites of passage', in McLeod,

Nonconformity had been the most popular religious tradition in towns in 1851, and was even more so by the 1880s, when nearly six in ten attenders were chapelgoers; only Bath and Hastings had more than half of their congregations in Anglican churches. Nevertheless, the Church of England remained the largest *single* denomination in most other towns and cities, reflecting its historical centrality. The major nonconformist groups (Wesleyan Methodists, Baptists and Congregationalists) outstripped the Anglicans in Leicester, Burnley and Bradford, but groups with humbler adherents, like the Primitive Methodists, were relatively weak in urban areas, except in Hull (the missionary headquarters of its joint-founder, William Clowes), and Scarborough (its outpost up the coast). Roman Catholicism was strongest in Liverpool (where it was the largest denomination) and in other areas in the West Midlands and North-West most subject to Irish immigration like Warrington, the Potteries and Barrow-in-Furness.[70]

If there was no simple relationship between religious attendance and the size of towns, marked contrasts *within* urban areas firmly support the notion of a clear relationship between religion and class. Towns were not undifferentiated wholes. Hence, as McLeod pointed out, in the 1880s' newspaper censuses low-status districts within cities had much lower church attendances than their high-status counterparts. Thus, elegant Edgbaston and insalubrious Saltley were very different within the overall 'Anglican' city of Birmingham, which had very low attendance rates (like the region of which it was part). Classy Clifton and 'poor and populous' St Philip and St Jacob, had contrasting, though high, rates, like their city, Bristol, and its region (compare numbers 2, 26, 39 and 45 on Figure 23.2). For similar reasons there were also important correspondences as regards denominational allegiances between high- and low-status areas of different towns. As Figure 23.2 suggests, attendance in high-status districts, wherever they were, tended disproportionally towards the established church (above all, in the examples given, in Birmingham's Moseley district, and in Hampstead), and towards the major nonconformist churches (in East Leicester particularly). By contrast, in low-status (working-class) areas Anglicanism was noticeably less

ed., *European Religion*, pp. 223, 233–4; Sarah C. Williams, *Religious Belief and Popular Culture in Southwark, c. 1880–1939* (Oxford, 1999); Geoffrey Robson, 'Between town and countryside: contrasting patterns of church-going in the early Victorian Black Country', in Baker, ed., *The Church in Town and Countryside*, pp. 401–14.
[70] Inglis, 'Patterns of religious worship in 1851', 85–6; McLeod, 'Class, community and region', pp. 46–7; Gill, *The Myth of the Empty Church*, p. 305; Hugh McLeod, *Religion and Society in England 1850–1914* (London, 1996), p. 34; Gilbert, *Religion and Society in Industrial England*, pp. 62–5; H. B. Kendall, *The Origin and History of the Primitive Methodist Church* (London, 1906), vol. I, pp. 361–409, II, pp. 111–14, 362–3, 458–63; Stubley, *A House Divided*, pp. 33–7, 57; Clive Field, 'The social structure of English Methodism, eighteenth–twentieth-centuries', *British Journal of Sociology*, 28 (1977), 199–225; David Hempton, *The Religion of the People* (London, 1996), p. 201; McLeod, 'New perspectives on Victorian working-class religion', 41–4.

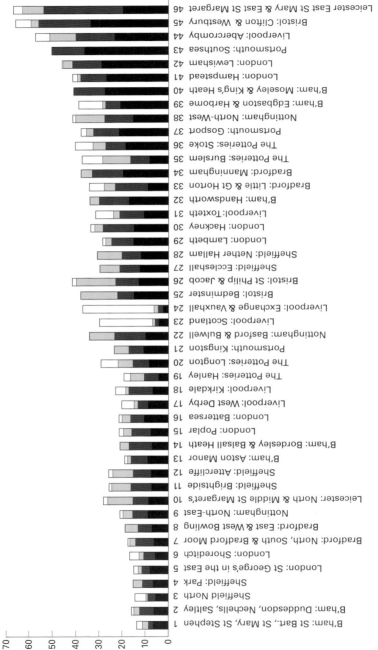

Figure 23.2 Urban religious differentiation: attendance rates in selected areas 1881

1–12 = low-status areas
13–26 = mainly working-class areas
27–38 = socially mixed areas
39–46 = high-status areas

Source: drawn from data in H. McLeod, 'Class, community and region; the religious geography of nineteenth-popular, and minor nonconformity was correspondingly stronger. Thus, major differences within urban areas certainly vindicate Mann with regards to the importance of class, and such findings are borne out by other detailed local studies of different parts of London. However, it is worth noticing that the strength of Roman Catholicism also implies the importance of religion as a symbol of national or sectarian rather than class identity – a factor which may also help to explain some of the social reach of Protestantism in Lancashire, and the vitality of separate Protestant and Catholic Whit Walks.[71]

(vii) BUILDING A RESPONSE

If class was the main factor conditioning non-churchgoing, how effective were the proposed solutions? Pew rents were both the immediate cause and symptom of the deeper social distinctions, argued Mann. There was much to this analysis, particularly in relation to the poorest, but the problem was not straightforward. Some form of income generation was an economic necessity (especially for the non-established churches lacking endowments), and pew rents were hallowed by time, and legitimate within the framework of an unequal society of ranks. Thus in Oldham and Saddleworth rents could be very low (a farthing per quarter in Saddleworth before 1850), were sometimes not rigidly enforced, and those who rented the cheaper pews felt that they were establishing their place in the parish. From this perspective it was not so shocking that 53 per cent of seats in English churches in 1851 were pew rented. However, rents were heavily criticised from the 1840s, by both evangelicals and Tractarians, as an 'intrusion of human pride' into God's House, and a reform campaign resulted, with early successes in Chesterfield, Pimlico and Clerkenwell. These criticisms represented a realisation – hastened by Chartist demonstrations early in the decade – that many had come to resent deeply such overt markers of their inferiority. The effect of class society was exemplified graphically by the case of the Glasgow 'city churches' of the Church of Scotland where pew-renting arrangements moved from being socially inclusive to exclusive in the first decades of the century. Middle-class demand pushed up the average rent to half-a-guinea for six months by 1832–3 – a trend reinforced by greater middle-class sensitivity to personal hygiene – and cheap seats were abandoned. It is easy to see how pew renting could alienate, though there was self- as well as enforced exclusion. Thus, even where new free seats were provided in other Glasgow churches poor parishioners rejected them – especially those who had known better times, and who

---

[71] McLeod, 'Class, community and region', pp. 31–43; *The Churchgoer, Being a Series of Sunday Visits to the Various Churches of Bristol* (Bristol, 1850 edn), pp. 84–5; cf. Thompson, 'The religious census of 1851', pp. 241–88; Cox, *The English Churches in a Secular Society*, pp. 31–3; Joyce, *Work, Society and Politics*, pp. 250–62; Neville Kirk, *The Growth of Working Class Reformism in Mid-Victorian England* (London, 1985), ch. 7.

therefore felt humiliated by the concession (a feeling reinforced by a lack of decent clothing). This sense of proud independence was impressively exemplified in certain other non-established Glasgow and Edinburgh churches where pew tariffs were fixed by congregational vote; here there were few seats at less than 3s., and the cheapest seats tended to go un-let. Thus, despite the indubitable off-putting effects of pew renting, analysis of the social composition of the membership of several Glasgow churches from the 1820s to the 1860s has demonstrated that at least 60 per cent, and sometimes as many as three-quarters, had working-class (particularly artisan) occupations. Consequently, in many places pew-rent reformers achieved little until the early 1900s, when the idea of abolition gained ground as parsons in the age of the 'social gospel' became uncomfortable with them – but also because mounting church debt prompted the adoption of different methods of fund raising, as in Halifax and Keighley. Yet, everywhere the damage done to church attendance was long since done, for neither the abolition of pew rents, nor their erosion through desertion of city-centre churches by the suburban-bound, restored those absolute falls in church attendance which were already becoming apparent by 1914. Furthermore, attendance rates in the Church of Scotland (whose male members suffered massive unemployment in the early thirties) held up much longer than those of its English counterpart, even though it enforced pew rents until the 1950s.[72]

Despite Mann's warnings, competitive campaigns of church building marked the decades after 1851, as nonconformist churches were built and rebuilt in a physical demonstration of the arrival to social power and influence of the previously excluded dissenters, and the establishment retaliated. Together they asserted the presence of religious authority in the urban landscape. Grand nonconformist chapels were the 'spiritual expressions of men who had . . . moulded . . . their towns', who built villas, banks, warehouses, town halls, YMCAs and

[72] Smith, *Religion in Industrial Society*, pp. 72–3; Wickham, *Church and People in an Industrial City*, pp. 88–9, 114–16, 142–3; Inglis, *Churches and the Working Classes*, pp. 49–52, 96; Dalton, 'Walter Farquhar Hook', 39–40; R. B. Walker, 'Religious changes in Liverpool in the nineteenth century', *JEcc.Hist.*, 19 (1968), 206, 208–9; Callum G. Brown, 'The costs of pew-renting: church management, church-going, and social class in nineteenth-century Glasgow', *JEcc.Hist.*, 38 (1987), esp. 355, 357; P. Hillis, 'Presbyterianism and social class in mid-nineteenth century Glasgow: a study of nine churches', *JEcc.Hist.*, 32 (1981), 55–6; W. R. Ward, 'The cost of Establishment: some reflections on church building in Manchester', in G. J. Cuming, ed., *Studies in Church History: Volume III* (Leiden, 1966), p. 287; Cox, *The English Churches in a Secular Society*, p. 103; Brown, *Social History of Religion in Scotland*, pp. 100, 153, 155–6, 165, 133, 141–2, 217–18; cf. A. A. McLaren, *Religion and Social Class: The Disruption Years in Aberdeen* (London, 1974), p. 135; Trainor, *Black Country Elites*, p. 183; Brown, 'Did urbanisation secularise Britain?', 4–5, 8–12; Eileen Yeo, 'Christianity in Chartist struggle 1838–1842', *P&P*, 91 (1981), 109–39, esp. 132–3; Lewis, *Lighten their Darkness*, pp. 109–10; Green, *Religion in the Age of Decline*, pp. 147–52, 164 esp. n.137, 364–5; Stephen Yeo, *Religion and Voluntary Organisations in Crisis, 1890–1914* (London, 1976), pp. 79–82; Nigel Yates, Robert Hume and Paul Hastings, *Religion and Society in Kent, 1640–1914* (Woodbridge, 1994), p. 81; Paul A. Welsby, 'Church and people in Victorian Ipswich', *Church Quarterly Review* (April–June 1963), 212–13.

Mechanics' Institutes as recreations of Rome, Florence or Milan: 'Halifax is a restless Renaissance city, with the Crossleys of Square Chapel as its Medici', writes Clyde Binfield. George Gilbert Scott's All Souls, Haley Hill, was the notable Anglican reply to Square Chapel's translation to Gothic magnificence in 1857. Glasgow saw the dominating Greek Presbyterian style of Alexander Thomson; London's East End got the imposing brick structures of James Brooks. The second major impetus to church building came from shifts in populations and property values. Thus Birmingham Baptists and Methodists built intensively in the suburbs between 1875 and 1888, with a grandeur reflecting the rise in the worldly fortunes of their congregations. 'Dissenting Gothic' was the style in Bowden, 'Manchester's most relaxed suburb'. Some suburban churches (like some public parks), may have been developed as speculative ventures, to improve the value of surrounding dwellings; like theatres, others moved to escape deterioration in their locality. The pace of building varied from town to town. In Birmingham the late 1860s saw ten new churches opened in five years. Between 1851 and 1901 the number of churches in Halifax quadrupled. In Glasgow nineteen suburban churches were built in the last five years of the century.[73]

The result was massive debts, and an increase in the costs and obligations of membership, one consequence of which was the annual resort to bazaars and sales of work from the 1870s. And the wasteful competition may have contributed to a demoralising feeling of decline because of the half-empty inner-urban churches. In contrast, Roman Catholicism built fewer churches, most of them were full, the congregation felt part of a thriving community and Catholicism was helped to its position as the denomination which resisted longest the tendency to attendance decline.[74]

The erection of new churches and chapels was complemented by the development of the mission hall. This occurred partly in a natural process as urban missionaries achieved some success and moved from evangelisation to pastoral care, and partly as a deliberate process of plantation, in recognition of the need to evangelise working-class communities from within to overcome the class gulfs

[73] Faucher, *Manchester in 1844*, p. 23 n. 8; Kendall, *Origin and History*, II, pp. 455–79; Clyde Binfield, *So Down to Prayers: Studies in English Nonconformity 1780–1920* (London, 1977), pp. 147, 171; Green, *Religion in the Age of Decline*, pp. 87–117, esp. 90 and 101–2; Dixon and Muthesius, *Victorian Architecture*, pp. 198, 216–17, 233–4; Ward, 'The cost of Establishment', pp. 282–3; R. Dennis, *English Industrial Cities of the Nineteenth Century* (Cambridge, 1984), pp. 158–9; *VCH*, Warwickshire, VII, pp. 354–96, 422; John H. Y. Briggs, 'Elite and proletariat in nineteenth-century Birmingham Nonconformity', in A. P. F. Sell, ed., *Protestant Nonconformists and the West Midlands of England* (Keele, 1996), p. 90; R. Q. Gray, 'Religion, culture and social class in late nineteenth and early twentieth century Edinburgh', in Crossick, ed., *The Lower Middle Class in Britain*, pp. 137–8; Brown, *Social History of Religion in Scotland*, pp. 177–8.
[74] Gill, *The Myth of the Empty Church*, pp. 79–80, 152, 155, 158–9, 180, 186–7, 237, 262–5; Green, *Religion in the Age of Decline*, pp. 165–76, 364; Royle, *The Victorian Church in York*, pp. 15–18; Brown, *Social History of Religion in Scotland*, pp. 178–9; H. A. Mess, *Industrial Tyneside* (London, 1928), p. 139.

between clergy and people tellingly emphasised by Mann. The former process is difficult to trace but it is noteworthy that by 1860 there were approximately half as many professional lay missionaries in London as there were clergymen. One of the problems for the established churches and respectable dissenting congregations in the new urban conditions was the relative fluidity of the industrial and service-class population as industries shifted and commerce and railways remade the character of central areas. The flexibility of small missions in rented premises helped to meet these conditions. Judging by the example of Birmingham, nonconformist churches were in the van of mission plantation, but, like the Anglicans, they too reached peaks of activity in the 1880s and 1890s. By 1900 Booth commented that London was 'dotted over' with 'shabby' mission halls, 'in almost every street' in the poorer parts, 'more numerous than schools or churches, and only less numerous than public-houses', preaching the Gospel, teaching children, guiding mothers, visiting the sick, relieving poverty and providing temperate 'social relaxation and enjoyment'. It is difficult not to be impressed by the ubiquity of these mission churches and their unsung contribution to the texture of life in poor districts.[75]

Institutional expansion was more than matched by church auxiliaries and associations so that by the last decades of the century the churches, collectively, had established themselves as among the most significant providers of community facilities. The initial rationale for this was to evangelise the 'home heathen', and to undertake 'practical Christianity', especially with 'the poor and lowly' and 'the hungry' (through coal clubs, clothing clubs, provident and sick societies, savings clubs, sewing classes, soup kitchens and medical missions), and thereby generally to increase the influence of religion upon society. To some extent nonconformity developed parochial attributes as a natural accompaniment of the transition that so many denominations were making in these decades from 'chapel' to 'church'. Similar developments took place in areas with strong Irish immigrant populations as a means of 'building the Catholic ghetto'.[76]

---

[75] Lewis, *Lighten their Darkness*, pp. 120, 132–3, 275–6; J. R. Kellett, *The Impact of Railways on Victorian Cities* (London, 1969), pp. 15–20, 287–376; Gilbert, *Religion and Society in Industrial England*, pp. 113–14, 147; *VCH*, Warwickshire, VII, pp. 360–96, 420–4, 434–42, 448–54; Briggs, 'Elite and proletariat in nineteenth-century Birmingham', pp. 79–80, 82–5; also Binfield, *So Down to Prayers*, pp. 201–2, for Kensington Congregational Church and Notting Dale Mission; Morris, *Religion and Urban Change*, p. 59; Green, *Religion in the Age of Decline*, p. 117; Booth, *Life and Labour of the People in London*, 3rd series, VII, pp. 270, 273, 289; C. Ward Davis, 'One man's answer', in W. S. F. Pickering, ed., *A Social History of the Diocese of Newcastle 1882–1982* (London, 1981), ch. 13. For insights into the contrasting styles of 'back street Bethels' and 'West End chapels' see Peter Ackers, 'West End Chapel, back street Bethel: labour and capital in the Wigan churches of Christ c. 1845–1945', *JEcc.Hist.*, 47 (1996), 298–329, and for the 'community' role of chapels in smaller towns see Ainsworth, 'Religion in the working-class community', 367–72 and McLeod, 'New perspectives on Victorian working-class religion', 41–3.

[76] Quotations from John M. Brindley, *Church Work in Birmingham* (Birmingham, 1880), pp. 144, 189; Reid, 'Labour, leisure and politics', pp. 130–9; Cox, *The English Churches in a Secular Society*,

However, the most popular church auxiliaries had been founded long before, namely the Sunday Schools. Their enrolments expanded from 38 per cent of the population of English under fifteens in 1851 to their peak of 53 per cent in 1901. Given similar trends in Scotland – 65 per cent belonged in Glasgow in 1890 – religion was thus at its most generally influential through Sunday Schools. From the mid-century, nonconformists, at least, began to see them as 'nurseries', especially through the development of the adolescent upper schools, Bible classes and (virtually all male) mutual improvement societies, which in Lancashire factory towns, in particular, were often deeply implicated in the development of popular party political activity. At a less committed level, it was said in Manchester that 'to the young people of the working classes it is their club; there they seek their diversions, form their friendships, and begin their courtings'.[77]

As Puritanism was reconsidered by leading clerics in the 1850s and 1860s, church-sponsored recreations grew apace, both with evangelical and moralising intent, but also as extensions of the increasing ambitions of their members – making 'rational recreations' really very popular. It has even been claimed that in Scotland they 'created a religious dominance of "respectable" urban culture in the mid-Victorian decades'. The result was a plethora of clubs and associations for adult men, young men, boys, girls and women, temperance clubs, Mothers' Meetings (a mixture of prayer, sewing, summer treats and tea), concerts, debating societies, gym or recreation classes, sports clubs and Christian Endeavour societies. Another important impulse was to induce young men to bridge the gap between Sunday School and church – the egalitarian Pleasant Sunday Afternoon movement (begun in West Bromwich in 1875), attracted four-figure attendance in numerous towns, though its success was also a measure of the social distance still felt between ordinary men and socially respectable churchgoers. Judging by evidence from Birmingham in 1880, Anglicanism was more conducive to both charitable and recreational auxiliaries. However, in 1900 Lambeth's nonconformists had left behind much of their puritan inheritance, having a higher proportion of recreational organisations than Lambeth's Anglican churches. A little further south into the suburbs, a typical Congregational church provided 'dances, socials, badminton tournaments, discussions and amateur

pp. 50–1, 56–8, 76–8; Brown, *Social History of Religion in Scotland*, pp. 143, 146–8; Morris, *Religion and Urban Change*, pp. 65, 84; Hugh McLeod, 'Building the "Catholic ghetto": Catholic organisations, 1870–1914', in W. J. Sheils and Diana Wood, eds., *Voluntary Religion* (Studies in Church History, 23, Oxford, 1986), pp. 411–44.

[77] Gill, *The Myth of the Empty Church*, p. 301; Gilbert, *Religion and Society in Industrial England*, pp. 201–2; Gill, 'Secularisation and census data', 96; Chadwick, *The Victorian Church*, II, pp. 257–62; David Hempton, *Methodism and Politics in British Society 1750–1850* (London, 1984), pp. 86–92; Brown, *Social History of Religion in Scotland*, p. 145; Callum Brown, 'Religion, class and church growth', in Fraser and Morris, eds., *People and Society in Scotland*, II, p. 328; Joyce, *Work, Society and Politics*, pp. 178–9, 246–50; John M. Elvey, *Recollections of the Cathedral and Parish Church of Manchester* ([Manchester], 1913), p. 61.

entertainments' to its younger members. And in Edinburgh's Morningside, the minister of St Matthew's Free Church depicted its social fellowships, guilds and societies (providing literary and dramatic activities, rambling, curling and golf), as valuable new 'links in the chain of full Church membership'. Thus, later nine-teenth-century suburban living tilted the role of the churches further towards associational and recreational objectives.[78]

Yet they were by no means purely absorbed in their own sense of mission and institutional developments, and the civic impact of the churches constitutes another major theme. The Scottish burgh councils had owned their churches since the Reformation, and were the earliest in Britain to develop a religious response to the new urban problems, playing an important role in coordinating educational, philanthropic and medical agencies. It is true that the removal of the parish vestry from the administration of poor relief in England in 1834, and in Scotland in 1845, represented a measure of institutional secularisation, yet the churches' role in education continued to expand into the second half of the century, and a more widely defined religiously inspired public welfare policy developed in the 1860s and 1870s as the intractability of the social and moral problems of the cities became apparent. As the discussion of parks and libraries illustrated, Buchanan in Glasgow, and Dawson and Dale in Birmingham, helped to moralise local politics. Although high church attempts to reform liturgical practice emphasised spiritual authority over a narrow field rather than over the wider society, evangelicals and broad churchmen within the Church of England did play a part in the quest for housing reform. It was thus at least partially as a result of the religious enthusiasm for social reform that the state became more important in the last third of the nineteenth century. The logical outcome of this approach was the vigorous slum clearance policy of Canon Charles Jenkinson as chairman of Leeds' Housing Committee (1932–5).[79]

[78] Reid, 'Labour, leisure and politics' pp. 102–16; Hewitt, *The Emergence of Stability in the Industrial City*, p. 167; Gray, 'Religion, culture and social class', pp. 143, 145–6; Brown, *Social History of Religion in Scotland*, pp. 134, 143, 145–8, 160–1, 175, 179–80, 183, 250–1; Mole 'Challenge to the Church. Birmingham, 1815–65', pp. 819–20; John Blackham, '"I remember". The true story of the P.S.A. Movement', *Birmingham Gazette and Express*, 6 Mar. 1908; Wickham, *Church and People in an Industrial City*, p. 158; Inglis, *Churches and the Working Classes*, pp. 79–85; McLeod, *Class and Religion*, pp. 65–6, 131 n. 133; Bradley, 'The English Sunday', 363; Kenward, *The Suburban Child*, p. 72; Besant, *London in the Nineteenth Century*, p. 30; John M. Brindley, *Church Work in Birmingham* (Birmingham, 1880), pp. 144, 189 and *passim*; Yeo, *Religion and Voluntary Organisations*, pp. 55–76; Cox, *The English Churches in a Secular Society*, pp. 48–89, 299–301; Morris, *Religion and Urban Change*, pp. 80–4; Rowntree, *Poverty*, pp. 324, 329–30; Royle, *Victorian Church in York*, pp. 22–4.

[79] J. Sandford, *Social Reforms; Or the Habits, Dwellings and Education of our People* (Birmingham, 1867); Roy Peacock, 'The Church of England and the working classes in Birmingham 1861–1905' (MPhil thesis, University of Aston, 1973), pp. 222ff.; Hennock, *Fit and Proper Persons*, pp. 61, 176; Callum G. Brown, 'A revisionist approach to religious change', in Bruce, ed., *Religion and Modernisation*, pp. 52–3; Alastair Mason, 'Jenkinson and Southcott', in Mason, ed., *Religion in Leeds*, pp. 143–50; Roger Lloyd, *The Church of England in the Twentieth Century* (London, 1946–50), vol. II, pp. 114–37.

Although there were periodic waves of evangelical activity between 1851 and 1900, the 1880s was a particularly significant decade. The 1850s had seen Anglican street preaching, the (female) Ranyard Bible Mission and the hiring of theatres for evangelism; the 1860s saw Methodist street-corner revivalism; the mid-1870s saw the enormous impact of the revivalist campaign of visiting American evangelists, Moody and Sankey, and the Salvation Army (which, after tumultuous opposition, stimulated another characteristic and lasting feature of street life, the Mission Band). However, the 1880s refocused the churches' attention even more on the problem of evangelising the poor. The local censuses showed little progress had been made in attracting the working classes, and the socio-economic impediments to religious faith were emphasised by several influential publications, in particular Rev. Andrew Mearns' sensational revelations of slum degradation, *The Bitter Cry of Outcast London* (1883) – all capped by economic depression in mid-decade, and the rebirth of socialism. The religious (and rational recreational) responses indicate that this was regarded as the most serious social crisis since the 1840s: university settlements (the first in Whitechapel in 1884), the Wesleyan Central Mission Hall movement (from 1885), the People's Palace movement (from 1887); the Anglican Christian Social Union (1889) and, as we have seen, innumerable church missions and parish auxiliaries. More specialised, but essentially part of the same movement to 'civilise' the working classes were the uniformed youth organisations: the Church Army (1882), the (Baptist) Boys' Brigade, formed in Glasgow in 1883, and its Anglican, Jewish and Roman Catholic counterparts, especially the very popular (Anglican) Church Lads' Brigade, established in London in 1891.[80]

Collectively then the churches developed the most extraordinary web of social institutions, and even when seen purely as voluntary organisations against other voluntary organisations their reach was impressive. For example, in Lambeth, in 1905 there were 172 churches, chapels and mission halls, attended by perhaps 17 per cent of the population, running numerous recreational

---

[80] Lewis, *Lighten their Darkness*, ch. 9; Winter, *London's Teeming Streets*, pp. 135–52; Brown, *Social History of Religion in Scotland*, pp. 138–9, 147, 159–60; Chadwick, *The Victorian Church*, II, p. 286; G. Stedman Jones, *Outcast London* (Oxford, 1971); A. Mearns, *The Bitter Cry of Outcast London* (London, 1883; new edn, ed. A. S. Wohl, Leicester, 1970); Victor Bailey, 'Salvation Army riots, the "Skeleton Army" and legal authority in the provincial town', in Donajgrodzki, ed., *Social Control*, pp. 231–53; Asa Briggs, 'The Salvation Army in Sussex 1883–1892', in Kitch, ed., *Studies in Sussex Church History*, pp. 189–208; Green, *Religion in the Age of Decline*, pp. 276–84; Inglis, *Churches and the Working Classes*, pp. 67–8, 70, 89–90, 92–3, 95–6, 98–9; McLeod, *Class and religion*, pp. 143–5; Morris, *Religion and Urban Change*, pp. 65–8, 80, 135–8; Gerald Parsons, 'A question of meaning: religion and working-class life', in G. Parsons, ed., *Religion in Victorian Britain*, vol. II: *Controversies* (Manchester, 1988), p. 74; S. Joyce, 'Castles in the air: the People's Palace, cultural reform and the East End working class', *Victorian Studies*, 39 (1996), 513–38; Elspeth King, *The People's Palace and Glasgow Green* (Glasgow, 1985); J. Springhall, *Youth, Empire and Society* (London, 1977), pp. 24–6, 37–8, *et passim*; John Springhall, *Sure & Steadfast: A History of the Boys' Brigade, 1883 to 1983* (London, 1983).

auxiliaries, as compared with 430 pubs and beerhouses. Their influence was much wider than indicated by snapshot census computations: through church day schools, and Sunday Schools, and post-Sunday School organisations, through their charitable and recreational ancillaries, through the popularity of religious festivals, through missions and street campaigns, and, indirectly but significantly, through the increasing proportion of women in most congregations, aspects of the Gospel message touched enormous numbers even of the working-class population.[81]

(viii) A FALLING AWAY

Nevertheless, if few historians would now maintain that urbanisation was comprehensively detrimental to habits of religious attendance, few would dissent from the view that formal religious adherence began to falter in the last two decades of the nineteenth century, and to decline absolutely early in the twentieth century. The local surveys conducted in the 1880s in large towns in both England and Scotland showed overall evidence of only a slight decline in the proportion of worshippers since mid-century. However, over the following twenty-five years there were very different results. Thus in 'metropolitan London' attendances fell by nearly a quarter, from 28.5 per cent to 22 per cent by 1902–3, and in eight northern and Midland towns in the early twentieth century were down to 27 per cent. Thus the rot had set in from the 1880s, or, judging by three censuses conducted in Liverpool between 1881 and 1901, mainly in the 1890s. Moreover, between 1902 and 1912 both Anglican and nonconformist attendance in Liverpool declined by 15 per cent, although Roman Catholic attendance continued to grow proportionately to the population. Where adequate *membership* figures exist for England as a whole (mostly for the Methodists), they also suggest the importance of the 1890s as the period when steady *relative* decline set in, though it should be stressed that *absolute* growth did not peak until 1906 for some Methodists and 1907 for English Baptists, and nonconformist confidence was hardly shaken until this period. Disruption to ordinary routines during the First World War had considerable effects on church attendance, and more than cancelled out the boost provided by anxious wartime worship, but afterwards Anglicans and Wesleyan Methodists, in particular, recovered somewhat, and reached their absolute peaks in the period 1927–34. In an

---

[81] Cox, *The English Churches in a Secular Society*, p. 24; McLeod, *Class and Religion*, pp. 30–1, 208–9, 308; Clive D. Field, 'Adam and Eve: gender in the English Free Church constituency', *JEcc.Hist.*, 44 (1993), 65–70; McLeod, *Religion and Society in England*, pp. 156–68; H. McLeod, *Piety and Poverty* (New York and London, 1995), pp. 149–63; Green, *Religion in the Age of Decline*, pp. 22, 205–9; see also Callum G. Brown and Jayne D. Stephenson, '"Sprouting wings?": women and religion in Scotland *c.* 1890–1950', in Esther Breitenbach and Eleanor Gordon, eds., *Women in Scottish Society 1800–1945* (Edinburgh, 1992), pp. 95–120.

indication of the strength of Scotland's Calvinist tradition, Presbyterian membership continued to grow (though much more slowly) well into the twentieth
century, despite *attendances* declining.[82]

Why did these declines occur? In order to begin answering this question it is
important to understand how they occurred: in other words, were there
differential falls between different social groups? The short answer is that the
'respectable classes' were those whose attendances showed the greatest falls. Thus
late nineteenth-century attendances in London declined most in the wealthiest
areas, especially in Hampstead, Kensington and Westminster, whereas in the
poorest areas the reduction was very limited; there was even an increase in attendances in the case of Bermondsey and Finsbury. In Lambeth, attendances of the
wealthier nonconformists, the Congregationalists and Wesleyans, 'declined most
rapidly'. And in Edwardian Liverpool attendance in the wealthiest suburbs fell
by a fifth, nearly twice as much as in the Protestant working-class areas.
Consequently, by the 1890s, even where attendance figures showed little diminution, as in Glasgow, there were difficulties in recruiting district visitors, and
Sunday School teachers – evidence of a lesser commitment to the churches by
the middle classes.[83]

Initially, at any rate, it is arguable that the decline in religious attendance was
more a consequence of apologies than of apostasy. In Lambeth, for instance,
morning attendances were particularly hit, which suggests that bicycling, or
boating or golf were becoming major disincentives to former 'twicers'. By 1914
motoring was noticed as a factor. In so far as the churches constituted 'clubs for
respectable people' competing attractions were becoming more powerful. Much
ink has been spilt trying to define the connection between the shaking of belief
by Biblical criticism, Darwinism, the repudiation of the doctrine of Hell and the
decline in church attendances. However, while not wishing to minimise unduly
the influence of intellectual doubt it seems likely that it was not the immediate
key to falls in church attendance, because, to put it at its simplest, and as we shall
see, it was possible to continue to believe in God while not feeling any urgent
need to go regularly to church. Rather, for the respectable classes, it was the
social incentives to go which were reducing while the incentives to be elsewhere

[82] Gilbert, *Religion and Society in Industrial England*, pp. 32, 37, 39; Gill, *The Myth of the Empty Church*,
pp. 161, 313, 322; McLeod, *Class and Religion*, pp. 231–2, 237–8, 265 n. 84; McLeod, 'White collar
values and the role of religion', pp. 87–8; D. C. Jones, ed., *Merseyside* (London, 1934), vol. III, p.
325; McLeod, *Religion and Society in England*, pp. 170–3; Cox, *The English Churches in a Secular
Society*, pp. 223–4; Currie, Gilbert and Horsley, *Churches and Church-Goers*, pp. 132–4, 142–4,
149–50, 163–5; Brown, *Social History of Religion in Scotland*, pp. 82–5, 88 n. 4; K. K. Harrison,
'The decline of Methodism in Kingston upon Hull in this century' (MA thesis, University of
Hull, 1973), pp. 59, 63, 72.
[83] McLeod, *Class and Religion*, pp. 237, 314; McLeod, 'White collar values and the role of religion',
pp. 87–8; Cox, *The English Churches in a Secular Society*, pp. 135, 140–1; Brown, *Social History of
Religion in Scotland*, pp. 170–1ff; Morris, *Religion and Urban Change*, p. 183.

were increasing. Intellectual doubt, not to mention a reaction against Puritanism and the churches which preached it, damaged the enthusiasm of religious adherents, but were solvents of religious beliefs in the *longer term*.[84]

Other social disincentives were consequent upon changes in the nature of the capitalist firm at the end of the nineteenth century, and in the loyalties of employees – by weakening the industrial paternalism which had formerly encouraged employers to emphasise churchgoing amongst their factory workers by the (sometimes coercive) force of their example. Reinforced by suburbanisation, the withdrawal of this 'Vice-Presidential class' from close involvement in factory district churches resulted in financial problems for them and their elaborate parish organisations, reducing their ability to compete with commercial leisure.[85]

The churches' increasing stress on the necessity of social reform meant that it came to be seen as a Christian's duty to pursue it, but by the end of the nineteenth century there were more effective channels for 'social service' than philanthropy, namely local sanitary boards, municipal councils, school boards and local education authorities. Simultaneously, the ideological challenge of collectivism reduced both the confidence and appeal of individualistic evangelicalism. The result was that the churches became marginalised – a process accelerated by wartime and post-war welfarism. More particularly, nonconformity was a victim of its own political success in eliminating discrimination against it. The integration of nonconformists into the governance of society inevitably eroded that sense of apartness which had sustained earlier generations of dissenters, and prosperous youngsters growing up in the last years of the nineteenth century saw less and less point in nonconformity in a society which had eradicated most of their civic and religious grievances. Some drifted to a looser religious affiliation with Anglicanism; others, affected by the theological liberalism characteristic of the more intellectual free churches, became susceptible to the appeal of alternative late nineteenth-century philosophies such as secularism and socialism. Paradoxically, 'men's meetings' and the (almost exclusively male) mutual improvement societies may have facilitated this kind of transition by developing the critical faculties as well as the social consciences of their members – in the case of Halifax's North End Unitarian Chapel, via the town's Labour Church (1893) to socialist politics. Amongst urban elites too the rise of class politics meant that it no longer mattered so much to them whether one was a nonconformist or an

---

[84] A. D. Gilbert, *The Making of Post-Christian Britain* (London, 1980), p. 95; Cox, *The English Churches in a Secular Society*, pp. 22, 35–6, 293; Gill, *The Myth of the Empty Church*, p. 192; Green, *Religion in the Age of Decline*, p. 366, cites 'clubs' quotation; Chadwick, *The Victorian Church*, chs. 1–3; Brown, *Social History of Religion in Scotland*, pp. 173–5; McLeod, *Religion and Society in England*, pp. 179–96; Inglis, *Churches and the Working Classes*, pp. 74–85.

[85] Yeo, *Religion and Voluntary Organisations in Crisis*, pp. 102–7; Cox, *The English Churches in a Secular Society*, pp. 22, 35–6, 293; Brown, *Social History of Religion in Scotland*, pp. 171–2, 175–7, 183; Green, *Religion in the Age of Decline*, pp. 65–71; cf. Wickham, *Church and People in an Industrial City*, pp. 146–7.

Anglican, and in interwar England nonconformity's remaining strength ebbed away from the once-Liberal industrial North to the more prosperous and Conservative South-East.[86]

In a pluralistic society religious organisations must 'recruit or die'. What incentives were there for the young to continue to join the churches? In so far as they appealed to young people's idealism regarding social reform the alternative practice of secular socio-political work and alternative ideal of socialism were damaging. Moreover, although the decline in numbers was led by the respectable classes, the gradual fall-off in urban immigration meant that the young urban populations were town bred, and therefore decreasingly likely to be reared as churchgoers, even in regions where churchgoing was higher. Consequently, when Sunday School attendances began gradually to decline (noticeably by 1921) the churches knew they were in trouble, especially as the birth rate decline meant proportionally fewer children from whom to recruit adult membership. However, real membership losses from Sunday Schools were smaller than those from adult church membership: there was a lag between rates of decline of adults and children. Therefore, one has to ask why were the churches unable to translate their popularity with children into popularity with adults? One reason is that like is not being compared with like. Many children must have been directed to Sunday School; when they became adults they could signify that status by choosing to 'put away childish things'. Beyond this explanation one comes to the issue of competition for time and newer, more compelling, sources of aspiration and identity. Involvement in increasingly multifarious church and chapel auxiliaries for charitable or sporting purposes absorbed energies and time, and tempted a lesser commitment to worship as they came to be seen as its religiously sanctioned surrogate. Although Sunday School leagues were still strong in the interwar period, especially in cricket, commentators in the 1920s were plausibly seeing football as an emotional substitute for religion.[87]

Missions, outgoing parsons, and philanthropic and recreational auxiliaries may

[86] Cox, *The English Churches in a Secular Society*, pp. 112–19, 228–30ff., 240, 252–3ff.; Binfield, *So Down to Prayers*, pp. 4, 20; Morris, *Religion and Urban Change*, chs. 6 and 7; S. J. D. Green, 'Religion and the rise of the common man: mutual improvement societies, religious associations and popular education in three industrial towns in the West Riding of Yorkshire c. 1850–1900', in Fraser, ed., *Cities, Class and Communication*, pp. 25–43; McLeod, *Religion and Society in England*, pp. 211–20, 223–4, 249 n. 58; Currie, Gilbert and Horsley, *Churches and Church-Goers*, pp. 203–12; Adrian Hastings, *A History of English Christianity* (London, 1986), pp. 265, 683 n. 7.

[87] Cox, *The English Churches in a Secular Society*, pp. 224–7, 307–8, tables 22–3; Gill, *The Myth of the Empty Church*, p. 301; Jeffrey Hill, '"First class" cricket and the leagues: some notes on the development of English cricket, 1900–40', *International Journal of the History of Sport*, 4 (1982), 68–81; David Bowker, 'Parks and baths: sport, recreation and municipal government in Ashton-under-Lyme between the wars', Jeffrey Hill, 'League cricket in the North and Midlands, 1900–1940', and Jack Williams, 'Recreational cricket in Bolton between the wars', all in Holt, ed., *Sport and the Working Class*, pp. 98, 111–16, 122; Fishwick, *English Football and Society*, pp. 12, 152; Jones, *Workers at Play*, pp. 55, 218 n. 87; McLeod, *Religion and Society in England*, p. 199.

have slowed down the decline a little (and certainly played a valuable part in the life of the new housing estates like Becontree, or North Hull) but some innovations ultimately made things worse. Thus, the association of the churches with youth organisations, especially the most popular, the Boy Scouts (from 1907), made them seem less relevant to adult men, just as the 'muscular Christianity' of the nineteenth century was put in the shade by 'the bonnet brigade' in the twentieth. In interwar Merseyside the Anglican female:male ratio at public worship was 163:100, and in Wallsend-on-Tyne reached 193:100. Furthermore, the recreational facilities offered by the churches began to pall against the plethora of offerings with no strings attached which could be increasingly afforded even by some of the poorest people after 1918. Increasing inability to recruit from outside the faithful led to a new inwardness and 'emphasis upon the appeal of belonging' rather than reaching out to the unconverted, making a vicious circle which encouraged further decline. Symptomatically, whereas the crude adult church attendance rate in York, was 35.5 per cent in 1901, by 1935 it had nearly halved, and by 1948 it stood at only 13 per cent; in High Wycombe, in Buckinghamshire, the rate was only 10.5 per cent. However, to put this in the perspective of other voluntary movements, it was still double the percentage of the population of Birmingham which belonged to sports clubs in the previous year.[88]

Moreover, institutional secularisation and declining church attendance rates did not necessarily carry implications for personal beliefs. The shallowness of the attendance test had been pointed out as long ago as 1903 by the perceptive district nurse, Margaret Loane; it was, she argued, 'a confusion of formal outward signs and inward spiritual graces'. Her experience of the urban poor was that most believed in a just and benevolent God who would recognise the essential goodness in people and reward it in Heaven, the hope of which was 'the only thing that made life tolerable to them both in its bitterest moments and in its long-drawn-out-struggles against weakness, poverty, ill-health, and sin'. This kind of belief was described as part of a 'diffusive Christianity' in 1903, and historians are now rightly paying it more attention. It accepted that the Bible had worthwhile teachings, especially for children, and the Christian ethic of 'doing the best you can and doing nobody any harm', but was uninterested in denominational dogmas and rejected the idea of Hell. Interestingly, Mass-Observation's study of a semi-suburban London borough ('Metrop') in 1948 independently reported very similar findings, showing considerable continuity from the later nineteenth century: about three-quarters of Mass-Observation's sample claimed

[88] Young, *Becontree and Dagenham*, pp. 42, 49–50, 66–8, 70–3, 81–3, 175, 182–9, 222–5, cf. 189–200; Harrison, 'The decline of Methodism in Kingston upon Hull', pp. 107–10; Cox, *The English Churches in a Secular Society*, pp. 215–18; Green, *Religion in the Age of Decline*, pp. 205–9, 369, 373–4; Jones, ed., *Merseyside*, II, pp. 330–41; Mess, *Industrial Tyneside*, pp. 19, 137; McLeod, *Religion and Society in England*, pp. 149–56; Gill, *The Myth of the Empty Church*, pp. 176–7; Currie, Gilbert and Horsley, *Churches and Church-Goers*, pp. 30–2, 35; Rowntree and Lavers, *English Life and Leisure*, pp. 342–3, 403–4; Sutcliffe and Smith, *History of Birmingham*, pp. 276, 295 n. 1.

to believe in God, although only one in ten went to church at all regularly. Few thought much about religion, though they wanted it taught in schools, but when they did it meant 'little more than being kind and neighbourly, doing good when opportunity arises'. While there was considerable anti-clericalism based on the class differences between clergy and people there was also regard for 'saintly' individual clergymen, and overt hostility to God and religion was rarer; however, both City missionary reports and subsequent oral history interviews do sometimes reveal a bitter rejection of an apparently uncaring deity.[89]

One of the most suggestive indications of a basic or residual religiosity was the reliance on the churches to sanctify life's crucial turning points, although there were often several layers of meaning invested in the rites of passage. In the 1920s two-thirds of all English infants were baptised, and more than two-thirds of all marriages were religiously solemnised, as were virtually all funerals. Thereafter the trend was downwards but only slowly. Although there were marginal groups such as nineteenth-century common lodging house dwellers for whom marriage was rare, among the majority of the domiciled poor it was the norm, and women particularly insisted that it should be solemnised in a church, thereby gaining access to both respectability and Divine blessing at an auspicious time in their lives. Superstitions regarding the power of the clergyman to intercede against malign fate also played their part in such rituals, as illustrated by the idea that the 'churching' ceremony for postpartum mothers would guard against an immediate subsequent pregnancy, or against a miscarriage – or with regard to 'Watch Night' services, the provision of which was sometimes forced upon unwilling clergy by rowdy East Enders in the 1890s. There was also a certain instrumentalism, such as the expectation of benefits from attendance at that late nineteenth-century urban paradox, the Harvest Festival: 'cadging' was deeply deplored by the consciously self-respecting but it was an inevitable feature of extremely poor districts in London, Liverpool and elsewhere, and still evident in 'Metrop' in 1948.[90]

[89] M. Loane, *The Queen's Poor: Life as they Find it in Town and Country* (London, 1905; 1998 edn), pp. 31, 33–4; McLeod, *Class and Religion*, pp. 49–52; Cox, *The English Churches in a Secular Society*, p. 94; Ainsworth, 'Religion in the working class community', esp. 363–5; McLeod, 'New perspectives on Victorian working-class religion', 33–5, 37–8; Lewis, *Lighten their Darkness*, p. 126; Mass-Observation, *Puzzled People: A Study in Popular Attitudes to Religion, Ethics, Progress and Politics in a London Borough* (London, 1948), pp. 12, 14, 21–2, 51, 85–90, 92, 157.

[90] Loane, *The Queen's Poor*, pp. 29, 32, 45–6; Currie, Gilbert and Horsley, *Churches and Church-Goers*, pp. 100–1, 223–9; Brown, *Social History of Religion in Scotland*, p. 87; McLeod, *Class and Religion*, pp. 51–7, 112–13; McKibbin, *Classes and Cultures*, pp. 289–90; Humphries, *Hooligans or Rebels?*, pp. 36–7; McLeod, 'New perspectives on Victorian working-class religion', 37; Booth, *Life and Labour of the People in London*, 3rd series, VII, p. 19; Cox, *The English Churches in a Secular Society*, pp. 91–5, 97–9, 101–3; Lewis, *Lighten their Darkness*, pp. 125–8; Ross, *Love and Toil*, pp. 132–3; John Kent, 'Feelings and festivals: an interpretation of some working-class religious attitudes', in Dyos and Wolff, eds., *The Victorian City*, II, pp. 855–72; Williams, 'Urban popular religion', pp. 223, 233; Walker, 'Religious changes in Liverpool', 208; McLeod, *Piety and Poverty*, pp. 180–5, 189; Green, *Religion in the Age of Decline*, pp. 334–7, 342–6; Mass-Observation, *Puzzled People*, pp. 12, 143.

(ix) CONCLUSION

Despite the common assumption that the world wars had a devastating effect on religious adherence, the later 1940s represented no particular landmark in Christian belief or church attendance. Mass-Observation concluded that few lost their faith directly, and some had theirs strengthened. And although the disruption caused by the war reduced church memberships they had recovered by 1948. Thereafter the moderate rate of decline of 1927-39 was resumed down to 1960, although in Scotland, where memberships had held up longer, they did begin to fall significantly in the 1950s. Many urban churches had suffered bomb damage, but this resulted in the unexpected bonus of financial compensation, enhancing their ability to meet the challenge of the outlying estates after the war. Nevertheless, it was a poignant moment in the history of urban nonconformity when Manchester's vast Union Chapel – 'the Nonconformist Cathedral of Lancashire' – was demolished in 1950, providing a mid-twentieth-century symbol of the fading vitality of the nineteenth-century religious institutional inheritance. By contrast, the late 1940s represented the zenith of many trends in the history of leisure since 1900: cinema reached its highest ever attendance, as did football and dog racing. There was a new 'hunger for pleasure' in the aftermath of war, with high purchasing power, continued rationing, few consumer durables available and greater time to seek it.[91]

There were as we have seen many links between urban and rural cultures, even though it is easier to pin down a distinctively urban culture in relation to leisure, primarily because of the commercial basis of so much modern recreational culture and because commerce gravitated towards the biggest markets. Concentration and diversity, attractivity and repulsion were keynotes of the urban culture of modern Britain – a culture symbolised physically in pubs, parks, picture halls and sports stadia, but also in spires, towers and humble mission halls. Contrary to dystopian visions of an atomised alienated metropolis many of the institutions of both religion and leisure affirmed the values of sociability and humanity, even if their aims and their trajectories were contrary (and the institutions themselves occasionally contradicted these values). If churches only attracted a tenth of the population to formal worship that was not negligible, and religion retained its capacity to contribute to community identities, whether on suburban church parades or Whit Walks, or on the terraces at Ibrox and Parkhead. And, in the 1950s the beginning of mass immigration from the Empire was soon to demonstrate that capacity once again, this time with many

[91] Mass-Observation, *Puzzled People*, pp. 22–3; Currie, Gilbert and Horsley, *Churches and Church-Goers*, pp. 30–2, 113–15; Sutcliffe and Smith, *History of Birmingham*, pp. 258–60; *Baptist Quarterly*, 13 (1951–2), 92–3, cited in Hastings, *A History of English Christianity*, p. 460; Zweig, *Labour, Life and Poverty*, pp. 49–52; Fishwick, *English Football and Society*, pp. 5–6; Browning and Sorrell, 'Cinemas and cinema-going', 134, 150–2, 170.

of the descendants of the 'heathens' the foreign missionary movement had attempted to evangelise in the nineteenth century. However, the decline of institutionalised Christianity was matched by the rise of leisure institutions to which many gave their energies and loyalties and from which they constructed, partially or substantially, secular social identities, for example as cinema goers, music lovers or sports fans. Thus one important aspect of the history of nineteenth- and twentieth-century towns and cities is that ordinary people achieved or received a massively expanded realm of choice about how to develop their humanity outside the necessity of making a living. There were, of course, still substantial constraints imposed by working and living conditions, as well as gender expectations, and much still to escape from, yet it is richly symbolic that in 1951 the fun-fair at Battersea turned out to be perhaps the most popular aspect of that icon of modernity the Festival of Britain.[92]

[92] Eric Hopkins, *The Rise and Decline of the English Working Classes 1918–1990* (London, 1991), p. 111; Becky Conekin, '"Here is the modern world itself": the Festival of Britain's representations of the future', in B. Conekin, Frank Mort and Chris Waters, eds., *Moments of Modernity: Reconstructing Britain 1945–1964* (London, 1999), pp. 228–46.

PART V

Images

24

The representation of the city in the visual arts

CAROLINE ARSCOTT

(i) HISTORICAL PATTERNS OF RESPONSE: CELEBRATION AND DESPAIR

ARTISTS' RESPONSES to the city in the nineteenth and twentieth centuries have to be understood in terms of social and political issues and debates. The prospect of ever-increasing urban populations, particularly in the metropolis and industrial centres of the North, elicited mixed feelings in contemporary commentary. For some the growth of cities was evidence of the prosperity and strength of the national or local community. The densely packed population represented unparalleled human resources, offering skills, industriousness and simple energy to push forward the manufacturing and trading enterprises that underpinned expansion. The pace and scale of construction of transport and other infrastructural facilities, industrial and commercial premises, residential and administrative buildings and centres for worship and the arts were a source of pride and wonder to those commentators who saw the modern city in a positive light. The modern city could be celebrated as a unique source of invention and harmony, in which the collective energy and intelligence of a democracy came into play. For others pride and wonder gave way to feelings of disquiet. Awe could tip over into terror if the massed population appeared uncontrollable or the environment seemed so huge and complex that the individual was dwarfed or lost. Lack of planning and sanitation became key policy issues as the conditions of slum dwellers were investigated. The city was regularly associated with vice and its smoke and dirt were connected with immorality and crime as well as disease. At an extreme the poorest elements of the urban population could be seen as degenerate and a threat to the breeding stock of the nation, undermining its military ambitions and international prowess. These

I would like to thank Juliet Hacking, Matthew Plampin and Sibylle Beck for editorial assistance and help with obtaining photographs and permissions.

different responses have been well documented.[1] A writer such as Robert Vaughan could make the case for cities with passion and clarity in 1845 in *The Age of Great Cities*. However, positions were not always so clearly polarised. In day-to-day discussions concerning specifics – whether the treatment of paupers, the launching of a provincial newspaper or the demolition of a group of old houses – assumptions came into play concerning the ethical status of the city, the tendency of urban development for good or ill and the disposition of the urban working class. We might say that depictions of the good and bad city fed into the rhetoric of modern politics and social comment. Political contests in which interests and status were at stake were fought out using the loaded terms of urban analysis but not necessarily in a coherent or consistent manner. Most often we see an eclectic mix of registers of response to the city in which enthusiastic excitement is allied to fear and disgust, or utopian visions of a controlled environment are mingled with unease at potential disruption.

The aesthetic is a key component of this discourse. Cities and city dwellers are not just good or bad they are beautiful, sublime, picturesque, quaint, hideous or beyond the limits of representation. The promise or threat of the city is couched in aesthetic terms whenever the experience of inhabiting the urban environment is summoned up. This complicates the task of surveying the visual imagery associated with the modern city, since the aesthetic might be said to be brought into play (at least) twice: once in terms of the picture itself (the visual format and effects of the image under consideration) and secondly in terms of the ethical/aesthetic registers of the city as it figures more generally, for instance in the realm of social policy. The two instances can only be separated artificially and there is, of course, considerable debate about the relationship of what is, at its crudest, text and context. None the less there is a point to be made about the way that, from the nineteenth century, the topic of the city is always saturated with aesthetic assumptions in a way that is perhaps only paralleled by discourses concerning the human body. Indeed, some of the most fascinating and surcharged visions of the city result from an identification of the (aestheticised) city with the (aestheticised) body when the city is seen in terms of the gender distinctions and the erotic potential of the human body.[2]

A third instance can also be drawn out. In architectural and town planning terms the city was subject to aesthetic criteria. Prestige developments were expected to display grandeur, logic and harmony of effect. The question of architectural aesthetics was closely entwined with moral categories in the nineteenth

---

[1] B. I. Coleman, *The Idea of the City in Nineteenth-Century Britain* (London, 1973); A. Lees, *Cities Perceived* (Manchester, 1985).

[2] See C. Gallagher, 'The body versus the social body in the works of Thomas Malthus and Henry Mayhew', in C. Gallagher and T. Laqueur, eds., *The Making of the Modern Body* (Berkeley, 1987), pp. 83–106; and E. Grosz, 'Bodies-cities', in B. Colomina, ed., *Sexuality and Space* (Princeton, N.J., 1992), pp. 191–233.

century; all the more so once John Ruskin's work on the relationship between style and political and moral vigour became widely known. The choice between a classical façade and gothic form became a vexed question. A beautiful vista or a fine building could figure prominently in an engraved or painted scene and lend the represented cityscape the aesthetic merits and ethical connotations of the environment or building. Or else an image could alter, cancel or marginalise the architectural components of the urban fabric. Once again we see that picture-makers had to negotiate a complex relationship with moralised aesthetics, here literally 'built in' to the city.[3]

The Victorian and Edwardian periods display a gradual transformation of attitudes to the city. The balance between celebration and despair could be said to shift decisively by the 1880s to a fairly bleak vision of urban alienation. The early period, up to 1845, is characterised by marked confidence in the achievements of urban development, despite pockets of strident criticism of city life. In the later 1840s and 1850s there was growing middle-class awareness of social problems in Britain and a fashion for social reportage developed. Concern about slum conditions and urban deprivation coexisted with faith in the efficacy of evangelical efforts or state intervention to improve affairs. There was an increasing emphasis on the punitive aspects of state intervention in the 1870s. From the 1880s into the pre-war period in the twentieth century gloom and anxiety about the state of urban life was offset by the emergence of utopian schemes for paternalistic or state-managed urban development.

I will be considering a range of visual material produced in the Victorian and Edwardian period. Many of my examples take aspects of London for their subject, some depict other urban areas such as Glasgow or Wigan. In a broad survey there is some justification in drawing mainly on London examples, since London was the centre of the British art world. I have been looking at this material in terms of attitudes to urban existence in the broadest possible terms, where the city is a concept that goes beyond the specifics of one or other place.[4]

(ii) THE URBAN FABRIC: CENTRE AND SUBURB

How then were the Victorian streets pictured? As cities grew in extent and density, it became necessary to map the developments in various ways. Every map defines an area, explicitly or otherwise, by centring, orientation, categorical

---

[3] See G. P. Landow, *The Aesthetic and Critical Theories of John Ruskin* (Princeton, N.J., 1971), and M. Wheeler, ed., *Ruskin and Environment* (Manchester, 1995).

[4] For an examination of the idea of the city in relation to specific locales see C. Arscott and G. Pollock, with J. Wolff, 'The partial view: the visual representation of the early nineteenth-century city' (on topographical views of Leeds and Manchester), in J. Wolff and J. Seed, eds., *The Culture of Capital* (Manchester, 1988), pp. 191–233; and C. Arscott, 'Victorian development and images of the past' (on lithographic views of Wakefield), in C. Shaw and M. Chase, eds., *The Imagined Past: History and Nostalgia* (Manchester, 1989), pp. 47–67.

positives and categorical exclusions.[5] Maps for tourists, travellers and business people needed to show transport routes, shopping streets, civic or governmental amenities, trading halls, religious edifices and centres of entertainment and leisure. These were the features highlighted by vignettes in the borders of street plans, emphasised or labelled in the all-inclusive sweep of panoramic views, and listed and illustrated systematically in town directories, railway guides and guide books. Factories, warehouses and showrooms might be of interest as tourist attractions, architectural features or for business inquiries. There was no need to show back courts, low lodging houses or small-scale workshops. A railway station, a bank, an arcade, a town hall, a cathedral, a theatre and a park – these were the defining aspects of most cities as represented for purposes that we can imagine falling somewhere between those represented today by a city's tourist board and the chamber of commerce. These were the functional components of the topographical grammar of the city and it becomes easy to recognise them in all sorts of topographical work, whether watercolour views for a private album, sets of engraved or lithographic prints published for collectors, or even in the paintings of specific cities that regularly appeared in public exhibitions.[6] We find that fine art forms are closely related to the more ephemeral images of the city produced for orientation, promotion or souvenir. Once the component parts have been recognised it is easier to appreciate the emphases; to understand the grammar of topography.

It made a considerable difference whether the array of significant routes and locations was centred on a church, for example, or an exhibition hall. The selection of St Paul's Cathedral as the vantage point for Hornor and Parris' panoramic view of London (exhibited from 1829 at the Colosseum, Regent's Park) lent an air of blessedness and authority to the view, but, beyond that, it put the City and the commercial world at the centre rather than the court and the fashionable West End. An aquatint of 1845 offered a fish-eye rendering of the panorama (Plate 28).[7] This anonymous print translated the large-scale popular installation into a two-dimensional format, adding a spin as the whole now suggests an orb that is both globe and eye. Clear lines of roads and river describe a whorl as they curve out from the centre to the margins. Just as London's commerce reaches to distant shores so the city spreads to the distant reaches of the globe. We are given the impression that city is in motion and that, as an eye, it consists of the essence of visibility. Nothing is assumed hidden or inaccessible. The sentient city is the

---

[5] On the ideological basis of map-making see J. B. Harley, 'Maps, knowledge, and power', in D. Cosgrove and S. Daniels, eds., *The Iconography of Landscape* (Cambridge, 1988), pp. 277–312.
[6] William Boyne of Leeds collected prints and watercolours for his (1877) grangerised edition of an earlier history of Leeds: R. Thoresby and T. Whitaker, *Ducatus Leodiensis*, 2nd edn (1816); grangerised edition, Leeds City Reference Library.
[7] R. Hyde, *The Fish-Eye View of London* (London, 1987), reprinted from *The Map Collector* (June 1987); Barbican Art Gallery, *Panoramania!*, exhibition catalogue (London, 1989); on the associations of St Paul's Cathedral see S. Daniels, *Fields of Vision* (Cambridge, 1993), ch. 1.

centre of knowledge and dynamism. The Church, with its links to the state, presides.

A comparison can be drawn between this and the painting of 1904 by Niels M. Lund, *The Heart of the Empire* (Plate 29). Here St Paul's sits at the centre of an urban environment that fills the picture space and, once again, the inference is that this city is so massive that it extends to the ends of the earth.[8] Yet here the power is vested not in clarity and living energy but in the somewhat grim compression of volumetric blocks of commercial, official and public premises. The view is taken from the roof of the Royal Exchange and we see Mansion House to the left. Where the buildings give way to the space of the intersection the vistas are not open; the space is crammed with minute dots of pedestrians and traffic. Birds fly up, and smoke blows sideways to fill the intervening space. Even the sky seems dense and heavy with smoke and massing cloud. It seems that the theme of the picture is the relationship between power and accumulation. The concentration of physical matter echoes the accumulation of capital. The wealth and influence of London and the nation are memorialised in a stern, insistent rhetoric.

These wide-ranging views of the city should be related to the systems of mapping that were developed in the nineteenth century. The spotty topographical lexicon that I have described gave way, as the century progressed, to a more inclusive vision. Street maps and atlases of the metropolis started to cater to strangers, in considerable detail, in 1851, at the moment when floods of visitors came to see the Great Exhibition at Crystal Palace.[9] The latter half of the nineteenth century saw governmental efforts to monitor the population in new and more sophisticated ways. As the Ordnance Survey produced its large-scale maps, a total and consistent ground survey of urban areas was available at a scale that permitted the noting of every lamp post and garden wall. Non-governmental investigations also found new ways of charting the spatial distribution of many elements of urban existence. Charles Booth's survey of London, *Life and Labour of the People in London*, presents an ambitious empirical framework for the apprehension of the total city.[10] Sets of maps that were issued with Booth's survey offer an extraordinarily inclusive cross-referencing of urban features, in an effort to map, analyse and indicate the potential for social intervention. A picture such as Lund's *The Heart of the Empire* assumes the existence of a density of data that can be implied even when it is not systematically noted.

In this context the artistic project of totalising the city took on a different quality. A concentric city of special features was giving way to a city to be understood as a conglomerate. Previously, the centre could embrace and energise the

[8] See Daniels, *Fields of Vision*, pp. 13–15; and Barbican Art Gallery, *The Image of London: Views by Travellers and Emigrées*, exhibition catalogue (London, 1987), p. 174.

[9] H. J. Dyos, 'A guide to the streets of Victorian London', in D. Cannadine and D. Reader, eds., *Exploring the Urban Past* (Cambridge, 1982), pp. 190–201.

[10] C. Booth, *Life and Labour of the People in London*, 17 vols. (London, 1889–1903).

periphery, now, at the turn of the century, the centre was felt to be compressed by the sheer burden of its annexations. The urban was experienced as a continuum. Consequently, it also became possible to experience a decentred city. In the late Victorian and Edwardian period the peripheral could typify the urban in a new way. Suburbs could be invoked, not as semi-rural retreats, but as the recurrent, sometimes dreary setting of quotidian city life. We can explore this point by comparing two very different views of north London localities. Ford Madox Brown completed his *An English Autumn Afternoon* in 1855 (Plate 30). A young couple and their dog are seated in the foreground, and beyond them stretches a vista of gardens and fields between the vantage point of Hampstead and Highgate Village in the distance. It is a modest subject. When he was criticised for the scene's lack of drama or notable features Brown declared that he painted the view just because it lay outside his window.[11] Amongst the variegated colours of foliage, patches of bonfire smoke and tiled roofs, Brown deliberately stresses the rectangles of gardens, neat paths and cultivated plots. The scene is not one of streets and rows of houses, but nor is it wild or natural. This suburban fringe is frankly artificial; the couple are settling to confined domestic existence like the doves whose manmade dovecote resembles the dwellings that we glimpse in the vicinity. The suburban environment is one in which the town can take pleasure in aspects of nature but the sway of the town is cheerfully asserted. The sensibility of many of the subjects completed by the artist W. R. Sickert from the 1880s and by his companions in the Camden Town Group from 1911 can be seen to be completely different. These late Victorian and Edwardian views resemble Brown's in that they take for their subject the immediate and unremarkable environment of the artist's dwelling or studio. Mornington Crescent was hardly rustic by the 1910s, and was arguably urban rather than suburban, but, unlike the City or the West End, it could not be taken as emblematic of London as the centre of fashion and power. Fairly leafy and somewhat shabby, the setting of Spencer Gore's *Mornington Crescent* of 1911 is presented as one aspect of the urban continuum (Plate 31). In comparison with the centrifugal optimism of Brown's suburban scene this is a subdued, even resigned work, that takes its place among the renderings of bedsits, teashops and street corners, quietly enjoying beauty where it presents itself, but not making any great claims.[12]

I have taken examples from each end of the period covered by this chapter to show that, throughout the period, the city could be the occasion of gentle observation just as much as of grand statements. However the ethos of the mid-nineteenth century was very different from that of the early twentieth century, and I have tried to draw attention to a decided change in inflection, discernible after 1880.

[11] Tate Gallery, *The Pre-Raphaelites*, exhibition catalogue (London, 1984); T. Newman and R. Watkinson, *Ford Madox Brown and the Pre-Raphaelite Circle* (London, 1991), p. 91.
[12] W. Baron, *The Camden Town Group* (London, 1979).

(iii) THE RIVER

In this section of this chapter I wish to explore ways in which the river was used as a motif of the city's potential for good and evil. In most industrial cities the main river or canal could figure as a gleaming highway or as a black stream of filth. London's Thames was the quintessential locus for these competing meanings. It was a favoured access route into the city, carrying a huge amount of traffic, and could be seen to unite the disparate faces of the city. Both the *Pictorial Times* and the *Illustrated London News* issued panoramic views of London in 1845, based on views along the Thames. The *Pictorial Times'* was updated and reissued by *Cassell's Illustrated Family News* in 1851.[13] Pleasure traffic mixes with commercial traffic the length of the panorama; coal and hay barges, paddle steamers, dredgers and rowing boats, ferries and sporting eights at the Westminster end are joined by masses of shipping below London Bridge. The variety and liveliness of the activity corresponds to the range of monuments and facilities picked out on the Middlesex side, where churches are slotted in alongside warehouses, factories, markets and government offices in a surprisingly non-hierarchical mix. Tricks of scale and lighting are not used to emphasise the centres of power. The river, calm and glassy at Westminster and brisk and choppy at The Isle of Dogs, seems to allow unimpeded access for one and all to the fun and the business of the metropolis. The democratic constituency of the illustrated press was being appealed to and pictured in this way. This presentation of the Thames is the key to many lively river scenes produced in a fine art context, in either oils or watercolour, such as those by James Wilson Carmichael, Joseph F. Ellis, Henry Dawson, Richard Drabble, James Barker Pyne and David Roberts.[14] The mood can vary from the placid to the frenetic but in every case the river caters to various social classes and brings together the grand and the quotidian in a pleasantly haphazard way. William Parrott's series of twelve lithographs, *London from the Thames* (1842), follows this formula and offers an exceptionally busy and cheerful vision of the city.[15] For instance, in the plate showing Southwark Bridge and St Paul's, lots of paddle steamers, large and small, cluster round the Old Swan Steps landing stage, emitting little puffs of smoke and visibly churning the water, while hundreds of tiny figures in neat coats and bright shawls stream down the walkways, crowd on to the landings and pack themselves on to the steamers,

---

[13] R. Hyde, introductory notes to *Grand Panorama of London from the Thames*, facsimile, Guildhall Library, Corporation of London, n.d.

[14] For example, J. W. Carmichael, *The Pool of London* (c. 1840), J. F. Ellis, *St Paul's Cathedral and the Thames* (before 1848), H. Dawson, *The New Houses of Parliament* (1858), R. Drabble, *Westminster and the Houses of Parliament* (exhibited Royal Academy 1863), J. B. Pyne, *View of London from Blackfriars Bridge* (c. 1840), D. Roberts, *The New Palace of Westminster, being No. 2 of a Series of Views of London on the River Thames* (exhibited Royal Academy 1862).

[15] W. Parrott, *London from the Thames* (1842), twelve plates without letterpress, details in B. Adams, *London Illustrated 1604–1851* (London, 1983), pp. 472–4.

which take off in procession into the clear water under the central arch of the bridge (Plate 32). Masts cut across warehouse façades, plumes of smoke from a steamer cut across the span of the bridge, a tall chimney cuts across the colonnaded side of the cathedral and another, beside it, gives out an energetic plume of smoke that bulks almost as large as the dome of St Paul's. In this context the factories and chimneys of the Surrey side are not alien to the solemn monumentality of St Paul's, but are incorporated into the overall picture of a working city that routinely takes on a carnival air.

Later in the century the Thames comes to figure more ambiguously as an amalgam of the debased and the aesthetic. When it provides the setting for the final scene in Augustus Egg's tripartite series, known as *Past and Present* (1858), the river stretches ahead of the outcast adulterous wife, who crouches under a bridge among the debris and wrecked boats of the muddy shore (Plate 33). The landing stage is deserted and the factories across the water stand dark and out of action. This is the lowest point of the city and she can only descend further by sinking to her death beneath the water. Yet a twinkling light fixed to the arch, and the radiant moon beyond, draw her gaze upwards; the effect of the light is to transform the grim industrial scene, to cast a golden sheen on the sewer/grave of the river and to illuminate the vaulting of the arch, rendering it somewhat church-like. Beauty can replace horror, just as grace can redeem sin.[16] Egg's ability to find an elevated aspect when confronting the sleaziest side of the city is taken up by Whistler in his *Thames Set* etchings (produced 1859–60, published as a set 1871) and in his Nocturnes of the 1870s.[17] Whistler was a pioneer in the transformation of artistic priorities in this period. There was a shift away from the moral and didactic and towards the formal and aesthetic. This was realised most completely in vanguard circles of the Aesthetic movement, but its effects were felt throughout the art world in the later Victorian period. Whistler explained that this Aesthetic attitude freed the artist from the slavish copying of the natural scene.

The artist's responsibility was not to bear witness to preordained truths, but to seek out beauty, and to use manipulation and selection to convey that beauty.[18] The Nocturnes consist of twilight or night-time views of the river where radical simplification of form is achieved through the elimination of detail and the restriction of palette (Plate 34). However, they share traits with the much more

[16] See L. Nead, *Myths of Sexuality* (Oxford, 1988), ch. 2.
[17] K. A. Lochnan, *The Etchings of James McNeill Whistler* (New Haven, 1984); Tate Gallery, *James McNeill Whistler*, exhibition catalogue, text by R. Dorment *et al.* (London, 1994).
[18] 'To say to the painter, that Nature is to be taken as she is, is to say to the player, that he may sit on the piano'; J. A. M. Whistler, *Ten O'Clock Lecture*, 1888, reprinted in J. A. M. Whistler, *The Gentle Art of Making Enemies*, 2nd edn (London, 1892), p. 143. For the transition to Aesthetic Movement attitudes see L. Merrill, *'A Pot Of Paint': Aesthetics on Trial in Whistler v. Ruskin* (Washington, 1992), and E. Prettejohn, *Rossetti and his Circle* (London, 1997).

detailed scenes of wharfside activity of Whistler's earlier Thames Set etchings (Plate 35). Both stress the grimy, industrial aspect of the river: whether factories and the rough and rowdy entertainment of Cremorne Gardens to the west of the city, or shipping and warehousing to the east. The etchings produce an overall sense of rhythm and design in the composition through their use of abrupt perspective and unusual viewpoints. I would suggest that the sense of the dreary and polluted aspect of the city is crucial to all this work by Whistler. His art effects a transformation into beauty but not an elimination of the dross. The example of the balance and resolution of the Nocturnes was decisive upon later artists' engagement with equivalent material. John Atkinson Grimshaw's moonlight scenes on the Thames of the 1880s display a degree of aesthetic serenity that is lacking in his earlier, more agitated dock and street scenes of Leeds, Liverpool and Glasgow.[19] William Wyllie, an artist who specialised in river and shipping themes from the 1870s and gained success and recognition in the 1880s, produced work that was more conventional in format, yet, nevertheless, has some affinities with the paradoxical exquisiteness of Whistler's Thames views. Wyllie's *Toil, Glitter, Grime and Wealth on a Flowing Tide* (1883) plays on the contrast between the sooty blackness of coal barges and steam tugs and the golden illumination of the pulsating river that bears this filthy traffic (Plate 36). The title makes explicit the kinship between wealth and dirt. Here the gleaming river and murky sky are not the elements that veil or compensate for the squalor of modernity: the poetry that cloaks life and allows an escape into aesthetic contemplation.[20] Instead, they are alternate versions of the same vital substance.

We have seen that the river can be seen to offer means of access and connection on one hand, and, on the other, the chance for tranquil contemplation within the city. The motif of the city street presented some analogous opportunities for the artist in terms of celebratory presentation of bustle and interchange, but it rarely figured as the setting for abstracted aesthetic musing. The street was almost invariably associated with its traffic and with a press of population. Thomas Hosmer Shepherd's steel engraved collections of views of metropolitan sites emphasise the splendid new developments and architectural achievements of the modern city by selecting the largely neoclassical schemes and new buildings. The prints depict their façades with crisp detail, and, at the same time, indicate an active throng at street level. Shepherd creates a complex sense of the city's criss-cross routes; the socially diverse crowd hurries in all

---

[19] A. Robertson, *Atkinson Grimshaw* (Oxford, 1988); Richard Green Gallery, *Atkinson Grimshaw*, exhibition catalogue (London, 1990); Richard Green Gallery, *John Atkinson Grimshaw*, exhibition catalogue (London, 1998).

[20] For the idea of the poetic veil over the city see Whistler, *The Gentle Art*, p. 144. Wyllie is discussed by W. Vaughan in I. B. Nadel and F. S. Schwarzbach, eds., *Victorian Artists and the City* (Elmsford, N.Y., and Oxford, 1979), pp. 74–5.

directions (Plate 37).[21] Thomas Shotter Boys, in the coloured lithographs of *London As It Is* (1842), articulates similar components to a rather different effect. His neoclassical elevations are stretched to a startling height and are bathed in clear, even light (Plate 38).[22] The city we are shown is certainly new and grand, the streets seem extraordinarily wide, but the pedestrians are not participants in, and beneficiaries of, the industrial and commercial dynamism in quite the same way that they are in Shepherd's views. The façades are very often angled so sharply that the architectural detail is compressed rather than laid out as an accessible and comprehensible system. Construction workers and their paraphernalia often block access for middle-class pedestrians, and the visual arrangement of perspectival depth also involves barriers which block imaginative access for middle-class viewers of the plates. Consequently, the city is presented as a clean, beautiful modern environment and a source of pride, but also, in part, as a troubling and potentially hazardous space.

(iv) URBAN FOLK

The 1850s saw the development of a form of genre painting that took as its subject the urban crowd. William Powell Frith, George Elgar Hicks and William Maw Egley produced multi-figure scenes that aimed to encompass the full range of social types and to evoke the unprecedented, impersonal crush of modern public places.[23] Human life and comic interaction took precedence over topographic presentation in these genre scenes, though the sites selected, for instance the General Post Office, Billingsgate Market and Paddington Station, were landmarks and tourist attractions in their own right, remarkable for the sheer quantity of business transacted and the startlingly modern technologies employed. The comedy depended on the frisson of excitement that unregulated social mixing inevitably produced. In these situations social contact and observable social conduct could move beyond the parameters of polite bourgeois interaction. Bourgeois behaviour might stray into the improper; working-class activity might be gross or criminal. Bourgeois bodies might be squashed, jostled, dirtied or infected. The example of Egley's *Omnibus Life in London* (1859) shows how these serious matters could produce a sort of muffled comedy (Plate 39). In this

[21] T. H. Shepherd, *Metropolitan Improvements* (London, 1827–30); T. H. Shepherd, *London in the Nineteenth Century* (London, 1830–1); T. H. Shepherd, *The World's Metropolis, or Mighty London* (London, 1854). The emphasis on cross-cutting routes has been pointed out and discussed in relation to a notion of the industrial sublime by A. Potts, 'Picturing the modern metropolis: images of London in the nineteenth century', *History Workshop Journal*, 26 (1988), pp. 28–56. See also J. F. C. Phillips, *Shepherd's London* (London, 1976).
[22] J. Roundell, *Thomas Shotter Boys* (London, 1974).
[23] E. D. H. Johnson, *Paintings of the British Social Scene from Hogarth to Sickert* (London, 1986); M. C. Cowling, *The Artist as Anthropologist* (Cambridge, 1989); Geffrye Museum, *George Elgar Hicks: Painter of Victorian Life*, exhibition catalogue (London, 1983).

picture the interior of an omnibus and its passengers are shown from the driver's end of the vehicle. In a constrained space various types are squashed close together: old and young, fat and thin, ladies and gentlemen, upper-middle-class and lower-middle-class figures. The viewer is encouraged to surmise that the contrasts extend to moral qualities too, and contemporary reviewers were ready to speculate as to the mingling of the foolish and the wise, the virtuous and the vicious, the honest and the criminal. The bus passengers do not communicate, they just stare rather suspiciously; their tension communicates itself to the picture's viewer but it also piques his or her sense of humour. The bus is already packed and yet more people want to get on. The final straw has to be the impossibility of accommodating the bulky crinoline of the fashionable young lady at the door. The sheer absurdity of the proposition allows the tension to be released in laughter.[24]

A decade or so later, the balance between anxiety and comedy was reversed. In the 1870s state policy concerning vagrancy and crime was being toughened up. There was a renewed effort to control urban populations, to limit workhouse expenditure, to identify perpetrators and punish crime. The phenomenon of city crowding, in these circumstances, tended to produce revulsion rather than amusement. With *London: A Pilgrimage* (1872), Gustave Doré and Blanchard Jerrold collaborated to produce a lavish publication, copiously illustrated by Doré's expressive woodcuts. London appears to be a place thronging with souls, a secular version of Dante's or Milton's heavenly or demonic realms.[25] Often the replication of figures in Doré's plates is macabre, whether in the wraithlike hordes of upper-class horse riders in the park, or the bulging proliferation of tottering infants in the streets of the slums. In 'Dudley Street, Seven Dials' in particular, these children seem to exist as unnaturally animated matter, rather than healthily burgeoning life (Plate 40). It appears that they have not been born, but have been reanimated in a godless resurrection from the tomb-like cellars. These cellars seem to announce their multiple interments by the fringe of sagging second-hand shoes arranged around every opening. *London: A Pilgrimage* offers a bleak vision, leavened by touches of humour or sentiment, and by the stubborn optimism of Jerrold's text. Where east end and west end are seen to mingle, as at the Boat Race, the anxiety is intense. In 'The River Bank – Under the Trees', dozens of ladies and gentlemen are gathered. Against a dark background the light catches the spectators. In the dark, upper part of the picture several working-class boys and a bearded man cling on to the overhanging branches, inches away from the middle-class crowd below. The viewer is acutely aware of

---

[24] See C. Arscott, 'Modern life subjects in British painting 1840–60' (PhD thesis, Dept of Fine Art, Leeds University, 1988); S. P. Casteras, 'Seeing the unseen: pictorial problematics and Victorian images of class, poverty, and urban life', in C. T. Christ and J. O. Jordan, eds., *Victorian Literature and the Victorian Visual Imagination* (Berkeley, 1995), pp. 264–88.
[25] Doré had illustrated Milton's *Paradise Lost* in 1866.

their lurking presence, but the figures on the ground appear unaware of the proximity.[26]

Throughout the Victorian period, and especially before 1880, urban settings provided the scenarios for sentimental dramas around the themes of poverty, charity and vice. The campaigning rhetoric of George Cruikshank's print series, *The Bottle* (1847) and *The Drunkard's Children* (1848), located the evils of drunkenness, improvidence, violence and prostitution in the working-class dwellings and resorts of the city. Starvation, murder and madness unfold in mean rooms, shabby saloons and, eventually, in the final plate of *The Drunkard's Children*, the gin-mad, prostitute daughter flings herself from a Thames bridge (Plate 41).[27] The propagandistic narrative was reversed in the before-and-after photographs that Dr Barnardo staged to attract support for his Home for Destitute Children from 1870. Wild street children are shown cleaned up, modest and contained, ready to take up useful employment.[28] The emotional landscape remained the same, however, and the highs and lows of the heart-rending and alarming poor proved a powerful resource for fine art. The genre paintings of Augustus Mulready show street-children as doe-eyed victims of circumstance, cowering in the gutter and mutely appealing for sympathy. Mingled responses of horror, erotic involvement, moral indignation and resolve to intervene charitably are mobilised in these apparently simple pictures.[29]

We have seen how the desolation of the Thames-side setting amplified the anguished finale of Egg's *Past and Present*. Dante Gabriel Rossetti worked on his major modern-life painting *Found* over an extended period (commenced 1854, unfinished) (Plate 42). It shows a woman who has become a prostitute sliding to the city pavement as she shrinks from an encounter. The country drover who has recognised her is a suitor from her virtuous rustic past. Like Egg, Rossetti was concerned to problematise the straightforward response of disgust and condemnation that the figure of the fallen woman was likely to provoke, but the image does not avoid the distasteful. The gutter, the city churchyard, the Thames bridge in the background, and even the allusion to the city cattle-market, combine to evoke the noisome environmental nuisances that campaigners for health and sanitation were endeavouring to redress. The woman with her fluid lines is the embodiment of effluent. Her proximity to the gravestones, the ghastly colour of her face and the identification between her and the tethered calf

[26] On Doré see I. B. Nadel, 'Gustave Doré: English art and London life', in Nadel and Schwarzbach, eds., *Victorian Artists*, pp. 152–62; G. Pollock, 'Vicarious excitements: *London: A Pilgrimage* by Gustave Doré and Blanchard Jerrold, 1872', *New Formations*, 4 (1988), 25–50.

[27] Manchester City Art Galleries, *Hard Times: Social Realism in Victorian Art*, exhibition catalogue, text by J. Treuherz (Manchester, 1987); R. L. Patten, *George Cruikshank: Life, Times and Art*, vol. II (Cambridge, 1996).

[28] National Portrait Gallery, *The Camera and Dr. Barnardo*, exhibition catalogue, text by V. Lloyd and G. Wagner (Hertford, 1974); J. Tagg, *The Burden of Representation* (London, 1988), ch. 3.

[29] C. Fox, *Londoners* (London, 1987).

heading for slaughter put her on the side of death. None the less, there is a lyr-
icism and life in the gentle floweriness of her dress, the soft curl of her hair, the
tender colours of the dawn and the strong yet gentle grasp of the man.
Repugnance, pity and love are aroused all at once. The city offers motifs that
reach the extremes of loathsomeness, but they are presented in an emotional and
ethical or religious framework that tempers distress.[30]

A heightening of beauty could be a signifier of emotional affect or religious
significance or, in the revised conditions of the latter part of the nineteenth
century, it could indicate an unmoralisable general spirituality, associated with
the aesthetic. Thomas Annan's photographs of Glasgow (1868–71) are haunting
images of disease-ridden crumbling alleyways destined for demolition. The
conundrum is the way the stained, seeping, closely spaced walls, signifiers of
overcrowding, foul air, sewage and disease, are rendered in visually arresting form
(Plate 43).[31] The many similar closes generate varied compositions which
balance blocks and patches of light and dark, the reflective and matt, and, above
all, differentiate the textures of the stonework that dominates the environment.
The set of photographs constitutes an investigation of the relationship between
randomness and pattern and of that between presence and absence. These issues
are explored in three different frameworks: first in a historic framework, in the
collection's reference to improvement, which involves the repatterning of the
environment and the physical displacement of people, secondly in a framework
of the self-referential, in the photographs' reflexive consideration of the technological aspects of the photographic process and finally in a framework of the aesthetic, in the pictures' exploration of form. Annan did not intend these images
to be reproduced; they were to be a unique record for the corporation. Public
interest in them was strong enough to convince him that the set was worthy of
publication and they survive as an outstanding example of the intersection
between the depiction of horrors and the perception of beauty in the city.[32]

The working-class population of the city appears regularly in the staffage of
the topographical work I have discussed, and is usually accorded a minor role in
genre subjects. Transport workers, street vendors, servants, delivery men and
building workers appear alongside beggars, thieves, prostitutes and urchins as
presences on the margins of visibility in middle-class zones. Their presence,

---

[30] A. I. Grieve, *The Art of Dante Gabriel Rossetti: 1. Found, 2. The Pre Raphaelite Modern Life Subject* (Norwich, 1976); Nead, *Myths of Sexuality*.

[31] There is a discussion of the omission of solid excrement and the depiction of liquid waste in these images in E. Handy, 'Dust piles and damp pavements: excrement, repression and the Victorian city in photography and literature', in Christ and Jordan, eds., *Victorian Literature*, pp. 111–33.

[32] T. Annan, *Photographs of Old Closes and Streets of Glasgow, Taken 1868–77*, Glasgow, City Improvement Trust, 1878/9; T. Annan, *Old Closes and Streets, a Series of Photogravures, 1868–1899*, Glasgow, James Maclehose, 1900. On Annan see A. V. Mozley's introduction to T. Annan, *Photographs of the Old Closes etc.* (New York, 1977); and S. Stevenson, *Thomas Annan 1829–1887* (Edinburgh, 1990).

though understated, was crucial to definitions of the modern urban. The focus on centre-stage destitute or fallen characters as the objects of moral concern was something of a novelty in the Victorian period, and there was an understanding that, with these subjects, the essence of the contemporary was being addressed. Prostitution was referred to as the 'great social evil', such themes constituted the 'modern moral subject'. Even newer and more unusual was the directing of attention to proletarian, or lumpen, figures as workers or as occupants of their own areas. Annan's inclusion of ranks of slum dwellers in his photographs, and Doré's depiction of East End enclaves followed on from avenues of social reportage that had been opened up by government investigations and journalistic surveys. Among the many middle-class exposés of industrial and urban conditions Henry Mayhew's *London Labour and the London Poor* was particularly influential. Mayhew's attention to the individuals encountered in his survey of street folk was exceptional. The apparently verbatim interviews and the individualised depictions in the engraved illustrations gave unparalleled representational presence to inferior social ranks. It became possible to present working people as genre figures in the visual arts without relying entirely on comic stereotypes of clumsy buffoonery.

Manual labour featured in Ford Madox Brown's *Work* (Plate 44). In this highly finished painting, a group of navvies engaged in excavation and construction work in connection with the water supply is placed at the centre of the composition and functions as the central example of healthy, moral, purposeful effort. Representative figures from the other ranks of society are arranged around this central motif. We are invited to consider the kind of work these other figures do or do not do, and they are implicitly compared to the reference point of the navvies.[33] William Bell Scott's *Iron and Coal* (1862) is another work which includes active, muscular industrial workers as central figures (Plate 45). This was the final canvas in a series produced as a decorative scheme for Wallington Hall and the theme of the history of the North-East runs through to this modern scene. The scale and might of the characteristic industries of Newcastle is emphasised and so the labourers figure more as allegorical embodiments of that general industrial achievement than as individually moralised characters.[34] By contrast the factory workers of Eyre Crowe's *The Dinner Hour, Wigan* (1874) are subject to our moral scrutiny (Plate 46). We are shown young women operatives gathering in the yard outside the factory in one of their breaks.[35] The space is hemmed in by the towering walls of the surrounding factories. The stark red-brick environment is relieved by the bright costumes and graceful movements

[33] Brown's pamphlet, produced for the exhibition of this picture, made the comparison explicit.
[34] On the allegorical status of this image see P. Usherwood, 'William Bell Scott's *Iron and Coal*: northern readings', in Laing Art Gallery, *Pre-Raphaelites: Painters and Patrons in the North East*, exhibition catalogue (Newcastle, 1989), pp. 39–56.
[35] See Manchester City Art Galleries, *Hard Times*.

of the young women, and our first impression is that this is a harmonious, well-fed, neatly dressed, attractive group of workers. The winning glance of the dark-haired beauty in the foreground could be assimilated to this generally favourable view of the benefits of the factory system, except that some of the less prominent figures, partly hidden behind the low wall, or else on the extreme edge of the picture, or in the shaded yard in the background, are engaged in dubious activities. A bottle of strong drink consumed, a transaction with a man, a meeting with a lover – all these scarcely decipherable motifs raise doubts about the moral health of the personnel and the suitability of paid work, large-scale workplaces and the urban environment itself for vulnerable, perhaps flighty, young women. Certainly, the vigilance of the tiny figure of the policeman in the road at the back is advisable. However, the picture does not convince us that his efforts are sufficient to seal off the workplace from the dangerous currents of the city. The women's beauty, then, is no longer simply a delight and a reassurance, it is also a source of anxiety.

In 1877, Adolphe Smith and John Thomson published a series of photographs of workers and the poor on the streets of London entitled *Street Life in London*.[36] They were, they said, producing an update on Mayhew's work, and Smith's text develops the personal stories of the people photographed by Thomson. In these stories we learn of the mutable fortunes of the characters and of the illusory or ephemeral quality of the goods that they trade: water-ice, advertising placards, patent medicines (Plate 47). The shots are taken out of doors and, while the main character may be posed and centred, additional figures and details creep into the composition, destabilising and blurring the arrangement. There is a strong sense of an environment in flux, and lives subject to uncontrollable forces. The themes of presence and absence that we discerned in Annan's photographic work appear here too, but the human life of the city, rather than the physical environment, is the major focus. The most prominent figure in the first picture of the book, 'London Nomades', is a woman on the steps of the van (Plate 48). We learn from the text that, two weeks after the photograph had been taken, she was found mysteriously murdered. We have to conclude that the evidence of our eyes, or the indexical record of the photograph, will not provide an adequate empirical basis for grasping the city. At this point, viewers could not rely, as the viewers of the 1850s and 1860s had done, on moral judgements based on careful looking and firm categorisation.[37] Smith and Thomson's work can be taken as a marker which indicates a loss of confidence with regard to the modern city.

---

[36] *Street Life in London* initially appeared in 1877 as a part-work and, later that year, as a bound volume.

[37] This kind of controlling vision has been associated with Foucault's notion of surveillance and the operations of the panopticon; M. Foucault, *Discipline and Punish: The Birth of the Prison*, trans. A. Sheridan (Harmondsworth, 1970). See G. Pollock, 'Power and visibility in the city' (review article), *Art History*, 11 (1988), 275–83; Tagg, *The Burden of Representation*; and T. Bennett, *The Birth of the Museum: History, Theory, Politics* (London and New York, 1995).

The impulse to control unruly phenomena and potentially dangerous populations through vigilant looking and effective categorisation did not vanish. The
pictures produced in the latter part of the nineteenth century are characterised,
rather, by a partial thwarting and a gradual diminution of that impulse. The
move to an aesthetic framework for the apprehension of modernity gave works
a melancholy cast, because the perception of beauty involved the renunciation
of interpretation and control. There was a submerged appreciation of the losses
that were entailed and, one might hypothesise, an acknowledgement that the
massive proportions of the city, its sheer extent and complexity, had forced this
abdication. The change of mood can perhaps be demonstrated by comparing
two works by John O'Connor, one from the 1870s and one from a decade later.
The Embankment (1874) is a bright sunny view from the promenade at Somerset
House, where a nursery maid is taking the air with her charges (Plate 49). We
look down the newly built embankment towards Cannon Street Station and St
Paul's Cathedral. It is a bright and lively prospect. A detachment of red-coated
soldiers march in neat formation, their bayonets glistening in the light. The light
also catches the regularly placed, new street lights. The even, uncongested road
stretches in a broad ribbon, leading the eye to a skyline that combines order and
tradition in the Temple, state and spiritual authority in St Paul's and the technological present and future in the gasometers (echoing the shape of St Paul's), the
smoking factory chimneys, the steaming railway train and the shining, new
railway shed. The fresh greenery of the young saplings and the glistening surface
of the river produce an extremely pleasant animation in the scene. The picture
manages to yoke together a series of apparently opposing terms: the lowly and
the grand, peace and military preparedness, the past and the future, leisure and
employment, freedom and order, the particular and the general, and the natural
and the manmade. The mood of the picture is so buoyant that the opposing
terms are not felt as sources of stress and potential rupture but as energising
differentials. The atmosphere of *From Pentonville Road Looking West: Evening*
(1884) is, by contrast, contemplative and melancholy (Plate 50). The view is
taken from a deserted rooftop on a damp and smoky evening as crowds of tiny
figures pack on to buses and hurry home along the street. They mainly head
downhill, westwards, towards the setting sun which illuminates the mist around
St Pancras, creating a glorious golden haze. In this romantic light the gothic pin-
nacles of the St Pancras frontage give it the appearance of a great cathedral,
despite the fact that it is just a station hotel. The railway shed extends across the
canvas, barely delineated and becoming ever fainter, but apparently extending
into infinity. The bare autumnal branches of the tree, the bell-tower of a church
and a jumble of empty and abandoned crates and baskets feature prominently at
viewing level. All these things combine to suggest the passing of time, loss and
the flight of the soul. We can therefore understand the evening rush of the city
folk as standing for something beyond their daily routine. They can be viewed

as humanity in general, rushing towards death, with their immortal fate ahead of them. The particular circumstances of the street: the mean shops and houses, the higgledy-piggledy chimneys, the pasted-over advertising notices, the *Daily News* prominent among them, all these things stand for the diurnal and are rendered insignificant in the light of eternity. The balanced polarities of O'Connor's earlier picture are torn apart. The symbolic presentation of the railway station as a gate to the afterlife is most unusual (though one thinks of the idea of the glory train) but the register of representation is entirely typical of the late nineteenth century. Modernity no longer lends itself to being experienced as an integrated phenomenon. The particular cannot easily be related to the whole; the city is experienced as random and unstable. The particular always threatens to stand as the banal and meaningless rather than the typical and informative. There is a sundering of the fragment from the totality.[38]

(v) LEISURE AND CONSUMPTION

In the final section of this chapter I wish to explore a further aspect of the city. Alongside the monumental fabric and the accumulation of slums and social problems, and interwoven with the city of congested traffic and drudgery, was the glittering city devoted to leisure and consumption. Upbeat images of shopping and middle-class leisure abound in the early Victorian period. The formative book of views by T. H. Shepherd, *Metropolitan Improvements* (1827–30), focused on Regent Street as the key part of what was to be the most splendid and ambitious building scheme for half a century. Shepherd produced images of Regent Street throughout his career and, in the Victorian period, the locale became a ubiquitous setting for images of fashionable display and luxurious consumption. In 1851, George Sidney Shepherd, the younger brother of Thomas, produced ten views for a large lithographic volume published by Ackermann, one of which was a view of Regent Street. Fashionably dressed bourgeois figures stand watching the display of ceremonial troops that ride past. The rival attraction is the prominent window of Ackermann's own print shop on the left where a multitude of brightly coloured views tempts the gathered ladies and gentlemen. It quite eclipses the Lace Warehouse two doors down. William McConnell and George Augustus Sala introduced Regent Street into the series of comic engravings by McConnell that illustrate the volume *Twice Round the Clock, or the Hours of the Day and Night in London* (1859) (Plate 51).[39] The pretensions of self-important carriage folk are gently satirised and the slightly alarming press of the city crowd is registered. Typically for the late 1850s, the crowd, which is mainly

[38] This might be thought to presage some of the features of the postmodern. See F. Jameson, *Postmodernism, or, the Cultural logic of Late Capitalism* (London, 1991).

[39] See P. Collins' introduction to G. A. Sala, *Twice Round the Clock, or the Hours of the Day and Night in London* (London, 1859; repr., Leicester, 1971).

composed of prosperous and respectable people, also includes a suspicious-looking street-vendor selling dogs, a blind beggar in the thick of the crowd and, on the right, a prostitute addressing a moustachioed man. In the accompanying text, Sala lists the huge variety of the street's luxury shops and notes the cachet given by their aristocratic patrons. His conclusion is that 'Regent Street is an avenue of superfluities – a great trunk road in Vanity Fair.'[40] This pulsing centre of fashion and upmarket retail activity inspires awe and promises pleasure, but pleasure, it seems, is not without its moral and physical dangers.

Ten years later we see Jacques Joseph Tissot, a specialist in the depiction of urban leisure, embarking on scenes of London life.[41] Tissot spent eleven years in London from 1871 and produced scenes of boating and picnicking, parties and balls, with figures lounging and chatting. The settings are the streets, drawing rooms and gardens of the city. These pictures show spacious and comfortable environments. Society beauties show off extravagantly gorgeous dresses and indulge in flirtation and dreamy silence. There is still room for social satire, though, for the most part, it does not play on the uncomfortable contrasts between respectable folk and the low-life characters around them, as it does in McConnell's engravings. The city induces less a sense of thrill and panic than a sense of alienation and boredom. In these social situations the atmosphere is heavy with innuendo, but the exact terms of the awkwardness, resentment or invitation are hard to decipher because this is a world of muffling upholstery and shining surfaces in which signals vanish or distort. An example of a picture that produces this kind of unease is Tissot's *London Visitors* (c. 1874) in which the severe classical lines of the portico of the National Gallery in London provide the chilly setting for a handful of figures (Plate 52). A woman at the exit on the left is being shown the way by a uniformed schoolboy and, in the foreground, his classmate stands on the steps on the right and stares out towards Trafalgar Square. Behind this boy is a couple. The woman gestures to the right with her umbrella or parasol and her companion leafs through his guide book. The viewer is struck by the way in which this woman's gaze does not follow her gesture. Instead she glances sideways and down the steps, without moving her head, apparently covertly looking in the direction of the viewer, or past the viewer to the left. The picture gives us a huge blank space on the left; the bare stone is grey and unyielding. Two versions of the city are superimposed here. In one the tourist sites are linked in logical order and the city is predictable and navigable with the aid of guides. In the other, represented by the gaze to the right, the environment appears inaccessible and even bewildering. Importantly, it contains the promise of sexual adventure. We assume that the lady's transgressive glance

[40] *Ibid.*, p. 157.
[41] See N. Marshall, '"Transcripts of modern life": the London pictures of James Tissot 1871–1882' (PhD thesis, Department of History of Art, Yale University, 1997).

has been drawn by a gentleman because there, on the empty steps, lies a cigar stub.

In the 1880s W. R. Sickert started to produce a series of paintings of music hall subjects.[42] These represent a major shift from the territory of Tissot's scenes of middle-class leisure. The music hall provided mass entertainment. Middle-class visitors would have been in the minority. Themes of alienation and indecipherability persist in this body of work, but they are worked through in relation to commercialised popular entertainment. These are, inescapably, scenes of city life and at this juncture urban life appears claustrophobic and joyless rather than seductive and thrilling. Very often the audience members appear blank and drab in comparison to the gaudy surroundings and the colourful spotlit stage performers. Sickert uses complex compositional systems involving mirrors and deceptive perspectival effects. The painting *The P.S. Wings in an O.P. Mirror* (*c.* 1889) is a condensed example of these features (Plate 53). We assume that the audience is assembled to watch the performance to the rear of the picture. Perplexingly, the spectators stare past the singer, while she projects into an unpeopled space above their heads. This seems very odd and produces an acute sense of dislocation. The puzzle can be resolved when we realise that this is a transverse image of the stage, seen in a mirror hanging to the left of the row of seats. None the less, the sense of dislocation remains because the spectators appear so shabby and grim; their gazes are fixed, their faces expressionless. This is absorption and, perhaps, intense excitement, but the spectacle seems to drain life and colour from the spectators. Sickert returned to this theme throughout his career. The music hall images take their place alongside his Mornington Crescent interiors of the 1900s and 1910s and the quietistic urban landscapes of the Camden Town school of the 1910s as some of the most compelling visions of modern city life at a moment when straightforward, optimistic celebration had ceased to be an option. At this point observation is aesthetically framed. In other words, Sickert was seeking beauty in the everyday rather than, on the one hand, selecting elevated subject matter which might be thought to bear with it a guarantee of its value as art, or, on the other hand, attending to the everyday primarily as a record maker or documentarist. Whistler felt that a veil had to be drawn over the city to render it beautiful. Sickert was prepared to find beauty without drawing a veil. The attention to banal surroundings is exercised from the protected vantage point of art. This makes it possible to view the sad, the impoverished and the seamy aspects of the city with a degree of detachment. The middle-class viewer willingly opens himself or herself up to the mood; he or she even empathises with the alienated social specimens on display. In this way, the turn-of-the-century viewer is

---

[42] See A. G. Robins, 'Sickert "painter-in-ordinary" to the music-hall', in Royal Academy of Arts, *Sickert: Paintings*, exhibition catalogue (London, 1992), pp. 13–24.

able to identify with the social other because it is understood that no harm will ensue, since this is the realm of art.

(vi) CONCLUSION

The music hall was the forerunner of, and closely entwined with, the most significant mass entertainment phenomenon of the twentieth century, the cinema. The Lumière Brothers in Lyons demonstrated the cinematographe in 1895. Early cinematic reels showed horses and carriages moving in the streets of Leeds. The excitement of the new form of representation was allied to the range of sights and entertainments available in the urban centres: traffic, eminent magicians and prize fights, for example. Soon these themes were supplemented by the whole range of fictional genres from the Biblical epic to the western. Experiments in France, England and the United States refined and advanced the technologies to the point that multi-reel features with continuous narrative, and such editing methods as close-ups and dissolves, were being produced in the 1910s. Political tensions in Europe and the outbreak of war in 1914 meant that the initiative in cinema shifted to the United States.

The First World War redrew the social map of Europe, and with it the social conventions and patterns of cultural consumption. The pre-1880 period was one in which the visual arts were relatively unified, in so far as the extensive middle-class public enthusiastically attended fine art exhibitions, purchased prints and pored over illustrated books and journals. The social groups addressed and the modes of reception required were comparable for diverse forms of visual representation. The gap between high and low art was relatively small and, among the bourgeoisie, there was considerable optimism concerning the social gains that could be made by encouraging the lower middle class and the working class to view fine art. The later Victorian period was marked by a polarisation within cultural production. Elite culture became walled around by specialist critical terms and the provision of entertainment for a working-class audience (which now had significant disposable income) became big business. The twentieth century saw the full-scale development of a culture industry and the increasing marginalisation of fine art production. Except in phases of heightened political consciousness the avant-garde practices of continental and British art movements were inaccessible to general audiences and deliberately restricted themselves to selected consumers. The texture of urban life, the pressure and pace and discontinuities of modernity and the delirium and despair to be found in the city were central themes of modernist art, surfacing, for example, in the abstraction of the Vorticists. As we have seen, they were also themes that ran through the topographical and anecdotal work of the Victorian period.

The modern city was an important motif in Victorian and Edwardian art. Across the period there were major shifts in artists' responses to urban phenomena, most notably, as I have demonstrated, a broad shift from expansive optimism to an inward-looking melancholy. Integrative vision gives way to fragmentary perception. The relationship of the middle-class viewer to other social orders in depiction also changed. Nineteenth-century viewers were particularly sensitive to situations that involved the mixing of different social classes. Spaces of the city might expose bourgeois figures to damaging or polluting contact with working-class inhabitants. The background to this sensitivity was an abiding anxiety concerning insurgent working-class populations. It might be argued that outright fear gave way, at the end of the century, to distaste tinged with pity for the mass. An artist like Sickert depicted working-class and lower-middle-class figures passively packed into the commercial facilities of the turn-of-the-century city. Earlier, mid-Victorian viewers had been attuned to a mingling of fear, disgust and sympathy, a vacillation between condemnation and the impulse to charitable intervention. The turn-of-the-century viewer was not barred from emotional affect, but was, nevertheless, less immediately driven to consider active intervention. We can discern a curious symmetry between the pictorial subject and the picture viewer. The draining of life and energy from the lower-class subjects of the picture (blank consumers subjected to entertainment), is mimicked by the resigned aestheticism of the high-art picture viewer.

At each historical moment urban experience had to be processed and assimilated. In the industrial era the modern city was recurrently experienced as gigantic, unprecedented and verging on the overwhelming. In retrospect the cities of the 1830s might seem fairly contained and manageable, but the early Victorians had to find terms and images to express the astonishing immensity and complexity of the city just as the late Victorians and the Edwardians had to. In this survey of visual imagery I have drawn attention to the constant reregistration of the city's wonders and horrors.

28 Anonymous, *An Anamorphic View of London and the Surrounding Country Taken from the Top of St Paul's Cathedral*, tinted aquatint, 75.5 cm diameter, *c.* 1845.

29 Niels Moeller Lund, *The Heart of the Empire*, oil on canvas, 137.2 × 182.9 cm, 1904.

30 Ford Madox Brown, *An English Autumn Afternoon, Hampstead – Scenery in 1853*, oil on canvas, 71.2 × 134.8 cm (oval), 1852–3; 1855.

31 Spencer Gore, *Mornington Crescent*, oil on canvas, 50.8 × 61.6 cm, c. 1911.

32 William Parrott, 'Southwark Bridge from London Bridge', lithograph, from W. Parrott, *London from the Thames*, 1842.

33 Augustus Leopold Egg, 'August the 4ᵗʰ. Have just heard that B—has been dead more than a fortnight, so his poor children have now lost both parents. I hear that she was seen on Friday last near the Strand, evidently without a place to lay her head. What a fall hers has been!', from the series known as Past and Present, no. 3, oil on canvas, 63.5×76.2 cm, 1858.

34 James Abbott McNeill Whistler, *Nocturne in Blue and Silver: Cremorne Lights*, oil on canvas, 50.2 × 74.3 cm, 1872.

35 James Abbott McNeill Whistler, 'Limehouse', etching, 1859, from J. A. M. Whistler, *Sixteen Etchings of Scenes on the Thames and Other Subjects (Thames Set) 1871*.

36 William Lionel Wyllie, *Toil, Glitter, Grime and Wealth on a Flowing Tide*, oil on canvas, 115.6 × 165.1 cm, 1883.

37 Thomas Hosmer Shepherd, 'Piccadilly from Coventry Street', engraving, from T. H. Shepherd, *London in the Nineteenth Century*, 1830–1.

38 Thomas Shotter Boys, 'Club Houses, Pall Mall', lithograph from T. S. Boys, *London As It Is*, 1842.

39 William Maw Egley, *Omnibus Life in London*, oil on canvas, 44.8×41.9 cm, 1859.

40 Gustave Doré, 'Dudley Street, Seven Dials', from G. Doré and B. Jerrold, *London: A Pilgrimage*, 1872.

41 George Cruikshank, 'The poor girl, homeless, friendless, deserted, and gin mad, commits self-murder', final plate from G. Cruikshank, *The Drunkard's Children*, 1848.

42 Dante Gabriel Rossetti, *Found*, oil on canvas, 91.4×80 cm, commenced
1854, unfinished.

43 Thomas Annan, 'Close No. 139, Saltmarket, Glasgow', from T. Annan, *Photographs of Old Closes, Streets &c. of Glasgow, Taken 1868–71, 1868/77*, albumen print, 28.5×23 cm, 1878/9, Glasgow City Improvement Trust.

44 Ford Madox Brown, *Work*, oil on canvas, 137 × 197.3 cm, 1852–63.

45 William Bell Scott, *The Nineteenth Century: Iron and Coal*, oil on canvas,
186.6×187.9 cm, 1861, Wallington Hall, The Trevelyan Collection (The
National Trust).

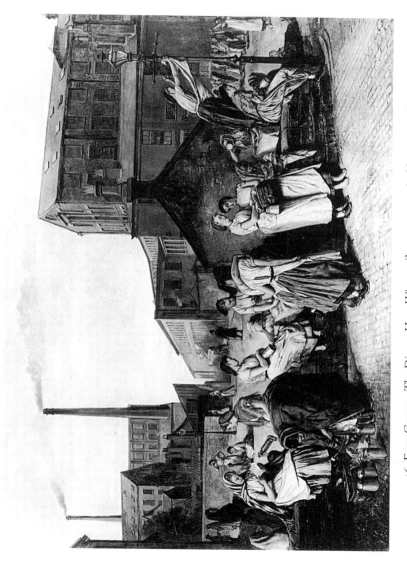

46 Eyre Crowe, *The Dinner Hour, Wigan*, oil on canvas, 76.3 × 107 cm, 1874.

47 John Thomson, 'Street advertising', woodburytype, 11 × 8.8 cm, from A. Smith and J. Thomson, *Street Life in London*, 1877.

48 John Thomson, 'London Nomades', woodburytype, 11×8.6 cm, from A. Smith and J. Thomson, *Street Life in London*, 1877.

49 John O'Connor, *The Embankment*, oil on canvas, 76.5 × 126.5 cm, 1874.

50 John O'Connor, *From Pentonville Road Looking West: Evening*, oil on canvas, 90.3 × 150.3 cm, 1884.

TWO O'CLOCK P.M.: REGENT STREET.

51 William McConnell, 'Two o'clock p.m.: Regent Street', from George Augustus Sala, *Twice Round the Clock, or the Hours of the Day and Night in London*, 1859.

52 Jacques Joseph Tissot, *London Visitors*, oil on canvas, 160 × 114.3 cm, *c*. 1874.

53 Walter Richard Sickert, *The P.S. Wings in an O.P. Mirror*, oil on canvas, 61 ×
51 cm, *c.* 1889.

· 25 ·

Epilogue

MARTIN DAUNTON

THE THIRD volume of the *Cambridge Urban History* comes to a close around 1950. It has explained how crisis and rupture in the second quarter of the nineteenth century were resolved in the later nineteenth century, through the creation of voluntary associations and an active municipal culture to deal with problems of 'free riders' and urban diseconomies, and to provide large-scale investment in the urban infrastructure. During much of this period, cities had powerful external economies, and allowed firms to operate with relatively weak internal systems of management. They accumulated considerable amounts of 'social capital' – webs of interconnections and sociability – which contributed to economic efficiency, social stability and political effectiveness. But the importance of cities slowly started to decline in the twentieth century. The power of the central state increased, taking an ever greater role in providing welfare and in offering financial assistance for local services. Municipal enterprises were nationalised, and local democratic control surrendered. Industrial concerns developed internal management systems, and were more concerned with national politics than with the municipality, with institutional investors in London than with networks of local reputation.

After 1950, it might be argued, an urban history of Britain is no longer feasible, and the urban variable lost any explanatory force it might once have possessed. On such an argument, there is no place for an urban history of Britain after 1950: Britain is an urban nation, and a separate urban history is no longer realistic. But should we so easily dismiss a continued interest in the history of British cities in the second half of the twentieth century and into the new millennium? Many of the issues considered in the present volume are in fact highly pertinent for the second half of the twentieth century. From the 1950s, British towns and cities underwent rapid change, introducing new variations on the debates of the previous hundred years. A sense of locality, the nature of the ecology of the city and the way that processes intersect to create a balance of

Martin Daunton

economies and diseconomies are as relevant in the later twentieth century as in the late nineteenth century. The issues of urban externalities, of systems of governance, of contesting claims on the urban environment are still important issues in contemporary Britain.

The difficulties of resolving these issues have been intensified by disruption of urban governance. The marginalisation of urban government in the last quarter century should not be read as a sign that urban history has lost its relevance. Rather, it should be seen in the same light as the disruption of urban government in the second quarter of the nineteenth century: there are serious problems to be resolved, without effective means of creating consensus and resolving conflicts. Local government at the end of the twentieth century attracts a very low turn-out in elections, in part reflecting reorganisation since the 1970s and the onslaught of the Thatcher government. The reforms of local government by the Heath administration in the early 1970s created large new metropolitan councils for Merseyside, Tyneside and so on, subsuming the old city councils and failing to develop a new sense of local identity. By the 1980s, so it appeared to many Conservatives, local government was out of control, in the hands of dangerous militants. Many officials in Whitehall were suspicious of the 'extravagance' of local government, and had little or no experience of the problems and difficulties facing councillors and officers in the town halls. Local government was seen as part of the problem of governance in the 1980s, rather than a means of resolving tensions over the nature of urban society.

The greatest irritant was the Greater London Council under the control of Ken Livingstone, who turned County Hall, at the other end of Westminster Bridge from the Commons, into a centre of opposition to Thatcherism, a constant and deliberate irritant. Abolition of the GLC meant that London, alone amongst the great capital cities of the world, had no overall political authority. Responsibility was left to the metropolitan boroughs which would consult over major issues, but there was a lack of real agreement. Outer London boroughs such as Croydon had little interest in the difficulties of desperately poor inner London boroughs such as Hackney. And many strategic issues were in the hands of unaccountable and anonymous officials in Whitehall, so removing problems such as an integrated transport system from the agenda for local or metropolitan politics. The privatisation of the railways and buses, and uncertainty over the status of the underground, caused additional complications. Redevelopment of the dock lands, one of the largest schemes of urban regeneration in Europe, was left to commercial concerns, with remarkably little public control over the provision of the infrastructure, and with a destructive competition with the City of London for the provision of new office space. In a longer-term perspective, the outcome was akin to the mid-nineteenth century: the forces of localism of the vestries, and the provision of metropolitan services by specific agencies such as the Metropolitan Commissioners of Sewers or the Metropolitan Police under the control of the Home Office. In the opinion of some critics, the outcome was unfortunate, and there was a serious deficit of democratic accountability – after all, the Metropolitan Police was the source of constant criticism as corrupt, racist and inefficient. The decision of the Blair government to create an elected mayor for London marks an attempt to recreate a political forum for resolving some of the problems of externalities and diseconomies in the metropolis.

The issue is not simply the creation of new systems of governance; finance is also vitally important. Nothing was done to widen the tax base of local government from dependence on the rates, which started to cause difficulties at the end of the nineteenth century. The alternatives of a local sales tax or income tax simply seemed too complex and the rates continued, with grants from central government. However, the politics of local government finance was to cause one of the gravest political problems of the Thatcher administration and contributed to her downfall. It had been accepted that the rates were regressive, so poor households were given rebates. Further, rateable values were periodically reassessed, so that some voters might find that their rate demands increased. These issues came together, and led to a revision of the entire system of local government finance. To many Conservatives, the existing fiscal system was the source of irresponsible urban government, for ratepayers were a minority of the electorate: only household heads paid, and even they might receive a rebate. The result, so they argued, was that most voters had an incentive to vote for expensive, irresponsible government. As a result – so the argument continued – a widow living alone would pay a large amount in rates, whereas a family of tenants on a council estate, with parents and children all earning, might pay less and vote for expensive policies. Here, it seemed, was the electoral basis for the schemes of the GLC or the left-wing Labour councils in Liverpool or Sheffield. One solution was to impose ever stricter controls over local spending, by 'capping' the rates and eroding the autonomy of local government. The permanent solution – so it was hoped – was to impose a flat-rate 'community charge' – the infamous poll tax – on all adults, so that all voters would be responsible. At least some advocates of the poll tax believed that it would recreate the conditions for efficient local government. In reality, the poll tax was highly unpopular, with a high level of non-payment which weakened local government finance. The picture of the poor widow could easily be countered by the millionaire in his mansion, paying less than a working-class family in a small inner-city terrace house. The failure of the poll tax meant a further undermining of local government autonomy. The result has been a disruption of urban governance and serious difficulties in resolving major debates over urban diseconomies.

In the 1990s, a beleaguered Minister of Transport faced great difficulties in allocating the costs of pollution and congestion, and the use of urban space continues to be contested. In the twentieth century, urban spaces were redesigned to separate traffic and create arterial roads. The approach reached its apogee – or nadir – with Colin Buchanan's report on traffic in towns, and the plans to construct a new road through Georgian Bath and a motorway 'box' around central London. The massive clearance schemes of the 1950s and 1960s far surpassed the efforts of the 1930s, with Harold Macmillan's pledge to build 300,000 new houses. The answer, so it seemed, was high-rise tower blocks and system building to increase productivity. Le Corbusier's image of the city was quite unlike that of the strolling, parading *boulevardier*: it was the street as 'a factory for producing traffic', of high-rise apartments as 'machines for living', separated by grass and linked by highways. In Marshall Berman's words, modernist architecture

> systematically attacked . . . the 'moving chaos' of nineteenth century urban life . . .
> In the new urban environment . . . the old modern street, with its volatile mixture
> of people and traffic, businesses and homes, rich and poor, is sorted out and split
> up into separate compartments, with exits and entrances strictly monitored and
> controlled, parking lots and underground garages the only mediation . . . The anar-
> chic, explosive forces that urban modernisation once brought together, a new wave
> of modernization, backed by an ideology of developing modernism, has pulled
> apart.[1]

The mall, with its private space and regulated behaviour, stands as the image of the new urban environment.

Although these schemes are often attacked as the product of arrogant architects and planners, or the greed of a new breed of property speculators, their vision of a new, modern city had considerable popular support. Indeed, in the 1960s local politicians were urged to press ahead with the building of high-rise flats by tenants, and in turn urged the central government to allow them to proceed. By the 1960s and 1970s, a reaction was already evident with the emergence of a powerful conservation movement to protect even mundane Georgian terraces from demolition. High-rise flats soon took on images of fear and alienation; the collapse of one block in east London was soon followed by a programme of deliberate demolition. The reaction was not simply against the form of housing erected by city councils; there was also an attack on council housing as a tenure. Tenants were given an absolute right to buy council houses, and the funds could not be spent on new public services. Any new social housing was to be provided by housing associations rather than local authorities which were no longer considered trustworthy. In fact, the stock of property for rent to low-income families was small, and homelessness became a serious political issue. Meanwhile, Britain was obsessed with buying and selling houses, with massive increases in prices as the market overheated and ran ahead of incomes. The political dangers of a subsequent fall in prices which would leave many people with 'negative equity', or of variations in interest rates which would affect mortgage repayments, were apparent.

[1] M. Berman, *All That is Solid Melts into Air* (New York, 1982), pp. 165–8

These tensions within the housing market may be explained in national terms, but they do have a local, urban dimension. The massive gap between house prices in different parts of the country is a serious constraint on the movement of labour, and affects accumulation of wealth. The owner of a house in Liverpool would scarcely be able to buy a house or flat in London – and would certainly not make the large, untaxed, capital gains experienced in the South-East of England. As the owner-occupiers of the 1930s died, their children inherited considerable sums of money. In inner London and, to an extent in other prosperous urban areas, 'gentrification' became an issue. In one of the first preservation battles, Richard Crossman – Minister of Housing and Local Government in the Labour government of 1964 – halted the bulldozers as they were razing swathes of Islington to the ground. As he realised, the main danger would be that the houses would soon be 'gentrified' and the working-class tenants displaced. The issue, as he saw it, was how to keep out the middle class. By the 1990s, his fears were realised, and the middle class was well entrenched in Islington. Working-class tenants survived in the remaining unmodernised properties, or inner-city council flats. These streets in Islington – where most of this volume was edited – may stand for a wider process of social change. They were built by a speculative builder in the 1840s and 1850s on 99 year leases. By the late nineteenth century, respectable city clerks had moved out to the newer suburbs, and the houses were subdivided with small workshops and factories inserted. Rent controls meant that little money was spent on maintenance, and damage during the war led to further decay. In the late 1940s, the freehold of the estate was purchased by the London and Manchester Insurance Company, which held the houses until the old tenants moved or died, when they could be renovated and sold to a new, affluent middle class. Different identities and subjectivities collide in the streets of Islington, and the urban environment was remade, with the profits of gentrification and redevelopment going to some interests and not others.

The pressure on the housing stock created political tensions over the location of new housing and planning controls over the green belt. Should the flight to the urban fringe for housing and out-of-town shopping be halted and building encouraged on 'brown' land within the city? Or should the green belt be sacrificed to the needs of housing and out-of-town shopping centres? These debates involve the economic interests of large builders and supermarket chains with their expectations of private profit – but there is also the matter of social costs, and how they should be balanced and by whom. Owners of shops in the city centre, or residents without access to motor transport, would have a different set of priorities. Many of the issues addressed in this third volume of the *Cambridge Urban History* remain relevant to these debates – and not least to Cambridge itself, where the editing has been completed. The sleepy market town of the nineteenth century has been transformed into one of the most prosperous cities in Britain, with the university generating science-based research. The strict limits of the green belt, and the conservation of the city centre, are creating pressure on the housing stock, with high prices and serious traffic problems. The debates over amenity and economic growth, over the desirability of controlling building or removing restrictions on the green belt, over the provision of improved public transport and limits on the private car, are simply further variations on the theme of urban externalities explored in this volume. The policy of containing urban England with a green belt, introduced in 1948, is now highly contentious, with implications for the allocation of profits from urban growth.

The creation of out-of-town shopping and new suburban estates has been countered by another trend, of regeneration of the inner city. In the 1950s and 1960s, cities were adapted to the motor car, with new roads and an insistence that new office buildings provide parking spaces. By the 1980s and 1990s, 'park and ride' schemes, pedestrianisation of city centres and the provision of new urban tram systems in a number of cities have taken a different approach. In some cases, the decline of inner-city shopping has been halted, and the vitality of the old city centre preserved or increased. One of the first triumphs of preservation was the old market at Covent Garden, which was renovated and converted into a centre for shops and restaurants and buskers, recreating in a sanitised way some of the 'moving chaos' celebrated by Marshall Berman. The process is highly commercial, a way of marketing the city and its bustle. In some cities – Glasgow, Leeds, Birmingham – a combination of public initiatives and commercial interests have invested in the central areas and given a new life to the Victorian city. In Birmingham, the symphony orchestra – the creation of an urban elite in the early twentieth century – is supported by the city as a sign of cultural confidence. The offices of the municipal gas undertaking – whose profits sustained the city's art gallery – has itself been converted into a new exhibition space, to host touring international exhibitions. A poster for the exhibition of paintings by Edward Burne-Jones – a native of the city – proudly announced it was visiting New York, Paris and Birmingham. Culture is a way of establishing status. On the old, derelict docks of London, Liverpool and Cardiff, massive investment has created new offices, housing and public buildings. In Saltaire and Halifax, the huge spinning mills of Titus Salt and the Crossleys have been converted into shops, galleries, restaurants, studios and offices for the new growth sectors of computing and design. The Bradford wool exchange, where Ruskin berated the philistines, is now a book shop, and Smithfield is far from the stench and stickiness of Dickens. The old meat warehouses have been converted into studios for architects and designers, chic restaurants and loft conversions. Clerkenwell, once the home of clock and scientific instrument makers as part of the web of interchange of skills and information has re-emerged as the base for design firms and consultants, who use the city in much the same way. Of course, other decayed industrial towns have been unable to transform themselves into sites of post-modernity – and loft conversions in mills and warehouses scarcely deal with the problems of deprivation in Liverpool or Bradford.

The issue of public investment in the urban infrastructure continues to be controversial. The redevelopment of the docklands in London was largely left to private enterprise, which was to take any profits – as well as the disastrous loss threatened when the property boom broke. The role of public investment was small, with a failure to provide adequate transport. Strict controls by central government over public investment by nationalised utilities meant a backlog of repairs and maintenance for sewers and water supply. Whether privatisation provided the answer was highly contentious. Essentially, the debates of the mid-nineteenth century, when public ownership started to replace regulated private monopolies, has been rerun, with a different outcome: competing suppliers can use the network of rails, cables, pipes to provide trains, gas, electricity and telephones, with prices and quality of service regulated by a public body. The current system of regulation is rather different from the maximum dividends or sliding scales introduced in the mid-nineteenth century, and gives more discretion to regulators to determine what is reasonable. What it does suggest is a continued concern with the allocation of monopoly profits between shareholders and consumers.

Since 1950, patterns of migration into cities have also changed. By 1950, migration into Britain from the Commonwealth was still small. The Jewish communities in London, Leeds and Manchester, the small black communities in Liverpool and Cardiff, were still unusual; perhaps more significant than racial tensions were the rivalries between Catholics and Protestants which still lingered in Glasgow and Liverpool. From the late 1940s, immigration from the Caribbean, the Indian sub-continent, and Cyprus marked a major change in the ethnic complexity of many British cities. Old inner-city districts were transformed, and serious tensions arose in the housing market. The limited stock of rented property led to conflict over access of housing, which contributed to riots in Notting Hill. A related issue was entitlement to welfare. Entry into the country gave access to many welfare services, in theory on an equal basis; in practice, the allocation of resources for health care was grossly unequal between areas, and many inner-city districts faced serious problems of ill-health, with high levels of infant mortality and the reappearance of tuberculosis. Local variations therefore continued in the provision of national services; and many services were still provided by local authorities. The most obvious was housing, and access to property might well exclude recent immigrants who would be forced into poor-quality housing as well as into poorly paid jobs. One result has been a revival of interest by the medical profession and social scientists in local variations in standards of mental and physical health, which has put the urban variable back on the agenda.

The flow of resources within the urban network continues to affect standards of well-being and prosperity. The economic regeneration of some towns rests on the arrival of investment from overseas, such as the Nissan car plant in Sunderland or Toyota in Derby, in place of the locally owned shipyards and railway workshops. Power within the urban network has moved to Tokyo and to a global economy. The result might be to create local employment; but ownership is elsewhere, and profits do not remain within the locality. The City of London itself – so often criticised for its destructive impact on investment in manufacturing industry – might not be immune. In 1950, it was a shadow of its former self, eclipsed by New York and constrained by exchange controls. It was reborn in the 1960s, as one of the three financial centres of the world economy: will it be able to sustain this role in the face of potential competition from European centres? However, the significance of local urban structures should not be dismissed. The economies of Cambridge or Oxford show the importance of knowledge and 'talk' for urban growth and dynamism, with spin-offs from university research laboratories into science parks. In some sectors of the economy, 'flexible specialisation' has re-emerged as efficient, with a positive role for external urban economies. Even in the poverty-stricken inner London borough of Hackney, the council is actively sponsoring small workshops, where independent designers make furniture or metalware for the affluent consumer market of London.

Indeed, the World Bank predicts that cities will be central to the changing political, economic and social structure of the coming century. The power of national governments is facing challenge from two directions, from the forces of globalisation and from a growing devolution to cities and provinces. The process of delegation of power to the localities allows for a degree of autonomy and participation, and might create more responsive and efficient local government. But it might also pose serious dangers, where local governments are spend-thrift and threaten macro-economic stability. The World Bank is also concerned about the social costs of urbanisation in developing countries, with serious problems of pollution and public health as a result of low levels of investment in the infrastructure. As the World Bank points out, similar problems in Europe and North America were overcome in the nineteenth century, as a result of processes analysed in this volume. Essentially, the problems of free riding and collective action were resolved. But the World Bank is less optimistic for the future, fearing that urban residents with higher incomes might be able to insulate themselves from urban problems through private provision, and so avoid collective action. The issues facing British cities in the nineteenth century have a new relevance to politicians and economists in the present, and urban historians should have something to contribute to the debate about long-term trends. At the very least, the realisation that cities are crucial to economic growth, stability and welfare should encourage historians to put the history of cities, and the issues considered in this volume, at the centre of their concerns.

Select bibliography

COMPILED BY ELEANOR O'KEEFFE

Abel-Smith, B., *The Hospitals 1800–1948: A Study in Social Administration in England and Wales* (London, 1964)

Abercrombie, P., *The Greater London Plan 1944* (London, 1945)

Adams, B., *Time and Social Theory* (London, 1990)

Adams, B., *Timewatch: The Social Analysis of Time* (London, 1995)

Adams, I. H., *The Making of Urban Scotland* (London, 1978)

Adams, T., 'Labour and the First World War: economy, politics and the erosion of local peculiarity?', *Journal of Regional and Local Studies*, 10 (1990)

Alborn, T. L., *Conceiving Companies: Joint-Stock Politics in Victorian England* (London, 1998)

Aldcroft, D. H., and Freeman, M. J., eds., *Transport in the Industrial Revolution* (Manchester, 1983)

Allan, C. M., 'The genesis of British urban redevelopment with special reference to Glasgow', *Ec.HR*, 2nd series, 18 (1965)

Allen, G., *et al.*, eds., *The Import Trade of the Port of Liverpool: Future Prospects* (Liverpool, 1946)

Allen, G. C., *The Industrial Development of Birmingham and the Black Country, 1860–1927* (London, 1929; repr., 1966)

Allen, R., *The Moving Pageant: A Literary Sourcebook on London Street-Life, 1700–1914* (London, 1998)

Anderson, A., 'Docker's culture in three north European port cities', in Holm and Edwards, eds., *North Sea Ports*

Anderson, G. L., *Victorian Clerks* (Manchester, 1976)

Anderson, M., 'The emergence of the modern life cycle in Britain', *Soc. Hist.*, 10 (1985)

Anderson, M., *Family Structure in Nineteenth-Century Lancashire* (Cambridge, 1971)

Anderson, M., 'Household structure and the Industrial Revolution: mid-nineteenth century Preston in comparative perspective', in Laslett and Wall, eds., *Household and Family in Past Time*

Anderson, M., 'The social implications of demographic change', in Thompson, ed., *Cambridge Social History of Britain*, II

Anderson, M., 'Urban migration in Victorian Britain: problems of assimilation?', in

Immigration et société urbaine en europe occidentale, XVIe–XXe siècle, sous la direction d'Etienne François (Paris, 1985)

Anderson, M., 'Urban migration in Victorian England', in Horn, ed., *Rise and Fall*

Anderson, M., ed., *British Population History: From the Black Death to the Present Day* (Cambridge, 1996)

Anderson, M., and Morse, D. J., 'High fertility, high emigration, low nuptiality: adjustment processes in Scotland's demographic experience, 1861–1914', Parts I and II, *Population Studies*, 47 (1993)

Anderson, R. D., *Education and Opportunity in Victorian Scotland: Schools and Universities* (Oxford, 1983; repr., Edinburgh, 1989)

Apperly, C. J. (pseud. Nimrod), *The Life of a Sportsman* (London, 1842)

Appleyard, D., 'The environment as a social symbol', *Journal of the American Planning Association*, 45 (1979)

Armstrong, J., 'Coastal shipping', in Aldcroft and Freeman, eds., *Transport in the Industrial Revolution*

Armstrong, J., 'The development of the Park Royal industrial estate in the inter-war period', *LJ*, 21 (1996)

Armstrong, W. A., 'The flight from the land', in G. Mingay, ed., *The Victorian Countryside*, vol. 1 (London, 1981)

Armstrong, W. A., 'The trend of mortality in Carlisle between the 1780s and 1840s: a demographic contribution to the standard of living debate', *Ec.HR*, 2nd series, 34 (1981)

Armstrong, W. A., ed., *The Economy of Kent 1640–1914* (Woodbridge, 1995)

Arnold, D., ed., *The Metropolis and Its Image: Constructing Identities for London, c. 1750–1950* (Oxford, 1999)

Arscott, C., and Pollock, G., with Wolff, J., 'The partial view: the visual representation of the early nineteenth-century city', in Wolff, and Seed, eds., *Culture of Capital*

Ashby, E., and Anderson, M., *The Politics of Clean Air* (Oxford, 1981)

Ashby, E., and Anderson, M., 'Studies in the politics of environmental protection: the historical roots of the British Clean Air Act, 1956. II. The ripening of public opinion, 1898–1952', *Interdisciplinary Science Reviews*, 2 (1977)

Ashford, D. E., *British Dogmatism and French Pragmatism: Central–Local Policy-Making in the Welfare State* (London, 1982)

Ashworth, W., *The Genesis of Modern British Town Planning* (London, 1954)

Aspinall, P., 'The internal structure of the housebuilding industry in nineteenth-century cities', in Johnson and Pooley, eds., *The Structure*

Aspinwall, B., 'Glasgow trams and American politics, 1894–1914', *SHR*, 56 (1976)

Aspinwall, B., *Portable Utopia: Glasgow and the United States, 1820–1920* (Aberdeen, 1984)

Atkins, P. J., 'The growth of London's railway milk trade, c. 1845–1914', *Journal of Transport History*, new series, 4 (1978)

Atkins, P. J., 'How the West End was won: the struggle to remove street barriers in Victorian London', *Journal of Historical Geography*, 19 (1993)

Atkins, P. J., 'The spatial configuration of class solidarity in London's West End, 1792–1939', *UHY*, 17 (1990)

Avebury, Lord, 'Municipal trading', *Contemporary Review*, 78 (1900)

Bagwell, P. S., *Doncaster: Town of Train Makers, 1853–1990* (Doncaster, 1991)

Bailey, B., 'The development of technical education, 1934–39', *History of Education*, 16 (1987)

Bailey, P., 'Champagne Charlie: performance and ideology in the music hall swell song', in Bratton, ed., *Music Hall*

Bailey, P., *Leisure and Class in Victorian England: Rational Recreation and the Contest for Control, 1830–1885* (London, 1978; 2nd edn, 1987)

Bailey, P., ed., *Music Hall: The Business of Pleasure* (Milton Keynes, 1986)

Baines, D. E., 'Merseyside in the British economy: the 1930s and the Second World War', in Lawton and Cunningham, eds., *Merseyside*

Baines, D. E., *Migration in a Mature Economy: Emigration and Internal Migration in England and Wales, 1861–1900* (Cambridge, 1985)

Baines, D. E., and Johnson, P., 'In search of the "traditional" working class: social mobility and occupational continuity in inter-war London', *Ec.HR*, 2nd series, 52 (1999)

Baker, D., ed., *The Church in Town and Countryside* (Oxford, 1979)

Balchin, P., *Housing Policy: An Introduction* (London, 1985)

Ball, M., *Housing Policy and Economic Power: The Political Economy of Owner Occupation* (London, 1983)

Banks, J. A., *Prosperity and Parenthood: A Study of Family Planning Among the Victorian Middle Classes* (London, 1954; repr., Aldershot, 1993)

Barber, B., 'Aspects of municipal government, 1835–1914', in Fraser, ed., *Leeds*

Barber, B., 'Municipal government in Leeds, 1835–1914', in Fraser, ed., *Municipal Reform*

Barbican Art Gallery, *The Edwardian Era*, exhibition catalogue, ed. J. Beckett and D. Cherry (London, 1987)

Barbican Art Gallery, *The Image of London: Views by Travellers and Emigrées*, exhibition catalogue (London, 1987)

Barke, M., 'The middle-class journey to work in Newcastle upon Tyne, 1850–1913', *Journal of Transport History*, 3rd series, 12 (1991)

Barker, R., 'The Metropolitan Railway and the making of Neasden', *Transport History*, 12 (1981)

Barker, T. C., 'Urban transport', in M. J. Freeman and D. H. Aldcroft, eds., *Transport in Victorian Britain* (Manchester, 1988)

Barker, T. C., and Gerhold, D., *The Rise and Rise of Road Transport, 1700–1990* (London, 1993)

Barker, T. C., and Harris, J. R., *A Merseyside Town in the Industrial Revolution: St. Helens, 1750–1900* (Liverpool, 1954)

Barker, T. C., and Robbins, M., *A History of London Transport*, vol. I: *The Nineteenth Century* (London, 1963)

Barker, T. C., and Robbins, M., *A History of London Transport*, vol. II: *The Twentieth Century to 1970* (London, 1974)

Barker, T. C., and Savage, C. I., *An Economic History of Transport in Britain*, 3rd edn (London, 1974)

Bartrip, P., 'Food for the body and food for the mind: the regulation of freshwater fisheries in the 1870's', *Victorian Studies*, 28 (1985)

Bassett, K., and Short, J. R., *Housing and Residential Structure: Alternative Approaches* (London, 1980)

Baugh, G. C., 'Government grants in aid of the rates in England and Wales, 1889–1990', *Bull. IHR*, 65 (1992)

Beattie, S., *A Revolution in London Housing: LCC Housing Architects and their Work, 1893–1914* (London, 1980)

Beaven, B., 'Re-constructing the business community: the small firm in the Coventry motor industry, 1896–1939', *Business Archives*, 72 (1996)

Beckett, J., ed., *A Centenary History of Nottingham* (Manchester, 1997)

Bédarida, F., 'Urban growth and social structure in nineteenth-century Poplar', *LJ*, 1 (1975)

Beevers, R., *The Garden City Utopia: A Critical Biography of Ebenezer Howard* (London, 1988)

Behagg, C., *Politics and Production in the Early Nineteenth Century* (London, 1990)

Behlmer, G. K., *Child Abuse and Moral Reform in England, 1870–1908* (Stanford, 1908)

Behlmer, G. K., *Friends of the Family: The English Home and its Guardians, 1850–1940* (Stanford, 1998)

Bell, Lady F., *At the Works: A Study of a Manufacturing Town (Middlesbrough)* (London, 1907)

Bell, F., and Millward, R., 'Public health expenditures and mortality in England and Wales, 1870–1914', *Continuity and Change*, 13 (1998)

Bellamy, C., *Administering Central–Local Relations, 1871–1919: The Local Government Board in its Fiscal and Cultural Context* (Manchester, 1988)

Bellamy, J., 'The Humber estuary and industrial development', in N. V. Jones, ed., *A Dynamic Estuary: Man, Nature and the Humber* (Hull, 1988)

Benson, J., *The Penny Capitalists: A Study of Nineteenth-Century Working-Class Entrepreneurs* (Dublin, 1983)

Benson, J., *The Rise of Consumer Society in Britain, 1880–1980* (London, 1994)

Benson, J., and Shaw, G., eds., *The Evolution of Retail Systems, c. 1800–1914* (Leicester, 1992)

Benwell Community Project, *The Final Report No. 6: The Making of a Ruling Class* (Newcastle-upon-Tyne, 1978)

Beresford, M. W., 'Prosperity Street and others: an essay in visible urban history', in M. W. Beresford and G. R. J. Jones, eds., *Leeds and its Region* (Leeds, 1967)

Berghoff, H., 'Regional variations in provincial business biography: the case of Birmingham, Bristol and Manchester, 1870–1914', *Business History*, 37 (1995)

Berghoff, H., 'The schooling of Kipps: the education of lower middle class boys in England, 1860–1918', in P. Searby, ed., *Educating the Victorian Middle Class* (Leicester, 1982)

Berman, M., *All That Is Solid Melts into Air: The Experience of Modernity* (New York, 1982; London, 1983)

Bernstein, G. L., 'Liberalism and the progressive alliance in the constituencies, 1900–1914: three case studies', *HJ*, 26 (1983)

Bernstein, H. T., 'The mysterious disappearance of Edwardian London fog', *LJ*, 2 (1975)

Best, G., *Mid-Victorian Britain 1851–75* (London, 1971; rev. edn, St Albans, 1973)

Best, R. H., *Land for New Towns: A Study of Land Use Densities and Agricultural Displacement* (London, 1964)

Bett, W. H., and Gillham, J. C., *Great British Tramway Networks* (London, 1967)

Biagini, E. F., 'Liberalism and direct democracy: John Stuart Mill and the model of ancient Athens', in E. F. Biagini, ed., *Citizenship and Community: Liberals, Radicals and Collective Identities in the British Isles, 1865–1931* (Cambridge, 1996)

Bijker, W. E., and Law, J., eds., *Shaping Technology/Building Society: Studies in Sociotechnical Change* (Cambridge, Mass., 1992)

Bijker, W. E., Hughes, T. P., and Pinch, T. J., eds., *The Social Construction of Technological Systems: New Directions in the Sociology and History of Technology* (Cambridge, Mass., 1987)

Bilsky, L. J., ed., *Historical Ecology: Essays on Environment and Social Change* (Port Washington, 1980)

Binfield, C. J., *George Williams and the YMCA: A Study in Victorian Social Attitudes* (London, 1973)

Binfield, C. J., *et al.*, eds., *The History of the City of Sheffield, 1843–1993* (Sheffield, 1993)

Birchall, J., 'Co-partnership housing and the garden city movement', *Planning Perspectives*, 10 (1995)

Bird, J. H., *The Geography of the Port of London* (London, 1957)

Bird, J. H., *The Major Seaports of the United Kingdom* (London, 1963)

Black, I. S., 'Geography, political economy and the circulation of finance capital in early industrial England', *Journal of Historical Geography*, 15 (1989)

Black, I. S., 'Money, information and space: banking in early nineteenth-century England and Wales', *Journal of Historical Geography*, 21 (1995)

Black, I. S., 'Re-building the heart of the empire: financial headquarters in the City of London, 1919–39', in Arnold, ed., *The Metropolis*

Black, I. S., 'Symbolic capital: the London and Westminster Bank headquarters, 1836–38', *Landscape Research*, 21 (1996)

Blackman, J., 'The development of the retail grocery trade in the nineteenth century', *Business History*, 9 (1957)

Blackman, J., 'The food supply of an industrial town: a study of Sheffield's public markets, 1780–1900', *Business History*, 5 (1963)

Boal, F., 'Territoriality and class: a study of two residential areas in Belfast', *Irish Geography*, 6 (1971)

Boddy, M., *The Building Societies* (London, 1980)

Bonfield, L., Smith, R., and Wrightson, K., eds., *The World We Have Gained: Histories of Population and Social Structure* (Oxford, 1986)

Bonsall, M., 'Local government initiatives in urban regeneration 1906–1932', *Planning History*, 10 (1988)

Boon, T., 'The smoke menace: cinema, sponsorship and the social relations of science in 1937', in Shortland, ed., *Science and Nature*

Borsay, P., *The Image of Georgian Bath, 1700–2000: Towns, Heritage, and History* (Oxford, 2000)

Borsay, P., ed., *The Eighteenth-Century Town: A Reader in English Urban History, 1688–1820* (London, 1990)

Bott, E., *Family and Social Network: Roles, Norms and External Relationships in Ordinary Urban Families* (London, 1957; 2nd edn, 1971)

Bourdieu, P., *Distinction: A Social Critique of the Judgement of Taste,* trans. R. Nice (London, 1984)

Bowler, C., and Brimblecombe, P., 'The difficulties of abating smoke in late Victorian York', *Atmospheric Environment*, 24B (1990)

Bowler, P. J., *The Fontana History of the Environmental Sciences* (London, 1992)

Bowlby, S., ed., 'Women and the environment', *Built Environment*, 10 (1984)

Bowley, M., *The British Building Industry: Four Studies in Response and Resistance to Change* (Cambridge, 1966)

Bradbury, J. B., 'The 1929 Local Government Act, the formulation and implementation of the poor law (health care) and exchequer grant reforms for England and Wales (outside London)' (PhD thesis, University of Bristol, 1990)

Branca, P., *Silent Sisterhood: Middle Class Women in the Victorian Home* (London, 1975)

Brantlinger, P., ed., *Energy and Entropy: Science and Culture in Victorian Britain: Essays from Victorian Studies* (Bloomington, Ind., 1989)

Bratton, J. S., ed., *Music Hall: Performance and Style* (Milton Keynes, 1986)

Brayshay, M., and Pointon, V., 'Migration and the social geography of mid-nineteenth century Plymouth', *The Devon Historian*, 28 (1984)

Brazell, J. H., *London Weather* (London, 1968)

Brendon, P., *Thomas Cook: 150 Years of Popular Tourism* (London, 1991)

Brenner, J. F., 'Nuisance law and the Industrial Revolution', *Journal of Legal Studies*, 3 (1974)

Briggs, A., *History of Birmingham*, vol. II: *Borough and City, 1865–1938* (Oxford, 1952)

Briggs, A., *Victorian Cities* (London, 1963)

Briggs, A., *Victorian Things* (London, 1988)

Brimblecombe, P., *The Big Smoke: A History of Air Pollution in London since Medieval Times* (London, 1987)

Broadberry, S. N., *The Productivity Race: British Manufacturing in International Perspective, 1850–1990* (Cambridge, 1997)

Broodbank, J., *History of the Port of London*, 2 vols. (London, 1921)

Brown, Alexander (pseud. Shadow) *Midnight Scenes and Social Photographs* (Glasgow, 1858; repr., Glasgow, 1976)

Brown, C., *Northampton, 1835–1985: Shoe Town, New Town* (Chichester, 1990)

Brown, C. G., 'Did urbanisation secularise Britain?', *UHY* (1988)

Brown, C. G., 'The mechanism of religious growth in urban societies: British cities since the eighteenth century', in H. McLeod, ed., *European Religion in the Age of Great Cities* (London, 1995)

Brown, C. G., *The Social History of Religion in Scotland since 1730* (London, 1987)

Brown, J., and Rose, M. B., eds., *Entrepreneurship, Networks, and Modern Business* (Manchester, 1993)

Brown, L., and Moore, E., 'The intra-urban migration process: a perspective', *Geografiska Annaler*, 52B (1970)

Brown, R., 'Cultivating a "green" image: oil companies and outdoor publicity in Britain and Europe, 1920–1936', *Journal of European Economic History*, 22 (1993)

Brown, R., *Waterfront Organization in Hull, 1870–1900* (Hull, 1972)

Brown, R. D., *The Port of London* (Lavenham, 1978)

Brownlow, J., *Melton Mowbray, Queen of the Shires* (Wymondham, 1980)

Bruce, F. E., 'Water supply and waste disposal', in T. I. Williams, ed., *A History of Technology*, vol. VII: *The Twentieth Century c. 1900 to c. 1950* (Oxford, 1958)

Bruce, S., ed., *Religion and Modernisation: Sociologists and Historians Debate the Secularization Thesis* (Oxford, 1992)

Bryant, C., and Jary, D., eds., *Giddens' Theory of Structuration: A Critical Appreciation* (London, 1991)

Bryder, L., 'The First World War: healthy or hungry?', *History Workshop Journal*, 24 (1987)

Buchanan, C., *Traffic in Towns* (London, 1963)

Buckley, R. J., *History of Tramways from Horse to Rapid Transit* (Newton Abbot, 1975)

Budge, I., and O'Leary, C., *Belfast: Approach to Crisis: A Study of Belfast Politics, 1613–1970* (London, 1973)

Bullock, I., 'The origins of economic growth on Teeside, 1851–1881', *NHist.*, 9 (1974)

Bullock, N., 'Ideas, priorities and harsh realities: reconstruction and the LCC, 1945–51', *Planning Perspectives*, 9 (1994)

Bulmer, M., *The Social Basis of Community Care* (London, 1987)

Bulmer, M., *et al.*, eds., *The Social Survey in Historical Perspective, 1880–1940* (Cambridge, 1991)

Bulpitt, J., *Territory and Power in the United Kingdom: An Interpretation* (Manchester, 1983)

Burgess, K. 'Authority relations and the division of labour in British industry, with special reference to Clydeside 1860–1930', *Soc. Hist.*, 11 (1986)

Burnett, J., *A Social History of Housing, 1815–1985*, 2nd edn (London, 1986)

Burns, W., *British Shopping Centres* (London, 1959)

Burt, R., 'Segmented capital markets and patterns of investment in late Victorian Britain: some evidence from the non-ferrous mining industry', *Ec.HR*, 2nd series, 51 (1998)

Butler, T., and Savage, M., eds., *Social Change and the Middle Classes* (London, 1995)

Butt, J., 'The changing character of urban employment 1901–1981', in Gordon, ed., *Perspectives*

Buttimer, A., 'Social space and the planning of residential areas', in A. Buttimer and D. Seaman, eds., *The Human Experience of Space and Place* (London, 1980)

Bynum, W. F., and Porter, R. S., eds., *Living and Dying in London, Medical History* (Supplement, 1991)

Cadman, D., and Catalano, A., *Property Development in the UK: Evolution and Change* (Reading, 1983)

Cage, R. A., 'Health in Glasgow', in Cage, ed., *The Working Class in Glasgow*

Cage, R. A., ed., *The Working Class in Glasgow 1750–1914* (London, 1987)

Cahill, M., and Jowitt, T., 'The new philanthropy: the emergence of the Bradford City Guild of Help', *Journal of Social Policy*, 9 (1980)

Cain, P. J., and Hopkins, A. G., 'Gentlemanly capitalism and British overseas expansion, II: New imperialism, 1850–1945', *Ec.HR*, 2nd series, 40 (1987)

Cairncross, A., 'Internal migration in Victorian England', in A. K. Cairncross, *Home and Foreign Investment 1870–1913* (Cambridge, 1953)

Cannadine, D., *Lords and Landlords: the Aristocracy and the Towns, 1774–1967* (Leicester, 1980)

Cannadine, D., 'The transformation of civic ritual in modern Britain: the Colchester oyster feast', *P&P*, 94 (1982)

Cannadine, D., 'Victorian cities: how different?', *Soc. Hist.*, 4 (1977)

Cannadine, D., ed., *Patricians, Power and Politics in Nineteenth-Century Towns* (Leicester, 1982)

Cannadine, D., and Reeder, D., eds., *Exploring the Urban Past: Essays in Urban History by H. J. Dyos* (Cambridge, 1982)

Capie, F., and Collins, M., 'Industrial lending by English commercial banks 1860s–1914. Why did banks refuse loans?', *Business History*, 38 (1996)

Carr, R. J. M., and Al Naib, S. K., eds., *Dockland: An Illustrated Historical Survey of Life and Work in East London* (London, 1986)

Carter, H., 'Cardiff, local, regional and national capital', in Gordon, ed., *Regional Cities*

Carter, H., *The Towns of Wales* (Cardiff, 1966)

Carter, H., and Lewis, C. R., *An Urban Geography of England and Wales in the Nineteenth Century* (London, 1990)

Carter, H., and Wheatley, S., *Merthyr Tydfil in 1851: A Study of the Spatial Structure of a Welsh Industrial Town* (Cardiff, 1982)

Cassell, M., *Long Lease!: The Story of Slough Estates, 1920–1991* (London, 1991)

Cassis, Y., 'Bankers in English society in the late nineteenth century', *Ec.HR*, 2nd series, 38 (1985)

Chalklin, C. W., *The Provincial Towns of Georgian England: A Study of the Building Process, 1740–1820* (London, 1974)

Chalmers, T., *The Christian and Civic Economy of Large Towns* (Edinburgh, 1821–6)

Chalmers, T., *The Health of Glasgow, 1818–1925: An Outline* (Glasgow, 1930)

Chaloner, W. H., *The Social and Economic Development of Crewe, 1780–1923* (Manchester, 1950)

Chamberlin, R., *The English Country Town* (Exeter, 1983)

Chandler, A. D., Jr, *Scale and Scope: The Dynamics of Industrial Capitalism* (Cambridge, Mass., 1990)

Chandler, T. J., *The Climate of London* (London, 1965)

Channon, G., 'The Aberdeenshire beef trade with London: a study in steamship and railway competition, 1850–69', *Transport History*, 2 (1969)

Chapman, S. D., ed., *The History of Working-Class Housing: A Symposium* (Newton Abbot, 1971)

Chartres, J., and Honeyman, K., eds., *Leeds City Business 1893–1993: Essays Marking the Centenary of the Incorporation* (Leeds, 1993)

Chatterton, D. A., 'State control of public utilities in the nineteenth century: the London gas industry', *Business History*, 14 (1972)

Checkland, O., *Philanthropy in Victorian Scotland: Social Welfare and the Voluntary Principle* (Edinburgh, 1983)

Checkland, O., and Lamb, M., eds., *Health Care as Social History: The Glasgow Case* (Aberdeen, 1982)

Checkland, S., *The Upas Tree: Glasgow 1875–1975: A Study in Growth and Contraction* (Glasgow, 1976)

Checkland, S., *The Upas Tree: Glasgow 1875–1975 – and after 1975–1980* (Glasgow, 1981)

Cherry, G., *Birmingham: A Study in Geography, History and Planning* (Chichester, 1994)

Cherry, G. E., *Cities and Plans: The Shaping of Urban Britain in the Nineteenth and Twentieth Centuries* (London, 1988)

Cherry, S., *Medical Services and the Hospitals in Britain, 1860–1939* (Cambridge, 1996)

Chinn, C., *They Worked All Their Lives: Women of the Urban Poor in England, 1880–1939* (Manchester, 1988)

Christ, C. T., and Jordan, J. O., eds., *Victorian Literature and the Victorian Visual Imagination* (Berkeley, 1995)

Church, R. A., *Economic and Social Change in a Midland Town: Victorian Nottingham 1815–1900* (London, 1966)

Church, R. A., *Herbert Austin: The British Motor Car Industry to 1941* (London, 1979)

Church, R. A., et al., *The History of the British Coal Industry*, vol. III: *1830–1913: Victorian Pre-Eminence* (Oxford, 1986)

Clapp, B. W., *An Environmental History of Britain since the Industrial Revolution* (London, 1994)

Clapson, M., 'Playing the system: the world of organised street betting in Manchester, Salford and Bolton, *c.* 1880 to 1939', in Davies and Fielding, eds., *Workers' Worlds*

Clark, P., ed., *The Transformation of English Provincial Towns, 1600–1800* (London, 1984)

Clark, P., and Corfield, P., eds., *Industry and Urbanisation in Eighteenth Century England: Papers from the ESRC Colloquia 1993–4* (Leicester, 1994)

Clark, P., and Hosking, J., *Population Estimates of English Small Towns, 1550–1851*, Centre for Urban History, University of Leicester, Working Paper, 5 (Leicester, 1993)

Clark, P., and Murfin, L., *The History of Maidstone: The Making of a Modern County Town* (Stroud, 1995)

Cleary, E. J., *The Building Society Movement* (London, 1965)

Clout, H., ed., *The Times London History Atlas* (London, 1997)

Clout, H., and Wood, P., eds., *London: Problems of Change* (Harlow, 1986)

Coleman, A., *Utopia on Trial: Vision and Reality in Planned Housing* (London, 1985)

Coleman, B. I., *The Idea of the City in Nineteenth-Century Britain* (London, 1973)

Collins, M., *Banks and Industrial Finance in Britain, 1800–1939* (Basingstoke, 1991)

Collins, M., and Hudson, P., 'Provincial bank lending: Yorkshire and Merseyside 1820–1860', *Bulletin of Economic Research*, 31 (1979)

Conway, H., *People's Parks: The Design and Development of Victorian Parks in Britain* (Cambridge, 1991)

Cook, C., *The Age of Alignment: Electoral Politics in Britain, 1922–1929* (London and Basingstoke, 1975)

Cook, C., 'Labour and the downfall of the Liberal party, 1906–1914', in A. Sked and C. Cook, eds., *Crisis and Controversy* (London, 1976)

Cook, C., 'Liberals, Labour and local elections', in G. Peele and C. Cook, eds., *The Politics of Reappraisal, 1918–39* (London, 1975)

Cooke, P., ed., *Localities: The Changing Face of Urban Britain* (London, 1989)

Cooter, R., ed., *In the Name of the Child: Health and Welfare in 1880–1940* (London, 1992)

Coppock, J. T., and Prince, H. C., eds., *Greater London* (London, 1964)

Corbin, A., *The Foul and the Fragrant: Odor and the French Social Imagination*, trans. M. L. Kochan (Leamington Spa, 1986)

Corfield, P. J., *The Impact of English Towns 1700–1800* (Oxford, 1982)

Cosgrove, D., and Daniels, S., eds., *The Iconography of Landscape: Essays on the Symbolic Representation, Design and Use of Past Environments* (Cambridge, 1988)

Cotter, E. P., *The Port of Liverpool, including Birkenhead and Garston: United States Department of Commerce and US Shipping Board Foreign Port Series No. 2* (Washington, 1929)

Cottrell, P. L., *Industrial Finance 1830–1914: The Finance and Organisation of English Manufacturing Industry* (London, 1980)

Cowen, P., et al., *The Office: A Facet of Urban Growth* (London, 1969)

Cowling, M. C., *The Artist as Anthropologist: The Representation of Type and Character in Victorian Art* (Cambridge, 1989)

Cox, J., *The English Churches in a Secular Society: Lambeth 1870–1930* (New York and Oxford, 1982)

Crafts, N. F. R., 'Some dimensions of the "quality of life" during the British Industrial Revolution', *Ec.HR*, 2nd series, 50 (1997)

Creaton, H., ed., *Bibliography of Printed Works on London History to 1939* (London, 1994)

Cross, G., *A Quest for Time: The Reduction of Work in Britain and France, 1840–1940* (London, 1989)

Cross, G., *Time and Money: The Making of Consumer Culture* (London, 1993)

Crossick, G., *An Artisan Elite in Victorian Society: Kentish London, 1840–1880* (London, 1978)

Crossick, G., 'Shopkeepers and the state in Britain, 1870–1914', in G. Crossick and H.-G. Haupt, eds., *Shopkeepers and Master Artisans in Nineteenth-Century Europe* (London, 1984)

Crossick, G., ed., *The Lower Middle Class in Britain, 1870–1914* (London, 1977)

Crossick, G., and Haupt, H.-G., *The Petite Bourgeoisie in Europe 1780–1914: Enterprise, Family and Independence* (London, 1995)

Crowther, M. A., *British Social Policy 1914–1939* (Basingstoke, 1988)

Crowther, M. A., 'Family responsibility and state responsibility in Britain before the welfare state', *HJ*, 25 (1982)

Crowther, M. A., 'Poverty, health and welfare', in Fraser and Morris, eds., *People and Society*, II

Crowther, M. A., *The Workhouse System, 1834–1929: The History of an English Social Institution* (London, 1981)

Cullingworth, J. B., *Environmental Planning, 1939–1969*, vol. I: *Reconstruction and Land Use Planning 1939–1947* (London, 1975)

Cullingworth, J. B., *Town and Country Planning in Britain* (London, 1964; 10th edn, 1988)

Cunningham, H., 'The employment and unemployment of children in England, c. 1680–1851', *P&P*, 126 (1990)

Cunningham, H., 'Leisure and culture', in Thompson, ed., *Cambridge Social History of Britain*, II

Cunningham, H., 'The metropolitan fairs: a case study in the social control of leisure', in A. P. Donajgrodzki, ed., *Social Control in Nineteenth Century Britain* (London, 1977)

Cunningham, H., 'Urban fairs and popular culture in nineteenth-century England', in L. H. van Voss and F. van Holthoon, eds., *Working Class and Popular Culture* (Amsterdam, 1988)

Daniels, P. W., *Office Location: An Urban and Regional Study* (London, 1975)

Daniels, S., *Fields of Vision: Landscape and National Identity in England and the United States* (Cambridge, 1993)

Daunton, M. J., *Coal Metropolis: Cardiff 1870–1914* (Leicester, 1977)

Daunton, M. J., 'Gentlemanly capitalism and British industry 1820–1914', *P&P*, 122 (1989)

Daunton, M. J., *House and Home in the Victorian City: Working-Class Housing 1850–1914* (London, 1983)

Daunton, M. J., ed., 'Industry in London: revisions and reflections', *LJ*, 21 (1996)

Daunton, M. J., 'Jack ashore: seamen in Cardiff before 1914', *Welsh History Review*, 9 (1978)

Daunton, M. J., 'Payment and participation: welfare and state formation in Britain 1900–1951', *P&P*, 150 (1996)

Daunton, M. J., *A Property-Owning Democracy?: Housing in Britain* (London, 1987)

Daunton, M. J., 'Public place and private space: the Victorian city and the working-class household', in Fraser and Sutcliffe, eds., *Pursuit of Urban History*

Daunton, M. J., 'Urban Britain', in T. R. Gourvish and A. O'Day, eds., *Later Victorian Britain, 1867–1900* (Basingstoke, 1988)

Daunton, M. J., ed., *Councillors and Tenants: Local Authority Housing in English Cities, 1919–1939* (Leicester, 1984)

Davidoff, L., *The Best Circles: Society, Etiquette and the Season* (London, 1973)

Davidoff, L., and Hall, C., *Family Fortunes: Men and Women of the English Middle Class 1780–1850* (London, 1987)

Davidoff, L., *et al.*, *The Family Story: Blood, Contract and Intimacy, 1830–1960* (London, 1999)

Davies, A., *Leisure, Gender and Poverty: Working-Class Culture in Salford and Manchester, 1900–1939* (Buckingham, 1992)

Davies, A., and Fielding, S., eds., *Workers' Worlds: Cultures and Communities in Manchester and Salford, 1880–1939* (Manchester, 1992)

Davies, J. C., and Brown, M. C., *Yesterday's Town: Market Harborough* (Buckingham, 1981)

Davis, J., 'Jennings' Buildings and the Royal Borough: the construction of the underclass in mid-Victorian England', in Feldman, and Stedman Jones, eds., *Metropolis*

Davis, J., 'Modern London 1850–1939', *LJ*, 20 (1995)

Davis, J., *Reforming London: The London Government Problem, 1855–1900* (Oxford, 1988)

Davis, J., and Tanner, D., 'The borough franchise after 1867', *HR*, 69 (1996)

Davison, G., 'The city as a natural system: theories of urban society in early nineteenth-century Britain', in Fraser and Sutcliffe, eds., *Pursuit of Urban History*

D'Cruze, S., 'Care, diligence and "Usfull Pride": gender, industrialisation and the domestic economy, *c.* 1770 to *c.* 1840', *Women's History Review*, 3 (1994)

Dean, D., and Jones, C., eds., *Parliament and Locality 1660–1939* (Edinburgh, 1998)

Dean, H., and Taylor-Gooby, P., *Dependency Culture: The Explosion of a Myth* (New York and London, 1992)

Dear, M., and Wolch, J., 'How territory shapes social life', in J. Wolch and M. Dear, eds., *The Power of Geography: How Territory Shapes Social Life* (Boston, 1989)

Dellheim, C. *The Face of the Past: The Preservation of the Medieval Inheritance of Victorian England* (Cambridge, 1982)

Dennis, R., *English Industrial Cities of the Nineteenth Century: A Social Geography* (Cambridge, 1984)

Dennis, R., 'The geography of Victorian values: philanthropic housing in London, 1840–1900', *Journal of Historical Geography*, 15 (1989)

Dennis, R., '"Hard to let" in Edwardian London', *Urban Studies*, 26 (1989)

Dennis, R., 'Intercensal mobility in a Victorian city', *Transactions of the Institute of British Geographers*, new series, 2 (1977)

Dennis, R., and Daniels, S., 'Community and the social geography of Victorian cities', *UHY* (1981)

Devine, T. M., *The Transformation of Rural Scotland: Social Change and the Agrarian Economy* (Edinburgh, 1994)

de Vries, J., *European Urbanisation 1500–1800* (London, 1984)

Dickinson, G. C., 'The development of suburban road passenger transport in Leeds, 1840–95', *Journal of Transport History*, 4 (1960)

Dickinson, G. C., and Longley, C. J., 'The coming of cheap transport – a study of tramway fares on municipal systems in British provincial towns, 1900–14', *Transport History*, 6 (1973)

Dickinson, G. C., and Longley, C. J., 'Twopence to the terminus? A study of tram and bus fares in Leeds during the interwar period', *Journal of Transport History*, 3rd series, 7 (1986)

Dickinson, R. E., *City and Region* (London, 1964)

Dickinson, R. E., 'The distribution and functions of the smaller urban settlements of East Anglia', *Geography*, 17 (1932)

Digby, A., *British Welfare Policy: Workhouse to Workfare* (London, 1989)

Dingle, A. E., '"The monster nuisance of all"; landowners, alkali manufacturers and air pollution 1828–1864', *Ec.HR*, 2nd series, 35 (1982)

Dintenfass, M., 'Coal masters and the culture of the middle class, c. 1890–1950', in Kidd and Nicholls, eds., *Making*

Dixon, C. H., 'Legislation and the seaman's lot', in P. Adam, ed., *Seamen in Society: Proceedings of the International Commission for Maritime History* (Paris, 1981)

Dixon, D. F., 'Petrol distribution in the UK, 1900–1950', *Business History*, 6 (1963)

Dobbin, F., *Forging Industrial Policy: The United States, Britain, and France in the Railway Age* (Cambridge, 1994)

Doherty, P., 'Ethnic segregation levels in the Belfast urban area', *Area*, 21 (1989)

Donzelot, J., *The Policing of Families* (New York, 1979)

Doré, G., and Jerrold, B., *London: A Pilgrimage* (London, 1872)

Doughty, M., ed., *Building the Industrial City* (Leicester, 1986)

Douglas, M., 'Environments at risk', in M. Douglas, *Implicit Meanings: Essays in Anthropology* (London, 1975)

Douglas, M., *Purity and Danger: An Analysis of the Concepts of Pollution and Taboo* (London, 1966)

Douglas, M., and Isherwood, B., *The World of Goods: Towards an Anthropology of Consumption* (London, 1979)

Douglas, M., and Wildavsky, A., *Risk and Culture: An Essay on the Selection of Technical and Environmental Dangers* (Berkeley and London, 1982)

Doyle, B. M., 'A conflict of interests? The local and national dimensions of middle class Liberalism, 1900–1935', in Dean and Jones, eds., *Parliament and Locality*

Doyle, B. M., 'Politics and middle class culture in Norwich 1900–1935', *HJ*, 38 (1995)

Doyle, B. M., 'The structure of elite power in the early twentieth-century city: Norwich, 1900–1935', *UH*, 24 (1997)

Doyle, B. M., 'Urban Liberalism and the "Lost Generation": politics and middle class culture in Norwich, 1900–1935', *HJ*, 38 (1995)

Dresser, M. and Ollerenshaw, P., eds., *The Making of Modern Bristol* (Tiverton, 1996)

Driver, F., 'Moral geographies: social science and the urban environment in mid-nineteenth century England', *Transactions of the Institute of British Geographers*, new series, 13 (1988)

Driver, F., *Power and Pauperism: The Workhouse System, 1834–84* (Cambridge, 1993)

Driver, F., and Gilbert, D., 'Heart of empire? Landscape, space and performance in imperial London', *Environment and Planning D: Society and Space*, 16 (1998)

Drummond, D. K., *Crewe: Railway Town, Company and People 1840–1914* (Aldershot, 1995)

Dunbabin, J. P. D., 'The politics of the establishment of county councils', *HJ*, 6 (1963)

Duncan, J., ed., *Housing and Identity: Cross-Cultural Perspectives* (London, 1981)

Dupree, M., *Family Structure in the Staffordshire Potteries, 1840–1880* (Oxford, 1995)

Durant, R., *Watling: A Survey of Social Life on a New Housing Estate* (London, 1939)

Dutton, H. I., and King, J. E., *Ten Per Cent and No Surrender: The Preston Strike, 1853–54* (Cambridge, 1981)

Dwork, D., *War is Good for Babies and Other Young Children: A History of the Infant and Child Welfare Movement in England 1898–1918* (London, 1987)

Dyos, H. J., 'Greater and Greater London: notes on metropolis and provinces in the nineteenth and twentieth centuries', in S. Bromley and E. H. Kossman, eds., *Britain and the Netherlands*, vol. IV: *Metropolis, Dominion and Providence* (The Hague, 1971)

Dyos, H. J., 'Railways and housing in Victorian London', *Journal of Transport History*, 2 (1955)

Dyos, H. J., 'The slums of Victorian London', *Victorian Studies*, 11 (1967)

Dyos, H. J., 'Some social costs of railway building in London', *Journal of Transport History*, new series, 3 (1957)

Dyos, H. J., 'Urban transformation: a note on the objects of street improvement in Regency and early Victorian London', *International Review of Social History*, 2 (1957)

Dyos, H. J., *Victorian Suburb: A Study of the Growth of Camberwell* (Leicester, 1961)

Dyos, H. J., 'Workmen's fares in south London, 1860–1914', *Journal of Transport History*, 1 (1953)

Dyos, H. J., ed., *The Study of Urban History* (London, 1968)

Dyos, H. J., and Aldcroft, D. H., *British Transport: An Economic Survey from the Seventeenth Century to the Twentieth* (Leicester, 1969)

Dyos, H. J., and Wolff, M., eds., *The Victorian City: Images and Realities*, 2 vols. (London, 1973)

Dyson, A. H., *Lutterworth* (London, 1913)

Edgerton, D., *Science, Technology and British Industrial 'Decline', 1870–1970* (Cambridge, 1996)

Elbaum, B., 'The persistence of apprenticeship in Britain and its decline in the United States', in Gospel, ed., *Industrial Training*

Elliott, A., 'Municipal government in Bradford in the mid-nineteenth century', in Fraser, ed., *Municipal Reform*

Elmsley, C., *The English Police: A Political and Social History*, 2nd edn (London, 1996)

Englander, D., *Landlord and Tenant in Urban Britain, 1838–1918* (Oxford, 1983)

Englander, D., and O'Day, R., eds., *Retrieved Riches: Social Investigation in Britain, 1840–1914* (Aldershot, 1995)

Erickson, C., *British Industrialists: Steel and Hosiery, 1850–1950* (Cambridge, 1959)

Errazurez, A., 'Some types of housing in Liverpool, 1785–1890', *Town Planning Review*, 19 (1943–7)

Evans, N., 'Urbanisation, elite attitudes and philanthropy: Cardiff, 1850–1914', *International Review of Social History*, 27 (1982)

Everitt, A., 'Country, county and town: patterns of regional evolution in England', *TRHS*, 5th series, 29 (1979)

Everitt, A., *Landscape and Community in England* (London, 1985)

Everitt, A., 'Town and country in Victorian Leicestershire: the role of the village carrier', in A. Everitt, ed., *Perspectives in English Urban History* (London, 1973)

Eyler, J. M., *Sir Arthur Newsholme and State Medicine, 1885–1935* (Cambridge, 1997)

Falkus, M., 'The development of municipal trading in the nineteenth century', *Business History*, 19 (1977)

Farnie, D. A., *The English Cotton Industry and the World Market, 1815–1896* (Oxford, 1979)

Farnie, D. A., *The Manchester Ship Canal and the Rise of the Port of Manchester, 1894–1975* (Manchester, 1980)

Fayle, C. E., *The War and the Shipping Industry* (London, 1927)

Fein, A., 'Victoria Park: its origins and history', *East London Papers*, 5 (1962)

Feinstein, C., 'Pessimism perpetuated: real wages and the standard of living in Britain during and after the Industrial Revolution', *Journal of Economic History*, 58 (1998)

Feldman, D., *Englishmen and Jews: Social Relations and Political Culture, 1840–1914* (London, 1994)

Feldman, D., and Stedman Jones, G., eds., *Metropolis – London: Histories and Representations since 1800* (London, 1989)

Field, J., 'Wealth, styles of life and social tone amongst Portsmouth's middle class, 1800–75', in Morris, ed., *Class, Power and Social Structure*

Fine, B., and Leopold, E., *The World of Consumption* (London, 1993)

Finer, H., *English Local Government* (London, 1933)

Finer, H., *Municipal Trading* (London, 1941)

Finer, S. E., *The Life and Times of Sir Edwin Chadwick* (London, 1952)

Finlayson, G. B. A. M., *Citizen, State and Social Welfare in Britain 1830–1990* (Oxford, 1994)

Fishwick, N., *English Football and Society, 1910–1950* (Manchester, 1989)

Fitzpatrick, D., 'A curious middle place: the Irish in Britain, 1871–1921', in Swift and Gilley, eds., *The Irish in Britain*

Fitzpatrick, D., 'Emigration, 1801–70', in W. E. Vaughan, ed., *A New History of Ireland*, vol. v: *Ireland under the Union, I, 1801–70* (Oxford, 1989)

Flick, C., 'The movement for smoke abatement in nineteenth-century Britain', *Technology and Culture*, 21 (1980)

Flintoff, F., and Millard, R., *Public Cleansing* (London, 1969)

Florence, P. S., *Investment, Location and Size of Plant* (Cambridge, 1948)

Floud, R., and McCloskey, D., eds., *The Economic History of Britain since 1700* (Cambridge, 1981; 2nd edn, 1994)

Floud, R., Wachter, K., and Gregory, A., *Height, Health and History: Nutritional Status in the United Kingdom, 1750–1980* (Cambridge, 1990)

Fogarty, J. P., *Prospects of the Industrial Areas of Great Britain* (London, 1945)

Foreman-Peck, J., 'Industry and industrial organisation in the inter-war years', in Floud and McCloskey, eds., *The Economic History of Britain*

Foreman-Peck, J., and Millward, R., *Public and Private Ownership of British Industry, 1820–1990* (Oxford, 1994)

Forman, C., *Industrial Town: Self Portrait of St Helens in the 1920s* (London, 1978; 2nd edn, 1979)

Forrest, R., and Murie, A., *Home Ownership: Differentiation and Fragmentation* (London, 1990)

Forrest, R., Williams, P., and Murie, A., 'Home ownership in recession', *Housing Studies*, 9 (1994)

Forrest, R., and Murie, A., *Selling the Welfare State: The Privatisation of Public Housing* (London, 1988)

Forshaw, J. H., and Abercrombie, P., *The County of London Plan* (London, 1943)

Foster, J., *Class Struggle and the Industrial Revolution: Early Industrial Capitalism in Three English Towns* (London, 1974)

Foster, J., 'Nineteenth-century towns – a class dimension', in Dyos, ed., *Study of Urban History*

Fowler, D., *The First Teenagers: The Lifestyle of Young Wage-Earners in Interwar Britain* (London, 1995)

Fox, A., 'Industrial relations in nineteenth-century Birmingham', *Oxford Economic Papers*, 7 (1955)

Fox, C., *Londoners* (London, 1987)

Francis, H. J. *A History of Hinckley* (Hinckley, 1930)

Fraser, D., 'The politics of Leeds water', *Proceedings of the Thoresby Society*, 3 (1970)

Fraser, D., *Power and Authority in the Victorian City* (Oxford, 1979)

Fraser, D., *Urban Politics in Victorian England: The Structure of Politics in Victorian Cities* (Leicester, 1976)

Fraser, D., ed., *A History of Modern Leeds* (Manchester, 1980)

Fraser, D., ed., *Municipal Reform and the Industrial City* (Leicester, 1982)

Fraser, D. and Sutcliffe, A., eds., *The Pursuit of Urban History* (London, 1983)

Fraser, W. H., *The Coming of the Mass Market, 1850–1914* (London, 1981)

Fraser, W. H., 'Municipal socialism and social policy', in Morris and Rodger, eds., *Victorian City*

Fraser, W. H., and Maver, I., eds., *Glasgow*, vol. II: *1830 to 1912* (Manchester, 1996)

Fraser, W. H., and Morris, R. J., eds., *People and Society in Scotland*, 2 vols. (Edinburgh, 1990)

Frewen, M., *Melton Mowbray and Other Memories* (London, 1924)

Fried, A., and Elman, R., eds., *Charles Booth's London* (London, 1969)

Friedlander, D., 'London's urban transition, 1851–1951', *Urban Studies*, 11 (1974)

Friedlander, D., and Roshier, R. J., 'A study of internal migration in England and Wales: Part 1', *Population Studies*, 19 (1966)

Gadian, D. S., 'Class consciousness in Oldham and other North-West industrial towns, 1830–1850', *HJ*, 21 (1978)

Gadian, D. S., 'Class formation and class action in North-West industrial towns, 1830–50', in Morris, ed., *Class, Power and Social Structure*

Gallagher, T., 'Protestant extremism in urban Scotland 1930–9', *SHR*, 64 (1985)

Gandy, M., *Recycling and the Politics of Urban Waste* (London, 1994)

Gandy, M., *Recycling and Waste: An Exploration of Contemporary Environmental Policy* (Aldershot, 1993)

Garrard, J., *Leadership and Power in Victorian Industrial Towns 1830–80* (Manchester, 1983)

Garrard, J., 'Urban elites, 1850–1914: the rule and decline of a new squirearchy?', *Albion*, 27 (1995)

Garrard, J., and Parrott, V., 'Craft, professional and middle-class identity: solicitors and gas engineers, *c.* 1850–1914', in Kidd and Nicholls, eds., *Making*

Garrett, E., 'The trials of labour: motherhood versus employment in a nineteenth-century textile centre', *Continuity and Change*, 5 (1990)

Garrett, E., and Reid, A., '"Satanic mills, pleasant lands"; spatial variation in women's work and infant mortality as viewed from the 1911 *Census*', *HR*, 68 (1994)

Garrett, E., Reid, A., Schurer, K., and Szreter, S., *Changing Family Size in England and Wales: Place, Class and Demography in England and Wales, 1891–1911* (Cambridge, forthcoming)

Garside, P. L., 'London and the Home Counties', in Thompson, ed., *Cambridge Social History of Britain*, 1

Garside, P. L., '"Unhealthy areas", town planning and eugenics in the slums 1890–1914', *Planning Perspectives*, 3 (1988)

Gartner, L., *The Jewish Immigrant in England, 1870–1914* (London, 1960)

Gaskell, S. M., 'Housing and the lower middle class, 1870–1914', in Crossick, ed., *The Lower Middle Class in Britain*

Gaskell, S. M., ed., *Slums* (Leicester, 1990)

Gatrell, V. A. C., 'Incorporation and the pursuit of Liberal hegemony in Manchester, 1790–1839', in Fraser, ed., *Municipal Reform*

Gauldie, E., *Cruel Habitations: A History of Working-Class Housing, 1780–1914* (London, 1973)

Geddes, P., *Cities in Evolution: An Introduction to the Town Planning Movement* (London, 1915)

Gellner, E., *Conditions of Liberty: Civil Society and its Rivals,* (London, 1994)

Gerrard, J., *Leadership and Power in Victorian Industrial Towns, 1830–80* (Manchester, 1983)

Gibb, A., *Glasgow: The Making of a City* (London, 1983)

Giddens, A., *The Constitution of Society: Outline of the Theory of Structuration* (Cambridge, 1984)

Gilbert, A. D., *Religion and Society in Industrial England: Church, Chapel and Social Change, 1740–1914* (London, 1976)

Gilbert, D., 'Community and municipalism: collective identity in late-Victorian and Edwardian mining towns', *Journal of Historical Geography*, 17 (1991)

Gillespie, J., 'Poplarism and proletarianism: unemployment and Labour politics in London, 1918–34', in Feldman, and Stedman Jones, eds., *Metropolis*

Gillett, E. E., *A History of Grimsby* (London, 1970)

Gillis, J. R., Tilly, L. A., and Levine, D., eds., *The European Experience of Declining Fertility, 1850–1970: The Quiet Revolution* (Oxford and Cambridge, Mass., 1992)

Glass, R., *et al.*, eds., *London: Aspects of Change* (London, 1964)

Glendinning, M., and Muthesius, S., *Tower Block: Modern Public Housing in England and Wales* (New Haven and London, 1994)

Glennie, P., 'Consumption, consumerism and urban form: historical perspectives', *Urban Studies*, 35 (1998)

Glick, T. F., 'Science, technology and the urban environment: the Great Stink of 1858', in Bilsky, ed., *Historical Ecology*

Goddard, N., '"A mine of wealth": the Victorians and the agricultural value of sewage', *Journal of Historical Geography*, 22 (1996)

Godley, A., 'Immigrant entrepreneurs and the emergence of London's East End as an industrial district', *LJ*, 21 (1996)

Gold, J. R. and Ward, S. V., eds., *Place Promotion: The Use of Publicity and Marketing to Sell Towns and Regions* (Chichester, 1994)

Golledge, R., 'A behavioural view of mobility and migration research', *Professional Geographer*, 31 (1980)

Goodacre, J., *The Transformation of a Peasant Economy: Townspeople and Villagers in the Lutterworth Area, 1500–1700* (Aldershot, 1994)

Gordon, G., ed., *Perspectives of the Scottish City* (Aberdeen, 1985)

Gordon, G., ed., *Regional Cities in the UK, 1890–1980* (London, 1986)

Gordon, G., and Dicks, B., eds., *Scottish Urban History* (Aberdeen, 1983)

Gorsky, M., *Patterns of Philanthropy: Charity and Society in Nineteenth-Century Bristol* (Woodbridge, 1999)

Gorz, A., ed., *The Division of Labour: The Labour Process and Class-Struggle in Modern Capitalism* (Hassocks, 1976)

Gosden, P. H. J. H., *Self Help* (London, 1973)

Gospel, H. F., *Markets, Firms, and the Management of Labour in Modern Britain* (Cambridge, 1992)

Gospel, H. F., ed., *Industrial Training and Technological Innovation: A Comparative and Historical Study* (London, 1991)

Gospel, H. F., and Littler, C. R., eds., *Managerial Strategies and Industrial Relations: An Historical and Comparative Study* (London, 1983)

Grant, R. K. J., 'Merthyr Tydfil in the mid-nineteenth century: the struggle for public health', *Welsh History Review*, 14 (1989)

Gray, R., 'The platform and the pulpit: cultural networks and civic identities in industrial towns, *c.* 1850–70', in Kidd and Nicholls, eds., *Making*

Gray, R. Q., *The Labour Aristocracy in Victorian Edinburgh* (Oxford, 1976)

Greig, T. Billington, *The Consumer in Revolt* (London, n.d., *c.* 1913)

Green, D. R., *From Artisans to Paupers: Economic Change and Poverty in London, 1790–1870* (Aldershot, 1995)

Green, D. R., 'Distance to work in Victorian London: a case study of Henry Poole, bespoke tailors', *Business History*, 30 (1988)

Green, D. R., 'The metropolitan economy: continuity and change 1800–1939', in K. Hoggart and D. R. Green, eds., *London: A New Metropolitan Geography* (London, 1991)

Green, D. R., 'The nineteenth-century metropolitan economy: a revisionist interpretation', *LJ*, 21 (1996)

Green, S. J. D., *Religion in the Age of Decline: Organisation and Experience in Industrial Yorkshire, 1870–1920* (Cambridge, 1996)

Green, S. J. D., 'In search of bourgeois civilisation: institutions and ideals in nineteenth-century Britain', *NHist.*, 28 (1992)

Greenwood, W., *Love on the Dole* (London, 1933)

Gregory, D., *Regional Transformation and Industrial Revolution: A Geography of the Yorkshire Woollen Industry* (London, 1982)

Gregory, D., 'Three geographies of industrialization', in R. A. Dodgshon and R. A. Butlin, *An Historical Geography of England and Wales* (London, 1990)

Gregory, D., and Urry, J., eds., *Social Relations and Spatial Structures* (Basingstoke, 1985)

Gregson, N., 'Structuration theory: some thoughts on the possibilities of empirical research', *Environment and Planning D: Society and Space*, 5 (1987)

Griffin, C. P., '"Three days down the pit and three days play": underemployment in the East Midlands coalfields between the wars', *International Review of Social History*, 38 (1993)

Griffith, J. A. G., *Central Departments and Local Authorities* (London, 1966)

Griffiths, T., 'Work, class and community: social identities and political change in the Lancashire coalfield, 1910–1939', in A. Campbell, N. Fishman, and D. Howell, eds., *Miners, Unions and Politics, 1910–47* (Aldershot, 1996)

Guagnini, A., 'The fashioning of higher technical education in Britain: the case of Manchester, 1851–1914', in Gospel, ed., *Industrial Training*

Guha, S., 'The importance of social intervention in England's mortality decline: the evidence reviewed', *Social History of Medicine*, 7 (1994)

Gunn, S., 'The failure of the Victorian middle class: a critique', in Wolff and Seed, eds., *Culture of Capital*

Gurney, P., *Co-operative Culture and the Politics of Consumption in England, 1870–1930* (Manchester, 1996)

Hagerstrand, T., 'Survival and arena: on the life history of individuals in relation to their geographic environment', in T. Carlstein, D. Parkes and N. Thrift, eds., *Timing Space and Spacing Time* (London, 1978)

Haigh, E. A., ed., *Huddersfield: A Most Handsome Town: Aspects of the History and Culture of a West Yorkshire Town* (Huddersfield, 1992)

Hall, J. A., ed., *Civil Society: Theory, History, Comparison* (Cambridge, 1995)

Hall, P., *The Industries of London since 1861* (London, 1962)

Hall, P., et al., *The Containment of Urban England*, 2 vols. (London, 1973)

Hallett, G., and Randall, P., *Maritime Industry and Port Development in South Wales* (Cardiff, 1970)

Halliday, S., *The Great Stink of London: Sir Joseph Bazalgette and the Cleaning of the Victorian Metropolis* (Stroud, 1999)

Hamlin, C., 'Edward Frankland's early career as London's official water analyst 1865–1876: the context of "previous sewage contamination"', *Bulletin of the History Medicine*, 56 (1982)

Hamlin, C., 'Edwin Chadwick and the engineers, 1842–1854: systems and anti-systems in the pipe-and-brick sewers war', *Technology and Culture*, 33 (1992)

Hamlin, C., 'Environmental sensibility in Edinburgh, 1839–1840: the fetid irrigation controversy', *JUH*, 20 (1994)

Hamlin, C., 'Muddling in bumbledom: on the enormity of large sanitary improvements in four British towns, 1855–1885', *Victorian Studies*, 33 (1988–9)

Hamlin, C., 'Providence and putrefaction: Victorian sanitarians and the natural theology of health and disease', *Victorian Studies*, 28 (1984–5)

Hamlin, C., *Public Health and Social Justice in the Age of Chadwick: Britain, 1800–54* (Cambridge, 1998)

Hamlin, C., *A Science of Impurity: Water Analysis in Nineteenth-Century Britain* (Bristol, 1990)

Hamlin, C., 'William Dibdin and the idea of biological sewage treatment', *Technology and Culture*, 29 (1988)

Hammond, J. L., and Hammond, B., *The Town Labourer* (London, 1911)

Hamnett, C., and Randolph, B., 'The rise and fall of London's purpose-built blocks of privately rented flats: 1853–1983', *LJ*, 11 (1985)

Handy, E., 'Dust piles and damp pavements: excrement, repression and the Victorian city in photography and literature', in C. T. Christ and J. O. Jordan, eds., *Victorian Literature and the Victorian Visual Imagination* (Berkeley, 1995)

Hannah, L., *Electricity before Nationalisation: A Study of the Development of the Electricity Supply Industry in Britain to 1948* (London, 1979)

Hannah, L., 'Mergers in manufacturing industry, 1880–1919', *Oxford Economic Papers*, 26 (1974)

Hannah, L., 'Public policy and the advent of large-scale technology: the case of electricity supply in the USA, Germany and Britain', in N. Horn and J. Kocka, eds., *Law and the Formation of Big Enterprises in the Nineteenth and Early Twentieth Centuries* (Göttingen, 1979)

Hannah, L., 'Visible and invisible hands in Great Britain', in A. Chandler and H. Daems, eds., *Managerial Hierarchies: Comparative Perspectives on the Rise of the Modern Industrial Enterprise* (Cambridge, Mass., 1980)

Hardman, M., *Ruskin and Bradford: An Experiment in Victorian Cultural History* (Manchester, 1986)

Hardy, A., *The Epidemic Streets: Infectious Disease and the Rise of Preventive Medicine 1856–1900* (Oxford, 1993)

Hardy, A., *Health and Medicine in Britain since 1860* (Basingstoke, 2000)

Hardy, A., 'Parish pump to private pipes: London's water supply in the nineteenth century', in Bynum and Porter, eds., *Living and Dying*

Hardy, A., 'Rickets and the rest: childcare, diet and the infectious children's diseases', *Social History of Medicine*, 5 (1992)

Hardy, A., 'Urban famine or urban crisis? Typhus in the Victorian city', *Medical History*, 32 (1988); repr. in Morris and Rodger, eds., *Victorian City*

Hardy, A., 'Water and the search for public health in London in the eighteenth and nineteenth centuries', *Medical History*, 28 (1984)

Harris, J., 'The transition to high politics in English social policy, 1880–1914', in M. Bentley, and J. Stevenson, eds., *High and Low Politics in Modern Britain* (Oxford, 1983)

Harrison, B., *Drink and the Victorians: The Temperance Question in England, 1815–72* (London, 1971)

Harrison, B., 'Pubs', in Dyos and Wolff, eds., *The Victorian City*, II

Harrison, C., and Reeder, D., 'The local economy', in D. Nash and D. Reeder, eds., *Leicester in the Twentieth Century* (Stroud, 1993)

Harrison, M., *Crowds and History: Mass Phenomena in English Towns, 1790–1835* (Cambridge, 1988)

Harrison, M., 'The ordering of the urban environment: time, work and the occurrence of crowds, 1790–1835', *P&P*, 110 (1986)

Harrison, M., 'Symbolism, ritualism and the location of crowds in early-nineteenth century English towns', in Cosgrove and Daniels, eds., *The Iconography of Landscape*

Hart, T., 'Urban growth and municipal government: Glasgow in a comparative context, 1846–1914', in A. Slaven and D. H. Aldcroft, eds., *Business, Banking and Urban History* (Edinburgh, 1982)

Harvey, C. E., and Press, J., 'Sir George White and the urban transport revolution in Bristol 1875–1916', in C. E. Harvey and J. Press, eds., *Studies in the Business History of Bristol* (Bristol, 1988)

Harvey, C. E., and Press, J., *William Morris: Design and Enterprise in Victorian England* (Manchester, 1991)

Harvey, D., 'Class structure in a capitalist society and the theory of residential differentiation', in R. Peel, *et al.*, eds., *Processes in Physical and Human Geography* (London, 1975)

Harvey, D., *The Condition of Postmodernity: An Enquiry into the Origins of Cultural Change* (Oxford, 1989)

Harvey, D., *Consciousness and the Urban Experience: Studies in the History and Theory of Capitalist Urbanization* (Oxford, 1985)

Harvey, D., *Justice, Nature and the Geography of Difference* (Oxford and Cambridge, Mass., 1996)

Harvey, D., *Social Justice and the City* (Oxford, 1973)

Harvey, D., *The Urbanization of Capital* (Oxford, 1985)

Hasegawa, J., *Replanning the Blitzed City Centre: A Comparative Study of Bristol, Coventry and Southampton 1941–50* (Milton Keynes, 1992)

Hassan, J. A., *Environmental and Economic History: Lessons from the Beaches?* (Manchester, 1995)

Hassan, J. A., 'The growth and impact of the British water industry in the nineteenth century', *Ec.HR*, 2nd series, 38 (1985)

Hassan, J. A., *A History of Water in Modern England and Wales* (Manchester, 1998)

Hassan, J. A., *Prospects for Economic and Environmental History* (Manchester, 1995)

Hassan, J. A., 'The water industry, 1900–1951: a failure of public policy?', in Millward and Singleton, eds., *Political Economy of Nationalisation*

Headrick, D. R., *The Tentacles of Progress: Technological Transfer in the Age of Imperialism, 1850–1940* (New York and Oxford, 1988)

Hebbert, M., *London: More by Fortune than Design* (Chichester, 1998)

Hebbert, M., 'London recent and present', *LJ*, 20 (1995)

Heim, C. E., 'Industrial organisation and regional development in inter-war Britain', *Journal of Economic History*, 43 (1983)

Heimann, H., 'Effects of air pollution on human health', in *Air Pollution*, World Health Organisation Monograph 46 (Geneva, 1961)

Hempton, D., *The Religion of the People: Methodism and Popular Religion c. 1750–1900* (London, 1996)

Hendrick, H., *Child Welfare: England, 1872–1989* (London, 1994)

Hennock, E. P., 'Finance and politics in urban local government in England, 1835–1900', *HJ*, 6 (1963)

Hennock, E. P., *Fit and Proper Persons: Ideal and Reality in Nineteenth-Century Urban Government* (London, 1973)

Hennock, E. P., 'The social compositions of borough councils in two large cities, 1835–1914', in Dyos, ed., *Study of Urban History*

Hennock, E. P., 'Technical education in England 1850–1926: the uses of a German model', *History of Education*, 19 (1990)

Hepburn, A., 'The Catholic community of Belfast, 1850–1940', in M. Engman, *et al.*, eds., *Ethnic Identity in Urban Europe* (Aldershot and New York, 1992)

Hewitt, M., *The Emergence of Stability in the Industrial City: Manchester, 1832–1867* (Aldershot, 1996)

Hewitt, M., 'The travails of domestic visiting: Manchester, 1830–70', *HR*, 71 (1998)

Hibbs, J., *The History of British Bus Services* (Newton Abbot, 1968)

Higgs, E., *Domestic Servants and Households in Rochdale* (New York, 1986)

Higgs, E., 'Domestic servants and households in Victorian England', *Soc. Hist.*, 8 (1983)

Higgs, E., 'Domestic service and household production', in John, ed., *Unequal Opportunities*

Hill, S., *The Dockers: Class and Tradition in London* (London, 1976)

Hilling, D., 'Socio-economic change in the maritime quarter: the demise of sailortown', in Hoyle, Pinder, and Husain, eds., *Revitalising the Waterfront*

Hillis, P., 'Presbyterianism and social class in mid-nineteenth century Glasgow: a study of nine churches', *J Ecc. Hist.*, 32 (1981)

Hillman, M., Adams, J., and Whitelegg, J., *One False Move: A Study of Children's Independent Mobility* (London, 1990)

Hills, P., 'Division and cohesion in the nineteenth-century middle class: the case of Ipswich, 1830–1870', *UHY* (1987)

Hinchcliffe, T., 'Highbury New Park: a nineteenth-century middle class suburb', *LJ*, 7 (1981)

HMSO, *Change and Decay: Final Report of the Liverpool Inner Area Study* (London, 1977)

Hoggart, R., *The Uses of Literacy* (London, 1957)

Hollis, P., *Ladies Elect: Women in English Local Government, 1865–1914* (Oxford, 1987)

Hollis, P., 'Women in council: separate spheres, public space', in J. Rendall, ed., *Equal or Different? Women's Politics 1800–1914* (Oxford, 1987)

Holm, P. and Edwards, J., eds., *North Sea Ports and Harbours – Adaptations to Change* (Esbjerg, 1992)

Holt, R., 'Football and the urban way of life in nineteenth-century Britain', in J. A. Mangan, ed., *Pleasure, Profit, Proselytism: British Culture and Sport at Home and Abroad, 1700–1914* (London, 1988)

Holt, R., *Sport and the British: A Modern History* (Oxford, 1989)

Holt, R., 'Working-class football and the city: the problem of continuity', *British Journal of Sports History*, 3 (1996)

Holt, R., ed., *Sport and the Working Class in Modern Britain* (Manchester, 1990)

Horn, P., ed., *The Rise and Fall of the Victorian Servant* (Dublin, 1975)

Hosgood, C. P., 'The "pigmies of commerce" and the working-class community: small shopkeepers in England 1870–1914', *Soc. Hist.* 22 (1989)

Hovey, J., *A Tale of Two Ports: London and Southampton* (London, 1990)

Howard, E., *Tomorrow: A Peaceful Path to Real Reform* (London, 1898)

Howe, A. C., *The Cotton Masters 1830–1860* (Oxford, 1984)

Howell, P., 'Public space and the public sphere: political theory and the historical geography of modernity', *Environment and Planning D: Society and Space*, 11 (1993)

Hoyle, B. S., and Pinder, D. A., eds., *Cityport Industrialization and Regional Development: Spatial Analysis and Planning Strategies* (Oxford, 1981)

Hoyle, B. S., and Pinder, D. A., eds., *European Port Cities in Transition* (London, 1992)

Hoyle, B. S., Pinder, D. A., and Husain, M. S., eds., *Revitalising the Waterfront: International Dimensions of Dockland Redevelopment* (London, 1988)

Huck, P., 'Infant mortality and living standards of English workers during the Industrial Revolution', *Journal of Economic History*, 55 (1995)

Hudson, P., 'Capital and credit in the West Riding wool textile industry c. 1750–1850', in Hudson, ed., *Regions and Industries*

Hudson, P., *The Genesis of Industrial Capital: A Study of the West Riding Wool Textile Industry, c. 1750–1850* (Cambridge, 1986)

Hudson, P., ed., *Regions and Industries: A Perspective on the Industrial Revolution in Britain* (Cambridge, 1989)

Hughes, C., *Lime, Lemon and Sarsparilla: The Italian Community in South Wales, 1881–1945* (Bridgend, 1991)

Hughes, T. P., 'British electrical industry lag: 1882–1888', *Technology and Culture*, 3 (1962)

Hughes, T. P., *Networks of Power: Electrification in Western Society, 1880–1930* (Baltimore, 1983)

Hugill, S., *Sailortown* (London, 1967)

Humphries, S., *Hooligans or Rebels? An Oral History of Working-Class Childhood and Youth, 1889–1939* (Oxford, 1981)

Humphries, S., and Taylor, J., *The Making of Modern London, 1945–1985* (London, 1986)

Hunt, E. H., *Regional Wage Variations in Britain, 1850–1914* (Oxford, 1973)

Hunter, J., *The Story of Slough* (Newbury, 1983)

Hurt, J. S., *Elementary Schooling and the Working Classes, 1860–1918* (London, 1979)

Hurt, J. S., ed., *Childhood, Youth and Education in the Late Nineteenth Century* (Leicester, 1981)

Husbands, C., 'East End racism, 1900–1980', *LJ*, 8 (1982)

Huxley, M., and Winchester, H., 'Residential differentiation and social reproduction: the inter-relations of class, gender and space', *Environment and Planning D: Society and Space*, 9 (1991)

Hyde, F. E., *Liverpool and the Mersey: The Development of a Port* (Newton Abbot, 1971)

Ingham, G., *Capitalism Divided? The City and Industry in British Social Development* (Basingstoke, 1984)

Inglis, K. S., *Churches and the Working Classes in Victorian England* (London, 1963)

Inwood, S., *A History of London* (London, 1998)

Irvine, J. W., *Lerwick: The Birth and Growth of an Island Town* (Lerwick, 1985)

Jackson, A. A., *The Middle Classes, 1900–1950* (Nairn, 1991)

Jackson, A. A., *Semi-Detached London: Suburban Development, Life and Transport, 1900–39* (London, 1973; 2nd edn, Didcot, 1991)

Jackson, G., *The History and Archaeology of Ports* (Tadworth, 1983)

Jackson, G., 'Shipowners and private dock companies: the case of Hull, 1770–1970', in L. M. Akveld, and J. R. Bruijn, eds., *Shipping Companies and Authorities in the 19th and 20th Centuries: Their Common Interest in the Development of Port Facilities* (The Hague, 1989)

Jahn, M., 'Suburban development in outer west London, 1850–1900', in Thompson, ed., *Rise of Suburbia*

Jarvis, A., *Liverpool Central Docks, 1799–1905: An Illustrated History* (Stroud, 1991)

Jeffery, T., 'A place in the nation: the lower-middle class in England', in R. Koshar, ed., *Splintered Classes: Politics and the Lower-Middle Classes in Europe* (New York, 1994)

Jeffery, T., 'The suburban nation: politics and class in Lewisham', in Feldman and Stedman Jones, eds., *Metropolis*

Jefferys, J. B., *Retail Trading in Britain, 1850–1950* (Cambridge, 1954)

Jenner, M., 'The politics of London air: John Evelyn's *Fumifugium* and the Restoration', *HJ*, 38 (1995)

Jevons, R. and Madge, J., *Housing Estates: A Study of Bristol Corporation Policy and Practice between the Wars* (Bristol, 1946)

Jevons, W. S., *The Coal Question* (London, 1866)

John, A. V., ed., *Unequal Opportunities: Women's Employment in England, 1800–1918* (Oxford, 1986)

Johnson, E. D. H., *Paintings of the British Social Scene from Hogarth to Sickert* (London, 1986)

Johnson, J. H., 'The suburban expansion of housing in London, 1918–1939', in Coppock and Prince, eds., *Greater London*

Johnson, J. H., and Pooley, C. G., eds., *The Structure of Nineteenth-Century Cities* (London, 1982)

Johnson, P., 'Economic development and industrial dynamism in Victorian London', *LJ*, 21 (1996)

Johnson, P., 'Conspicuous consumption and working-class culture in late Victorian and Edwardian Britain', *TRHS*, 5th series, 38 (1988)

Johnson, P., *Saving and Spending: The Working-Class Economy in Britain 1870–1939* (Oxford, 1985)

Jones, D. C., ed., *Merseyside. The Social Survey of Merseyside*, 3 vols. (Liverpool, 1934)

Jones, G., and Rose, M. B., 'Family capitalism', *Business History*, 35 (1993)

Jones, G. W., ed., *New Approaches to the Study of Central–Local Government Relationships* (Farnborough, 1980)

Jones, H., *Health and Society in Twentieth-Century Britain* (London, 1994)

Jones, L. J., 'Public pursuit of private profit? Liberal businessmen and municipal politics in Birmingham, 1845–1900', *Business History*, 25 (1983)

Jones, M., 'The economic history of the regional problem in Britain, 1920–1938', *Journal of Historical Geography*, 10 (1984)

Jones, P., 'Perspective, sources and methodology in a comparative study of the middle class in nineteenth-century Leicester and Peterborough', *UHY* (1987)

Jones, P., 'The recruitment of office holders in Leicester, 1861–1931', *Transactions Leicestershire Archaeological and Historical Society*, 58 (1981/2)

Jones, R., 'Country town survival: some Anglo-Australian comparisons', in M. R. Wilson, ed., *Proceedings of the Prairie Division, Canadian Association of Geographers* (Saskatoon, 1992)

Jones, S. G., *Workers at Play: A Social and Economic History of Leisure, 1918–1939* (London, 1986)

Jones, S. G., 'Working-class sport in Manchester between the wars', in Holt, ed., *Sport and the Working Class*

Jordan, E., 'The exclusion of women from industry in nineteenth-century Britain', *Comparative Studies in Society and History*, 31 (1989)

Joyce, P., *Work, Society and Politics: The Culture of the Factory in Later Victorian England* (Brighton, 1980)

Joyce, P., *Visions of the People: Industrial England and the Question of Class, 1840–1914* (Cambridge, 1991)

Kargon, R. H., *Science in Victorian Manchester: Enterprise and Expertise* (Manchester, 1977)

Karn, V., Kemeny, J., and Williams, P., *Home Ownership in the Inner City: Salvation or Despair?* (Aldershot, 1986)

Katznelson, I., *Marxism and the City* (Oxford, 1992)

Kay, J. P., *The Moral and Physical Condition of the Working Classes Employed in the Cotton Manufacture in Manchester* (Manchester, 1832)

Kearns, G., 'Cholera, nuisances and environmental management in Islington, 1830–1855', in Bynum and Porter, eds., *Living and Dying*

Kearns, G., and Withers, C. W. J., eds., *Urbanising Britain: Essays on Class and Community in the Nineteenth Century* (Cambridge, 1991)

Keating, M., *The City that Refused to Die: Glasgow: The Politics of Urban Regeneration* (Aberdeen, 1988)

Keeble, D., 'Small firms, new firms, and uneven regional development in the United Kingdom', *Area*, 22 (1990)

Keith-Lucas, B., *English Local Government in the Nineteenth and Twentieth Centuries* (London, 1977)

Keith-Lucas, B., and Richards, P. G., *A History of Local Government in the Twentieth Century* (London, 1976)

Kellett, J. R., *The Impact of Railways on Victorian Cities* (London, 1969)

Kellett, J. R., 'Municipal socialism, enterprise and trading in the Victorian city', *UHY* (1978)

Kelly, T., *A History of Public Libraries in Great Britain, 1845–1966* (London, 1973)

Kenwood, A. G., 'Port investment in England and Wales, 1851–1913', *Yorkshire Bulletin of Economic and Social Research,* 17 (1965)

Kidd, A., 'Charity organisation and the unemployed in Manchester c. 1870–1914', *Soc. Hist.*, 9 (1984)

Kidd, A., and Nicholls, D., eds., *The Making of the British Middle Class? Studies of Regional and Cultural Diversity since the Eighteenth Century* (Stroud, 1998)

Kidd, A. J., and Roberts, K. W., eds., *City, Class and Culture: Studies of Cultural Production and Social Policy in Victorian Manchester* (Manchester, 1985)

Kiernan, K., 'The boundaries between marriage, non-marriage, and parenthood: changes in behaviour and policy in postwar Britain', *Journal of Family History*, 21 (1996)

Kinchin, P., *Tea and Taste: The Glasgow Tea Rooms 1875–1975* (Wendlebury, 1991)

Kinealy, C. 'The role of the poor law during the famine', in C. Poirteir, ed., *The Great Irish Famine* (Cork, 1995)

King, A. D., *Global Cities: Post-Imperialism and the Internationalization of London* (London, 1990)

King, A. D., ed., *Buildings and Society: Essays on the Social Development of the Built Environment* (London, 1980)

King, E., 'Popular culture in Glasgow', in Cage, ed., *Working Class in Glasgow*

Kinvig, R. H., Smith, J. G., and Wise, M. J., eds., *Birmingham and its Regional Setting: A Scientific Survey* (Birmingham, 1950)

Kleinmann, M., 'Large scale transfers of council housing to new landlords. Is British social housing becoming more European?', *Housing Studies*, 8 (1993)

Knox, P., *Urban Social Geography: An Introduction* (London, 1982; 3rd edn, Harlow, 1995)

Knox, V., 'The economic effects of the Tramways Act of 1870', *Economic Journal*, 11 (1901)

Koditschek, T., *Class Formation and Urban Industrial Society: Bradford, 1750–1850* (Cambridge, 1990)

Koven, S., and Michel, S., 'Womanly duties, maternalist policies and the origins of welfare states in France, Germany, Great Britain and the United States, 1880–1920', *American Historical Review*, 95 (1900)

Koven, S., and Michel, S., eds., *Mothers of a New World: Maternalist Politics and the Origins of Welfare States* (London and New York, 1993)

Kynaston, D., *The City of London*, vol. I: *A World of its Own, 1815–1890* (London, 1994)

Kynaston, D., *The City of London*, vol. II: *Golden Years, 1890–1914* (London, 1995)

La Gory, M., and Pipkin, J., *Urban Social Space* (Belmont, Calif., 1981)

Lambert, R., *Sir John Simon 1816–1904 and English Social Administration* (London, 1963)

Lancaster, B., and Maguire, P., eds., *Towards the Co-operative Commonwealth* (Loughborough, 1996)

Lancaster, B., and Mason, T., eds., *Life and Labour in a Twentieth Century City: The Experience of Coventry* (Coventry, 1986)

Langton, J., 'The Industrial Revolution and the regional geography of England', *Transactions of the Institute of British Geographers*, new series, 9 (1984)

Langton, J., and Morris, R. J., eds., *Atlas of Industrialising Britain, 1780–1914* (London, 1986)

Lash, S., and Urry, J., *Economies of Signs and Space* (London, 1994)

Laslett, P., and Wall, R., eds., *Household and Family in Past Time* (Cambridge, 1972)

Law, C. M., 'The growth of urban population in England and Wales, 1801–1911', *Transactions, Institute of British Geographers*, 41 (1967)

Lawrence, J., 'Class and gender in the making of urban Toryism, 1880–1914', *English Historical Review*, 108 (1993)

Lawrence, J., 'Popular politics and the limitations of party: Wolverhampton, 1867–1900', in E. F. Biagini and A. J. Reid, eds., *Currents of Radicalism: Popular Radicalism, Organised Labour and Party Politics in Britain, 1850–1914* (Cambridge, 1991)

Lawrence, J., 'Geographical space, social space and the realm of the department store', *UH*, 19 (1992)

Lawton, R., 'Mobility in nineteenth-century British cities', *Geographical Journal*, 145 (1979)

Lawton, R., 'Population changes in England and Wales in the later nineteenth century: an analysis of trends by registration district', *Transactions of the Institute of British Geographers*, 44 (1968)

Lawton, R., 'From the Port of Liverpool to the Conurbation of Merseyside', in W. T. S. Gould and A. G. Hodgkiss, eds., *The Resources of Merseyside* (Liverpool, 1982)

Lawton, R., ed., *The Rise and Fall of Great Cities: Aspects of Urbanization in the Western World* (London, 1989)

Lawton, R., and Cunningham, C. M., eds., *Merseyside: Social and Economic Studies* (Liverpool, 1970)

Lawton, R., and Pooley, C. G., *Britain 1740–1950: An Historical Geography* (London, 1992)

Lawton, R., and Pooley, C. G., *The Social Geography of Merseyside in the Nineteenth Century* (Final report to the SSRC, 1976)

Lawton, R., and Pooley, C. G., 'The social geography of nineteenth-century cities: a review', in D. Denecke and G. Shaw, eds., *Urban Historical Geography: Recent Progress in Britain and Germany* (Cambridge, 1988)

Laybourn, K., 'The Guild of Help and the changing face of Edwardian philanthropy', *UH*, 20 (1993)

Lazonick, W., *Competitive Advantage on the Shop Floor* (Cambridge, Mass., 1990)

Lee, C. H., 'Regional growth and structural change in Victorian Britain', *Ec.HR*, 2nd series, 34 (1981)

Lee, C. H., 'Regional inequalities in infant mortality in Britain, 1871–1971: patterns and hypotheses', *Population Studies*, 45 (1991)

Lee, C. H., 'The service sector, regional specialisation and economic growth in the Victorian economy', *Journal of Historical Geography*, 10 (1984)

Lee, J. M., 'The rise and fall of a market town: Castle Donnington in the nineteenth century', *Transactions of the Leicestershire Archaeological and Historical Society*, 32 (1956)

Lee, J. M., *Social Leaders and Public Persons: A Study of County Government in Cheshire since 1888* (Oxford, 1963)

Lees, A., *Cities Perceived: Urban Society in European and American Thought, 1820–1940* (Manchester, 1985)

Lees, L. H., *Exiles of Erin: Irish Migrants in Victorian London* (Manchester, 1979)

Lees, L. H., *The Solidarities of Strangers: The English Poor Laws and the People, 1700–1948* (Cambridge, 1998)

Lees, L. H., 'The study of social conflict in English industrial towns', *UHY* (1980)

Lees, L. H., and Modell, J., 'The Irish countryman urbanized: a comparative perspective on the famine migration', *JUH*, 3 (1977)

Lemire, B., *Fashion's Favourite: The Cotton Trade and the Consumer in Britain, 1660–1800* (Oxford, 1991)

Levitt, I., *Poverty and Welfare in Scotland 1890–1948* (Edinburgh, 1988)

Lewis, C. R., 'A stage in the development of an industrial town: a case study of Cardiff, 1845–1875', *Transactions of the Institute of British Geographers*, new series, 4 (1979)

Lewis, D. M., *Lighten their Darkness: The Evangelical Mission to Working-Class London, 1828–1860* (New York, 1986)

Lewis, J., 'Agents of health care: the relationship between family, professionals and the state in the mixed economy of welfare in twentieth-century Britain', in J. Woodward and R. Jutte, eds., *Coping with Sickness: Perspectives on Health Care, Past and Present* (Sheffield, 1996)

Lewis, J., 'The boundary between voluntary and statutory social service in the later nineteenth and early twentieth centuries', *HJ*, 39 (1996)

Lewis, J., 'Family provision of health and welfare in the mixed economy of care in the late nineteenth and twentieth centuries', *Social History of Medicine*, 8 (1995)

Lewis, J., 'Gender, the family and women's agency in the building of "Welfare States": the British case', *Soc. Hist.*, 19 (1994)

Lewis, J., *The Politics of Motherhood: Child and Maternal Welfare in England, 1900–39* (London, 1980)

Lewis, J. P., *Building Cycles and Britain's Growth* (London, 1965)

Lewis, R. A., *Edwin Chadwick and the Public Health Movement, 1832–1854* (London, 1952)

Liebenau, J., ed., *The Challenge of New Technology: Innovation in British Business since 1850* (Aldershot, 1988)

Lipman, V. D., *Local Government Areas, 1834–1945* (Oxford, 1949; repr., Westport, Conn., 1976)

Litchfield, R. B., 'The family and the mill: cotton mill work, family work patterns and fertility in mid-Victorian Stockport', in Wohl, ed., *The Victorian Family*

Liverpool University, Department of Social Science, *The Dock Worker: An Analysis of Conditions of Employment in the Port of Manchester* (Liverpool, 1956)

Liverpool University, Department of Social Science, *Survey of Merseyside,* vol. II (Liverpool, 1969)

Lloyd-Jones, R., and Lewis, M. J., *Manchester and the Age of the Factory: The Business Structure of Cottonopolis in the Industrial Revolution* (Manchester, 1988)

Lockwood, D., *The Blackcoated Worker: A Study in Class Consciousness* (London, 1958; 2nd edn, Oxford, 1989)

Loebl, H., *Government Factories and the Origins of British Regional Policy, 1934–1948* (London, 1948)

Loudon, I., *Death in Childbirth: An International Study of Maternal Care and Maternal Mortality, 1800–1950* (Oxford, 1992)

Lovell, J., *Stevedores and Dockers* (London, 1969)

Lowe, R., *The Welfare State in Britain since 1945* (Basingstoke, 1993)

Lowe, S., and Hughes, D., eds., *A New Century of Social Housing* (Leicester, 1991)

Luckin, B., 'Death and survival in the city', *UHY* (1980)

Luckin, B., 'Evaluating the sanitary revolution: typhus and typhoid in London, 1851–1900', in Woods and Woodward, eds., *Urban Disease*

Luckin, B., *Pollution and Control: A Social History of the Thames in the Nineteenth Century* (Bristol, 1986)

Luckin, B., and Mooney, G., 'Urban history and historical epidemiology: the case of London, 1860–1920', *UH*, 24 (1997)

McCallum, J. D., 'The development of British regional policy', in D. Maclennan and J. Parr, eds., *Regional Policy: Past Experience and New Directions* (Oxford, 1979)

McClaren, J. P. S., 'Nuisance law and the Industrial Revolution: some lessons from social history', *Oxford Journal of Legal Studies*, 3 (1983)

McClelland, W. G., *Studies in Retailing* (Oxford, 1963)

McCloskey, D. N., and Sandberg, L. G., 'From damnation to redemption: judgements on the late-Victorian entrepreneur', *Explorations in Economic History*, 9 (1971)

McCord, N., *North East England: An Economic and Social History* (London, 1979)

McCrone, G., *Regional Policy in Britain* (London, 1969)

McCrone, D., and Elliot, B., 'The decline of landlordism: property rights and relationships in Edinburgh', in R. Rodger, ed., *Scottish Housing in the Twentieth Century* (Leicester, 1989)

MacDonagh, O., *A Pattern of Government Growth 1800–60: The Passenger Acts and their Enforcement* (London, 1961)

McDowell, L., 'Space, place and gender relations. Parts 1 and 2', *Progress in Human Geography*, 17 (1993)

Mace, R., *Trafalgar Square: Emblem of Empire* (London, 1976)

McFarlane, N., 'Hospitals, housing and tuberculosis in Glasgow, 1911–51', *Social History of Medicine*, 2 (1989)

MacGregor, A., *Public Health in Glasgow, 1905–46* (Edinburgh, 1967)

McKay, J. P., *Tramways and Trolleys: The Rise of Urban Mass Transport in Europe* (Princeton, 1976)

McKenna, M., 'The suburbanisation of the working-class population of Liverpool between the wars', *Soc. Hist.*, 16 (1991)

MacKenzie, J. M., ed., *Imperialism and Popular Culture* (Manchester, 1986; repr., 1998)

McKibbin, R., *Classes and Cultures: England 1918–51* (Oxford, 1998)

McKibbin, R., *The Ideologies of Class: Social Relations in Britain, 1880–1950* (Oxford, 1990; repr., 1994)

McKichan, F., 'A burgh's response to the problems of industrial growth: Stirling, 1780–1880', *SHR*, 57 (1978)

McKinley, A., 'A certain short-sightedness: metal working, innovation, and apprenticeship 1897–1939', in Gospel, ed., *Industrial Training*

McLaren, A. A., *Religion and Social Class: The Disruption Years in Aberdeen* (London, 1974)

Macleod, D. S., *Art and the Victorian Middle Class: Money and the Making of Cultural Identity* (Cambridge, 1996)

McLeod, H., 'Class, community and region: the religious geography of nineteenth-century England', in M. Hill, ed., *A Sociological Yearbook of Religion in Britain* (London, 1973)

McLeod, H., *Class and Religion in the Late Victorian City* (London, 1974)

McLeod, H., *Piety and Poverty: Working-Class Religion in Berlin, London and New York, 1870–1914* (New York and London, 1995)

MacLeod, R. M., 'The Alkali Acts administration, 1863–84: the emergence of the civil scientist', *Victorian Studies*, 9 (1965)

MacLeod, R. M., 'Government and resource conservation: the Salmon Acts Administration, 1860–1886', *Journal of British Studies*, 8 (1968)

Madanipour, A., *Design of Urban Space: An Enquiry into Socio-Spatial Process* (Chichester, 1996)

Malchow, H. L., *Gentleman Capitalists: The Social and Political World of the Victorian Businessman* (London, 1991)

Malcolmson, P., 'Getting a living in the slums of Victorian Kensington', *LJ*, 1 (1975)

Malcolmson, R. W., *Popular Recreations in English Society, 1700–1850* (Cambridge, 1973)

Manchester City Art Galleries, *Hard Times: Social Realism in Victorian Art*, exhibition catalogue, text by J. Treuherz (Manchester, 1987)

Mandler, P., 'Against "Englishness": English culture and the limits to rural nostalgia, 1850–1940', *TRHS*, 6th series, 7 (1997)

Mandler, P., 'Politics and the English landscape since the First World War', *Huntington Library Quarterly*, 55 (1992)

Mandler, P., *The Rise and Fall of the Stately Home* (New Haven, 1997)

Marks, L., *Metropolitan Maternity: Maternal and Infant Welfare Services in Early Twentieth Century London* (Amsterdam and Atlanta, 1996)

Marks, L., *Model Mothers: Jewish Mothers and Maternity Provision in East London, 1870–1939* (Oxford, 1994)

Marland, H., *Medicine and Society in Wakefield and Huddersfield, 1780–1870* (Cambridge, 1987)

Marland, H., 'A pioneer in infant welfare: the Huddersfield scheme, 1903–1920', *Social History of Medicine*, 6 (1993)

Marriott, J., *The Culture of Labourism: The East End between the Wars* (Edinburgh, 1991)

Marriott, J., 'West Ham: London's industrial centre and gateway to the world. 1: industrialisation, 1840–1910', *LJ*, 13 (1987–8)

Marriott, O., *The Property Boom* (London, 1967)

Marshall, A., *Industry and Trade: A Study of Industrial Technique and Business Organization* (London, 1919)

Marshall, J., *The History of the Great West Road: Its Social and Economic Influence on the Surrounding Area* (Hounslow, 1995)

Marshall, J. D., *Furness and the Industrial Revolution* (Barrow-in-Furness, 1958)

Marshall, J. D., 'The rise and transformation of the Cumbrian market town, 1660–1900', *NHist.*, 19 (1983)

Marshall, W. A. L., *A Century of London Weather* (London, 1952)

Mason, M., *The Making of Victorian Sexual Attitudes* (Oxford, 1994)

Mason, T., *Association Football and English Society, 1863–1915* (Brighton, 1980)

Massey, D., *Space, Place and Gender* (Cambridge, 1994)

Massey, D., *Spatial Divisions of Labour: Social Structures and the Geography of Production* (London, 1984; 2nd edn, 1995)

Massey, D., and Catalano, A., *Capital and Land: Landownership by Capital in Great Britain* (London, 1978)

Mass-Observation, *Browns and Chester* (London, 1947)

Mathias, P., *Retailing Revolution: A History of Multiple Retailing in the Food Trades Based upon the Allied Suppliers Group of Companies* (London, 1967)

Matthews, D., 'Laissez-faire and the London gas industry in the nineteenth century: another look', *Ec.HR*, 2nd series, 39 (1986)

Mayhew, H., *London Labour and the London Poor* (London, 1851; repr., New York, 1967)

Mayne, A., *The Imagined Slum: Newspaper Representation in Three Cities, 1870–1914* (Leicester, 1993)

Meacham, S., 'Raymond Unwin, 1863–1940: designing for democracy in Edwardian England', in S. Pedersen and P. Mandler, eds., *After the Victorians: Private Conscience and Public Duty* (London, 1994)

Mearns, A., *The Bitter Cry of Outcast London,* (London, 1883; new edn, ed. A. S. Wohl, Leicester, 1970)

Meller, H. E., *Leisure and the Changing City, 1870–1914* (London, 1976)

Meller, H. E., *Patrick Geddes: Social Evolutionist and City Planner* (London, 1990)

Meller, H. E., *Towns, Plans and Society in Modern Britain* (Cambridge, 1997)

Meller, H. E., 'Urban renewal and citizenship: the quality of life in British cities, 1890–1990', *UH*, 22 (1995)

Melling, J., *Housing, Social Policy and the State* (London, 1980)

Melling, J., '"Non-commissioned officers": British employers and their supervisory workers, 1880–1920', *Soc. Hist.*, 5 (1980)

Melling, J., *Rent Strikes: People's Struggle for Housing in West Scotland 1890–1916* (Edinburgh, 1983)

Mercer, A., *Disease, Mortality and Population in Transition: Epidemiological-Demographic Change in England since the Eighteenth Century as Part of a Global Phenomenon* (Leicester, 1990)

Merrett, S., *Owner-Occupation in Britain* (London, 1982)

Merrett, S., *State Housing in Britain* (London, 1979)

Mess, H. A., *Industrial Tyneside: A Social Survey* (London, 1928)

Michie, R. C., *The City of London: Continuity and Change, 1850–1990* (London, 1992)

Michie, R. C., 'London and the process of economic growth since 1750', *LJ*, 22 (1997)

Midwinter, E., 'The sectarian troubles and the Police Inquiry of 1909–10', in E. Midwinter, *Old Liverpool* (Newton Abbot, 1971)

Miles, A., *Social Mobility in Nineteenth- and Early Twentieth-Century England* (Basingstoke, 1999)

Miller, D., *Material Culture and Mass Consumption* (Oxford, 1987)

Miller, M., 'The elusive green background: Raymond Unwin and the Greater London Regional Plan', *Planning Perspectives*, 4 (1989)

Miller, M., 'Raymond Unwin', in G. E. Cherry, ed., *Pioneers in British Planning* (London, 1981)

Miller, M., and Gray, A., *Hampstead Garden Suburb* (Chichester, 1992)

Miller, W., 'Politics in the Scottish city, 1832–1982', in Gordon, ed., *Perspectives*

Millward, R., 'The emergence of gas and water monopolies in nineteenth-century Britain: contested markets and public control', in J. Foreman-Peck, ed., *New Perspectives on the Late Victorian Economy: Essays in Quantitative Economic History: 1860–1914* (Cambridge, 1991)

Millward, R., and Sheard, S., 'The urban fiscal problem, 1870–1914: government expenditure and finances in England and Wales', *Ec.HR*, 2nd series, 48 (1995)

Millward, R., and Singleton, J., eds., *The Political Economy of Nationalisation, 1920–1950* (Cambridge, 1995)

Millward, R., and Ward, R., 'The costs of public and private gas enterprises in late nineteenth-century Britain', *Oxford Economic Papers*, 39 (1987)

Millward, R., and Ward, R., 'From private to public ownership of gas undertakings in England and Wales, 1851–1947: chronology, incidence and causes', *Business History*, 35 (1993)

Minford, P., Peel, M., and Ashton, P., *The Housing Morass: Regulation, Immobility and Unemployment: An Economic Analysis of the Consequences of Government Regulation, with Proposals to Restore the Market in Rented Housing* (London, 1987)

Monkhouse, F. J., *A Survey of Southampton and its Region* (Southampton, 1964)

Mooney, G., 'Did London pass the "sanitary test"? Seasonal infant mortality in London, 1870–1914', *Journal of Historical Geography*, 20 (1994)

Morgan, N. J., 'Hugh Kennedy', in A. Slaven and S. Checkland, eds., *Dictionary of Scottish Business Biography 1860–1960*, vol. II (Aberdeen, 1990)

Morris, J. N., *Religion and Urban Change: Croydon, 1840–1914* (Woodbridge, 1992)

Morris, R. J., *Cholera 1832: The Social Response to an Epidemic* (London, 1976)

Morris, R. J., *Class and Class Consciousness in the Industrial Revolution, 1780–1850* (London, 1979)

Morris, R. J., *Class, Sect and Party: The Making of the British Middle Class, Leeds 1820–1850* (Manchester, 1990)

Morris, R. J., 'Clubs, societies and associations', in Thompson, ed., *Cambridge Social History of Britain*, III

Morris, R. J., 'Externalities, the market, power structure and the urban agenda', *UHY*, 17 (1990)

Morris, R. J., 'The middle class and British towns and cities of the industrial revolution, 1780–1870', in Fraser and Sutcliffe, eds., *Pursuit* (London, 1983)

Morris, R. J., 'The middle class and the property cycle during the Industrial Revolution', in T. C. Smout, ed., *The Search for Wealth and Stability* (London, 1979)

Morris, R. J., 'Middle-class culture, 1700–1914', in Fraser, ed., *Leeds*

Morris, R. J., 'Urbanisation and Scotland', in Fraser and Morris, eds., *People and Society*, II

Morris, R. J., 'Voluntary societies and British urban elites, 1780–1850: an analysis', *HJ*, 26 (1983)

Morris, R. J., ed., *Class, Power and Social Structure in British Nineteenth-Century Towns* (Leicester, 1986)

Morris, R. J. and Rodger, R., eds., *The Victorian City: A Reader in British Urban History 1820–1914* (London, 1993)

Morris, R. J., and Smyth, J., 'Paternalism as an employer strategy, 1800–1960', in J. Rubery and F. Wilkinson, eds., *Employer Strategy and the Labour Market* (Oxford, 1994)

Morris, R. J., and Trainor, R. H., eds., *Urban Governance: Britain and Beyond since 1750* (Aldershot, 2000)

Mort, F., *Cultures of Consumption: Masculinities and Social Space in Late Twentieth-Century Britain* (London, 1996)

Mortimore, M. J., 'Landownership and urban growth in Bradford and its environs in the West Riding conurbation, 1850–1950', *Transactions of the Institute of British Geographers*, 46 (1969)

Moser, C. A., and Scott, W., *British Towns: A Statistical Study of their Social and Economic Differences* (Edinburgh, 1961)

Moss, M. S., 'William Todd Lithgow: founder of a fortune', *SHR*, 62 (1983)

Mulley, C., 'The background to bus regulation in the 1930 Road Traffic Act: economic, political and personal influences in the 1920s', *Journal of Transport History*, 3rd series, 4 (1983)

Murphy, S. J., *Continuity and Change: Building in the City of London 1834–1984* (London, 1984)

Muthesius, S., *The English Terraced House* (London and New Haven, 1982)

Nadel, I. B., and Schwarzbach, F. S., eds., *Victorian Artists and the City: A Collection of Critical Essays* (Elmsford, N.Y., and Oxford, 1979)

Naismith, R. J., *The Story of Scotland's Towns* (Edinburgh, 1989)

National Maritime Museum, *London and the Thames: Paintings of Three Centuries*, exhibition catalogue (London, 1977)

Nava, M., and O'Shea, A., eds., *Modern Times: Reflections on a Century of English Modernity* (London, 1996)

Nead, L., *Myths of Sexuality: Representation of Women in Victorian Britain* (Oxford, 1988)

Neal, F., *Sectarian Violence: The Liverpool Experience, 1819–1914* (Manchester, 1987)

Neale, R. S., *Bath, 1680–1850: A Social History Or, A Valley of Pleasure, Yet a Sink of Iniquity* (London, 1981)

Neeson, J. M., *Commoners: Common Right, Enclosure and Social Change in England, 1700–1820* (Cambridge, 1993)

Nenadic, S., 'Businessmen, the urban middle classes, and the "dominance" of manufacturers in nineteenth-century Britain', *Ec.HR*, 2nd series, 44 (1991)

Nenadic, S., 'The life-cycle of firms in late nineteenth-century Britain', in P. Jobert and M. Moss, eds., *The Birth and Death of Companies: An Historical Perspective* (Carnforth, 1990)

Nenadic, S., 'The small family firm in Victorian Britain', *Business History*, 35 (1993)

Nenadic, S., 'The Victorian middle classes', in Fraser and Maver, eds., *Glasgow*, II

Newell, E. 'Atmospheric pollution and the British copper industry, 1690–1920', *Technology and Culture*, 38 (1997)

Newton, L., 'Regional bank–industry relations during the mid-nineteenth century: links between bankers and manufacturing in Sheffield, *c.* 1850 to *c.* 1885', *Business History*, 38 (1996)

Newton, R., *Victorian Exeter, 1837–1914* (Leicester, 1968)

Nicholas, T., 'Wealthmaking in nineteenth- and early twentieth-century Britain: industry v. commerce and finance', *Business History*, 41 (1999)

Norcliffe, G., Bassett, K., and Hoare, T., 'The emergence of postmodernism on the urban waterfront: geographical perspectives on changing relationships', *Journal of Transport Geography*, 4 (1996)

Nord, D. E., *Walking the Victorian Streets: Women, Representation and the City* (Ithaca, 1995)

Nossiter, T. J., *Influence, Opinion and Political Idioms in Reformed England: Case Studies from the North East, 1832–1874* (Brighton, 1975)

Niven, D., *The Development of Housing in Scotland* (London, 1979)

O'Brien, J. V. *'Dear Dirty Dublin': A City in Distress, 1899–1916* (Berkeley, 1982)

O'Brien, P., and Keyder, C., *Economic Growth in Britain and France, 1780–1914: Two Paths to the Twentieth Century* (London, 1978)

O'Carroll, A. 'Tenements to bungalows: class and the growth of home ownership before "World War II"', *UH*, 24 (1997)

O'Connell, S., *The Car and British Society: Class, Gender and Motoring 1896–1939* (Manchester, 1998)

O'Connell, S., 'Taste, status and middle class motoring in interwar Britain', in D. Thoms, *et al.*, eds., *The Motor Car and Popular Culture in the Twentieth Century* (Aldershot, 1998)

Ochojna, A. D., 'The influence of local and national politics on the development of urban passenger transport in Britain 1850–1900', *Journal of Transport History*, new series, 4 (1978)

Offer, A., *Property and Politics, 1870–1914: Landownership, Law, Ideology and Urban Development in England* (Cambridge, 1981)

Olechnowicz, A., *Working-Class Housing in England between the Wars: The Becontree Estate* (Oxford, 1997)

Oliver, P., Davis, I., and Bentley, I., *Dunroamin: The Suburban Semi and its Enemies* (London, 1981)

Olsen, D. J., *The City as a Work of Art: London, Paris, Vienna* (London and New Haven, 1986)

Olsen, D. J., *The Growth of Victorian London* (London, 1976)

Olsen, D. J., *Town Planning in London: The Eighteenth and Nineteenth Centuries* (New Haven, 1964; 2nd edn, London, 1982)

Osborn, F. J., and Whittick, A., *New Towns: Their Origins, Achievements and Progress* (London, 1977)

Owen, D., *The Government of Victorian London, 1855–1889: The Metropolitan Board of Works, the Vestries and the City Corporation* (Cambridge, Mass., and London, 1982)

Owen, D. J., *The Origins and Development of the Ports of the United Kingdom* (London, 1939; 2nd rev. edn, London, 1948)

Owen, J. R., 'Defending the county? The reorganisation of local government in England and Wales, 1935–1950' (PhD thesis, University of Bristol, 1990)

Palmer, S., 'From London to Tilbury – the Port of London since 1945', in Holm and Edwards, eds., *North Sea Ports*

Palmer, S., 'Seamen ashore in late nineteenth-century London: protection from the crimps', in P. Adam, ed., *Seamen in Society* (Paris, 1980)

Park, R., and Burgess, E., eds., *The City* (Chicago, 1967)

Payne, P. L., 'The emergence of the large scale company in Great Britain, 1870–1914', *Ec.HR*, 2nd series, 20 (1967)

Pearce, C. J., *The Machinery of Change in Local Government, 1888–1974: A Study of Central Involvement* (London, 1980)

Pedersen, S., *Family, Dependence and the Origins of the Welfare State: Britain and France, 1914–45* (Cambridge, 1993)

Pennybacker, S., '"The millennium by return of post": reconsidering London progressivism, 1889–1907', in Feldman and Stedman Jones, eds., *Metropolis*

Pennybacker, S. D., *A Vision for London, 1889–1914: Labour, Everyday Life and the LIC Experiment* (London, 1995)

Peretz, E. P., 'Infant welfare between the wars', in Whiting, ed., *Oxford*

Peretz, E. P., 'A maternity service for England and Wales: local authority maternity care in the interwar period in Oxfordshire and Tottenham', in J. Garcia, R. Kilpatrick and M. Richards, eds., *The Politics of Maternity Care* (Oxford, 1990)

Petrow, S., *Policing Morals: The Metropolitan Police and the Home Office, 1870–1914* (Oxford, 1994)

Pfister, C., and Brimblecombe, P., eds., *The Silent Countdown: Essays in European Environmental History* (Berlin, 1990)

Phillips, C. B., and Smith, J. H., *Lancashire and Cheshire from AD 1540* (London, 1994)

Phillips, D., *Crime and Authority in Victorian England* (London, 1977)

Phillips, G., and Whiteside, N., *Casual Labour: The Unemployment Question in the Port Transport Industry, 1880–1970* (Oxford, 1985)

Philo, C., ed., *New Words, New Worlds: Reconceptualising Social and Cultural Geography* (Lampeter, 1991)

Pick, D., *Faces of Degeneration: A European Disorder, c. 1848–c. 1918* (Cambridge, 1989)

Pickstone, J. V., *Medicine and Industrial Society: A History of Hospital Development in Manchester and its Region* (Manchester, 1985)

Pilgrim Trust, *Men without Work* (Cambridge, 1938)

Pitfield, D. E., 'Labour migration and the regional problem in Britain, 1920–39' (PhD thesis, University of Stirling, 1973)

Plowden, W., *The Motor Car and Politics 1896–1970* (London, 1971)

Pollard, S., *A History of Labour in Sheffield* (Liverpool, 1959)

Pollock, G., 'Power and visibility in the city', *Art History*, 11 (1988)

Pollock, G., 'Vicarious excitements: *London: a Pilgrimage*, by Gustave Doré and Blanchard Jerrold, 1872', *New Formations*, 4 (1988)

Poole, R., *Popular Leisure and the Music Hall in Nineteenth-Century Bolton* (Lancaster, 1982)

Pooley, C. G., 'Choice and constraint in the nineteenth-century city: a basis for residential differentiation', in Johnson and Pooley, eds., *The Structure*

Pooley, C. G., 'Residential differentiation in Victorian cities: a reassessment', *Transactions of the Institute of British Geographers*, new series, 9 (1984)

Pooley, C. G., 'Residential mobility in the Victorian city', *Transactions of the Institute of British Geographers*, new series, 4 (1979)

Pooley, C. G., and Harmer, M., *Property Ownership in Britain, 1850–1965: The Role of the Bradford and Bingley Building Society in the Development of Homeownership* (Bingley, 1997)

Pooley, C. G., and Irish, S., 'Access to housing on Merseyside', *Transactions of the Institute of British Geographers*, new series, 12 (1987)

Pooley, C. G., and Irish, S., *The Development of Corporation Housing in Liverpool, 1869–1945* (Lancaster, 1984)

Pooley, C. G., and Irish, S., 'Housing and health in Liverpool, 1870–1940', *Transactions of the Historic Society of Lancashire and Cheshire*, 143 (1994)

Pooley, C. G., and Turnbull, J., 'Counterurbanization: the nineteenth-century origins of a late twentieth-century phenomenon', *Area*, 28 (1996)

Pooley, C. G., and Turnbull, J., 'Migration and mobility in Britain from the eighteenth to the twentieth centuries', *Local Population Studies*, 57 (1996)

Pooley, C. G., and Whyte, I. D., *Migrants, Emigrants and Immigrants: A Social History of Migration* (London, 1991)

Port, M. H., *Imperial London: Civil Government Building in London, 1850–1915* (New Haven and London, 1995)

Porter, D., '"Enemies of the Race": biologism, environmentalism and public health in Edwardian England', *Victorian Studies*, 34 (1991)

Porter, R., *London: A Social History* (London, 1994)

Potts, A., 'Picturing the modern metropolis: images of London in the nineteenth century', *History Workshop Journal*, 4 (1988)

Poulsen, C., *Victoria Park: A Study in the History of East London* (London, 1976)

Powell, M., 'An expanding service: municipal acute medicine in the 1930s', *Twentieth Century British History*, 8 (1997)

Powell, M., 'Did politics matter? Municipal public health expenditure in the 1930s', *UH*, 22 (1995)

Powell, M., 'Hospital provision before the NHS: territorial justice or inverse care law?', *Journal of Social Policy*, 21 (1992)

Pratt, G., 'The house as an expression of social worlds', in Duncan, ed., *Housing and Identity*

Pratt, G., and Hanson, S., 'Gender, class and space', *Environment and Planning D: Society and Space*, 6 (1988)

Pred, A., *City Systems in Advanced Economies* (New York, 1977)

Pred, A., *Making Histories and Constructing Human Geographies: The Local Transformation of Practice, Power Relations and Consciousness* (Boulder, 1990)

Prest, J., *Liberty and Locality: Parliament, Permissive Legislation and Ratepayers' Democracies in the Nineteenth Century* (Oxford, 1990)

Price, R., *Masters, Unions and Men: Work Control in Building and the Rise of Labour, 1830–1914* (Cambridge, 1980)

Price, S., *Building Societies: Their Origin and History* (London, 1958)

Priestley, J. B., *English Journey* (London, 1934)

Pritchard, R., *Housing and the Spatial Structure of the City* (Cambridge, 1976)

Prochaska, F. K., 'Female philanthropy and domestic service in Victorian England', *Bull. IHR*, 54 (1981)

Prochaska, F. K., *Philanthropy and the Hospitals of London: The King's Fund, 1897–1990* (Oxford, 1992)

Quail, J. M., 'From personal patronage to public school privilege: social closure in the recruitment of managers in the United Kingdom from the late nineteenth century to 1930', in Kidd and Nicholls, eds., *Making*

Rappaport, E., '"The halls of temptation": gender, politics and the construction of the department store in late Victorian London', *Journal of British Studies*, 35 (1996)

Rappaport, E., '"A husband and his wife's dresses": consumer credit and the debtor family in England, 1864–1914', in V. De Grazia and E. Furlough, eds., *The Sex of Things: Gender and Consumption in Historical Perspective* (Berkeley and London, 1996)

Rappaport, E., *Shopping for Pleasure: Women in the Making of London's West End* (Princeton, 2000)

Raven, N., 'Occupational structures of three north Essex towns: Halstead, Braintree and Great Coggeshall, *c.* 1780–1880. Research in progress', *Urban History Newsletter*, 12 (1992)

Ravenstein, E. G., 'The laws of migration', *Journal of the Royal Statistical Society* (1885)

Ravetz, A., *Model Estate: Planned Housing at Quarry Hill* (London, 1974)

Redfern, P., *The Consumer's Place in Society* (Manchester, 1920)

Redford, A., *Labour Migration in England, 1800–1850* (Manchester, 1926; 2nd edn, 1964)

Redford, A., and Russell, I. S., *The History of Local Government in Manchester*, vol. III: *The Last Half Century* (London, 1940)

Redlich, J., and Hirst, F. W., *Local Government in England*, 2 vols. (London, 1903)

Reeder, D., 'The politics of urban leaseholds in late Victorian Britain', *International Review of Social History*, 6 (1961)

Reeder, D., 'A recurring debate. Education and industry', in G. Bernbaum, ed., *Schooling in Decline* (London, 1979)

Reeder, D., and the London Topographical Society, *Charles Booth's Descriptive Map of London Poverty 1889* (London, 1987)

Rees, R., 'The South Wales copper-smoke dispute, 1833–1895', *Welsh History Review*, 10 (1981)

Reid, D. A., 'The decline of Saint Monday', *P&P*, 71 (1976)

Reid, D. A., 'Interpreting the festival calendar: wakes and fairs as carnivals', in Storch, ed., *Popular Culture and Custom*

Reid, D. A., 'The "iron roads" and "the happiness of the working classes": the early development and social significance of the railway excursion', *Journal of Transport History*, 3rd series, 17 (1996)

Reid, D. A., 'Labour, leisure, and politics in Birmingham *c.* 1800–1875' (PhD thesis, University of Birmingham, 1985)

Reid, D. A., 'Weddings, weekdays, work and leisure in urban England, 1791–1911: the decline of Saint Monday revisited', *P&P*, 153 (1996)

Reilly, M. D., 'Urban electric railway management and operation in Britain and America, 1900–1914', *UHY* (1989)

Relph, E., *Place and Placelessness* (London, 1976)

Reynolds, J., *The Great Paternalist: Titus Salt and the Growth of Nineteenth-Century Bradford* (London, 1983)

Rhodes, R. A. W., *Control and Power in Central–Local Government Relationships* (Farnborough, 1981)

Richards, J., *The Age of the Dream Palace: Cinema and Society in Britain 1930–1939* (London, 1984)

Richards, J., 'The cinema and cinema going in Birmingham in the 1930s', in Walton and Walvin, eds., *Leisure in Britain*

Richards, J., and MacKenzie, J. M., *The Railway Station: A Social History* (Oxford, 1986)

Richardson, H. W., and Aldcroft, D. H., *Building in the British Economy between the Wars* (London, 1968)

Riley, C., *Sick Not Dead: The Health of British Workingmen during the Mortality Decline* (Baltimore and London, 1997)

Riley, R. C., and Smith, J. L., 'Industrialization in naval ports: the Portsmouth case', in Hoyle and Pinder, eds., *Cityport Industrialization*

Ritchie-Noakes, N., *Liverpool's Historic Waterfront: The World's First Mercantile Dock System* (Liverpool, 1984)

Roberts, E., *A Woman's Place: An Oral History of Working-Class Women 1890–1940* (Oxford, 1984)

Roberts, E., *Women's Work, 1840–1940* (Basingstoke, 1988; 2nd edn, Cambridge, 1995)

Roberts, E., 'Working-class standards of living in Barrow and Lancaster, 1890–1914', *Ec.HR*, 2nd series, 30 (1977)

Roberts, R., *The Classic Slum* (Manchester, 1971)

Roberts, R., 'The corporation as impresario: the municipal provision of entertainment in Victorian and Edwardian Bournemouth', in Walton and Walvin, eds., *Leisure in Britain*

Robinson, R., 'The development of the British North Sea steam trawling fleet 1877–1900', in L. U. Scholl and J. Edwards, eds., *The North Sea, Resource and Seaway* (Aberdeen, 1996)

Robinson, R., *A History of the Yorkshire Coast Fishing Industry, 1780–1914* (Hull, 1987)

Robson, B. 'Coming full circles: London versus the rest, 1890–1980', in Gordon, ed., *Regional Cities*

Robson, B. T., *Urban Growth: An Approach* (London, 1973)

Robson, W. A., *The Development of Local Government* (London, 1931; 3rd edn, 1954)

Robson, W. A., *The Government and Misgovernment of London* (London, 1939; 2nd edn, 1948)

Rodger, R., 'Concentration and fragmentation: capital, labour, and the structure of mid-Victorian Scottish industry', *JUH*, 14 (1988)

Rodger, R., 'Employment, wages and poverty in the Scottish cities, 1841–1914', in Gordon, ed., *Perspectives*, and in Morris and Rodger, eds., *Victorian City*

Rodger, R., 'The evolution of Scottish town planning', in Gordon and Dicks, eds., *Scottish Urban History*

Rodger, R., 'Rents and ground rents: housing and the land market in nineteenth century Britain', in Johnson and Pooley, eds., *The Structure*

Rodger, R., 'Urbanisation in twentieth-century Scotland', in T. M. Devine and R. J. Finlay, eds., *Scotland in the Twentieth Century* (Edinburgh, 1996)

Rodger, R., 'The Victorian building industry and the housing of the Scottish working class', in Doughty, ed., *Building the Victorian City*

Rodger, R., ed., *Scottish Housing in the Twentieth Century* (Leicester, 1989)

Rodgers, H. B., 'The suburban growth of Victorian Manchester', *Transactions of the Manchester Geographical Society*, 58 (1961–2)

Roper, M., and Tosh, J., eds., *Manful Assertions: Masculinities in Britain since 1800* (London, 1991)

Rose, D., 'Rethinking gentrification', *Environment and Planning D: Society and Space*, 2 (1984)

Rose, G., 'Imagining Poplar in the 1920s: contested concepts of community', *Journal of Historical Geography*, 19 (1990)

Rose, G., 'Locality, politics, and culture: Poplar in the 1920s', *Environment and Planning D: Society and Space*, 6 (1988)

Rose, J., *The Dynamics of Urban Property Development* (London, 1985)

Rose, M. E., 'Rochdale man and the Stalybridge riot: the relief and control of the unemployed during the Lancashire cotton famine', in A. P. Donajgrodzki, ed., *Social Control in Nineteenth-Century Britain* (London, 1977)

Rose, M. E., 'Settlement, removal and the New Poor Law', in D. Fraser, ed., *The New Poor Law in the Nineteenth Century* (London, 1976)

Rose, M. E., ed., *The Poor and the City: The English Poor Law in its Urban Context, 1834–1914* (Leicester, 1985)

Rosen, G., 'Disease, debility and death', in Dyos and Wolff, eds., *Victorian City*, II

Rosevear, S., 'Balancing business and the regions: British distribution of industry policy and the Board of Trade, 1945–1951', *Business History*, 40 (1998)

Ross, D. M., 'The unsatisfied fringe in Britain, 1930s–1980s', *Business History*, 38 (1996)

Ross, E., *Love and Toil: Motherhood in Outcast London, 1870–1918* (New York and Oxford, 1993)

Ross, E., 'Survival networks – women's neighbourhood sharing in London before World War I', *History Workshop*, 15 (1983)

Rotenberg, R., and McDonogh, G., eds., *The Cultural Meaning of Urban Space* (Westport, Conn., 1993)

Royle, S. A., 'The development of Coalville, Leicestershire, in the nineteenth century', *East Midland Geographer*, 7 (1978)

Royle, S. A., '"The spiritual destitution is excessive – the poverty overwhelming": Hinckley in the mid-nineteenth century', *Transactions, Leicestershire Archaeology and Historical Society*, 54 (1979–80)

Rubinstein, D., *School Attendance in London, 1870–1914: A Social History* (Hull, 1969)

Rubinstein, W. D., 'Britain's elites in the interwar period, 1918–1939', in Kidd and Nicholls, eds., *Making*

Rubinstein, W. D., *Elites and the Wealthy in Modern British History: Essays in Social and Economic History* (Brighton, 1987)

Rubinstein, W. D., *Men of Property: The Very Wealthy in Britain since the Industrial Revolution* (London, 1981)

Rubinstein, W. D., 'The size and distribution of the English middle classes in 1860', *HR*, 61 (1988)

Rubinstein, W. D., 'The Victorian middle classes: wealth, occupation, and geography', *Ec.HR*, 2nd series, 30 (1977)

Rubinstein, W. D., 'Wealth, elites and the class structure of modern Britain', *P&P*, 76 (1977)

Rudé, G., *The Crowd in History: A Study of Popular Disturbances in France and England, 1730–1848* (London, 1981)

Russell, D., *Popular Music in England, 1840–1914: A Social History* (Manchester, 1987)

Russell, D., '"Sporadic and curious": the emergence of rugby and soccer zones in Yorkshire and Lancashire, c. 1860–1914', *International Journal of History of Sport*, 5 (1988)

Sabel, C., and Zeitlin, J., 'Historical alternatives to mass production: politics, markets and technology in nineteenth-century industrialisation', *P&P*, 108 (1985)

Saint, A., ed., *Politics and the People of London: The London County Council, 1889–1965* (London, 1989)

Sala, G. A., *Twice Round the Clock, or the Hours of the Day and Night in London* (London, 1859; repr., Leicester, 1971)

Samuel, R., 'Comers and goers', in Dyos and Wolff, eds., *Victorian City*, 1

Samuel, R., 'The workshop of the world: steam power and hand technology in mid-Victorian Britain', *History Workshop Journal*, 3 (1977)

Sanderson, M., 'The professor as industrial consultant: Oliver Arnold and the British steel industry, 1900–1914', *Ec.HR*, 2nd series, 3 (1978)

Sanderson, M., *The Universities and British Industry 1850–1970* (London, 1972)

Saul, S. B., 'House-building in England, 1890–1914', *Ec.HR*, 2nd series, 15 (1962)

Saul, S. B., 'The market and the development of the mechanical engineering industries in Britain, 1860–1914', *Ec.HR*, 2nd series, 20 (1967)

Saunders, P., *A Nation of Home Owners* (London, 1990)

Savage, M., 'Career, mobility and class formation: British banking workers and the lower middle class', in A. G. Miles and D. Vincent, eds., *Building European Society: Occupational and Social Mobility in Europe, 1840–1940* (Manchester, 1993)

Savage, M., 'Discipline, surveillance and the "career": employment on the Great Western Railway, 1833–1914', in A. McKinlay and K. Starkey, eds., *Foucault, Management and Organization Theory* (London, 1998)

Savage, M., *The Dynamics of Working-Class Politics: The Labour Movement in Preston, 1880–1940* (Cambridge, 1987)

Savage, M., 'Trade unionism, sex segregation, and the state: women's employment in "new" industries in inter-war Britain', *Soc. Hist.*, 13 (1988)

Savage, M., 'Urban history and social class: two paradigms', *UH*, 20 (1993)

Savage, M., 'Urban politics and the rise of the Labour party, 1919–39', in L. Jamieson and H. Corr, eds., *State, Private Life and Political Change* (Basingstoke, 1990)

Savage, M., and Miles, A., *The Remaking of the British Working Class, 1840–1940* (London, 1994)

Savage, M., and Warde, A., *Urban Sociology, Capitalism and Modernity* (Basingstoke, 1993)

Savage, M., et al., *Property, Bureaucracy and Culture: Middle-Class Formation in Contemporary Britain* (London, 1992)

Saville, J., *Rural Depopulation in England and Wales, 1851–1951* (London, 1957)

Schaffer, F., *The New Town Story* (London, 1970)

Schivelbusch, W., *The Railway Journey: Trains and Travel in the Nineteenth Century* (Oxford, 1980)

Schlör, J., *Nights in the Big City: Paris, Berlin, London, 1840–1930* (London, 1998)

Schoenwald, R. L., 'Training urban man', in Dyos and Wolff, eds., *Victorian City*, II

Scola, R., *Feeding the Victorian City: The Food Supply of Manchester, 1770–1870* (Manchester, 1992)

Scott, P., 'Dispersion versus decentralisation: British location of industry policies and regional development 1945–1960', *Economy and Society*, 26 (1997)

Scott, P., 'Learning to multiply: the property market and the growth of multiple retailing in Britain, 1919–1939', *Business History*, 36 (1994)

Scott, P., 'Planning for profit: the Garden City concept and private sector industrial estate development during the inter-war years', *Planning History*, 16 (1994)

Scott, P., *Property Masters: A History of the British Commercial Property Sector* (London, 1996)

Scott, P., 'The worst of both worlds: British regional policy, 1951–1964', *Business History*, 38 (1996)

Seccombe, W., *Weathering the Storm: Working-Class Families from the Industrial Revolution to the Fertility Decline* (London, 1993)

Seed, J., 'Theologies of power: Unitarianism and the social relations of religious discourse, 1800–1850', in Morris, ed., *Class, Power and Social Structure*

Seed, J., 'Unitarianism, political economy and the antinomies of liberal culture in Manchester, 1830–50', *Soc. Hist.*, 7 (1982)

Sell, A. P. F., ed., *Protestant Nonconformists and the West Midlands of England* (Keele, 1996)

Sennett, R., *Flesh and Stone: The Body and the City in Western Civilisation* (London, 1994)

Shanes, E., *Impressionist London* (London and New York, 1994)

Shapely, P., 'Charity, status and leadership: charitable service and the Manchester man', *Journal of Social History*, 32 (1998)

Shaw, G., 'Changes in consumer demand and food supply in nineteenth-century British cities', *Journal of Historical Geography*, 11 (1985)

Shaw, G., 'The evolution and impact of large-scale retailing in Britain', in Benson and Shaw, eds., *Evolution of Retail Systems*

Shaw, G., 'Industrialisation, urban growth and the city economy', in Lawton, ed., *Rise and Fall of Great Cities*

Shaw, G., and Wild, M. T., 'Retail patterns in the Victorian city', *Transactions of the Institute of British Geographers,* new series, 4 (1979)

Shaw, M., 'The ecology of social change: Wolverhampton, 1851–1871', *Transactions of the Institute of British Geographers*, new series, 2 (1977)

Sheail, J., 'Planning, water supplies and ministerial power in inter-war Britain', *Public Administration*, 61 (1983)

Sheail, J., 'Public interest and self-interest: the disposal of trade effluent in inter-war Britain', *Twentieth Century British History*, 4 (1993)

Sheail, J., *Rural Conservation in Inter-War Britain* (Oxford, 1981)

Sheail, J., 'Sewering the English suburbs: an inter-war perspective', *Journal of Historical Geography*, 19 (1993)

Sheail, J., 'Taken for granted: the inter-war West Middlesex Drainage Scheme', *LJ*, 18 (1993)

Sheail, J., 'Town wastes, agricultural sustainability and Victorian sewage', *UH*, 23 (1996)

Sheppard, F., *London: A History* (Oxford, 1998)

Shields, R., ed., *Lifestyle Shopping: The Subject of Consumption* (London, 1992)

Shields, R., *Places on the Margin: Alternative Geographies of Modernity* (London, 1991)

Shortland, M., ed., *Science and Nature: Essays in the History of the Environmental Sciences* (Stamford in the Vale, 1993)

Shurmer-Smith, P., and Hannam, K., *Worlds of Desire, Realms of Power: A Cultural Geography* (London, 1994)

Sibley, D., *Geographies of Exclusion: Societies and Difference in the West* (London, 1995)

Sigsworth, M., and Worboys, M., 'The public's view of public health in mid-Victorian Britain', *UH*, 21 (1994)

Simey, M., *Charity Rediscovered: A Study of Philanthropic Effort in Nineteenth-Century Liverpool* (originally published as: *Charitable Effort in Liverpool in the Nineteenth Century*, 1951; repr., Liverpool, 1992)

Simmons, J., *The Railway in Town and Country, 1830–1914* (Newton Abbot, 1986)

Simon, C. J., and Nardinelli, C., 'The talk of the town: human capital, information and the growth of English cities, 1861–1961', *Explorations in Economic History*, 33 (1996)

Simpson, M., 'Urban transport and the development of Glasgow's West End', *Journal of Transport History*, new series, 1 (1972)

Simpson, M. A. and Lloyd, T. H., eds., *Middle Class Housing in Britain* (Newton Abbot, 1977)

Sindall, R., *Street Violence in the Nineteenth Century: Media Panic or Real Danger?* (Leicester, 1990)

Skilleter, K. J., 'The role of public utility societies in early British town planning and housing reform, 1901–1936', *Planning Perspectives*, 8 (1993)

Slater, T., ed., *The Built Form of Western Cities: Essays for M. R. G. Conzen on the Occasion of his Eightieth Birthday* (Leicester, 1990)

Smailes, A. E., 'The urban hierarchy in England and Wales', *Geography*, no. 144, vol. 29, pt 2 (1944)

Smith, D., *Conflict and Compromise: Class Formation in English Society, 1830–1914: A Comparative Study of Birmingham and Sheffield* (London, 1982)

Smith, F. B., *The People's Health, 1830–1910* (London, 1979)

Smith, J., 'Class, skill and sectarianism in Glasgow and Liverpool, 1880–1914', in Morris, ed., *Class, Power and Social Structure*

Smith, M., *Religion in Industrial Society: Oldham and Saddleworth, 1740–1865* (Oxford, 1994)

Smith, P. J., 'The foul burns of Edinburgh: public health attitudes and environmental change', *Scottish Geographical Magazine*, 91 (1975)

Smith, P. J., 'The legislated control of river pollution in Victorian Scotland', *Scottish Geographical Magazine*, 98 (1982)

Smith, S., *Crime, Space and Society* (Cambridge, 1986)

Snell, K. D. M., *Annals of the Labouring Poor* (Cambridge, 1985)

Snell, K. D. M., *Church and Chapel in the North Midlands: Religious Observance in the Nineteenth Century* (Leicester, 1991)

Southall, H. R., 'The origins of the depressed areas: unemployment, growth and regional economic structure before 1914', *Ec.HR*, 2nd series, 41 (1988)

Southall, H. R., 'The tramping artisan revisits: labour mobility and economic distress in early Victorian England', *Ec.HR*, 2nd series, 44 (1991)

Spalding, F., *British Art since 1900* (London, 1986)

Springett, J., 'Building development on the Ramsden estate, Huddersfield', *Journal of Historical Geography*, 8 (1982)

Springhall, J., *Youth, Empire and Society: British Youth Movements, 1883–1940* (London, 1977)

Stacey, M., *Tradition and Change: A Study of Banbury* (London, 1960)

Stapleton J., *Englishness and the Study of Politics: The Social and Political Thought of Ernest Barker* (Cambridge, 1994)

Stedman Jones, G., *Outcast London: A Study in the Relationship between Classes in Victorian Society* (Oxford, 1971)

Stedman Jones, G., 'Working-class culture and working-class politics in London, 1870–1900: notes on the remaking of a working class', *Journal of Social History*, 7 (1974)

Steedman, C., *Policing and the Victorian Community: The Formation of English Provincial Police Forces, 1856–80* (London, 1984)

Stenhouse, D. K., 'Liverpool's office district, 1875–1905', *Historical Society of Lancashire and Cheshire*, 133 (1984)

Stephens, W. B., 'Illiteracy in provincial maritime districts and among seamen in early and mid-nineteenth-century England', in E. Jenkins, ed., *Studies in the History of Education* (Leeds, 1995)

Storch, R. D., 'The plague of the blue locusts: police reform and popular resistance in northern England, 1840–57', *International Review of Social History*, 20 (1975)

Storch, R. D., 'Police control of street prostitution in Victorian London: a study in the context of police action', in D. H. Bayley, ed., *Police and Society* (Beverly Hills, 1977)

Storch, R. D., 'The policeman as domestic missionary: urban discipline and popular culture in northern England, 1850–80', in Morris and Rodger, eds., *Victorian City*

Storch, R. D., ed., *Popular Culture and Custom in Nineteenth-Century England* (London, 1982)

Stovel, K., Savage, M., and Bearman, P., 'Ascription into achievement: models of career systems at Lloyds Bank, 1890–1970', *American Journal of Sociology*, 102 (1996)

Summerfield, P., and Evans, E. J., eds., *Technical Education and the State since 1850* (Manchester, 1990)

Summerson, J., *The London Building World of the Eighteen-Sixties* (London, 1973)

Summerson, J., 'The Victorian rebuilding of the City of London', *LJ*, 3 (1977)

Sutcliffe, A., 'Britain's first town planning act: a review of the 1909 achievement', *Town Planning Review*, 59 (1988)

Sutcliffe, A., *Towards the Planned City: Germany, Britain, United States and France, 1780–1914* (Oxford, 1981)

Sutcliffe, A., ed., *British Town Planning: The Formative Years* (Leicester, 1981)

Sutcliffe, A., ed., *Metropolis, 1890–1940* (London, 1984)

Sutcliffe, A., ed., *Multi-Storey Living* (London, 1974)

Sutcliffe, A., and Smith, R., *History of Birmingham*, vol. iii: *Birmingham 1939–1970* (London, 1974)

Sutherland, G., *Policy-Making in Elementary Education, 1870–1895* (Oxford, 1973)

Swenarton, M., *Homes Fit for Heroes: The Politics and Architecture of Early State Housing in Britain* (London, 1981)

Swenarton, M., and Taylor, S., 'The scale and nature of the growth of owner-occupation in Britain between the wars', *Ec.HR*, 2nd series, 38 (1985)

Swift, R., and Gilley, S., eds., *The Irish in Britain, 1815–1939* (London, 1989)

Swift, R., and Gilley, S., eds., *The Irish in the Victorian City* (London, 1985)

Szreter, S., 'Economic growth, disruption, deprivation, disease and death: on the importance of the politics of public health for development', *Population and Development Review*, 23 (1997)

Szreter, S., *Fertility, Class and Gender in Britain, 1860–1940* (Cambridge, 1996)

Szreter, S., 'The importance of social intervention in Britain's mortality decline, c. 1850–1914: a reinterpretation of the role of public health', *Social History of Medicine*, 1 (1988)

Szreter, S., 'Mortality in England in the eighteenth and nineteenth centuries: a reply to Sumit Guha', *Social History of Medicine*, 7 (1994)

Szreter, S., and Mooney, G., 'Urbanisation, mortality and the standard of living debate: new estimates of the expectation of life at birth in nineteenth-century British cities', *Ec.HR*, 2nd series, 51 (1998)

Tagg, J., *The Burden of Representation: Essays on Photographies and Histories* (London, 1988)

Takel, R. E., 'The spatial demands of ports and related industry and their relationships with the community', in Hoyle and Pinder, eds., *Cityport*

Taplin, E. L., *Liverpool Dockers and Seamen, 1870–90* (Hull, 1974)

Tarn, J. N., *Five Per Cent Philanthropy: An Account of Housing in Urban Areas between 1840 and 1914* (Cambridge, 1973)

Taylor, D., *The New Police in Nineteenth-Century England: Crime, Conflict and Control* (Manchester, 1997)

Taylor, I., 'The court and cellar dwelling: the eighteenth-century origin of the Liverpool slum', *Transactions of the Historical Society of Lancashire and Cheshire*, 122 (1970)

Taylor, S., 'A study of post-war office developments', *Journal of the Town Planning Institute*, 52 (1966)

Tebbutt, M., *Making Ends Meet: Pawnbroking and Working-Class Credit* (Leicester, 1983)

Temple Patterson, A., 'Southampton in the eighteenth and nineteenth centuries', in F. J. Monkhouse, ed., *A Survey of Southampton and its Region* (Southampton, 1964)

Thane, P., 'Women in the British Labour Party and the construction of state welfare 1906–1939', in Koven and Michel, eds., *Mothers of a New World*

Thomas, K., *Man and the Natural World: Changing Attitudes in England 1500–1800* (London, 1983)

Thomas, W. A., *The Provincial Stock Exchanges* (London, 1973)

Thompson, B., 'Infant mortality in nineteenth-century Bradford', in Woods and Woodward, eds., *Urban Disease*

Thompson, E. P., 'Time, work discipline and industrial capitalism', *P&P*, 37 (1967)

Thompson, F. M. L., *Hampstead: The Building of a Borough* (London, 1974)

Thompson, F. M. L., 'The land market in the nineteenth century', in W. E. Michinton, ed., *Essays in Agrarian History*, vol. II (Newton Abbot, 1968)

Thompson, F. M. L., 'Nineteenth-century horse sense', *Ec.HR*, 2nd series, 29 (1976)

Thompson, F. M. L., *The Rise of Respectable Society: A Social History of Victorian Britain 1830–1900* (London, 1988)

Thompson, F. M. L., ed., *The Cambridge Social History of Britain, 1750–1950*, vol. I: *Regions and Communities*, vol. II: *People and their Environment*, vol. III: *Social Agencies and Institutions* (Cambridge, 1990)

Thompson, F. M. L., ed., *The Rise of Suburbia* (Leicester, 1982)

Thoms, D. W., 'Market forces and recruitment to technical education: the example of the junior technical schools', *History of Education*, 10 (1981)

Thoms, D. W., and Donnelly, T., 'Coventry's industrial economy, 1880–1980', in Lancaster and Mason, eds., *Life and Labour in a Twentieth Century City*

Thomson, J., and Smith, A., *Street Life in London* (East Ardsley, 1973)

Thorne, R., 'Places of refreshment in the nineteenth-century city', in King, ed., *Buildings and Society*

Thorne, R., 'The White Hart Lane estate: an LCC venture in suburban development', *LJ*, 12 (1986)

Thrift, N., 'The arts of living, the beauty of the dead: anxieties of being in the work of Anthony Giddens', *Progress in Human Geography*, 17 (1993)

Timmins, J. G., 'Concentration and integration in the Sheffield crucible steel industry', *Business History*, 24 (1982)

Timms, D. W. G., *The Urban Mosaic: Towards a Theory of Residential Differentiation* (London, 1971)

Tiratsoo, N., *Reconstruction, Affluence and Labour Politics: Coventry 1945–60* (London, 1990)

Tomes, N., '"A torrent of abuse": crimes of violence between working-class men and women in London, 1840–1875', *Journal of Social History*, 11 (1978)

Tomkins, S. M., 'The failure of expertise: public health policy in Britain during the 1918–19 influenza epidemic', *Social History of Medicine*, 5 (1992)

Toms, S., 'Windows of opportunity in the textile industry: the business strategy of Lancashire entrepreneurs, 1880–1914', *Business History*, 40 (1998)

Topalov, C., 'The city as terra incognita: Charles Booth's poverty survey and the people of London, 1886–1891', *Planning Perspectives*, 8 (1993)

Tosh, J., *A Man's Place: Masculinity and the Middle-Class Home in Victorian England* (New Haven, 1999)

Trainor, R. H., *Black Country Elites: The Exercise of Authority in an Industrialized Area, 1830–1900* (Oxford, 1993)

Trainor, R. H., 'The elite', in Fraser and Maver, eds., *Glasgow*, II

Trainor, R. H., 'The gentrification of Victorian and Edwardian industrialists', in A. L. Beier, D. Cannadine and J. M. Rosenheim, eds., *The First Modern Society: Essays in English History in Honour of Lawrence Stone* (Cambridge, 1989)

Trainor, R. H., 'Neither metropolitan nor provincial: the interwar middle class', in Kidd and Nicholls, eds., *Making*

Trainor, R. H., 'Urban elites in Victorian Britain', *UHY* (1985)

Treble, J., *Urban Poverty in Britain, 1830–1914* (London, 1979)

Trentmann, F., 'Civilisation and its discontents: English neo-romanticism and the transformation of anti-modernism in twentieth-century western culture', *Journal of Contemporary History*, 29 (1994)

Trinder, B., *The Making of the Industrial Landscape* (London, 1982; 3rd edn, 1997)

Trotter, D., *Circulation: Defoe, Dickens and the Economies of the Novel* (Basingstoke, 1988)

Turnbull, G. L., *Traffic and Transport: An Economic History of Pickfords* (London, 1979)

Turnbull, P., and Weston, S., 'Employment regulation, state intervention and the economic performance of European ports', *Cambridge Journal of Economics*, 16 (1992)

Turton, B. J., 'The railway towns of southern England', *Transport History*, 2 (1969)

Turvey, R., 'London lifts and hydraulic power', *Transactions of the Newcomen Society*, 65 (1993–4)

Turvey, R., 'Street mud, dust and noise', *LJ*, 21 (1996)

Tweedale, G., *Steel City: Entrepreneurship, Strategy, and Technology in Sheffield, 1743–1993* (Oxford, 1995)

Urry, J., *Consuming Places* (London and New York, 1994)

Utton, M. A., 'Some features of the early merger movements in British manufacturing industry', *Business History*, 14 (1972)

Vamplew, W., *Pay Up and Play the Game: Professional Sport in Britain, 1875–1914* (Cambridge, 1988)

Ville, S., ed., *Shipbuilding in the United Kingdom in the Nineteenth Century: A Regional Approach* (St Johns, Newfoundland, 1993)

Vincent, D., *Poor Citizens: The State and the Poor in Twentieth-Century Britain* (London, 1991)

Voigt, W., 'The garden city as an eugenic utopia', *Planning Perspectives*, 4 (1989)

Waddington, K., *Charity and the London Hospitals, 1850–1898* (Woodbridge, 2000)

Walby, S., *Patriarchy at Work: Patriarchal and Capitalist Relations in Employment* (Cambridge, 1986)

Walker, F., *The Bristol Region* (London, 1972)

Walker, R. B., 'Religious changes in Liverpool in the nineteenth century', *JEcc.Hist.* 19 (1968)

Walkowitz, J., *City of Dreadful Delight: Narratives of Sexual Danger in Late-Victorian London* (London, 1992)

Walkowitz, J., *Prostitution and Victorian Society: Women, Class and the State* (Cambridge, 1980)

Wall, R., 'The age at leaving home', *Journal of Family History*, 3 (1978)

Wall, R., 'Work, welfare and the family: an illustration of the adaptive family economy', in Bonfield, Smith and Wrightson, eds., *The World We Have Gained*

Waller, P. J., *Democracy and Sectarianism: A Political and Social History of Liverpool, 1868–1939* (Liverpool, 1981)

Waller, P. J., *Town, City and Nation: England, 1850–1914* (Oxford, 1983)

Waller, R., *The Dukeries Transformed: The Social and Political Development of a Twentieth Century Coalfield* (Oxford, 1983)

Walton, J. K., *Blackpool* (Edinburgh, 1998)

Walton, J. K., 'The demand for working-class seaside holidays in Victorian England', *Ec.HR*, 2nd series, 34 (1981)

Walton, J. K., *The English Seaside Resort: A Social History, 1750–1914* (Leicester, 1983)

Walton, J. K., *Fish and Chips and the British Working Class, 1870–1940* (Leicester, 1992)

Walton, J. K., 'Municipal government and the holiday industry in Blackpool, 1876–1914', in Walton and Walvin, eds., *Leisure in Britain*

Walton, J. K., and Walvin, J., eds., *Leisure in Britain, 1780–1939* (Manchester, 1983)

Wannop, U., 'Glasgow/Clydeside: a century of metropolitan evolution', in Gordon, ed., *Regional Cities*

Ward, C., and Hardy, D., *Goodnight Campers: The History of the British Holiday Camp* (London, 1986)

Ward, D., 'A comparative historical geography of streetcar suburbs in Boston, Massachusetts and Leeds, England, 1850–1920', *Annals of the Association of American Geographers*, 54 (1964)

Ward, D., 'Environs and neighbours in the "Two Nations": residential differentiation in mid-nineteenth century Leeds', *Journal of Historical Geography*, 6 (1980)

Ward, D., 'Victorian cities: how modern?', *Journal of Historical Geography*, 1 (1975)

Ward, S. V., *The Geography of Inter-War Britain: The State and Uneven Development* (London, 1988)

Ward, S. V., 'Local industrial promotion and development policies', *Local Economy*, 5 (1990)

Ward, S. V., *Planning and Urban Change* (London, 1994)

Watterson, P., 'The role of the environment in the decline of infant mortality: an analysis of the 1911 census of England and Wales', *Journal of Biosocial Science*, 18 (1986)

Webster, C., 'Conflict and consensus: explaining the British health service', *Twentieth Century British History*, 1 (1990)

Webster, C., *The Health Service since the War*, vol. 1 (London, 1988)

Webster, C., 'Health, welfare and unemployment during the Depression', *P&P*, 109 (1985)

Webster, C., 'Healthy or hungry thirties?', *History Workshop Journal*, 13 (1982)

Weightman, G., and Humphries, S., *The Making of Modern London 1914–1939* (London, 1984)

Wheeler, A., *The Tidal Thames: The History of a River and its Fishes* (London, 1979)

Wheeler, M., ed., *Ruskin and Environment: The Storm-Cloud of the Nineteenth Century* (Manchester, 1995)

Whipp, R., *Patterns of Labour: Work and Social Change in the Pottery Industry* (London, 1990)

White, J., 'Police and people in London in the 1930s', *Oral History*, 11 (1983)

White, J., *Rothschild Buildings: Life in an East End Tenement Block 1887–1920* (London, 1980)

White, J., *The Worst Street in North London: Campbell Bunk, Islington, Between the Wars* (London, 1986)

Whitehand, J. W. R., *The Changing Face of Cities: A Study of Development Cycles and Urban Form* (Oxford, 1987)

Whitehouse, B. P., *Partners in Property* (London, 1964)

Whiteside, N., *Bad Times: Unemployment in British Social and Political History* (London, 1991)

Whiteside, N., 'Private agencies for public purposes: some new perspectives on policy making in health insurance between the wars', *Journal of Social Policy*, 12 (1983)

Whiting, R. C., ed., *Oxford: Studies in the History of a University Town since 1800* (Manchester, 1993)

Wickham, E. R., *Church and People in an Industrial City* (London, 1957)

Williams, K., *From Pauperism to Poverty* (London, 1981)

Williams, N., 'Death in its season: class, environment and the mortality of infants in nineteenth-century Sheffield', *Social History of Medicine*, 5 (1992)

Williams, N., and Galley, C., 'Urban–rural differentials in infant mortality in Victorian England', *Population Studies*, 49 (1995)

Williams, N., and Mooney, G., 'Infant mortality in "an age of great cities": London and the English provincial cities compared, *c.* 1840–1910', *Continuity and Change*, 9 (1994)

Williams, R., *The Country and the City* (London, 1973)

Williamson, J. G., *Coping with City Growth during the British Industrial Revolution* (Cambridge, 1990)

Willmott, P., and Young, M., *Family and Class in a London Suburb* (London, 1960; 2nd edn, 1971)

Wilson, A., 'Technology and municipal decision-making: sanitary systems in Manchester, 1868–1910' (PhD thesis, University of Manchester, 1990)

Wilson, C., *First with the News: The History of W. H. Smith, 1792–1972* (London, 1985)

Wilson, E., *The Sphinx in the City: Urban Life, the Control of Disorder, and Women* (London, 1991)

Winstanley, M. J., 'Concentration and competition in the retail sector, *c.* 1800–1990', in M. W. Kirby and M. B. Rose, eds., *Business Enterprise in Modern Britain: From the Eighteenth to the Twentieth Century* (London, 1994)

Winstanley, M. J., *The Shopkeeper's World 1830–1914* (Manchester, 1983)

Winter, J., *London's Teeming Streets, 1830–1914* (London, 1993)

Winter, J. M., *The Great War and the British People* (Basingstoke, 1986)

Withers, C. W. J., 'Class, culture and migrant identity: Gaelic Highlanders in urban Scotland', in Kearns and Withers, eds., *Urbanising Britain*

Withers, C. W. J., and Watson, A. J., 'Stepwise migration and Highland migration to Glasgow, 1852–1898', *Journal of Historical Geography*, 17 (1991)

Wohl, A. S., *Endangered Lives: Public Health in Victorian Britain* (London, 1983)

Wohl, A. S., *The Eternal Slum: Housing and Social Policy in Victorian London* (London, 1977)

Wohl, A. S., ed., *The Victorian Family: Structures and Stresses* (London, 1978)

Wolff, J., and Seed, J., eds., *The Culture of Capital: Art, Power and the Nineteenth-Century Middle Class* (Manchester, 1988)

Wolpert, J., 'Behavioural aspects of the decision to migrate', *Papers and Proceedings of the Regional Science Association*, 15 (1965)

Wood, L. B., *The Restoration of the Tidal Thames* (Bristol, 1982)

Woods, R., *The Demography of Victorian England and Wales* (Cambridge, 2000)

Woods, R., and Shelton, N., *An Atlas of Victorian Mortality* (Liverpool, 1997)

Woods, R., Watterson, P. A., and Woodward, J., 'The causes of rapid infant mortality decline in England and Wales, 1861–1921', *Population Studies*, Part I, 42 (1988), Part II, 43 (1989)

Woods, R., and Woodward, J., eds., *Urban Disease and Mortality in Nineteenth-Century England* (London, 1984)

Wright, N. R., *Lincolnshire Towns and Industry, 1700–1914* (Lincoln, 1982)

Wrigley, E. A., *Continuity, Chance and Change: The Character of the Industrial Revolution in England* (Cambridge, 1988)

Wrigley, E. A., 'Men on the land and men in the countryside: employment in agriculture in early nineteenth-century England', in Bonfield, Smith and Wrightson, eds., *The World We Have Gained*

Wrigley, E. A., *People, Cities, and Wealth: The Transformation of Traditional Society* (Oxford, 1987)

Van Vugt, W. E., 'Running from ruin? The emigration of British farmers to the U.S.A. in the wake of the repeal of the Corn Laws', *Ec.HR*, 2nd series, 41 (1988)

Vogele, J., *Urban Mortality Change in England and Germany, 1870–1913* (Liverpool, 1998)

Yeadall, M., 'Building societies in the West Riding of Yorkshire and their contribution to housing provision in the nineteenth century', in Doughty, ed., *Building the Industrial City*

Yelling, J. A., 'Expensive land, subsidies, and mixed development in London, 1943–56', *Planning Perspectives*, 9 (1994)

Yelling, J. A., 'Planning and the land question', *Planning History*, 16 (1994)

Yelling, J. A., *Slums and Redevelopment: Policy and Practice in England, 1918–45, with Particular Reference to London* (London, 1992)

Yelling, J. A., *Slums and Slum Clearance in Victorian London* (London, 1986)

Yeo, E. J., *The Contest for Social Science: Relations and Representations of Gender and Class* (London, 1996)

Yeo, S., *Religion and Voluntary Organisations in Crisis, 1890–1914* (London, 1976)

Yeo, S., ed., *New Views of Co-operation* (London, 1988)

Young, K., *Local Politics and the Rise of Party: The London Municipal Society and the Conservative Intervention in Local Elections, 1894–1963* (Leicester, 1975)

Young, K., and Garside, P., *Metropolitan London: Politics and Urban Change, 1837–1981* (London, 1982)

Young, M., and Willmott, P., *Family and Kinship in East London* (London, 1957)

Young, M., and Willmott, P., *The Symmetrical Family* (London, 1973)

Zimmeck, M., 'Jobs for the girls: the expansion of clerical work for women 1850–1914', in John, ed., *Unequal Opportunities*

Index

Note: page numbers in italic refer to Tables and Figures; only those Plates mentioned in the text are indexed

building industry 499, 501, 580–1
  boom (1930s) 511
  boom (1950s) 519–20
  craft traditions in 606
  cyclical nature of 471, 472, 486, 499
  employment in 499, 511, 519, 562
  recession (1900s) 471, 472, 484
building licences 516, 517, 519, 521
building materials
  post-war shortages 516, 517
  reinforced concrete 501
  steel-framing 501, 505–6, 512
  technological developments 501–2, 505–6,
    836
  transport of 233, 408
building quality 547, 836
  council housing 455, 457, 462, 463–4
  early developments 475–6
building regulations 49, 453, 474
building societies 110, 308, 516
  cheap mortgages 202–3, 445
  credit facilities 386, 446–7
  loans for development 497, 516
Building Societies Act (1874) 497
buildings
  commercial 29, 37–8, 499, 501–3, 507, 508–9
  community 538, 539
  factories 37, 505–6
  historic 519
  industrial, redevelopment of 838–9
  institutional 499, 506
  public 36–7, 471
  see also architecture; housing; office
    buildings; shops
bulk processing 37, 144
bull-running 9, 758, 759
Bungay 154, 173, 181
burghs of barony (Scotland) 264, 798
burial societies 360, 374
Burnley 655, 679, 775, 791
Burslem 623
Burton-on-Trent 647, 653
Burton's, tailors 503, 510
  and men's fashions 739–40
Bury 359, 362, 655, 659, 661
Busby, William, trams 236
buses
  horse 9–10, 230, 236, 404, 437
  licensing of 254–5
  London, privatised 834
  motor 252–3, 254–5
  operating costs 252–3
  trolley 242, 252
business organisations, influence in local
  politics 307–8
businesses 25, 328, 619, 708
  company headquarters in London 129–30,
    417, 512, 520, 583–4

corporate structure 578, 583–5, 610
development of formal offices 500
family firms 556, 578, 583, 584–5
internal labour markets 45, 54
internalised supplies 584
local links severed 583–4, 585, 609, 833
managerial structure 18, 38, 416, 584, 610, 620
mergers 578, 583, 610
mining companies 613
multi-national 417
national organisation of 416–17, 503, 583–4,
  609
need for stable workforce 601, 613
new forms of organisation 578, 610, 802,
  833
public corporations 316, 347, 349
run from home 29, 495, 500, 523, 725
small firms 44–5, 555, 578–9
structure of 18, 25, 44–5, 833
see also property development
Bute family, Cardiff 80, 143
by-law housing 7, 31, 718
  see also council housing
by-laws
  to regulate trams 323
  on smoke pollution 211

cabaret 783
Cadman Report (1938) 347
Caernarfon 154, 181, 182
Caernarfonshire 158
Caerphilly 154, 169
cafés 736
Caithness 169
Cambridge 276, 678
  modern 837–8
  science-based industry 838, 840
Camden Town Group of artists 816, 829
canals 76, 78, 140, 233
Canterbury 84, 647, 652, 760
capital 352
  flows 18, 83
  knowledge-based human 554
  local supplies 578, 584
  mobility of 66, 78–9, 418–19
capital costs 320, 335–6, 337
capital investment
  by family firms 578
  funding for 12, 321
  in industrialising regions 76, 77–8
  in ports 137–9
capitalism
  dynamic nature of 66, 124
  and house ownership 452–3
  and linkages 63
  and modernity 398
  and social structure 398
  and urbanisation 73, 431–2

charities (*cont.*)
  trusts and foundations 44, 374
  urban focus of 409–10
  see also voluntary organisations
charity
  exhortations to 742
  impulse to intervention 831
Charity Organisation Society (COS) 310, 362, 363
  cooperation with poor law guardians 367, 371–2, 373–4
  coordination role 367, 371
Charlton, fair 759
Chartism 67, 81, 605
  demonstrations 118, 163, 759, 762; Kennington Common 118, 762, 765
Chatham, naval base 135
Chelmsford *154*, 181
Cheltenham 623, *690*
chemical industry 5, 574, 587
Chepstow *154*, 168
Cheshire 158
Chesser, Eustace, urban anthropology 667
Chester 50, 71, 334, *654*
  shopping areas 724, 736
  wealth *690*
Chester Gaslight Company 318
Chesterfield 793
Cheyne Investments Ltd 510
Chicago School of urban ecology 431, 439
Chichester *154*, 168, 334, 678
children 8, 311, 375, 376
  childcare 35, 664
  compulsory education 46, 292, 600, 657
  consumer expenditure on 740
  as consumers 719, 740–1
  costs of childrearing 657, 664, 666
  deaths: from disease 631–2, 634 and n, 671; in hospitals 645
  employment of 46, 598–9, 600, 601
  playgrounds 256, 766
  portrayed in London scenes 821–2
  on suburban council estates 463
Children's Act (1948) 286n
Children's Care Committee 311
Chingford, urban growth 436
Chiozza Money, Leo 468
choice
  consumer 722–3, 742
  in urban life 396, 410, 425, 807
cholera 213, 222
choral societies 780–1
Chorley 406
Church Army 799
Church of England 19, 84, 785, 802
  and class 791, 793
  and housing reform 798
  pew rents 788, 793–4

recreational clubs 797, 799
urban attendance 789
as urban landowner 495
urban ministry 786–7
and urban missions 796
see also churches and religious groups; evangelicalism
Church Lads' Brigade 799
Church of Scotland 793, 794
churches and religious groups
  attendance: census of (1851) 787–91; falling 711, 713, 745, 800–5, 806
  City Missions 787
  and education 309–10
  evangelising role 787, 795, 796
  income 793, 794, 795
  influence in local politics 307–8, 706, 802–3
  lay leadership positions in 699, 706, 711
  lay workers' societies 787, 796
  membership 800–1, 803, 804; failure to retain young 803–4
  and moralism 310, 742
  national networks of 709
  new urban 785–6, 794–5
  popular alienation 787, 788–9
  revivalism 787, 799
  and rites of passage 805
  social facilities 773, 787, 799, 803–4
  social functions of 745–6, 787, 796
  and social life 695, 706, 711, 780
  in suburbs 795
  voluntary organisations 372, 799
  welfare provision 373, 796, 802; poor relief 360, 372, 796; unemployment 383
  see also Church of England; evangelicalism; Methodism; nonconformity; religion; Roman Catholics
Churchill, Winston 199
cinemas 51, 422, 718, 737, 778
  development of 830
  expansion of 770–1, 785
  and film stars 740, 776
  and licensing 52–3
  popularity of 776–7
  Sunday opening 752–3
circulation
  'continuous' 5–7, 12
  of information 6, 13, 396
  restricted 1–2, 3
cisterns, public water 323
cities *see* towns and cities
City and Guilds of London Institute qualifications 588
City of London Real Property Ltd 501
City of Manchester Plan (1945) 491–2
City Offices Company 129, 501
civic culture 412, 585

Index

Dickens, Charles 1, 5, 48, 146, 600
  on urban experience 423–4
diet
  among poor 727, 730
  effect on health 633–4, 649 and n
Dingwall *154*, 178
dioceses, reorganised 19
diseases 593, 811
  asthma 209, 224, 227
  bronchitis 209, 224, 227, 640
  cancer 640, 646–7
  chronic and degenerative 631, 640–1, 646–7
  diarrhoea: epidemic 213, 638; infant 632 and n, 638
  germ theory of 213
  improved diagnosis 640, 646–7
  industrial 641
  of infant mortality 632 and n, 638
  infectious 8–9; diphtheria 632, 637; falling mortality from 632–3, 671; measles 631–2, 637; scarlet fever 631, 632, 637; smallpox 631, 632; typhus 632; whooping cough 631–2, 637
  late-onset diabetes 646
  miasma theory 213
  and need for sunlight 222–3, 224
  pneumonia 209, 224, 227, 643
  polio (1950s) 219, 220
  and pollution 209, 210, 224, 642
  respiratory 642, 643–4
  rickets 5, 224, 642
  Spanish influenza (1918) 644
  transmitted syphilis 638
  tuberculosis 32, 291, 631, 632, 637, 642, 643–5; reappearance of 839
  water-borne 209, 210, 213; cholera 213, 220, 227, 631; typhoid 31, 213, 215, 220, 227, 632
dispensaries 363, 364, 374
Diss *154*, 173, 181
dissenters *see* nonconformity
Distressed Areas, residential segregation in 536
distribution
  networks 575
  retailing 18, 40
  transport and 235, 513
Distribution of Industry Acts (1945 and 1950) 591
district councils (second tier), proposed (1888) 270
district nursing 364, 384
District Provident Societies 787
district visiting, by charitable societies 362
dividends
  10 per cent limit 26, 322, 839
  Co-op 727
do-it-yourself 740
dock workers 147, 148–9, 405, 596–7, 601

docks
  in art 819
  financial performance of municipal *340*
  investment *319*
  redevelopment of xx, 834, 838
dockyards, naval 564
doctors 16
  powers of 8–9
  see also medical officers of health
dogs, strays destroyed 7
Dolgellau *154*, 161, 182
Dollan, P. J., Glasgow 420
domesticity, ideology of 377, 403–4
  as middle-class aspiration 693, 725
  and middle-class career structure 621
  welfare provision to support 667
Donald, R., on costs 335
Doncaster 251, 277, 293
  revenues 295, *331*
Dorchester, as 'Casterbridge' 164
Doré, Gustave 824
  London: A Pilgrimage (1872) 821 and Plate 40
  'The River Bank – Under the Trees' 821–2
Dorset 158
Dover 91, 134
Drabble, Richard, artist 817
drink and drunkenness 290, 310
  beer consumption 727, 767
  at fairs and festivals 754–5
  portrayed by Cruickshank 822
  see also public houses
Dublin 89, 660
Duckworth, Mr, Rochdale 300
Dudley 303, 651, *653*, *690*, 705
Dudley Report, on design of dwellings (1944) 492
Dulwich 781
Duncan, Andrew, chairman of CEB 343
Dundee 71, 661
  economy 422, 571
  occupational structure *566*, *568*, *570*; female employment 564, 565n
  recreation 774, 777
  utilities 219, 339
  wealth *690*
Dunfermline 76, 414, 661
dungheaps 2
Dunlop, relocation to Speke (Liverpool) 590
Durant, Ruth 203
Durham 627, 628, 678
Dyos, H. J. xxi, xxii, 245, 247

Ealing Tenants' Society 534
East Anglia 18, 89, 178, 181
East Hoathly (Sussex) 184
East India Company 2, 6
Eastbourne 50, 198, 662, 708
  population, marriage and fertility *652*, 664

901

Index

industrial estates 115, 514, *515*; on arterial roads 575; Great West Road 115, 125, 512
industry: geographical trends 124–5; New Towns factory development 522; small-scale 44, 121, 122–3, 838; in suburbs 109, 115; workshop production 45, 359, 840
infrastructure 88; disposal of household waste 221, 234; sewers 3n, 12, 102; *see also* utilities (*below*)
international role 18, 81, 91, 127
Islington 32, 236, 837
journeys to work 231; *see also* transport
Kennington Common 9, 118, 765
Kensington 250, 392, 616, 801
Kingston By-Pass 115
Kingsway-Aldwych 130
Knightsbridge 110
Lambeth 797, 799–800, 801
Lea Valley, industry 124
Lewisham 713, 781
livery companies 495, 602
Marylebone, poor law 371, 372
May Day celebrations 759
Mayfair, Grosvenor estate 477
metropolitan boroughs 102, 103, 289, 303; after GLC 834; conflict with LCC 20, 28; housing policies 115–16; municipalisation of utilities 324; and voluntary organisations 392
Metropolitan Railway 108–9
middle classes 662, 677, 678; compared with provinces 675, 680, 688–9; occupations 679
Millbank council estate 114
Mornington Crescent 816 and Plate 31
New Oxford Street 50, 246
Noel Park suburb 110
North Circular Road 115
North Kensington, slums 110
office buildings 37, 126, 520; *see also* City (*above*)
Pall Mall 119, 121
parliamentary boroughs 102
Piccadilly Circus 12, 771
Pimlico 112, 116, 793
politics: Labour Party 124; Liberals 113; Progressives 100, 114; radical Liberalism 124; working-class 123–4
poor relief 363–4, 367; administration 371, 372; charities 363–4; COS coordination role in 371; poor law rebellion 389, 417
Poplar 247–8, 250, 389, 417, 419
population 69, 229, 436, 522; 1911 census 652, 769; decline in central districts 198; growth 102; Irish immigrants 194, 357; Jewish immigrants 198; life expectancy 648; marriage and fertility 652, 661; migrants 189; mortality rates 637, 645,

infant 209, 638, maternal 391–2, 640, *641*, share of 81, 98, *see also* size (*below*)
port 134, 139, 143, 145; cargo handling 138; dock labour 596–7; and Port of London Authority (PLA) 137; proportion of trade 93, 135, 140–1; transport links 140; volume of trade 91–2, 146
predominance 18, 65–6, 81, 97–8; imperial capital 125–30; perceptions of 98–9; as world city 18, 93
Queen's Hall 121, 781
Queen's Park 110
recreation, church facilities 797, 799–800; sports 421, 759, 775; suburbs 783–4, 785
Regent Street 247, 827–8
Regent's Park 50, 765
relations with regions 81–6, 97–8, 421; provincial urban elites and 708–9
Ritz Hotel, steel-framed 501
Rotherhithe Tunnel 114
Royal Colonial Institute 127
Royal Docks 109
St Helier industrial estate 115
St James Park 50
St Pancras station 249, 826
St Paul's Cathedral 814–15 and Plate 28
Savoy Theatre 768
Shaftesbury Avenue 12, 102, 770
Shaftesbury Park suburb 110
shopping districts 720, 723, 724
Shoreditch, theatre 770
size 18, 96, 229, 436; boundaries 96, *97*; expansion 71, 110, 204
Smithfield 5, 838
social geography 95–6, 104–17; Booth's poverty maps 105, *106–7*, 108
Somers Town 116
Southall, trams 239
Spa Fields 9
Stepney 391–2
Strand 127, 247
Stratford 109, 124
Streatham Street, model dwellings 111–12
streets 100–1; new 112, 246; surfaces 11, 244
suburbs: Highbury New Park 244–5; recreation 783–4, 785
Tate Gallery 126
Tottenham 392, *653*; trading profits *331*
Tower Hamlets 114
trade: coal supplies 233; connections 126–7; share 129; warehouses 37–8
Trafalgar Square 119
transport 100, 238, 834, 836; cabs 230; hackney carriages 230; horse buses 230; motor buses 252; road accidents 254; trams 114, 236, 238, 239; underground railways 240–1, 249, 834; *see also* railways
Tyburn 9

917